Metaphysics

BLACKWELL PHILOSOPHY ANTHOLOGIES

Each volume in this outstanding new series provides an authoritative and comprehensive collection of the essential primary readings from philosophy's main fields of study. Designed to complement the *Blackwell Companions to Philosophy* series, each volume represents an unparalleled resource in its own right, and will provide the ideal platform for course use.

Metaphysics
An Anthology

Edited by *Jaegwon Kim* and *Ernest Sosa*
Brown University

Copyright © Blackwell Publishers Ltd, 1999

First published 1999

2 4 6 8 10 9 7 5 3 1

Blackwell Publishers Inc.
350 Main Street
Malden, Massachusetts 02148
USA

Blackwell Publishers Ltd
108 Cowley Road
Oxford OX4 1JF
UK

Library of Congress Cataloging-in-Publication Data

Metaphysics / edited by Jaegwon Kim and Ernest Sosa.
      p.   cm. — (Blackwell philosophy anthologies)
  Includes bibliographical references and index.
  ISBN 0–631–20278–1 (alk. paper). — ISBN 0–631–20279–X (pbk. : alk. paper)
  1. Metaphysics. I. Kim, Jaegwon. II. Sosa, Ernest. III. Series.
BD111. M55 1999
  110–dc21   98–8538
                                              CIP

British Library Cataloguing in Publication Data

A CIP catalogue record for this book is available from the British Library

Typeset in 9 on 11 pt Ehrhardt by Pure Tech India Ltd, Pondicherry
http://www.puretech.com.
Printed in Great Britain by T. J. International, Padstow, Cornwall

This book is printed on acid-free paper

Contents

Contents

Contents

Preface

Metaphysics is a philosophical inquiry into the most basic and general features of reality and our place in it. Because of its very subject matter, metaphysics is often philosophy at its most theoretical and abstract. But, as the works in this book show, simple, intuitive reflections on our familiar experiences of everyday life and the concepts that we use to describe them can lead us directly to some of the most profound and intractable problems of metaphysics.

This anthology, intended as a companion to Blackwell's *A Companion to Metaphysics*, is a collection of writings chosen to represent the state of discussion on the central problems of contemporary metaphysics. Many of the selections are "contemporary classics," and many of the rest will likely join the ranks of the "classics" in due course. Throughout the selection process we tried to be responsive to the needs of students who are relatively new to metaphysics. Given the overall aim of the volume and the nature of the field, it is unavoidable that some of the writings included contain somewhat technical parts that demand close study; however, we believe that most of the essential selections are accessible to the attentive reader without an extensive background in metaphysics or technical philosophy.

The selections are grouped in nine parts. Each part is preceded by a brief editorial introduction, including a list of works for further reading. These introductions are not intended as comprehensive surveys and discussions of the problems, positions, and arguments on the topic of each part; for such guidance the reader is encouraged to consult *A Companion to Metaphysics*. Rather, their aim is to give the reader some orientation, by indicating the scope of the problems dealt with in the works included in that section, and what their authors attempt to accomplish.

Part I, on the nature of existence, deals with the question of what it is for something to exist and what it is for us to acknowledge something as existing. Part II concerns the problem of identity – whether qualitative indiscernibility entails identity, whether identity is always necessary or can be contingent, whether identity is relative to sortals, and so on. Part III is on "modal" concepts like necessity and possibility, essence and essential property, necessary and contingent truth, and "possible worlds." The part that follows is devoted to age-old issues concerning universals, properties, and kinds – the items in terms of which we characterize things of this world. The central question of Part V is what it is for something to be a "thing," and, in particular, what makes one thing at one time to be "the same thing" as something at another time. This part is followed by a group of writings addressing the same question for persons: there is a clear and deep difference, most of us would feel, between our continuing to live till tomorrow and our being replaced by an exact "molecule-for-molecule" duplicate in our sleep tonight; but in what does this difference consist? Part VII is devoted to the nature of causation, the relation that David Hume famously called "the cement of the universe." Major contemporary accounts of the nature of causation are represented here. This is followed by a part concerning the ways (besides the causal relation) in which things and phenomena of this world may hang together, and the topics dealt with here – emergence, reduction, and supervenience – are of critical importance to current debates in philosophy of mind and philosophy of science. The issue of realism/antirealism has lately returned as a major philosophical problem, and the final part of the book includes discussions of realism and its major contemporary alternatives. It was often difficult to neatly segregate the works into separate parts; the reader should be aware that many of the selections are of relevance to problems dealt with in more than one part. This is especially true of the chapters in Parts II and III, and those in Parts V and VI.

The topics represented in this book by no means exhaust the field of metaphysics. For reasons of space, we have had to leave out many important topics, among them the following: facts, events, and tropes; primary and secondary qualities; the status of abstract entities; parts and wholes; the objective and the subjective; time and becoming; determinism and agency; and the nature and possibility of metaphysics. Even on the topics included here, many important and worthy works have had to be left out, either on account of limited space or because of the difficulty of extracting from them something of reasonable length that would be self-contained. In choosing the works to be included, our primary focus has been on seminal primary literature that represents the major contemporary positions on the issues involved. In consequence,

we have had to forgo many valuable follow-up discussions and elaborations, objections and replies, and expository surveys. We hope that the interested reader will pursue the threads of discussion inspired by the materials included here.

During much of the middle half of the century, metaphysics was in the doldrums, at least within the analytic tradition. This was largely due to the anti-metaphysical influence of the two then dominant philosophical trends. Logical positivism and its formalistic, hyper-empiricist legacies lingered through the 1950s and 1960s in the United States, nourishing an atmosphere that did not encourage serious metaphysics, while in Britain the anti-metaphysical animus derived from "ordinary language" philosophy and the later works of Wittgenstein. However, metaphysics began a surprisingly swift, robust comeback in the 1960s, and since then has been among the most active and productive areas of philosophy. It is now flourishing as never before, showing perhaps that our need for metaphysics is as basic as our need for philosophy itself. We believe that this collection gives a broad glimpse of metaphysics during the century that is now about to close.

Maura Geisser, Brie Gertler, and Matt McGrath have helped us with this project in various ways, and we have received valuable advice from our Brown colleagues Victor Caston and Jamie Dreier. Also helpful were the comments and suggestions by the anonymous readers of the preliminary plan we submitted to Blackwell. Steve Smith, our editor, has been unfailingly supportive and helpful. We owe thanks to them all.

Jaegwon Kim
Ernest Sosa
October 1998

Acknowledgments

The authors and publishers would like to thank the following for permission to use copyright material:
American Philosophical Quarterly for chapters 27, 32;
The American Philosophy Association and William P. Alston for chapter 46;
Blackwell Publishers for chapters 13 (with David Lewis), 30, 47 (with Simon Blackburn);
Cambridge University Press for chapters 25, 42;
Columbia University for chapters 5, 10, 14, 24, 31, 33, 34 (with David Lewis), 38, 41, 45 (with Ernest Sosa);
Cornell University Press for chapters 6, 8, 28, 29;
Harvard University Press for chapter 22;
Kluwer Academic Publishers for chapters 4, 9, 18, 19, 20, 23, 39, 43;
La Trobe University and David Lewis for chapter 17;
New York University Press for chapter 7;
Open Court, a division of Carus Publishing, for chapters 21, 26, 44;
Oxford University Press for chapter 11;
Philosophy and Phenomenological Research and Brown University for chapter 40;
Princeton University Press for chapter 35;
Review of Metaphysics for chapter 1;
Routledge and Kegan Paul for chapter 37;
The Bertrand Russell estate for chapter 3;
University of Calgary Press for chapters 15, 36;
University of Chicago Press for chapter 2;
University of Minnesota Press for chapters 12, 48;
Westview Press for chapter 16.
Every effort has been made to trace the copyright holders, but if any have been inadvertently overlooked, the publishers will be pleased to make the necessary arrangements at the first opportunity.

PART I

Existence

Introduction

The concept of existence is probably basic and primitive in the sense that it is not possible to produce an informative definition of it in terms that are more clearly understood and that would tell us something important and revealing about what it is for something to exist. Rather, the primary conceptual question about existence has been this: What *kind* of concept is expressed by "existence" and its cognates? When we say of something that it exists, are we attributing to that thing a certain *property*, the property of existing, much in the way we attribute the property red to this apple when we say it is red? Something is red as opposed to yellow or black – or, at any rate, not red. But something exists as opposed to what? Being non-existent? But how is that possible? Is it coherent to suppose that some things exist and some things don't exist? As Quine says in his "On What There Is" (chapter 1), isn't it a truism that everything exists, and nothing else does?

But this doesn't seem to make the issues go away. For, as Terence Parsons points out in "Referring to Nonexistent Objects" (chapter 4), our ordinary discourse is full of apparent references to things that do not exist, like fictional characters (Sherlock Holmes, Hamlet), mythological creatures (Pegasus, centaurs), and the fountain of youth that Ponce de León sought to find. It seems natural and intelligible to say that *there are* things, like centaurs and the fountain of youth, that do not exist. Moreover, we apparently can say things that are true of them and things that are false of them. It seems true to say that centaurs are mythical animals, that Sherlock Holmes was a detective and lived on Baker Street, and so on; and it seems false to say that Sherlock Holmes was a baseball player, or that the golden mountain is in Argentina. But how is it possible for us to refer to them to begin with – things with which we have no causal or epistemic contact? Are we forced to countenance these nonexistent objects as denizens of our ontology, or is it possible to explain them away by paraphrasing statements that are apparently about them into statements that are free of such references? These are among the questions addressed in the selections by Bertrand Russell and Terence Parsons.

Quine's "On What There Is" and Carnap's "Empiricism, Semantics, and Ontology" (chapter 2) address some fundamental issues about what it is for something to exist, and, more importantly, what it is for us, or our theory, to recognize something as existing. Carnap's distinction between "internal questions" and "external questions" about existence – that is, questions about whether something exists *within* a scheme of language, on the one hand, and questions about whether or not to accept a scheme that posits its existence, on the other – introduces pragmatic and relativistic dimensions into questions of existence. This question of the possible relativity of ontology to conceptual schemes is the topic of Quine's "Ontological Relativity" (chapter 5).

Further reading

Alston, William P., "Ontological commitment," *Philosophical Studies* 9 (1958), pp. 8–17.

Butchvarov, Panayot, *Being Qua Being* (Bloomington: Indiana University Press, 1979).

Chisholm, Roderick M., "Beyond being and nonbeing," *Philosophical Studies* 24 (1973), pp. 245–57.

Evans, Gareth, *The Varieties of Reference* (Oxford: Oxford University Press, 1982).

Fine, Kit, "The problem of non-existence: I. Internalism," *Topoi* 1 (1982), pp. 97–140.

Katz, Jerrold J., "Names without bearers," *Philosophical Review* 103 (1994), pp. 1–39.

Lewis, David, "Truth in fiction," in *Philosophical Papers*, vol. 1 (New York: Oxford University Press, 1983).

Moore, G. E., "Is existence a predicate?," repr. in *Philosophical Papers* (London: Allen and Unwin, 1959).

Parsons, Terence, *Nonexistent Objects* (New Haven, Conn.: Yale University Press, 1980).

Routley, Richard, *Exploring Meinong's Jungle and Beyond* (Canberra: Australian National University, 1980).

Russell, Bertrand, "On denoting," repr. in R. C. Marsh (ed.), *Logic and Knowledge* (London: George, Allen and Unwin, 1956).

Walton, Kendall, *Mimesis as Make-Believe* (Cambridge, Mass.: Harvard University Press, 1990).

Williams, C. J. F., *What Is Existence?* (Oxford: Oxford University Press, 1981).

1

On What There Is

W. V. Quine

A curious thing about the ontological problem is its simplicity. It can be put in three Anglo-Saxon monosyllables: 'What is there?' It can be answered, moreover, in a word – 'Everything' – and everyone will accept this answer as true. However, this is merely to say that there is what there is. There remains room for disagreement over cases; and so the issue has stayed alive down the centuries.

Suppose now that two philosophers, McX and I, differ over ontology. Suppose McX maintains there is something which I maintain there is not. McX can, quite consistently with his own point of view, describe our difference of opinion by saying that I refuse to recognize certain entities. I should protest, of course, that he is wrong in his formulation of our disagreement, for I maintain that there are no entities, of the kind which he alleges, for me to recognize; but my finding him wrong in his formulation of our disagreement is unimportant, for I am committed to considering him wrong in his ontology anyway.

When *I* try to formulate our difference of opinion, on the other hand, I seem to be in a predicament. I cannot admit that there are some things which McX countenances and I do not, for in admitting that there are such things I should be contradicting my own rejection of them.

It would appear, if this reasoning were sound, that in any ontological dispute the proponent of the negative side suffers the disadvantage of not being able to admit that his opponent disagrees with him.

This is the old Platonic riddle of nonbeing. Nonbeing must in some sense be, otherwise what is it that there is not? This tangled doctrine might be nicknamed *Plato's beard*; historically it has proved tough, frequently dulling the edge of Occam's razor.

It is some such line of thought that leads philosophers like McX to impute being where they might otherwise be quite content to recognize that there is nothing. Thus, take Pegasus. If Pegasus *were* not, McX argues, we should not be talking about anything when we use the word; therefore it would be nonsense to say even that Pegasus is not. Thinking to show thus that the denial of Pegasus cannot be coherently maintained, he concludes that Pegasus is.

McX cannot, indeed, quite persuade himself that any region of space-time, near or remote, contains a flying horse of flesh and blood. Pressed for further details on Pegasus, then, he says that Pegasus is an idea in men's minds. Here, however, a confusion begins to be apparent. We may for the sake of argument concede that there is an entity, and even a unique entity (though this is rather implausible), which is the mental Pegasus-idea; but this mental entity is not what people are talking about when they deny Pegasus.

McX never confuses the Parthenon with the Parthenon-idea. The Parthenon is physical; the Parthenon-idea is mental (according anyway to McX's version of ideas, and I have no better to offer). The Parthenon is visible; the Parthenon-

Originally published in the *Review of Metaphysics* 2/1 (Sept. 1948), reprinted with permission.

idea is invisible. We cannot easily imagine two things more unlike, and less liable to confusion, than the Parthenon and the Parthenon-idea. But when we shift from the Parthenon to Pegasus, the confusion sets in – for no other reason than that McX would sooner be deceived by the crudest and most flagrant counterfeit than grant the nonbeing of Pegasus.

The notion that Pegasus must be, because it would otherwise be nonsense to say even that Pegasus is not, has been seen to lead McX into an elementary confusion. Subtler minds, taking the same precept as their starting point, come out with theories of Pegasus which are less patently misguided than McX's, and correspondingly more difficult to eradicate. One of these subtler minds is named, let us say, Wyman. Pegasus, Wyman maintains, has his being as an unactualized possible. When we say of Pegasus that there is no such thing, we are saying, more precisely, that Pegasus does not have the special attribute of actuality. Saying that Pegasus is not actual is on a par, logically, with saying that the Parthenon is not red; in either case we are saying something about an entity whose being is unquestioned.

Wyman, by the way, is one of those philosophers who have united in ruining the good old word 'exist'. Despite his espousal of unactualized possibles, he limits the word 'existence' to actuality – thus preserving an illusion of ontological agreement between himself and us who repudiate the rest of his bloated universe. We have all been prone to say, in our common-sense usage of 'exist', that Pegasus does not exist, meaning simply that there is no such entity at all. If Pegasus existed he would indeed be in space and time, but only because the word 'Pegasus' has spatio-temporal connotations, and not because 'exists' has spatio-temporal connotations. If spatio-temporal reference is lacking when we affirm the existence of the cube root of 27, this is simply because a cube root is not a spatio-temporal kind of thing, and not because we are being ambiguous in our use of 'exist'.[1] However, Wyman, in an ill-conceived effort to appear agreeable, genially grants us the nonexistence of Pegasus and then, contrary to what *we* meant by nonexistence of Pegasus, insists that Pegasus *is*. Existence is one thing, he says, and subsistence is another. The only way I know of coping with this obfuscation of issues is to *give* Wyman the word 'exist'. I'll try not to use it again; I still have 'is'. So much for lexicography; let's get back to Wyman's ontology.

Wyman's overpopulated universe is in many ways unlovely. It offends the aesthetic sense of us who have a taste for desert landscapes, but this is not the worst of it. Wyman's slum of possibles is a breeding ground for disorderly elements. Take, for instance, the possible fat man in that doorway; and, again, the possible bald man in that doorway. Are they the same possible man, or two possible men? How do we decide? How many possible men are there in that doorway? Are there more possible thin ones than fat ones? How many of them are alike? Or would their being alike make them one? Are no *two* possible things alike? Is this the same as saying that it is impossible for two things to be alike? Or, finally, is the concept of identity simply inapplicable to unactualized possibles? But what sense can be found in talking of entities which cannot meaningfully be said to be identical with themselves and distinct from one another? These elements are well-nigh incorrigible. By a Fregean therapy of individual concepts, some effort might be made at rehabilitation; but I feel we'd do better simply to clear Wyman's slum and be done with it.

Possibility, along with the other modalities of necessity and impossibility and contingency, raises problems upon which I do not mean to imply that we should turn our backs. But we can at least limit modalities to whole statements. We may impose the adverb 'possibly' upon a statement as a whole, and we may well worry about the semantical analysis of such usage; but little real advance in such analysis is to be hoped for in expanding our universe to include so-called *possible entities*. I suspect that the main motive for this expansion is simply the old notion that Pegasus, for example, must be because otherwise it would be nonsense to say even that he is not.

Still, all the rank luxuriance of Wyman's universe of possibles would seem to come to naught when we make a slight change in the example and speak not of Pegasus but of the round square cupola on Berkeley College. If, unless Pegasus were, it would be nonsense to say that he is not, then by the same token, unless the round square cupola on Berkeley College were, it would be nonsense to say that it is not. But, unlike Pegasus, the round square cupola on Berkeley College cannot be admitted even as an unactualized *possible*. Can we drive Wyman now to admitting also a realm of unactualizable impossibles? If so, a good many embarrassing questions could be asked about them. We might hope even to trap Wyman in contradictions, by getting him to admit that certain of these entities are at once round and square. But the wily Wyman chooses the other horn of the dilemma and concedes that it is nonsense to say that the round square cupola on Berkeley College is not. He says that the phrase 'round square cupola' is meaningless.

Wyman was not the first to embrace this alternative. The doctrine of the meaninglessness of contradictions runs away back. The tradition survives, moreover, in writers who seem to share none of Wyman's motivations. Still, I wonder whether the first temptation to such a doctrine may not have been substantially the motivation which we have observed in Wyman. Certainly the doctrine has no intrinsic appeal; and it has led its devotees to such quixotic extremes as that of challenging the method of proof by *reductio ad absurdum* – a challenge in which I sense a *reductio ad absurdum* of the doctrine itself.

Moreover, the doctrine of meaninglessness of contradictions has the severe methodological drawback that it makes it impossible, in principle, ever to devise an effective test of what is meaningful and what is not. It would be forever impossible for us to devise systematic ways of deciding whether a string of signs made sense – even to us individually, let alone other people – or not. For it follows from a discovery in mathematical logic, due to Church,[2] that there can be no generally applicable test of contradictoriness.

I have spoken disparagingly of Plato's beard, and hinted that it is tangled. I have dwelt at length on the inconveniences of putting up with it. It is time to think about taking steps.

Russell, in his theory of so-called singular descriptions, showed clearly how we might meaningfully use seeming names without supposing that there be the entities allegedly named. The names to which Russell's theory directly applies are complex descriptive names such as 'the author of *Waverley*', 'the present King of France', 'the round square cupola on Berkeley College'. Russell analyzes such phrases systematically as fragments of the whole sentences in which they occur. The sentence 'The author of *Waverley* was a poet', for example, is explained as a whole as meaning 'Someone (better: something) wrote *Waverley* and was a poet, and nothing else wrote *Waverley*'. (The point of this added clause is to affirm the uniqueness which is implicit in the word 'the', in '*the* author of *Waverley*'.) The sentence 'The round square cupola on Berkeley College is pink' is explained as 'Something is round and square and is a cupola on Ber-

keley College and is pink, and nothing else is round and square and a cupola on Berkeley College'.

The virtue of this analysis is that the seeming name, a descriptive phrase, is paraphrased *in context* as a so-called incomplete symbol. No unified expression is offered as an analysis of the descriptive phrase, but the statement as a whole which was the context of that phrase still gets its full quota of meaning – whether true or false.

The unanalyzed statement 'The author of *Waverley* was a poet' contains a part, 'the author of *Waverley*', which is wrongly supposed by McX and Wyman to demand objective reference in order to be meaningful at all. But in Russell's translation, 'Something wrote *Waverley* and was a poet and nothing else wrote *Waverley*', the burden of objective reference which had been put upon the descriptive phrase is now taken over by words of the kind that logicians call bound variables, variables of quantification: namely, words like 'something', 'nothing', 'everything'. These words, far from purporting to be names specifically of the author of *Waverley*, do not purport to be names at all; they refer to entities generally, with a kind of studied ambiguity peculiar to themselves. These quantificational words or bound variables are, of course a basic part of language, and their meaningfulness, at least in context, is not to be challenged. But their meaningfulness in no way presupposes there being either the author of *Waverley* or the round square cupola on Berkeley College or any other specifically preassigned objects.

Where descriptions are concerned, there is no longer any difficulty in affirming or denying being. 'There *is* the author of *Waverley*' is explained by Russell as meaning 'Someone (or, more strictly, something) wrote *Waverley* and nothing else wrote *Waverley*'. 'The author of *Waverley* is not' is explained, correspondingly, as the alternation 'Either each thing failed to write *Waverley* or two or more things wrote *Waverley*'. This alternation is false, but meaningful; and it contains no expression purporting to name the author of *Waverley*. The statement 'The round square cupola on Berkeley College is not' is analyzed in similar fashion. So the old notion that statements of nonbeing defeat themselves goes by the board. When a statement of being or nonbeing is analyzed by Russell's theory of descriptions, it ceases to contain any expression which even purports to name the alleged entity whose being is in question, so that the meaningfulness of the statement no longer can be thought to presuppose that there be such an entity.

Now what of 'Pegasus'? This being a word rather than a descriptive phrase, Russell's argument does not immediately apply to it. However, it can easily be made to apply. We have only to rephrase 'Pegasus' as a description, in any way that seems adequately to single out our idea; say, 'the winged horse that was captured by Bellerophon'. Substituting such a phrase for 'Pegasus', we can then proceed to analyze the statement 'Pegasus is', or 'Pegasus is not', precisely on the analogy of Russell's analysis of 'The author of *Waverley* is' and 'The author of *Waverley* is not'.

In order thus to subsume a one-word name or alleged name such as 'Pegasus' under Russell's theory of description, we must, of course, be able first to translate the word into a description. But this is no real restriction. If the notion of Pegasus had been so obscure or so basic a one that no pat translation into a descriptive phrase had offered itself along familiar lines, we could still have availed ourselves of the following artificial and trivial-seeming device: we could have appealed to the *ex hypothesi* unanalyzable, irreducible attribute of *being Pegasus*, adopting, for its expression, the verb 'is-Pegasus', or 'pegasizes'. The noun 'Pegasus' itself could then be treated as derivative, and identified after all with a description: 'the thing that is-Pegasus', 'the thing that pegasizes'.

If the importing of such a predicate as 'pegasizes' seems to commit us to recognizing that there is a corresponding attribute, pegasizing, in Plato's heaven or in the minds of men, well and good. Neither we nor Wyman nor McX have been contending, thus far, about the being or nonbeing of universals, but rather about that of Pegasus. If in terms of pegasizing we can interpret the noun 'Pegasus' as a description subject to Russell's theory of descriptions, then we have disposed of the old notion that Pegasus cannot be said not to be without presupposing that in some sense Pegasus is.

Our argument is now quite general. McX and Wyman supposed that we could not meaningfully affirm a statement of the form 'So-and-so is not', with a simple or descriptive singular noun in place of 'so-and-so', unless so-and-so is. This supposition is now seen to be quite generally groundless, since the singular noun in question can always be expanded into a singular description, trivially or otherwise, and then analyzed out *à la* Russell.

We commit ourselves to an ontology containing numbers when we say there are prime numbers larger than a million; we commit ourselves to an ontology containing centaurs when we say there are

centaurs; and we commit ourselves to an ontology containing Pegasus when we say Pegasus is. But we do not commit ourselves to an ontology containing Pegasus or the author of *Waverley* or the round square cupola on Berkeley College when we say that Pegasus or the author of *Waverley* or the cupola in question is *not*. We need no longer labor under the delusion that the meaningfulness of a statement containing a singular term presupposes an entity named by the term. A singular term need not name to be significant.

An inkling of this might have dawned on Wyman and McX even without benefit of Russell if they had only noticed – as so few of us do – that there is a gulf between *meaning* and *naming* even in the case of a singular term which is genuinely a name of an object. The following example from Frege will serve.[3] The phrase 'Evening Star' names a certain large physical object of spherical form, which is hurtling through space some scores of millions of miles from here. The phrase 'Morning Star' names the same thing, as was probably first established by some observant Babylonian. But the two phrases cannot be regarded as having the same meaning; otherwise that Babylonian could have dispensed with his observations and contented himself with reflecting on the meanings of his words. The meanings, then, being different from one another, must be other than the named object, which is one and the same in both cases.

Confusion of meaning with naming not only made McX think he could not meaningfully repudiate Pegasus; a continuing confusion of meaning with naming no doubt helped engender his absurd notion that Pegasus is an idea, a mental entity. The structure of his confusion is as follows. He confused the alleged *named object* Pegasus with the *meaning* of the word 'Pegasus', therefore concluding that Pegasus must be in order that the word have meaning. But what sorts of things are meanings? This is a moot point; however, one might quite plausibly explain meanings as ideas in the mind, supposing we can make clear sense in turn of the idea of ideas in the mind. Therefore Pegasus, initially confused with a meaning, ends up as an idea in the mind. It is the more remarkable that Wyman, subject to the same initial motivation as McX, should have avoided this particular blunder and wound up with unactualized possibles instead.

Now let us turn to the ontological problem of universals: the question whether there are such entities as attributes, relations, classes, numbers, functions. McX, characteristically enough, thinks

W. V. Quine

there are. Speaking of attributes, he says: 'There are red houses, red roses, red sunsets; this much is prephilosophical common sense in which we must all agree. These houses, roses, and sunsets, then, have something in common; and this which they have in common is all I mean by the attribute of redness.' For McX, thus, there being attributes is even more obvious and trivial than the obvious and trivial fact of there being red houses, roses, and sunsets. This, I think, is characteristic of metaphysics, or at least of that part of metaphysics called ontology: one who regards a statement on this subject as true at all must regard it as trivially true. One's ontology is basic to the conceptual scheme by which he interprets all experiences, even the most commonplace ones. Judged within some particular conceptual scheme – and how else is judgment possible? – an ontological statement goes without saying, standing in need of no separate justification at all. Ontological statements follow immediately from all manner of casual statements of commonplace fact, just as – from the point of view, anyway, of McX's conceptual scheme – 'There is an attribute' follows from 'There are red houses, red roses, red sunsets'.

Judged in another conceptual scheme, an ontological statement which is axiomatic to McX's mind may, with equal immediacy and triviality, be adjudged false. One may admit that there are red houses, roses, and sunsets, but deny, except as a popular and misleading manner of speaking, that they have anything in common. The words 'houses', 'roses', and 'sunsets' are true of sundry individual entities which are houses and roses and sunsets, and the word 'red' or 'red object' is true of each of sundry individual entities which are red houses, red roses, red sunsets; but there is not, in addition, any entity whatever, individual or otherwise, which is named by the word 'redness', nor, for that matter, by the word 'household', 'rosehood', 'sunsethood'. That the houses and roses and sunsets are all of them red may be taken as ultimate and irreducible, and it may be held that McX is no better off, in point of real explanatory power, for all the occult entities which he posits under such names as 'redness'.

One means by which McX might naturally have tried to impose his ontology of universals on us was already removed before we turned to the problem of universals. McX cannot argue that predicates such as 'red' or 'is-red', which we all concur in using, must be regarded as names each of a single universal entity in order that they be meaningful at all. For we have seen that being a name of something is a much more special feature than being meaningful. He cannot even charge us – at least not by *that* argument – with having posited an attribute of pegasizing by our adoption of the predicate 'pegasizes'.

However, McX hits upon a different strategem. 'Let us grant,' he says, 'this distinction between meaning and naming of which you make so much. Let us even grant that "is red", "pegasizes", etc., are not names of attributes. Still, you admit they have meanings. But these *meanings*, whether they are *named* or not, are still universals, and I venture to say that some of them might even be the very things that I call attributes, or something to much the same purpose in the end.'

For McX, this is an unusually penetrating speech; and the only way I know to counter it is by refusing to admit meanings. However, I feel no reluctance toward refusing to admit meanings, for I do not thereby deny that words and statements are meaningful. McX and I may agree to the letter in our classification of linguistic forms into the meaningful and the meaningless, even though McX construes meaningfulness as the *having* (in some sense of 'having') of some abstract entity which he calls a meaning, whereas I do not. I remain free to maintain that the fact that a given linguistic utterance is meaningful (or *significant*, as I prefer to say so as not to invite hypostasis of meanings as entities) is an ultimate and irreducible matter of fact; or, I may undertake to analyze it in terms directly of what people do in the presence of the linguistic utterance in question and other utterance similar to it.

The useful ways in which people ordinarily talk or seem to talk about meanings boil down to two: the *having* of meanings, which is significance, and *sameness* of meaning, or synonymy. What is called *giving* the meaning of an utterance is simply the uttering of a synonym, couched, ordinarily, in clearer language than the original. If we are allergic to meanings as such, we can speak directly of utterances as significant or insignificant, and as synonymous or heteronymous one with another. The problem of explaining these adjectives 'significant' and 'synonymous' with some degree of clarity and rigor – preferably, as I see it, in terms of behavior – is as difficult as it is important.[4] But the explanatory value of special and irreducible intermediary entities called meanings is surely illusory.

Up to now I have argued that we can use singular terms significantly in sentences without presupposing that there are the entities which those terms purport to name. I have argued further that we can use general terms, for example, predicates, without conceding them to be names of abstract entities. I have argued further that we can view utterances as significant, and as synonymous or heteronymous with one another, without countenancing a realm of entities called meanings. At this point McX begins to wonder whether there is any limit at all to our ontological immunity. Does *nothing* we may say commit us to the assumption of universals or other entities which we may find unwelcome?

I have already suggested a negative answer to this question, in speaking of bound variables, or variables of quantification, in connection with Russell's theory of descriptions. We can very easily involve ourselves in ontological commitments by saying, for example, that *there is something* (bound variable) which red houses and sunsets have in common; or that *there is something* which is a prime number larger than a million. But this is, essentially, the *only* way we can involve ourselves in ontological commitments: by our use of bound variables. The use of alleged names is no criterion, for we can repudiate their namehood at the drop of a hat unless the assumption of a corresponding entity can be spotted in the things we affirm in terms of bound variables. Names are, in fact, altogether immaterial to the ontological issue, for I have shown, in connection with 'Pegasus' and 'pegasize', that names can be converted to descriptions, and Russell has shown that descriptions can be eliminated. Whatever we say with the help of names can be said in a language which shuns names altogether. To be assumed as an entity is, purely and simply, to be reckoned as the value of a variable. In terms of the categories of traditional grammar, this amounts roughly to saying that to be is to be in the range of reference of a pronoun. Pronouns are the basic media of reference; nouns might better have been named propronouns. The variables of quantification, 'something', 'nothing', 'everything', range over our whole ontology, whatever it may be; and we are convicted of a particular ontological presupposition if, and only if, the alleged presupposition has to be reckoned among the entities over which our variables range in order to render one of our affirmations true.

We may say, for example, that some dogs are white and not thereby commit ourselves to recognizing either doghood or whiteness as entities. 'Some dogs are white' says that some things that are dogs are white; and, in order that this statement be true, the things over which the bound variable 'something' ranges must include some white dogs, but need not include doghood or whiteness. On the other hand, when we say that some zoological species are cross-fertile, we are committing ourselves to recognizing as entities the several species themselves, abstract though they are. We remain so committed at least until we devise some way of so paraphrasing the statement as to show that the seeming reference to species on the part of our bound variable was an avoidable manner of speaking.[5]

Classical mathematics, as the example of primes larger than a million clearly illustrates, is up to its neck in commitments to an ontology of abstract entities. Thus it is that the great medieval controversy over universals has flared up anew in the modern philosophy of mathematics. The issue is clearer now than of old, because we now have a more explicit standard whereby to decide what ontology a given theory or form of discourse is committed to: a theory is committed to those and only those entities to which the bound variables of the theory must be capable of referring in order that the affirmations made in the theory be true.

Because this standard of ontological presupposition did not emerge clearly in the philosophical tradition, the modern philosophical mathematicians have not on the whole recognized that they were debating the same old problem of universals in a newly clarified form. But the fundamental cleavages among modern points of view on foundations of mathematics do come down pretty explicitly to disagreements as to the range of entities to which the bound variables should be permitted to refer.

The three main medieval points of view regarding universals are designated by historians as *realism*, *conceptualism*, and *nominalism*. Essentially these same three doctrines reappear in twentieth-century surveys of the philosophy of mathematics under the new names *logicism, intuitionism,* and *formalism*.

Realism, as the word is used in connection with the medieval controversy over universals, is the Platonic doctrine that universals or abstract entities have being independently of the mind; the mind may discover them but cannot create them. *Logicism*, represented by Frege, Russell, Whitehead, Church, and Carnap, condones the use of bound variables to refer to abstract entities known and unknown, specifiable and unspecifiable, indiscriminately.

Conceptualism holds that there are universals but they are mind-made. *Intuitionism*, espoused in modern times in one form or another by Poincaré, Brouwer, Weyl, and others, countenances the use of bound variables to refer to abstract entities only when those entities are capable of being cooked up individually from ingredients specified in advance. As Fraenkel has put it, logicism holds that classes are discovered while intuitionism holds that they are invented – a fair statement indeed of the old opposition between realism and conceptualism. This opposition is no mere quibble; it makes an essential difference in the amount of classical mathematics to which one is willing to subscribe. Logicists, or realists, are able on their assumptions to get Cantor's ascending orders of infinity; intuitionists are compelled to stop with the lowest order of infinity, and, as an indirect consequence, to abandon even some of the classical laws of real numbers. The modern controversy between logicism and intuitionism arose, in fact, from disagreements over infinity.

Formalism, associated with the name of Hilbert, echoes intuitionism in deploring the logicist's unbridled recourse to universals. But formalism also finds intuitionism unsatisfactory. This could happen for either of two opposite reasons. The formalist might, like the logicist, object to the crippling of classical mathematics; or he might, like the *nominalists* of old, object to admitting abstract entities at all, even in the restrained sense of mind-made entities. The upshot is the same: the formalist keeps classical mathematics as a play of insignificant notations. This play of notations can still be of utility – whatever utility it has already shown itself to have as a crutch for physicists and technologists. But utility need not imply significance, in any literal linguistic sense. Nor need the marked success of mathematicians in spinning out theorems, and in finding objective bases for agreement with one another's results, imply significance. For an adequate basis for agreement among mathematicians can be found simply in the rules which govern the manipulation of the notations – these syntactical rules being, unlike the notations themselves, quite significant and intelligible.[6]

I have argued that the sort of ontology we adopt can be consequential – notably in connection with mathematics, although this is only an example. Now how are we to adjudicate among rival ontologies? Certainly the answer is not provided by the semantical formula 'To be is to be the value of a variable'; this formula serves rather, conversely, in testing the conformity of a given remark or doctrine to a prior ontological standard. We look to bound variables in connection with ontology not in order to know what there is, but in order to know what a given remark or doctrine, ours or someone else's, *says* there is; and this much is quite properly a problem involving language. But what there is is another question.

In debating over what there is, there are still reasons for operating on a semantical plane. One reason is to escape from the predicament noted at the beginning of this essay: the predicament of my not being able to admit that there are things which McX countenances and I do not. So long as I adhere to my ontology, as opposed to McX's, I cannot allow my bound variables to refer to entities which belong to McX's ontology and not to mine. I can, however, consistently describe our disagreement by characterizing the statements which McX affirms. Provided merely that my ontology countenances linguistic forms, or at least concrete inscriptions and utterances, I can talk about McX's sentences.

Another reason for withdrawing to a semantical plane is to find common ground on which to argue. Disagreement in ontology involves basic disagreement in conceptual schemes; yet McX and I, despite these basic disagreements, find that our conceptual schemes converge sufficiently in their intermediate and upper ramifications to enable us to communicate successfully on such topics as politics, weather, and, in particular, language. Insofar as our basic controversy over ontology can be translated upward into a semantical controversy about words and what to do with them, the collapse of the controversy into question-begging may be delayed.

It is no wonder, then, that ontological controversy should tend into controversy over language. But we must not jump to the conclusion that what there is depends on words. Translatability of a question into semantical terms is no indication that the question is linguistic. To see Naples is to bear a name which, when prefixed to the words 'sees Naples', yields a true sentence; still there is nothing linguistic about seeing Naples.

Our acceptance of an ontology is, I think, similar in principle to our acceptance of a scientific theory, say a system of physics: we adopt, at least insofar as we are reasonable, the simplest conceptual scheme into which the disordered fragments of raw experience can be fitted and arranged. Our ontology is determined once we have fixed upon the over-all conceptual scheme which is to accommodate science in the broadest sense; and the considerations which determine a reasonable construction of any part of that conceptual scheme, for example, the biological or the physical part, are not different in kind from the considerations which determine a reasonable construction of the whole. To whatever extent the adoption of any system of scientific theory may be said to be a matter of language, the same – but no more – may be said of the adoption of an ontology.

But simplicity, as a guiding principle in constructing conceptual schemes, is not a clear and unambiguous idea; and it is quite capable of presenting a double or multiple standard. Imagine, for example, that we have devised the most economical set of concepts adequate to the play-by-play reporting of immediate experience. The entities under this scheme – the values of bound variables – are, let us suppose, individual subjective events of sensation or reflection. We should still find, no doubt, that a physicalistic conceptual scheme, purporting to talk about external objects, offers great advantages in simplifying our over-all reports. By bringing together scattered sense events and treating them as perceptions of one object, we reduce the complexity of our stream of experience to a manageable conceptual simplicity. The rule of simplicity is indeed our guiding maxim in assigning sense-data to objects: we associate an earlier and a later round sensum with the same so-called penny, or with two different so-called pennies, in obedience to the demands of maximum simplicity in our total world-picture.

Here we have two competing conceptual schemes, a phenomenalistic one and a physicalistic one. Which should prevail? Each has its advantages; each has its special simplicity in its own way. Each, I suggest, deserves to be developed. Each may be said, indeed, to be the more fundamental, though in different senses: the one is epistemologically, the other physically, fundamental.

The physical conceptual scheme simplifies our account of experience because of the way myriad scattered sense events come to be associated with single so-called objects; still there is no likelihood that each sentence about physical objects can actually be translated, however deviously and complexly, into the phenomenalistic language. Physical objects are postulated entities which round out and simplify our account of the flux of experience, just as the introduction of irrational numbers simplifies laws of arithmetic. From the point of view of the conceptual scheme of the elementary arithmetic of rational numbers alone, the broader arithmetic of rational and irrational numbers would have the status of a convenient myth, simpler than the literal truth (namely, the arithmetic of rationals) and yet containing that literal truth as a scattered part. Similarly, from a phenomenalistic point of view, the conceptual scheme of physical objects is a convenient myth, simpler than the literal truth and yet containing that literal truth as a scattered part.[7]

Now what of classes or attributes of physical objects, in turn? A platonistic ontology of this sort is, from the point of view of a strictly physicalistic conceptual scheme, as much a myth as that physicalistic conceptual scheme itself is for phenomenalism. This higher myth is a good and useful one, in turn, insofar as it simplifies our account of physics. Since mathematics is an integral part of this higher myth, the utility of this myth for physical science is evident enough. In speaking of it nevertheless as a myth, I echo that philosophy of mathematics to which I alluded earlier under the name of formalism. But an attitude of formalism may with equal justice be adopted toward the physical conceptual scheme, in turn, by the pure aesthete or phenomenalist.

The analogy between the myth of mathematics and the myth of physics is, in some additional and perhaps fortuitous ways, strikingly close. Consider, for example, the crisis which was precipitated in the foundations of mathematics, at the turn of the century, by the discovery of Russell's paradox and other antinomies of set theory. These contradictions had to be obviated by unintuitive, *ad hoc* devices; our mathematical myth-making became deliberate and evident to all. But what of physics? An antinomy arose between the undular and the corpuscular accounts of light; and if this was not as out-and-out a contradiction as Russell's paradox, I suspect that the reason is that physics is not as out-and-out as mathematics. Again, the second great modern crisis in the foundations of mathematics – precipitated in 1931 by Gödel's proof that there are bound to be undecidable statements in arithmetic[8] – has its companion piece in physics in Heisenberg's indeterminacy principle.

In earlier pages I undertook to show that some common arguments in favor of certain ontologies are fallacious. Further, I advanced an explicit standard whereby to decide what the ontological commitments of a theory are. But the question what ontology actually to adopt still stands open, and the obvious counsel is tolerance and an experimental spirit. Let us by all means see how much of the physicalistic conceptual scheme can be reduced to a phenomenalistic one; still, physics also naturally demands pursuing, irreducible *in toto* though it be. Let us see how, or to what degree, natural science may be rendered independent of platonistic mathematics; but let us also pursue mathematics and delve into its platonistic foundations.

From among the various conceptual schemes best suited to these various pursuits, one – the phenomenalistic – claims epistemological priority. Viewed from within the phenomenalistic conceptual scheme, the ontologies of physical objects and mathematical objects are myths. The quality of myth, however, is relative; relative, in this case, to the epistemological point of view. This point of view is one among various, corresponding to one among our various interests and purposes.

Notes

1 The impulse to distinguish terminologically between existence as applied to objects actualized somewhere in space-time and existence (or subsistence or being) as applied to other entities arises in part, perhaps, from an idea that the observation of nature is relevant only to questions of existence of the first kind. But this idea is readily refuted by counter-instances such as 'the ratio of the number of centaurs to the number of unicorns'. If there were such a ratio, it would be an abstract entity, viz., a number. Yet it is only by studying nature that we conclude that the number of centaurs and the number of unicorns are both 0 and hence that there is no such ratio.

2 Alonzo Church, 'A note on the *Entscheidungsproblem*', *Journal of Symbolic Logic* 1 (1936), pp. 40–1, 101–2.

3 Gottlob Frege, 'On sense and nominatum', in Herbert Feigl and Wilfrid Sellars (eds), *Readings in Philosophical Analysis* (New York: Appleton-Century-Crofts, 1949), pp. 85–102.

4 See 'Two dogmas of empiricism' and 'The problem of meaning in linguistics', in W. V. Quine, *From a Logical Point of View* (Cambridge, Mass.: Harvard University Press, 1953).

5 W. V. Quine, 'Logic and the reification of universals', in *From a Logical Point of View*.

6 See Nelson Goodman and W. V. Quine, 'Steps toward a constructive nominalism', *Journal of Symbolic Logic* 12 (1947), pp. 105–22.

7 The arithmetical analogy is due to Philip Frank, *Modern Science and its Philosophy* (Cambridge, Mass.: Harvard University Press, 1949), pp. 108f.

8 Kurt Gödel, 'Über formal unertscheidbare Sätze der Principia Mathematica und verwandter Systeme', *Monatshefte für Mathematik und Physik* 38 (1931), pp. 173–98.

2

Empiricism, Semantics, and Ontology

Rudolf Carnap

1   The Problem of Abstract Entities

Empiricists are in general rather suspicious with respect to any kind of abstract entities like properties, classes, relations, numbers, propositions, etc. They usually feel much more in sympathy with nominalists than with realists (in the medieval sense). As far as possible they try to avoid any reference to abstract entities and to restrict themselves to what is sometimes called a nominalistic language, i.e., one not containing such references. However, within certain scientific contexts it seems hardly possible to avoid them. In the case of mathematics, some empiricists try to find a way out by treating the whole of mathematics as a mere calculus, a formal system for which no interpretation is given or can be given. Accordingly, the mathematician is said to speak not about numbers, functions, and infinite classes, but merely about meaningless symbols and formulas manipulated according to given formal rules. In physics it is more difficult to shun the suspected entities, because the language of physics serves for the communication of reports and predictions and hence cannot be taken as a mere calculus. A physicist who is suspicious of abstract entities may perhaps try to declare a certain part of the language of physics as uninterpreted and uninterpretable, that part which

Originally published in *Meaning and Necessity* (Chicago: University of Chicago Press, 1956), pp. 205–21. Reprinted by permission of the University of Chicago Press.

refers to real numbers as space-time coordinates or as values of physical magnitudes, to functions, limits, etc. More probably he will just speak about all these things like anybody else but with an uneasy conscience, like a man who in his everyday life does with qualms many things which are not in accord with the high moral principles he professes on Sundays. Recently the problem of abstract entities has arisen again in connection with semantics, the theory of meaning and truth. Some semanticists say that certain expressions designate certain entities, and among these designated entities they include not only concrete material things but also abstract entities, e.g., properties as designated by predicates and propositions as designated by sentences.[1] Others object strongly to this procedure as violating the basic principles of empiricism and leading back to a metaphysical ontology of the Platonic kind.

It is the purpose of this article to clarify this controversial issue. The nature and implications of the acceptance of a language referring to abstract entities will first be discussed in general; it will be shown that using such a language does not imply embracing a Platonic ontology but is perfectly compatible with empiricism and strictly scientific thinking. Then the special question of the role of abstract entities in semantics will be discussed. It is hoped that the clarification of the issue will be useful to those who would like to accept abstract entities in their work in mathematics, physics, semantics, or any other field; it may help them to overcome nominalistic scruples.

2 Linguistic Frameworks

Are there properties, classes, numbers, propositions? In order to understand more clearly the nature of these and related problems, it is above all necessary to recognize a fundamental distinction between two kinds of questions concerning the existence or reality of entities. If someone wishes to speak in his language about a new kind of entities, he has to introduce a system of new ways of speaking, subject to new rules; we shall call this procedure the construction of a linguistic *framework* for the new entities in question. And now we must distinguish two kinds of questions of existence: first, questions of the existence of certain entities of the new kind *within the framework*; we call them *internal questions*; and second, questions concerning the existence or reality *of the system of entities as a whole*, called *external questions*. Internal questions and possible answers to them are formulated with the help of the new forms of expressions. The answers may be found either by purely logical methods or by empirical methods, depending upon whether the framework is a logical or a factual one. An external question is of a problematic character which is in need of closer examination.

The world of things. Let us consider as an example the simplest kind of entities dealt with in the everyday language: the spatio-temporally ordered system of observable things and events. Once we have accepted the thing language with its framework for things, we can raise and answer internal questions, e.g., "Is there a white piece of paper on my desk?," "Did King Arthur actually live?," "Are unicorns and centaurs real or merely imaginary?," and the like. These questions are to be answered by empirical investigations. Results of observations are evaluated according to certain rules as confirming or disconfirming evidence for possible answers. (This evaluation is usually carried out, of course, as a matter of habit rather than a deliberate, rational procedure. But it is possible, in a rational reconstruction, to lay down explicit rules for the evaluation. This is one of the main tasks of a pure, as distinguished from a psychological, epistemology.) The concept of reality occurring in these internal questions is an empirical, scientific, nonmetaphysical concept. To recognize something as a real thing or event means to succeed in incorporating it into the system of things at a particular space-time position so that it fits together with the other things recognized as real, according to the rules of the framework.

From these questions we must distinguish the external question of the reality of the thing world itself. In contrast to the former questions, this question is raised neither by the man in the street nor by scientists, but only by philosophers. Realists give an affirmative answer, subjective idealists a negative one, and the controversy goes on for centuries without ever being solved. And it cannot be solved because it is framed in a wrong way. To be real in the scientific sense means to be an element of the system; hence this concept cannot be meaningfully applied to the system itself. Those who raise the question of the reality of the thing world itself have perhaps in mind not a theoretical question, as their formulation seems to suggest, but rather a practical question, a matter of a practical decision concerning the structure of our language. We have to make the choice whether or not to accept and use the forms of expression in the framework in question.

In the case of this particular example, there is usually no deliberate choice because we all have accepted the thing language early in our lives as a matter of course. Nevertheless, we may regard it as a matter of decision in this sense: we are free to choose to continue using the thing language or not; in the latter case we could restrict ourselves to a language of sense-data and other 'phenomenal' entities, or construct an alternative to the customary thing language with another structure, or, finally, we could refrain from speaking. If someone decides to accept the thing language, there is no objection against saying that he has accepted the world of things. But this must not be interpreted as if it meant his acceptance of a *belief* in the reality of the thing world; there is no such belief or assertion or assumption, because it is not a theoretical question. To accept the thing world means nothing more than to accept a certain form of language, in other words, to accept rules for forming statements and for testing, accepting, or rejecting them. The acceptance of the thing language leads, on the basis of observations made, also to the acceptance, belief, and assertion of certain statements. But the thesis of the reality of the thing world cannot be among these statements, because it cannot be formulated in the thing language or, it seems, in any other theoretical language.

The decision of accepting the thing language, although itself not of a cognitive nature, will nevertheless usually be influenced by theoretical knowledge, just like any other deliberate decision concerning the acceptance of linguistic or other rules. The purposes for which the language is intended to be used, for instance, the purpose of communicating factual knowledge, will determine which factors are relevant for the decision. The efficiency, fruitfulness, and simplicity of the use of the thing language may be among the decisive factors. And the questions concerning these qualities are indeed of a theoretical nature. But these questions cannot be identified with the question of realism. They are not yes–no questions but questions of degree. The thing language in the customary form works indeed with a high degree of efficiency for most purposes of everyday life. This is a matter of fact, based upon the content of our experiences. However, it would be wrong to describe this situation by saying: "The fact of the efficiency of the thing language is confirming evidence for the reality of the thing world"; we should rather say instead: "This fact makes it advisable to accept the thing language."

The system of numbers. As an example of a system which is of a logical rather than a factual nature let us take the system of natural numbers. The framework for this system is constructed by introducing into the language new expressions with suitable rules: (1) numerals like "five" and sentence forms like "there are five books on the table"; (2) the general term "number" for the new entities, and sentence forms like "five is a number"; (3) expressions for properties of numbers (e.g., "odd," "prime"), relations (e.g., "greater than"), and functions (e.g., "plus"), and sentence forms like "two plus three is five"; (4) numerical variables ("m," "n," etc.) and quantifiers for universal sentences ("for every n, . . .") and existential sentences ("there is an n such that . . .") with the customary deductive rules.

Here again there are internal questions, e.g., "Is there a prime number greater than a hundred?" Here, however, the answers are found, not by empirical investigation based on observations, but by logical analysis based on the rules for the new expressions. Therefore the answers are here analytic, i.e., logically true.

What is now the nature of the philosophical question concerning the existence or reality of numbers? To begin with, there is the internal question which, together with the affirmative answer, can be formulated in the new terms, say, by "There are numbes" or, more explicitly, "There is an n such that n is a number." This statement follows

from the analytic statement "five is a number" and is therefore itself analytic. Moreover, it is rather trivial (in contradistinction to a statement like "There is a prime number greater than a million," which is likewise analytic but far from trivial), because it does not say more than that the new system is not empty; but this is immediately seen from the rule which states that words like "five" are substitutable for the new variables. Therefore nobody who meant the question "Are there numbers?" in the internal sense would either assert or even seriously consider a negative answer. This makes it plausible to assume that those philosophers who treat the question of the existence of numbers as a serious philosophical problem and offer lengthy arguments on either side, do not have in mind the internal question. And, indeed, if we were to ask them: "Do you mean the question as to whether the framework of numbers, *if* we were to accept it, would be found to be empty or not?," they would probably reply: "Not at all; we mean a question *prior* to the acceptance of the new framework." They might try to explain what they mean by saying that it is a question of the ontological status of numbers; the question whether or not numbers have a certain metaphysical characteristic called reality (but a kind of ideal reality, different from the material reality of the thing world) or subsistence or status of "independent entities." Unfortunately, these philosophers have so far not given a formulation of their question in terms of the common scientific language. Therefore our judgment must be that they have not succeeded in giving to the external question and to the possible answers any cognitive content. Unless and until they supply a clear cognitive interpretation, we are justified in our suspicion that their question is a pseudo-question, that is, one disguised in the form of a theoretical question while in fact it is non-theoretical; in the present case it is the practical problem whether or not to incorporate into the language the new linguistic forms which constitute the framework of numbers.

The system of propositions. New variables, "p," "q," etc., are introduced with a rule to the effect that any (declarative) sentence may be substituted for a variable of this kind; this includes, in addition to the sentences of the original thing language, also all general sentences with variables of any kind which may have been introduced into the language. Further, the general term "proposition" is introduced. "p is a proposition" may be defined by "p or not p" (or by any other sentence form yielding only analytic sentences). Therefore, every sentence of the form "... is a proposition" (where any sentence may stand in the place of the dots) is analytic. This holds, for example, for the sentence:

(a) "Chicago is large is a proposition."

(We disregard here the fact that the rules of English grammar require not a sentence but a that–clause as the subject of another sentence; accordingly, instead of (a) we should have to say "That Chicago is large is a proposition".) Predicates may be admitted whose argument expressions are sentences; these predicates may be either extensional (e.g., the customary truth-functional connectives) or not (e.g., modal predicates like "possible," "necessary," etc.). With the help of the new variables, general sentences may be formed, e.g.,

(b) "For every p, either p or not-p."
(c) "There is a p such that p is not necessary and not-p is not necessary."
(d) "There is a p such that p is a proposition."

(c) and (d) are internal assertions of existence. The statement "There are propositions" may be meant in the sense of (d); in this case it is analytic (since it follows from (a)) and even trivial. If, however, the statement is meant in an external sense, then it is noncognitive.

It is important to notice that the system of rules for the linguistic expressions of the propositional framework (of which only a few rules have here been briefly indicated) is sufficient for the introduction of the framework. Any further explanations as to the nature of the propositions (i.e., the elements of the system indicated, the values of the variables "p," "q," etc.) are theoretically unnecessary because, if correct, they follow from the rules. For example, are propositions mental events (as in Russell's theory)? A look at the rules shows us that they are not, because otherwise existential statements would be of the form: "If the mental state of the person in question fulfils such and such conditions, then there is a p such that ...." The fact that no references to mental conditions occur in existential statements (like (c), (d), etc.) shows that propositions are not mental entities. Further, a statement of the existence of linguistic entities (e.g., expressions, classes of expressions, etc.) must contain a reference to a language. The fact that no such reference occurs in the existential statements here shows that propositions are not linguistic entities. The fact that in these statements no reference to a subject (an observer or knower) occurs (nothing like: "There is a p which is necessary for Mr X") shows that the propositions (and their properties, like necessity, etc.) are not subjective. Although characterizations of these or similar kinds are, strictly speaking, unnecessary, they may nevertheless be practically useful. If they are given, they should be understood, not as ingredient parts of the system, but merely as marginal notes with the purpose of supplying to the reader helpful hints or convenient pictorial associations which may make his learning of the use of the expressions easier than the bare system of the rules would do. Such a characterization is analogous to an extra-systematic explanation which a physicist sometimes gives to the beginner. He might, for example, tell him to imagine the atoms of a gas as small balls rushing around with great speed, or the electromagnetic field and its oscillations as quasi-elastic tensions and vibrations in an ether. In fact, however, all that can accurately be said about atoms or the field is implicitly contained in the physical laws of the theories in question.[2]

The system of thing properties. The thing language contains words like "red," "hard," "stone," "house," etc., which are used for describing what things are like. Now we may introduce new variables, say "f," "g," etc., for which those words are substitutable and furthermore the general term "property." New rules are laid down which admit sentences like "Red is a property," "Red is a color," "These two pieces of paper have at least one color in common" (i.e., "There is an f such that f is a color, and ..."). The last sentence is an internal assertion. It is of an empirical, factual nature. However, the external statement, the philosophical statement of the reality of properties – a special case of the thesis of the reality of universals – is devoid of cognitive content.

The systems of integers and rational numbers. Into a language containing the framework of natural numbers we may introduce first the (positive and negative) integers as relations among natural numbers and then the rational numbers as relations among integers. This involves introducing new types of variables, expressions substitutable for them, and the general terms "integer" and "rational number."

The system of real numbers. On the basis of the rational numbers, the real numbers may be introduced as classes of a special kind (segments) of rational numbers (according to the method developed by Dedekind and Frege). Here again a new type of variables is introduced, expressions substitutable for them (e.g., "$\sqrt{2}$"), and the general term "real number."

The spatio-temporal coordinate system for physics. The new entities are the space-time points. Each is an ordered quadruple of four real numbers, called its coordinates, consisting of three spatial and one temporal coordinates. The physical state of a spatio-temporal point or region is described either with the help of qualitative predicates (e.g., "hot") or by ascribing numbers as values of a physical magnitude (e.g., mass, temperature, and the like). The step from the system of things (which does not contain space-time points but only extended objects with spatial and temporal relations between them) to the physical coordinate system is again a matter of decision. Our choice of certain features, although itself not theoretical, is suggested by theoretical knowledge, either logical or factual. For example, the choice of real numbers rather than rational numbers or integers as coordinates is not much influenced by the facts of experience but mainly due to considerations of mathematical simplicity. The restriction to rational coordinates would not be in conflict with any experimental knowledge we have, because the result of any measurement is a rational number. However, it would prevent the use of ordinary geometry (which says, e.g., that the diagonal of a square with the side 1 has the irrational value $\sqrt{2}$) and thus lead to great complications. On the other hand, the decision to use three rather than two or four spatial coordinates is strongly suggested, but still not forced upon us, by the result of common observations. If certain events allegedly observed in spiritualistic séances, e.g., a ball moving out of a sealed box, were confirmed beyond any reasonable doubt, it might seem advisable to use four spatial coordinates. Internal questions are here, in general, empirical questions to be answered by empirical investigations. On the other hand, the external questions of the reality of physical space and physical time are pseudo-questions. A question like "Are there (really) space-time points?" is ambiguous. It may be meant as an internal question; then the affirmative answer is, of course, analytic and trivial. Or it may be meant in the external sense: "Shall we introduce such and such forms into our language?"; in this case it is not a theoretical but a practical question, a matter of decision rather than assertion, and hence the proposed formulation would be misleading. Or finally, it may be meant in the following sense: "Are our experiences such that the use of the linguistic forms in question will be expedient and fruitful?" This is a theoretical question of a factual, empirical nature. But it concerns a matter of degree; therefore a formulation in the form "real or not?" would be inadequate.

3 What does Acceptance of a Kind of Entities Mean?

Let us now summarize the essential characteristics of situations involving the introduction of a new kind of entities, characteristics which are common to the various examples outlined above.

The acceptance of a new kind of entities is represented in the language by the introduction of a framework of new forms of expressions to be used according to a new set of rules. There may be new names for particular entities of the kind in question; but some such names may already occur in the language before the introduction of the new framework. (Thus, for example, the thing language contains certainly words of the type of "blue" and "house" before the framework of properties is introduced; and it may contain words like "ten" in sentences of the form "I have ten fingers" before the framework of numbers is introduced.) The latter fact shows that the occurrence of constants of the type in question – regarded as names of entities of the new kind after the new framework is introduced – is not a sure sign of the acceptance of the new kind of entities. Therefore the introduction of such constants is not to be regarded as an essential step in the introduction of the framework. The two essential steps are rather the following. First, the introduction of a general term, a predicate of higher level, for the new kind of entities, permitting us to say of any particular entity that it belongs to this kind (e.g., "Red is a *property*," "Five is a *number*"). Second, the introduction of variables of the new type. The new entities are values of these variables; the constants (and the closed compound expressions, if any) are substitutable for the variables.[3] With the help of the variables, general sentences concerning the new entities can be formulated.

After the new forms are introduced into the language, it is possible to formulate with their help internal questions and possible answers to them. A question of this kind may be either empirical or logical; accordingly a true answer is either factually true or analytic.

From the internal questions we must clearly distinguish external questions, i.e., philosophical questions concerning the existence or reality of the total system of the new entities. Many philosophers regard a question of this kind as an ontological question which must be raised and answered *before* the introduction of the new language forms. The latter introduction, they believe, is legitimate only if it can be justified by an ontological insight supplying an affirmative answer to the question of reality. In contrast to this view, we take the position that the introduction of the new ways of speaking does not need any theoretical justification because it does not imply any assertion of reality. We may still speak (and have done so) of "the acceptance of the new entities," since this form of speech is customary; but one must keep in mind that this phrase does not mean for us anything more than acceptance of the new framework, i.e., of the new linguistic forms. Above all, it must not be interpreted as referring to an assumption, belief, or assertion of "the reality of the entities." There is no such assertion. An alleged statement of the reality of the system of entities is a pseudo-statement without cognitive content. To be sure, we have to face at this point an important question; but it is a practical, not a theoretical question; it is the question of whether or not to accept the new linguistic forms. The acceptance cannot be judged as being either true or false because it is not an assertion. It can only be judged as being more or less expedient, fruitful, conducive to the aim for which the language is intended. Judgments of this kind supply the motivation for the decision of accepting or rejecting the kind of entities.[4]

Thus it is clear that the acceptance of a linguistic framework must not be regarded as implying a metaphysical doctrine concerning the reality of the entities in question. It seems to me due to a neglect of this important distinction that some contemporary nominalists label the admission of variables of abstract types as "Platonism."[5] This is, to say the least, an extremely misleading terminology. It leads to the absurd consequence that the position of everybody who accepts the language of physics with its real number variables (as a language of communication, not merely as a calculus) would be called Platonistic, even if he is a strict empiricist who rejects Platonic metaphysics.

A brief historical remark may here be inserted. The noncognitive character of the questions which we have called here external questions was recognized and emphasized already by the Vienna Circle under the leadership of Moritz Schlick, the group from which the movement of logical empiricism originated. Influenced by ideas of Ludwig Wittgenstein, the Circle rejected both the thesis of the reality of the external world and the thesis of its irreality as pseudo-statements;[6] the same was the case for both the thesis of the reality of universals (abstract entities, in our present terminology) and the nominalistic thesis that they are not real and that their alleged names are not names of anything but merely *flatus vocis*. (It is obvious that the apparent negation of a pseudo-statement must also be a pseudo-statement.) It is therefore not correct to classify the members of the Vienna Circle as nominalists, as is sometimes done. However, if we look at the basic anti-metaphysical and pro-scientific attitude of most nominalists (and the same holds for many materialists and realists in the modern sense), disregarding their occasional pseudo-theoretical formulations, then it is, of course, true to say that the Vienna Circle was much closer to those philosophers than to their opponents.

4 Abstract Entities in Semantics

The problem of the legitimacy and the status of abstract entities has recently again led to controversial discussions in connection with semantics. In a semantical meaning analysis certain expressions in a language are often said to designate (or name or denote or signify or refer to) certain extra-linguistic entities.[7] As long as physical things or events (e.g., Chicago or Caesar's death) are taken as designata (entities designated), no serious doubts arise. But strong objections have been raised, especially by some empiricists, against abstract entities as designata, e.g., against semantical statements of the following kind:

(1) "The word 'red' designates a property of things."
(2) "The word 'color' designates a property of properties of things."
(3) "The word 'five' designates a number."
(4) "The word 'odd' designates a property of numbers."
(5) "The sentence 'Chicago is large' designates a proposition."

Those who criticize these statements do not, of course, reject the use of the expressions in question, like "red" or "five"; nor would they deny that these expressions are meaningful. But to be meaningful, they would say, is not the same as having a meaning in the sense of an entity designated. They reject the belief, which they regard as implicitly presupposed by those semantic statements, that to each expression of the types in question (adjectives like "red," numerals like "five," etc.) there is a particular real entity to which the expression stands in the relation of designation. This belief is rejected as incompatible with the basic principles of empiricism or of scientific thinking. Derogatory labels like "Platonic realism," "hypostatization," or "'Fido'–Fido principle" are attached to it. The latter is the name given by Gilbert Ryle to the criticized belief, which, in his view, arises by a naïve inference of analogy: just as there is an entity well known to me, viz., my dog Fido, which is designated by the name "Fido," thus there must be for every meaningful expression a particular entity to which it stands in the relation of designation or naming, i.e., the relation exemplified by "Fido"–Fido.[8] The belief criticized is thus a case of hypostatization, i.e., of treating as names expressions which are not names. While "Fido" is a name, expressions like "red," "five," etc. are said not to be names, not to designate anything.

Our previous discussion concerning the acceptance of frameworks enables us now to clarify the situation with respect to abstract entities as designata. Let us take as an example the statement:

(a)   "'Five' designates a number."

The formulation of this statement presupposes that our language L contains the forms of expressions which we have called the framework of numbers, in particular, numerical variables and the general term "number." If L contains these forms, the following is an analytic statement in L:

(b)   "Five is a number."

Further, to make the statement (a) possible, L must contain an expression like "designates" or "is a name of" for the semantic relation of designation. If suitable rules for this term are laid down, the following is likewise analytic:

(c)   "'Five' designates five."

(Generally speaking, any expression of the form "'...' designates..." is an analytic statement provided the term "..." is a constant in an accepted framework. If the latter condition is not fulfilled, the expression is not a statement.) Since (a) follows from (c) and (b), (a) is likewise analytic.

Thus it is clear that *if* someone accepts the framework of numbers, then he must acknowledge (c) and (b) and hence (a) as true statements. Generally speaking, if someone accepts a framework for a certain kind of entities, then he is bound to admit the entities as possible designata. Thus the question of the admissibility of entities of a certain type or of abstract entities in general as designata is reduced to the question of the acceptability of the linguistic framework for those entities. Both the nominalistic critics, who refuse the status of designators or names to expressions like "red," "five," etc., because they deny the existence of abstract entities, and the skeptics, who express doubts concerning the existence and demand evidence for it, treat the question of existence as a theoretical question. They do, of course, not mean the internal question; the affirmative answer to *this* question is analytic and trivial and too obvious for doubt or denial, as we have seen. Their doubts refer rather to the system of entities itself; hence they mean the external question. They believe that only after making sure that there really is a system of entities of the kind in question are we justified in accepting the framework by incorporating the linguistic forms into our language. However, we have seen that the external question is not a theoretical question but rather the practical question whether or not to accept those linguistic forms. This acceptance is not in need of a theoretical justification (except with respect to expediency and fruitfulness), because it does not imply a belief or assertion. Ryle says that the "Fido"–Fido principle is "a grotesque theory." Grotesque or not, Ryle is wrong in calling it a theory. It is rather the practical decision to accept certain frameworks. Maybe Ryle is historically right with respect to those whom he mentions as previous representatives of the principle, viz., John Stuart Mill, Frege, and Russell. If these philosophers regarded the acceptance of a system of entities as a theory, an assertion, they were victims of the same old, metaphysical confusion. But it is certainly wrong to regard *my* semantic method as involving a belief in the reality of abstract entities, since I reject a thesis of this kind as a metaphysical pseudo-statement.

The critics of the use of abstract entities in semantics overlook the fundamental difference between the acceptance of a system of entities and an internal assertion, e.g., an assertion that there are elephants or electrons or prime numbers greater than a million. Whoever makes an internal assertion is certainly obliged to justify it by providing evidence, empirical evidence in the case of electrons, logical proof in the case of the prime numbers. The demand for a theoretical justification, correct in the case of internal assertions, is sometimes wrongly applied to the acceptance of a system of entities. Thus, for example, Ernest Nagel asks for "evidence relevant for affirming with warrant that there are such entities as infinitesimals or propositions."[9] He characterizes the evidence required in these cases – in distinction to the empirical evidence in the case of electrons – as "in the broad sense logical and dialectical." Beyond this no hint is given as to what might be regarded as relevant evidence. Some nominalists regard the acceptance of abstract entities as a kind of superstition or myth, populating the world with fictitious or at least dubious entities, analogous to the belief in centaurs or demons. This shows again the confusion mentioned, because a superstition or myth is a false (or dubious) internal statement.

Let us take as example the natural numbers as cardinal numbers, i.e., in contexts like "Here are three books." The linguistic forms of the framework of numbers, including variables and the general term "number," are generally used in our common language of communication; and it is easy to formulate explicit rules for their use. Thus the logical characteristics of this framework are sufficiently clear (while many internal questions, i.e., arithmetical questions, are, of course, still open). In spite of this, the controversy concerning the external question of the ontological reality of the system of numbers continues. Suppose that one philosopher says: "I believe that there are numbers as real entities. This gives me the right to use the linguistic forms of the numerical framework and to make semantical statements about numbers as designata of numerals." His nominalistic opponent replies: "You are wrong; there are no numbers. The numerals may still be used as meaningful expressions. But they are not names, there are no entities designated by them. Therefore the word 'number' and numerical variables must not be used (unless a way were found to introduce them as merely abbreviating devices, a way of

translating them into the nominalistic thing language)." I cannot think of any possible evidence that would be regarded as relevant by both philosophers, and therefore, if actually found, would decide the controversy or at least make one of the opposite theses more probable than the other. (To construe the numbers as classes or properties of the second level, according to the Frege–Russell method, does, of course, not solve the controversy, because the first philosopher would affirm and the second deny the existence of the system of classes or properties of the second level.) Therefore I feel compelled to regard the external question as a pseudo-question, until both parties to the controversy offer a common interpretation of the question as a cognitive question; this would involve an indication of possible evidence regarded as relevant by both sides.

There is a particular kind of misinterpretation of the acceptance of abstract entities in various fields of science and in semantics that needs to be cleared up. Certain early British empiricists (e.g., Berkeley and Hume) denied the existence of abstract entities on the ground that immediate experience presents us only with particulars, not with universals, e.g., with this red patch, but not with Redness or Color-in-General; with this scalene triangle, but not with Scalene Triangularity or Triangularity-in-General. Only entities belonging to a type of which examples were to be found within immediate experience could be accepted as ultimate constituents of reality. Thus, according to this way of thinking, the existence of abstract entities could be asserted only if one could show either that some abstract entities fall within the given, or that abstract entities can be defined in terms of the types of entity which are given. Since these empiricists found no abstract entities within the realm of sense-data, they either denied their existence, or else made a futile attempt to define universals in terms of particulars. Some contemporary philosophers, especially English philosophers following Bertrand Russell, think in basically similar terms. They emphasize a distinction between the data (that which is immediately given in consciousness, e.g., sense-data, immediately past experiences, etc.) and the constructs based on the data. Existence or reality is ascribed only to the data; the constructs are not real entities; the corresponding linguistic expressions are merely ways of speech not actually designating anything (reminiscent of the nominalists' *flatus vocis*). We shall not criticize here this general conception. (As far as it is a principle of accepting certain entities and not accepting others, leaving aside any ontological, phenomenalistic, and nominalistic pseudo-statements, there cannot be any theoretical objection to it.) But if this conception leads to the view that other philosophers or scientists who accept abstract entities thereby assert or imply their occurrence as immediate data, then such a view must be rejected as a misinterpretation. References to space-time points, the electromagnetic field, or electrons in physics, to real or complex numbers and their functions in mathematics, to the excitatory potential or unconscious complexes in psychology, to an inflationary trend in economics, and the like, do not imply the assertion that entities of these kinds occur as immediate data. And the same holds for references to abstract entities as designata in semantics. Some of the criticisms by English philosophers against such references give the impression that, probably due to the misinterpretaion just indicated, they accuse the semanticist not so much of bad metaphysics (as some nominalists would do) but of bad psychology. The fact that they regard a semantical method involving abstract entities not merely as doubtful and perhaps wrong, but as manifestly absurd, preposterous and grotesque, and that they show a deep horror and indignation against this method, is perhaps to be explained by a misinterpretation of the kind described. In fact, of course, the semanticist does not in the least assert or imply that the abstract entities to which he refers can be experienced as immediately given either by sensation or by a kind of rational intuition. An assertion of this kind would indeed be very dubious psychology. The psychological question as to which kinds of entities do and which do not occur as immediate data is entirely irrelevant for semantics, just as it is for physics, mathematics, economics, etc., with respect to the examples mentioned above.[10]

5 Conclusion

For those who want to develop or use semantical methods, the decisive question is not the alleged ontological question of the existence of abstract entities but rather the question whether the use of abstract linguistic forms or, in technical terms, the use of variables beyond those for things (or phe-

nomenal data) is expedient and fruitful for the purposes for which semantical analyses are made, viz., the analysis, interpretation, clarification, or construction of languages of communication, especially languages of science. This question is here neither decided nor even discussed. It is not a question simply of yes or no, but a matter of degree. Among those philosophers who have carried out semantical analyses and thought about suitable tools for this work, beginning with Plato and Aristotle and, in a more technical way on the basis of modern logic, with C. S. Peirce and Frege, a great majority accepted abstract entities. This does, of course, not prove the case. After all, semantics in the technical sense is still in the initial phases of its development, and we must be prepared for possible fundamental changes in methods. Let us therefore admit that the nominalistic critics may possibly be right. But if so, they will have to offer better arguments than they have so far. Appeal to ontological insight will not carry much weight. The critics will have to show that it is possible to construct a semantical method which avoids all references to abstract entities and achieves by simpler means essentially the same results as the other methods.

The acceptance or rejection of abstract linguistic forms, just as the acceptance or rejection of any other linguistic forms in any branch of science, will finally be decided by their efficiency as instruments, the ratio of the results achieved to the amount and complexity of the efforts required. To decree dogmatic prohibitions of certain linguistic forms instead of testing them by their success or failure in practical use, is worse than futile; it is positively harmful because it may obstruct scientific progress. The history of science shows examples of such prohibitions based on prejudices deriving from religious, mythological, metaphysical, or other irrational sources, which slowed up the developments for shorter or longer periods of time. Let us learn from the lessons of history. Let us grant to those who work in any special field of investigation the freedom to use any form of expression which seems useful to them; the work in the field will sooner or later lead to the elimination of those forms which have no useful function. *Let us be cautious in making assertions and critical in examining them, but tolerant in permitting linguistic forms.*

Notes

1 The terms "sentence" and "statement" are here used synonymously for declarative (indicative, propositional) sentences.

2 In my book *Meaning and Necessity* (Chicago: University of Chicago Press, 1947) I have developed a semantical method which takes propositions as entities designated by sentences (more specifically, as intensions of sentences). In order to facilitate the understanding of the systematic development, I added some informal, extra-systematic explanations concerning the nature of propositions. I said that the term "proposition" "is used neither for a linguistic expression nor for a subjective, mental occurrence, but rather for something objective that may or may not be exemplified in nature.... We apply the term 'proposition' to any entities of a certain logical type, namely, those that may be expressed by (declarative) sentences in a language" (p. 27). After some more detailed discussions concerning the relation between propositions and facts, and the nature of false propositions, I added: "It has been the purpose of the preceding remarks to facilitate the understanding of our conception of propositions. If, however, a reader should find these explanations more puzzling than clarifying, or even unacceptable, he may disregard them" (p. 31) (that is, disregard these extra-systematic explanations, not the whole theory of the propositions as intensions of sentences, as one reviewer understood). In spite of this warning, it seems that some of those readers who were puzzled by the explanations, did not disregard them but thought that by raising objections against them they could refute the theory. This is analogous to the procedure of some laymen who by (correctly) criticizing the ether picture or other visualizations of physical theories, thought they had refuted those theories. Perhaps the discussions in the present paper will help in clarifying the role of the system of linguistic rules for the introduction of a framework for entities on the one hand, and that of extra-systematic explanations concerning the nature of the entities on the other.

3 W. V. Quine was the first to recognize the importance of the introduction of variables as indicating the acceptance of entities. "The ontology to which one's use of language commits him comprises simply the objects that he treats as falling... within the range of values of his variables" (W. V. Quine, "Notes on existence and necessity," *Journal of Philosophy* 40 (1943), pp. 113–27, at p. 118; compare also his "Designation and existence," *Journal of Philosophy* 36 (1939), pp. 702–9, and "On universals," *Journal of Symbolic Logic* 12 (1947), pp. 74–84.

4 For a closely related point of view on these questions see the detailed discussions in Herbert Feigl, "Existential hypotheses," *Philosophy of Science* 17 (1950), pp. 35–62.

5 Paul Bernays, "Sur le platonisme dans les mathématiques," *L'Enseignement math.* 34 (1935), pp. 52–69. W. V. Quine, see previous note and a recent paper "On what there is," this volume, ch. 1, Quine does not acknowledge the distinction which I emphasize above, because according to his general conception there are no sharp boundary lines between logical and factual truth, between questions of meaning and questions of fact, between the acceptance of a language structure and the acceptance of an assertion formulated in the language. This conception, which seems to deviate considerably from customary ways of thinking, will be explained in his article "Semantics and abstract objects," *Proceedings of the American Academy of Arts and Sciences* 80 (1951), pp. 90–6. When Quine in the above article classifies my logicistic conception of mathematics (derived from Frege and Russell) as "platonic realism" (p. 9), this is meant (according to a personal communication from him) not as ascribing to me agreement with Plato's metaphysical doctrine of universals, but merely as referring to the fact that I accept a language of mathematics containing variables of higher levels. With respect to the basic attitude to take in choosing a language form (an "ontology" in Quine's terminology, which seems to me misleading), there appears now to be agreement between us: "the obvious counsel is tolerance and an experimental spirit" (ibid., p. 12).

6 See Rudolf Carnap, *Scheinprobleme in der Philosophie; das Fremdpsychische und der Realismusstreit* (Berlin, 1928); Moritz Schlick, *Positivismus und Realismus*, repr. in *Gesammelte Aufsätze* (Vienna: 1938).

7 See Rudolf Carnap, *Introduction to Semantics* (Cambridge, Mass.: Harvard University Press, 1942); *idem*, *Meaning and Necessity*. The distinction I have drawn in the latter book between the method of the name-relation and the method of intension and extension is not essential for our present discussion. The term "designation" is used in the present article in a neutral way; it may be understood as referring to the name-relation or to the intension-relation or to the extension-relation or to any similar relations used in other semantical methods.

8 Gilbert Ryle, "Meaning and necessity," *Philosophy* 24 (1949), pp. 69–76.

9 Ernest Nagel, review of Rudolf Carnap, *Meaning and Necessity*, 1st edn, *Journal of Philosophy* 45 (1948), pp. 467–72.

10 Wilfrid Sellars, "Acquaintance and description again," *Journal of Philosophy* 46 (1949), pp. 496–504, at pp. 502 f. analyzes clearly the roots of the mistake "of taking the designation relation of semantic theory to be a reconstruction of *being present to an experience*."

3

Existence and Description

Bertrand Russell

1 General Propositions and Existence

I am going to speak today about general propositions and existence. The two subjects really belong
together; they are the same topic, although it might
not have seemed so at the first glance. The propositions and facts that I have been talking about
hitherto have all been such as involved only perfectly definite particulars, or relations, or qualities,
or things of that sort, never involved the sort of
indefinite things one alludes to by such words as
'all', 'some', 'a', 'any', and it is propositions and
facts of that sort that I am coming on to today.

Really all the propositions of the sort that I mean
to talk of today collect themselves into two groups –
the *first* that are about 'all', and the *second* that are
about 'some'. These two sorts belong together;
they are each other's negations. If you say, for
instance, 'All men are mortal', that is the negative
of 'Some men are not mortal'. In regard to general
propositions, the distinction of affirmative and
negative is arbitrary. Whether you are going to
regard the propositions about 'all' as the affirmative
ones and the propositions about 'some' as the negative ones, or vice versa, is purely a matter of taste.
For example, if I say 'I met no one as I came along',
that, on the face of it, you would think is a negative

proposition. Of course, that is really a proposition
about 'all', i.e., 'All men are among those whom I
did not meet'. If, on the other hand, I say 'I met a
man as I came along', that would strike you as
affirmative, whereas it is the negative of 'All men
are among those I did not meet as I came along'.
If you consider such propositions as 'All men
are mortal' and 'Some men are not mortal',
you might say it was more natural to take the
general propositions as the affirmative and the
existence-propositions as the negative, but, simply
because it is quite arbitrary which one is to choose,
it is better to forget these words and to speak only
of general propositions and propositions asserting
existence. All general propositions deny the existence of something or other. If you say 'All men are
mortal', that denies the existence of an immortal
man, and so on.

I want to say emphatically that general propositions are to be interpreted as not involving existence. When I say, for instance, 'All Greeks are
men', I do not want you to suppose that that
implies that there are Greeks. It is to be considered
emphatically as not implying that. That would
have to be added as a separate proposition. If you
want to interpret it in that sense, you will have to
add the further statement 'and there are Greeks'.
That is for purposes of practical convenience. If
you include the fact that there are Greeks, you are
rolling two propositions into one, and it causes
unnecessary confusion in your logic, because the
sorts of propositions that you want are those that do
assert the existence of something and general

'Existence and description' is a new title for lectures V
and VI of 'The Philosophy of Logical Atomism', first published in *The Monist* (1918), and reprinted with permission of the author's estate.

propositions which do not assert existence. If it happened that there were no Greeks, both the proposition that 'All Greeks are men' and the proposition that 'No Greeks are men' would be true. The proposition 'No Greeks are men' is, of course, the proposition 'All Greeks are not-men'. Both propositions will be true simultaneously if it happens that there are no Greeks. All statements about all the members of a class that has no members are true, because the contradictory of any general statement does assert existence and is therefore false in this case. This notion, of course, of general propositions not involving existence is one which is not in the traditional doctrine of the syllogism. In the traditional doctrine of the syllogism, it was assumed that when you have such a statement as 'All Greeks are men', that implies that there are Greeks, and this produced fallacies. For instance, 'All chimeras are animals, and all chimeras breathe flame, therefore some animals breathe flame.' This is a syllogism in Darapti, but that mood of the syllogism is fallacious, as this instance shows. That was a point, by the way, which had a certain historical interest, because it impeded Leibniz in his attempts to construct a mathematical logic. He was always engaged in trying to construct such a mathematical logic as we have now, or rather such a one as Boole constructed, and he was always failing because of his respect for Aristotle. Whenever he invented a really good system, as he did several times, it always brought out that such moods as Darapti are fallacious. If you say 'All A is B and all A is C, therefore some B is C' – if you say this, you incur a fallacy, but he could not bring himself to believe that it was fallacious, so he began again. That shows you that you should not have too much respect for distinguished men.[1]

Now when you come to ask what really is asserted in a general proposition, such as 'All Greeks are men' for instance, you find that what is asserted is the truth of all values of what I call a propositional function. A *propositional function* is simply *any expression containing an undetermined constituent, or several undetermined constituents, and becoming a proposition as soon as the undetermined constituents are determined*. If I say 'x is a man' or 'n is a number', that is a propositional function; so is any formula of algebra, say $(x + y)(x - y) = x^2 - y^2$. A propositional function is nothing, but, like most of the things one wants to talk about in logic, it does not lose its importance through that fact. The only thing really that you can do with a propositional function is to assert either that it is

always true, or that it is sometimes true, or that it is never true. If you take:

'If x is a man, x is mortal',

that is always true (just as much when x is not a man as when x is a man); if you take:

'x is a man',

that is sometimes true; if you take:

'x is a unicorn',

that is never true.

One may call a propositional function

necessary, when it is always true;
possible, when it is sometimes true;
impossible, when it is never true.

Much false philosophy has arisen out of confusing propositional functions and propositions. There is a great deal in ordinary traditional philosophy which consists simply in attributing to propositions the predicates which only apply to propositional functions, and, still worse, sometimes in attributing to individuals predicates which merely apply to propositional functions. This case of *necessary, possible, impossible*, is a case in point. In all traditional philosophy there comes a heading of 'modality', which discusses *necessary, possible*, and *impossible* as properties of propositions, whereas in fact they are properties of propositional functions. Propositions are only true or false.

If you take 'x is x', that is a propositional function which is true whatever 'x' may be, i.e., a necessary propositional function. If you take 'x is a man', that is a possible one. If you take 'x is a unicorn', that is an impossible one.

Propositions can only be true or false, but propositional functions have these three possibilities. It is important, I think, to realize that the whole doctrine of modality only applies to propositional functions, not to propositions.

Propositional functions are involved in ordinary language in a great many cases where one does not usually realize them. In such a statement as 'I met a man', you can understand my statement perfectly well without knowing whom I met, and the actual person is not a constituent of the proposition. You are really asserting there that a certain propositional function is sometimes true, namely the propositional function 'I met x and x is human'. There is at least one value of x for which that is true, and that therefore is a possible propositional function. Whenever you get such words as 'a', 'some', 'all', 'every', it is always a mark of the presence of a propositional function, so that these things are not, so to speak, remote or recondite: they are obvious and familiar.

A propositional function comes in again in such a statement as 'Socrates is mortal', because 'to be mortal' means 'to die at some time or other'. You mean there is a time at which Socrates dies, and that again involves a propositional function, namely, that 't is a time, and Socrates dies at t' is possible. If you say 'Socrates is immortal', that also will involve a propositional function. That means that 'If t is any time whatever, Socrates is alive at time t', if we take immortality as involving existence throughout the whole of the past as well as throughout the whole of the future. But if we take immortality as only involving existence throughout the whole of the future, the interpretation of 'Socrates is immortal' becomes more complete, viz., 'There is a time t, such that if t' is any time later than t, Socrates is alive at t''. Thus when you come to write out properly what one means by a great many ordinary statements, it turns out a little complicated. 'Socrates is mortal' and 'Socrates is immortal' are not each other's contradictories, because they both imply that Socrates exists in time, otherwise he would not be either mortal or immortal. One says, 'There is a time at which he dies', and the other says, 'Whatever time you take, he is alive at that time', whereas the contradictory of 'Socrates is mortal' would be true if there is not a time at which he lives.

An undetermined constituent in a propositional function is called *a variable*.

Existence

When you take any propositional function and assert of it that it is possible, that it is sometimes true, that gives you the fundamental meaning of 'existence'. You may express it by saying that there is at least one value of x for which that propositional function is true. Take 'x is a man'; there is at least one value of x for which this is true. That is what one means by saying that 'There are men', or that 'Men exist'. Existence is essentially a property of a propositional function. It means that that propositional function is true in at least one instance. If you say 'There are unicorns', that will mean that 'There is an x, such that x is a unicorn'. That is

written in phrasing which is unduly approximated to ordinary language, but the proper way to put it would be '(x is a unicorn) is possible'. We have got to have some idea that we do not define, and one takes the idea of 'always true', or of 'sometimes true', as one's undefined idea in this matter, and then you can define the other one as the negative of that. In some ways it is better to take them both as undefined, for reasons which I shall not go into at present. It will be out of this notion of *sometimes*, which is the same as the notion of *possible*, that we get the notion of existence. To say that unicorns exist is simply to say that '(x is a unicorn) is possible'.

It is perfectly clear that when you say 'Unicorns exist', you are not saying anything that would apply to any unicorns there might happen to be, because as a matter of fact there are not any, and therefore if what you say had any application to the actual individuals, it could not possibly be significant unless it were true. You can consider the proposition 'Unicorns exist' and can see that it is false. It is not nonsense. Of course, if the proposition went through the general conception of the unicorn to the individual, it could not be even significant unless there were unicorns. Therefore when you say 'Unicorns exist', you are not saying anything about any individual things, and the same applies when you say 'Men exist'. If you say that 'Men exist, and Socrates is a man, therefore Socrates exists', that is exactly the same sort of fallacy as it would be if you said 'Men are numerous, Socrates is a man, therefore Socrates is numerous', because existence is a predicate of a propositional function, or derivatively of a class. When you say of a propositional function that it is numerous, you will mean that there are several values of x that will satisfy it, that there are more than one; or, if you like to take 'numerous' in a larger sense, more than ten, more than twenty, or whatever number you think fitting. If x, y, and z all satisfy a propositional function, you may say that that proposition is numerous, but x, y, and z severally are not numerous. Exactly the same applies to existence, that is to say that the actual things that there are in the world do not exist, or, at least, that is putting it too strongly, because that is utter nonsense. To say that they do not exist is strictly nonsense, but to say that they do exist is also strictly nonsense.

It is of propositional functions that you can assert or deny existence. You must not run away with the idea that this entails consequences that it does not entail. If I say 'The things that there are in the world exist', that is a perfectly correct state-ment, because I am there saying something about a certain class of things; I say it in the same sense in which I say 'Men exist'. But I must not go on to 'This is a thing in the world, and therefore this exists'. It is there the fallacy comes in, and it is simply, as you see, a fallacy of transferring to the individual that satisfies a propositional function a predicate which only applies to a propositional function. You can see this in various ways. For instance, you sometimes know the truth of an exist-ence-proposition without knowing any instance of it. You know that there are people in Timbuctoo, but I doubt if any of you could give me an instance of one. Therefore you clearly can know existence-propositions without knowing any individual that makes them true. Existence-propositions do not say anything about the actual individual but only about the class or function.

It is exceedingly difficult to make this point clear as long as one adheres to ordinary language, because ordinary language is rooted in a certain feeling about logic, a certain feeling that our pri-meval ancestors had, and as long as you keep to ordinary language you find it very difficult to get away from the bias which is imposed upon you by language. When I say, e.g., 'There is an x such that x is a man', that is not the sort of phrase one would like to use. 'There is an x' is meaningless. What is 'an x' anyhow? There is not such a thing. The only way you can really state it correctly is by inventing a new language *ad hoc*, and making the statement apply straight off to 'x is a man', as when one says '(x is a man) is possible', or invent a special symbol for the statement that 'x is a man' is sometimes true.

I have dwelt on this point because it really is of very fundamental importance. I shall come back to existence in my next lecture: existence as it applies to descriptions, which is a slightly more complic-ated case than I am discussing here. I think an almost unbelievable amount of false philosophy has arisen through not realizing what 'existence' means.

As I was saying a moment ago, a propositional function in itself is nothing: it is merely a schema. Therefore in the inventory of the world, which is what I am trying to get at, one comes to the ques-tion: What is there really in the world that corre-sponds with these things? Of course, it is clear that we have general *propositions*, in the same sense in which we have atomic propositions. For the moment I will include existence-propositions with general propositions. We have such propositions as 'All men are mortal' and 'Some men are Greeks'. But you have not only such *propositions*; you have also such *facts*, and that, of course, is where you get back to the inventory of the world: that, in addition to particular facts, which I have been talking about in previous lectures, there are also general facts and existence-facts; that is to say, there are not merely *propositions* of that sort but also *facts* of that sort. That is rather an important point to realize. You cannot ever arrive at a general fact by inference from particular facts, however numerous. The old plan of complete induction, which used to occur in books, which was always supposed to be quite safe and easy as opposed to ordinary induction, that plan of complete induction, unless it is accompan-ied by at least one general proposition, will not yield you the result that you want. Suppose, for example, that you wish to prove in that way that 'All men are mortal', you are supposed to proceed by complete induction, and say 'A is a man that is mortal', 'B is a man that is mortal', 'C is a man that is mortal', and so on until you finish. You will not be able, in that way, to arrive at the proposition. 'All men are mortal' unless you know when you have finished. That is to say that, in order to arrive by this road at the general proposition 'All men are mortal', you must already have the general propo-sition 'All men are among those I have enumer-ated'. You never can arrive at a general proposition by inference from particular propositions alone. You will always have to have at least one general proposition in your premises. That illustrates, I think, various points. One, which is epistemologi-cal, is that if there is, as there seems to be, know-ledge of general propositions (I mean by that, knowledge of general propositions which is not obtained by inference), because if you can never infer a general proposition except from premises of which one at least is general, it is clear that you can never have knowledge of such propositions by inference unless there is knowledge of some general propositions which is not by inference. I think that the sort of way such knowledge – or rather the belief that we have such knowledge – comes into ordinary life is probably very odd. I mean to say that we do habitually assume general propositions which are exceedingly doubtful; as, for instance, one might, if one were counting up the people in this room, assume that one could see all of them, which is a general proposition, and very doubtful as there may be people under the tables. But, apart from that sort of thing, you do have in any empirical verification of general propositions some kind of assumption that amounts to this, that what you do not see is not there. Of course, you would not put it so strongly as that, but you would assume that, with certain limitations and certain qualifications, if a thing does not appear to your senses, it is not there. That is a general proposition, and it is only through such propositions that you arrive at the ordinary empirical results that one obtains in ordinary ways. If you take a census of the country, for instance, you assume that the people you do not see are not there, provided you search properly and carefully, otherwise your census might be wrong. It is some assumption of that sort which would underline what seems purely empirical. You could not prove empirically that what you do not perceive is not there, because an empirical proof would consist in perceiving, and by hypothesis you do not perceive it, so that any proposition of that sort, if it is accepted, has to be accepted on its own evidence. I only take that as an illustration. There are many other illustrations one could take of the sort of propositions that are commonly assumed, many of them with very little justification.

I come now to a question which concerns logic more nearly, namely, the reasons for supposing that there are general facts as well as general propositions. When we were discussing molecular propositions I threw doubt upon the supposition that there are molecular facts, but I do not think one can doubt that there are general facts. It is perfectly clear, I think, that when you have enumerated all the atomic facts in the world, it is a further fact about the world that those are all the atomic facts there are about the world, and that is just as much an objective fact about the world as any of them are. It is clear, I think, that you must admit general facts as distinct from and over and above particular facts. The same thing applies to 'All men are mortal'. When you have taken all the particular men that there are, and found each one of them severally to be mortal, it is definitely a new fact that all men are mortal; how new a fact, appears from what I said a moment ago, that it could not be inferred from the mortality of the several men that there are in the world. Of course, it is not so difficult to admit what I might call existence-facts – such facts as 'There are men', 'There are sheep', and so on. Those, I think, you will readily admit as separate and distinct facts over and above the atomic facts I spoke of before. Those facts have got to come into the inventory of the world, and in that way propositional functions come in as involved in the study of general facts. I do not profess to know what the right analysis of general facts is. It is an exceedingly difficult question, and one which I should very much like to see studied. I am sure that, although the convenient technical treatment is by means of propositional functions, that is not the whole of the right analysis. Beyond that I cannot go.

There is one point about whether there are molecular facts. I think I mentioned, when I was saying that I did not think there were disjunctive facts, that a certain difficulty does arise in regard to general facts. Take 'All men are mortal'. That means:

> ' "x is a man" implies
> "x is a mortal" whatever
> x may be.'

You can see at once that it is a hypothetical proposition. It does not imply that there are any men, nor who are men, and who are not; it simply says that if you have anything which is a man, that thing is mortal. As Mr Bradley has pointed out in the second chapter of his *Principles of Logic*, 'Trespassers will be prosecuted' may be true even if no one trespasses, since it means merely that, *if* any one trespasses, he will be prosecuted. It comes down to this that

> ' "x is a man" implies "x is a mortal" is always true'

is a fact. It is perhaps a little difficult to see how that can be true if one is going to say that ' "Socrates is a man" implies "Socrates is a mortal" ' is not itself a fact, which is what I suggested when I was discussing disjunctive facts. I do not feel sure that you could not get round that difficulty. I only suggest it as a point which should be considered when one is denying that there are molecular facts, since, if it cannot be got round, we shall have to admit molecular facts.

Now I want to come to the subject of *completely general* propositions and propositional functions. By those I mean propositions and propositional functions that contain only variables and nothing else at all. This covers the whole of logic. Every logical proposition consists wholly and solely of variables, though it is not true that every proposition consisting wholly and solely of variables is logical. You can consider stages of generalizations as, e.g.,

'Socrates loves Plato'

'x loves Plato'

'x loves y'

'$x R y$.'

There you have been going through a process of successive generalization. When you have got to xRy, you have got a schema consisting only of variables, containing no constants at all, the pure schema of dual relations, and it is clear that any proposition which expresses a dual relation can be derived from xRy by assigning values to x and R and y. So that that is, as you might say, the pure form of all those propositions. I mean by the form of a proposition that which you get when for every single one of its constituents you substitute a variable. If you want a different definition of the form of a proposition, you might be inclined to define it as the class of all those propositions that you can obtain from a given one by substituting other constituents for one or more of the constituents the proposition contains. E.g., in 'Socrates loves Plato', you can substitute somebody else for Socrates, somebody else for Plato, and some other verb for 'loves'. In that way there are a certain number of propositions which you can derive from the proposition 'Socrates loves Plato', by replacing the constituents of that proposition by other constituents, so that you have there a certain class of propositions, and those propositions all have a certain form, and one can, if one likes, say that the form they all have is the class consisting of all of them. That is rather a provisional definition, because as a matter of fact, the idea of form is more fundamental than the idea of class. I should not suggest that as a really good definition, but it will do provisionally to explain the sort of thing one means by the form of a proposition. The form of a proposition is that which is in common between any two propositions of which the one can be obtained from the other by substituting other constituents for the original ones. When you have got down to those formulas that contain only variables, like xRy, you are on the way to the sort of thing that you can assert in logic.

To give an illustration, you know what I mean by the domain of a relation: I mean all the terms that have that relation to something. Suppose I say: 'xRy implies that x belongs to the domain of R', that would be a proposition of logic and is one that contains only variables. You might think it contains such words as 'belong' and 'domain', but that is an error. It is only the habit of using ordinary language that makes those words appear. They are not really

there. That is a proposition of pure logic. It does not mention any particular thing at all. This is to be understood as being asserted whatever x and R and y may be. All the statements of logic are of that sort.

It is not a very easy thing to see what are the constituents of a logical proposition. When one takes 'Socrates loves Plato', 'Socrates' is a constituent, 'loves' is a constituent, and 'Plato' is a constituent. Then you turn 'Socrates' into x, 'loves' into R, and 'Plato' into y. x and R and y are nothing, and they are not constituents, so it seems as though all the propositions of logic were entirely devoid of constituents. I do not think that can quite be true. But then the only other thing you can seem to say is that the *form* is a constituent, that propositions of a certain form are always true: that *may* be the right analysis, though I very much doubt whether it is.

There is, however, just this to observe, viz., that the form of a proposition is never a constituent of that proposition itself. If you assert that 'Socrates loves Plato', the form of that proposition is the form of the dual relation, but this is not a constituent of the proposition. If it were, you would have to have that constituent related to the other constituents. You will make the form much too substantial if you think of it as really one of the things that have that form, so that the form of a proposition is certainly not a constituent of the proposition itself. Nevertheless it may possibly be a constituent of general statements about propositions that have that form, so I think it is *possible that* logical propositions might be interpreted as being about forms.

I can only say, in conclusion, as regards the constituents of logical propositions, that it is a problem which is rather new. There has not been much opportunity to consider it. I do not think any literature exists at all which deals with it in any way whatever, and it is an interesting problem.

I just want now to give you a few illustrations of propositions which can be expressed in the language of pure variables but are not propositions of logic. Among the propositions that are propositions of logic are included all the propositions of pure mathematics, all of which cannot only be expressed in logical terms but can also be deduced from the premisses of logic, and therefore they are logical propositions. Apart from them there are many that can be expressed in logical terms, but cannot be proved from logic, and are certainly not propositions that form part of logic. Suppose you take such a proposition as: 'There is at least one thing in the world'. That is a proposition that you can express in logical terms. It will mean, if you like, that the propositional function '$x = x$' is a possible one. That is a proposition, therefore, that you can express in logical terms; but you cannot know from logic whether it is true or false. So far as you do know it, you know it empirically, because there might happen not to be a universe, and then it would not be true. It is merely an accident, so to speak, that there is a universe. The proposition that there are exactly 30,000 things in the world can also be expressed in purely logical terms, and is certainly not a proposition of logic but an empirical proposition (true or false), because a world containing more than 30,000 things and a world containing fewer than 30,000 things are both possible, so that if it happens that there are exactly 30,000 things, that is what one might call an accident and is not a proposition of logic. There are again two propositions that one is used to in mathematical logic, namely, the multiplicative axiom and the axiom of infinity. These also can be expressed in logical terms, but cannot be proved or disproved by logic. In regard to the axiom of infinity, the impossibility of logical proof or disproof may be taken as certain, but in the case of the multiplicative axiom, it is perhaps still open to some degree to doubt. Everything that is a proposition of logic has got to be in some sense or other like a tautology. It has got to be something that has some peculiar quality, which I do not know how to define, that belongs to logical propositions and not to others. Examples of typical logical propositions are:

'If p implies q and q implies r, then p implies r.'
'If all a's are b's and all b's are c's, then all a's are c's.'
'If all a's are b's, and x is an a, then x is a b.'

Those are propositions of logic. They have a certain peculiar quality which marks them out from other propositions and enables us to know them a priori. But what exactly that characteristic is, I am not able to tell you. Although it is a necessary characteristic of logical propositions that they should consist solely of variables, i.e., that they should assert the universal truth, or the sometimes-truth, of a propositional function consisting wholly of variables – although that is a necessary characteristic, it is not a sufficient one. I am sorry that I have had to leave so many problems unsolved. I always have to make this apology, but the world really is rather puzzling and I cannot help it.

Discussion

Question: Is there any word you would substitute for 'existence' which would give existence to individuals? Are you applying the word 'existence' to two ideas, or do you deny that there are two ideas?

Mr Russell: No, there is not an idea that will apply to individuals. As regards the actual things there are in the world, there is nothing at all you can say about them that in any way corresponds to this notion of existence. It is a sheer mistake to say that there is anything analogous to existence that you can say about them. You get into confusion through language, because it is a perfectly correct thing to say 'All the things in the world exist', and it is so easy to pass from this to 'This exists because it is a thing in the world'. There is no sort of point in a predicate which could not conceivably be false. I mean, it is perfectly clear that, if there were such a thing as this existence of individuals that we talk of, it would be absolutely impossible for it not to apply, and that is the characteristic of a mistake.

2 Descriptions and Incomplete Symbols

I am proposing to deal this time with the subject of descriptions, and what I call 'incomplete symbols', and the existence of described individuals. You will remember that last time I dealt with the existence of *kinds* of things, what you mean by saying 'There are men' or 'There are Greeks' or phrases of that sort, where you have an existence which may be plural. I am going to deal today with an existence which is asserted to be singular, such as 'The man with the iron mask existed' or some phrase of that sort, where you have some object described by the phrase 'The so-and-so' in the singular, and I want to discuss the analysis of propositions in which phrases of that kind occur.

There are, of course, a great many propositions very familiar in metaphysics which are of that sort: 'I exist' or 'God exists' or 'Homer existed', and other such statements are always occurring in metaphysical discussions, and are, I think, treated in ordinary metaphysics in a way which embodies a simple logical mistake that we shall be concerned with today, the same sort of mistake that I spoke of last week in connection with the existence of kinds of things. One way of examining a proposition of that sort is to ask yourself what would happen if it were false. If you take such a proposition as

'Romulus existed', probably most of us think that Romulus did not exist. It is obviously a perfectly significant statement, whether true or false, to say that Romulus existed. If Romulus himself entered into our statement, it would be plain that the statement that he did not exist would be nonsense, because you cannot have a constituent of a proposition which is nothing at all. Every constituent has got to be there as one of the things in the world, and therefore if Romulus himself entered into the propositions that he existed or that he did not exist, both these propositions could not only not be true, but could not be even significant, unless he existed. That is obviously not the case, and the first conclusion one draws is that, although it *looks* as if Romulus were a constituent of that proposition, that is really a mistake. Romulus does not occur in the proposition 'Romulus did not exist'.

Suppose you try to make out what you do mean by that proposition. You can take, say, all the things that Livy has to say about Romulus, all the properties he ascribes to him, including the only one probably that most of us remember, namely, the fact that he was called 'Romulus'. You can put all this together, and make a propositional function saying '*x* has such-and-such properties', the properties being those you find enumerated in Livy. There you have a propositional function, and when you say that Romulus did not exist you are simply saying that that propositional function is never true, that it is impossible in the sense I was explaining last time, i.e., that there is no value of *x* that makes it true. That reduces the non-existence of Romulus to the sort of non-existence I spoke of last time, where we had the non-existence of unicorns. But it is not a *complete* account of this kind of existence or non-existence, because there is one other way in which a described individual can fail to exist, and that is where the description applies to more than one person. You cannot, e.g., speak of '*The* inhabitant of London', not because there are none, but because there are so many.

You see, therefore, that this proposition 'Romulus existed' or 'Romulus did not exist' does introduce a propositional function, because the name 'Romulus' is not really a name but a sort of truncated description. It stands for a person who did such-and-such things, who killed Remus, and founded Rome, and so on. It is short for that description; if you like, it is short for 'the person who was called "Romulus"'. If it were really a name, the question of existence could not arise, because a name has got to name something or it is

not a name, and if there is no such person as Romulus, there cannot be a name for that person who is not there, so that this single word 'Romulus' is really a sort of truncated or telescoped description, and if you think of it as a name, you will get into logical errors. When you realize that it is a description, you realize therefore that any proposition about Romulus really introduces the propositional function embodying the description, as (say) '*x* was called "Romulus"'. That introduces you at once to a propositional function, and when you say 'Romulus did not exist', you mean that this propositional function is not true for one value of *x*.

There are two sorts of descriptions, what one may call 'ambiguous descriptions', when we speak of '*a* so-and-so', and what one may call 'definite descriptions', when we speak of '*the* so-and-so' (in the singular). Instances are:

Ambiguous: A man, a dog, a pig, a Cabinet Minister.
Definite: The man with the iron mask.
　　　　　The last person who came into this room.
　　　　　The only Englishman who ever occupied the Papal See.
　　　　　The number of the inhabitants of London.
　　　　　The sum of 43 and 34.

(It is not necessary for a description that it should describe an individual: it may describe a predicate or a relation or anything else.)

It is phrases of that sort, definite descriptions, that I want to talk about today. I do not want to talk about ambiguous descriptions, as what there was to say about them was said last time.

I want you to realize that the question whether a phrase is a definite description turns only upon its form, not upon the question whether there is a definite individual so described. For instance, I should call 'The inhabitant of London' a definite description, although it does not in fact describe any definite individual.

The first thing to realize about a definite description is that it is not a name. We will take 'The author of *Waverley*'. That is a definite description, and it is easy to see that it is not a name. A name is a simple symbol (i.e., a symbol which does not have any parts that are symbols), a simple symbol used to designate a certain particular or by extension an object which is not a particular but is treated for the moment as if it were, or is falsely believed to be a particular, such as a person. This sort of phrase, 'The author of *Waverley*', is not a name because it is a complex symbol. It contains parts which *are* symbols. It contains four words, and the meanings of those four words are already fixed, and they have fixed the meaning of 'The author of *Waverley*' in the only sense in which that phrase does have any meaning. In that sense, its meaning is already determinate, i.e., there is nothing arbitrary or conventional about the meaning of that whole phrase, when the meanings of 'the', 'author', 'of', and '*Waverley*' have already been fixed. In that respect, it differs from 'Scott', because when you have fixed the meaning of all the other words in the language, you have done nothing toward fixing the meaning of the name 'Scott'. That is to say, if you understand the English language, you would understand the meaning of the phrase 'The author of *Waverley*' if you had never heard it before, whereas you would not understand the meaning of 'Scott' if you had never heard the word before because to know the meaning of a name is to know who it is applied to.

You sometimes find people speaking as if descriptive phrases were names, and you will find it suggested, e.g., that such a proposition as 'Scott is the author of *Waverley*' really asserts that 'Scott' and the 'the author of *Waverley*' are two names for the same person. That is an entire delusion; first of all, because 'the author of *Waverley*' is not a name, and, secondly, because, as you can perfectly well see, if that were what is meant, the proposition would be one like 'Scott is Sir Walter', and would not depend upon any fact except that the person in question was so called, because a name is what a man is called. As a matter of fact, Scott was the author of *Waverley* at a time when no one called him so, when no one knew whether he was or not, and the fact that he was the author was a physical fact, the fact that he sat down and wrote it with his own hand, which does not have anything to do with what he was called. It is in no way arbitrary. You cannot settle by any choice of nomenclature whether he is or is not to be the author of *Waverley*, because in actual fact he chose to write it and you cannot help yourself. That illustrates how 'the author of *Waverley*' is quite a different thing from a name. You can prove this point very clearly by formal arguments. In 'Scott is the author of *Waverley*' the 'is', of course, expresses identity, i.e., the entity whose name is Scott is identical with the author of *Waverley*. But, when I say 'Scott is mortal', this 'is' is the 'is' of predication, which is quite different from the 'is' of identity. It is a mistake to interpret 'Scott is mortal' as meaning 'Scott is identical with one among mortals', because (among

other reasons) you will not be able to say what 'mortals' are except by means of the propositional function '*x* is mortal', which brings back the 'is' of predication. You cannot reduce the 'is' of predication to the other 'is'. But the 'is' in 'Scott is the author of *Waverley*' is the 'is' of identity and not of predication.[2]

If you were to try to substitute for 'the author of *Waverley*' in that proposition any name whatever, say '*c*', so that the proposition becomes 'Scott is *c*', then if '*c*' is a name for anybody who is not Scott, that proposition would become false, while if, on the other hand, '*c*' is a name for Scott, then the proposition will become simply a tautology. It is at once obvious that if '*c*' were 'Scott' itself, 'Scott is Scott' is just a tautology. But if you take any other name which is just a name for Scott, then if the name is being used *as* a name and not as a description, the proposition will still be a tautology. For the name itself is merely a means of pointing to the thing, and does not occur in what you are asserting, so that if one thing has two names, you make exactly the same assertion whichever of the two names you use, provided they are really names and not truncated descriptions.

So there are only two alternatives. If '*c*' is a name, the proposition 'Scott is *c*' is either false or tautologous. But the proposition 'Scott is the author of *Waverley*' is neither, and therefore is not the same as any proposition of the form 'Scott is *c*', where '*c*' is a name. That is another way of illustrating the fact that a description is quite a different thing from a name.

I should like to make clear what I was saying just now, that if you substitute another name in place of 'Scott' which is also a name of the same individual, say, 'Scott is Sir Walter', then 'Scott' and 'Sir Walter' are being used as names and not as descriptions, your proposition is strictly a tautology. If one asserts 'Scott is Sir Walter', the way one would mean it would be that one was using the names as descriptions. One would mean that the person called 'Scott' is the person called 'Sir Walter', and 'the person called "Scott"' is a description, and so is 'the person called "Sir Walter".' So that would not be a tautology. It would mean that the person called 'Scott' is identical with the person called 'Sir Walter'. But if you are using both as names, the matter is quite different. You must observe that the name does not occur in that which you assert when you use the name. The name is merely that which is a means of expressing what it is you are trying to assert, and when I say 'Scott wrote *Waverley*', the name 'Scott' does not occur in the thing I am asserting. The thing I am asserting is about the person, not about the name. So if I say 'Scott is Sir Walter', using these two names *as* names, neither 'Scott' nor 'Sir Walter' occurs in what I am asserting, but only the person who has these names, and thus what I am asserting is a pure tautology.

It is rather important to realize this about the two different uses of names or of any other symbols: the one when you are talking about the symbol and the other when you are using it *as* a symbol, as a means of talking about something else. Normally, if you talk about your dinner, you are not talking about the word 'dinner' but about what you are going to eat, and that is a different thing altogether. The ordinary use of words is as a means of getting through to things, and when you are using words in that way the statement 'Scott is Sir Walter' is a pure tautology, exactly on the same level as 'Scott is Scott'.

That brings me back to the point that when you take 'Scott is the author of *Waverley*' and you substitute for 'the author of *Waverley*' a name in the place of a description, you get necessarily either a tautology or a falsehood – a tautology if you substitute 'Scott' or some other name for the same person, and a falsehood if you substitute anything else. But the proposition itself is neither a tautology nor a falsehood, and that shows you that the proposition 'Scott is the author of *Waverley*' is a different proposition from any that can be obtained if you substitute a name in the place of 'the author of *Waverley*'. That conclusion is equally true of any other proposition in which the phrase 'the author of *Waverley*' occurs. If you take any proposition in which that phrase occurs and substitute for that phrase a proper name, whether that name be 'Scott' or any other, you will get a different proposition. Generally speaking, if the name that you substitute is 'Scott', your proposition, if it was true before will remain true, and if it was false before will remain false. But it is a *different* proposition. It is not *always* true that it will remain true or false, as may be seen by the example: 'George IV wished to know if Scott was the author of *Waverley*'. It is not true that George IV wished to know if Scott was Scott. So it is even the case that the truth or the falsehood of a proposition is sometimes changed when you substitute a name of an object for a description of the same object. But in any case it is always a different proposition when you substitute a name for a description.

Identity is a rather puzzling thing at first sight. When you say 'Scott is the author of *Waverley*', you are half-tempted to think there are two people, one of whom is Scott and the other the author of *Waverley*, and they happen to be the same. That is obviously absurd, but that is the sort of way one is always tempted to deal with identity.

When I say 'Scott is the author of *Waverley*' and that 'is' expresses identity, the reason that identity can be asserted there truly and without tautology is just the fact that the one is a name and the other a description. Or they might both be descriptions. If I say 'The author of *Waverley* is the author of *Marmion*', that, of course, asserts identity between two descriptions.

Now the next point that I want to make clear is that when a description (when I say 'description' I mean, for the future, a *definite* description) occurs in a proposition, there is no constituent of that proposition corresponding to that description as a whole. In the true analysis of the proposition, the description is broken up and disappears. That is to say, when I say 'Scott is the author of *Waverley*', it is a wrong analysis of that to suppose that you have there three constituents, 'Scott', 'is', and 'the author of *Waverley*'. That, of course, is the sort of way you might think of analysing. You might admit that 'the author of *Waverley*' was complex and could be further cut up, but you might think the proposition could be split into those three bits to begin with. That is an entire mistake. 'The author of *Waverley*' is not a constituent of the proposition at all. There is no constituent really there corresponding to the descriptive phrase. I will try to prove that to you now.

The first and most obvious reason is that you can have significant propositions denying the existence of 'the so-and-so'. 'The unicorn does not exist.' 'The greatest finite number does not exist.' Propositions of that sort are perfectly significant, are perfectly sober, true, decent propositions, and that could not possibly be the case if the unicorn were a constituent of the proposition, because plainly it could not be a constituent as long as there were not any unicorns. Because the constituents of propositions, of course, are the same as the constituents of the corresponding facts, and since it is a fact that the unicorn does not exist, it is perfectly clear that the unicorn is not a constituent of that fact, because if there were any fact of which the unicorn was a constituent, there would be a unicorn, and it would not be true that it did not exist. That applies in this case of descriptions particularly. Now since it is possible for 'the so-and-so' not to exist and yet for propositions in which 'the so-and-so' occurs to be significant and even true, we must try to see what is meant by saying that the so-and-so does exist.

The occurrence of tense in verbs is an exceedingly annoying vulgarity due to our preoccupation with practical affairs. It would be much more agreeable if they had no tense, as I believe is the case in Chinese, but I do not know Chinese. You ought to be able to say 'Socrates exists in the past', 'Socrates exists in the present' or 'Socrates exists in the future', or simply 'Socrates exists', without any implication of tense, but language does not allow that, unfortunately. Nevertheless, I am going to use language in this tenseless way: when I say 'The so-and-so exists', I am not going to mean that it exists in the present or in the past or in the future, but simply that it exists, without implying anything involving tense.

'The author of *Waverley* exists': there are two things required for that. First of all, what is 'the author of *Waverley*'? It is the person who wrote *Waverley*, i.e., we are coming now to this, that you have a propositional function involved, viz., '*x* writes *Waverley*', and the author of *Waverley* is the person who writes *Waverley*, and in order that the person who writes *Waverley* may exist, it is necessary that this propositional function should have two properties:

1 It must be true for *at least* one *x*.
2 It must be true for *at most* one *x*.

If nobody had ever written *Waverley*, the author could not exist, and if two people had written it, *the* author could not exist. So that you want these two properties, the one that it is true for at least one *x*, and the other that it is true for at most one *x*, both of which are required for existence.

The property of being true for at least one *x* is the one we dealt with last time: what I expressed by saying that the propositional function is *possible*. Then we come on to the second condition, that it is true for at most one *x*, and that you can express in this way: 'If *x* and *y* wrote *Waverley*, then *x* is identical with *y*, whatever *x* and *y* may be.' That says that at most one wrote it. It does not say that anybody wrote *Waverley* at all, because if nobody had written it, that statement would still be true. It only says that at most one person wrote it.

The first of these conditions for existence fails in the case of the unicorn, and the second in the case of the inhabitant of London.

We can put these two conditions together and get a portmanteau expression including the meaning of both. You can reduce them both down to this: that '("*x* wrote *Waverley*" is equivalent to "*x* is *c*" whatever *x* may be) is possible in respect of *c*'. That is as simple, I think, as you can make the statement.

You see, that means to say that there is some entity *c*, we may not know what it is, which is such that when *x* is *c*, it is true that *x* wrote *Waverley*, and when *x* is not *c*, it is not true that *x* wrote *Waverley*, which amounts to saying that *c* is the only person who wrote *Waverley*; and I say there is a value of *c* which makes that true. So that this whole expression, which is a propositional function about *c*, is *possible* in respect of *c* (in the sense explained last time).

That is what I mean when I say that the author of *Waverley* exists. When I say 'The author of *Waverley* exists', I mean that there is an entity *c* such that '*x* wrote *Waverley*' is true when *x* is *c*, and is false when *x* is not *c*. 'The author of *Waverley*' as a constituent has quite disappeared there, so that when I say 'The author of *Waverley* exists', I am not saying anything about the author of *Waverley*. You have instead this elaborate to-do with propositional functions, and 'the author of *Waverley*' has disappeared. That is why it is possible to say significantly 'The author of *Waverley* did not exist'. It would not be possible if 'the author of *Waverley*' were a constituent of propositions in whose verbal expression this descriptive phrase occurs.

The fact that you can discuss the proposition 'God exists' is a proof that 'God', as used in that proposition, is a description and not a name. If 'God' were a name, no question as to existence could arise.

I have now defined what I mean by saying that a thing described exists. I have still to explain what I mean by saying that a thing described has a certain property. Supposing you want to say 'The author of *Waverley* was human', that will be represented thus: '("*x* wrote *Waverley*" is equivalent to "*x* is *c*" whatever *x* may be, and *c* is human) is possible with respect to *c*.'

You will observe that what we gave before as the meaning of 'The author of *Waverley* exists' is part of this proposition. It is part of any proposition in which 'the author of *Waverley*' has what I call a 'primary occurrence'. When I speak of a 'primary occurrence', I mean that you are not having a proposition about the author of *Waverley* occurring as a part of some larger proposition, such as

'I believe that the author of *Waverley* was human' or 'I believe that the author of *Waverley* exists'. When it is a primary occurrence, i.e., when the proposition concerning it is not just part of a larger proposition, the phrase which we defined as the meaning of 'The author of *Waverley* exists' will be part of that proposition. If I say the author of *Waverley* was human, or a poet, or a Scotsman, or whatever I say about the author of *Waverley* in the way of a primary occurrence, always this statement of his existence is part of the proposition. In that sense all these propositions that I make about the author of *Waverley* imply that the author of *Waverley* exists. So that any statement in which a description has a primary occurrence implies that the object described exists. If I say 'The present King of France is bald', that implies that the present King of France exists. If I say, 'The present King of France has a fine head of hair', that also implies that the present King of France exists. Therefore unless you understand how a proposition containing a description is to be denied, you will come to the conclusion that it is not true either that the present King of France is bald or that he is not bald, because if you were to enumerate all the things that are bald you would not find him there, and if you were to enumerate all the things that are not bald, you would not find him there either. The only suggestion I have found for dealing with that on conventional lines is to suppose that he wears a wig. You can only avoid the hypothesis that he wears a wig by observing that the denial of the proposition 'The present King of France is bald' will not be 'The present King of France is not bald', if you mean by that 'There is such a person as the King of France and that person is not bald'. The reason for this is that when you state that the present King of France is bald, you say 'There is a *c* such that *c* is now King of France and *c* is bald', and the denial is not 'There is a *c* such that *c* is now King of France and *c* is not bald'. It is more complicated. It is: 'Either there is not a *c* such that *c* is now King of France, or, if there is such a *c*, then *c* is not bald.' Therefore you see that, if you want to deny the proposition. 'The present King of France is bald', you can do it by denying that he exists, instead of by denying that he is bald. In order to deny this statement that the present King of France is bald, which is a statement consisting of two parts, you can proceed by denying either part. You can deny the one part, which would lead you to suppose that the present King of France exists but is not bald, or the other part,

which will lead you to the denial that the present King of France exists; and either of those two denials will lead you to the falsehood of the proposition 'The present King of France is bald'. When you say 'Scott is human', there is no possibility of a double denial. The only way you can deny 'Scott is human' is by saying 'Scott is not human'. But where a descriptive phrase occurs, you do have the double possibility of denial.

It is of the utmost importance to realize that 'the so-and-so' does not occur in the analysis of propositions in whose verbal expression it occurs; that when I say 'The author of *Waverley* is human', 'the author of *Waverley*' is not the subject of that proposition, in the sort of way that Scott would be if I said 'Scott is human', using 'Scott' as a name. I cannot emphasize sufficiently how important this point is, and how much error you get into in metaphysics if you do not realize that when I say 'The author of *Waverley* is human', that is not a proposition of the same form as 'Scott is human'. It does not contain a constituent 'the author of *Waverley*'. The importance of that is very great for many reasons, and one of them is this question of existence. As I pointed out to you last time, there is a vast amount of philosophy that rests upon the notion that existence is, so to speak, a property that you can attribute to things, and that the things that exist have the property of existence and the things that do not exist do not. That is rubbish, whether you take kinds of things, or individual things described. When I say, e.g., 'Homer existed', I am meaning by 'Homer' some description, say 'the author of the Homeric poems', and I am asserting that those poems were written by one man, which is a very doubtful proposition; but if you could get hold of the actual person who did actually write those poems (supposing there was such a person), to say of him that he existed would be uttering nonsense, not a falsehood but nonsense, because it is only of persons described that it can be significantly said that they exist. Last time I pointed out the fallacy in saying 'Men exist, Socrates is a man, therefore Socrates exists'. When I say 'Homer exists, this is Homer, therefore this exists', that is a fallacy of the same sort. It is an entire mistake to argue: 'This is the author of the Homeric poems and the author of the Homeric poems exists, therefore this exists'. It is only where a prepositional function comes in that existence may be significantly asserted. You can assert 'The so-and-so exists', meaning that there is just one *c* which has those properties, but when you get hold of a *c* that has them, you cannot say of this *c* that it exists, because that is nonsense: it is not false, but it has no meaning at all.

So the individuals that there are in the world do not exist, or rather it is nonsense to say that they exist and nonsense to say that they do not exist. It is not a thing you can say when you have named them, but only when you have described them. When you say 'Homer exists', you mean 'Homer' is a description which applies to something. A description when it is fully stated is always of the form 'the so-and-so'.

The sort of things that are like these descriptions in that they occur in words in a proposition, but are not in actual fact constituents of the proposition rightly analysed, things of that sort I call 'incomplete symbols'. There are a great many sorts of incomplete symbols in logic, and they are sources of a great deal of confusion and false philosophy, because people get misled by grammar. You think that the proposition 'Scott is mortal' and the proposition 'The author of *Waverley* is mortal' are of the same form. You think that they are both simple propositions attributing a predicate to a subject. That is an entire delusion: one of them is (or rather might be), and one of them is not. These things, like 'the author of *Waverley*', which I call incomplete symbols, are things that have absolutely no meaning whatsoever in isolation, but merely acquire a meaning in a context. 'Scott' taken as a name has a meaning all by itself. It stands for a certain person, and there it is. But 'the author of *Waverley*' is not a name, and does not all by itself mean anything at all, because

when it is rightly used in propositions, those propositions do not contain any constituent corresponding to it.

There are a great many other sorts of incomplete symbols besides descriptions. These are classes, which I shall speak of next time, and relations taken in extension, and so on. Such aggregations of symbols are really the same thing as what I call 'logical fictions', and they embrace practically all the familiar objects of daily life: tables, chairs, Piccadilly, Socrates, and so on. Most of them are either classes, or series, or series of classes. In any case they are all incomplete symbols; i.e., they are aggregations that only have a meaning in use, and do not have any meaning in themselves.

It is important, if you want to understand the analysis of the world, or the analysis of facts, or if you want to have any idea what there really is in the world, to realize how much of what there is in phraseology is of the nature of incomplete symbols. You can see that very easily in the case of 'the author of *Waverley*' because 'the author of *Waverley*' does not stand simply for Scott, nor for anything else. If it stood for Scott, 'Scott is the author of *Waverley*' would be the same proposition as 'Scott is Scott', which it is not, since George IV wished to know the truth of the one and did not wish to know the truth of the other. If 'the author of *Waverley*' stood for anything other than Scott, 'Scott is the author of *Waverley*' would be false, which it is not. Hence you have to conclude that 'the author of *Waverley*' does not, in isolation, really stand for anything at all; and that is the characteristic of incomplete symbols.

Notes

1 Cf. Louis Couturat, *La Logique de Leibniz* (Paris: F. Alean, 1901).

2 The confusion of these two meanings of 'is' is essential to the Hegelian conception of identity- in-difference.

4

Referring to Nonexistent Objects

Terence Parsons

This paper has three parts. In part I I'm going to argue that there's a big difference between the way English speakers treat empty singular terms and the way they treat singular terms that refer to objects that don't exist. That is, the data of linguistic behavior suggest that referring to something that doesn't exist is very different from failing to refer to anything at all. Most Anglo-American philosophers haven't believed in nonexistent objects, and so they've generally tried to treat singular terms which refer to nonexistent objects as if they were singular terms which fail to refer to anything at all. And I think that that is wrong; I'm going to argue that it's wrong in part I of the paper.

In part II of the paper I'm going to describe for you a theory about nonexistent objects. I think people are generally opposed to nonexistent objects because they don't understand them, and because such objects have gotten a bad press from people like Russell and Quine, people who argue very eloquently. But I think that if we had a better understanding of nonexistent objects, then we wouldn't be persuaded by these arguments against them. So I am trying to bring about such an understanding by sketching a theory about nonexistent objects. The present paper only contains a *sketch* of such a theory; a more comprehensive development will be given elsewhere.[1]

Originally published in *Theory and Decision* 11 (1979), pp. 95–110. Copyright © by Reidel Publishing Company. Reprinted by permission of Kluwer Academic Publishers.

Finally, in part III I'm going to sketch a theory of singular terms. According to this theory, some of these terms will refer to existing objects, some of them will refer to nonexistent objects, and some of them just won't refer at all.

Part 1: Referring to Nonexistent Objects isn't Failing to Refer

The first point I'd like to make is that people behave differently when they fail to refer than when they refer to something that doesn't exist – that is, they react differently when they realize what they've done in each case. I'm going to give you two conversations. In each conversation there are two characters, *A* and *B*, plus one outsider. In the first conversation speaker *B* plays the devil's advocate; you're supposed to find speaker *A*'s reactions normal.

> *A*: "The man in the doorway over there looks pretty silly."
>
> *Outsider*: "But there is no man in the doorway over there."
>
> *A*: (*Looks again*) "Oh! I thought there was; I was wrong."
>
> *B*: "Does he look anything like your department chairman?"
>
> *A*: "Who?"
>
> *B*: "The man in the doorway over there."
>
> *A*: "There isn't any man there; I was mistaken about that."

B: "Well, he doesn't exist, but he's there, isn't he?"

A: "Look, I was talking about a guy who exists; that is I thought I was, but I was wrong, I wasn't talking about anybody. I can't tell you what 'he' looks like because there's no 'he' to describe."

Now that was supposed to be a case of failure of reference. The speaker was trying to refer to someone, but he just made a mistake and failed to do so. When confronted with questions about the object he was referring to he treats the questions as spurious (i.e., he does this once he realizes his mistake). Now here's another case:

A: "The unicorn I dreamed about last night looked pretty silly."

Outsider: "But there are no unicorns."

A: "So what?"

Outsider: "Well there aren't any unicorns, so there couldn't be any such thing as the unicorn you dreamed about last night, so 'it' couldn't possibly have looked silly."

A: "Come on, it's not a real unicorn, it's one I dreamed about."

B: "Did it look anything like your department chairman?"

A: "No, actually it looked a little bit like my hairdresser."

In this conversation speaker *A* rejects the contention that he had failed to refer to anything, though he grants that what he is referring to doesn't exist. And he treats questions about it as perfectly reasonable. Some philosophers would criticize *A* for this; they'll say that he should have rejected the questions. But that won't work. The question was reasonable, and it *had* an answer, which *A* communicated to *B*.

Now I know what many of you are thinking: sure, *A* managed to communicate some information to *B*, but did he do it by referring to a nonexistent object? The grammatical form of the English sentences being used suggests yes, but as Russell, and the early Wittgenstein, and Carnap, and Ryle, and Quine, and Chisholm, and half the rest of the philosophical world have been telling us for ages now, you can't trust the "surface" grammatical form of a sentence to reveal what's really going on. Since there aren't any nonexistent objects to be referred to, *A*'s sentences must have a different logical form than their grammatical form suggests. And what we need to do to account for

what's going on is merely to show how to *paraphrase A*'s sentences in such a way that we eliminate the *apparent* reference to an unreal object.

Well I hate to be a spoilsport, but, as various people have pointed out, there's one major flaw in this idea: nobody knows how to produce the paraphrases. It hasn't been done. None of you know how to do it either. So here's the situation: speakers of English act as if they sometimes refer to nonexistent objects. We either have to take this at face value or explain it away. Nobody knows how to explain it away.

I've tried to illustrate the situation with reference to a couple of lifelike conversations. If you're willing to supply the lifelike contexts yourselves, there are lots of other examples. You are all probably willing to assert each of the following sentences:

(1) Ironically, a certain fictional detective (namely, Sherlock Holmes) is much more famous than any real detective, living or dead.

(2) Certain Greek gods were also worshipped by the Romans, though they called them by different names. For example, the Romans worshipped Zeus, though they called him "Jupiter."

(3) Any good modern criminologist knows much more about chemical analysis than Sherlock Holmes knew.

(4) Pegasus is the winged horse of Greek mythology.

(5) Pegasus is not the chief Greek deity; Zeus is.

I suggest that you are not only willing to assert these sentences, but you are also prepared to treat the singular terms in them as if they referred; you are willing to "refer back" to previous utterances of "Zeus" with pronouns, and you do not treat questions about the chief Roman deity as spurious; many of them you're willing to answer.

Of course, I certainly haven't shown that all of this apparent reference to the nonexistent *can't* be paraphrased away. But some of the best minds have been trying for over fifty years now, without success. Maybe it's time to stop beating our heads against that wall. Besides, there's another wall that's more fun.

Part 2: A Quasi-Meinongian View

Alexius Meinong is perhaps the most infamous believer in nonexistent objects. The theory to be sketched here was inspired by him, though I think there are ways in which it diverges from his views.[2]

I am going to assume that no two existing objects have exactly the same properties. This is not so much an assumption about the paucity of existing objects as it is an assumption about the variety of properties; in particular I assume that for any existing object there is at least one property (and probably many) that it has and that no other existing object has. Anyway, given this assumption, there's a natural one–one correlation between real, existing objects and certain non-empty sets of properties. For example, Madame Curie is a real object, and correlated with her is the set of properties that she has:

Madame Curie $\{p: \text{Madame Curie has } p\}$

Now, make a list of all existing objects. Correlated with each one is a set of properties – the set of all the properties it has:

REAL OBJECTS	SETS OF PROPERTIES
0_1	$\{p: 0_1 \text{ has } p\}$
0_2	$\{p: 0_2 \text{ has } p\}$
.	.
.	.
.	.
0_α	$\{p: 0_\alpha \text{ has } p\}$

The left-hand list now exhausts the ontology that people like Russell, Quine, Frege, and most of us find acceptable; the existing objects constitute all there is. But the theory now being presented says that there's a *lot* more, and it goes like this. It's not clear how to continue the left-hand list (that's our goal), but you can easily see how to continue the right-hand list – just write down any other non-empty set of properties. For example, write down:

$$\{\text{goldenness, mountainhood,} \dots\}$$

filling in whatever properties for the dots that you like. Now the theory under discussion says that for any such set in the right-hand list, there is correlated with it exactly one object. So write in "$0_{\alpha+1}$" in the left-hand list:

$0_{\alpha+1}$	$\{\text{goldenness, mountainhood,} \dots\}$

The object $0_{\alpha+1}$ can't be an existing object, because it has the properties goldenness and mountainhood – it's a gold mountain – and there aren't any real gold mountains. But, as Meinong pointed out, that

doesn't stop there from being *unreal* gold mountains; although certain narrow-minded people object to this, that's just because they're prejudiced! (He called this 'the prejudice in favor of the actual.')

It's clear how to extend the right-hand list – just include *any* set of properties that isn't already there. Corresponding to each such set is a unique object, and vice versa – i.e., each object appears only once in the left-hand list. The two lists extend our original correlation, so that it is now a correlation between *all* objects and the sets of properties that they have.

Actually we can dispense with talk of lists and correlations and present the theory in a more direct manner in terms of two principles. For reasons that will become apparent shortly, let me call the properties I have been discussing *nuclear* properties. The principles are:

1   No two objects (real *or* unreal) have exactly the same nuclear properties.
2   For any set of nuclear properties, some object has all of the properties in that set and no other nuclear properties.

Principle 2 does most of the work; it's a sort of "comprehension" principle for objects. Notice that principle 2 does not require that objects be "logically closed"; e.g., an object may have the property of being blue and the property of being square without having the property of being blue-and-square. This lack of logical closure is important in certain applications of the theory, particularly applications to fictional objects and objects in dreams.[3]

Many nonexistent objects will be *incomplete*. By calling an object 'complete,' I mean that for any nuclear property, the object either has that property or it has its negation. This characterization presupposes that it makes sense to talk of the 'negation" of a nuclear property in a somewhat unusual sense. The assumption is that for any nuclear property, p, there is another nuclear property, q, which (necessarily) is had by all and only those *existing* objects which don't have p, and which I call the *negation* of p. The negation of a nuclear property, p, will *not* be a property that any object has if and only if it does not have p, for *no* nuclear property fits that description (by principle 2 any nuclear property, q, is such that some object has both p and q).[4]

Given this account of nuclear property negation, all existing objects are complete. Some nonexistent objects are complete too, but some aren't. Consider the object whose sole nuclear properties are goldenness and mountainhood. It does not have the property of blueness, nor does it have the property of nonblueness either; I will say that it is *indeterminate* with respect to blueness. That object will in fact be indeterminate with respect to every nuclear property except goldenness and mountainhood. (The object in question *may* be the one that Meinong was referring to when he used the words "the gold mountain"; whether this is so or not involves questions of textual interpretation that I am unsure about.)

Completeness is different from logical closure. Consider the set of properties got by taking all of my properties and replacing "hazel-eyed" by "non-hazel-eyed." According to principle 2 there is an object which has the resulting properties and no others. This object will be complete, but it will not be logically closed. For example, it has brown-hairedness and it has non-hazel-eyedness, but it does not have the nuclear property of being both-brown-haired-and-non-hazel-eyed.

To get an object which is logically closed yet incomplete, add to "the gold mountain" all nuclear properties that are entailed by goldenness and mountainhood. Then it will have, e.g., the property of either-being-located-in-North-America-or-not-being-located-in-North-America, but it will not have either of those disjuncts; it will be indeterminate with respect to being located in North America.

Some objects are impossible. By calling an object, *x*, *possible*, I mean that it is possible that there exists an object which has all of *x*'s nuclear properties (and perhaps more besides).[5] All existing objects are automatically possible objects by this definition. And some unreal ones are too, e.g., "the gold mountain." But consider the object whose sole nuclear properties are roundness and squareness (this may be Meinong's famous "round square"). This is an impossible object, since there could not be an *existing* object which has both of these properties. Still, as Meinong pointed out, that doesn't prevent there from being an impossible object which has them.

Principles 1 and 2 yield a theory that has an important virtue: they not only tell us that there are nonexistent objects, they also in part tell us *what* nonexistent objects there are, and they tell us what properties they have. *Nuclear* properties anyway, which brings us to the following point:

Not all predicates can stand for nuclear properties.

Take "exists." In the theory I've sketched, if we allowed "exists" to stand for a nuclear property, there would be trouble. Because, suppose it did stand for a nuclear property, existence. Now consider this set of properties:

{goldenness, mountainhood, existence}

If existence were a nuclear property, then there would be an object correlated with this set of properties; call it "the existent gold mountain." Then the existent gold mountain would turn out to have the property existence; that is, the existent gold mountain would exist. But that's just false.

Initially we were troubled by there being a gold mountain; Meinong placated us by pointing out that it's only an unreal object, it doesn't exist. But in the case of the *existent* gold mountain, this option doesn't seem open. Conclusion: "exists," at least as it is used above, does *not* stand for a nuclear property. I'll call "exists" an *extranuclear* predicate, and in general I'll divide predicates into two categories, those which stand for nuclear properties, which I'll call nuclear predicates, and the others, which I'll call extranuclear.

Which are which? First, here are some examples:

NUCLEAR PREDICATES:
"is blue," "is tall," "kicked Socrates," "was kicked by Socrates," "kicked somebody," "is golden," "is a mountain," . . .

EXTRANUCLEAR PREDICATES:

Ontological:	"exists," "is mythical," "is fictional," . . .
Modal:	"is possible," "is impossible," . . .
Intentional:	"is thought about by Meinong," "is worshipped by someone," . . .
Technical:	"is complete," . . .

I'd like to emphasize that this division of predicates into nuclear and extranuclear is not peculiar to Meinong at all, it's an old and familiar one. People like Frege and Russell distinguish predicates that stand for properties of individuals from those that don't. The extranuclear predicates listed above are mostly ones that Frege and Russell have been telling us all along do not stand for properties of individuals. For example, is "exists" a predicate? Some people say flatly "no." Frege tells us that it is a predicate, but not a predicate of individuals; it's a higher-order predicate, a predicate of concepts. Likewise, we all know that "is possible" is either not a predicate at all, or it's a predicate not of individuals but of propositions or sentences. With the intentional predicates we're not sure *what* to say, but we are sure that there's trouble in supposing them to be properties of individuals.

Our historical situation yields a very rough kind of decision procedure for telling whether a predicate is nuclear or extranuclear. It's this: if everyone agrees that the predicate stands for an ordinary property of individuals, then it's a nuclear predicate, and it stands for a nuclear property. On the other hand, if everyone agrees that it doesn't stand for an ordinary property of individuals (for whatever reason), or if there's a history of controversy about whether it stands for a property of individuals, then it's an extranuclear predicate, and it does not stand for a nuclear property.

Of course, this "decision procedure" is a very imperfect one. Probably its main virtue is to give us enough clear cases of nuclear and extranuclear predicates for us to develop an intuitive feel for the distinction, so that we can readily classify new cases. I find that I have such a feel, and that other people pick it up quite readily, and even those who are skeptical about the viability of the distinction seem to agree about which predicates are supposed to be which.

The theory itself will help by putting severe constraints on what can be nuclear. For example, it is a thesis of the theory that no nuclear property, F, satisfies:

$$(\exists X) \, (X \text{ is a set of nuclear properties } \& \, F \notin X \\ \& \, (x) \, (x \text{ has every member of } X \supset x \text{ has } F)).$$

This is because if F is nuclear and $F \notin X$, then the object which has exactly those nuclear properties in X has every member of X without having F. For similar reasons, no nuclear property, F, satisfies:

$$(\exists X) \, (X \text{ is a set of nuclear properties } \& \, F \notin X \\ \& \, (x) \, (x \text{ has every member of } X \supset x \text{ lacks } F)).$$

If we make some minimal assumptions about nuclear properties, then these principles will show that lots of properties are extranuclear. For example, suppose that we assume the following to be nuclear: being a unicorn, being a ball bearing, being round, being square. Then we can show that all of the paradigm extranuclear predicates listed above are indeed extranuclear. For example, for $F = $ existence, pick as X the unit set of being a unicorn. Every object that has every member of X,

i.e., every object that is a unicorn, lacks existence. So existence is extranuclear. For each of the following choices of F, the corresponding choice of X can be used in one of the above theses to show that F is extranuclear:[6]

F	X
is mythical, is fictional	{is a ball bearing}
is possible, is impossible	{is round, is square}
is thought about by Meinong	{p: Jimmy Carter has p}
is worshipped by someone	{is a ball bearing}
is complete	{p: Madame Curie has p}

Part 3:   Singular Terms

Now let me turn to singular terms, specifically definite descriptions and proper names. Ideally I would discuss these within the context of ordinary language, but I find it too complicated to say anything both precise and general and brief in that context. So instead I'll talk about a certain artificial language, one that's designed to allow us a lot of talk about objects. The language will look very much like the predicate calculus, and that's good, because we all know how to symbolize lots of English in that language. There are problems here, of course; for example, whether the English "if...then..." means the same as the material conditional. But most of my examples will deal with atomic sentences, so we can avoid many of these issues.

In fact, to avoid complexity, I'll just talk about the monadic part of the language.[7] Here's what it looks like:

We have *nuclear predicates*: P^N, Q^N, R^N,...; they are supposed to stand for nuclear properties.

We have *extranuclear predicates*: P^E, Q^E, R^E,..., and they are supposed to stand for extranuclear properties.

And we have *object names* and *object variables*: a, b, c,..., x, y, z,...; these are supposed to stand for objects.

I've called a, b, c,... object "names," but don't take that too seriously because I really don't think that they behave very much like *English* proper names (one reason is that they're not allowed to lack reference, like Russellian "logically proper names"). In fact, eventually I won't use them at all; they're just a temporary expedient to help out in my exposition.

We make sentences as in the predicate calculus. For example, suppose that

D^N stands for being a detective,
E^E stands for existing, and
    s stands for Sherlock Holmes.

Then we can write:

$D^N s$ for "Holmes is a detective" (which is true), and
$E^E s$ for "Holmes exists" (which is false).

I suppose that we also have some connectives, so that we can write things like: $(D^N s \& \sim E^E s)$, meaning that Sherlock Holmes is a detective who doesn't exist. And this is a truth of the simplest sort; the name, s, refers to Sherlock Holmes, and we say of him, of that object, that he's a detective and that he doesn't exist.

Quantifiers are nice to have too, so I'll suppose we have quantifiers. They range over objects, *all* objects of course, not just the ones that exist. So we can truly say things like: $(\exists x)(D^N x \& E^E x) \& (\exists x)(D^N x \& \sim E^E x)$, that is, "some detectives exist, and some don't."

Now a certain amount of care is needed in symbolizing English here. For sometimes we don't say literally quite all that we mean. For example, forgetting nonexistent objects for the moment, if I tell someone "Every dish is broken," it would be wrong to symbolize this as $(x)(Dx \supset Bx)$; because *that* says that every dish in the universe is broken, and I certainly didn't mean that. I only had *certain* dishes in mind. We can capture this by using a special predicate to symbolize my use of "dish," or else we can display what's going on by "expanding" the symbolization, something like this: $(x)(Dx \& Ox \supset Bx$, which says "Every dish that we own is broken." Now we sometimes have to do something like this with respect to existence. For example, we are sometimes inclined to say "There are winged horses (Pegasus for example)," and this is easy to symbolize; it's: $(\exists x)(W^N x \& H^N x)$. But we're also sometimes inclined to say "There are no winged horses," and I don't think that we then contradict what we said earlier. We use the same words, but we mean something different. We mean, I suppose, that there are no *existent* winged horses: $\sim (\exists x)(E^E x \& W^N x \& H^N x)$.

Well now let me turn to definite descriptions. I'm going to write them just like everybody else, namely, if you have a formula, $\emptyset$, then you can put an ιx in front of it like this: $(\iota x)\emptyset$, and you read it 'the thing such that $\emptyset$,' or words to this effect. For example, you read:

$(\iota x)(Wx \& Hx)$

as "the thing such that it's winged and it's a horse," or just "the winged horse." And my semantical account of these definite descriptions is pretty ordinary: $(\iota x)\emptyset$ refers to the unique object that satisfies $\emptyset$, if there is one, and otherwise $(\iota x)\emptyset$ just doesn't refer at all.

Now we can make sentences with these things, and I'm going to do something just slightly unorthodox here – it's really just heuristic and not a matter of logic or semantics at all – but I want to put definite descriptions in *front* of the predicates they combine with, as we do it in English. So if we want to write "The man in the doorway is clever," we can write:

$(\iota x)(M^N x \& I^N x)C^N.$

Now actually that isn't the way I'd be inclined to symbolize that English sentence if someone used it in an ordinary real-life situation. Because, if you remember how big our ontology is, you'll realize that there are *lots* of men in the doorway – and this is partly in answer to Quine's worries about what he called "the possible man in the doorway";[8] there's no such thing as *the* possible man in the doorway, because there are lots of men there. There are fat men in the doorway, skinny ones, bald ones, and so on. But probably if I say, in real life, "The man in the doorway is clever," I'm not talking about, *them* – they're all nonexistent men, and I'm talking about an existing one. So the right way to symbolize the most natural use of the sentence is like we did with the winged horses earlier, namely:

$(\iota x)(M^N x \& I^N x \& E^E x)C^N;$

that is, "The existing man in the doorway is clever," but I don't *say* "existing" when I talk, because content makes it clear that that's what I mean. And now if I'm lucky, my definite description will refer to someone, and that will happen if there's an existing man there, and if he's alone there (except for the unreal men who are there). And then maybe what I say will be true. When will it be true? Well this much is clear: if $(\iota x)\emptyset$ refers to an object, then a sentence of the form $(\iota x)\emptyset F$ will be true if the object referred to has property F, and false if it lacks property F. (It doesn't matter here whether F is nuclear or extranuclear.) But what if the definite description fails to refer? Well, for sure the sentence is untrue, but is it untrue because it's false, or untrue because it lacks truth-value altogether? Oh, I don't know. The data doesn't seem to tell us. I've said that the linguistic data tell us this: that if we believe that "the $\emptyset$" fails to refer, and if someone asks us whether the $\emptyset$ is F, then we generally regard the question as spurious; we won't answer it. But there are two ways this might be explained. First, maybe simple sentences with non-referring definite descriptions lack truth-value; that would explain why the question is spurious – it has no true or false answer. But maybe instead of lacking truth-value such sentences are false, automatically false, because of the failure of reference. Then literally the question has an answer – the answer is "no" – but the speaker will be reluctant to say this, for fear of encouraging the impression that the $\emptyset$ has some property incompatible with F. In the first conversation I gave you, maybe speaker A won't say 'no' when speaker B asks if the man in the doorway looks like A's department chairman for fear of conveying the impression that the man in the doorway looks different from his department chairman. If this explanation were correct, it would be OK for A to precede his answer with the word "no," just as long as he went on to explain that there was no such man. And I think it would be natural for him to do this, but that doesn't show he thinks there literally *is* an answer to B's question, because we often say "no" just as a kind of generalized protest reaction.

So I don't know what the right thing is to say here, but for present purposes I think I can remain neutral on this issue. So let me just stick with saying that when $(\iota x)\emptyset$ fails to refer, then $(\iota x)\emptyset F$ is automatically untrue, without committing myself to which sort of untruth is in question. And that's really all I need to illustrate how failing to refer is different from referring to something nonexistent, because, for example, we can truly say that the fictional detective who lived at 221B Baker Street was clever, but we can't ever say truly that the man in the doorway (i.e., the existing man in the doorway) is clever, when there exists no man in the doorway. (We can't even truly say that "he" is a man.)

Before moving on to names, I should say one more thing about descriptions. Suppose that we have in our language some verbs of propositional attitude, such as *believes* or *wonders whether*. Then, as lots of people have pointed out, a sentence like:

Agatha believes the tallest spy is a spy

is ambiguous. It has a *de dicto* reading, which can be symbolized:

$$aB\{(\iota x)\emptyset S\}$$

where $(\iota x)\emptyset$ stands for "the tallest spy" (I don't really have the resources in this monadic fragment to represent the superlative construction, so just suppose it's done somehow). But the sentence also has a *de re* reading; Agatha believes *of* the tallest spy that he or she is a spy. So how is this to be written? Well, I'll use a technique here that Ron Scales has made much of.[9] First, we use abstraction to symbolize the *de re* property of being believed by Agatha to be a spy:

$$[\lambda x a B\{Sx\}]$$

and then we say that the tallest spy has that property:

$$(\iota x)\emptyset[\lambda x a B\{Sx\}].$$

This gives us the effect of descriptions having scope, but without forcing us to consider them to be incomplete symbols. And that in turn lets us solve one of Russell's problems, a problem that Russell himself failed to solve; namely, we can symbolize the *de dicto* reading of "George IV wondered whether the author of *Waverley* was such-and-such" as:

g wondered whether $\{(\iota x)\ (x$ authored *Waverley*$)$ was such-and-such$\}$

without insisting that this means the same as "George IV wondered whether one and only one person authored *Waverley*", and was such-and-such."[10]

Finally, what about proper names? Let me symbolize them with capital letters: $A, B, C, \ldots$, and put them in sentences in the same places where definite descriptions go, just as in English. So we write "Pegasus flies" just as PF. Semantically, some names refer, and some don't; of those that refer, some refer to existing objects, and some to nonexistent objects. The rest of their semantics is just like definite descriptions.

Now I want to deny some of the popular things that have been said recently about proper names. Well first I'll say (I've already said) that, contrary to popular opinion, names like "Pegasus" and "Sherlock Holmes" *do* refer; they refer to nonexistent objects. The former refers to a certain winged horse that appears in Greek mythology, and the latter to a certain fictional detective.

My second denial: I deny that whether or not a name refers depends on whether our use of it can be traced back by means of a causal chain to something like a dubbing that takes place in the presence of its referent. I'm denying a popular version of the causal theory of names. Though in fact I think that the causal theory may come very close to being right in these cases; it only makes a *small* mistake (maybe) that isn't really relevant to the spirit of the theory. The mistake is to suppose that the referent of a name must itself be a causal agent in the chain. I don't think that's right even in the case of certain existing things. For example, the novel *The Wind in the Willows* has a certain name (namely, "*The Wind in the Willows*"); but if we trace back our present use of that name *causally*, we don't come to the *novel*, but rather to a *copy* of the novel. The novel itself is not a physical object, and doesn't enter into causal relations. But coming to a copy of the novel is good enough; we need one more link in the chain, but it's not a causal one; rather it consists of something like exemplification, or tokening. I think that reference to Sherlock Holmes is like this. We trace the name back causally to the Conan Doyle novels, but then instead of encountering what Keith Donnellan[11] calls a "block," which is sort of like a break in the chain, we make one more *non*-causal step to Sherlock Holmes.[12] If we couldn't reach Holmes through the novels in this way, probably we couldn't refer to him.

Third, I have heard some people recently say that proper names do not manifest *de re*/*de dicto* ambiguities. This is thought to follow from the claim that they are rigid designators. But it doesn't follow. A rigid designator is a name that names the same object in every possible world. But all that follows from this is that proper names do not manifest *de re*/*de dicto* ambiguities with respect to modal operators. It says nothing about what they do in the presence of, say, epistemic words. Agatha can believe *de dicto* that Plato is a famous philosopher without having any *de re* beliefs about Plato at all. Conversely, she can believe of Tully (i.e., *de re*) that he did such and such without believing *de dicto* that Tully did such and such.

Lastly, I want to say that proper names have sense. Or at least they're as good candidates for having sense as any other kind of word in our language. Their having sense would explain how it's possible for Agatha to believe (*de dicto*) that Cicero did such and such without her believing (again *de dicto*) that Tully did. The reason people have thought that proper names lacked sense is that they seem to think that if proper names do have sense, then they must be synonymous with certain definite descriptions. But there's no good reason to think this, any more than you should think that if definite descriptions have sense, then they must be synonymous with certain names. I know that both Frege and Russell suggested this – that names are synonymous with descriptions – and recently this has been rejected. And the view that names have sense has been maligned by being associated with this view. But it's a classic case of guilt by association. I think that people have failed to notice the need for senses because of their preoccupation with modalities, and the view that names are rigid designators.

Notes

Work on this paper was supported by the University of Massachusetts and by a grant from the National Endowment for the Humanities. I am indebted to the University of California at Irvine for providing office facilities, and to Karel Lambert, Kit Fine, and David Woodruff Smith for criticism. A draft of this paper was read at a conference at Arizona State University, Tempe.

1 Preliminary work on such a theory is found in my "A prolegomenon to Meinongian semantics," *Journal of Philosophy* 71/16 (1974), pp. 561–80, hereafter PMS; "A Meinongian analysis of fictional objects," *Grazer Philosophische Studien* 1 (1975), pp. 73–86, hereafter MAFO; and "Nuclear and extranuclear properties,

Meinong and Leibniz," *Nous* 12 (1978), pp. 147–51. A more comprehensive treatment is being developed in a book entitled *Nonexistent Objects* (New Haven: Yale University Press, 1980), hereafter NO. In none of these works are objects taken to *be* sets of properties.

2 Many of Meinong's views can be found in A. Meinong, "The theory of objects," in R. Chisholm (ed.) *Realism and the Background of Phenomenology* (Glencoe, Ill.: Free Press, 1960), and in J. Findlay, *Meinong's Theory of Objects and Values* (Oxford: Clarendon Press, 1963). For purposes of comparing my views with Meinong's, interpret my "exists" as his "exists or subsists".

3 Cf. MAFO and NO, 3 and 7.

4 Perhaps for this reason I shouldn't use the term "negation," but should use something like "complement." It isn't certain that "the" negation of p is unique, but the discussion of incomplete objects in the text doesn't suffer from this. Cf. NO, chs 5 and 6.

5 Many other notions may have an equal right to the title "possible." E.g., we might want to reserve the term for objects which are both possible in the sense defined and also complete. Or we might use it to denote those objects which are such that they might have existed (in a *de re* sense of "might have"). Cf. NO, chs 1 and 5.

6 By "is mythical" I mean "occurs in an actual myth"; similarly for "is fictional." For certain of the predicates we might have to appeal to the stronger, modalized principle:

$(\exists X)$ (X is a set of nuclear properties & $F \notin X$ & possibly (x) (x has every member of $X \supset x$ lacks F)).

Ultimately the distinction between nuclear and extranuclear properties should gain viability by being incorporated into a general theory of objects and properties; that is the task of most of NO.

7 Relations are very important; they, together with the other constructions discussed below in the text, are developed throughout NO.

8 In W. V. Quine, *From a Logical Point of View* (New York: Harper & Row, 1961), p. 4.

9 R. Scales, "Attribution and existence" (Ph.D. diss., University of California, Irvine, 1969).

10 Cf. L. Linsky, *Referring* (London: Routledge and Kegan Paul, 1967).

11 K. Donnellan, "Speaking of nothing," *Philosophical Review* 83 (1974), pp. 3–32, sect. 6.

12 The nature of the noncausal step from the story to Sherlock Holmes is discussed tersely in MAFO and in somewhat more detail in NO, ch. 7.

5

Ontological Relativity

W. V. Quine

I

I listened to Dewey on Art as Experience when I was a graduate student in the spring of 1931. Dewey was then at Harvard as the first William James Lecturer. I am proud now to be at Columbia as the first John Dewey Lecturer.

Philosophically I am bound to Dewey by the naturalism that dominated his last three decades. With Dewey I hold that knowledge, mind, and meaning are part of the same world that they have to do with, and that they are to be studied in the same empirical spirit that animates natural science. There is no place for a prior philosophy.

When a naturalistic philosopher addresses himself to the philosophy of mind, he is apt to talk of language. Meanings are, first and foremost, meanings of language. Language is a social art which we all acquire on the evidence solely of other people's overt behavior under publicly recognizable circumstances. Meanings, therefore, those very models of mental entities, end up as grist for the behaviorist's mill. Dewey was explicit on the point: "Meaning . . . is not a psychic existence; it is primarily a property of behavior."[1]

Once we appreciate the institution of language in these terms, we see that there cannot be, in any useful sense, a private language. This point was

Originally published in W. V. Quine Ontological Relativity and other Essays (1969), pp. 26–68. Copyright © by W. V. Quine. Reprinted by permission of Columbia University Press.

stressed by Dewey in the twenties. "Soliloquy," he wrote, "is the product and reflex of converse with others."[2] Further along he expanded the point thus: "Language is specifically a mode of interaction of at least two beings, a speaker and a hearer; it presupposes an organized group to which these creatures belong, and from whom they have acquired their habits of speech. It is therefore a relationship."[3] Years later, Wittgenstein likewise rejected private language. When Dewey was writing in this naturalistic vein, Wittgenstein still held his copy theory of language.

The copy theory in its various forms stands closer to the main philosophical tradition, and to the attitude of common sense today. Uncritical semantics is the myth of a museum in which the exhibits are meanings and the words are labels. To switch languages is to change the labels. Now the naturalist's primary objection to this view is not an objection to meanings on account of their being mental entities, though that could be objection enough. The primary objection persists even if we take the labeled exhibits not as mental ideas but as Platonic ideas or even as the denoted concrete objects. Semantics is vitiated by a pernicious mentalism as long as we regard a man's semantics as somehow determinate in his mind beyond what might be implicit in his dispositions to overt behavior. It is the very facts about meaning, not the entities meant, that must be construed in terms of behavior.

There are two parts to knowing a word. One part is being familiar with the sound of it and being able to reproduce it. This part, the phonetic part, is achieved by observing and imitating other people's behavior, and there are no important illusions about the process. The other part, the semantic part, is knowing how to use the word. This part, even in the paradigm case, is more complex than the phonetic part. The word refers, in the paradigm case, to some visible object. The learner has now not only to learn the word phonetically, by hearing it from another speaker; he also has to see the object; and in addition to this, in order to capture the relevance of the object to the word, he has to see that the speaker also sees the object. Dewey summed up the point thus: "The characteristic theory about B's understanding of A's sounds is that he responds to the thing from the standpoint of A."[4] Each of us, as he learns his language, is a student of his neighbor's behavior; and conversely, insofar as his tries are approved or corrected, he is a subject of his neighbor's behavioral study.

The semantic part of learning a word is more complex than the phonetic part, therefore, even in simple cases: we have to see what is stimulating the other speaker. In the case of words not directly ascribing observable traits to things, the learning process is increasingly complex and obscure; and obscurity is the breeding place of mentalistic semantics. What the naturalist insists on is that, even in the complex and obscure parts of language learning, the learner has no data to work with but the overt behavior of other speakers.

When with Dewey we turn thus toward a naturalistic view of language and a behavioral view of meaning, what we give up is not just the museum figure of speech. We give up an assurance of determinacy. Seen according to the museum myth, the words and sentences of a language have their determinate meanings. To discover the meanings of the native's words, we may have to observe his behavior, but still the meanings of the words are supposed to be determinate in the native's *mind*, his mental museum, even in cases where behavioral criteria are powerless to discover them for us. When on the other hand we recognize with Dewey that "meaning... is primarily a property of behavior," we recognize that there are no meanings, nor likenesses nor distinctions of meaning, beyond what are implicit in people's dispositions to overt behavior. For naturalism the question whether two expressions are alike or unlike in meaning has no determinate answer, known or unknown, except insofar as the answer is settled in principle by people's speech dispositions, known or unknown. If by these standards there are indeterminate cases, so much the worse for the terminology of meaning and likeness of meaning.

To see what such indeterminacy would be like, suppose there were an expression in a remote language that could be translated into English equally defensibly in either of two ways, unlike in meaning in English. I am not speaking of ambiguity within the native language. I am supposing that one and the same native use of the expression can be given either of the English translations, each being accommodated by compensating adjustments in the translation of other words. Suppose both translations, along with these accommodations in each case, accord equally well with all observable behavior on the part of speakers of the remote language and speakers of English. Suppose they accord perfectly not only with behavior actually observed, but with all dispositions to behavior on the part of all the speakers concerned. On these assumptions it would be forever impossible to know of one of these translations that it was the right one, and the other wrong. Still, if the museum myth were true, there would be a right and wrong of the matter; it is just that we would never know, not having access to the museum. See language naturalistically, on the other hand, and you have to see the notion of likeness of meaning in such a case simply as nonsense.

I have been keeping to the hypothetical. Turning now to examples, let me begin with a disappointing one and work up. In the French construction "ne ... rien" you can translate "rien" into English as "anything' or as "nothing" at will, and then accommodate your choice by translating "ne" as "not" or by construing it as pleonastic. This example is disappointing because you can object that I have merely cut the French units too small. You can believe the mentalistic myth of the meaning museum and still grant that "rien" of itself has no meaning, being no whole label; it is part of "ne ... rien," which has its meaning as a whole.

I began with this disappointing example because I think its conspicuous trait – its dependence on cutting language into segments too short to carry meanings – is the secret of the more serious cases as well. What makes other cases more serious is that the segments they involve are seriously long: long enough to be predicates and to be true of things and hence, you would think, to carry meanings.

An artificial example which I have used elsewhere[5] depends on the fact that a whole rabbit is present when and only when an undetached part of a rabbit is present; also when and only when a temporal stage of a rabbit is present. If we are wondering whether to translate a native expression "gavagai" as "rabbit" or as "undetached rabbit part" or as "rabbit stage," we can never settle the matter simply by ostension – that is, simply by repeatedly querying the expression "gavagai" for the native's assent or dissent in the presence of assorted stimulations.

Before going on to urge that we cannot settle the matter by non-ostensive means either, let me belabor this ostensive predicament a bit. I am not worrying, as Wittgenstein did, about simple cases of ostension. The color word "sepia," to take one of his examples,[6] can certainly be learned by an ordinary process of conditioning, or induction. One need not even be told that sepia is a color and not a shape or a material or an article. True, barring such hints, many lessons may be needed, so as to eliminate wrong generalizations based on shape, material, etc., rather than color, and so as to eliminate wrong notions as to the intended boundary of an indicated example, and so as to delimit the admissible variations of color itself. Like all conditioning, or induction, the process will depend ultimately also on one's own inborn propensity to find one stimulation qualitatively more akin to a second stimulation than to a third; otherwise there can never be any selective reinforcement and extinction of responses.[7] Still, in principle nothing more is needed in learning "sepia" than in any conditioning or induction.

But the big difference between "rabbit" and "sepia" is that whereas "sepia" is a mass term like "water," "rabbit" is a term of divided reference. As such it cannot be mastered without mastering its principle of individuation: where one rabbit leaves off and another begins. And this cannot be mastered by pure ostension, however persistent.

Such is the quandary over "gavagai": where one gavagai leaves off and another begins. The only difference between rabbits, undetached rabbit parts, and rabbit stages is in their individuation. If you take the total scattered portion of the spatio-temporal world that is made up of rabbits, and that which is made up of undetached rabbit parts, and that which is made up of rabbit stages, you come out with the same scattered portion of the world each of the three times. The only difference is in how you slice it. And how to slice it is what ostension or simple conditioning, however persistently repeated, cannot teach.

Thus consider specifically the problem of deciding between "rabbit" and "undetached rabbit part" as translation of "gavagai." No word of the native language is known, except that we have settled on some working hypothesis as to what native words or gestures to construe as assent and dissent in response to our pointings and queryings. Now the trouble is that whenever we point to different parts of the rabbit, even sometimes screening the rest of the rabbit, we are pointing also each time to the rabbit. When, conversely, we indicate the whole rabbit with a sweeping gesture, we are still pointing to a multitude of rabbit parts. And note that we do not have even a native analogue of our plural ending to exploit, in asking "gavagai?" It seems clear that no even tentative decision between "rabbit" and "undetached rabbit part" is to be sought at this level.

How would we finally decide? My passing mention of plural endings is part of the answer. Our individuating of terms of divided reference, in English, is bound up with a cluster of interrelated grammatical particles and constructions: plural endings, pronouns, numerals, the "is" of identity, and its adaptations "same" and "other." It is the cluster of interrelated devices in which quantification becomes central when the regimentation of symbolic logic is imposed. If in his language we could ask the native "Is this *gavagai* the same as that one?" while making appropriate multiple ostensions, then indeed we would be well on our way to deciding between "rabbit," "undetached rabbit part," and "rabbit stage." And of course the linguist does at length reach the point where he can ask what purports to be that question. He develops a system for translating our pluralizations, pronouns, numerals, identity, and related devices contextually into the native idiom. He develops such a system by abstraction and hypothesis. He abstracts native particles and constructions from observed native sentences and tries associating these variously with English particles and constructions. Insofar as the native sentences and the thus associated English ones seem to match up in respect of appropriate occasions of use, the linguist feels confirmed in these hypotheses of translation – what I call *analytical hypotheses*.[8]

But it seems that this method, though laudable in practice and the best we can hope for, does not in principle settle the indeterminacy between "rabbit," "undetached rabbit part," and "rabbit stage." For if one workable overall system of analytical hypotheses provides for translating a given native expression into "is the same as," perhaps another equally workable but systematically different system would translate that native expression rather into something like "belongs with." Then, when in the native language we try to ask, "Is this *gavagai* the same as that?," we could as well be asking "Does this *gavagai* belong with that?" Insofar, the native's assent is no objective evidence for translating "gavagai" as "rabbit" rather than "undetached rabbit part" or "rabbit stage."

This artificial example shares the structure of the trivial earlier example "ne ... rien." We were able to translate "rien" as "anything" or as "nothing," thanks to a compensatory adjustment in the handling of "ne." And I suggest that we can translate "gavagai" as "rabbit" or "undetached rabbit part" or "rabbit stage," thanks to compensatory adjustments in the translation of accompanying native locutions. Other adjustments still might accommodate translation of "gavagai" as "rabbithood," or in further ways. I find this plausible because of the broadly structural and contextual character of any considerations that could guide us to native translations of the English cluster of interrelated devices of individuation. There seem bound to be systematically very different choices, all of which do justice to all dispositions to verbal behaviour on the part of all concerned.

An actual field linguist would of course be sensible enough to equate "gavagai" with "rabbit," dismissing such perverse alternatives as "undetached rabbit part" and "rabbit stage" out of hand. This sensible choice and others like it would help in turn to determine his subsequent hypotheses as to what native locutions should answer to the English apparatus of individuation, and thus everything would come out all right. The implicit maxim guiding his choice of "rabbit," and similar choices for other native words, is that an enduring and relatively homogeneous object, moving as a whole against a contrasting background, is a likely reference for a short expression. If he were to become conscious of this maxim, he might celebrate it as one of the linguistic universals, or traits of all languages, and he would have no trouble pointing out its psychological plausibility. But he would be wrong; the maxim is his own imposition, toward settling what is objectively indeterminate. It is a very sensible imposition, and I would recommend no other. But I am making a philosophical point.

It is philosophically interesting, moreover, that what is indeterminate in this artificial example is not just meaning, but extension; reference. My remarks on indeterminacy began as a challenge to likeness of meaning. I had us imagining "an expression that could be translated into English equally defensibly in either of two ways, unlike in meaning in English." Certainly likeness of meaning is a dim notion, repeatedly challenged. Of two predicates which are alike in extension, it has never been clear when to say that they are alike in meaning and when not; it is the old matter of featherless bipeds and rational animals, or of equiangular and equilateral triangles. Reference, extension, has been the firm thing; meaning, intension, the infirm. The indeterminacy of translation now confronting us, however, cuts across extension and intension alike. The terms "rabbit," "undetached rabbit part," and "rabbit stage" differ not only in meaning; they are true of different things. Reference itself proves behaviorally inscrutable.

Within the parochial limits of our own language, we can continue as always to find extensional talk clearer than intensional. For the indeterminacy between "rabbit," "rabbit stage," and the rest depended only on a correlative indeterminacy of translation of the English apparatus of individuation – the apparatus of pronouns, pluralization, identity, numerals, and so on. No such indeterminacy obtrudes so long as we think of this apparatus as given and fixed. Given this apparatus, there is no mystery about extension; terms have the same extension when true of the same things. At the level of radical translation, on the other hand, extension itself goes inscrutable.

My example of rabbits and their parts and stages is a contrived example and a perverse one, with which, as I said, the practicing linguist would have no patience. But there are also cases, less bizarre ones, that obtrude in practice. In Japanese there are certain particles, called "classifiers," which may be explained in either of two ways. Commonly they are explained as attaching to numerals, to form compound numerals of distinctive styles. Thus take the numeral for 5. If you attach one classifier to it, you get a style of "5" suitable for counting animals; if you attach a different classifier, you get a style of "5" suitable for counting slim things like pencils and chopsticks; and so on. But another way of viewing classifiers is to view them not as constituting part of the numeral, but as constituting part of the term – the term for "chopsticks" or "oxen" or whatever. On this view the classifier does the individuative job that is done in English by "sticks of" as applied to the mass term "wood," or "head of" as applied to the mass term "cattle."

What we have on either view is a Japanese phrase tantamount say to "five oxen," but consisting of three words;[9] the first is in effect the neutral numeral "5," the second is a classifier of the animal kind, and the last corresponds in some fashion to "ox." On one view the neutral numeral and the classifier go together to constitute a declined numeral in the "animal gender," which then modifies "ox" to give, in effect, "five oxen." On the other view the third Japanese word answers not to the individuative term "ox" but to the mass term "cattle"; the classifier applies to this mass term to produce a composite individuative term, in effect "head of cattle"; and the neutral numeral applies directly to all this without benefit of gender, giving "five head of cattle," hence again in effect "five oxen."

If so simple an example is to serve its expository purpose, it needs your connivance. You have to understand "cattle" as a mass term covering only bovines, and "ox" as applying to all bovines. That these usages are not the invariable usages is beside the point. The point is that the Japanese phrase comes out as "five bovines," as desired, when parsed in either of two ways. The one way treats the third Japanese word as an individuative term true of each bovine, and the other way treats that word rather as a mass term covering the unindividuated totality of beef on the hoof. These are two very different ways of treating the third Japanese word; and the three-word phrase as a whole turns out all right in both cases only because of compensatory differences in our account of the second word, the classifier.

This example is reminiscent in a way of our trivial initial example, "ne ... rien." We were able to represent "rien" as "anything" or as "nothing," by compensatorily taking "ne" as negative or as vacuous. We are able now to represent a Japanese word either as an individuative term for bovines or as a mass term for live beef, by compensatorily taking the classifer as declining the numeral or as individuating the mass term. However, the triviality of the one example does not quite carry over to the other. The early example was dismissed on the ground that we had cut too small; "rien" was to short for significant translation on its own, "and 'ne ... rien' was the significant unit. But you cannot dismiss the Japanese example by saying that the third word was too short for significant translation on its own and that only the whole three-word phrase, tantamount to "five oxen," was the significant unit. You cannot take this line unless you are prepared to call a word too short for significant translation even when it is long enough to be a term and carry denotation. For the third Japanese word is, on either approach, a term: on one approach a term of divided reference, and on the other a mass term. If you are indeed prepared thus to call a word too short for significant translation even when it is a denoting term, then in a back-handed way you are granting what I wanted to prove: the inscrutability of reference.

Between the two accounts of Japanese classifiers there is no question of right and wrong. The one account makes for more efficient translation into idiomatic English; the other makes for more of a feeling for the Japanese idiom. Both fit all verbal behavior equally well. All whole sentences, and even component phrases like "five oxen," admit of the same net overall English translations on either account. This much is invariant. But what is philosophically interesting is that the reference or extension of shorter terms can fail to be invariant. Whether that third Japanese word is itself true of each ox, or whether on the other hand it is a mass term which needs to be adjoined to the classifier to make a term which is true of each ox – here is a question that remains undecided by the totality of human dispositions to verbal behavior. It is indeterminate in principle; there is no fact of the matter. Either answer can be accommodated by an account of the classifier. Here again, then, is the inscrutability of reference – illustrated this time by a humdrum point of practical translation.

The inscrutability of reference can be brought closer to home by considering the word "alpha," or again the word "green." In our use of these words and others like them there is a systematic ambiguity. Sometimes we use such words as concrete general terms, as when we say the grass is green, or that some inscription begins with an alpha. Sometimes, on the other hand, we use them as abstract singular terms, as when we say that green is a color and alpha is a letter. Such ambiguity is encouraged by the fact that there is nothing in ostension to distinguish the two uses. The pointing that would be done in teaching the concrete general term "green" or "alpha" differs none from the pointing that would be done in teaching the abstract singular term "green" or "alpha." Yet the objects referred to by the word are very different under the two uses; under the one use the word is true of many concrete objects, and under the other use it names a single abstract object.

We can of course tell the two uses apart by seeing how the word turns up in sentences: whether it takes an indefinite article, whether it takes a plural ending, whether it stands as singular subject, whether it stands as modifier, as predicate complement, and so on. But these criteria appeal to our special English grammatical constructions and particles, our special English apparatus of individuation, which, I already urged, is itself subject to indeterminacy of translation. So, from the point of view of translation into a remote language, the distinction between a concrete general and an abstract singular term is in the same predicament as the distinction between "rabbit," "rabbit part," and "rabbit stage." Here then is another example of the inscrutability of reference, since the difference between the concrete general and the abstract singular is a difference in the objects referred to.

Incidentally we can concede this much indeterminacy also to the "sepia" example, after all. But this move is not evidently what was worrying Wittgenstein.

The ostensive indistinguishability of the abstract singular from the concrete general turns upon what may be called "deferred ostension," as opposed to direct ostension. First let me define direct ostension. The *ostended point*, as I shall call it, is the point where the line of the pointing finger first meets an opaque surface. What characterizes *direct ostension*, then, is that the term which is being ostensively explained is true of something that contains the ostended point. Even such direct ostension has its uncertainties, of course, and these are familiar. There is the question how wide an environment of the ostended point is meant to be covered by the term that is being ostensively explained. There is the question how considerably an absent thing or substance might be allowed to differ from what is now ostended, and still be covered by the term that is now being ostensively explained. Both of these questions can in principle be settled as well as need be by induction from multiple ostensions. Also, if the term is a term of divided reference like "apple," there is the question of individuation: the question where one of its objects leaves off and another begins. This can be settled by induction from multiple ostensions of a more elaborate kind, accompanied by expressions like "same apple" and "another," if an equivalent of this English apparatus of individuation has been settled on; otherwise the indeterminacy persists that was illustrated by "rabbit," "undetached rabbit part," and "rabbit stage."

Such, then, is the way of direct ostension. Other ostension I call *deferred*. It occurs when we point at the gauge, and not the gasoline, to show that there is gasoline. Also it occurs when we explain the abstract singular term "green" or "alpha" by pointing at grass or a Greek inscription. Such pointing is direct ostension when used to explain the concrete general term "green" or "alpha," but it is deferred ostension when used to explain the abstract singular terms; for the abstract object which is the color green or the letter alpha does not contain the ostended point, nor any point.

Deferred ostension occurs very naturally when, as in the case of the gasoline gauge, we have a correspondence in mind. Another such example is afforded by the Gödel numbering of expressions. Thus if 7 has been assigned as Gödel number of the letter alpha, a man conscious of the Gödel numbering would not hesitate to say "Seven" on pointing to an inscription of the Greek letter in question. This is, on the face of it, a doubly deferred ostension: one step of deferment carries us from the inscription to the letter as abstract object, and a second step carries us thence to the number.

By appeal to our apparatus of individuation, if it is available, we can distinguish between the concrete general and the abstract singular use of the word "alpha"; this we saw. By appeal again to that apparatus, and in particular to identity, we can evidently settle also whether the word "alpha" in its abstract singular use is being used really to name the letter or whether, perversely, it is being used to name the Gödel number of the letter. At any rate we can distinguish these alternatives if also we have located the speaker's equivalent of the numeral "7" to our satisfaction; for we can ask him whether alpha *is* 7.

These considerations suggest that deferred ostension adds no essential problem to those presented by direct ostension. Once we have settled upon analytical hypotheses of translation covering identity and the other English particles relating to individuation, we can resolve not only the indecision between "rabbit" and "rabbit stage" and the rest, which came of direct ostension, but also any indecision between concrete general and abstract singular, and any indecision between expression and Gödel number, which come of deferred ostension. However, this conclusion is too sanguine. The inscrutability of reference runs deep, and it persists in a subtle form even if we accept identity and the rest of the apparatus of individuation as fixed and settled; even, indeed, if we forsake radical translation and think only of English.

Consider the case of a thoughtful protosyntactician. He has a formalized system of first-order proof theory, or protosyntax, whose universe comprises just expressions, that is, strings of signs of a specified alphabet. Now just what sorts of things, more specifically, are these expressions? They are types, not tokens. So, one might suppose, each of them is the set of all its tokens. That is, each expression is a set of inscriptions which are variously situated in space-time but are classed together by virtue of a certain similarity in shape. The concatenate $x \frown y$ of two expressions x and y, in a given order, will be the set of all inscriptions each of which has two parts which are tokens respectively of x and y and follow one upon the other in that order. But $x \frown y$ may then be the null set, though x and y are not null; for it may be that inscriptions belonging to x and y happen to turn up head to tail nowhere, in the past, present, or future. This danger increases with the lengths of x and y. But it is easily seen to violate a law of protosyntax which says that $x = z$ whenever $x \frown y = z \frown y$.

Thus it is that our thoughtful protosyntactician will not construe the things in his universe as sets of inscriptions. He can still take his atoms, the single signs, as sets of inscriptions, for there is no risk of nullity in these cases. And then, instead of taking his strings of signs as sets of inscriptions, he can invoke the mathematical notion of sequence and take them as sequences of signs. A familiar way of taking sequences, in turn, is as a mapping of things on numbers. On this approach an expression or string of signs becomes a finite set of pairs each of which is the pair of a sign and a number.

This account of expressions is more artificial and more complex than one is apt to expect who simply says he is letting his variables range over the strings of such and such signs. Moreover, it is not the inevitable choice; the considerations that motivated it can be met also by alternative constructions. One of these constructions is Gödel numbering itself, and it is temptingly simple. It uses just natural numbers, whereas the foregoing construction used sets of one-letter inscriptions and also natural numbers and sets of pairs of these. How clear is it that at just *this* point we have dropped expressions in favor of numbers? What is clearer is merely that in both constructions we were artificially devising models to satisfy laws that expressions in an unexplicated sense had been meant to satisfy.

So much for expressions. Consider now the arithmetician himself, with his elementary number theory. His universe comprises the natural numbers outright. Is it clearer than the protosyntactician's? What, after all, is a natural number? There

are Frege's version, Zermelo's, and von Neumann's, and countless further alternatives, all mutually incompatible and equally correct. What we are doing in any one of these explications of natural number is to devise set-theoretic models to satisfy laws which the natural numbers in an unexplicated sense had been meant to satisfy. The case is quite like that of protosyntax.

It will perhaps be felt that any set-theoretic explication of natural number is at best a case of *obscurum per obscurius*; that all explications must assume something, and the natural numbers themselves are an admirable assumption to start with. I must agree that a construction of sets and set theory from natural numbers and arithmetic would be far more desirable than the familiar opposite. On the other hand, our impression of the clarity even of the notion of natural number itself has suffered somewhat from Gödel's proof of the impossibility of a complete proof procedure for elementary number theory, or, for that matter, from Skolem's and Henkin's observations that all laws of natural numbers admit nonstandard models.[10]

We are finding no clear difference between *specifying* a universe of discourse – the range of the variables of quantification – and *reducing* that universe to some other. We saw no significant difference between clarifying the notion of expression and supplanting it by that of number. And now to say more particularly what numbers themselves are is in no evident way different from just dropping numbers and assigning to arithmetic one or another new model, say in set theory.

Expressions are known only by their laws, the laws of concatenation theory, so that any constructs obeying those laws – Gödel numbers, for instance – are *ipso facto* eligible as explications of expression. Numbers in turn are known only by their laws, the laws of arithmetic, so that any constructs obeying those laws – certain sets, for instance – are eligible in turn as explications of number. Sets in turn are known only by their laws, the laws of set theory.

Russell pressed a contrary thesis, long ago. Writing of numbers, he argued that for an understanding of number the laws of arithmetic are not enough; we must know the applications, we must understand numerical discourse embedded in discourse of other matters. In applying number, the key notion, he urged, is *Anzahl*: there are n so-and-so's. However, Russell can be answered. First take, specifically, *Anzahl*. We can define "there are n so-and-so's" without ever deciding what numbers are, apart from their fulfillment of arithmetic.

That there are n so-and-so's can be explained simply as meaning that the so-and-so's are in one-to-one correspondence with the numbers up to n.[11]

Russell's more general point about application can be answered too. Always, if the structure is there, the applications will fall into place. As paradigm it is perhaps sufficient to recall again this reflection on expressions and Gödel numbers: that even the pointing out of an inscription is no final evidence that our talk is of expressions and not of Gödel numbers. We can always plead deferred ostension.

It is in this sense true to say, as mathematicians often do, that arithmetic is all there is to number. But it would be a confusion to express this point by saying, as is sometimes said, that numbers are any things fulfilling arithmetic. This formulation is wrong because distinct domains of objects yield distinct models of arithmetic. Any progression can be made to serve; and to identify all progressions with one another, e.g., to identify the progression of odd numbers with the progression of evens, would contradict arithmetic after all.

So, though Russell was wrong in suggesting that numbers need more than their arithmetical properties, he was right in objecting to the definition of numbers as any things fulfilling arithmetic. The subtle point is that any progression will serve as a version of number so long and only so long as we stick to one and the same progression. Arithmetic is, in this sense, all there is to number: there is no saying absolutely what the numbers are; there is only arithmetic.[12]

II

I first urged the inscrutability of reference with the help of examples like the one about rabbits and rabbit parts. These used direct ostension, and the inscrutability of reference hinged on the indeterminacy of translation of identity and other individuative apparatus. The setting of these examples, accordingly, was radical translation: translation from a remote language on behavioral evidence, unaided by prior dictionaries. Moving then to deferred ostension and abstract objects, we found a certain dimness of reference pervading the home language itself.

Now it should be noted that even for the earlier examples the resort to a remote language was not really essential. On deeper reflection, radical translation begins at home. Must we equate our neighbor's English words with the same strings of phonemes in our own mouths? Certainly not; for sometimes we do not thus equate them. Sometimes we find it to be in the interests of communication to recognize that our neighbor's use of some word, such as "cool" or "square" or "hopefully," differs from ours, and so we translate that word of his into a different string of phonemes in our idiolect. Our usual domestic rule of translation is indeed the homophonic one, which simply carries each string of phonemes into itself; but still we are always prepared to temper homophony with what Neil Wilson has called the "principle of charity."[13] We will construe a neighbor's word heterophonically now and again if thereby we see our way to making his message less absurd.

The homophonic rule is a handy one on the whole. That it works so well is no accident, since imitation and feedback are what propagate a language. We acquired a great fund of basic words and phrases in this way, imitating our elders and encouraged by our elders amid external circumstances to which the phrases suitably apply. Homophonic translation is implicit in this social method of learning. Departure from homophonic translation in this quarter would only hinder communication. Then there are the relatively rare instances of opposite kind, due to divergence in dialect or confusion in an individual, where homophonic translation incurs negative feedback. But what tends to escape notice is that there is also a vast mid-region where the homophonic method is indifferent. Here, gratuitously, we can systematically reconstrue our neighbor's apparent references to rabbit stages, and his apparent references to formulas as really references to Gödel numbers, and vice versa. We can reconcile all this with our neighbor's verbal behavior, by cunningly readjusting our translations of his various connecting predicates so as to compensate for the switch of ontology. In short, we can reproduce the inscrutability of reference at home. It is of no avail to check on this fanciful version of our neighbor's meanings by asking him, say, whether he really means at a certain point to refer to formulas or to their Gödel numbers; for our question and his answer – "By all means, the numbers" – have lost their title to homophonic translation. The problem at home differs none from radical translation ordinarily so called except in the willfulness of this suspension of homophonic translation.

I have urged in defense of the behavioral philosophy of language, Dewey's, that the inscrutability of reference is not the inscrutability of a fact; there is no fact of the matter. But if there is really no fact of the matter, then the inscrutability of reference can be brought even closer to home than the neighbor's case; we can apply it to ourselves. If it is to make sense to say even of oneself that one is referring to rabbits and formulas and not to rabbit stages and Gödel numbers, then it should make sense equally to say it of someone else. After all, as Dewey stressed, there is no private language.

We seem to be maneuvering ourselves into the absurd position that there is no difference on any terms, interlinguistic or intralinguistic, objective or subjective, between referring to rabbits and referring to rabbit parts or stages; or between referring to formulas and referring to their Gödel numbers. Surely this is absurd, for it would imply that there is no difference between the rabbit and each of its parts or stages, and no difference between a formula and its Gödel number. Reference would seem now to become nonsense not just in radical translation but at home.

Toward resolving this quandary, begin by picturing us at home in our language, with all its predicates and auxiliary devices. This vocabulary includes "rabbit," "rabbit part," "rabbit stage," "formula," "number," "ox," "cattle"; also the two-place predicates of identity and difference, and other logical particles. In these terms we can say in so many words that this is a formula and that a number, this a rabbit and that a rabbit part, this and that the same rabbit, and this and that different parts. *In just those words.* This network of terms and predicates and auxiliary devices is, in relativity jargon, our frame of reference, or coordinate system. Relative to *it* we can and do talk meaningfully and distinctively of rabbits and parts, numbers and formulas. Next, as in recent paragraphs, we contemplate alternative denotations for our familiar terms. We begin to appreciate that a grand and ingenious permutation of these denotations, along with compensatory adjustments in the interpretations of the auxiliary particles, might still accommodate all existing speech dispositions. This was the inscrutability of reference, applied to ourselves; and it made nonsense of reference. Fair enough; reference *is* nonsense except relative to a coordinate system. In this principle of relativity lies the resolution of our quandary.

It is meaningless to ask whether, in general, our terms "rabbit," "rabbit part," "number," etc. really refer respectively to rabbits, rabbit parts, numbers, etc., rather than to some ingeniously permuted denotations. It is meaningless to ask this absolutely; we can meaningfully ask it only relative to some background language. When we ask, "Does 'rabbit' really refer to rabbits?," someone can counter with the question: "Refer to rabbits in what sense of 'rabbits'?," thus launching a regress; and we need the background language to regress into. The background language gives the query sense, if only relative sense; sense relative in turn to it, this background language. Querying reference in any more absolute way would be like asking absolute position, or absolute velocity, rather than position or velocity relative to a given frame of reference. Also it is very much like asking whether our neighbour may not systematically see everything upside down, or in complementary color, forever undetectably.

We need a background language, I said, to regress into. Are we involved now in an infinite regress? If questions of reference of the sort we are considering make sense only relative to a background language, then evidently questions of reference for the background language make sense in turn only relative to a further background language. In these terms the situation sounds desperate, but in fact it is little different from questions of position and velocity. When we are given position and velocity relative to a given coordinate system, we can always ask in turn about the placing of origin and orientation of axes of that system of coordinates; and there is no end to the succession of further coordinate systems that could be adduced in answering the successive questions thus generated.

In practice of course we end the regress of coordinate systems by something like pointing. And in practice we end the regress of background languages, in discussions of reference, by acquiescing in our mother tongue and taking its words at face value.

Very well; in the case of position and velocity, in practice, pointing breaks the regress. But what of position and velocity apart from practice? what of the regress then? The answer, of course, is the relational doctrine of space; there is no absolute position or velocity; there are just the relations of coordinate systems to one another, and ultimately of things to one another. And I think that the parallel question regarding denotation calls for a parallel answer, a relational theory of what the objects of a theories are. What makes sense is to say not what the objects of a theory are, absolutely speaking, but how one theory of objects is interpretable or reinterpretable in another.

The point is not that bare matter is inscrutable: that things are indistinguishable except by their properties. That point does not need making. The present point is reflected better in the riddle about seeing things upside down, or in complementary colors; for it is that things can be inscrutably switched even while carrying their properties with them. Rabbits differ from rabbit parts and rabbit stages not just as bare matter, after all, but in respect of properties; and formulas differ from numbers in respect of properties. What our present reflections are leading us to appreciate is that the riddle about seeing things upside down, or in complementary colors, should be taken seriously and its moral applied widely. The relativistic thesis to which we have come is this, to repeat: it makes no sense to say what the objects of a theory are, beyond saying how to interpret or reinterpret that theory in another. Suppose we are working within a theory and thus treating of its objects. We do so by using the variables of the theory, whose values those objects are, though there be no ultimate sense in which that universe can have been specified. In the language of the theory there are predicates by which to distinguish portions of this universe from other portions, and these predicates differ from one another purely in the roles they play in the laws of the theory. Within this background theory we can show how some subordinate theory, whose universe is some portion of the background universe, can by a reinterpretation be reduced to another subordinate theory whose universe is some lesser portion. Such talk of subordinate theories and their ontologies *is* meaningful, but only relative to the background theory with its own primitively adopted and ultimately inscrutable ontology.

To talk thus of theories raises a problem of formulation. A theory, it will be said, is a set of fully interpreted sentences. (More particularly, it is a deductively closed set: it includes all its own logical consequences, insofar as they are couched in the same notation.) But if the sentences of a theory are fully interpreted, then in particular the range of values of their variables is settled. How then can there be no sense in saying what the objects of a theory are?

My answer is simply that we cannot require theories to be fully interpreted, except in a relative sense, if anything is to count as a theory. In specifying a theory we must indeed fully specify, in our own words, what sentences are to comprise the theory, and what things are to be taken as values of the variables, and what things are to be taken as satisfying the predicate letters; insofar we do fully interpret the theory, *relative* to our own words and relative to our overall home theory which lies behind them. But this fixes the objects of the described theory only relative to those of the home theory; and these can, at will, be questioned in turn.

One is tempted to conclude simply that meaninglessness sets in when we try to pronounce on everything in our universe; that universal predication takes on sense only when furnished with the background of a wider universe, where the predication is no longer universal. And this is even a familiar doctrine, the doctrine that no proper predicate is true of everything. We have all heard it claimed that a predicate is meaningful only by contrast with what it excludes, and hence that being true of everything would make a predicate meaningless. But surely this doctrine is wrong. Surely self-identity, for instance, is not to be rejected as meaningless. For that matter, any statement of fact at all, however brutally meaningful, can be put artificially into a form in which it pronounces on everything. To say merely of Jones that he sings, for instance, is to say of everything that it is other than Jones or sings. We had better beware of repudiating universal predication, lest we be tricked into repudiating everything there is to say.

Carnap took an intermediate line in his doctrine of universal words, or *Allwörter*, in *The Logical Syntax of Language*. He did treat the predicating of universal words as "quasi-syntactical" – as a predication only by courtesy, and without empirical content. But universal words were for him not just any universally true predicates, like "is other than Jones or sings." They were a special breed of universally true predicates, ones that are universally true by the sheer meanings of their words and no thanks to nature. In his later writing this doctrine of universal words takes the form of a distinction between "internal" questions, in which a theory comes to grips with facts about the world, and "external" questions, in which people come to grips with the relative merits of theories.

Should we look to these distinctions of Carnap's for light on ontological relativity? When we found there was no absolute sense in saying what a theory is about, were we sensing the in-factuality of what Carnap calls "external questions"? When we found that saying what a theory is about did make sense against a background theory, were we sensing the factuality of internal questions of the background theory? I see no hope of illumination in this quarter. Carnap's universal words were not just any universally true predicates, but, as I said, a special breed; and what distinguishes this breed is not clear. What I said distinguished them was that they were universally true by sheer meanings and not by nature; but this is a very questionable distinction. Talking of "internal" and "external" is no better.

Ontological relativity is not to be clarified by any distinction between kinds of universal predication – unfactual and factual, external and internal. It is not a question of universal predication. When questions regarding the ontology of a theory are meaningless absolutely, and become meaningful relative to a background theory, this is not in general because the background theory has a wider universe. One is tempted, as I said a little while back, to suppose that it is; but one is then wrong.

What makes ontological questions meaningless when taken absolutely is not universality but circularity. A question of the form "What is an F?" can be answered only by recourse to a further term: "An F is a G." The answer makes only relative sense: sense relative to the uncritical acceptance of "G."

We may picture the vocabulary of a theory as comprising logical signs such as quantifiers and the signs for the truth functions and identity, and in addition descriptive or nonlogical signs, which, typically, are singular terms, or names, and general terms, or predicates. Suppose next that in the statements which comprise the theory, that is, are true according to the theory, we abstract from the meanings of the nonlogical vocabulary and from the range of the variables. We are left with the logical form of the theory, or, as I shall say, the *theory form*. Now we may interpret this theory form anew by picking a new universe for its variables of quantification to range over, and assigning objects from this universe to the names, and choosing subsets of this universe as extensions of the one-place predicates, and so on. Each such interpretation of the theory form is called a model of it, if it makes it come out true. Which of these models is meant in a given actual theory cannot, of course, be guessed from the theory form. The intended references of the names and predicates have to be learned rather by ostension, or else by paraphrase in some antecedently familiar vocabulary. But the first of these two ways has proved inconclusive, since, even apart from indeterminacies of translation affecting identity and other logical vocabulary, there is the problem of deferred ostension. Para-phrase in some antecedently familiar vocabulary, then, is our only recourse; and such is ontological relativity. To question the reference of all the terms of our all-inclusive theory becomes meaningless, simply for want of further terms relative to which to ask or answer the question.

It is thus meaningless within the theory to say which of the various possible models of our theory form is our real or intended model. Yet even here we can make sense still of there being many models. For we might be able to show that for each of the models, however unspecifiable, there is bound to be another which is a permutation or perhaps a diminution of the first.

Suppose, for example, that our theory is purely numerical. Its objects are just the natural numbers. There is no sense in saying, from within that theory, just which of the various models of number theory is in force. But we can observe even from within the theory that, whatever 0, 1, 2, 3, etc. may be, the theory would still hold true if the 17 of this series were moved into the role of 0, and the 18 moved into the role of 1, and so on.

Ontology is indeed doubly relative. Specifying the universe of a theory makes sense only relative to some background theory, and only relative to some choice of a manual of translation of the one theory into the other. Commonly of course the background theory will simply be a containing theory, and in this case no question of a manual of translation arises. But this is after all just a degenerate case of translation still – the case where the rule of translation is the homophonic one.

We cannot know what something is without knowing how it is marked off from other things. Identity is thus of a piece with ontology. Accordingly it is involved in the same relativity, as may be readily illustrated. Imagine a fragment of economic theory. Suppose its universe comprises persons, but its predicates are incapable of distinguishing between persons whose incomes are equal. The interpersonal relation of equality of income enjoys, within the theory, the substitutivity property of the identity relation itself; the two relations are indistinguishable. It is only relative to a background theory, in which more can be said of personal identity than equality of income, that we are able even to appreciate the above account of the fragment of economic theory, hinging as the account does on a contrast between persons and incomes.

A usual occasion for ontological talk is reduction, where it is shown how the universe of some theory can by a reinterpretation be dispensed with in favor of some other universe, perhaps a proper part of the first. I have treated elsewhere[14] of the reduction of one ontology to another with help of a *proxy function:* a function mapping the one universe into part or all of the other. For instance, the function "Gödel number of" is a proxy function. The universe of elementary proof theory or protosyntax, which consists of expressions or strings of signs, is mapped by this function into the universe of elementary number theory, which consists of numbers.

The proxy function used in reducing one ontology to another need not, like Gödel numbering, be one-to-one. We might, for instance, be confronted with a theory treating of both expressions and ratios. We would cheerfully reduce all this to the universe of natural numbers, by invoking a proxy function which enumerates the expressions in the Gödel way and enumerates the ratios by the classical method of short diagonals. This proxy function is not one-to-one, since it assigns the same natural number both to an expression and to a ratio. We would tolerate the resulting artificial convergence between expressions and ratios, simply because the original theory made no capital of the distinction between them; they were so invariably and extravagantly unlike that the identity question did not arise. Formally speaking, the original theory used a two-sorted logic.

For another kind of case where we would not require the proxy function to be one-to-one, consider again the fragment of economic theory lately noted. We would happily reduce its ontology of persons to a less numerous one of incomes. The proxy function would assign to each person his income. It is not one-to-one; distinct persons give way to identical incomes. The reason such a reduction is acceptable is that it merges the images of only such individuals as never had been distinguishable by the predicates of the original theory. Nothing in the old theory is contravened by the new identities.

If on the other hand the theory that we are concerned to reduce or reinterpret is straight protosyntax, or a straight arithmetic of ratios or of real numbers, then a one-to-one proxy function is mandatory. This is because any two elements of such a theory are distinguishable in terms of the theory. This is true even for the real numbers, even though not every real number is uniquely specifiable; any two real numbers x and y are still distinguishable, in that $x < y$ or $y < x$ and never $x < x$. A proxy function that did not preserve the distinctness of

the elements of such a theory would fail of its purpose of reinterpretation.

One ontology is *always* reducible to another when we are given a proxy function f that is one-to-one. The essential reasoning is as follows. Where P is any predicate of the old system, its work can be done in the new system by a new predicate which we interpret as true of just the correlates fx of the old objects x that P was true of. Thus suppose we take fx as the Gödel number of x, and as our old system we take a syntactical system in which one of the predicates is "is a segment of." The corresponding predicate of the new or numerical system, then, would be one which amounts, so far as its extension is concerned, to the words "is the Gödel number of a segment of that whose Gödel number is." The numerical predicate would not be given this devious form, of course, but would be rendered as an appropriate purely arithmetical condition.

Our dependence upon a background theory becomes especially evident when we reduce our universe U to another V by appeal to a proxy function. For it is only in a theory with an inclusive universe, embracing U and V, that we can make sense of the proxy function. The function maps U into V and hence needs all the old objects of U as well as their new proxies in V.

The proxy function need not exist as an object in the universe even of the background theory. It may do its work merely as what I have called a "virtual class,"[15] and Gödel has called a "notion."[16] That is to say, all that is required toward a function is an open sentence with two free variables, provided that it is fulfilled by exactly one value of the first variable for each object of the old universe as value of the second variable. But the point is that it is only in the background theory, with its inclusive universe, that we can hope to write such a sentence and have the right values at our disposal for its variables.

If the new objects happen to be among the old, so that V is a subclass of U, then the old theory with universe U can itself sometimes qualify as the background theory in which to describe its own ontological reduction. But we cannot do better than that; we cannot declare our new ontological economies without having recourse to the uneconomical old ontology.

This sounds, perhaps, like a predicament: as if no ontological economy is justifiable unless it is a false economy and the repudiated objects really exist after all. But actually this is wrong; there is no more cause for worry here than there is in *reductio ad absurdum*, where we assume a falsehood that we are out to disprove. If what we want to show is that the universe U is excessive and that only a part exists, or need exist, then we are quite within our rights to assume all of U for the space of the argument. We show thereby that if all of U were needed, then not all of U would be needed; and so our ontological reduction is sealed by *reductio ad absurdum*.

Toward further appreciating the bearing of ontological relativity on programs of ontological reduction, it is worthwhile to reexamine the philosophical bearing of the Löwenheim–Skolem theorem. I shall use the strong early form of the theorem,[17] which depends on the axiom of choice. It says that if a theory is true and has an indenumerable universe, then all but a denumerable part of that universe is dead wood, in the sense that it can be dropped from the range of the variables without falsifying any sentences.

On the face of it, this theorem declares a reduction of all acceptable theories to denumerable ontologies. Moreover, a denumerable ontology is reducible in turn to an ontology specifically of natural numbers, simply by taking the enumeration as the proxy function, if the enumeration is explicitly at hand. And even if it is not at hand, it exists; thus we can still think of all our objects as natural numbers, and merely reconcile ourselves to not always knowing, numerically, which number an otherwise given object is. May we not thus settle for an all-purpose Pythagorean ontology outright?

Suppose, afterward, someone were to offer us what would formerly have qualified as an ontological reduction – a way of dispensing in future theory with all things of a certain sort S, but still leaving an infinite universe. Now in the new Pythagorean setting his discovery would still retain its essential content, though relinquishing the form of an ontological reduction; it would take the form merely of a move whereby some numerically unspecified numbers were divested of some property of numbers that corresponded to S.

Blanket Pythagoreanism on these terms is unattractive, for it merely offers new and obscurer accounts of old moves and old problems. On this score again, then, the relativistic proposition seems reasonable: that there is no absolute sense in speaking of the ontology of a theory. It very creditably brands this Pythagoreanism itself as meaningless. For there is no absolute sense in saying that all the objects of a theory are numbers, or that they are sets, or bodies, or something else; this makes no sense unless relative to some background theory. The relevant predicates – "number," "set," "body," or whatever – would be distinguished from *one another* in the background theory by the roles they play in the laws of that theory.

Elsewhere I urged in answer to such Pythagoreanism that we have no ontological reduction in an interesting sense unless we can specify a proxy function. Now where does the strong Löwenheim–Skolem theorem leave us in this regard? If the background theory assumes the axiom of choice and even provides a notation for a general selector operator, can we in these terms perhaps specify an actual proxy function embodying the Löwenheim–Skolem argument?

The theorem is that all but a denumerable part of an ontology can be dropped and not be missed. One could imagine that the proof proceeds by partitioning the universe into denumerably many equivalence classes of indiscriminable objects, such that all but one member of each equivalence class can be dropped as superfluous; and one would then guess that where the axiom of choice enters the proof is in picking a survivor from each equivalence class. If this were so, then with help of Hilbert's selector notation we could indeed express a proxy function. But in fact the Löwenheim–Skolem proof has another structure. I see in the proof even of the strong Löwenheim–Skolem theorem no reason to suppose that a proxy function can be formulated anywhere that will map an indenumerable ontology, say the real numbers, into a denumerable one.

On the face of it, of course, such a proxy function is out of the question. It would have to be one-to-one, as we saw, to provide distinct images of distinct real numbers; and a one-to-one mapping of an indenumerable domain into a denumerable one is a contradiction. In particular it is easy to show in the Zermelo–Fraenkel system of set theory that such a function would neither exist nor admit even of formulation as a virtual class in the notation of the system.

The discussion of the ontology of a theory can make variously stringent demands upon the background theory in which the discussion is couched. The stringency of these demands varies with what is being said about the ontology of the object theory. We are now in a position to distinguish three such grades of stringency.

The least stringent demand is made when, with no view to reduction, we merely explain what things a theory is about, or what things its terms denote. This amounts to showing how to translate part or all of the object theory into the background theory. It is a matter really of showing how we *propose*, with some arbitrariness, to relate terms of the object theory to terms of the background theory; for we have the inscrutability of reference to allow for. But there is here no requirement that the background theory have a wider universe or a stronger vocabulary than the object theory. The theories could even be identical; this is the case when some terms are clarified by definition on the basis of other terms of the same language.

A more stringent demand was observed in the case where a proxy function is used to reduce an ontology. In this case the background theory needed the unreduced universe. But we saw, by considerations akin to *reductio ad absurdum*, that there was little here to regret.

The third grade of stringency has emerged now in the kind of ontological reduction hinted at by the Löwenheim–Skolem theorem. If a theory has by its own account an indenumerable universe, then even by taking that whole unreduced theory as background theory we cannot hope to produce a proxy function that would be adequate to reducing the ontology to a denumerable one. To find such a proxy function, even just a virtual one, we would need a background theory essentially stronger than the theory we were trying to reduce. This demand cannot, like the second grade of stringency above, be accepted in the spirit of *reductio ad absurdum*. It is a demand that simply discourages any general argument for Pythagoreanism from the Löwenheim–Skolem theorem.

A place where we see a more trivial side of ontological relativity is in the case of a finite universe of named objects. Here there is no occasion for quantification, except as an inessential abbreviation; for we can expand quantifications into finite conjunctions and alternations. Variables thus disappear, and with them the question of a universe of values of variables. And the very distinction between names and other signs lapses in turn, since the mark of a name is its admissibility in positions of variables. Ontology thus is emphatically meaningless for a finite theory of named objects, considered in and of itself. Yet we are now talking meaningfully of such finite ontologies. We are able to do so precisely because we are talking, however vaguely and implicitly, within a broader containing theory. What the objects of the finite theory are, makes sense only as a statement of the background theory in its own referential idiom. The answer to the question depends on the background theory, the finite foreground theory, and, of course, the particular manner in which we choose to translate or embed the one in the other.

Ontology is internally indifferent also, I think, to any theory that is complete and decidable. Where we can always settle truth values mechanically, there is no evident internal reason for interest in the theory of quantifiers nor, therefore, in values of variables. These matters take on significance only as we think of the decidable theory as embedded in a richer background theory in which the variables and their values are serious business.

Ontology may also be said to be internally indifferent even to a theory that is not decidable and does not have a finite universe, if it happens still that each of the infinitely numerous objects of the theory has a name. We can no longer expand quantifications into conjunctions and alternations, barring infinitely long expressions. We can, however, revise our semantical account of the truth conditions of quantification, in such a way as to turn our backs on questions of reference. We can explain universal quantifications as true when true under all substitutions; and correspondingly for existential. Such is the course that has been favored by Leśniewski and by Ruth Marcus.[18] Its nonreferential orientation is seen in the fact that it makes no essential use of namehood. That is, additional quantifications could be explained whose variables are place-holders for words of any syntactical category. *Substitutional* quantification, as I call it, thus brings no way of distinguishing names from other vocabulary, nor any way of distinguishing between genuinely referential or value-taking variables and other place-holders. Ontology is thus meaningless for a theory whose only quantification is substitutionally construed; meaningless, that is, insofar as the theory is considered in and of itself. The question of its ontology makes sense only relative to some translation of the theory into a background theory in which we use referential quantification. The answer depends on both theories and, again, on the chosen way of translating the one into the other.

A final touch of relativity can in some cases cap this, when we try to distinguish between substitutional and referential quantification. Suppose again a theory with an infinite lot of names, and suppose that, by Gödel numbering or otherwise, we are treating of the theory's notations and proofs within the terms of the theory. If we succeed in showing that every result of substituting a name for the variable in a certain open sentence is true in the theory, but at the same time we disprove the universal quantification of the sentence,[19] then certainly we have shown that the universe of the theory contained some nameless objects. This is a case where an absolute decision can be reached in favor of referential quantification and against substitutional quantification, without ever retreating to a background theory.

But consider now the opposite situation, where there is no such open sentence. Imagine on the contrary that, whenever an open sentence is such that each result of substituting a name in it can be proved, its universal quantification can be proved in the theory too. Under these circumstances we can construe the universe as devoid of nameless objects and hence reconstrue the quantifications as substitutional, but we need not. We could still construe the universe as containing nameless objects. It could just happen that the nameless ones are *inseparable* from the named ones, in this sense: it could happen that all properties of nameless objects that we can express in the notation of the theory are shared by named objects.

We could construe the universe of the theory as containing, e.g., all real numbers. Some of them are nameless, since the real numbers are indenumerable while the names are denumerable. But it could still happen that the nameless reals are inseparable from the named reals. This would leave us unable within the theory to prove a distinction between referential and substitutional quantification.[20] Every expressible quantification that is true when referentially construed remains true when substitutionally construed, and vice versa.

We might still make the distinction from the vantage point of a background theory. In it we might specify some real number that was nameless in the object theory; for there are always ways of strengthening a theory so as to name more real numbers, though never all. Further, in the background theory, we might construe the universe of the object theory as exhausting the real numbers. In the background theory we could, in this way, clinch the quantifications in the object theory as referential. But this clinching is doubly relative: it is relative to the background theory and to the interpretation or translation imposed on the object theory from within the background theory.

One might hope that this recourse to a background theory could often be avoided, even when the nameless reals are inseparable from the named reals in the object theory. One might hope by indirect means to show within the object theory that there are nameless reals. For we might prove within the object theory that the reals are indenumerable and that the names are denumerable and hence that there is no function whose arguments are names and whose values exhaust the real numbers. Since the relation of real numbers to their names would be such a function if each real number had a name, we would seem to have proved within the object theory itself that there are nameless reals and hence that quantification must be taken referentially.

However, this is wrong; there is a loophole. This reasoning would prove only that a relation of all real numbers to their names cannot exist as an entity in the universe of the theory. This reasoning denies no number a name in the notation of the theory, as long as the name relation does not belong to the universe of the theory. And anyway we should know better than to expect such a relation, for it is what causes Berry's and Richard's and related paradoxes.

Some theories can attest to their own nameless objects and so claim referential quantification on their own; other theories have to look to background theories for this service. We saw how a theory might attest to its own nameless objects, namely, by showing that some open sentence became true under all constant substitutions but false under universal quantification. Perhaps this is the only way a theory can claim referential import for its own quantifications. Perhaps, when the nameless objects happen to be inseparable from the named, the quantification used in a theory cannot meaningfully be declared referential except through the medium of a background theory. Yet referential quantification is the key idiom of ontology.

Thus ontology can be multiply relative, multiply meaningless apart from a background theory. Besides being unable to say in absolute terms just what the objects are, we are sometimes unable even to distinguish objectively between referential quantification and a substitutional counterfeit. When we do relativize these matters to a background theory, moreover, the relativization itself has two components: relativity to the choice of background theory and relativity to the choice of how to translate the object theory into the background theory. As for the ontology in turn of the background theory, and even the referentiality of its quantification – these matters can call for a background theory in turn.

There is not always a genuine regress. We saw that, if we are merely clarifying the range of the variables of a theory or the denotations of its terms, and are taking the referentiality of quantification itself for granted, we can commonly use the object theory itself as background theory. We found that when we undertake an ontological reduction, we must accept at least the unreduced theory in order to cite the proxy function; but this we were able cheerfully to accept in the spirit of *reductio ad absurdum* arguments. And now in the end we have found further that if we care to question quantification itself, and settle whether it imports a universe of discourse or turns merely on substitution at the linguistic level, we in some cases have genuinely to regress to a background language endowed with additional resources. We seem to have to do this unless the nameless objects are separable from the named in the object theory.

Regress in ontology is reminiscent of the now familiar regress in the semantics of truth and kindred notions – satisfaction, naming. We know from Tarski's work how the semantics, in this sense, of a theory regularly demands an in some way more inclusive theory. This similarity should perhaps not surprise us, since both ontology and satisfaction are matters of reference. In their elusiveness, at any rate – in their emptiness now and again except relative to a broader background – both truth and ontology may in a suddenly rather clear and even tolerant sense be said to belong to transcendental metaphysics.[21]

Note added in proof. Besides such ontological reduction as is provided by proxy functions (cf. pp. 55–7), there is that which consists simply in dropping objects whose absence will not falsify any truths expressible in the notation. Commonly this sort of deflation can be managed by proxy functions, but R. E. Grandy has shown me that sometimes it cannot. Let us by all means recognize it then as a further kind of reduction. In the background language we must, of course, be able to say what class of objects is dropped, just as in other cases we had to be able to specify the proxy function. This requirement seems sufficient still to stem any resurgence of Pythagoreanism on the strength of the Löwenheim–Skolem theorem.

Notes

1 J. Dewey, *Experience and Nature* (La Salle, Ill.: Open Court, 1925; repr. 1958), p. 179.

2 Ibid., p. 170.

3 Ibid., p. 185.

4 Ibid., p. 178.

5 W. V. Quine, *Word and Object* (Cambridge, Mass.: MIT Press, 1960), sect. 12.

6 L. Wittgenstein, *Philosophical Investigations* (New York: Macmillan, 1953), p. 14.

7 Cf. Quine, *Word and Object*, sect. 17.

8 Quine, *Word and Object*, sect. 15. For a summary of the general point of view see also sect. 1 of "Speaking of objects," in W. V. Quine, *Ontological Relativity and Other Essays* (New York: Columbia University Press, 1969).

9 To keep my account graphic, I am counting a certain postpositive particle as a suffix rather than a word.

10 See Leon Henkin, "Completeness in the theory of types," *Journal of Symbolic Logic* 15 (1950), pp. 81–91, and references therein.

11 For more on this theme see W. V. Quine, *Set Theory and its Logic* (Cambridge, Mass.: Harvard University Press, 1963, repr. 1969), sect. 11.

12 Paul Benacerraf, "What numbers cannot be," *Philosophical Review* 74 (1965), pp. 47–73, develops this point. His conclusions differ in some ways from those I shall come to.

13 N. L. Wilson, "Substances without substrata," *Review of Metaphysics* 12 (1959), pp. 521–39, at p. 532.

14 W. V. Quine, *The Ways of Paradox* (New York: Random House, 1966), pp. 204ff; or see "Ontological reduction and the world of numbers," this volume, ch. 38.

15 Quine, *Set Theory and its Logic*, sects 2f.

16 Kurt Gödel, *The Consistency of the Continuum Hypothesis* (Princeton: Princeton University Press, 1940), p. 11.

17 Thoralf Skolem, "Logisch-kombinatorische Untersuchungen über die Erfüllbarkeit oder Beweisbarkeit mathematischer Sätze nebst einem Theorem über dichte Mengen," *Skrifter utgit av Videnskapsselskapet i Kristiania* (1919); trans. in Jean van Heijenoort (ed.) *From Frege to Gödel: Source Book in the History of Mathematical Logic* (Cambridge, Mass.: Harvard University Press, 1967), pp. 252–63.

18 Ruth B. Marcus, "Modalities and intensional languages," *Synthese* 13 (1961), pp. 303–22. I cannot locate an adequate statement of Stanisław Leśniewski's philosophy of quantification in his writings; I have it from his conversations. E. C. Luschei, in

The Logical Systems of Leśniewski (Amsterdam: North-Holland, 1962), pp. 108f, confirms my attribution but still cites no passage. On this version of quantification see further "Existence and quantification," in Quine, *Ontological Relativity and Other Essays*.

19 Such is the typical way of a numerically insegregative system, misleadingly called "ω-inconsistent." See W. V. Quine, *Selected Logic Papers* (New York: Random House, 1966), pp. 118f, or "ω-inconsistency and a so-called axiom of infinity," *Journal of Symbolic Logic* 18 (1953), pp. 122f.

20 This possibility was suggested by Saul Kripke.

21 In developing these thoughts I have been helped by discussions with Saul Kripke, Thomas Nagel, and especially Burton Dreben.

PART II

Identity

Introduction

On the face of it, identity seems like the simplest of concepts: everything is identical with itself and with nothing else. But, as philosophers have long been aware, the concept of identity gives rise to some complex and difficult problems. One of these is the so-called Leibniz' law, or the identity of indiscernibles: Things with the same properties are one and the same. (The converse of this principle, also sometimes called "Leibniz' law," is uncontroversial: Identical things have the same properties.) In his "The Identity of Indiscernibles" (chapter 6), Max Black presents a possible objection to Leibniz' law, by presenting a by-now famous counterexample involving two distinct spheres that nonetheless appear to have exactly the same properties. (Black's example is discussed further by A. J. Ayer and D. J. O'Connor; see Further reading, below.)

Another question that has recently been much discussed is whether all statements of identity are metaphysically necessary or whether they can be contingent. The Evening Star is identical with the Morning Star. Given this, could or might the Evening Star not have been the Morning Star? It was long assumed that some identities, especially those that can be known only empirically, were only contingently true or contingently false, not necessarily true or necessarily false. Saul Kripke's challenge to this assumption, in "Identity and Necessity" (chapter 7), is among the more important developments in contemporary metaphysics, and has generated much discussion.

In "The Same *F*" (chapter 8), John Perry explores the claim, due to Peter Geach (see Further reading), that identities are relative to a *sortal*. That is, it is not proper to say simply '*x* is identical with *y*'; one should rather say 'x is *the same F* as y," where '*F*' is a sortal term denoting a kind. The following sort of example has been used in support of the doctrine of 'relative identity': although the chairman of the school board is not *the same official* as the postmaster, they are *the same person*. (This issue is further discussed in works by Fred Feldman and David Wiggins; see Further reading.)

In "Contingent Identity" (chapter 9), Allan Gibbard makes a case for contingent identities, and carefully and systematically investigates some complex issues involved in allowing identities that are not necessary. The issue of sortal relativity of identity reappears in this context. Stephen Yablo, too, is concerned, in his "Identity, Essence, and Indiscernibility" (chapter 10), with the problem of making sense of identities and related relations that are not necessary, and develops a scheme that is interestingly different from that of Gibbard. The distinction between essential and contingent properties of an object plays a large role in Yablo, and his distinctions between "categorical" and "hypothetical" properties, and between "coincidence" and "identity," are worthy of note. (Modal concepts, such as necessity and contingency, which are used prominently in some of the chapters in this section, are treated more fully in Part III, "Modalities and Possible Worlds.")

Further reading

Ayer, A. J., "The identity of indiscernibles," in *Philosophical Essays* (New York: St Martin's Press; London: Macmillan, 1954).

Cartwright, Richard, "Identity and substitutivity," in *Philosophical Essays* (Cambridge, Mass.: MIT Press, 1987).

Feldman, Fred, "Geach and relative identity," *Review of Metaphysics* 22 (1968/9), pp. 547–55.

Geach, Peter, "Identity" and "Identity – a reply," in *Logic Matters* (Oxford: Basil Blackwell, 1972).

Kripke, Saul, *Naming and Necessity* (Cambridge, Mass.: Harvard University Press, 1980).

Lowe, E. J., "What is a criterion of identity?," *Philosophical Quarterly* 39 (1989), pp. 1–21.

O'Connor, D. J., "The identity of indiscernibles," *Analysis* 14 (1954), pp. 102–10.

Salmon, Nathan, *Frege's Puzzle* (Cambridge, Mass.: MIT Press, 1986).

Wiggins, David, *Sameness and Substance* (Cambridge, Mass.: Harvard University Press, 1980).

6

The Identity of Indiscernibles

Max Black

A: The principle of the Identity of Indiscernibles seems to me obviously true. And I don't see how we are going to define identity or establish the connection between mathematics and logic without using it.

B: It seems to me obviously false. And your troubles as a mathematical logician are beside the point. If the principle is false, you have no right to use it.

A: You simply *say* it's false – and even if you said so three times, that wouldn't make it so.

B: Well, you haven't done anything more yourself than assert the principle to be true. As Bradley once said, 'assertion can demand no more than counter-assertion; and what is affirmed on the one side, we on the other can simply deny.'

A: How will this do for an argument? If two things, *a* and *b*, are given, the first has the property of being identical with *a*. Now *b* cannot have this property, for else *b* would be *a*, and we should have only one thing, not two as assumed. Hence *a* has at least one property, which *b* does not have, that is to say the property of being identical with *a*.

B: This is a roundabout way of saying nothing, for '*a* has the property of being identical with *a*' means no more than '*a* is *a*'. When you begin to say '*a* is . . .' I am supposed to know what thing you are referring to as '*a*', and I expect to be told something about that thing. But when you end the sentence

with the words ' . . . is *a*', I am left still waiting. The sentence '*a* is *a*' is a useless tautology.

A: Are you as scornful about difference as about identity? For *a* also has, and *b* does not have, the property of being different from *b*. This is a second property that the one thing has but not the other.

B: All you are saying is that *b* is different from *a*. I think the form of words '*a* is different from *b*' does have the advantage over '*a* is *a*' that it might be used to give information. I might learn from hearing it used that '*a*' and '*b*' were applied to different things. But this is not what you want to say, since you are trying to use the names, not mention them. When I already know what '*a*' and '*b*' stand for, '*a* is different from *b*' tells me nothing. It, too, is a useless tautology.

A: I wouldn't have expected you to treat 'tautology' as a term of abuse. Tautology or not, the sentence has a philosophical use. It expresses the necessary truth that different things have at least one property not in common. Thus different things must be discernible; and hence, by contraposition, indiscernible things must be identical. Q.E.D.

B: Why obscure matters by this old-fashioned language? By 'indiscernible' I suppose you mean the same as 'having all properties in common' Do you claim to have proved that two things having all their properties in common are identical?

A: Exactly.

B: Then this is a poor way of stating your conclusion. If *a* and *b* are identical, there is just one thing having the two names '*a*' and '*b*'; and in that case it is absurd to say that *a* and *b* are two. Conversely, once you have supposed there are *two*

Originally published in *Mind 51* (1952), and reprinted in Max Black, *Problems of Analysis* (1954), pp. 204–16.

things having all their properties in common, you can't without contradicting yourself say that *they* are 'identical'.

A: I can't believe you were really misled. I simply meant to say it is logically impossible for two things to have all their properties in common. I showed that *a* must have at least two properties – the property of being identical with *a* and the property of being different from *b* – neither of which can be a property of *b*. Doesn't this prove the principle of identity of indiscernibles?

B: Perhaps you have proved something. If so, the nature of your proof should show us exactly what you have proved. If you want to call 'being identical with *a*' a 'property' I suppose I can't prevent you. But you must then accept the consequences of this way of talking. All you mean when you say '*a* has the property of being identical with *a*' is that *a* is *a*. And all you mean when you say '*b* does not have the property of being identical with *a*' is that *b* is not *a*. So what you have 'proved' is that *a* is *a* and *b* is not *a*; that is to say, *b* and *a* are different. Similarly, when you said that *a*, but not *b*, had the property of being different from *b*, you were simply saying that *a* and *b* were different. In fact you are merely redescribing the hypothesis that *a* and *b* are different by calling it a case of 'difference of properties'. Drop the misleading description and your famous principle reduces to the truism that different things are different. How true! And how uninteresting!

A: Well, the properties of identity and difference may be uninteresting, but they *are* properties. If I had shown that grass was green, I suppose you would say I hadn't shown that grass was coloured.

B: You certainly would not have shown that grass had any colour *other than* green.

A: What it comes to is that you object to the conclusion of my argument *following* from the premiss that *a* and *b* are different.

B: No, I object to the triviality of the conclusion. If you want to have an interesting principle to defend, you must interpret 'property' more narrowly – enough so, at any rate, for 'identity' and 'difference' not to count as properties.

A: Your notion of an interesting principle seems to be one which I shall have difficulty in establishing. Will you at least allow me to include among 'properties' what are sometimes called 'relational characteristics' – like *being married to Caesar* or *being at a distance from London*?

B: Why not? If you are going to defend the principle, it is for you to decide what version you wish to defend.

A: In that case, I don't need to count identity and difference as properties. Here is a different argument that seems to me quite conclusive. The only way we can discover that two different things exist is by finding out that one has a quality not possessed by the other or else that one has a relational characteristic that the other hasn't.

If *both* are blue and hard and sweet and so on, and have the same shape and dimensions and are in the same relations to everything in the universe, it is logically impossible to tell them apart. The supposition that in such a case there might really be two things would be unverifiable *in principle*. Hence it would be meaningless.

B: You are going too fast for me.

A: Think of it this way. If the principle were false, the fact that I can see only two of your hands would be no proof that you had just two. And even if every conceivable test agreed with the supposition that you had two hands, you might all the time have three, four, or any number. You might have nine hands, different from one another and all indistinguishable from your left hand, and nine more all different from each other but indistinguishable from your right hand. And even if you really did have just two hands, and no more, neither you nor I nor anybody else could ever know that fact. This is too much for me to swallow. This is the kind of absurdity you get into, as soon as you abandon verifiability as a test of meaning.

B: Far be it from me to abandon your sacred cow. Before I give you a direct answer, let me try to describe a counter-example.

Isn't it logically possible that the universe should have contained nothing but two exactly similar spheres? We might suppose that each was made of chemically pure iron, had a diameter of one mile, that they had the same temperature, colour, and so on, and that nothing else existed. Then every quality and relational characteristic of the one would also be a property of the other. Now if what I am describing is logically possible, it is not impossible for two things to have all their properties in common. This seems to me to *refute* the Principle.

A: Your supposition, I repeat, isn't verifiable and therefore can't be regarded as meaningful. But supposing you *have* described a possible world, I still don't see that you have refuted the principle. Consider one of the spheres, *a*, . . .

B: How can I, since there is no way of telling them apart? *Which* one do you want me to consider?

A: This is very foolish. I mean either of the two spheres, leaving you to decide which one you wished to consider. If I were to say to you 'Take any book off the shelf', it would be foolish on your part to reply 'Which?'

B: It's a poor analogy. I know how to take a book off a shelf, but I don't know how to identify one of two spheres supposed to be alone in space and so symmetrically placed with respect to each other that neither has any quality or character the other does not also have.

A: All of which goes to show as I said before, the unverifiability of your supposition. Can't you imagine that one sphere has been designated as '*a*'?

B: I can imagine only what is logically possible. Now it is logically possible that somebody should enter the universe I have described, see one of the spheres on his left hand and proceed to call it '*a*'. I can imagine that all right, if that's enough to satisfy you.

A: Very well, now let me try to finish what I began to say about *a* . . .

B: I still can't let you, because you, in your present situation, have no right to talk about *a*. All I have conceded is that if something were to happen to introduce a change into my universe, so that an observer entered and could see the two spheres, one of them could then have a name. But this would be a different supposition from the one I wanted to consider. My spheres don't yet have names. If an observer were to enter the scene, he could perhaps put a red mark on one of the spheres. You might just as well say 'By "*a*" I mean the sphere which would be the first to be marked by a red mark if anyone were to arrive and were to proceed to make a red mark!' You might just as well ask me to consider the first daisy in my lawn that would be picked by a child, if a child were to come along and do the picking. This doesn't now distinguish any daisy from the others. You are just pretending to use a name.

A: And I think you are just pretending not to understand me. All I am asking you to do is to think of one of your spheres, no matter which, so that I may go on to say something about it when you give me a chance.

B: You talk as if naming an object and then thinking about it were the easiest thing in the world. But it isn't so easy. Suppose I tell you to name any spider in my garden: if you can catch one first or describe one uniquely, you can name it easily enough. But you can't pick one out, let alone 'name' it, by just thinking. You remind me of the mathematicians who thought that talking about an Axiom of Choice would really allow them to choose a single member of a collection when they had no criterion of choice.

A: At this rate you will never give me a chance to say anything. Let me try to make my point without using names. Each of the spheres will surely differ from the other in being at some distance from that other one, but at no distance from itself – that is to say, it will bear at least one relation to itself – *being at no distance from*, or *being in the same place as* – that it does not bear to the other. And this will serve to distinguish it from the other.

B: Not at all. *Each* will have the relational characteristic *being at a distance of two miles*, say, *from the centre of a sphere one mile in diameter*, etc. And each will have the relational characteristic (if you want to call it that) of *being in the same place as itself*. The two are alike in this respect as in all others.

A: But look here. Each sphere occupies a different place; and this at least will distinguish them from one another.

B: This sounds as if you thought the places had some independent existence, though I don't suppose you really think so. To say the spheres are in 'different places' is just to say that there is a distance between the two spheres; and we have already seen that that will not serve to distinguish them. Each is at a distance – indeed the same distance – from the other.

A: When I said they were at different places, I didn't mean simply that they were at a distance from one another. That one sphere is in a certain place does not entail the existence of any *other* sphere. So to say that one sphere is in its place, and the other in its place, and then to add that these places are different seems to me different from saying the spheres are at a distance from one another.

B: What does it mean to say 'a sphere is in its place'? Nothing at all, so far as I can see. Where else could it be? *All* you are saying is that the spheres are in different places.

A: Then my retort is, What does it mean to say 'Two spheres are in different places'? Or, as you so neatly put it, 'Where else could they be?'

B: You have a point. What I should have said was that your assertion that the spheres occupied different places said nothing at all, unless you were drawing attention to the necessary truth that different physical objects must be in different places. Now if two spheres must be in different places, as indeed they must, to say that the spheres occupy different places is to say no more than they are two spheres.

A: This is like a point you made before. You won't allow me to deduce anything from the supposition that there are two spheres.

B: Let me put it another way. In the two–sphere universe, the only reason for saying that the places occupied were different would be that different things occupied them. So in order to show the places were different, you would first have to show, in some other way, that the spheres were different. You will never be able to distinguish the spheres by means of the places they occupy.

A: A minute ago, you were willing to allow that somebody might give your spheres different names. Will you let me suppose that some traveller has visited your monotonous 'universe' and has named one sphere 'Castor' and the other 'Pollux'?

B: All right – provided you don't try to use those names yourself.

A: Wouldn't the traveller, at least, have to recognize that *being at a distance of two miles from Castor* was not the same property as being at a distance of two miles *from Pollux*?

B: I don't see why. If he were to see that Castor and Pollux had exactly the same properties, he would see that 'being at a distance of two miles from Castor' meant exactly the same as 'being at a distance of two miles from Pollux'.

A: They couldn't mean the same. If they did, *'being at a distance of two miles from Castor and at the same time not being at a distance of two miles from Pollux'* would be a self-contradictory description. But plenty of bodies could answer to this description. Again, if the two expressions meant the same, anything which was two miles from Castor would have to be two miles from Pollux – which is clearly false. So the two expressions don't mean the same, and the two spheres have at least two properties not in common.

B: Which?

A: *Being at a distance of two miles from Castor* and *being at a distance of two miles from Pollux*.

B: But now you are *using* the words 'Castor' and 'Pollux' as if they really stood for something. They are just our old friends '*a*' and '*b*' in disguise.

A: You surely don't want to say that the arrival of the name-giving traveller creates spatial properties? Perhaps we can't name your spheres and therefore can't name the corresponding properties; but the properties must be there.

B: What can this mean? The traveller has not visited the spheres, and the spheres have no names – neither 'Castor', nor 'Pollux', nor '*a*', nor '*b*', nor any others. Yet you still want to say they

have certain properties which cannot be referred to without using names for the spheres. You want to say 'the property of being at a distance from Castor', though it is logically impossible for you to talk in this way. You can't speak, but you won't be silent.

A: How eloquent, and how unconvincing! But since you seem to have convinced yourself, at least, perhaps you can explain another thing that bothers me: I don't see that you have a right to talk as you do about places or spatial relations in connection with your so-called universe. So long as we are talking about our own universe – *the* universe – I know what you mean by 'distance', 'diameter', 'place' and so on. But in what you want to call a universe, even though it contains only two objects, I don't see what such words could mean. So far as I can see, you are applying these spatial terms in their present usage to a hypothetical situation which contradicts the presuppositions of that usage.

B: What do you mean by 'presupposition'?

A: Well, you spoke of measured distances, for one thing. Now this presupposes some means of measurement. Hence your 'universe' must contain at least a third thing – a ruler or some other measuring device.

B: Are you claiming that a universe must have at least three things in it? What is the least number of things required to make a world?

A: No, all I am saying is that you cannot describe a configuration as *spatial* unless it includes at least three objects. This is part of the meaning of 'spatial' – and it is no more mysterious than saying you can't have a game of chess without there existing at least thirty-five things (thirty-two pieces, a chessboard, and two players).

B: If this is all that bothers you, I can easily provide for three or any number of things without changing the force of my counter-example. The important thing, for my purpose, was that the configuration of two spheres was symmetrical. So long as we preserve this feature of the imaginary universe, we can now allow any number of objects to be found in it.

A: You mean any *even* number of objects.

B: Quite right. Why not imagine a plane running clear through space, with everything that happens on one side of it always exactly duplicated at an equal distance in the other side.

A: A kind of cosmic mirror producing real images.

B: Yes, except that there wouldn't be any mirror! The point is that in *this* world we can imagine any degree of complexity and change to occur. No reason to exclude rulers, compasses and weighing machines. No reason, for that matter, why the Battle of Waterloo shouldn't happen.

A: Twice over, you mean – with Napoleon surrendering later in two different places simultaneously!

B: Provided you wanted to call both of them 'Napoleon'.

A: So your point is that everything could be duplicated on the other side of the non-existent Looking Glass. I suppose whenever a man got married, his identical twin would be marrying the identical twin of the first man's fiancée?

B: Exactly.

A: Except that 'identical twins' wouldn't be *numerically* identical?

B: You seem to be agreeing with me.

A: Far from it. This is just a piece of gratuitous metaphysics. If the inhabitants of your world had enough sense to know what was sense and what wasn't, they would never suppose all the events in their world were duplicated. It would be much more sensible for them to regard the 'second' Napoleon as a mere mirror image – and similarly for all the other supposed 'duplicates'.

B: But they could walk through the 'mirror' and find water just as wet, sugar just as sweet, and grass just as green on the other side.

A: You don't understand me. They would not postulate 'another side'. A man looking at the 'mirror' would be seeing *himself*, not a duplicate. If he walked in a straight line toward the 'mirror', he would eventually find himself back at his starting point, not at a duplicate of his starting point. This would involve their having a different geometry from ours – but that would be preferable to the logician's nightmare of the reduplicated universe.

B: They might think so – until the twins really began to behave differently for the first time!

A: Now it's you who are tinkering with your supposition. You can't have your universe and change it too.

B: All right, I retract.

A: The more I think about your 'universe', the queerer it seems. What would happen when a man crossed your invisible 'mirror'? While he was actually crossing, his body would have to change shape, in order to preserve the symmetry. Would it gradually shrink to nothing and then expand again?

B: I confess I hadn't thought of that.

A: And here is something that explodes the whole notion. Would you say that one of the two Napoleons in your universe had his heart in the right place – literally, I mean?

B: Why, of course.

A: In that case his 'mirror-image' twin would have the heart on the opposite side of the body. One Napoleon would have his heart on the left of his body, and the other would have it on the right of his body.

B: It's a good point, though it would still make objects like spheres indistinguishable. But let me try again. Let me abandon the original idea of a *plane* of symmetry and suppose instead that we have only a *centre* of symmetry. I mean that everything that happened at any place would be exactly duplicated at a place an equal distance on the opposite side of the centre of symmetry. In short, the universe would be what the mathematicians call 'radially symmetrical'. And to avoid complications, we could suppose that the centre of symmetry itself was physically inaccessible, so that it would be impossible for any material body to pass through it. Now in *this* universe, identical twins would have to be either both right-handed or both left-handed.

A: Your universes are beginning to be as plentiful as blackberries. You are too ingenuous to see the force of my argument about verifiability. Can't you see that your supposed description of a universe in which everything has its 'identical twin' doesn't describe anything verifiably different from a corresponding universe without such duplication? This must be so, no matter what kind of symmetry your universe manifested.

B: You are assuming that in order to verify that there are two things of a certain kind, it must be possible to show that one has a property not possessed by the other. But this is not so. A pair of very close but similar magnetic poles produce a characteristic field of force which assures me that there are two poles, even if I have no way of examining them separately. The presence of two exactly similar stars at a great distance might be detected by some resultant gravitational effect or by optical interference – or in some such similar way – even though we had no way of inspecting one in isolation from the other. Don't physicists say something like this about the electrons inside an atom? We can verify *that* there are two, that is to say a certain property of the whole configuration, even though there is no way of detecting any character that uniquely characterises any element of the configuration.

A: But if you were to approach your two stars one would have to be on your left and one on the right'. And this would distinguish them.

B: I agree. Why shouldn't we say that the two stars are distinguishable – meaning that it would be possible for an observer to see one on his left and the other on his right, or more generally, that it would be *possible* for one star to come to have a relation to a third object that the second star would not have to that third object.

A: So you agree with me after all.

B: Not if you mean that the two stars do not have all their properties in common. All I said was that it was logically possible for them to enter into different relationships with a third object. But this would be a change in the universe.

A: If you are right, nothing unobserved would be observable. For the presence of an observer would always change it, and the observation would always be an observation of something else.

B: I don't say that every observation changes what is observed. My point is that there isn't any *being to the right* or *being to the left* in the two-sphere universe until an observer is introduced, that is to say until a real change is made.

A: But the spheres themselves wouldn't have changed.

B: Indeed they would: they would have acquired new relational characteristics. In the absence of any asymmetric observer, I repeat, the spheres would have all their properties in common (including, if you like, the power to enter into different relations with other objects). Hence the principle of identity of indiscernibles is false.

A: So perhaps you really do have twenty hands after all?

B: Not a bit of it. Nothing that I have said prevents me from holding that we can verify *that* there are exactly two. But we could know *that* two things existed without there being any way to distinguish one from the other. The Principle is false.

A: I am not surprised that you ended in this way, since you assumed it in the description of your fantastic 'universe'. Of course, if you began by assuming that the spheres were numerically different though qualitatively alike, you could end by 'proving' what you first assumed.

B: But I wasn't 'proving' anything. I tried to support my contention that it is logically possible for two things to have all their properties in common by giving an illustrative description. (Similarly, if I had to show it is logically possible for nothing at all to be seen, I would ask you to imagine a universe in which everybody was blind.) It was for you to show that my description concealed some hidden contradiction. And you haven't done so.

A: All the same I am not convinced.

B: Well, then, you ought to be.

7

Identity and Necessity

Saul Kripke

A problem which has arisen frequently in contemporary philosophy is: "How are *contingent* identity statements possible?" This question is phrased by analogy with the way Kant phrased his question "How are synthetic a priori judgments possible?" In both cases, it has usually been taken for granted in the one case by Kant that synthetic a priori judgments were possible, and in the other case in contemporary philosophical literature that contingent statements of identity are possible. I do not intend to deal with the Kantian question except to mention this analogy: After a rather thick book was written trying to answer the question how synthetic a priori judgments were possible, others came along later who claimed that the solution to the problem was that synthetic a priori judgments were, of course, impossible and that a book trying to show otherwise was written in vain. I will not discuss who was right on the possibility of synthetic a priori judgments. But in the case of contingent statements of identity, most philosophers have felt that the notion of a contingent identity statement ran into something like the following paradox. An argument like the following can be given against the possibility of contingent identity statements:[1]

First, the law of the substitutivity of identity says that, for any objects x and y, if x is identical to y, then if x has a certain property F, so does y:

Originally published in Milton K. Munitz (ed.), *Identity and Individuation* (1971), pp. 135–64. Reprinted by permission of New York University Press © Copyright by New York University.

(1) $(x)(y)[(x = y) \supset (Fx \supset Fy)]$

On the other hand, every object surely is necessarily self-identical:

(2) $(x)\Box(x = x)$

But

(3) $(x)(y)(x = y) \supset [\Box(x = x) \supset \Box(x = y)]$

is a substitution instance of (1), the substitutivity law. From (2) and (3), we can conclude that, for every x and y, if x equals y, then, it is necessary that x equals y:

(4) $(x)(y)((x = y) \supset \Box(x = y))$

This is because the clause $\Box(x = x)$ of the conditional drops out because it is known to be true.

This is an argument which has been stated many times in recent philosophy. Its conclusion, however, has often been regarded as highly paradoxical. For example, David Wiggins, in his paper, "Identity-Statements," says:

> Now there undoubtedly exist contingent identity-statements. Let $a = b$ be one of them. From its simple truth and (5) [=(4) above] we can derive "$\Box(a = b)$". But how then can there be any contingent identity-statements?[2]

He then says that five various reactions to this argument are possible, and rejects all of these reactions, and reacts himself. I do not want to discuss all the possible reactions to this statement, except to mention the second of those Wiggins rejects. This says:

> We might accept the result and plead that provided '*a*' and '*b*' are proper names nothing is amiss. The consequence of this is that no contingent identity-statements can be made by means of proper names.

And then he says that he is discontented with this solution, and many other philosophers have been discontented with this solution, too, while still others have advocated it.

What makes the statement (4) seem surprising? It says, for any objects x and y, if x is y, then it is necessary that x is y. I have already mentioned that someone might object to this argument on the grounds that premise (2) is already false, that it is not the case that everything is necessarily self-identical. Well, for example, am I myself necessarily self-identical? Someone might argue that in some situations which we can imagine I would not even have existed, and therefore the statement "Saul Kripke is Saul Kripke" would have been false, or it would not be the case that I was self-identical. Perhaps, it would have been neither true nor false, in such a world, to say that Saul Kripke is self-identical. Well, that may be so, but really it depends on one's philosophical view of a topic that I will not discuss: that is, what is to be said about truth-values of statements mentioning objects that do not exist in the actual world or any given possible world or counterfactual situation. Let us interpret necessity here weakly. We can count statements as necessary if, whenever the objects mentioned therein exist, the statement would be true. If we wished to be very careful about this, we would have to go into the question of existence as a predicate and ask if the statement can be reformulated in the form: For every x it is necessary that, if x exists, then x is self-identical. I will not go into this particular form of subtlety here because it is not going to be relevant to my main theme. Nor am I really going to consider formula (4). Anyone who believes formula (2) is, in my opinion, committed to formula (4). If x and y are the same things and we can talk about modal properties of an object at all, that is, in the usual parlance, we can speak of modality *de re* and an object *necessarily* having certain properties as such, then formula (1), I think, has to hold. Where x is any

property at all, including a property involving modal operators, and if x and y are the same object and x had a certain property F, then y has to have the same property F. And this is so even if the property F is itself of the form of necessarily having some other property G, in particular that of necessarily being identical to a certain object. Well, I will not discuss the formula (4) itself because by itself it does not assert, of any particular true statement of identity, that it is necessary. It does not say anything about *statements* at all. It says for every *object* x and *object* y, if x and y are the same object, then it is necessary that x and y are the same object. And this, I think, if we think about it (anyway, if someone does not think so, I will not argue for it here), really amounts to something very little different from the statement (2). Since x, by definition of identity, is the only object identical with x, "$(y)(y = x \supset Fy)$" seems to me to be little more than a garrulous way of saying "Fx," and thus $(x)(y)(y = x \supset Fx)$ says the same as $(x)Fx$ no matter what "F" is – in particular, even if "F" stands for the property of necessary identity with x. So if x has this property (of necessary identity with x), trivially everything identical with x has it, as (4) asserts. But, from statement (4) one may apparently be able to deduce that various particular statements of identity must be necessary, and this is then supposed to be a very paradoxical consequence.

Wiggins says, "Now there undoubtedly exist contingent identity-statements." One example of a contingent identity statement is the statement that the first Postmaster General of the United States is identical with the inventor of bifocals, or that both of these are identical with the man claimed by the *Saturday Evening Post* as its founder (*falsely* claimed, I gather, by the way). Now some such statements are plainly contingent. It plainly is a contingent fact that one and the same man both invented bifocals and took on the job of Postmaster General of the United States. How can we reconcile this with the truth of statement (4)? Well, that, too, is an issue I do not want to go into in detail except to be very dogmatic about it. It was, I think, settled quite well by Bertrand Russell in his notion of the scope of a description. According to Russell, one can, for example, say with propriety that the author of *Hamlet* might not have written *Hamlet*, or even that the author of *Hamlet* might not have been the author of *Hamlet*. Now here, of course, we do not deny the necessity of the identity of an object with itself; but we say it is true concerning a certain man that he in fact was the unique person to have written *Hamlet* and secondly that the man, who in fact was the man who wrote *Hamlet*, might not have written *Hamlet*. In other words, if Shakespeare had decided not to write tragedies, he might not have written *Hamlet*. Under these circumstances, the man who in fact wrote *Hamlet* would not have written *Hamlet*. Russell brings this out by saying that in such a statement, the first occurrence of the description "the author of *Hamlet*" has large scope.[3] That is, we say, "The author of *Hamlet* has the following property: that he might not have written *Hamlet*." We *do not* assert that the following statement might have been the case, namely that the author of *Hamlet* did not write *Hamlet*, for that is not true. That would be to say that it might have been the case that someone wrote *Hamlet* and yet did not write *Hamlet*, which would be a contradiction. Now, aside from the details of Russell's particular formulation of it, which depends on his theory of descriptions, this seems to be the distinction that any theory of descriptions has to make. For example, if someone were to meet the President of Harvard and take him to be a Teaching Fellow, he might say: "I took the President of Harvard for a Teaching Fellow." By this he does not mean that he took the proposition "The President of Harvard is a Teaching Fellow" to be true. He could have meant this, for example, had he believed that some sort of democratic system had gone so far at Harvard that the President of it decided to take on the task of being a Teaching Fellow. But that probably is not what he means. What he means instead, as Russell points out, is "Someone is President of Harvard and I took him to be a Teaching Fellow." In one of Russell's examples someone says, "I thought your yacht is much larger than it is." And the other man replies, "No, my yacht is not much larger than it is."

Provided that the notion of modality *de re*, and thus of quantifying into modal contexts, makes any sense at all, we have quite an adequate solution to the problem of avoiding paradoxes if we substitute descriptions for the universal quantifiers in (4) because the only consequence we will draw,[4] for example, in the bifocals case, is that there is a man who both happened to have invented bifocals and happened to have been the first Postmaster General of the United States, and is necessarily self-identical. There is an object x such that x invented bifocals, and as a matter of contingent fact an object y, such that y is the first Postmaster General of the United States, and finally, it is necessary, that x is y. What are x and y here? Here, x and y are both

Benjamin Franklin, and it can certainly be necessary that Benjamin Franklin is identical with himself. So, there is no problem in the case of descriptions if we accept Russell's notion of scope.[5] And I just dogmatically want to drop that question here and go on to the question about names which Wiggins raises. And Wiggins says he might accept the result and plead that, provided *a* and *b* are proper names, nothing is amiss. And then he reject this.

Now what is the special problem about proper names? At least if one is not familiar with the philosophical literature about this matter, one naïvely feels something like the following about proper names. First, if someone says "Cicero was an orator," then he uses the name "Cicero" in that statement simply to pick out a certain object and then to ascribe a certain property to the object, namely, in this case, he ascribes to a certain man the property of having been an orator. If someone else uses another name, such as, say, "Tully," he is still speaking about the same man. One ascribes the same property, if one says "Tully is an orator," to the same man. So to speak, the fact, or state of affairs, represented by the statement is the same whether one says "Cicero is an orator" or one says "Tully is an orator." It would, therefore, seem that the function of names is *simply* to refer, and not to describe the objects so named by such properties as "being the inventor of bifocals" or "being the first Postmaster General." It would seem that Leibniz' law and the law (1) should not only hold in the universally quantified form, but also in the form "if $a = b$ and Fa, then Fb," wherever "a" and "b" stand in place of names and "F" stands in place of a predicate expressing a genuine property of the object:

$$(a = b \cdot Fa) \supset Fb$$

We can run the same argument through again to obtain the conclusion where "a" and "b" replace any names, "If $a = b$, then necessarily $a = b$." And so, we could venture this conclusion: that whenever "a" and "b" are proper names, if a is b, that it is necessary that a is b. Identity statements between proper names have to be necessary if they are going to be true at all. This view in fact has been advocated, for example, by Ruth Barcan Marcus in a paper of hers on the philosophical interpretation of modal logic.[6] According to this view, whenever, for example, someone makes a correct statement of identity between two names, such as, for example, that Cicero is Tully, his statement has to be necessary if it is true. But such a conclusion *seems* plainly to be false. (I, like other philosophers, have a habit of understatement in which "it seems plainly false" means "it is plainly false." Actually, I think the view is true, though not quite in the form defended by Mrs Marcus.) At any rate, it seems plainly false. One example was given by Professor Quine in his reply to Professor Marcus at the symposium: "I think I see trouble anyway in the contrast between proper names and descriptions as Professor Marcus draws it. The paradigm of the assigning of proper names is tagging. We may tag the planet Venus some fine evening with the proper name 'Hesperus'. We may tag the same planet again someday before sunrise with the proper name 'Phosphorus'." (Quine thinks that something like that actually was done once.) "When, at last, we discover that we have tagged the same planet twice, our discovery is empirical, and not because the proper names were descriptions." According to what we are told, the planet Venus seen in the morning was originally thought to be a star and was called "the Morning Star," or (to get rid of any question of using a description) was called "Phosphorus." One and the same planet, when seen in the evening, was thought to be another star, the Evening Star, and was called "Hesperus." Later on, astronomers discovered that Phosphorus and Hesperus were one and the same. Surely no amount of a priori ratiocination on their part could conceivably have made it possible for them to deduce that Phosphorus is Hesperus. In fact, given the information they had, it might have turned out the other way. Therefore, it is argued, the statement "Hesperus is Phosphorus" has to be an ordinary contingent, empirical truth, one which might have come out otherwise, and so the view that true identity statements between names are necessary has to be false. Another example which Quine gives in *Word and Object* is taken from Professor Schrödinger, the famous pioneer of quantum mechanics: A certain mountain can be seen from both Tibet and Nepal. When seen from one direction, it was called "Gaurisanker"; when seen from another direction, it was called "Everest"; and then, later on, the empirical discovery was made that Gaurisanker *is* Everest. (Quine further says that he gathers the example is actually geographically incorrect. I guess one should not rely on physicists for geographical information.)

Of course, one possible reaction to this argument is to deny that names like "Cicero," "Tully," "Gaurisanker," and "Everest" really are proper names. Look, someone might say (someone has said it: his name was "Bertrand Russell"), just because statements like "Hesperus is Phosphorus" and "Gaurisanker is Everest" are contingent, we can see that the names in question are not really purely referential. You are not, in Mrs Marcus's phrase, just "tagging" an object; you are actually describing it. What does the contingent fact that Hesperus is Phosphorus amount to? Well, it amounts to the fact that *the* star in a certain portion of the sky in the evening is *the* star in a certain portion of the sky in the morning. Similarly, the contingent fact that Guarisanker is Everest amounts to the fact that the mountain viewed from such and such an angle in Nepal is the mountain viewed from such and such another angle in Tibet. Therefore, such names as "Hesperus" and "Phosphorus' can only be abbreviations for descriptions. The term "Phosphorus" *has* to mean "the star seen...," or (let us be cautious because it actually turned out not to be a star), "the *heavenly body* seen from such and such a position at such and such a time in the morning," and the name "Hesperus" has to mean "the heavenly body seen in such and such a position at such and such a time in the evening." So, Russell concludes, if we want to reserve the term "name" for things which really just name an object without describing it, the only real proper names we can have are names of our own immediate sense-data, objects of our own "immediate acquaintance." The only such names which occur in language are demonstratives like "this" and "that." And it is easy to see that this requirement of necessity of identity, understood as exempting identities between names from all imaginable doubt, can indeed be guaranteed only for demonstrative names of immediate sense-data; for only in such cases can an identity statement between two different names have a general immunity from Cartesian doubt. There are some other things Russell has sometimes allowed as objects of acquaintance, such as one's self; we need not go into details here. Other philosophers (for example, Mrs Marcus in her reply, at least in the verbal discussion as I remember it – I do not know if this got into print, so perhaps this should not be "tagged" on her[7]) have said, "If names are really just tags, genuine tags, then a good dictionary should be able to tell us that they are names of the same object." You have an object *a* and an object *b* with names "John" and "Joe." Then, according to Mrs Marcus, a dictionary should be able to tell you whether or not "John" and "Joe" are names of the same object.

Of course, I do not know what ideal dictionaries should do, but ordinary proper names do not seem to satisfy this requirement. You certainly *can*, in the case of ordinary proper names, make quite empirical discoveries that, let's say, Hesperus is Phosphorus, though we thought otherwise. We can be in doubt as to whether Gaurisanker is Everest or Cicero is in fact Tully. Even now, we could conceivably discover that we were wrong in supposing that Hesperus was Phosphorus. Maybe the astronomers made an error. So it seems that this view is wrong and that if by a name we do not mean some artificial notion of names such as Russell's, but a proper name in the ordinary sense, then there can be contingent identity statements using proper names, and the view to the contrary seems plainly wrong.

In recent philosophy a large number of other identity statements have been emphasized as examples of contingent identity statements, different, perhaps, from either of the types I have mentioned before. One of them is, for example, the statement "Heat is the motion of molecules." First, science is supposed to have discovered this. Empirical scientists in their investigations have been supposed to discover (and, I suppose, they did) that the external phenomenon which we call "heat" is, in fact, molecular agitation. Another example of such a discovery is that water is H_2O, and yet other examples are that gold is the element with such and such an atomic number, that light is a stream of photons, and so on. These are all in some sense of "identity statement" identity statements. Second, it is thought, they are plainly contingent identity statements, just because they were scientific discoveries. After all, heat might have turned out not to have been the motion of molecules. There were other alternative theories of heat proposed, for example, the caloric theory of heat. If these theories of heat had been correct, then heat would not have been the motion of molecules, but instead, some substance suffusing the hot object, called "caloric." And it was a matter of course of science and not of any logical necessity that the one theory turned out to be correct and the other theory turned out to be incorrect.

So, here again, we have, apparently, another plain example of a contingent identity statement. This has been supposed to be a very important example because of its connection with the mind –body problem. There have been many philosophers who have wanted to be materialists, and to be materialists in a particular form, which is known today as "the identity theory." According to this theory, a certain mental state, such as a person's being in pain, is identical with a certain state of his brain (or, perhaps, of his entire body, according to some theorists), at any rate, a certain material or neural state of his brain or body. And so, according to this theory, my being in pain at this instant, if I were, would be identical with my body's being or my brain's being in a certain state. Others have objected that this cannot be because, after all, we can imagine my pain existing even if the state of the body did not. We can perhaps imagine my not being embodied at all and still being in pain, or, conversely, we could imagine my body existing and being in the very same state even if there were no pain. In fact, conceivably, it could be in this state even though there were no mind "back of it," so to speak, at all. The usual reply has been to concede that all of these things might have been the case, but to argue that these are irrelevant to the question of the identity of the mental state and the physical state. This identity, it is said, is just another contingent scientific identification, similar to the identification of heat with molecular motion, or water with H_2O. Just as we can imagine heat without any molecular motion, so we can imagine a mental state without any corresponding brain state. But, just as the first fact is not damaging to the identification of heat and the motion of molecules, so the second fact is not at all damaging to the identification of a mental state with the corresponding brain state. And so, many recent philosophers have held it to be very important for our theoretical understanding of the mind–body problem that there can be contingent identity statements of this form.

To state finally what *I* think, as opposed to what seems to be the case, or what others think, I think that in both cases, the case of names and the case of the theoretical identifications, the identity statements are necessary and not contingent. That is to say, they are necessary if *true*; of course, false identity statements are not necessary. How can one possibly defend such a view? Perhaps I lack a complete answer to this question, even though I am convinced that the view is true. But to begin an answer, let me make some distinctions that I want to use. The first is between a *rigid* and a *nonrigid designator*. What do these terms mean? As an example of a nonrigid designator, I can give an expression such as "the inventor of bifocals." Let us suppose it was Benjamin Franklin who invented bifocals, and so the expression, "the inventor of bifocals," designates or refers to a certain man, namely, Benjamin Franklin. However, we can easily imagine that the world could have been different, that under different circumstances someone else would have come upon this invention before Benjamin Franklin did, and in that case, *he* would have been the inventor of bifocals. So, in this sense, the expression "the inventor of bifocals' is non-rigid: Under certain circumstances one man would have been the inventor of bifocals; under other circumstances, another man would have. In contrast, consider the expression "the square root of 25." Independently of the empirical facts, we can give an arithmetical proof that the square root of 25 is in fact the number 5, and because we have proved this mathematically, what we have proved is necessary. If we think of numbers as entities at all, and let us suppose, at least for the purpose of this lecture, that we do, then the expression "the square root of 25" necessarily designates a certain number, namely 5. Such an expression I call "a *rigid* designator." Some philosophers think that anyone who even uses the notions of rigid or nonrigid designator has already shown that he has fallen into a certain confusion or has not paid attention to certain facts. What do I mean by "rigid designator"? I mean a term that designates the same object in all possible worlds. To get rid of one confusion, which certainly is not mine, I do not use "might have designated a different object" to refer to the fact that language might have been used differently. For example, the expression "the inventor of bifocals" might have been used by inhabitants of this planet always to refer to the man who corrupted Hadleyburg. This would have been the case, if, first, the people on this planet had not spoken English, but some other language, which phonetically overlapped with English; and if, second, in that language the expression "the inventor of bifocals" meant the "man who corrupted Hadleyburg." Then it would refer, of course, in their language, to whoever in fact corrupted Hadleyburg in this counterfactual situation. That is not what I mean. What I mean by saying that a description might have referred to something different, I mean that in *our* language as *we* use it in describing a counterfactual situation, there might have been a different object satisfying the descriptive conditions *we* give for reference. So, for example, we use the phrase "the inventor of bifocals," when we are talking about another possible world or a counterfactual situation, to refer to whoever in that counterfactual situation would have invented bifocals, not to the person whom people *in* that counterfactual situation would have called "the inventor of bifocals." *They* might have spoken a

different language which phonetically overlapped with English in which "the inventor of bifocals" is used in some other way. I am *not* concerned with that question here. For that matter, they might have been deaf and dumb, or there might have been no people at all. (There still could have been an inventor of bifocals even if there were no people – God, or Satan, will do.)

Second, in talking about the notion of a rigid designator, I do not mean to imply that the object referred to has to exist in all possible worlds, that is, that it has to necessarily exist. Some things, perhaps mathematical entities such as the positive integers, if they exist at all, necessarily exist. Some people have held that God both exists and necessarily exists; others, that he contingently exists; others, that he contingently fails to exist; and others, that he necessarily fails to exist:[8] all four options have been tried. But at any rate, when I use the notion of rigid designator, I do not imply that the object referred to necessarily exists. All I mean is that in any possible world where the object in question *does* exist, in any situation where the object *would* exist, we use the designator in question to designate that object. In a situation where the object does not exist, then we should say that the designator has no referent and that the object in question so designated does not exist.

As I said, many philosophers would find the very notion of rigid designator objectionable *per se*. And the objection that people make may be stated as follows: Look, you're talking about situations which are counterfactual, that is to say, you're talking about other possible worlds. Now these worlds are completely disjoint, after all, from the actual world which is not just another possible world; it is the actual world. So, before you talk about, let us say, such an object as Richard Nixon in another possible world at all, you have to say which object in this other possible world would *be* Richard Nixon. Let us talk about a situation in which, as *you* would say, Richard Nixon would have been a member of SDS. Certainly the member of SDS you are talking about is someone very different in many of his properties from Nixon. Before we even can say whether this man would have been Richard Nixon or not, we have to set up criteria of identity across possible worlds. Here are these other possible worlds. There are all kinds of objects in them with different properties from those of any actual object. Some of them resemble Nixon in some ways, some of them resemble Nixon in other ways. Well, which of these objects is

Nixon? One has to give a criterion of identity. And this shows how the very notion of rigid designator runs in a circle. Suppose we designate a certain number as the number of planets. Then, if that is our favorite way, so to speak, of designating this number, then in any other possible worlds we will have to identify whatever number is the number of planets with the number 9, which in the actual world is the number of planets. So, it is argued by various philosophers, for example, implicitly by Quine, and explicitly by many others in his wake, we cannot really ask whether a designator is rigid or nonrigid because we first need a criterion of identity across possible worlds. An extreme view has even been held that, since possible worlds are so disjoint from our own, we cannot really say that any object in them is the *same* as an object existing now but only that there are some objects which resemble things in the actual world, more or less. We, therefore, should not really speak of what would have been true of Nixon in another possible world but, only of what "counterparts" (the term which David Lewis uses[9]) of Nixon there would have been. Some people in other possible worlds have dogs whom they call "Checkers." Others favor the ABM but do not have any dog called Checkers. There are various people who resemble Nixon more or less, but none of them can really be said to be Nixon; they are only *counterparts* of Nixon, and you choose which one is the best counterpart by noting which resembles Nixon the most closely, according to your favorite criteria. Such views are widespread, both among the defenders of quantified modal logic and among its detractors.

All of this talk seems to me to have taken the metaphor of possible worlds much too seriously in some way. It is as if a "possible world" were like a foreign country, or distant planet way out there. It is as if we see dimly through a telescope various actors on this distant planet. Actually David Lewis's view seems the most reasonable if one takes this picture literally. No one far away on another planet can be strictly identical with someone here. But, even if we have some marvelous methods of transportation to take one and the same person from planet to planet, we really need some epistemological criteria of identity to be able to say whether someone on this distant planet is the same person as someone here.

All of this seems to me to be a totally misguided way of looking at things. What it amounts to is the view that counterfactual situations have to be described purely qualitatively. So, we cannot say, for example, "If Nixon had only given a sufficient bribe to Senator X, he would have gotten Carswell through," because that refers to certain people, Nixon and Carswell, and talks about what things would be true of them in a counterfactual situation. We must say instead "If a man who has a hairline like such and such, and holds such and such political opinions had given a bribe to a man who was a senator and had such and such other qualities, then a man who was a judge in the South and had many other qualities resembling Carswell would have been confirmed." In other words, we must describe counterfactual situations purely qualitatively and then ask the question, "Given that the situation contains people or things with such and such qualities, which of these people is (or is a counterpart of) Nixon, which is Carswell, and so on?" This seems to me to be wrong. Who is to prevent us from saying "Nixon might have gotten Carswell through had he done certain things"? We are speaking of *Nixon* and asking what, in certain counterfactual situations, would have been true of *him*. We can say that if Nixon had done such and such, he would have lost the election to Humphrey. Those I am opposing would argue, "Yes, but how do you find out if the man you are talking about is in fact Nixon?" It would indeed be very hard to find out, if you were looking at the whole situation through a telescope, but that is not what we are doing here. Possible worlds are not something to which an epistemological question like this applies. And if the phrase "possible worlds" is what makes anyone think some such question applies, he should just *drop* this phrase and use some other expression, say "counterfactual situation," which might be less misleading. If we say "If Nixon had bribed such and such a senator, Nixon would have gotten Carswell through," what is *given* in the very description of that situation is that it is a situation in which we are speaking of Nixon, and of Carswell, and of such and such a senator. And there seems to be no less objection to *stipulating* that we are speaking of certain *people* than there can be objection to stipulating that we are speaking of certain *qualities*. Advocates of the other view take speaking of certain qualities as unobjectionable. They do not say, "How do we know that this quality (in another possible world) is that of redness?" But they do find speaking of certain *people* objectionable. But I see no more reason to object in the one case than in the other. I think it really comes from the idea of possible worlds as existing out there, but very far off, viewable only through a special telescope. Even more objectionable is the view of David Lewis. According to Lewis, when we say "Under certain circumstances Nixon would have gotten Carswell through," we really mean "Some man, other than Nixon but closely resembling him, would have gotten some judge, other than Carswell but closely resembling him, through." Maybe that is so, that some man closely resembling Nixon could have gotten some man closely resembling Carswell through. But *that* would not comfort either Nixon or Carswell, nor would it make Nixon kick himself and say "*I* should have done such and such to get Carswell through." The question is whether under certain circumstances Nixon *himself* could have gotten *Carswell* through. And I think the objection is simply based on a misguided picture.

Instead, we can perfectly well talk about rigid and nonrigid designators. Moreover, we have a simple, intuitive test for them. We can say, for example, that the number of planets might have been a different number from the number it in fact is. For example, there might have been only seven planets. We can say that the inventor of bifocals might have been someone other than the man who *in fact* invented bifocals.[10] We cannot say, though, that the square root of 81 might have been a different number from the number it in fact is, for that number just has to be 9. If we apply this intuitive test to proper names, such as for example "Richard Nixon," they would seem intuitively to come out to be rigid designators. First, when we talk even about the counterfactual situation in which we suppose Nixon to have done different things, we assume we are still talking about Nixon himself. We say, "If Nixon had bribed a certain senator, he would have gotten Carswell through," and we assume that by "Nixon" and "Carswell" we are still referring to the very same people as in the actual world. And it seems that we cannot say "Nixon might have been a different man from the man he in fact was," unless, of course, we mean it metaphorically: He might have been a different *sort* of person (if you believe in free will and that people are not inherently corrupt). You might think the statement true in that sense, but Nixon could not have been in the other literal sense a different person from the person he, in fact, is, even though the thirty-seventh President of the United States might have been Humphrey. So the phrase "the thirty-seventh President" is nonrigid, but "Nixon," it would seem, is rigid.

Let me make another distinction before I go back to the question of identity statements. This dis-

tinction is very fundamental and also hard to see through. In recent discussion, many philosophers who have debated the meaningfulness of various categories of truths, have regarded them as identical. Some of those who identify them are vociferous defenders of them, and others, such as Quine, say they are all identically meaningless. But usually they're not distinguished. These are categories such as "analytic," "necessary," "a priori," and sometimes even "certain." I will not talk about all of these but only about the notions of aprioricity and necessity. Very often these are held to be synonyms. (Many philosophers probably should not be described as holding them to be synonyms; they simply *use* them interchangeably.) I wish to distinguish them. What do we mean by calling a statement *necessary*? We simply mean that the statement in question, first, is true, and, second, that it could not have been otherwise. When we say that something is *contingently* true, we mean that, though it is in fact the case, it could have been the case that things would have been otherwise. If we wish to assign this distinction to a branch of philosophy, we should assign it to metaphysics. To the contrary, there is the notion of an *a priori truth*. An a priori truth is supposed to be one which can be *known* to be true independently of all experience. Notice that this does not in and of itself say anything about all possible worlds, unless this is put into the definition. All that it says is that it can be known to be true of the actual world, independently of all experience. It may, by some philosophical argument, follow from our knowing, independently of experience, that something is true of the actual world, that it has to be known to be true also of all possible worlds. But if this is to be established, it requires some philosophical argument to establish it. Now, *this* notion, if we were to assign it to a branch of philosophy, belongs, not to metaphysics, but to epistemology. It has to do with the way we can know certain things to be in fact true. Now, it may be the case, of course, that anything which is necessary is something which *can* be known a priori. (Notice, by the way, the notion a priori truth as thus defined has in it *another* modality: it *can* be known independently of all experience. It is a little complicated because there is a double modality here.) I will not have time to explore these notions in full detail here, but one thing we can see from the outset is that these two notions are by no means trivially the same. If they are coextensive, it takes some philosophical argument to establish it. As stated, they belong to different domains of philosophy. One of them has something to do with *knowledge*, of what can be known in certain ways about the *actual* world. The other one has to do with *metaphysics*, how the world *could* have been; given that it is the way it is, could it have been otherwise, in certain ways? Now I hold, as a matter of fact, that neither class of statements is contained in the other. But all we need to talk about here is this: Is everything that is necessary knowable a priori or known a priori? Consider the following example: the Goldbach conjecture. This says that every even number is the sum of two primes. It is a mathematical statement, and if it is true at all, it has to be necessary. Certainly, one could not say that though in fact every even number is the sum of two primes, there could have been some extra number which was even and not the sum of two primes. What would that mean? On the other hand, the answer to the question whether every even number *is* in fact the sum of two primes is unknown, and we have no method at present for deciding. So we certainly do not know, a priori or even a posteriori, that every even number is the sum of two primes. (Well, perhaps we have some evidence in that no counterexample has been found.) But we certainly do not know a priori anyway, that every even number is, in fact, the sum of two primes. But, of course, the definition just says "*can* be known independently of experience," and someone might say that if it is true, we *could* know it independently of experience. It is hard to see exactly what this claim means. It might be so. One thing it might mean is that if it were true we could *prove* it. This claim is certainly wrong if it is generally applied to mathematical statements and we have to work within some fixed system. This is what Gödel proved. And even if we mean an "intuitive proof in general," it might just be the case (at least, this view is as clear and as probable as the contrary) that though the statement is true, there is just no way the human mind could ever prove it. Of course, one way an *infinite* mind might be able to prove it is by looking through each natural number one by one and checking. In this sense, of course, it can, perhaps, be known a priori, but only by an infinite mind, and then this gets into other complicated questions. I do not want to discuss questions about the conceivability of performing an infinite number of acts like looking through each number one by one. A vast philosophical literature has been written on this: Some have declared it is logically impossible; others that it is logically possible; and some do not know. The

main point is that it is not trivial that just because such a statement is necessary it can be known a priori. Some considerable clarification is required before we decide that it can be so known. And so this shows that even if everything necessary is a priori in some sense, it should not be taken as a trivial matter of definition. It is a substantive philosophical thesis which requires some work.

Another example that one might give relates to the problem of essentialism. Here is a lectern. A question which has often been raised in philosophy is: What are its essential properties? What properties, aside from trivial ones like self-identity, are such that this object has to have them if it exists at all,[11] are such that if an object did not have it, it would not be this object?[12] For example, being made of wood, and not of ice, might be an essential property of this lectern. Let us just take the weaker statement that it is not made of ice. That will establish it as strongly as we need it, perhaps as dramatically. Supposing this lectern is in fact made of wood, could this very lectern have been made from the very beginning of its existence from ice, say frozen from water in the Thames? One has a considerable feeling that it could *not*, though in fact one certainly could have made a lectern of water from the Thames, frozen it into ice by some process, and put it right there in place of this thing. If one had done so, one would have made, of course, a *different* object. It would not have been *this very lectern*, and so one would not have a case in which this very lectern here was made of ice, or was made from water from the Thames. The question of whether it could afterward, say in a minute from now, turn into ice is something else. So, it would seem, if an example like this is correct – and this is what advocates of essentialism have held – that this lectern could not have been made of ice, that is in any counterfactual situation of which we would say that this lectern existed at all, we would have to say also that it was not made from water from the Thames frozen into ice. Some have rejected, of course, any such notion of essential property as meaningless. Usually, it is because (and I think this is what Quine, for example, would say) they have held that it depends on the notion of identity across possible worlds, and that this is itself meaningless. Since I have rejected this view already, I will not deal with it again. We can talk about *this very object*, and whether it could have had certain properties which it does not in fact have. For example, it could have been in another room from the room it in fact is in, even at this very time, but it could not have been made from the very beginning from water frozen into ice.

If the essentialist view is correct, it can only be correct if we sharply distinguish between the notions of a posteriori and a priori truth on the one hand, and contingent and necessary truth on the other hand, for although the statement that this table, if it exists at all, was not made of ice, is necessary, it certainly is not something that we know a priori. What we know is that first, lecterns usually are not made of ice, they are usually made of wood. This looks like wood. It does not feel cold, and it probably would if it were made of ice. Therefore, I conclude, probably this is not made of ice. Here my entire judgment is a posteriori. I could find out that an ingenious trick has been played upon me and that, in fact, this lectern is made of ice; but what I am saying is, given that it is in fact not made of ice, in fact is made of wood, one cannot imagine that under certain circumstances it could have been made of ice. So we have to say that though we cannot know a priori whether this table was made of ice or not, given that it is not made of ice, it is *necessarily* not made of ice. In other words, if P is the statement that the lectern is not made of ice, one knows by a priori philosophical analysis, some conditional of the form "if P, then necessarily P." If the table is not made of ice, it is necessarily not made of ice. On the other hand, then, we know by empirical investigation that P, the antecedent of the conditional, is true – that this table is not made of ice. We can conclude by *modus ponens*:

$$P \supset \Box P$$
$$\frac{P}{\Box P}$$

The conclusion – "$\Box P$" – is that it is necessary that the table not be made of ice, and this conclusion is known a posteriori, since one of the premises on which it is based is a posteriori. So, the notion of essential properties can be maintained only by distinguishing between the notions of a priori and necessary truth, and I do maintain it.

Let us return to the question of identities. Concerning the statement "Hesperus is Phosphorus" or the statement "Cicero is Tully," one can find all of these out by empirical investigation, and we might turn out to be wrong in our empirical beliefs. So, it is usually argued, such statements must therefore be contingent. Some have embraced the other side of the coin and have held "Because of

this argument about necessity, identity statements between names have to be knowable a priori, so, only a very special category of names, possibly, really works as names; the other things are bogus names, disguised descriptions, or something of the sort. However, a certain very narrow class of statements of identity are known a priori, and these are the ones which contain the genuine names." If one accepts the distinctions that I have made, one need not jump to either conclusion. One can hold that certain statements of identity between names, though often known a posteriori, and maybe not knowable a priori, are in fact necessary, if true. So, we have some room to hold this. But, of course, to have some room to hold it does not mean that we should hold it. So let us see what the evidence is. First, recall the remark that I made that proper names seem to be rigid designators, as when we use the name "Nixon" to talk about a certain man, even in counterfactual situations. If we say, "If Nixon had not written the letter to Saxbe, maybe he would have gotten Carswell through," we are in this statement talking about Nixon, Saxbe, and Carswell, the very same men as in the actual world, and what would have happened to them under certain counterfactual circumstances. If names are rigid designators, then there can be no question about identities being necessary, because "a" and "b" will be rigid designators of a certain man or thing x. Then even in every possible world, a and b will both refer to this same object x, and to no other, and so there will be no situation in which a might not have been b. That would have to be a situation in which the object which we are also now calling "x" would not have been identical with itself. Then one could not possibly have a situation in which Cicero would not have been Tully or Hesperus would not have been Phosphorus.[13]

Aside from the identification of necessity with a priority, what has made people feel the other way? There are two things which have made people feel the other way.[14] Some people tend to regard identity statements as metalinguistic statements, to identify the statement "Hesperus is Phosphorus" with the metalinguistic statement " 'Hesperus' and 'Phosphorus' are names of the same heavenly body." And that, of course, might have been false. We might have used the terms "Hesperus" and "Phosphorus" as names of *two* different heavenly bodies. But, of course, this has nothing to do with the necessity of identity. In the same sense "$2 + 2 = 4$" might have been false. The phrases

"2 + 2" and "4" might have been used to refer to two different numbers. One can imagine a language, for example, in which "+," "2," and "=" were used in the standard way, but "4" was used as the name of, say, the square root of minus 1, as we should call it, "*i*." Then "2 + 2 = 4" would be false, for 2 plus 2 is not equal to the square root of minus 1. But this is not what we want. We do not want just to say that a certain statement which we in fact use to express something true could have expressed something false. We want to use the statement in *our* way and see if it could have been false. Let us do this. What is the idea people have? They say, 'Look, Hesperus might not have been Phosphorus. Here a certain planet was seen in the morning, and it was seen in the evening; and it just turned out later on as a matter of empirical fact that they were one and the same planet. If things had turned out otherwise, they would have been two different planets, or two different heavenly bodies, so how can you say that such a statement is necessary?'

Now there are two things that such people can mean. First, they can mean that we do not know a priori whether Hesperus is Phosphorus. This I have already conceded. Second, they may mean that they can actually imagine circumstances that they would call circumstances in which Hesperus would not have been Phosphorus. Let us think what would be such a circumstance, using these terms here as *names* of a planet. For example, it could have been the case that Venus did indeed rise in the morning in exactly the position in which we saw it, but that on the other hand, in the position which is in fact occupied by Venus in the evening, Venus was not there, and Mars took its place. This is all counterfactual because in fact Venus is there. Now one can also imagine that in this counterfactual other possible world, the Earth would have been inhabited by people and that they should have used the names "Phosphorus" for Venus in the morning and "Hesperus" for Mars in the evening. Now, this is all very good, but would it be a situation in which Hesperus was not Phosphorus? Of course, it is a situation in which people would have been able to *say*, truly, "Hesperus is not Phosphorus"; but we are supposed to describe things in our language, not in theirs. So let us describe it in our language. Well, how could it actually happen that Venus would not be in that position in the evening? For example, let us say that there is some comet that comes around every evening and yanks things over a little bit. (That would be a very simple scientific way of imagining

it: not really too simple – that is very hard to imagine actually.) It just happens to come around every evening, and things get yanked over a bit. Mars gets yanked over to the very position where Venus is, then the comet yanks things back to their normal position in the morning. Thinking of this planet which we now call "Phosphorus," what should we say? Well, we can say that the comet passes it and yanks Phosphorus over so that it is not in the position normally occupied by Phosphorus in the evening. If we do say this, and really use "Phosphorus" as the name of a planet, then we have to say that, under such circumstances, Phosphorus in the evening would not be in the position in where we, in fact, saw it; or alternatively, Hesperus in the evening would not be in the position in which we, in fact, saw it. We might say that under such circumstances, we would not have called Hesperus "Hesperus" because Hesperus would have been in a different position. But that still would not make Phosphorus different from Hesperus; what would then be the case instead is that Hesperus would have been in a different position from the position it in fact is and, perhaps, not in such a position that people would have called it "Hesperus." But that would not be a situation in which Phosphorus would not have been Hesperus.

Let us take another example which may be clearer. Suppose someone uses "Tully" to refer to the Roman orator who denounced Cataline and uses the name 'Cicero' to refer to the man whose works he had to study in third-year Latin in high school. Of course, he may not know in advance that the very same man who denounced Cataline wrote these works, and that is a contingent statement. But the fact that this statement is contingent should not make us think that the statement that Cicero is Tully, if it is true, and it is in fact true, is contingent. Suppose, for example, that Cicero actually did denounce Cataline, but thought that this political achievement was so great that he should not bother writing any literary works. Would we say that these would be circumstances under which he would not have been Cicero? It seems to me that the answer is no, that instead we would say that, under such circumstances, Cicero would not have written any literary works. It is not a necessary property of Cicero – the way the shadow follows the man – that he should have written certain works; we can easily imagine a situation in which Shakespeare would not have written the works of Shakespeare, or one in which Cicero would not have written the works of Cicero. What may be the case is that we *fix the reference* of the term "Cicero" by use of some descriptive phrase, such as "the author of these works." But once we have this reference fixed, we then use the name "Cicero" *rigidly* to designate the man who in fact we have identified by his authorship of these works. We do not use it to designate whoever would have written these works in place of Cicero, if someone else wrote them. It might have been the case that the man who wrote these works was not the man who denounced Cataline. Cassius might have written these works. But we would not then say that Cicero would have been Cassius, unless we were speaking in a very loose and metaphorical way. We would say that Cicero, whom we may have identified and come to know by his works, would not have written them, and that someone else, say Cassius, would have written them in his place.

Such examples are not grounds for thinking that identity statements are contingent. To take them as such grounds is to misconstrue the relation between a *name* and a *description used to fix its reference*, to take them to be *synonyms*. Even if we fix the reference of such a name as "Cicero" as the man who wrote such and such works, in speaking of counterfactual situations, when we speak of Cicero, we do not then speak of whoever in such counterfactual situations *would* have written such and such works, but rather of Cicero, whom we have identified by the contingent property that he is the man who in fact, that is, in the actual world, wrote certain works.[15]

I hope this is reasonably clear in a brief compass. Now, actually I have been presupposing something I do not really believe to be, in general, true. Let us suppose that we do fix the reference of a name by a description. Even if we do so, we do not then make the name *synonymous* with the description, but instead we use the name *rigidly* to refer to the object so named, even in talking about counterfactual situations where the thing named would not satisfy the description in question. Now, this is what I think in fact is true for those cases of naming where the reference is fixed by description. But, in fact, I also think, contrary to most recent theorists, that the reference of names is rarely or almost never fixed by means of description. And by this I do not just mean what Searle says: "It's not a single description, but rather a cluster, a family of properties which fixes the reference." I mean that properties in this sense are not used *at all*. But I do not have the time to go into this here. So, let us suppose that at least one half of prevailing views about

naming is true, that the reference is fixed by descriptions. Even were that true, the name would not be synonymous with the description, but would be used to *name* an object which we pick out by the contingent fact that it satisfies a certain description. And so, even though we can imagine a case where the man who wrote these works would not have been the man who denounced Cataline, we should not say that that would be a case in which Cicero would not have been Tully. We should say that it is a case in which Cicero did not write these works, but rather that Cassius did. And the identity of Cicero and Tully still holds.

Let me turn to the case of heat and the motion of molecules. Here, surely, is a case that is contingent identity! Recent philosophy has emphasized this again and again. So, if it is a case of contingent identity, then let us imagine under what circumstances it would be false. Now, concerning this statement I hold that the circumstances philosophers apparently have in mind as circumstances under which it would have been false are not in fact such circumstances. First, of course, it is argued that "Heat is the motion of molecules" is an a posteriori judgment; scientific investigation might have turned out otherwise. As I said before, this shows nothing against the view that it is necessary – at least if I am right. But here, surely, people had very specific circumstances in mind under which, so they thought, the judgment that heat is the motion of molecules would have been false. What were these circumstances? One can distill them out of the fact that we found out empirically that heat is the motion of molecules. How was this? What did we find out first when we found out that heat is the motion of molecules? There is a certain external phenomenon which we can sense by the sense of touch, and it produces a sensation which we call "the sensation of heat." We then discover that the external phenomenon which produces this sensation, which we sense, by means of our sense of touch, is in fact that of molecular agitation in the thing that we touch, a very high degree of molecular agitation. So, it might be thought, to imagine a situation in which heat would not have been the motion of molecules, we need only imagine a situation in which we would have had the very same sensation and it would have been produced by something other than the motion of molecules. Similarly, if we wanted to imagine a situation in which light was not a stream of photons, we could imagine a situation in which we were sensitive to something else in exactly the same way, producing what we call visual experiences, though not through a stream of photons. To make the case stronger, or to look at another side of the coin, we could also consider a situation in which we *are* concerned with the motion of molecules but in which such motion does not give us the sensation of heat. And it might also have happened that we, or, at least, the creatures inhabiting this planet, might have been so constituted that, let us say, an increase in the motion of molecules did not give us this sensation but that, on the contrary, a slowing down of the molecules did give us the very same sensation. This would be a situation, so it might be thought, in which heat would not be the motion of molecules, or, more precisely, in which temperature would not be mean molecular kinetic energy.

But I think it would not be so. Let us think about the situation again. First, let us think about it in the actual world. Imagine right now the world invaded by a number of Martians, who do indeed get the very sensation that we call "the sensation of heat" when they feel some ice which has slow molecular motion, and who do not get a sensation of heat – in fact, maybe just the reverse – when they put their hand near a fire which causes a lot of molecular agitation. Would we say, "Ah, this casts some doubt on heat being the motion of molecules, because there are these other people who don't get the same sensation"? Obviously not, and no one would think so. We would say instead that the Martians somehow feel the very sensation we get when we feel heat when they feel cold, and that they do not get a sensation of heat when they feel heat. But now let us think of a counterfactual situation.[16] Suppose the earth had from the very beginning been inhabited by such creatures. First, imagine it inhabited by no creatures at all: then there is no one to feel any sensations of heat. But we would not say that under such circumstances it would necessarily be the case that heat did not exist; we would say that heat might have existed, for example, if there were fires that heated up the air.

Let us suppose the laws of physics were not very different: Fires do heat up the air. Then there would have been heat even though there were no creatures around to feel it. Now let us suppose evolution takes place, and life is created, and there are some creatures around. But they are not like us, they are more like the Martians. Now would we say that heat has suddenly turned to cold, because of the way the creatures of this planet

sense it? No, I think we should describe this situation as a situation in which, though the creatures on this planet got our sensation of heat, they did not get it when they were exposed to heat. They got it when they were exposed to cold. And that is something we can surely well imagine. We can imagine it just as we can imagine our planet being invaded by creatures of this sort. Think of it in two steps. First there is a stage where there are no creatures at all, and one can certainly imagine the planet still having both heat and cold, though no one is around to sense it. Then the planet comes through an evolutionary process to be peopled with beings of different neural structure from ourselves. Then these creatures could be such that they were insensitive to heat; they did not feel it in the way we do; but on the other hand, they felt cold in much the same way that we feel heat. But still, heat would be heat, and cold would be cold. And particularly, then, this goes in no way against saying that in this counterfactual situation heat would still *be* the molecular motion, *be* that which is produced by fires, and so on, just as it would have been if there had been no creatures on the planet at all. Similarly, we could imagine that the planet was inhabited by creatures who got visual sensations when there were sound waves in the air. We should not therefore say, "Under such circumstances, sound would have been light." Instead we should say, "The planet was inhabited by creatures who were in some sense visually sensitive to sound, and may be even visually sensitive to light." If this is correct, it can still be and will still be a necessary truth that heat is the motion of molecules and that light is a stream of photons.

To state the view succinctly: we use both the terms "heat" and "the motion of molecules" as rigid designators for a certain external phenomenon. Since heat is in fact the motion of molecules, and the designators are rigid, by the argument I have given here, it is going to be *necessary* that heat is the motion of molecules. What gives us the illusion of contingency is the fact we have identified the heat by the contingent fact that there happen to be creatures on this planet – (namely, ourselves) who are sensitive to it in a certain way, that is, who are sensitive to the motion of molecules or to heat – these are one and the same thing. And this is contingent. So we use the description, 'that which causes such and such sensations, or that which we sense in such and such a way,' to identify heat. But in using this fact we use a contingent property of heat, just as we use the contingent property of Cicero as having written such and such works to identify him. We then use the terms "heat" in the one case and "Cicero" in the other *rigidly* to designate the objects for which they stand. And of course the term "the motion of molecules" is rigid; it always stands for the motion of molecules, never for any other phenomenon. So, as Bishop Butler said, "everything is what it is and not another thing." Therefore, "Heat is the motion of molecules" will be necessary, not contingent, and one only has the *illusion* of contingency in the way one could have the illusion of contingency in thinking that this table might have been made of ice. We might think one could imagine it, but if we try, we can see on reflection that what we are really imagining is just there being another lectern in this very position here which was in fact made of ice. The fact that we may identify this lectern by being the object we see and touch in such and such a position is something else.

Now how does this relate to the problem of mind and body? It is usually held that this is a contingent identity statement just like "Heat is the motion of molecules." That cannot be. It cannot be a contingent identity statement just like "Heat is the motion of molecules" because, if I am right, "Heat is the motion of molecules" is not a contingent identity statement. Let us look at this statement. For example, "My being in pain at such and such a time is my being in such and such a brain state at such and such a time," or "Pain in general is such and such a neural (brain) state."

This is held to be contingent on the following grounds. First, we can imagine the brain state existing though there is no pain at all. It is only a scientific fact that whenever we are in a certain brain state we have a pain. Second, one might imagine a creature being in pain, but not being in any specified brain state at all, maybe not having a brain at all. People even think, at least prima facie, though they may be wrong, that they can imagine totally disembodied creatures, at any rate certainly not creatures with bodies anything like our own. So it seems that we can imagine definite circumstances under which this relationship would have been false. Now, if these circumstances are circumstances, notice that we cannot deal with them simply by saying that this is just an illusion, something we can apparently imagine, but in fact cannot in the way we thought erroneously that we could imagine a situation in which heat was not the motion of molecules. Because although we can say that we pick out heat contingently by the contingent prop-

erty that it affects us in such and such a way, we cannot similarly say that we pick out pain contingently by the fact that it affects us in such and such a way. On such a picture there would be the brain state, and we pick it out by the contingent fact that it affects us as pain. Now that might be true of the brain state, but it cannot be true of the pain. The experience itself has to be *this experience*, and I cannot say that it is a contingent property of the pain I now have that it is a pain.[17] In fact, it would seem that the terms "my pain" and "my being in such and such a brain state" are, first of all, both rigid designators. That is, whenever anything is such and such a pain, it is essentially that very object, namely, such and such a pain, and wherever anything is such and such a brain state, it is essentially that very object, namely, such and such a brain state. So both of these are rigid designators. One cannot say this pain might have been something else, some other state. These are both rigid designators.

Second, the way we would think of picking them out – namely, the pain by its being an experience of a certain sort, and the brain state by its being the state of a certain material object, being of such and such molecular configuration – both of these pick out their objects essentially and not accidentally, that is, they pick them out by essential properties. Whenever the molecules *are* in this configuration, we *do* have such and such a brain state. Whenever you feel *this*, you do have a pain. So it seems that the identity theorist is in some trouble, for, since we have two rigid designators, the identity statement in question is necessary. Because they pick out their objects essentially, we cannot say the case where you seem to imagine the identity statement false is really an illusion like the illusion one gets in the case of heat and molecular motion, because that illusion depended on the fact that we pick out heat by a certain contingent property. So there is very little room to maneuver; perhaps none.[18] The identity theorist, who holds that pain is the brain state, also has to hold that it necessarily is the brain state. He therefore cannot concede, but has to deny, that there would have been situations under which one would have had pain but not the corresponding brain state. Now usually in arguments on the identity theory, this is very far from being denied. In fact, it is conceded from the outset by the materialist as well as by his opponent. He says, "Of course, it *could* have been the case that we had pains without the brain states. It is a contingent identity." But that cannot be. He has to hold that we are under some illusion in thinking that we can imagine that there could have been pains without brain states. And the only model I can think of for what the illusion might be, or at least the model given by the analogy the materialists themselves suggest, namely, heat and molecular motion, simply does not work in this case. So the materialist is up against a very stiff challenge. He has to show that these things we think we can see to be possible are in fact not possible. He has to show that these things which we can imagine are not in fact things we can imagine. And that requires some very dif-ferent philosophical argument from the sort which has been given in the case of heat and molecular motion. And it would have to be a deeper and subtler argument than I can fathom and subtler than has ever appeared in any materialist literature that I have read. So the conclusion of this investigation would be that the analytical tools we are using go against the identity thesis and so go against the general thesis that mental states are just physical states.[19]

The next topic would be my own solution to the mind–body problem, but that I do not have.

Notes

1 This paper was presented orally, without a written text, to the New York University lecture series on identity which makes up the volume *Identity and Individuation*. The lecture was taped, and the present paper represents a transcription of these tapes, edited only slightly with no attempt to change the style of the original. If the reader imagines the sentences of this paper as being delivered, extemporaneously, with proper pauses and emphases, this may facilitate his comprehension. Nevertheless, there may still be passages which are hard to follow, and the time allotted necessitated a condensed presentation of the argument. (A longer version of some of these views, still rather compressed and still representing a transcript of oral remarks, has appeared in Donald Davidson and Gilbert Harman (eds), *Semantics of Natural Language* (Dordrecht: Reidel, 1972).) Occasionally, reservations, amplifications, and gratifications of my remarks had to be repressed, especially in the discussion of theoretical identification and the mind–body problem. The notes, which were added to the original, would have become even more unwieldly if this had not been done.

2 R. J. Butler (ed.), *Analytical Philosophy, Second Series* (Oxford: Blackwell, 1965), p. 41.

3 The second occurrence of the description has small scope.

4 In Russell's theory, $F(\imath x Gx)$ follows from $(x)Fx$ and $(\exists! x)$ Gx, provided that the description in $F(\imath x Gx)$ has the entire context for its scope (in Russell's 1905 terminology, has a "primary occurrence"). Only then is $F(\imath x Gx)$ "about" the denotation of "$\imath x Gx$." Applying this rule to (4), we get the results indicated in the text. Notice that, in the ambiguous form $\square(\imath x Gx = \imath x Hx)$, if one or both of the descriptions have "primary occurrences," the formula does not assert the necessity of $\imath x Gx = \imath x Hx$; if both have secondary occurrences, it does. Thus in a language without explicit scope indicators, descriptions must be construed with the smallest possible scope – only then will $\sim A$ be the negation of A, $\square A$ the necessitation of A, and the like.

5 An earlier distinction with the same purpose was, of course, the medieval one of *de dicto–de re*. That Russell's distinction of scope eliminates model paradoxes has been pointed out by many logicians, especially Smullyan.

So as to avoid misunderstanding, let me emphasize that I am of course not asserting that Russell's notion of scope solves Quine's problem of "essentialism", what it does show, especially in conjunction with modern model-theoretic approaches to modal logic, is that quantified modal logic need not deny the truth of all instances of $(x)(y)(x = y \cdot \supset \cdot Fx \supset Fy)$, nor of all instances of "$(x)(Gx \supset Ga)$" (where "a" is to be replaced by a nonvacuous definite description whose scope is all of "Ga"), in order to avoid making it a necessary truth that one and the same man invented bifocals and headed the original Postal Department. Russell's contextual definition of description need not be adopted in order to ensure these results; but other logical theories, Fregean or other, which take descriptions as primitive must somehow express the same logical facts. Frege showed that a simple, non-iterated context containing a definite description with small scope, which cannot be interpreted as being "about" the denotation of the description, can be interpreted as about its "sense." Some logicians have been interested in the question of the conditions under which, in an intensional context, a description with small scope is equivalent to the same one with large scope. One of the virtues of a Russellian treatment of descriptions in modal logic is that the answer (roughly that the description be a "rigid designator" in the sense of this lecture) then often follows from the other postulates for quantified modal logic: no special postulates are needed, as in Hintikka's treatment. Even if descriptions are taken as primitive, special postulation of when scope is irrelevant can often be deduced from more basic axioms.

6 R. B. Marcus, "Modalities and intensional languages," in *Boston Studies in the Philosophy of Science*, vol. 1 (New York: Humanities Press, 1963), pp. 71ff. See also the "Comments" by Quine and the ensuing discussion.

7 It should. See her remark in *Boston Studies in the Philosophy of Science*, vol. 1, p. 115, in the discussion following the papers.

8 If there is no deity, and especially if the nonexistence of a deity is *necessary*, it is dubious that we can use "he" to refer to a deity. The use in the text must be taken to be nonliteral.

9 David K. Lewis, "Counterpart theory and quantified modal logic," *Journal of Philosophy* 65 (1968), pp. 113ff.

10 Some philosophers think that definite descriptions, in English, are ambiguous, that sometimes "the inventor of bifocals" rigidly designates the man who in fact invented bifocals. I am tentatively inclined to reject this view, construed as a thesis about English (as opposed to a possible hypothetical language), but I will not argue the question here.

What I do wish to note is that, contrary to some opinions, this alleged ambiguity cannot replace the Russellian notion of the scope of a description. Consider the sentence "The number of planets might have been necessarily even." This sentence plainly can be read so as to express a truth; had there been eight planets, the number of planets would have been necessarily even. Yet without scope distinctions, both a "referential" (rigid) and a nonrigid reading of the description will make the statement false. (Since the number of planets is the rigid reading amounts to the falsity that 9 might have been necessarily even.)

The "rigid" reading is equivalent to the Russellian primary occurrence; the nonrigid, to innermost scope – some, following Donnellan, perhaps loosely, have called this reading the "attributive" use. The possibility of intermediate scopes is then ignored. In the present instance, the intended reading of $\Diamond \Box$ (the number of planets is even) makes the scope of the description $\Box$ (the number of planets is even), neither the largest nor the smallest possible.

11 This definition is the usual formulation of the notion of essential property, but an exception must be made for existence itself: on the definition given, existence would be trivially essential. We should regard existence as essential to an object only if the object necessarily exists. Perhaps there are other recherché properties, involving existence, for which the definition is similarly objectionable. (I thank Michael Slote for this observation.)

12 The two clauses of the sentence noted give equivalent definitions of the notion of essential property, since $\Box((\exists x)(x = a) \supset Fa)$ is equivalent to $\Box(x)(\sim Fx \supset x = a)$. The second formulation, however, has served as a powerful seducer in favor of theories of "identification across possible worlds." For it sug-

gests that we consider 'an object *b* in another possible world' and test whether it is identifiable with *a* by asking whether it lacks any of the essential properties of *a*. Let me therefore emphasize that, although an essential property is (trivially) a property without which an object cannot be *a*, it by no means follows that the essential, purely qualitative properties of *a* jointly form a sufficient condition for being *a*, nor that *any* purely qualitative conditions are sufficient for an object to be *a*. Further, even if necessary and sufficient qualitative conditions for an object to be Nixon may exist, there would still be little justification for the demand for a purely qualitative description of all counterfactual situations. We can ask whether Nixon might have been a Democrat without engaging in these subtleties.

13 I thus agree with Quine, that "Hesperus is Phosphorus" is (or can be) an empirical discovery; with Marcus, that it is necessary. Both Quine and Marcus, according to the present standpoint, err in identifying the epistemological and the metaphysical issues.

14 The two confusions alleged, especially the second, are both related to the confusion of the metaphysical question of the necessity of "Hesperus is Phosphorus" with the epistemological question of its aprioricity. For if Hesperus is identified by its position in the sky in the evening, and Phosphorus by its position in the morning, an investigator may well know, in advance of empirical research, that Hesperus is Phosphorus if and only if one and the same body occupies position x in the evening and position y in the morning. The a priori material equivalence of the two statements, however, does not imply their strict (necessary) equivalence. (The same remarks apply to the case of heat and molecular motion.) Similar remarks apply to some extent to the relationship between "Hesperus is Phosphorus" and " 'Hesperus' and 'Phosphorus' name the same thing." A confusion that also operates is, of course, the confusion between what *we* say of a counterfactual situation and how people *in* that situation would have described it; this confusion, too, is probably related to the confusion between aprioricity and necessity.

15 If someone protests, regarding the lectern, that it *could* after all have *turned out* to have been made of ice, and therefore could have been made of ice, I would reply that what he really means is that a *lectern* could have looked just like this one, and have been placed in the same position as this one, and yet have been made of ice. In short, I could have been in the *same epistemological situation* in relation to *a lectern made of ice* as I actually am in relation to *this* lectern. In the main text, I have argued that the same reply should be given to protests that Hesperus could have turned out to be other than Phosphorus, or Cicero other than Tully. Here, then, the notion of "counterpart" comes into its own. For it is not this table, but an epistemic "counterpart," which was hewn from ice; not

Hesperus–Phosphorus–Venus, but two distinct counterparts thereof, in two of the roles Venus actually plays (that of Evening Star and Morning Star), which are different. Precisely because of this fact, it is not *this table* which could have been made of ice. Statements about the modal properties of *this table* never refer to counterparts. However, if someone confuses the epistemological and the metaphysical problems, he will be well on the way to the counterpart theory Lewis and others have advocated.

16 Isn't the situation I just described also counterfactual? At least it may well be, if such Martians never in fact invade. Strictly speaking, the distinction I wish to draw compares how we *would* speak *in* a (possibly counterfactual) situation, *if* it obtained, and how we *do* speak *of* a counterfactual situation, knowing that it does not obtain – i.e., the distinction between the language we would have used in a situation and the language we *do* use to describe it. (Consider the description: "Suppose we all spoke German." This description is in English.) The former case can be made vivid by imagining the counterfactual situation to be actual.

17 The most popular identity theories advocated today explicitly fail to satisfy this simple requirement. For these theories usually hold that a mental state is a brain state, and that what makes the brain state into a mental state is its "causal role," the fact that it tends to produce certain behavior (as intentions produce actions, or pain, pain behavior) and to be produced by certain stimuli (e.g., pain, by pinpricks). If the relations between the brain state and its causes and effects are regarded as contingent, then *being such-and-such-a-mental-state* is a contingent property of the brain state. Let X be a pain. The causal-role identity theorist holds (1) that X is a brain state, (2) that the fact that X is a pain is to be analyzed (roughly) as the fact that X is produced by certain stimuli and produces certain behavior. The fact mentioned in (2) is, of course, regarded as contingent; the brain state X might well exist and not tend to produce the appropriate behavior in the absence of other conditions. Thus (1) and (2) assert that a certain pain X might have existed, yet not have been a pain. This seems to me self-evidently absurd. Imagine any pain: is it possible that *it itself* could have existed, yet not have been a pain?

If $X = Y$, then X and Y share all properties, including modal properties. If X is a pain and Y the corresponding brain state, then *being a pain* is an essential property of X, and *being a brain state* is an essential property of Y. If the correspondence relation is, in fact, identity, then it must be *necessary* of Y that it corresponds to a pain, and *necessary* of X that it correspond to a brain state, indeed to this particular brain state, Y. Both assertions seem false; it *seems* clearly possible that X should have existed without the corresponding brain state; or that the brain state

should have existed without being felt as pain. Identity theorists cannot, contrary to their almost universal present practice, accept these intuitions; they must deny them, and explain them away. This is none too easy a thing to do.

18 A brief restatement of the argument may be helpful here. If "pain" and "C-fiber stimulation" are rigid designators of phenomena, one who identifies them must regard the identity as necessary. How can this necessity be reconciled with the apparent fact that C-fiber stimulation might have turned out not to be correlated with pain at all? We might try to reply by analogy to the case of heat and molecular motion; the latter identity, too, is necessary, yet someone may believe that, before scientific investigation showed otherwise, molecular motion might have turned out not to be heat. The reply is, of course, that what really is possible is that people (or some rational or sentient beings) could have been in the *same epistemic situation* as we actually are, and identify *a phenomenon* in the same way we identify heat, namely, by feeling it by the sensation we call "the sensation of heat," without the phenomenon being molecular motion. Further, the beings might not have been sensitive to molecular motion (i.e., to heat) by any neural mechanism whatsoever. It is impossible to explain the apparent possibility of C-fiber stimulations not having been pain in the same way. Here, too, we would have to suppose that we could have been in the same epistemological situation, and identify something in the same way we identify pain, without its corresponding to C-fiber stimulation. But the way we identify pain is by feeling it, and if a C-fiber stimulation could have occurred without our feeling any pain, then the C-fiber stimulation would have occurred without there *being* any pain, contrary to the necessity of the identity. The trouble is that although "heat" is a rigid designator, heat is picked out by the contingent property of its being felt in a certain way; pain, on the other hand, is picked out by an essential (indeed necessary and sufficient) property. For a sensation to be *felt* as pain is for it to *be* pain.

19 All arguments against the identity theory which rely on the necessity of identity, or on the notion of essential property, are, of course, inspired by Descartes's argument for his dualism. The earlier arguments which superficially were rebutted by the analogies of heat and molecular motion, and the bifocals inventor who was also Postmaster General, had such an inspiration: and so does my argument here. R. Albritton and M. Slote have informed me that they independently have attempted to give essentialist arguments against the identity theory, and probably others have done so as well.

The simplest Cartesian argument can perhaps be restated as follows: Let "A" be a *name* (rigid designator) of Descartes's body. Then Descartes argues that since he could exist even if A did not, $\Diamond$ (Descartes $\neq A$), hence Descartes $\neq A$. Those who have accused him of a modal fallacy have forgotten that "A" is rigid. His argument is valid, and his conclusion is correct, provided its (perhaps dubitable) premise is accepted. On the other hand, provided that Descartes is regarded as having ceased to exist upon his death, "Descartes $\neq A$" can be established without the use of a modal argument; for if so, no doubt A survived Descartes when A was a corpse. Thus A had a prop-

erty (existing at a certain time) which Descartes did not. The same argument can establish that a statue is not the hunk of stone, or the congery, of molecules, of which it is composed. Mere non-identity, then, may be a weak conclusion. (See D. Wiggins, *Philosophical Review* 77 (1968), pp. 90ff.) The Cartesian modal argument, however, surely can be deployed to maintain relevant stronger conclusions as well.

8

The Same *F*

John Perry

In several places Peter Geach has put forward the view that "it makes *no sense* to judge whether *x* and *y* are 'the same'... unless we add or understand some general term – the same *F*."[1] In this paper I discuss just what Geach's view comes to; I argue that there are no convincing reasons for adopting it and quite strong reasons for rejecting it.

I agree with criticisms of Geach made by David Wiggins in his recent book, *Identity and Spatio-Temporal Continuity*,[2] some of which are repeated here. I hope, however, to shed more light than he has on the motivations for Geach's view, and to state somewhat more systematically an opposing one. This is possible in part because of an article by Geach[3] on this topic which has appeared since Wiggins's book.

I

Geach generally develops his view of identity in conscious opposition to Frege; he emphasizes that his view is the result of noticing an important fact that he thinks Frege missed:

> I am arguing for the thesis that identity is relative. When one says "*x* is identical with *y*," this, I hold, is an incomplete expression; it is short for "*x* is the same *A* as *y*," where "*A*" repre-

Originally published in *Philosophical Review* 79 (1970), pp. 181–200. Reprinted by permission of Cornell University.

sents some count noun understood from the context of utterance – or else, it is just a vague expression of some half-formed thought. Frege emphasized that "*x* is *one*" is an incomplete way of saying "*x* is one *A*, a single *A*," or else has no clear sense; since the connection of the concepts *one* and identity comes out just as much in the German "*ein und dasselbe*" as in the English "one and the same," it has always surprised me that Frege did not similarly maintain the parallel doctrine of relativized identity, which I have just briefly stated.[4]

I maintain it makes no sense to judge whether *x* and *y* are "the same" or whether *x* remains "the same" unless we add or understand some general term – the same *F*. That in accordance with which we thus judge as to the identity, I call a criterion of identity; ... Frege sees clearly that "one" cannot significantly stand as a predicate of objects unless it is (at least understood as) attached to a general term; I am surprised he did not see that this holds for the closely allied expression "the same."[5]

Frege has clearly explained that the predication of "one endowed with wisdom'... does not split up into predications of "one" and "endowed with wisdom." ... It is surprising that Frege should on the contrary have constantly assumed that "*x* is the same *A* as *y*" does split up into "*x* is an *A* (and *y* is an *A*)" and "*x* is the same as ... *y*." We have already by implication rejected this analysis.[6]

We can best see what Geach's view of identity amounts to, and what considerations might weigh in favor of it, by seeing just how he disagrees with Frege. What does Geach mean by denying that, for example, "being the same horse as" "splits up" into "being the same as" and "being a horse'? We can better understand the disagreement if we first list the points on which Frege and Geach might agree.

First, I think that Frege could agree with Geach that an utterance of the grammatical from "*x* and *y* are the same" might not have a clear truth-value, and that this situation might be remedied by adding a general term after the word "same.'[7] For instance, the utterance "What I bathed in yesterday and what I bathed in today are the same" might not have a clear truth-value in a certain situation, although "What I bathed in yesterday and what I bathed in today are the same river" or "What I bathed in yesterday and what I bathed in today are the same water" do have clear truth-values. And Frege would further agree, I believe, that the truth-values of the last two statements might differ: it might be true that I bathed in the same river on both days, but false that I bathed in the same water.

Second, I think Frege could agree that in adding the general term after the word "same," one could be said to convey a criterion of identity, and that the original utterance is deficient in that no criterion of identity is conveyed.

And, finally, I think Frege might agree with reservations in saying that, in supplying a general term and conveying a criterion of identity, one is making clear which relation is asserted to hold between the referents of the statement. Frege must admit that the truth-values of "*x* and *y* are the same *F*" and "*x* and *y* are the same *G*" may differ. For instance, "Cassius Clay and Muhammed Ali are the same man" is true, but "Cassius Clay and Muhammed Ali are the same number" is not true. This shows that "being the same man as" and "being the same number as" are not extensionally equivalent, and therefore do not express the same relation. But, having admitted this, Frege might add that, in an important sense, one relation is asserted in both cases. And this is where Frege and Geach disagree. To see how the relations might be said to be the same in each statement after all, let us compare a case Frege might regard as analogous.

Consider "being a left-handed brother of" and "being a red-haired brother of." These quite obviously express different relations, for they are not extensionally equivalent. But these relations differ in a way that leaves them intimately connected. "Being a left-handed brother of" clearly splits up into "being a brother of" and "being left-handed." To say that Jim is a left-handed brother of Mike is to say no more or less than that Jim is a brother of Mike and Jim is left-handed. And the same thing is true of "being a red-haired brother of." The two relations involved do not differ, we might say, in being two different kinds of brotherhood, left-handed and red-haired. The job of the words "red-haired" and "left-handed" is not to tell us what kind of brotherhood is being asserted. Rather, they assert something about the first referent in addition to the relation asserted. In such a case, it is very natural to say that the relations are in a sense the same, for the words "left-handed brother of" and "red-haired brother of" express a conjunction of two conditions, only one of which is relational. And that condition which is relational is the same in both cases – namely, *being a brother of*. One important consequence of this is that it follows from "*x* is a left-handed brother of *y*" and "*x* is red-haired" that "*x* is a red-haired brother of *y*." We can express this by saying that "is a red-haired brother of" and "is a left-handed brother of" express *restrictions* of the relation "being a brother of" to, respectively, the domains of the left-handed and the red-haired.

Now compare with this the difference between the relations expressed by "being a better golfer than" and "being a better swimmer than." These are different relations. But they do not differ in the way those just examined differ. "Being a better golfer than" does not break up into "being better than" and "being a golfer." There is no such thing as just *being better than*. This is the reason that it does not follow from "*x* is a better golfer than *y*" and "*x* is a swimmer" that "*x* is a better swimmer than *y*."

Frege's position is that "being the same *F* as," like "being a red-haired brother of," splits up into a general relation and an assertion about the referent; it breaks up into "being the same as" and "being an *F*.'[8] This is what Geach denies. He thinks that "being the same *F* as," like "being a better golfer than," does not split up. Just as there is no such thing as being just "better than," Geach says that "there is no such thing as being just 'the same'. . . ."[9]

This then is the difference of opinion between Frege and Geach. Geach's succinct statement of his view is: "it makes no sense to judge whether *x* and *y* are 'the same' . . . unless we add or understand some general term – the same *F*." But this disguises the real nature of the dispute. Frege would not deny, and I will not deny, that in all significant judgments of identity a general term that conveys a criterion of identity will be implicitly or explicitly available. I shall not try to refute Geach by producing a case of being the same that is not a case of being the same F for some general term "F." That is not the issue. The issue is the role of the general term and the criterion of identity that it conveys.

The view I advocate, and which I believe to be Frege's, is that the role of the general term is to identify the referents – not to identify the "kind of identity" asserted. According to this view, x and y cannot be the same F, but different G's; if x and y are the same F, then the relation of identity obtains between x and y, and any statement that denies this is false. In particular, no denial of identity of the form "x and y are different G's" can be true. Frege cannot allow the possibility that x and y are the same F but different G's.[10] But, on Geach's view, there is no objection to such a case. On his view, just as it does not follow that Jones is a better golfer than Smith from the fact that he is a better swimmer than Smith and is a golfer, so too it does not follow that x is the same G as y from the fact that x is the same F as y and is a G. Thus Geach says, "On my own view of identity I could not object in principle to different A's being one and the same B; . . . as different official personages may be one and the same man."[11] If we can find an example in which x and y are the same F but x and y are different G's, we shall have to admit Geach is right in rejecting Frege's view, just as if there were cases of people who are left-handed and brothers but not left-handed brothers, we should have to give up the view that "being a left-handed brother" splits up into "being left-handed" and "being a brother."

Before considering some examples that seem to be of this form, I would like to point out an interesting consequence of Geach's view. Geach's view differs from Frege's in allowing the possibility of true statements of the form "x and y are the same F but x and y are different G's." But if we can find a counterexample of this form, we shall have to give up more than Frege's view. We shall have to give up some principles about identity that seem very plausible.

If we are going to view a statement of the form "x is the same F as y" as asserting some relation expressed by "is the same F as" of the referents of "x" and "y," then this relation should behave, on Frege's view, as a restriction of the general relation of identity to a specific kind of object. As such, it

should share some of the properties ordinarily attributed to identity: transitivity, symmetry, and substitutivity. Reflexivity is lost: every object need not be the same F as itself, for all objects are not F's. But these relations should be at least *weakly* reflexive: any object that is the same F as some object must be the same F as itself. But any counterexample to Frege will also be a counterexample to some of these principles. Consider any such counterexample. It is in the form of a conjunction. The second conjunct says that x and y are different G's. If we make the substitution in this conjunct that the first conjunct licenses us to make, the result is "x and x are different G's." To accept this result is to deny that the relation expressed by "the same G" is even weakly reflective, which requires either that such relations are not transitive or not symmetrical. To deny the substitution is to deny that these relations confer substitutivity. If we accept Geach's view, we shall have to abandon some traditional and rather plausible logical doctrines.

II

In "Identity," a recent article from which some of the earlier quotations were drawn, Geach has explained his views at greater length than before. At first glance, the views expressed in that article may seem difficult to reconcile with those I have just attributed to him; it is a difficult article. Although Geach says that "at first sight" his own view seems to conflict with "classical identity theory" – the view that identity is a reflexive relation that confers substitutivity – he never points out in so many words that it will have to be abandoned if his theory of identity is correct. Nevertheless, the view Geach expounds does turn out to be, when carefully examined, just the view I have attributed to him, and does have the consequences I said it had.

Geach's view is best understood, I think, by looking first at his examples, and then considering the rather involved argument and doctrine those examples are supposed to illustrate. These examples, as interpreted by Geach, are of just the sort we found required to refute Frege's view.

Consider the following list of words:

A. Bull
B. Bull
C. Cow

How many words are on the list? It has often been pointed out that such a question is ambiguous; the right answer might be "two" or it might be "three." One explanation of this ambiguity is that the answer depends on what kind of object we are counting, word *types* or word *tokens*; there are three word tokens, but only two word types on the list. But this is not the way Geach looks at the matter. According to him, there are not two kinds of objects to be counted, but two different ways of counting the same objects. And the reason there are two ways of counting the objects is that there are two different "criteria of relative identity." The number of words on the list depends on whether *A* and *B* are counted as one and the same word; they are counted the same according to the criteria of relative identity expressed by "word type," but not according to the one expressed by "word token." Geach's claim is then that the conjunction.

(1)   *A* is the same word type as *B*, but *A* and *B* are different word tokens

is true. And this conjunction seems to be just the sort of counterexample required to prove Frege wrong.

The rather involved and difficult doctrine that precedes such alleged counterexamples as this in Geach's article seems to me best viewed as an attempt to undermine some distinctions implicit in fairly obvious objections to such an example. I will now state those objections, and in the next section explain how Geach seeks to undermine them.

First, in order to be of the form "*x* and *y* are the same *F*, but *x* and *y* are different *G*'s," the referring expressions in the example that correspond to "*x*" and "*y*" will have to refer to the same objects in the first and second conjuncts. The sameness of expression is not sufficient. If it were, the true statement "John Adams was the father of John Adams" would be of the form "*x* was the father of *x*" and a counterexample to a principle of genealogy. It seems a plausible criticism of Geach's proposed counterexample that it fails for just this reason; in the first conjunct of (1) "*A*" and "*B*" refer to word types, in the second to word tokens. Indeed, the role of the general terms "word token" and "word type" is just to tell us what objects – the types or the tokens – those expressions do refer to.

One might reply to this objection by saying that the fact expressed by (1) could as well have been expressed by

(2)   *A* and *B* are different word tokens, but the same word type.

In (2) the expressions "*A*" and "*B*" appear only once; it might be claimed that it becomes very dubious, in virtue of this single appearance, to claim that four references to three referents take place within (2).

But there is a second criticism. Even if the occurrences of "*A*" and "*B*" are interpreted as referring to the same objects in both conjuncts of (1), or as not being multiply referential in (2), it is still far from clear that either (1) or (2) is a good counterexample. There is a further requirement. It is not sufficient, for a statement to be what Frege, or most other philosophers, would call an *identity* statement, that it contain the word "same," or be of the verbal form "*x* and *y* are the same *F*." For example, "Sarah and Jimmy are members of the same family" is not an identity statement; no one would suppose its truth required that everything true of Sarah be true of Jimmy. Nor are "The couch and the chair are the same color" or "Tommy is the same age as Jimmy" identity statements. These statements are of course closely related to identity statements; the first two, for example, are equivalent to "The family of Jimmy is identical with the family of Sarah" and "The color of the couch is identical with the color of the chair." But as they are, they are *not* identity statements: the relation of identity is not asserted to obtain between the subjects of the statements – Jimmy and Sarah, the couch and the chair. Yet it is clearly a further requirement of a counterexample to Frege that both conjuncts be identity statements in the relevant sense. That is, the conjunct that says "*x* and *y* are the same *G*'s" must be an assertion of identity, and the conjunct that says "*x* and *y* are different *G*'s" must be a denial of identity. For example, no one should suppose that "The couch and the chair are the same color, but different pieces of furniture" would be a good counterexample to Frege.

It seems clear to me that if we assume that "*A*" and "*B*" refer to word tokens throughout (1), then the first conjunct of (1), is not an assertion of identity, but merely an assertion that *A* and *B* are similar in a certain respect, or have some property in common; they are both tokens of the same type, they have the same shape, they are "equiform." Note that this conjunct could be more naturally expressed "*A* and *B* are *of* the same type" or "*A* and *B* are tokens of the same type." In this way the conjunct resembles the statement "The couch and the chair are the same color" which could more naturally be put "The couch and the chair have the same color" or "The couch and the chair are of the same color." But identity statements are not more naturally expressed in such ways; we feel no temptation to say that Lyndon Johnson and LBJ are *of* the same man, or have the same man.

Thus Geach's counterexample seems open to the following objection. If "*A*" and "*B*" refer to the same objects throughout (1), the first conjunct of (1) is not an identity statement, and the counterexample fails. If both conjuncts are identity statements in the required sense, "*A*" and "*B*" must refer to word types in the first conjunct and word tokens in the second, and the counterexample fails.

III

We find in "Identity" a rather abstract line of argument which, if correct, will show the criticism I have just made of Geach's counterexample to be based on untenable or at least unnecessary notions: the notion of word types as a kind of object different from word tokens and the notion of a statement of identity ("absolute" identity) as opposed to a resemblance or common property statement ("relative" identity). The only distinction needed, according to Geach, is between different kinds of "relative" identity:[12] being-the-same-word-type and being-the-same-word-token.

To understand Geach's argument, we must first notice a rather interesting point. A great many propositions are *about* particular things. For instance, the proposition "The pen I am writing with is blue" is about a particular object – the pen in my hand – which is referred to by the subject term. An assertion of the proposition can be looked upon as asserting of that pen that it has a certain property – being blue – which is expressed by the predicate. Now part of understanding an utterance that expresses such a proposition is understanding under what conditions the proposition expressed would be true. The interesting point to which I wish to call attention is just that this element in, or requirement of understanding the utterance, does not generally require knowing which object the subject term of the proposition refers to, and exactly what the predicate asserts of it.

A simple example will establish this. Consider the sentence "*Pa*" in the language *L*. I inform you that the utterance "*Pa*" is true if and only if the word in the box stands for a much misunderstood notion.

You understand the English; you now know the truth-conditions of "*Pa*." But my explanation has not determined the referent of "*a*" or the condition expressed by "*P*—." Even if we take the English sentence

The word in the box stands for a much misunderstood notion

as a translation of "*Pa*," nothing has been said about which parts of the English sentence correspond to which parts of "*Pa*." Different translations of the elements seem equally allowable:

a : the word in the box
P—:— stands for a much misunderstood notion

a : the box
P—: the word in—stands for a much misunderstood notion.

It is possible, in certain easily imagined cases, to know the truth-conditions of a great many sentences of some such language, without being clear about the proper interpretations of their parts. Suppose "*Pa*" is true if and only if the type of which the word in the box is a token is often misspelled. On the basis of this information, two interpretations of "*P*—" and "*a*" seem allowable:

a : the type of which the word in the box is a token.
P—:—is often misspelled.

a : the word in the box
P—:—is a token of a type that is often misspelled.

We might be told the truth-conditions of a great many sentences containing "*P*—" and "*a*," and still be in the dark as to their proper interpretation. For example, we might be told that "*Fa*" is true if and only if the type of the token in the box is often capitalized; that "*Pc*" is true if and only if the first word on the author's copy of this page is often misspelled, and so forth. This additional information about further sentences would not resolve the problem of interpretation.

The relation between the referring expressions, "the token in the box" and "the type of the token in the box," is that the latter refers to an object which is identified by means of a reference to the object identified by the former. Thus "the type of the token in the circle" identifies the same type as "the type of the token in the box" – although the tokens are different.

Identity

Suppose we were told that "*Pb*" were true if and only if the type of the token in the circle were often misspelled. Then, clearly, "*Pb*" is equivalent to "*Pa*." But is *a* identical with *b*? This is just the question of the proper interpretation. If "*P*—" means "—is often misspelled," then "*a*" and "*b*" refer to the same word type. If "*P*—" means "—is a token of a type that is often misspelled," then "*a*" and "*b*" refer to different word tokens (of the same type).

To show that *a* is not identical with *b*, it would be necessary only to establish that *a* has some property *b* lacks; if *a* and *b* are identical, they must share their properties. Suppose there is some predicate "*S*—" in *L*, such that "*Sa*" has a different truth-value than "*Sb*." Clearly, we could conclude that *a* is not identical with *b*; that *a* and *b* are different tokens, not one and the same type.

Suppose we are told that "*R(a,b)*" is true if and only if the token in the circle and the token in the box are tokens of the same type. Then there seem to be two possible interpretations of "*R(a,b)*":

a: the type of the token in the box.
b: the type of the token in the circle.
R (—,—): — and — are identical.
a: the token in the box.
b: the token in the circle.
R (—,—): — and — are equiform.

Which should we choose? Well, if we choose the first interpretation, then everything true of *a* will have to be true of *b*. So if there is some predicate "*S*—" in *L* such that the truth-values of "*Sa*" and "*Sb*" are different, the second interpretation would have to be chosen. If not, it would seem that we were free to choose the first.

Suppose, however, there are no such predicates. Would that fact be *sufficient* justification for interpreting "*R* (—,—)" as "is identical with"? In a sense, it would not *force* us to do so. Even if there were no predicate like "*S*—" in *L*, it still *might* be that "*R* (—,—)" did not mean identity. It might be just *accidental* that there are no such predicates; perhaps the speakers of *L* have not yet *noticed* any properties that distinguish word tokens, or think them unworthy of expression in their language.

To have the formal properties required to express identity, an expression "*R*—,—" in *L* need satisfy only the following two conditions:[13] (*i*) for any referring expression α in *L*, "*R* α, α" is true; (*ii*) for any referring expressions α and β, and any predicate Φ in *L*, if "*R* α, β" is true, "$\Phi\alpha$" and "$\Phi\beta$" are materially equivalent. The force of the last paragraph is that these necessary conditions for expressing identity are not logically sufficient. "*R*—,—" might satisfy these conditions and *not* express identity – but just the kind of similarity (or relative identity) appropriate to the objects in the domain of *L*.

Now let us make a rough distinction between an object of a kind *K* and an occurrence of a kind *K*. An occurrence of a kind *K* is an object which, although it is not itself a *K*, is the sort of object, or one sort of object, which would ordinarily be employed in ostensively identifying a *K*. For example, a word token is an occurrence of a word type, because we ostensively identify word types by pointing to a word token and saying "the type of which that is a token" or even "that type." Surfaces or physical objects are occurrences of colors, because we ostensively identify colors by pointing at surfaces and saying "the color of that" or "that color.'

Our choice in interpreting "*R(a,b)*" is just this: to interpret "*a*" and "*b*" as references to word types and "*R*(—,—)" as "is identical with," or to interpret "*a*" and "*b*" as references to *occurrences* of word types (which is to say, as references to word tokens), and "*R*(—,—)" as expressing one kind of what Geach calls "relative identity" – namely, "is equiform with."

Geach's argument, as I understand it, is this. We might very well have a reason to choose the second interpretation – for example, that there is in *L* a predicate "*S*—" such that "*Sa* & ~ *Sb*" is true. Moreover, even if we do not have such a predicate in *L*, we might choose to add one in the future, and should not close this option ('limit our ideology'). But no circumstances are conceivable in which we are forced to choose the first interpretation. We are always theoretically free to take the second. Moreover, there is a general reason for not choosing the first: in doing so we multiply the entities to which we allow references (types now as well as tokens) and thereby "pollute our ontology." But then there is never any good reason to interpret a predicate in *L* as expressing identity, rather than some form of relative identity, and never any good reason to interpret the references in *L* to be to things which have occurrences, rather than to occurrences themselves. But then are not the very notions of identity, and of a reference to such an object, suspect? And if this is so, are we not justified in waiving the criticisms made of the counterexample to Frege in section II, since those criticisms are completely based on these notions?

IV

The charges that the interpretation of "$R (—,—)$" as "is identical with" would restrict ideology while polluting the universe are completely unfounded.

Consider the language $L+$, which contains all of the sentences of L, plus sentences composed of the predicate "$K (—,—)$" and the referring expressions of L. The sentences of $L +$ which are also sentences of L have the same truth-conditions in $L + $ as in L. "$K(a,b)$" is true if and only if the word token on page 94 is more legible than the word token on page 95. Then clearly, "$R (—,—)$" does not express identity in $L +$. "$R(a, b)$" is true, but "$K(a, b)$" and "$K(a, a)$" are not materially equivalent, or so we shall suppose.

Now all of this does not in the least show that "$R (—,—)$" does not express identity in L. The facts that "$R (—,—)$" does not express identity in $L +$, and that the symbols used in L and $L +$ are largely the same, and that the truth-conditions of the shared sentences are the same in each, do not entail that the shared expressions have the same interpretation.

If, however, we think of L and $L+$ as successive states of the same language, actually employed by humans, then the evidence that "$R (—,—)$" does not confer substitutivity in $L+$ is grounds for thinking it is only an accident that it did in L – the earlier state; perhaps no one had conceptualized the relation *being more legible than*, or any other property capable of distinguishing tokens. This seems to be Geach's view: as our language grows, what now has the formal properties ascribed by the classical view to identity (is an "I-predicable" in Geach's terminology) may cease to have them. To pick out any one stage of the language and say that those expressions that are I-predicable at that point must always be, are somehow necessarily, in virtue of their meaning, I-predicable is to "freeze" the language – to prohibit it from growing in certain directions.

This argument is confused. Suppose we interpret "$R (—,—)$" as expressing identity, and take L to have as its domain word types. We are in no way

blocked from adding the predicate "is more legible than" to L. It would be a futile gesture unless some names for word tokens were also added, but there is also no objection to doing that. In that case we have not $L+$, but $L + +- L$ plus "$K (——)$" plus some names for word tokens. Nothing in L prevents us from taking "$R (—,—)$" as expressing identity; in so doing we do not block the development of L to $L + +$.

What about the claim that interpreting "$R(—,—)$" as expressing identity will "pollute our ontology"? To make this point, Geach introduces another example; a look at it will indicate the sorts of confusion that underlie this charge.

> As I remarked years ago when criticizing Quine, there is a certain set of predicables that are true of men but do not discriminate between two men of the same surname. If the ideology of a theory T is restricted to such predicables, the ontology of T calls into being a universe of androids (as science fiction fans say) who differ from men in just this respect, that two different ones cannot share the same surname. I call these androids surmen; a surman is in many ways very much like a man, e.g., he has brains in his skull and a heart in his breast and guts in his belly. The universe now shows itself as a baroque Meinongian structure, which hardly suits Quine's expressed preference for desert landscapes.[14]

Here we have a language fragment whose predicates are such that all the same predicates apply to me, my father, my brother, and the rest of the Perrys, and the same is true of the Smiths and the Joneses, and so forth. If the words in this language fragment corresponded to English, then there would be nothing to stop us, says Geach, from interpreting "has the same last name" as expressing identity; this would be an I-predicable in the rump language. Then, he suggests, the names in the language fragment will have to be reinterpreted as names of surmen, which are queer and objectionable entities.

But as far as I can see, nothing more objectionable than families would emerge from this reinterpretation. I cannot see why Geach thinks it should require androids. The entity that has all the persons with a certain last name as occurrences (parts or members) is clearly something like a family, and not anything like an android. Moreover, this example is not analogous to the theoretical descriptions Geach gives in his abstract arguments; here we go from the richer language to the leaner; it is not clear how the predicates (such as "has guts in his belly') are to be reinterpreted in such a case, and Geach gives us no directions.

It seems to me that any cogency that attaches to Geach's claim of pollution can be traced to a confusion of his position with some sort of nominalism. Geach's position seems to presuppose nominalism: the thesis that, in our terminology, only occurrences are ultimately real. But it amounts to far more. The nominalist would claim that "being of the same type" is analyzable in terms of "equiformity" and that references to types are in some sense eliminable; Geach seems to claim that they are not only eliminable, but never occur in the first place.

The disadvantages of interpreting a predicate like "*R* (—,—)" as identity are thus illusory; are there any advantages?

The most obvious is that if we interpret "*R* (—, —)" as "equiform" even though there are no predicates in *L* that discriminate between tokens, then we seem to be granting that the speakers of *L* refer to a kind of objects, tokens, between which they have no means of distinguishing. But if tokens cannot be individuated in *L*, is it really reasonable to suppose that the users of *L* are actually talking about tokens, but have just not bothered to express in the language any of the ways they use to tell them apart?

This point does not have its full weight with the example of *L*. *L*, a language with a restricted subject matter of the sort dealt with only by those with access to a richer language, presents itself as an artificial language. It clearly might be reasonable for someone to stipulate that the referring expressions in some artificial language he is discussing should be construed as referring to tokens even if they *could* be construed as referring to types; he might, for example, want to compare *L* with wider languages such as *L*+, and this might be more conveniently done if *L* is so construed.

But suppose an anthropologist should have the following worry. He arrives at a coherent and plausible translation scheme for a certain out-of-the-way language. In this scheme a certain predicate "*R* (—,—)" is translated "— is identical with —." In the thousands of conversations he has recorded and studied he has found no cases in which natives would deny that an object had the relation expressed by this predicate to itself; he has found that, in every case, once natives find objects have this relation, they are willing to infer that what

is true of one is true of the other. In a murder trial, the prosecution tries to prove, and the defense to disprove, that this relation obtains between the defendant and the murderer. But our anthropologist is a Geachian. He worries, Does "*R* (—, —)" really express identity? Do they really talk about people, or only stages of people? This is absurd. Some internally consistent theory about the natives' beliefs and linguistic practices could be formulated that casts this sort of metaphysical doubt on any entry in the anthropologist's dictionary. He need not have any special worries about identity; in the situation described, there is no real room for doubt.

With regard to one's own language, it seems clear that we can pick out predicates – for example, "is one and the same as" – which, in some sense I shall not here try to analyze, owe their logical properties (transitivity, symmetry, and so forth) to their meaning, and could not lose them merely by virtue of additions to the ideology of the language, or changes in the state of the nonlinguistic world. Such predicates express the concept of identity.

Thus, as far as I can see, Geach has no effective arguments against the dilemma posed in section II for any counterexample to Frege. Until some counterexample is put forward to which those objections do not apply, we have no reason to reject this part of Frege's account of identity. In the next section, I shall examine an example of the required form which may seem more powerful than the one discussed thus far.

V

Suppose Smith offered Jones \$5,000 for a clay statue of George Washington. Jones delivers a statue of Warren Harding he has since molded from the same clay, and demands payment, saying, "That's the same thing you bought last week."

It is the same piece of clay, but a different statue. It seems then that we can form the awkward but true conjunction

> This is the same piece of clay as the one you bought last week, but this is a different statue from the one you bought last week.

What are we to say of this sentence?[15]

Following the criticisms of such counterexamples outlined in section II, we could either say that "this" and "the one you bought last week" refer to pieces of clay in the first conjunct and statues in the second, or that one or the other of the conjuncts does not assert or deny identity.

To maintain the first criticism, we must claim that "this statue" and "this clay" would not in this situation refer to one and the same object; that the clay and the statue are not identical. This view seems paradoxical to some, but I think it can be reasonably defended. There are things true of the one not true of the other (for example, the piece of clay was bought in Egypt in 1956, but not the statue), and the piece of clay may remain with us long after the statue is destroyed. There is clearly a rather intimate relation between the two; I would argue that this relation is that the current "stage" of the piece of clay and the current "stage" of the statue are identical. We might well reserve the phrase "are the same *thing*" for this relation, while using "identical', "are the same object," "are the same entity," and so forth, for the notion whose logical properties were formulated by Leibniz and Frege. But the point I wish to insist on at present is simply that there is nothing paradoxical about maintaining that the clay and the statue are not identical, and a great deal that is problematical about maintaining the opposite.

If all the references are to the statue, then "being the same piece of clay" simply amounts to "being made of the same piece of clay" and does not express identity. If all the references are to the clay, then "— is a different statue from —" should be construed as meaning "— is a different statue than — was," which amounts to "— is formed into a statue that is not identical with the statue – was formed into."

Having these alternative unobjectionable analyses of the apparent counterexample does not constitute an *embarras des richesses*. The speaker's intention to refer to the clay or the statues, or the clay in one conjunct and the statues in the other, might be revealed by later turns in the conversation. But he need not have any such intentions, just as when I say "This is brown" with a gesture toward my desk, I need not have decided whether I am referring to the desk or its color.

VI

Let me then summarize my position. (1) In identity statements like "This is the same river as that" the general term plays the same role as it does in "This river is the same as that river'; it identifies the referents, and not the "kind of identity" being asserted. (2) Apparent counterexamples to the equivalence of "x and y are the same F" and "x and y are F's, and are the same," of the form "x is the same F as y, but x and y are different G's," err either because (i) they have the grammatical, but not the logical, form of a counterexample, since the referring expressions do not have the same referents in both conjuncts, or (ii) one of the conjuncts does not assert or deny identity, but one of the other relations often expressed by phrases of the form "is the same F as." (3) Geach's criticisms of the distinctions implicit in (i) and (ii) are unfounded.[16]

Notes

1 Peter Geach, *Reference and Generality* (Ithaca, NY: Cornell University Press, 1962), p. 39.

2 David Wiggins, *Identity and Spatio-Temporal Continuity* (Oxford: Blackwell, 1967), pt. 1.

3 Peter Geach, "Identity," *Review of Metaphysics* 21 (1967–8), pp. 3–12.

4 Ibid., p. 3.

5 Geach, *Reference and Generality*, p. 39.

6 Ibid., pp. 151–2.

7 I base my remarks about what Frege could say and would say on his general view of these matters as expressed in various writings, and not on any specific discussion of *this* problem. My general view about identity owes much to Frege's remarks in his *Grundlagen der Arithmetik* (Breslau: W. Kolbner, 1884), sects. 62ff, and those expressed by W. V. Quine in *From a Logical Point of View* (Cambridge, Mass.: Harvard University Press, 1953), pp. 65ff.

8 It should be pointed out that Frege would not regard this equivalence as a helpful *analysis* of "being the same *F*." See the remarks cited in n. 7.

9 Peter Geach, *Mental Acts* (New York: Humanities Press, 1957), p. 69.

10 This may seem inconsistent with the view I attributed to Frege with respect to the bathing example. The river I bathed in yesterday and the river I bathed in today are water, and they are the same. Shouldn't it follow that they are the same water? Well, in the sense in which the rivers *are* water, they *are* the same water, and *were* the same water yesterday – although the river I bathed in today *is* not the water the river I bathed in yesterday *was*. Two confusions need to be

avoided. First, the statement in question, that the river I bathed in yesterday and the river I bathed in today are the same water, is not an identity statement (see below). Second, the truth of this statement in no way conflicts with the falsity of "The water I bathed in yesterday and the water I bathed in today are the same," which, on one interpretation, is what "What I bathed in yesterday and what I bathed in today are the same water" amounts to in the example in question.

11 Geach, *Reference and Generality*, p. 157.

12 It is important to see that statements of "relative" identity are not what I have called "identity statements" at all, but rather what I would prefer to call "statements of resemblance" or "common property statements." The statements on p. 93 above, for example, are what Geach calls statements of relative identity. *Relative* identity should not be confused with *restricted* identity (see p. 9 above). On my view, a restricted identity statement can be reworded without changing referents, as a clear identity statement: to say "Leningrad and Stalingrad are the same city" is just to say "The city of Leningrad is identical with the city of Stalingrad." This is not true of statements of relative identity – and that is why they are not identity statements.

13 Double quotes occasionally function as quasi-quotes. I am ignoring problems of nonextensional contexts.

14 Geach, "Identity," p. 10.

15 An example like this is discussed by Wiggins, *Identity*, pp. 8ff.

16 I am grateful to a number of persons for commenting on earlier versions of this paper; I would particularly like to thank Keith Donnellan and Wilfrid Hodges.

9

Contingent Identity

Allan Gibbard

This brief for contingent identity begins with an example. Under certain conditions, I shall argue, a clay statue is identical with the piece of clay of which it is made – or at least it is plausible to claim so. If indeed the statue and the piece of clay are identical, I shall show, then the identity is contingent: that is to say, where s is the statue and c the piece of clay.

$$(1) \quad s = c \ \& \ \lozenge \ (s \text{ exists } \& \ c \text{ exists } \& \ s \neq c)$$

This claim of contingent identity, if true, has important ramifications. Later I shall develop theories of concrete things and proper names which are needed to fit the claim. These theories together form a coherent alternative to theories which hold that all true identities formed with proper names are necessary – a plausible alternative, I shall argue, with many advantages.

Most purported examples of such contingent identity fail: that much, I think, has been shown by Saul Kripke's recent work.[1] Kripke's work has transformed the subjects of necessity and reference, and the usual examples of contingent identity depend on accounts of those subjects which Kripke's attacks undermine. Take, for instance, one of Frege's examples of *a posteriori* identity, somewhat reworded:[2]

(2) If Hesperus exists, then Hesperus = Phosphorus.

On the account of necessity which prevailed before Kripke, a truth is necessary only if it can be known a priori. Now as Frege pointed out, (2) is clearly a posteriori, since it reports a discovery which could only have been made by observation. On the old account, then, (2), although true, is not a necessary truth. Kripke's attacks undermine this account of necessary truth as a priori truth. Whether something is a necessary truth, he argues, is not a matter of how we can know it, but of whether it might have been false if the world had been different: a proposition is a necessary truth if it would have been true in any possible situation. The necessary–contingent distinction and the a priori–a posteriori distinction, then, are not drawn in the same way, and to prove a truth contingent, it is not enough simply to show that it is a posteriori.[3]

Kripke's attacks also undermine accounts of reference which would make (2) a contingent truth. On both Russell's theory of descriptions[4] and the later "cluster" theory, a name gets its reference in some way from the beliefs of the person who uses it. On Russell's view, the heavenly body Hesperus of which the ancients spoke would be the thing which fitted certain beliefs they had about Hesperus; on the cluster theory, it would be the thing which fitted a preponderance of their beliefs about it. Now the ancients" beliefs about Hesperus and their beliefs about Phosphorus were such that, in some possible worlds, one thing would fit the former and another the latter. On such an

Originally published in *Journal of Philosophical Logic* 4 (1975), pp. 187–221. Copyright © by D. Reidel Publishing Company. Reprinted by permission of Kluwer Academic Publishers.

account of proper names, then, (2) would be false in some possible worlds, and is therefore contingent.

I shall not repeat Kripke's attacks on the description and cluster theories of proper names.[5] My purpose here is to argue that even if these attacks are successful, there may well remain some contingent identities consisting of proper names. The identity of Hesperus and Phosphorus is not contingent, on the theories I shall develop, but I shall give an example which is. Kripke's attacks, if I am right, transform the subject of contingent identity, but they do not eliminate it.

I

In what sort of case might a statue *s* be identical with the piece of clay, *c*, of which it is made? Identity here is to be taken in a strict, timeless sense, not as mere identity during some period of time. For two things to be strictly identical, they must have all properties in common. That means, among other things, that they must start to exist at the same time and cease to exist at the same time. If we are to construct a case in which a statue is identical with a piece of clay, then, we shall need persistence criteria for statues and pieces of clay – criteria for when they start to exist and when they cease to exist.

Take first the piece of clay. Here I do not mean the portion of clay of which the piece consists, which may go on existing after the piece has been broken up or merged with other pieces. I shall call this clay of which the piece consists a *portion* of clay; a portion of clay, as I am using the term, can be scattered widely and continue to exist. Here I am asking about a *piece* or *lump* of clay.

A lump sticks together: its parts stick to each other, directly or through other parts, and no part of the lump sticks to any portion of clay which is not part of the lump. The exact nature of this sticking relation will not matter here; it is a familiar relation which holds between parts of a solid object, but not between parts of a liquid, powder, or heap of solid objects. We know, then, what it is for two portions of clay to be parts of the same lump of clay at a time *t*, and if they are, I shall say that they are *stuck to* each other *at t*.

For how long, then, does a piece of clay persist? As a first approximation, the criteria might be put as follows. A piece of clay consists of a portion *P* of clay. It comes into existence when all the parts of *P* come to be stuck to each other, and cease to be stuck to any clay which is not part of *P*. It ceases to exist when the parts of *P* cease to be stuck to each other or come to be stuck to clay which is not in *P*. Thus a piece of clay can be formed either by sticking smaller pieces of clay together or by breaking it off a larger piece of clay, and it can be destroyed either by breaking it apart or by sticking it to other pieces of clay.

This standard is probably too strict; we ought to allow for such things as wear and the adherence of clay dust to a wet piece of clay. Nothing will change, though, for my purposes, if we allow the portion of clay which composes a piece of clay to change slowly over time. In the actual world, then, a piece of clay might be characterized by a function **P** from instants to portions of clay. In order for it to characterize a piece of clay, the function **P** would have to satisfy the following conditions.

(a) The domain of **P** is an interval of time *T*.
(b) For any instant *t* in *T*, **P**(*t*) is a portion of clay the parts of which, at *t*, are both stuck to each other and not stuck to any clay particles which are not part of **P**(*t*).
(c) The portions of clay **P**(*t*) change with *t* only slowly, if at all. (I shall give no exact standard of slowness here, but one might be stipulated if anything hinged on it.)
(d) No function **P*** which satisfies (a), (b), and (c) *extends* **P**, in the sense that the domain of **P*** properly includes the domain of **P** and the function **P** is **P*** with its domain restricted.

Both on this standard, then, and on the earlier, stricter one, a piece of clay comes into existence when parts in it are stuck to each other and unstuck from all other clay, and goes out of existence when its parts cease to be stuck to each other or become stuck to other clay. That is what I shall need for what follows.

What, now, are the persistence criteria for clay statues? By a statue here, I do not mean a shape of which there could be more than one token, but a concrete particular thing: distinct clay statues, as I am using the term, may come out of the same mold. A clay statue consists of a piece of clay in a specific shape. It lasts, then, as long as the piece of clay lasts and keeps that shape. It comes into being when the piece of clay first exists and has that shape, and it goes out of existence as soon as the piece of clay ceases to exist or to have that shape.

These criteria too may be overly strict: again we may want to allow for slow changes of shape from wear, accretion, and slight bending. So let us say, a clay statue persists as long as the piece of clay it is made of persists and changes shape only slowly.

I do not claim that the criteria I have given are precisely set forth that way in our conceptual scheme. I do think that the criteria I have given fit at least roughly what we say about statues and pieces of clay. My argument will depend on no such claim, though, and for all I shall have to say, the criteria I have given might have been purely stipulative. I do need to make one claim for those criteria: I claim that as I have defined them, pieces of clay and clay statues are objects. That is to say, they can be designated with proper names, and the logic we ordinarily use will still apply. That is all, strictly speaking, that I need to claim for the criteria I have given.

Now we are in a better position to ask, are a clay statue and the piece of clay of which it is made identical? The persistence criteria I have given make it clear that often the two are distinct. In a typical case, a piece of clay is brought into existence by breaking it off from a bigger piece of clay. It then gets shaped, say, into the form of an elephant. With the finishing touches, a statue of an elephant comes into being. The statue and the piece of clay therefore have different properties: the times they start to exist are different, and whereas the statue has the property of being elephant-shaped as long as it exists, the piece of clay does not. Since one has properties the other lacks, the two are not identical.[6]

Suppose, though, a clay statue starts to exist at the same time as the piece of clay of which it is made, and ceases to exist at the same time as the piece of clay ceases to exist. Will the statue then be identical with the piece of clay? It is indeed possible for a statue to endure for precisely the same period of time as its piece of clay, as the persistence criteria I have given make clear. Consider the following story.

I make a clay statue of the infant Goliath in two pieces, one the part above the waist and the other the part below the waist. Once I finish the two halves, I stick them together, thereby bringing into existence simultaneously a new piece of clay and a new statue. A day later I smash the statue, thereby bringing to an end both statue and piece of clay. The statue and the piece of clay persisted during exactly the same period of time.

Here, I am tempted to say, the statue and the piece of clay are identical. They began at the same time, and on any usual account, they had the same shape, location, color, and so forth at each instant in their history; everything that happened to one happened to the other; and the act that destroyed the one destroyed the other. If the statue is an entity over and above the piece of clay in that shape, then statues seem to take on a ghostly air. No doubt other explanations of what the statue is can be offered, but the hypothesis that the statue and piece of clay are identical seems well worth exploring.

If indeed the statue and piece of clay are the same thing, then their identity is contingent. It is contingent, that is to say in the sense of (1) at the beginning of this paper. (1) uses proper names, and so let me name the statue and the lump: the statue I shall call "*Goliath*"; the piece of clay, "Lumpl." Naming the piece of clay, to be sure, seems strange, but that, presumably, is because it is unusual to name pieces of clay, not because pieces of clay are unnamable. With these names, (1) becomes

(3) *Goliath* = Lumpl & ◊ (*Goliath* exists & Lumpl exists & *Goliath* ≠ Lumpl).

It is in this sense that I want to claim that *Goliath* = Lumpl contingently.

Suppose, then, that *Goliath* = Lumpl. Then their identity is contingent in the sense of (3). For suppose I had brought Lumpl into existence as *Goliath*, just as I actually did, but before the clay had a chance to dry, I squeezed it into a ball. At that point, according to the persistence criteria I have given, the statue *Goliath* would have ceased to exist, but the piece of clay Lumpl would still exist in a new shape. Hence Lumpl would not be *Goliath*, even though both existed. We would have

Lumpl exists & *Goliath* exists & *Goliath* ≠ Lumpl.

If in fact, then, *Goliath* = Lumpl, then here is a case of contingent identity. In fact *Goliath* = Lumpl, but had I destroyed the statue *Goliath* by squeezing it, then it would have been the case that, although both existed, *Goliath* ≠ Lumpl. The identity is contingent, then, in the sense given in (3).

II

The claim that *Goliath* = Lumpl, then, has important consequences for the logic of identity. How can the claim be evaluated?

Initially, at least, the claim seems plausible. *Goliath* and Lumpl exist during precisely the same period of time, and at each instant during that period, they have, it would seem, the same shape, color, weight, location, and so forth: they share all their obvious properties.

The claim that *Goliath* = Lumpl, moreover, fits a systematic account of statues and piece of clay. A clay statue ordinarily begins to exist only after its piece of clay does. In such cases, it seems reasonable to say, the statue is a temporal segment of the piece of clay – a segment which extends for the period of time during which the piece of clay keeps a particular, statuesque shape. Here, then, is a systematic account of the relation between a statue and its piece of clay. By that account, however, there will be cases in which a clay statue is identical with its piece of clay. For in some cases the very temporal segment of the piece of clay which constitutes the statue extends for the entire life of the piece of clay. In such a case, the segment is the piece of clay in its entire extent: the statue and the piece of clay are identical.[7]

That leads to my main reason for wanting to say that *Goliath* = Lumpl. Concrete things, like statues and pieces of clay, are a part of the physical world, and we ought, it seems to me, to have a systematic physical account of them. Concrete things, I want to maintain, are made up in some simple, canonical way from fundamental physical entities. Now what I have said of the relation between a statue and its piece of clay fits such a general view of concrete things. Suppose, for example, we take point-instants to be our fundamental physical entities, and let a concrete thing be a set of point-instants. In that case, *Goliath* = Lumpl simply because they are the same set of point-instants. Suppose instead we take particles to be our fundamental physical entities, and let a concrete thing be a changing set of particles – which might mean a function from instants in time to sets of particles. Then again, *Goliath* = Lumpl, because at each instant they consist of the same set of particles. Now particles and point-instants are the sorts of things we might expect to appear in a well-confirmed fundamental physics – in that part of an eventual physics which gives the fundamental laws of the universe. A system according to which *Goliath* = Lumpl, then, may well allow concrete things to be made up in a simple way from entities that appear in well-confirmed fundamental physics. Concrete things, then, can be given a place in a comprehensive view of the world.

In the rest of this paper, then, I shall work out a theory according to which *Goliath* = Lumpl. Concrete things, for all I shall say, may be either sets of point-instants or changing sets of particles. The sections which follow develop a theory of proper names and a theory of modal and dispositional properties for concrete things.

III

If, as I want to claim, *Goliath* = Lumpl, then how do proper names like "*Goliath*" and "Lumpl" work? Kripke gives an account of proper names from which it follows that *Goliath* cannot be identical with Lumpl; thus if Kripke's were the only plausible account of proper names, then the claim that *Goliath* = Lumpl would have to be abandoned. In fact, though, accepting that *Goliath* = Lumpl leads to an alternative account of proper names, which, I shall argue, is fully coherent and at least at plausible as Kripke's.

Kripke's account of proper names is roughly this. We in the actual world use proper names both to talk about the actual world and to talk about ways the world might have been. According to Kripke, if a proper name denotes a thing in the actual world, then in talk of non-actual situations, the name, if it denotes at all, simply denotes that same thing. A proper name is a *rigid designator*: it refers to the same thing in talk of any possible world in which that thing exists, and in talk of any other possible world, it refers to nothing in that world.[8]

Now if all proper names are rigid designators, then *Goliath* cannot be identical with Lumpl as I have claimed. For suppose they are identical. Call the actual world W_0 and the world as it would be if I had squeezed the clay into a ball W'; then

(i) In W_0, *Goliath* = Lumpl,

but as I have shown,

(ii) In W', *Goliath* $\neq$ Lumpl.

Now if the names "*Goliath*" and "Lumpl" are both rigid designators, then (i) and (ii) cannot both hold. For suppose (i) is true. Then the names "*Goliath*" and "Lumpl" both denote the same thing in W_0. Hence if they are both rigid designators, they both denote that thing in every possible world in which it exists, and denote nothing otherwise. Since they each denote something in W', they must therefore both denote the same thing in W', and thus (ii) must be false.

The claim that $Goliath$ = Lumpl, then, is incompatible with Kripke's account of proper names. Suppose, then, that $Goliath$ is indeed identical with Lumpl; what view of proper names emerges? How, on that supposition, could we decide whether the name "$Goliath$" is a rigid designator? Consider the situation. In the actual world, "$Goliath$" refers to a thing which I made and then broke, which is both a statue and a piece of clay. Hence the name "$Goliath$" is a rigid designator if it refers to that same thing in any possible situation in which the thing exists, and refers to nothing otherwise.

What, though, would constitute "that same thing" if the statue and the piece of clay were different? Take the situation in W': suppose instead of breaking the statue, as I actually did, I had squeezed the clay into a ball. Would that single thing which in fact I made and then broke – which in fact was both a piece of clay and a statue – then be the statue $Goliath$ which I squeezed out of existence, or the piece of clay Lumpl which went on existing after I squeezed it?

I can find no sense in the question. To ask meaningfully what that thing would be, we must designate it either as a statue or as a piece of clay. It makes sense to ask what the statue $Goliath$ would be in that situation: it would be a statue; likewise, it makes sense to ask what the piece of clay Lumpl would be in that situation: it would be a piece of clay. What that thing would be, though, apart from the way it is designated, is a question without meaning.

A rough theory begins to emerge from all this. If $Goliath$ and Lumpl are the same thing, asking what that thing would be in W' apart from the way the thing is designated, makes no sense. Meaningful cross-world identities of such things as statues, it begins to seem, must be identities qua something: qua statue or qua lump,[9] qua $Goliath$ or qua Lumpl. It makes sense to talk of the "same statue" in different possible worlds, but no sense to talk of the 'same thing.'

Put more fully, what seems to be happening is this. Proper names like "$Goliath$" or "$Lumpl$" refer to a thing as a thing of a certain kind: "$Goliath$" refers to something as a statue; "$Lumpl$," as a lump. For each such kind of thing, there is a set of persistence criteria, like the ones I gave for statues and for lumps.[10] In rare cases, at least, one thing will be of two different kinds, with different persistence criteria, and whereas one proper name refers to it as a thing of one kind, another proper name will refer to it as a thing of another kind. In such cases, the identity formed with those names is contingently true. It is true because the two names designate the same thing, which ceases to exist at the same time on both sets of criteria. It is contingent because if the world had gone differently after the thing came into existence, the thing might have ceased to exist at different times on the two sets of criteria: it would have been one thing on one set of persistence criteria, and another thing – perhaps a temporal segment of the first – on the second set of criteria.

If all that is so, it makes no sense to call a designator rigid or nonrigid by itself. A designator may be rigid with respect to a sortal: it may be statue-rigid, as "$Goliath$" is, or it may be lump-rigid, as "$Lumpl$" is. A designator, for instance, is $statue$-$rigid$ if it designates the same statue in every possible world in which that statue exists and designates nothing in any other possible world. What is special about proper names like "$Goliath$" and "$Lumpl$" is not that they are rigid designators. It is rather that each is rigid with respect to the sortal it invokes. "$Goliath$" refers to its bearer as a statue and is statue-rigid; "$Lumpl$" refers to its bearer as a lump and is lump-rigid.

In short, then, if we accept that $Goliath$ = Lumpl and examine the situation, a rough theory of proper names emerges. A proper name like "$Goliath$" denotes a thing in the actual world, and invokes a sortal with certain persistence criteria. It then denotes the same thing-of-that-sort in every possible world in which it denotes at all. The name "$Goliath$" itself, for instance, denotes a lump of clay and invokes the sortal $statue$; hence it denotes the same statue in every possible world in which that statue exists.

That leaves two questions unanswered. First, how does a name like "$Goliath$" get its reference in the actual world? Second, what makes a thing in another possible world "the same statue" as the one which in fact I made and then broke? I shall tackle this second question first.

Once I made my statue, that statue existed, and nothing that happened from then on could change the fact that it had existed or the way it had come to exist. It would be that same statue whether I subsequently broke it, squeezed it, or sold it. Its origin, then, makes a statue the statue that it is, and if statues in different possible worlds have the same beginning, then they are the same statue.

The name "*Goliath*" picks out in W' the one statue which begins in W' like *Goliath* in W_0. Consider the case more fully. The world W' bears an important relation to W_0 and the statue *Goliath* in W_0: W' *branches* from W_0 after *Goliath* begins to exist; that is, until some time after *Goliath* begins to exist in W_0, the histories of W_0 and W' are exactly the same. In the branching world W', then, *Goliath* is the statue which has exactly the same history before the branching as *Goliath* in W_0. The name "Lumpl" too picks out a thing in W' which begins exactly like the statue *Goliath* in W_0. "Lumpl," though, picks out, not the unique statue in W' which begins that way, but the unique piece of clay in W' which begins that way. Since that piece of clay in W' is distinct from that statue in W', the two names pick out different things in W' – different things which both start out in the same way.

Here, then, is a theory of reference for the special case of branching possible worlds. Let proper name α denote a thing X in the actual world W_0; the theory will apply to any possible world W which branches from W_0 after X begins to exist in W_0. According to the theory, α not only denotes X in W_0, but also invokes a set C of persistence criteria which X satisfies in W_0. The reference of α in W, then, is the thing in W which has the same history before the branching as X has in W_0 and which satisfies the persistence criteria in set C.

According to the theory, then, the reference of a name in branching world W depends on two things: its reference in the actual world, and the persistence criteria it invokes. The reference of the name in the actual world determines how the thing it denotes in W begins; the persistence criteria it invokes determine which of the various things that begin that way in W the name denotes.

That leaves the problem of possible worlds which do not branch from the actual world, or which branch too early. How to handle reference to things in such obdurate worlds I do not know. Perhaps the best course is to deny that any such reference is possible. The clearest cases of reference by a speaker in one possible world to a thing in another are ones like the clay statue case, where a world branches from the actual one after the thing to which reference is made starts to exist. I am inclined, then, for the sake of clarity, to rule out any other sort of reference to concrete entities in other possible worlds. If, though, a clear criterion which allowed such reference were devised, that criterion could probably be adopted without much changing the system I am proposing.

There remains the question of how a name gets its reference in the actual world. Its reference in branching worlds, I have said, depends partly on its reference in the actual world. Until we say how a name gets its reference in the actual world, then, even the theory of reference for branching worlds is incomplete. Nothing I have said about the names "*Goliath*" and "Lumpl" has any direct bearing on the question of reference in the actual world. The account Kripke gives[11] seems plausible to me, and everything I have said in this paper is compatible with it.

On that account, a name gets its reference from a causal chain that connects the person who uses the name with the thing denoted. In my mouth and in the mouth of anyone else who uses the names "*Goliath*" and "Lumpl," those names denote the actual thing they do because I applied those names to it directly and others got the names from me. Other people, then, are connected to that clay statue by a tradition through which the name was handed down; I am connected more directly, by having perceived the thing and named it.

Persistence criteria play a role in starting the tradition. I named the thing I did by pointing to it and invoking persistence criteria: "I name this statue '*Goliath*,'" I said, "and this piece of clay 'Lumpl.'" The name "*Goliath*," then, denoted the unique thing at which I was pointing which satisfied the persistence criteria for statues – that is, the unique statue at which I was pointing. Since the same thing satisfied both the criteria for statues and the criteria for pieces of clay, both names denoted the same thing, but if I had invoked different persistence criteria, I might have named a different thing. When I pointed at the statue, I pointed at a number of things of various durations. I pointed, for instance, at the portion of clay which made up the statue. I might have said, "I name the portion of clay which makes up this statue 'Portia.'" If I had done so, I would have named a portion of clay which survived the breaking of the statue. Thus when the tradition is started which gives a name a concrete reference in the actual world, the persistence criteria invoked help determine what entity bears that name.

I have given a theory of proper names, and on that theory, it is clear why the identity "*Goliath* = Lumpl" is contingent. It is equally clear, on that theory, why the identity "Hesperus = Phosphorus" is necessary, in the sense that it holds in any possible world in which Hesperus exists. At least, it is clear if identity of concrete things across possible worlds is confined to branching cases in the way I have described. Both names, "Hesperus" and "Phosphorus," invoke the persistence criteria for heavenly bodies. Both refer to Venus. Hence in any possible world W which branches from the actual world after Venus begins to exist, they both refer to the heavenly body in W which starts out in W like Venus in W_0. Both, then, refer to the same thing in W. On the theory here, then, as on Kripke's theory, the identity "Hesperus = Phosphorus," even though a posteriori, is a necessary truth: it would hold in any situation in which Hesperus or Phosphorus existed.

In short, then, if we accept that *Goliath* = Lumpl, the following theory of proper names for concrete objects emerges. The reference of a name in the actual world is fixed partly by invoking a set of persistence criteria which determine what thing it names. The name may then be passed on through a tradition, and the reference is fixed by the origin of that tradition. The name can also be used to refer to a thing in a possible world which branches from the actual world after the thing named in the actual world begins to exist. In that case the name refers to the unique thing in that possible world which both satisfies the persistence criteria the name invokes and starts out exactly like the bearer of the name in the actual world.

IV

Kripke's theory of proper names is incompatible with the theory I have developed, and Kripke gives a number of forceful arguments for his theory. Do any of those arguments tell against the theory here? Let me try to pick out arguments Kripke gives which are germane.

According to the theory here, it makes no sense to call a designator rigid and leave it at that, because it makes no strict sense to call things in different possible worlds identical and leave it at that: identity across possible worlds makes sense only with respect to a sortal. According to Kripke, qualms about identity across possible worlds are unfounded, and plain talk of rigid designators makes perfectly good sense. What Kripke says most directly on this point, however, shows no more than what I have already accepted: that it makes sense to call a designator rigid with respect to a sortal, like *statue, number* or *man*. "... we can perfectly well talk about rigid and nonrigid designators. Moreover, we have a simple, intuitive test

for them. We can say, for example, that the number of planets might have been a different number from the number it in fact is." The designator "the number of planets," then, is nonrigid. "If we apply this intuitive test to proper names, such as for example 'Richard Nixon,' they would seem intuitively to come out as rigid designators. ... It seems that we cannot say 'Nixon might have been a different man from the man he in fact was,' unless, of course, we mean it metaphorically."[12]

Does it make sense, then, to call a designator "rigid" independently of a sortal it invokes? Kripke's examples here prove no such thing. Nixon indeed could not have been a different *man* from the man he in fact is. That, however, shows only that the designator "Nixon" is rigid with respect to the sortal *man*, not that it is rigid independently of any sortal. To show it rigid independently of any sortal, one would have to go beyond what Kripke says in the passage I have quoted, and show that Nixon could not have been a different *entity* from the one he in fact is.

For that purpose, the "simple, intuitive test" Kripke offers will not help. We speak and think of "the same person" but not of "the same entity." The point at issue is how everyday talk of "the same person" best fits into systematic talk of "entities." To this issue, everyday intuitions about entities, if we had them, would be irrelevant: the matter has to be settled by working out rival systems and comparing their implications.

Kripke attacks qualms about cross-world identity in another way: those qualms, he says, may just grow out of a confusion about what possible worlds are. Talk of "possible worlds" suggests that they are like distant planets to be explored. If that were what they were like, I might explore a possible world and discover someone who looked like Benjamin Franklin; I would then have to determine whether it actually was Franklin I had discovered, or just someone who looked like him.[13]

Instead, according to Kripke, possible worlds are situations which we stipulate – "counterfactual situations" may be the best term. What thing is what in a counterfactual situation is not something I find out; it is part of what I stipulate: it is "given in the very description" of the stipulated situation. "And there seems to be no less objection to *stipulating* that we are speaking of certain *people* than there can be to stipulating that we are speaking of certain *qualities*."[14]

Is that so? The statue example seems to provide an objection – an objection, at least, to stipulating that we are speaking of certain *entities*. In that example, a possible situation was stipulated, just as Kripke demands. "For suppose I had brought Lumpl into existence as *Goliath*, just as I actually did, but before the clay had a chance to dry, I squeezed it into a ball." In this stipulated situation, I showed, there are two distinct things, a statue and a piece of clay. It might be tempting to ask which of the two is the one thing which, in the actual world, I made and then broke. To that question, though, there is no plain answer – or so I argued. Now the problem is not one of understipulation. It is not as if the thing I actually made could appear in two different possible situations in which I squeezed it: in one as a statue that ceased to exist when squeezed, and in another as a piece of clay which persisted after it was squeezed. After I made that thing, I held it in my hands and I could have squeezed it; if I suppose that I did squeeze it, I have stipulated as much about the identities of the things in that supposed situation as can be stipulated. A situation, then, can be fully stipulated even though questions of identity across possible worlds remain unsettled.

Kripke agrees to something like this. "Given certain counterfactual vicissitudes in the history of the molecules of a table, T, one may ask whether T would exist, in that situation, or whether a certain bunch of molecules, which in that situation would constitute a table, constitute the very same table T." Such a conception of "transworld identification," he says, "differs considerably from the usual one"; for one thing, "the attempted notion deals with criteria of identity of particulars in terms of other particulars, not qualities" – in terms of particular molecules, that is to say.[15] This qualification, though, has no bearing on the point in question here. Take a possible world in which I squeeze Lumpl into a ball, and suppose all the molecules involved are clearly identified. There are still two distinct things in that world, the statue *Goliath* which I destroy by squeezing, and the piece of clay Lumpl which survives the squeezing. The question remains, then, which of those two distinct things in that possible world is the single thing which in fact I made and then broke. There is, in short, a genuine problem with cross-world identification – Kripke's arguments notwithstanding.

V

The most prominent objection to contingent identity remains to be tackled: the objection that it violates Leibniz' Law. If *Goliath* is contingently identical with Lumpl, then although

(4) $\Box$(Lumpl exists $\rightarrow$ Lumpl = Lumpl)

is true,

(5) $\Box$(Lumpl exists $\rightarrow$ *Goliath* = Lumpl)

is false. Yet (5) is derived from (4) and

(6)   *Goliath* = Lumpl

by substitutivity of identicals. Thus, the objection goes, *Goliath* cannot be contingently identical with Lumpl.

The usual answer will serve my purpose here. Leibniz' Law settles very little by itself: put as a general law of substitutivity of identicals, it is just false; in its correct version, it is a law about properties and relations: *If $x = y$, then for any property, if x has it, then y has it, and for any relation and any given things, if x stands in that relation to those things, then y stands in that relation to those things.* The law so stated yields substitutivity of identicals only for contexts that attribute properties and relations. (5) follows from (4) and (6) by Leibniz' Law, then, only if the context

(7) $\Box$(Lumpl exists $\rightarrow$ — = Lumpl)

attributes a property. We can block the inference to (5), then, simply by denying that the context (7) attributes a property.

It may seem arbitrary to deny that (7) attributes a property, but whether it does is the very point in question here. A property, if it is to be a property, must apply or not apply to a thing independently of the way the thing is designated. (7) gives a property, then, only if it gives something that is true of Lumpl or false of Lumpl independently of the way Lumpl is designated, and whether it does is the point in question.

The proponent of contingent identity, then, has a reasonable, consistent position open to him – a position that is familiar in the literature on the subject.[16] Expressions constructed with modal operators, he can say, simply do not give properties of *concrete things*, such as statues and pieces of clay. Modal expressions do not apply to concrete things independently of the way they are designated. Lumpl, for instance, is the same thing as *Goliath*: it is a clay statue of the infant *Goliath* which I put

Allan Gibbard

together and then broke. Necessary identity to
Lumpl, though, is not a property which that
thing has or lacks, for it makes no sense to ask
whether that thing, as such, is necessarily identical
with Lumpl. Modal contexts, then, do not attribute
properties or relations to concrete things – so the
proponent of contingent identity can respond to
Leibniz' Law.

Now this response comes at a stiff price. Quantificational contexts must attribute properties or
relations; they must be true or false of things independently of the way those things are designated. If
modal contexts do not attribute properties or relations to concrete things, it follows that such contexts are not open to quantification with variables
whose values are concrete things. A large number
of formulas, then, must be ruled out as ill formed.

Although, for instance, the sentence

$$\Diamond \,(\text{Lumpl exists} \; \& \; \textit{Goliath} \neq \text{Lumpl})$$

is well formed, the expression

(8) $\Diamond \,(\text{Lumpl exists} \; \& \; x \neq \text{Lumpl})$

turns out to be ill formed – at least, that is, if the
variable x can take *Goliath* as a value. Now on the
basis of what I have said, that seems reasonable.
Take the expression (8), and consider the thing I
made and then broke, which is both a statue and a
lump. There is no apparent way of saying that (8) is
true or false of that thing; it is true of it *qua* statue
but not *qua* piece of clay. By that test, the free
variable x does not belong in its context in (8) if it
takes concrete things like statues and lumps among
its values.

Here, then, may be a telling objection to contingent identity: if in order to maintain contingent
identity we must restrict quantification so drastically, the objector can argue, we shall be unable to
say many of the things we need to say, both in
scientific talk and in daily life. Concrete things
will have no modal properties: there will, that is,
be no such thing as *de re* modality for concrete
things. Indeed on some accounts, there will also
be problems with dispositions – as I shall later
show. Perhaps we can maintain contingent identity
only at the cost of tying our tongues, and that, if it
is true, might be a strong reason for rejecting contingent identity.

The remainder of my argument for the plausibility of the system I am advocating will concern
this issue. I shall give devices which I think will

enable us to say anything that we ought seriously to
regard as meaningful, and say it in the system I am
advocating. What I have to say will center around
the system Carnap proposed in *Meaning and Necessity* for quantifying into modal contexts.[17] Carnap's
system, I think, is the best one for handling quantified modal talk of concrete things. In what follows, I shall draw loosely both on Carnap's system
and on Aldo Bressan's extension of it[18] to give ways
of saying what we need to say.

Carnap's system has many advantages. It fits my
claim that *Goliath* = Lumpl, and it allows variables
in any context in which a proper name can appear.
Indeed on Carnap's account, variables in modal
contexts act almost exactly as proper names do on
the account in section III of this paper. Carnap, in
short, gives a clear, consistent theory which fits
what I have been saying.

There is, to be sure, a price for all this: Carnap
gives a nonstandard account of the way predicates
and variables behave in modal contexts. The
account he gives, though, makes sense, and it
departs from the standard account of quantifiers
in much the same way as I departed in section III
from the standard account of proper names. It is
nonstandard, then, in ways that fit nicely the theory in this paper.

Carnap's treatment of variables is suggested by
part of Frege's treatment of proper names. According to Frege,[19] a proper name in a modal context
refers *obliquely*: its reference there is its usual sense.
Hence in

(9) $\Diamond \,(\text{Lumpl exists} \; \& \; \text{Goliath} \neq \text{Lumpl}),$

the name "*Goliath*" refers, not to a statue, but to a
statue-concept which is the normal sense of the
name. Any other name with that same normal
sense could be substituted for "*Goliath*" in (9)
without changing its truth-value. This part of Frege's account fits what I have said of proper names,
as I shall later illustrate.

Now just as, on Frege's account, proper names
shift their reference in modal contexts, on Carnap's
account, variables in modal contexts shift their
range of values: they range over senses. In the
formula

$$\Diamond \,(\text{Lumpl exists} \; \& \; x \neq \text{Lumpl}),$$

then, x ranges not over concrete things, like statues
and pieces of clay, but over what Carnap calls
"individual concepts" – including statue-concepts

and lump-concepts. Call things of the kind the variables take as values in nonmodal contexts *individuals*: an *individual concept* is a function whose domain is a set of possible worlds, and which assigns to each world W in its domain an individual that exists in W.

I spell out what is roughly Carnap's proposal in the appendix;[20] here I give it by example. Let the individuals in the system be concrete things, like statues and lumps. Let "E" in nonmodal contexts be the predicate *exists*, and let "H" in such contexts be the predicate *is humanoid*, by which I shall mean *is human-shaped throughout its early history*. Then in the formula

(10) $\Box(Ex \rightarrow Hx)$,

on Carnap's proposal, both the variable and the predicates make a shift. The variable x in (10) now ranges over individual concepts, and the predicates in (10) make compensating shifts as follows: "E" now means not *exists*, but rather *is a concept of an individual that exists*. "H" now means not *is humanoid*, but rather *is a concept of an individual that is humanoid*. For any possible world W and individual concept f, that is to say, "H" in modal contexts is true of f in W if and only if the individual f assigns to W is humanoid in W.[21]

That gives (10) a clear interpretation: the open sentence (10) is true of any individual concept f such that for every world W, if f assigns an individual to W, then f assigns to W an individual that is humanoid in W. In particular, then, (10) is true of the *Goliath*-concept – the individual concept that assigns the statue *Goliath* to each possible world in which that statue exists, and assigns nothing to any other possible world. For *Goliath* in any possible world, according to the theory I have given, is humanoid: in any world in which it exists, it starts out in the shape of the actual *Goliath*, and changes shape only slowly. (10) is false of the Lumpl-concept correspondingly defined, since in possible worlds in which I squeeze Lumpl into a ball, Lumpl loses its human shape during its early history, and thus is not humanoid in the stipulated sense. To such a possible world, then, the Lumpl-concept does not assign an individual which is humanoid.

Variables on this proposal work very much like proper names on my account of them in section III. Just as on that earlier account,

(11) $\Box(E \, Goliath \rightarrow H \, Goliath)$

is true and

(12) $\Box(E \, Lumpl \rightarrow H \, Lumpl)$

is false, so on the Carnapian account I am now giving, the open sentence $\Box(Ex \rightarrow Hx)$ is true of the *Goliath*-concept and false of the Lumpl-concept.

Indeed, just as, on Carnap's account, variables in modal contexts range over individual concepts, so on the account in section III, proper names in modal contexts can be construed as denoting individual concepts. Proper names work, in other words, roughly as Frege claims. Let the name "*Goliath*" in (11), for instance, denote the *Goliath*-concept, and suppose predicates shift in modal contexts as Carnap suggests. Then (11) attributes to the *Goliath*-concept the property

$\Box(E \underline{\quad} \rightarrow H \underline{\quad})$,

that in every possible world W, if it assigns to W an existing individual, then it assigns to W an individual that is humanoid. The *Goliath*-concept has that property, and so (11) on this construal is true. The Lumpl-concept does not have that property, and so (12) on this construal is false. That is as it should be on the account in section III. Modal properties can be construed as attributing properties and relations to individual concepts, much as Frege claims.

VI

What happens to identity on this account? Identity of individual concepts x and y is not now expressed as "$x = y$"; that, in modal contexts, means just that x and y are concepts of the same individual. The way to say that x and y are the same individual concept is

$\Box[(Ex \lor Ey) \rightarrow x = y]$.

I shall abbreviate this "$x \equiv y$".

It could now be objected that the thesis of contingent identity has collapsed. Identity in the system here, it seems, is given not by "$=$," but by "$\equiv$" and the relation "$\equiv$" is never contingent: if it holds between two individual concepts, then it holds between them in every possible world. No genuine relation of identity, then, is contingent; the illusion that there are contingent identities came from using the identity sign "=" to mean something other than true identity.

To this objection the following answer can be given. "=" indeed is the identity sign for individuals in the system, and if I am right that a piece of clay is an individual in the Carnapian sense, then "=" is the identity sign for pieces of clay. For consider: in nonmodal contexts, I stipulated, the variables range over individuals. Now "=" in such contexts holds only for identical individuals; it is the relation a piece of clay, for instance, bears to itself and only to itself. Moreover, applied to individuals, "=" satisfies Leibniz' Law: individuals related by it have the same properties in the strict sense, and stand in the same relations in the strict sense. The contexts where "=" is not an identity sign are modal contexts, but there the variables range not over individuals, but over individual concepts. "=" in the system, then, is the identity sign for individuals, and according to the system, "=" can hold contingently for individuals: A sentence of the form "$a = b$," then, asserts the identity of two individuals, and it may be contingent.

Quine would object to this answer. It depends on a "curious double interpretation of variables": outside modal contexts they are interpreted as ranging over individuals; inside modal contexts, over individual concepts. "This complicating device," Quine says, "has no essential bearing, and is better put aside."[22] "Since the duality in question is a peculiarity of a special metalinguistic idiom and not of the object-language itself, there is nothing to prevent our examining the object-language from the old point of view and asking what the values of its variables are in the old-fashioned non-dual sense of the term."[23] The values in the old-fashioned sense, Quine says, are individual concepts, for "$(\forall x) \equiv$" is a logical truth, and on "the old point of view," that means that entities between which the relation $\equiv$ fails are distinct entities. In all contexts, then, the values of the variables are individual concepts, and identity is given by "$\equiv$."

All this can be accepted, however, and the point I have made stands: "=" in the system expresses identity of individuals. "$a = b$," on Quine's interpretation, says that a and b are concepts of the same individual. That amounts to saying that the individual of which a is the concept is identical with the individual of which b is the concept. Even on Quine's interpretation, then, "$a = b$" in effect asserts the identity of individuals, and does so in the most direct way the system allows.

On either Quine's interpretation or Carnap's, then, to assert

(13)   *Goliath* = Lumpl

is in effect to assert the identity of an individual. For all Carnap's system says, (13) may be true, though *Goliath* might not have been identical with Lumpl. If (13) is true but contingent, then it seems reasonable to call it a contingent identity. The claim that there are contingent identities in a natural sense, then, is consistent with Carnap's modal system on either Carnap's or Quine's interpretation of values of variables.

VII

One further Quinean objection needs to be answered. I am embracing "essentialism" for individual concepts. Essentialism, if I understand Quine, is the view that necessity properly applies "to the fulfillment of conditions by objects . . . apart from special ways of specifying them."[24] Now what I have said, as I shall explain, requires me to reject essentialism for concrete things but accept it for individual concepts. That discriminatory treatment needs to be justified.

First, a more precise definition of essentialism: *Essentialism for* a class of entities U, I shall say, is the claim that for any entity e in U and any condition ϕ which e fulfills, the question of whether e necessarily fulfills ϕ has a definite answer apart from the way e is specified.[25]

Now according to what I have said, essentialism for the class of concrete things is false. In the clay statue example, I said, the same concrete thing fulfills the condition

$$E \_\_ \to H \_\_$$

necessarily under the specification "*Goliath*" and only contingently under the specification "Lumpl"; whether that thing, apart from any special designation, necessarily fulfills that condition is a meaningless question.

Essentialism for the class of individual concepts, on the other hand, must be true if Carnap's system is to work. That is so because Carnap's system allows quantification into modal contexts without restriction. For let ϕ be a condition and e an individual concept which fulfills ϕ. Then $\square\phi x$ is well formed and the variable "x" ranges over individual concepts, so that e is in the range of "x." Thus e either definitely satisfies the formula $\Box\phi x$ or definitely fails to satisfy it. The question of whether e necessarily fulfills ϕ must have a definite answer even apart from the way e is specified. Thus essentialism holds for individual concepts.

Why this discriminatory treatment? Why accept essentialism for individual concepts and reject it for individuals? The point of doing so is this: my arguments against essentialism for concrete things rested not on general logical considerations, but on considerations that apply specifically to concrete things. I argued that it makes no sense to talk of a concrete thing as fulfilling a condition ϕ in every possible world – as fulfilling ϕ necessarily, in other words – apart from its designation. Essentialism, then, is false for concrete things because apart from a special designation, it is meaningless to talk of the same concrete thing in different possible worlds.

For this last, I had two arguments, both of which apply specifically to concrete things. First I considered the clay statue example, gave reasons for saying that *Goliath* is identical to Lumpl, and showed that the same statue in a different situation would not be the same piece of clay. Second, in section III, I gave a theory of identity of concrete things across certain possible worlds, according to which such identity made sense only with respect to a kind. These arguments applied only to concrete things.[26]

It makes good sense, on the other hand, to speak of the same individual concept in different possible worlds. An individual concept is just a function which assigns to each possible world in a set an individual in that world. There is no problem of what that function would be in a possible world different from the actual one. Whereas, then, there is no good reason for rejecting essentialism indiscriminately, there are strong grounds for rejecting essentialism for concrete things.

VIII

An objection broached in section V remains to be tackled. There is, according to the system here, no such thing as *de re* modality for concrete things: in a formula of the form $\Box Fx$, the variable ranges over individual concepts rather than concrete things. Now without *de re* modality for concrete things, the objection goes, our tongues will be tied: we will be left unable to say things that need to be said, both for scientific and for daily purposes.

In fact, though, the system here ties our tongues very little. It allows concrete things to have modal properties of a kind, and those permissible modal properties will do any job that *de re* modalities could reasonably be asked to do. To see how such legitimate modal properties can be constructed, return to the statue example.

According to the theory given here, the concrete thing *Goliath* or Lumpl has neither the property of being essentially humanoid nor the property of being possibly nonhumanoid. There is a modal property, though, which it does have: it is essentially humanoid *qua* statue. That can be expressed in the Carnapian system I have given. Let δ be the predicate "is a statue-rigid individual concept." δ is intensional, then, in the sense that it applies to individual concepts, so that variables in its scope take individual concepts as values, just as they do in the scope of a modal operator. The sentence

x is essentially humanoid *qua* statue,

then, means this:

$$(14) \quad (\exists y)[y = x \mathbin{\&} \delta y \mathbin{\&} \Box(Ey \rightarrow Hy)].^{27}$$

Here the variable y is free within the scope of a modal operator, and hence ranges over individual concepts; but x occurs only outside the scope of modal operators, and hence ranges over individuals. In "$y = x$," then, the predicate "$=$" makes a compensating shift of the kind shown in section V, but only in its left argument. Thus "$y = x$" here means that y is a concept of an individual identical to x – in other words, y is a concept of x. (14), then, says the following: "There is an individual concept y which is a statue-concept, and is a concept of something humanoid in any possible world in which it is a concept of anything." That gives a property which applies to concrete things: only the variable x is free in (14), and since it occurs only outside the scope of modal operators, it ranges over individuals. (14), then, gives a property of the concrete thing Lumpl, a property which we might call "being essentially humanoid *qua* statue."

Concrete things, then, in the system given here, have no *de re* modal properties – no properties of the form $\Box F$. They do, however, have modal properties of a more devious kind: modal properties *qua* a sortal. Such properties should serve any purpose for which concrete things really need modal properties.

IX

Dispositional properties raise problems of much the same kind as do modal properties. At least one promising account of dispositions is incompatible with the system given here.

Here is the account. A disposition like solubility is a property which applies to concrete things, and it can be expressed as a counterfactual conditional: "x is soluble" means "If x were placed in water, then x would dissolve." This counterfactual conditional in turn means something like this: "In the possible world which is, of all those worlds in which x is in water, most like the actual world, x dissolves."[28]

Now this account is incompatible with the system I have given, because it requires identity of concrete things across possible worlds. For without such cross-world identity, it makes no sense to talk of "the possible world which is, of all those worlds in which x is in water, most like the actual world." For such talk makes sense only if there is a definite set of worlds in which x is in water, and there is such a definite set only if for each possible world, either x is some definite entity in that world – so that it makes definite sense to say that x is in water in that world – or x definitely does not exist in that world. The account of dispositions I have sketched, then, requires identity of concrete things across possible worlds, which on the theory in this paper is meaningless.

The point is perhaps most clear in the statue example. It makes no sense to say of the concrete thing *Goliath*, or Lumpl, that if I squeezed it, it would cease to exist. If I squeezed the statue *Goliath*, *Goliath* would cease to exist, but if I squeezed the piece of clay Lumpl, Lumpl would go on existing in a different shape. Take, then, the property "If I squeezed x, then x would cease to exist," which I shall write

(15) I squeeze x $\square\!\!\!\rightarrow$ x ceases to exist.

That is not a property which the single concrete thing, *Goliath* or Lumpl, either has or straightforwardly lacks.

Counterfactual properties, then, have much the same status as modal properties. A concrete thing – a piece of salt, for instance – cannot have the counterfactual property

x is in water $\square\!\!\!\rightarrow$ x dissolves,

or as I shall write it,

(16) Wx $\square\!\!\!\rightarrow$ Dx.

Put more precisely, the point is this: a concrete thing can have no such property if, first, the account of counterfactuals which I have given is correct and, second, identity of concrete things across possible worlds makes no sense. Call a property of the form given in (15) and (16) a *straightforward counterfactual property*; then on the theories I have given, concrete things can have no straightforward counterfactual properties.

Individual concepts, in contrast, can perfectly well have straightforward counterfactual properties, since they raise no problems of identity across possible worlds. Indeed we can treat the connective "$\square\!\!\!\rightarrow$" as inducing the same shifts as do modal operators: making the variables in its scope range over individual concepts, and shifting the predicates appropriately. On that interpretation, (15) is true of the *Goliath*-concept but false of the Lumpl-concept; (15) says, "In the possible world which, of all those worlds in which I squeeze the thing picked out by concept x, is most like the actual world, the thing picked out by x ceases to exist." That holds of the *Goliath*-concept but not of the Lumpl-concept. Likewise on this interpretation, (16) is true not of a piece of salt, but of a piece-of-salt individual concept. (16) now says the following: "In the possible world which is, of all those worlds in which the thing picked out by x is in water, most like the actual world, the thing picked out by x dissolves."

So far the situation is grave. The moral seems to be this: concrete things have no dispositional properties, but individual concepts do. Water-solubility, or something like it, may be a property of a piece-of-salt individual concept, but it cannot be a property of the concrete thing, that piece of salt. That is a sad way to leave the matter. On close examination, many seeming properties look covertly dispositional – mass and electric charge are prime examples. Strip concrete things of their dispositional properties, and they may have few properties left.

Fortunately, though, individuals do turn out to have dispositional properties of a kind. The device used for modal properties in the last section works here too. A concrete thing like a piece of salt cannot, it is true, have the straightforward counterfactual property Wx $\square\!\!\!\rightarrow$ Dx. Only an individual concept could have that property. A piece of salt does, though, have the more devious counterfactual property given by "*Qua* piece of salt, if x were in water then x would dissolve," which I shall write

(17) $(x \ qua \ \text{piece})[Wx \ \Box\!\!\rightarrow Dx]$.

This expands as follows: let $\mathscr{P}$ mean "is a piece-rigid individual concept"; then (17) means

(18) $(\exists y)[y = x \ \& \mathscr{P}y(Wy \ \Box\!\!\rightarrow Dy)]$.

As in the corresponding formula (14) for modal properties, "x" here is free of modal entanglements, and so it ranges over concrete things. (18) seems a good way to interpret water solubility as a property of pieces of salt.

Concrete things, then, can have dispositional properties. The dispositional property *is water-soluble* is not the straightforward counterfactual property given by (16), but the more devious counterfactual property given by (18). A system with contingent identity can still allow dispositions to be genuine properties of concrete things.

X

From the claim that *Goliath* = Lumpl, I think I have shown, there emerges a coherent system which stands up to objections. Why accept this system? In section II, I gave one main reason: the system lets concrete things be made up in a simple way from entities that appear in fundamental physics. It thus gives us machinery for putting into one coherent system both our beliefs about the fundamental constitution of the world and our everyday picture of concrete things.

Another important reason for accepting the system is one of economy. I think I have shown how to get along without *de re* modality for concrete things and still say what needs to be said about them. That may be especially helpful when we deal with causal necessity; indeed, the advantages of doing without *de re* causal necessity go far beyond mere economy. What I have said in this paper about plain necessity applies equally well to causal necessity, and the notion of causal necessity seems especially unobjectionable – even Quine thinks it may be legitimate.[29] Causally necessary truths are what scientists are looking for when they look for fundamental scientific laws, and it surely makes sense to look for fundamental scientific laws. Now we might expect fundamental scientific laws to take the form $\Box_c \phi$, "It is causally necessary that ϕ," where ϕ is extensional – contains no modal operators. If so, then scientific laws contain *de dicto* causal necessity, but no *de re* necessity. To get significant *de re*

causal necessities, we would need to make metaphysical assumptions with no grounding in scientific law. If we can get along without *de re* physical necessity, that will keep puzzling metaphysical questions about essential properties out of physics. The system here shows how to do that.

None of the reasons I have given in favor of the system here are conclusive. The system has to be judged as a whole: it is coherent and withstands objections; the remaining question is whether it is superior to its rivals. What, then, are the alternatives?

Kripke gives an alternative formal semantics,[30] but no systematic directions for applying it. To use Kripke's semantics, one needs extensive intuitions that certain properties are essential and others accidental. Kripke makes no attempt to say how concrete things might appear in a theory of fundamental physics; whether such an account can be given in Kripke's system remains to be seen.

One other alternative to the theory in this paper is systematic: statues and pieces of clay can be taken, not to be "individuals" in the Carnapian sense of the term which I have been using, but to be Carnapian "individual concepts." They may be regarded, that is, as functions from possible worlds, whose values are Carnapian individuals.[31] On such a view, a Carnapian individual would be regarded as a sort of "proto-individual" from which concrete things are constructed.

Such a view has its advantages: it allows standard quantification theory, with no Carnapian shift of the range of variables in modal contexts. Indeed, as Quine points out, a Carnapian semantics can be interpreted so that variables always range over individual concepts.[32]

One reason for preferring the Carnapian system is this. I expect that the variables used in expressing fundamental laws can most simply be interpreted as ranging over Carnapian individuals. If so, then I would be reluctant to regard those Carnapian individuals as mere proto-individuals, with genuine individuals as functions which take these proto-individuals as values at possible worlds. Fundamental physics, I would like to say, deals with genuine individuals.

If the system I have given is accepted, the ramifications are wide. Take just one example: the question of whether a person is identical with his body. If there is no consciousness after death, then, it would seem, a person ceases to exist when he dies. A person's body normally goes on existing after he dies. Ordinarily, then, a person is not identical with his body. In some cases, however, a person's body is destroyed when he dies. In such cases, according to the system in this paper, there is no purely logical reason against saying the following: the person in this case is identical with his body, but had he died a normal death, he would have been distinct from his body. If there are reasons against such a view, they must be nonlogical reasons.

Whether or not the system I have advocated is the best one, I have at least done the following. First, I have shown that there is a problem with identity across possible worlds, even in the simple case of possible worlds which branch after the entity in question begins to exist. In such cases, I

have shown, certain assumptions, not easily refuted, lead to contingent identity. Second, I have given a theory of proper names which fits much of what Kripke says about proper names when he considers examples, and which, in rare cases, allows contingent identity. Finally, I have shown how, while accepting contingent identity and rejecting *de re* modality for concrete things, we can still allow concrete things to have modal and dispositional properties.

The system I advocate is worked out in more detail in the appendix.[33] In that system, I think, concrete things and possible worlds lose some of their mystery: they arise naturally from a systematic picture of the physical world.

Notes

I am grateful for the comments and criticisms of many people. I was helped in the early stages of revision by discussion at the University of Pittsburgh philosophy colloquium, by the written comments of Richard Gale and Paul Teller, and by discussion with Allen Hazen, Robert Kraut, and Storrs McCall. I am especially grateful to Anil Gupta for his extensive help, both in the early and the late stages of revision.

1 Saul Kripke, "Identity and necessity," this volume, ch. 7; *idem*, "Naming and necessity," in D. Davidson and G. Harman (eds), *Semantics of Natural Language* (Dordrecht: Reidel, 1972).
2 Gottlob Frege, "On sense and reference," trans. M. Black, in P. Geach and M. Black, *Translations from the Philosophical Writings of Gottlob Frege* (Oxford: Blackwell, 1966), pp. 55–78, at p. 57; orig. German pub. 1892.
3 This volume, pp. 74–5; Kripke, "Naming and necessity," pp. 260–4.
4 Bertrand Russell, "On denoting," in Robert Marsh (ed.), *Logic and Knowledge* (New York: Macmillan, 1956), pp. 41–56; orig. pub. 1905.
5 Kripke, "Naming and necessity," pp. 254–60, 284–308.
6 W. V. O. Quine, "Identity, ostension, and hypostasis," this volume, ch. 22, sect. 1.
7 This fits the view put forth in ibid.
8 Kripke, "Naming and necessity," pp. 269–70.
9 David Lewis, "Counterparts of persons and their bodies," *Journal of Philosophy* 68 (1971), pp. 203–11, gives a theory very much like this. There are, according to Lewis, a diversity of counterpart relations which hold between entities in different possible worlds – the "personal" counterpart relation and the "bodily" counterpart relation are two (p. 208). The counterpart relation appropriate to a given modal

context may be selected by a term, such as "I" or "my body," or it may be selected by a phrase, "regarded as a —," which works like one of my "qua" phrases. In these respects, then, my theory fits Lewis's. In other respects, it differs. My relation of being an *F*-counterpart is an equivalence relation, and it holds between any two entities in different worlds which are both *F*'s and which share a common past. Lewis's counterpart relations "are a matter of overall resemblance in a variety of respects" (p. 208), and are not equivalence relations (p. 209).
10 Peter Geach *Reference and Generality* (Ithaca, NY: Cornell University Press, 1962), sect. 34, contends that a proper name conveys a "nominal essence" – "requirements as to identity" that can be expressed by a common noun. The name "Thames," for instance, conveys the nominal essence expressed by the common noun "river." In this respect, my theory follows Geach's. Geach, however, (sect. 31), thinks that even in the actual world, identity makes no sense except with respect to a general term. According to the theory in this paper, non-relative identity makes sense in talk of any one possible world; it is only cross-world identity that must be made relative to a sortal.
11 Kripke, "Naming and necessity," pp. 298–9.
12 This volume, p. 74.
13 Kripke, "Naming and necessity," p. 268.
14 This volume, p. 74.
15 Kripke, "Naming and necessity," pp. 271–2.
16 Cf. W. V. O. Quine, "Reference and modality," in *From a Logical Point of View*, 2nd edn (New York: Harper & Row, 1961), pp. 139–59, sect. 2.
17 See esp. Rudolf Carnap, *Meaning and Necessity* (Chicago: University of Chicago Press, 1947), sect. 41. I shall not follow Carnap in detail, nor, for the most part, shall I try to say in what precise ways I follow him and in what ways I deviate from what he says.

18 Aldo Bressan, *A General Interpreted Modal Calculus* (New Haven, Conn.: Yale University Press, 1972).

19 Frege, "On sense and reference," p. 59.

20 The original paper included an appendix, omitted here.

21 The talk of "shifts" is not Carnap's; it is part of my own informal reading of Carnap's semantics. Carnap does think "that individual variables in modal sentences . . . must be interpreted as referring, not to individuals, but to individual concepts" (*Meaning and Necessity*, p. 180). He does not, however, allow variables to shift their ranges of values within a single language. Rather, he constructs two languages, a non-modal language S_1 in which variables range over individuals and a modal language S_2 in which variables range over individual concepts. Any sentence of S_1 is a sentence of S_2 and is its own translation into S_2 (see ibid., pp. 200–2). The semantics I give in the Appendix (not included in this volume) is roughly that of Carnap's S_2 (see ibid., pp. 183–4). In informal discussion in the body of this paper, though, I take a variable to range over individuals whenever such an interpretation is possible.

Carnap does not talk of predicates shifting in the way I describe, but once variables are taken to range over individual concepts, such a reinterpretation of predicates allows a straightforward reading of Carnap's semantics. Quine discussed this point in his letter to Carnap (*Meaning and Necessity*, p. 197).

22 Quine, "Reference and modality," p. 153.

23 Letter in Carnap, *Meaning and Necessity*, p. 196.

24 Quine, "Reference and modality," p. 151.

25 For other characterizations of essentialism, see Terence Parsons, "Essentialism and quantified modal logic," *Philosophical Review* 78 (1969), pp. 35–52, sect. 2.

26 Quine objects to essentialism even for abstract entities. "Essentialism," he writes, "is abruptly at variance with the idea, favored by Carnap, Lewis, and others, of explaining necessity by analyticity" ("Reference and modality," p. 155). That, however, cannot be true: Carnap does explain his system in terms of analyticity, and his system involves essentialism, as I have explained. Carnap's system is thus a counterexample to Quine's claim; it shows that one can consistently both accept essentialism for individual concepts and explain necessity by analyticity.

27 Anil Gupta has shown me a formula similar to this one, which he attributes to Nuel Belnap.

28 See Robert Stalnaker, "A theory of conditionals," in *Studies in Logical Theory*, American Philosophical Quarterly Monograph Series, no. 2 (1968), and Stalnaker and Richmond Thomason, "A semantic analysis of conditional logic," *Theoria* 36 (1970), pp. 23–42. For a somewhat different theory which raises similar problems, see David K. Lewis, *Counterfactuals* (Oxford: Blackwell, 1973).

29 See Quine, "Reference and modality," pp. 158–9.

30 Saul Kripke, "Semantical considerations on modal logic," *Acta philosophica Fennica* 16 (1963), pp. 83–94.

31 See Richmond Thomason and Robert Stalnaker, "Modality and reference," *Nous* 2 (1968) pp. 359–72.

32 Letter in Carnap, *Meaning and Necessity*, p. 196.

33 See n. 20 above.

10

Identity, Essence, and Indiscernibility

Stephen Yablo

Can things be identical *as a matter of fact* without
being *necessarily* identical? Until recently it seemed
they could, but now "the dark doctrine of a relation
of 'contingent identity' "[1] has fallen into disrepute.
In fact, the doctrine is worse than disreputable. By
most current reckonings, it is refutable. That is,
philosophers have *discovered* that things can never
be contingently identical. Appearances to the contrary, once thought plentiful and decisive, are
blamed on the befuddling influence of a powerful
alliance of philosophical errors. How has this come
about? Most of the credit goes to a simple argument
(original with Ruth Marcus, but revived by Saul
Kripke) purporting to *show* that things can never be
only contingently identical. Suppose that α and β
are identical. Then they share all their properties.
Since one of β's properties is that necessarily it is
identical with β, this must be one of α's properties
too. So necessarily α is identical with β, and it
follows that α and β cannot have been only contingently identical.[2]

1 A Paradox of Essentialism

Despite the argument's simplicity and apparent
cogency, somehow, as Kripke observes, "its conclusion . . . has often been regarded as highly paradoxical."[3] No doubt there are a number of bad
reasons for this (Kripke himself has exposed sev-

Originally published in *Journal of Philosophy* 84 (1987),
pp. 293–314. Copyright © by Journal of Philosophy, Inc.
Reprinted by permission of Columbia University.

eral), but there is also a good one: essentialism
without some form of contingent identity is an
untenable doctrine, because essentialism has a
shortcoming that only some form of contingent
identity can rectify. The purpose of this paper is
to explain, first, why contingent identity is
required by essentialism and, second, how contingent identity is permitted by essentialism.

Essentialism's problem is simple. Identicals are
indiscernible, and so discernibles are distinct.
Thus, if α has a property necessarily which β has
only accidentally, then α is distinct from β. In the
usual example, there is a bust of Aristotle, and it is
formed of a certain hunk of wax. (Assume for the
sake of argument that the hunk of wax composes
the bust throughout their common duration, so
that temporal differences are not in question.) If
the bust of Aristotle is *necessarily* a bust of Aristotle
and if the hunk of wax is only *accidentally* a bust of
Aristotle, then the bust and the hunk of wax are not
the same thing. Or suppose that Jones drives home
at high speed. Assuming that her speeding home is
something *essentially* done at high speed, whereas
her driving home only *happens* to be done at high
speed, her speeding home and her driving home are
distinct.

So far, so good, maybe; but it would be incredible to call the bust and the wax, or the driving
home and the speeding home, distinct, and leave
the matter there. In the first place, that would be to
leave relations between the bust and the hunk of
wax on a par with either's relations to the common
run of *other* things, for example, the Treaty of
Versailles. Secondly, so far it seems an extraordi-

narily baffling metaphysical coincidence that bust and wax, though entirely distinct, nevertheless manage to be *exactly alike* in almost every ordinary respect: size, weight, color, shape, location, smell, taste, and so on indefinitely. If distinct *statues* (say) were as similar as this, we would be shocked and amazed, not to say incredulous. How is such a coincidence possible? And, thirdly, if the bust and the wax are distinct (pure and simple), how is it that the number of middle-sized objects on the marble base is not (purely and simply) 2 (or more)? Ultimately, though, none of these arguments is really needed: that the bust and the wax are in *some* sense the same thing is perfectly obvious.

Thus, if essentialism is to be at all plausible, nonidentity had better be compatible with intimate identity-*like* connections. But these connections threaten to be inexplicable on essentialist principles, and essentialists have so far done nothing to address the threat.[4] Not *quite* nothing, actually; for essentialists have tried to understand certain (special) of these connections in a number of (special) ways. Thus, it has been proposed that the hunk of wax *composes* the bust; that the driving home *generates* the speeding home; that a neural event *subserves* the corresponding pain; that a computer's structural state *instantiates* its computational state; that humankind *comprises* personkind; and that a society is *nothing over and above* its members. Now all these are important relations, and each is importantly different from the others. But it is impossible to ignore the fact that they seem to reflect something quite general, something not adequately illuminated by the enumeration of its special cases, namely, the phenomenon of things' being distinct *by nature* but the same *in the circumstances*. And what is that if not the – arguably impossible – phenomenon of things" being contingently identical but not necessarily so? The point is that, if essentialism is true, then many things that are obviously in *some* sense the same will emerge as strictly distinct; so essentialism must at least provide for the possibility of intimate identity-*like* connections between distinct things; and such connections seem to be ways of being contingently identical. Essentialism, if it is to be plausible, has to be tempered by some variety of contingent identity.

Hence, essentialism is confronted with a kind of paradox: to be believable, it needs contingent identity; yet its principles appear to entail that contingent identity is not possible. To resolve the paradox, we have to ask: What is the "nature" of a particular thing?

2   Essence

Begin with a particular thing α. How should α be characterized? That is, what style of characterization would best bring out "what α is"? Presumably a characterization of any sort will be via certain of α's properties. But which ones?

Why not begin with the set of all α's properties whatsoever, or what may be called the *complete profile* of α? Since α's properties include, among others, that of being identical with α, there can be no question about the sufficiency of characterization by complete profile. But there may be doubt about its philosophical interest. For the properties of α will generally be of two kinds: those which α had to have and those which it merely happens to have. And, intuitively, the properties α merely happens to have reveal nothing of what α is, as contrasted with what it happens to be like. As Antoine Arnauld explains in a letter to Leibniz,

> ... it seems to me that I must consider as contained in the individual concept of myself only that which is such that I should no longer be me if it were not in me: and that all that is to the contrary such that it could be or not be in me without my ceasing to be me, cannot be considered as being contained in my individual concept.[5]

(Adding: "That is my idea, which I think conforms to everything which has ever been believed by all the philosophers in the world"!) If α's nonnecessary properties reveal nothing about what α is, nothing will be lost if they are struck from its characterization.

Dropping α's nonnecessary properties from its complete profile yields the set of all properties that α possesses essentially, or what can be called the *complete essence* of α.[6] Since α is essentially identical with α, the property of so being will be included in α's complete essence; so the sufficiency of the characterization is again beyond doubt. Nor can there be much question that complete essences do better than complete profiles at showing what particulars are by nature. But worries about philosophical interest remain.

In the first place, the essence of an entity ought, one feels, to be an assortment of properties *in virtue of which* it is the entity in question. But this requirement is trivialized by the inclusion, in essences, of identity properties, like that of being identical with California. A thing does not get to be identical with California by having the property, alike, by having certain *other* properties. And it is these other properties that really belong in a thing's characterization. Another way of putting what is probably the same point is that identity properties and their ilk are not "ground floor," but dependent or supervenient. As a kind of joke, someone I know explains the difference between his two twin collies like this: "It's simple: *this* one's *Lassie*, and *that* one's *Scottie*." What makes this a joke is that that cannot be all there is to it; and the reason is that identity properties are possessed not *simpliciter*, but dependently on other properties. It is only these latter properties that ought, really, to be employed in a thing's characterization.

Secondly, the essence of a thing is supposed to be a measure of *what is required* for it to be that thing. But, intuitively, requirements can be more or less. If the requirements for being β are stricter than the requirements for being α, then β ought to have a "bigger" essence than α. To be the Shroud of Turin, for instance, a thing has to have everything it takes to be the associated piece of cloth, *and* it has to have enshrouded Jesus Christ (this is assuming that the Cloth of Turin did, in fact, enshroud Jesus Christ). Thus, more is essential to the Shroud of Turin than to the piece of cloth, and the Shroud of Turin ought accordingly to have the bigger essence. So, if essences are to set out the requirements for being their possessors, it should be possible for one thing's essence to include another's.[7] What is perhaps surprising, however, is that this natural perspective on things will not survive the introduction of identity properties and their ilk into individual essences. Think of the piece of cloth that makes up the Shroud of Turin (call it "the Cloth of Turin"): if the property of being identical with the Cloth of Turin is in the Cloth of Turin's essence, then, since that property is certainly not in the *Shroud* of Turin's essence, the inclusion is lost. Equivalently, it ought to be possible to start with the essence of the Cloth of Turin, *add* the property of having served as the burial shroud of Jesus Christ (along perhaps with others this entails), and wind up with the essence of the Shroud of Turin. But, if the property of being identical to the Cloth of Turin is allowed into the Cloth of Turin's essence, then adding the property of having served as Jesus's burial shroud produces a

sort of contradiction; for, obviously, *nothing* is both identical to the Cloth of Turin and necessarily possessed of a property – having served as Jesus's burial shroud – which the Cloth of Turin possesses only contingently. And the argument is perfectly general: if identity properties (or others like them) are allowed into things' essences, then distinct things' essences will always be incomparable.[8]

Implicit in the foregoing is a distinction between two types of property. On the one hand, there are properties that can only 'build up' the essences in which they figure. Since to include such properties in an essence is not (except trivially) to keep any other property out, they will be called *cumulative*. On the other hand, there are properties that exercise an inhibiting effect on the essences to which they belong. To include this sort of property in an essence is always to block the entry of certain of its colleagues. Properties like these – identity properties, kind properties, and others – are *restrictive*. If restrictive properties are barred from essences, that will ensure that essences are comparable, and so preserve the intuition that each essence specifies what it takes to be the thing that has it.

Essences constrained to include only cumulative properties will have two advantages. First, they will determine their possessors' inessential properties negatively, not by what they include but by what they leave out; and, as a result, things' essences will be amenable to expansion into the larger essences of things it is "more difficult to be," thus preserving the intuition that a thing's essence specifies what it takes to be that thing. And, second, things will be the things they are *in virtue of* having the essences they have. To put it approximately but vividly, they will be what they are because of what they are like (see Prop. 4).[9] Our tactic will be to look first for properties suited to inclusion in cumulative essences and then to show that, under reasonable further assumptions, identity supervenes on cumulative essence.

3   Modeling Essence

To find a set of properties suitable for the construction of cumulative essences, one needs to know what "properties" are; especially because a totally unrestricted notion of property is incoherent, as Richard's and Grelling's paradoxes show.[10] So it makes sense to look for a sharper formulation of the notion of property before pushing ahead with the search for cumulative essence. Such a formulation is provided by the apparatus of possible worlds.

Let $\mathscr{L}$ be an ordinary first-order language with identity, and let $\mathscr{L}(\Box)$ be $\mathscr{L}$ supplemented with the sentential necessity operator "$\Box$." To a first approximation, a model of $\mathscr{L}(\Box)$ is just a set $\mathscr{W}$ of models W of $\mathscr{L}$ (to be thought of as possible worlds). But there is a qualification. Traditionally, a model's domain is simultaneously the set of things that *can be talked about* and the set of things that *exist*, i.e., the domain of *discourse* and the *ontological* domain. But, since one can talk about things that do not exist, W's domain of discourse should be allowed to contain things not in its ontological domain; and since there are not, mystical considerations to the side, things about which one cannot talk, W's ontological domain should be a subset of its domain of discourse. What this means formally is that with each model W in $\mathscr{W}$ is associated a subset $\mathscr{D}(W)$ of its domain (intuitively, the set of things existing in W). Let W thus supplemented be known as a *free model* of $\mathscr{L}$. For simplicity's sake, every member of $\mathscr{W}$ will have the same domain $\mathscr{D}$, and $\mathscr{D}$ will be the union of the $\mathscr{D}(W)$'s. And now a model of $\mathscr{L}(\Box)$ can be defined as a set $\mathscr{W}$ of free models of $\mathscr{L}$, such that the domain of discourse of each is the union of all their ontological domains.[11]

Tempting though it is to define a property as any function P from worlds W to subsets $P(W)$ of $\mathscr{D}$, there is reason not to. For when will α have P necessarily: when it has P in every world, or when it has it in every world in which it exists? Not the former, because then everything necessarily exists.[12] Nor the latter, first, because it permits a thing to possess only accidentally a property it must perish to lose and, second, because it upsets the principle that essence varies inversely with existence; i.e., the fewer the worlds a thing exists in, the more properties it has essentially. What this in fact points up is a difference between two kinds of characteristic: being human in every world where you exist is sufficient for being human everywhere (almost all characteristics are like this), but existing in every world where you exist is obviously not sufficient for existing everywhere (apparently only existence and characteristics involving existence are like this). From now on, an *attribute* is a function from worlds W to subsets of $\mathscr{D}$, and a *property* is an attribute P such that anything having it wherever it exists has it everywhere. In general, an attribute is necessary to a thing if it attaches to the thing in every possible world (preserving the intuition that existence is sometimes contingent). If the attribute is also a property, this reduces to the thing's having the attribute wherever it exists (preserving the intuition that humanity is necessary to Socrates if he cannot exist without it). In what follows, properties (rather than attributes in general) are the items under investigation.

From the definition of property, it follows that, if P is a property, then so are $P^{\Box} : W \to \{\alpha\epsilon\mathscr{D} \mid \forall W'\alpha\epsilon P(W')\}$ (the property of being essentially P, or P's *essentialization*); $P^{\Diamond} : W \to \{\alpha\epsilon\mathscr{D} \mid \exists W' \alpha\epsilon P(W')\}$ (the property of being possibly P, or P's *possibilization*); and $P^{\triangle} : W \to \{\alpha\epsilon P(W) \mid \exists W'\alpha \notin P(W')\}$ (the property of being accidentally P, henceforth P's *accidentalization*). The essentialization $X^{\Box}$ (accidentalization $X^{\triangle}$) of a set X of properties is the set of its members' essentializations (accidentalizations). If α is in $P(W)$ and exists in W, then it is in $P[W]$ (note the square brackets). If for each P in X $\alpha\epsilon P(W)$, then $\alpha\epsilon X(W)$; if, in addition, α exists in W, then it is in $X[W]$. A set Y of properties is *satisfiable* in W, written Sat $[Y, W]$, iff there is something in $\cap_{P\epsilon Y}P[W]$. Given a set X of properties, a thing α's X-*essence* $\mathbb{E}_x(\alpha)$ is the set of all P in X which α possesses essentially, or $\{P\epsilon X \mid \exists W(\alpha\epsilon P^{\Box}(W))\}$. β is an X-*refinement* of α, written $\alpha \leq \beta(X)$ – or just $\alpha \leq \beta$ if X is clear from context – iff α's X-essence is a subset of β's, i.e., if $\mathbb{E}_x(\alpha) \subseteq \mathbb{E}_x(\beta)$.

That essences drawn from X should be amenable to expansion is a condition not on X alone, but on X and $\mathscr{W}$ taken together: X and $\mathscr{W}$ must be so related that suitably expanding the X-essence of any thing in any world in $\mathscr{W}$ always produces the X-essence of some other thing existing in that same world. Let $\Omega =\; <\mathscr{W}, X>$ be a *property-model* of $\mathscr{L}(\Box)$ if $\mathscr{W}$ is a model of $\mathscr{L}(\Box)$ and X is a set of properties on $\mathscr{W}$. A property-model Ω is *upward-closed*, or *u-closed*, iff:

$$\text{(U)} \quad \forall\alpha\forall Y \subseteq X - \mathbb{E}_x(\alpha)\forall W[\alpha\epsilon Y^{\triangle}[W]$$
$$\Rightarrow (\exists\beta \geq \alpha)\beta\epsilon Y^{\Box}[W]]$$

In words, given any α, given any set Y of properties not essential to α, and given any world W, if α exists in W and has Y there, then it has a refinement β which exists in W and has Y essentially there. (For future reference, (U) is provably equivalent to the simpler statement that $\forall Z \subseteq X \; \forall W \; [\text{Sat}[Z, W] \Rightarrow \text{Sat}[Z^{\Box}, W]]$.)

Upward closure requires that any existing α possessing (suitable) properties inessentially be refinable into an existing β that possesses those properties essentially. The converse is intuitive too: if there exists a β refining α which essentially possesses (suitable) properties not essential to α, then α should exist and possess those same properties accidentally. Thus, if the Shroud of Turin exists in a world W, then not only should the Cloth of Turin exist in W, but it should serve as Jesus's burial shroud in W. Not only is this plausible on the face of it, but otherwise it is hard to see what separates the worlds in which the Cloth occurs by itself from those in which it occurs together with the Shroud; whereas surely the difference is that in the latter, but not the former, the Cloth serves as Jesus's burial shroud. And, in general, if β refines α, then surely what separates worlds in which α exists without β from those in which α exists with β is that, in the latter worlds, α possesses the difference between their X-essences, whereas in the former it does not. Specifically, if β refines α, then (1) α exists wherever β does, (2) in worlds where both exist, α accidentally possesses every property in $\mathbb{E}_x(\beta) - \mathbb{E}_x(\alpha)$, i.e., every property in the difference between their essences, and (3) in worlds where just β exists, α does not possess all the properties in $\mathbb{E}_x(\beta) - \mathbb{E}_x(\alpha)$. All of these follow on the addition of a requirement of *downward closure*, literally the converse of the upward closure enforced above:

(D) $\forall \alpha \forall Y \subseteq X - \mathbb{E}_x(\alpha) \forall W [(\exists \beta \geq \alpha)$
$\beta \epsilon Y^{\square}[W] \Rightarrow \alpha \epsilon Y^{\triangle}[W]]$

In words, for anything α, any properties Y not essential to it, and any world, if α has an existing refinement β possessing Y essentially, then α exists and possesses Y accidentally. Property-models satisfying both (U) and (D) are *closed*.

Prop. 1 Let Ω be closed. If $\alpha \leq \beta$, then

(1) $\mathcal{W}(\beta) \subseteq \mathcal{W}(\alpha)$

(2) $\forall W \epsilon \mathcal{W}(\beta) [\alpha \epsilon (\mathbb{E}_x(\beta) - \mathbb{E}_x(\alpha))^{\triangle}(W)]$

(3) $\forall W \epsilon \mathcal{W}(\alpha) - \mathcal{W}(\beta)[\alpha \notin (\mathbb{E}_x(\beta)$
$- \mathbb{E}_x(\alpha))^{\triangle}(W)]$

Proof: For (1), observe first that $\Lambda[W] = \Lambda(W) \cap \mathcal{D}(W) = \mathcal{D} \cap \mathcal{D}(W) = \mathcal{D}(W)$ (because the null intersection is everything, in this case $\mathcal{D}$). By (D), $\beta \epsilon \mathcal{D}(W) \Rightarrow \beta \epsilon \; \Lambda[W] \Rightarrow \beta \epsilon \Lambda^{\square}[W] \Rightarrow \alpha \epsilon \Lambda^{\triangle}[W] \Rightarrow \alpha \epsilon \Lambda[W] \Rightarrow \alpha \epsilon \mathcal{D}(W)$.

For (2), just let Z be $\mathbb{E}_x(\beta) - \mathbb{E}_x(\alpha)$. For (3), suppose that β does not exist in W, and suppose *per absurdum* that α accidentally possesses, in W, the difference between its X-essence and β's. By upward closure, α has a refinement γ which exists in W and which possesses the whole lot, i.e., all of $\mathbb{E}_x(\beta)$, essentially. But then γ refines β; so, by (1), β exists in W after all. Contradiction.

4   Contingent Identity

Things that disagree in any of their properties are not identical. The Shroud of Turin, which (let us suppose) *had* to enshroud Jesus, is thus distinct from the Cloth of Turin, which did not. But, as we said, there is something deeply troubling about leaving matters thus. After all, the Shroud of Turin is also distinct from the Treaty of Versailles. Do we really want to leave the Shroud's relations with the Cloth on the same level as its relations with the Treaty of Versailles? And the trouble does not stop here. The Cloth and the Shroud differ, it is true, but it must also be said that their differences are of a somewhat recherché variety. In every *ordinary* respect the two are exactly alike. And this is on the face of it a rather extraordinary coincidence. That the Cloth and the Shroud are specially connected seems undeniable, but something must be done to demystify the connection. If it is not identity, what is it?

Maybe the answer is that it *is* identity, but identity of a different, less demanding, character. In the terms of a currently unpopular theory – and notwithstanding the argument that seems to rule it out – it is 'contingent identity,' or (the more neutral term) "coincidence."[13] Despite the once widespread enthusiasm for contingent identity, it seems to me that the idea never received a satisfactory formulation. Specifically, all the analyses I have seen have a drawback in common: they (sometimes explicitly, sometimes in effect) treat things as strung together out of their modal manifestations (states, slices, stages), and call them coincident in a world if their manifestations in that world are properly identical. There are two objections to this kind of explication. The first is that it relies, ultimately, on the notion to be explicated; for one has little idea what a thing's state or manifestation in a world is, if not something whose nature is exhausted by its being exactly like the thing so far as the relevant world is concerned, i.e., by its being contingently identical with the thing in that world.

Even more important, intuitively, things (e.g., animals) are *not* strung together out of their modal manifestations in this way, and proper identity of modal manifestations is not what is meant by contingent identity. Intuitively, things are just, well, *things*, and coincidence is a matter of things' circumstantial sameness.

How, then, is circumstantial sameness to be separated out from total sameness? What marks off the "ordinary" respects in which the Cloth and the Shroud are alike from the "extraordinary" respects in which they differ? Let us start with Dana Scott's idea that "two individuals that are generally distinct might share all the same properties (of a certain kind!) with respect to the present world."[14] Probably the most obvious way of elucidating this would be to say the following: α and β are contingently identical (in a world) if and only if they have the same *contingent properties* (in that world). So, for example, the bust and the hunk of wax agree in their size, weight, color, and so on – and all these are, of course, properties they have contingently. Maybe contingent identity is sameness of contingent properties.

That that cannot be right follows from the fact that, if anything has a property contingently, then it has all its stronger properties contingently too. (Suppose α has P contingently; then there is a world in which α lacks P; but if Q is stronger than P, α also lacks Q there; and, since α has Q, it has it contingently.) So, for example, if Paris is only contingently romantic, then it is only contingently identical-to-Paris-and-romantic. But that means that anything that has the same contingent properties that Paris has is (among other things) identical with Paris. And that already shows that Paris is the only thing with exactly its contingent properties. Thus, if contingent identity is treated as sameness of contingent properties, contingent identity collapses into identity proper.

Still, from a certain perspective, this first analysis might be only a little way off the mark. To the question, What makes a thing's possession of a property *circumstantial*? it seems natural to reply that the possession is circumstantial if it depends on *how matters actually stand with the thing*. But now notice that this is ambiguous. Depends *how*: *partly* or *wholly*? If you answer "partly," then you get the thing's *contingent* properties. But, if you answer "wholly," you get the properties the thing has *entirely* in virtue of how matters actually stand with it; and these properties, what can be called the *categorical* properties, seem intuitively to be the ones in question.[15] For if two things agree in all their categorical properties (in a world), then *so far as that world and it alone* is concerned, the two things are just the same. And that is what was meant by "contingent identity." So contingent identity is categorical indiscernibility.

To come to this conclusion from a different direction, consider again the driving home and the speeding home. What separates the "ordinary" respects in which these two are alike from the "extraordinary" respects in which they differ? For a start, the driving home could have been done slowly, but not so the speeding home; the driving home had higher prior probability than the speeding home; if the driving home had not occurred, Jones would have taken the bus home, but the same cannot be said of the speeding home; and the speeding home, rather than the driving home as such, caused Jones's accident. Thus, the driving home and the speeding home differ in – among other things – their modal, probabilistic, counterfactual, and causal properties. Now what is special about modal, probabilistic, counterfactual, and causal properties? Primarily this: they are grounded not just in how a thing *actually* is, but on how it *would* or *could* have been if circumstances had been different. All a thing's other properties, by contrast, are grounded entirely in how it is in the circumstances that happen to obtain. The former properties are a thing's *hypothetical* properties, the latter its *categorical* properties. Now the contingent identity of the driving home with the speeding home seems intuitively to be a matter of their sharing such properties as speed, place, time, etc., regardless of their modal, causal, probabilistic, and counterfactual differences; that is, their contingent identity seems to be a matter of their sharing their categorical properties, irrespective of their hypothetical differences.

How are a thing's categorical properties to be found? (Actually it will be simplest if we look for properties categorical *as such*, i.e., properties that can only be had in a manner independent of what would or could have happened.) Why not take the intuitive notion that a property is categorical just in case a thing's having it is independent of what goes on in nonactual worlds, and try to turn this into a definition? The problem is that such a definition would be circular. Suppose it is a categorical property of this hunk of clay that it is spherical. How can that depend on how the clay comports itself in other worlds? But, if you think about it, it does, in that the clay's being spherical in this world depends on its being, in those worlds, such that in *this* world it is spherical. The problem is that being such that, in this world, it is spherical, is a hypothetical property of the clay. So, apparently, what we really meant to say was that a property is categorical if it attaches to a thing regardless of its *categorical properties* in other worlds. And that is clearly circular.[16]

Somehow the circularity has to be circumvented. Things are going to be coincident in a world iff they have exactly the same categorical properties there. But maybe this can be turned around: the categorical properties are exactly those which cannot tell coincident things apart.

Postpone for a moment the question of how that would help, and ask, instead, is it even true? That is, *are* the categorical properties the properties insensitive to the difference between coincidents? This will be the case only if coincidence is compatible with every kind of hypothetical variation, i.e., if, for every hypothetical property, coincidents can be found that disagree on it. But it is clear that ordinary things do not exhibit the hypothetical variety that this would require. Among ordinary things, coincidents never differ on (e.g.) the score of fragility (if the statue is fragile, then so is the piece of clay); among ordinary things, one never finds one thing accidentally juvenile, or mature, and another, coincident with the first, essentially so (simply because *no* ordinary thing is essentially juvenile, or mature).

So much for ordinary things. But what about things as seen from the vantage point of metaphysics? Metaphysics aspires to understand reality as it is in itself, independently of the conceptual apparatus observers bring to bear on it. Even if we do not ourselves recognize essentially juvenile or mature entities, it is not hard to imagine others who would;[17] and to someone who, in addition to the statue and the piece of clay, discerned a statue-cum-shards, not everything coincident with the statue would be fragile. Conversely, we recognize things, say, essentially suitable for playing cribbage, or cutting grass, which others do not, or might not have. To insist on the credentials of the things *we* recognize against those which others do, or might, seems indefensibly parochial. In metaphysics, unusual hypothetical coloring can be no ground for exclusion.[18] Since this is metaphysics, everything up for recognition must actually be recognized; and, when this is done, there are coincidents enough to witness the hypotheticality of every hypothetical property.[19]

Given information about what was coincident with what, the categorical properties could be identified: they would be the properties insensitive to the difference between coincidents. Now, as of yet, there *is* no information about what is coincident with what (that is why we were looking for the categorical properties in the first place). But that is not to say that none can be obtained; and, in fact, *certain* cases of coincidence – enough to weed out all the noncategoricals – are discoverable in advance.

To find these cases, try to imagine pairs of things that differ as little as possible from being strictly identical (for things almost identical will be contingently identical if any things are). Trivially, if α and β are strictly identical, α will exist in exactly the same possible worlds as β, and α will be coincident with β in all of them. To arrange for the least possible departure from this, let α exist in a few more worlds than β, but otherwise leave everything unchanged, i.e., let them be coincident in all the worlds where both exist. As it happens, that is exactly how it is with the driving home and the speeding home. Wherever the speeding home occurs, the driving home occurs too, and is coincident with the speeding home. But there will also be worlds in which the driving home is done at a reasonable speed, and in such worlds the speeding home does not occur.

Still, none of this helps with the project of explicating contingent identity, unless there is a way of characterizing the given relation – the relation between the driving home and the speeding home – which does not itself rely on the notion of contingent identity. But there is: it is the relation of refinement. Although only a fraction of all coincidents stand in the relation of refinement, this fraction is enough to weed out all the noncategorical properties.[20] With the noncategorical properties weeded out, the categorical properties are isolated. And with the categorical properties in hand, contingent identity is at last explicable: things are contingently identical in a world if they have the same categorical properties there.

Trivial cases aside, things contingently identical will not be identical as a matter of necessity. But then what about the argument that purported to show that identities obtained necessarily if at all? Was the argument invalid? No; it showed that *something* was impossible. The question is, was the refuted possibility really that of contingent identity? Looking back at the argument, the crucial assumption was this: to be contingently identical, things have to have *all* their properties, up to and including properties of the form *necessary identity with such and such*, in common. If that is right, then contingent identity is, as argued, impossible. So the question is, *do* contingently identical things have to have all their properties, not only categorical but hypothetical as well, in common?

They do not. To agree that they did would be to concede the very point of contingent identity and to frustrate the clear intent of its advocates, which was that it was to be a relation *compatible* with counterfactual divergence. Understanding contingent identity as sameness of nonhypothetical properties, on the other hand, preserves its point and sustains it against the "proof" of its impossibility. Still, why did it even *seem* that contingent identity entailed absolute indiscernibility? Probably because it was taken for granted that contingently identical things were (at least) *properly* identical, only – and this was their distinction – *not necessarily so*.[21] (And the expression "contingent identity" can certainly be faulted for encouraging this interpretation.) Admittedly, contingent identity in *this* sense is not possible.[22] But there is a better and more generous way of understanding contingent identity: strict and contingent identity are different relations, and, because of their differences as relations, one can obtain contingently whereas the other cannot. It only remains to spell out the formal details.

5 Modeling Contingent Identity

Formally, a property P is *categorical* iff necessarily, if α and β are related by refinement, then α has P iff β does, i.e., if

$$(\forall W)(\forall \alpha, \beta \epsilon \mathcal{D}(W))(\alpha \le \beta \Rightarrow (\alpha \epsilon P(W) \Leftrightarrow \beta \epsilon P(W)))$$

What is the relation between the cumulative properties and the categorical properties? Closure implies a partial answer.

Prop. 2 If Ω is closed, then every cumulative property is categorical.

Proof: Let $P \epsilon X$, and let $\alpha, \beta \epsilon \mathcal{D}(W), \alpha \le \beta$. By u-closure, there are α^* and β^* in $\mathcal{D}(W)$ such that $\forall P \epsilon X(\alpha \epsilon P[W] \Rightarrow \alpha^* \epsilon P^\square[W])$ and $\forall P \epsilon X(\beta \epsilon P[W] \Rightarrow \beta^* \epsilon P^\square[W])$. We show that $\alpha \epsilon P[W] \Leftrightarrow \beta \epsilon P[W]$. Since $\alpha \le \beta \le \beta^*, \alpha \le \beta^*$. Therefore,

$\beta \epsilon P[W] \Rightarrow \beta^* \epsilon P^\square[W] \Leftrightarrow \alpha \epsilon P[W]$ (by d-closure). For the converse, notice first that $\beta \le \alpha^*$. For if $Q \epsilon \mathbb{E}_x(\beta)$, then, by d-closure, $\alpha \epsilon Q[W]$; whence $Q \epsilon \mathbb{E}_x(\alpha^*)$. Since $\beta \le \alpha^*, \alpha \epsilon P[W] \Rightarrow \alpha^* \epsilon P^\square[W] \Rightarrow \beta \epsilon P[W]$ (by d-closure).

Things are *coincident* in W – written $\alpha \approx \beta$ – if they have the same categorical properties there. But, for the definition of categoricity to achieve its purpose, the system of coincidents has to be *full* or *complete*. Informally, this means that every point in the logical space of possible coincidents must actually be occupied; formally, for any (partial) function f from worlds W to things existing in W, there is a thing existing, and coincident with $f(W)$, in exactly the worlds in f's domain. Ω is *full* if it satisfies

$$(F) \quad \forall f : W \epsilon \mathcal{W} \to f(W) \epsilon \mathcal{D}(W) \exists \alpha [\mathcal{W}(\alpha) = \text{dom}(f) \,\&\, \forall W \epsilon \mathcal{W}(\alpha) \alpha \approx_w f(W)]$$

Prop. 2 showed that, if Ω is closed, then every cumulative property is categorical. For the converse, let Ω be *maximal closed* if

$$(M) \quad \Omega = \langle \mathcal{W}, X \rangle \text{ is closed, and there is no } X' \text{extending } X \text{ such that} \langle \mathcal{W}, X' \rangle \text{is closed.}$$

If Ω is maximal closed and full, then every categorical property is cumulative. In other words, a property is cumulative if and only if it is categorical.

Prop. 3 Let Ω be maximal closed and full. Then

$$\forall P[P \text{is cumulative} \Leftrightarrow P \text{is categorical}]$$

Proof: [$\Rightarrow$] This is just Prop. 2. [$\Leftarrow$] Let P be categorical. I claim that $< \mathcal{W}, X + P >$ is closed. For u-closure, let $Z \subseteq X$ and suppose that α has $Z + P$ in W. By fullness, there is an α^* which exists in W only and which is coincident with respect to (X) with α in W. Since α^* exists in W only, it has all its properties essentially. In particular, α^* has all of α's categorical (w.r.t. X) properties essentially, and so (by Prop. 2) α^* refines α (w.r.t. X). Since P is categorical (w.r.t. X), α^* has P in W too, and so it has P essentially in W. Thus α^* has $(Z + P)^\square$ in W. For d-closure, let $Z \subseteq X$ and let $\alpha \le \beta \epsilon (Z + P)^\square[W]$. By the d-closure of Ω, $\alpha \epsilon Z[W]$, and, since P is categorical (w.r.t. X), $\alpha \epsilon P[W]$ too. Since $< \mathcal{W}, X + P >$ is both u-closed and d-closed, P is in X.[23]

6 Essence and Identity

Can distinct things have the same cumulative essence? So far, nothing prevents it. For example, there is nothing to rule out the following: there are exactly two possible worlds, W and W', α and β exist in both worlds; γ exists in W alone; and γ' exists in W' alone. In this situation γ will have to refine both α and β in W, and γ' will refine both α and β in W'. From the fact that α and β have a common refinement in each world, it quickly follows that they are coincident, i.e., have the same categorical properties, in each world. But, by Prop. 3, the categorical properties are exactly the cumulative properties; and, if α and β share their cumulative properties in every world, how can they have different cumulative essences?

Actually, this raises the critical question, avoided until now, of how coincidence and identity are related. Can α and β exist in the same worlds, be coincident in all of them, and still be distinct? It is hard to imagine how they could. For, presumably, distinct items differ in one or another of two ways. Either they exist in different worlds, or they exist in the same worlds and are unlike, i.e., have different categorical properties, in at least one of them. Between distinct things, that is, there have got to be either intra-world or extra-world differences.

But what is the argument for this? If things exist in the same worlds, then, unless they have different categorical properties in at least one of them, the hypothesis of their distinctness can find no foothold. Take the standard example of 'indiscernible' spheres afloat in otherwise empty space (suppose for argument's sake that they exist in no other world). If the spheres were in *exactly the same place*, could they still be reckoned distinct? A hypothesis *so* gratuitous is beyond not only our powers of belief, but even our powers of stipulation. If, on the other hand, the spheres are in different places, then they differ on the (presumably categorical) properties of being in those places. (The properties have to be different, because they map the world in question to different spheres.)[24]

Call a property-model *separable* if it satisfies

$$(S) \quad \forall\alpha\forall\beta[(\mathscr{W}(\alpha) = \mathscr{W}(\beta) \ \& \ \forall W \epsilon \mathscr{W}(\alpha)\cup \\ \mathscr{W}(\beta)\alpha \approx_w \beta) \Rightarrow \alpha = \beta]$$

The last proposition shows that, if Ω is (besides being closed) separable, then things with the same cumulative essence are identical.

Prop. 4 Let Ω be closed and separable. Then

$$\forall\alpha\forall\beta[\mathbb{E}_x(\alpha) = \mathbb{E}_x(\beta) \Rightarrow \alpha = \beta]$$

Proof: Let α and β have the same X-essence. Since α and β X-refine each other, by Prop. 1 they exist in the same worlds. By the definition of X-categoricity, in each of these worlds any X-categorical property attaching to either attaches also to the other. Thus α and β have the same X-categorical properties, and so coincide, in every world where they exist. By separability, α is identical with β.

To this extent, essence determines identity.[25]

7 Applications

(A) Treating contingent identity as sameness of categorical properties goes *part* of the way toward solving a problem David Wiggins raises for relative identity in *Sameness and Substance*. He argues there that, since (i) what sets identity relations apart from the common run of equivalence relations is their satisfaction of Leibniz's law, and (ii) no variety of relative identity can satisfy (an unrestricted version of) Leibniz's law, (iii) relations of relative identity are not identity relations (pending discovery of a suitably restricted form of Leibniz's law). To answer this argument, one would need an uncontrived law of the form: if α is the same f as β, then α and β have thus-and-such properties in common. However, Wiggins thinks such a law will prove impossible to formulate:

> It seems that the very least we shall require is more information about the case of the *restricted* congruence that results from the g-identity, for *some one* sortal concept g, of x and y. No stable formulation of restricted congruence is available, however. Nor, I suspect, will it ever be given.[26]

But, if contingent identicals are seen as the *same concrete thing*, then a rigorous restriction of Leibniz's law is at hand: if α and β are the same concrete thing, then they have the same categorical properties.[27]

(B) Nearly everyone's gut reaction to functionalism is that *phenomenal* properties, at any rate, cannot be functional, because nothing functional can attain to the "manifest" character of felt experience. Perhaps this idea finds support in the categorical/hypothetical distinction. The property of playing functional role R is the property of bearing certain complicated counterfactual relations to inputs, outputs, and the players of various other functional roles. Details aside, such a property is obviously hypothetical. But the property of painfulness (note: not the property of causing pain, but that of being pain) *seems* to be a categorical property *par excellence*. Therefore, painfulness is not a functional property. (Note that this affects only the version of functionalism that flatly identifies mental properties with functional properties.)

(C) That mental and physical events are not properly identical is argued not only by their essential differences (emphasized by Kripke), but also by their causal differences. Suppose Smith's pain is identical with neural event ν, which causes neural event ε. Then the strict identity theorist will have to say that Smith's pain caused ε; but that seems questionable, because ν's *being* Smith's pain contributed nothing to its production of ε (one wants to say: even if ν had not been Smith's, or any, pain,

ε would still have eventuated). If Smith's pain and ν are only coincident, on the other hand, then *naturally* they will have different causal powers and susceptibilities; and a sensitive counterfactual theory of causation might be able to *exploit* their essential differences to predict their causal differences.[28] Irrelevant qualifications aside, an event α causes an event β only if it is *required* for β, in the following sense: given any (actually occurring) event $\gamma \approx \alpha$ whose essence does not include α's, if γ had occurred in α's absence, β would not have occurred; and only if it is *enough* for β, in the following sense: given any (actually occurring) event $\gamma \approx \alpha$ whose essence is not included in α's, γ is not required for β. As for Smith's pain (call it π), that ε would have occurred even in π's absence, provided that ν had still occurred, shows that π is not required for ε; and that ν is (let us assume) required for ε shows that π is not enough for ε either. Complementary considerations show how it can be Smith's decision, rather than the corresponding neural event, that causes her action.

NOTES

Donald Davidson, Sally Haslanger, Kit Fine, David Kaplan, Noa Latham, Shaughan Lavine, Barry Loewer, George Myro, Sydney Shoemaker, Robert Stalnaker, and David Velleman all made comments that helped me with the writing of this paper.

1 Saul Kripke, *Naming and Necessity* (Cambridge, Mass.: Harvard University Press, 1980), p. 4.
2 In the prevailing necessitarian euphoria, it has become difficult to recapture the atmosphere of a few years back, when contingent identity was a commonplace of logical and metaphysical theorizing. To cite just two examples, Dana Scott's "Advice on modal logic," in Karel Lambert (ed.), *Philosophical Problems in Logic* (Boston: Reidel, 1970), urged that "two individuals that are generally distinct might share all the same properties (of a certain kind!) with respect to the present world ... Hence they are equivalent or *incident* at the moment. Relative to other points of reference they may cease to be incident" (p. 165). And most of the early mind/body-identity theorists – U. T. Place, J. J. C. Smart, Thomas Nagel, among others – took themselves to be asserting the contingent identity of mental and physical entities. Smart, for instance, says very explicitly that "on the brain-process thesis the identity between the brain process and the experience is a contingent one" ("Sensations and brain processes," *Philosophical Review*, 68, 2 (April 1959), pp. 141–56, at p. 152). There is a ques-

tion, actually, how it is that so many people *thought* that an impossible thing was possible. One hypothesis – maybe it is Kripke's hypothesis – is that these people were just very mixed up. And, in fact, it does seem that to varying degrees they were. Ruth Marcus once described W. V. Quine as thinking that modal logic was conceived in sin, the sin of confusing use and mention. Contingent identity had, if anything, even shadier beginnings, because at least three separate sins attended at its conception. Contingency was routinely identified with (or at least thought to follow from) a posteriority; particular identity statements (like "This pain is identical to that brain-event") were insufficiently distinguished from general identity statements (like "Consciousness is a process in the brain"); and the contingent truth of an identity statement was equated with the contingency of the asserted identity, guaranteeing that contingent coincidence of concepts would be taken for the contingent identity of the things specified. So evidence for the confusion hypothesis is not lacking. The other hypothesis is, of course, that people recognized, confusedly perhaps, something sensible and defensible in the notion that things can be identical as a matter of fact. Philosophically, it does not much matter which of these hypotheses is correct. There *is* something sensible and defensible in the idea of contingent identity, whether its advocates recognized it or not. Or so I hope to show.

3 Kripke, "Identity and necessity," this volume, p. 72. Let me say at the outset that, as far as I can see, Kripke's argument does succeed in establishing what it claims to establish: namely, that identity, in the strict sense, can never obtain contingently. If the conclusion seems paradoxical, as it surely does, that is because people are confusing it with the genuinely paradoxical thesis that there can be *no* relation with the characteristics traditionally associated with "contingent identity." Speaking more generally, what Kripke says about identity is important and correct, and not questioned here; but people may have thought that his conclusions closed off certain avenues of investigation which are in fact still open. And that is perhaps why some of those conclusions have seemed hard to accept.

4 Observing that not only modal but temporal differences "establish that a statue is not the hunk of stone, or the congery of molecules, of which it is composed," Kripke allows that "mere non-identity...may be a weak conclusion" (this volume, p. 89). *Extremely* weak, from the point of view of philosophical materialism. That pains were not identical with neural stimulations seemed to be a powerfully antimaterialistic result; but now it turns out to be compatible with pains and neural stimulations being as tightly bound up with one another as statues and their clay. And what materialist would not be delighted with that result? On the other hand, "The Cartesian modal argument...surely can be deployed to maintain relevant stronger conclusions as well" (ibid.). Possibly this means that the statue is "nothing over and above" its matter, whereas the same cannot be said of a person; in the sense that necessarily, the statue (but not the person) exists if its matter does, and with a certain organization (*Naming and Necessity*, p. 145). But it seems doubtful whether the statue *is* "nothing over and above" its matter *in that sense* (what if the statue's matter had gathered together by chance, before the earth was formed? what if a different sculptor had organized the matter?); and the subtler the sense in which a statue really is "nothing over and above" its matter, the less implausible it becomes that, in a substantially similar sense, a person is "nothing over and above" *its* matter. So there may still be room for doubt whether modal arguments establish significantly more difference between a person and her matter than between a statue and its.

5 H. T. Mason (ed.), *The Leibniz–Arnauld Correspondence* (Manchester: Manchester University Press, 1967), p. 30.

6 In some contexts it is useful to distinguish between essential and necessary and between accidental and contingent properties. For example, someone might think that, whereas Socrates is essentially human, he is only necessarily Greek-or-not. The distinction is intuitive but irrelevant to our purposes.

7 Where *kinds* of things are concerned, this is comparatively uncontroversial: the essence attaching to the kind *cow* strictly includes the essence attaching to the kind *animal*. But, as Leibniz noticed, individuals can be thought of as instancing smallest or least kinds, what we might call *individual kinds* (what sets *individual* kinds apart is that in each possible world at most one thing instances them): "...since St Thomas could maintain that every separate intelligence differed in kind from every other, what evil will there be in saying the same of every person and in conceiving individuals as final species" (G. R. Montgomery (ed.), *Discourse on Metaphysics, Correspondence with Arnauld, Monadology* (La Salle, Ill.: Open Court, 1908), p. 237). Now just as the essences of general kinds can be comparable, so can the essences of an individual and a general kind (*Bossie*'s essence includes that of *cow*). But then why should the essences of individual kinds not be comparable too? There is every reason to see the relation between the Shroud of Turin and the piece of cloth as continuous with that between cow and animal: just as it is harder to be a cow than an animal, it is harder to be the Shroud of Turin than the piece of cloth, and just as nothing can be a cow without being an animal (but not conversely), nothing can be the Shroud of Turin without being the piece of cloth (but not conversely). So there seems to be a strong case for extending the familiar doctrine that the essence of one kind can include that of another to individual kinds, and, what comes to the same, to individuals themselves. (Incidentally, I am assuming that the Shroud of Turin could not have been made of anything other than that piece of cloth. Something made of another piece of cloth might have been called "the Shroud of Turin," but it would not have been our Shroud of Turin.)

8 Identity properties are by no means the only properties that lead to these difficulties. Kind properties, for example, are just as bad. If the property of being a piece of cloth (i.e., being of the *kind* piece of cloth) is included in the Cloth of Turin's essence, then adding on the property of having served as Jesus's burial shroud (along with perhaps some others) can no longer yield the essence of the Shroud of Turin. For it is never essential to any piece of cloth that it should have been used in any particular way (necessarily, any piece of cloth could have been destroyed moments after its fabrication). Incidentally, kind properties are disqualified by the first argument too: like identity properties, they are possessed not *simpliciter*, but dependently on other properties. It defies credulity that two things should be indiscernible up to this detail, that one is a collie and the other is not. (Thinking of identity and kind properties as *classificatory*, rather than *characterizing*, the above becomes the truism that a thing's classification depends entirely on what the thing is like.)

9 Although this is probably overstating it, at least as far as what is actually established goes (see Prop. 4 below). See also David Wiggins, *Sameness and Substance* (Cambridge, Mass.: Harvard University Press, 1980), and Robert M. Adams, "Primitive thisness and primitive identity," this volume, ch. 14, in both of which the sufficiency of "quality" for "quiddity" is considered and rejected. Wiggins's opinion is that " ... to make clear which thing a thing is, it is not enough (*pace* the friends of the logically particularized essence) to say however lengthily that it is *such*, or *so and so*. We have to say that it is *this* or *that such*. This is perfectly obvious when we think of trying to determine one entity by mentioning short or simple predicates (other than *identical with x* or suchlike). But it is difficult to see any reason to believe that by making ordinary predicates ever longer and more complicated we shall be able to overcome the obvious nonsufficiency or nonnecessity for identity with just *x* that infects all the relatively simple predicates true of *x*" (pp. 104–5).

10 See Peter Geach, "Identity," in his *Logic Matters* (Oxford: Blackwell, 1972). Baruch Brody asserts that his theory, according to which items are identical if and only if they are indiscernible over "all" properties, "is not ruled out by its leading to any paradoxes" (*Identity and Essence* (Princeton: Princeton University Press, 1980), p. 18). But he does not satisfactorily explain why not.

11 The accessibility relation is omitted; in effect, every world has access to every other.

12 The problem existence raises for the definition of "essential" is not unfamiliar. Kripke alludes to it in "Identity and necessity": "Here is a lectern. A question which has often been raised in philosophy is: What are its essential properties? What properties ... are such that this object has to have them if it exists at all ... [Footnote:] This definition is the usual formulation of the notion of essential property, but an exception must be made for existence itself: on the definition given, existence would be trivially essential. We should regard existence as essential to an object only if the object necessarily exists" (this volume, pp. 80, 87).

13 Another reason for preferring "coincident" to "contingently identical" is that properly identical things will also be coincident, indeed necessarily so, and it sounds funny to say that they are *necessarily* contingently identical. But I continue to use the term, partly for shock value, and partly for reasons to be given presently.

14 Scott, "Advice on modal logic," p. 165.

15 To be absolutely clear about the difference between contingency and categoricity, consider their complements. Where a thing has its noncontingent properties *necessarily*, it has its noncategorical properties *hypothetically*.

16 Two remarks. As a characterization of the categorical properties, the foregoing is circular. But it does have the virtue of illustrating why not *every* property can be hypothetical (as is sometimes suggested). For a property to be hypothetical, whether a thing has it must depend on the things" *categorical* properties in other worlds; and that shows that no property can be hypothetical unless at least some properties are categorical. And, since it is relatively unproblematic that categorical properties give rise to hypothetical properties (given the present broadly essentialist assumptions), neither category can be emptied without emptying the other. So a skeptic about the distinction should maintain that no property is of *either* kind, not that all (some) properties are of one kind and none are of the other. [For example, Sydney Shoemaker's theory of properties as "second-order powers," though it might seem to imply that all properties are hypothetical, or, on another reading, that all properties are categorical, is perhaps better read as rejecting the distinction altogether. See "Causality and properties," this volume, ch. 20, and "Identity, properties, and causality," in *Identity, Cause, and Mind* (New York: Cambridge University Press, 1984).] Second, in rejecting the proposed account of categoricity on grounds of circularity, I do not mean to imply that the account I finally give is not itself ultimately circular. Given the cumulative properties, the categorical properties can be noncircularly specified; but the cumulative properties themselves cannot be noncircularly specified, in particular not by the formal conditions laid down above.

17 To get a sense of what it might be like to countenance a creature coming into existence "in mid-life," consider Jane Eyre's reflections on the eve of her (anticipated) marriage to Mr Rochester: "Mrs Rochester! She did not exist: she would not be born till tomorrow, sometime after eight o'clock A.M.; and I would wait to be assured she had come into the world alive before I assigned her all that property." For a creature that stops existing "in mid-life," there are the opening lines of Neil Young's "A child's claim to fame': "I am a child / I last a while.'

18 Less dogmatically, there are two kinds of metaphysics: descriptive and transcendental. In descriptive metaphysics one is interested in reality as people see it; in transcendental metaphysics one tries to abstract to the largest extent possible from the human contribution. Pretty clearly, the distinction is relative. All metaphysics is somewhat transcendental (metaphysicians do not spend much time thrashing out the nature of time zones), but probably the present approach is more transcendental than most.

19 To say that everything up for recognition is actually recognized, is to say the following: given any set of worlds, and given an assignment to each of categorical properties satisfiable therein, there is something that exists in those worlds exactly and possesses in each the

associated categorical properties. Call this the requirement of *fullness*.

20 To see *why* the properties insensitive to the difference between things related by refinement can be relied on to be exactly the categoricals: Call these properties the *provisionally* categorical properties, and call things indiscernible with respect to these properties *provisionally* coincident. The problem is really to prove that every provisionally categorical property is genuinely categorical (the converse is clear). Let P be provisionally categorical. Then, by the definition of provisional coincidence, P cannot distinguish provisionally coincident things. Suppose toward a contradiction that P is not genuinely categorical. Then there are α and W such that α possesses P in W, but its possession of P in W depends on what worlds (other than W) it inhabits or on its genuinely categorical properties in those worlds. Thus, if there were something genuinely coincident with α in W, but differing from α in the worlds (other than W) it inhabited, or the genuinely categorical properties it had in them, that thing would lack P in W. Specifically, something existing in worlds $W, W', W'' \ldots$, and possessing the genuinely categorical properties Y in W (Y is the set of α's genuinely categorical properties in W), Y' in W', Y'' in $W'' \ldots$, would lack P in W. To produce such a thing, let $\gamma (= \alpha), \gamma', \gamma''' \ldots$ be entities satisfying $Y, Y', Y'', \ldots$ in $W, W', W'' \ldots$ If $Z, Z', Z'' \ldots$ are the sets of provisionally categorical properties possessed by $\gamma, \gamma', \gamma'', \ldots$ in $W, W', W'' \ldots$, then, by fullness (see the preceding note), there is a β existing in exactly $W, W', W'' \ldots$, and possessing Z in W, Z' in W', Z'' in $W'' \ldots$. Since a thing's provisionally categorical properties include its genuinely categorical properties, β meets the conditions laid down above for lacking P in W. But, by its definition, β is provisionally coincident with α in W. Since P distinguishes provisional coincidents, it is not provisionally categorical after all. Q.E.D.

21 True, Smart does go out of his way to emphasize that "the brain-process doctrine asserts identity in the *strict* sense" ('Sensations and brain processes," p. 145). But by this he seems to mean that he is not talking about the relation that one thing bears to another when they are "time slice[s] of the same four-dimensional object" or when they are "spatially or temporally continuous" (ibid.). Certainly there is nothing to suggest that he had in mind a contrast between "strict identity" and coincidence. What is clear is that he took "strict identity" to be a relation fully compatible with hypothetical dissimilarity.

22 Although some philosophers would say that identity *itself* can obtain contingently. *To some extent*, such philosophers can be seen as questioning the notion that is here called "identity proper" and as taking something *roughly* analogous to what is here called "coincidence" to be all the identity there is. Since this relation, which, relative to their schemes, probably

deserves to be called "identity proper," can obtain contingently, the kind(s) of contingent identity they advocate is (are) in a certain sense more radical than the kind assayed here. See, e.g. Allan Gibbard, "Contingent identity," this volume, ch. 9; David Lewis, "Counterpart theory and quantified modal logic," *Journal of Philosophy*, 65/5 (7 Mar. 1968), pp. 113–26; and *idem, Counterfactuals* (Cambridge, Mass.: Harvard University Press, 1973); and Robert Stalnaker, "Counterparts and identity," *Midwest Studies in Philosophy*, (1986). (Take note: as a descriptive account of these authors' theories, which are anyway not very similar to one another, the above is not reliable.)

23 Although it is wrong to try to *explicate* contingent identity in terms of identity of modal states (the notion of modal state depending on that of contingent identity), Prop. 3 suggests a way to define modal states so that the equation comes out true. Call $\alpha^* \alpha$'s *state* in W iff α^*s cumulative essence is exactly the set of α's categorical properties in W. To see that if α exists in W, its state in W exists too: By fullness, there is a β existing in W alone and coincident with α there. Thus β's categorical properties in W are exactly α's. By Prop. 3, β's cumulative properties in W are exactly α's categorical properties in W. Since β has all its properties essentially, β's cumulative essence is the set of α's categorical properties in W. Now it is easy to verify that things are coincident in a world iff they have strictly identical states there: α coincides with β in W iff α and β have the same categorical properties in W iff anything whose cumulative essence is the set of α's categorical properties is also something whose cumulative essence is the set of β's categorical properties iff any state of α in W is a state of β in W. (For the uniqueness of α's state in W, see Prop. 4.)

24 Granted, one cannot identify these properties without appeal to the objects that have them; but the claim was that they have different categorical properties, not that one can distinguish them by their categorical properties. Granted also, except in connection with the world in question, the properties' extensions will be to a large extent arbitrary (when is something in this world in the same place as the first sphere in that one?); but that does not matter, so long as the arbitrary choices are made in such a way that the resulting properties are categorical.

25 Even if this result is accepted, there is plenty of room for doubt about its precise significance. Briefly, one worry is that to distinguish α's cumulative essence from β's, one would already have to be able to distinguish α from β. But this seems to confuse the metaphysical thesis that distinct things have different essences with the epistemological doctrine that distinct things can always be *distinguished* by their essences. Second, not everything here called a "property" – basically, functions from worlds to extensions – is a *genuine property*. If this means that genuine

properties are not functions, this is granted; but it does not matter, if, for every world-to-extension function, there is some genuine property such that the function takes each world to the set of things possessing that property therein. But the criticism survives in the form: not all world-to-extension functions (not even all cumulative ones) *are* induced in this way by genuine properties. And that is undeniable. Further progress depends on figuring out what makes genuine properties genuine. (For more on the difference between genuine and pseudo properties, see the articles by Sydney Shoemaker mentioned in n. 16 above.)

26 Wiggins, *Sameness and Substance*, p. 39.
27 Whether this helps with the general problem of saying what properties relative identicals must have in common is another question, but one perhaps worth exploring. See also Nicholas Griffin, *Relative Identity* (New York: Oxford University Press, 1975), sects 1.2 and 8.5.
28 Thanks to Barry Loewer for talking to me about this; he and Paul Boghossian are working along similar lines.

PART III

Modalities and Possible Worlds

Introduction

Modalities in the present sense used to be called "modes" of truth. Some propositions, like "There are horses" and "Socrates is wise," are true but only contingently so. That is, they might have been false: the world might have been such that there were no horses, and Socrates was a fool. Or, as one is apt to say today, there are "possible worlds" in which horses don't exist and those in which Socrates is not wise. On the other hand, some truths seem necessary; for example, "Horses are animals" and "$2 + 1 = 3$." Nothing *could* count as a horse unless it was an animal; a world without animals is *ipso facto* one without horses. Might there be a world in which 2 plus 1 isn't 3? It's difficult – in fact, it does not seem possible – to think of such a world. What could such a world be like? Perhaps there is a world in which 2 plus 1 equals 4? But where would 3 fit into the number series in that world? Perhaps 3 would immediately follow 4, in which case 3 would be $4 + 1$. But wouldn't that make 4 an odd number and 3 an even number? This doesn't make sense. Or perhaps there is a world in which our 3 is missing, and 4 is the immediate successor of 2? But these things don't seem to make much sense: what makes a natural number the number it is, is its position in the number series, and if *per impossibile* 3 and 4 switched their places, 4 would now just be 3 (that is, the number that follows 2 would still be 3) and 3 would now be 4, and nothing would have changed – or so it seems. The reader is invited to explore further consequences of supposing that 2 plus 1 doesn't equal 3.

In "Modalities: Basic Concepts and Distinctions" (chapter 11), Alvin Plantinga elucidates the basic modal concepts, including those of necessity and possibility, and explains the important distinction between *de re* and *de dicto* modalities, defending the coherence of *de re* modal concepts against some influential objections. Briefly, *de dicto* modalities apply to *dicta* – that is, statements, sentences, propositions, and the like – and *de re* modalities pertain not to *dicta* but directly to objects in the world. So when we say that the proposition that horses are animals is *necessary*, the modality involved is *de dicto*. When we say that Socrates is necessarily a person but only contingently a husband, we are attributing the modal properties of being necessarily a person and of being contingently a husband to Socrates, the person, not to any linguistic/conceptual item. We are saying of Socrates, by whatever name he is picked out, that he could not have been something other than a person (a world without persons is *ipso facto* one in which Socrates does not exist), but that he might not have married (there is a possible world in which he stays a bachelor).

But this convenient and often perspicuous way of explaining *de re* modalities seems to assume that Socrates, the very same person, could inhabit different possible worlds, having different properties in different worlds. How is this possible? In "Identity through Possible Worlds" (chapter 12), Roderick Chisholm forcefully brings out a difficulty ('Chisholm's paradox') involved in the assumption that one and the same object can be in different possible worlds. One possible response to this problem is David Lewis's "counterpart theory." According to Lewis, individuals can each inhabit only a single world. But they can have "counterparts" in other worlds, and to say that Socrates is possibly rich is to say that there is a possible world in which Socrates' counterpart is rich. In "Counterparts or Double Lives?" (chapter 13), Lewis gives detailed discussions of many issues involved in the controversy between positions that allow different worlds to share common parts and those that do not.

In "Primitive Thisness and Primitive Identity" (chapter 14), Robert M. Adams takes up an important related issue: Is a world constituted exclusively by pure qualities, or do individuals as such ("thisness") have part in shaping it? This is the age-old question of haecceitism, a question addressed by Lewis as well.

Talk of possible worlds, nonactual but possible individuals, and the like strikes some philosophers as highly dubious – metaphysics at its speculative extreme. In "The Nature of Possibility" (chapter 15), D. M. Armstrong undertakes to construct possible worlds on a naturalistically acceptable basis. His basic idea, derived from Wittgenstein, is to generate possible worlds by combining and recombining the materials that exist in the actual world. Whether these combinatorial possible worlds can fully serve to explicate all of our modal notions remains an open question.

Further reading

Adams, Robert M., "Actualism and thisness," *Synthese* 49 (1981), pp. 3–42.

——, "Theories of actuality," *Nous* 8 (1974), pp. 211–31.

Armstrong, David, *A Combinatorial Theory of Possibility* (Cambridge: Cambridge University Press, 1989).

Forbes, Graeme, *The Metaphysics of Modality* (Oxford: Oxford University Press, 1985).

Jubien, Michael, "Problems with possible worlds," in D. F. Adams (ed.), *Philosophical Analysis* (Dordrecht: Reidel, 1988).

Kim, Jaegwon, "Possible worlds and Armstrong's combinatorialism," *Canadian Journal of Philosophy* 16 (1986), pp. 595–612.

Lewis, David, *On the Plurality of Worlds* (Oxford: Blackwell).

Loux, Michael (ed.), *The Possible and the Actual* (Ithaca, NY: Cornell University Press, 1979).

Lycan, William, "The trouble with possible worlds," in Loux (ed.).

Marcus, Ruth Barcan, *Modalities* (Oxford: Oxford University Press, 1993).

Prior, A. N., and Fine, Kit, *Worlds, Times, and Selves* (Amherst, Mass.: University of Massachusetts Press, 1977).

Stalnaker, Robert, "Counterparts and identity," *Midwest Studies in Philosophy* 11 (1986): 121–40.

——, "Possible worlds," *Nous* 10 (1976), pp. 65–75.

Van Fraassen, Bas, "All necessity is verbal necessity," *Journal of Philosophy* 74 (1977), pp. 71–85.

11

Modalities: Basic Concepts and Distinctions

Alvin Plantinga

1 Preliminary Distinctions and Remarks

A. Necessity circumscribed

The distinction between necessary and contingent truth is as easy to recognize as it is difficult to explain to the sceptic's satisfaction. Among true propositions[1] we find some, like

(1)   The average annual rainfall in Los Angeles is about 12 inches

that are contingent, while others, like

(2) $7 + 5 = 12$

or

(3)   If all men are mortal and Socrates is a man, then Socrates is mortal

that are necessary.

But what exactly do these words – 'necessary' and 'contingent' – mean? What distinction do they mark? Just what is supposed to be the difference between necessary and contingent truths? We can hardly explain that p is necessary if and only if its denial is impossible; this is true but insufficiently enlightening. It would be a peculiar philosopher who had the relevant concept of impossibility well

Originally published in A. Plantinga, *The Nature of Necessity* (Oxford: Clarendon Press, 1974), chs 1, 2. Copyright © by Oxford University Press. Reprinted by permission of Oxford University Press.

in hand but lacked that of necessity. Instead, we must give examples and hope for the best. In the first place, truths of logic – truths of propositional logic and first-order quantification theory, let us say – are necessary in the sense in question. Such truths are logically necessary in the narrow sense; (3) above would be an example. But the sense of necessity in question – call it 'broadly logical necessity' – is wider than this. Truths of set theory, arithmetic and mathematics generally are necessary in this sense, as are a host of homelier items such as

No one is taller than himself
Red is a colour
If a thing is red, then it is coloured
No numbers are human beings

and

No prime minister is a prime number.

And of course there are many propositions debate about whose status has played an important role in philosophical discussion – for example,

Every person is conscious at some time or other
Every human person has a body
No one has a private language
There never was a time when there was space but no material objects

and

There exists a being than which it is not possible that there be a greater.

So the sense of necessity in question is wider than that captured in first-order logic. On the other hand, it is narrower than that of *causal* or *natural* necessity.

Voltaire once swam the Atlantic

for example is surely implausible. Indeed, there is a clear sense in which it is impossible. Eighteenth-century intellectuals (as distinguished from dolphins) simply lacked the physical equipment for this kind of feat. Unlike Superman, furthermore, the rest of us are incapable of leaping tall buildings at a single bound, or (without auxiliary power of some kind) travelling faster than a speeding bullet. These things are impossible for us; but not in the broadly logical sense. Again, it may be necessary – causally necessary – that any two material objects attract each other with a force proportional to their mass and inversely proportional to the square of the distance between them; it is not necessary in the sense in question.

Another notion that must carefully be distinguished from necessity is what (for want of a better name) we might call 'unrevisability' or perhaps 'ungiveupability'. Some philosophers hold that *no* proposition – not even the austerest law of logic – is in principle immune from revision. The future development of science (though presumably not that of theology) could lead us rationally to abandon any belief we now hold, including the law of non-contradiction and *modus ponens* itself. So Quine:

> ... it becomes folly to seek a boundary between synthetic statements which hold contingently on experience, and analytic statements, which hold come what may. Any statement can be held come what may, if we make drastic enough adjustments elsewhere in the system. Even a statement very close to the periphery can be held true in the face of recalcitrant experience by pleading hallucination or by amending certain statements of the kind called logical laws. Conversely, by the same token, no statement is immune to revision. Revision even of the logical law of excluded middle has been proposed as a means of simplifying quantum mechanics; and what difference is there in principle between such a shift and the shift whereby Kepler superseded Ptolemy, or Einstein Newton, or Darwin Aristotle?[2]

Giving up a truth of logic – *modus ponens*, let us say – in order to simplify physical theory may strike us

as like giving up a truth of arithmetic in order to simplify the Doctrine of the Trinity. In any event, Quine's point is that no statement is immune from revision; for each there are circumstances under which (perhaps with a reluctant wave) we should give it up, and do so quite properly.

Here Quine may or may not be right. But suppose we temporarily and irenically concede that every statement, *modus ponens* included, is subject to revision. Are we then obliged to follow those who conclude that there are no genuinely necessary propositions? No; for their conclusion displays confusion. To say of *modus ponens* that it (or its corresponding conditional) is a necessary truth is not, of course, to say that people will never give it up, as if necessity were a trait conferred by long-term popular favour. I may be unprepared to give up the belief that I am a fine fellow in the face of even the most recalcitrant experience; it does not follow either that this belief is necessarily true or that I take it to be so. Nor would the unlikely event of everyone's sharing my truculence on this point make any difference. Just as obviously, a proposition might be necessarily true even if most people thought it false or held no opinion whatever on the matter.

So necessity has little or nothing to do with what people would *in fact* give up under various happy or unhappy circumstances. But it must also be distinguished from what cannot be *rationally* rejected. For clearly a proposition might be both necessary and such that on a given occasion the rational thing to do is to give up or deny it. Suppose I am a mathematical neophyte and have heard and accepted rumours to the effect that the continuum hypothesis has been shown to be independent of Zermelo–Fraenkel set theory. I relate this rumour to a habitually authoritative mathematician, who smiles indulgently and produces a subtly fallacious argument for the opposite conclusion – an argument which I still find compelling after careful study. I need not be irrational in believing him and accepting his argument, despite the fact that in this instance his usual accuracy has deserted him and he has told me what is necessarily false. To take a more homely example: I have computed the sum $97 + 342 + 781$ four times running, and each time got the answer 1120; so I believe, naturally enough, that $97 + 342 + 781 = 1120$. The fact, however, is that I made the same mistake each time – carried a '1' instead of a '2' in the third column. But my belief may none the less be rational. I do not know whether circumstances could arise in which the reasonable thing to do would be to give up *modus ponens*; but if such circumstances could and did arise, it would not follow that *modus ponens* is not a necessary truth. Broadly logical necessity, therefore, must be distinguished from unrevisability as well as from causal necessity and logical necessity strictly so called.

It must also be distinguished from the *self-evident* and the a priori. The latter two are epistemological categories, and fairly vaporous ones at that. But consider the first. What does self-evidence come to? The answer is by no means easy. In so far as we can make rough and intuitive sense of this notion, however, to say that a proposition *p* is self-evident is to answer the question 'how do you know that *p*?' It is to claim that *p* is utterly obvious – obvious to anyone or nearly anyone who understands it. If *p* is self-evident, then on understanding it we simply see that it is true; our knowledge of *modus ponens* may be cited as of this sort. Now obviously many questions arise about this notion; but in so far as we do apprehend it, we see that many necessary propositions are not thus transparent. $97 + 342 + 781 = 1220$ is indeed necessary, but certainly not self-evident – not to most of us, at any rate.

Still, perhaps we could say that this truth is self-evident in an extended sense: it is a consequence of self-evident truths by argument forms whose corresponding conditionals are themselves self-evident. Could we add that all necessary truths are self-evident in this extended sense? Not with any show of plausibility. The axiom of choice and the continuum hypothesis are either necessarily true or necessarily false; there is little reason to think that either of these, or either of their denials, are deducible from self-evident propositions by self-evident steps. You may think it inappropriate to speak of truth in connection with such an item as, say, the continuum hypothesis. If so, I disagree; I think this proposition just as true or just as false as the commonest truths and falsities of arithmetic. But no matter; there are simpler and more obvious examples. Each of Goldbach's conjecture and Fermat's last theorem, for example, is either necessarily true or necessarily false; but each may turn out to be such that neither it nor its denial is self-evident in the extended sense. That is to say, for all I know, and, so far as I know, for all *anyone* knows, this may be so. I do not mean to assert that this is *possibly* so, in the broadly logical sense; for (as could plausibly be argued) where *S* is the set of self-evident propositions and *R* that of self-evident argument

forms, a proposition *p* *possibly* follows from *S* by *R* only if *p* *actually*, and, indeed, *necessarily* thus follows. And since I do not know whether Goldbach's conjecture or Fermat's theorem *do* follow from *S* by *R*, I am not prepared to say that it is *possible* that they do so. My point is only that the question whether, for example, Goldbach's conjecture is self-evident in the extended sense is distinct from the question whether it is a necessary truth.

So not all necessary propositions are self-evident. What about the converse? Are some contingent propositions self-evident? The question is vexed, and the answer not obvious. Is the proposition I express by saying '$2 + 2 = 4$ is self-evident for me now' self-evident for me now? Perhaps so, perhaps not. Perhaps the idea of self-evidence is not sharp enough to permit an answer. What is once more important is that a negative answer is not immediate and obvious; self-evidence must be distinguished, initially, at least, from necessity.

Not strictly to the point but worth mentioning is the fact that some propositions *seem* or *appear* to be self-evident although they are not necessarily true or, for that matter, true at all. Some of the best examples are furnished by the Russellian paradoxes. It seems self-evident that for every condition or property *P* there is the set of just those things displaying *P*; it seems equally self-evident that there is such a condition or property as that of *being non-self-membered*. But of course these (together with some other apparently self-evident propositions) self-evidently yield the conclusion that there is a set that is and is not a member of itself; and this is self-evidently false. Some may see in this the bankruptcy of self-evidence. It is not my purpose, in these introductory pages, to defend self-evidence or answer the question how we know the truth of such propositions as *modus ponens*. Still, the conclusion is hasty. Our embarrassment in the face of such paradoxes shows that a proposition may seem to be self-evident when in fact it is false. How does it follow that *modus ponens*, for example, is not self-evident, or that there is some other or better answer to the question of how we know that it is true? The senses sometimes deceive us; square towers sometimes appear round. It does not follow either that we do not know the truth of such propositions as *The Empire State Building is rectangular* or that we have some non-empirical method of determining its truth.

Finally, the distinction between the necessary and the contingent must not be confused with the alleged cleavage between the a priori and the a posteriori. The latter distinction, indeed, is shrouded in obscurity. But given the rough and intuitive understanding we have of the terms involved, it is clear that the distinction they mark, like that between what is self-evident and what is not (and unlike that between the necessary and contingent), is *epistemological*. Furthermore, the relation between what is known a priori and what is necessarily true is by no means simple and straightforward. It is immediately obvious that not all necessary truths are known a priori; for there are necessary truths – Fermat's last theorem or its denial, for example – that are not known at all, and *a fortiori* are not known a priori. Is it rather that every necessary truth that is known, is known a priori? This question divides itself: (*a*) is every necessary truth that is known, known a priori to everyone who knows it? and (*b*) is every necessary truth that is known to someone or other, known a priori to some one or other? The answer to (*a*) is clear. Having taken the trouble to understand the proof, you may know a priori that the Schroeder–Bernstein theorem is a consequence of some standard formulation of set theory. If I know that you are properly reliable in these matters and take your word for it, then I may know that truth a posteriori – as I may if I've forgotten the proof but remember having verified that indeed there is one. To learn the value of the sine of 54 degrees, I consult a handy table of trigonometric functions: my knowledge of this item is then a posteriori. In the same way, even such simple truths of arithmetic as that $75 + 36 = 111$ can be known a posteriori. So the answer to (*a*) is obvious. The answer to question (*b*) is perhaps not quite so clear; but elsewhere give some examples of truths that are necessary but probably not known *a priori* to any of us.[3]

So necessity cannot be identified with what is known a priori. Should we say instead that a proposition is necessary if and only if it is know*able* a priori? But by whom? We differ widely in our ability to apprehend necessary truths; and no doubt some are beyond the grasp of even the best of us. Is the idea, then, that a proposition is necessarily true, if and only if it is *possible*, in the broadly logical sense, that some person, human or divine, knows it a priori? Perhaps this is true. Indeed, perhaps every truth whatever is possibly known a priori to some person – to God if not to man. But suppose we avoid the turbid waters of speculative theology and restrict our question to *human* knowledge: must a contingent proposition, if known, be known a posteriori? The question is as vexed as the notion

of a priori knowledge is obscure. What is known a priori is known independently, somehow or other, of experience. My knowledge of *modus ponens* or that $7 + 5 = 12$ would be cited by way of example. But how about my knowledge that I do know that $7 + 5 = 12$? Is that independent of experience in the requisite fashion? Suppose

(4)   I know that $7 + 5 = 12$;

cannot I know a priori that (4) is true? And this despite the contingency of (4)? Perhaps you will say that I know (4) only if I know

(4')   I believe that $7 + 5 = 12$;

and perhaps you will add that knowledge of this last item must be a posteriori. But is this really true? On a strict construction of 'independent of experience' it may seem so; for surely I must have had *some* experience to know that I thus believe – if only that needed to acquire the relevant concepts. But on such a strict construction it may seem equally apparent that I know no truths at all a priori; even to know that $7 + 5 = 12$, I must have had some experience. There is no specific *sort* of experience I need, to know that $7 + 5 = 12$; and this (subject, of course, to all the difficulty of saying what counts as a *sort* here) is perhaps what distinguishes my knowledge of this truth as a priori. But the same thing holds for my knowledge of (4'). Belief is not (*pace* Hume) a special brilliance or vividness of idea or image; there is no specific sort of experience I must have to know that I believe that $7 + 5 = 12$. So perhaps I know a priori that I believe that $7 + 5 = 12$. If so, then I have a priori knowledge of a contingent truth. Similarly, perhaps my knowledge that I *exist* is a priori. For perhaps I know a priori that I believe that I exist; I also know a priori that if I believe that I exist, then indeed I do exist. But then nothing but exceptional obtuseness could prevent my knowing a priori that I exist, despite the contingency of that proposition.

It is fair to say, therefore, that I probably know some contingent truths a priori. At any rate it seems clearly *possible* that I do so. So necessity cannot be identified with what is knowable a priori.[4] Unrevisability, self-evidence, and a priori knowledge are difficult notions; but conceding that we do have a grasp – one that is perhaps halting and infirm – of these notions, we must also concede that the notion of necessary truth coincides with none of them.

B. *Modality* de dicto *and modality* de re

I have spoken of necessity as a property or trait of *propositions* and tried to distinguish it from others sometimes confused with it. This is the idea of modality *de dicto*. An assertion of modality *de dicto*, for example

(5)   necessarily nine is composite

predicates a modal property – in this instance *necessary truth* – of another *dictum* or proposition:

(6)   nine is composite.

Much traditional philosophy, however, bids us distinguish this notion from another. We may attribute necessary truth to a proposition; but we may also ascribe to some object – the number 9, let us say – the *necessary* or *essential possession* of such a property as that of *being composite*. The distinction between modality *de dicto* and modality *de re* is apparently embraced by Aristotle, who observes (*Prior Analytics*, i. 9) that 'It happens sometimes that the conclusion is necessary when only one premiss is necessary; not, however, either premiss taken at random, but the major premiss'.[5] Here Aristotle means to sanction such inferences as

(7)   Every human being is necessarily rational
(8)   Every animal in this room is a human being

so

(9)   Every animal in this room is necessarily rational;

he means to reject such inferences as

(10)   Every rational creature is in Australia
(11)   Every human being is necessarily a rational creature

so

(12)   Every human being is necessarily in Australia.

Now presumably Aristotle would accept as sound the inference of (9) from (7) and (8) (granted the truth of (8)). If he is right, therefore, then (9) is not to be read as

(9′)   It is necessarily true that every animal in this room is rational;

for (9′) is clearly false. Instead, (9) must be construed (if Aristotle is correct) as the claim that each animal in this room has a certain property – the property of being rational – *necessarily* or *essentially*. That is to say, (9) must be taken as an expression of modality *de re* rather than modality *de dicto*. And what this means is that (9) is not the assertion that a certain *dictum* or proposition – *every animal in this room is rational* – is necessarily true, but is instead the assertion that each *res* of a certain kind has a certain property essentially or necessarily – or, what comes to the same, the assertion that each such thing has the modal property of being essentially rational.

In *Summa contra Gentiles*, St Thomas considers the question whether God's foreknowledge of human action – a foreknowledge that consists, according to St Thomas, in God's simply *seeing* the relevant action's taking place – is consistent with human freedom. In this connection he inquires into the truth of

(13)   What is seen to be sitting is necessarily sitting.

For suppose at t_1 God sees that Theaetetus is sitting at t_2. If (13) is true, then presumably Theaetetus is *necessarily* sitting at t_2, in which case he was not free, at that time, to do anything *but* sit.

St Thomas concludes that (13) is true taken *de dicto* but false taken *de re*; that is

(13′)   It is necessarily true that whatever is seen to be sitting is sitting

is true but

(13″)   Whatever is seen to be sitting has the property of sitting necessarily or essentially

is false. The deterministic argument, however, requires the truth of (13″); and hence that argument fails. Like Aristotle, then, Aquinas appears to believe that modal statements are of two kinds. Some predicate a modality of another statement (modality *de dicto*); but others predicate of an object the necessary or essential possession of a property; and these latter express modality *de re*.

But what is it, according to Aristotle and Aquinas, to say that a certain object has a certain property essentially or necessarily? That, presumably, the object in question could not conceivably have lacked the property in question; that under no possible circumstances could that object have failed to possess that property. Here, as in the case of modality *de dicto*, no mere definition is likely to be of much use; what we need instead is example and articulation. I am thinking of the number 5; what I am thinking of then, is prime. *Being prime*, furthermore, is a property that it could not conceivably have lacked. Of course, the proposition

(14)   What I am thinking of is prime

is not necessarily true. This has no bearing on the question whether what I am thinking of could have failed to be prime; and indeed it could not. No doubt the number 5 could have lacked many properties that in fact it has: the property of numbering the fingers on a human hand would be an example. But that it should have lacked the property of being prime is quite impossible. And a statement of modality *de re* asserts of some object that it has some property essentially in this sense.

Aquinas points out that a given statement of modality *de dicto* – (13') for example – may be true when the corresponding statement of modality *de re* – (13'') in this instance – is false. We might add that in other such pairs the *de dicto* statement is false but the *de re* statement true; if I am thinking of the number 17, then

(15)   What I am thinking of is essentially prime

is true, but

(15')   Necessarily, what I am thinking of is prime
       is false.

The distinction between modality *de re* and modality *de dicto* is not confined to ancient and medieval philosophy. G. E. Moore discusses the idealistic doctrine of internal relations;[6] he concludes that it is false or confused or perhaps both. What is presently interesting is that he takes this doctrine to be the claim that all relational properties are *internal* – which claim, he thinks, is just the proposition that every object has each of its relational properties essentially in the above sense. The doctrine of internal relations, he says, 'implies, in fact, quite generally, that any term which does in fact have a particular relational property, could not have existed without having that property. And in

saying this it obviously flies in the face of common sense. It seems quite obvious that in the case of many relational properties which things have, the fact that they have them is a mere matter of fact; that the things in question might have existed without having them.'[7] Now Moore is prepared to concede that objects do have some of their relational properties essentially. Like Aristotle and Aquinas, therefore, Moore holds that some objects have some of their properties essentially and others non-essentially or accidentally.

One final example: Norman Malcolm believes that the Analogical Argument for other minds requires the assumption that one must learn what, for example, *pain* is 'from his own case'. But, he says, 'if I were to learn what pain is from perceiving my own pain then I should, necessarily, have learned that pain is something that exists only when I feel pain. For the pain that serves as my paradigm of pain (i.e. my own) has the property of existing only when I feel it. That property is essential, not accidental; it is nonsense to suppose that the pain I feel could exist when I did not feel it.'[8] This argument appears to require something like the following premiss:

(16)   If I acquire my concept of *C* by experiencing objects and all the objects that serve as my paradigms have a property *P* essentially, then my concept of *C* is such that the proposition *Whatever is an instance of C has P* is necessarily true.

Is (16) true? I shall not enter that question here. But initially, at least, it looks as if Malcolm means to join Aristotle, Aquinas and Moore in support of the thesis that objects typically have both essential and accidental properties; apparently he means to embrace the conception of modality *de re*.

There is a prima facie distinction, then, between modality *de dicto* and modality *de re*. This distinction, furthermore, has a long and distinguished history. Many contemporary philosophers who find the idea of modality *de dicto* tolerably clear, however, look utterly askance at that of modality *de re*, suspecting it a source of boundless confusion. Indeed, there is abroad the subtle suggestion that the idea of modality *de re* is not so much confused as vaguely immoral or frivolous – as if to accept or employ it is to be guilty of neglecting serious work in favour of sporting with Amaryllis in the shade. In the next section, therefore, we shall examine objections to modality *de re*.

2 Modality *De Re*: Objections

A. *The problem*

One who accepts the idea of modality *de re* typically holds that some objects – 9, for example – have some of their properties – being composite, for example – *essentially* or *necessarily*.[9] That is to say, 9 has this property and could not conceivably have lacked it. And here the force of 'could have' is that broadly logical notion of possibility outlined in section 1. This is a notion of possibility broader than that of *casual* or *natural* possibility: it is causally impossible that David should have the attribute of travelling from Boston to Los Angeles at a velocity greater than the speed of light, but not impossible in the sense in question. On the other hand, this sense is narrower than that of logical possibility strictly so called. That someone should have the attribute of knowing that 7+5 = 13 is impossible, and impossible in the sense in question; the resources of logic alone, however, do not suffice to demonstrate this impossibility. The claim that objects have some of their properties essentially or necessarily is part of what we may call *essentialism*. To this contention the essentialist, as I shall understand him, adds the claim that objects have accidental as well as essential properties. Socrates, for example, has self-identity essentially, but is accidentally snub-nosed; while he could not have been self-diverse, he could have been non-snub-nosed. Still further, essentialism (as here understood) includes the idea that some properties are essential to some but not all objects; thus 9 but not 5 is essentially composite. So the essentialist holds that objects have both essential and accidental properties; and that some properties are had essentially by some but not all objects.

According to Quine, essentialism 'is the doctrine that some of the attributes of a thing (quite independently of the language in which the thing is referred to, if at all) may be essential to the thing and others accidental'.[10] I take the point to be this. When the essentialist says of something x that it has a certain property P essentially, he means to be predicating a property of x – a property distinct from P.[11] For every property P there is the property of having P essentially; and if x has P essentially, then x has the property *having P essentially*. This has two important consequences. In the first place, a proposition of the form x has P *essentially* entails that *something* has P essentially and is therefore properly subject to existential generalization.

To say that 9 is essentially composite is to predicate a property – that of being essentially composite – of 9; hence

(1) 9 is essentially composite

entails

(2) There is at least one thing that is essentially composite.

A second consequence: if x has P essentially, then the same claim must be made for anything identical with x. If 9 is essentially composite, so is Paul's favourite number, that number being 9. This follows from the principle sometimes called 'Leibniz's Law' or 'The Indiscernibility of Identicals':

(3) For any property P and any objects x and y, if x is identical with y, then x has P if and only if y has P.

Like Caesar's wife Calpurnia, this principle is entirely above reproach.[12] But then, if an object x has a property P essentially, it has the property of having P essentially; by (3), therefore, anything identical with x shares that distinction with it. Accordingly, if an object has a property essentially, so does anything identical with it. *Having P essentially* is a property of an object x; it is not, for example, a three-termed relation involving x, P, and (say) some description of x.

The essentialist, therefore, holds that some objects have both accidental and essential properties – properties not everything has essentially. He adds that where P is a property, so is *having P essentially*. And many philosophers view these claims with suspicion, if not outright disdain. What are the objections to it?

B. *Essentialism and set-theoretical reduction*

Some who accept essentialism point, by way of illustration, to the fact that the number 9 has the property *being composite* essentially or necessarily. Gilbert Harman is unsympathetic to this notion.[13] Arguing that 'the claim that numbers have such essential properties is incompatible with the familiar idea that number theory can be reduced to set theory in various ways',[14] he taxes those who accept *de re* modality with putting forward this idea 'less as an empirical hypothesis than as a metaphysical or religious doctrine';[15] and he rhetorically asks 'Why should we take them seriously?'

While I have no ready answer to this last question, I do feel that the theory of *de re* modality, taken as a religious doctrine, is a bit thin. It will never replace the Heidelberg Catechism, or even Supralapsarianism. What is presently interesting, however, is Harman's argument for the thesis that 9's being essentially composite *is* incompatible with this familiar idea. How does it go? According to the familiar idea, says Harman,

> the natural numbers can be identified with any of various sequences of sets. Zero might be identified with the null set, and each succeeding natural number with the set whose only member is the set identified with the previous number. Or a natural number might be identified with the set of all natural numbers less than it. And there are an infinity of other possible identifications all of which allow the full development of number theory.[16]

So far, so good. That the natural numbers can be identified, in this fashion, with various distinct set-theoretical structures is indeed a familiar idea. But of course there is no reason to stick thus unimaginatively to sets; we may, if we wish, identify President Nixon with zero and the remaining numbers with propositions about him: *Nixon is less than one foot tall, Nixon is less than two feet tall,...* All we need for such 'identification' is a countably infinite set of objects together with a relation[17] under which they form an infinite sequence or progression. Since practically any object you please is the tenth element in some progression, any object you please can be 'identified', in this fashion, with 9.

'But', continues Harman, 'being a composite number is not an essential property of any set. Therefore', he says, 'if numbers can be identified with sets and *de re* necessity is in question, no number is necessarily a composite number. Being a composite number is not an essential property of any number.'[18]

Here there may be less than meets the eye. How, exactly, are we to construe this argument? Taken at face value, it appears to involve an application of Leibniz's Law; perhaps we can outline it as follows:

(4) No set is essentially a composite number,

that is,

(5) No set has the property of being essentially composite.

But

(6) Numbers can be identified with sets.

Therefore (given Leibniz's Law),

(7) No number has the property of being essentially composite.

Put thus baldly, this argument, obviously, is about as imperforate as an afghan knitted by an elephant. We might as well argue that 9 does not have the property of being divisible by 3, since Nixon does not, and it can be identified with him.

The point is this. That number theory can be reduced to set theory in various ways is indeed, in Harman's words, a familiar idea. It is widely recognized and accepted as accurate and as part of the current lore about numbers and sets. And according to this familiar idea, a given number can be 'identified' with any of many distinct sets. But what this comes to (in so far as the idea in question *is* widely accepted) is only this: there are many denumerable families of sets that form a progression under some (recursive) relation. Accordingly, for any number n, there are many distinct sets each of which is the $n+$ 1st element in some progression and can therefore play the role of n in some set-theoretical development of number theory. But of course the fact that numbers can be identified in *this* sense with Nixon or with various distinct set-theoretical objects does not suggest that any number is in fact *identical with* Nixon or some set; it is this latter, however, that is required for an application of Leibniz's Law.

C. *Essentialism and the number of apostles*

According to the essentialist, for each property P there is the property of having P essentially – a property an object has (if at all) in itself, regardless of how it may be described or referred to. If 9 is essentially composite, so is Paul's favourite number, that number being 9. The essentialist therefore rejects the idea that 9 *qua*, as they say, Paul's favourite number has the property of being his favourite number essentially, but *qua* the successor of 8 has that property accidentally, this would be to say that *being essentially Paul's favourite number* is not a property at all but perhaps a relation involving 9, the property of being Paul's favourite number, and a designation of 9. He holds instead that such an item as *being essentially composite* is a property – in this case, one enjoyed by 9; hence it is a property of Paul's favourite number, if indeed Paul's favourite number is 9.

It is here that he makes his mistake, according to William Kneale.[19] For, says Kneale, an object does not have a property *P* essentially *just as an object* (to speak oracularly); instead it has *P* essentially (if at all) *relative to* certain ways of specifying or selecting it for attention – and perhaps accidentally, relative to other ways. When we say that *x* has *P* essentially or necessarily, this must be construed as 'an elliptical statement of relative necessity';[20] that is, as short for something like '*x* has *P* necessarily relative to *D*' where *D* is some description. Of course if *P* is a *truistic* property – one which, like *is red or is not red*, is had necessarily by every object relative to every way of describing it, then this reference to ways of selecting *x* may perhaps be suppressed without undue impropriety, so that we may say *simpliciter* that *P* is essential to *x*. In these cases, then, the reference to a description is otiose; but where *P* is not truistic, such a reference is crucial, even if implicit. Fundamentally, therefore, Kneale holds that there is no such thing, for a property *P*, as the property of having *P* essentially; these are only three-termed relations involving *P*, an object *x*, and the various ways of selecting *x* for attention.

But why so? The opposite view, he says, is based on the mistaken assumption that

> properties may be said to belong to individuals necessarily or contingently, as the case may be, without regard to the ways in which the individuals are selected for attention. It is no doubt true to say that the number 12 is necessarily composite, but it is certainly not correct to say that the number of apostles is necessarily composite, unless the remark is to be understood as an elliptical statement of relative necessity. And again, it is no doubt correct to say that this at which I am pointing is contingently white, but it is certainly not correct to say that the white paper at which I am looking is contingently white, unless again, the remark is to be understood as elliptical.[21]

Kneale's argument does not wear its structure upon its sleeve. How, exactly, does it go? What are the premises? The *conclusion*, pretty clearly, is that an object does not have a property necessarily *in itself* or just as an object; it has it necessarily or

contingently, as the case may be, *relative to* certain descriptions of the object. There is no such thing as the property of being necessarily composite; and a proposition like

(8) The number 12 is necessarily composite

does not predicate a property of 12; instead it predicates a relation of 12, the property of being composite, and a 'way of selecting 12 for attention'. But why should we think so? How are we to construe the argument? Perhaps it has something like the following premises:

(9)   12 = the number of apostles.
(8)   The number 12 is necessarily composite.
(10) If (8), then if there is such a property as *being necessarily composite*, 12 has it.
(11) The number of apostles is not necessarily composite.
(12) If (11), then if there is such a property as *being necessarily composite*, the number of the apostles lacks it.

It therefore follows that there is no such property as *being necessarily composite*; hence, it is false that for any property *P*, there is the property of having *P* essentially or necessarily; and hence the essentialist thesis is mistaken.

Now clearly Kneale's argument requires Leibniz's Law as an additional premiss – a principle the essentialist will be happy to concede. And if we add this premiss, then the argument is apparently valid. But why should we accept (11)? Consider an analogous argument for the unwelcome conclusion that *necessary truth* or *being necessarily true* is not a property that a proposition has in itself or just as a proposition, but only relative to certain descriptions of it:

(13) The proposition that $7 + 5 = 12$ is necessarily true.
(14) The proposition I am thinking of is not necessarily true.
(15) The proposition that $7 + 5 = 12$ is identical with the proposition I am thinking of.

Therefore

(16) *Being necessarily true* is not a property.

This argument is feeble and unconvincing; if (15) is true, then (14) must be false. But is not the very same comment appropriate to (11) and (9)? If (9) is true, then presumably (11) is false. And so the question becomes acute: why *does* Kneale take (11) to be true? The answer, I suspect, is that he reads (11) as

(11′)   The proposition *the number of apostles is composite* is not necessarily true.

More generally, Kneale seems to think of sentences of the form '— has ... essentially' (where the first blank is filled by a singular term and the second by an expression denoting a property) as short for or a stylistic variant of the corresponding sentences of the form 'the proposition — has ... is necessarily true'; where α ranges over singular terms and 'B' over expressions denoting properties, Kneale apparently means to ascribe something like the following definitional schema to the essentialist:

D$_1$ $\ulcorner \alpha$ has B essentially $\urcorner$ = def. $\ulcorner$The proposition α *has* B is necessarily true$\urcorner$.

But this ascription is at best uncharitable as an account of what the essentialist means by his characteristic assertions. As noted above, the latter holds that a proposition like

(17)   12 is essentially composite

predicates a property of 12, and hence entails (by way of existential generalization)

(18)   There is at least one object x such that x is essentially composite.

Applying D$_1$ (and making appropriate grammatical adjustments) we have

(19)   There is at least one object x such that the proposition x *is composite* is necessarily true.

But of course (19) as it stands is grotesque; there is no such thing as the proposition x *is composite*; the words 'x is composite' do not express a proposition. The essentialist may be benighted, but he does not confound (18), which he accepts, with such a darkling hodge-podge as (19).

Fundamentally, however, to saddle the essentialist with D$_1$ is to ignore his claim that an item like (17) is a *de re* assertion that predicates a *property* of the number 12. If he accepts (17), then he will also hold that the number of apostles is essentially

composite; and he will be utterly unshaken by the *de dicto* truth that

(11′)   *the number of apostles is composite* is not necessarily true.

A central feature of his programme, after all, is to distinguish such *de re* propositions as (17) from such *de dicto* items as (11′); and to ascribe D$_1$ to him is to ignore, not discredit, his claim that there is such a distinction to be drawn.

But perhaps we were being hasty. Suppose we look again at Kneale's argument. Perhaps he does not mean to ascribe D$_1$ to the essentialist: perhaps we are to understand his argument as follows. We have been told that 'x has P essentially' means that it is impossible or inconceivable that x should have lacked P; that there is no conceivable set of circumstances such that, should they have obtained, x would not have had P. Well, consider the number 12 and the number of apostles. Perhaps it *is* impossible that *the number 12* should have lacked the property of being composite; but it is certainly possible that *the number of apostles* should have lacked it; for clearly the number of apostles could have been 11, in which case it would not have been composite. Hence *being essentially composite* is not a property, and the essentialist thesis fails.

How could the defender of essentialism respond? The relevant portion of the argument may perhaps be stated as follows:

(20)   The number of apostles could have been 11.
(21)   If the number of apostles had been 11, then the number of apostles would have been prime.

Hence

(22)   It is possible that the number of apostles should have been prime

and therefore

(23)   The number of apostles is not essentially composite.

But the essentialist has an easy retort. The argument is successful only if (23) is construed as the assertion *de re* that a certain number – 12 as it happens – does not have the property of being essentially composite. Now (22) can be read *de dicto* as

(22a) The proposition *the number of apostles is prime* is possible;

it may also be read *de re*, that is, as

(22b) The number that numbers the apostles (that is, the number that *as things in fact stand* numbers the apostles) could have been prime.

The latter entails (23); the former, of course, does not. Hence to preserve the argument we must take (22) as (22b). Now consider (20). The same *de re/ de dicto* ambiguity is once again present. Read *de dicto* it makes the true (if unexciting) assertion that

(20a) The proposition *there are just 11 apostles* is possible.

Read *de re*, however – that is, as

(20b) The number that (as things in fact stand) numbers the apostles could have been 11

— it will be indignantly repudiated by the essentialist; for the number that numbers the apostles is 12, and accordingly could not have been 11. We must therefore take (20) as (20a).

This brings us to (21). If (20a) and (21) are to entail (22b), then (21) must be construed as

(21a) If the proposition *the number of apostles is 11* had been true, then the number that (as things in fact stand) numbers the apostles would not have been composite.

But surely this is false. For what it says is that if there had been 11 apostles, then the number that in fact does number the apostles – the number 12 – would not have been composite; and at best this is outrageous. No doubt any inclination to accept (21a) may be traced to an unremarked penchant for confusing it with

(24) If the proposition *the number of apostles is 11* had been true, then the number that *would have* numbered the apostles would have been prime.

(24), of course, though true, is of no use to Kneale's argument. Accordingly, Kneale's objection to essentialism is at best inconclusive.

D. Essentialism and the mathematical cyclist

Let us therefore turn to a different but related complaint. Quine argues that talk of a difference between necessary and contingent attributes of an object is baffling:

> Perhaps I can evoke the appropriate sense of bewilderment as follows. Mathematicians may conceivably be said to be necessarily rational and not necessarily two-legged; and cyclists necessarily two-legged and not necessarily rational. But what of an individual who counts among his eccentricities both mathematics and cycling? Is this concrete individual necessarily rational and contingently two-legged or vice versa? Just insofar as we are talking referentially of the object, with no special bias towards a background grouping of mathematicians as against cyclists or vice versa, there is no semblance of sense in rating some of his attributes as necessary and others as contingent. Some of his attributes count as important and others as unimportant, yes, some as enduring and others as fleeting; but none as necessary or contingent.[22]

Noting the existence of a philosophical tradition in which this distinction *is* made, Quine adds that one attributes it to Aristotle 'subject to contradiction by scholars, such being the penalty for attributions to Aristotle'. None the less, he says, the distinction is 'surely indefensible'.

Now this passage reveals that Quine has little enthusiasm for the distinction between essential and accidental attributes; but how exactly are we to understand him? Perhaps as follows. The essentialist, Quine thinks, will presumably accept

(25) Mathematicians are necessarily rational but not necessarily bipedal

and

(26) Cyclists are necessarily bipedal but not necessarily rational.

But now suppose that

(27) Paul K. Zwier is both a cyclist and a mathematician.

From these we may infer both that

(28) Zwier is necessarily rational but not necessarily bipedal

and

(29) Zwier is necessarily bipedal but not necessarily rational

which appear to contradict each other twice over: (28) credits Zwier with the property of being necessarily rational, while (29) denies him that property; (29) alleges that he has the property of being essentially bipedal, an allegation disputed by (28).

This argument is unsuccessful as a refutation of the essentialist, whatever its merits as an evocation of a sense of bewilderment. For consider the inference of (29) from (26) and (27). (29) is a conjunction, as are (26) and (27). And presumably its first conjunct

(30) Zwier is necessarily bipedal

is supposed to follow from the first conjuncts of (26) and (27), viz.

(31) Cyclists are necessarily bipedal

and

(32) Zwier is a cyclist.

But sensitive, as by now we are, to *de re/ de dicto* ambiguity, we see that (31) can be read *de dicto* as

(31a) Necessarily, all cyclists are bipedal

or *de re* as

(31b) Every cyclist has the property of being necessarily bipedal.

And if (30) is to follow from (32) and (31), the latter must be seen as predicating of every cyclist the property (30) ascribes to Zwier; (31), that is, must be read as (31 b). So taken, there is less than a ghost of a chance the essentialist will accept it. No doubt he will concede the necessary truth of

(33) All (well-formed) cyclists are bipedal

and thus the truth of (31a); he will accept no obligation to infer that such well-formed cyclists as Zwier are essentially bipedal. And the same

comments apply, *mutatis mutandis*, to the inference of the second conjunct of (29) from those of (26) and (27). Accordingly, (26) is true but of no use to the argument if we read it *de dicto*; read *de re*, it will be repudiated by the essentialist.

Taken as a refutation of the essentialist, therefore, this passage misses the mark; but perhaps we should emphasize its second half and take it instead as an expression of a sense of bewildered puzzlement as to what *de re* modality might conceivably be. Similar protestations may be found elsewhere in Quine's works:

> An object, of itself and by whatever name or none, must be seen as having some of its traits necessarily and others contingently, despite the fact that the latter traits follow just as analytically from some ways of specifying the object as the former do from other ways of specifying it.

And

> This means adapting an invidious attitude towards certain ways of specifying x ... and favouring other ways ... as somehow better revealing the 'essence' of the object.

But 'such a philosophy', he says, 'is as unreasonable by my lights as it is by Carnap's or Lewis's'.[23]

Here Quine's central complaint is this: a given object, according to the essentialist, has *some* of its properties essentially and others accidentally, despite the fact that the latter follow from certain ways of specifying the object just as the former do from others. So far, fair enough. Snub-nosedness (we may suppose) is not one of Socrates' essential attributes; none the less it follows (in the sense in question) from the description 'the snub-nosed teacher of Plato'. As we construe him, furthermore, the essentialist holds that among the essential attributes of an object are certain non-truistic properties – properties which, unlike the property of being red or not red, do not follow from every description; so it will indeed be true, as Quine suggests, that ways of uniquely specifying an object are not all on the same footing. Those from which each of its essential properties follows must be awarded the accolade as best revealing the essence of the object.

But what, exactly, is 'unreasonable' about this? And how, precisely, is it baffling? The real depth of Quine's objection, as I understand it, is this: he holds that 'A's are necessarily B's' must, if it means anything at all, mean something like 'necessarily, A's are B's'; for 'necessity resides in the way we talk about things, not in the things we talk about'. And hence the bafflement in asking, of some specific individual who is both cyclist and mathematician, whether he is essentially rational and contingently two-legged, or vice versa. Perhaps the claim is, finally, that while we can make a certain rough sense of modality *de dicto*, we can understand modality *de re* only if we can explain it in terms of the former.

Notes

1 Necessity, truth and allied properties are at bottom (as I see it) properties of propositions, not sentences. A sentence is true, on a given occasion of its use, if on that occasion it expresses a true proposition. My conception of proposition as non-linguistic entity expressed by but distinct from sentences parallels Moore's idea of proposition, Frege's of *Gedanke*, and Bolzano's of *Satz*. Some find propositions objectionable – on the grounds, apparently, that they lack 'a clear criterion of identity'. In so far as the alleged debility can be made tolerably clear, it is one that propositions share with electrons, mountains, wars – and sentences.

2 W. V. O. Quine, 'Two dogmas of empiricism', in *From a Logical Point of View*, 2nd edn (Cambridge, Mass.: Harvard University Press, 1961), p. 43.

3 See A. Plantinga, *The Nature of Necessity* (Oxford: Clarendon Press, 1974), ch. 5, sect. 2. See also *idem*, 'World and essence', *Philosophical Review* 79 (1970), p. 481.

4 In 'Naming and necessity', in D. Davidson and G. Harman (eds), *Semantics of Natural Language* (Dordrecht: Reidel, 1972, p. 253), Saul Kripke suggests that another kind of proposition is contingent but knowable a priori. Suppose, he says, that I fix the reference of the term 'one metre' as the length of a certain stick (call it S) at a time t. Then 'one metre' is not synonymous with the phrase 'the length of S at t' but is instead a proper name or 'rigid designator' of the length S actually has at t. And under these conditions, he adds, my knowledge of the proposition *S is one metre long at t* is a priori despite the contingency of that proposition. 'If he used stick S to fix the reference of the term "one metre"', then as a result of this kind of "definition" (which is not an abbreviative or synonymous definition) he knows automatically without further investigation, that S is one metre long' (p. 275). Here we may have doubts. Suppose I have never seen S and hold no views as to its length. I propose none the less to use 'one metre' as a rigid designator of the length, whatever it is, that S actually displays at t. After thus determining the reference of 'one metre', I know that the *sentence* 'S is one metre long at t' expresses a truth in my language; the truth it does express, however, is one I neither know nor believe. So my thus determining the reference of 'one metre' is not sufficient for my knowing a priori that S is one metre long.

What I do know a priori (or so it seems to me) is that if I use 'one metre' as a rigid designator of the length of S (and given the appropriate function of the phrase 'S is . . . long at t'), then the sentence 'S is one metre long at t' expresses a truth in my language. This conditional, however, is necessary rather than contingent.

The issues here are complex, and much more must be said; unfortunately 'Naming and necessity' came into my hands too late for the detailed consideration I should like to have given this and other issues it raises.

5 Quoted by William Kneale in 'Modality *de dicto* and *de re*', in E. Nagel, P. Suppes, and A. Tarski (eds), *Logic, Methodology, and Philosophy of Science* (Stanford, Calif.: Stanford University Press, 1962), p. 623.

6 G. E. Moore, *Philosophical Studies* (London: Routledge & Kegan Paul, 1951), p. 276.

7 Ibid., p. 289.

8 Norman Malcolm, 'Wittgenstein's *Philosophical Investigations*', *Philosophical Review* 63 (1954); repr. in *idem*, *Knowledge and Certainty* (Englewood Cliffs, NJ: Prentice-Hall Inc., 1963). The quoted passage is on p. 105 of the latter volume.

9 In speaking of the view in question, I use the words 'necessarily' and 'essentially' as synonyms. Of course I neither assume nor suggest that these words are in fact synonyms as ordinarily employed. See R. Marcus, 'Essential attribution', *Journal of Philosophy* 68 (Apr. 1971), p. 193.

10 W. V. O. Quine, 'Three grades of modal involvement', in *The Ways of Paradox* (New York: Random House, 1966), p. 173.

11 Alternatively, we might take it that what he asserts is a proposition predicating of x and P a special relation of *property-inherence*: that in which an object and a of property stand if the former has the latter essentially. Such a proposition, presumably, will be equivalent to one predicating of x the property of having P essentially.

12 Apparently Leibniz himself did not clearly distinguish (3) from:

(3′) Singular terms denoting the same object can replace each other in any context *salva veritate*, a 'principle' that does not hold for such excellent examples of language as English.

13 Gilbert Harman, 'A nonessential property', *Journal of Philosophy* 67 (Apr. 1970), p. 183.

14 Ibid., p. 184.

15 Ibid., p. 185.

16 Ibid., p. 184.

17 Perhaps recursive; see Paul Benacerraf, 'What numbers could not be', *Philosophical Review* 74 (1965), p. 51.

18 Harman, 'Nonessential property', p. 184.

19 Kneale, 'Modality *de dicto* and *de re*', p. 622.

20 Ibid., p. 629.

21 Ibid.

22 W. V. Quine, *Word and Object* (Cambridge, Mass.: MIT Press, 1960), p. 199.

23 *From a Logical Point of View*, 2nd edn (New York: Harper & Row, 1963), pp. 155–6.

24 Quine, *Ways of Paradox*, p. 174.

12

Identity through Possible Worlds

Roderick M. Chisholm

It is now easy to see a simple way of avoiding undesirable existential generalizations in epistemic contexts. Existential generalization with respect to a term – say b – is admissible in such contexts if b refers to one and the same man in all the "possible worlds" we have to consider.[1]

In an article on Hintikka's *Knowledge and Belief*, I suggested that certain difficult questions come to mind when we consider the thought that an individual in one possible world might be identical with an individual in another possible world.[2] The present paper is written in response to the editor's invitation to be more explicit about these questions.

Let us suppose, then, that the figure of an infinity of possible worlds makes good sense and let us also suppose, for simplicity of presentation, that we have a complete description of this one. We may consider some one of the entities of this world, alter its description slightly, adjust the descriptions of the other entities in the world to fit this alteration, and then ask ourselves whether the entity in the possible world that we thus arrive at is identical with the entity we started with in this world. We start with Adam, say; we alter his description slightly and allow him to live for 931 years instead

of for only 930; we then accommodate our descriptions of the other entities of the world to fit this possibility (Eve, for example, will now have the property of being married to a man who lives for 931 years instead of that of being married to a man who lives for only 930); and we thus arrive at a description of another possible world.[3]

Let us call our present world "W¹" and the possible world we have just indicated "W²." Is the Adam of our world W¹ the same person as the Adam of the possible world W²? In other words, is Adam such that he lives for just 930 years in W¹ and for 931 in W²? And how are we to decide?

One's first thought might be that the proposition that Adam is in both worlds is incompatible with the principle of the indiscernibility of identicals. How could our Adam be identical with that one if ours lives for just 930 years and that one for 931? Possibly this question could be answered in the following way:

"Compare the question: How can Adam at the age of 930 be the same person as the man who ate the forbidden fruit, if the former is old and the latter is young? Here the proper reply would be: it is not true that the old Adam has properties that render him discernible from the young Adam; the truth is, rather, that Adam has the property of being young when he eats the forbidden fruit and the property of being old in the year 930, and that these properties, though different, are not incompatible. And so, too, for the different possible worlds: It is not true that the Adam of W¹ has properties that render him discernible from the

Originally published in *Nous* (1967). Reprinted here from Roderick M. Chisholm, *On Metaphysics* (Minneapolis: University of Minnesota Press, 1989), pp. 19–24, by permission of the University of Minnesota Press.

Adam of W^2; the truth is, rather, that Adam has the property of living for 930 years in W^1 and the property of living for 931 in W^2, and that these properties, though different, are not incompatible."

I think it is clear that we must deal with the old Adam and the young Adam in the manner indicated; but in this case, one could argue, we know independently that the same Adam is involved throughout. But are we justified in dealing in a similar way with the Adam of W^1 and the Adam of W^2? In this latter case, one might say, we do not know independently that the same Adam is involved throughout. Here, then, is one of the questions that I do not know how to answer. Let us suppose, however, that we answer it affirmatively.

The Adam of this world, we are assuming, is identical with the Adam of that one. In other words, Adam is such that he lives for only 930 years in W^1 and for 931 in W^2. Let us now suppose further that we have arrived at our conception of W^2, not only by introducing alterations in our description of the Adam of W^1, but also by introducing alterations in our description of the Noah of W^1. We say: "Suppose Adam had lived for 931 years instead of 930 and suppose Noah had lived for 949 years instead of 950." We then arrive at our description of W^2 by accommodating our descriptions of the other entities of W^1 in such a way that these entities will be capable of inhabiting the same possible world as the revised Noah and the revised Adam. Both Noah and Adam, then, may be found in W^2 as well as in W^1.

Now let us move from W^2 to still another possible world W^3. Once again, we will start by introducing alterations in Adam and Noah and then accommodate the rest of the world to what we have done. In W^3 Adam lives for 932 years and Noah for 948. Then moving from one possible world to another, but keeping our fingers, so to speak, on the same two entities, we arrive at a world in which Noah lives for 930 years and Adam for 950. In that world, therefore, Noah has the age that Adam has in this one, and Adam has the age that Noah has in this one; the Adam and Noah that we started with might thus be said to have exchanged their ages. Now let us continue on to still other possible worlds and allow them to exchange still other properties. We will imagine a possible world in which they have exchanged the first letters of their names, then one in which they have exchanged the second, then one in which they

have exchanged the fourth, with the result that Adam in this new possible world will be called "Noah" and Noah "Adam." Proceeding in this way, we arrive finally at a possible world W^n which would seem to be exactly like our present world W^1, except for the fact that the Adam of W^n may be traced back to the Noah of W^1 and the Noah of W^n may be traced back to the Adam of W^1.

Should we say of the Adam of W^n that he is identical with the Noah of W^1 and should we say of the Noah of W^n that he is identical the Adam of W^1? In other words, is there an x such that x is Adam in W^1 and x is Noah in W^n, and is there a y such that y is Noah in W^1 and y is Adam in W^n? And how are we to decide?

But let us suppose that somehow we have arrived at an affirmative answer. Now we must ask ourselves: How is one to tell the difference between the two worlds W^1 and W^n? Shall we say that, though they are diverse, they are yet indiscernible from each other – or, at any rate, that the Adam of W^1 is indiscernible from the Adam of W^n (who is in fact the Noah of W^1) and that the Noah of W^1 is indiscernible from the Noah of W^n (who is in fact the Adam of W^1)? There is a certain ambiguity in "discernible" and in "indiscernible." The two Adams could be called "discernible" in that the one has the property of being Noah in the other world and the other does not, and similarly for the two Noahs. But in the sense of "indiscernible" that allows us to say that "indiscernibles are identical" tells us more than merely "identicals are identical," aren't the two Adams, the two Noahs, and the two worlds indiscernible? Could God possibly have had a sufficient reason for creating W^1 instead of W^n?

If W^1 and W^n are two different possible worlds, then, of course, there are indefinitely many others, equally difficult to distinguish from each other and from W^1 and W^n. For what we have done to Adam and Noah, we can do to any other pair of entities. Therefore, among the possible worlds that would seem to be indiscernible from this one, there are those in which you play the role that I play in this one and in which I play the role that you play in this one.[4] (If this is true, there may be good ground for the existentialist's *angst*; since, it would seem, God could have had no sufficient reason for choosing the world in which you play your present role instead of one in which you play mine.)

Is there really a good reason for saying that this Adam and Noah are identical, respectively, with that Noah and Adam? We opened the door to this conclusion by assuming that Adam could be found in more than one possible world – by assuming that there is an x such that x is Adam in W^1 and lives here for 930 years and x is also Adam in W^2 and lives there for 931. If it is reasonable to assume that Adam retains his identity through the relatively slight changes involved in the transition from W^1 to W^2, and so, too, for Noah, then it would also seem reasonable to assume that each retains his identity through the equally slight changes involved in all the other transitions that took us finally to W^n. (These transitions, of course, may be as gradual as one pleases. Instead of it being a year that we take away from Noah in our first step and give to Adam, it could be only a day, or a fraction of a second.) But identity is transitive. And therefore, one might argue, once we allow Adam to exist in more than one possible world, we commit ourselves to affirmative answers to the puzzling questions we have encountered.

Is there a way, then, in which we might reasonably countenance identity through possible worlds and yet avoid such extreme conclusions? The only way, so far as I can see, is to appeal to some version of the doctrine that individual things have essential properties. One possibility would be this:

For every entity x, there are certain properties N and certain properties E such that: x has N in some possible worlds and x has non-N in others; but x has E in every possible world in which x exists; and, moreover, for every y, if y has E in any possible world, then y is identical with x. (If "being identical with x" refers to a property of x, then we should add that E includes certain properties other than that of being identical with x.) The properties E will thus be *essential* to x and the properties N *nonessential*, or accidental.[5]

To avoid misunderstanding, we should contrast this present use of "essential property" with two others.

(1) Sometimes the "essential properties" of a thing are said to be just those properties that the thing has *necessarily*. But it is not implausible to say that there are certain properties which are such that *everything* has those properties necessarily; the properties, the example, of being either red or non-red, of being colored if red, and of being self-identical.[6] Thus the Eiffel Tower is necessarily red or non-red, necessarily colored if red, and necessarily self-identical; and so is everything else.[7]

(2) And sometimes it is said (most unfortunately, it seems to me) that each individual thing is such that it has certain properties that are essential or

necessary to it "under certain descriptions of it" and that are not essential or necessary to it "under certain other descriptions of it." Thus "under one of his descriptions," the property of being President is said to be essential to Mr Johnson, whereas "under that description" the property of being the husband of Lady Bird is not; and "under another one of his descriptions," it is the other way around. Presumably *every* property P of every individual thing x is such that, "under some description of x," P is essential or necessary to x.

But if E is the set of properties that are essential to a given thing x, in the sense of "essential" that we have defined above, then: E will not be a universal property (indeed, *nothing* but x will have E); some of the properties of x will not be included in E; and E will not be such that there are descriptions of x "under which" E is not, in the sense defined, essential to x.

If we accept this doctrine of essential properties, we may say, perhaps, that the property of living for just 930 years is essential to Adam and therefore that he may inhabit other possible worlds without living for just 930 years in each of them. And so, too, perhaps, for having a name which, in English, ends with the letter "m." But, we may then go on to say, somewhere in the journey from W^1 to W^n, we left the essential properties of Adam (and therefore Adam himself) behind. But where? What *are* the properties that are essential to Adam? Being the first man? Having a name which, in English, begins with the first letter of the alphabet? But why *these* properties? If we can contemplate Adam with slightly different properties in another possible world, why can't we think of him as having ancestors in some possible worlds and as having a different name in others? And similarly for any other property that might be proposed as being thus essential to Adam.

It seems to me that even if Adam does have such essential properties, there is no procedure at all for finding out what they are. And it also seems to me that there is no way of finding out whether he *does* have any essential properties. Is there really a good reason, then, for supposing that he does?

The distinction between essential and nonessential properties seems to be involved in one of the traditional ways of dealing with the problem of *knowing who*.[8] If this way of dealing with that problem were satisfactory, then the doctrine of essential properties might have a kind of independent confirmation. But I am not sure that is satisfactory. The problem of *knowing who* may be illustrated in this way. I do not know who it was who robbed the bank this morning, but I do know, let us assume, that there is someone who robbed the bank and I also know that that person is the man who drove off from the bank at 9:20 A.M. in a Buick sedan. For me to know *who* he is, therefore, it is not enough for me to have information enabling me to characterize him uniquely. What kind of information, then, *would* entitle me to say that I know who he is? The essentialistic answer would be: "You *know who* the bank robber is, provided that there is a certain set of properties E which are essential to the x such that x robbed the bank and you know that x has E and x robbed the bank." But if my doubts about essential properties are well-founded, this solution to the problem of knowing who would imply that the police, though they may finally "learn the thief's identity," will never know that they do. For to *know that one knows who* the thief is (according to the proposed solution), one must know what properties are essential to the thief; and if what I have said is correct, we have no way of finding out what they are. How are the police to decide that they know who the thief is if they have no answer to the metaphysical question 'What are the essential properties of the man we have arrested?'[9]

It is assumed, in many writings on modal logic, that "Necessarily, for every x, x is identical with x"

implies "For every x, necessarily x is identical with x," and therefore also "For every x and y, if x is identical with y, then necessarily x is identical with y." But is the assumption reasonable? It leads us to perplexing conclusions: for example, to the conclusion that *every* entity exists in *every* possible world and therefore, presumably, that everything is an *ens necessarium*.

Why assume that necessarily the evening star is identical with the evening star? We should remind ourselves that "The evening star is identical with the evening star" is not a logical truth, for it implies the contingent proposition "There is an evening star," and that its negation is not "The evening star is diverse from the evening star." Wouldn't it be simpler to deny that "Necessarily, for every x, x is identical with x" implies "For every x, necessarily x is identical with x"? Then we could deny the principle *de dicto*, "Necessarily the evening star is identical with the evening star," and also deny the principle, *de re*, "The evening star is necessarily identical with the evening star."[10] We could still do justice to the necessity that is here involved, it seems to me, provided we continued to affirm such principles, *de dicto*, as "Necessarily, for every x, x is identical with x" and "Necessarily, for every x and y, if x is identical with y then y is identical with x," and such principles, *de re*, "The evening star, like everything else, is necessarily self-identical."

Notes

1 Jaakko Hintikka, *Knowledge and Belief: An Introduction to the Logic of the Two Notions* (Ithaca, NY: Cornell University Press, 1962), p. 152.
2 Roderick M. Chisholm, "The logic of knowing," *Journal of Philosophy* 60 (1963), pp. 773–95; see esp. pp. 787–95.
3 It should be noted that the possible world in question is not one that Hintikka would call *epistemically* possible, for it could be said to contain certain states of affairs (Adam living for 931 years) that are incompatible with what we know to hold of this world; hence it is not one of the worlds Hintikka is concerned with in the passage quoted above. But it is *logically* possible, and that is all that matters for purposes of the present discussion.
4 "She (Ivich) looked at the glass, and Mathieu looked at her. A violent and undefined desire had taken possession of him; a desire to *be* for one instant that unconsciousness... to feel those long slender arms from within...To be Ivich and not to cease to be himself" (Sartre, *The Age of Reason*, trans. E. Sutton

(New York: Vintage Books, 1973). Compare N. L. Wilson, "Substance without substrata," *Review of Metaphysics* 12 (1959), and A. N. Prior, "Identifiable individuals," *Review of Metaphysics* 13 (1960).
5 We could put the doctrine more cautiously by saying that the distinction between the two types of property holds, not for *every* entity x, but only for *some* entities x. But what reason could there be for thinking that it holds of some entities and not of others?
6 Sometimes these properties are called "analytic properties" or "tautological properties"; but the property of being colored if red should not be so-called if, as some have argued, "Everything that is red is colored" is not analytic.
7 From the proposition that the Eiffel Tower is red and necessarily colored if red, it would be fallacious to infer that the Eiffel Tower is necessarily colored; this is the fallacy of inferring *necessitate consequentis* from *necessitate consequentiae*. And from the proposition that the Eiffel Tower is necessarily red or non-red, it would be fallacious to infer that the proposition

that the Eiffel Tower is red or non-red is a necessary proposition; the proposition could hardly be necessary, for it implies the contingent proposition that there is an Eiffel Tower. This latter fallacy might be called the fallacy of inferring *necessitate de dicto* from *necessitate de re*.

8 Compare Aristotle, *De Sophisticis Elenchis*, 179b3; Petrus Hispanus, *Summulae Logicales*, ed. I. M. Bochenski (Turin: La Scuola, 1947), 7.41; Franz Brentano, *Kategorienlehre* (Leipzig: Felix Meiner Verlag, 1933), p. 165.

9 Hintikka says that we know who the thief is provided that there exists an *x* such that we know that the thief is identical with *x* (*Knowledge and Belief*, p. 153). But under what conditions may it be said that there exists an *x* such that we know that the thief is identical with *x*? Presumably, if ever, when we catch him in the act – when we *see* him steal the money. But the teller saw him steal the money, and *she* doesn't know who he is.

I have suggested elsewhere a slightly different way of looking at these questions; compare "Believing and intentionality," *Philosophy and Phenomenological Research* 25 (1964), pp. 266–9, esp. p. 268.

10 I have discussed this possibility in "Query on substitutivity," in Robert S. Cohen and Marx W. Wartofsky (eds.), *Boston Studies in the Philosophy of Science*, vol. 2 (New York: Humanities Press, 1965), pp. 275–8.

If we deny that "Necessarily, for every *x*, *x* is F" implies "For every *x*, necessarily *x* is F," then presumably we should also deny that "It is possible that there exists an *x* such that *x* is F" implies "There exists an *x* such that it is possible that *x* is F." But isn't this what we should do? One could hold quite consistently, it seems to me, that though it is possible that there exists something having the properties that Christians attribute to God, yet nothing that does exist is such that it is possible that *that* thing has the properties that Christians attribute to God.

13

Counterparts or Double Lives?

David Lewis

1 Good Questions and Bad

Peter van Inwagen has written that anyone who is rightly taught – that is, anyone who has read Plantinga –

> will see that there is no problem of trans-world identity. He will find that all attempts he knows of to formulate the supposed problem are either incoherent or else have such obvious 'solutions' that they do not deserve to be called problems. He will realize that it was all done with mirrors – that is, with empty words and confused pictures. There is, therefore, no longer any excuse for talking as if there were a 'problem of trans-world identity'.[1]

Nevertheless, I shall devote the whole of this chapter to the problem of trans-world identity.

Still, to a great extent I agree with van Inwagen's harsh judgement. Very often we do meet formulations that probably manifest confusion, and that are apt to cause it. I shall begin by separating questions. I think there are some good ones to be found, as well as the incoherent ones and the ones with uncontroversial 'solutions'.

The first thing to say is that our topic, like the Holy Roman Empire, is badly named; we may continue to use the customary name, but only if we are careful not to take it seriously. In the first

Originally published in David Lewis, *On the Plurality of Worlds* (Oxford: Blackwell, 1986), ch. 4. Reprinted by permission of the author.

place we should bear in mind that Trans-World Airlines is an intercontinental, but not as yet an interplanetary, carrier. More important, we should not suppose that we have here any problem about *identity*.

We never have. Identity is utterly simple and unproblematic. Everything is identical to itself; nothing is ever identical to anything else except itself. There is never any problem about what makes something identical to itself; nothing can ever fail to be. And there is never any problem about what makes two things identical; two things never can be identical. There might be a problem about how to define identity to someone sufficiently lacking in conceptual resources – we note that it won't suffice to teach him certain rules of inference – but since such unfortunates are rare, even among philosophers, we needn't worry much if their condition is incurable.

We *do* state plenty of genuine problems in terms of identity. But we *needn't* state them so. Therefore they are not problems about identity. Is it ever so that an F is identical to a G? That is, is it ever so that the same thing is an F, and also a G? More simply, is it ever so that an F is a G? The identity drops out. Thus it is a good question whether a river is something you can bathe in twice; or whether a restaurant is something that can continue to exist through a simultaneous change in ownership and location and name; or whether numbers are von Neumann ordinals; or whether there is something that all charged particles have in common; or whether there could be a time traveller who meets his younger self; or whether there was ever a genuine nation that included both Austria and Hungary. All of these questions could be stated in terms of identity – harmlessly, unless that way of stating the questions confused us about where to seek for answers.

Likewise for the question whether worlds ever overlap; that is, whether two worlds ever have a common part; that is, whether any part of one world is ever part of another as well; that is, whether there is ever identity between parts of different worlds. This is a good question, but not a question about identity. Or rather, it is a good question for genuine modal realists; it makes little sense as a question for ersatzers. I consider this question in section 2, where I shall defend a qualified negative answer.

It is also a good question, but it is a different good question, whether there is anything that overlaps two different worlds, and so is in both in the way that a highway may be in two different states. Again, I could state it in terms of identity: is there ever identity between things that are (partly) in different worlds? Really it is not a question about identity, but about mereology: is there any reason to restrict mereological summation so that several things have a mereological sum only if all of them are parts of a single world? The follow-up question concerns semantics: if summation is unrestricted, so that indeed there are trans-world individuals, are these mere oddities? Are they nameless, do they fall outside the extensions of ordinary predicates and the domains of ordinary quantification? Or do they include things of importance to us, such as ourselves? I consider these questions in section 3, where I shall acknowledge the existence of trans-world individuals but dismiss them as oddities.

It is yet another good question, and this time it is a good question for genuine modal realists and ersatzers alike, whether it ever happens that anything exists according to two different (genuine or ersatz) worlds. If you like, I can state this question too in terms of identity: does it ever happen that something which exists according to one world and something which exists according to another are identical? The answer to that ought to be uncontroversial: yes, that very often happens. Take our world-mate Hubert Humphrey, for instance. The Humphrey who exists according to our world and the Humphrey who exists according to some other worlds are identical. (It is too bad that grammar demands the plural.) That is, Humphrey exists according to many different (genuine or ersatz) worlds. According to ours, he exists and he lost the presidential election; according to others, he exists and he won. This is a question that, as van Inwagen says, does not deserve to be called a problem.

But what *does* deserve to be called a problem is the follow-up question: what is it for Humphrey to exist according to a world? What is representation *de re*? How does a world, genuine or ersatz, represent, concerning Humphrey, that he exists? This one is *not* a question for genuine modal realists and ersatzers alike. Or rather, it is not *one* question for both. The available answers for genuine and for ersatz worlds will look quite different.

A genuine world might do it by having Humphrey himself as a part. That is how our own world represents, concerning Humphrey, that he exists. But for other worlds to represent in the same way that Humphrey exists, Humphrey would have to be a common part of many overlapping worlds, and somehow he would have to have different properties in different ones. I reject such overlap, for reasons to be considered shortly. There is a better way for a genuine world to represent, concerning Humphrey, that he exists. Humphrey may be represented *in absentia* at other worlds, just as he may be in museums in this world. The museum can have a waxwork figure to represent Humphrey, or better yet an animated simulacrum. Another world can do better still: it can have as part a Humphrey of its own, a flesh-and-blood counterpart of our Humphrey, a man very like Humphrey in his origins, in his intrinsic character, or in his historical role. By having such a part, a world represents *de re*, concerning Humphrey – that is, the Humphrey of our world, whom we as his worldmates may call simply Humphrey – that he exists and does thus-and-so. By waving its arm, the simulacrum in the museum represents Humphrey as waving his arm; by waving his arm, or by winning the presidential election, the other-worldly Humphrey represents the this-worldly Humphrey as waving or as winning. That is how it is that Humphrey – our Humphrey – waves or wins according to the other world. This is counterpart theory, the answer I myself favour to the question how a world represents *de re*.[2]

(The same goes in reverse. Our Humphrey is a counterpart of many Humphreys of many other worlds. I deny that the counterpart relation is always symmetrical, but surely it often is. So here are many other-worldly Humphreys who win the presidency, but who lose according to this world. They are represented as losing by the presence here of Humphrey the loser.)

There are various ways that an ersatz world might represent, concerning Humphrey, that he exists, or that he waves, or that he wins. It depends on what sort of ersatz world we are dealing with. A linguistic ersatz world might include English sentences that mention Humphrey by name: 'Humphrey exists', 'Humphrey waves', 'Humphrey wins'. Or it might include sentences of some other world-making language, which mention Humphrey by some other name. Or it might instead include sentences of the world-making language which say explicitly that there is someone of a certain description who exists, and waves, and wins; and this could qualify as representation *de re* concerning Humphrey if the description sufficiently resembles the description of Humphrey as he actually is. Or, instead of saying explicitly that there is someone of the appropriate description, a linguistic ersatz world might say it implicitly, by means of many sentences having to do with the vacancy or occupation of space-time points, or with the instantiating of various elementary universals by various elementary particulars. A pictorial ersatz world might have a part which is a picture, made out of stuff that is in some mysterious sense abstract, of Humphrey waving and winning. A magical ersatz world might represent that Humphrey exists and waves and wins by having some ineffable distinctive intrinsic nature. Or it might do it by means of brute necessary connections: necessarily, if some simple element stands in some unanalysable relation to the concrete world, then Humphrey exists and waves and wins.

It is sometimes thought that ersatzism is better off than counterpart theory in respecting certain intuitions: intuitions that *de re* modality has to do with the *res* itself, not some imitation or substitute or counterpart. Thus Kripke makes his famous complaint that on my view

> ... if we say 'Humphrey might have won the election (if only he had done such-and-such)', we are not talking about something that might have happened to *Humphrey*, but to someone else, a 'counterpart'. Probably, however, Humphrey could not care less whether someone *else*, no matter how much resembling him, would have been victorious in another possible world.[3]

Coming from an advocate of genuine modal realism with overlap, this complaint might have some force. But here it comes only a page away from Kripke's equally famous remark that

> A possible world isn't a distant country that we are coming across, or viewing through a telescope.[4]

Joking aside (he does say that 'another possible world is too far away'), Kripke's point seems to be that we are supposed to respect Humphrey's intuition that it is *he himself* who would have been victorious in another world, and we are supposed to do this by declining to think of that other world as the sort of thing that he himself could even be part of! What is going on?

I think counterpart theorists and ersatzers are in perfect agreement that there are other worlds (genuine or ersatz) *according to* which Humphrey – he himself! (stamp the foot, bang the table) – wins the election. And we are in equal agreement that Humphrey – he himself – is not *part* of these other worlds. Somehow, perhaps by containing suitable constituents or perhaps by magic, but anyhow not by containing Humphrey himself, the other world represents him as winning. If there were any genuine modal realists who believed in overlap of worlds, they would indeed be in a position to insist that at another world we have Humphrey himself winning the presidency. That might indeed be a point in their favour. But it is not a point in favour of any other view but theirs, and in particular it is not a point in favour of any kind of ersatzism.

Counterpart theory does say (and ersatzism does not) that someone else – the victorious counterpart – enters into the story of how it is that another world represents Humphrey as winning, and thereby enters into the story of how it is that Humphrey might have won. In so far as the intuitive complaint is that someone else gets into the act, the point is rightly taken. But I do not see why that is any objection, any more than it would be an objection against ersatzism that some abstract whatnot gets into the act. What matters is that the someone else, or the abstract whatnot, should not crowd out Humphrey himself. And there all is well. Thanks to the victorious counterpart, Humphrey himself has the requisite modal property: we can truly say that *he* might have won. There is no need to deny that the victorious counterpart also makes true a second statement describing the very same possibility: we can truly say that a Humphrey-like counterpart might have won. The two statements are not in competition. Therefore we need not suppress the second (say, by forbidding any mixture of ordinary modal language with talk of counterparts) in order to safeguard the first.[5]

I said that counterpart theory and ersatzism are alike in denying that Humphrey himself is part of the other world which represents him as winning. But that was a little too quick. Counterpart theory and ersatzism are also alike in having trick ways to dodge the conclusion. In both cases there is a loophole to exploit, but exploiting the loophole does nothing to satisfy the alleged intuition that it must be Humphrey himself who wins. For the counterpart theorist, the trick is to say that 'Humphrey' names not the Humphrey of our world, and not the Humphrey of another, but rather the trans-world individual who is the mereological sum of all these local Humphreys. If that is what Humphrey is (but I shall argue in section 3 that it isn't), then indeed he himself is partly in this world and partly in that and not wholly in any. Part of him loses, and part of him wins. But presumably the losing part cares what might have happened to *it*; it could not care less what happens to some *other* slice off the same great salami – unless, of course, the world containing that other-worldly slice of Humphrey can be taken as a world that represents the this-worldly slice as winning.

For the ersatzer (of the linguistic persuasion) the trick is to remember that anything you please can serve as a word of the world-making language. Humphrey might as well be used as his own name, in Lagadonian fashion. Then he will be, if not a part, at least a set-theoretic constituent of the ersatz world which is a set of sentences saying *inter alia* that he wins. So what? Presumably he could not care less what words of what languages are assembled with him into what set-theoretic structures – unless, of course, we get a linguistic structure that represents him as winning. Let him by all means care how he can be consistently represented, but not about the words of the representation. It is perfectly arbitrary whether he serves as a word. And if he does, it is perfectly arbitrary what he means. If Humphrey is to be made a word, there is no need to make him be his own name. He would do just as well as a name for Checkers, or as a preposition or adverb. Or he could be the negation sign in a sentence that denies his existence.

There are at least two more good questions that can be extracted from the topic of trans-world identity, though again they have nothing special to do with identity. I merely state these questions here; I shall take them up in sections 4 and 5.[6] Again they are questions for genuine modal realists and ersatzers alike. For the sake of neutrality, I shall formulate them in terms of representation *de re*; that is, in terms of truth according to a world, genuine or ersatz, concerning some actual individual such as Humphrey.

One is the question of haecceitism. We can distinguish representation of the way things are qualitatively (in a broad sense of that word) from representation *de re*. It may be the case according to a world that there are things of certain kinds, arranged in certain ways, and with certain causal relationships; these are matters of qualitative character. But also it may be the case, according to a world, concerning the individual Humphrey, that he exists and waves and wins. Can these two kinds of representation vary independently? Or does what a world represents concerning matters of qualitative character determine what that world represents *de re*?

The other is the question of constancy. Do we have a settled answer, fixed once and for all, about what is true concerning a certain individual according to a certain (genuine or ersatz) world? Or can different answers be right in different contexts? Can two opposed answers even be right together, in a single context? Can it happen sometimes that no answer is determinately right?

2 Against Overlap

The simplest way that part of another world could represent Humphrey – our Humphrey – is by identity. He might lead a double life, in two worlds at once. He himself, who is part of the actual world, might be part of the other world as well. He could be a common part of both, in the same way that a shared hand might be a common part of two Siamese twins. The other world represents him as existing because he is part of it. He exists at the other world because, restricting our quantification to the parts of that world, he exists. This leading of double lives is what best deserves to be called 'trans-world identity'.

I cannot name one single philosopher who favours trans-world identity, thus understood. The philosophers' chorus on behalf of 'trans-world identity' is merely insisting that, for instance, it is Humphrey himself who might have existed under other conditions, who might have been different, who might have won the presidency, who exists according to many worlds and wins according to some of them. All that is uncontroversial. The controversial question is *how* he manages to have these modal properties. The answer now mooted is that he has them by being a shared part common to many worlds, and by having different properties relative to different worlds that he is part of. Despite its lack of supporters, this answer deserves our attention. First, because it is agreeably simple. Second, because it is the only view that fully respects the 'he himself' intuition: rival views say that Humphrey himself *might* have won, and that he himself is somehow *represented* as winning, but only this view says that he himself *does* win. And third, because it is congenial to haecceitism; but I shall postpone that issue to section 4.[7]

The advantages are genuine. Nevertheless, trans-world identity, in the sense of overlap of worlds, is to be rejected. Or rather, it is to be rejected as a general theory of representation *de re*. There are one or two special cases of overlap that might be tolerated, but they fall far short of meeting all our needs for representation *de re*.

My main problem is not with the overlap itself. Things do have shared parts in common, as in the case of the Siamese twins' hand. Given the unrestricted mereology I favour, sharing of parts is altogether commonplace. Indeed, any part of any world is part of countless mereological sums that extend beyond that world. But what I do find problematic – inconsistent, not to mince words – is the way the common part of two worlds is supposed to have different properties in one world and in the other.

Hubert Humphrey has a certain size and shape, and is composed of parts arranged in a certain way. His size and shape and composition are intrinsic to him. They are simply a matter of the way he is. They are not a matter of his relations to other things that surround him in this world. Thereby they differ from his extrinsic properties, such as being popular, being Vice-President of the United States, wearing a fur hat, inhabiting a planet with a moon, or inhabiting a world where nothing goes faster than light. Also, his size and shape and composition are accidental, not essential, to him. He could have been taller, he could have been slimmer, he could have had more or fewer fingers on his hands.[8]

Consider the last. He could have had six fingers on his left hand. There is some other world that so represents him. We are supposing now that representation *de re* works by trans-world identity. So Humphrey, who is part of this world and there has five fingers on the left hand, is also part of some other world and there has six fingers on his

left hand. *Qua* part of this world he has five fingers, *qua* part of that world he has six. He himself – one and the same and altogether self-identical – has five fingers on the left hand, and he has not five but six. How can this be? You might as well say that the shared hand of the Siamese twins has five fingers as Ted's left hand, but it has six fingers as Ned's right hand! That is double-talk and contradiction. Here is the hand. Never mind what else it is part of. How many fingers does it have? What shape is it?

(You might say that five fingers and the palm are common to Ted and Ned, however the sixth finger belongs to Ned alone; and likewise with Humphrey. But no: a proper five-fingered hand differs in shape and composition from a proper six-fingered hand less one of its fingers, and likewise a proper six-fingered hand differs from a proper five-fingered hand with an extra finger stuck on.)

I expect protest: though it would be contradiction to say, simply, that Humphrey had five fingers on the left hand and also that he had not five but six, that is *not* what was said. He has five *at this world*; he has six *at that world*. – But how do the modifiers help? There are several ways for modifiers to remove a contradiction. But none of them apply here.

(1) If a tower is square on the third floor and round on the fourth floor, no worries; it's just that one segment differs in cross-sectional shape from another. The modifiers direct us to consider the shapes of the segments, not of the whole tower. But the thesis we are considering is that the *whole* of Humphrey is part of different worlds, with different properties at different ones. It is exactly the trans-world identity that spoils this way out.

(2) If a man is honest according to the *News* and crooked according to *The Times*, no worries; different papers tell different stories about him, they represent him differently, and at least one of them gets it wrong. But the thesis we are considering is a form of genuine, not ersatz, modal realism: the way that Humphrey has a property according to a world is that Humphrey himself, having that very property, is a part of that world.

(3) If a man is father of Ed and son of Fred, no worries; he bears different relations to different individuals, and the extrinsic properties he thereby has – being a father, being a son – are compatible. Likewise if the wisest man in the village is by no means the wisest man in the nation. But our problem does not concern Humphrey's relationships to the things that accompany him in one or another

world. Rather, we are dealing with his intrinsic nature; and the only relations relevant to that are those that obtain between his own parts. (And if he is part of two worlds, so in turn are his parts.) If you say that Humphrey has five fingers at this world and six fingers at that, and you take the modifiers to cure the contradiction, most likely you mean to suggest that having five or six fingers is not an intrinsic property after all, but a relation. (And an external relation − not one that supervenes on the intrinsic properties of the *relata*.) Then the right thing to say would be that Humphrey bears the five-finger relation to this world and the six-finger relation to that world. Or you might say it by coining transitive verbs: he five-fingers this world, but he six-fingers that world. But what are these relations? I know what to say if I want to make-believe formally that shapes are relations rather than intrinsic properties, but I know better. If you say that a shape − sphericity, or five-fingeredness − is just what we always thought it was, except that it is a relation which something may bear to some but not all of the wholes of which it is part, that will not do. What would it be to five-finger one thing while six-fingering another? How can these supposed relations be the shape of something?

They cannot be; and so there is no solution. If indeed Humphrey − he himself, the whole of him − is to lead a double life as part of two different worlds, there is no intelligible way for his intrinsic properties to differ from one world to the other. And it will not do just to declare, when we know better, that such things as his size and shape and composition are after all not among his intrinsic properties.

Call this *the problem of accidental intrinsics*. It would not arise for Humphrey's essential properties, however intrinsic. For the problem is how he can have different properties as part of different worlds, and in the case of essential properties there is no variation to worry about. It is very hard to see how Humphrey could be a man as part of one world and an angel as part of another; but if he is essentially human, that difficulty does not arise.

Neither would it arise for Humphrey's extrinsic properties, however accidental. There are two ways to think of his extrinsic properties: as relations in disguise, or as genuine properties.[9] First, take them as relations. He is related to his surroundings, and we are not supposing that his surroundings also are common from world to world. Perhaps he owns four dogs who are part of this world, and he owns only three dogs who are part of that other world. That is how the accidental extrinsic 'property' of owning four dogs can be a property that he has at this world, but lacks at that other world of which he is also a part. Owning four dogs is covertly a relation: Humphrey bears it to the worlds that have himself and four dogs he owns as parts, and not to any other worlds. It is as easy for him to have this 'property' at one world and not another as it is for a man to be father of Ed and not of Fred.

Second, take his extrinsic properties instead as genuine properties. Then he has them *simpliciter*, and they cannot vary from world to world. But what can vary from world to world is the way we name them, and predicate them of him − which may give an illusion that the properties themselves vary. Thus he has, *simpliciter*, the extrinsic property of owning four dogs who are part of this world; and he has, *simpliciter*, the property of not owning four dogs who are part of that world. These properties are compatible, if indeed there is overlap; having both of them is part of what it is to lead a double life in two worlds. But the restricting modifier 'at this world' or 'at that world' enables us to refer to these two extrinsic properties by shortened names. In the scope of 'at this world', we can drop the final clause from the name 'the property of owning four dogs who are part of this world', and in the scope of 'at that world', we can likewise drop the final clause from the name 'the property of not owning four dogs who are part of that world', and that is how it can be true at this world that he has the property of owning four dogs, and true at that world that he has the property of not owning four dogs, although his extrinsic properties − properties rightly speaking, as opposed to disguised relations − do not vary from world to world.

There is no problem of accidental intrinsics for rival theories. Not for my own theory, genuine modal realism with counterparts instead of overlap: counterparts need not be exact intrinsic duplicates, so, of course, Humphrey and his counterparts can differ in their intrinsic properties. Not for the theory that Humphrey is a vast trans-world individual, composed of distinct parts from different worlds: one part of the vast Humphrey can differ in its intrinsic properties from other parts. Not for any sort of ersatzism: in whatever way it is that ersatz worlds represent or misrepresent Humphrey, they can misrepresent him as having intrinsic properties that in fact he does not have, just as lying newspapers can do.

David Lewis

Our question of overlap of worlds parallels the this-worldly problem of identity through time; and our problem of accidental intrinsics parallels a problem of temporary intrinsics, which is the traditional problem of change.[10] Let us say that something *persists* iff, somehow or other, it exists at various times; this is the neutral word. Something *perdures* iff it persists by having different temporal parts, or stages, at different times, though no one part of it is wholly present at more than one time; whereas it *endures* iff it persists by being wholly present at more than one time. Perdurance corresponds to the way a road persists through space; part of it is here and part of it is there, and no part is wholly present at two different places. Endurance corresponds to the way a universal, if there are such things, would be wholly present wherever and whenever it is instantiated. Endurance involves overlap: the content of two different times has the enduring thing as a common part. Perdurance does not.

(There might be mixed cases: entities that persist by having an enduring part and a perduring part. An example might be a person who consisted of an enduring entelechy ruling a perduring body; or an electron that had a universal of unit negative charge as a permanent part, but did not consist entirely of universals. But here I ignore the mixed cases. And when I speak of ordinary things as perduring, I shall ignore their enduring universals, if such there be.)

Discussions of endurance versus perdurance tend to be endarkened by people who say such things as this: 'Of course you are wholly present at every moment of your life, except in case of amputation. For at every moment all your parts are there: your legs, your lips, your liver....' These endarkeners may think themselves partisans of endurance, but they are not. They are perforce neutral, because they lack the conceptual resources to understand what is at issue. Their speech betrays – and they may acknowledge it willingly – that they have no concept of a temporal part. (Or at any rate none that applies to a person, say, as opposed to a process or a stretch of time.) Therefore they are on neither side of a dispute about whether or not persisting things are divisible into temporal parts. They understand neither the affirmation nor the denial. They are like the people – fictional, I hope – who say that the whole of the long road is in their little village, for not one single lane of it is missing. Meaning less than others do by 'part', since they omit parts cut crosswise, they also mean less than

others do by 'whole'. They say the 'whole' road is in the village; by which they mean that every 'part' is; but by that, they only mean that every part cut lengthwise is. Divide the road into its least lengthwise parts; they cannot even raise the question whether those are in the village wholly or only partly. For that is a question about crosswise parts, and the concept of a crosswise part is what they lack. Perhaps 'crosswise part' really does sound to them like a blatant contradiction. Or perhaps it seems to them that they understand it, but the village philosophers have persuaded them that really they couldn't, so their impression to the contrary must be an illusion. At any rate, *I* have the concept of a temporal part; and for some while I shall be addressing only those of you who share it.[11]

Endurance through time is analogous to the alleged trans-world identity of common parts of overlapping worlds; perdurance through time is analogous to the 'trans-world identity', if we may call it that, of a trans-world individual composed of distinct parts in non-overlapping worlds. Perdurance, which I favour for the temporal case, is closer to the counterpart theory which I favour for the modal case; the difference is that counterpart theory concentrates on the parts and ignores the trans-world individual composed of them.

The principal and decisive objection against endurance, as an account of the persistence of ordinary things such as people or puddles, is the problem of temporary intrinsics. Persisting things change their intrinsic properties. For instance, shape: when I sit, I have a bent shape; when I stand, I have a straightened shape. Both shapes are temporary intrinsic properties; I have them only some of the time. How is such change possible? I know of only three solutions.

(It is *not* a solution just to say how very commonplace and indubitable it is that we have different shapes at different times. To say that is only to insist – rightly – that it must be possible somehow. Still less is it a solution to say it in jargon – as it might be, that bent-on-Monday and straight-on-Tuesday are compatible because they are 'time-indexed properties'–if that just means that, somehow, you can be bent on Monday and straight on Tuesday.)

First solution: contrary to what we might think, shapes are not genuine intrinsic properties. They are disguised relations, which an enduring thing may bear to times. One and the same enduring thing may bear the bent-shape relation to some times, and the straight-shape relation to others. In itself, considered apart from its relations to other things, it has no shape at all. And likewise for all other seeming temporary intrinsics; all of them must be reinterpreted as relations that something with an absolutely unchanging intrinsic nature bears to different times. The solution to the problem of temporary intrinsics is that there aren't any temporary intrinsics. This is simply incredible, if we are speaking of the persistence of ordinary things. (It might do for the endurance of entelechies or universals.) If we know what shape is, we know that it is a property, not a relation.

Second solution: the only intrinsic properties of a thing are those it has at the present moment. Other times are like false stories; they are abstract representations, composed out of the materials of the present, which represent or misrepresent the way things are. When something has different intrinsic properties according to one of these ersatz other times, that does not mean that it, or any part of it, or anything else, just *has* them – no more so than when a man is crooked according to *The Times*, or honest according to the *News*. This is a solution that rejects endurance, because it rejects persistence altogether. And it is even less credible than the first solution. In saying that there are no other times, as opposed to false representations thereof, it goes against what we all believe. No man, unless it be at the moment of his execution, believes that he has no future; still less does anyone believe that he has no past.

Third solution: the different shapes, and the different temporary intrinsics generally, belong to different things. Endurance is to be rejected in favour of perdurance. We perdure; we are made up of temporal parts, and our temporary intrinsics are properties of these parts, wherein they differ one from another. There is no problem at all about how different things can differ in their intrinsic properties.

Some special cases of overlap of worlds face no problem of accidental intrinsics. One arises on the hypothesis that there are universals, wholly present recurrently as non-spatio-temporal parts of all their particular instances. If so, these universals must recur as freely between the worlds as they do within a world. For there is qualitative duplication between the worlds, by the principle of recombination; and universals are supposed to recur whenever there is duplication. Doubtless there are electrons in other worlds than ours. If a universal

of unit negative charge is part of each and every this-worldly electron, then equally it is part of the other-worldly electrons; in which case, since parthood is transitive, it is a common part of all the worlds where there are electrons; and that is overlap. We expect trouble with the accidental intrinsic properties of the common part. But what are those properties in this case? I cannot think of any. There isn't much to the intrinsic nature of a universal. Maybe it's intrinsically simple, or maybe it's intrinsically composed, somehow, of other universals; but if so, that seems to be an essential matter, so we still have no intrinsic accidents to trouble us. (Likewise there seem to be no temporary intrinsics to trouble us, so there is no problem about universals enduring through time.) If indeed there are no accidental intrinsics to raise a problem, then overlap confined to the sharing of universals seems entirely innocent. And also it seems inevitable, if there are universals at all. So my rejection of overlap must be qualified: whatever the universals may do, at any rate no two worlds have any particular as a common part.

If there are universals, identical between worlds as they are between instances within a world, then for them we may as well help ourselves to the simplest method of representation *de re*: what is true of a universal according to a world is what is true of *it*, when we restrict quantifiers to that world. What is true of it at a world will then be, first, that it has its constant essential intrinsic nature; and, second, that it has various relationships – notably, patterns of instantiation – to other things of that world. For instance, it will be true of unit negative charge, at one world, that it is instantiated by exactly seventeen things, which are close together; and at another world, that it is instantiated by infinitely many widely scattered things. Thus its extrinsic 'properties', taken as disguised relations, vary. Its extrinsic properties, properly speaking, do not. But the way we name them does, so that for instance we can say that at one world but not the other, the universal has the property of being instantiated by seventeen close-together things.[12]

Another special case of overlap would be, if not altogether innocent, at least safe from the problem of accidental intrinsics. This is simply the case in which something does have accidental intrinsic properties, but they are constant within a limited range of worlds, and the proposed overlap is confined to the worlds in that limited range. Such limited overlap could not give us all we

David Lewis

need by way of representation *de re*. For the thing does have some accidental intrinsic properties; so there must be some world which represents it as lacking some of these properties; that must be a world outside the limited range of overlap; so when that world represents the thing as lacking the properties, that representation *de re* must work not by trans-world identity but in some other way. Limited overlap would have to be combined with some other treatment of representation *de re*, presumably some form of counterpart theory.

Even so, limited overlap might be wanted. The most likely case would be limited overlap when branching worlds share a common initial segment. I distinguish *branching* of worlds from *divergence*. In branching, worlds are like Siamese twins. There is one initial spatio-temporal segment; it is continued by two different futures – different both numerically and qualitatively – and so there are two overlapping worlds. One world consists of the initial segment plus one of its futures; the other world consists of the identical initial segment plus the other future.

In divergence, on the other hand, there is no overlap. Two worlds have two duplicate initial segments, not one that they share in common. I, and the world I am part of, have only one future. There are other worlds that diverge from ours. These worlds have initial segments exactly like that of our world up to the present, but the later parts of these worlds differ from the later parts of ours. (Or we could make it relativistic: what is duplicated is the past cone from some space-time point, as it might be from here and now.) Not I, but only some very good counterparts of me, inhabit these other worlds.

I reject genuine branching in favour of divergence. However, there might be some reason to go the other way. Consider the philosophers who say that the future is unreal. It is hard to believe they mean it. If ever anyone is right that there is no future, then that very moment is his last, and what's more is the end of everything. Yet when these philosophers teach that there is no more time to come, they show no trace of terror or despair! When we see them planning and anticipating, we might suspect that they believe in the future as much as anyone else does. Maybe they only insist on restricting their quantifiers, and all they mean is that nothing future is present? – No, for they seem to think that what they are saying is controversial. What is going on?

Perhaps their meaning is clearer when they turn linguistic, and say that there is no determinate truth about the future. A modal realist who believed in genuine branching, in which his world overlaps with others by having initial segments in common, could agree with that. To have determinate truth about the future, it helps to have a future; but also, it helps to have only one future. If there are two futures, and both are equally mine with nothing to choose between them, and one holds a sea fight and the other doesn't, what could it mean for me to say that *the* future holds a sea fight? Not a rhetorical question: we have three options. (1) It is false that the future holds a sea fight, because 'the future' is a denotationless improper description. (2) It is true that the future holds a sea fight, because 'the future' denotes neither of the two partial futures but rather their disunited sum, which does hold a sea fight. (3) It is neither true nor false that the future holds a sea fight, because 'the future' has indeterminate denotation, and we get different truth-values on different resolutions of the indeterminacy. Offhand, the third option – indeterminacy – seems best. (At least it lets us talk in the ordinary way about matters on which the futures do not differ; what has the same truth-value on all resolutions is determinately true or false.) But whichever way we go, our customary thought about 'the' future is in bad trouble. Against the common-sense idea that we have one single future, advocates of many may join forces with advocates of none; but the advocates of many have the better of it, for they have no cause to despair. I do not suggest that philosophers of the unreal or indeterminate future are, in fact, modal realists who accept branching. But modal realists can make good sense of much that they say. So whatever motivates these philosophers to deny that we have a single future might equally motivate a modal realist to accept branching.

Why not, given that the overlap is limited enough not to raise the problem of accidental intrinsics? Well, one man's reason is another man's *reductio*. The trouble with branching exactly is that it conflicts with our ordinary presupposition that we have a single future. If two futures are equally mine, one with a sea fight tomorrow and one without, it is nonsense to wonder which way it will be – it will be both ways – and yet I do wonder. The theory of branching suits those who think this wondering *is* nonsense. Or those who think the wondering makes sense only if reconstrued: you have leave to wonder about the sea fight, pro-

vided that really you wonder not about what tomorrow will bring but about what today predetermines. But a modal realist who thinks in the ordinary way that it makes sense to wonder what *the* future will bring, and who distinguishes this from wondering what is already predetermined, will reject branching in favour of divergence. In divergence also there are many futures; that is, there are many later segments of worlds that begin by duplicating initial segments of our world. But in divergence, only one of these futures is truly ours. The rest belong not to us but to our other-worldly counterparts. Our future is the one that is part of the same world as ourselves. It alone is connected to us by the relations – the (strictly or analogically) spatio-temporal relations, or perhaps natural external relations generally – that unify a world. It alone is influenced causally by what we do and how we are in the present. We wonder which one is the future that has the special relation to ourselves. We care about it in a way that we do not care about all the other-worldly futures. Branching, and the limited overlap it requires, are to be rejected as making nonsense of the way we take ourselves to be related to our futures; and divergence without overlap is to be preferred.[13]

There is a less weighty argument against branching, and indeed against overlap generally. What unifies a world, I suggested, is that its parts stand in suitable external relations, preferably spatio-temporal. But if we have overlap, we have spatio-temporal relations between the parts of different worlds. For instance, let P be the common part – say, a shared initial segment – of two different worlds W_1 and W_2, let R_1 be the remainder of W_1 and let R_2 be the remainder of W_2. Then the appropriate unifying relations obtain between P and R_1, and also between P and R_2. But now the relations obtain between parts of two different worlds: between P, which is *inter alia* a part of the world W_1 and R_2, which is part of the different world W_2.

Of course, it is also true that P and R_2 are parts of a single world W_2. So at least we can still say that whenever two things are appropriately related, there is some world they are both parts of, even if they may be parts of other worlds besides. Or can we say even that? In a sense, even R_1 and R_2 are related, in a stepwise back-and-forward way, via P. For instance, R_1 and R_2 might stand to one another in the complex temporal relation: successor-of-a-predecessor-of. Yet R_1 and R_2 are not both parts of any one world. Thus overlap complicates what we

must say in explaining how worlds are unified by spatio-temporal interrelation, and thereby differ from trans-world individuals composed of parts of several worlds. The complication is unwelcome, but I think it's nothing worse. Overlap spoils the easiest account of how worlds are unified by interrelation: namely, the mereological analogue of the definition of equivalence classes. But alternative accounts are available (as in the parallel problem about time discussed in my 'Survival and identity')[14], so I presume that a modal realist who wished to accept overlap would not be in serious difficulty on this score. Still less is there any problem if the only overlap we accept is the sharing of universals; we need only say that a world is unified by the spatio-temporal (or whatever) interrelation of its *particular* parts.

If we stay with the simple account of how worlds are unified, we will conclude that where there is branching, there is one single world composed of all the branches. That would not be branching *of* worlds, but branching *within* worlds; and so the overlap of branches would not be overlap of worlds. Branching within worlds, I think, is to be accepted: it is possible that the space-time of a world might have such a shape, and if that is a possible way for a world to be, then it is a way that some world is. Some world; but there is no reason to think that such a world is ours. Respect for common sense gives us reason to reject any theory that says that we ourselves are involved in branching, or that if we are not, that can only be because (contrary to accepted theory) our world is governed by deterministic laws. But we needn't reject the very possibility that a world branches. The unfortunate inhabitants of such a world, if they think of 'the future' as we do, are of course sorely deceived, and their peculiar circumstances do make nonsense of how they ordinarily think. But that is their problem; not ours, as it would be if the worlds generally branched rather than diverging.

I noted that our special cases of trans-world identity, sharing of universals and sharing of initial segments in branching, avoid the problem of accidental intrinsics. They avoid another well-known problem as well. A friend of overlap might wish to say that trans-world identity follows lines of qualitative similarity. Or he might not; whether to say this is part of the topic of haecceitism, to be considered in section 4.[15] But if he does, his problem is that identity is transitive, similarity in general is not. But it is *approximate* similarity that fails to be transitive; whereas the supposed sharing of universals, and likewise the supposed sharing of initial segments in branching, would follow lines of *exact* similarity. When we have the exact similarity in a respect between two instances of unit negative charge, or the perfect match when two worlds start out exactly alike in their history, there is no discrepancy of formal character to stop us from taking these as cases of trans-world identity.

3 Against Trans-World Individuals

The Hume Highway runs between the capital cities of two adjacent states. Thus it is present in one state and in the other. Call this a case of 'interstate identity' if you like: a highway that runs through one state is identical with a highway that runs through the other; there is one highway that runs through them both. But the states do not overlap thereby; they share no (particular) part in common. The highway consists of parts, one part in one state and another in the other. It is partly in each state. The parts are not identical; they don't even overlap. But the highway which includes the one part is identical with the highway which includes the other. More simply: there is a highway they are both parts of.

Likewise Hume (no relation) runs between 1711 and 1776. He is present in the early half of the century and in the later half. Call this a case of 'identity over time' if you like: a man who runs through the early years is identical with a man who runs through the later years, there is one man who lives both early and late. But the times do not overlap thereby; they share no (particular) part in common. Hume consists of parts, different parts in different times. He is partly in each of the times during his life. The parts of him are not identical; they don't even overlap. But the man which includes one part is identical with the man which includes the other. More simply: there is a man they are both parts of.

Or so say I. (And he.) Of course, this account of Hume's perdurance through time is controversial; many would favour the view that he endures, wholly present at every time of his life, so that those times do overlap by having him as a shared part. That would be 'identity over time' in a truer sense. Such endurance may appeal to intuition, but – so I argued in the previous section – it creates a disastrous problem about Hume's temporary intrinsic properties. The enduring Hume, multiply located in time, turns out to be intrinsically shape-

less; he bent-shapes one time, he straight-shapes another, but these relations are no part of the way he is, considered in himself. I call that a *reductio*. Likewise 'trans-world identity' in the truest sense – overlap of worlds – creates a disastrous problem about the accidental intrinsic properties of the alleged common parts. But when we therefore reject overlap of worlds, we need not reject trans-world identity in the lesser sense which corresponds to the interstate identity of the Hume Highway or to (what I take to be) the identity over time of Hume.

I shall argue that indeed there are things that enjoy trans-world identity in this sense. But then I shall argue that we ourselves, and other things that we ordinarily name, or classify under predicates, or quantify over, are not among them. So I oppose trans-world individuals not by denying their existence – not when I quantify without restriction – but rather by denying that they deserve our attention.

I do not deny the existence of trans-world individuals, and yet there is a sense in which I say that they cannot possibly exist. As should be expected, the sense in question involves restricted quantification. It is possible for something to exist iff it is possible for the whole of it to exist. That is, iff there is a world at which the whole of it exists. That is, iff there is a world such that, quantifying only over parts of that world, the whole of it exists. That is, iff the whole of it is among the parts of some world. That is, iff it is part of some world – and hence not a trans-world individual. Parts of worlds are *possible* individuals; trans-world individuals are therefore *impossible* individuals.

To call the trans-world individuals 'impossible' in this sense is not an argument for ignoring them – that comes later. It is only a terminological stipulation. If we thought they should not be ignored, perhaps because we thought that we ourselves were trans-world individuals, it would be appropriate and easy to give 'possible individual' a more inclusive sense. We could say that an individual exists at a world iff, quantifying only over parts of that world, *some part* of that individual exists – that way, the trans-world individuals would count as possible.[16]

I claim that mereological composition is unrestricted: any old class of things has a mereological sum. Whenever there are some things, no matter how disparate and unrelated, there is something composed of just those things. Even a class of things out of different worlds has a mereological sum. That sum is a trans-world individual. It overlaps each world that contributes a part of it, and so is partly in each of many worlds.

We are happy enough with mereological sums of things that contrast with their surroundings more than they do with one another; and that are adjacent, stick together, and act jointly. We are more reluctant to affirm the existence of mereological sums of things that are disparate and scattered and go their separate ways. A typical problem case is a fleet: the ships contrast with their surroundings more than with one another, they act jointly, but they are not adjacent, nor do they stick together. A class of things from different worlds might do well on the first *desideratum*, but it will fail miserably on the other three. Far from being adjacent, these things will not be spatio-temporally related in any way; they can exert no cohesive forces whatever on one another, nor can they have any joint effects. So if composition could be restricted in accordance with our intuitions about this-worldly cases, then doubtless trans-world composition would fall under the ban.

But composition cannot be restricted in accordance with our intuitions about this-worldly cases, as I shall shortly argue. Therefore a ban on trans-world composition, though unproblematic in itself, would be unmotivated and gratuitous. The simple principle of absolutely unrestricted composition should be accepted as true.[17]

The trouble with restricted composition is as follows. It is a vague matter whether a given class satisfies our intuitive *desiderata* for composition. Each *desideratum* taken by itself is vague, and we get still more vagueness by trading them off against each other. To restrict composition in accordance with our intuitions would require a vague restriction. It's not on to say that somewhere we get just enough contrast with the surroundings, just enough cohesion, . . . to cross a threshold and permit composition to take place, though if the candidate class had been just a little worse it would have remained sumless. But if composition obeys a vague restriction, then it must sometimes be a vague matter whether composition takes place or not. And that is impossible.

The only intelligible account of vagueness locates it in our thought and language. The reason it's vague where the outback begins is not that there's this thing, the outback, with imprecise borders; rather there are many things, with different borders, and nobody has been fool enough to try to

enforce a choice of one of them as the official referent of the word 'outback'[18] Vagueness is semantic indecision. But not all of language is vague. The truth-functional connectives aren't, for instance. Nor are the words for identity and difference, and for the partial identity of overlap. Nor are the idioms of quantification, so long as they are unrestricted. How could any of these be vague? What would be the alternatives between which we haven't chosen?

The question whether composition takes place in a given case, whether a given class does or does not have a mereological sum, can be stated in a part of language where nothing is vague. Therefore it cannot have a vague answer. There is such a thing as the sum, or there isn't. It cannot be said that, because the *desiderata* for composition are satisfied to a borderline degree, there sort of is and sort of isn't. What is this thing such that it sort of is so, and sort of isn't, that there is any such thing? No restriction on composition can be vague. But unless it is vague, it cannot fit the intuitive *desiderata*. So no restriction on composition can serve the intuitions that motivate it. So restriction would be gratuitous. Composition is unrestricted, and so there are trans-world individuals.

(To be sure, a ban against trans-world composition would not itself be a vague restriction, so it would not fall victim to the argument just given. But taken by itself it would be unmotivated. To motivate it, we have to subsume it under a broader restriction. Which can't be done, because a well-motivated broader restriction *would* be vague.)

Restrict quantifiers, not composition. Vague existence, speaking unrestrictedly, is unintelligible; vague existence, speaking restrictedly, is unproblematic. Is it so, ignoring things that don't measure up to certain standards of unification of their parts, that this class has a mereological sum? Definitely yes, if the sum definitely does measure up; definitely no, if it definitely doesn't; not definitely one way or the other, if the sum, is a borderline case with respect to unification. There is a sum, unrestrictedly speaking, but it can perfectly well be a vague matter whether this sum falls within a vaguely restricted domain of quantification. Speaking restrictedly, of course we can have our intuitively motivated restrictions on composition. But not because composition ever fails to take place; rather, because we sometimes ignore some of all the things there really are.

We have no name for the mereological sum of the right half of my left shoe plus the Moon plus the sum of all Her Majesty's ear-rings, except for the long and clumsy name I just gave it; we have no predicates under which such entities fall, except for technical terms like 'physical object' (in a special sense known to some philosophers) or blanket terms like 'entity' and maybe 'thing', we seldom admit it to our domains of restricted quantification. It is very sensible to ignore such a thing in our everyday thought and language. But ignoring it won't make it go away. And really making it go away without making too much else go away as well – that is, holding a theory according to which classes have mereological sums only when we intuitively want them to – turns out not to be feasible.

If unrestricted composition is granted, I can reformulate counterpart theory in terms of trans-world individuals. This will begin as an exercise in definition-mongering, nothing more. For the time being, I shall continue to suppose that ordinary individuals – we ourselves, and other things we have ordinary names and predicates and quantified variables for – never exist at more than one world. Of course, an ordinary individual will exist *according to* other worlds, thanks to its other-worldly counterparts. Still, it is a part of one world only, and neither the whole nor any (particular) part of it is part of any other world. In short: my usual doctrines. Only the formulation will change.

(*Almost* my usual doctrines. For simplicity I shall impose one extra assumption: that the counterpart relation is symmetric. Also, I shall leave one assumption in force that I would sometimes be willing to drop: that nothing is a counterpart of anything else in its own world. I take both of these assumptions to be correct for some but not all reasonable candidate counterpart relations, so that imposing them amounts to somewhat narrowing down what the counterpart relation might be, and thus giving up a little of the built-in flexibility of counterpart theory.)

As suggested above, let us call an individual which is wholly part of one world a *possible* individual.[19] If a possible individual X is part of a trans-world individual Y, and X is not a proper part of any other possible individual that is part of Y, let us call X a *stage* of Y. The stages of a trans-world individual are its maximal possible parts; they are the intersections of it with the worlds which it overlaps. It has at most one stage per world, and it is the mereological sum of its stages. Sometimes one stage of a trans-world individual will be a counterpart of another. If all stages of a trans-

world individual Y are counterparts of one another, let us call Y *counterpart-interrelated*. If Y is counterpart-interrelated, and not a proper part of any other counterpart-interrelated trans-world individual (i.e., if Y is maximal counterpart-interrelated), then let us call Y a *-possible* individual.

Given any predicate that applies to possible individuals, we can define a corresponding starred predicate that applies to *-possible individuals relative to worlds. A *-possible individual is a *-man* at W iff it has a stage at W that is a man; it *-wins the presidency* at W iff it has a stage at W that wins the presidency; it is a *-ordinary individual* at W iff it has a stage at W that is an ordinary individual. It *-exists* at world W iff it has a stage at W that exists; likewise it *-exists in its entirety* at world W iff it has a stage at W that exists in its entirety, so – since any stage at any world does exist in its entirety – a *-possible individual *-exists in its entirety at any world where it *-exists at all. (Even though it does not exist in its entirety at any world.) It *-is not a trans-world individual* at W iff it has a stage at W that is not a trans-world individual, so every *-possible individual (although it *is* a trans-world individual) also *-is not a trans-world individual at any world. It is a *-possible individual* at W iff it has a stage at W that is a possible individual, so something is a *-possible individual *simpliciter* iff it is a *-possible individual at every world where it *-exists. Likewise for relations. One *-possible individual *-kicks* another at world W iff a stage at W of the first kicks a stage at W of the second; two *-possible individuals are *-identical* at W iff a stage at W of the first is identical to a stage at W of the second; and so on.

Two further conventions for the starred language. I shall often omit 'at W' when the world in question is ours; and I shall use starred pronouns as variables over *-possible individuals, saying, as it might be, that if one *-man *-kicks *-another, then the *-latter *-kicks *-him back.

To any name of a possible individual, there corresponds a predicate: 'Humphrey' and 'is Humphrey', or 'Socrates' and 'Socratizes'. Our schema for defining starred predicates applies as much to these predicates as to any other. A *-possible individual *-is Humphrey* at W iff it has a stage at W that is Humphrey. If 'Humphrey' names our Humphrey and not his other-worldly counterparts, this means that a *-possible individual *-is Humphrey iff Humphrey is its stage at the actual world. We could try defining names for *-possible individuals, saying for instance that *-*Humphrey* is the one that *-is Humphrey. The problem is that, since Humphrey has twin counterparts at some worlds, many different possible individuals *-are Humphrey, and so are equally candidates to bear the name '*-Humphrey'. We can say in the plural that all of them are *-Humphreys. As for the name in the singular, let us regard it as ambiguous: its different disambiguations make it name different *-Humphreys. But often its ambiguity will not matter. The *-Humphreys, though different, are all *-identical at this world. Therefore all or none of them are *-men at this world, all or none of them *-win the presidency at this world, and so on. The things we might say using the starred name in non-modal contexts will have the same truth-value on all disambiguations. Such a sentence is true, or is false, for every way of disambiguating its starred names. (For short: *every way*.) For instance it is true, every way, that *-Humphrey is a *-man. It is false, every way, that *-Humphrey *-wins.

As for modal contexts, we should note that two possible individuals are counterparts iff there is some *-possible individual of which they both are stages. (Here I use the two simplifying assumptions I imposed on the counterpart relation.) Then Humphrey has some other-worldly stage as a counterpart iff, for some way of disambiguating the starred name (for short: *some way*) that stage belongs to *-Humphrey. I would ordinarily say that Humphrey might have won iff he has some counterpart who wins; and that he is essentially a man iff all his counterparts are men. Now I can say, equivalently, that Humphrey might have won iff, some way, there is a world where *-Humphrey *-wins; and he is essentially a man iff, every way, *-Humphrey is a *-man at every world where *-he *-exists.

But 'might have won' and 'is essentially a man' are predicates that apply to possible individuals. So we can star them: a *-possible individual *-*might have won* at world W iff it has a stage at W that might have won; a *-possible individual is *-*essentially a man* at world W iff it has a stage there that is essentially a man. Now we can say that *-Humphrey *-might have won iff, some way, there is a world where *-Humphrey *-wins; and *-Humphrey is *-essentially a man iff, every way, *-Humphrey is a *-man at every world where *-he *-exists.

We have very little remaining use for the unstarred predicates and names and pronouns of ordinary things, since we can use the starred vocabulary even when talking entirely about what goes on at this world.[20] At this point somebody – as it

might be, the long-suffering compositor – might be heard to suggest a new convention for our language, at least when it is used outside the philosophy room: leave off all the stars. Do it: then here are some doctrines I take to be true.

Humphrey is a possible individual; he is an ordinary individual; he is not a trans-world individual. He exists; he exists at many worlds; he exists in his entirety at any world where he exists at all. He is a man; he is essentially a man because, every way, he is a man at every world where he exists. He lost; but he might have won because, some way, there is a world where he wins. Every way, Humphrey is identical to Humphrey. But, some way, there are some worlds where Humphrey is not identical to Humphrey.

I dare say a fan of 'trans-world identity' might like this new theory better than he liked counterpart theory. That would be a mistake. It *is* counterpart theory.[21] New terminology is not a new theory. Saying that a horse's tail is a leg does not make five-legged horses. Saying that Humphrey exists in his entirety at many worlds does not make overlap of worlds. I told you just what my words were meant to mean, and I'm their master, so you needn't hope that really they mean something else.

There's a question whether this fan of trans-world identity ought to like counterpart theory any better when he finds out how it can be restated. Probably not. Sometimes it can indeed enhance the plausibility of a theory to gain verbal agreement with what opponents want to say, even at the cost of a bit of gentle reinterpretation, but in the case at hand the reinterpretation is much too violent to buy any plausibility. Further, if what's wanted is trans-world identity, I have all along agreed to it in the uncontroversial sense: Humphrey – he himself, the whole of him – exists (in his entirety) *according to* many worlds. Many worlds represent *de re* of him that he exists. They do it by counterparts, but they do it. This is a less devious way to give the fan what he says he wants.

So far, counterpart theory reworded, first harmlessly and then deceptively. But now someone might say that I have made one mistake, as follows. When I worked my way around to the starless abbreviation of the starred language, I did *not* forge a deceptive imitation of our ordinary language. Rather, *that* was our ordinary language. I returned home and knew the place for the first time. We ourselves, and other things that we ordinarily name, or classify under predicates, or quantify over, *are* trans-world individuals unified by counterpart relations. It is quite wrong to ignore such things; we would be ignoring, *inter alia*, ourselves. If anything, it is the stages that we should ignore and leave out of our restricted quantifying.

The theory that ordinary things are trans-world individuals, unified by counterpart relations among their stages, really is a different theory from mine. But the difference is limited. There is no disagreement about what there is; there is no disagreement about the analysis of modality. Rather, there is extensive *semantic* disagreement. It is a disagreement about which of the things my opponent and I both believe in are rightly called persons, or sticks, or stones.

In his 'Worlds away', Quine portrays a form of modal realism that treats ordinary things as trans-world individuals, perduring through nonoverlapping worlds in just the way they perdure through time and space. It isn't that he advocates such a view; rather, he takes for granted that this is what modal realism would be.[22] The reason is that he takes the analogy of time and modality as his guide. In the case of time we do not think of ourselves as momentary stages, but rather as trans-time sums of stages. (I agree.) So we should say the same in the case of modality. (Why?) But it turns out that the analogy is not so very good after all; the unification of the sums is much more problematic for modality than it is for time. (Again I agree.) So much the worse for modal realism. (No – so much the worse for following the analogy wherever it may lead.)

Grant me, what is controversial, that we perdure through time by having distinct temporal stages at different times; else Quine's analogy of time and modality doesn't even begin. (Then if in addition we are trans-world individuals, there is a double summation: we are composed of stages at different worlds, which stages in turn are composed of stages at different times within the same world. And of course those are composed in turn of spatial parts.) Even so, the unification of the sums would be more problematic for modality than it is for time, in three different ways.

(1) The temporal parts of an ordinary thing that perdures through time are united as much by relations of causal dependence as by qualitative similarity. In fact, both work together: the reason the thing changes only gradually, for the most part, is

that the way it is at any time depends causally on the way it was at the time just before, and this dependence is by and large conservative. However, there can be no trans-world causation to unite counterparts. Their unification into a trans-world individual can only be by similarity.

(2) To the extent that unification by similarity does enter into perdurance through time, what matters is not so much the long-range similarity between separated stages, but rather the linkage of separated stages by many steps of short-range similarity between close stages in a one-dimensional ordering. Change is mostly gradual, but not much limited overall. There is no such one-dimensional ordering given in the modal case. So any path is as good as any other; and what's more, in logical space anything that can happen does. So linkage by a chain of short steps is too easy: it will take us more or less from anywhere to anywhere. Therefore it must be disregarded; the unification of trans-world individuals must be a matter of direct similarity between the stages. (Quine rests his objection on this point.)

(3) In the case of temporal perdurance, it is possible to get pathological cases: fission, fusion, and people who gradually turn into different people. These arise when the relation that unites the stages is intransitive, so that different perduring people overlap. Then what do we say when a stage shared between two (or more) people is present? Strictly speaking, two people are present there by way of that one stage, but the fact that there are two is extrinsic to the time in question. It seems for all the world that there is only one. We will have to say something counter-intuitive, but we get a choice of evils. We could say that there are two people; or that there is one, but really we're counting stages rather than people; or that there is one, and we're counting people, but we're not counting all the people who are present; or that there is one, and we're counting people, but we're not counting them by identity.[23] It really isn't nice to have to say any of these things – but after all, we're talking about something that doesn't really ever happen to people except in science fiction stories and philosophy examples, so is it really so very bad that peculiar cases have to get described in peculiar ways? We get by because ordinary cases are not pathological. But modality is different: pathology is everywhere. Whenever something in this world has two counterparts that are not counterparts of each other, we get two different maximal counterpart-interrelated trans-world individuals which share a

common stage at this world. That could happen because the this-worldly stage has twin counterparts at some world – and I'd like to know how *anything* could ever fail to have twin counterparts somewhere, except under some very restrictive notion about what eligible candidates for a counterpart relation there are. Or it could happen still more easily that something has two counterparts at different worlds that are not counterparts of each other. The counterpart relation is a matter of some sort of similarity, little differences add up to big differences, so of course there is intransitivity. So the modal case will always, or almost always, give us the same choice of evils about how to count that the temporal case gives us only in connection with far-fetched stories. If trans-world individuals are oddities we mostly ignore, no harm done if we have puzzles about how to count them from the standpoint of a world where they share stages. But if they are said to be ordinary things that we cannot ignore, then these puzzles are much more obnoxious.

These three considerations are general. They apply against the doctrine that we ourselves are trans-world individuals, and equally against the doctrine that sticks and stones are trans-world individuals. But in the case of ourselves, there is a fourth consideration. Consider the various desires of my various temporal stages in this world. They differ, of course; but there is plenty of common purpose to it. To some extent, stages want to fulfil the remembered desires of earlier stages: I strive for something today mainly because I wanted it yesterday.

That is what it means not to be a quitter. To a greater extent, stages want to fulfil the foreseen desires of later stages: that is prudence. It isn't quite all for one and one for all, of course – how I envy my future self who is sending this manuscript away! – but it is so to a great extent. Even if it is in the first instance the momentary stages that do the desiring, still a person perduring through time is capable of collective self-interest. Not so across worlds. My this-worldly self has *no* tendency to make the purposes of its other-worldly counterparts its own. Far from wishing good fortune to all the counterparts alike, what it wants is that it should be one of the most fortunate among them. There is no common purpose. The supposed trans-world person, no matter how well unified by counterpart relations, is not the sort of integrated self that is capable of self-interest. How could it be, in view of the absolute lack of causal connection between its parts, and the non-contingency of its total allotment of good and ill fortune? It would be strange and pointless to think of the trans-world sums in the way we are accustomed to think of ourselves. That is further reason to set the trans-world individuals aside as oddities best ignored.

The final, and simplest, reason is that a modal realism which makes ordinary things out to be trans-world individuals disagrees gratuitously with common opinion. After all, not all of us are modal realists; and those who are not (even the ersatzers) couldn't possibly think of ordinary things as having parts in many worlds. Surely it is better for modal realists if they can think of people, sticks, and stones exactly as others do.

Notes

1 Peter van Inwagen, 'Plantinga on trans-world identity' in J. Tomberlin and P. van Inwagen (eds), *Alvin Plantinga: A Profile* (Dordrecht: Reidel, 1985), p. 101.
2 See my 'Counterpart theory and quantified modal logic', *Journal of Philosophy* 65 (1968), pp. 113–26; *idem*, 'Counterparts of persons and their Bodies', *Journal of Philosophy* 68 (1971), pp. 203–11; and *idem*, *Counterfactuals* (Oxford: Blackwell, 1973), pp. 39–43; also David Kaplan, 'Transworld heir lines', in Michael Loux (ed.) *The Possible and the Actual* (Ithaca, NY: Cornell University Press, 1979).
3 Saul Kripke, *Naming and Necessity* (Cambridge, Mass.: Harvard University Press, 1980), p. 45.
4 Ibid., p. 44.
5 Here I am indebted to Fabrizio Mondadori; see his 'Counterpartese, counterpartese*, Counterpartese', *Histoire, epistemologie, langage* 5 (1983), pp. 69–94. But I disagree with him at one point. He grants that I may truly say that Humphrey himself might have won; but then he insists that if we ask 'who would have had the property of *winning*', my answer must be 'not Humphrey, but one of his counterparts' (p. 81). Not so. The modal predicate 'would have had the property of winning' is on a par with the modal predicate 'might have won'. I can apply either predicate in one sense to Humphrey, in another sense to the victorious counterpart. If there is an objection to be raised, it must be that I *can* say unwanted things, not that I *cannot* say *wanted* things. I reply that the unwanted things are not seriously objectionable in the way that the lack of the wanted things would be.

6 These sections are omitted in this volume; see David Lewis, *On the Plurality of Worlds* (Oxford: Blackwell, 1986), pp. 220–63.

7 Omitted in this volume; see ibid., pp. 220–48.

8 The next several paragraphs are mostly adapted from my 'Individuation by acquaintance and by stipulation', pp. 21–2, with the kind permission of the editors of *Philosophical Review* 92 (1983), pp. 3–32, at *Philosophical Review*.

9 See my discussion in ibid., sect. 1.5 (pp. 50–69) of 'properties' that are had relative to this or that.

10 My discussion of this parallel problem is much indebted to D. M. Armstrong, 'Identity through time', and to Mark Johnston. I follow Johnston in terminology. In, Peter van Inwagen (ed.) *Time and Cause*, (Dordrecht: Reidel, 1980).

11 I attempt to explain it to others in *Philosophical Papers* (Oxford: Oxford University Press, 1983), vol. 1, pp. 76–7. But I have no great hopes, since any competent philosopher who does not understand something will take care not to understand anything else whereby it might be explained.

12 A universal can safely be part of many worlds because it hasn't any accidental intrinsics. But mightn't the same be said of some simple particulars – tropes, if such there be, or fundamental particles, or momentary slices thereof? Maybe these things have no accidental intrinsic properties – it certainly seems hard to think of plausible candidates. If they haven't, then they too could safely be shared between overlapping worlds. We would not face a problem of accidental intrinsics. But I suggest that we would face a parallel problem of accidental external relations. Suppose we have a pair of two of these simple particulars A and B, both of which are common parts of various worlds. A and B are a certain distance apart. Their distance, it seems, is a relation of A and B and nothing else – it is not really a three-place relation of A, B, and this or that world. That means that A and B are precisely the same distance apart in all the worlds they are both part of. That means (assuming that we explain representation *de re* in terms of trans-world identity when we can) that it is impossible that A and B should both have existed and been a different distance apart. That seems wrong: it is hard to suppose that the distance is essential to the pair, equally hard to suppose that distance is not the plain two-place relation that it seems to be. So trans-world identity, even for simple particulars without accidental intrinsic properties, is prima facie trouble. An advocate of it will have some explaining to do, both as to how he gets around the problem of accidental external relations, and also as to what motivates it when it cannot provide a fully general account of representation *de re*. Such explaining may be found in Mark Johnston, 'Particulars and Persistence' (Ph.D. diss., Princeton University, 1983), ch. 4.

13 In his 'Theories of actuality', *Nous* 8 (1974), pp. 211–31, Robert M. Adams makes the same point; but while I use it in favour of modal realism without overlap, Adams uses it in favour of ersatzism.

14 In Amélie O. Rorty (ed.) *The Identities of Persons*, (Berkeley: University of California Press, 1976); repr., with added postscripts, in Lewis, *Philosophical Papers*, vol. 1.

15 Omitted in this volume; see Lewis, *Plurality*, pp. 220–48.

16 Indeed, I think that in this sense, there would be no impossible individuals. No individual is wholly distinct from all the worlds; so every individual is divisible into parts which are parts of worlds. What of an individual that stands in none of the external relations that unify worlds? – According to what I said in *Plurality*, sect. 1.6, it cannot be a worldmate of anything else; but without worldmates it can still be a world all on its own. Or, if its parts are not suitably interrelated, it can divide into several individuals each of which is a world all on its own.

17 I really do mean *absolutely* unrestricted – for instance, I see no bar to composition of sets with individuals, or particulars with universals, or casts with numbers. But here it will be enough to consider the composition of particular individuals.

18 I realize that one can construct a so-called vague object as a class of precise objects – i.e., objects *simpliciter* – and then quantify over these classes. I take that project to be part of an analysis of vagueness in language, not an alternative to it.

19 I avoid the convenient phrase 'world-bound individual' because it often seems to mean an individual that exists *according to* one world only, and I very much doubt that there are any such individuals.

20 At this point, we have something resembling various systems of quantified modal logic that quantify over individual concepts: functions from worlds to individuals. Carnap's *Meaning and Necessity* system is of this kind; but there is more of a resemblance to later systems that quantify only over certain selected individual concepts. See, for instance, Kaplan, 'Transworld heir lines'; Richmond Thomason, 'Modal logic and metaphysics', in Karel Lambert (ed.), *The Logical Way of Doing Things*, (New Haven, Conn.: Yale University Press, 1969) (the system Q3); Gibbard, this volume, ch. 9; and many papers by Hintikka from the sixties and seventies. If worlds never overlap, then there is a one-to-one correspondence between my trans-world individuals and functions from worlds to parts of themselves. So if those functions were the only individual concepts we wanted to quantify over, we might as well replace set-theoretic construction by mereology. It is sometimes hard to tell how these systems are meant to be understood – whether ordinary things are supposed to be the world-to-individual functions or the values of those functions, whether the worlds or the individuals or both are supposed to be ersatz.

21 Plus unrestricted composition, plus two slightly restrictive assumptions on the counterpart relation.

22 W. V. Quine, 'Worlds away', *Journal of Philosophy* 73 (1976), pp. 859–63, appears to be about genuine modal realism. There is no connection with the mathematical construction of ersatz worlds he had considered in 'Propositional objects', in Quine, *Ontological Relativity and other Essays* (New York: Columbia University Press, 1969), unless it be a subterranean connection by way of Pythagorean reduction and ontological relativity.

23 See my 'Survival and identity'.

14

Primitive Thisness and Primitive Identity

Robert M. Adams

Is the world – and are all possible worlds – constituted by purely qualitative facts, or does thisness hold a place beside suchness as a fundamental feature of reality? Some famous philosophers – Leibniz, Russell, and Ayer, for example – have believed in a purely qualitative constitution of things; others, such as Scotus, Kant, and Peirce, have held to primitive thisness. Recent discussions of direct, nondescriptive reference to individuals have brought renewed interest in the idea of primitive, nonqualitative thisness.

I am inclined to accept primitive thisness, but for reasons that do not depend very heavily on recent semantics. In the present essay I will try to justify my position – but even more to sort out some issues that are easily and often confused. I will begin (in section 1) by trying to elucidate some terms that will be important in the discussion. Leibniz will be discussed in section 2 as the archetypal believer in a purely qualitative universe. I will argue that his position is not inconsistent with the semantics of direct reference, and that proponents of primitive thisness must attack rather a certain doctrine of the Identity of Indiscernibles. Two types of argument against that doctrine will be analyzed and defended in sections 3 and 4.

Primitive thisness has been associated or even identified, in recent discussion, with primitive identity and non-identity of individuals in different possible worlds.[1] The association is appropriate,

but the main issue about primitive transworld identity is quite different from that about primitive thisness, as will be argued in section 5, where I will also defend the primitiveness of transworld identity. The sixth and final section of the paper will be devoted to some problems about necessary connections between qualitative properties and primitive thisnesses.

1 Thisness and Suchness

Three notions that we will use call for some elucidation at the outset. They are the notions of an *individual*, of a *thisness*, and of a purely qualitative property or (as I shall call it) a *suchness*.

By "individual" here I mean particulars such as persons, physical objects, and events. It is assumed that numbers and universals are not individuals in this sense, and that particular places and times are individuals if they have an absolute being and identity independent of their relation to particular physical objects and events.

A thisness[2] is the property of being identical with a certain particular individual – not the property that we all share, of being identical with some individual or other, but my property of being identical with me, your property of being identical with you, etc. These properties have recently been called "essences,"[3] but that is historically unfortunate; for essences have normally been understood to be constituted by qualitative properties, and we are entertaining the possibility of non-qualitative thisnesses. In defining "thisness" as I

Originally published in *Journal of Philosophy* 76 (1979), pp. 5–26. Copyright © by Journal of Philosophy, Inc. Reprinted by permission of Columbia University.

have, I do not mean to deny that universals have analogous properties – for example, the property of being identical with the quality red. But since we are concerned here principally with the question whether the identity and distinctness of individuals is purely qualitative or not, it is useful to reserve the term "thisness" for the identities of individuals.

It may be controversial to speak of a "property" of being identical with me. I want the word "property" to carry as light a metaphysical load here as possible. "Thisness" is intended to be a synonym or translation of the traditional term "haecceity" (in Latin, *haecceitas*), which so far as I know was invented by Duns Scotus. Like many medieval philosophers, Scotus regarded properties as components of the things that have them. He introduced haecceities (thisness), accordingly, as a special sort of metaphysical component of individuals.[4] I am not proposing to revive this aspect of his conception of a haecceity, because I am not committed to regarding properties as components of individuals. To deny that thisnesses are purely qualitative is not necessarily to postulate "bare particulars," substrata without qualities of their own, which would be what was left of the individual when all its qualitative properties were subtracted. Conversely, to hold that thisnesses are purely qualitative is not to imply that individuals are nothing but bundles of qualities, for qualities may not be components of individuals at all.

We could probably conduct our investigation, in somewhat different terms, without referring to thisnesses as properties; but the concept of a *suchness* is not so dispensable. Without the distinction between the qualitative and the nonqualitative, the subject of this paper does not exist. I believe the concept, and the distinction, can be made clear enough to work with, though not, I fear, clear enough to place them above suspicion.

We might try to capture the idea by saying that a property is purely qualitative – a suchness – if and only if it could be expressed, in a language sufficiently rich, without the aid of such referential devices as proper names, proper adjectives and verbs (such as "Leibnizian" and "pegasizes"), indexical expressions, and referential uses of definite descriptions. That seems substantially right, but may be suspected of circularity, on the ground that the distinction between qualitative and nonqualitative might be prior to the notions of some of those referential devices. I doubt that it really is circular, in view of the separation between semantical and metaphysical issues for which I shall argue

in section 2; but it would take us too far afield to pursue the issue of circularity here.

There is another and possibly more illuminating approach to the definition of "suchness". All the properties that are, in certain senses, general (capable of being possessed by different individuals) and nonrelational are suchnesses. More precisely, let us say that a *basic suchness* is a property that satisfies the following three conditions. (1) It is not a thisness and is not equivalent to one. (2) It is not a property of being related in one way or another to one or more particular individuals (or to their thisnesses). This is not to deny that some basic suchnesses are in a sense relational (and thus do not fall in the Aristotelian category of Quality, though they count as "purely qualitative" for present purposes). An example may help to clarify this. The property of owning the house at 1011 Rose Avenue, Ann Arbor, Michigan, is not a basic suchness, although several different individuals have had it, because it involves the thisness of that particular house. But the property of being a home-owner is a basic suchness, although relational, because having it does not depend on which particular home one owns. (3) A basic suchness is not a property of being identical with or related in one way or another to an extensionally defined set that has an individual among its members, or among its members' members, or among its members' members' members, etc. Thus, if being an American is to be analyzed as a relation to a set of actual people and places, it is not a basic suchness.

These three conditions may be taken as jointly sufficient for being a suchness, but it is not clear that they are also necessary for being a suchness. For it seems intuitively that any property that is constructed by certain operations out of purely qualitative properties must itself be purely qualitative. The operations I have in mind for the construction are of two sorts. (1) They may be logical, such as those expressed by "not", "or", and $\lceil (\exists x)\phi(\,,x)\rceil$, where the property ascribed to x by $\lceil (\exists y)\phi(y,x)\rceil$ is a basic suchness or constructed by allowed operations out of basic suchnesses. Or (2) they may be epistemic, such as those expressed by $\lceil$ believes that $p\rceil$ and $\lceil$ wishes that $p\rceil$, where p is a proposition constructed, by allowed operations, solely out of basic suchnesses. So if your thisness, or a property equivalent to the property of being (identical with) you, could be constructed in these ways as a complex of basic suchnesses, it would seem intuitively to be a suchness, although (by definition) it is not a *basic* suchness. Indeed, as we shall see, this is precisely the way in which Leibniz attempts to account for individuality in a purely qualitative universe.

So as not to beg the question against him, let us define a *suchness* as a property that is either a basic suchness or constructed out of basic suchnesses in such a way as I have indicated. This recursive definition of "suchness" seems to me to capture the notion I want to discuss; but it depends on notions of property construction and of being a relation to a particular individual which may themselves be somewhat unclear or otherwise debatable. In any event, I am prepared to accept the notion of a suchness, and related notions of qualitativeness of facts, similarities, differences, etc., as primitive if they cannot be satisfactorily defined. Some philosophers may entirely reject this distinction between the qualitative and the nonqualitative, or may doubt that there are any properties that really ought to count as suchnesses under it. We shall not be concerned here with these doubts, but rather with what can be said, within the framework of the distinction, against those philosophers who think that all properties are suchnesses and all facts purely qualitative.

2 The Leibnizian Position

Leibniz held, as I have suggested, that the thisness of each particular individual *is* a suchness. "Singulars," he said, "are in fact *infimae species*," the lowest or final species, the most specific members of the system of kinds. In this, as he sometimes remarked, he was extending to all individuals the doctrine of Thomas Aquinas about angels, that each one constitutes a separate species.[5]

The idea behind this claim is fairly simple, though the structure it postulates for thisnesses is infinitely complex. According to Leibniz, the terms of all propositions, at least as they are apprehended by the omniscience of God, are analyzable into simple, purely qualitative concepts. The construction of complex concepts out of simple ones is by logical operations; Leibniz thinks principally of conjunction and negation. The concept of an individual, which as we may put it expresses the property of being that individual, differs from more general concepts in being *complete*.[6] What makes a thing an individual, in other words, is that, in the logical construction of its concept, differentia is added to differentia until a concept is reached so

specific that no new content can consistently be added to it.

Leibniz expresses this notion of completeness by saying that the concept of an individual implies every predicate of the individual. He inferred, notoriously, that alternative careers cannot be possible for the same individual. If a man never marries, for example, the concept of him must contain the predicate of never marrying, and so it would have been contradictory for *him* to have married.[7] I see no need to incorporate this implausible thesis in the theory of purely qualitative thisnesses. For if God can form complete concepts in the way that Leibniz supposes, he can also form the concept of a being that satisfies *either* one *or* another *or* another ... of them.[8] If individuals are defined by disjunctive concepts of the latter sort, there are alternative careers, in different possible worlds, that they could have had. And if Leibnizian complete concepts are purely qualitative, so are disjunctions of them. The completeness of individual concepts, at least in the form actually maintained by Leibniz, is therefore not to be regarded as an integral part of the "Leibnizian position" under discussion here.

If we want an up-to-date argument for primitive, *non*qualitative thisnesses, we may be tempted to seek it in the semantics of direct reference. Several philosophers have made a persuasive case for the view that we often succeed in referring to a particular individual without knowing any clearly qualitative property, or even any disjunction of such properties, that a thing must possess in order to be that individual. Such direct reference is commonly effected by the use of proper names and indexical expressions, and sometimes by what has been called the "referential" use of descriptions.[9] If these claims are correct (as I believe they are), doesn't it follow that thisnesses are primitive and nonqualitative?

Yes and no. It follows that thisnesses are *semantically* primitive – that is, that we can express them (and know that we express them) without understanding each thisness (the property of being this or that individual) in terms of some other property or properties, better known to us, into which it can be analyzed or with which it is equivalent. But it does not follow that thisnesses *are* not analyzable into, equivalent with, or even identical with, purely qualitative properties or suchnesses, as claimed by Leibniz. Thus it does not follow that we are entitled to say that thisnesses are *metaphysically* primitive in the sense that interests us here, or (more precisely) that they are non-qualitative.

For Leibniz could certainly accept direct reference without giving up his conception of thisnesses as qualitative properties. All he must say is that we can refer to individuals, and thus express their thisnesses, without understanding the analyses that show the thisnesses to be qualitative. And that he believed in any case. On his view the complete, definitive concept of an individual is infinitely complex and, therefore, cannot be distinctly apprehended by any finite mind, but only by God. Hence *we* must refer to the concept of the individual by reference to the individual (as "the individual notion or haecceity of Alexander,"[10] for example), rather than referring to the individual as the one who satisfies the concept.

We may rely intuitively on direct reference in arguing for nonqualitative thisnesses, but the issue of direct reference is not the center of our metaphysical inquiry. The purely qualitative conception of individuality stands or falls, rather, with a certain doctrine of the Identity of Indiscernibles.

The Identity of Indiscernibles might be defined, in versions of increasing strength, as the doctrine that no two distinct individuals can share (1) all their properties, or (2) all their suchnesses, or (3) all their nonrelational suchnesses. Leibniz takes no pains to distinguish these three doctrines, because he holds all of them; but it is only the second that concerns us here. The first is utterly trivial. If thisnesses are properties, of course two distinct individuals, Castor and Pollux, cannot have all their properties in common. For Castor must have the properties of being identical with Castor and not being identical with Pollux, which Pollux cannot share.[11] The third doctrine, rejecting the possibility of individuals differing in relational suchnesses alone, is a most interesting thesis, but much more than needs to be claimed in holding that reality must be purely qualitative. Let us therefore here reserve the title "Identity of Indiscernibles" for the doctrine that any two distinct individuals must differ in some suchness, *either* relational *or* nonrelational.

I say, the doctrine that they *must* so differ. Leibniz commonly states this principle, and the stronger principle about relations, in the language of necessity. And well he might; for he derives them from his theory of the nature of an individual substance, and ultimately from his conception of the nature of truth, which he surely regarded as absolutely necessary.[12] He was not perfectly consistent about this. He seemed to admit to Clarke that there could have been two perfectly indiscernible things. But, as Clarke remarked, some of Leibniz's arguments require the claim of necessity.[13] And it is only if necessity is claimed, that philosophically interesting objections can be raised to the Identity of Indiscernibles. For surely we have no reason to believe that there actually are distinct individuals that share all their qualitative properties, relational as well as nonrelational.

Here we are concerned with the necessary connection between the Identity of Indiscernibles, in the sense I have picked out, and Leibniz's conception of thisnesses as suchnesses. If individuals are *infimae species*, then "the principle of individuation is always some specific difference";[14] individuals must be distinguished by their suchnesses. Conversely, the clearest way of proving the distinctness of two properties is usually to find a possible case in which one would be exemplified without the other. In order to establish the distinctness of thisnesses from all suchnesses, therefore, one might try to exhibit possible cases in which two things would possess all the same suchnesses, but with different thisnesses. That is, one might seek counterexamples to refute the Identity of Indiscernibles.

Indeed a refutation of that doctrine is precisely what is required for the defense of nonqualitative thisnesses. For suppose the Identity of Indiscernibles is true. And suppose further, as Leibniz did and as believers in the doctrine may be expected to suppose, that it is true of possible worlds as well as of individuals, so that no two possible worlds are exactly alike in all qualitative respects. Then for each possible individual there will be a suchness of the disjunctive form:

having suchnesses S_{i1} in a world that has suchnesses $S_{\omega1}$, *or*
having suchnesses S_{i2} in a world that has suchnesses $S_{\omega2}$, *or* ...

which that individual will possess in every world in which it occurs, and which no other individual will possess in any possible world.[15] This suchness will, therefore, be necessarily equivalent to the property of being that individual, and, since there will be such a suchness for every individual, it follows that every individual's thisness will be equivalent to a suchness.

Perhaps it does not follow immediately that every possible individual's thisness will *be* a suchness. If being an even prime and being the successor of 1 may be distinct though necessarily equivalent properties, some thisness and some suchness might also be distinct though necessarily equivalent. But if *every* thisness must be necessarily equivalent to a suchness, it will be hard to show that thisnesses distinct from suchnesses cannot be dispensed with, or that possible worlds cannot all be constituted purely qualitatively.

On the other hand, if it is possible for there to be distinct but qualitatively indiscernible individuals, it is possible for there to be individuals whose thisnesses are both distinct from all suchnesses and necessarily equivalent to no suchness. And in that case there is some point to distinguishing the thisnesses of individuals systematically from their suchnesses. For it is plausible to suppose that the structure of individuality is sufficiently similar in all cases that, if in some possible cases thisnesses would be distinct from all suchnesses, then thisnesses are universally distinct from suchnesses – even if some thisnesses (including, for all we know, those of all actual individuals) are necessarily equivalent to some suchnesses.

3   The Dispersal Arguments against the Identity of Indiscernibles

The standard argument against the Identity of Indiscernibles, going back at least to Kant,[16] is from spatial dispersal. Max Black's version[17] is fairly well known. We are to imagine a universe consisting solely of two large, solid globes of iron. They always have been, are, and always will be exactly similar in shape (perfectly spherical), size, chemical composition, color – in short, in every qualitative respect. They even share all their relational suchnesses; for example, each of them has the property of being two diameters from another iron globe similar to itself. Such a universe seems to be logically possible; hence it is concluded that there could be two qualitatively indiscernible things and that the Identity of Indiscernibles is false.

Similar arguments may be devised using much more complicated imaginary universes, which may have language-users in them. Such universes may be perfectly symmetrical about a central point, line, or plane, throughout their history. Or they may always repeat themselves to infinity in every direction, like a monstrous three-dimensional wallpaper pattern.

The reason that is assumed to show that the indiscernibles in these imaginary universes are not identical is not that they have different properties, but that they are spatially dispersed, spatially distant from one another. The axiom about identity that is used here is not that the same thing cannot both have and lack the same property, but that the same thing cannot be in two places at once – that is, cannot be spatially distant from itself.[18]

An argument for the possibility of non-identical indiscernibles, very similar to the argument from spatial dispersal, and as good, can also be given from *temporal* dispersal. For it seems that there could be a perfectly cyclical universe in which each event was preceded and followed by infinitely many other events qualitatively indiscernible from itself. Thus there would be distinct but indiscernible *events*, separated by temporal rather than spatial distances. And depending on our criteria of transtemporal identity, it might also be argued that there would be indiscernible persons and physical objects, similarly separated by temporal distances.

In a recent interesting article Ian Hacking argues that "it is vain to contemplate possible spatiotemporal worlds to refute or establish the identity of indiscernibles."[19] He holds that

> Whatever God might create, we are clever enough to describe it in such a way that the identity of indiscernibles is preserved. This is a fact not about God but about description, space, time, and the laws that we ascribe to nature.[20]

The dichotomy between what God might create and our descriptions is important here. Hacking allows that there are consistent descriptions of non-identical indiscernibles and that there are possible states of affairs in which those descriptions would not exactly be false. On the other hand, he thinks that those same possible states of affairs could just as truly (not more truly, but just as truly) be described as containing only one thing in place of each of the sets of indiscernibles. The two descriptions are very different, but there is no difference at all in the possible reality that they represent. Thus Hacking is not exactly asserting the Identity of Indiscernibles. But his rejection of primitive, nonqualitative thisness runs at least as deep as Leibniz's. He thinks that there cannot be any objective fact of the matter about how many individuals are present in the cases that seem to be counterexamples to the Identity of Indiscernibles. And on his view the constitution of reality, of what

"God might create," as distinct from our descriptions of it, is purely qualitative.

Hacking's criticisms are directed against both the spatial- and the temporal-dispersal arguments for the possibility of non-identical indiscernibles. The most telling point he makes against them is that they overlook the possibility of alternative geometries and chronometries. If we have a space or time that is curved, then an individual can be spatially or temporally distant from itself, and distance does not prove distinctness. Hacking makes this point most explicitly about time,[21] but he could also use it to criticize the spatial argument, as follows: "The most that God could create of the world imagined by Black is a globe of iron, having internal qualities Q, which can be reached by traveling two diameters in a straight line from a globe of iron having qualities Q. This possible reality can be described as two globes in Euclidean space, or as a single globe in a non-Euclidean space so tightly curved that the globe can be reached by traveling two diameters in a straight line from itself. But the difference between these descriptions represents no difference in the way things could really be."

There are at least two possible replies to Hacking. (1) He acknowledges that if "absolute space-time" is accepted, the spatial and temporal dispersal arguments are quite successful in refuting the Identity of Indiscernibles. But to hold, as he seems to,[22] that no weaker assumption would vindicate the arguments is to demand more than is needed. The dispersal arguments hold up very well even if places and times are defined in terms of relations of objects, provided that certain spatiotemporal relational properties of objects are accepted as primitive. For example, if it is a primitive feature of a possible reality that an iron globe such as Black describes can be reached by traveling some distance in one direction on a *Euclidean* straight line from an exactly similar globe, then non-identical indiscernibles are possible in reality and not just in description.

In order to reply to Hacking in this way, one must assume that a difference in geometries makes, in its own right, a difference in possible worlds, so the same paths in the same universe could not be described, without error, both as Euclidean straight paths and as non-Euclidean straight paths. One must assume that facts about what geometry the universe has are not reducible to facts about what laws of nature best explain other, more primitive facts about objects in space; in particular, one must assume that what geometry the universe has does not depend on a determination of the number of objects in space. Some philosophers may accept these assumptions, and I do not have any better than intuitive grounds for rejecting them. Like Hacking, nonetheless, I am inclined to reject them.

(2) The most obvious and fundamental difference between Black's imaginary Euclidean (or gently Riemannian) two-globe universe and its tightly curved one-globe counterpart seems to be that in one of them there are two iron globes, and in the other only one. Why can't that be a difference between possible realities in its own right? Indeed, I think it is extremely plausible to regard it so.[23]

To give this answer, of course, is to hold that the thisnesses of the two globes are metaphysically primitive. The function of the imaginary spatiotemporal world here is not to show how individual distinctness can be explained by spatiotemporal relations; no such explanation is needed if thisnesses are metaphysically primitive. The imaginary world simply provides an example in which it seems intuitively that two individuals would be distinct although it is clear that they would have all the same suchnesses.

The intuition involved here is akin to those which support belief in direct reference. This will be clearer if we imagine that we are on one of the two globes, with indiscernible twins on the other, so that the use of demonstratives will be possible. Then we can appeal to the intuition that it means something, which we understand quite well and which if true expresses a metaphysical reality, to say that this globe is not identical with that one, even in a situation in which we are not able to distinguish them qualitatively. But the argument goes beyond direct reference in one important respect: it incorporates a judgment that the assertion of individual distinctness is not only intelligible independently of qualitative difference, but also consistent with the assumption that there is no qualitative difference.

4 Arguments from the Possibility of Almost Indiscernible Twins

We may just have an intuition that there could be distinct, though indiscernible, globes in these circumstances. But there may also be an argument for this view – which will depend in turn on other intuitions, like all arguments in these matters. The argument might rest on an intuition that the possibility of there being two objects in a given spatiotemporal relation to each other is not affected by any slight changes in such features as the color or chemical composition of one or both objects.[24] If we accept that intuition, we can infer the possibility of indiscernible twins from the uncontroversial possibility of *almost* indiscernible twins. No one doubts that there could be a universe like the universe of our example in other respects, if one of the two globes had a small chemical impurity that the other lacked. Surely, we may think, the absence of the impurity would not make such a universe impossible.

Spatiotemporal dispersal still plays a part in this argument. But one can argue against the Identity of Indiscernibles from the possibility of almost indiscernible twins in quite a different way, using an example that has to do primarily with minds rather than with bodies. Suppose I have an almost indiscernible twin. The only qualitative difference between him and me, and hence between his part of the universe and mine, is that on one night of our lives (when we are 27 years old) the fire-breathing dragon that pursues me in my nightmare has ten horns, whereas the monster in his dream has only seven. I assume that the number of horns is little noted nor long remembered, and that any other, causally associated differences between his and my lives and parts of the world are slight and quite local. No doubt there is a possible world (call it w) in which there are almost indiscernible twins of this sort; it is only an expository convenience to assume that I am one of them and that w is actual. But if such a world is even possible, it seems to follow that a world with perfectly indiscernible twins is also possible. For surely I could have existed, and so could my twin, if my monster had had only seven horns, like his. And that could have been even if there were no other difference from the lives we live in w, except in the details causally connected with the number of horns in my dream. In that case we would have been distinct but qualitatively indiscernible – a relation which seems therefore to be logically possible.

Several points in this argument call for further mention or explanation. (1) The non-identity obtaining between me and my twin in w is proved by a qualitative difference between us there. (2) The argument depends on an intuition of transworld identity – that in a possible world (call it w'), otherwise like w, but in which my dragon has only seven horns, there could exist an individual identical with me and an individual identical with my twin, even though we would not be qualitatively different in that case. (3) The transitivity of identity is relied on in arguing that since my twin and I are not identical in w (as shown by the difference in our suchnesses there), it follows that we are not identical in any possible world, and therefore are distinct in w', if we both exist in it.

(4) Because differences in modal properties can be purely qualitative, the conclusion that my twin and I would be qualitatively indiscernible in w' depends, additionally, on the assumption that in w' he as well as I would be a person who could have dreamed of a ten-horned monster in the circumstances in which I did in w. In other words, it is assumed that if w and w' are possible, so is a world w'' just like w except that in w'' it is my twin's beast that has ten horns and mine that has seven. (More precisely, it is assumed that w and w'' would be equally possible if w' were actual.) The implications of the supposition that there are possible worlds that differ, as w and w'' do, only by a transposition of individuals will be studied further in section 5 below.

(5) But we may notice here a consideration about time that seems to me to support assumptions (2) and (4). The mutual distinctness of two individual persons already existing cannot depend on something that has not yet happened. The identity and non-identity of most individuals, and surely of persons, are conceived of as determined, at any time of their existence, by their past and present. This is doubtless connected with the importance that origins seem to have in questions of transworld identity. Consider the state of w when my twin and I are 22, five years before the distinctive dreams. We are already distinct from each other, though nothing has yet happened to distinguish us qualitatively. I think it follows that our mutual distinctness is independent of the qualitative difference arising from our later dreams. We would be distinct, therefore, even if our dreams did not differ at age 27 – that is, even if we were perfectly indiscernible qualitatively, as we would be in w'. Moreover, since my twin and I have our identities already established by age 22, which of us is which cannot depend on which has which dream five years later; it is possible that the seven-horned monster trouble my sleep, and the ten-horned his, when we are 27, as in w''. This argument depends, of course, on the assumption that in w my twin and I have histories that differ qualitatively during a certain period after we are 22, but not before then. It follows that w is not completely deterministic,

but that does not keep w from being at least logically possible.[25]

5 Primitive Trans-world Identity

Issues of modality *de re* turn on identity questions. To say that a certain individual is only contingently a parent, but necessarily an animal, for example, is to say that there could have been a nonparent, but not a non-animal, that would have been the same individual as that one. It has become customary, and has been at least heuristically helpful, to represent such identities as identities of individuals in different possible worlds – "transworld identities" for short – although (as we have just seen) modal claims *de re* can be understood as identity claims even without the imagery of possible worlds. Whether modality *de re* really adds anything important to the stock of modal facts depends, I think, on whether there are transworld identities or non-identities, and if so, whether they are primitive or are rather to be analyzed in terms of some more fundamental relation(s) among possible worlds. I will try to show here that, if we are prepared to accept nonqualitative thisnesses, we have a very plausible argument for primitive transworld identities and non-identities.

It might be thought, indeed, that we would have a more than plausible argument – that if, by refuting the Identity of Indiscernibles, we can show that thisnesses are metaphysically primitive, it will follow trivially that transworld identity of individuals is also primitive. For the property of being identical with (for example) Aristotle is the same property in every possible world in which it occurs. Hence it cannot be distinct from all suchnesses when possessed by a famous philosopher in the actual world if it is identical with a suchness when possessed by one of Alexander the Great's tax collectors in some other possible world.

This argument is correct insofar as it makes the point that the thisness or identity of a particular individual is nonqualitative either at all places, times, and possible worlds at which it occurs, or at none of them. By the same token, however, there is nothing special about transworld identity in this connection. But the issue on which I wish to focus here is specifically about the primitiveness of *transworld* identities. It therefore cannot be the issue of whether they are purely qualitative.

When we ask about the primitiveness of a kind of identity, we typically want to know, about a certain range of cases, whether the belonging of two properties to a single subject can be explained as consisting in other, more basic relations obtaining between distinct subjects of the same or related properties.[26] Thus Aristotle is the subject of the diverse properties expressed by "is a philosopher" and "could have been a tax collector". In asking whether the identity of the actual philosopher with the possible tax collector is primitive, we want to know whether it consists in some more fundamental relation between Aristotle's actual career and a career in which he would have been a tax collector. This issue is quite distinct from that of the qualitative or nonqualitative character of Aristotle's identity, in the same or in different worlds, as may be seen by reflecting on some other sorts of identity.

The claim that there are nonqualitative thisnesses does not clearly entail that *transtemporal* identity, for example, is primitive. For suppose there are two persisting individuals, Indi and Scerni, acknowledged to be qualitatively indiscernible, and therefore to possess nonqualitative thisnesses. It is not obvious that the identity of Indi at time t_1 with Indi at time t_2 (or the belonging of Indi's t_1 states and t_2 states to a single individual) cannot be explained as consisting in other, more basic relations among successive events or states or stages of Indi, without presupposing the transtemporal identity of any individual. Perhaps this can be done in terms of spatiotemporal continuity or memory links or causal connections or some other relation. The property of being Indi at any given time would still not be equivalent to any suchness. It could be analyzed in terms of the more basic relations among Indi's temporal stages. But the distinctness of those stages from the corresponding stages of Scerni would still be irreducibly nonqualitative, and this nonqualitative character would be passed on to the property of being Indi (at any time). The transtemporal aspect of Indi's identity, however, would not be indispensably primitive. In the present state of philosophical research it is probably unclear whether any transtemporal identity is indeed primitive; my point here is just that the thesis of the nonqualitativeness of thisnesses can be separated from that of the primitiveness of transtemporal identity.

If, to complete the separation of issues, we seek an example of a philosopher who is committed, with apparent consistency, both to the purely qualitative character of all thisnesses and to the primitiveness of some sort of individual identity, we can find it in Leibniz. He regards thisnesses as conjunctions of simpler, logically independent suchnesses. That the combination of properties is effected by the logical operation of conjunction is an essential part of his conceptual atomism. He assumes that there are some cases in which the instantiation of a conjunction of properties cannot be analyzed as consisting in any more fundamental fact. But if it is a primitive fact that the property F and G is instantiated, the identity of some possessor of F with a possessor of G must also be primitive, rather than analyzable as consisting in some more basic relation obtaining between distinct possessors of F and of G or related properties. The primitiveness of identity in such cases is in no way inconsistent with Leibniz's opinion that thisnesses are suchnesses; it is indeed required by the way in which he thinks thisnesses are constructed out of simpler suchnesses.

The primitive identities for Leibniz would probably not be transtemporal, and would certainly not be transworld. But no distance in space, time, or "logical space" is needed for questions of identity. Suppose one of Aristotle's momentary perceptual states includes both tasting an olive and hearing a bird sing. In this supposition it is implied, and not yet explained by any more basic relation, that some individual that is tasting an olive is *identical* with one that is hearing a bird sing. And it seems that this sort of identity (identity of the individual subject of simultaneous qualities) could be primitive in a purely qualitative construction of reality.

So questions of the primitiveness of identity relations are in general distinct from the question of the qualitativeness or nonqualitativeness of thisnesses. But, in the case of transworld identity in particular, I think that primitive identities are much more plausible if nonqualitative thisnesses are accepted than if they are rejected. Suppose, on the one hand, that all thisnesses are purely qualitative. Then the thisness of any individual can be constructed as a disjunction of suchnesses, each suchness representing one possible career of the individual (as explained in section 2 above). It seems quite possible that in every case the grouping of disjuncts as alternative careers of a single individual could be explained by general principles about transworld identity of one or another kind of individuals, and the transworld identity of the particular individual could be analyzed as consisting in the satisfaction of the general principles by the relevant disjuncts. And if there should be borderline cases, in which the issue of transworld

identity is not settled by general principles, one might well conclude that transworld identity or non-identity is undefined, rather than primitive, in those cases.

If, on the other hand, we reject the Identity of Indiscernibles in favor of nonqualitative thisnesses, it will not be hard to find examples that will provide support of great intuitive plausibility for primitive transworld identities and non-identities. Consider, again, a possible world w_1 in which there are two qualitatively indiscernible globes; call them Castor and Pollux.[27] Being indiscernible, they have of course the same duration; in w_1 both of them have always existed and always will exist. But it seems perfectly possible, logically and metaphysically, that either or both of them cease to exist. Let w_2 then, be a possible world just like w_1 up to a certain time t at which in w_2 Castor ceases to exist while Pollux goes on forever; and let w_3 be a possible world just like w_2 except that in w_3 it is Pollux that ceases to exist at t while Castor goes on forever. That the difference between w_2 and w_3 is real, and could be important, becomes vividly clear if we consider that, from the point of view of a person living on Castor before t in w_1 and having (of course) an indiscernible twin on Pollux, it can be seen as the difference between being annihilated and somebody else being annihilated instead. But there is no qualitative difference between w_2 and w_3. And there are no qualitative necessary and sufficient conditions for the transworld identity or non-identity of Castor and Pollux; for every qualitative condition satisfied by Castor in w_2 is satisfied by Pollux in w_1 and vice versa.[28]

A similar example can be constructed for transworld identity of *events*. Suppose all that happens in w_1 is that Castor and Pollux approach and recede from each other in an infinite series of indiscernible pulsations of the universe. In w_1 their pulsations go on forever, but they might not have. For every pair of them there is surely a possible world in which one member of the pair is the last pulsation, and a different possible world in which the other is the last pulsation. But there is no qualitative difference between these possible worlds; each contains the same number ($\aleph_0$ the first infinite number) of exactly similar pulsations. There are therefore no qualitative necessary and sufficient conditions for the transworld identities and non-identities of the events in these possible worlds.

Any case of this sort, in which two possible worlds differ in the transworld identities of their individuals but not in their suchnesses, provides us at once with a clearer proof of a primitive trans-world identity than has yet been found for a primitive transtemporal identity.[29] For the geometrical, topological, psychological, and causal relations out of which philosophers have hoped to construct transtemporal identity do not obtain among the alternative possible careers of an individual. 'Logical space' is not a space to which the concepts of physical space apply literally. There is no causal interaction between different possible worlds. One cannot remember events in another possible world in the same sense in which one's memory of events in the actual past might be important to personal identity. The most important transworld relations of individuals, which seem to be the foundation of all their other transworld relations, are qualitative similarity – which cannot explain different transworld identities in worlds that are qualitatively indiscernible – and identity itself. One might try to analyze the transworld identity of an individual in terms of qualitative similarities plus having the same parts, or the same parents; but then the transworld identity of some individuals (the parts or the parents) is presupposed. If the Identity of Indiscernibles is rejected, there seems to be no plausible way of analyzing transworld identity and non-identity in general in terms of other, more basic relations.

6   Thisness and Necessity

I have argued that there are possible cases in which no purely qualitative conditions would be both necessary and sufficient for possessing a given thisness. It may be thought that this is too cautious a conclusion – that if thisnesses are nonqualitative, there cannot be any qualitative necessary conditions at all for possessing them. The following argument could be given for this view.

Let T be a thisness, and let S be a suchness. Many philosophers have believed that all necessary truths are *analytic*, in the sense that they are either truths of formal logic or derivable by valid logical rules from correct analyses of concepts or properties. This may be regarded as a broadly Leibnizian conception of necessity. Suppose it is right; and suppose that thisnesses are irreducibly nonqualitative. We may well wonder, then, how it could be a necessary truth that whatever has T has S. For it is surely not a truth of formal logic. And suchnesses are not analyzable in terms of thisnesses; so if thisnesses are not analyzable in terms of such-

nesses, how can any connection between T and S fail to be synthetic?

The conclusion, that there cannot be any purely qualitative necessary condition for the possession of any given thisness, is absurd, however. It implies that you and I, for example, could have been individuals of any sort whatever – plutonium atoms, noises, football games, places, or times, if those are all individuals.[30] If we cannot trust our intuition that we could not have been any of those things, then it is probably a waste of time to study *de re* modalities at all. If there are any transworld identities and non-identities, there are necessary connections between thisnesses and some suchnesses.

But it is difficult to understand what makes these connections necessary; and that difficulty has doubtless motivated some philosophical doubts about *de re* modality.[31] Those who accept nonqualitative thisnesses but cling to the dogma that all necessary truths are analytic in the sense explained above may suppose that every nonqualitative thisness that is necessarily connected with suchnesses is analyzable as a conjunction of some or all of the suchnesses it implies, plus a relation to one or more particular individuals of some more fundamental sort. Either the latter individuals (or others still more basic to which one would come by recursive applications of the view) would have no qualitative necessary conditions of their identity at all, or there would be an infinite regress (perhaps virtuous) of thisnesses analyzable in terms of more fundamental thisnesses. Neither alternative seems particularly plausible.

It is better to abandon the identification of necessity with analyticity and suppose that necessities *de re* are commonly synthetic. Perhaps the best answer that can be given to the question, What makes it necessary that Jimmy Carter (for example) is not a musical performance? is this: It is a fact, which we understand very well to be true, though not analytic, that Jimmy Carter is a person. And there are necessary conditions of intra- and transworld identity which follow (analytically, indeed) from the concept or property of being a person and which entail that no individual that is in fact a person could under any circumstances be a musical performance.

There are many notoriously perplexing questions about what suchnesses belong necessarily to which individuals. "Could Cleopatra have been male?" "Could I (who am blue-eyed) have been brown-eyed?" And so forth. It may be that some of these questions call for conceptual legislation rather than metaphysical discovery, for some of our concepts of kinds of individual may be somewhat vague with respect to necessary conditions of transworld identity. The acceptance of nonqualitative thisnesses does not oblige us to settle doubtful cases in favor of contingency. Indeed, I am inclined to decide a very large proportion of them in favor of necessity (or impossibility, as the case may be).

If a name is desired for the position I have defended here, according to which thisnesses and transworld identities are primitive but logically connected with suchnesses, we may call it *Moderate Haecceitism*.

Notes

Versions of this paper were read to colloquia at UCLA, UC Irvine, and Stanford. I am indebted to many, and particularly to Marilyn Adams, Kit Fine, Dagfinn Føllesdal, Ian Hacking, Robert Hambourger, David Kaplan, Kenneth Olson, John Perry, and Peter Woodruff, for discussion that helped in writing and rewriting the paper. My interest in the project grew out of discussions with Kaplan.

1 See David Kaplan, "How to Russell a Frege-Church," *Journal of Philosophy* 72 (1975, Nov. 6), pp. 716–29, at pp. 722–7.
2 "Thisness" is the inevitable and historic word here. But we must not suppose that everything important that is expressed by a demonstrative is caught up in the relevant thisness. You might know many facts involving the thisness (in my sense) of Gerald Ford, for example, and yet be ignorant that *that* man (disappearing over the hill in a golf cart) is Ford. I believe this is a translation into my terminology of a point John Perry has made; see his "Frege on demonstratives," *Philosophical Review* 86/4 (Oct. 1977), pp. 474–97, and "Indexicality and belief," unpublished.
3 E.g., by Alvin Plantinga, *The Nature of Necessity* (Oxford; Clarendon Press, 1974), pp. 71f.
4 Johannes Duns Scotus, *Quaestiones in libros metaphysicorum*, VII. xii. schol. 3; cf. *Ordinatio*, II. 3. 1. 2, 57. I am indebted to Marilyn McCord Adams for acquainting me with these texts and views of Scotus, and for much discussion of the topics of this paragraph.
5 Gottfried Wilhelm Leibniz, *Fragmente zur Logik*, ed. Franz Schmidt (Berlin: Akademie-Verlag, 1960), p. 476; cf. Leibniz, *Discourse on Metaphysics*, trans. P. G. Lucas and L. Griut (Manchester: Manchester University Press, 1953), sect. 9. This is not the place to debate points of interpretation, and I will sometimes speak of "properties" where Leibniz usually restricts himself to "concept" and "predicate"; but I think I do not substantially misrepresent him on the points that concern us.
6 *Discourse on Metaphysics*, sect. 8.
7 See Leibniz's letter of 4/14 July, 1686 to Antoine Arnauld, in *The Leibniz–Arnaud Correspondence*, trans. H. T. Mason, (Manchester: Manchester University Press, 1967), pp. 53–66.

8 This point could also be put in terms of constructing complete concepts from predicates that are indexed to possible worlds. This possible amendment of Leibniz's position, and its analogy with Leibniz's commitment to the indexing of predicates to times, were noted by Benson Mates, "Individuals and modality in the philosophy of Leibniz," *Studia Leibnitiana* 4 (1972), p. 109.
9 Cf. Keith S. Donnellan, "Reference and definite descriptions," *Philosophical Review*, 75/3 (July 1966), pp. 281–304, and *idem*, "Proper names and identifying descriptions," in D. Davidson and G. Harman (eds), *The Semantics of Natural Languages*, 2nd edn. (Boston: Reidel, 1972), pp. 356–79; Saul Kripke, "Naming and necessity," in Davidson and Harman (eds), pp. 253–355.
10 Leibniz, *Discourse on Metaphysics*, sect. 8.
11 This way of establishing a trivial version of the Identity of Indiscernibles was noticed by Whitehead and Russell, *Principia Mathematica*, vol. 1, 2nd edn. (Cambridge: Cambridge University Press, 1957), p. 57. It is the initial topic in Max Black's "The identity of indiscernibles," this volume, ch. 6, and I think that Black does not quite distinguish it from any interesting version of the doctrine, because he does not explicitly distinguish relational properties that are suchnesses from those which are not.
12 See esp. his famous paper "First truths," and his *Discourse on Metaphysics*, sects. 8, 9.
13 *The Leibniz–Clarke Correspondence*, ed. H. G. Alexander (Manchester: Manchester University Press, 1956), Leibniz's fifth letter, sects. 25, 26, and Clarke's fifth reply, sects. 21–5 and 26–32. Clarke could not have seen the papers in which Leibniz most clearly implied the claim of necessity.
14 Leibniz, *Fragmente zur Logik*, p. 476.
15 Of course the suchness will be constituted by a single disjunct if, as Leibniz held, each individual exists in only one possible world.
16 Immanuel Kant, *Critique of Pure Reason*, A263f = B319f.
17 This volume, ch. 6, pp. 66ff.
18 This axiom might be doubted, but I simply assume it here. Occam denied that it is a necessary truth (*Reportatio*, IV, q. 4N and q. 5), in *Opera Plurima* (Lyon,

1494–6); I am indebted to Marilyn Adams for this information).

19 Ian Hacking, "The identity of indiscernibles," *Journal of Philosophy* 72, 9 (8 May 1975), pp. 249–56, at p. 249.

20 Ibid., pp. 255–6.

21 Ibid., p. 255. The point was also suggested, about space, by Black, this volume, ch. 6.

22 Hacking, "Identity of indiscernibles," pp. 251f, 254f.

23 Strictly speaking, I think it is highly plausible to regard it so *if* physical objects are accepted as primitive features of reality. Like Leibniz, I am inclined to take a phenomenalistic view of physical objects, and hence doubt the primitiveness of *their* thisnesses. Unlike Leibniz, I think there could be distinct but indiscernible sentient beings and mental events; cases that help to show the plausibility of this view may be provided by temporal dispersal arguments, or by another type of argument to be discussed in section 4 below.

24 If we assume that differences in color or chemical composition necessarily involve microscopic differences in spatiotemporal configuration, the intuition would have to be that slight differences of that sort do not affect the logical or metaphysical possibility of a given macroscopic configuration of objects.

25 I do not claim that Leibniz would accept this judgment of possibility.

26 Cf. John Perry, "Can the self divide?," *Journal of Philosophy* 59/6 (7 Sept. 1972), pp. 463–88, at pp. 466–8.

27 The question may be raised whether giving names to the globes is consistent with their qualitative indiscernibility (cf. Black, this volume, ch. 6). Two answers may be given. The imaginative answer is that we may suppose that the globes have (indiscernible) societies of language-users on them and we are speaking the language of the Castor-dwellers; in the language of the Pollux-dwellers, of course, "Castor" names Pollux and "Pollux" Castor, but that does not keep Castor from *being* Castor and Pollux Pollux. The

sober answer is that "Castor" and "Pollux" are informal equivalents of variables bound by the existential quantifiers that would be used to introduce the example in a formal way.

28 We rely here on an intuition that the Castor-dweller can refer directly to the same individual (namely herself) in different possible worlds, despite the absence of qualitative necessary and sufficient conditions for the identity. This is related, in ways that should by now be familiar to us, to intuitions that have been used to support the semantics of direct reference – as, for example, that when we say, "Nixon might have lost the 1968 election," we refer to the actual individual, Nixon, in a non-actual situation even if we do not know any clearly qualitative property that the possible loser must have in order to be identical with the actual President. (The example is Kripke's; see his "Naming and necessity," pp. 264ff.)

29 It is not essential to the argument to start from a world in which (as in w_1) there are non-identical indiscernibles. An essentially similar argument can be based on the case presented in section 4 above, in which I have an *almost* indiscernible twin. But, since the crux of the argument will be that every qualitative condition satisfied by me in w is satisfied by him in w'', and vice versa, we must still be prepared to accept non-qualitative thisnesses. And, as we saw in section 4, the case can also be used to argue for the possibility of a world containing perfectly indiscernible twins.

30 In his *Examination of McTaggart's Philosophy*, vol. 1 (Cambridge: Cambridge University Press, 1933), p. 177, C. D. Broad pointed out that rejection of the Identity of Indiscernibles does not imply "that it is logically possible that [a particular] P, which *in fact has* the nature N, should *instead* have had some other nature N′; e.g., that I might have been born in Rome in 55 BC, or that the Albert Memorial might have been a volcano in South America."

31 Cf. W. V. Quine, *From a Logical Point of View*, 2nd edn (New York: Harper Torchbooks, 1963), p. 155.

15

The Nature of Possibility

D. M. Armstrong

1 Introductory

I want to defend a *combinatorial* theory of possibility. Such a view traces the very idea of possibility to the idea of the combinations – *all* the combinations which respect a certain simple form – of given, actual, elements. Combination is to be understood widely enough to cover the notions of *expansion* and *contraction*. (My central metaphysical hypothesis is that all there is, is the world of space and time. It is this world which is to supply the actual elements for the totality of combinations. So what is proposed is a *naturalistic* form of a combinatorial theory.)

The combinatorial idea is not new, of course. Wittgenstein gave a classical exposition of it in the *Tractatus*. Perhaps its charter is 3.4: 'A proposition determines a place in logical space. The existence of this logical place is guaranteed by *the mere existence of the constituents*.'[1] There is a small additional combinatorial literature. I myself was converted to a combinatorial view by Brian Skyrms' brief but fascinating article 'Tractarian nominalism'.[2]

It is convenient to develop the position in stages. I begin in Wittgensteinian fashion with a world of simple objects whose recombinations determine the possibilities. After that, ladders have to be kicked away. Expansion and contraction have to be allowed for, as does the (at least doxastic) possibility that there are no simple objects in the world.

2 Ontological Sketch

The world that I begin with contains a number of simple individuals, a, b, c, ... The number is not specified. It might be finite, or be one of the infinite cardinals. It is an a posteriori, scientific question how many individuals the world contains.

These individuals may have indefinitely many properties, and stand in indefinitely many relations to other individuals. Their simplicity is constituted by the fact that they have no proper parts, where parts of individuals are individuals. Candidates for such individuals would be propertied point-instants.

The world also contains, in finite or infinite number, simple properties, F, G, H, . . . and simple relations, R, S, T, . . . (Their simplicity is constituted by the fact that they have no properties or relations as proper parts.) The relations may be dyadic, triadic, . . . n-adic. In agreement with Skyrms, these properties and relations are conceived of as *universals*. The identical property F can be possessed by two or more distinct individuals. The identical dyadic relation R can hold between two or more distinct pairs.

I pause here to indicate briefly some of my views on universals. The central contention is that there is no automatic inference from n-adic *predicates* to n-adic *universals*. What universals, what true properties and relations, the world contains is not to be

Originally published in *Canadian Journal of Philosophy* 16 (1986), pp. 575–94. Reprinted by permission of the University of Calgary.

determined a priori on a semantic basis. The question must rather be settled a posteriori on the basis of total science.

If U_1 and U_2 are universals, then the predicate $\lceil U_1 \vee U_2 \rceil$ will apply truly to various individuals. But there is no universal *Either U_1 or U_2*. Similarly, it is likely that the predicate $\lceil Not\text{-}U_1 \rceil$ will apply truly to some individuals. But there is no universal *Not being U_1*. This latter contention, worked out before I arrived at my combinatorial view, turns out to be a vital part of a combinatorialism involving universals.[3] For U_1 and Not-U_1 is an impossible combination. But what resource would there be in combinatorialism to exclude it?

Conjunctions of universals, however, seem to be acceptable (complex) universals. Provided only that some individual exists which is both F and G, and these are universals, then we can treat $F \wedge G$ as a universal, identical in different instances. The same holds for the very important category of *structural* universal. If a compound individual consists of an F-part having R to a G-part, with F, R and G universals, then the individual instantiates the structural universal *an F having R to a G*.

I have postulated individuals, properties and relations, the latter two being monadic and polyadic universals respectively (forming, if the hypothesis of naturalism is correct, a single spatio-temporal system). But this may suggest that I am thinking of reality, of actuality, like a tinker-toy construction from three different parts. Instead, I hold that these 'elements' are essentially aspects of, abstractions from, what Wittgenstein and Skyrms call *facts* and what I shall call *states of affairs*: a's being F, b's having R to c, and so on, constitute states of affairs. If it is simples that we are dealing with the whole time, then we can speak of these as *atomic* states of affairs.

The choice between the phrases 'states of affairs' and 'facts' is a little delicate. 'Facts' may seem to have the advantage that there cannot be false facts, whereas language does permit talk of non-existent states of affairs. But, as we shall see shortly, this apparent advantage is not really an advantage. It is in fact useful to have a relaxed sense of 'state of affairs' in which one can speak of states of affairs that are non-existent.

Now consider the totality of atomic states of affairs. As Skyrms suggests, we may think of an individual, such as a, as no more than an *abstraction* from all those states of affairs in which a figures, F an abstraction from all those states of affairs in which F figures, and similarly for relation R. By

'abstraction' is not meant that a, F and R are in any way other-worldly, still less 'mental' or unreal. What is meant is that, while by an act of selective attention they may be *considered* apart from the states of affairs in which they figure, they have no existence outside states of affairs.

Properties may be thought of as *ways* that (some) individuals are, and relations as *ways* that individuals stand to each other. This makes it clear why they exist in states of affairs, and so why there can be no uninstantiated properties and relations. A *possible* property or relation, even if empirically possible, is not *ipso facto* a property or relation.

To be individuals, individuals must be *an* individual, must be *one* thing. But this demands that they 'fall under a concept' as Frege would put it, that they have some unit-making property. Hence, I think, we can reject bare individuals as well as uninstantiated properties and relations. States of affairs rule.

3 The Wittgenstein Worlds

Given the notion of an atomic state of affairs, we can introduce the notion of a *molecular* state of affairs. These are confined to *conjunctive* states of affairs. Disjunctive and negative states of affairs are not admitted. But the conjunctions may be infinite. The world is a certain conjunction of states of affairs, perhaps an infinite one.

We can also introduce the notion of a *possible* atomic state of affairs, and, in particular, a *merely* possible atomic state of affairs. The world 'possible' here modifies the sense of the phrase 'state of affairs'. For, as the phrase was introduced in the previous section, all states of affairs are actual.

The notion of a possible state of affairs is introduced semantically, via the notion of an atomic *statement*. Suppose that a is F, but is not G. Consider the statements 'a is F' and 'a is G'. The former is true, and may be called an atomic statement. But the latter may *also* be called an atomic statement. For while failing to correspond to an atomic state of affairs, it does respect the *form* of an atomic state of affairs.

I pause here to note that no particular knowledge of what in fact these individuals and properties are is assumed. What we have here is a thought-experiment in which we imagine ourselves formulating a false atomic statement. In my view, Wittgenstein's avowal of ignorance here was a stroke of genius, and not, as is often thought, a cowardly evasion. It pays tribute to the fact that we have no a priori insight into, and, even nowadays, only a little a posteriori insight into, the building-blocks of the world, in particular the true properties and relations. What does somewhat muddy Wittgenstein's insight is the thought that it should still be possible, by logical analysis alone, to get from *ordinary* true or false statements down to the atomic bed-rock. This in turn is connected with the idea that necessities must one and all be analytic or tautological. Kripke has shown us the way ahead here. Some of his ideas about necessities of identity that are established a posteriori seem to cast much light on the situation.

Returning to the line of the argument, '*a* is G' is a false atomic statement. What it states, that *a* is G, is false. But we can also say that *a*'s being G is a possible (merely possible) atomic state of affairs. A merely possible state of affairs does not exist, subsist, or have any sort of being. It is no addition to our ontology. But we can refer to it, or, better, make *ostensible* reference to it.

Now that we have the notion of molecular or conjunctive states of affairs, and of possible atomic states of affairs, we can form the notion of conjunctions, including infinite conjunctions, of possible atomic states of affairs, that is, molecular possible states of affairs.

The simple individuals, properties and relations may be combined in *all* ways to yield possible atomic states of affairs, provided only that the form of atomic facts is respected. That is the combinatorial idea. Such possible atomic states of affairs may then be combined in *all* ways to yield possible molecular states of affairs. If such a possible molecular state of affairs is thought of as the totality of being, then it is a *possible world*.

Wittgenstein, besides postulating a world of simple objects (whether they included universals is unclear) also adopted what Skyrms calls a 'fixed domain' account of possible worlds. Putting it into our terms, for him each possible world must contain *each* simple individual, property and relation and no others. I will call such worlds *Wittgenstein worlds*. It is convenient to start from this set of worlds, and then consider what sorts of world require to be added to give *all* possible worlds.

It is to be noted also that Wittgenstein holds (as does Skyrms) that first-order objects combined into first-order facts (states of affairs) are all that we need postulate. I think that that is too optimistic. Properties and relations *of* properties and relations may well be required for a satisfactory ontology. Again, states of affairs concerning states

of affairs may be required. Indeed, as Russell in effect pointed out, just to say that a certain conjunction of states of affairs exhausts the world is not something which can itself be analyzed purely in terms of first-order states of affairs. The notion of a possible world is not a first-order notion.

But in this paper I propose to prescind from these complications. My hope and trust is that, from the point of view of a combinatorial theory, they are *mere* complications.

4 Haecceities and Quiddities

Suppose, then, that one is a *naturalist*, believing that the space-time world is all there is. Suppose further that one holds that this space-time world has an ultimate structure: individuals having (universal) properties and relations, the identification of these universals being an a posteriori matter. Suppose, finally, that one holds a *combinatorial* theory of possibility, holding in particular that all *mere* possibilities are recombinations of actual elements.

Two difficulties present themselves. First, is it not possible that there should be individuals which are neither identical with actual individuals, nor composed of actual individuals. Following Lewis,[4] call such individuals *alien* individuals. Second, is it not possible that there should be universals which are neither identical with actual, that is, instantiated, universals, nor composed of actual universals? Call such universals alien universals. Alien universals and individuals seem to be ruled out by our original premises.

Skyrms, in his 1981 paper, says that to deal with these alien possibilities we must desert combination for 'analogy'. Analogy, as he explains it, turns out to be the use of the existential quantifier. Can we not understand the statement that there might have been individuals which are neither identical with, nor composed of, actual individuals? Can we not understand the statement that there might have been universals which are neither identical with, nor composed of, actual universals? Such alien individuals and universals would be *like* actual individuals and universals in being individuals and universals (that, I take it, is the 'analogy'), even if unlike them in being 'other'.

In the case of universals, at least, I do not think that this treatment will serve. In particular, it will involve deserting naturalism. Suppose that it is said that actually existing individual *a* might have had an alien property. What is it in the world that makes this statement true? What is its truth-maker, or ontological ground? If alien properties are possible, then each of them will have its own nature, its *quiddity* as we may put it. (Suppose *a* had had an alien property, and *b* had had another. The supposition that *a* had the property *b* had while *b* had *a*'s property will be a different supposition. Each alien property must have its own nature.) But these natures, these quiddities, are not to be found in the space-time world. Lewis can instantiate them in other possible worlds. A Platonist could give them uninstantiated existence 'alongside' the natural world. But what can the naturalist-combinatorialist do? For universals, I think the way of analogy fails.

It might be suggested that one might use actual universals to 'triangulate' alien universals. The inspiration is Hume's 'missing shade of blue'. Consider the (putative) universals, red, orange, yellow, and again red, purple, blue. Suppose orange to have never been instantiated. Would it not then have been alien? But, even so, could we not 'fix' it as the property between red and yellow, in the same way that purple is between red and blue?

The first point to notice, in criticism of this suggestion, is that the ploy is of limited value only. Orange would not be totally alien (orange is a *colour*). By hypothesis, the *totally* alien could not be triangulated thus.

But in any case I doubt whether orange is in *any* degree alien relative to the other colours. If a physicalist reduction of some sort gives the true nature of colour, as I believe to be the case, then the colours are different positions on a scale or scales of quantities. Quantities in turn are structural properties, and a 'missing structure' can be constructed directly from instantiated structures.

Sterner measures are necessary for genuine aliens. I believe that a naturalist–combinatorialist should deny the possibility of genuinely alien universals. For a combinatorialist, the possible is determined by the actual. So the actual universals set a limit, a limit given by the totality of their recombinations, to the possible universals. It may be allowed that alien universals are conceivable, that is, doxastically possible, in the same sort of way that the falsity of Goldbach's conjecture is conceivable. But just as (it may be) that Goldbach's conjecture is a necessary truth, so the denial of alien universals is a necessary truth.

The strongest way to mobilize intuition in favour of alien universals is this. Consider a 'con-

tracted' world, contracted by removing, say, certain simple properties from this world. From the standpoint of this contracted world, these simple properties will be alien properties. But if, relative to a contracted world, properties in our world could be alien, are there not possible worlds relative to which *our* world is contracted, contracted with respect to universals? Such a world will contain alien universals, alien, that is, to our world.

But this line of thought covertly depends upon taking all worlds as equal. The *combinatorialist* is an actual world chauvinist. The actual world, and it alone, is genuinely a world. The possible is determined by the actual, and so, saving recombination, cannot outrun the actual. To consider a contracted world is to suppose, falsely suppose, that the actual world is contracted. If the possible is determined by the actual, with the actual supposed contracted, the possible must be supposed contracted, and certain actual universals supposed alien. But that does not licence expanded worlds.

What then of alien *individuals*? Here the problem for the combinatorialist is rather more severe. It seems very hard to deny that it is possible that the world should contain more individuals than it actually contains. There is no mouse in my study. Nevertheless, it is possible that there should be one. But why does this mouse have to be one of the world's mice? Why not an additional mouse? And if additional, why not made up of particles (I assume a materialist theory of mice) which are additional to the world's particles? The supposition is much less recherché than the supposition of alien universals. It seems to be a genuine possibility.

What I want to suggest is that in the case of alien individuals Skyrm's appeal to 'analogy' can be upheld. But in order to uphold it, it is necessary to reject a doctrine that Skyrms accepts (for actual individuals): the doctrine of *haecceitism*. So first a discussion of that doctrine.

Let us use as an example a contracted world, as a substitute for our actual rich and complicated world, which contains nothing but the simple individuals *a* and *b*, along with the properties, also simple, F and G. The world is exhausted by the states of affairs:

I   F*a* & G*b*.

What will the combinatorialist say are the possible worlds relative to actuality thus thinly conceived? Omitting further contractions, for simplicity, we seem to have:

II Ga & Fb
III Fa & Ga & Fa
IV Fa & Fb & Gb
V Fa & Ga & Gb
VI Ga & Fb & Gb
VII Fa & Ga & Fb & Gb

Consider now the pairs I and II, III and IV, V and VI. Carnap would say that, although the members of each pair had different *state-descriptions*, they had the same *structure-description*. The question is: are I and II the very same world differently described, or are they the same world? The same question holds for the other two pairs. A haecceitist holds that the members of each pair differ from each other. The anti-haecceitist denies it. A combinatorialist anti-haecceitist therefore allows *fewer possible worlds* than the haecceitist does.

The haecceitist holds that, apart from repeatable properties (F and G), *a* and *b* each have a unique inner essence, a metaphysical signature tune as it were, which distinguishes *a* and *b*. Even abstracted from their repeatable properties, *a* and *b* differ in nature.

The anti-haecceitist denies this. Notice that there could be a *strong* and a *weak* anti-haecceitism. A strong anti-haecceitism denies that individuals are anything more than the 'bundles' of their properties. For the strong haecceitist 'world' VII would collapse into a one-individual world, the individual having the properties F and G. (The 'two' bundles are the same bundle.) I reject strong haecceitism, for a number of reasons, but am inclined to accept the weak version.[5]

Haecceitism for individuals is parallel to quidditism for universals. Furthermore, haecceitism united with a naturalist-combinatorialism appears to make alien individuals impossible, just as quidditism makes alien universals impossible. For the alien individual must be supposed to have some definite haecceity, different from, and not obtainable from, actual haecceities. But how can a naturalist provide a truth-maker for the statement that alien individuals, with their alien haecceities, are possible?

But the rub is that, while we perhaps can deny the possibility of truly alien universals, truly alien individuals seem straightforwardly possible.

I suggest that the naturalist-combinatorialist should move to a (weak) anti-haecceitist position. I think that this is a natural and comfortable view. And then, I hope, we can revive the Skyrms doctrine of 'analogy' in more favourable circumstances.

The idea is quite simple. If weak anti-haecceitism is true, then individuals, *qua* individuals, are merely, barely, numerically different from each other. They are *simply* other. (Unlike properties and relations.) This concept of otherness is derivable from actuals. When applied to further, alien, individuals, it encompasses the whole of their nature *qua* particulars. Nothing is missing, as it would be missing if haecceitism were true. So we can form a *fully determinate* concept of an indefinite number of alien individuals 'by analogy'. They are then available to form worlds additional to the Wittgenstein worlds. This *is* a qualification of combinatorialism. But, I hope, 'only a little one'.

5 Contracted Worlds

So the Wittgenstein worlds require to be supplemented by worlds which contain further individuals, but not by worlds which contain further simple universals.

But there is more to be done. Not only must we allow this limited expansion, but, as already anticipated in the previous section, we must also countenance contraction. If there is no contraction, then every actual individual, and every simple universal, will appear in every possible world. As has often been noted, that would make both the individuals and the universals necessary beings. Of any individual in the actual world, it seems true to say that it might not have existed. Of any universal in the actual world, it seems true to say that it might not have been instantiated (at any time), and so, for a naturalist, that it might not have existed.

The obvious solution is to allow contraction in the forming of possible worlds. Any given individual is contingent. That is, there are worlds which omit this individual. Any universal is contingent. Such contraction does not seem unreasonable. Why, one may ask, in combining elements into states of affairs, and then conjoining these states of affairs to make possible worlds, are we forced to make use of *every* simple individual, property and relation? Why not a proper subset?

However, while there seems to be no particular difficulty about the contraction of individuals, the contraction of universals does raise problems for combinatorialism. The difficulty was noted by W. G. Lycan, who refers to Philip Quinn.[6]

As the modal logicians say, the Wittgenstein worlds are all 'accessible' to each other. That is, each of them is a possible world *relative to all the others*. In this respect, they form an equivalence class. The relation of accessibility is reflexive, transitive and symmetrical, and so is governed by an S5 modal logic. Given an anti-haecceitist account of individuals, the situation does not change if worlds are added which add and/or subtract individuals.

But suppose that we consider a contracted world, W_c, contracted by the absence of the simple property F, relative to a Wittgenstein world, W_w, which contains F's. W_c is accessible from W_w, that is, is a possible world relative to W_w. However, given combinatorial theory, W_w is not accessible from W_c. This is because, relative to W_c, F is an alien property. Symmetry of accessibility thus fails. For a set of worlds which contains both W_w and W_c we must content ourselves with an *S4* modal logic, with accessibility reflexive and transitive, but not symmetrical.

I do not think that this is too difficult to hold. What we must, but I think can, accept about the simple property F is this. F might not have existed, so it is a contingent being. But from the standpoint of a 'world' where F does not exist, it is impossible that it should exist. When we go down to the F-less world, W_c, then we are pretending that that world is the actual world. Now if W_c is taken as the actual world, then F *is* alien to it. So why should we not say that *in that world* F could not exist? F is actual, of course. But our supposition was that it is not actual. That is a new game. The new point of view makes it unactual, and so alien, and so impossible.

The central point is this. On the view being put forward, the possible is determined by the actual. Suppose the actual reduced. Then the sphere of the possible is also reduced.

But before concluding this section, I note that there is an ultimate contraction which a combinatorial theory cannot accept. It cannot countenance the empty world. The reason is that the empty world is not a construction from given elements. For the combinatorialist, then, it is necessary that there be something. Of course, there is no particular something which it is necessary that there be. I do not think that there is any particular paradox in this rejection of the possibility of the empty world.

6 What If There Are No Atoms?

The combinatorial scheme, as so far developed, postulates a world of simples: simple individuals, simple properties and simple relations, all conceived of as abstractions from atomic states of affairs. But is the world made up of simples in this way?

May it not be that some, or all, individuals have proper parts which in turn have proper parts, *ad infinitum*. And may it not be that this process fails to reach simple individuals *even at infinity*?

It may be that the property F is nothing but the conjunction of two wholly distinct properties, G and H, that G and H, in their turn, are conjunctions of properties, and so on *ad infinitum*. This progression, it may be, does not even end 'at infinity'. There are no simple properties involved, even at the end of an infinite road.

Or, again, it may be that the property F dissolves into a structure. To be an F may be nothing but to be a G standing in relation R to an H. To be a G may be a matter of being a J standing in relation S to a K. And so on forever. Structures all the way down, and no escape even at infinity.

The same may be true of some, or all, relations. For R to hold may be a matter of S and T both holding. S and T may dissolve similarly, with simple relations never reached.

Is it a *contingent* matter whether a certain individual, property or relation is, or is not, indefinitely complex in the way just described? I once said this about properties and relations.[7] But I now think that this was a bad mistake. I am not sure what to say about individuals, so will leave them aside here. But that a certain universal is or is not simple now seems to me to be a necessary truth. Certainly, it may be a question to be decided a posteriori to the extent that it can be decided. But it is not a contingent matter. It is what we might call a Kripkean necessity.

Here is the simple *reductio ad absurdum* argument for this new position. Suppose that it is contingent whether property F is simple or not. There will then be a possible world where F exists (is instantiated, presumably) and is simple. There will be another possible world where F will be identical with, say, the conjunction G & H. But this is absurd. What *identity* across possible worlds do we have here? Simple F in W_1 is identical with G & H in W_2! Why not with any other universal, simple, conjunctive or structural?

Here is what seems the best that one can do for the contingency thesis. In the actual world, say, a certain class of individuals has the simple property F. Properties G and H are not instantiated in this world. (In order to avoid difficulties about alien properties, let G and H both be complex properties.) In a certain possible world, the individuals that are F in the actual world (or their counterparts, if you prefer) lack F but do have G & H. The worlds do not differ in any other way at all.

We may say that F in our world, and G & H in another world, play exactly the same role. This includes *causal* role. Possession of F in this world, and G & H in the other, has just the same causes and just the same effects, including effects upon perceivers and, more generally, minds.

F in this world, G & H in the other, are set in exactly the same environment. But can one say that F *is* G & H? I do not see how we can. They may be said to be identical for all practical purposes. But I do not see how a philosopher, at least, can say that they are really identical. At best, they are counterparts of each other.

I conclude that we do have a necessity here, even if one which has to be established a posteriori. The conclusion to be drawn is that if there are simple universals, or if all universals are ultimately made up of simple universals, then this is a matter of necessity. The structure, or make-up, of a universal cannot change from one possible world to another. I should add that to concede a Kripkean necessity here does not commit one to underwriting all the alleged Kripkean necessities. For instance, I am very dubious about necessities of origin for individuals.

Nevertheless, it remains *doxastically* open, a matter to be decided by natural science if decided at all, whether or not the world reduces to genuinely atomic states of affairs. So our theory of possibility had better be equipped to deal with the doxastic possibility that there are no atomic individuals, properties or relations.

We may so equip the theory by introducing the notion of *relative atoms*. Let the states of affairs whose conjunction makes up the world involve certain individuals, properties and relations. They may or may not be simple (doxastic 'may'). The totality of recombinations of these 'atoms' yields a set of possible worlds, which can in addition be 'expanded' and 'contracted' in the usual way. If the atoms are genuine atoms, then no more remains to be done. But if the atoms are not genuinely atomic, then this set is a mere subset of the worlds which can be formed. With one or more of the 'atoms' broken up, we can go on to an enlarged set of worlds. If the breaking-up goes on forever, and reaches no genuine atoms even at infinity, then at each point in the break-up new worlds emerge.

Perhaps all this seems too easy. But a vital condition has to be placed upon the relative atoms, a condition which is satisfied automatically in the atomic universes which we have considered up to this point. The relative atoms – the individuals, the properties, the relations – must not merely be distinct from each other, they must be *wholly distinct*. Only if the atoms are wholly distinct will each different recombination yield a different possible world.

We must distinguish, then, between distinct and wholly distinct, and demand the latter for our relative atoms. To give examples: the property *F*, the conjunctive property *F & G*, the conjunctive property *F & H*, and the structural property *made up of an F-part having R to a G-part*, are all distinct (different) properties. But they are not *wholly* distinct. F is a proper part of *F & G* and *F & H*. It is also a proper part, in a somewhat different fashion, of the structural property. *F & G* and *F & H* are distinct, but have overlapping parts. And so on. This distinction between mere distinctness and being wholly distinct is a *mereological* distinction. Instead of distinct/wholly distinct, we could speak of *partial* and *complete* non-identity.

This leads on to a point of the most far-reaching importance. When we come in practice to assert that P is a possible state of affairs, we may assume that the requirement of wholly distinct relative atoms is satisfied when in fact it is not. Here is a schematic case.

Suppose that there is a set of individuals which has the conjunctive property *F & G*, a wholly disjoint set which has *G & H*, and a third wholly disjoint set which has *F & H*. Suppose, however, that these properties present themselves to us, say in perception, as different, but unanalysed (and so for all we know simple) properties. Suppose that we give them the names 'A', 'B' and 'C'. Taking A, B and C as property-atoms, as we might feel entitled to do, we can form the set of possible properties, {A, B, C, AB, BC, AC, ABC} which individuals might have. Combinatorialism has given us distinct, if not wholly distinct, properties.

But suppose that we now feed in the (previously supposed unknown) analysis of A, B and C. Substituting in our set of possible properties, we get {FG, GH, FH, FGH, FGH, FGH, FGH}. The last four terms are identical. Whatever we might have thought originally, before being given the constitution of A, B and C, recombination in fact yields only four distinct properties.

Nevertheless, given that one cannot analyse properties A, B and C into their constituents, will we not naturally form the notion of seven distinct combinations? This in turn allows us to form the conception of worlds which are epistemically distinct, or, better, doxastically distinct, but which are *in fact not distinct*. (Consider, for instance, worlds where AB was instantiated, but not AC, BC and ABC, but contrast with others where BC was instantiated but not AB, AC and ABC.) These doxastically distinct worlds are not a subset of the possible worlds. The possible worlds are a subset of them!

Suppose that we consider the *nomically* possible worlds. Here the *laws of nature* are held fixed, but anything else which can be recombined (expanded, contracted, etc.) is so. Taking the laws of nature to be contingent (on combinatorial grounds!), then the nomically possible worlds are a proper subset of the possible worlds. The same sort of situation holds if we keep fixed, not the laws of nature, but what we *know* about the world. But we must not assume that all 'qualified' types of possibility involve cutting down on the possible worlds in this way. On the contrary, as we have just seen, there may be more doxastically possible worlds than possible worlds.

Doxastically possible worlds may even be impossible worlds. If combinatorialism is correct, then all distinct simple properties and, more generally, all wholly distinct properties, are compossible. But, as will emerge in the next section, in the case of structural properties, combinatorialism permits distinct but incompatible properties. However, if it is not known that the properties involved are incompatible, impossible combinations may be formed.

I suggest that this is a cause for rejoicing rather than dismay. We want impossible worlds. For example, they are required in mathematics where we want to say, for instance, that it is 'possible' that Goldbach's conjecture that every number is the sum of two primes is false, but also 'possible' that it is true. That we can get them so easily shows the power of the combinatorial conception. Of course, impossible worlds would be very bad news for a *realistic* theory of these worlds. We could then only accommodate impossible worlds by holding that some worlds contain objective contradictions. But the view being espoused is that possible worlds are fictions. Impossible worlds are just impossible fictions.

A thoroughgoing scientific realism about *this* world gives us, I hope, enough realistic capital to cover our expenses for the unreal possible worlds. There are no ideal gases, but it is very convenient, in investigating the behaviour of actual gases, to compare their behaviour to an ideal gas. For the latter is like a real gas, but is one from which certain complicating features have been stripped. There are no worlds over and above the actual one, but it is very convenient, in many philosophical investigations, to speak of these extra worlds and hold them up against the actual world. The worlds are 'constructed' in certain ways from the materials provided by the actual world. And it is useful, for certain purposes, to move beyond possible worlds to merely doxastically distinct worlds, and even to impossible worlds.

At this point we are in a position to explain why the postulation of alien universals seems so attractive. I argued that they are impossible, because combinatorially inaccessible from the actual world. But, without rejecting that result, we can now see that such universals are doxastically possible. After all, we have no a priori insight into the extent of the realm of universals. The known universals, if any are known, may be all the universals that there are. (Remember that the only universals are the instantiated ones.) Their recombinations will then exhaust the realm of the possible. But it is at least *doxastically* possible ('conceivable') that there exist universals completely different, completely alien, from the known universals.

We could introduce symbols for such unknown universals, or refer to them indeterminately by using existential quantifiers. As a result, they could figure in doxastically possible worlds. Yet, it might be, there are no such universals. In that case, the doxastically possible worlds would be impossible worlds. But that these universals would be doxastically possible, together with the fact that their genuine impossibility could not be established a priori, would convincingly explain why they seemed to be genuinely possible.

7 A Major Difficulty

I finish this paper by considering what appears to be a major difficulty for the view put forward.

The combinatorialist scheme depends upon all combinations of universals being compossible. A single individual can instantiate any such combination, provided only that the universals so combined are *wholly distinct*. For if we do not have this promiscuous compatibility, then we get logical incompatibility not envisaged by the theory.

However, if we consider what pass for properties (and relations) in our *ordinary* thinking, then we find that failures of compossibility abound. Consider properties. These characteristically appear in *ranges*, so that they form classes of determinates falling under the one determinable. An individual can, at one time, instantiate only one member of a given range. The colour-compatibilities are a notorious instance of this phenomenon. Historically, they seem to have furnished one of the reasons Wittgenstein had for abandoning the metaphysics of the *Tractatus*.

I make no promise to solve the problem in a definitive way. Here the combinatorial theory goes on the defensive. But I hope to show that the incompatibility problem does not refute combinatorialism. I would then appeal to the other merits of the theory, in particular its subordination of the possible of the actual.

Of importance here is the already introduced notion of a *structural* property. Structural properties are a species of complex property. But it makes for ease of exposition if we work with simple *individuals*. Suppose, then, that atomic a is F, atomic b is F, and that a has R to b. F and R are universals. Now consider the compound individual $[a + b]$. Call it 'c'. c has the complex property of being made up of two wholly distinct F-parts which stand in the relation R. Call this property of c 'S'. S is a good example of a structural property.

Let there be another compound individual, d, but this time made up of *three* atomic individuals, each of which is F, and where the first atom has R to the second, and the second has R to the third. Call this structural property of d 'T'.

Now consider combinatorially formed possible worlds. Properties S and T are not suitable properties for such combinatorial operations. For although they are distinct properties, *they are not wholly distinct*. Furthermore, they are not-wholly-distinct properties of a sort which cannot be bestowed on the same individual. For the individual would have to be just two-atomed (to be S) and just three-atomed (to be T).[8] The point can be put the other way round. For all possible worlds, for all individuals x and y, if x has S and y has T, then x and y are distinct (but not in all cases wholly distinct) individuals.

A treatment of this sort may perhaps be extracted from Wittgenstein's remark in the *Tractatus*, 6.3751. He writes:

For example, the simultaneous presence of two colours at the same place in the visual field is impossible, in fact logically impossible, since it is ruled out by the logical structure of colour.

Let us think how this contradiction appears in physics: more or less as follows – a particle cannot have two velocities at the same time; that is to say, particles that are in different places at the same time cannot be identical.

Our present concern is with the second paragraph. Suppose that at a certain instant a moves with uniform velocity in a straight line for a second and covers a distance of two inches. At the same instant b moves with uniform velocity in a straight line for a second and covers a distance of one inch. a now has the relational property of being two inches from where it was a second before. But b has the relational property of being one inch from where it was a second before.

These relational properties, however, involve a structural element. A two-inch distance is made up of two numerically distinct one-inch distances. As a result, the properties are incompatible. If a and b have the two properties at the same instant, then a and b must be different. This, I take it, is the sort of reasoning that Wittgenstein had in mind. The numerical difference of a and b is built into the distinct, but not wholly distinct, properties.

I suggest that this is the solution to the problem for combinatorialism posed by the typical cases of incompatible properties. Such properties are structural properties. In many cases they fall into ranges of properties: they are determinates falling under a common determinable. Furthermore, it is the nature of the structure that it involves numerically different individuals (a two-inch long thing is a compound individual made up of two wholly distinct one-inch things). As a result, these properties are not compossible. Individuals instantiating both of a pair of such properties will never appear in possible worlds, that is, in recombinations of *wholly distinct* 'atoms'.

It would seem that the *quantities* which natural science deals so extensively in, and in particular the quantities recognized in physics, can, in many cases, be treated as structural properties of this sort. At any rate, such treatment seems a promising research programme. These quantities are among the best candidates that we have for organized classes of universals. Their ranges are a fruitful source of incompatibilities.

But how are we going to deal with the *colour-incompatibilities*? Wittgenstein in the passage quoted suggests that they can be assimilated to the velocity case. I have interpreted him as adumbrating a solution to the latter in terms of structural properties. To complete the solution, a link has to be forged between colour and structural properties.

What I suggest, and what I think Wittgenstein was also suggesting, is that the colours *are* suitable structural properties. As a result, they immediately yield the required incompatibilities. But, and here is an epistemological point, in perception it is not given to us that they are such structures. The identity is established a posteriori by empirical and other scientific reasoning.

We have in fact already envisaged situations of this sort, where a conjunction of properties, F and G say, is perceived as a single 'gestalt' property, A. The epistemology of the situation does not seem to raise great difficulties. We can understand how F and G might both be required to stimulate a single, all-or-nothing, reaction in a perceiver. As a result, an ontologically complex property would be epistemically simple. Structural properties of the sort discussed could be plugged into this account without difficulty. Research into the physical basis of colour seems at present so controversial that it is unwise to speculate just what these properties are.

There are *phenomenological* objections to even an a posteriori identification of colours (*seen* colours) with physical bases of the colours. But without discussing the matter here, I will say that I think both that such objections are overrated, and that, in any case, some rough justice can be done to them.[9]

If colour can be dealt with in this way, so, presumably, can other cases of incompatibility involving the other secondary qualities. It may be noted that we seem to be (a little vaguely) *aware* of the incompatibilities while having no idea, in the state of nature, of their suggested structural basis. This again seems to be a mere epistemic difficulty. It seems that we can fairly easily conceive how a perceptual processing of properties could yield an awareness of incompatibility without an awareness of the basis of the incompatibility. (Cf. 'I know that something has been disarranged, although I am unable to spot the nature of the disarrangement.')

A combinatorial theory of possibility raises other questions, and involves further difficulties which require discussion. But let this suffice for the present.

Notes

1 L. Wittgenstein, *Tractatus Logico-Philosophicus*, trans. D. Pears and B. F. McGuiness (London: Routledge and Kegan Paul 1922); my italics.

2 B. Skyrms, 'Tractarian nominalism', *Philosophical Studies* 40 (1981), pp. 199–206.

3 See D. M. Armstrong, *Universals and Scientific Realism*, vol. 2: *A Theory of Universals* (Cambridge: Cambridge University Press, 1978), ch. 14.

4 David Lewis, *On the Plurality of Worlds* (Oxford: Blackwell, 1986).

5 See D. M. Armstrong, *Universals and Scientific Realism*, vol. 1: *Nominalism and Realism* (Cambridge: Cambridge University Press, 1978), ch. 9.

6 W. G. Lycan, 'The trouble with possible worlds', in M. J. Loux (ed.) *The Possible and the Actual* (Ithaca, NY: Cornell University Press, 1979), pp. 274–316, 307n.

7 Armstrong, *Theory of Universals*, ch. 15, sect. 1.

8 What is the basis of this impossibility? I think it is reasonable to say that this mereological truth is purely analytic. We see that it holds if we understand what it means to say that something is a proper part of a whole.

9 See D. M. Armstrong and Norman Malcolm, *Consciousness and Causality* (Oxford: Blackwell, 1984), pp. 180–1.

Universals, Properties, Kinds

Introduction

There are individual red things: this paint patch here, the apple over there, and so on. But, in addition to these particular red objects, is there also *redness*, something had in common by all and only red things? In general, in addition to particulars that are *F*, is there also such a thing as *F*-ness, a "universal," shared by all and only *F*-things? If there are such universals, what sort of thing are they? Is there a universal corresponding to every meaningful predicative expression ("red," "not red," "red or large," "located ten miles due north of Providence," "being sought by Ponce de León," ....)? Are there genuine properties and kinds in nature independently of languages and systems of concepts? Are there "natural kinds," kinds that reflect genuine similarities and differences in nature? These are some of the central questions about universals, properties, and kinds that have occupied philosophers.

In "Universals as Attributes" (chapter 16), D. M. Armstrong elucidates his conception of universals as attributes that are instantiated by particulars. He defends a "sparse" theory that does not allow a universal for every meaningful predicate, and also disallows "negative" and "disjunctive" universals, although he does allow conjunctive universals.

David Lewis, in "New Work for a Theory of Universals" (chapter 17), argues that, although we may not need Armstrong's universals themselves, we need entities that will do their work. What we need, according to Lewis, are *natural classes of*

possibilia, and he claims that these can help solve a variety of philosophical problems, including the problem of "the One over Many," of defining duplicate, determinism and materialism, of analyzing causation, lawlikeness, and other important concepts.

In "Natural Kinds" (chapter 18), W. V. Quine explains how our innate sensory quality space gets progressively sharpened by experience and scientific theorizing into a group of properties we recognize as natural kinds, inductively projectable properties in terms of which we formulate our theories of the world. The idea of qualitative similarity receives a good deal of attention from Quine.

Hilary Putnam, too, subscribes to the "sparse" ontology of properties, sharply distinguishing properties from predicates and concepts. In "On Properties" (chapter 19), he argues that properties are indispensable to science, and critically discusses various proposals for an identity criterion for properties. His own positive proposals are grounded in considerations of the properties and magnitudes of fundamental physical theory.

In "Causality and Properties" (chapter 20), Sydney Shoemaker tackles the same question: How do we individuate properties? His answer is a causal theory of properties: the identity of properties consists in the identity of the causal powers that the properties confer on objects that have them. This approach, if not Shoemaker's specific proposals, has come to be widely accepted, and it is now a commonplace closely to associate, or even identify, properties with causal powers.

Further reading

Armstrong, D. M., *Nominalism and Realism* (Cambridge: Cambridge University Press, 1978).
——, *A Theory of Universals* (Cambridge: Cambridge University Press, 1978).
——, *A World of States of Affairs* (Cambridge: Cambridge University Press, 1997).
Bealer, George, *Quality and Concept* (Oxford: Clarendon Press, 1982).
Jubien, Michael, "On properties and property theory," in G. Chierchia and B. H. Partee (eds), *Properties, Types and Meaning* (Dordrecht: Kluwer, 1989).
Loux, Michael J., *Substance and Attribute* (Dordrecht: Reidel, 1978).
Mellor, D. H., "Properties and predicates," in K. Mulligan (ed.), *Language, Truth and Ontology* (Dordrecht: Kluwer, 1992).

Mellor, D. H., and Oliver, Alex (eds), *Properties* (Oxford: Oxford University Press, 1997).
Oliver, Alex, "The metaphysics of properties," *Mind* 105 (1996), pp. 1–80.
Shoemaker, Sydney, "Identity, properties and causality," in *Identity, Cause and Mind* (Cambridge: Cambridge University Press, 1984).
Sober, Elliott, "Evolutionary theory and the ontological status of properties," *Philosophical Studies* 40 (1981), pp. 147–76.
Swoyer, Chris, "Theories of properties: from plenitude to paucity," *Philosophical Perspectives* 10 (1962), pp. 244–64.
Wilson, Mark, "Predicate meets property," *Philosophical Review* 91 (1982), pp. 549–90.

16

Universals as Attributes

D. M. Armstrong

1 Uninstantiated Universals?

If we abandon the idea that particulars are nothing but bundles of universals but still want to recognize universals, then we must return to the traditional view that particulars, tokens, *instantiate* universals: having properties and standing to each other in relations. If we do this, then there are a number of controversial questions that have to be settled. One key question is this. Should we, or should we not, accept a Principle of Instantiation for universals? That is, should we, or should we not, demand that every universal be instantiated? That is, for each property universal must it be the case that it is a property of some particular? For each relation universal must it be the case that there are particulars between which the relation holds?

We certainly should not demand that every universal should be instantiated *now*. It would be enough if a particular universal was not instantiated now, but was instantiated in the past, or would be instantiated in the future. The Principle of Instantiation should be interpreted as ranging over all time: past, present, and future. But should we uphold the principle even in this relatively liberal form?

This is a big parting of the ways. We can call the view that there are uninstantiated universals the Platonist view. It appears to have been the view

Originally published in D. M. Armstrong, *Universals: An Opinionated Introduction* (1989), ch. 5. Copyright © by Westview Press. Reprinted by permission of the publisher.

held by Plato, who was also, apparently, the first philosopher to introduce universals. (He spoke of Forms or Ideas – but there was nothing psychological about the Ideas.)

Once you have uninstantiated universals, you need somewhere special to put them, a "Platonic heaven," as philosophers often say. They are not to be found in the ordinary world of space and time. And since it seems that any instantiated universal might have been uninstantiated – for example, there might have been nothing past, present, or future that had that property – then if uninstantiated universals are in a Platonic heaven, it will be natural to place all universals in that heaven. The result is that we get two realms: the realm of universals and the realm of particulars, the latter being ordinary things in space and time. Such universals are often spoken of as *transcendent*. (A view of this sort was explicitly held by Russell in his earlier days before he adopted a bundle-of-universals view.[1] Instantiation then becomes a very big deal: a relation between universals and particulars that crosses realms. The Latin tag used by the Scholastics for a theory of this sort is *universalia ante res*, "universals before things." Such a view is unacceptable to Naturalists, that is, to those who think that the space-time world is all the world that there is. This helps to explain why Empiricists, who tend to be sympathetic to Naturalism, often reject universals.

It is interesting to notice that a separate-realm theory of universals permits of a blob as opposed to a layer-cake view of particulars. For on this view, what is it for a thing to have a property? It is not the thing's having some internal feature, but rather its having a relationship, the instantiation relationship, to certain universals or Forms in another realm. The thing itself could be bloblike. It is true that the thing could also be given a property structure. But then the properties that make up this structure cannot be universals but must be particulars. They would have to be tropes. The particular involves property tropes, but these property tropes are put into natural classes by their instantiating a certain universal in the realm of the universals. At any rate, without bringing in tropes in addition, it seems that Platonic theories of universals have to treat particulars as bloblike rather than layer-caked. I think that this is an argument against Platonic theories.

If, however, we reject uninstantiated universals, then we are at least in a position, if we want to do it, to bring the universals down to earth. We can adopt the view whose Latin tag is *universalia in rebus*, "universals in things." We can think of a thing's properties as constituents of the thing and think of the properties as universals. This may have been the position of Aristotle. (The scholars differ. Some make him a Nominalist. Some think he believed in this-worldly universals. Certainly, he criticized Plato's other worldly universals.) *Universalia in rebus* is, of course, a layer-cake view, with properties as universals as part of the internal structure of things. (Relations will be *universalia inter res*, "universals between things."[2]

There are difficulties in this position, of course, objections that can be brought, as with every other solution to the Problem of Universals. One thing that has worried many philosophers, including perhaps Plato, is that on this view we appear to have multiple location of the same thing. Suppose *a* is F and *b* is also F, with F a property universal. The very same entity has to be part of the structure of two things at two places. How can the universal be in two places at once? I will come back to this question later.

Just to round things off, I will mention the third Scholastic tag: *universalia post res*, "universals after things." This was applied to Nominalist theories. It fits best with Predicate or Concept Nominalism, where properties, etc. are as it were created by the classifying mind: shadows cast on things by our predicates or concepts.

But our present task is to decide whether or not we ought to countenance uninstantiated universals. The first point to be made is that the onus of proof seems to be firmly on the side of the Platonists. It can hardly be doubted that there is a world of space

and time. But a separate realm of universals is a mere hypothesis, or postulation. If a postulation has great explanatory value, then it may be a good postulation. But it has to prove itself. Why should we postulate uninstantiated universals?

One thing that has moved many philosophers is what we may call the argument from the meaning of general terms. Plato, in his *Republic*, had Socrates say, "shall we proceed as usual and begin by assuming the existence of a single essential nature or Form for every set of things which we call by the same name?"[3] Socrates may have been thinking along the following lines. Ordinary names, that is, proper names, have a bearer of the name. If we turn to general terms – words like 'horse' and 'triangular' that apply to many different things – then we need something that stands to the word in the same general sort of relation that the bearer of the proper name stands to the proper name. There has to be an object that constitutes or corresponds to the meaning of the general word. So there has to be something called horseness and triangularity. But now consider a general word that applies to nothing particular at all, a word like 'unicorn' for instance. It is perfectly meaningful. And if it is meaningful, must there not be something in the world that constitutes or corresponds to the word? So there must be uninstantiated universals.

This "argument from meaning" is a very bad argument. (In fairness to Socrates, it is not clear whether he was using it. Other philosophers have, though, often at a rather unself-conscious level.) The argument depends on the assumption that in every case where a general word has meaning, there is something in the world that constitutes or corresponds to that meaning. Gilbert Ryle spoke of this as the 'Fido'–Fido fallacy. Fido corresponds to the word 'Fido', but there does not have to be some single thing corresponding to a general word.

To go along with the argument from meaning is to be led into a very promiscuous theory of universals. If it is correct, then we know a priori that for each general word with a certain meaning, there exists a universal. This lines up predicates and properties in a nice neat way, but it is a way that we ought to be very suspicious of. Is it that easy to discover what universals there are?

Plato had another line of thought that led him toward uninstantiated universals. This is the apparent failure of things in the ordinary world to come up to exact standards. It seems that nothing in the world is perfectly straight or circular, yet in geometry we discuss the properties of perfectly straight lines or perfect circles. Again, no thing is perfectly changeless. Yet again, it may well be that no act is perfectly just. Certainly no person is perfectly virtuous, and no state is perfectly just. Yet in ethical and political discussion (e.g., in the *Republic*) we can discuss the nature of virtue and justice. In general, we perceive the world as falling short of certain standards. This can be explained if, whether we know it or not, we are comparing ordinary things to Forms, which the ordinary things can never fully instantiate. (This can lead one, and perhaps led Plato, to the difficult notion of degrees of instantiation, with the highest degree never realized.)

It is interesting to notice that this argument did not quite lead Plato where he wanted to go in every case. Consider geometry. In geometry one might wish to consider the properties of, say, two intersecting circles. These circles will be perfectly circular. But also, of course, there is only *one* Form of the circle. So what are these two perfect circles? Plato, apparently, had to introduce what he called the Mathematicals. Like the mathematical Forms they were perfect and thus were unlike ordinary things. But unlike the Forms, there could be many tokens of the same type, and in this they were like ordinary things. They were particulars, although perfect particulars. But if this is so, though perhaps the falling away from standards gave Plato an argument for the Mathematicals, it is not clear that it is any argument for the Forms.

But in any case, cannot ideal standards simply be things that we merely think of? We can quite knowingly form thoughts of that which does not exist. In the case of ideal standards nothing comes up to the standard, but by extrapolating from ordinary things that approximate to the standard in different degrees, we can form the thought of something that does come up to the standard. It turns out to be useful to do so. Why attribute metaphysical reality to such standards? They could be useful fictions. As a matter of fact, in the geometrical case it appears that such notions as that of a perfectly straight line or a perfectly circular object may be acquired directly in experience. For cannot something look perfectly straight or perfectly circular, even if it is not in fact so?

One should note that one thing that seems to keep a theory of uninstantiated universals going is the widespread idea that it is sufficient for a universal to exist if it is merely possible that it should be instantiated. I have found in discussion that this idea has particular appeal if it is empirically possible (that is, compatible with the laws of nature) that the alleged universal should have actual instances. Suppose, for instance, that somebody describes a very complex pattern of wallpaper but does not ever sketch the pattern or manufacture the wallpaper. Suppose nobody else does either in the whole history of the universe. It is clear that there was nothing in the laws of nature that prevented the pattern's ever having an instance, from ever having a token of the type. But is not that pattern a monadic universal, a complex and structural universal to be sure, but a universal nonetheless?

In this way, apparently, it is natural for philosophers to argue. But for myself I do not see the force of the argument. Philosophers do not reason that way about particulars. They do not argue that it is empirically possible that present-day France should be a monarchy and therefore that the present king of France exists, although, unfortunately for French royalists, he is not instantiated. Why argue in the same way about universals? Is it that philosophers think that universals are so special that they can exist whether or not particular things, which are contingent only, exist? If so, I think that this is no better than a prejudice, perhaps inherited from Plato.

There is one subtle variation of the argument to uninstantiated universals from their empirical possibility that I think has more weight. It has been developed by Michael Tooley.[4] However, it depends upon deep considerations about the nature of the laws of nature, which cannot be discussed here. And in any case, the argument depends upon the laws' being found to have a very special structure, which it is unlikely that they actually have. As a result, it seems that the best that the argument shows is that uninstantiated universals are possible rather than actual. And even this conclusion may be avoidable.[5]

It may also be thought that considerations from mathematics, and the properties and relations postulated by mathematicians, push toward the recognition of uninstantiated universals. However, the whole project of bringing together the theory of universals with the disciplines of mathematics, although very important, cannot be undertaken here. I have sketched out, rather broadly, the way that I think it ought to go in a book on the nature of possibility.[6]

From this point on, therefore, I am going to assume the truth of the Principle of Instantiation. As already noted, this does not compel one to abandon a two-realm doctrine. It does not compel one to bring the universals down among ordinary things. But it does *permit* one to do this, and to do so seems the natural way to develop the theory once one rejects uninstantiated universals.

2 Disjunctive, Negative, and Conjunctive Universals

For simplicity, in this section I will consider property universals only. But the points to be made appear to apply to relations also. We have already rejected uninstantiated universals. But it seems that the potential class of universals needs to be cut down a great deal further if we are to get a plausible theory. I will begin by giving reasons for rejecting disjunctive property universals. By a *disjunctive property* I mean a disjunction of (property) universals. Let us assume that particular electric charges and particular masses are universals. Then having charge C or having mass M (with C and M dummies for determinate, that is, definite values) would be an example of a disjunctive property. Why is it not a universal? Consider two objects. One has charge C but lacks mass M. The other lacks charge C but has mass M. So they have the disjunctive property having charge C or having mass M. But surely that does not show that, in any serious sense, they thereby have something identical? The whole point of a universal, however, is that it should be identical in its different instances.

There is another reason to deny that a disjunction of universals is a universal. There is some very close link between universals and causality. The link is of this nature. If a thing instantiates a certain universal, then, in virtue of that, it has the power to act in a certain way. For instance, if a thing has a certain mass, then it has the power to act upon the scalepan of a balance, or upon scales, in a certain way. Furthermore, different universals bestow different powers. Charge and mass, for instance, manifest themselves in different ways. I doubt if the link between universals and powers is a necessary one, but it seems real. Moreover, if, as seems abstractly possible, two different universals bestowed the very same powers, how could one ever know that they were two different universals? If they affect all apparatus, including our brains, in exactly the same way, will we not judge that we are dealing with one universal only?

Now suppose that a thing has charge C but lacks mass M. In virtue of charge C, it has certain powers

to act. For instance, it repels things with like charge. Possession of the disjunctive property C or M adds nothing to its power. This suggests that while C may be a genuine universal, C or M is not.

So I think that we should reject disjunctive universals. A similar case seems to hold against negative universals: the lack or absence of a property is not a property. If having charge C is the instantiation of a universal, then not having C is not the instantiating of a universal.

First, we may appeal to identity again. Is there really something in common, something identical, in everything that lacks charge C? Of course, there might be some universal property that just happened to be coextensive with lacking charge C. But the lack itself does not seem to be a factor found in each thing that lacks charge C.

Second, causal considerations seem to point in the same direction. It is a strange idea that lacks or absences do any causing. It is natural to say that a thing acts in virtue of positive factors alone. This also suggests that absences of universals are not universals.

It is true that there is some linguistic evidence that might be thought to point the other way. We do say things like "lack of water caused his death." At the surface, the statement says that a lack of water caused an absence of life. But how seriously should we take such ways of expressing ourselves? Michael Tooley has pointed out that we are unhappy to say "lack of poison causes us to remain alive." Yet if the surface way of understanding the first statement is correct, then the second statement should be understood in the same way and thought to be true. Certain counterfactual statements are true in both cases: If he had had water, then he would (could) have still been alive; if we had taken poison, we would have been dead now. These are causal truths. But they tell us very little about the actual causal factors operative in the two cases. We believe, I think, that these actual causal factors could be spelled out in purely positive terms.

It is interesting to notice that conjunctions of universals (having both charge C and mass M) escape the two criticisms leveled against disjunctive and negative universals. With conjunctions we do have identity. The very same conjunction of factors is present in each instance. There is no problem about causality. If a thing instantiates the conjunction, then it will have certain powers as a consequence. These powers will be different from those that the thing would have had if it had had just one of the conjuncts. It may even be that the conjunction can do more than the sum of what each property would do if each was instantiated alone. (As scientists say: There could be synergism. The effect could be more than the sum of each cause acting by itself.)

But there is one condition that ought to be put on conjunctive universals. Some thing (past, present, future) must actually have both properties and at the same time. This, of course, is simply the Principle of Instantiation applied to conjunctive universals.

3 Predicates and Universals

What has been said about uninstantiated universals, and also about disjunctions and negations of universals, has brought out a most important point. It is that there is no automatic passage from predicates (linguistic entities) to universals. For instance, the expression "either having charge C or having mass M" is a perfectly good predicate. It could apply to, or be true of, innumerable objects. But as we have seen, this does not mean that there is a universal corresponding to this predicate.

Wittgenstein made a famous contribution to the Problem of Universals with his discussion of *family resemblances*. Wittgenstein was an anti-metaphysician, and his object was to dissolve rather than to solve the Problem of Universals. He seems to have thought that what he said about family resemblances was (among other things) a step toward getting rid of the problem. But I think that the real moral of what he said is only that predicates and universals do not line up in any simple way.

In his *Philosophical Investigations* he considered the notion of a *game*. He had this to say about it:[7]

66. Consider for example the proceedings that we call "games." I mean board-games, card-games, ball-games, Olympic games, and so on. What is common to them all? – Don't say: "There *must* be something common, or they would not be called 'games'" – but *look and see* whether there is anything common to all – For if you look at them you will not see something that is common to *all*, but similarities, relationships, and a whole series of them at that. To repeat: don't think, but look! – Look for example at board-games, with their multifarious relationships. Now pass to card-games; here you find many correspondences with the first group, but many common features drop out, and others appear. When we pass next to ball-games, much that is common is retained, but much is lost. – Are they all "amusing"? Compare chess with noughts and crosses. Or is there always winning and losing, or competition between players? Think of patience. In ball games there is winning and losing; but when a child throws his ball at the wall and catches it again, this feature has disappeared. Look at the parts played by skill and luck; and at the difference between skill in chess and skill in tennis. Think now of games like ring-a-ring-a-roses; here is the element of amusement, but how many other characteristic features have disappeared! And we can go through the many, many other groups of games in the same way; we can see how similarities crop up and disappear.

And the result of this examination is: we see a complicated network of similarities overlapping and criss-crossing: sometimes overall similarities, sometimes similarities of detail.

67. I can think of no better expression to characterize these similarities than "family resemblances"; for the various resemblances between members of a family: build, features, colour of eyes, gait, temperament, etc. etc. overlap and criss-cross in the same way. – And I shall say: "games" form a family.

This has been a very influential passage. Wittgenstein and his followers applied the point to all sorts of notions besides those of a game, including many of the central notions discussed by philosophers. But what should a believer in universals think that Wittgenstein has shown about universals?

Let us agree, as we probably should, that there is no universal of gamehood. But now what of this "complicated network of similarities overlapping and criss-crossing" of which Wittgenstein speaks? All the Realist has to do is to analyze each of these similarities in terms of common properties. That analysis of similarity is not a difficult or unfamiliar idea, though it is an analysis that would be contested by a Nominalist. But there will not be any property that runs through the whole class and makes them all games. To give a crude and oversimplified sketch, the situation might be like this:

Particulars:	*a*	*b*	*c*	*d*	*e*
Their properties:	FGHJ	GHJK	HJKL	JKLM	KLMN

Here F to M are supposed to be genuine property universals, and it is supposed that the predicate "game" applies in virtue of these properties. But the class of particulars {a ... e}, which is the class of all tokens of games, is a family in Wittgenstein's sense. Here, though, I have sketched an account of such families that is completely compatible with Realism about universals.

However, Wittgenstein's remarks do raise a big question. How does one decide whether one is or is not in the presence of a genuine property or relation? Wittgenstein says of games, "don't think, but look!" As a general recipe, at least, that seems far too simple.

I do not think that there is any infallible way of deciding what are the true universals. It seems clear that we must not look to semantic considerations. As I said in section 1, those who argue to particular universals from semantic data, from predicates to a universal corresponding to that predicate, argue in a very optimistic and unempirical manner. I call them *a priori realists*. Better, I think, is *a posteriori realism*. The best guide that we have to just what universals there are is total science.

For myself, I believe that this puts physics in a special position. There seem to be reasons (scientific, empirical, a posteriori reasons) to think that physics is *the* fundamental science. If that is correct, then such properties as mass, charge, extension, duration, space-time interval, and other properties envisaged by physics may be the true monadic universals. (They are mostly ranges of quantities. Quantities raise problems that will need some later discussion.) Spatiotemporal and causal relations will perhaps be the true polyadic universals.

If this is correct, then the ordinary types – the type red, the type horse, in general, the types of the manifest image of the world – will emerge as preliminary, rough-and-ready classifications of reality. For the most part they are not false, but they are rough-and-ready. Many of them will be family affairs, as games appear to be. To the one type will correspond a whole family of universals and not always a very close family. And even where the ordinary types do carve the beast of reality along its true joints, they may still not expose those joints for the things that they are. But let it be emphasized that any identification of universals remains rather speculative. In what I have just been saying I have been trying to combine a philosophy of universals with Physicalism. Others may have other ideas.

4   States of Affairs

In the Universals theory that we are examining, particulars instantiate properties, pairs of particulars instantiate (dyadic) relations, triples of particulars instantiate (triadic) relations, and so on as far as is needed. Suppose that *a* is F, with F a universal, or that *a* has R to *b*, with R a universal. It appears that we are required to recognize *a*'s being F and *a*'s having R to *b* as items in our ontology. I will speak of these items as *states of affairs*. Others have called them facts.[8]

Why do we need to recognize states of affairs? Why not recognize simply particulars, universals (divided into properties and relations), and, perhaps, instantiation? The answer appears by considering the following point. If *a* is F, then it is entailed that *a* exists and that the universal F exists. However, *a* could exist, and F could exist, and yet it fail to be the case that *a* is F (F is instantiated, but instantiated elsewhere only). *a*'s being F involves something more than *a* and F. It is no good simply adding the fundamental tie or nexus of instantiation to the sum of *a* and F. The existence of *a*, of instantiation, and of F does not amount to *a*'s being F. The something more must be *a*'s being F – and this is a state of affairs.

This argument rests upon a general principle, which, following C. B. Martin, I call the truthmaker principle. According to this principle, for every contingent truth at least (and perhaps for all truths contingent or necessary) there must be something in the world that makes it true. "Something" here may be taken as widely as may be wished. The "making" is not causality, of course: Rather, it is that in the world in virtue of which the truth is true. Gustav Bergmann and his followers have spoken of the "ontological ground" of truths, and I think that this is my "something in the world" that makes truths true. An important point to notice is that different truths may all have the same truth-maker, or ontological ground. For instance, that this thing is colored, is red, and is scarlet are all made true by the thing's having a particular shade of color.

The truth-maker principle seems to me to be fairly obvious once attention is drawn to it, but I do not know how to argue for it further. It is to be noted, however, that some of those who take perfectly seriously the sort of metaphysical investigation that we are here engaged upon nevertheless reject the principle.[9]

Accepting the truth-maker principle will lead one to reject Quine's view[10] that *predicates* do not have to be taken seriously in considering the onto-logical implications of statements one takes to be true. Consider the difference between asserting that a certain surface is red and asserting that it is green. An upholder of the truth-maker principle will think that there has to be an ontological ground, a difference in the world, to account for the difference between the predicate 'red' applying to the surface and the predicate 'green' so applying. Of course, what that ontological ground is, is a further matter. There is no high road from the principle to universals and states of affairs.

Returning now to states of affairs, it may be pointed out that there are some reasons for accepting states of affairs even if the truth-maker principle is rejected. First, we can apparently refer to states of affairs, preparatory to saying something further about them. But it is generally, if not universally, conceded by philosophers that what can be referred to exists. Second, states of affairs are plausible candidates for the terms of causal relations. The state of affairs of a's being F may be the cause of b's being G. Third, as we shall see in section 8, states of affairs can help to solve a fairly pressing problem in the theory of universals: how to understand the multiple location of property universals and the nonlocation of relation universals.

It is interesting to see that states of affairs seem not to be required by a Class Nominalist or a Resemblance Nominalist, and of course that is an important economy for their respective theories. The Class Nominalist analyzes a's being F as a's being a member of a class (or natural class) containing $\{a, b, c, \ldots\}$. But here we have simply a and the class. The class-membership relation is internal, dictated by the nature of the terms. So we need not recognize it as something additional to the terms. The terms by themselves are sufficient truth-makers. Hence we do not need states of affairs.

The Resemblance Nominalist analyzes a's being F as a matter of resemblance relations holding between a and, say, suitable paradigm Fs. But that relation is also internal, dictated by what I called the particularized nature of a and the paradigm objects. Once again, states of affairs are not needed.

(But it seems that a Predicate Nominalist *will* require states of affairs. a's being F is analyzed as a's falling under the predicate F. But how can the falling under be dictated simply by a and the linguistic object F? Falling under is an external relation.)

Now for something very important. States of affairs have some rather surprising characteristics. Let us call a, b, F, R, etc. the constituents of states of affairs. It turns out that it is possible for there to be two different states of affairs that nevertheless have *exactly the same constituents*.

Here is a simple example. Let R be a nonsymmetrical relation (for instance, loves). Let it be the case, contingently, that a has R to b and b has R to a. Two distinct states of affairs exist: a's having R to b, and b's having R to a (a's loving b and b's loving a). Indeed, these states of affairs are *wholly* distinct, in the sense that it is possible for either state of affairs to fail to obtain while the other exists. Yet the two states of affairs have exactly the same constituents.

You can get the same phenomenon with properties as well as relations.[11] Assume, as I think it is correct to assume, that a conjunction of states of affairs is itself a state of affairs. Then consider (1) a's being F and b's being G; and (2) a's being G and b's being F. Two wholly distinct states of affairs, it may be, but the very same constituents.

At this point, it is worth realizing that states of affairs may be required not simply by those who recognize universals but also by any philosophy that recognizes properties and relations, whether as universals or as particulars. This is very important, because we saw in examining Natural Class and Resemblance theories what difficulties there are in denying properties and relations (in espousing a blob view).

Suppose that a has R_1 to b, with R_1 a particular, but a nonsymmetrical, relation. If b has 'the same' relation to a, then, on a philosophy of tropes, we have b's having R_2 to a: two states of affairs with different (though overlapping) constituents. For the loving that holds between a and b is a different object from the loving that holds between b and a. Nevertheless, a's having R_1 to b entails the existence of constituents a, R_1, and b, but the existence of these constituents does not entail that a has R_1 to b. So states of affairs still seem to be something more than their constituents.

With tropes, you never get different states of affairs constructed out of exactly the same constituents. But given just one set of constituents, more than one state of affairs having just these constituents is *possible*. From a, trope R_1, and b, for instance, we could get a's having R_1 to b or b's having R_1 to a. There is a way for a philosophy of tropes to avoid having to postulate states of affairs. But let us leave that aside for now.

I have spoken of the constituents of states of affairs. Could we also think and speak of them as *parts* of states of affairs? I think that it would be very unwise to think and speak of them in this way. Logicians have paid some attention to the notions of whole and part. They have worked out a formal calculus for manipulating these notions, which is sometimes called the calculus of individuals or, better, *mereology* (in Greek *meros* means a part). One philosopher who helped to work this out was Nelson Goodman, and in his book *The Structure of Appearance* an account of mereology is given.[12] There is one mereological principle that is very important for us here: If there are a number of things, and if they have a sum, that is, a whole of which they are parts, then they have just one sum.

I say *if* they have a sum, because it is controversial whether a number of things *always* have a sum. Do the square root of 2 and the Sydney Opera House have a sum? Philosophers differ on how permissive a mereology should be, that is, on whether there are limits to what you can sum, and if there are limits, where the limits fall. I myself would accept total permissiveness in summing. But all that is needed here is something that is agreed by all: where things can be summed, for each collection of things there is just one sum. We have just seen, however, that the complete constituents of a state of affairs are capable of being, and may actually even be, the complete constituents of a different state of affairs. Hence constituents do not stand to states of affairs as parts to whole.

It is worth noticing that complex universals have constituents rather than parts. At any rate this is so if we accept the Principle of Instantiation. Consider, for instance, conjunctive universals. If being P and Q is a conjunctive universal, then there must exist some particular, x, such that x is both P and Q. But to say that is to say that there exists at least one state of affairs of the form x is P and x is Q. For the conjunctive universal to exist is for there to be a state of affairs of a certain sort. As a result, it is misleading to say that P and Q are *parts* of the conjunctive universal, a thing that I myself did say in the past.[13]

A very important type of complex universal is a *structural* property. A structural property involves a thing instantiating a certain pattern, such as a flag. Different parts (mereological parts) of the thing that instantiates the structural property will have certain properties. If the structural property involves relations, as a flag does, some or all of these parts will be related in various ways. It is

easy to see that states of affairs must be appealed to. If a has P, and b has Q, and a has R to b, then and only then the object $[a + b]$ has the structural property that may be presented in a shorthand way as P-R-Q.

A final point before leaving this particularly important section. The fact that states of affairs, if they exist, have a nonmereological mode of composition may have consequences for the view that particulars are no more than bundles of universals. (I understand that this point comes from Mark Johnston.) We have seen that different states of affairs can have exactly the same constituents (a's loving b, and b's loving a). We have previously argued against the Bundle theory that two bundles containing exactly the same universals are impossible. They would be the very same bundle. Yet, considering the matter independently of the Bundle theory, why should not two different particulars be exactly alike? But now suppose that, as is plausible, we treat a bundling of universals as a state of affairs. Why should not exactly the same universals be bundled up in different ways?

In reply, I think it must be admitted that this is conceivable. But it would depend upon the Bundle theorist's working out a scheme that allowed for different bundling of the very same things. This is not provided for in the actual Bundle theories that have been developed. So if they want to take this path, then the onus is on Bundle theorists to try to develop their theory in a new way.

5 A World of States of Affairs?

In the previous section it was argued that a philosophy that admits both particulars and universals ought to admit states of affairs (facts), which have particulars and universals as constituents (not as parts). As a matter of fact, we saw that to introduce properties and relations at all, even as particulars, would apparently involve states of affairs. But our present concern is with universals.

The suggestion to be put forward now is that we should think of the world as a world of states of affairs, with particulars and universals only having existence within states of affairs. We have already argued for a Principle of Instantiation for universals. If this is a true principle, then the way is open to regard a universal as an identical element present in certain states of affairs. A particular that existed outside states of affairs would not be clothed in any properties or relations. It may be called a *bare*

particular. If the world is to be a world of states of affairs, we must add to the Principle of Instantiation a Principle of the Rejection of Bare Particulars.

This second principle looks plausible enough. In a Universals theory, it is universals that give a thing its nature, kind, or sort. A bare particular would not instantiate any universals, and thus would have no nature, be of no kind or sort. What could we make of such an entity? Perhaps a particular need not have any relations to any other particular – perhaps it could be quite isolated. But it must instantiate at least one property.

6   The Thin and the Thick Particular

Here is a problem that has been raised by John Quilter.[14] He calls it the "Antinomy of Bare Particulars." Suppose that particular a instantiates property F. a is F. This "is" is obviously not the "is" of identity, as in a is a or F is F. a and F are different entities, one being a particular, the other a universal. The "is" we are dealing with is the "is" of instantiation – of a fundamental tie between particular and property. But if the "is" is not the "is" of identity, then it appears that a considered in itself is really a bare particular lacking any properties. But in that case a has not got the property F. The property F remains outside a – just as transcendent forms remain outside the particular in Plato's theory.

I believe that we can at least begin to meet this difficulty by drawing the important distinction between the *thin* and the *thick* particular.[15] The thin particular is a, taken apart from its properties (substratum). It is linked to its properties by instantiation, but it is not identical with them. It is not bare, because to be bare it would have to be not instantiating any properties. But though clothed, it is thin.

However, this is not the only way that a particular can be thought of. It can also be thought of as involving its properties. Indeed, that seems to be the normal way that we think of particulars. This is the thick particular. But the thick particular, because it enfolds both thin particulars and properties, held together by instantiation, can be nothing but a state of affairs.

Suppose that a instantiates F, G, H, ... They comprise the totality of a's (nonrelational) properties. Now form the conjunctive property F & G & H.... Call this property N, where N is meant to be short for a's nature. a is N is true, and a's being N

is a (rather complex) state of affairs. It is also the thick particular. *The thick particular is a state of affairs.* The properties of a thing are "contained within it" because they are constituents of this state of affairs. (Notice that states of affairs, such as a's being N, are not repeatable. So, along with thin particulars, they can be called particulars also.)

Therefore, in one sense a particular is propertyless. That is the thin particular. In another sense it enfolds properties within itself. In the latter case it is the thick particular and is a state of affairs. I think that this answers the difficulty raised by the Antinomy of Bare Particulars.

Two points before leaving this section: First, the distinction between thin and thick particulars does not depend upon a doctrine of properties as universals. It does presuppose a substance-attribute account of a particular, rather than a bundle view. But we have already seen that it is possible to take a substance-attribute view with the attributes as particulars, that is, as tropes. The thin particular remains the particular with its attributes abstracted away. The thick particular is again a state of affairs: the thin particular's having the (particular) attributes that it has.

Second, the thin and the thick particular are really the two ends of a scale. In between is the particular clothed with some, but only some, of its properties. They may be properties that are, for one reason or another, particularly important. This intermediate particular will, of course, be a state of affairs, but a less comprehensive one than the state of affairs that is the thick particular.

7   Universals as Ways

The discussion in the previous section is not entirely satisfactory as it stands. It still leaves us with a picture of the thin particular and its properties as distinct metaphysical nodules that are linked together in states of affairs to form the thick particular. This makes the Principles of Instantiation and of the Rejection of Bare Particulars seem a bit arbitrary. Why must the nodules occur together? Could they not come apart? But would they then not be those unwanted creatures: uninstantiated universals and bare particulars?

Here I turn to a suggestion that has often been in the air, but had not, I think, been expounded systematically before David Seargent's book on Stout's theory of universals.[16] Unlike Stout, Seargent accepts universals, and in chapter 4 he argues that we should think of them as *ways*. Properties are ways things are. The mass or charge of an electron is a way the electron is (in this case, a way that any electron is). Relations are ways things stand to each other.

If a property is a way that a thing is, then this brings the property into very intimate connection with the thing, but without destroying the distinction between them. One can see the point of thinking of instantiation as a fundamental connection, a tie or nexus closer than mere relation. Nor will one be much tempted by the idea of an uninstantiated property. A way that things are could hardly exist on its own.

Again, one will not be tempted by the idea that the way a thing stands to other things, a relation, could exist on its own, independent of the things. (Not that the idea was ever very tempting! It is easier to substantialize properties than relations.)

It may be objected that the phrases "ways things are" and "ways things stand to each other" beg the question against uninstantiated universals. Should I not have spoken of ways things could be and ways things could stand to each other, thus canceling the implication that the ways must be the ways of actual things?

However, my argument is not attempting to take advantage of this semantic point. My contention is that once properties and relations are thought of not as things, but as ways, it is profoundly unnatural to think of these ways as floating free from things. Ways, I am saying, are naturally construed only as ways actual things are or ways actual things stand to each other. The idea that properties and relations can exist uninstantiated is nourished by the idea that they are not ways but things.

Before concluding this section, I should like to note that the conception of properties and relations as ways does not depend upon taking them as universals. We can still think of *a*'s property as a way that *a* is, even if the property is particular, a trope. It will just be the case that no other thing besides *a* can be that way. Similarly, a relation holding between *a* and *b* can still be a way *a* and *b* stand to each other, even if this way is non-repeatable.

It is very important to realize that the notions of states of affairs and their constituents, the distinction between the thin and the thick particular, and the conception of properties and relations as ways things are and ways things stand to other things are available, if desired, to a philosophy of tropes as much as to a philosophy of universals.

8 Multiple Location

To bring universals from a Platonic realm down to earth, down to space-time, seems to involve saying something rather strange. It seems to follow that universals are, or may be, multiply located. For are they not to be found wherever the particulars that instantiate them are found? If two different electrons each have charge *e*, then *e*, one thing, a universal, is to be found in two different places, the places where the two electrons are, yet entirely and completely in each place. This has seemed wildly paradoxical to many philosophers.

Plato appears to be raising this difficulty in the *Philebus*, 15b–c. There he asked about a Form: "Can it be as a whole outside itself, and thus come to be one and identical in one thing and in several at once – a view which might be thought to be the most impossible of all?"[17] A theory that kept universals in a separate realm from particulars would at least avoid this difficulty!

You might try just accepting the multiple location of universals. Some philosophers have. But then a difficulty can be raised: What about relations? Perhaps one can give *properties* a multiple location. But just where will you locate the "multiply located" relations? In the related things? That does not sound right. If *a* precedes *b*, is the relation in both *a* and *b*? Or in the thing [*a* + *b*]? Neither answer sounds right. But if it is not in the things, where is it?

I am inclined to meet the difficulty by saying that talk of the location of universals, while better than placing them in another realm, is also not quite appropriate. What should be said first, I think, is that the world is a world of states of affairs. These states of affairs involve particulars having properties and standing in relations to each other. The properties and relations are universals, which means both that different particulars can have the very same property and that different pairs, triples, . . . , of particulars can stand in the very same relation to each other. I do not think that all that is too startling a claim.

But if Naturalism is true, then the world is a single spatiotemporal manifold. What does this come to in terms of the states of affairs theory? That is, how do we reconcile Naturalism with the view sketched in the previous paragraph? It would be an enormous undertaking, presumably involving both fundamental science and philosophy, to give an answer involving even the sketchiest detail. All that can be said here is that the space-time world would have to be an enormous plurality or conjunction of states of affairs, with all the particulars that feature in the states of affairs linked up together (in states of affairs) by spatiotemporal relations.

To talk of locating universals in space-time then emerges as a crude way of speaking. Space-time is not a box into which universals are put. Universals are constituents of states of affairs. Space-time is a conjunction of states of affairs. In that sense universals are "in" space-time. But they are in it as helping to constitute it. I think that this is a reasonable understanding of *universalia in rebus*, and I hope that it meets Plato's objection.[18]

Notes

It is suggested that ch. 11 of D. M. Armstrong's *Nominalism and Realism* (Cambridge: Cambridge University Press, 1978) and chs 13–17 of his *A Theory of Universals* (Cambridge: Cambridge University Press, 1978) be used as companion readings to this chapter.

1 See his introductory book *The Problems of Philosophy* (London: Williams and Norgate, 1912), chs 9 and 10.
2 F. E. Abbott, *Scientific Theism* (London: Macmillan, 1886).
3 Plato, *Republic*, trans. F. M. Cornford (New York: Oxford University Press, 1947), p. 595.
4 Michael Tooley, *Causation* (Oxford: Clarendon Press, 1987), sects 3.1.4 and 3.2.
5 See D. M. Armstrong, *What is a Law of Nature?* (Cambridge: Cambridge University Press, 1983), ch. 8.
6 D. M. Armstrong, *A Combinatorial Theory of Possibility* (Cambridge: Cambridge University Press, 1989), ch. 10.
7 L. Wittgenstein, *Philosophical Investigations* (Oxford: Blackwell, 1953), sects 66 and 67.
8 E.g., L. Wittgenstein, *Tractatus Logico-Philosophicus* (Oxford: Blackwell, 1961); B. Skyrms, "Tractarian nominalism," *Philosophical Studies* 40 (1981).

9 See in particular David Lewis, "New work for a theory of universals," this volume, ch. 17.
10 W. V. Quine, "On what there is," this volume, ch. 1.
11 As pointed out by David Lewis, "Comment on Forrest and Armstrong," *Australasian Journal of Philosophy* 64 (1986).
12 Nelson Goodman, *The Structure of Appearance* (Cambridge, Mass.: Harvard University Press, 1966).
13 Armstrong, *Theory of Universals*, ch. 15, sect. 2.
14 John Quilter, "What has properties?," *Proceedings of the Russellian Society* (Sydney University, Philosophy Dept., 1985), p. 10.
15 This distinction is discussed in greater detail in D. M. Armstrong's *Universals: An Opinionated Introduction* (Boulder, Colo.: Westview Press, 1989), from which the present selection is taken.
16 D. A. J. Seargent, *Plurality and Continuity, an Essay on G. F. Stout's Theory of Universals* (Martinus Nijhoff, 1985).
17 Plato, *Philebus*, trans. A. E. Taylor.
18 For more on this topic see my "Can a naturalist believe in universals?", in E. Ullmann-Margalit (ed.), *Science in Reflection*, (Kluwer Academic Publishers, 1988); together with critical comment in the same volume by Gilead Bar-Elli.

New Work for a Theory of Universals

David Lewis

Introduction

D. M. Armstrong offers a theory of universals as the only adequate answer to a compulsory question for systematic philosophy: the problem of One over Many.[1] I find this line of argument unpersuasive. But I think there is more to be said for Armstrong's theory than he himself has said. For as I bear it in mind considering various topics in philosophy, I notice time and again that it offers solutions to my problems. Whatever we may think of the problem of One over Many, universals can earn their living doing other much-needed work.

I do not say that they are indispensable. The services they render could be matched using resources that are Nominalistic in letter, if perhaps not in spirit.[2] But neither do I hold any presumption against universals, to the effect that they are to be accepted only if we have no alternative. I therefore suspend judgement about universals themselves. I only insist that, one way or another, their work must be done.

I shall investigate the benefits of adding universals to my own usual ontology. That ontology, though Nominalistic, is in other respects generous. It consists of *possibilia* – particular, individual things, some of which comprise our actual world and others of which are unactualized[3] – together with the iterative hierarchy of classes built up from

Originally published in *Australasian Journal of Philosophy* 61 (1983), pp. 343–77. Reprinted with permission of the author and La Trobe University, Bundoora.

them. Thus I already have at my disposal a theory of properties as classes of *possibilia*. Properties, so understood, are not much like universals. Nor can they, unaided, take over the work of universals. Nevertheless, they will figure importantly in what follows, since for me they are part of the environment in which universals might operate.

The friend of universals may wonder whether they would be better employed not as an addition to my ontology of *possibilia* and classes, but rather as a replacement for parts of it. A fair question, and an urgent one; nevertheless, not a question considered in this paper.

In the next section, I shall sketch Armstrong's theory of universals, contrasting universals with properties understood as classes of *possibilia*. Then I shall say why I am unconvinced by the One over Many argument. Then I shall turn to my principal topic: how universals could help me in connection with such topics as duplication, supervenience, and divergent worlds; a minimal form of materialism; laws and causation; and the content of language and thought. Perhaps the list could be extended.

Universals and Properties

Language offers us several more or less interchangeable words: 'universal'; 'property', 'quality', 'attribute', 'feature', and 'characteristic'; 'type', 'kind', and 'sort'; and perhaps others. And philosophy offers us several conceptions of the entities that such words refer to. My purpose is not to fix on one of these conceptions; but rather to distinguish two (at opposite extremes) and contemplate helping myself to both. Therefore some regimentation of language is called for; I apologize for any inconvenience caused. Let me reserve the word 'universal' for those entities, if such there be, that mostly conform to Armstrong's account. And let me reserve the word 'property' for classes – any classes, but I have foremost in mind classes of things. To have a property is to be a member of the class.[4]

Why call them 'properties' as well as 'classes'? – Just to underline the fact that they need not be classes of *actual* things. The property of being a donkey, for instance, is the class of *all* the donkeys. This property belongs to – this class contains – not only the actual donkeys of this world we live in, but also all the unactualized, otherworldly donkeys.

Likewise I reserve the word 'relation' for arbitrary classes of ordered pairs, triples, ... Thus a relation among things is a property of 'tuples of things. Again, there is no restriction to actual things. Corresponding roughly to the division between properties and relations of things, we have the division between 'monadic' and 'polyadic' universals.

Universals and properties differ in two principal ways. The first difference concerns their instantiation. A universal is supposed to be wholly present wherever it is instantiated. It is a constituent part (though not a spatiotemporal part) of each particular that has it. A property, by contrast, is spread around. The property of being a donkey is partly present wherever there is a donkey, in this or any other world. Far from the property being part of the donkey, it is closer to the truth to say that the donkey is part of the property. But the precise truth, rather, is that the donkey is a member of the property.

Thus universals would unify reality[5] in a way that properties do not. Things that share a universal have not just joined a single class. They literally have something in common. They are not entirely distinct. They overlap.

By occurring repeatedly, universals defy intuitive principles. But that is no damaging objection, since plainly the intuitions were made for particulars. For instance, call two entities *copresent* if both are wholly present at one position in space and time. We might intuit offhand that copresence is transitive. But it is not so, obviously, for universals. Suppose for the sake of argument that there are

universals: round, silver, golden. Silver and round are copresent, for here is a silver coin; golden and round are copresent, for there is a gold coin; but silver and golden are not copresent. Likewise, if we add universals to an ontology of *possibilia*, for the relation of being part of the same possible world.[6] I and some otherworldly dragon are not worldmates; but I am a worldmate of the universal golden, and so is the dragon. Presumably I needed a mixed case involving both universals and particulars. For why should any two universals ever fail to be worldmates? Lacking such failures, the worldmate relation among universals alone is trivially transitive.

The second difference between universals and properties concerns their abundance. This is the difference that qualifies them for different work, and thereby gives rise to my interest in having universals and properties both.

A distinctive feature of Armstrong's theory is that universals are sparse. There are the universals that there must be to ground the objective resemblances and the causal powers of things, and there is no reason to believe in any more. All of the following alleged universals would be rejected:

not golden,	first examined before 2000 AD;
golden or wooden,	being identical,
metallic,	being alike in some respect,
self-identical,	being exactly alike,
owned by Fred,	being part of,
belonging to class C,	owning,
grue,	being paired with by some pair in R

(where C and R are utterly miscellaneous classes). The guiding idea, roughly, is that the world's universals should comprise a minimal basis for characterizing the world completely. Universals that do not contribute at all to this end are unwelcome, and so are universals that contribute only redundantly. A satisfactory inventory of universals is a non-linguistic counterpart of a primitive vocabulary for a language capable of describing the world exhaustively.

(That is rough: Armstrong does not dismiss redundant universals out of hand, as the spirit of his theory might seem to demand. Conjunctive universals – as it might be, golden-and-round – are accepted, though redundant; so are analysable structural universals. The reason is that if the world were infinitely complex, there might be no way to cut down to a minimal basis. The only alternative to redundancy might be inadequacy, and if so, we had better tolerate redundancy. But the redundancy is mitigated by the fact that complex universals consist of their simpler – if perhaps not absolutely simple – constituents. They are not distinct entities.[7]

It is quite otherwise with properties. Any class of things, be it ever so gerrymandered and miscellaneous and indescribable in thought and language, and be it ever so superfluous in characterizing the world, is nevertheless a property. So there are properties in immense abundance. (If the number of things, actual and otherwise, is beth-2, an estimate I regard as more likely low than high, then the number of properties of things is beth-3. And that is a big infinity indeed, except to students of the outer reaches of set theory.) There are so many properties that those specifiable in English, or in the brain's language of synaptic interconnections and neural spikes, could be only an infinitesimal minority.

Because properties are so abundant, they are undiscriminating. Any two things share infinitely many properties, and fail to share infinitely many others. That is so whether the two things are perfect duplicates or utterly dissimilar. Thus properties do nothing to capture facts of resemblance. That is work more suited to the sparse universals. Likewise, properties do nothing to capture the causal powers of things. Almost all properties are causally irrelevant, and there is nothing to make the relevant ones stand out from the crowd. Properties carve reality at the joints – and everywhere else as well. If it's distinctions we want, too much structure is no better than none.

It would be otherwise if we had not only the countless throng of all properties, but also an élite minority of special properties. Call these the *natural* properties.[8] If we had properties and universals both, the universals could serve to pick out the natural properties. Afterwards the universals could retire if they liked, and leave their jobs to the natural properties. Natural properties would be the ones whose sharing makes for resemblance, and the ones relevant to causal powers. Most simply, we could call a property *perfectly* natural if its members are all and only those things that share some one universal. But also we would have other less-than-perfectly natural properties, made so by families of suitable related universals.[9] Thus we might have an imperfectly natural property of being metallic, even if we had no such single universal as metallic, in virtue of a close-knit family of genuine universals one or another of which is instantiated by any metallic thing. These imperfectly natural properties would be natural to varying degrees.

Let us say that an *adequate* theory of properties is one that recognizes an objective difference between natural and unnatural properties; preferably, a difference that admits of degree. A combined theory of properties and universals is one sort of adequate theory of properties.

But not the only sort. A Nominalistic theory of properties could achieve adequacy by other means. Instead of employing universals, it could draw primitive distinctions among particulars. Most simply, a Nominalist could take it as a primitive fact that some classes of things are perfectly natural properties; others are less-than-perfectly natural to various degrees; and most are not at all natural. Such a Nominalist takes 'natural' as a primitive predicate, and offers no analysis of what he means in predicating it of classes. His intention is to select the very same classes as natural properties that the user of universals would select. But he regards the universals as idle machinery, fictitiously superimposed on the primitive objective difference between the natural properties and the others.[10]

Alternatively, a Nominalist in pursuit of adequacy might prefer to rest with primitive objective resemblance among things. (He might not think that 'natural' was a very natural primitive, perhaps because it is to be predicated of classes.) Then he could undertake to define natural properties in terms of the mutual resemblance of their members and the failure of resemblance between their members and their non-members. Unfortunately, the project meets with well-known technical difficulties. These can be solved, but at a daunting price in complexity and artificiality of our primitive. We cannot get by with the familiar dyadic 'resembles'. Instead we need a predicate of resemblance that is both contrastive and variably polyadic. Something like

$x_1, x_2, \ldots$ resemble one another and do not likewise resemble any of $y_1, y_2, \ldots$

(where the strings of variables may be infinite, even uncountable) must be taken as understood without further analysis.[11] If adequate Nominalism requires us to choose between this and a primitive predicate of classes, we might well wonder whether the game is worth the candle. I only say we might wonder; I know of no consideration that seems to me decisive.

At this point, you may see very well why it could be a good idea to believe in universals as well as properties; but you may see no point in having properties as well as universals. But properties have work of their own, and universals are ill-suited to do the work of properties.

It is properties that we need, sometimes natural and sometimes not, to provide an adequate supply of semantic values for linguistic expressions. Consider such sentences as these:

(1) Red resembles orange more than it resembles blue.
(2) Red is a colour.
(3) Humility is a virtue.
(4) Redness is a sign of ripeness.

Prima facie, these sentences contain names that cannot be taken to denote particular, individual things. What is the semantic role of these words? If we are to do compositional semantics in the way that is best developed, we need entities to assign as semantic values to these words, entities that will encode their semantic roles. Perhaps sometimes we might find paraphrases that will absolve us from the need to subject the original sentence to semantic analysis. That is the case with (1), for instance.[12] But even if such paraphrases sometimes exist – even if they *always* exist, which seems unlikely – they work piecemeal and frustrate any systematic approach to semantics.

Armstrong takes it that such sentences provide a subsidiary argument for universals, independent of his main argument from the One over Many problem.[13] I quite agree that we have here an argument for something. But not for universals as opposed to properties. Properties can serve as the requisite semantic values. Indeed, properties are much better suited to the job than universals are. That is plain even from the examples considered. It is unlikely that there are any such genuine universals as the colours (especially determinable colours, like red, rather than determinate shades), or ripeness, or humility. Armstrong agrees[14] that he cannot take (1)–(4) as straightforwardly making reference to universals. He must first subject them to paraphrase. Even if there always is a paraphrase that does refer to, or quantify over, genuine universals, still the need for paraphrase is a threat to systematic semantics. The problem arises exactly because universals are sparse. There is no corresponding objection if we take the requisite semantic values as properties.

Other sentences make my point more dramatically.

(5) Grueness does not make for resemblance among all its instances.
(6) What is common to all who suffer pain is being in some or another state that occupies the pain role, presumably not the same state in all cases.

The point is not that these sentences are true – though they are – but that they require semantic analysis. (It is irrelevant that they are not ordinary language.) A universal of grueness would be anathema; as would a universal such that, necessarily, one has it if he is in some state or other that occupies the pain role in his case.[15] But the corresponding properties are no problem.

Indeed, we have a comprehension schema applying to any predicate phrase whatever, however complicated. (Let it even be infinitely long; let it even include imaginary names for entities we haven't really named.) Let x range over things, P over properties (classes) of things. Then:

$$\exists_1 P \Box \forall x (x \text{ has } P \equiv \phi x).$$

We could appropriately call this 'the property of ϕ-ing' in those cases where the predicate phrase is short enough to form a gerund, and take this property to be the semantic value of the gerund. Contrast this with the very different relationship of universals and predicates set forth in *Universals*, vol. 2, pp. 7–59.

Consider also those sentences which prima facie involve second-order quantification. From *Universals*, vol. 1, p. 62, and 'Against "ostrich" nominalism' we have these:

(7) He has the same virtues as his father.
(8) The dresses were of the same colour.
(9) There are undiscovered fundamental physical properties.
(10) Acquired characteristics are never inherited.
(11) Some zoological species are cross-fertile.

Prima facie, we are quantifying either over properties or over universals. Again, paraphrases might defeat that presumption, but in a piecemeal way that threatens systematic semantics. In each case, properties could serve as the values of the variables of quantification. Only in case (9) could universals serve equally well. To treat the other cases, not to mention

(12)   Some characteristics, such as the colours, are more disjunctive than they seem

as quantifications over universals, we would again have to resort to some preliminary paraphrase.[16] This second semantic argument, like the first, adduces work for which properties are better qualified than universals.

Which is not to deny that a partnership might do better still. Let it be granted that we are dealing with quantifications over properties. Still, these quantifications – like most of our quantifications – may be tacitly or explicitly restricted. In particular, they usually are restricted to natural properties. Not to perfectly natural properties that correspond to single universals, except in special cases like (9), but to properties that are at least somewhat more natural than the great majority of the utterly miscellaneous. That is so for all our examples, even (12). Then even though we quantify over properties, we still need either universals or the resources of an adequate Nominalism in order to say which of the properties we mostly quantify over.

I also think that it is properties that we need in characterizing the content of our intentional attitudes. I believe, or I desire, that I live in one of the worlds in a certain class, rather than any world outside that class. This class of worlds is a property had by worlds. I believe, or I desire, that my world has that property. (The class of worlds also may be called a *proposition*, in one of the legitimate senses of that word, and my 'propositional attitude' of belief or desire has this proposition as its 'object'.) More generally, subsuming the previous case, I believe or I desire that I myself belong to a certain class of *possibilia*. I ascribe a certain property to myself, or I want to have it. Or I might ascribe a property to something else, or even to myself, under a relation of acquaintance I bear to that thing.[17] Surely the properties that give the content of attitudes in these ways cannot be relied on to be perfectly natural, hence cannot be replaced by universals. It is interesting to ask whether there is any lower limit to their naturalness (see the final section), but surely no very exacting standard is possible. Here again properties are right for the job, universals are not.

One Over Many

Armstrong's main argument for universals is the 'One over Many'. It is because I find this argument

unconvincing that I am investigating alternative reasons to accept a theory of universals.

Here is a concise statement of the argument, taken by condensation from 'Against "ostrich" nominalism', pp. 440–1. A very similar statement could have been drawn from the opening pages of *Universals*.

> I would wish to start by saying that many different particulars can all have what appears to be the same nature and draw the conclusion that, as a result, there is a *prima facie* case for postulating universals. We are continually talking about different things having the same property or quality, being of the same sort of kind, having the same nature, and so on. Philosophers draw the distinction between sameness of token and sameness of type. But they are only making explicit a distinction which ordinary language (and so, ordinary thought) perfectly recognizes. I suggest that the fact of sameness of type is a Moorean fact: one of the many facts which even philosophers should not deny, whatever philosophical account or analysis they give of such facts. Any comprehensive philosophy must try to give some account of Moorean facts. They constitute the compulsory questions in the philosophical examination paper.

From this point of departure, Armstrong makes his case by criticizing rival attempts to answer the compulsory question, and by rejecting views that decline to answer it at all.

Still more concisely, the One over Many problem is presented as the problem of giving some account of Moorean facts of apparent sameness of type. Thus understood, I agree that the question is compulsory; I agree that Armstrong's postulation of shared universals answers it; but I think that an adequate Nominalism also answers it.

An effort at systematic philosophy must indeed give an account of any purported fact. There are three ways to give an account. (1) 'I deny it' – this earns a failing mark if the fact is really Moorean. (2) 'I analyse it thus' – this is Armstrong's response to the facts of apparent sameness of type. Or (3) 'I accept it as primitive'. Not every *account* is an *analysis*! A system that takes certain Moorean facts as primitive, as unanalysed, cannot be accused of failing to make a place for them. It neither shirks the compulsory question nor answers it by denial. It does give an account.

An adequate Nominalism, of course, is a theory that takes Moorean facts of apparent sameness of type as primitive. It predicates mutual resemblance of the things which are apparently of the same type; or it predicates naturalness of some property that they all share, i.e., that has them all as members; and it declines to analyse these predications any further. That is why the problem of One over Many, rightly understood, does not provide more than a prima facie reason to postulate universals. Universals afford one solution, but there are others.

I fear that the problem does not remain rightly understood. Early in *Universals* it undergoes an unfortunate double transformation. In the course of a few pages[18] the legitimate demand for an account of Moorean facts of apparent sameness of type turns into a demand for an analysis of predication in general. The analysandum becomes the schema '*a* has the property *F*'. The turning point takes only two sentences:

> How is [the Nominalist] to account for the apparent (if usually partial) identity of numerically different particulars? How can two different things both be white or both be on a table?[19]

And very soon, those who 'refuse to countenance universals but who at the same time see no need for any reductive analyses [of the schema of predication]', those according to whom 'there are no universals but the proposition that *a* is *F* is perfectly all right as it is', stand accused of dodging the compulsory question.[20]

When the demand for an account – for a place in one's system – turned into a demand for an analysis, then I say that the question ceased to be compulsory. And when the analysandum switched, from Moorean facts of apparent sameness of type to predication generally, then I say that the question ceased to be answerable at all. The transformed problem of One over Many deserves our neglect. The ostrich that will not look at it is a wise bird indeed.

Despite his words, I do not think that Armstrong really means to demand, either from Nominalists or from himself, a *fully* general analysis of predication. For none is so ready as he to insist that not just any shared predicate makes for even apparent sameness of type. (That is what gives his theory its distinctive interest and merit.) It would be better to put the transformed problem thus: one way or another, all predication is to be analysed. Some predications are to be analysed away in terms of others. Here we have one-off analyses for specific predicates – as it might be, for 'grue'. But all those predications that remain, after the one-off analyses are finished, are to be analysed wholesale by means of a general analysis of the schema '*a* has property *F*'.

There is to be no unanalysed predication. Time and again, Armstrong wields this requirement against rival theories. One theory after another falls victim to the 'relation regress': in the course of analysing other predications, the theory has resort to a new predicate that cannot, on pain of circularity, be analysed along with the rest. So falls Class Nominalism (including the version with primitive naturalness that I deem adequate): it employs predications of class membership, which predications it cannot without circularity analyse in terms of class membership. So falls Resemblance Nominalism: it fails to analyse predications of resemblance. So fall various other, less deserving Nominalisms. And so fall rival forms of Realism, for instance Transcendent, Platonic Realism: this time, predications of participation evade analysis. Specific theories meet other, specific objections; suffice it to say that I think these inconclusive against the two Nominalisms that I called adequate. But the clincher, the one argument that recurs throughout the many refutations, is the relation regress. And this amounts to the objection that the theory under attack does not achieve its presumed aim of doing away with all unanalysed predication and therefore fails to solve the transformed problem of One over Many.

Doing away with all unanalysed predication is an unattainable aim, and so an unreasonable aim. No theory is to be faulted for failing to achieve it. For how could there be a theory that names entities, or quantifies over them, in the course of its sentences, and yet altogether avoids primitive predication? Artificial tricks aside,[21] the thing cannot be done.

What's true is that a theory may be faulted for its overabundant primitive predications, or for unduly mysterious ones, or for unduly complicated ones. These are not fatal faults, however. They are to be counted against a theory, along with its faults of overly generous ontology or of disagreement with less-than-Moorean commonsensical opinions. Rival philosophical theories have their prices, which we seek to measure. But it's all too clear that for philosophers, at least, there ain't no such thing as a free lunch.

How does Armstrong himself do without primitive predication? – He doesn't. Consider the predicate 'instantiates' (or 'has'), as in 'particular *a* instantiates universal *F*' or 'this electron has unit charge'. No one-off analysis applies to this specific predicate. 'Such identity in nature [as results from the having of one universal in many particulars] is literally inexplicable, in the sense that it cannot be further explained.'[22] Neither do predications of 'instantiates' fall under Armstrong's general analysis of (otherwise unanalysed) predication. His is a *non-relational* Realism: he declines, with good reason, to postulate a dyadic universal of instantiation to bind particulars to their universals. (And if he did, it would only postpone the need for primitive predication.) So let all who have felt the bite of Armstrong's relation regress rise up and cry '*Tu quoque!*' And let us mark well that Armstrong is prepared to give *one* predicate 'what has been said to be the privilege of the harlot: power without responsibility. The predicate is informative, it makes a vital contribution to telling us what is the case, the world is different if it is different, yet ontologically it is supposed not to commit us. Nice work: if you can get it.'[23]

Let us dump the project of getting rid of primitive predication, and return to the sensible – though not compulsory – project of analysing Moorean facts of apparent sameness of type. Now does the relation regress serve Armstrong better? I think not. It does make better sense within the more sensible project, but it still bites Armstrong and his rivals with equal force. Let the Nominalist say 'These donkeys resemble each other, so likewise do those stars, and there analysis ends.' Let the Platonist say 'This statue participates in the Form of beauty, likewise that lecture participates in the Form of truth, and there analysis ends.' Let Armstrong say 'This electron instantiates unit charge, likewise that proton instantiates tripartiteness, and there analysis ends.' It is possible to complain in each case that a fact of sameness of type has gone unanalysed, the types being respectively resemblance, participation, and instantiation. But it is far from evident that the alleged facts are Moorean, and still less evident that the first two are more Moorean than the third. None of them are remotely the equals of the genuine Moorean fact that, in some sense, different lumps of gold are the same in kind.

Michael Devitt has denounced the One over Many problem as a mirage better left unseen.[24] I have found Devitt's discussion instructive, and I agree with much of what he says. But Devitt has joined Armstrong in transforming the One over Many problem. He takes it to be the problem of analysing the schema

> *a* and *b* have the same property (are of the same type), *F*-ness

otherwise than by means of a one-off analysis for some specific *F*. To that problem it is fair to answer as he does that

> *a* is *F*; *b* is *F*

is analysis enough, once we give over the aim of doing without primitive predication. But Devitt has set himself too easy a problem. If we attend to the modest, untransformed One over Many problem, which is no mirage, we will ask about a different analysandum:

> *a* and *b* have some common property (are somehow of the same type)

in which it is not said what *a* and *b* have in common. This less definite analysandum is not covered by what Devitt has said. If we take a clearly Moorean case, he owes us an account: either an analysis or an overt resort to primitive predication of resemblance.

Duplication, Supervenience, and Divergent Worlds

Henceforth I shall speak only of my need for the distinction between natural and unnatural, or more and less natural, properties. It is to be understood that the work I have in store for an adequately discriminatory theory of properties might be new work for a theory of universals, or it might instead be work for the resources of an adequate Nominalism.

I begin with the problem of analysing duplication. We are familiar with cases of approximate duplication, e.g., when we use copying machines. And we understand that if these machines were more perfect than they are, the copies they made would be perfect duplicates of the original. Copy and original would be alike in size and shape and chemical composition of the ink marks and the paper, alike in temperature and magnetic alignment and electrostatic charge, alike even in the exact arrangement of their electrons and quarks. Such duplicates would be exactly alike, we say.

They would match perfectly, they would be qualitatively identical, they would be indiscernible.

But they would not have exactly the same properties, in my sense of the word. As in the case of any two things, countless class boundaries would divide them. Intrinsically, leaving out their relations to the rest of the world, they would be just alike. But they would occupy different spatio-temporal positions; and they might have different owners, be first examined in different centuries, and so on.

So if we wish to analyse duplication in terms of shared properties, it seems that we must first distinguish the *intrinsic* (or 'internal') properties from the *extrinsic* (or 'external' or 'relational') properties. Then we may say that two things are duplicates iff they have precisely the same intrinsic properties, however much their extrinsic properties might differ. But our new problem of dividing the properties into intrinsic and extrinsic is no easier than our original problem of analysing duplication. In fact, the two problems are joined in a tight little circle of interdefinability. Duplication is a matter of sharing intrinsic properties; intrinsic properties are just those properties that never differ between duplicates. Property P is intrinsic iff, for any two duplicate things, not necessarily from the same world, either both have P or neither does. P is extrinsic iff there is some such pair of duplicates of which one has P and the other lacks P.[25]

If we relied on our physical theory to be accurate and exhaustive, we might think to define duplication in physical terms. We believe that duplicates must be alike in the arrangement of their electrons and quarks – why not put this forward as a definition? But such a 'definition' is no analysis. It presupposes the physics of our actual world; however physics is contingent and known a posteriori. The definition does not apply to duplication at possible worlds where physics is different, or to duplication between worlds that differ in their physics. Nor does it capture what those ignorant of physics mean when they speak – as they do – of duplication.

The proper course, I suggest, is to analyse duplication in terms of shared properties; but to begin not with the intrinsic properties but rather with natural properties. Two things are qualitative duplicates if they have exactly the same perfectly natural properties.[26]

Physics is relevant because it aspires to give an inventory of natural properties – not a complete inventory, perhaps, but a complete enough inventory to account for duplication among actual things. If physics succeeds in this, then duplication within our world amounts to sameness of physical description. But the natural properties themselves are what matter, not the theory that tells us what they are. If Materialism were false and physics an utter failure, as is the case at some deplorable worlds, there would still be duplication in virtue of shared natural properties.

On my analysis, all perfectly natural properties come out intrinsic. That seems right. The converse is not true. Intrinsic properties may be disjunctive and miscellaneous and unnatural, so long as they never differ between duplicates. The perfectly natural properties comprise a basis for the intrinsic properties; but arbitrary Boolean compounds of them, however unnatural, are still intrinsic. Hence if we adopt the sort of adequate Nominalism that draws a primitive distinction between natural and unnatural properties, that is not the same thing as drawing a primitive distinction between intrinsic and extrinsic properties. The former distinction yields the latter, but not vice versa.

Likewise if we adopt the sort of adequate Nominalism that begins with a suitable relation of partial resemblance, that is not the same thing as taking duplication itself as primitive. Again, the former yields the latter, but not vice versa.

If instead we reject Nominalism, and we take the perfectly natural properties to be those that correspond to universals (in the sense that the members of the property are exactly those things that instantiate the universal), then all the properties that correspond to universals are intrinsic. So are all the Boolean compounds – disjunctions, negations, etc. – of properties that correspond to universals. The universals themselves are intrinsic *ex officio*, so to speak.

But here I must confess that the theory of universals for which I offer new work cannot be exactly Armstrong's theory. For it must reject extrinsic universals; whereas Armstrong admits them, although not as irreducible.[27] I think he would be better off without them, given his own aims. (1) They subvert the desired connection between sharing of universals and Moorean facts of partial or total sameness of nature. Admittedly, there is such a thing as resemblance in extrinsic respects: things can be alike in the roles they play *vis-à-vis* other things, or in the origins they spring from. But such resemblances are not what we mean when we say of two things that they are of the same kind, or have the same nature. (2) They subvert the desired immanence of universals: if something instantiates an extrinsic universal, that is not a fact just about that thing. (3) They are not needed for Armstrong's theory of laws of nature; any supposed law connecting extrinsic universals of things can be equivalently replaced by a law connecting intrinsic structures of larger systems that have those things as parts.

Thus I am content to say that if there are universals, intrinsic duplicates are things having exactly the same universals. We need not say '...exactly the same *intrinsic* universals,' because we should not believe in any other kind.

Not only is duplication of interest in its own right; it also is needed in dealing with other topics in metaphysics. Hence such topics create a derived need for natural properties. I shall consider two topics where I find need to speak of duplication: supervenience and divergent worlds.

First, supervenience. A supervenience thesis is a denial of independent variation. Given an ontology of *possibilia*, we can formulate such theses in terms of differences between possible individuals or worlds. To say that so-and-so supervenes on such-and-such is to say that there can be no difference in respect of so-and-so without difference in respect of such-and-such. Beauty of statues supervenes on their shape, size, and colour, for instance, if no two statues, in the same or different worlds, ever differ in beauty without also differing in shape or size or colour.[28]

A supervenience thesis is, in a broad sense, reductionist. But it is a stripped-down form or reductionism, unencumbered by dubious denials of existence, claims of ontological priority, or claims of translatability. One might wish to say that in some sense the beauty of statues is nothing over and above the shape and size and colour that beholders appreciate, but without denying that there is such a thing as beauty, without claiming that beauty exists only in some less-than-fundamental way, and without undertaking to paraphrase ascriptions of beauty in terms of shape, etc. A supervenience thesis seems to capture what the cautious reductionist wishes to say.

Even if reductionists ought to be less cautious and aim for translation, still it is a good idea to attend to the question of supervenience. For if supervenience fails, then no scheme of translation can be correct, and we needn't go on Chisholming away in search of one. If supervenience succeeds, on the other hand, then some correct scheme must exist; the remaining question is whether there exists a correct scheme that is less than infinitely

complex. If beauty is supervenient on shape, etc., the worst that can happen is that an ascription of beauty is equivalent to an uncountably infinite disjunction of maximally specific descriptions of shape, etc., which descriptions might themselves involve infinite conjunctions.

Interesting supervenience theses usually involve the notion of qualitative duplication that we have just considered. Thus we may ask what does or doesn't supervene on the qualitative character of the entire world, throughout all of history. Suppose that two possible worlds are perfect qualitative duplicates – must they then also have exactly the same distributions of objective probability, the same laws of nature, the same counterfactuals and causal relations? Must their inhabitants have the same *de re* modal properties? If so, it makes sense to pursue such projects as a frequency analysis of probability, a regularity analysis of laws of nature, or a comparative similarity analysis of causal counterfactuals and *de re* modality. If not, such projects are doomed from the start, and we needn't look at the details of the attempts. But we cannot even raise these questions of supervenience unless we can speak of duplicate worlds. And to do that, I have suggested, we need natural properties.

(Note that if possible worlds obey a principle of identity of qualitative indiscernibles, then all these supervenience theses hold automatically. If no two worlds are duplicates, then *a fortiori* no two are duplicates that differ in their probabilities, laws, ... or anything else.)

We might also ask whether qualitative character supervenes on anything less. For instance, we might ask whether global qualitative character supervenes on local qualitative character. Say that two worlds are *local duplicates* iff they are divisible into corresponding small parts in such a way that (1) corresponding parts of the two worlds are duplicates, and (2) the correspondence preserves spatio temporal relations. (The exact meaning depends, of course, on what we mean by 'small'.) If two worlds are local duplicates, then must they be duplicates *simpliciter*? Or could they differ in ways that do not prevent local duplication – e.g., in external relations, other than the spatio temporal relations themselves, between separated things? Again, we must make sense of duplication – this time, both in the large and in the small – even to ask the question.[29]

Next, divergent worlds. I shall say that two possible worlds *diverge* iff they are not duplicates but they do have duplicate initial temporal segments. Thus our world and another might match perfectly up through the year 1945, and go their separate ways thereafter.

Note that we need no identity of times across worlds. Our world through our 1945 duplicates an initial segment of the other world; that otherworldly segment ends with a year that indeed resembles our 1945, but it is part of otherworldly time, not part of our time. Also, we need no separation of time and space that contravenes Relativity – we have initial temporal segments, of this or another world, if we have spatio temporal regions bounded by space like surfaces that cut the world in two.

I distinguish *divergence* of worlds from *branching* of worlds. In branching, instead of duplicate segments, one and the same initial segment is allegedly shared as a common part by two overlapping worlds. Branching is problematic in ways that divergence is not. First, because an inhabitant of the shared segment cannot speak unequivocally of *the* world he lives in. What if he says there will be a sea fight tomorrow, meaning of course to speak of the future of his own world, and one of the two worlds he lives in has a sea fight the next day and the other doesn't? Second, because overlap of worlds interferes with the most salient principle of demarcation for worlds, viz., that two possible individuals are part of the same world iff they are linked by some chain of external relations, e.g., of spatio temporal relations. (I know of no other example.) Neither of these difficulties seems insuperable, but both are better avoided. That makes it reasonable to prefer a theory of non-overlapping divergent worlds to a theory of branching worlds. Then we need to be able to speak of qualitative duplication of world-segments, which we can do in terms of shared natural properties.

Divergent (or branching) worlds are of use in defining Determinism. The usual definitions are not very satisfactory. If we say that every event has a cause, we overlook probabilistic causation under Indeterminism. If we speak of what could be predicted by a superhuman calculator with unlimited knowledge of history and the laws of nature, we overlook obstacles that might prevent prediction even under Determinism, or else we try to make non-vacuous sense of counterfactuals about what our predictor could do if he had some quite impossible combination of powers and limitations.

A better approach is as follows. First, a system of laws of nature is Deterministic iff no two divergent worlds both conform perfectly to the laws of that system. Second, a world is Deterministic iff its laws comprise a Deterministic system. Third, Determinism is the thesis that our world is Deterministic.[30]

(Alternative versions of Determinism can be defined in similar fashion. For instance, we could strengthen the first step by prohibiting convergence as well as divergence of law-abiding worlds. Or we could even require that no two law-abiding worlds have duplicate momentary slices without being duplicates throughout their histories. Or we could define a weaker sort of Determinism: we could call a world *fortuitously* Deterministic, even if its laws do not comprise a Deterministic system, iff no world both diverges from it and conforms to its laws. The laws and early history of such a world suffice to determine later history, but only because the situations in which the laws fall short of Determinism never arise. We might equivalently define fortuitous Determinism as follows: for any historical fact F and any initial segment S of the world, there are a true proposition H about the history of S and a true proposition L about the laws of nature, such that H and L together strictly imply F.[31] Does this definition bypass our need to speak of duplication of initial segments? Not so, for we must ask what it means to say that H is about the history of S. I take that to mean that H holds at both or neither of any two worlds that both begin with segments that are duplicates of S.)

Divergent worlds are important also in connection with the sort of counterfactual conditional that figures in patterns of causal dependence. Such counterfactuals tend to be temporally asymmetric, and this is what gives rise to the asymmetry of causation itself. Counterfactuals of this sort do not 'backtrack': it is not to be said that if the present were different, a different past would have led up to it, but rather that if the present were different, the same past would have had a different outcome. Given a hypothesized difference at a certain time, the events of future times normally would be very different indeed, but the events of past times (except perhaps for the very near past) would be no different. Thus actuality and its counterfactual alternatives are divergent worlds, with duplicate initial segments.[32]

Minimal Materialism

There is a difficulty that arises if we attempt to formulate certain reductionist views, for instance

Materialism, as supervenience theses. A solution to this difficulty employs natural properties not only by way of duplication but in a more direct way also.

Roughly speaking, Materialism is the thesis that physics – something not too different from present-day physics, though presumably somewhat improved – is a comprehensive theory of the world, complete as well as correct. The world is as physics says it is, and there's no more to say. World history written in physical language is all of world history. That is rough speaking indeed; our goal will be to give a better formulation. But before I try to say more precisely what Materialism is, let me say what it is not. (1) Materialism is not a thesis of finite translatability of all our language into the language of physics. (2) Materialism is not to be identified with any one Materialist theory of mind. It is a thesis that motivates a variety of theories of mind: versions of Behaviourism, Functionalism, the mind–body identity theory, even the theory that mind is all a mistake. (3) Materialism is not just the theory that there are no things except those recognized by physics. To be sure, Materialists don't believe in spirits, or other such non-physical things. But anti-materialists may not believe in spirits either – their complaint needn't be that physics omits some of the things that there are. They may complain instead that physics overlooks some of the ways there are for physical things to differ; for instance, they may think that physical people could differ in what their experience is like. (4) That suggests that Materialism is, at least in part, the thesis that there are no natural properties instantiated at our world except those recognized by physics. That is better, but I think still not right. Couldn't there be a natural property X (in the nature of the case, it is hard to name an example!) which is shared by the physical brains in worlds like ours and the immaterial spirits that inhabit other worlds? Or by this-worldly quarks and certain otherworldly particles that cannot exist under our physics? Physics could quite properly make no mention of a natural property of this sort. It is enough to recognize the special case applicable to our world, X-cum-physicality, brainhood or quarkhood as it might be. Then if by physical properties we mean those properties that are mentioned in the language of physics, a Materialist ought not to hold that all natural properties instantiated in our world are physical properties.

At this point, it ought to seem advisable to formulate Materialism as a supervenience thesis: no difference without physical difference. Or, contra-posing: physical duplicates are duplicates *simpliciter*. *A fortiori*, no mental difference without physical difference; physical duplicates are mental duplicates. The thesis might best be taken as applying to whole possible worlds, in order to bypass such questions as whether mental life is to some extent extrinsic to the subject. So we have this first of several attempted formulations of Materialism:

M1: Any two possible worlds that are exactly alike in all respects recognized by physics are qualitative duplicates.

But this will not do. In making Materialism into a thesis about how just any two worlds can and cannot differ, M1 puts Materialism forward as a necessary truth. That is not what Materialists intend. Materialism is meant to be a contingent thesis, a merit of our world that not all other worlds share. Two worlds could indeed differ without differing physically, if at least one of them is a world where Materialism is false. For instance, our Materialistic world differs from a non-materialistic world that is physically just like ours but that also contains physically epiphenomenal spirits.

There is a non-contingent supervenience thesis nearby that might appeal to Materialists:

M2: There is no difference, *a fortiori* no mental difference, without some non-mental difference. Any two worlds alike in all non-mental respects are duplicates, and in particular do not differ in respect of the mental lives of their inhabitants.

This seems to capture our thought that the mental is a pattern in a medium, obtaining in virtue of local features of the medium (neuron firings) and perhaps also very global features (laws of nature) that are too small or too big to be mental themselves. But M2 is not Materialism. It is both less and more. Less, obviously, because it never says that the medium is physical. More, because it denies the very possibility of what I shall call *Panpsychistic* Materialism.

It is often noted that psychophysical identity is a two-way street: if all mental properties are physical, then some physical properties are mental. But perhaps not just some but *all* physical properties might be mental as well; and indeed every property of anything might be at once physical and mental. Suppose there are indeed worlds where this is so. If so, presumably there are many such worlds, not all duplicates, differing *inter alia* in the mental lives of their inhabitants. But all differences between such worlds are mental (as well as physical), so none are non-mental. These worlds will be vacuously alike in all non-mental respects, for lack of any non-mental respects to differ in. Then M2 fails. And not just at the trouble-making worlds; M2 is non-contingent, so if it fails at any worlds, it fails at all – even decent Materialistic worlds like ours. Maybe Panpsychistic Materialism is indeed impossible – how do you square it with a broadly functional analysis of mind? – but a thesis that says so is more than just Materialism.

A third try. This much is at least true:

M3: No two Materialistic worlds differ without differing physically; any two Materialistic worlds that are exactly alike physically are duplicates.

But M3 is not a formulation of Materialism, for the distinction between Materialistic and other worlds appears within M3. All we learn is that the Materialistic worlds comprise a class within which there is no difference without physical difference. But there are many such classes. In fact, any world, however spirit-ridden, belongs to such a class.

A fourth try. Perhaps we should confine our attention to nomologically possible worlds, thus:

M4: Among worlds that conform to the actual laws of nature, no two differ without differing physically; any two such worlds that are exactly alike physically are duplicates.

But again we have something that is both less and more than Materialism: less, because M4 could hold at a world where Materialism is false but where spiritual phenomena are correlated with physical phenomena according to strict laws; more, because M4 fails to hold at a Materialistic, spirit-free world if the laws of that world do not preclude the existence of epiphenomenal spirits. Our world might be such a world, a world where spirits are absent but not outlawed.[33]

So far, a supervenience formulation of Materialism seems elusive. But I think we can succeed if we join the idea of supervenience with the idea that a non-materialistic world would have something extra, something that a Materialistic world lacks. It might have spirits; or it might have physical things that differ in non-physical ways, for instance

in what their experience is like. In either case there are extra natural properties, properties instantiated in the non-materialistic world but nowhere to be found in the Materialistic world. Let us say that a property is *alien* to a world iff (1) it is not instantiated by any inhabitant of that world, and (2) it is not analysable as a conjunction of, or as a structural property constructed out of, natural properties all of which are instantiated by inhabitants of that world. (I need the second clause because I am following Armstrong, *mutatis mutandis*, in declining to rule out perfectly natural properties that are conjunctive or structurally complex.[34] It would be wrong to count as alien a complex property analysable in terms of non-alien constituents.) If our world is Materialistic, then it is safe to say that some of the natural properties instantiated in any non-materialistic world are properties alien to our world. Now we can proceed at last to formulate Materialism as a restricted and contingent supervenience thesis:

M5: Among worlds where no natural properties alien to our world are instantiated, no two differ without differing physically; any two such worlds that are exactly alike physically are duplicates.[35]

We took Materialism to uphold the comprehensiveness of 'something not too different from present-day physics, though presumably somewhat improved'. That was deliberately vague. Materialist metaphysicians want to side with physics, but not to take sides within physics. Within physics, more precise claims of completeness and correctness may be at issue. Physics (ignoring latter-day failures of nerve) is the science that aspires to comprehensiveness, and particular physical theories may be put forward as fulfilling that aspiration. If so, we must again ask what it means to claim comprehensiveness. And again, the answer may be given by a supervenience formulation: no difference without physical difference as conceived by such-and-such grand theory. But again it must be understood as a restricted and contingent supervenience thesis, applying only among worlds devoid of alien natural properties.

Thus the business of physics is not just to discover laws and causal explanations. In putting forward as comprehensive theories that recognize only a limited range of natural properties, physics proposes inventories of the natural properties instantiated in our world. Not complete inventories, perhaps, but complete enough to account for all the duplications and differences that could arise in the absence of alien natural properties. Of course, the discovery of natural properties is inseparable from the discovery of laws. For an excellent reason to think that some hitherto unsuspected natural properties are instantiated – properties deserving of recognition by physics, the quark colours as they might be – is that without them, no satisfactory system of laws can be found.

This is reminiscent of the distinctive a posteriori, scientific character of Armstrong's Realism.[36] But in the setting of an ontology of *possibilia*, the distinction between discovering what universals or natural properties there actually are and discovering which ones are actually instantiated fades away. And the latter question is a posteriori on any theory. What remains, and remains important, is that physics discovers properties. And not just any properties – natural properties. The discovery is, for instance, that neutrinos are not all alike. That is not the discovery that different ones have different properties in my sense, belong to different classes. We knew that much a priori. Rather, it is the surprising discovery that some *natural* property differentiates some neutrinos from others. That discovery has in fact been made; I should like to read an account of it by some philosopher who is not prepared to adopt a discriminatory attitude toward properties and who thinks that all things are equally similar and dissimilar to one another.

Laws and Causation

The observation that physics discovers natural properties in the course of discovering laws may serve to introduce our next topic: the analysis of what it is to be a law of nature. I agree with Armstrong that we need universals, or at least natural properties, in explaining what lawhood is, though I disagree with his account of how this is so.

Armstrong's theory, in its simplest form,[37] holds that what makes certain regularities lawful are second-order states of affairs $N (F, G)$ in which the two ordinary, first-order universals F and G are related by a certain dyadic second-order universal N. It is a contingent matter which universals are thus related by the lawmaker N. But it is necessary – and necessary *simpliciter*, not just nomologically necessary – that if $N (F, G)$ obtains, then F and G are constantly conjoined. There is a necessary con-

nection between the second-order state of affairs $N(F, G)$ and the first-order lawful regularity $\forall x(Fx \supset Gx)$; and likewise between the conjunctive state of affairs $N(F, G)$ & Fa and its necessary consequence Ga.

A parallel theory could be set up with natural properties in place of Armstrong's first- and second-order universals. It would have many of the attractive features that Armstrong claims on behalf of his theory, but at least one merit would be lost. For Armstrong, the lawful necessitation of Ga by Fa is a purely local matter: it involves only a, the universals F and G that are present in a, and the second-order law-making universal that is present in turn in (or between) these two universals. If we replace the universals by properties, however natural, that locality is lost. For properties are classes with their membership spread around the worlds, and are not wholly present in a. But I do not think this a conclusive objection, for our intuitions of locality often seem to lead us astray. The selective regularity theory I shall shortly advocate also sacrifices locality, as does any regularity theory of law.

What leads me (with some regret) to reject Armstrong's theory, whether with universals or with natural properties, is that I find its necessary connections unintelligible. Whatever N may be, I cannot see how it could be absolutely impossible to have $N(F, G)$ and Fa without Ga. (Unless N just *is* constant conjunction, or constant conjunction plus something else, in which case Armstrong's theory turns into a form of the regularity theory he rejects.) The mystery is somewhat hidden by Armstrong's terminology. He uses 'necessitates' as a name for the law-making universal N; and who would be surprised to hear that if F 'necessitates' G and a has F, then a must have G? But I say that N deserves the name of 'necessitation' only if, somehow, it really can enter into the requisite necessary connections. It can't enter into them just by bearing a name, any more than one can have mighty biceps just by being called 'Armstrong'.

I am tempted to complain in Humean fashion of alleged necessary connections between distinct existences, especially when first-order states of affairs in the past supposedly join with second-order states of affairs to necessitate first-order states of affairs in the future. That complaint is not clearly right: the sharing of universals detracts from the distinctness of the necessitating and the necessitated states of affairs. But I am not appeased. I conclude that necessary connections can be unintelligible even when they are supposed to obtain between existences that are not clearly and wholly distinct.[38]

Thus I do not endorse Armstrong's way of building universals, or alternatively natural properties, into the analysis of lawhood. Instead I favour a regularity analysis. But I need natural properties even so.

Certainly not just any regularity is a law of nature. Some are accidental. So an adequate regularity analysis must be selective. Also, an adequate analysis must be collective. It must treat regularities not one at a time, but rather as candidates to enter into integrated systems. For a given regularity might hold either as a law or accidentally, depending on whether other regularities obtain that can fit together with it in a suitable system. (Thus I reject the idea that lawhood consists of 'lawlikeness' plus truth.) Following Mill and Ramsey,[39] I take a suitable system to be one that has the virtues we aspire to in our own theory building, and that has them to the greatest extent possible given the way the world is. It must be entirely true; it must be closed under strict implication; it must be as simple in axiomatization as it can be without sacrificing too much information content; and it must have as much information content as it can have without sacrificing too much simplicity. A law is any regularity that earns inclusion in the ideal system. (Or, in case of ties, in every ideal system.) The ideal system need not consist entirely of regularities; particular facts may gain entry if they contribute enough to collective simplicity and strength. (For instance, certain particular facts about the Big Bang might be strong candidates.) But only the regularities of the system are to count as laws.

We face an obvious problem. Different ways to express the same content, using different vocabulary, will differ in simplicity. The problem can be put in two ways, depending on whether we take our systems as consisting of propositions (classes of worlds) or as consisting of interpreted sentences. In the first case, the problem is that a single system has different degrees of simplicity relative to different linguistic formulations. In the second case, the problem is that equivalent systems, strictly implying the very same regularities, may differ in their simplicity. In fact, the content of any system what ever may be formulated very simply indeed. Given system S, let F be a predicate that applies to all and only things at worlds where S holds. Take F as primitive, and axiomatize S (or an equivalent thereof) by the single axiom $\forall x Fx$. If utter simplicity is so easily attained, the ideal theory may as

well be as strong as possible. Simplicity and strength needn't be traded off. Then the ideal theory will include (its simple axiom will strictly imply) all truths, and a fortiori all regularities. Then, after all, every regularity will be a law. That must be wrong.

The remedy, of course, is not to tolerate such a perverse choice of primitive vocabulary. We should ask how candidate systems compare in simplicity when each is formulated in the simplest eligible way; or, if we count different formulations as different systems, we should dismiss the ineligible ones from candidacy. An appropriate standard of eligibility is not far to seek: let the primitive vocabulary that appears in the axioms refer only to perfectly natural properties.

Of course, it remains an unsolved and difficult problem to say what simplicity of a formulation is. But it is no longer the downright insoluble problem that it would be if there were nothing to choose between alternative primitive vocabularies.

(One might think also to replace strict implication by deducibility in some specified calculus. But this second remedy seems unnecessary given the first, and seems incapable of solving our problem by itself.)

If we adopt the remedy proposed, it will have the consequence that laws will tend to be regularities involving natural properties. Fundamental laws, those that the ideal system takes as axiomatic, must concern perfectly natural properties. Derived laws that follow fairly straightforwardly also will tend to concern fairly natural properties. Regularities concerning unnatural properties may indeed be strictly implied, and should count as derived laws if so. But they are apt to escape notice even if we someday possess a good approximation to the ideal system. For they will be hard to express in a language that has words mostly for not-too-unnatural properties, as any language must. (See the next section.) And they will be hard to derive, indeed they may not be finitely derivable at all, in our deductive calculi. Thus my account explains, as Armstrong's does in its very different way, why the scientific investigation of laws and of natural properties is a package deal; why physicists posit natural properties such as the quark colours in order to posit the laws in which those properties figure, so that laws and natural properties get discovered together.

If the analysis of lawhood requires natural properties, then so does the analysis of causation. It is fairly uncontroversial that causation involves laws. That is so according to both of the leading theories of causation: the deductive-nomological analysis, on which the laws are applied to the actual course of events with the cause and effect present; and the counterfactual analysis that I favour, on which the laws are applied to counterfactual situations with the cause hypothesized away. These counterfactual alternatives may need to break actual laws at the point where they diverge from actuality, but the analysis requires that they evolve thereafter in accordance with the actual laws.[40]

According to my counterfactual analysis, causation involves natural properties in a second way too. We need the kind of counterfactuals that avoid backtracking; or else the analysis faces fatal counterexamples involving epiphenomenal side-effects or cases of causal pre-emption. As I have already noted, these counterfactuals are to be characterized in terms of divergent worlds, hence in terms of duplicate initial world-segments, hence in terms of shared natural properties.

Causation involves natural properties in yet another way. (Small wonder that I came to appreciate natural properties after working on the analysis of causation!) Causation holds between events. Unless we distinguish genuine from spurious events, we will be left with too many putative causes. You put a lump of butter in a skillet, and the butter melts. What event causes this? There is one event that we can call a moving of molecules. It occurs in the region where the skillet is, just before the butter melts. This is an event such that, necessarily, it occurs in a spatiotemporal region only if that region contains rapidly moving molecules. Surely this event is a cause of the melting of the butter.

Heat is that phenomenon, whatever it may be, that manifests itself in certain familiar characteristic ways. Let us say: heat is that which occupies the heat-role. (It won't matter whether we take the definite description plain, as I prefer, or rigidified.) In fact, but contingently, it is molecular motion that occupies the heat-role. It might have been molecular non-motion, or 'caloric fluid, or what you will. Now consider an alleged second event, one that we may call a having-the-occupant-of-the-heat-role. This second event occurs just when and where the first does, in the region where the hot skillet is. It occurs there in virtue of the two facts (1) that the skillet's molecules are moving rapidly, and (2) that the region in question is part of a world where molecular motion is what occupies the heat-

role. But this second event differs from the first. The necessary conditions for its occurrence are different. Necessarily, it occurs in a region only if that region contains whatever phenomenon occupies the heat-role in the world of which that region is part. So in those worlds where caloric fluid occupies the heat-role and molecular motion does not, the first event occurs only in regions with molecular motion whereas the second occurs only in regions with caloric fluid.

Certainly the first event causes the melting of the butter, but shall we say that the second event does so as well? No; that seems to multiply causes beyond belief by playing a verbal trick. But if there really are two events here, I cannot see why the second has less of a claim than the first to be a cause of the melting of the butter. It is out of the question to say that the first and the second events are one and the same – then this one event would have different conditions of occurrence from itself. The best solution is to deny that the alleged second event is a genuine event at all. If it isn't, of course it can't do any causing.

Why is the first event genuine and the second spurious? Compare the properties involved: containing rapidly moving molecules versus containing whatever phenomenon occupies the heat-role. (I mean these as properties of the spatiotemporal region; other treatments of events would take instead the corresponding properties of the skillet, but my point would still apply.) The first is a fairly natural, intrinsic property. The second is highly disjunctive and extrinsic. For all sorts of different phenomena could occupy the heat-role; and whether the phenomenon going on in a region occupies the role depends not only on what goes on in the region but also on what goes on elsewhere in the same world. Thus the distinction between more and less natural properties gives me the distinction between genuine and spurious events that I need in order to disown an overabundance of causes. If a property is too unnatural, it is inefficacious in the sense that it cannot figure in the conditions of occurrence of the events that cause things.[41]

The Content of Language and Thought

Hilary Putnam has given an argument which he regards as a refutation of a 'radically non-epistemic' view of truth, but which I regard rather as a *reductio* against Putnam's premisses.[42] In particular, it refutes his assumption that '*we* interpret our languages or nothing does',[43] so that any constraint on reference must be established by our own stipulation in language or thought. Gary Merrill has suggested that Putnam may be answered by appeal to a constraint that depends on an objective structure of properties and relations in the world.[44] I agree, and find here another point at which we need natural properties.

Putnam's argument, as I understand it, is as follows. First, suppose that the only constraint on interpretation of our language (or perhaps our language of thought) is given by a description theory of reference of a global and futuristic sort. An 'intended interpretation' is any interpretation that satisfies a certain body of theory: viz., the idealized descendant of our current total theory that would emerge at the end of enquiry, an ideal theory refined to perfection under the guidance of all needed observation and our best theoretical reasoning. If so, intended interpretations are surprisingly abundant. For *any* world can satisfy *any* theory (ideal or not), and can do so in countless very different ways, provided only that the world is not too small and the theory is consistent. Beyond that, it doesn't matter what the world is like or what the theory says. Hence we have radical indeterminacy of reference. And we have the coincidence that Putnam welcomes between satisfaction under all intended intrepretations and 'epistemic truth'. For the ideal theory is the whole of 'epistemic truth', the intended interpretations are just those interpretations of our language that satisfy the ideal theory, and (unless the world is too small or ideal theory is inconsistent) there are some such interpretations.

I take this to refute the supposition that there are no further constraints on reference. But Putnam asks: how *could* there be a further constraint? How could we ever establish it? By stipulation, by saying or thinking something. But whatever we say or think will be in language (or language of thought) that suffers from radical indeterminacy of interpretation. For the saving constraint will not be there until we succeed in establishing it. So the attempted stipulation must fail. The most we can do is to contribute a new chapter to current and ideal theory, a chapter consisting of whatever we said or thought in our stipulation. And this new theory goes the way of all theory. So we cannot establish a further constraint; and '*we* interpret our language or nothing does'; so there cannot be any further constraint. We cannot lift ourselves by our bootstraps, so we must still be on the ground.

Indeed we cannot lift ourselves by our bootstraps, but we are off the ground, so there must be another way to fly. Our language does have a fairly determinate interpretation (a Moorean fact!) so there must be some constraint not created *ex nihilo* by our stipulation.

What can it be? Many philosophers would suggest that it is some sort of causal constraint. If so, my case is made, given my arguments in the previous section: we need natural properties to explain determinacy of interpretation. But I doubt that it really is a causal constraint, for I am inclined to think that the causal aspect of reference *is* established by what we say and think. Thus: I think of a thing as that which I am causally acquainted with in such-and-such way, perhaps perceptually or perhaps through a channel of acquaintance that involves the naming of the thing and my picking up of the name. I refer to that thing in my thought, and derivatively in language, because it is the thing that fits this causal and egocentric description extracted from my theory of the world and of my place in the world.[45]

I would instead propose that the saving constraint concerns the referent – not the referrer, and not the causal channels between the two. It takes two to make a reference, and we will not find the constraint if we look for it always on the wrong side of the relationship. Reference consists in part of what we do in language or thought when we refer, but in part it consists in eligibility of the referent. And this eligibility to be referred to is a matter of natural properties.

That is the suggestion Merrill offers. (He offers it not as his own view, but as what opponents of Putnam ought to say; and I gratefully accept the offer.) In the simplest case, suppose that the interpretation of the logical vocabulary somehow takes care of itself, to reveal a standard first-order language whose non-logical vocabulary consists entirely of predicates. The parts of the world comprise a domain; and sets, sets of pairs, . . . , from this domain are potential extensions for the predicates. Now suppose we have an all-or-nothing division of properties into natural and unnatural. Say that a set from the domain is *eligible* to be the extension of a one-place predicate iff its members are just those things in the domain that share some natural property; and likewise for many-place predicates and natural relations. An *eligible interpretation* is one that assigns none but eligible extensions to the predicates. A so-called 'intended' interpretation is an eligible interpretation that satisfies the ideal theory. (But the name is misleading: it is not to be said that our intentions establish the constraint requiring eligibility. That way lies the futile bootstrap tugging that we must avoid.) Then if the natural properties are sparse, there is no reason to expect any overabundance of intended interpretations. There may even be none. Even ideal theory runs the risk of being unsatisfiable, save in 'unintended' ways. Because satisfaction is not guaranteed, we accomplish something if we manage to achieve it by making a good fit between theory and the world. All this is as it should be.

The proposal calls for refinement. First, we need to provide for richer forms of language. In this we can be guided by familiar translations, for instance between modal language with higher-order quantification and first-order language that explicitly mentions *possibilia* and classes built up from them. Second, it will not do to take naturalness of properties as all-or-nothing. Here, above all, we need to make naturalness – and hence eligibility – a comparative matter, or a matter of degree. There are salient sharp lines, but not in the right places. There is the line between the perfectly natural properties and all the rest, but surely we have predicates for much-less-than-perfectly natural properties. There is the line between properties that are and that are not finitely analysable in terms of perfectly natural properties, but that lets in enough highly unnatural properties that it threatens not to solve our problem. We need gradations; and we need some give and take between the eligibility of referents and the other factors that make for 'intendedness', notably satisfaction of appropriate bits of theory. (Ideal theory, if we keep as much of Putnam's story as we can.) Grueness is not an absolutely ineligible referent (as witness my reference to it just now), but an interpretation that assigns it is to that extent inferior to one that assigns blueness instead. *Ceteris paribus*, the latter is the 'intended' one, just because it does better on eligibility.

Naturalness of properties makes for differences of eligibility not only among the properties themselves, but also among things. Compare Bruce with the cat-shaped chunk of miscellaneous and ever-changing matter that follows him around, always a few steps behind. The former is a highly eligible referent, the latter is not. (I haven't succeeded in referring to it, for I didn't say just which such chunk 'it' was to be.) That is because Bruce, unlike the cat-shaped chunk, has a boundary well demarcated by differences in highly natural properties.

Where Bruce ends, there the density of matter, the relative abundance of the chemical elements, . . . abruptly change. Not so for the chunk. Bruce is also much more of a locus of causal chains than is the chunk; this too traces back to natural properties, by the considerations of the previous section. Thus naturalness of properties sets up distinctions among things. The reverse happens also. Once we are away from the perfectly natural properties, one thing that makes for naturalness of a property is that it is a property belonging exclusively to well-demarcated things.

You might well protest that Putnam's problem is misconceived, wherefore no need has been demonstrated for resources to solve it. Putnam seems to conceive of language entirely as a repository of theory, and not at all as a practice of social interaction. We have the language of the encyclopedia, but where is the language of the pub? Where are the communicative intentions and the mutual expectations that seem to have so much to do with what we mean? In fact, where is thought? It seems to enter the picture, if at all, only as the special case where the language to be interpreted is hard-wired, unspoken, hidden, and all too conjectural.

I think the point is well taken, but I think it doesn't matter. If the problem of intentionality is rightly posed, there will still be a threat of radical indeterminacy, there will still be a need for saving constraints, there will still be a remedy analogous to Merrill's suggested answer to Putnam, and there will still be a need for natural properties.

Set language aside and consider instead the interpretation of thought. (Afterward we can hope to interpret the subject's language in terms of his beliefs and desires regarding verbal communication with others.) The subject is in various states, and could be in various others, that are causally related to each other, to the subject's behaviour, and to the nearby environment that stimulates his senses. These states fit into a functional organization, they occupy certain causal roles. (Most likely they are states of the brain. Maybe they involve something that is language-like but hard-wired, maybe not. But the nature of the states is beside the point.) The states have their functional roles in the subject as he now is, and in the subject as he is at other times and as he might have been under other circumstances, and even in other creatures of the same kind as the subject. Given the functional roles of the states, the problem is to assign them content. Propositional content, some would say;

but I would agree only if the propositions can be taken as egocentric ones, and I think an 'egocentric proposition' is simply a property. States indexed by content can be identified as a belief that this, a desire for that, a perceptual experience of seeming to confront so-and-so, an intention to do such-and-such. (But not all ordinary ascriptions of attitudes merely specify the content of the subject's states. Fred and Ted might be alike in the functional roles of their states, and hence have states with the same content in the narrowly psychological sense that is my present concern, and hence believe alike, e.g., by each believing himself to have heard of a pretty town named 'Castlemaine'. Yet they might be acquainted via that name with different towns, at opposite ends of the earth, so that Fred and not Ted believes that Castlemaine, Victoria, is pretty.) The problem of assigning content to functionally characterized states is to be solved by means of constraining principles. Foremost among these are principles of fit. If a state is to be interpreted as an intention to raise one's hand, it had better typically cause the hand to go up. If a state (or complex of states) is to be interpreted as a system of beliefs and desires – or better, degrees of belief and desire – according to which raising one's hand would be a good means to one's ends, and if another state is to be interpreted as an intention to raise one's hand, then the former had better typically cause the latter. Likewise on the input side. A state typically caused by round things before the eyes is a good candidate for interpretation as the visual experience of confronting something round; and its typical impact on the states interpreted as systems of belief ought to be interpreted as the exogenous addition of a belief that one is confronting something round, with whatever adjustment that addition calls for.

So far, so good. But it seems clear that preposterous and perverse misinterpretations could nevertheless cohere, could manage to fit the functional roles of the states because misassignment of content at one point compensates for misassignment at another. Let us see just how this could happen, at least under an oversimplified picture of interpretation as follows. An interpretation is given by a pair of functions C and V. C is a probability distribution over the worlds, regarded as encapsulating the subject's dispositions to form beliefs under the impact of sensory evidence: if a stream of evidence specified by proposition E would put the subject into a total state S – for short, if E yields S – we interpret S to consist in part of the belief

system given by the probability distribution $C(-/E)$ that comes from C by conditionalizing on E. V is a function from worlds to numerical desirability scores, regarded as encapsulating the subject's basic values: if E yields S, we interpret S to consist in part of the system of desires given by the $C(-/E)$-expectations of V. Say that C and V *rationalize* behaviour B after evidence E iff the system of desires given by the $C(-/E)$-expectations of V ranks B at least as high as any alternative behaviour. Say that C and V *fit* iff, for any evidence-specifying E, E yields a state that would cause behaviour rationalized by C and V after E. That is our only constraining principle of fit. (Where did the others go? – We built them into the definitions whereby C and V encapsulate an assignment of content to various states.) Then any two interpretations that always rationalize the same behaviour after the same evidence must fit equally well. Call two worlds *equivalent* iff they are alike in respect of the subject's evidence and behaviour, and note that any decent world is equivalent *inter alia* to horrendously counterinductive worlds and to worlds where everything unobserved by the subject is horrendously nasty. Fit depends on the total of C for each equivalence class, and on the C-expectation of V within each class, but that is all. Within a class, it makes no difference which world gets which pair of values of C and V. We can interchange equivalent worlds *ad lib* and preserve fit. So, given any fitting and reasonable interpretation, we can transform it into an equally fitting perverse interpretation by swapping equivalent worlds around so as to enhance the probabilities of counterinductive worlds, or the desirabilities of nasty worlds, or both. *Quod erat demonstrandum.*

(My simplifications were dire: I left out the egocentricity of belief and desire and evidence, the causal aspect of rationalized behaviour, the role of intentions, change of basic values, limitations of logical competence, ... But I doubt that these omissions matter to my conclusion. I conjecture that if they were remedied, we could still transform reasonable interpretations into perverse ones in a way that preserves fit.)

If we rely on principles of fit to do the whole job, we can expect radical indeterminacy of interpretation. We need further constraints, of the sort called principles of (sophisticated) charity, or of 'humanity'.[46] Such principles call for interpretations according to which the subject has attitudes that we would deem reasonable for one who has lived the life that he has lived. (Unlike principles of crude charity, they call for imputations of error if he has lived under deceptive conditions.) These principles select among conflicting interpretations that equally well conform to the principles of fit. They impose a priori – albeit defeasible – presumptions about what sorts of things are apt to be believed and desired; or rather, about what dispositions to develop beliefs and desires, what inductive biases and basic values, someone may rightly be interpreted to have.

It is here that we need natural properties. The principles of charity will impute a bias toward believing that things are green rather than grue, toward having a basic desire for long life rather than for long-life-unless-one-was-born-on-Monday-and-in-that-case-life-for-an-even-number-of-weeks. In short, they will impute eligible content, where ineligibility consists in severe unnaturalness of the properties the subject supposedly believes or desires or intends himself to have. They will impute other things as well, but it is the imputed eligibility that matters to us at present.

Thus the threat of radical indeterminacy in the assignment of content to thought is fended off. The saving constraint concerns the content – not the thinker, and not any channels between the two. It takes two to index states with content, and we will not find the constraint if we look for it always on the wrong side of the relationship. Believing this or desiring that consists in part in the functional roles of the states whereby we believe or desire, but in part it consists in the eligibility of the content. And this eligibility to be thought is a matter, in part, of natural properties.

Consider the puzzle whereby Kripke illustrates Wittgenstein's paradox that 'no course of action could be determined by a rule, because every course of action can be made out to accord with the rule'.[47] A well-educated person working arithmetic problems intends to perform addition when he sees the '+' sign. He does not intend to perform quaddition, which is just like addition for small numbers but which yields the answer 5 if any of the numbers to be quadded exceeds a certain bound. Wherefore does he intend to add and not to quadd? Whatever he says and whatever is written in his brain can be perversely (mis)interpreted as instructing him to quadd. And it is not enough to say that his brain state is the causal basis of a disposition to add. Perhaps it isn't. Perhaps if a test case arose, he would abandon his intention, he would neither add nor quadd but instead would put his homework aside and complain that the problems are too hard.

The naïve solution is that adding means going on in the same way as before when the numbers get big, whereas quadding means doing something different; there is nothing present in the subject that constitutes an intention to do different things in different cases; therefore he intends addition, not quaddition. We should not scoff at this naïve response. It is the correct solution to the puzzle. But we must pay to regain our naïveté. Our theory of properties must have adequate resources to somehow ratify the judgement that instances of adding are all alike in a way that instances of quadding are not. The property of adding is not perfectly natural, of course, not on a par with unit charge or sphericality. And the property of quadding is not perfectly unnatural. But quadding is worse by a disjunction. So quaddition is to that extent less of a way to go on doing the same, and therefore it is to that extent less of a way to go on doing the same, and therefore it is to that extent less of an eligible thing to intend to do.

It's not that you couldn't possibly intend to quadd. You could. Suppose that today there is as much basis as there ever is to interpret you as intending to add and as meaning addition by your word 'addition' and quaddition by 'quaddition'; and tomorrow you say to yourself in so many words that it would be fun to tease the philosophers by taking up quaddition henceforth, and you make up your mind to do it. But you have to go out of your way. Adding and quadding aren't on a par. To intend to add, you need only have states that would fit either interpretation and leave it to charity to decree that you have the more eligible intention. To intend to quadd, you must say or think something that creates difficulties of fit for the more eligible intention and thereby defeats the presumption in its favour. You must do something that, taking principles of fit and presumptions of eligibility and other principles of charity together, tilts the balance in favour of an interpretation on which you intend to quadd. How ironic that we were worried to find nothing positive to settle the matter in favour of addition! For the lack of anything positive that points either way just *is* what it takes to favour addition. Quaddition, being less natural and eligible, needs something positive in its favour. Addition can win by default.

What is the status of the principles that constrain interpretation, in particular the charitable presumption in favour of eligible content? We must shun several misunderstandings. It is not to be said (1) that as a contingent psychological fact, the contents of our states turn out to be fairly eligible, we mostly believe and desire ourselves to have not-too-unnatural properties. Still less should it be said (2) that we should daringly presuppose this in our interpreting of one another, even if we haven't a shred of evidence for it. Nor should it be said (3) that as a contingent psychological fact we turn out to have states whose content involves some properties rather than others, and that is what makes it so that the former properties are more natural. (This would be a psychologistic theory of naturalness.) The error is the same in all three cases. It is supposed, wrongly as I think, that the problem of interpretation can be solved without bringing to it the distinction between natural and unnatural properties; so that the natural properties might or might not turn out to be the ones featured in the content of thought according to the correct solution, or so that they can afterward be defined as the ones that are so featured. I think this is over-optimistic. We have no notion how to solve the problem of interpretation while regarding all properties as equally eligible to feature in content. For that would be to solve it without enough constraints. Only if we have an independent, objective distinction among properties, and we impose the presumption in favour of eligible content a priori as a constitutive constraint, does the problem of interpretation have any solution at all. If so, then any correct solution must automatically respect the presumption. There's no contingent fact of psychology here to be believed, either on evidence or daringly.

Compare our selective and collective theory of lawhood: lawhood of a regularity just consists in its fitting into an ideally high-scoring system, so it's inevitable that laws turn out to have what it takes to make for high scores. Likewise, I have suggested, contenthood just consists in getting assigned by a high-scoring interpretation, so it's inevitable that contents tend to have what it takes to make for high scores. And in both cases, I've suggested that part of what it takes is naturalness of the properties involved. The reason natural properties feature in the contents of our attitudes is that naturalness is part of what it is to feature therein. It's not that we're built to take a special interest in natural properties, or that we confer naturalness on properties when we happen to take an interest in them.

Notes

I am indebted to comments by Gilbert Harman, Lloyd Humberstone, Frank Jackson, Mark Johnston, Donald Morrison, Kim Sterelny, and others; and especially to discussion and correspondence with D. M. Armstrong over several years, without which I might well have believed to this day that set theory applied to *possibilia* is all the theory of properties that anyone could ever need.

1 D. M. Armstrong, *Universals and Scientific Realism* (Cambridge: Cambridge University Press, 1978), henceforth cited as *Universals*; see also his 'Against "ostrich" nominalism: a reply to Michael Devitt.' *Pacific Philosophical Quarterly* 61 (1980), pp. 440–9.

2 Here I follow Armstrong's traditional terminology: 'universals' are repeatable entities, wholly present wherever a particular instantiates them; 'Nominalism' is the rejection of such entities. In the conflicting modern terminology of Harvard, classes count as 'universals' and 'Nominalism' is predominantly the rejection of classes. Confusion of the terminologies can result in grave misunderstanding; see W. V. Quine, 'Soft impeachment disowned', *Pacific Philosophical Quarterly* 61 (1980), pp. 450–1.

3 Among 'things' I mean to include all the gerrymandered wholes and undemarcated parts admitted by the most permissive sort of mereology. Further, I include such physical objects as spatiotemporal regions and force fields, unless an eliminative reduction of them should prove desirable. Further, I include such non-physical objects as gods and spooks, though not – I hope – as parts of the same world as us. Worlds themselves need no special treatment. They are things – big ones, for the most part.

4 My conception of properties resembles the doctrine of Class Nominalism considered in *Universals*, vol. 1, pp. 28–43. But, strictly speaking, a Class Nominalist would be someone who claims to solve the One over Many problem simply by means of properties taken as classes, and that is far from my intention.

5 *Universals*, vol. 1, p. 109.

6 If universals are to do the new work I have in store for them, they must be capable of repeated occurrence not only within a world but also across worlds. They would then be an exception to my usual principle – meant for particulars, of course – that nothing is wholly present as part of two different worlds. But I see no harm in that. If two worlds are said to overlap by having a coin in common, and if this coin is supposed to be wholly round in one world and wholly octagonal in the other, I stubbornly ask what shape it

is, and insist that shape is not a relation to worlds. (See my 'individuation by acquaintance and by stipulation', *Philosophical Review* 92 (1983), pp. 3–32.) I do not see any parallel objection if worlds are said to overlap by sharing a universal. What contingent, non-relational property of the universal could we put in place of shape of the coin in raising the problem? I cannot think of any.

7 See *Universals*, vol. 2, pp. 30–42 and 67–71.

8 See ibid., vol. 1, pp. 38–41; Anthony Quinton, 'Properties and classes', *Proceedings of the Aristotelian Society* 48 (1957), pp. 33–58; and W. V. Quine, 'Natural kinds', this volume, ch. 18. See also George Bealer, *Quality and Concept* (Oxford: Oxford University Press, 1982), esp. pp. 9–10 and 177–87. Like me, Bealer favours an inegalitarian twofold conception of properties: there are abundant 'concepts' and sparse 'qualities', and the latter are the ones that 'determine the logical, causal, and phenomenal order of reality' (p. 10). Despite this point of agreement, however, Bealer's views and mine differ in many ways.

9 Here I assume that some solution to the problem of resemblance of universals is possible, perhaps along the lines suggested by Armstrong in *Universals*, vol. 2, pp. 48–52 and 101–31; and that such a solution could be carried over into a theory of resemblance of perfectly natural properties, even if we take naturalness of properties as primitive.

10 This is the Moderate Class Nominalism considered in ibid., vol. 1, pp. 38–41. It is akin to the view of Quinton, 'Properties and classes'; but plus the unactualized members of the natural classes, and minus any hint that 'natural' could receive a psychologistic analysis.

11 Such a theory is a form of Resemblance Nominalism, in Armstrong's classification, but it is unlike the form that he principally considers. See *Universals*, vol. 1, pp. 44–63. For discussions of the problem of defining natural classes in terms of resemblance, and of the trickery that proves useful in solving this problem, see Nelson Goodman, *The Structure of Appearance* (Cambridge, Mass.: Harvard University Press, 1951), chs 4–6; Quine, this vol., ch. 18; and Adam Morton, 'Complex individuals and multigrade relations', *Nous* 9 (1975), pp. 309–18.

To get from primitive resemblance to perfectly natural properties, I have in mind a definition as follows. We begin with R as our contrastive and variably polyadic primitive. We want it to turn out that $x_1, x_2, \ldots R y_1, y_2, \ldots$ iff some perfectly natural property is shared by all of $x_1, x_2, \ldots$ but by none of $y_1, y_2, \ldots$ We want to define N, another variably polyadic predicate, so that it will turn out that $N x_1, x_2, \ldots$ iff $x_1, x_2, \ldots$ are all and only the members of some perfectly natural property. Again we must allow for, and expect, the case where there are infinitely many x's. We define $N x_1, x_2, \ldots$ as:

$$\exists y_1, y_2, \ldots, \forall z (z, x_1, x_2, \ldots R y_1, y_2, \ldots \equiv z = x_1 \vee z = x_2 \vee \ldots).$$

Then we finish the job by defining a perfectly natural property as a class such that, if $x_1, x_2, \ldots$ are all and only its members, then $N x_1, x_2, \ldots$

We might have taken N as primitive instead of R. But would that have been significantly different, given the interdefinability of the two? On the other hand, taking N as primitive also seems not significantly different from taking perfect naturalness of classes as primitive. It is only a difference between speaking in the plural of individuals and speaking in the singular of their classes, and that seems no real difference. Is plural talk a disguised form of class talk? Or vice versa? (See the discussion in *Universals*, vol. 1, pp. 32–4; also Max Black, 'The elusiveness of sets', *Review of Metaphysics* 24 (1971), pp. 614–36; Eric Stenius, 'Sets', *Synthese* 27 (1974), pp. 161–88; and Kurt Gödel, 'Russell's mathematical Logic', in P. A. Schilpp (ed.), *The Philosophy of Bertrand Russell* (Cambridge: Cambridge University Press, 1944).) At any rate, it is not at all clear to me that Moderate Class Nominalism and Resemblance Nominalism in its present form are two different theories, as opposed to a single theory presented in different styles.

12 In virtue of the close resemblance of red and orange, it is possible for a red thing to resemble an orange one very closely; it is not possible for a red thing to resemble a blue one quite so closely. Given our ontology of *possibilia*, all possibilities are realized. So we could paraphase (1) by

(1′) Some red thing resembles some orange thing more than any red thing resembles any blue thing.

so long as it is understood that the things in question needn't be part of our world, or of any one world. Or if we did not wish to speak of unactualized things, but we were willing to take ordinary-language modal idioms as primitive, we could instead give the paraphrase:

(1″) A red thing can resemble an orange thing more closely than a red thing can resemble a blue thing.

It is necessary to use the ordinary-language idioms, or some adequate formalization of them, rather than standard modal logic. You cannot express (1″) in modal logic (excluding an enriched modal logic that would defeat the point of the paraphrase by quantifying over degrees of resemblance or whatnot) because you cannot express cross-world relations, and in particular cannot express the needed cross-world comparison of similarity.

13 *Universals*, vol. 1, pp. 58–63; also his 'Against "ostrich" nominalism'. He derives the argument, and a second semantic argument to be considered shortly, from Arthur Pap, 'Nominalism, empiricism, and universals: I, *Philosophical Quarterly* 9 (1959), pp. 330–40, and F. C. Jackson, 'Statements about universals', *Mind* 86 (1977), pp. 427–9.

14 *Universals*, vol. 1, p. 61.

15 Or better, in the case of creatures of his kind. See my 'Mad pain and Martian pain', in Ned Block (ed.) *Readings in Philosophy of Psychology*, vol. 1 (Cambridge, Mass.: Harvard University Press, 1980).

16 Armstrong again agrees: *Universals*, vol. 1, p. 63.

17 See my 'Attitudes *de dicto* and *de se*', *Philosophical Review* 88 (1979), pp. 513–43; and 'Individuation by acquaintance and by stipulation'.

18 *Universals*, vol. 1, pp. 11–16.

19 Ibid., p. 12.

20 Ibid., pp. 16–17.

21 Let S be the syntactic category of sentences, let N be the category of names, and for any categories x and y, let x/y be the category of expressions that attach to y-expressions to make x-expressions. Predicates, then, are category S/N. (Or $(S/N)/N$ for two-place predicates, and so on.) To embed names (or variables in the category of names) into sentences without primitive predication, take any category Q which is neither S nor N, nor S/N, and let there be primitives of categories Q/N and S/Q. Or take Q_1 and Q_2, different from S and N and S/N and each other, and let the primitives be of categories Q_1/N, Q_2/Q_1, and S/Q_2. Or . . . I cannot see how this trickery could be a genuine alternative to, rather than a disguise for, primitive predication.

22 *Universals*, vol. 1, p. 109.

23 Compare Armstrong on Quine's treatment of predication, 'Against "ostrich" nominalism', p. 443.

24 Michael Devitt, ' "Ostrich nominalism" or "mirage realism"?', *Pacific Philosophical Quarterly* 61 (1980), pp. 433–9. Devitt speaks on behalf of Quine as well as himself; Quine indicates agreement with Devitt in 'Soft impeachment disowned'.

25 Given duplication, we can also subdivide the extrinsic properties, distinguishing pure cases from various mixtures of extrinsic and intrinsic. Partition the things, of this and other worlds, into equivalence classes under the relation of duplication. A property may divide an equivalence class, may include it, or may exclude it. A property P is extrinsic, as we said, if it divides at least some of the classes. We have four subcases. (1) P divides every class; then we may call P *purely extrinsic*. (2) P divides some classes, includes some, and excludes none; then P is the disjunction of an intrinsic property and a purely extrinsic property. (3) P divides some, excludes some, and includes none; then P is the conjunction of an intrinsic property and a purely extrinsic property. (4) P divides some, includes some, and excludes some; then P is the con-

junction of an intrinsic property and an impurely extrinsic property of the sort considered in the second case, or equivalently is the disjunction of an intrinsic property and an impurely extrinsic property of the sort considered in the third case.

We can also classify relations as intrinsic or extrinsic, but in two different ways. Take a dyadic relation, i.e. a class or ordered pairs. Call the relation *intrinsic to its relata* iff, whenever a and a' are duplicates (or identical) and b and b' are duplicates (or identical), then both or neither of the pairs $\langle a, b \rangle$ and $\langle a', b' \rangle$ stand in the relation. Call the relation *intrinsic to its pairs* iff, whenever the pairs $\langle a, b \rangle$ and $\langle a', b' \rangle$ themselves are duplicates, then both or neither of them stand in the relation. In the second case, a stronger requirement is imposed on the pairs. For instance they might fail to be duplicate pairs because the distance between a and b differs from the distance between a' and b', even though a and a' are duplicates and b and b' are duplicates. In traditional terminology, 'internal relations' are intrinsic to their *relata*; 'external relations' are intrinsic to their pairs but not to their *relata*; and relations extrinsic even to their pairs, such as the relation of belonging to the same owner, get left out of the classification altogether.

Our definition of intrinsic properties in terms of duplication closely resembles the definition of 'differential properties' given by Michael Slote in 'some thoughts on Goodman's riddle', *Analysis* 27 (1967), pp. 128–32, and in *Reason and Scepticism* (London: George Allen & Unwin, 1970). But where I quantify over *possibilia*, Slote applies modality to ordinary, presumably actualist, quantifiers. That makes a difference. An extrinsic property might differ between duplicates, but only when the duplicates inhabit different worlds; then Slote would count the property as differential. An example is the property of being a sphere that inhabits a world where there are pigs or a cube that inhabits a world without pigs.

See my 'Extrinsic properties', *Philosophical Studies* 44 (1983), pp. 197–200; repr. in *On the Plurality of Worlds* (Oxford: Blackwell, 1994), ch. 5, for further discussion of the circle from duplication to intrinsicness and back.

26 Likewise $\langle a, b \rangle$ and $\langle a', b' \rangle$ are duplicate pairs iff a and a' have exactly the same perfectly natural properties, and so do b and b', and also the perfectly natural relations between a and b are exactly the same as those between a' and b'.

27 See *Universals*, vol. 2, pp. 78–9.

28 For a general discussion of supervenience, see Jaegwon Kim, 'Supervenience and nomological incommensurables', *American Philosophical Quarterly* 15 (1978), pp. 149–56.

29 Such a thesis of supervenience of the global on the local resembles the 'holographic hypothesis' considered and rejected by Saul Kripke in 'Identity through Time', presented at the 1979 conference of the Amer-

ican Philosophical Association, Eastern Division, and elsewhere.

30 This approach is due, in essence, to Richard Montague, 'Deterministic theories', in *Decisions, Values and Groups*, vol. 2 (Oxford: Pergamon Press, 1962), and in his *Formal Philosophy* (New Haven: Yale University Press, 1974). But Montague did not speak as I have done of duplication of initial segments of worlds in virtue of the sharing of certain élite properties. Instead, he used sameness of description in a certain vocabulary, which vocabulary was left as an unspecified parameter of his analysis. For he wrote as a logician obliged to remain neutral on questions of metaphysics.

31 A closely related definition appears in Peter van Inwagen, 'The incompatibility of free will and determinism', *Philosophical Studies* 27 (1975), pp. 185–99.

32 See my 'Counterfactual dependence and time's arrow', *Nous* 13 (1979), pp. 455–76; Jonathan Bennett's review of my *Counterfactuals, Canadian Journal of Philosophy* 4 (1974), pp. 381–402; P. B. Downing, 'Subjunctive conditionals, time order, and causation', *Proceedings of the Aristotelian Society* 59 (1959), pp. 125–40; Allan Gibbard and William Harper, 'Counterfactuals and two kinds of expected utility', in C. A. Hooker, J. T. Leach, and E. F. McClennen (eds), *Foundations and Applications of Decision Theory* (Dordrecht: Reidel, 1978), and in W. L. Harper, R. Stalnaker, and G. Pearce (eds), *Ifs* (Dordrecht: Reidel, 1981); and Frank Jackson, 'A causal theory of counterfactuals', *Australasian Journal of Philosophy* 55 (1977), pp. 3–21.

33 This objection against M4 as a formulation of 'the ontological primacy of the microphysical' appears in Terence Horgan, 'Supervenience and microphysics', *Pacific Philosophical Quarterly* 63 (1982), pp. 29–43.

34 See *Universals*, vol. 2, pp. 30–42 and 67–71.

35 This formulation resembles one proposed by Horgan, 'Supervenience and microphysics'. The principal difference is as follows. Horgan would count as alien (my term, not his) any property cited in the fundamental laws of otherworldly microphysics that is not also explicitly cited in the fundamental laws of thisworldly microphysics. Whether the property is instantiated in either world doesn't enter into it. But must an alien property figure in laws of otherworldly *physics*? Must it figure in any otherworldly laws at all? It seems that a Materialistic world might differ without differing physically from a world where there are properties alien in my sense but not in Horgan's – perhaps a world where laws are in short supply.

36 *Universals*, vol. 1, pp. 8–9 and *passim*.

37 Ibid., vol. 2, pp. 148–57. A more developed form of the theory appears in D. M. Armstrong, *What Is a Law of Nature?* (Cambridge: Cambridge University Press, 1983). Similar theories have been proposed in Fred I. Dretske, 'Laws of nature', *Philosophy of Science* 44 (1977), pp. 248–68, and in Michael Tooley,

'The nature of laws', *Canadian Journal of Philosophy* 4 (1977), pp. 667–98.

38 Armstrong's more developed theory in *What Is a Law of Nature?* complicates the picture in two ways. First, the second-order state of affairs $N(F, G)$ is itself taken to be a universal, and its presence in its instances detracts yet further from the distinctness of the necessitating and the necessitated states of affairs. Second, all laws are defeasible. It is possible after all to have $N(F, G)$ and Fa without Ga, namely if we also have $N(E \& F, H)$ and Ea, where H and G are incompatible. (The law that F's are G's might be *contingently* indefeasible, if no such defeating state of affairs $N(E \& F, H)$ obtains; but no law has its indefeasibility built in essentially.) It remains true that there are alleged necessary connections that I find unintelligible, but they are more complicated than before. To necessitate a state of affairs, we need not only the first- and second-order states of affairs originally considered, but also a negative existential to the effect that there are no further states of affairs of the sort that could act as defeaters.

39 John Stuart Mill, *A System of Logic* (London: Parker, 1843), bk III, ch. 4, sect. 1; F. P. Ramsey, 'Universals of law and of fact', in his *Foundations* (London: Routledge & Kegan Paul, 1978). Ramsey regarded this theory of law as superseded by the different theory in his 'General propositions and causality', also in *Foundations*, but I prefer his first thoughts to his second. I present a theory of lawhood along the lines of Ramsey's earlier theory in my *Counterfactuals* (Oxford: Blackwell, 1973), pp. 73–5. A revision to that discussion is needed in the probabilistic case, which I here ignore.

40 See my 'Causation', this volume, ch. 34.

41 See the discussion of impotence of dispositions in Elizabeth W. Prior, Robert Pargetter, and Frank Jackson, 'Three theses about dispositions', *American Philosophical Quarterly* 19 (1982), pp. 251–7. If a disposition is not identified with its actual basis, there is a threat of multiplication of putative causes similar to that in my example. We would not wish to say that the breaking of a struck glass is caused both by its fragility and by the frozen-in stresses that the fragility is inefficacious because it is too unnatural a property, too disjunctive and extrinsic, to figure in the conditions of occurence of any event.

42 Hilary Putnam, 'Realism and reason', in his *Meaning and the Moral Sciences* (London: Routledge & Kegan Paul, 1978), and 'Models and reality', *Journal of Symbolic Logic* 45 (1980), pp. 464–82. The reader is warned that the argument as I present it may not be quite as Putnam intended it to be. For I have made free in reading between the lines and in restating the argument in my own way.

43 Putnam, 'Models and reality', p. 482.

44 G. H. Merrill, 'The model-theoretic argument against realism', *Philosophy of Science* 47 (1980), pp. 69–81.

David Lewis

45 See Stephen Schiffer, 'The basis of reference', *Erkenntnis* 13 (1978), pp. 171–206.

46 See my 'Radical interpretation', *Synthese* 23 (1974), pp. 331–44; and Richard E. Grandy, 'Reference, meaning and belief', *Journal of Philosophy* 70 (1973), pp. 439–52.

47 See Saul A. Kripke, 'Wittgenstein on rules and private language: an elementary exposition', in Irving Block (ed.), *Perspectives on Wittgenstein* (Oxford: Blackwell, 1981).

18

Natural Kinds

W. V. Quine

What tends to confirm an induction? This question has been aggravated on the one hand by Hempel's puzzle of the non-black non-ravens,[1] and exacerbated on the other by Goodman's puzzle of the grue emeralds.[2] I shall begin my remarks by relating the one puzzle to the other, and the other to an innate flair that we have for natural kinds. Then I shall devote the rest of the paper to reflections on the nature of this notion of natural kinds and its relation to science.

Hempel's puzzle is that just as each black raven tends to confirm the law that all ravens are black, so each green leaf, being a non-black non-raven, should tend to confirm the law that all non-black things are non-ravens, that is, again, that all ravens are black. What is paradoxical is that a green leaf should count toward the law that all ravens are black.

Goodman propounds his puzzle by requiring us to imagine that emeralds, having been identified by some criterion other than color, are now being examined one after another, and all up to now are found to be green. Then he proposes to call anything *grue* that is examined today or earlier and found to be green or is not examined before tomorrow and is blue. Should we expect the first one examined tomorrow to be green, because all examined up to now were green? But all examined up to

now were also grue; so why not expect the first one tomorrow to be grue, and therefore blue?

The predicate "green," Goodman says,[3] is *projectible*; "grue" is not. He says this by way of putting a name to the problem. His step toward solution is his doctrine of what he calls entrenchment,[4] which I shall touch on later. Meanwhile the terminological point is simply that projectible predicates are predicates ζ and η whose shared instances all do count, for whatever reason, toward confirmation of $\lceil$All ζ are $\eta\rceil$.

Now I propose assimilating Hempel's puzzle to Goodman's by inferring from Hempel's that the complement of a projectible predicate need not be projectible. "Raven" and "black" are projectible; a black raven does count toward "All ravens are black." Hence a black raven counts also, indirectly, toward "All non-black things are non-ravens," since this says the same thing. But a green leaf does not count toward "All non-black things are non-ravens," nor, therefore, toward "All ravens are black"; "non-black" and "non-raven" are not projectible. "Green" and "leaf" are projectible, and the green leaf counts toward "All leaves are green" and "All green things are leaves"; but only a black raven can confirm "All ravens are black," the complements not being projectible.

If we see the matter in this way, we must guard against saying that a statement $\lceil$All ζ are $\eta\rceil$ is lawlike only if ζ and η are projectible. "All non-black things are non-ravens" is a law despite its non-projectible terms, since it is equivalent to "All ravens are black." Any statement is lawlike that is

Originally published in Nicholas Rescher et al. (eds), *Essays in Honor of Carl G. Hempel* (Dordrecht: Reidel, 1969). Copyright © W. V. Quine. Reprinted with permission of Kluwer Academic Publishers.

logically *equivalent* to ⌈All ζ are η⌉ for some projectible ζ and η.[5]

Having concluded that the complement of a projectible predicate need not be projectible, we may ask further whether there is *any* projectible predicate whose complement is projectible. I can conceive that there is not, when complements are taken strictly. We must not be misled by limited or relative complementation; "male human" and "non-male human" are indeed both projectible.

To get back now to the emeralds, why do we expect the next one to be green rather than grue? The intuitive answer lies in similarity, however subjective. Two green emeralds are more similar than two grue ones would be if only one of the grue ones were green. Green things, or at least green emeralds, are a kind.[6] A projectible predicate is one that is true of all and only the things of a kind. What makes Goodman's example a puzzle, however, is the dubious scientific standing of a general notion of similarity, or of kind.

The dubiousness of this notion is itself a remarkable fact. For surely there is nothing more basic to thought and language than our sense of similarity; our sorting of things into kinds. The usual general term, whether a common noun or a verb or an adjective, owes its generality to some resemblance among the things referred to. Indeed, learning to use a word depends on a double resemblance: first, a resemblance between the present circumstances and past circumstances in which the word was used, and second, a phonetic resemblance between the present utterance of the word and past utterances of it. And every reasonable expectation depends on resemblance of circumstances, together with our tendency to expect similar causes to have similar effects.

The notion of a kind and the notion of similarity or resemblance seem to be variants or adaptations of a single notion. Similarity is immediately definable in terms of kind; for, things are similar when they are two of a kind. The very words for "kind" and "similar" tend to run in etymologically cognate pairs. Cognate with "kind" we have "akin" and "kindred." Cognate with "like" we have "ilk." Cognate with "similar" and "same" and "resemble" there are "*sammeln*" and "assemble," suggesting a gathering into kinds.

We cannot easily imagine a more familiar or fundamental notion than this, or a notion more ubiquitous in its applications. On this score it is like the notions of logic: like identity, negation, alternation, and the rest. And yet, strangely, there is something logically repugnant about it. For we are baffled when we try to relate the general notion of similarity significantly to logical terms. One's first hasty suggestion might be to say that things are similar when they have all or most or many properties in common. Or, trying to be less vague, one might try defining comparative similarity – "*a* is more similar to *b* than to *c*" – as meaning that *a* shares more properties with *b* than with *c*. But any such course only reduces our problem to the unpromising task of settling what to count as a property.

The nature of the problem of what to count as a property can be seen by turning for a moment to set theory. Things are viewed as going together into sets in any and every combination, describable and indescribable. Any two things are joint members of any number of sets. Certainly then, we cannot define "*a* is more similar to *b* than to *c*" to mean that *a* and *b* belong jointly to more sets than *a* and *c* do. If properties are to support this line of definition where sets do not, it must be because properties do not, like sets, take things in every random combination. It must be that properties are shared only by things that are significantly similar. But properties in such a sense are no clearer than kinds. To start with such a notion of property, and define similarity on that basis, is no better than accepting similarity as undefined.

The contrast between properties and sets which I suggested just now must not be confused with the more basic and familiar contrast between properties, as intensional, and sets as extensional. Properties are intensional in that they may be counted as distinct properties even though wholly coinciding in respect of the things that have them. There is no call to reckon kinds as intensional. Kinds can be seen as sets, determined by their members. It is just that not all sets are kinds.

If similarity is taken simple-mindedly as a yes-or-no affair, with no degrees, then there is no containing of kinds within broader kinds. For, as remarked, similarity now simply means belonging to some one same kind. If all colored things comprise a kind, then all colored things count as similar, and the set of all red things is too narrow to count as a kind. If on the other hand the set of all red things counts as a kind, then colored things do not all count as similar, and the set of all colored things is too broad to count as a kind. We cannot have it both ways. Kinds can, however, overlap; the red things can comprise one kind, the round another.

When we move up from the simple dyadic relation of similarity to the more serious and useful triadic relation of comparative similarity, a correlative change takes place in the notion of kind. Kinds come to admit now not only of overlapping but also of containment one in another. The set of all red things and the set of all colored things can now both count as kinds; for all colored things can now be counted as resembling one another more than some things do, even though less, on the whole, than red ones do.

At this point, of course, our trivial definition of similarity as sameness of kind breaks down; for almost any two things could count now as common members of some broad kind or other, and anyway we now want to define comparative or triadic similarity. A definition that suggests itself is this: *a* is more similar to *b* than to *c* when *a* and *b* belong jointly to more kinds than *a* and *c* do. But even this works only for finite systems of kinds.

The notion of kind and the notion of similarity seemed to be substantially one notion. We observed further that they resist reduction to less dubious notions, as of logic or set theory. That they at any rate be definable each in terms of the other seems little enough to ask. We just saw a somewhat limping definition of comparative similarity in terms of kinds. What now of the converse project, definition of kind in terms of similarity?

One may be tempted to picture a kind, suitable to a comparative similarity relation, as any set which is "qualitatively spherical" in this sense: it takes in exactly the things that differ less than so-and-so much from some central norm. If without serious loss of accuracy we can assume that there are one or more actual things (*paradigm cases*) that nicely exemplify the desired norm, and one or more actual things (*foils*) that deviate just barely too much to be counted into the desired kind at all, then our definition is easy: *the kind with paradigm a and foil b* is the set of all the things to which *a* is more similar than *a* is to *b*. More generally, then, a set may be said to be a *kind* if and only if there are *a* and *b*, known or unknown, such that the set is the kind with paradigm *a* and foil *b*.

If we consider examples, however, we see that this definition does not give us what we want as kinds. Thus take red. Let us grant that a central shade of red can be picked as norm. The trouble is that the paradigm cases, objects in just that shade of red, can come in all sorts of shapes, weights, sizes, and smells. Mere degree of overall similarity to any one such paradigm case will afford little evidence of degree of redness, since it will depend also on shape, weight, and the rest. If our assumed relation of comparative similarity were just comparative chromatic similarity, then our paradigm-and-foil definition of kind would indeed accommodate red-kind. What the definition will not do is distill purely chromatic kinds from mixed similarity.

A different attempt, adapted from Carnap, is this: a set is a kind if all its members are more similar to one another than they all are to any one thing outside the set. In other words, each nonmember differs more from some member than that member differs from any member. However, as Goodman showed in a criticism of Carnap,[7] this construction succumbs to what Goodman calls the difficulty of imperfect community. Thus consider the set of all red round things, red wooden things, and round wooden things. Each member of this set resembles each other member somehow: at least in being red, or in being round, or in being wooden, and perhaps in two or all three of these respects or others. Conceivably, moreover, there is no one thing outside the set that resembles every member of the set to even the least of these degrees. The set then meets the proposed definition of kind. Yet surely it is not what any one means by a kind. It admits yellow croquet balls and red rubber balls while excluding yellow rubber balls.

The relation between similarity and kind, then, is less clear and neat than could be wished. Definition of similarity in terms of kind is halting, and definition of kind in terms of similarity is unknown. Still the two notions are in an important sense correlative. They vary together. If we reassess something *a* as less similar to *b* than to *c*, where it had counted as more similar to *b* than to *c*, surely we will correspondingly permute *a*, *b*, and *c* in respect of their assignment to kinds; and conversely.

I have stressed how fundamental the notion of similarity or of kind is to our thinking, and how alien to logic and set theory. I want to go on now to say more about how fundamental these notions are to our thinking, and something also about their non-logical roots. Afterward I want to bring out how the notion of similarity or of kind changes as science progresses. I shall suggest that it is a mark of maturity of a branch of science that the notion of similarity or kind finally dissolves, so far as it is relevant to that branch of science. That is, it ultimately submits to analysis in the special terms of that branch of science and logic.

For deeper appreciation of how fundamental similarity is, let us observe more closely how it figures in the learning of language. One learns by *ostension* what presentations to call yellow; that is, one learns by hearing the word applied to samples. All he has to go on, of course, is the similarity of further cases to the samples. Similarity being a matter of degree, one has to learn by trial and error how reddish or brownish or greenish a thing can be and still be counted yellow. When he finds he has applied the word too far out, he can use the false cases as samples to the contrary; and then he can proceed to guess whether further cases are yellow or not by considering whether they are more similar to the in-group or the out-group. What one thus uses, even at this primitive stage of learning, is a fully functioning sense of similarity, and relative similarity at that: *a* is more similar to *b* than to *c*.

All these delicate comparisons and shrewd inferences about what to call yellow are, in Sherlock Holmes's terminology, elementary. Mostly the process is unconscious. It is the same process by which an animal learns to respond in distinctive ways to his master's commands or other discriminated stimulations.

The primitive sense of similarity that underlies such learning has, we saw, a certain complexity of structure: *a* is more similar to *b* than to *c*. Some people have thought that it has to be much more complex still: that it depends irreducibly on *respects*, thus similarity in color, similarity in shape, and so on. According to this view, our learning of yellow by ostension would have depended on our first having been told or somehow apprised that it was going to be a question of color. Now hints of this kind are a great help, and in our learning we often do depend on them. Still one would like to be able to show that a single general standard of similarity, but of course comparative similarity, is all we need, and that respects can be abstracted afterward. For instance, suppose the child has learned of a yellow ball and block that they count as yellow, and of a red ball and block that they do not, and now he has to decide about a yellow cloth. Presumably he will find the cloth more similar to the yellow ball and to the yellow block than to the red ball or red block; and he will not have needed any prior schooling in colors and respects. Carnap undertook to show long ago how some respects, such as color, could by an ingenious construction be derived from a general similarity notion;[8] however, this development is challenged, again, by Goodman's difficulty of imperfect community.

A standard of similarity is in some sense innate. This point is not against empiricism; it is a com-

monplace of behavioral psychology. A response to a red circle, if it is rewarded, will be elicited again by a pink ellipse more readily than by a blue triangle; the red circle resembles the pink ellipse more than the blue triangle. Without some such prior spacing of qualities, we could never acquire a habit; all stimuli would be equally alike and equally different. These spacings of qualities, on the part of men and other animals, can be explored and mapped in the laboratory by experiments in conditioning and extinction.[9] Needed as they are for all learning, these distinctive spacings cannot themselves all be learned; some must be innate.

If then I say that there is an innate standard of similarity, I am making a condensed statement that can be interpreted, and truly interpreted, in behavioral terms. Moreover, in this behavioral sense it can be said equally of other animals that they have an innate standard of similarity too. It is part of our animal birthright. And, interestingly enough, it is characteristically animal in its lack of intellectual status. At any rate we noticed earlier how alien the notion is to mathematics and logic.

This innate qualitative spacing of stimulations was seen to have one of its human uses in the ostensive learning of words like "yellow." I should add as a cautionary remark that this is not the only way of learning words, nor the commonest; it is merely the most rudimentary way. It works when the question of the reference of a word is a simple question of spread: how much of our surroundings counts as yellow, how much counts as water, and so on. Learning a word like "apple" or "square" is more complicated, because here we have to learn also where to say that one apple or square leaves off and another begins. The complication is that apples do not add up to an apple, nor squares, generally, to a square. "Yellow" and "water" are mass terms, concerned only with spread; "apple" and "square" are terms of divided reference, concerned with both spread and individuation. Ostension figures in the learning of terms of this latter kind too, but the process is more complex.[10] And then there are all the other sorts of words, all those abstract and neutral connectives and adverbs and all the recondite terms of scientific theory; and there are also the grammatical constructions themselves to be mastered. The learning of these things is less direct and more complex still. There are deep problems in this domain, but they lie aside from the present topic.

Our way of learning "yellow," then, gives less than a full picture of how we learn language. Yet more emphatically, it gives less than a full picture of the human use of an innate standard of similarity, or innate spacing of qualities. For, as remarked, every reasonable expectation depends on similarity. Again on this score, other animals are like man. Their expectations, if we choose so to conceptualize their avoidance movements and salivation and pressing of levers and the like, are clearly dependent on their appreciation of similarity. Or, to put matters in their methodological order, these avoidance movements and salivation and pressing of levers and the like are typical of what we have to go on in mapping the animals' appreciation of similarity, their spacing of qualities.

Induction itself is essentially only more of the same: animal expectation or habit formation. And the ostensive learning of words is an implicit case of induction. Implicitly the learner of "yellow" is working inductively toward a general law of English verbal behavior, though a law that he will never try to state; he is working up to where he can in general judge when an English speaker would assent to "yellow" and when not.

Not only is ostensive learning a case of induction; it is a curiously comfortable case of induction, a game of chance with loaded dice. At any rate this is so if, as seems plausible, each man's spacing of qualities is enough like his neighbor's. For the learner is generalizing on his yellow samples by similarity considerations, and his neighbors have themselves acquired the use of the word "yellow," in their day, by the same similarity considerations. The learner of "yellow" is thus making his induction in a friendly world. Always, induction expresses our hope that similar causes will have similar effects; but when the induction is the ostensive learning of a word, that pious hope blossoms into a foregone conclusion. The uniformity of people's quality spaces virtually assures that similar presentations will elicit similar verdicts.

It makes one wonder the more about other inductions, where what is sought is a generalization not about our neighbor's verbal behavior but about the harsh impersonal world. It is reasonable that our quality space should match our neighbor's, we being birds of a feather; and so the general trustworthiness of induction in the ostensive learning of words was a put-up job. To trust induction as a way of access to the truths of nature, on the other hand, is to suppose, more nearly, that our quality space matches that of the cosmos. The brute irrationality of our sense of similarity, its irrelevance to anything in logic and mathematics, offers little

reason to expect that this sense is somehow in tune with the world – a world which, unlike language, we never made. Why induction should be trusted, apart from special cases such as the ostensive learning of words, is the perennial philosophical problem of induction.

One part of the problem of induction, the part that asks why there should be regularities in nature at all, can, I think, be dismissed. *That* there are or have been regularities, for whatever reason, is an established fact of science; and we cannot ask better than that. *Why* there have been regularities is an obscure question, for it is hard to see what would count as an answer. What does make clear sense is this other part of the problem of induction: why does our innate subjective spacing of qualities accord so well with the functionally relevant groupings in nature as to make our inductions tend to come out right? Why should our subjective spacing of qualities have a special purchase on nature and a lien on the future?

There is some encouragement in Darwin. If people's innate spacing of qualities is a gene-linked trait, then the spacing that has made for the most successful inductions will have tended to predominate through natural selection.[11] Creatures inveterately wrong in their inductions have a pathetic but praiseworthy tendency to die before reproducing their kind.

At this point let me say that I shall not be impressed by protests that I am using inductive generalizations, Darwin's and others, to justify induction, and thus reasoning in a circle. The reason I shall not be impressed by this is that my position is a naturalistic one; I see philosophy not as an a priori propaedeutic or groundwork for science, but as continuous with science. I see philosophy and science as in the same boat – a boat which, to revert to Neurath's figure as I so often do, we can rebuild only at sea while staying afloat in it. There is no external vantage point, no first philosophy. All scientific findings, all scientific conjectures that are at present plausible, are therefore in my view as welcome for use in philosophy as elsewhere. For me, then, the problem of induction is a problem about the world: a problem of how we, as we now are (by our present scientific lights), in a world we never made, should stand better than random or coin-tossing chances of coming out right when we predict by inductions which are based on our innate, scientifically unjustified similarity standard. Darwin's natural selection is a plausible partial explanation.

It may, in view of a consideration to which I next turn, be almost explanation enough. This consideration is that induction, after all, has its conspicuous failures. Thus take color. Nothing in experience, surely, is more vivid and conspicuous than color and its contrasts. And the remarkable fact, which has impressed scientists and philosophers as far back at least as Galileo and Descartes, is that the distinctions that matter for basic physical theory are mostly independent of color contrasts. Color impresses man; raven black impresses Hempel; emerald green impresses Goodman. But color is cosmically secondary. Even slight differences in sensory mechanisms from species to species, Smart remarks,[12] can make overwhelming differences in the grouping of things by color. Color is king in our innate quality space, but undistinguished in cosmic circles. Cosmically, colors would not qualify as kinds.

Color is helpful at the food-gathering level. Here it behaves well under induction, and here, no doubt, has been the survival value of our color-slanted quality space. It is just that contrasts that are crucial for such activities can be insignificant for broader and more theoretical science. If man were to live by basic science alone, natural selection would shift its support to the color-blind mutation.

Living as he does by bread and basic science both, man is torn. Things about his innate similarity sense that are helpful in the one sphere can be a hindrance in the other. Credit is due man's inveterate ingenuity, or human sapience, for having worked around the blinding dazzle of color vision and found the more significant regularities elsewhere. Evidently natural selection has dealt with the conflict by endowing man doubly: with both a color-slanted quality space and the ingenuity to rise above it.

He has risen above it by developing modified systems of kinds, hence modified similarity standards for scientific purposes. By the trial-and-error process of theorizing he has regrouped things into new kinds which prove to lend themselves to many inductions better than the old.

A crude example is the modification of the notion of fish by excluding whales and porpoises. Another taxonomic example is the grouping of kangaroos, opossums, and marsupial mice in a single kind, marsupials, while excluding ordinary mice. By primitive standards the marsupial mouse is more similar to the ordinary mouse than to the kangaroo; by theoretical standards the reverse is true.

A theoretical kind need not be a modification of an intuitive one. It may issue from theory full-blown, without antecedents; for instance the kind which comprises positively charged particles.

We revise our standards of similarity or of natural kinds on the strength, as Goodman remarks,[13] of second-order inductions. New groupings, hypothetically adopted at the suggestion of a growing theory, prove favorable to inductions and so become "entrenched." We newly establish the projectibility of some predicate, to our satisfaction, by successfully trying to project it. In induction nothing succeeds like success.

Between an innate similarity notion or spacing of qualities and a scientifically sophisticated one, there are all gradations. Sciences, after all, differ from common sense only in degree of methodological sophistication. Our experiences from earliest infancy are bound to have overlaid our innate spacing of qualities by modifying and supplementing our grouping habits little by little, inclining us more and more to an appreciation of theoretical kinds and similarities, long before we reach the point of studying science systematically as such. Moreover, the later phases do not wholly supersede the earlier; we retain different similarity standards, different systems of kinds, for use in different contexts. We all still say that a marsupial mouse is more like an ordinary mouse than a kangaroo, except when we are concerned with genetic matters. Something like our innate quality space continues to function alongside the more sophisticated regroupings that have been found by scientific experience to facilitate induction.

We have seen that a sense of similarity or of kinds is fundamental to learning in the widest sense – to language learning, to induction, to expectation. Toward a further appreciation of how utterly this notion permeates our thought, I want now to point out a number of other very familiar and central notions which seem to depend squarely on this one. They are notions that are definable in terms of similarity, or kinds, and further irreducible.

A notable domain of examples is the domain of dispositions, such as Carnap's example of solubility in water. To say of some individual object that it is soluble in water is not to say merely that it always dissolves when in water, because this would be true by default of any object, however insoluble, if it merely happened to be destined never to get into water. It is to say rather that it *would* dissolve if it were in water; but this account brings small comfort, since the device of a subjunctive conditional involves all the perplexities of disposition terms and more. Thus far I simply repeat Carnap.[14] But now I want to point out what could be done in this connection with the notion of kind. Intuitively, what qualifies a thing as soluble though it never gets into water is that it is of the same kind as the things that actually did or will dissolve; it is similar to them. Strictly we can't simply say "*the* same kind," nor simply "similar," when we have wider and narrower kinds, less and more similarity. Let us then mend our definition by saying that the soluble things are the common members of *all* such kinds. A thing is soluble if *each* kind that is broad enough to embrace all actual victims of solution embraces it too.

Graphically the idea is this: we make a set of all the some-time victims, all the things that actually did or will dissolve in water, and then we add just enough other things to round the set out into a kind. This is the water-soluble kind.

If this definition covers just the desired things, the things that are really soluble in water, it owes its success to a circumstance that could be otherwise. The needed circumstance is that a sufficient variety of things actually get dissolved in water to assure their not all falling under any one kind narrower than the desired water-soluble kind itself. But it is a plausible circumstance, and I am not sure that its accidental character is a drawback. If the trend of events had been otherwise, perhaps the solubility concept would not have been wanted.

However, if I seem to be defending this definition, I must now hasten to add that of course it has much the same fault as the definition which used the subjunctive conditional. This definition uses the unreduced notion of kind, which is certainly not a notion we want to rest with either; neither theoretical kind nor intuitive kind. My purpose in giving the definition is only to show the link between the problem of dispositions and the problem of kinds.

As between theoretical and intuitive kinds, certainly the theoretical ones are the ones wanted for purposes of defining solubility and other dispositions of scientific concern. Perhaps "amiable" and "reprehensible" are disposition terms whose definitions should draw rather on intuitive kinds.[15]

· Another dim notion, which has intimate connections with dispositions and subjunctive conditionals, is the notion of cause; and we shall see that it too turns on the notion of kinds. Hume explained cause as invariable succession, and this makes sense as long as the cause and effect are referred to by general terms. We can say that fire causes heat, and we can mean thereby, as Hume would have it, that each event classifiable under the head of fire is followed by an event classifiable under the head of heat, or heating up. But this account, whatever its virtues for these general causal statements, leaves singular causal statements unexplained.

What does it mean to say that the kicking over of a lamp in Mrs Leary's barn caused the Chicago fire? It cannot mean merely that the event at Mrs Leary's belongs to a set, and the Chicago fire belongs to a set, such that there is invariable succession between the two sets: every member of the one set is followed by a member of the other. This paraphrase is trivially true and too weak. Always, if one event happens to be followed by another, the two belong to *certain* sets between which there is invariable succession. We can rig the sets arbitrarily. Just put any arbitrary events in the first set, including the first of the two events we are interested in; and then in the other set put the second of those two events, together with other events that happen to have occurred just after the other members of the first set.

Because of this way of trivialization, a singular causal statement says no more than that the one event was followed by the other. That is, it says no more if we use the definition just now contemplated; which, therefore, we must not. The trouble with that definition is clear enough: it is the familiar old trouble of the promiscuity of sets. Here, as usual, kinds, being more discriminate, enable us to draw distinctions where sets do not. To say that one event caused another is to say that the two events are of *kinds* between which there is invariable succession. If this correction does not yet take care of Mrs Leary's cow, the fault is only with invariable succession itself, as affording too simple a definition of general causal statements; we need to hedge it around with provisions for partial or contributing causes and a good deal else. That aspect of the causality problem is not my concern. What I wanted to bring out is just the relevance of the notion of kinds, as the needed link between singular and general causal statements.

We have noticed that the notion of kind, or similarity, is crucially relevant to the notion of disposition, to the subjunctive conditional, and to singular causal statements. From a scientific point of view these are a pretty disreputable lot. The notion of kind, or similarity, is equally disreputable. Yet some such notion, some similarity sense, was seen to be crucial to all learning, and central in particular to the processes of inductive generalization and prediction which are the very life of science. It appears that science is rotten to the core.

Yet there may be claimed for this rot a certain undeniable fecundity. Science reveals hidden mysteries, predicts successfully, and works technological wonders. If this is the way of rot, then rot is rather to be prized and praised than patronized.

Rot, actually, is not the best model here. A better model is human progress. A sense of comparative similarity, I remarked earlier, is one of man's animal endowments. Insofar as it fits in with regularities of nature, so as to afford us reasonable success in our primitive inductions and expectations, it is presumably an evolutionary product of natural selection. Secondly, as remarked, one's sense of similarity or one's system of kinds develops and changes and even turns multiple as one matures, making perhaps for increasingly dependable prediction. And at length standards of similarity set in which are geared to theoretical science. This development is a development away from the immediate, subjective, animal sense of similarity to the remoter objectivity of a similarity determined by scientific hypotheses and posits and constructs. Things are similar in the later or theoretical sense to the degree that they are interchangeable parts of the cosmic machine revealed by science.

This progress of similarity standards, in the course of each individual's maturing years, is a sort of recapitulation in the individual of the race's progress from muddy savagery. But the similarity notion even in its theoretical phase is itself a muddy notion still. We have offered no definition of it in satisfactory scientific terms. We of course have a behavioral definition of what counts, for a given individual, as similar to what, or as more similar to what than to what; we have this for similarity old and new, human and animal. But it is no definition of what it means really for a to be more similar to b than to c; really, and quite apart from this or that psychological subject.

Did I already suggest a definition to this purpose, metaphorically, when I said that things are similar to the extent that they are interchangeable parts of the cosmic machine? More literally, could things be said to be similar in proportion to how much of scientific theory would remain true on interchanging those things as objects of reference in the theory? This only hints a direction; consider

for instance the dimness of "how much theory." Anyway the direction itself is not a good one; for it would make similarity depend in the wrong way on theory. A man's judgments of similarity do and should depend on his theory, on his beliefs; but similarity itself, what the man's judgments purport to be judgments of, purports to be an objective relation in the world. It belongs in the subject matter not of our theory of theorizing about the world, but of our theory of the world itself. Such would be the acceptable and reputable sort of similarity concept, if it could be defined.

It does get defined in bits: bits suited to special branches of science. In this way, on many limited fronts, man continues his rise from savagery, sloughing off the muddy old notion of kind or similarity piecemeal, a vestige here and a vestige there. Chemistry, the home science of water-solubility itself, is one branch that has reached this stage. Comparative similarity of the sort that matters for chemistry can be stated outright in chemical terms, that is, in terms of chemical composition. Molecules will be said to *match* if they contain atoms of the same elements in the same topological combinations. Then, in principle, we might get at the comparative similarity of objects a and b by considering how many pairs of matching molecules there are, one molecule from a and one from b each time, and how many unmatching pairs. The ratio gives even a theoretical measure of relative similarity, and thus abundantly explains what it is for a to be more similar to b than to c. Or we might prefer to complicate our definition by allowing also for degrees in the matching of molecules; molecules having almost equally many atoms, or having atoms whose atomic numbers or atomic weights are almost equal, could be reckoned as matching better than others. At any rate a lusty chemical similarity concept is assured.

From it, moreover, an equally acceptable concept of kinds is derivable, by the paradigm-and-foil definition noted early in this paper. For it is a question now only of distilling purely chemical kinds from purely chemical similarity; no admixture of other respects of similarity interferes. We thus exonerate water-solubility, which, the last time around, we had reduced no further than to an unexplained notion of kind. Therewith also the associated subjunctive conditional, "If this were in water, it would dissolve," gets its bill of health.

The same scientific advances that have thus provided a solid underpinning for the definition of solubility in terms of kinds, have also, ironically enough, made that line of definition pointless by providing a full understanding of the mechanism of solution. One can redefine water-solubility by simply describing the structural conditions of that mechanism. This embarrassment of riches is, I suspect, a characteristic outcome. That is, once we can legitimize a disposition term by defining the relevant similarity standard, we are apt to know the mechanism of the disposition, and so bypass the similarity. Not but that the similarity standard is worth clarifying too, for its own sake or for other purposes.

Philosophical or broadly scientific motives can impel us to seek still a basic and absolute concept of similarity, along with such fragmentary similarity concepts as suit special branches of science. This drive for a cosmic similarity concept is perhaps identifiable with the age-old drive to reduce things to their elements. It epitomizes the scientific spirit, though dating back to the pre-Socratics: to Empedocles with his theory of four elements, and above all to Democritus with his atoms. The modern physics of elementary particles, or of hills in space-time, is a more notable effort in this direction.

This idea of rationalizing a single notion of relative similarity, throughout its cosmic sweep, has its metaphysical attractions. But there would remain still need also to rationalize the similarity notion more locally and superficially, so as to capture only such similarity as is relevant to some special science. Our chemistry example is already a case of this, since it stops short of full analysis into neutrons, electrons, and the other elementary particles.

A more striking example of superficiality, in this good sense, is afforded by taxonomy, say in zoology. Since learning about the evolution of species, we are in a position to define comparative similarity suitably for this science by consideration of family trees. For a theoretical measure of the degree of similarity of two individual animals we can devise some suitable function that depends on proximity and frequency of their common ancestors. Or a more significant concept of degree of similarity might be devised in terms of genes. When kind is construed in terms of any such similarity concept, fishes in the corrected, whale-free sense of the word qualify as a kind, while fishes in the more inclusive sense do not.

Different similarity measures, or relative similarity notions, best suit different branches of science; for there are wasteful complications in providing for finer gradations of relative similarity than matter for the phenomena with which the particular science is concerned. Perhaps the branches of science could be revealingly classified by looking to the relative similarity notion that is appropriate to each. Such a plan is reminiscent of Felix Klein's so-called *Erlangerprogramm* in geometry, which involved characterizing the various branches of geometry by what transformations were irrelevant to each. But a branch of science would only qualify for recognition and classification under such a plan when it had matured to the point of clearing up its similarity notion. Such branches of science would qualify further as unified, or integrated into our inclusive systematization of nature, only insofar as their several similarity concepts were *compatible*; capable of meshing, that is, and differing only in the fineness of their discriminations.

Disposition terms and subjunctive conditionals in these areas, where suitable senses of similarity and kind are forthcoming, suddenly turn respectable; respectable and, in principle, superfluous. In other domains they remain disreputable and practically indispensable. They may be seen perhaps as unredeemed notes; the theory that would clear up the unanalyzed underlying similarity notion in such cases is still to come. An example is the disposition called intelligence – the ability, vaguely speaking, to learn quickly and to solve problems. Sometime, whether in terms of proteins or colloids or nerve nets or overt behavior, the relevant branch of science may reach the stage where a similarity notion can be constructed capable of making even the notion of intelligence respectable. And superfluous.

In general we can take it as a very special mark of the maturity of a branch of science that it no longer needs an irreducible notion of similarity and kind. It is that final stage where the animal vestige is wholly absorbed into the theory. In this career of the similarity notion, starting in its innate phase, developing over the years in the light of accumulated experience, passing then from the intuitive phase into theoretical similarity, and finally disappearing altogether, we have a paradigm of the evolution of unreason into science.

Notes

1 C. G. Hempel, *Aspects of Scientific Explanation and Other Essays* (New York: Free Press, 1965), p. 15.

2 Nelson Goodman, *Fact, Fiction, and Forecast* (1st edn, Cambridge, Mass.: Harvard University Press, Indianapolis: 1955; 2nd edn,: Bobbs-Merrill, 1965), p. 74. I am indebted to Goodman and to Burton Dreben for helpful criticisms of earlier drafts of the present paper.

3 Goodman, *Fact*, pp. 82f.

4 Ibid., pp. 95ff.

5 I mean this only as a sufficient condition of lawlikeness. See Donald Davidson, "Emeroses by other names," *Journal of Philosophy* 63 (1966), pp. 778–80.

6 This relevance of kind is noted by Goodman, *Fact*, 1st edn, pp. 119f; 2nd edn, pp. 121f.

7 Nelson Goodman, *The Structure of Appearance*, 2nd edn (Indianapolis: Bobbs-Merrill, 1966), pp. 163f.

8 Rudolf Carnap, *The Logical Structure of the World* (Berkeley: University of California Press, 1967), pp. 141–7 (German edn, 1928).

9 See my *Word and Object* (Cambridge, Mass.: MIT Press, 1960), pp. 83f, for further discussion and references.

10 See ibid., pp. 90–5.

11 This was noted by S. Watanabe on the second page of his paper "Une Explication mathématique du classement d'objects," in S. Dockx and P. Bernays (eds), *Information and Prediction in Science* (New York: Academy Press, 1965).

12 J. J. C. Smart, *Philosophy and Scientific Realism* (New York: Humanities Press, 1963), pp. 68–72.

13 Goodman, *Fact*, pp. 95ff.

14 Rudolf Carnap, "Testability and meaning," *Philosophy of Science* 3 (1936), pp. 419–71; 4 (1937), pp. 1–40.

15 Here there followed, in previous printings, 26 lines which I have deleted. They were concerned with explaining certain subjunctive conditionals on the basis of the notion of kind. Paul Berent pointed out to me that the formulation was wrong, for it would have equated those conditionals to their converses.

19

On Properties

Hilary Putnam

It has been maintained by such philosophers as Quine and Goodman that purely 'extensional' language suffices for all the purposes of properly formalized scientific discourse. Those entities that were traditionally called 'universals' – properties, concepts, forms, etc. – are rejected by these extensionalist philosophers on the ground that 'the principle of individuation is not clear'. It is conceded that science requires that we allow something tantamount to quantification over non-particulars (or, anyway, over things that are not material objects, not space-time points, not physical fields, etc.), but, the extensionalists contend, quantification over *sets* serves the purposes nicely. The 'ontology' of modern science, at least as Quine formalizes it, comprises material objects (or, alternatively, space-time points), sets of material objects, sets of sets of material objects, . . . , but no *properties, concepts,* or *forms.* Let us thus examine the question: can the principle of individuation for properties ever be made clear?

1 Properties and Reduction

It seems to me that there are at least two notions of 'property' that have become confused in our minds. There is a very old notion for which the

Originally published in N. Rescher et al. (eds), *Essays in Honor of Carl G. Hempel* (Dordrecht: Reidel, 1969). Reprinted by permission of Kluwer Academic Publishers.

word 'predicate' used to be employed (using 'predicate' as a term only for *expressions* and never for properties is a relatively recent mode of speech: 'Is existence a predicate?' was not a *syntactical* question), and there is the notion for which I shall use the terms 'physical property', 'physical magnitude', 'physical relation', etc., depending on whether the object in question is one-place, a functor, more than one-place, etc. Ignore, if possible the connotations of 'physical', which are rather misleading (I would be pleased if someone suggested a better terminology for the distinction that I wish to draw), and let me try to tell you what distinction it is that I mean to mark by the use of the terms 'predicate' (which I shall revive, in its classical sense) and 'physical property'.

The principle of individuation for predicates is well known: the property of being P (where 'property' is understood in the sense of 'predicate') is one and the same property as the property of being Q – i.e., to say of something that it is P and to say of something else that it is Q is to apply the *same predicate* to the two things – just in case 'x is P' is *synonymous* (in the wide sense of 'analytically equivalent to') 'x is Q'. Doubt about the clarity of the principle of individuation for predicates thus reduces to doubt about the notion of synonymy. While I share Quine's doubts about the existence of a clear notion of synonymy, I have more hope than he does that a satisfactory concept can be found, although that is not to be the subject of this paper.

Consider, however, the situation which arises when a scientist asserts that temperature *is* mean molecular kinetic energy. On the face of it, this is a statement of identity of properties. What is being asserted is that the *physical property* of having a particular temperature is *really* (in some sense of 'really') the *same property* as the property of having a certain molecular energy; or (more generally) that the *physical magnitude* temperature is one and the same physical magnitude as mean molecular kinetic energy. If this is right, then, since '*x* has such-and-such a temperature' is not *synonymous* with '*x* has bla-bla mean molecular kinetic energy', even when 'bla-bla' is the value of molecular energy that corresponds to the value 'such-and-such' of the temperature, it must be that what the physicist means by a 'physical magnitude' is something quite other than what philosophers have called a 'predicate' or a 'concept'.

To be specific, the difference is that, whereas synonymy of the expressions '*x* is *P*' and '*x* is *Q*' is required for the predicates *P* and *Q* to be the 'same', it is not required for the physical property *P* to be the same physical property as the physical property *Q*. Physical properties can be 'synthetically identical'.

This fact is closely connected with *reduction*. 'Temperature is mean molecular kinetic energy' is a classical example of a reduction of one physical magnitude to another; and the problem of stating a 'principle of individuation' for physical properties, magnitudes, etc., reduces, as we shall see, to the problem of describing the methodological constraints on reduction. Not all reductions involve properties or magnitudes; for example, 'Water is H_2O' asserts the identity of each body of water with a certain aggregation of H_2O molecules, give or take some impurities, not the identity of 'the property of being water' and 'the property of being H_2O' – although one might assert that those are the same physical property, too – but many reductions do: e.g., the reduction of gravitation to space-time curvature, of surface tension to molecular attraction, and so on.

I shall suppose, then, that there is a notion of property – for which I use the adjective 'physical', mainly because 'physical magnitude' already exists with a use similar to the use I wish to make of 'physical property', which satisfies the condition that the property *P* can be synthetically identical with the property *Q*, the criterion being that this is said to be true just in case *P* 'reduces' (in the sense of empirical reduction) to *Q*, or *Q* to *P*, or both *P* and *Q* 'reduce' to the same *R*.

2 Can one get an Extensional Criterion for the Identity of Properties?

The criterion for the identity of properties just given is not extensional, because the relation of reduction is not extensional. Water reduces to H_2O, and H_2O is coextensive with (H_2O ∨ Unicorn), but water does not reduce to (H_2O ∨ Unicorn). The difficulty is simply that

$$(x)(x \text{ is water} \equiv x \text{ is an aggregation of } H_2O \text{ molecules})$$

is not merely true but nomological ('lawlike'), while

$$(x)(x \text{ is water} \equiv x \text{ is an aggregation of } H_2O \text{ molecules} \vee x \text{ is a unicorn})$$

is extensionally true (assuming there are no unicorns), but not lawlike (unless the non-existence of unicorns is a law of nature, in which case things become still more complicated).

This raises the question: can one hope to get a criterion for the identity of properties (in the sense of 'physical property') expressible in an extensional language? The problem is related to such problems as the problem of getting a necessary and sufficient condition for 'nomological', and of getting one for causal statements, expressible in an extensional language, and what I shall say about this problem is closely related to the way in which I propose to treat those other problems.

3 Fundamental Magnitudes

For reasons which will become clear later, I wish to begin by discussing the notion of a fundamental magnitude in physics. It seems clear that no *analytic* necessary and sufficient condition for something to be a fundamental magnitude can be given. At any rate, I shall not even try to give one. But just how serious is this? There do seem to be methodological principles, albeit vague ones, governing the physicist's decision to take certain terms as fundamental magnitude terms and not others. Relying on these principles, and on his scientific intuition, the physicist arrives at a list of 'fundamental magnitudes'. At this point he *has* a necessary and sufficient condition for something to be a fundamental magnitude – his list. To be sure, this is an *empirical* necessary and sufficient condition, not an analytic one. But so what? If one has a confirmation procedure, even a vague one, for a term T, and by using that procedure one can arrive at a biconditional of the form $(x)\,(T(x) \equiv \ldots x \ldots)$ that one accepts as empirically true (and the condition $\ldots x \ldots$ occurring on the right side of the biconditional is precise), then what problem of 'explicating the notion of T-hood' remains? Such a term T may be regarded as a *programmatic* term: we introduce it not by a definition, but by a trial-and-error procedure (often an implicit one); and the program is (using the trial-and-error procedure) to find an empirically correct necessary and sufficient condition for 'T-hood' which is precise. If this is successful, then the notion of 'T-hood' is precise enough for all scientific purposes. Even if it is unsuccessful, one might succeed in discovering in each individual case whether T applies or not without ever obtaining any general necessary and sufficient condition: if even *this* is unsuccessful, someone is sure to propose that we drop the notion T altogether.

Even if it is not reasonable to ask for an analytic necessary and sufficient condition in the case of programmatic terms, it is surely reasonable to ask for some indication of the associated trial-and-error procedure, provided that we do not demand more precision in the reply than can reasonably be expected in descriptions of the scientific method at the present stage of knowledge. What is the associated 'trial-and-error procedure', or 'confirmation procedure', in the case of the term 'fundamental magnitude'?

One obvious condition is that fundamental magnitude terms must be 'projectible' in the sense of Goodman. Since this is a general requirement on all terms in empirical science, except complex-compound expressions, and since discussing it properly involves (as Goodman rightly stresses), attacking the whole problem of induction, I shall simply take it for granted. (Goodman's solution is, in effect, to say that a term is projectible if we do in fact project it sufficiently often. This leaves the whole problem of why we project some terms to begin with and not others up to psychology. I am inclined to believe that this, far from being a defect in Goodman's approach, is its chief virtue. It is hard to see, once one has passed Goodman's 'intelligence test for philosophers' (as Ullian has described Goodman's discussion of *green* and *grue*), how this question could be anything but a question for psychology. But anyone who feels that there is *some further* philosophical work to be done here is welcome to do it; my feeling is that what we have here is not so much an unsolved philosophical problem as an undefined one.)

A second condition is that these terms must characterize all things – i.e., all particles, in a particle formulation of physics, and all space-time points, in a field formulation of physics. (I believe that one will get different, though interdefinable, lists of fundamental magnitudes depending on which of these two types of formulation one chooses for physics.)

A third condition is that one of these terms must be 'distance', or a term with the aid of which 'distance' is definable, and that the positions of things must be predictable from the values of the fundamental magnitudes at a given time by means of the assumed laws. (This last requirement applies only before 'quantization'.)

A fourth condition is that the laws must assume an especially simple form – say, differential equations (and linear rather than nonlinear, first-order rather than second-order, etc., as far as possible), if these terms are taken as primitive.

Looking over these conditions, we see that what one has is not one trial-and-error procedure but two. For the laws (or, rather, putative laws) of physics are not fixed in advance, but are to be discovered at the same time as the fundamental magnitudes. If we assume, however, that the laws are to be expressible in a reasonably simple way as differential equations in the fundamental magnitudes, and that statistics enter (in fundamental particle physics) only through the procedure of passing from a deterministic theory to a corresponding quantum-mechanical theory (the so-called procedure of 'quantization'), then the double trial-and-error procedure is reasonably clear. What one does is to simultaneously look for laws expressible in the form specified (which will predict the position of particles), and to look for terms which are 'projectible' and by means of which such laws can be formulated.

To avoid misunderstandings, let me make it clear that I am *not* claiming that it is 'part of the concept' (as people say) of a fundamental law that it *must* be a differential equation, etc. I am saying that that is what we in fact look for *now*. If it turns out that we cannot *get* that, then we will look for the next best thing. We do not know now what the next best thing would be; partly this is a question of psychology, and partly it depends on what mathematical forms for the expressions of laws have actually been thought of at the time. I deny that the double trial-and-error procedure is fixed by *rules* (or, at least, it is a daring and so far unsupported guess that it *is* fixed by rules), unless one is willing to count 'look for laws in a form that seems simple and natural' as a *rule*. But the procedure *is* 'fixed' by the *de facto* agreement of scientists on what is a simple and natural form for the formulation of physical laws. It seems to me to be a great mistake in the philosophy of science to overplay the importance of *rules*, and to underestimate the importance of *regularities* Regularities in what scientists take to be 'simple' and 'natural' may be a matter of psychology rather than methodology; but (a) the line between methodology and psychology is not at all that sharp; and (b) methodology may well *depend* on such psychological regularities.

4 A Criterion for the Identity of 'Physical₂' Properties

H. Feigl has distinguished two notions of the 'physical'. In Feiglese, every scientific predicate is 'physical₁', i.e., 'physical' in the sense of having something to do with causality, space, and time; but only the predicates of *physics* are physical in the narrower sense, 'physical₂'. In this terminology, what I have been calling 'physical properties' should have been called 'physical₁ properties'. Our problem is to find a criterion for the identity of physical₁ properties. In this section I shall approach this problem by discussing the special problem of a criterion of identity for physical₂ properties. Assuming that the presently accepted list of fundamental magnitudes is complete, i.e., that there are no further fundamental magnitudes to be discovered, the natural procedure is to correlate physical₂ properties with equivalence classes of predicates definable with the aid of the fundamental magnitude terms. Each defined term in the vocabulary of physics (i.e., of elementary particle physics) corresponds to a physical₂ property, and vice versa; two terms correspond to the same physical₂ property just in case they belong to the same equivalence class. But what should the equivalence relation be?

There are *two* natural proposals, I think, leading to two quite different notions of physical₂ property. One proposal, which I shall not investigate here, would be to take *nomological coextensiveness* as the equivalence relation; the other would be to take *logical equivalence*. I shall choose logical equivalence, because, although we want to allow 'synthetic identities' between physical₂ properties and, for example, observation properties (e.g., temperature

is mean molecular kinetic energy), it does not seem natural or necessary to consider two terms as corresponding to the same physical₂ property when both are already 'reduced' (i.e., expressed in terms of the fundamental magnitude terms), and in their reduced form they are not logically equivalent.

How shall we understand 'logical equivalence', however? I propose to understand 'logical equivalence' as meaning logical equivalence in the narrower sense (not allowing considerations of 'synonymy'); so that P_1 and P_2 will be regarded as corresponding to the same physical₂ property only if: (a) P_1 and P_2 are built up out of fundamental magnitude terms alone with the aid of logical and mathematical vocabulary; and (b) $(x)(P_1(x) \equiv P_2(x))$ is a truth of pure logic or mathematics. (The criterion as just given is for one-place predicates; it should be obvious how it is intended to be extended to relations and functors.)

The proposed criterion of identity implicitly takes the stand that *no* relations among the fundamental magnitudes should be considered as 'analytic'. This seems reasonable to me in view of the strongly 'law-cluster' character of the fundamental magnitude terms, but a word of explanation may be in order. Consider, for the sake of an example or two, some of the relations among the fundamental magnitude terms that have seemed analytic in the past. For 'distance' ('$d(x, y)$'), the following relation has often been considered to be 'part of the meaning'; $(d(x, y)$ is not equal to zero unless $x = y$. Yet just this relation is given up (for 'space-time distance', at least) by the Minkowskian metric for space-time. Similarly, that $d(x, y)$ has no upper bound is given up when we go over from Euclidean to Riemannian geometry. These examples indicate, to me at any rate, that, when fundamental magnitude terms are involved, it is foolish to regard *any* statement (outside of a logical or mathematical truth) as 'analytic'.

But is it safe to regard even logic and mathematics as analytic? The answer seems to depend on just what is being packed into the notion 'analytic'. If 'analytic' is a covert way of saying 'true by linguistic convention alone', then the view that logic and mathematics are 'analytic' is highly suspect. Certainly I do not presuppose this view (which I do not in any case accept) here. But if 'analytic' means 'true by virtue of linguistic convention *and* logic or mathematics', then trivially all truths of logic or mathematics are 'analytic'. But this thesis is compatible, for example, with the radical thesis that logic and mathematics are empirical, subject to revision for experimental reasons, etc. I do not wish to rule out this attitude towards logic and mathematics (which, in fact, I hold). Thus, when I say that *logical equivalence* is the criterion for the identity of physical$_2$ properties, I do not mean logical equivalence according to what we today take to be the laws of logic and mathematics; I simply mean equivalence according to whatever may in fact be the truths of logic. If we change our logic, then we may have to change our minds about what physical$_2$ properties are in fact identical; but the *criterion* of identity will not have changed; it will just be that we made a mistake in its application in some particular cases.

5 Basic Terms of 'Non-fundamental' Disciplines

The issues involved in the reduction of theoretical terms in 'non-fundamental' disciplines to physical$_2$ terms are so well known by now, that I shall be very brief. (I shall lean on the discussion by Kemeny and Oppenheim, which I regard as still being the best paper on the subject,[1] and on the subsequent paper by Oppenheim and myself.[2] The basic requirement in every reduction, as enunciated by Kemeny and Oppenheim, is that all the observable phenomena explainable by means of the reduced theory should be explainable by means of the reducing theory. This means that the observation terms must be counted as part of the reducing theory – in the present case, physics – and that we must suppose that we have at least one true biconditional of the form $(x)(O(x) \equiv P(x))$, where P is a physical$_2$ term, for each undefined observation term O. (This requirement is not made by Kemeny and Oppenheim, but it seems the simplest way of ensuring that the maximum possible observational consequences will be derivable from the reducing theory.)

In the paper by Oppenheim and Putnam mentioned above, it is stressed that the reduction at issue need not be made *directly* to physics; if, for example, the laws of psychology are ever reduced to those of cell biology (explanation in terms of reverberating circuits of neurons, etc.), while the laws of biology are reduced to laws of physics and chemistry, which is itself reduced to physics, then *the laws of psychology will have been reduced to those of physics* from the point of view of the logician of science, even if no one should ever care to write out the definition of a single psychological term directly in physical$_2$ language.

Once one has found a way of explaining the phenomena in physical$_2$ terms (in the sense just explained), then the next step is to see if anything can be found (from the standpoint of the new explanation of the phenomena directly by means of the laws of physics) which answers to the old theoretical primitives. It is not necessary for this purpose that the old laws should be *exactly* derivable from the proposed identification. If we can find a relative interpretation of the old theories into the theory consisting of the laws of physics plus the 'bridge laws' connecting physical$_2$ terms with observation terms, which permits the deduction of a good approximation theory to the old theories, then we identify the things and properties referred to by the basic terms of the old theories with the things and properties$_1$ referred to by the corresponding physical$_2$ terms (even if some conventional extension of meaning is involved, as in the case of 'water' and 'hot').

On the other hand, it may happen that some basic term of the old theories does not answer to *anything* (in the light of our new way of explaining the phenomena). In this case, we simply *drop* the old theories (or those laws involving the term in question, at any rate) and explain the phenomena by means of 'lower'-level theories, including, in the last resort, direct explanation by means of physics plus bridge laws.

The second case is classified by Kemeny and Oppenheim as *reduction by replacement*; the first case is classified as *reduction by means of biconditionals*. Both types of reduction are exemplified in science, and in some cases it is arguable whether, in view of the shifts of meaning involved, a given reduction should be classified as a reduction by replacement or by means of biconditionals. The important point is that *after* the reduction of a discipline, those basic terms that *remain*, that are still regarded as corresponding to 'physical properties' (in the sense of 'physical$_1$') at all, are reduced by means of biconditionals (or identity-signs, as in the case of 'Temperature *is* mean molecular kinetic energy'). For terms which are 'reduced by replacement' are *dropped*, so that the only basic terms that survive are the ones that we reduce by the other method.

6 Psychological Properties

What first led me to write a paper on the topic of 'properties' was the desire to study reduction in the case of *psychology*. I am inclined to hold the view that psychological properties would be reduced not to physical$_2$ properties in the usual sense (i.e., first-order combinations of fundamental magnitudes), but to *functional states*, where crude examples of the kinds of properties I call 'functional states' would be (a) the property of being a finite automaton with a certain machine table; and (b) the property of being a finite automaton with a certain machine table *and* being in the state described in a certain way in the table. To say that a finite automaton has a certain machine table is to say that *there are properties* (in the sense of physical$_1$ properties) which the object has (i.e., it always has one of them), and which succeed each other in accordance with a certain rule. Thus the property of having a certain machine table is a *property of having properties which*... – although a property of the first level (a property of things), it is of 'second order' in the old Russell – Whitehead sense, in that its definition involves a quantification over (first-order) physical$_1$ properties. This is a general characteristic of all 'functional' properties, as I use the term: although physical$_1$ properties in a wide sense, they are *second-order* physical$_1$ properties. How then should a reduction to such properties be analyzed – e.g., *pain* to a certain functional state (as I proposed in an earlier paper)?

The answer is, that if we are willing to accept the hypothesis that all *first-order* physical$_1$ properties will turn out to be reducible to physical$_2$ properties, then all second-order physical$_1$ properties will automatically reduce to *second-order* physical$_2$ properties. If we succeed in reducing psychological properties to properties of the form: *the property (of second-order) of having (first-order) physical$_1$ properties which*..., then we make the further reduction to (second-order) physical$_2$ properties by simply making the theoretical identification of the foregoing physical$_1$ property with the corresponding physical$_2$ property, that is, with *the (second-order) physical$_2$ property of having (first-order) physical$_2$ properties which*...

It is likely, however, that this unusual type of reduction will have to be combined with the more familiar type if psychology is ever to be reduced. For, although a reduction of psychological states to properties of the kind just described would enable us to predict many of the aspects of the behavior of the corresponding species and to understand the functional organization of that behavior, there are undoubtedly aspects of human behavior whose explanation will require a reference not just to the functional organization of the human brain and nervous system, but to the details of the physical realization of that functional organization. An analogous complication has already appeared in the case of the reduction of chemistry to physics, and is beginning to appear in the case of molecular biology. Although many chemical phenomena can be explained 'at the chemical level', in some cases it is necessary to descend to the level of elementary particle physics, even to explain such familiar facts as the liquidity of water and the hardness of diamond; and although many cellular phenomena can be explained at the level of whole cells, nuclei, etc., in the most important cases it is necessary to 'descend' to explanation directly in physical-chemical terms.

It should be noted that if we accept the strict extensionalism which is urged by Quine, then all questions of reduction of properties trivialize upon the passing-over to corresponding questions about *sets*. *Temperature* as a physical magnitude which is not intrinsically quantified has no place in Quine's scheme: instead, we are urged to take as primitive 'temperature-in-degrees-centigrade', or some such. And the statement that temperature *is* mean molecular kinetic energy passes over into the harmless statement that 'temperature in degrees centigrade is directly proportional to mean molecular kinetic energy in c.g.s. units'. I have discussed this difficulty with Quine, and he has suggested meeting it by saying that 'temperature in degrees centigrade *is a quantification of* mean molecular kinetic energy'. (This would indicate the question '*Why* is temperature in degrees centigrade directly proportional to mean molecular kinetic energy in c.g.s. units?' is not a happy question.) Discussing this move would involve discussing: (a) whether it is really satisfactory to think of mean molecular kinetic energy as a class of equivalence-classes as Quine also suggests; and (b) whether the relation 'the function f is a quantification of S' does not, on the natural understanding of such phrases as 'a quantification of kinetic energy', turn out to be an *intensional* one. Of course, one *can* take the relation extensionally as meaning that temperature is a one–one function of the equivalence-classes, subject to a continuity condition; but then one will not have distinguished between the cases in which one magnitude is a *function* of another, and the cases in which one magnitude *reduces* to another, which is just our problem.

In the same way, there would be no sense, if Quine were right, in discussing whether pain is a brain state, or a functional state, or yet another kind of state. 'Pain' is construed by Quine as a predicate whose arguments are an organism and a time; if the set of ordered pairs (O, t) such that O is in pain at t is identical with the set of ordered pairs (O, t) such that O satisfies some other condition at t, then *pain* (the relation) *is* (extensionally) the relation that holds between an organism and a time just in case the organism satisfies that other condition. Pain could be *both* a brain state and a functional state. In some world, pain could even be 'identical' with pricking one's finger – if the organisms in that world experienced pain when and only when they pricked a finger.

Quine does not find this result counterintuitive, because he does not find intensional differences 'philosophically explanatory'. I believe that pointing to differences that are there *is* philosophically explanatory; and it seems to me that these particular differences are 'there'. But I do not expect that either of us will succeed in convincing the other.

7 Prospect for an Extensional Criterion for the Identity of Properties

In the light of the foregoing discussion, I can give a brief answer to the question: can we get a criterion for the identity of properties (in the sense of physical$_1$ properties) which is expressible in extensional language? The answer is that we cannot *today*, as far as I am aware, but that prospects seem reasonably good for obtaining one eventually. The reduction of those observation terms that one might want to take as undefined terms in a reasonable formalization of science seems fully possible, not withstanding some formidable complexities still to be unraveled. Also, it is assumed in present science that the number of fundamental magnitudes *is* finite (since there are assumed to be only four fundamental kinds of forces); and the assumption that the basic terms of the 'non-fundamental' disciplines will eventually be reduced is at least reasonable.

Of course, the present discussion is entirely empirical in spirit. Indeed, my whole purpose is to break away from two recent traditions ('recent tradition' is deliberate) which seem to me to be sterile and already exhausted: the tradition of 'explication' and the tradition of 'ordinary language analysis'. It may turn out that the number of fundamental magnitudes is infinite; or that some properties other than the ones studied in physics have also to be taken as 'fundamental' (although it is easy

to see how the discussion should be modified in this case); or that there are *no* fundamental properties (e.g., there is a level still more 'fundamental' than the level of elementary particles, and a level still more 'fundamental' than that, etc.) If any one of these possibilities turns out to be real, then I am content to leave it to some philosopher of that future to reopen this discussion! The philosophical point that I wish to make is that at present, when we do *not* have a criterion for the identity of arbitrary physical$_1$ properties that is expressible in extensional language, we are still not all that badly off. We do have a criterion for the identity of physical$_2$ properties, as we presently conceive physical$_2$ properties, and this criterion can be extended to other physical$_1$ properties just as rapidly as we succeed in reducing the disciplines in which the corresponding physical$_1$ terms appear to physics. It does not appear unreasonable that we should be unable, in the case of physical$_1$ properties which have not been reduced, to answer the question of identity or non-identity with any certainty prior to the reduction. Of course, in some cases we *can* answer it; for example, properties which are not coextensive are certainly not identical.

8 Are Properties Dispensable?

That there are many assertions that scientists make that we do not know how to render in a formalized notation without something tantamount to quantification over properties is easily seen. First, consider the question we have mentioned several times: whether there are any fundamental magnitudes not yet discovered. Second, consider the scientist who utters a conjecture of the form 'I think that there is a single property, not yet discovered, which is responsible for such-and-such'. Thirdly, consider the assertion that two things have an unspecified observable property in common.

I believe that all of these cases really reduce to the second: the case of saying that something's having a property P *is responsible for* (or 'causes', etc.) such-and-such. Let us call a description of the form 'the property P, the presence of which (in such-and-such cases) is responsible for (or causes, etc.) such-and-such', a *causal description* of a property. Let us call a description of the form 'the property of being P' a *canonical description* of a property. Then the difficulty is basically this: that there are properties for which we know a causal description but no canonical description. And when we wish to speak of such properties, an existential quantifier over all properties seems unavoidable.

Consider the first case: the case of saying that there is a fundamental magnitude not yet discovered. This comes down to saying that there are phenomena (which itself involves a quantifier over observable properties!) for which some property P is responsible, such that the property P is not definable (in some specified way) in terms of the properties currently listed as 'fundamental'. Consider the third case: quantifying over observable properties. This might be handled in the case of humans by giving a list of all observable properties (although the impracticality of this proposal is obvious); but we also talk of properties that other species can observe and we cannot. But presumably this comes down to talking of those properties P that act as the stimuli for certain responses, and this could presumably be construed as a reference to the properties satisfying certain causal descriptions. Probably, then (although I do not feel absolutely sure of this), it is ultimately only in causal contexts that quantification over properties is indispensable.

One proposal which has been made for handling such references in an extensional way is this: the assertion that 'A's having the property P at t_1 is the cause of B's having the property Q at t_1', for example, is handled by saying that '$P(A, t_0)$' is part of an *explanans*, whose corresponding *explanandum* is '$Q(B, t_1)$'. The 'explanans' and the 'explanandum' are respectively the premise and the conclusion in an argument which meets the conditions for an explanation as set forth in the familiar covering-law model. Does this obviate the need for property-talk?

I do not wish to discuss here the familiar objections to handling causal statements via the covering-law model (e.g., Bromberger's ingenious objection that this model would permit one to say that the period of a pendulum's being so-and-so *caused* the string to have such-and-such a length). But even without going into the adequacy of this model itself, two points need to be made.

First of all, the proposed analysis of causal statements only works when the properties in question are specified by canonical descriptions. When the property hypothesized to be the cause is mentioned only by a causal description – when part of the *explanans* is that there *exists* a property with certain causal efficacies – then this analysis does not apply. Of course, one could treat such explanations as programmatic: when the scientist says, 'I hypothesize that there is a property which is responsible for

such-and-such, and which obeys some law of the following form', one could 'translate' this by 'I propose to introduce a new primitive P into the language of science, and I suggest that some theory containing the term P in such-and-such a way will turn out to be confirmed'; but this is clearly inadequate. (The theory might never be confirmed, because, for example, the money to perform the experiments was not forthcoming, and it might still be true that there *was* a property P which . . . , etc.) Or one might propose to substitute 'is true' for 'will turn out to be confirmed'; but then one runs into the difficulty that one is speaking of 'truth' in a language which contains a primitive one cannot translate into one's metalanguage (and which has not, indeed, been given any precise meaning). Or one might say that the scientist has not made any *statement* at all; that he has just said, in effect '*Let's look for a new theory of the following kind . . .*'; but this seems just plain false.

Secondly, the covering-law theory of explanation uses the term 'nomological' ('lawlike') which has admittedly never been explicated. What are the prospects for an explication of this term, in comparison with the prospects of the notion 'property'?

The following would be my program for arriving at a more precise description of the class of 'nomological statements': first, I think that we should try to formulate a hypothesis as to the *form* in which the fundamental laws can be written. This is a much weaker requirement than the requirement that we actually find the laws. The same mathematical form – for example, differential equations in the 'fundamental magnitudes' of classical physics – can be used for the laws of both classical physics and relativity physics. If one takes '$d(x, y)$' (the distance from x to y, where x and y are spatial points at one time) as primitive, then, indeed, this is context-dependent in relativity physics (i.e., $d(x, y)$, or even what x's and y's are spatial points *at one time*, is relative to the reference system), but this is irrelevant to the statement of the *laws*, since these are the same in all reference systems. The change in the geometry is just a change in the laws obeyed by $d(x, y)$; but laws are still expressible as differential equations valid at all points of space and time, and involving only the fundamental magnitudes. Conversely, it seems reasonable to say that any physical relation that can be expressed as a differential equation without boundary conditions, valid at *all* points in space and time, and in just the fundamental magnitudes, should count as a law. Once such a form has been found, the true statements of that form are defined to be the 'nomological' statements of physics. Secondly, as soon as one succeeds in reducing the basic terms of some 'non-fundamental' discipline to physics, one can define the concept 'nomological' for that discipline: namely, a statement in the vocabulary of that discipline is nomological if and only if it is equivalent, via the accepted reducing biconditionals, to a nomological statement of physics.

It should not be supposed from the foregoing that I think that 'law of nature' *means* 'statement which is reducible to (or which itself is) a nomological statement of physics'. Rather, the situation seems to me to be as follows. Each of the scientific disciplines has pretty much its own list of 'fundamental magnitudes' and its own preferred form or forms for the expression of 'laws'. Thus the discussion in the section of this paper headed 'Fundamental Magnitudes' could be repeated, with suitable modifications, for each of the other disciplines. In each case there seem to be certain magnitudes which are 'dependent', in the sense that it is the business of the discipline (at least prima facie – a discipline may, of course, change its mind about what its 'business' is) to predict their time-course, and certain magnitudes which are independent, in the sense that they are introduced in order to help predict the values of the dependent magnitudes. In physics, for example, it was the position of particles that was, above all, dependent. In economics it would be prices and amounts of production. In each case the scientist looks for a set of properties including his 'dependent variables' which are 'projectible', and which will suffice for the statement of 'laws' – i.e., in order for properties to be accepted as the 'fundamental' ones, it must be possible to formulate (hopefully) true general statements in terms of those properties, which have one of the forms recognized as a form for the expression of laws at that stage in the development of science, and which will predict, at least statistically, the time-course of the dependent variables.

As we mentioned just before in the case of physics, it may be that one cannot *get* true general statements which will do what one wants in the form that one originally takes to be the preferred form for the expression of laws. For example, although the laws of relativity theory can be stated as differential equations in the classical 'fundamental magnitudes', just as the laws of classical physics were, the laws of quantum mechanics require additional 'fundamental magnitudes' (e.g., *spin*), and a more complex mathematical form – one

has to introduce operators on Hilbert spaces. Similarly, it might be that the form preferred for the expression of laws in, say, economics at a particular time is too restrictive. When this turns out to be the case, one goes to the 'next best' form, where what is 'next best' is determined by the scientists in the field on the basis of their scientific intuition, in the light of the mathematical methods available at the time for their purposes.

The foregoing suggests that one might seek to explicate the notion of a fundamental law for each of the basic scientific disciplines, and then define a 'nomological statement' simply as a statement which is either itself a fundamental law of one of these disciplines, or which follows from the fundamental laws of one or more disciplines. However, this approach seems to overlook something.

What is overlooked is the enormous impact that the successes of reduction are having on our concept of a natural law. Thus, suppose the Weber–Fechner Law is true without exception (which it in fact is not), and that it is in terms of 'fundamental magnitudes' of psychology, and of the right form to be a 'psychological law'. Then, if it were not for the strong tendency in science in the direction of physicalistic reduction, there would be no question but that it is a 'law of nature'. But let us suppose that when we possess reduction-biconditionals for the concepts involved, we find that the equivalent statement of physics is *not* 'necessary' at the level of physics, and that this is so because there is a perfectly possible mutation such that, if it took place, then the 'Weber–Fechner Law' would fail. In that case, it seems to me that we would not conclude that the 'Weber–Fechner Law' was a natural law, albeit one with an unstated scope limitation (although some ordinary language philosophers have urged such a course), but rather that it was not a law at all, but a good approximation to a more complex statement which *is* a law. It seems to me, in short, that a decisive condition for a statement's being law *is* that the 'equivalent' physical$_2$ statement be a law of physics, although this decisive condition is itself not part of the 'meaning' of the *word* 'law', but rather a condition erected by science relatively recently. (Actually, things are much more complicated than the foregoing suggests. For the reductive definitions of the basic terms of the 'non-fundamental' disciplines are themselves selected largely on the basis that they *enable us to derive the laws* of those disciplines. On the other hand, once a reduction has been accepted, there is a great reluctance to change it.)

It is on the basis of the considerations just reviewed that I earlier advanced the suggestion that the following be our program for gaining a precise description of the class of nomological statements: to first try to specify a form in which all the fundamental laws of physics (and only laws, though not necessarily only fundamental ones) can be written; and then to characterize the nomological statements as the statements which follow from true statements of that form together with empirical reduction–biconditionals. (The remaining part of this program – finding a suitable characterization of the law of physics – say, that they all be differential equations in the fundamental magnitudes, valid at every point of space and time, at least 'before quantization' – and finding the empirical reduction–biconditionals – is, of course, a task for science and not for philosophy. In a sense, that is the whole point of this paper.)

It is evident that if this particular program for characterizing the nomological statements ever succeeds, so must the program for characterizing 'identity of properties'. Indeed, the program for characterizing the nomological statements is in one way harder of fulfillment than the program for characterizing identity of properties, in that the latter program requires only that we know the reduction–biconditionals (and reduction–identities) and the fundamental magnitudes of physics, but not that we ever have a suitable characterization of the form of the physical laws.

What of the more conventional program for explicating 'nomological', as represented by the writings of Reichenbach, Goodman, et al.? This program is to characterize fundamental laws (in all disciplines at once) as *true generalizations of a certain form*, where the specification of the form involves not only considerations of logical form in the usual sense, but such restrictions on the choice of the predicates as Goodman's requirement of projectibility. It is, further, a part of this program to be independent of the sorts of empirical considerations that I have constantly been bringing up – one is apparently to discover a form in which all and only laws of nature can be written (i.e., no *true* statement can have the form in question and not be a law of nature), and to do this by reflection on the

meaning of 'law' (and, perhaps, on the methodology of science) alone. In short, what I hope scientists may be able to do empirically in the next couple of hundred years, these philosophers would like to do a priori. Good luck to them!

It should be noted that if these philosophers ever succeed, then they will also succeed in providing us with one criterion for the identity of properties (though not the one I have suggested): for *nomological equivalence*, in spite of some counter-intuitive consequences, is another criterion for the identity of physical$_1$ properties that I think would be workable (if one were willing to change one's intuitions a bit), and that deserves further investigation. Moreover, if one *could* 'explicate "nomological"', then one should also be able to explicate 'reduction law', and hence to explicate the criterion for the identity of physical$_1$ properties suggested in this paper.

In terms of the foregoing discussion, my answer to the question of whether quantification over properties is indispensable goes as follows. First, there are important locutions which are most naturally formalized as quantifications over properties, and for which there is no obvious formalization today in extensional language. Secondly, the concept of a property is intimately connected with the notions *nomological, explanation, cause*, etc., and even comes close to being definable in terms of these notions. Yet these notions are generally admitted to be indispensable in science, even by those philosophers who reject *analytic, necessary, synonymy*, etc. (i.e., the notions most closely connected with the *other* concept of property mentioned at the beginning of this paper, the concept of a predicate, or the concept of a concept). The notion *is* indispensable, then, in the sense in which any notion is (i.e., we might use different *words*, but we would have to somehow be able to get the notion expressed); and, if the discussion of the prospects for a criterion of identity earlier in this paper was not unduly optimistic, science is well on its way to giving us as precise a criterion for identity of properties as we could ask for. Let us, then, keep our properties, while not in any way despising the useful work performed for us by our classes!

Notes

1 John Kemeny and Paul Oppenheim, 'On reduction,' *Philosophical Studies* 7 (1956), pp. 6–19.
2 Paul Oppenheim and Hilary Putnam, 'Unity of science as a working hypothesis,' in *Minnesota Studies in the Philosophy of Science*, vol. 2 (Minneapolis: University of Minnesota Press, 1958), pp. 8–36.

20

Causality and Properties

Sydney Shoemaker

I

It is events, rather than objects or properties, that are usually taken by philosophers to be the terms of the causal relationship. But an event typically consists of a change in the properties or relationships of one or more objects, the latter being what Jaegwon Kim has called the "constituent objects" of the event.[1] And when one event causes another, this will be in part because of the properties possessed by their constituent objects. Suppose, for example, that a man takes a pill and, as a result, breaks out into a rash. Here the cause and effect are, respectively, the taking of the pill and the breaking out into a rash. Why did the first event cause the second? Well, the pill was pencillin, and the man was allergic to penicillin. No doubt one could want to know more – for example, about the biochemistry of allergies in general and this one in particular. But there is a good sense in which what has been said already explains why the one event caused the other. Here the pill and the man are the constituent objects of the cause event, and the man is the constituent object of the effect event. Following Kim we can also speak of events as having "constituent properties" and "constituent times." In this case the constituent property of the cause event is the relation expressed by the verb "takes", while the constituent property of the effect event is

expressed by the predicate "breaks out into a rash". The constituent times of the events are their times of occurrence. Specifying the constituent objects and properties of the cause and effect will tell us what these events consisted in, and together with a specification of their constituent times will serve to identify them; but it will not, typically, explain why the one brought about the other. We explain this by mentioning certain properties of their constituent objects. Given that the pill was penicillin, and that the man was allergic to penicillin, the taking of the pill by the man was certain, or at any rate very likely, to result in an allergic response like a rash. To take another example, suppose a branch is blown against a window and breaks it. Here the constituent objects include the branch and the window, and the causal relationship holds because of, among other things, the massiveness of the one and the fragility of the other.

It would appear from this that any account of causality as a relation between events should involve, in a central way, reference to the properties of the constituent objects of the events. But this should not encourage us to suppose that the notion of causality is to be analyzed away, in Humean fashion, in terms of some relationship between properties – for example, in terms of regularities in their instantiation. For as I shall try to show, the relevant notion of a property is itself to be explained in terms of the notion of causality in a way that has some strikingly non-Humean consequences.

Originally published in Peter van Inwagen (ed.), *Time and Cause* (Dordrecht: Reidel, 1980). Reprinted by permission of Kluwer Academic Publishers.

253

II

Philosophers sometimes use the term "property" in such a way that for every predicate F true of a thing there is a property of the thing which is designated by the corresponding expression of the form "being F". If "property" is used in this broad way, every object will have innumerable properties that are unlikely to be mentioned in any causal explanation involving an event of which the object is a constituent. For example, my typewriter has the property of being over one hundred miles from the current heavyweight boxing champion of the world. It is not easy to think of a way in which its having this property could help to explain why an event involving it has a certain effect, and it seems artificial, at best, to speak of my typewriter's acquisition of this property as one of the causal effects of the movements of the heavyweight champion.

It is natural, however, to feel that such properties are not "real" or "genuine" properties. Our intuitions as to what are, and what are not, genuine properties are closely related to our intuitions as to what are, and what are not, genuine changes. A property is genuine if and only if its acquisition or loss by a thing constitutes a genuine change in that thing. One criterion for a thing's having changed is what Peter Geach calls the "Cambridge criterion." He formulates this as follows: "The thing called 'x' has changed if we have '$F(x)$' at time t' true and '$F(x)$' at time $t^{1'}$ false, for some interpretations of 'F,' 't,' and 't^1.' "[2] But, as Geach points out, this gives the result that Socrates undergoes a change when he comes to be shorter than Theaetetus in virtue of the latter's growth, and even that he undergoes a change every time a fresh schoolboy comes to admire him. Such "changes", those that intuitively are not genuine changes, Geach calls "mere 'Cambridge' changes." For Geach, real changes are Cambridge changes, since they satisfy the Cambridge criterion, but some Cambridge changes, namely those that are *mere* Cambridge changes, fail to be real changes. Since it is mere Cambridge changes, rather than Cambridge changes in general, that are to be contrasted with real or genuine changes, I shall introduce the hyphenated expression "mere-Cambridge" to characterize these. And I shall apply the terms "Cambridge" and "mere-Cambridge" to properties as well as to changes. Mere-Cambridge properties will include such properties as being "grue" (in Nelson Goodman's sense), historical properties like being over twenty years old and having been slept in by George Washington, relational properties like being fifty miles south of a burning barn,[3] and such properties as being such that Jimmy Carter is President of the United States.

It is worth mentioning that in addition to distinguishing between real and mere-Cambridge properties and changes, we must also distinguish between real and mere-Cambridge resemblance or similarity, and between real and mere-Cambridge differences. Cambridge similarities hold in virtue of the sharing of Cambridge properties. And mere-Cambridge similarities hold in virtue of the sharing of mere-Cambridge properties: there is such a similarity between all grue things; there is one between all things fifty miles south of a burning barn; there is one between all beds slept in by George Washington; and there is one between all things such that Jimmy Carter is President of the United States. It will be recalled that the notion of similarity, or resemblance, plays a prominent role in Hume's account of causality. His first definition of *cause* in the *Treatise* is "an object precedent and contiguous to another, and where all the objects resembling the former are plac'd in a like relation of priority and contiguity to those objects, that resemble the latter."[4] Hume clearly regarded the notion of resemblance as quite unproblematical and in no need of elucidation.[5] Yet it is plain that he needs a narrower notion of resemblance than that of Cambridge resemblance if his definition of causality is to have the desired content. Cambridge resemblances are too easily come by; any two objects share infinitely many Cambridge properties, and so "resemble" one another in infinitely many ways. There are also infinitely many Cambridge differences between any two objects. What Hume needs is a notion of resemblance and difference which is such that some things resemble a given thing more than others do, and such that some things may resemble a thing exactly (without being numerically identical to it) while others resemble it hardly at all. Only "real" or "genuine" resemblance will serve his purposes. If it turns out, as I think it does, that in order to give a satisfactory account of the distinction between real and mere-Cambridge properties, changes, similarities, and differences, we must make use of the notion of causality, the Humean project of defining causality in terms of regularity or "constant conjunction", notions that plainly involve the notion of resemblance, is seriously undermined.

I have no wish to legislate concerning the correct use of the terms "property", "changes", "similar", and so forth. It would be rash to claim that the accepted use of the term "property" is such that what I have classified as mere-Cambridge properties are not properties. But I do think that we have *a* notion of what it is to be a property which is such that this is so – in other words, which is such that not every phrase of the form "being so and so" stands for a property which something has just in case the corresponding predicate of the form "is so and so" is true of it, and is such that sometimes a predicate is true of a thing, not because (or only because) of any properties *it* has, but because something else, perhaps something related to it in certain ways, has certain properties. It is this narrow conception of what it is to be a property, and the correlative notions of change and similarity, that I am concerned to elucidate in this essay. (I should mention that I am concerned here only with the sorts of properties with respect to which change is possible; my account is not intended to apply to such properties of numbers as being even and being prime.)

III

John Locke held that "*Powers make a great part of our complex* Ideas *of substances.*"[6] And there is one passage in which Locke seems to suggest that all qualities of substances are powers; he says, in explanation of his usage of the term 'quality', that "the Power to produce any *Idea* in our mind, I call *quality* of the Subject wherein that power is."[7] This suggests a theory of properties, namely that properties are causal powers, which is akin to the theory I shall be defending. As it happens, this is not Locke's view. If one ascribed it to him on the basis of the passage just quoted, one would have to ascribe to him the view that all qualities are what he called 'secondary qualities' – powers to produce certain mental effects ('ideas') in us. But Locke recognized the existence of powers that are not secondary qualities, namely powers (for example, the power in the sun to melt wax) to produce effects in material objects. These have been called 'tertiary qualities'. And he distinguished both of these sorts of powers from the 'primary qualities' on which they 'depend'. Nevertheless, the view which Locke's words unintentionally suggest is worth considering.

What would seem to be the same view is sometimes put by saying that all properties are dispositional properties. But as thus formulated, this view seems plainly mistaken. Surely we make a distinc-

tion between dispositional and nondispositional properties, and can mention paradigms of both sorts. Moreover, it seems plain that what dispositional properties something has, what powers it has, depends on what nondispositional properties it has – just as Locke thought that the powers of things depend on their primary qualities and those of their parts.

In fact, I believe, there are two different distinctions to be made here, and these are often conflated. One is not a distinction between kinds of *properties* at all, but rather a distinction between kinds of *predicates*. Sometimes it belongs to the meaning, or sense, of a predicate that if it is true of a thing, then under certain circumstances the thing will undergo certain changes or will produce certain changes in other things. This is true of what are standardly counted as dispositional predicates, for example, 'flexible', 'soluble', 'malleable', 'magnetized', and 'poisonous'. Plainly not all predicates are of this sort. Whether color predicates are is a matter of controversy. But whatever we say about this, it seems plain that predicates like 'square', 'round' and 'made of copper' are not dispositional in this sense. There are causal powers associated with being made of copper – for example, being an electrical conductor. But presumably this association is not incorporated into the meaning of the term 'copper'.

The first distinction, then, is between different sorts of predicates, and I think that the term 'dispositional' is best employed as a predicate of predicates, not of properties. A different distinction is between powers, in a sense I am about to explain, and the properties in virtue of which things have the powers they have.[8] For something to have a power, in this sense, is for it to be such that its presence in circumstances of a particular sort will have certain effects.[9] One can think of such a power as a function from circumstances to effects. Thus if something is poisonous, its presence in someone's body will produce death or illness; in virtue of this, being poisonous is a power. Here it is possible for things to have the same power in virtue of having very different properties. Suppose that one poisonous substance kills by affecting the heart, while another kills by directly affecting the nervous system and brain. They produce these different effects in virtue of having very different chemical compositions. They will of course differ in their powers as well as in their properties, for one will have the power to produce certain physiological effects in the nervous system, while the other will have the power to produce quite different physiological effects in the heart. But there is one power they will share, in virtue of having these different powers, namely that of producing death if ingested by a human being. Properties here play the role, vis-à-vis powers, that primary qualities play in Locke; it is in virtue of a thing's properties that the thing has the powers (Locke's secondary and tertiary qualities) that it has.

There is a rough correspondence between this distinction between powers and properties and the earlier distinction between dispositional and non-dispositional predicates. By and large, dispositional predicates ascribe powers, while nondispositional monadic predicates ascribe properties that are not powers in the same sense.

IV

On the view of properties I want to propose, while properties are typically not powers of the sort ascribed by dispositional predicates, they are related to such powers in much the way that such powers are related to the causal effects which they are powers to produce. Just as powers can be thought of as functions from circumstances to causal effects, so the properties on which powers depend can be thought of as functions from properties to powers (or, better, as functions from sets of properties to sets of powers). One might even say that properties are second-order powers; they are powers to produce first-order powers (powers to produce certain sorts of events) if combined with certain other properties. But the formulation I shall mainly employ is this: what makes a property the property it is, what determines its identity, is its potential for contributing to the causal powers of the things that have it. This means, among other things, that if under all possible circumstances properties X and Y make the same contribution to the causal powers of the things that have them, X and Y are the same property.

To illustrate this, let us take as our example of a property the property of being 'knife-shaped' – I shall take this to be a highly determinate property which belongs to a certain knife in my kitchen and to anything else of exactly the same shape. Now if all that I know about a thing is that it has this property, I know nothing about what will result from its presence in any circumstances. What has the property of being knife-shaped could be a knife, made of steel, but it could instead be a piece of balsa wood, a piece of butter, or even an oddly shaped cloud of some invisible gas. There is no power which necessarily belongs to all and only the things having this property. But if this property is combined with the property of being knife-sized and the property of being made of steel, the object having these properties will necessarily have a number of powers. It will have the power of cutting butter, cheese, and wood, if applied to these substances with suitable pressure, and also the power of producing various sorts of sense-impressions in human beings under appropriate observational conditions, and also the power of leaving an impression of a certain shape if applied to soft wax and then withdrawn, and so on. The combination of the property of being knife-shaped with the property of being made of glass will result in a somewhat different set of powers, which will overlap with the set which results from its combination with the property of being made of steel. Likewise with its combination with the property of being made of wood, the property of being made of butter, and so on.

Let us say that an object has power P conditionally upon the possession of the properties in set Q if it has some property r such that having the properties in Q together with r is causally sufficient for having P, while having the properties in Q is not by itself causally sufficient for having P. Thus, for example, a knife-shaped object has the power of cutting wood conditionally upon being knife-sized and made of steel; for it is true of knife-shaped things, but not of things in general, that if they are knife-sized and made of steel, they will have the power to cut wood. When a thing has a power conditionally upon the possession of certain properties, let us say that this amounts to its having a *conditional power*. Our knife-shaped object has the conditional power of being able to cut wood if knife-sized and made of steel. The identity condition for conditional powers is as follows: if A is the conditional power of having power P conditionally upon having the properties in set Q, and B is the conditional power of having P' conditionally upon having the properties in set Q', then A is identical to B just in case P is identical to P' and Q is identical to Q'. Having introduced this notion of a conditional power, we can express my view by saying that properties are clusters of conditional powers. (I shall count powers *simpliciter* as a special case of conditional powers.) I have said that the identity of a property is determined by its causal potentialities, the contributions it is capable of making to the causal powers of things that have it. And the causal potentialities that are essential to a property correspond to the conditional powers that make up the cluster with which the property can be identified; for a property to have a causal potentiality is for it to be such that whatever has it has a certain conditional power.

This account is intended to capture what is correct in the view that properties just are powers, or that all properties are dispositional, while acknowledging the truth of a standard objection to that view, namely that a thing's powers or dispositions are distinct from, because 'grounded in', its intrinsic properties.[10]

Before I give my reasons for holding this view, I should mention one prima facie objection to it. Presumably the property of being triangular and the property of being trilateral do not differ in the contributions they make to the causal powers of the things that have them, yet it is natural to say that these, although necessarily coextensive, are different properties. It seems to me, however, that what we have good reason for regarding as distinct are not these properties, as such, but rather the concepts of triangularity and trilaterality, and the meanings of the expressions 'triangular' and 'trilateral'. If we abandon, as I think we should, the idea that properties are the meanings of predicate expressions, and if we are careful to distinguish concepts from what they are concepts of, I see no insuperable obstacle to regarding the properties themselves as identical.

V

My reasons for holding this theory of properties are, broadly speaking, epistemological. Only if some causal theory of properties is true, I believe, can it be explained how properties are capable of engaging our knowledge, and our language, in the way they do.

We know and recognize properties by their effects, or, more precisely, by the effects of the events which are the activations of the causal powers which things have in virtue of having the properties. This happens in a variety of ways. Observing something is being causally influenced by it in certain ways. If the causal potentialities involved in the possession of a property are such that there is a fairly direct causal connection between the possession of it by an object and the sensory states of an observer related to that object

in certain ways, e.g., looking at it in good light, we say that the property itself is observable. If the relationship is less direct, e.g., if the property can affect the sensory states of the observer only by affecting the properties of something else which the observer observes, a scientific instrument, say, we speak of inferring that the thing has the property from what we take to be the effects of its possession. In other cases we conclude that something has a property because we know that it has other properties which we know from other cases to be correlated with the one in question. But the latter way of knowing about the properties of things is parasitic on the earlier ways; for unless the instantiation of the property had, under some circumstances, effects from which its existence could be concluded, we could never discover laws or correlations that would enable us to infer its existence from things other than its effects.

Suppose that the identity of properties consisted of something logically independent of their causal potentialities. Then it ought to be possible for there to be properties that have no potential whatever for contributing to causal powers, i.e., are such that under no conceivable circumstances will their possession by a thing make any difference to the way the presence of that thing affects other things or to the way other things affect it. Further, it ought to be possible that there be two or more different properties that make, under all possible circumstances, exactly the same contribution to the causal powers of the things that have them. Further, it ought to be possible that the potential of a property for contributing to the production of causal powers might change over time, so that, for example, the potential possessed by property A at one time is the same as that possessed by property B at a later time, and that possessed by property B at the earlier time is the same as that possessed by property A at the later time. Thus a thing might undergo radical change with respect to its properties without undergoing any change in its causal powers, and a thing might undergo radical change in its causal powers without undergoing any change in the properties that underlie these powers.

The supposition that these possibilities are genuine implies, not merely (what might seem harmless) that various things might be the case without its being in any way possible for us to know that they are, but also that it is impossible for us to know various things which we take ourselves to know. If there can be properties that have no potential for contributing to the causal powers of the things that have them, then nothing could be good evidence that the overall resemblance between two things is greater than the overall resemblance between two other things; for even if *A* and *B* have closely resembling effects on our senses and our instruments while *C* and *D* do not, it might be (for all we know) that *C* and *D* share vastly more properties of the causally impotent kind than do *A* and *B*. Worse, if two properties can have exactly the same potential for contributing to causal powers, then it is impossible for us even to know (or have any reason for believing) that two things resemble one another by sharing a single property. Moreover, if the properties and causal potentialities of a thing can vary independently of one another, then it is impossible for us to know (or have any good reason for believing) that something has retained a property over time, or that something has undergone a change with respect to the properties that underlie its causal powers. On these suppositions, there would be no way in which a particular property could be picked out so as to have a name attached to it; and even if, *per impossibile*, a name did get attached to a property, it would be impossible for anyone to have any justification for applying the name on particular occasions.

It may be doubted whether the view under attack has these disastrous epistemological consequences. Surely, it may be said, one can hold that it is a contingent matter that particular properties have the causal potentialities they have, and nevertheless hold, compatibly with this, that there are good theoretical reasons for thinking that as a matter of fact different properties differ in their causal potentialities, and that any given property retains the same potentialities over time. For while it is logically possible that the latter should not be so, according to the contingency view, the simplest hypothesis is that it is so; and it is reasonable to accept the simplest hypothesis compatible with the data.

Whatever may be true in general of appeals to theoretical simplicity, this one seems to me extremely questionable. For here we are not really dealing with an explanatory hypothesis at all. If the identity of properties is made independent of their causal potentialities, then in what sense do we explain sameness or difference of causal potentialities by positing sameness or difference of properties? There are of course cases in which we explain a constancy in something by positing certain underlying constancies in its properties. It is genuinely explanatory to say that something retained

the same causal power over time because certain of its properties remained the same. And this provides, *ceteris paribus*, a simpler, or at any rate more plausible, explanation of the constancy than one that says that the thing first had one set of underlying properties and then a different set, and that both sets were sufficient to give it that particular power. For example, if the water supply was poisonous all day long, it is more plausible to suppose that this was due to the presence in it of one poisonous substance all day rather than due to its containing cyanide from morning till noon and strychnine from noon till night. But in such cases we presuppose that the underlying property constancies carry with them constancies in causal potentialities, and it is only on this presupposition that positing the underlying constancies provides the simplest explanation of the constancy to be explained. Plainly this presupposition cannot be operative if what the 'inference to the best explanation' purports to explain is, precisely, that sameness of property goes with sameness of causal potentialities. It is not as if a property had the causal potentialities in question as a result of having yet *other* causal potentialities, the constancy of the latter explaining the constancy of the former. This disassociation of property identity from identity of causal potentiality is really an invitation to eliminate reference to properties from our explanatory hypotheses altogether; if it were correct, then we could, to use Wittgenstein's metaphor, 'divide through' by the properties and leave the explanatory power of what we say about things untouched.

It might be objected that even if my arguments establish that the causal potentialities of a genuine property cannot change over time, they do not establish that these causal potentialities are essential to that property, in the sense of belonging to it in all possible worlds. The immutability of properties with respect to their causal potentialities, it might be said, is simply a consequence of the immutability of laws – of the fact that it makes no sense to speak of a genuine law holding at one time and not at another. And from the fact that the laws governing a property cannot change over time, it does not follow, it may be said, that the property cannot be governed by different laws in different possible worlds.

Let me observe first of all that in conceding that the immutability of the causal potentialities of genuine properties is a consequence of the immutability of laws, the objection concedes a large part of what I want to maintain. It is not true in general of mere-Cambridge properties that their causal potentialities cannot change over time; for example, this is not true of *grueness* on the Barker–Achinstein definition of *grue*, where something is grue just in case it is green and the time is before T (say AD 2000) or it is blue and the time is T or afterwards.[11] That genuine properties are marked off from mere-Cambridge properties by their relation to causal laws (and that it is nonsense to speak of a world in which it is the mere-Cambridge properties rather than the genuine ones that are law-governed in a way that makes their causal potentialities immutable) is a central part of my view.

There is, moreover, a prima facie case for saying that the immutability of the causal potentialities of a property does imply their essentiality; or in other words, that if they cannot vary across time, they also cannot vary across possible worlds. Most of us do suppose that *particulars* can (or do) have different properties in different possible worlds. We suppose, for example, that in some possible worlds I am a plumber rather than a philosopher, and that in some possible worlds my house is painted yellow rather than white. But it goes with this that particulars can change their properties over time. It is possible that I, the very person who is writing this essay, might have been a plumber, because there is a possible history in which I start with the properties (in this case relational as well as intrinsic) which I had at some time in my actual history, and undergo a series of changes which result in my eventually being a plumber. If I and the world were never such that it was then possible for me to *become* a plumber, it would not be true that I might have been a plumber, or (in other words) that there is a possible world in which I am one. There is, in short, a close linkage between identity across time and identity across possible worlds; the ways in which a given thing can be different in different possible worlds depend on the ways in which such a thing can be different at different times in the actual world. But now let us move from the case of particulars to that of properties. There is no such thing as tracing a property through a series of changes in its causal potentialities – not if it is a genuine property, i.e., one of the sort that figures in causal laws. And so there is no such thing as a possible history in which a property starts with the set of causal potentialities it has in the actual world and ends with a different set. To say the least, this calls into question the intelligibility of the suggestion that the very properties we designate with words like 'green', 'square', 'hard', and so

on, might have had different causal potentialities than they in fact have.

However, this last argument is not conclusive. My earlier arguments, if sound, establish that there is an intimate connection between the identity of a property and its causal potentialities. But it has not yet been decisively established that *all* of the causal potentialities of a property are essential to it. The disastrous epistemological consequences of the contingency view would be avoided if for each property we could identify a proper subset of its causal potentialities that are essential to it and constitutive of it, and this would permit some of a property's causal potentialities, those outside the essential cluster, to belong to it contingently, and so not belong to it in some other possible worlds. There would, in this case, be an important difference between the trans-world identity of properties and that of particulars – and it is a difference which there is in my own view as well. If, as I believe, the assertion that a certain particular might have had different properties than it does in the actual world (that in some other possible world it does have those properties) implies that there is a possible history 'branching off' from the history of the actual world in which it acquires those properties, this is because there is, putting aside historical properties and 'identity properties' (like being identical to Jimmy Carter), no subset of the properties of such a thing which constitutes an individual essence of it, i.e., is such that, in any possible world, having the properties in that subset is necessary *and sufficient* for being that particular thing. To put this otherwise, the reason why the possible history in which the thing has different properties must be a branching-off from the history of the actual world is that the individual essence of a particular thing must include historical properties. Now I am not in a position to object to the suggestion that properties differ from particulars in having individual essences which do not include historical properties and which are sufficient for their identification across possible worlds; for I hold that the totality of a property's causal potentialities constitutes such an individual essence. So a possible alternative to my view is one which holds that for each property there is a proper subset of its causal potentialities that constitutes its individual essence. Such a view has its attractions, and is compatible with much of what I say in this essay; in particular, it is compatible with the claim that within any possible world properties are identical just in case they have the same causal potentialities.

But I shall argue in section IX that this view is unworkable, and that there is no acceptable alternative to the view that all of the causal potentialities of a property are essential to it.

VI

As was intended, my account of properties does not apply to what I have called mere-Cambridge properties. When my table acquired the property of being such that Gerald Ford is President of the United States, which it did at the time Nixon resigned from the presidency, this presumably had no effect on its causal powers. Beds that were slept in by George Washington may command a higher price than those that lack this historical property, but presumably this is a result, not of any causal potentialities in the beds themselves, but of the historical beliefs and interests of those who buy and sell them. And grueness, as defined by Goodman, is not associated in the way greenness and blueness are with causal potentialities. (In this sense, which differs from that invoked in section V, something is grue at a time just in case it is green at that time and is first examined before T, say, AD 2000, or is blue at that time and is not first examined before T.) It can happen that the only difference between something that is grue and something that is not is that one of them has and the other lacks the historical property of being (or having been) first examined before the time T mentioned in Goodman's definition of *grue*; and presumably this does not in itself make for any difference in causal potentialities. It can also happen that two things share the property of being grue in virtue of having properties that have different potentialities – that is, in virtue of one of them being green (and examined before T) and the other being blue (and not so examined).

There is an epistemological way of distinguishing genuine and mere-Cambridge properties that is prima facie plausible. If I wish to determine whether an emerald is green at t, the thing to do, if I can manage it, is to examine the emerald at t. But examination of a table will not tell me it is such that Gerald Ford is President of the United States, or whether it is fifty miles south of a burning barn. And if I am ignorant of the date, or if t is after T (the date in Goodman's definition), examination of an emerald will not tell me whether it is grue. Likewise, while scrutiny of a bed may reveal a plaque claiming that it was slept in by George Washington, it will not tell me whether this claim is true. Roughly, if a question about whether a thing has a property at a place and time concerns a genuine nonrelational property, the question is most directly settled by observations and tests in the vicinity of that place and time, while if it concerns a mere-Cambridge property it may be most directly settled by observations and tests remote from that place and time, and observations and tests made at that place and time will either be irrelevant (as in the case of the property of being such that Jimmy Carter is President) or insufficient to settle the question (as in the case of grue).

It would be difficult to make this into a precise and adequate criterion of genuineness of property, and I do not know whether this could be done. But I think that to the extent that it is adequate, its adequacy is explained by my account of properties in terms of causal powers. Properties reveal their presence in actualizations of their causal potentialities, a special case of this being the perception of a property. And the most immediate and revealing effects of an object's having a property at a particular place and time are effects that occur in the immediate vicinity of that place and time. To be sure, we cannot rule out on purely philosophical grounds the possibility of action at a spatial and/or temporal distance. And the more prevalent such action is, the less adequate the proposed epistemological criterion will be. But there do seem to be conceptual limitations on the extent to which causal action can be at a spatial or temporal distance. It is doubtful, to say the least, whether there could be something whose causal powers are *all* such that whenever any of them is activated the effects of its activation are spatially remote from the location of the thing at that time, or occur at times remote from the time of activation.

Causation and causal powers are as much involved in the verification of ascriptions of mere-Cambridge properties as in the verification of ascriptions of genuine ones. But in the case of mere-Cambridge properties some of the operative causal powers will either belong to something other than the object to which the property is ascribed, or will belong to that object at a time other than that at which it has that property. Thus if I verify that a man has the property of being fifty miles south of a burning barn, it will be primarily the causal powers of the barn, and of the intervening stretch of land (which, we will suppose, I measure), rather than the causal powers of the man, that will be responsible for my verifying observations.

VII

It will not have escaped notice that the account of properties and property identity I have offered makes free use of the notion of a property and the notion of property identity. It says, in brief, that properties are identical, whether in the same possible world or in different ones, just in case their coinstantiation with the same properties gives rise to the same powers. This is, if anything, even more circular than it looks. For it crucially involves the notion of sameness of powers, and this will have to be explained in terms of sameness of circumstances and sameness of effects, the notions of which both involve the notion of sameness of property. And of course there was essential use of the notion of a property in my explanation of the notion of a conditional power.

It is worth observing that there is a distinction between kinds of powers that corresponds to the distinction, mentioned earlier, between genuine and mere-Cambridge properties.[12] Robert Boyle's famous example of the key can be used to illustrate this.[13] A particular key on my key chain has the power of opening locks of a certain design. It also has the power of opening my front door. It could lose the former power only by undergoing what we would regard as real change, for example, a change in its shape. But it could lose the latter without undergoing such a change; it could so do in virtue of the lock on my door being replaced by one of a different design. Let us say that the former is an intrinsic power and the latter a mere-Cambridge power. It is clear that in my account of properties the word 'power' must refer only to intrinsic powers. For if it refers to mere-Cambridge powers as well, then what seems clearly to be a mere-Cambridge property of my key, namely being such that my door has a lock of a certain design, will make a determinate contribution to its having the powers it has, and so will count as a genuine property of it. But it seems unlikely that we could explain the distinction between intrinsic and mere-Cambridge powers without making use of the notion of a genuine change and that of a genuine property. And so again my account of the notion of a property in terms of the notion of a power can be seen to be circular.

How much do these circularities matter? Since they are, I think, unavoidable, they preclude a reductive analysis of the notion of a property in terms of the notion of causality. But they by no means render my account empty. The claim that the causal potentialities of a property are essential to it, and that properties having the same causal potentialities are identical, is certainly not made vacuous by the fact that the explanation of the notion of a causal potentiality, or a conditional power, must invoke the notion of a property. As I see it, the notion of a property and the notion of a causal power belong to a system of internally related concepts, no one of which can be explicated without the use of the others. Other members of the system are the concept of an event, the concept of similarity, and the concept of a persisting substance. It can be worthwhile, as a philosophical exercise, to see how far we can go in an attempt to reduce one of these concepts to others – for both the extent of our success and the nature of our failures can be revealing about the nature of the connections between the concepts. But ultimately such attempts must fail. The goal of philosophical analysis, in dealing with such concepts, should not be reductive analysis but rather the charting of internal relationships. And it is perfectly possible for a "circular" analysis to illuminate a network of internal relationships and have philosophically interesting consequences.

VIII

According to the theory of properties I am proposing, all of the causal potentialities possessed by a property at any time in the actual world are essential to it and so belong to it at all times and in all possible worlds. This has a very strong consequence, namely that causal necessity is just a species of logical necessity. If the introduction into certain circumstances of a thing having certain properties causally necessitates the occurrence of certain effects, then it is impossible, logically impossible, that such an introduction could fail to have such an effect, and so logically necessary that it has it. To the extent that causal laws can be viewed as propositions describing the causal potentialities of properties, it is impossible that the same properties should be governed by different causal laws in different possible worlds, for such propositions will be necessarily true when true at all.

It is not part of this theory, however, that causal laws are analytic or knowable a priori. I suppose that it is analytic that flexible things bend under suitable pressure, that poisonous things cause injury to those for whom they are poisonous, and so on. But I do not think that it is analytic that copper is an electrical conductor, or that knife-shaped things, if knife-sized and made of steel, are capable of cutting butter. Nor does it follow from the claim that such truths are necessary that they are analytic. Kripke has made a compelling case for the view that there are propositions that are necessary a posteriori, that is, true in all possible worlds but such that they can only be known empirically.[14] And such, according to my theory, is the status of most propositions describing the causal potentialities of properties. The theory can allow that our knowledge of these potentialities is empirical, and that it is bound to be only partial. But in order to show how, in the theory, such empirical knowledge is possible, I must now bring out an additional way in which the notion of causality is involved in the notion of a property.

One of the formulations of my theory says that every property is a cluster of conditional powers. But the converse does not seem to me to hold; not every cluster of conditional powers is a property. If something is both knife-shaped and made of wax, then it will have, among others, the following conditional powers: the power of being able to cut wood conditionally upon being knife-sized and made of steel (this it has in virtue of being knife-shaped), and the power of being malleable conditionally upon being at a temperature of 100°F (this it has in virtue of being made of wax). Intuitively, these are not common components of any single property. By contrast, the various conditional powers a thing has in virtue of being knife-shaped – for example, the power of being able to cut wood conditionally upon being knife-sized and made of steel, the power of being able to cut butter conditionally upon being knife-sized and made of wood, the power of having a certain visual appearance conditionally upon being green, the power of having a certain other visual appearance conditionally upon being red, and so on – are all constituents of a single property, namely the property of being knife-shaped. The difference, I think, is that in the one case the set of conditional powers has, while in the other it lacks, a certain kind of causal unity. I shall now try to spell out the nature of this unity.

Some subsets of the conditional powers which make up a genuine property will be such that it is a consequence of causal laws that whatever has any member of the subset necessarily has all of its members. Thus, for example, something has the power of leaving a six-inch-long knife-shaped impression in soft wax conditionally upon being six inches long if and only if it has the power of leaving an eight-inch-long knife-shaped impression in soft wax conditionally upon being eight inches long. Now some conditional powers will belong to more than one property cluster; thus, for example, there are many different-shape properties that give something the power of being able to cut wood conditionally upon being made of steel. But where a conditional power can be shared by different properties in this way, it will belong to a particular property cluster only if there is another member of that cluster which is such that it is a consequence of causal laws that whatever has that other member has the conditional power in question. And at the core of each cluster there will be one or more conditional powers which are such that as a consequence of causal laws whatever has any of them has all of the conditional powers in the cluster. For example, if something has, conditionally upon being made of steel, the power of leaving a knife-shaped impression in soft wax, then it cannot fail to be knife-shaped, and so cannot fail to have all of the other conditional powers involved in being knife-shaped. I suggest, then, that conditional powers X and Y belong to the same property if and only if it is a consequence of causal laws that either (1) whatever has either of them has the other, or (2) there is some third conditional power such that whatever has it has both X and Y.

Returning now to the conditional power of being able to cut wood conditionally upon being made of steel and the conditional power of being malleable conditionally upon being at a temperature of 100°F, it seems to me that these do not qualify under the proposed criterion as belonging to a common property. It is obviously not true that whatever has one of them must have the other. And it does not appear that there is any third conditional power which is such that whatever has it must have the two conditional powers in question.

If I am right in thinking that the conditional powers constituting a property must be causally unified in the way indicated, it is not difficult to see how knowledge of the causal potentialities of properties can develop empirically. The behavior of objects, that is, the displays of their powers, will reveal that they have certain conditional powers. Once it is discovered that certain conditional powers are connected in a lawlike way, we can use these to 'fix the reference' of a property term to the cluster containing those conditional powers and whatever other conditional powers are related to them in the appropriate lawlike relationships.[15] And we can then set about to determine empirically what the other conditional powers in the cluster are.

IX

As I observed earlier, my theory appears to have the consequence that causal laws are logically necessary, and that causal necessity is just a species of logical necessity. While to some this may be an attractive consequence, to many it will seem counterintuitive. It does seem to most of us that we can conceive of possible worlds which resemble the actual world in the kinds of properties that are instantiated in them, but differ from it in the causal laws that obtain. My theory must maintain either that we cannot really conceive of this or that conceivability is not proof of logical possibility.

Anyone who finds both of these alternatives unacceptable, but is persuaded by the arguments in section V that the identity of properties is determined by their causal potentialities, will look for ways of reconciling that conclusion with the view that there can be worlds in which some of the causal laws are different from, and incompatible with, those that obtain in the actual world. I want now to consider two ways in which one might attempt to achieve such a reconciliation. First, it might be held that while propositions describing the causal potentialities of properties are necessarily true if true at all, there are other lawlike propositions, namely those asserting lawlike connections between conditional powers, which are contingent and so true in some possible worlds and false in others. According to this view, when we seem to be conceiving of worlds in which the same properties are governed by different laws, what we are really conceiving of are worlds in which the same conditional powers stand to one another in different lawlike connections than they do in the actual world, and so are differently clustered into properties. Second, it might be held that my condition for the identity of properties across possible worlds is too strict. The theory I have advanced might be called the 'total cluster theory'; it identifies a property with a cluster containing all of the conditional powers which anything has in virtue of having that property, and maintains that in any possible world anything that has that property must have all of the members of that cluster. One might attempt to replace this with a 'core

cluster theory', which identifies the property with some proper subset of the conditional powers something has in virtue of having that property. On this theory, it is only some of the causal potentialities possessed by a property in the actual world, namely those constituted by the conditional powers in its core cluster, that are essential to it – so it is possible for the same property to have somewhat different causal potentialities in different possible worlds, because of different laws relating the conditional powers in its core cluster with other conditional powers.

I do not believe, however, that either of these attempted reconciliations is successful. The first involves the suggestion that it is at least sometimes a contingent matter whether two conditional powers belong to the same property, and hence that there could be a world in which some of the same conditional powers are instantiated as in this world, but in which, owing to the holding of different laws, these are differently clustered into properties. The difficulty with this is that the specification of a conditional power always involves, in two different ways, reference to properties that are instantiated in our world and which, *ex hypothesi*, would not be instantiated in the alternative world in question. It involves reference to the properties on which the power is conditional, and also to the properties in the instantiation of which the exercise of the power would result. For example, one of the conditional powers in the property of being knife-shaped is the power, conditionally upon being made of steel, of leaving a knife-shaped impression if pressed into soft wax and then withdrawn. This conditional power, although not by itself identical to the property of being knife-shaped, could not be exercised without that property being instantiated. Neither could it be exercised without the property of being made of steel being instantiated. And a conditional power could not be instantiated in a world in which the causal laws would not allow an exercise of it. So in general, a conditional power could not be instantiated in a world in which the causal laws did not permit the instantiation of the properties whose instantiation would be involved in its instantiation or in its exercise.

Nothing I have said precludes the possibility of there being worlds in which the causal laws are different from those that prevail in this world. But it seems to follow from my account of property identity that, if the laws are different, then the properties will have to be different as well. And it does not appear that we have the resources for describing a world in which the properties that can be instantiated differ from what I shall call the 'actual world properties', that is, those that can be instantiated in the actual world. We have just seen that we cannot do this by imagining the conditional powers that exist in this world to be governed by different laws, and so to be differently grouped into properties.

It might seem that we can at least imagine a world in which *some* of the properties that can be instantiated are actual world properties while others are not. But a specification of the causal potentialities of one property will involve mention of other properties, a specification of the causal potentialities of those other properties will involve mention of still other properties, and so on. If there could be a world in which some but not all of the actual world properties can be instantiated, this could only be because those properties were causally insulated, as it were, from the rest – that is, were such that their causal potentialities could be fully specified without reference to the rest and vice versa. It seems unlikely that any proper subset of the actual world properties is causally insulated in this way – and any that are insulated from all properties we know about are thereby insulated from our knowledge and our language. But could there be a world in which the properties that can be instantiated include all of the actual world properties plus some others? This would be possible only if the two sets of properties, the actual world properties and the properties that cannot be instantiated in the actual world, were causally insulated from one another. And because of this, it would be impossible for us to say anything about the properties that cannot be instantiated in the actual world; for what we can describe is limited to what can be specified in terms of properties that can be so instantiated. What we could describe of such a world would have to be compatible with the laws that specify the causal potentialities of the actual world properties and, what we have found to be inseparable from these, the laws describing the lawlike connections between the conditional powers that constitute these properties.

Now let us consider the second attempt to reconcile the claim that the identity of a property is determined by its causal potentialities with the apparent conceivability of worlds in which the causal laws that obtain are different from, and incompatible with, those that obtain in the actual world. This involves the proposal that we adopt a 'core cluster theory' in place of the 'total cluster theory', and make the identity of a property depend on a proper subset, rather than on the totality, of the causal potentialities it has in the actual world. Like the first attempted reconciliation, this involves the idea that at least some of the lawlike connections between conditional powers hold only contingently; it is this that is supposed to make it possible for the composition of the total cluster associated with a property to differ from one possible world to another, owing to different conditional powers being causally linked with the conditional powers in the property's essential core cluster. But it would seem that the lawlike connections between those conditional powers included in the essential core cluster will have to hold of logical necessity, i.e., in all possible worlds. For if they held only contingently, then in some possible worlds they would not hold. In such a world, the individual conditional powers which in the actual world constitute the essential core of the property could be instantiated, but the property itself could not be instantiated. Even if these conditional powers could be instantiated together in such a world, their coinstantiation would not count as the instantiation of a property, and so of that property, since the requisite causal unity would be lacking. But I have already argued, in discussing the first attempted reconciliation, that it is not possible that there should be a world in which conditional powers that are instantiated in the actual world can be instantiated while actual world properties cannot be instantiated.

But if, as I have just argued, the lawlike connections between conditional powers within the essential core cluster will have to hold of logical necessity, then we are faced with a problem. Some lawlike connections between conditional powers will hold contingently (according to the core cluster theory), while others will hold as a matter of logical necessity. How are we to tell which are which? It does not appear that we can distinguish these lawlike connections epistemologically, i.e., by the way in which they are known. For if, as I am assuming, there are truths that are necessary a posteriori, the fact that a connection is discovered empirically is no guarantee that it does not hold necessarily. Nor can it be said that we identify the necessary connections by the fact that they hold between conditional powers belonging to some property's essential core cluster; for this presupposes that we have some way of identifying essential core clusters, and how are we to do this if we do not already know which connections between conditional powers are necessary and which are contingent?

It might be suggested that what constitutes a set of conditional powers as constituting an essential core cluster is just its being a lawlike truth that whatever has any of its members has all of them, and that it is by discovering such lawlike truths that we identify essential core clusters. Given that the lawlike connections between members of essential core clusters hold of logical necessity, this would amount to the claim that if two conditional powers are so related that the possession of either of them is both causally necessary and causally sufficient for the possession of the other, then the lawlike connection between them holds as a matter of logical necessity, while if the possession of one is causally sufficient but not causally necessary for the possession of the other, then the lawlike connection may be contingent. I have no knock-down argument against this view, but it seems to me implausible. If it is possible for it to be a contingent fact that the possession of one conditional power is causally sufficient for the possession of another, then it seems to me that it ought to be possible for it to be a contingent fact that the possession of one conditional power is both causally necessary and causally sufficient for the possession of another; that is, it ought to be possible for it to be contingently true of two conditional powers that the possession of either of them is causally sufficient for the possession of the other. So if we deny that the latter is a possibility, we should also deny that the former is.

It may be suggested that it is our linguistic conventions that make certain causal potentialities essential to a property, and so determine the makeup of a property's essential core cluster. But this cannot be so. It may in some cases belong to the conventionally determined sense of a property word that the property it designates has certain causal potentialities; while I think there is no need for property words to have such Fregean senses, and think that such words often function much as Kripke thinks natural kind terms do, I have no wish to deny that a property word can have a conventionally determined sense. But there is only so much that linguistic conventions can do; and one thing they cannot do is to dictate to reality, creating lawlike connections and *de re* necessities. Having discovered that certain conditional powers necessarily go together, and so are appropriately related for being part of an essential core cluster, we can lay down the convention that a certain word applies, in any possible world, to those and only those things having those conditional powers. But this leaves open the question of how we know that the conditional powers in question are appropriately related – that they must go together in any world in which either can be instantiated. And here appeal to convention cannot help us.

It begins to appear that if we hold that some lawlike connections are contingent, there is no way in which we could discover which of the lawlike connections between conditional powers are logically necessary and which are logically contingent, and so no way in which we could identify the essential core clusters of properties. This means that when we conceive, or seem to be conceiving, of a possible world in which the actual world properties are governed by somewhat different laws, there is no way in which we can discover whether we are conceiving of a genuine possibility. All that any of our empirical investigations can tell us is what lawlike connections obtain in the actual world; and without some way of telling which of these connections are contingent and which necessary, this gives us no information about what can be the case in other possible worlds. This makes all talk about what logically might be and might have been completely idle, except where questions of logical possibility can be settled a priori. If the core cluster theory makes the modal status of causal connections, their being necessary or contingent, epistemologically indeterminate in this way, it does not really save the intuitions which lead us to resist the total cluster theory, according to which all such connections are necessary. Unless we are prepared to abandon altogether the idea that there is a 'fact of the matter' as to whether there are logically possible circumstances in which a given property would make a certain contribution to the causal powers of its subject, I think we must accept the total cluster theory and its initially startling consequence that all of the causal potentialities of a property are essential to it.

X

If, as my theory implies, there are no situations that are logically but not causally possible, how is it that we are apparently able to conceive or imagine such situations? Saul Kripke has suggested one answer to a very similar question.[16] He holds that it is a necessary truth that heat is molecular motion, but recognizes that it seems as if we can imagine heat turning out to be something other than this. According to Kripke, this appearance of conceivability is something to be explained away, and he explains it away by claiming that the seeming conceivability of heat turning out not to be molecular motion consists in the actual conceivability of something else: namely, of sensations of a certain sort, those that we in fact get from heat, turning out to be caused by something other than molecular motion. The latter really is conceivable, he holds, and for understandable reasons we mistake its conceivability for the conceivability of something that is in fact not conceivable.

But if conceivability is taken to imply possibility, this account commits one to the possibility that the sensations we get from heat might standardly be caused by something other than molecular motion (and so something other than heat); more than that, it commits one to the possibility that this might be so and that these sensations might be related to other sensations and sense experiences in all the ways they are (or have been to date) in the actual world. And since the property of having such sensations is one that is actualized in this world, this would commit one, in my view, to the claim that it is compatible with the laws of nature that prevail in the actual world that these sensations should be so caused and so related to other experiences. Now this claim may be true – if 'may be' is used epistemically. But it is hard to see how we are entitled to be confident that it is. For might there not be laws, unknown to us, that make it impossible that the standard cause of these sensations should be anything other than it is, given the way they are related to the rest of our experience? If the seeming conceivability of heat turning out to be something other than molecular motion does not prove the actual possibility of this, why should the seeming conceivability of certain sensations being caused by something other than molecular motion prove the actual, and so causal, possibility of that? And if seeming conceivability no more proves possibility in the latter case than in the former, there seems little point in distinguishing between conceivability and seeming conceivability; we may as well allow that it is conceivable (and not just seemingly conceivable) that heat should turn out to be molecular motion, and then acknowledge that conceivability is not conclusive proof of possibility. We could use the term 'conceivable' in such a way that it is conceivable that P just in case not-P is not provable a priori. Or we could use it in such a way that it is conceivable that P just in case it is epistemically possible that it is possible that P should be the case – that is, just in case P's being possible is compatible, for all we know, with what we know. These uses of 'conceivable' are not equivalent, but on both of them it is possible to conceive of what is not possible.

XI

Although many of the implications of the account I have advanced are radically at odds with Humean views about causality, it does enable us to salvage one of the central tenets of the Humean view: namely, the claim that singular causal statements are 'implicitly general'. As I see it, the generality of causal propositions stems from the generality of properties, that is, from the fact that properties are universals, together with the fact which I began this essay by pointing out: namely, that causal relations hold between particular events in virtue of the properties possessed by the constituent objects of those events, and the fact, which I have tried to establish in the essay, that the identity of a property is completely determined by its potential for contributing to the causal powers of the things that have it. If I assert that one event caused another, I imply that the constituent objects of the cause event had properties which always contribute in certain ways to the causal powers of the things that have them, and that the particular episode of causation at hand was an actualization of some of these potentialities. I may of course not know what the relevant properties of the cause event were; and if I do know this, I may know little about their causal potentialities. This is closely related to the now familiar point that in claiming to know the truth of a singular causal statement one is not committed to knowing the laws in virtue of which it holds.[17] Moreover, a singular causal statement does not commit one to the claim that the instantiation of the relevant properties in relevant similar circumstances always produces the effect that it did in the case at hand, for the laws governing these properties may be statistical; the powers to which the properties contribute may, accordingly, be statistical tendencies or propensities, and the causation may be nonnecessitating. Also, the claim that singular causal statements are implicitly general does not, as here interpreted, imply anything about how such statements are known – in particular, it does not imply the Humean view that causal relationships can only be discovered via the discovery of regularities or 'constant con-junctions'. But where the present theory differs most radically from theories in the Humean tradi-tion is in what it claims about the modality of the general propositions, the laws, that explain the truth of singular causal propositions; for whereas on the Humean view the truth of these propositions is contingent, on my view it is logically necessary. I thus find myself, in what I once would have regarded as reactionary company, defending the very sort of 'necessary connection' account of causality which Hume is widely applauded for having refuted.

Postscript[18]

Richard Boyd has offered the following as a counterexample to the account of properties proposed in this essay. Imagine a world in which the basic physical elements include substances A, B, C, and D. Suppose that X is a compound of A and B, and Y is a compound of C and D. We can suppose that it follows from the laws of nature governing the elements that these two compounds, although composed of different elements, behave exactly alike under all possible circumstances – so

that the property of being made of X and the property of being made of Y share all of their causal potentialities. (This means, among other things, that it follows from the laws that once a portion of X or Y is formed, it cannot be decomposed into its constituent elements.) It would follow from my account of properties that being made of X and being made of Y are the same property. And this seems counterintuitive. If, as appears, X and Y would be different substances, the property of being composed of the one should be different from the property of being composed of the other.

I think that this example does show that my account needs to be revised. I propose the follow-ing as a revised account which is still clearly a causal account of properties: for properties F and G to be identical, it is necessary *both* that F and G have the same causal potentialities *and* (this is the new requirement) that whatever set of circum-stances is sufficient to cause the instantiation of F is sufficient to cause the instantiation of G, and vice versa. This amounts to saying that properties are individuated by their possible causes as well as by their possible effects. No doubt Boyd's example shows that other things I say in the essay need to be amended.

Notes

1 See Jaegwon Kim, "Causation, nomic subsumption, and the concept of event," *Journal of Philosophy* 70 (1973), pp. 27–36. I should mention that it was reflec-tion on this excellent paper that first led me to the views developed in the present one.

2 Peter Geach, God *and the Soul* (London: Routledge and Kegan Paul, 1969), p. 71. See also Jaegwon Kim, "Non-causal connections", *Noûs* 8 (1974), pp. 41–52, and *idem*, "Events as property exemplifications," in M. Brand and D. Walton (eds), *Action Theory* (Dordrecht: Reidel, 1976), pp. 159–77.

3 I take this example from Kim, "Causation, nomic subsumption, and the concept of event."

4 David Hume, *A Treatise of Human Nature*, ed. L. A. Selby-Bigge (Oxford: Clarendon Press, 1888), p. 170 (bk I, pt iii, sect. 14).

5 "When any objects *resemble* each other, the resemb-lance will at first strike the eye, or rather the mind, and seldom requires a second examination" (ibid., p. 70 (bk I, pt iii, sect. 1)).

6 John Locke, *Essay Concerning Human Understanding*, ed. Peter H. Nidditch (Oxford: Clarendon Press, 1975), p. 300 (bk II, ch. 23, sect. 8).

7 Ibid., p. 134 (bk II, ch. 8, sect. 8).

8 What does 'in virtue of' mean here? For the moment we can say that a thing has a power in virtue of having certain properties if it is a lawlike truth that whatever has those properties has that power. On the theory I shall be defending, it turns out that this is a matter of the possession of the properties entailing the posses-sion of the power (i.e., its being true in all possible worlds that whatever has the properties has the power).

9 In speaking of "circumstances" I have in mind the relations of the object to other objects; instead of speaking of "presence in circumstances of a particular sort" I could instead speak of "possession of parti-cular relational properties." Being in such and such circumstances is a mere-Cambridge property of an object, not a genuine (intrinsic) property of it.

10 After this was written, I found that Peter Achinstein has advanced a causal account of property identity which, despite a different approach, is in some ways similar to the account proposed here. See his "The identity of properties," *American Philosophical Quar-terly* II (1974), pp. 257–76. There are also similarities, along with important differences, between my views and those presented by D. H. Mellor in "In defense of

dispositions," *Philosophical Review* 83 (1974), pp. I57–81, and those presented by R. Harré and E. H. Madden in *Causal Powers: A Theory of Natural Necessity* (Oxford: Clarendon Press, 1975).

11 See S. F. Barker and P. Achinstein, "On the new riddle of induction," *Philosophical Review* 69 (1960), pp. 511–22. The definition given there is not equivalent to that originally given by Goodman, in *Fact, Fiction and Forecast*, 3rd edn (Indianapolis: Bobbs-Merrill, 1975), p. 74, and it is the latter which is employed elsewhere in the present essay.

12 This was called to my attention by Nicholas Sturgeon.

13 See Boyle, "The origins and forms of qualities," in *The Works of the Honourable Robert Boyle* (5 vols, London, 1744), vol. 2, pp. 461ff.

14 See Saul Kripke, "Naming and necessity," in D. Davidson and G. Harman (eds), *Semantics of Natural Language* (Dordrecht: Reidel, 1972), pp. 253–355.

15 For the notion of 'reference fixing', see ibid., pp. 269–75.

16 Ibid., pp. 331–42.

17 See, e.g., Donald Davidson, "Causal relations," this volume, ch. 33.

18 This was appended to the original publication of this essay as a "Note added in proof."

PART V

Things and their Persistence

Introduction

Things change over time. At least, that is what we ordinarily believe. To say that something has changed must mean that it had a certain property, F, at an earlier time, t_1, that it does not now have, at t_2. This seems to imply that the thing that had F at t_1 is the very thing that has non-F at t_2. Rivers flow, trees grow, and mountains erode. But we can track the same rivers, trees, and mountains over time. Or at least, so we think.

In "Identity through Time" (chapter 21), Roderick Chisholm sets out the classic problems associated with the idea that things persist through time. More specifically, the main question he is concerned with is how a thing can persist as "the same thing" in spite of changes in its constituent parts. This is the famous problem of the "Ship of Theseus," a ship all of whose wooden planks are replaced one by one, over a long time (say, one plank a day). Is the ship made of entirely new wood the same ship we began with? What if the old planks have been saved and assembled into a ship, with each plank placed in its original place in relation to other planks? Which ship is the original ship identical with?

Chisholm systematically works out and defends the view, which originated with Bishop Butler, that in the strict sense ordinary material things, such as ships, tables, and trees, do not persist through time. There is no real identity over time; rather, we only "feign" identity. (As we will see in the section that follows, Chisholm argues that, unlike material things, we, as persons, do persist through time.)

W. V. Quine, in his "Identity, Ostension, and Hypostasis" (chapter 22), brings a different perspective to persistence. Different masses of water pass through a river, but the river persists nonetheless, since it *is* something constituted by these passing river stages. An approach like this is called a "four-dimensional" or "time-slice" view of persisting things: things persists over time by having different "temporal parts" at different times, just as a table is one thing in spite of – in fact, in virtue of – having different spatial parts in different places. On this approach, a thing is a four-dimensional object constituted by temporal parts. If you begin with these temporal parts or stages as the basic items in your ontology, you face the question: Under what conditions does a sum of such temporal stages count as an enduring object? Quine defends an essentially pragmatic answer to this question.

In general, views concerning persisting things fall in two groups: the continuant theories and the temporal-part (or four-dimensional) theories. The former explain persistence in terms of the same three-dimensional objects being "fully" present at each moment of their existence; it is only that they have different properties at different times. Theories of the latter type explain a persisting object as a series of temporal parts. It is therefore a four-dimensional object consisting of temporal stages. Where the continuant theorist will say "Object O has property F at time t," the temporal-part theorist will say "The temporal part of O at t has property F."

My summer suit comes in two separate parts, a jacket and a pair of trousers. I keep the jacket in my office, but my trousers are at home, a mile away. My suit, therefore, is a "scattered object" – scattered spatially. Richard Cartwright (chapter 23) explores the nature of such objects and the principles that govern them, arguing that these objects should be recognized as genuine things of the world.

Judith Jarvis Thomson, in her "Parthood and Identity across Time", (chapter 24), begins with a problem Cartwright considers in his piece concerning persisting objects. Her essay is a sustained argument against the four-dimensional, temporal-parts view of persisting things, and she proposes an account of her own without recourse to temporal parts. Mark Heller's "Temporal Parts of Four-Dimensional Objects" (chapter 25) can be taken as a response to Thomson. While acknowledging that our ordinary ("folk") metaphysics views persisting things as continuants, Heller believes that continuant theories face serious difficulties, and that the revisionist four-dimensionalism gives us a more defensible metaphysics of persistence.

Most of the items in the next part, "The Persistence of the Self," are directly relevant to the issues discussed in the present section.

Further reading

Forbes, Graeme, "Is there a problem about persistence?," *Proceedings of the Aristotelian Society*, suppl. vol. 61 (1987), pp. 137–55.

Hirsch, Eli, *The Concept of Identity* (New York: Oxford University Press, 1982).

Hoffman, Joshua, and Rosenkrantz, Gary S., *Substance: Its Nature and Existence* (London and New York: Routledge, 1997).

Johnston, Mark, "Is there a problem about persistence?," *Proceedings of the Aristotelian Society*, suppl. vol. 61 (1987), pp. 107–35.

Loux, Michael J., *Substance and Attribute* (Dordrecht: Reidel, 1978).

Odeberg, David S., *The Metaphysics of Identity Over Time* (New York: St Martin's Press, 1993).

Quinton, Anthony, *The Nature of Things* (London: Routledge and Kegan Paul, 1973).

Simons, Peter, *Parts: A Study in Ontology* (Oxford: Clarendon Press, 1987).

Strawson, P. F., *Individuals* (London: Methuen, 1959).

Van Cleve, James, "Mereological essentialism, mereological conjunctivism, and identity through time," *Midwest Studies in Philosophy* 11 (1986), pp. 141–56.

Van Inwagen, Peter, *Material Things* (Ithaca, NY: Cornell University Press, 1990).

21

Identity through Time

Roderick M. Chisholm

The identity of a person is a perfect identity; wherever it is real, it admits of no degrees; and it is impossible that a person should be in part the same, and in part different... For this cause, I have first considered personal identity, as that which is perfect in its kind, and the natural measure of that which is imperfect.

Thomas Reid[1]

1 The Ship of Theseus

To understand the philosophical problems involved in persistence, in the fact that one and the same thing may endure through a period of time, we will begin with what Reid would have called the 'imperfect' cases and remind ourselves of some ancient philosophical puzzles. One such puzzle is suggested by the familiar dictum of Heraclitus: 'You could not step twice in the same river; for other and yet other waters are ever flowing on.'[2] Another is the problem of the Ship of Theseus.[3]

Updating the latter problem somewhat, let us imagine a ship – the Ship of Theseus – that was made entirely of wood when it came into being. One day a wooden plank is cast off and replaced by an aluminum one. Since the change is only slight, there is no question as to the survival of the Ship of Theseus. We still have the ship we had before; that is to say, the ship that we have now is identical with

Originally published in Roderick M. Chisholm, *Person and Object* (1976), ch. 3. Reprinted by permission of Open Court, a division of Canis Publishing.

the ship we had before. On another day, another wooden plank is cast off and also replaced by an aluminum one. Still the same ship, since, as before, the change is only slight. The changes continue, in a similar way, and finally the Ship of Theseus is made entirely of aluminum. The aluminum ship, one may well argue, *is* the wooden ship we started with, for the ship we started with survived each particular change, and identity, after all, is transitive.

But what happened to the discarded wooden planks? Consider this possibility, suggested by Thomas Hobbes: 'If some man had kept the old planks as they were taken out, and by putting them afterwards together in the same order, had again made a ship of them, this, without doubt, had also been the same numerical ship with that which was at the beginning; and so there would have been two ships numerically the same, which is absurd.'[4] Assuming, as perhaps one has no right to do, that each of the wooden planks survived intact throughout these changes, one might well argue that the reassembled wooden ship *is* the ship we started with. 'After all, it is made up of the very same parts, standing in the very same relations, whereas that ugly aluminum object doesn't have a single part in common with our original ship.'

To compound the problem still further, let us suppose that the captain of the original ship had solemnly taken the vow that, if his ship were ever to go down, he would go down with it. What, now, if the two ships collide at sea and he sees them start to sink together? Where does his duty lie – with the aluminum ship or with the reassembled wooden ship?

'The carriage' is another ancient version of the problem. Socrates and Plato change the parts of their carriages piece by piece until, finally, Socrates' original carriage is made up of all the parts of Plato's carriage and Plato's carriage is made up of all the parts of Socrates' original carriage. Have they exchanged their carriages or not, and if so, at what point?

Perhaps the essence of the problem is suggested by an even simpler situation. Consider a child playing with his blocks. He builds a house with ten blocks, uses it as a garrison for his toy soldiers, disassembles it, builds many other things, then builds a house again, with each of the ten blocks occupying the position it had occupied before, and he uses it again as a garrison for his soldiers. Was the house that was destroyed the same as the one that subsequently came into being?

These puzzles about the persistence of objects through periods of time have their analogues for the extension of objects through places in space. Consider the river that is known in New Orleans as 'the Mississippi'. Most of us would say that the source of the river is in northern Minnesota. But what if one were to argue instead that the source is in Montana, where it is known as 'the Missouri'? Or that its source is in Pittsburgh, where it is known as 'the Ohio', or that its source is farther back where it is called 'the Allegheny', or in still another place where it is called 'the Mononga-hela'?[5]

The accompanying diagram (Fig. 21.1) provides us with a schematic illustration.

Of the river that has its central point at (d), one might wonder whether it flows south-easterly from (a), or due south from (b), or south-westerly from (c). (For simplicity, we ignore the Allegheny and the Monongahela.) If we are puzzled about the beginning of the Mississippi, we should be equally puzzled about the end of the Rhine. Reading our diagram from bottom to top (and again oversimplifying), we could say that if the Rhine begins at (d), then it ends either with the Maas at (a), or with the Waal at (b), or with the Lek at (c).[6]

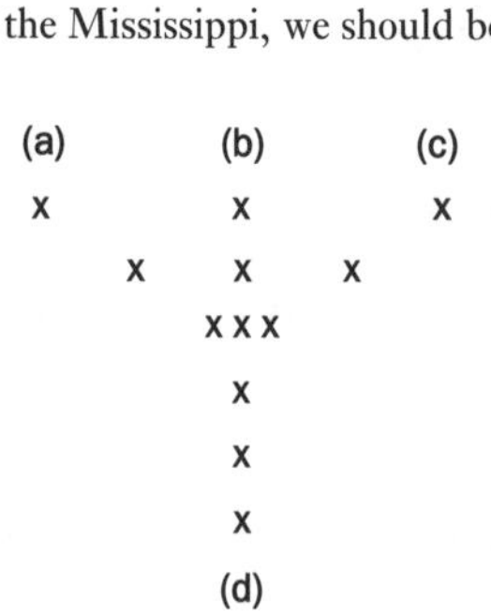

Perhaps we can imagine three philosophers looking down at the river(s) that end(s) at (d). One insists that the river flows between (a) and (d), another that it flows between (b) and (d) and the third that it flows between (c) and (d); and each insists that, since the arms (or tributaries) to which the other two philosophers refer are distinct not only from each other but from the river itself, neither of the other two can be right. Their dispute, clearly, would be analogous in significant respects to the problem of the Ship of Theseus.

What are we to say of such puzzles? We might follow the extreme course that Carneades took and simply deny the principle of the transitivity of identity.[7] In other words, we might say that things identical with the same thing need not be identical with each other. But if we thus abandon reason and logic at the very outset, we will have no way of deciding at the end what is the most reasonable thing to say about ourselves and *our* persistence through time.

We might be tempted to deny the possibility of alteration. Thus one could say: 'Strictly speaking, nothing alters – nothing is such that at one time it has one set of properties and at another time it has another set of properties. What happens is, rather, that at one time there is a thing having the one set of properties and at the other time there is another thing having the other set of properties.' But this supposition, if we apply it to ourselves, is inconsistent with the data with which we have begun. Each of us knows with respect to himself that he now has properties he didn't have in the past and that formerly he had properties he doesn't have now. ('But a thing *x* isn't identical with a thing *y* unless they have all their properties in common. And if the present you has one set of properties and the past you another, how can they be the same thing?') The answer is, of course, that there aren't two you's, a present one having one set of properties and a past one having another. It is rather that you *are* now such that you have these properties and lack those, whereas formerly you *were* such that you had those properties and lacked these. The 'former you' *has* the same properties that the 'present you' now has, and the 'present you' *had* the same properties that the 'former you' then had.[8]

```
        (a)          (b)          (c)
         x            x            x
              x       x       x
                   x x x
                     x
                     x
                     x
                    (d)
```

Figure 21.1

Bishop Butler suggested that it is only in 'a loose and popular sense' that we may speak of the persistence of such familiar things as ships, plants and houses. And he contrasted this 'loose and popular sense' with 'the strict and philosophical sense' in which we may speak of the persistence of *persons*.[9] Let us consider these suggestions.

2 Playing Loose with the 'Is' of Identity

We will not pause to ask what Butler meant in fact. Let us ask what he could have meant. He suggested that there is a kind of looseness involved when we say that such things as the Ship of Theseus persist through time. What kind of looseness is this?

It could hardly be that the Ship of Theseus, in contrast with other things, is only loosely identical with itself. Surely one cannot say that, while some things are only loosely identical with themselves, other things are tightly identical with themselves.[10] The statement 'This thing is more loosely identical with itself than that thing', if it says anything at all, tells us only that the first thing is more susceptible than the second to loss of identity, and this means only that the first is more readily perishable than the second.

We should construe Butler's remark as saying, not that there is a loose kind of identity, but rather that there is a loose sense of 'identity' – a loose (and popular) use of the 'is' of identity.

What would be a *loose* sense of 'A is B', or 'A is identical with B' – a sense of 'A is B' which is consistent with a denial of the *strict* sense of 'A is B'? I suggest this: we use the locution 'A is B', or 'A is identical with B', in a *loose* sense, if we use it in such a way that it is consistent with saying 'A has a certain property that B does not have' or 'Some things are true of A that aren't true of B'.

Do we ever use the locution 'A is B' in this loose way? It would seem, unfortunately, that we do.

I will single out five different types of such misuse.

(1)   One may say: 'Route 6 is Point Street in Providence and is Fall River Avenue in Seekonk.' Here we would seem to have the 'is' of identity, since it is followed in each occurrence by a term ('Point Street' and 'Fall River Avenue') and not by a predicate expression. But since Point Street and Fall River Avenue have different properties (one is in Providence and not in Seekonk, and the other is

in Seekonk and not in Providence), the statement may be said to play loose with 'is'.

As our brief discussion of the rivers may make clear, this use of 'is' is readily avoided. We have only to replace 'is' by 'is part of' and then switch around the terms, as in: 'Point Street in Providence is part of Route 6 and Fall River Avenue in Seekonk is part of Route 6.' Or we could also say, of course: 'Point Street is part of Route 6 in Providence and Fall River Avenue is part of Route 6 in Seekonk.'[11]

(2)   One may say 'This train will be two trains after Minneapolis', or, traveling in the other direction, 'Those two trains will be one train after Minneapolis'. In the first case ('fission'), we are not saying that there is one thing which will subsequently be identical with two things. We are saying, rather, that there is one thing which will be divided into two things, neither of them being identical with the original thing, but each of them being a part of the original thing. And in the second case ('fusion'), we are not saying that there are two things which are subsequently to become identical with each other, or with a third thing. We are saying rather that there are two things which will both become parts of a third thing. (Why not cite an amoeba as an instance of 'fission'? There is the offchance that amoebas are persons, or at least may be thought to be persons, and in such a case, as we shall see, our treatment would have to be somewhat different.)

(3)   One may say: 'The President of the United States was Eisenhower in 1955, Johnson in 1965, and Ford in 1975.'[12] Here one may seem to be saying that there is, or was, something – namely, the President of the United States – which was identical with Eisenhower in 1955, with Johnson in 1965, and with Ford in 1975. And so, given that Eisenhower, Johnson and Ford were three different people, one may seem to be saying that there is one thing which has been identical with three different things. But this talk, too, is readily avoided. We have only to reformulate the original sentence in such a way that the temporal expression ('in 1955', 'in 1965' and 'in 1975') may be seen to modify, not the verb 'was', but the term 'the President of the United States'. Thus we could say: 'The President of the United States in 1955 (the person who officially presided over the United States in 1955) was Eisenhower; the President of the United States in 1965 was Johnson; and the President of the United States in 1975 was Ford.'[12]

(4)   Pointing to a musical instrument, one man may say to another: 'What you have there is the same instrument that I play, but the one that I play isn't as old as that one.' The first 'is' might be taken to be the 'is' of identity, for it would seem to be followed by a term ('the same instrument that I play'), but the man is saying, of the thing designated by the first term ('what you have there'), that it is older than the thing designated by the second. But of course he didn't need to talk that way. He could have said: 'What you have there is an instrument of the same sort as the one that I play.'

We note a second example of this way of playing loose with 'is' – not because the example introduces any new considerations (for it doesn't), but because it has attracted the attention of philosophers.

Consider the following list:

Socrates is mortal.
Socrates is mortal.

How many sentences have been listed? We could say either 'exactly one' or 'exactly two'. That these incompatible answers are both possible indicates that the question is ambiguous. And so it has been suggested that, to avoid the ambiguity, we introduce the terms 'sentence-token' and 'sentence-type' and then say 'There are two sentence-tokens on the list and one sentence-type'. But if we say this, then we can say: 'The first item on the list is the same sentence-type as the second (for they are syntactically just alike and say the same thing), but the two are different sentence-tokens (for they are two, one being in one place and the other in another).' Here, once again, we are playing loose with 'is'.[14] We needn't speak this way in order to deal with the ambiguity of 'How many sentences are there?' We could say there *are* two sentence-tokens and they are tokens *of* the same (sentence-)type. The example does not differ in principle, then, from 'The instrument Jones plays is the same as the one Smith plays but is somewhat older'.

It is sometimes said that we should distinguish the two locutions 'A is identical with B and A is a so-and-so' and 'A is the same so-and-so as B'. It has even been suggested that, for purposes of philosophy, the first of these two locutions should be abandoned in favour of the second.[15] According to this suggestion, we should never say, simply and absolutely, 'A is identical with B'; we should 'relativize the ascription of identity to a sortal', and say something of the form 'A is the same so-and-so as

B', where the expression replacing 'so-and-so' is a count-term, or sortal, such as 'man', 'dog', 'horse'. But this suggestion has point only if we can find instances of the following:

A is the same so-and-so as B, and A is a such-and-such but is not the same such-and-such as B.

Are there really any such A's and B's?

What would be an instance of the above formula? In other words, what would be an instance of an A which is 'the same so-and-so' as something B, but which is not 'the same such-and-such' as B? The only instances which have ever been cited, in defending this doctrine of 'relativized identity', would seem to be instances of one or the other of the four ways of playing loose with 'is' that we have just distinguished. For example: 'Different official personages may be one and the same man' or 'This is the same word as that'. What the suggestion comes to, then, is that we abandon the strict use of 'is' and replace it by one or more of the loose uses just discussed. There may be advantages to this type of permissiveness, but it will not help us with our philosophical problems.[16]

Do these ways of playing loose with 'is' suggest a true interpretation of the thesis we have attributed to Bishop Butler – the thesis according to which it is only in 'a loose and popular sense' that we may speak of the persistence through time of such familiar physical things as ships, plants and houses? Is it only by playing loose with 'is' that we may say, of the Ship of Theseus, that it is one and the same thing from one period of time to another?

We *can*, of course, play loose with 'is' in one or another of these ways when we talk about the Ship of Theseus. Knowing that it is going to be broken up into two ships, we might say: 'It's going to be two ships.' Or knowing that it was made by joining two other ships, we might say: 'Once it had been two ships.' Or knowing that it makes the same ferry run as does the Ship of Callicles, we might say: 'The Ship of Theseus and the Ship of Callicles are the same ferry.' But the Ship of Theseus doesn't have to be talked about in these loose and popular ways any more than anything else does.

(5)   It may be that the Ship of Theseus and the carriage and other familiar things involve still another way of playing loose with 'is'. Thus Hume said that it is convenient to 'feign identity' when we speak about things which, though they 'are sup-

posed to continue the same, are such only as consist of succession of parts, connected together by resemblance, contiguity, or causation'.[17] What Hume here has in mind by 'feigning' may have been put more clearly by Thomas Reid. (Though Reid and Hume were far apart with respect to most of the matters that concern us here, they seem to be together with respect to this one.) Reid wrote:

All bodies, as they consist of innumerable parts that may be disjoined from them by a great variety of causes, are subject to continual changes of their substance, increasing, diminishing, changing insensibly. When such alterations are gradual, because language could not afford a different name for every different state of such a changeable being, it retains the same name, and is considered as the same thing. Thus we say of an old regiment that it did such a thing a century ago, though there now is not a man alive who then belonged to it. We say a tree is the same in the seed-bed and in the forest. A ship of war, which has successively changed her anchors, her tackle, her sails, her masts, her planks, and her timbers, while she keeps the same name is the same.[18]

I believe that Reid is here saying two things. The first is that, whenever there is a change of parts, however insignificant the parts may be, then some old thing ceases to be, and some new thing comes into being. This presupposes that, strictly speaking, the parts of a thing are essential to it, and therefore when, as we commonly say, something loses a part, then that thing strictly and philosophically ceases to be.[19]

The second thing I take Reid to be saying is this. If, from the point of view of our practical concerns, the new thing that comes into being upon the addition of parts is sufficiently similar to the old one, then it is much more convenient for us to treat them as if they were one than it is for us to take account of the fact that they are diverse. This point could also be put by saying that such things as the Ship of Theseus and indeed most familiar physical things are really 'fictions', or as we would say today, 'logical constructions'. They are logical constructions upon things which *cannot* survive the loss of their parts.

If Reid is right, then, 'The Ship of Theseus was in Athens last week and will be in Kerkyra Melaina next week' need not be construed as telling us that there *is* in fact a certain ship that was in Athens last week and will be in Kerkyra Melaina next week. It does not imply that any ship that was in the one place is identical with any ship that will be in the other place. And so if this is true, and if all the same we say 'A ship that was in Athens last week is identical with a ship that will be in Kerkyra Melaina next week', then, once again, we are playing loose with the 'is' of identity.

3 An Interpretation of Bishop Butler's Theses

We have found a way, then, of interpreting Bishop Butler's two theses.

According to the first, familiar physical things such as trees, ships, bodies and houses persist 'only in a loose and popular sense'. This thesis may be construed as presupposing that these things are 'fictions', logical constructions or *entia per alio*. And it tells us that, from the fact that any such physical thing may be said to exist at a certain place P at a certain time *t* and also at a certain place Q at a certain other time *t*, we may *not* infer that what exists at P at *t* is identical with what exists at Q at *t'*.

According to the second thesis, persons persist 'in a striot and philosophical sense'. This may be construed as telling us that persons are not thus 'fictions', logical constructions or *entia per alio*. And so it implies that, if a person may be said to exist at a certain place P at a certain time *t* and also at a certain place Q at a certain other time *t'*, then we *may* infer that something existing at P at *t* is identical with something existing at Q at *t'*.

We now consider the two theses in turn.

4 Feigning Identity

Could we think of familiar physical things, such as ships and trees and houses, as being logical constructions? Let us consider just one type of physical thing, for what we say about it may be applied, *mutatis mutandis*, to the others (see Fig. 21.2)

Mon	AB
Tue	BC
Wed	CD

Figure 21.2

Consider the history of a very simple table. On Monday it came into being when a certain thing A was joined with a certain other thing B. On Tuesday A was detached from B and C was joined to B, these things occurring in such a way that a table was to be found during every moment of the process. And on Wednesday B was detached from C and D was joined with C, these things, too, occurring in such a way that a table was to be found during every moment of the process. Let us suppose that no other separating or joining occurred.

I suggest that in this situation there are the following three wholes among others: AB, that is, the thing made up of A and B; BC, the thing made up of B and C; and CD, the thing made up of C and D. I will say that AB 'constituted' our table on Monday, that BC 'constituted' our table on Tuesday, and that CD 'constituted' our table on Wednesday. Although AB, BC and CD are three different things, they all constitute the same table. We thus have an illustration of what Hume called 'a succession of objects'.[20]

One might also say, of each of the three wholes, AB, BC and CD, that it 'stands in for' or 'does duty for' our table on one of the three successive days. Thus if we consider the spatial location of the three wholes, we see that the place of the table was occupied by AB on Monday, by BC on Tuesday, and by CD on Wednesday. Again, the table was red on Monday if and only if AB was red on Monday, and it weighed 10 pounds on Monday if and only if AB weighed 10 pounds on Monday. And analogously for BC on Tuesday and for CD on Wednesday.

The situation may seem to involve two somewhat different types of individual thing. On the one hand, there is what might be called the *ens successivum* – the 'successive table' that is made up of different things at different times.[21] And on the other hand, there are the things that do duty on the different days for the successive table: namely, AB, BC and CD. But any *ens successivum* may be viewed as a logical construction upon the various things that may be said to do duty for it.

Considering, then, just the simple situation I have described, can we express the information we have about the *ens successivum* in statements that refer only to the particular things that stand in or do duty for it? It should be clear that we can, but let us consider the situation in some detail.

Looking back to our diagram, we can see that Monday's table evolved into Tuesday's table, and that Tuesday's table evolved into Wednesday's

table. We began with AB; then A was separated from B and replaced by C, but in such a way that there was a table to be found at every moment during the process; then, in a similar way, B was separated from C and replaced by D. We could say, then, that BC was a 'direct table successor' of AB and that CD was a 'direct table successor' of AB.

Making use of the undefined concept of *part*, or *proper part*, we may define the concept of 'table successor' in the following way:

D. III. 1 x is at t a direct table successor of y at $t' =$ Df (i) t does not begin before t'; (ii) x is a table at t and y is a table at t'; and (iii) there is a z, such that z is a part of x at t and a part of y at t', and at every moment between t' and t, inclusive, z is itself a table.

Thus z is a table which is a proper part of a table. (If we cut off a small part of a table, we may still have a table left. But if the thing that is left is a table, then, since it was there before, it was then a table that was a proper part of a table.) The concept *part*, as it is understood here, is discussed in detail in Appendix B ('Mereological essentialism').[22]

We may also say, more generally, that the CD of Wednesday is a 'table successor' of the AB of Monday, even though CD is not a *direct* table successor of AB. The more general concept is this:

D. III. 2 x is at t a table successor of y at $t' =$ Df (i) t does not begin before t'; (ii) x is a table at t, and y is a table at t'; and (iii) x has at t every property P such that (a) y has P at t' and (b) all direct table successors of anything having P have P.

The definition assures us that a direct table successor of a direct table successor is a table successor; so, too, for a direct table successor of a direct table successor . . . of a direct table successor.[23]

We may now say that things that are thus related by table succession 'constitute the same successive table'.

D. III. 3 x constitutes at t the same successive table that y constitutes at $t' =$ Df either (a) x and only x is at t a table successor of y at t', or (b) y and only y is at t' a table successor of x at t.

Each such thing may be said to 'constitute a successive table'.

D. III. 4 x constitutes at t a successive table $=$ Df There are a y and a t' such that y is other than x, and x constitutes at t the same table that y constitutes at t'.

We are on the way, then, to reducing our successive table to those things that are said to constitute it.

Certain propositions, ostensibly about the successive table, may be reduced in a straightforward way to propositions about the things that are said to constitute it. For example:

D. III. 5   There is exactly one successive table at place P at time t $=$ Df There is exactly one thing at place P at time t that constitutes a successive table at t.

Our definition of 'constituting the same successive table' (D. III. 3) assures us that nothing will constitute more than one successive table at any given time.

Some of the properties that the table has at any given time are thus such that the table borrows them from the thing that constitutes it at that time; but others are not. An example of a property of the first sort may be that of *being red*; an example of a property of the second sort may be that of *having once been blue*. How are we to mark off the former set of properties?

Some properties may be said to be 'rooted outside the times at which they are had'. Examples are the property of *being a widow* and the property of *being a future President*. If we know of anything that it has the former property at any given time, then we can deduce that the thing existed prior to that time. And if we know of anything that it has the latter property at any given time, then we can deduce that the thing continues to exist after that time. Let us say:

D. III. 6   G is rooted outside times at which it is had $=$ Df Necessarily, for any x and for any period of time t, x has the property G throughout t only if x exists at some time before or after t.

Some properties may – but need not – be rooted outside the times at which they are had. An example is the property of *being such that it is or was red*.

Our successive table may derive this from its present constituent – if its present constituent is red. But it may derive it from a former constituent – if its present constituent is not red. The definition of this type of property is straightforward:

D. III. 7   G may be rooted outside times at which it is had $=$ Df G is equivalent to a disjunction of two properties one of which is, and the other of which is not, rooted outside times at which it is had.

Some properties, finally, are *not* such that they may be rooted outside the times at which they are had.[24] An example is *being red*.

Of the properties that our successive table has at any given time, which are the ones that it borrows from the thing that happens to constitute it at that time? The answer is: those of its properties which are *not* essential to it, and those of its properties which are *not* such that they may be rooted outside the times at which they are had. But the essential properties of the successive table – e.g., that it *is* a successive table – and those of its properties which may be rooted outside the times at which they are had – e.g., that it was blue or that it was or will be blue – are not such that, for any time, they are borrowed from the thing that constitutes the successive table at that time.

We may say, more generally, of the *ens successivum* and the thing that constitutes it at any given time, that they are exactly alike at that time with respect to all those properties which are such that they are not essential to either and they may not be rooted outside the times at which they are had.

Consider now the following definitional schema:

D. III. 8   The successive table that is at place P at time t is F at t $=$ Df There is exactly one thing at place P at t that constitutes a successive table at t, and that thing is F at t.

This definition is applicable only if the predicates that replace the schematic letter 'F' are properly restricted. For the properties designated by such predicates should be those which are not essential to either and are not such that they may be rooted outside the times at which they are had. Hence acceptable replacements for 'F' would be: 'red', '10 feet square', and 'such that it weighs 10 pounds'.

But not all the properties of the successive table are derivable in this straightforward way from the properties of things that constitute it. For example, if AB ceased to be after Monday, we could say of the successive table on Monday, but not of AB, that it was going to persist through Wednesday. Or if CD came into being on Wednesday, we could say of the successive table on Wednesday, but not of CD, that it is at least two days old. Moreover, on Monday, the successive table, but not AB, was such that it would be constituted by CD on Wednesday; while on Wednesday, the successive table, but not CD, was such that it was constituted by AB on Monday.

Nevertheless all such truths about the successive table may be reduced to truths about AB, BC and CD. That this is so should be apparent from these definitions.

D. III. 9   The successive table that is at place P at time t has existed for at least three days $=_{Df}$ There is exactly one x such that x is at place P at time t and x constitutes a successive table at t; there are a y and a time t' such that x is at t a table-successor of y at t'; and t and t' are separated by a period of three days.

This definition tells us, then, what it is for a successive table to persist through time. And the following definition suggests the way in which, at any time, the successive table may borrow its properties from things that constitute it at *other* times:

D. III. 10   The successive table that is at place P at time t is constituted by x at $t' =_{Df}$ There is a y such that y is at place P at time t; y constitutes a successive table at t; and either x is identical with y, and t is identical with t', or y constitutes at t the same successive table that x constitutes at t'.

It should now be obvious how to say such things as 'the successive table is red on Monday and green on Wednesday'.

One may object, 'You are committed to saying that AB, BC, CD, and our table are four different things. It may well be, however, that each of the three things AB, BC, CD satisfies the conditions of any acceptable definition of the term "table". Indeed your definitions presuppose that each of them *is* a table. Hence you are committed to saying that, in the situation described, there are *four* tables. But this is absurd; for actually you have described only *one* table.'

We will find a reply to this objection, if we distinguish the strict and philosophical sense of such expressions as 'There are four tables' from their ordinary, or loose and popular, sense. To say that there are four tables, in the strict and philosophical sense, is to say that there are four different things, each of them a table. But from the fact that there are four tables, in this strict and philosophical sense, it will not follow that there are four tables in the ordinary, or loose and popular, sense. If there are to be four tables in the ordinary, or loose and popular, sense, it must be the case that there are four things, not only such that each constitutes a table, but also such that no two of them constitute the same table. In other words, there must be four *entia successiva*, each of them a table.

We may, therefore, explicate the ordinary, or loose and popular, sense of 'There are n so-and-so's at t' (or 'The number of so-and-so's at t is n') in the following way:

D. III. 11   There are, in the loose and popular sense, n so-and-so's at $t =_{Df}$ There are n things each of which constitutes a so-and-so at t, and no two of which constitute the same so-and-so at t.

The term 'so-and-so' in this schematic definition may be replaced by any more specific count-term, e.g., 'table' or 'ship'. And the *definiendum* could be replaced by 'The number of successive so-and-so's at t is n'.

Hence the answer to the above objection is this: in saying that there are exactly *three* tables in the situation described, one is speaking in the strict and philosophical sense and not in the loose and popular sense. In saying that there is exactly *one* table, one is speaking in the loose and popular sense and not in the strict and philosophical sense. But the statement that there are *four* tables – AB, BC, CD and the successive table – is simply the result of confusion. One is trying to speak both ways at once.[25] The sense in which we may say that there *is* the successive table is not the sense in which we may say that there *is* the individual thing AB, or BC, or CD.[26]

The foregoing sketch, then, makes clear one way in which we may feign identity when what we are dealing with is in fact only a 'succession of related objects'. The ways in which we do thus feign identity are considerably more subtle and complex. Playing loose with 'is' and 'same', we may even speak of the sameness of a table when we are dealing with successions of objects which are related, not by what I have called table succession, but in much more tenuous ways. Nevertheless, it should be clear that if we are saying something we really know, when we thus speak of the sameness of a table, what we are saying could be re-expressed in such a way that we refer only to the related objects and not to the ostensible entities we think of them as making up. And so, too, for other familiar things – ships and trees and houses – that involve successions of related objects that stand in or do duty for them at different times.

We could say, then, that such things are *entia per alio*. They are ontological parasites that derive all their properties from other things – from the various things that do duty for them. An *ens per alio* never is or has anything on its own. It is what it is in virtue of the nature of something other than itself. At every moment of its history an *ens per alio* has something other than itself as its stand-in.

But if there are *entia per alio*, then there are also *entia per se*.

Notes

1 Thomas Reid, *Essays on the Intellectual Powers of Man*, essay III, ch. 14 in Sir William Hamilton (ed.), *The Works of Thomas Reid, D. D.* (Edinburgh: Maclachlan & Stewart, 1854), p. 345.

2 Fragment 41–2, as translated in Milton C. Nahm, *Selections from Early Greek Philosophy* (New York: F. S. Crofts, 1934), p. 91.

3 See Plato, *Phaedo*, 58A, and Xenophon, *Memorabilia*, 4. 8. 2. Leibniz speaks of the Ship of Theseus in *New Essays Concerning Human Understanding*, II, ch. 27, sect. 4, noting that any ordinary physical body may be said to be 'like a river which always changes its water, or like the ship of Theseus which the Athenians were always repairing' (Open Court edn), p. 240.

4 Thomas Hobbes, *Concerning Body*, ch. 11 ('Of identity and difference'), sect. 7.

5 Cf. W. V. Quine: 'Thus take the question of the biggest fresh lake. Is Michigan-Huron admissible, or is it a pair of lakes?...Then take the question of the longest river. Is the Mississippi-Missouri admissible, or is it a river and a half?' (*Word and Object* (New York: John Wiley, 1960), p. 128).

6 Using terms not commonly applied to rivers, we may note for future reference that when our diagram is read from top to bottom it illustrates *fusion* and when it is read from bottom to top it illustrates *fission*.

7 See note c of the article 'Carneades' in Pierre Bayle's *A General Dictionary: Historical and Critical*, trans. Rev. J. P. Bernard, Rev. Thomas Birch, John Locke-man et al. (10 vols, London: James Bettenham, 1734–41): 'He found uncertainty in the most evident notions. All logicians know that the foundation of the syllogism, and consequently the faculty of reasoning, is built on this maxim: Those things which are identical with a third are the same with each other (*Quae sunt idem uno tertio sunt idem inter se*). It is certain that Carneades opposed it strongly and displayed all his subtleties against it.'

8 Further aspects of this kind of problem are discussed in Roderick M. Chisholm, *Person and Object* (La Salle, Ill.: Open Court, 1976), Appendix A ('The Doctrine of Temporal Parts').

9 Dissertation 1, in *The Whole Works of Joseph Butler, LL.D.* (London: Thomas Tegg, 1839), pp. 263–70. But compare Locke's third letter to the Bishop of Worcester: 'For it being his body both before and after the resurrection, everyone ordinarily speaks of his body as the same, though, in a strict and philosophical sense, as your lordship speaks, it be not the very same.'

10 I have heard it suggested, however, that (a) whereas the evening star is strictly identical with the evening star, nevertheless (b) the evening star is identical but not strictly identical with the morning star. The facts of the matter would seem to be only these: the evening star (i.e., the morning star) is necessarily self-identical; it is not necessarily such that it is visible in the evening or in the morning; it would be contradictory to say that the evening star exists and is not identical with the evening star, or that the morning star exists and is not identical with the morning star; but it would not be contradictory to say that the morning star exists and the evening star exists and the morning star is not identical with the evening star; and whatever is identical with the evening star (i.e., with the morning star) has all the properties that it does.

11 This example of the roads, like that of the rivers above ('the Mississippi-Missouri'), may suggest that the key to our puzzles about identity through time may be found in the doctrine of 'temporal parts'. According to this doctrine, every individual thing *x* is such that, for every period of time through which *x* exists, there is a set of parts which are such that *x* is made up of them at that time and they do not exist at any other time. (Compare: every individual thing *x* is such that, for every portion of space that *x* occupies at any time, there is at that time a set of parts of *x* which then occupy that place and no other place.) I consider this doctrine in detail in *Person and Object*, Appendix A. I there conclude that it will not help us with our

problems about identity through time and that there is no sufficient reason for accepting it.

12 Contrast P. T. Geach, *Reference and Generality* (Ithaca, NY: Cornell University Press, 1962), p. 157: '...different official personages may be one and the same man.' Possibly an illustration would be: 'The fire-chief isn't the same personage as the Sunday-school superintendent (for one is charged with putting out fires and the other with religious instruction); yet Jones is both.' But here one seems to be playing loose with 'isn't', for what one has in mind, presumably, is something of this sort: 'Being the fire- chief commits one to different things than does being the Sunday-school superintendent, and Jones is both.'

13 There may be temptations in thus playing loose with 'is'. Suppose there were a monarchy wherein the subjects found it distasteful ever to affirm that the monarch vacated his throne. Instead of saying that there have been so many dozen kings and queens in the history of their country, they will say that the monarch has now existed for many hundreds of years and has had so many dozen different names. At certain times it has been appropriate that these names be masculine, like 'George' and 'Henry', and at other times it has been appropriate that they be feminine, like 'Victoria' and 'Elizabeth'. What, then, if we knew about these people and were to hear such talk as this: 'There has existed for many hundreds of years an x such that x is our monarch; x is now feminine, though fifty years ago x was masculine, and fifty years before that x was feminine'? We should not conclude that there was in that land a monarch who is vastly different from any of the people in ours. We should conclude rather that the speakers were either deluded or pretending.

14 Other examples are suggested by: 'He has a copy of *The Republic* on his desk and another on the table, and he doesn't have any other books. How many books does he have?' 'He played the *Appassionata* once in the afternoon and once again in the evening, but nothing further. How many sonatas did he play?'

15 Compare P. T. Geach in *Logic Matters* (Berkeley and Los Angeles: University of California Press, 1972), pp. 238–49; and *Reference and Generality*, pp. 149ff. The suggestion is criticized in detail by David Wiggins, in *Identity and Spatio-Temporal Continuity* (Oxford: Blackwell, 1967), pp. 1–26. Compare W. V. Quine in a review of *Reference and Generality* in *Philosophical Review*, 73 (1964), pp. 100–4, and Fred Feldman, 'Geach and relativized identity', *Review of Metaphysics* 22 (1968), pp. 547–55.

16 Compare P. T. Geach: 'Even if the man Peter Geach is the same person as the man Julius Caesar, they are certainly different men; they were for example born at different times to a different pair of parents' (*God and the Soul* (London: Routledge & Kegan Paul, 1969), p. 6). John Locke says very similar things; see the Fraser

edn of the *Essay Concerning Human Understanding*, pp. 445, 450ff.

17 David Hume, *A Treatise of Human Nature*, bk I, sect. 6; L. A. Selby-Bigge edn, (Oxford: Clarendon Press, 1896), p. 255.

18 Reid, *Essays on the Intellectual Powers of Man*, p. 346.

19 This thesis is discussed and defended in my *Person and Object*, Appendix B ('Mereological essentialism').

20 See Hume, *Treatise of Human Nature*, bk I, pt iv, sect. 6 (Selby-Bigge edn, p. 255): 'all objects, to which we ascribe identity, without observing their invariableness and uninterruptedness, are such as consist of a succession of related objects.' In this same section. Hume affirms a version of the principle of mereological essentialism.

21 We could define an *ens successivum* by saying, with St Augustine, that it is 'a single thing...composed of many, all of which exist not together'; see *Confessions*, bk IV, ch. 11. St Thomas says in effect that a *successivum* is a thing such that some of its parts do not coexist with others of its parts ('una pars non est cum alia parte'); see the *Commentary on the Sentences*, bk I, dist. VIII, Q. 2, Art. 1, ad 4. The term *ens successivum* has traditionally been applied to such things as periods of time (e.g., days, weeks, months) and events; compare Aristotle's *Physics*, bk III, ch. 6, 206a.

22 See Chisholm, *Person and Object*.

23 Definition D. III. 2 thus makes use of the general device by means of which Frege defined the ancestral relation; see G. Frege, *The Foundations of Arithmetic* (Oxford: Blackwell, 1950), sect. 79. A more intuitive reading of clause (iii) might be: '(iii) x belongs at t to every class c which is such that (a) y belongs to c at t' and (b) all direct table successors of anything belonging to c belong to c.'

24 The distinction among these several types of property are used in my *Person and Object*, ch. 4, to mark off those states of affairs that are *events*. (We had noted in the previous chapter that, although 'John is walking' refers to an event, 'John will walk' and 'John is such that either he is walking or he will walk' do not refer to events.)

25 Compare Hume: 'Tho' we commonly be able to distinguish pretty exactly betwixt numerical and specific identity, yet it sometimes happens that we confound them, and in our thinking and reasoning employ the one for the other. (*Treatise of Human Nature*, bk I, pt iv, sect. 6 ('Of Personal Identity'), Selby-Bigge edn, pp. 257–8.

26 It may be noted that we have defined the loose and popular sense of the expression 'There are n so-and-so's at t' and not the more general 'The number of so-and-so's that there ever will have been is n'. For the loose and popular sense of this latter expression is not sufficiently fixed to be explicated in any strict and philosophical sense. The following example may make this clear. In the infantry of the United States

Army during World War II each private carried materials for half a tent – something like one piece of canvas, a pole and ropes. Two privates could then assemble their materials and create a tent which would be disassembled in the morning. On another night the two privates might find different tent companions. Occasionally when the company was in camp, the various tent parts were collected, stored away, and then reissued, but with no attempt to assign particular parts to their former holders. Supposing, to simplify the matter considerably, that all the tents that there ever will have been were those that were created by the members of a certain infantry company, how, making use of our ordinary criteria, would we go about answering the question 'Just how many tents *have* there been?' Would an accounting of the history of the joinings of the various tent parts be sufficient to give us the answer?

22

Identity, Ostension, and Hypostasis

W. V. Quine

I

Identity is a popular source of philosophical perplexity. Undergoing change as I do, how can I be said to continue to be myself? Considering that a complete replacement of my material substance takes place every few years, how can I be said to continue to be I for more than such a period at best?

It would be agreeable to be driven, by these or other considerations, to belief in a changeless and therefore immortal soul as the vehicle of my persisting self-identity. But we should be less eager to embrace a parallel solution of Heracleitus's parallel problem regarding a river: 'You cannot bathe in the same river twice, for new waters are ever flowing in upon you.'

The solution of Heracleitus's problem, though familiar, will afford a convenient approach to some less familiar matters. The truth is that you *can* bathe in the same *river* twice, but not in the same river stage. You can bathe in two river stages which are stages of the same river, and this is what constitutes bathing in the same river twice. A river is a process through time, and the river stages are its momentary parts. Identification of the river bathed in once with the river bathed in again is just what determines our subject matter to be a river process as opposed to a river stage.

Let me speak of any multiplicity of water molecules as a *water*. Now a river stage is at the same time a water stage, but two stages of the same river are not in general stages of the same water. River stages are water stages, but rivers are not waters. You may bathe in the same river twice without bathing in the same water twice, and you may, in these days of fast transportation, bathe in the same water twice while bathing in two different rivers.

We begin, let us imagine, with momentary things and their interrelations. One of these momentary things, called *a*, is a momentary stage of the river Caÿster, in Lydia, around 400 BC. Another, called *b*, is a momentary stage of the Caÿster two days later. A third, *c*, is a momentary stage, at this same latter date, of the same multiplicity of water molecules which were in the river at the time of *a*. Half of *c* is in the lower Caÿster valley, and the other half is to be found at diffuse points in the Aegean Sea. Thus *a*, *b*, and *c* are three objects, variously related. We may say that *a* and *b* stand in the relation of river kinship, and that *a* and *c* stand in the relation of water kinship.

Now the introduction of rivers as single entities, namely, processes or time-consuming objects, consists substantially in reading identity in place of river kinship. It would be wrong, indeed, to say that *a* and *b* are identical; they are merely river-kindred. But if we were to point to *a*, and then wait the required two days and point to *b*, and affirm identity of the objects pointed to, we should thereby show that our pointing was intended not as a pointing to two kindred river stages but as a pointing to a single river which included them both. The imputation of identity is essential, here, to fixing the reference of the ostension.

These reflections are reminiscent of Hume's account of our idea of external objects. Hume's theory was that the idea of external objects arises from an error of identification. Various similar impressions separated in time are mistakenly treated as identical; and then, as a means of resolving this contradiction of identifying momentary events which are separated in time, we invent a new non-momentary object to serve as subject matter of our statement of identity. Hume's charge of erroneous identification here is interesting as a psychological conjecture on origins, but there is no need for us to share that conjecture. The important point to observe is merely the direct connection between identity and the positing of processes, or time-extended objects. To impute identity rather than river kinship is to talk of the river Caÿster rather than of a and b.

Pointing is of itself ambiguous as to the temporal spread of the indicated object. Even given that the indicated object is to be a process with considerable temporal spread, and hence a summation of momentary objects, still pointing does not tell us *which* summation of momentary objects is intended, beyond the fact that the momentary object at hand is to be in the desired summation. Pointing to a, if construed as referring to a time-extended process and not merely to the momentary object a, could be interpreted either as referring to the river Caÿster of which a and b are stages, or as referring to the water of which a and c are stages, or as referring to any one of an unlimited number of further less natural summations to which a also belongs.

Such ambiguity is commonly resolved by accompanying the pointing with such words as 'this river', thus appealing to a prior concept of a river as one distinctive type of time-consuming process, one distinctive form of summation of momentary objects. Pointing to a and saying 'this river' – or ὅ δε ὅ ποταμός, since we are in 400 BC – leaves no ambiguity as to the object of reference if the word 'river' itself is already intelligible. 'This river' means 'the riverish summation of momentary objects which contains this momentary object'.

But here we have moved beyond pure ostension and have assumed conceptualization. Now suppose instead that the general term 'river' is not yet understood, so that we cannot specify the Caÿster by pointing and saying 'This river is the Caÿster'. Suppose also that we are deprived of other descrip-

tive devices. What we may do then is point to a and two days later to b and say each time, 'This is the Caÿster'. The word 'this' so used must have referred not to a nor to b, but beyond to something more inclusive, identical in the two cases. Our specification of the Caÿster is not yet unique, however, for we might still mean any of a vast variety of other collections of momentary objects, related in other modes than that of river kinship; all we know is that a and b are among its constituents. By pointing to more and more stages additional to a and b, however, we eliminate more and more alternatives, until our listener, aided by his own tendency to favor the most natural groupings, has grasped the idea of the Caÿster. His learning of this idea is an induction: from our grouping the sample momentary objects a, b, d, g, and others under the head of Caÿster, he projects a correct general hypothesis as to what further momentary objects we would also be content to include.

Actually there is in the case of the Caÿster the question of its extent in space as well as in time. Our sample pointings need to be made not only on a variety of dates, but at various points up and down stream, if our listener is to have a representative basis for his inductive generalization as to the intended spatiotemporal spread of the four-dimensional object Caÿster.

In ostension, spatial spread is not wholly separable from temporal spread, for the successive ostensions which provide samples over the spatial spread are bound to consume time. The inseparability of space and time characteristic of relativity theory is foreshadowed, if only superficially, in this simple situation of ostension.

The concept of identity, then, is seen to perform a central function in the specifying of spatiotemporally broad objects by ostension. Without identity, n acts of ostension merely specify up to n objects, each of indeterminate spatiotemporal spread. But when we affirm identity of object from ostension to ostension, we cause our n ostensions to refer to the same large object, and so afford our listener an inductive ground from which to guess the intended reach of that object. Pure ostension plus identification conveys, with the help of some induction, spatiotemporal spread.

II

Now between what we have thus far observed and the ostensive explanation of *general* terms, such as 'red' or 'river', there is an evident similarity. When I point in a direction where red is visible and say 'This is red', and repeat the performance at various places over a period of time, I provide an inductive basis for gauging the intended spread of the attribute of redness. The difference would seem to be merely that the spread concerned here is a conceptual spread, generality, rather than spatiotemporal spread.

And is this really a difference? Let us try shifting our point of view so far as to think of the word 'red' in full analogy to 'Cayster'. By pointing and saying 'This is Cayster' at various times and places, we progressively improve our listener's understanding as to what portions of space-time we intend our word 'Cayster' to cover; and by pointing and saying 'This is red' at various times and places, we progressively improve our listener's understanding as to what portions of space-time we intend our word 'red' to cover. The regions to which 'red' applies are indeed not continuous with one another as those are to which 'Cayster' applies, but this surely is an irrelevant detail; 'red' surely is not to be opposed to 'Cayster', as abstract to concrete, merely because of discontinuity in geometrical shape. The territory of the United States including Alaska is discontinuous, but it is nonetheless a single concrete object; and so is a bedroom suite, or a scattered deck of cards. Indeed, every physical object that is not subatomic is, according to physics, made up of spatially separated parts. So why not view 'red' quite on a par with 'Cayster', as naming a single concrete object extended in space and time? From this point of view, to say that a certain drop is red is to affirm a simple spatiotemporal relation between two concrete objects; the one object, the drop, is a spatiotemporal part of the other, red, just as a certain waterfall is a spatiotemporal part of Cayster.

Before proceeding to consider how it is that a general equating of universals to particulars breaks down, I want to go back and examine more closely the ground we have already been over. We have seen how identity and ostension are combined in conceptualizing extended objects, but we have not asked why. What is the survival value of this practice? Identity is more convenient than river kinship or other relations, because the objects related do not have to be kept apart as a multiplicity. As long as what we may propose to say about the river Cayster does not in itself involve distinctions between momentary stages a, b, etc., we gain formal simplicity of subject matter by representing

our subject matter as a single object, Cayster, instead of a multiplicity of objects a, b, etc., in river kinship. The expedient is an application, in a local or relative way, of Occam's razor: the entities concerned in a particular discourse are reduced from many, a, b, etc., to one, the Cayster. Note, however, that from an overall or absolute point of view the expedient is quite opposite to Occam's razor, for the multiple entities a, b, etc., have not been dropped from the universe; the Cayster has simply been added. There are contexts in which we shall still need to speak differentially of a, b, and others rather than speaking indiscriminately of the Cayster. Still the Cayster remains a convenient addition to our ontology because of the contexts in which it does effect economy.

Consider, somewhat more generally, a discourse about momentary objects all of which happen still to be river stages, but not entirely river-kindred. If it happens in this particular discourse that whatever is affirmed of any momentary object is affirmed also of every other which is river-kindred to it, so that no distinctions between stages of the same river are relevant, then clearly we can gain simplicity by representing our subject matter as comprising a few rivers rather than the many river stages. Diversities remain among our new objects, the rivers, but no diversities remain beyond the needs of the discourse with which we are occupied.

I have been speaking just now of integration of momentary objects into time-consuming wholes, but it is clear that similar remarks apply to integration of individually indicable localities into spatially extensive wholes. Where what we want to say about certain broad surfaces does not concern distinctions between their parts, we simplify our discourse by making its objects as few and large as we can – taking the various broad surfaces as single objects.

Analogous remarks hold, and very conspicuously, for conceptual integration – the integrating of particulars into a universal. Suppose a discourse about person stages, and suppose that whatever is said about any person stage, in this particular discourse, applies equally to all person stages which make the same amount of money. Our discourse is simplified, then, by shifting its subject matter from person stages to income groups. Distinctions immaterial to the discourse at hand are thus extruded from the subject matter.

In general we might propound this maxim of the *identification of indiscernibles*: Objects indistinguishable from one another within the terms of a given discourse should be construed as identical for that discourse. More accurately: the references to the original objects should be reconstrued for purposes of the discourse as referring to other and fewer objects, in such a way that indistinguishable originals give way each to the same new object.

For a striking example of the application of this maxim, consider the familiar so-called propositional calculus. To begin with, let us follow the lead of some modern literature by thinking of the 'p', 'q', etc. of this calculus as referring to propositional concepts, whatever they may be. But we know that propositional concepts alike in truth-value are indistinguishable within the terms of this calculus, interchangeable so far as anything expressible in this calculus is concerned. Then the canon of identification of indiscernibles directs us to reconstrue 'p', 'q', etc. as referring merely to truth-values – which, by the way, was Frege's interpretation of this calculus.

For my own part, I prefer to think of 'p', 'q', etc. as schematic letters standing in place of statements but not referring at all. But if they are to be treated as referring, the maxim is in order.

Our maxim of identification of indiscernibles is relative to a discourse, and hence vague insofar as the cleavage between discourses is vague. It applies best when the discourse is neatly closed, like the propositional calculus; but discourse generally departmentalizes itself to some degree, and this degree will tend to determine where and to what degree it may prove convenient to invoke the maxim of identification of indiscernibles.

III

Now let us return to our reflections on the nature of universals. Earlier we represented this category by the example 'red', and found this example to admit of treatment as an ordinary spatiotemporally extended particular on a par with the Caÿster. Red was the largest red thing in the universe – the scattered total thing whose parts are all the red things. Similarly, in the recent example of income groups, each income group can be thought of simply as the scattered total spatiotemporal thing which is made up of the appropriate person stages, various stages of various persons. An income group is just as concrete as a river or a person, and, like a person, it is a summation of person stages. It differs from a person merely in that the person stages

which go together to make up an income group are another assortment than those which go together to make up a person. Income groups are related to persons much as waters are related to rivers; for it will be recalled that the momentary object a was part in a temporal way both of a river and of a water, while b was a part of the same river but not of the same water, and c was a part of the same water but not of the same river. Up to now, therefore, the distinction between spatiotemporal integration and conceptual integration appears idle; all is spatiotemporal integration.

Now let me switch to a more artificial example. Suppose our subject matter consists of the visibly outlined convex regions, small and large, in figure 22.1. There are 33 such regions. Suppose further that we undertake a discourse relatively to which any geometrically similar regions are interchangeable. Then our maxim of identification of indiscernibles directs us for purposes of this discourse to speak not of similarity but of identity; to say not that x and y are similar but that $x = y$, thus reconstruing the objects x and y as no longer regions but shapes. The subject matter then shrinks in multiplicity from 33 to 5: the isosceles right triangle, the square, the two-to-one rectangle, and two forms of trapezoid.

Each of these five is a universal. Now just as we have reconstrued the color red as the total spatiotemporal thing made up of all the red things, so suppose we construe the shape square as the total region made up by pooling all the five square regions. Suppose also we construe the shape isosceles right triangle as the total region made up by pooling all the 16 triangular regions. Similarly suppose we construe the shape two-to-one rectangle as the total region made up by pooling the four two-to-one rectangular regions; and similarly for the two trapezoidal shapes. Clearly this leads to trouble, for our five shapes then all reduce to one, the total region. Pooling all the triangular regions gives simply the total square region; pooling all the

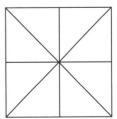

Figure 22.1

square regions gives the same; and similarly for the other three shapes. We should end up, intolerably, by concluding identity among the five shapes.

So the theory of universals as concrete, which happened to work for red, breaks down in general.[1] We can imagine that universals in general, as entities, insinuated themselves into our ontology in the following way. First we formed the habit of introducing spatiotemporally extended concrete things, according to the pattern considered earlier. Red entered with Caÿster and the others as a concrete thing. Finally triangle, square, and other universals were swept in on a faulty analogy with red and its ilk.

Purely as philosophical sport, without supposing there to be any serious psychological or anthropological import in our reflections, let us now go back to Hume's theory of external objects and carry it a step further. Momentary impressions, according to Hume, are wrongly identified with one another on the basis of resemblance. Then, to resolve the paradox of identity among temporally disparate entities, we invent time-consuming objects as objects of the identity. Spatial spread, beyond what is given momentarily in an impression, may be supposed introduced in similar fashion. The entity red, call it a universal or a widespread particular as you please, may be viewed as entering by the same process (though we are now beyond Hume). Momentary localized red impressions are identified one with another, and then a single entity red is appealed to as vehicle of these otherwise untenable identities. Similarly for the entity square, and the entity triangle. Square impressions are identified with one another, and then the single entity square is imported as vehicle for the identity; and correspondingly for triangle.

So far, no difference is noted between the introduction of particulars and universals. But in retrospect we have to recognize a difference. If square and triangle were related to the original square and triangular particulars in the way in which concrete objects are related to their momentary stages and spatial fragments, then square and triangle would turn out to be identical with each other – as lately observed in terms of our artificial little universe of regions.

Therefore we come to recognize two different types of association: that of concrete parts in a concrete whole, and that of concrete instances in an abstract universal. We come to recognize a divergence between two senses of 'is': 'This is the Caÿster' versus 'This is square'.

IV

Interrupting this speculative psychology, let us return to our analysis of ostension of spatiotemporally extended objects, and see how it differs from what may be called the ostension of irreducible universals such as square and triangle. In ostensively explaining the Caÿster, we point to *a*, *b*, and other stages, and say each time 'This is the Caÿster', identity of indicated object being understood from each occasion to the next. In ostensively explaining 'square', on the other hand, we point to various particulars and say each time 'This is square' *without* imputing identity of indicated object from one occasion to the next. These various latter pointings give our listener the basis for a reasonable induction as to what we might in general be willing to point out as square, just as our various former pointings gave him the basis for a reasonable induction as to what we might willingly point to as the Caÿster. The difference in the two cases is merely that in the one case an identical indicated object is supposed, and in the other case not. In the second case what is supposed to be identical from pointing to pointing is not the indicated object, but, at best, an attribute squareness which is *shared by* the indicated objects.

Actually there is no need, up to this point, to suppose such entities as attributes at all in our ostensive clarification of 'square'. We are clarifying, by our various pointings, our use of the words 'is square'; but neither is an object squareness supposed as object pointed to, nor need it be supposed available as reference of the word 'square'. No more need be demanded, in explication of 'is square' or any other phrase, than that our listener learn when to expect us to apply it to an object and when not; there is no need for the phrase itself to be a name in turn of a separate object of any kind.

These contrasts, then, have emerged between general terms and singular terms. First, the ostensions which introduce a general term differ from those which introduce a singular term in that the former do not impute identity of indicated object between occasions of pointing. Second, the general term does not, or need not, purport to be a name in turn of a separate entity of any sort, whereas the singular term does.

These two observations are not independent of each other. The accessibility of a term to identity contexts was urged by Frege as the standard by which to judge whether that term is being used as a name.[2] Whether or not a term is being used as naming an entity is to be decided, in any given context, by whether or not the term is viewed as subject in that context to the algorithm of identity: the law of putting equals for equals.

It is not to be supposed that this doctrine of Frege's is connected with a repudiation of abstract entities. On the contrary, we remain free to admit names of abstract entities; and, according to Frege's criterion, such admission will consist precisely in admitting abstract terms to identity contexts subject to the regular laws of identity. Frege himself, incidentally, was rather a Platonist in his own philosophy.

It is clearest, I think, to view this step of hypostasis of abstract entities as an additional step which follows after the introduction of the corresponding general terms. First we may suppose the idiom 'This is square', or '*x* is square', introduced – perhaps by ostension as previously considered, or perhaps by other channels, such as the usual geometrical definition in terms of prior general terms. Then as a separate step we derive the attribute *squareness*, or, what comes to much the same thing, *the class of squares*. A new fundamental operator 'class of', or '-ness', is appealed to in this step.

I attach much importance to the traditional distinction between general terms and abstract singular terms, 'square' versus 'squareness', because of the ontological point: use of the general term does not of itself commit us to the admission of a corresponding abstract entity into our ontology; on the other hand, the use of an abstract singular term, subject to the standard behavior of singular terms such as the law of putting equals for equals, flatly commits us to an abstract entity named by the term.

It is readily conceivable that it was precisely because of failure to observe this distinction that abstract entities gained their hold upon our imaginations in the first place. Ostensive explanation of general terms such as 'square' is, we have seen, much like that of concrete singular terms such as 'Caÿster', and indeed there are cases such as 'red' where no difference need be made at all. Hence the natural tendency not only to introduce general terms along with singular ones, but to treat them on a par as names each of a single entity. This tendency is no doubt encouraged by the fact that it is often convenient for purely syntactical reasons, reasons, for example, of word order or cross-reference, to handle a general term like a proper name.

V

The conceptual scheme in which we grew up is an eclectic heritage, and the forces which conditioned its evolution from the days of Java man onward are a matter of conjecture.[3] Expressions for physical objects must have occupied a focal position from the earliest linguistic periods, because such objects provided relatively fixed points of reference for language as a social development. General terms also must have appeared at an early stage, because similar stimuli tend psychologically to induce similar responses; similar objects tend to be called by the same word. We have seen, indeed, that the ostensive acquisition of a concrete general term proceeds in much the same way as that of a concrete singular term. The adoption of abstract singular terms, carrying with it the positing of abstract entities, is a further step and a philosophically revolutionary one; yet we have seen how this step in turn could have been made without conscious invention.

There is every reason to rejoice that general terms are with us, whatever the cause. Clearly language would be impossible without them, and thought would come to very little. On the admission of abstract entities, however, as named by abstract singular terms, there is room for divergent value judgements. For clarity it is important in any case to recognize in their introduction an additional operator, 'class of' or '-ness'. Perhaps, as just now suggested, it was failure to appreciate the intrusion of such an additional unexplained operator that engendered belief in abstract entities. But this genetic point is independent of the question whether abstract entities, once with us, are not a good thing from the point of view of conceptual convenience after all – happy accident though their adoption may have been.

Anyway, once abstract entities are admitted, our conceptual mechanism goes on and generates an unending hierarchy of further abstractions as a matter of course. For, it must be noted to begin with that the ostensive processes which we have been studying are not the only way of introducing terms, singular or general. Most of us will agree that such introduction is fundamental; but once a fund of ostensively acquired terms is at hand, there is no difficulty in explaining additional terms discursively, through paraphrase into complexes of the terms already at hand. Now discursive explanation, unlike ostension, is just as available for defining new general terms applicable to abstract entities, for example, 'shape' or 'zoological species', as for defining general terms applicable to concrete entities. Applying then the operator '-ness' or 'class of' to such abstract general terms, we get second-level abstract singular terms, purporting to name such entities as the attribute of being a shape or zoological species, or the class of all shapes or zoological species. The same procedure can be repeated for the next level, and so on, theoretically without end. It is in these higher levels that mathematical entities such as numbers, functions of numbers, etc. find their place, according to the analyses of the foundations of mathematics which have been usual from Frege onward through Whitehead and Russell.

The fundamental-seeming philosophical question, How much of our science is merely contributed by language and how much is a genuine reflection of reality? is perhaps a spurious question which itself arises wholly from a certain particular type of language. Certainly we are in a predicament if we try to answer the question; for to answer the question, we must talk about the world as well as about language, and to talk about the world we must already impose upon the world some conceptual scheme peculiar to our own special language.

Yet we must not leap to the fatalistic conclusion that we are stuck with the conceptual scheme that we grew up in. We can change it bit by bit, plank by plank, though meanwhile there is nothing to carry us along but the evolving conceptual scheme itself. The philosopher's task was well compared by Neurath to that of a mariner who must rebuild his ship on the open sea.

We can improve our conceptual scheme, our philosophy, bit by bit while continuing to depend on it for support; but we cannot detach ourselves from it and compare it objectively with an unconceptualized reality. Hence it is meaningless, I suggest, to inquire into the absolute correctness of a conceptual scheme as a mirror of reality. Our standard for appraising basic changes of conceptual scheme must be, not a realistic standard of correspondence to reality, but a pragmatic standard.[4] Concepts are language, and the purpose of concepts and of language is efficacy in communication and in prediction. Such is the ultimate duty of language, science, and philosophy, and it is in relation to that duty that a conceptual scheme has finally to be appraised.

Elegance, conceptual economy, also enters as an objective. But this virtue, engaging though it is, is secondary – sometimes in one way and sometimes in another. Elegance can make the difference between a psychologically manageable conceptual scheme and one that is too unwieldy for our poor minds to cope with effectively. Where this happens, elegance is simply a means to the end of a pragmatically acceptable conceptual scheme. But elegance also enters as an end in itself – and quite properly so as long as it remains secondary in another respect; namely, as long as it is appealed to only in choices where the pragmatic standard prescribes no contrary decision. Where elegance doesn't matter, we may and shall, as poets, pursue elegance for elegance's sake.

Notes

1 Nelson Goodman, *The Structure of Appearance* (Cambridge, Mass.: Harvard University Press, 1951), pp. 46–51.

2 Gottlob Frege, 'On sense and nominatum', in H. Feigl and W. Sellars (eds), *Readings in Philosophical Analysis* (New York: Appleton-Century-Crofts, 1949).

3 The unrefined and sluggish mind
  Of *Homo javanensis*
  Could only treat of things concrete
  And present to the senses.

4 On this theme see Pierre Duhem, *La Théorie physique: son object et sa structure* (Paris, 1906), pp. 34, 280, 347; or Armand Lowinger, *The Methodology of Pierre Duhem* (New York: Columbia University Press, 1941), pp. 41, 121, 145.

23

Scattered Objects

Richard Cartwright

According to Hobbes, "a body is that, which having no dependence on our thought, is coincident or coextended with some part of space."[1] Bodies in Hobbes's sense are material objects in ours; so at any rate I shall assume. And I shall assume also that his definition is correct at least in its implication that coincidence with some part of space is required of anything that is to count as a material object. But what is to count as a part of space?

By a *region of space*, or simply a *region*, let us agree to understand any set of points of space. And by a *receptacle* let us understand a region of space with which it is possible some material object should be, in Hobbes's phrase, coincident or coextended. Plainly, not every region is a receptacle. The null region is not; neither is any region that consists of a single point or, for that matter, of any finite number of points. Nor are higher cardinalities by themselves sufficient: no region exceeds a straight line in sheer number of members;[2] yet straight lines, along with curves and surfaces, are not receptacles. How, then, are receptacles to be characterized?

Let p be any point of space. By an *open sphere about p* is meant a region the members of which are all and only those points that are less than some fixed distance from p. In other words, a region A is an open sphere about the point p if and only if there

is a positive real number r such that A is the set of all those points whose distance from p is less than r. A region that is an open sphere about some point or other is called simply an *open sphere*.

Every open sphere is, I suggest, a receptacle. There are of course neither minimal nor maximal open spheres: given any open sphere, no matter how large or small, there is a larger and a smaller. My suggestion will thus disturb those for whom material objects are "moderate-sized specimens of dry goods."[3] But surely not all material objects *are* moderate-sized. Heavenly bodies are bodies, some of them very large; and antibodies are bodies, extremely small ones. Given these actualities, why impose bounds on the possibilities?

Others will be disturbed because they think of receptacles as closed. Let me explain. A point p is said to be a *boundary point* of a region A if and only if every open sphere about p has a non-null intersection with both A and the complement of A (where the *complement* of a region is the set of points of space not in the region). Otherwise put, p is a boundary point of A just in case every open sphere about p has in it points of A and points of the complement of A. To illustrate, let S be the open sphere of radius r about p, and let q be a point whose distance from p is exactly r. Then, every open sphere about q will intersect both S and the complement of S; and hence q is a boundary point of S. In fact, the boundary points of S are precisely those points that are like q in that their distance from p is exactly r. A point whose distance from p is less than r will be the center of an open sphere

Originally published in Keith Lehrer (ed.), *Analysis and Metaphysics* (Dordrecht: Reidel, 1975), pp. 153–71. Reprinted by permission of Kluwer Academic Publishers.

included in S; and a point whose distance from p is greater than r will be the center of an open sphere included in the complement of S. Now, a region, spherical or otherwise, is said to be *open* just in case none of its boundary points is a member of it and *closed* just in case all its boundary points are members of it. We have just seen that an open sphere is, appropriately enough, an open region: an open sphere and its surface have no points in common. And it is precisely this that will cause some to resist the suggestion that every open sphere is a receptacle. Their intuitions tell them that a receptacle should be closed. Descartes's told him otherwise. After explaining that what he calls the "external place" of a body is "the superficies of the surrounding body," he remarks that "by superficies we do not here mean any portion of the surrounding body, but merely the extremity which is between the surrounding body and that surrounded."[4] I shall follow Descartes, though I should have no idea how to defend my choice; indeed, the issue seems hardly worthy of serious dispute. There is, however, a possible misconception that needs to be cleared away, a misconception perhaps latent in Descartes's use of 'between'. If receptacles are open, it might seem that bodies never touch, since something – if only a very fine something – is always in between. But this *is* a misconception. On either view body x touches body y when and only when at least one boundary point of the region occupied by x is also a boundary point of the region occupied by y. The only issue is whether such a boundary point must belong to the regions occupied by x and y. And it is this issue that seems hardly worthy of serious dispute.

I shall assume, then, that every receptacle is an open region. But not every receptacle is an open sphere; bodies do, after all, come in other shapes. To allow for the endless possibilities, it will perhaps be suggested that an open region be counted a receptacle provided only that it is non-null. Receptacles would thus come to be identified with non-null open regions, spherical or otherwise. A good many unwanted regions would thereby be excluded: regions with only a finite number of points, curves, and surfaces, for example. But the suggestion will not do. Consider a region the members of which are all the points of an open sphere S save for a single point p. Consider, that is, $S - \{p\}$, where S is an open sphere and p is a point in S. We are reluctant, I think, to suppose this a receptacle. Surely no material object could occupy all the points of an open sphere save one. It is not that

objects never have holes; it is rather that holes are never so small. Yet $S - \{p\}$ is open, for it contains none of its boundary points.

Only some, then, among open regions are receptacles. Which ones? To investigate the question, we shall need the notions of the interior and the closure of a region. By the *interior* of a region is meant the set of all points in the region that are not boundary points of the region. Note that a region is open if and only if it is identical with its interior, for no boundary point of an open region is a member of the region and interiors themselves are always open. The *closure* of a region is the union of the region with the set of all its boundary points. Just as a region is open if and only if it is identical with its interior, so a region is closed if and only if it is identical with its closure; for a closed region includes the set of its boundary points and closures themselves are always closed. Now consider again the region $S - \{p\}$. The point p is a boundary point of the region, for every open sphere about p intersects both $S - \{p\}$ and its complement. But as boundary points go, p is peculiarly situated, for it is also a member of the interior of the closure of $S - \{p\}$. Close $S - \{p\}$ and you pick up p along with the points on the surface of S; take the interior of the resulting region and you keep p, though you lose the points on the surface of S. In view of this peculiarity of situation, let us say that p is an 'inner' boundary point of $S - \{p\}$, where in general an *inner boundary point* of a region is a boundary point of the region that is also a member of the interior of the closure of the region. It is possession of an inner boundary point that leads us to exclude the region $S - \{p\}$ from the class of receptacles; and, accordingly, I suggest that at least a necessary condition for a non-null open region to qualify as a receptacle is that it have no inner boundary points.

It is easily shown that open regions having no inner boundary points are precisely those regions that are identical with the interiors of their closures. And a region that is identical with the interior of its closure is known as an *open domain*.[5] So the present suggestion comes to this: a region of space is a receptacle only if it is a non-null open domain. Another example may serve to clarify the suggestion. Imagine an open sphere cut by a plane. Let the open region on one side of the plane be A and that on the other be B. Both A and B are open domains, but their union is not; for the points on the plane other than those on the surface of the sphere are inner boundary points of $A \cup B$. Otherwise put, since the points on the plane that are not on the surface of the sphere are members of the interior of the closure of $A \cup B$ but not of $A \cup B$, $A \cup B$ is not identical with the interior of its closure and is therefore not an open domain.[6] Thus $A \cup B$ is not a receptacle: no object can be coincident or coextended with it. This is not to exclude the possibility of cracks; it is simply to insist that cracks are never so fine. Of course, the interior of the closure of $A \cup B$ is a receptacle. It is in fact the open sphere with which we began. Thus a body can occupy a region that *includes* $A \cup B$. But such a region must include as well the set of inner boundary points of $A \cup B$.

The proposition that every receptacle is a non-null open domain is not apt to meet with serious opposition. But what of its converse? Is every non-null open domain a receptacle? Here there is likely to be controversy. The issue turns on the notion of connectedness, and we therefore need to see exactly what this notion is.

It is customary to say that two regions are *separated* if and only if the intersection of either with the closure of the other is null. Thus, in the example just discussed, the regions A and B are separated: take the closure of either, and you pick up no points of the other. That is, no point or boundary point of either is a member of the other. Obviously, if two regions are separated, their intersection is null. But two regions with a null intersection need not be separated. Thus the intersection of A with the closure of B is null; yet A and the closure of B are not separated, for there are boundary points of A in the closure of B. Now, a region is said to be *disconnected* if and only if it is the union of two non-null separated regions; and a region is *connected* if and only if it is not disconnected. Thus, keeping to the same example, $A \cup B$ is disconnected. In contrast, the interior of the closure of $A \cup B$ is connected, for there do not exist two non-null separated regions of which it is the union. It is a connected open domain. But it is by no means the case that all open domains are connected. Consider, for example, two open spheres that touch at a single point. The closure of either intersected with the other is null, and the two are therefore separated. Hence their union is disconnected. But it is an open domain: none of its boundary points is inner, even the point of contact. Or consider two open spheres situated at some distance from each other. Their union is evidently a disconnected open domain.

Connected open domains, as long as they are non-null, presumably present no problems. Each is a receptacle. But disconnected open domains are

another matter. Are they receptacles? I shall defend the position that they are, though admittedly I have no conclusive argument.

Let us say that a material object is *scattered* just in case the region of space it occupies is disconnected. That there are scattered material objects seems to me beyond reasonable doubt. If natural scientists are to be taken at their word, all the familiar objects of everyday life are scattered. But I have in mind nothing so esoteric. Rather, it seems to me a matter of simple observation that among material objects some are scattered. Consider, for example, my copy of McTaggart's *The Nature of Existence*. There surely *is* such a thing; and it is a *material* thing, even a moderate-sized specimen of dry goods. After all, it is made of paper and certain other materials; it weighs roughly three and a quarter pounds; it is bound in a hard black cover; it occupies a certain region of space, into which it was recently moved; and so on. But it is scattered, for volume 1 is in Cambridge and volume 2 is in Boston. Each volume occupies, or at least to the ordinary eye appears to occupy, a connected open domain; but these regions are separated, and hence their union is disconnected. This example will bring to mind hosts of similar ones. Let me mention two others of a somewhat different kind. There is at the moment a pipe on my desk. Its stem has been removed, but it remains a pipe for all that; otherwise no pipe could survive a thorough cleaning. So at the moment the pipe occupies a disconnected region of space, a region which appears to common sense to be the disconnected open domain that is the union of the connected open domains occupied by the two parts. Consider, finally, some printed inscription: the token of 'existence' on the title page of my copy of McTaggart's *The Nature of Existence*, for example. Presumably it is a material object – a "mound of ink," as some say. But evidently it occupies a disconnected region of space.

If there are scattered objects, then some disconnected open domains are receptacles. It does not follow that all are. Still, once some have been admitted, it seems arbitrary to exclude any – just as it seems arbitrary to impose limits on the size or shape of receptacles. And it should be remembered that to call a region a receptacle is not to say that some object is in fact coincident or coextended with it, but only to say that this is not impossible. All this inclines me to identify receptacles with non-null open domains.[7]

An interesting question remains, however. To introduce it, let me mention an objection that is apt to be brought against the contention that my copy of *The Nature of Existence* is a scattered material object. Some will be inclined to say, with Leibniz, that my copy of *The Nature of Existence* is a "being by aggregation," not a "true unity."[8] Leibniz would not himself have taken this to imply that it is not a material object – only that it is not what he called an "individual substance." His notion of individual substance aside, however, some will still be inclined to say that my copy of *The Nature of Existence* is a mere 'plurality' or 'aggregate' or 'assemblage' of material objects and not properly speaking a single material object in its own right. It is no more correct, they will say, to suppose there is one thing composed or made up of my copy of volume 1 and my copy of volume 2 than to suppose there is one thing composed or made up of, say, the Eiffel Tower and Old North Church. We do speak of my copy of *The Nature of Existence* as if it were a single thing, and there is no parallel to this in the case of the Eiffel Tower and Old North Church. But it will be claimed that this is reflective merely of our special human interests, not of the metaphysical status of the entities involved. The two volumes are a mere assemblage, just as are the tower and the church.

The obscurity of the objection makes a direct response difficult. What exactly is meant by "a mere plurality or aggregate or assemblage"? And what sense is to be made of the claim that my copy of *The Nature of Existence* – or anything else, for that matter – is not 'one' thing? Furthermore, one wonders how far the objection is to be carried. The alleged defect in my copy of *The Nature of Existence* is surely not simply that the region occupied by volume 1 is at some distance from that occupied by volume 2. Even were the two volumes side by side, separated only by a plane, they would presumably still be said not to constitute or compose a single material object. The interior of the closure of the union of the region occupied by the one volume with that occupied by the other would be a receptacle, but an unoccupied one. But then why not argue, as Leibniz did, that *no* material thing is properly speaking *one* thing? Any connected open domain can be cut by a plane in such a way as to leave two open domains whose union is disconnected. Therefore, Leibniz reasoned, every corporeal object is in theory divisible, and what is in theory divisible is only a being by aggregation.[9]

In spite of its obscurity and the uncertainty of its extent of applicability, the objection brings to the surface a question of some interest. *Is* there a material object composed of the Eiffel Tower and Old North Church? In general, is it the case that for each non-null set of material objects there is a material object composed of the members of the set? The question needs sharper formulation, and for that some additional technical terminology is required.

A set *M* of material objects will be said to *cover* a region *A* if and only if *A* is included in the union of the receptacles occupied by members of *M*. If *A* simply is that union, then obviously *M* covers *A*. For example, the set the members of which are the Eiffel Tower and Old North Church covers the region which is the union of the receptacle occupied by the Eiffel Tower and the receptacle occupied by Old North Church. In particular, if *x* is any material object, the set having *x* as sole member covers the region occupied by *x*. Clearly, if *M* covers *A*, then *M* covers any region included in *A*. Hence a given region may be covered by more than one set. The region occupied by Old North Church, for example, is covered by the set having Old North Church as sole member and also by the set the members of which are the Eiffel Tower and Old North Church. If *M* covers *A*, then *A* is included in the interior of the closure of the union of the receptacles occupied by members of *M*. But notice that *M* may cover *A* and yet fail to cover the interior of the closure of *A*. Thus, although a set the members of which are two books situated side by side covers the union of the receptacles occupied by the books, it does not cover the interior of the closure of that union.

If and only if a set covers a region, the region itself will be said to be *covered*. It should be noticed that if each member of a collection of regions is covered, so is the union of the collection. Indeed, so is any region included in the union of the collection.

Given the notion of a covered region, a proposition I shall call the Covering Principle can be formulated: *If A is any non-null covered open region, there exists exactly one material object x such that the region occupied by x is the interior of the closure of A.* Our question is whether this principle, or more especially a certain consequence of it, is true.

A preliminary word of explanation. Given a non-null covered open region *A*, the Covering Principle guarantees that *A* is the region occupied by a unique material object if and only if *A* is the interior of its closure, that is, if and only if *A* is an open domain. This accords with our requirement that only open domains be counted receptacles. It is in fact easily shown that the Covering Principle runs no risk of violating that requirement; for the interior of the closure of any set is an open domain. But then, it may be asked, why limit the principle to non-null covered *open* regions? The answer is that otherwise there would be a conflict with the requirement that receptacles be non-null; for the interior of the closure of a non-open region may well be the null set.[10]

Notice now the power of the principle. To use a familiar and convenient metaphor, it provides for the generation by composition of new objects from old in somewhat the fashion of the Power Set Axiom in Set Theory. Given three objects in separated receptacles A, B, and C, there will exist four others. For if A, B and C are covered, so are each of $A \cup B$, $A \cup C$, $B \cup C$, and $A \cup B \cup C$; and if A, B, and C are separated, these unions are distinct from one another and from each of A, B, and C. In general, given a set M of n objects situated in pairwise separated receptacles, there will exist $2^n - (n + 1)$ further objects, each compounded of members of m. A dozen dollar bills in your wallet makes for 4,083 additional objects in your wallet – none of them dollar bills, however. And this is by no means the end. For the Covering Principle provides for generation of objects by division as well as by composition. Let A be a covered receptacle, and for purposes of simplification suppose it connected. Then A is the interior of the closure of the union of two connected and separated receptacles B and C, so situated that B lies on one side of a plane that intersects A while C lies on the other. Clearly, the same is in turn true of B and C, and of the receptacles into which they are thus divided, and so on without end. So there corresponds to A an infinity of connected and pairwise separated receptacles each of which is covered. The Covering Principle provides that each of these receptacles is the region of space occupied by a unique material object. Now, it is easily seen that if any region is covered, at least one connected receptacle is covered. Hence, by the Covering Principle, if there is one material object, there are infinitely many.[11]

Our present concern is less with division than composition. It will therefore be of use to extract from the Covering Principle an appropriately weaker principle, one directed squarely at the issue of scattered objects. First a definition. A material object x will be said to *fuse* a set M of material objects just in case the receptacle occupied by x meets two conditions: (i) it includes the receptacles occupied by members of M, and (ii) it

is included in every receptacle that includes the receptacles occupied by members of M. More simply, x fuses M if and only if the region occupied by x is the smallest receptacle that includes the receptacles occupied by members of M. In the case of any collection of receptacles, there is always a smallest receptacle that includes each member of the collection – namely, the interior of the closure of the union of the collection. So we might as well have said: x fuses M if and only if the region occupied by x is precisely the interior of the closure of the union of the receptacles occupied by members of M. My copy of *The Nature of Existence*, for example, fuses the set whose members are my copy of volume 1 and my copy of volume 2; and the object, if such there be, composed of the Eiffel Tower and Old North Church fuses the set whose members are the Eiffel Tower and Old North Church. Notice that any material object fuses the set having that object as sole member. And notice also a sort of transitivity: if x fuses a set the members of which in turn fuse other sets, x fuses the union of those other sets.

Can distinct objects fuse the same set? Not if the Covering Principle is true. If x and y fuse M, the receptacle occupied by x is the very same as that occupied by y; and the Covering Principle tells us that no receptacle is the region occupied by more than one object. Can there be a non-null set of material objects which no material object fuses? Again, not if the Covering Principle is true. For the union of the receptacles occupied by members of the set is a covered non-null open region the interior of the closure of which is the smallest receptacle that includes the receptacles occupied by members of the set. Thus the Covering Principle entails what I shall call the Fusion Principle: *If M is any non-null set of material objects, there is exactly one material object x such that x fuses M.* According to this principle, each non-null set of material objects has a unique *fusion*: a material object so situated that its receptacle is the interior of the closure of the union of the receptacles occupied by members of the set. If the Fusion Principle is true, there really is a material object – exactly one, in fact – composed of the Eiffel Tower and Old North Church. It is composed of them in the sense that the region it covers is the union of the regions they cover.

I have taken the word 'fusion' from the exposition given by Leonard and Goodman of the so-called calculus of individuals.[12] And it may be instructive at this point to digress briefly from our main concerns in order to make contact with the principal ideas of that calculus.

Let E be a non-empty set, and let R be a relation that is reflexive in E, antisymmetric in E, and transitive in E. (We are to think of R as a part–whole relation among elements of E, though of course that plays no role in the abstract development.) Two elements of E are said to *overlap* just in case they have a part in common; that is, if x and y are in E, x overlaps y if and only if some element of E bears R to both x and y. Now, the ordered pair (R, E) is a *mereology* just in case two further conditions are satisfied: (i) if x and y are members of E such that every member of E that overlaps x also overlaps y, then x is part of y; (ii) there exists a function f from the collection of non-empty subsets of E into E such that, for each non-empty subset A of E, a member of E overlaps $f(A)$ if and only if it overlaps some member of A.[13] As thus defined, mereologies are natural models of the Leonard–Goodman calculus.

Examples of mereologies are readily available. In fact, if B is the set of non-zero elements of a complete Boolean algebra and R is the inclusion relation among elements of B, (B, R) is a mereology in which the Boolean join plays the part of the mereological function f.[14] More pertinent examples are provided by the following small theorem:

Let N be a non-empty family of non-empty open domains of a topological space. And suppose N is such that (i) the interior of the closure of the union of each non-empty subset of N is itself in N; (ii) if A and B are members of N such that $A - B$ is non-empty, then the interior of the closure of $A - B$ is in N. Then $(N, \subseteq)$ is a mereology with respect to which the mereological function f is the function that assigns to each non-empty subset of N the interior of the closure of its union.

Notice that the theorem holds for any topological space – that is, for any space defined simply via a specification of the subsets that are to count as open, where the notion of an open set is subject only to the usual condition that among the open sets are to be found all unions of collections of open sets and all intersections of finite collections of open sets. Of greater interest for our purposes is the following corollary. Assume the Covering Principle; and assume that each material object occupies a unique receptacle, where receptacles are non-empty open domains of a topological space.

Let M be a non-empty set of material objects that satisfies two closure conditions: (i) the fusion of each non-empty subset of M is itself in M; (ii) if x and y are elements of M such that the receptacle of x minus the receptacle of y is non-empty, then the material object that occupies the interior of the closure of the receptacle of x minus the receptacle of y is in M. (Note that the existence of this object is a consequence of the Covering Principle.) Then, if P is the relation that an element x of M bears to an element y of M just in case the receptacle of x is included in the receptacle of y, (M, P) is a mereology with respect to which the mereological function f is the function that assigns to each non-empty subset of M its fusion.

So much for connections with the calculus of individuals. Let us return to our main themes.

As already noticed, every material object is the fusion of at least one set: namely, the set having that object as sole member. Commonly, an object will be the fusion of others sets as well. A scattered object, for example, will be the fusion of the set having itself as sole member; but it will also be the fusion of the set of those objects that occupy maximal connected receptacles included in the receptacle of the scattered object. Indeed, if the Covering Principle is true, every object will be the fusion of endlessly many sets. The Covering Principle provides for fission as well as fusion, and what is obtained at any stage by fission is a set of which the original object is the fusion. Any given object occupies a receptacle; and covered receptacles are, as we have seen, endlessly divisible into further covered receptacles. The given object will be the fusion of the set of objects occupying the subreceptacles obtained at any stage of the division – provided, of course, the division is exhaustive, in the sense that the receptacle occupied by the object is the interior of the closure of the union of those subreceptacles. To think of an object in this way will seem more or less natural depending on our willingness to count as genuine the alleged occupants of the various subreceptacles. Two halves of an intact baseball will perhaps seem material objects only in some contrived sense, and the baseball itself will then not naturally be thought of as the fusion of a set the members of which are the two halves. Similarly with bottles, doughnuts, and sheets of paper. But it is otherwise with automobiles, books of matches, and salami sandwiches. In these cases we take rather easily to the idea that the object is the fusion of a set of other objects – not just any set of alleged objects yielded by the Covering Principle, of course, but a set consisting of what are in the natural way thought of as parts of the object.

To become quite specific, consider some particular book of matches, and for ease of reference call it 'Charlie'. It is altogether natural to think of Charlie as consisting of twenty matches, a paper base to which they are attached, a surrounding paper cover, and an appropriately placed metal staple. That is to say, Charlie is quite naturally thought of as the fusion of the set that has these various objects as members. Thus, calling the set in question 'A', we are inclined to assert

(1) Charlie $=$ the fusion of A.

Of course, we are not prepared to regard every set the members of which are twenty matches, a paper cover, and so on as having a book of matches as its fusion. The objects in the set must be properly put together. But the objects in A are properly put together. And the region of space Charlie occupies is the interior of the closure of the union of the receptacles occupied by members of A.

But now let us remove a single match from Charlie and place it some distance from him, while putting him back where he was – that is, putting him in a receptacle properly included in the receptacle he earlier occupied. Charlie, we should all agree, has undergone a change. He has lost a part, as material objects often do. He now consists of the various objects he consisted of before, save for the removed match. The receptacle he now occupies is the interior of the closure of the union of the receptacles occupied by members of $A - \{z\}$, where z is the match that has been removed. Just as we were earlier inclined to assert (1), so we are now inclined to assert

(2) Charlie $=$ the fusion of $(A - \{z\})$.

But we can hardly deny

(3) The fusion of $A \neq$ the fusion of $(A - \{z\})$.

And so we seem to be in violation of the principle that no one thing is identical with diverse things.

It will no doubt be suggested at once that the appearance of paradox is removed once time is properly taken into account. Charlie *was* identical with the fusion of A but is *now* identical with the fusion of $(A - \{z\})$; or, avoiding tensed verbs:

(4) At t, Charlie $=$ the fusion of A,

whereas

(5) At t', Charlie $=$ the fusion of $(A - \{z\})$,

where it is to be understood that t' is appropriately later than t. If it is pointed out that (3), (4), and (5) together entail

(6) At t', Charlie $\neq$ the fusion of A,

the response will be that this is no cause for alarm, since (4) and (6) are perfectly compatible.

But is it really possible for both (4) and (6) to be true? Their conjunction appears to imply that there is a certain object – namely, the fusion of A – with which Charlie is identical at t but not at t'. And this surely is impossible. It is impossible for Charlie to have been identical with one object, the fusion of A, and then to have become identical with another object, the fusion of $(A - \{z\})$. No object can be identical with something for a while and then become identical with something else. Once identical with one thing, never identical with another.[15]

It will be pointed out that the conjunction of (4) and (6) does not imply that there is an object with which Charlie is identical at t but not at t'. According to (4), Charlie has at t the property of being sole fuser of A; and according to (6), he lacks that property at t'. But this no more requires Charlie to have been temporarily identical with the fusion of A than the fact that Lyndon Johnson had and then lost the property of being president of the United States requires him to have been temporarily identical with a certain object with which Richard Nixon became identical. Thus (4) amounts to

(7) $(x)(x$ fuses A at t iff $x =$ Charlie$)$,

(5) amounts to

(8) $(x)(x$ fuses $(A - \{z\})$ at t' iff $x =$ Charlie$)$,

and (6) amounts to

(9) $\sim (x)(x$ fuses A at t' iff $x =$ Charlie$)$.

And it is evidently quite possible that all these should be true.

There is reason to doubt, however, whether this ends the matter. If the Fusion Principle is true, some object is the fusion of A at t', a certain scattered object we may call 'Harry'. Now why should we not say that Harry fused A at t? We have treated Charlie as a continuant, an object that endures for a period of time during which it undergoes change. It would seem only fair to treat Harry in the same way. Like Charlie, Harry underwent a certain change. He occupied a connected receptacle at t and a disconnected one at t'. Harry became a scattered object.

It would appear, then, that Harry has as good a claim to having been sole fuser of A at t as does Charlie. If (7) is true, so, it would appear, is

(10) $(x)(x$ fuses A at t iff $x =$ Harry$)$.

Now, from (7) and (10) it presumably follows that at t Charlie and Harry were identical. But they are not identical now. And so once more we seem to have on our hands a temporary identity.

And another is in the offing. For consider Sam, the object which at t occupied the receptacle now occupied by Charlie. Sam is right where he was at t. He has of course undergone a change: at t he and z were in contact, the boundaries of their receptacles intersected; and this is no longer the case. But his position has not changed. The receptacle he now occupies is the one he occupied at t – namely, the interior of the closure of the union of the receptacles occupied by members of $A - \{z\}$. In short, Sam is at t' the fusion of $(A - \{z\})$. Or, to adopt the preferred form,

(11) $(x)(x$ fuses $(A - \{z\})$ at t' iff $x =$ Sam$)$.

But from (8) and (11) it presumably follows that at t' Charlie and Sam are identical, which they certainly were not at t. Though now identical, Charlie and Sam were once diverse. Or so it seems.

How are these temporary identities to be avoided? Perhaps some will say that there really is no such object as Harry: Charlie exists and so does the removed match, but those two objects do not compose or make up a single scattered object. But if there are scattered objects at all – and I have urged that there are – why object to Harry? There would appear to be no difference in principle between Harry, on the one hand, and my copy of *The Nature of Existence*, on the other. It has to be conceded that there is no readily available response to a request to say what sort or kind of object Harry is. But it is not clear to me that this is indicative of anything more than a paucity of readily available schemes of classification, a paucity resulting from quite parochial concerns of human beings. It is not out of the

question that objects composed in the way Harry is should come to be of some interest; we should not then be at a loss to find an appropriate kind or sort.

Short of denying outright the existence of Harry, it might be contended that he begins to exist only at t', that he starts his career with Charlie's loss of z. This suggestion does have the merit of preserving the Fusion Principle while removing the necessity to puzzle over the apparent temporary identity of Charlie with Harry. But I see nothing else to be said for it. Bodies do from time to time become scattered. What reason is there to suppose this is not the situation with Harry? And in any case, what is to be done about Sam? There is no plausibility at all in an outright denial of his existence, and it seems obvious enough that his duration coincides with Charlie's. To deny the existence of Harry or to claim that he begins to exist only upon z's removal from Charlie simply leaves the problem of Sam untouched.

An alternative suggestion, one that not only preserves the Fusion Principle but also has the required generality, is that Charlie is really identical with Harry. On this view, Charlie fuses A at t and also at t'. He does not lose a part; he becomes scattered. As for Sam, well, once Charlie is thought of as scattered at t', we are free to think of Sam as fusing $A - \{z\}$ at t' without thereby implying a temporary identity of Sam with Charlie. There is simply no time at which Charlie and Sam occupy the same receptacle.

In spite of its neatness, I think this view will seem less than wholly satisfactory. We are all, I believe, inclined to think that after the removal of z Charlie survives as a nonscattered object. If asked to give his present location, we should indicate a certain connected receptacle, the one occupied by Sam. Perhaps our stake in Charlie's nonscattered persistence is not especially great, but it is there all the same; and certainly in other, analogous cases the view under discussion would seem quite unacceptable. If a branch falls from a tree, the tree does not thereby become scattered; and a human body does not become scattered upon loss of a bit of fingernail.

At this point some will despair of preserving the Fusion Principle. They will see no alternative to saying that Charlie and Harry, though distinct, nevertheless occupy the same receptacle at t and that Charlie and Sam, though again distinct objects, share a receptacle at t'. To take this position is to sacrifice the Fusion Principle by denying that exactly *one* thing fuses a given non-empty set of material objects. Both Charlie and Harry, according to this view, fuse A at t; neither has the property of being *sole* fuser of A at t. Similarly, neither Charlie nor Sam is sole fuser of $A - \{z\}$ at t'; for at t' Charlie and Sam are spatially coincident.

This view seems to me to put undue strain on one's metaphysical imagination. Locke wrote: "...never finding, nor conceiving it possible, that two things of the same kind should exist in the same place at the same time, we rightly conclude, that, whatever exists anywhere at any time, excludes all of the same kind, and is there itself alone."[16] Are not Charlie and Harry two things of some one appropriate kind? Notice, furthermore, that it is not that just *two* material objects will, on this view, occupy the same receptacle at the same time; for it takes only a little ingenuity to find material objects other than Charlie and Harry with an equal claim to occupancy of that receptacle at t. To give some indication of the procedure involved, let us remove a second match from Charlie, place it some distance from z and from Charlie, and again put Charlie back where he was. Charlie has lost another part. In thus putting Charlie back where he was while leaving the position of z unchanged, we have also put Harry back where *he* was; he now occupies a receptacle properly included in the receptacle he occupied at t'. Harry too has lost a part. As a result, he has lost the property, which he had at t', of being sole fuser of A. But something now has that property, a certain scattered object whose receptacle is the union of two receptacles: the one occupied by Harry and the one occupied by the second removed match. Let us call that object 'Bill'. Now, there is no more reason to suppose that Bill just now came into existence than there is to suppose that Harry came into existence at t'. Indeed, there is no reason to deny that there is a material object which occupied a connected receptacle at t, became somewhat scattered at t', and has just now had its degree of scatter

increased. Bill has as good a claim to occupancy of Charlie's receptacle at t as do Charlie and Harry. So, if Charlie and Harry shared a receptacle at t, they shared it with Bill.

If the Fusion Principle is to be retained, is there an alternative to acquiescence in the view that Charlie fails to survive in nonscattered form? I think there is. The view I have in mind involves recourse to what are sometimes called 'temporal parts' or 'stages' of objects. In the case at hand the suggestion would be that although Charlie and Harry are distinct objects, as is revealed by their divergent careers, a certain temporal part of Charlie is identical with a certain temporal part of Harry: Charlie's t-stage, as we might call it, is identical with Harry's t-stage. Similarly, although Charlie and Sam are distinct objects, Charlie's t'-stage is identical with Sam's t'-stage. No stage of Sam is identical with any stage of Harry, though it happens that each stage of Harry has some stage of Sam as a spatial part. What was loosely spoken of earlier as the fusion of A at t is now to be thought of as the fusion of the set of t-stages of members of A; and this object is simply Charlie's t-stage – that is, Harry's t-stage. Similarly, Harry's t'-stage is the fusion of the set of t'-stages of members of A; and Sam's t'-stage – that is, Charlie's t'-stage – is the fusion of the set of t'-stages of members of $A - \{z\}$. Charlie, Harry, and Sam thus come to be conceived as distinct four-dimensional objects, which happen on occasion to share a common temporal part.

Philosophers as divergent in their outlooks as McTaggart and Quine have found the doctrine of temporal parts congenial or even obviously true.[17] But there are others who exhibit something less than overwhelming enthusiasm for it.[18] To these latter I can say only that if they are drawn to the Fusion Principle and are at the same time reluctant to think that Charlie fails to survive in nonscattered form, they had better learn to live with temporal parts.

Notes

1 Thomas Hobbes, *De corpore*, 2. 8. 1.

2 Georg Cantor, "Ein Beitrag zur Mannigfaltigkeitslehre," *Journal für die reine und angewandte Mathematik* 84 (1878), pp. 242–58.

3 The phrase, though not the view, is J. L. Austin's. See *Sense and Sensibilia* (Oxford: Clarendon Press, 1962), p. 8.

4 René Descartes, *Principles of Philosophy*, pt 2, principle 15; trans. Elizabeth S. Haldane and G. R. T. Ross (Cambridge: Cambridge University Press, 1967).

5 K. Kuratowski, *Topology*, vol. 1 (New York: Academic Press, 1966), p. 75. A common alternative is 'regular open set'.

6 Compare Paul R. Halmos, *Lectures on Boolean Algebras* (Princeton, NJ: Van Nostrand, 1963), p. 14.

7 The identification of receptacles with non-null open domains was suggested to me by remarks made by Alfred Tarski in "Foundations of the geometry of solids," included in his *Logic, Semantics, and Metamathematics* (Oxford: Clarendon Press, 1956), pp. 24–9.

8 See, e.g., his letter to Arnauld, 30 Apr. 1687, in George R. Montgomery (trans) *Leibniz: Discourse on Metaphysics, Correspondence with Arnauld, and Monadology* (La Salle, Ill.: Open Court, 1945), esp. pp. 189–91.

9 "Every extended mass may be considered as a composite of two or of a thousand others, and the only extension there is, is that by contact. Consequently, we shall never find a body of which we can say that it is really one substance; it will always be an aggregate of several" (Leibniz, draft of the letter of 28 Nov.–8 Dec. 1686 to Arnauld, in Montgomery, *Leibniz*, pp. 149–57; the quotation is from pp. 154–5).

10 For instance, the interior of the closure of a region containing a single point. Any set the interior of the closure of which is null is called *nowhere dense*.

11 "The least corpuscle is actually subdivided *in infinitum* and contains a world of other creatures which would be wanting in the universe if that corpuscle was an atom, that is, a body of one entire piece without subdivision" (Leibniz, fourth letter to Clarke, in Leroy E. Loemaker (trans. and ed), *Leibniz: Philosophical Papers and Letters*, 2nd edn (Dordrecht: Reidel, 1970), pp. 687–91; the quotation is from p. 691).

12 Henry S. Leonard and Nelson Goodman, "The calculus of individuals and its uses," *Journal of Symbolic Logic* 5 (1940), pp. 45–55. I have not had access to the earlier expositions given by Lesniewski, for references to which see the bibliography in Eugene C. Luschei, *The Logical Systems of Lesniewski* (Amsterdam: North-Holland, 1962).

13 More economical characterizations are known. See, for instance, Tarski's "Foundations of the geometry of solids."

14 See Tarski, *Logic, Semantics, and Metamathematics*, p. 333n.

15 Compare David Wiggins, *Identity and Spatio-Temporal Continuity* (Oxford: Blackwell, 1967), p. 68.

16 John Locke, *Essay Concerning Human Understanding*, bk 2, ch. 27, sect. 1. And compare Aquinas: "nec est possibile, secundum naturam, duo corpora esse simul in eodem loco, qualiacumque corpora sint" (*Summa theologiae*, 1, q. 67, a. 2, *in corpore*.) See also Aristotle, *Physics*, 209a6.

17 See J. M. E. McTaggart, *The Nature of Existence*, vol. 1 (Cambridge: Cambridge University Press, 1921), p. 176; W. V. Quine, *From a Logical Point of View*, 2nd edn, rev. (New York: Harper and Row, 1963), pp. 65–79.

18 Thus C. D. Broad: "It is plainly contrary to common sense to say that the phases in the history of a thing are parts of the thing" (*Examination of McTaggart's Philosophy*, vol. 1 (Cambridge: Cambridge University Press, 1933), pp. 349–50).

24

Parthood and Identity Across Time

Judith Jarvis Thomson

Temporal parts have come in handy in a number of areas in philosophy.[1] Let us take a close look at one use to which some may be inclined to want to put them.

I

Suppose I own some Tinkertoys. I make a house out of them, finishing the task at 1:00. I put the house, which I shall call "H," on an otherwise empty shelf. Since H is the only Tinkertoy house now on the shelf, and since also the time now is 1:15, we may truly say

(1) H = the Tinkertoy house on the shelf at 1:15.

A Tinkertoy house is made of Tinkertoys. And surely a Tinkertoy house is made only of Tinkertoys: surely it has no additional ingredients, over and above the Tinkertoys it is made of. (Perhaps there is such an entity as "house-shape." Even if there is, it certainly is not literally part of any Tinkertoy house.)

It is an attractive idea that the logic of parthood is the Leonard–Goodman Calculus of Individuals,[2] which takes "$x \, \mathrm{D} \, y$" (read: x is discrete from y) as primitive, defines "$x < y$" (read: x is part of y) and "$x \, \mathrm{O} \, y$" (read: x overlaps y) as follows:

Originally published in *Journal of Philosophy* 80 (1983), pp. 201–20. Copyright © by Journal of Philosophy, Inc. Reprinted by permission of Columbia University.

$$x < y =_{\mathrm{df}} (z)(z \, \mathrm{D} \, y \supset z \, \mathrm{D} \, x)$$
$$x \, \mathrm{O} \, y =_{\mathrm{df}} (\exists z)(z < x \, \& \, z < y)$$

and contains the following distinctive axioms:

(CI$_1$) $(x = y) \equiv (x < y \, \& \, y < x)$ identity axiom

(CI$_2$) $(x \, \mathrm{O} \, y) \equiv -(x \, \mathrm{D} \, y)$ overlap axiom

(CI$_3$) $(\exists x)(x \in S) \supset (\exists y)(y \, \mathrm{Fu} \, S)$ fusion axiom

where "$x \, \mathrm{Fu} \, S$" (read: x fuses, S, or the Ss, or the members of S) is defined as follows:

$$x \, \mathrm{Fu} \, S =_{\mathrm{df}} (y)[y \mathrm{D} x \equiv (z)(z \in S \supset y \mathrm{D} z)]$$

(Another way in which we might have defined "x fu S" is this: x fuses S just in case a thing y is part of x if and only if every part of y overlaps a member of S.)

It is worth stressing that the fusion axiom says only that, if anything is a member of S, then there is a thing that fuses the Ss. What I shall call *the fusion principle*[3] says that if anything is a member of S, then there is a unique thing that fuses the Ss.

$$(\exists x)(x \in S) \supset (E!y)(y \, \mathrm{Fu} \, S) \quad \text{fusion principle}$$

Or, as we may put it: if anything is a member of S, then there is such a thing as *the fusion of* the Ss. The fusion principle is provable in the Calculus of Individuals.

I said it is an attractive idea that the logic of parthood is the Leonard–Goodman Calculus of

Individuals. If the axioms are true under their intended interpretation, then so is the fusion principle. There are Tinkertoys on the shelf at 1:15; so the fusion principle tells us that there is such a thing as the fusion of the Tinkertoys on the shelf at 1:15. I shall call it "W"; so we can say

(2) $W =$ the fusion of the Tinkertoys on the shelf at 1:15.

Surely a Tinkertoy house is made only of Tinkertoys. The Tinkertoys H is made of are the Tinkertoys on the shelf at 1:15. So it very naturally suggests itself that we should say

(3) $H = W$.

So far so good; no problem yet.

II

But we should take note of the fact that that fusion axiom makes some people feel nervous. Few, I think, feel nervous about the definitions or about the identity and overlap axioms, but many object to the idea that there is something that fuses (as it might be) the set whose members are all giraffes and all apples. They think the fusion axiom grossly overstrong.

But why? The fusion axiom does commit us to the existence of some pretty odd things, but, so far as I can see, their oddity is no objection to them.

Never mind: the problem I want to set before you arises even if we reject the fusion axiom.

For suppose you have some bits of wood in your hand now; doesn't it follow that there is such a thing as *the wood* in your hand now?

There are some Tinkertoys on the shelf at 1:15, and, since Tinkertoys are bits of wood, it seems right to say there therefore is such a thing as the wood on the shelf at 1:15. Let us call it "W'"; so we can say

(2') $W' =$ the wood on the shelf at 1:15.

Surely a Tinkertoy house is made only of Tinkertoys. The Tinkertoys H is made of are the Tinkertoys on the shelf at 1:15. The Tinkertoys on the shelf at 1:15 are themselves bits of wood. So it very naturally suggests itself that we should say

(3') $H = W'$.

If the fusion principle is true, then there is such a thing as the fusion of the Tinkertoys on the shelf at 1:15. I gave that thing the name "W". If there is such a thing as W, it seems plausible to suppose that W' is identical with it; i.e., it seems plausible to suppose that the wood on the shelf at 1:15 *is* the fusion of the Tinkertoys on the shelf at 1:15.

Even if the fusion principle is not true – in that the fusion axiom is overstrong – it seems plausible to suppose that there is such a thing as W, and that W' is identical with it; i.e., even if the fusion principle is not (in general) true, it seems plausible to suppose that there is such a thing as the fusion of the Tinkertoys on the shelf at 1:15, and that the wood on the shelf at 1:15 is identical with it.

But whether or not there is such a thing as W, it really does seem plausible to suppose that there is such a thing as W', the wood on the shelf at 1:15. *And* that the Tinkertoy house H is identical with it. That will suffice for generating the problem I want to set before you.

III

For let us give the name "alpha" to one of the sticks that help attach the roof of the house to its front wall. At 1:30, I remove alpha; I then replace alpha with a new stick, beta, and I throw alpha on the floor. Shortly thereafter, the time is 1:45. Is H still on the shelf at 1:45? That is, can we truly say

(4) H is on the shelf at 1:45?

Most of us are, I think, inclined to think we can: most of us are inclined to think that H survives replacement of alpha by beta and is still on the shelf at 1:45.

Now there is trouble. For the conjunction of (3') and (4) entails

(5') W' is on the shelf at 1:45,

which is not true, for W' is only partly on the shelf at 1:45 – the wood on the shelf at 1:15 is partly on the floor at 1:45, since alpha is on the floor at 1:45.

So also of course the conjunction of (3) and (4) entails

(5) W is on the shelf at 1:45,

which is also not true, even if there is such a thing as W. For W is only partly on the shelf at 1:45 – the fusion of the Tinkertoys on the shelf at 1:15 is partly on the floor at 1:45, since alpha is on the floor at 1:45.

What to do? Something has to give.

Well, we really must retain (4). Surely that *is* H on the shelf at 1:45. (This *is* the typewriter I bought five years ago, though I've had a key replaced.)

So it is the identity sentences (3) and (3′) which have to go. But it seemed intuitively right to say that a Tinkertoy house is made only of Tinkertoys. It was that intuition which led us to identify H first with W and then, anyway, with W′. There has got to be something right in that intuition; but what is the something right in it, if (3) and (3′) are not true? How *is* H related to W′ – and to W, if there is such a thing as W?

David Wiggins,[4] I think, would say that W, or anyway W′, *constitutes* H at 1:15, and that that is the most that can be retained of the intuition that a Tinkertoy house is made only of Tinkertoys. He may be right. But we cannot tell until we are made clearer than Wiggins makes us about just what it is for a thing x to constitute a thing y at a time t.

Richard Cartwright[5] draws attention to a solution that appeals to temporal parts. By hypothesis, H came into existence at 1:00, and alpha was removed from H at 1:30. H was in existence throughout that time; and suppose we allow ourselves to say that H therefore had a temporal part that came into existence at 1:00 and went out of existence at 1:30. If you like the fusion principle, you will think there is such a thing as W. It too was in existence throughout that time; and suppose we allow ourselves to conclude that it too had a temporal part that came into existence at 1:00 and went out of existence at 1:30. Let us call these entities, respectively, "H-from-1:00-to-1:30" and "W-from-1:00-to-1:30." Friends of temporal parts take it that the temporal parts of a thing are, literally, parts of it; so we should say

H-from-1:00-to-1:30 is part of H

and

W-from-1:00-to-1:30 is part of W.

A Tinkertoy house is made only of Tinkertoys. Throughout 1:00 to 1:30, H was made of the Tinkertoys that W fuses; so shouldn't we say

H-from-1:00-to-1:30 = W-from-1:00- to-1:30,

and thus that H and W share a part – that they literally overlap? Tinkertoy houses may be made of different Tinkertoys at different times, however; so don't we preserve as much as anyone could want of the spirit of "A Tinkertoy house is made only of Tinkertoys" if we say, quite generally, that, for every temporal part x of a Tinkertoy house, there is a Tinkertoy fusion y such that x is identical with, or at least overlaps, some temporal part of y?

Of course you may not think there is any such thing as W. Then you are cordially invited to rewrite the preceding paragraph, replacing "W" by "W′", and making the necessary changes elsewhere in it.

But what exactly *are* these putative entities H-from-1:00-to-1:30 and W-from-1:00-to-1:30? Friends of "temporal parts" do seem to be just a bit casual about the manner in which they explain their use of that term; and a number of people have, rightly, complained that we are owed something more careful in the way of an account of them than we are commonly given.

IV

There are a number of different ways of defining the expression "temporal part". I shall try to define it in such a way as to lend the greatest possible plausibility to the metaphysical theses commonly asserted by use of it.

What we are interested in here is physical objects and their parts. Could I have said, more briefly, that what we are interested in here is physical objects? That is, is *not* every part of a physical object itself a physical object? I should think so. But let us not assume this. (I shall come back to it below.) Let us take the variables "x", "y", etc. to range over physical objects and their parts. Then the first of the metaphysical theses that must be accommodated is this:

(M₁) If x is a temporal part of y, then x is part of y.

As I said, friends of temporal parts take it that the temporal parts of a thing are *literally* part of it.

Or at least I think they do. For all I know, there may be those who think that the temporal parts of a thing are not parts of it, but only parts of something else, perhaps of the thing's history. I shall ignore that idea. (In any case, it is not clear exactly how appeal to temporal parts is to help anyone see how

H is related to W and W' if their temporal parts are not among their parts.)

I should think that M_1 rules out taking the temporal parts of a physical object to be sets. Thus the temporal parts of my chair, for example, cannot be identified (as it might be) with the sets whose members are the chair and a time-point or time-stretch at or through which the chair exists, for I should think that no set is literally part of my chair.

What I suggest we do is attend to places as well as times. We have the idea that no two things can occupy the same place at the same time. Well, I hope that on reflection we shall conclude that that idea is false. But if two things occupy the same place at the same time, then don't they at least overlap? Don't they literally share a part? That at any rate is the root idea that generates the definitions I shall give.

It will be simplest if we can make a certain assumption: viz., that every physical object, and every part of every physical object, exactly occupies exactly one place at every time-point at which it exists. I mean to include among "places," of course, discontinuous places, since there are physical objects that occupy such places now – for example, my suit now occupies a discontinuous place, the jacket being on one hanger and the skirt on another.

On one way of construing "places", that is a strong, and presumably false, assumption. Suppose we take places to have "sharp boundaries." (Because they are sets of space-points? Because they are fusions of sets of space-points? No matter.) Common-or-garden physical objects presumably do not have sharp spatial boundaries. (What *exactly* are the spatial boundaries of my chair now?) But let us simply ignore the questions raised here. Let us take places to have sharp boundaries, and ignore the fact that making the assumption therefore involves spatial idealizing.

We are letting "x", "y", etc. range over physical objects and their parts. Let "P" range over places. Let t range over time-points, and "T" over times. I include time-stretches among the times. I also include time-points among the times, since many (most? all?) friends of temporal parts take it that physical objects have temporal parts that exist only at a time-point – i.e., that physical objects have temporal "slices" as well as temporal "chunks." (So the range of "t" is included in the range of "T".)

We go in two steps. Let us say, first,

x is a cross-sectional temporal part of $y = _{df}$
$(\exists T)$ [y and x exist through T & no part of x

exists outside T & (t) (t is in $T \supset (P)$ (y exactly occupies P at $t \supset x$ exactly occupies P at t))].

Consider again the Tinkertoy house H. It existed through the time-stretch 1:00 to 1:30. If there is an x such that x exists through that time-stretch and such that no part of x exists outside that time-stretch and such that, for all time-points in that time-stretch, if H exactly occupies a place, then x exactly occupies it too – *if* there is such an x, then this definition tells us that x is a cross-sectional temporal part of H. The definition does not tell us that there is such an x. The friends of temporal parts, of course, think there is; but telling us there is is the job, not of any definition, but of a second metaphysical thesis: viz.,

(M_2) (T) [y exists through $T \supset (\exists x)$ (x exists through T & no part of x exists outside T & (t) (t is in $T \supset (P)$ (y exactly occupies P at $t \supset x$ exactly occupies P at t))].

Consider again alpha, the stick that was in H until I removed it at 1:30. M_2 tells us that alpha had a cross-sectional temporal part that existed only from 1:00 to 1:30. Shouldn't all cross-sectional temporal parts of alpha which existed only during that time be temporal parts not merely of alpha, but also of H itself? Presumably they should; so let us say

x is a temporal part of $y = _{df}$
$(\exists T)$ [y and x exist through T & no part of x exists outside T & (t) (t is in $T \supset (P)$ (y exactly occupies P at $t \supset x$ exactly occupies P, or a place in P, at t))].

This definition tells us that cross-sectional temporal parts of alpha which exist only during 1:00 to 1:30 are temporal parts of alpha – and of H.

Nothing so far said ensures uniqueness. For example, nothing so far said ensures that, if H exists through 1:00 to 1:30, then there is *exactly one* x such that x exists through that time-stretch and such that no part of x exists outside that time-stretch and such that, for all time-points in that time-stretch, if H exactly occupies a place, then x exactly occupies it too. But shouldn't uniqueness be ensured? I think that friends of temporal parts would like it ensured; indeed, I think they accept a third metaphysical thesis: viz.,

(M_3) If x is part of y and y is part of x, then x is identical with y.[6]

Between them, M_1 and M_3 ensure the desired uniqueness. For suppose, for example, that x and x' both have that rather complicated relation to H which I just drew attention to. Then x and x' have it to each other. Then x and x' are cross-sectional temporal parts of each other and, hence, temporal parts of each other and, hence, by M_1, parts of each other. It follows, by M_3 that x is identical with x'.

M_3 is obviously a consequence of the identity axiom

$$(x = y) \equiv (x < y) \,\&\, (y < x)$$

of the Calculus of Individuals under its intended interpretation. Friends of temporal parts need not assent to all the axioms of that calculus: for all I know, some of them reject the fusion axiom as too strong. (So far as I can see, there is nothing in the metaphysic of temporal parts which commits its adherents to the existence of a thing that fuses the set whose members are all giraffes and all apples.) But I think they are all of them happy to assent to the identity axiom.

M_2 tells us that there is an x that is a cross-sectional temporal part of alpha lasting only from 1:00 to 1:05 and that there is a y that is a cross-sectional temporal part of H lasting only from 1:10 to 1:15; and the definition of "temporal part" tells us that both x and y are temporal parts of H. Does it follow that there is an entity that fuses x and y? I think that even those friends of temporal parts who think that the fusion axiom is not (in general) true would assent to

If x is a temporal part of z and y is a temporal part of z, then there is a z' that fuses the set whose members are x and y.

If this is true, then (in light of what precedes) they can say that there is exactly one such z' and that it is, itself, a temporal part of z. But I do not give this further metaphysical thesis a name, since I suppose it is just barely possible that some friend of temporal parts thinks that even *this* "fusion thesis" is too strong.

I have obviously been so using the expression "is part of" to stand for a reflexive relation: I have been throughout using it in such a way as to make it true to say that everything is part of itself. I think all friends of temporal parts use the expression "is a

temporal part of" in that way too – i.e., in such a way as to make their fourth and final metaphysical thesis

(M_4) x is a temporal part of x

true.

That looks at first glance like an uninteresting metaphysical thesis; so it pays us to take note of the fact that it is very strong indeed.

In the first place, with M_4 in hand we can now easily deduce that every physical object, and every part of every physical object, is the fusion of its temporal parts. But after all, that consequence is presumably just as it should be – the friends of temporal parts would welcome it.

In the second place, we should ask: do "times" have "sharp boundaries"? If so, something that is presumably false now follows. Consider a common-or-garden physical object – my chair, for example. M_4 tells us it is a temporal part of itself. The definition of "temporal part" tells us that this means there is a time T such that my chair exists through T and such that no part of my chair exists outside T, and so, in particular, such that my chair itself does not exist outside T. But is there? Is there a time-point t such that my chair was in existence at t and at no time before t? Or a time-point t such that my chair was not in existence at or before t, but was in existence at times as close after t as you like? I should think not: I should think there is no such thing as the *exact* temporal boundary of a chair.

Well, temporal idealizing is presumably no worse than spatial idealizing, and those who are still reading are already engaging in the latter activity – see p. 304 above.

The third consequence is far more serious. M_4 tells us that my chair is a temporal part of itself, and this means there is a time T such that my chair exists through T and such that no part of my chair exists outside T, and so, in particular, such that my chair exists through and only through T and no part of it exists before T. Now my chair was made out of wood: four wooden legs, a wooden seat, and a wooden back were screwed together to make that chair. So the legs, seat, and back existed before the chair existed; so neither the legs, seat, nor back of the chair are parts of the chair. What an absurd result to have arrived at!

"No doubt it sounds odd," says the friend of temporal parts with a sigh. "But it can be lived with. For keep this in mind: if the legs, seat, and back of the chair are not themselves parts of the chair, they do at all events overlap the chair – since they have temporal parts that are temporal parts of the chair."

And perhaps the friend of temporal parts doesn't even sigh. A Tinkertoy house is made only of Tinkertoys; and isn't a chair made only of bits of wood, metal, cloth, etc.? And how is this intuition to be more tidily accommodated than by saying that every temporal part of a chair overlaps a temporal part of one or other of the bits of wood, metal, cloth, etc. of which it is made – and that the chair itself just is the fusion of its temporal parts?

More precisely: by saying that every temporal part of a chair overlaps a temporal part of one or other of the bits of wood, etc., of which the chair is at some time or other made. A Tinkertoy house is made only of Tinkertoys, but it may be made of different Tinkertoys at different times – remember the replacement of beta for alpha in H. Similarly, a chair may be made of different bits of wood, etc. at different times. How better to capture what goes on when a chair or house is made or when a bit of stuff is replaced in a chair or house, than by adoption of the metaphysic of temporal parts?

V

It seems to me a crazy metaphysic – obviously false. But it seems to me also that there is no such thing as a *proof* that it is false.[7]

Some people have the idea that it follows from this metaphysic that the world is static, that nothing changes, and that, that being false, the metaphysic must be false. But why should we think that this does follow? A thing changes if and only if it has a feature at an earlier time which it lacks at a later time. And a friend of temporal parts says that changes take place all the time, but that a thing does have a feature at an earlier time which it lacks at a later time if and only if earlier cross-sectional temporal parts of the thing have it and later cross-sectional temporal parts of the thing lack it.

Again, some people object to the fact that this metaphysic yields that more than one thing can occupy a given place at a given time – e.g., the cross-sectional temporal part of H which exists only from 1:00 to 1:30 occupies the very same place at 1:15 as H itself occupies at 1:15. But should we take this seriously? On reflection, it does not appear to be a conclusive objection. For after all, the metaphysic also yields that those two things,

though not identical, are not discrete – it yields that the former is part of the latter.

I have deliberately refrained from including among the metaphysical theses anything that says that the temporal parts of a thing are ontologically or epistemologically "prior" to it. These are dark notions; but I think we have *some* grip on what they are, enough perhaps to be able to construct a (more or less messy) argument to the effect that the temporal parts of a physical object are not ontologically or epistemologically prior to it. No matter. What concerns me now is not their priority, but their very existence.

Why should we accept this metaphysic? I am inclined to think that the friends of temporal parts are largely motivated by two things: one, the fact that so many problems in philosophy having to do with identity across time can be so tidily solved by appeal to them, and, two, what might be called "the spatial analogy." I shall come back to the first later; let us attend now to the second.

Suppose I have a piece of chalk in my hands now, one end in my right hand, the other in my left. It is a plausible idea that there is such a thing as the "right-hand half" of the bit of chalk. (No part of it is in my left hand.) If there is such a thing, we might as well call it "Alfred."

Friends of temporal parts say that, analogously, there is such a thing as the "later half" of the bit of chalk. (No part of it existed when the chalk first came into existence.) If there is such a thing, we might as well call it "Bert."

I think it is not merely plausible to think that there is such a thing as Alfred, but that we are under considerable pressure to say that there is. For I can break the bit of chalk in half. (Actually, it isn't easy to break a bit of chalk *exactly* in half, but I might be lucky.) If I do, I will have something in my right hand which is white, roughly cylindrical in shape, dusty, etc.; and it could hardly be said that that thing will come into existence at breaking-time – surely the thing does exist before I break it off (note that "it") off. And surely the thing does exist now, even if I never break it off.

There is no analogous pressure to say that there is such a thing as Bert. (Homework: try breaking a bit of chalk into its two temporal halves.)

Friends of temporal parts are quite unmoved by this difference. They say: No doubt there are differences, but why shouldn't we take lasting through time to be analogous with extending through space? Why shouldn't we say that, just as there is Alfred, so also there is Bert?

Let us look at the consequences for Bert of the idea that Bert is to be Alfred's temporal analogue.

Is Alfred a physical object? It would presumably be wrong to say that Alfred is a bit or piece or chunk of chalk. If I break Alfred off, Alfred will become a bit of chalk; but I have not in fact broken Alfred off. It is an interesting and not easily answerable question why Alfred is not now a bit of chalk. The point isn't that Alfred isn't independently movable, for you can glue two bits of wood together, which are then two bits of wood that are not independently movable. (Of course you could break off one of the bits of wood; but so could you break Alfred off.) And I think the point isn't that Alfred is continuous with more chalk; for if Alfred had been broken off and were now being held carefully in place again, it is arguable that Alfred would have been a bit of chalk continuous with another bit of chalk. No matter: as things stand, Alfred is not a bit or piece or chunk of chalk.

Something similar should presumably be said of Bert, viz., that it too is not a bit or piece or chunk of chalk. (For temporal parts come and go during a time in which I have only one bit of chalk in my hand.)

Now perhaps it may be thought that a thing is not a physical object unless it is a bit or piece or chunk of stuff of some kind. It would be no surprise if one who took this view thought that neither Alfred nor Bert is a physical object. It was to allow for the possibility that someone might take this view that I said we should take "x", "y", etc. to range not merely over physical objects, but also over anything that is part of a physical object.

What are Alfred and Bert then? Well, perhaps it will be said that they are quantities[8] of chalk. Or portions[9] of chalk. Which leaves it open for them to be perfectly respectable entities, with any number of ordinary physical properties. Thus Alfred presumably is white, roughly cylindrical in shape, and dusty; if the bit of chalk now weighs three ounces, then Alfred presumably now weighs an ounce and a half; and so on. And shouldn't we say, analogously, that Bert is white, roughly cylindrical in shape, and dusty? Perhaps by the time Bert comes into existence, the bit of chalk will weigh less than three ounces; but surely Bert will have some weight or other at every time at which it exists – just as Alfred does. If Alfred and Bert are not bits of chalk, and therefore not physical objects, they are anyway, both of them, surely *chalk*.

If Bert has not got these properties, then it is very obscure what Bert is, and hard to see why drawing our attention to Alfred should incline us to think there is such a thing as Bert.

I said this seems to me a crazy metaphysic. It seems to me that its full craziness comes out only when we take the spatial analogy seriously. The metaphysic yields that if I have had exactly one bit of chalk in my hand for the last hour, then there is something in my hand which is white, roughly cylindrical in shape, and dusty, something which also has a weight, something which is chalk, which was not in my hand three minutes ago, and indeed, such that no part of it was in my hand three minutes ago. As I hold the bit of chalk in my hand, new stuff, new chalk keeps constantly coming into existence *ex nihilo*. That strikes me as obviously false.

At a minimum, we ought to see whether there isn't some less extravagant way of solving the problem with which we began.

VI

What exactly is the problem? Whether or not there is such a thing as W (the fusion of the Tinkertoys on the shelf at 1:15), there is such a thing as W' (the wood on the shelf at 1:15). A Tinkertoy house is made only of Tinkertoys; that is an intuition we should like to preserve. Tinkertoys are bits of wood. So it seems right to say that the Tinkertoy house H is identical with W'. But at 1:30, I remove alpha from H, and then replace it with beta. H is on the shelf at 1:45, but W' is not then on the shelf, for alpha is on the floor at 1:45. So how *is* H related to W'?

I spoke earlier of alpha's having been "in H" until 1:30, when I removed it from H and replaced it with beta. I have been trying throughout (not without difficulty) to avoid speaking as common sense speaks. Common sense says: alpha was part of H, and then ceased to be; beta was not part of H, but became part of H.

It really is the most obvious common sense that a physical object can acquire and lose parts. Parthood surely is a three-place relation, among a pair of objects and a time. If you want to construe parthood as a two-place relation, you really will have to indulge in temporal parts to accommodate what common sense calls acquisition and loss of parts. But why should anyone want to?

If parthood is a three-place relation, then it is not possible to read the expression "$x < y$" of the Calculus of Individuals as: x is part of y. And it cannot be said that the logic of parthood is the Calculus of Individuals.

But we can easily construct a Cross-temporal Calculus of Individuals, by emending the Leonard–Goodman definitions and axioms. I think it pays us to do so.

Let us take as primitive "$x\,\mathrm{D}\,y\,@\,t$", and read it as: x is discrete from y at t.[10]

But we cannot move on just yet. For the intended interpretation of "$x\,\mathrm{D}\,y\,@\,t$" to be fixed, it has to be fixed for all threesomes of a pair of objects and a time-point which make "$x\,\mathrm{D}\,y\,@\,t$" true and which make it false. There is no difficulty if both objects exist at the time-point: your nose is now discrete from my nose, your nose is not now discrete from your face, and so on. But what if one or more of the objects does not exist at the time-point? Is Caesar's nose now discrete from your nose?

Looking ahead, we know that the intended interpretation of "$x\,\mathrm{D}\,y\,@\,t$" is to be such as to link it with parthood-at-a-time. For example, the threesome containing A, B, and 9 p.m. should make "$x\,\mathrm{D}\,y\,@\,t$" true if and only if A and B have no part in common at 9 p.m. More precisely; if and only if there is no z such that z is part of A at 9 p.m. and z is part of B at 9 p.m. Well, is there a z such that z is *now* part of Caesar's nose? After all, Caesar's nose does not exist now. I think it will seem right to say: if x does not exist at t, then there is no z such that z is part of x at t. (If my car goes out of existence at midnight tonight, nothing will be part of it tomorrow.) If we do adopt this view, we are committed to saying that there is no z that is now part of Caesar's nose and, therefore, no z that is now part of both Caesar's nose and your nose and, thus, that Caesar's nose is now discrete from your nose. More generally, adopting this view is adopting an existence principle expressible as follows:

x does not exist at $t \supset (y)(x\,\mathrm{D}\,y\,@\,t)$

first existence principle

I think it really does seem right to say these things – until it strikes us that it follows that not even Caesar's nose is now part of Caesar's nose and that Caesar's nose is now discrete even from itself. There is no entirely happy alternative in the offing here. We might weaken the first existence principle; e.g., we might choose to say, instead,

x does not exist at $t \supset (y)(x\,\mathrm{D}\,y\,@\,t \equiv y \neq x)$.

But this has its own unhappy consequence: viz., that a thing is atomic at all times at which it does not exist; and choosing it would impose complications elsewhere. So I suggest we accept the unhappy consequences of what I called the "first existence principle," and take it to control the intended interpretation of "$x\,\mathrm{D}\,y\,@\,t$".

We should surely say also that, if everything is now discrete from a thing, then that thing does not now exist – more generally, that

$(y)(x\,\mathrm{D}\,y\,@\,t) \supset x$ does not exist at t

second existence principle

The conjunction of the first and second existence principles is

x does not exist at $t \equiv (y)(x\,\mathrm{D}\,y\,@\,t)$

or, alternatively,

x exists at $t \equiv\, \sim (y)(x\,\mathrm{D}\,y\,@\,t)$.

So we may introduce "$x\,E\,@\,t$" (read: x exists at t) by definition as follows:

$x\,E\,@\,t =_{\mathrm{df}} \sim (y)(x\,\mathrm{D}\,y\,@\,t)$

"$x < y\,@\,t$" (read: x is part of y at t) and "$x\mathrm{O}y\,@\,t$" (read: x overlaps y at t) are now definable as follows:

$$x < y\,@\,t =_{\mathrm{df}} x\,E\,@\,t\ \&\ y\,E\,@\,t\ \&$$
$$(z)(z\,\mathrm{D}\,y\,@\,t \supset z\,\mathrm{D}\,x\,@\,t)$$
$$x\,\mathrm{O}\,y\,@\,t =_{\mathrm{df}} (\exists z)(z < x\,@\,t\ \&\ z < y\,@\,t)$$

The old overlap axiom is easy enough to emend: what we want is

(CCI$_2$) $(x\,\mathrm{O}\,y\,@\,t) \equiv\, \sim(x\,\mathrm{D}\,y\,@\,t)$

new overlap axiom

The old identity axiom is not so easily emended, however. That is, we obviously cannot replace it with

$(x = y) \equiv (x < y\,@\,t\ \&\ y < x\,@\,t)$,

for this tells us that, whatever time you choose, x is identical with y only if x is part of y at that time and y is part of x at that time and, thus (by the definition of "$x < y\,@\,t$"), only if x and y exist at that time. That is far too restrictive. Caesar's nose is surely identical with Caesar's nose, even if it does not exist now.

What we want is instead this: x is identical with y if and only if for all times t such that one or the other of them exists at t, x is part of y at t, and y is part of x at t – i.e.,

$$(\text{CCI}_1) \quad (x = y) \equiv (t)[(x\,\text{E}\,@\,t \ \vee\ y\,\text{E}\,@\,t) \supset$$
$$(x < y\,@\,t \ \& \ y < x\,@\,t)]$$

new identity axiom

A great many analogues of theorems of the Calculus of Individuals are now provable in the Cross-temporal Calculus of Individuals. It is perhaps just worth drawing attention to the fact that, although "$x < x$" is provable in the Calculus of Individuals, "$x < x\,@\,t$" is not provable in the Cross-temporal Calculus of Individuals. But it plainly ought not be; for what it tells us is that, whatever time you choose, x is part of itself at that time and thus (by the definition of "$x < y\,@\,t$") that everything exists all the time. What is provable in the Cross-temporal Calculus of Individuals is, instead, this:

$$x\,\text{E}\,@\,t \equiv x < x\,@\,t,$$

which says only that, whatever time you choose, x is part of itself at that time if and only if it exists at that time.

The old fusion axiom presents a different kind of problem. If things can have different parts at different times, then a thing can fuse one set at one time and a different set at a different time. Indeed, fusing has to be regarded as relativized to times, and I suggest we redefine it as follows:

$$x\,\text{Fu}\,S\,@\,t =_{\text{df}}$$
$$x\,\text{E}\,@\,t \ \& \ (y)[y\,\text{D}\,x\,@\,t \equiv (z)[(z \in S \ \& \ z\,\text{E}\,@\,t)$$
$$\supset t\,\text{D}\,z\,@\,t]]$$

One possible analogue of the old fusion axiom is, then, this:

$$(\text{CCI}_3)(\exists x)(x \in S \ \& \ x\,\text{E}\,@\,t) \supset (\exists y)(y\,\text{Fu}\,S\,@\,t).$$

But that is only one of the possibilities. It is, after all, rather weak. It allows us to say, for example, that there is something that fuses Caesar's nose in 44 BC and that there is something that fuses Nixon's nose in 1979; but it does not allow us to conclude that there is something that both fuses Caesar's nose in 44 BC and fuses Nixon's nose in

1979. Admirers of the Calculus of Individuals will surely want that there be such a thing and will, therefore, regard the axiom I set out as too weak to be regarded as the appropriate analogue of the old fusion axiom.

There are a number of available middle grounds, but I suspect that the truly devoted friends of fusions will want to go the whole distance. The simplest way of expressing their view is to take them to say that there is not one fusion axiom in the Cross-temporal Calculus of Individuals, but indefinitely many, the procedure for generating them being this. Take any set of n sets $S_1 \ldots S_n$. For $n = 1$, write what I earlier called (CCI_3). For $n = 2$, write

$$[t_1 \neq t_2 \ \& \ (\exists x)(x \in S_1 \ \& \ x\,\text{E}\,@\,t_1) \ \&$$
$$(\exists y)(y \in S_2 \ \& \ y\,\text{E}\,@\,t_2)] \supset (\exists z)(z\,\text{Fu}\,S_1\,@\,t_1$$
$$\& \ z\,\text{Fu}\,S_2\,@\,t_2)$$

and so on. For my own part, I have no objection – it seems to me that one has only to live with fusions for a while to come to love them. But I shall not argue for all or even any of these fusion axioms. I do not know what an argument for them would look like. By the same token, however, I do not know what an argument against them would look like, "What an odd entity!" not seeming to me to count as an argument. So I shall leave it open which fusion axiom or axioms should be regarded as replacing the old fusion axiom.

More precisely, I shall leave it open which fusion axiom or axioms should be regarded as replacing the old fusion axiom, so long as the axiom or axioms chosen do not guarantee the uniqueness of fusions. For we do not want an analogue of what I earlier called "the fusion principle" to be provable in the Cross-temporal Calculus of Individuals. The fusion principle, it will be remembered, says that, if anything is a member of S, then there is a unique thing that fuses the Ss. We do not want to have it provable that if anything is a member of S and exists at t, then there is a unique entity that fuses the Ss at t: we want, precisely, to leave open that there may be more than one. My reason for saying that issues from the use to which I would like to be able to put these notions. Consider again the Tinkertoy house H. A Tinkertoy house is made only of Tinkertoys; and H is, at 1:15, made only of the Tinkertoys on the shelf at 1:15. I would like, therefore, to be able to say that H fuses, at 1:15, the Tinkertoys on the shelf at 1:15. And what about

W', the wood on the shelf at 1:15? I would like to be able to say that that too fuses the Tinkertoys on the shelf at 1:15. But nothing can be true if it licenses our concluding from this that H is identical with W'.

With fusions now relativized to times, we cannot single out a thing to call "W" as I did in section I above:

(2) W = the fusion of the Tinkertoys on the shelf at 1:15

now lacks a sense, for there now is no fusing *simpliciter*, there is only fusing-at-a-time. And, without an analogue of the fusion principle, we cannot even single out a thing to call "W" by drawing attention to the fact that there is something that fuses, at 1:15, the Tinkertoys on the shelf at 1:15: i.e., we cannot replace (2) with

W = the unique thing that fuses, at 1:15, the Tinkertoys on the shelf at 1:15,

for there may be more than one thing that does this. Indeed, I suggest we agree that there are at least two things which do this, viz., H and W'.

Perhaps you have no taste for fusions, and regard the new fusion axioms (like the old one) as grossly overstrong. All the same, the difficulty we began with can be eliminated, and without appeal to temporal parts, if we say that parthood is a three-place relation[11] and that the new identity axiom (interpreted as I indicated) is true. How is H related to W'? We can say, quite simply, that

$$H < W' @ t \ \& \ W' < H @ t$$

is true for all times t between 1:00 and 1:30 (which was when alpha was removed from H); but that it is not true for any other times t. Since H and W' exist at times at which it is not true, H is not identical with W'.[12]

More generally, a Tinkertoy house is made only of Tinkertoys, and Tinkertoys are bits of wood; so, at every time throughout its life, a Tinkertoy house is part of, and contains as part, the wood it is made of at that time.

VII

There is a difficulty analogous to the one we began with, which I suggest we look at briefly.

Let us supply the Tinkertoy house H with a different history. Suppose H came into existence on a shelf at 1:00 and that all the Tinkertoys it was then made of, indeed, all the bits of wood, indeed, all of the stuff it was then made of, came into existence at 1:00 along with H. Suppose that the whole thing rested quietly on the shelf until 5:00, and then everything – house, bits of wood, stuff – all went out of existence together. Let W' be, as before, the wood on the shelf at 1:15. Now we can say more than that W' is part of H from 1:00 to 1:30, and H part of W' from 1:00 to 1:30: we can say that, for all times t such that either of them exists at t, W' and H are parts of each other at t. It follows, by the new identity axiom, that H is identical with W'.

Is that an acceptable conclusion? I am sure that there are those who will say it is not. For isn't it true of W', and false of H, that W' could have failed to have the form of a house? Can't wood come into existence in ship-shape as well as in house-shape? But houses can't.

But is that a possible history? Normally, a house that *is* made of Tinkertoys *was* made of Tinkertoys; i.e., normally, the Tinkertoys existed before the house did, and the house was then built out of them. Could a house, and the Tinkertoys it is made of, come into existence together?

Again, could some wood have come into existence *ex nihilo*? (Compare the temporal parts of the bit of chalk.)

Well, I was being unfair to those who think there is a problem in the offing here. Let us suppose I make a house, not out of Tinkertoys, but out of ice. I do so, not by fitting bits of ice together, but by pouring water into a house-shaped ice-tray, and freezing it. Four hours later, I melt the whole thing down, and throw out the water. Worries about temporal idealizing apart, we can say that the house and the ice it was made of came into existence (and went out of existence) together. And the ice didn't come into existence *ex nihilo* – it came into existence *ex aqua*. But surely (it will be said) the house is not identical with the ice. For the ice, but not the house, could have failed to have the form of a house. I could have poured that very same water into a ship-shaped ice-tray instead.

I don't myself find it obvious that a piece of house-shaped ice could have been a piece of ship-shaped ice; but my informants tell me it could have been. If they are right, we must give up the Cross-temporal Calculus of Individuals, because we must give up the new identity axiom.[13]

Suppose they are right. Then we must take the logic of parthood to be a modal logic, which might be called the Modal Cross-temporal Calculus of Individuals.

I shall not construct such a logic, since I think it does not pay to rehearse the alternative possible replacements for the fusion axiom or axioms. What matters for present purposes, in any case, is really only what should be said about identity. It seems to me, however, that that is plain enough: we should replace CCI$_1$ with:

$$(\text{MCCI}')(x = y) \equiv \Box(t)[(x\,\text{E}\,@\,t \vee y\,\text{E}\,@\,t) \supset$$
$$(x < y\,@\,t \,\&\, y < x\,@\,t)]$$

That eliminates the difficulty. Let "House" be the name of the house, and "Ice" be the name of the ice

it is made of. Then (if my informants are right) there is a world, and a time t in that world, such that

$$\text{Ice E}\,@\,t$$

is true, and (since House does not exist in that world)

$$\text{Ice} < \text{House}\,@\,t \,\&\, \text{House} < \text{Ice}\,@\,t$$

is false. That being so, MCCI$_1$ tells us that House is not identical with Ice.

But this is of interest only if my informants are right about this case, or would be right about a better case.

Notes

I am grateful to George Boolos, Paul Horwich, Fred Katz, and Sydney Shoemaker for comments on an earlier draft.

1 It is familiar enough that they have been used by those interested in the metaphysics of matter. But so also have they been used by those interested in philosophy of mind (cf., e.g., David Lewis, "Survival and identity," repr. in A. O. Rorty (ed.), *The Identities of Persons* (Berkeley: University of California Press, 1976)), and even by moral philosophers (cf., e.g., Allan Gibbard, "Natural property rights," *Nous* 10/1 (Mar. 1976), pp. 77–88, and the views of Jonathan Edwards on moral responsibility, described by Roderick Chisholm in Appendix A of his *Person and Object* (London: Allen & Unwin, 1976)).

2 Henry S. Leonard and Nelson Goodman, "The calculus of individuals and its uses," *Journal of Symbolic Logic* 5/2 (June 1940), pp. 45–55. For perspicuousness in the discussion to come, I have strengthened their identity axiom.

3 Following Richard Cartwright, in "Scattered objects," this volume, ch. 23.

4 David Wiggins, *Sameness and Substance* (Cambridge, Mass.: Harvard University Press, 1980), pp. 30ff.

5 Cartwright, "Scattered objects," this volume, ch. 23.

6 But see section VII, n. 13 in particular.

7 But see section VII, n. 13 in particular.

8 In the sense singled out by Helen Morris Cartwright, in "Quantities," *Philosophical Review*, 79/1 (Jan. 1970), pp. 25–42.

9 Following Allan Gibbard, in "Contingent Identity," this volume, ch. 9.

10 The variables of the Calculus of Individuals range only over existing entities. In the same spirit, the variables "x", "y", etc. of the Cross-temporal Calculus of Individuals are to range only over entities that exist at some time or other.

11 Unlike physical objects, events really do have temporal parts (though the term must be defined differently for events); hence there is no need to use tenses in ascribing parthood relations to events. We can take events to be a model of the Cross-temporal Calculus of Individuals (reading x E $@\,t$ as: x is occurring at t). But the event-identities so obtained would be the same as those I obtained (in *Acts and Other Events* (Ithaca, NY: Cornell University Press, 1977) by taking events to be a model of the simpler Calculus of Individuals.

12 David Wiggins would say that W' *constitutes H* at 1:15 – see p. 303 above. I said: fine, but what is it for a thing x to constitute a thing y at a time t? I have no great confidence in the likelihood of his accepting the gift, but I offer him the following:

$$x \text{ constitutes } y \text{ at } t =_{\text{df}} x < y\,@\,t \,\&\, y < x\,@\,t.$$

On this account of the matter, H constitutes W' at 1:15 if W' constitutes H at 1:15; but that strikes me as harmless.

13 If my informants are right, then the friends of temporal parts must give up metaphysical thesis M$_j$ and, therefore, the old identity axiom and, therefore, the Calculus of Individuals. They can still construe parthood as a two-place relation; but they must take identity to be governed, instead, by

$$(x = y) \equiv \Box[(x < y) \,\&\, (y < x)]$$

25

Temporal Parts of Four-Dimensional Objects

Mark Heller

1   The General Camp

The ontology of physical objects I will defend in
this work is that of four-dimensional hunks of
matter. Some of these hunks are temporal parts of
others. Thus, I place myself in the same general
camp as Willard Van Orman Quine, John Perry,
and David Lewis.[1] Lewis mentions a common
objection to such an ontology, and begins to answer
it:

> Some would protest that they do not know what
> I mean by 'more or less momentary person-
> stages, or time-slices of continuant persons, or
> persons-at-times.' ... [This] objection is easy to
> answer, especially in the case where the stages
> are less momentary rather than more. Let me
> consider that case only, though I think that
> instantaneous stages also are unproblematic; I
> do not really need them. A person-stage is a
> physical object, just as a person is. (If persons
> had a ghostly part as well, so would person-
> stages.) It does many of the same things that a
> person does: it talks and walks and thinks, it has
> beliefs and desires, it has a size and shape and
> location. It even has a temporal duration. But
> only a brief one, for it does not last long. (We
> can pass over the question how long it can last
> before it is a segment rather than a stage, for

that question raises no objection of principle.) It
begins to exist abruptly, and it abruptly ceases
to exist soon after. Hence a stage cannot do
everything that a person can do, for it cannot
do those things that a person does over a longish
interval.[2]

In spite of its insightfulness, this brief response
may not be completely satisfactory to those who do
not already understand the notion of a person-
stage. The primary goal of this chapter is to
develop a clear account of the nature of temporal
parts. (Notice that temporal parts, unlike Lewis's
stages, are not vague.) Once this account is developed, I will attempt to answer some criticisms of an
ontology that includes temporal parts.

The confusion over the nature of temporal parts
is increased by the fact that such phrases as 'temporal part', 'temporal phase', and 'temporal slice'
have been used in ways that suggest such varied
purported objects as processes, events, ways things
are, sets, and portions of careers or histories. Judith
Jarvis Thomson, not herself a friend of temporal
parts, makes a reasonable attempt to get clear about
the notion.[3] (In the following read '$\leq$' as 'is earlier
than or simultaneous with', and read '$\geq$' as 'is later
than or simultaneous with'.) Consider an object O
which exists from time t_0 to t_3. On Thomson's
account, a temporal part of O, call it P, is an object
that comes into existence at some time $t_1 \geq t_0$ and
goes out of existence at some time $t_2 \leq t_3$ and takes
up some portion of the space that O takes up for all
the time that P exists. (This might better have been
called a spatiotemporal part.)

Originally published in Mark Heller, *The Ontology of
Physical Objects* (Cambridge: Cambridge University
Press, 1990), ch. 1. Reprinted by permission of Cam-
bridge University Press.

2 Unpleasant Alternatives

As she begins to explain the inner workings of her notion of a temporal part, the existence of such objects begins to look implausible. The basic problem with Thomson's account is that it seems to be developed against the background of an unhelpful presupposition about the nature of physical objects. She seems to think of physical objects as being three-dimensional and enduring through time. I am prepared to admit from the outset that this is our normal philosophical way of thinking of physical objects.[4] But it is this way of thinking that makes temporal parts seem implausible. I see nothing in favor of it other than the fact that it is our standard view, and I put very little weight on this advantage.

Furthermore, the three-dimensional view of objects in general leads to having to choose between what I take to be unpleasant alternatives. The alternatives are:

(a) there is no such physical object as my body,
(b) there is no physical object in the space that we would typically say is now exactly occupied by all of me other than my left hand,
(c) no physical object can undergo a loss of parts,
(d) there can be distinct physical objects exactly occupying the same space at the same time,
(e) identity is not transitive.

To deny each of these alternatives and to accept three-dimensional enduring objects would lead to a contradiction. To show this I present a slightly altered version of an argument of Peter van Inwagen's.[5] If we deny alternative (a), then there is such an object as my body. Call it 'Body'. If we deny alternative (b), then there is an object that is all of me other than my left hand. Call that object 'Body-minus'. Now consider some time t at which my left hand is cut off. This does not affect Body-minus, so:

(1) the thing that, before t, is Body-minus = the thing that, after t, is Body-minus.

If we also deny alternative (c), then my losing my hand does not end my body's existence, so:

(2) the thing that, after t, is Body = the thing that, before t, is Body.

Further, if we deny (d), it *seems* to follow that:

(3) the thing that, after t, is Body-minus = the thing that, after t, is Body.

If we then deny (e), by transitivity of identity it follows that:

(4) the thing that, before t, is Body-minus = the thing that, before t, is Body.

But since Body was bigger before t than Body-minus was before t:

(5) the thing that, before t, is Body-minus $\neq$ the thing that, before t, is Body,

and (5) contradicts (4).

In the end, Thomson's preferred way of avoiding this contradiction is to accept (d).[6] In contrast, van Inwagen avoids the contradiction by accepting (b).[7] Roderick Chisholm instead accepts (c).[8] And Peter Geach seems to accept (e), or at least something that will have the same effect for this argument as accepting (e).[9] My way of avoiding the contradiction is to claim that (3) does not follow from the denial of (d) unless we accept the additional thesis that physical objects are three-dimensional and endure through time. I will deny this additional thesis. Doing so will allow me to claim that Body and Body-minus are distinct objects that, even after t, do not occupy the same space at the same time. It is incumbent upon me, then, to offer a reasonable alternative to the three-dimensional view of physical objects.

3 Four-Dimensional Objects

I propose that a physical object is not an enduring spatial hunk of matter, but is, rather, a spatiotemporal hunk of matter. Instead of thinking of matter as filling up regions of space, we should think of matter as filling up regions of space-time. A physical object is the material content of a region of space-time.

Just as such an object has spatial extent, it also has temporal extent – it extends along four dimensions, not just three. To see the contrast clearly, consider an object that is created at noon and destroyed at one. If we think of the object as three-dimensional and enduring through time, it would be appropriate to say that the object exists at different times; the same object exists at noon and at one. Such an object has boundaries along only three dimensions. The whole object is that hunk of matter that entirely fills up those boundaries. The whole object, therefore, exists at noon and still exists at one.

A four-dimensional object, on the other hand, has boundaries along an additional dimension. The whole object must fill up all of its boundaries and, therefore, does not exist at a single moment. If we accept that physical objects are four-dimensional, the appropriate thing to say about the object under consideration is that it takes up more than an instantaneous region of time. It does not exist *at* noon and *at* one; rather, it exists *from* noon *until* one. Thinking of it as an enduring three-dimensional object, we might still say that it exists from noon until one, but only because we would say that it exists *at* every time between noon and one. Instead of thinking of an object as existing at various times, we should, adopting the four-dimensional stance, think of it as existing within regions of time.

Insofar as time is just one more dimension, roughly alike in kind to the three spatial dimensions, we should expect that our claims about an object's spatial characteristics have analogues with respect to its temporal characteristics. For instance, just as we might talk about the distance between two points along a line in space, we can also talk about the distance between two points in time. This allows us to understand the notion of temporal boundaries as analogous to that of spatial boundaries. Furthermore, there is an analogy with respect to the part/whole relationship. Just as a spatial part fills up a subregion of the space occupied by the whole, a temporal part fills up a subregion of the time occupied by the whole.

Another important analogy is that, for both spatial and temporal parts, we can point at or perceive or name a whole by pointing at, perceiving, or indicating a part. When naming a person at birth, I might place my finger on that person's chest and say, "Let us call this Kaitlin" or "This is Kaitlin." In doing so, I did not name the piece of skin directly beneath my finger, nor did I name the chest, nor the surface of the baby. I named the whole person. It is an interesting question as to how this is done, but it is not one that must be taken up here. The point is that on the four-dimensional view there is an analogy. 'Kaitlin' does not name a temporally tiny four-dimensional object that exists for just the amount of time that I am pointing or for just as long as it takes for me to utter my naming sentence. I named the whole person.

It should be noted that an object's temporal characteristics are not completely analogous to its spatial characteristics. This is because time is not completely alike in kind to the three spatial dimensions. Time, for instance, seems to have a direction to it. Also, our perception along the temporal dimension is only one-directional (memory) and is discontinuous (I can remember things that happened on my third and fourth birthdays without remembering anything that happened between them). Furthermore, temporal units of measurement are not of the same kind as spatial units of measurement. These disanalogies will not have any significance for the present work.

One question about four-dimensional objects is whether it is possible to have zero extent along the temporal dimension – Can there be instantaneous objects? I do not have a strong opinion about this one way or the other. What should be noted is that this is no more an issue with respect to the temporal dimension than with any of the spatial dimensions – again we have an analogy. Could there be a physical object such as the surface of a cube? Thinking according to our standard three-dimensional picture, such an object would have zero extent along one of the spatial dimensions. It could, therefore, be called a two-dimensional object. According to our new four-dimensional picture, such an object would still have zero extent along one of the spatial dimensions. It could, therefore, be called a three-dimensional object, one of the three being the temporal dimension. I emphasize that, because a thing's parts are no more ontologically fundamental than the thing itself, existence of four-dimensional objects in no way depends upon their being built up out of instantaneous objects.

4 Refinements

I do not pretend to be in a position to evaluate scientific theses. The ontology I present should end up being consistent with any plausible story that the scientist might tell us about the inner workings of the world. If it turns out that matter just is space-time (perhaps any bit of space-time is matter, or perhaps only bits with a certain shape), then physical objects just are pieces of space-time. (I am prepared to set aside the question of how much the scientific proclamation is really based upon controversial philosophy.) Along these same lines, though for simplicity's sake I assume throughout this book that all nonrelational properties of an object are a function of the configuration of that object's parts, I am prepared to revise my claims if scientists should determine that there really are irreducible properties (for instance, the flavor of a quark may be such a property).

In saying that a physical object is the material content of a region of space-time, I do not mean to suppose that there are any empty regions. Nor do I mean to suppose the opposite. My point is simply that if there are any regions that do not contain matter, then they do not contain any physical objects. What of a region that is empty in parts and full in other parts? Such a region can be divided into two subregions (perhaps they are scattered subregions), the one that is full and the one that is empty. If the full one is the right shape (perhaps every shape is right, perhaps not), then it contains an object, and, therefore, so does the original region that is partly full. The empty subregion does not contain an object nor any part of an object. So, for instance, if there really is empty space between the parts of an atom, then atoms are really scattered objects, since the region of space that an atom exactly fills at any given time is not connected. Similarly, those everyday objects around us that are composed of atoms are also, on the present hypothesis, scattered objects; the region that a given object exactly fills (the region that contains that object, no other matter, and no empty space) is really a lot smaller than we had thought.

It is not part of my account of the nature of four-dimensional objects to suppose that such an object must stand out from its surroundings in some significant way. Nor is it part of my account to suppose the opposite. The notion of four-dimensional objects can be understood without answering the question of which filled regions of space-time contain such objects. In particular, we do not have to answer such questions as whether a statue can exist inside a boulder, just waiting to be carved out. I would in fact argue that for *every* filled region there is one object that exactly fills it.[10] But this should not be built into the very concept of a four-dimensional object.

The claim that every filled region of spacetime is exactly filled by a physical object presupposes a clear distinction between those regions that are full and those that are not. However, contemporary physics raises a problem for that supposition. Quantum mechanics seems to tell us that when we get down to a small enough level, there just is no fact of the matter as to where a given particle is,

and therefore, it would seem, no fact of the matter as to whether a certain region is full. (Again, I am prepared to set aside the question of how much of this scientific proclamation is really based upon controversial philosophy.) I am prepared to accept this little bit of imprecision into my ontology. I accept this imprecision, not because it is so small, but because it is the right thing to do. If there is real indeterminacy in the world, if there really is no fact of the matter as to whether a given region of space-time is full, then the world is really imprecise, and that must be reflected in the true ontology. This is a very different sort of imprecision from that which is involved in the vagueness of our everyday objects (as I will argue later); the imprecision here arises from the structure of the world, not just from our way of conceptualizing the world.

But there are other ways to raise doubts about my assumption that for every region there is a determinate fact as to whether that region is exactly filled. If matter is just space-time of a certain shape, so that not all space-time counts as matter, then 'filled' is, in effect, a shape predicate. As such, it may very well be vague. There may be no precise line between those shapes that count as a region's being full and those that count as the region's not being full. It could be that certain regions are shaped in such a way that they neither count as full nor count as not full.

This proposal has the presupposition that matter is space-time. Thus, given what I have said above, the physical objects proposed by my theory are themselves regions of space-time. If it should turn out that 'filled' is a vague shape predicate, then I should revise my ontology by allowing every region of space-time to be a physical object, not just the filled regions. Perhaps I could not continue to call these objects *physical*, since some of the space-time regions included are clearly empty (they are not among the borderline cases of being empty), and it seems inappropriate to say that an empty region of space-time contains a physical object. (For a region of space-time to contain a physical object, on the present proposal, is just for it to be a physical object.) Instead I would be offering an ontology of spatiotemporal objects, to be distinguished, perhaps, from such purported nonspatiotemporal objects as mental entities and abstract entities.

But suppose that it turns out that 'filled' is a vague predicate even without equating matter with space-time. That is, suppose that it turns out that matter is distinct from the spatiotemporal regions that it fills, that it does not fill all regions, and that there are some regions for which, for reasons having nothing to do with quantum mechanics, there is no fact of the matter as to whether those regions are full or not. In this case expanding my ontology to include objects that are in clearly empty regions would seem very odd. Even an empty region would contain an object, and here "contains" is not just another word for "be". I could avoid the apparent oddness by simply stipulating that "contains" is another word for "be" in this context, stipulating that matter is space-time. But that is not the sort of thing that should be built into an ontology by stipulation. That is the sort of thing we should wait for science to rule upon.

I do not think I need to be forced into such a strange-sounding position. For a spatiotemporal region to be full, in the sense in which I am using that term, is just for it to contain no empty subregions. Because what it is for one spatiotemporal region to contain another is not in any way vague, 'full' is only as vague as 'empty'. And 'empty' seems to be a paradigm non-vague term. If a region can possibly contain less than it does in fact contain, then it is not empty. Thus the only way for 'empty' to be vague is for there to be cases in which it is indeterminate whether a given region can possibly contain less than it does. And it seems unlikely that there will be any way for this to be indeterminate other than the two that I have already discussed, or relatives of those two: the first being real physical indeterminacy as posited by quantum mechanics and the second being an indeterminacy due to the fact that the supposed filler (i.e., matter) is just space-time of a certain sort.

It should be noted that while I talk of matter as the ultimate filler, I would be prepared to accept that matter is itself composed of particles. The question of which is more basic (in the sense of which is composed of which), stuff or things, is one to be answered by scientists, not philosophers. Perhaps matter is composed of particles that are themselves composed of matter that is itself composed of smaller particles, and on and on. Regardless of which proves to be the basic one, and even if the series continues *ad infinitum*, there should still be a determinate fact for any specified region whether that region could have less in it than it does (barring the two options for letting in indeterminacy that I discuss above).

It could turn out that every particle is itself composed of particles that are spread out in space-time. If this is the case, then any continuous region that is extended along all four dimensions will contain some empty space-time, and hence, there will be no full extended regions. The terms 'empty' and 'full' do not seem to be applicable to nonextended regions, but the supposition that all particles are composed of separated particles does seem to require a distinction between two kinds of points, a distinction that is analogous to that between 'full' and 'empty'. Using the terms in an expanded sense, then, we could say that some points are full, and, further, that some discontinuous regions of space-time are full. In the kind of world now being considered, four-dimensional physical objects turn out to be scattered in the extreme. The region exactly containing a physical object will be a collection of discrete points.

It is crucial for my overall project that the object of my ontology have precise boundaries; for any of the objects in my proposed ontology there is a unique and determinate region that that object exactly fills. Given my characterization of a four-dimensional object as the material content of a filled region of space-time, and given that there is a determinate fact as to which regions are full and which are not, four-dimensional objects can have the precision that I require. I do not deny, however, that there could be other ways of characterizing four-dimensional objects that do not imply their having precise boundaries. In principle, precise boundaries need be no more a part of the concept of a four-dimensional object than it is part of the concept of a three-dimensional object. However, I will build this precision into my concept of a four-dimensional object.[11]

Given the precision of four-dimensional objects and the apparent imprecision of the objects of our standard ontology, there are serious questions about the relationship between the two kinds of objects. For the remainder of this essay I will set aside any further discussion of imprecision and will pretend that either the boundaries of our standard objects are as precise as those of my four-dimensional objects or the boundaries of the four-dimensional objects are as imprecise as those of our standard objects.

5 Parts

A four-dimensional object is the material content of a filled region of space-time. A spatiotemporal part of such an object is the material content of a subregion of the space-time occupied by the whole. For instance, consider a particular object O and the region R of space-time that O fills. A spatiotemporal part of O is the material content of a subregion of R. A spatiotemporal part, as long as it has greater than zero extent along every dimension, is itself a four-dimensional physical object. A spatiotemporal part is not a set or a process or a way something is at a place and time. It, like the object it is part of, is a hunk of matter.

If Heller is a physical object, then so is Heller's-left-hand-from-(1:00 p.m, 3 January, 1990)-to-(1:01 p.m. 3 January, 1990). This spatiotemporal part of me could have, between 1:00 p.m. and 1:01 p.m. on 3 January, 1990, been felt, seen, heard, smelled, and, if need be, tasted. It had weight and volume. Thinking of spatiotemporal parts as physical objects corresponds to the way we ordinarily think of parts on our old three-dimensional picture. When not being swayed by specific philosophical arguments, we have no doubt that my hand is a physical object. Accepting the account of four-dimensional objects presented here, we may continue to hold the general principle that a part of a physical object is itself a physical object.

The fact that any part of O is the material content of a subregion of R does not entail that every filled subregion of R contains a part of O. This point directly parallels the fact that it is not part of the concept of a four-dimensional object that every filled region contains such an object. One could consistently accept all three of the following:

(i)   there are four-dimensional objects and spatiotemporal parts of such objects,

(ii) not every filled region of space-time contains a physical object,

(iii) even for a region of space-time that does contain a physical object, not every subregion contains a spatiotemporal part of that object.

I take it that typically someone who accepts all three of these would be accepting (iii) for the same reasons that he accepts (ii). Someone might accept (ii) if he thought that there is good reason to reject scattered objects. Or (ii) might be accepted if independent grounds could be found for some claim like 'every object must contain its principle of unity within itself' (whatever that might mean). My immediate goal is not to supply a means for answering every question of the form 'Is there a spatiotemporal part here?', but rather to make clear the concept of spatiotemporal parthood.

It is now easy to understand the notion of a temporal part. Any proper part of a four-dimensional object is smaller than the whole object along at least one dimension. A proper temporal part is smaller along just one dimension, the temporal dimension. A temporal part of O is a spatiotemporal part that is the same spatial size as O for as long as that part exists, though it may be a smaller temporal size. Let us suppose that object O exactly fills the temporal region from t_0 to t_3. That is, the region of space-time filled by O, namely region R, has the temporal boundaries t_0 and t_3. Now consider a certain subregion of R the temporal boundaries of which are $t_1 \geq t_0$ and $t_2 \leq t_3$ and the spatial boundaries of which are just the spatial boundaries of R from t_1 to t_2 Call this subregion S. If the material content of S is an object, then it is a temporal part of O. In general, using the single letters as variables rather than names, a temporal part of O is the material content of a temporal subregion of R. 'Temporal subregion of R' means spatiotemporal subregion that shares all of R's spatial boundaries within that subregion's temporal boundaries. A temporal part of me which exists from my fifth birthday to my sixth is the same spatial size that I am from age five to age six.

6   Strictly Speaking

One matter of detail that is particularly important for temporal parts specifically and four-dimensional objects in general is how to understand such phrases as '— exists in region—' or '— exists at time —'. Physical objects are four-dimensional hunks of matter. They therefore have precise spatiotemporal boundaries. Consider a particular physical object, this piece of paper (assuming that this piece of paper does have precise boundaries). Call this object 'Whitey'. Whitey has certain spatiotemporal boundaries – there is a region that it exactly occupies. But we also think it is true to say that Whitey now exists. This way of talking may be misleading. If Whitey exists now and existed a minute ago, then it is the same object that exists at both times. But this suggests the old three-dimensional picture that we have been denying.

This confusion is easily avoided. When we say that Whitey exists now, this should be taken as a loose way of saying that part of Whitey exists now. If we meant strictly that Whitey exists now, we would be saying something false. Whitey names the whole piece of paper, and that object does not exist now. Strictly speaking, Whitey is temporally too large to exist now.[12] Here, then, is the major difference between the three-dimensional and four-dimensional viewpoints. On the three-dimensional picture, if we said that Whitey exists now and really meant it, we would be saying something true. It is Whitey that exists at different times. On the other hand, on the four-dimensional picture Whitey does not, strictly speaking, exist at different times. Whitey's parts exist at different times (different parts at different times), and in virtue of this fact, we say, in our loose way of speaking, that Whitey exists at those times.

This can be made clearer by considering a spatial analogy. Put Whitey mostly in a drawer, but leave a small corner sticking out. Now if asked where Whitey is, you will answer that it is in the drawer. Strictly speaking, however, your answer would be false. Even on the three-dimensional picture, part of Whitey is not in the drawer. But 'Whitey' names the whole piece of paper, so if it is not the whole piece in the drawer, then it is not Whitey in the drawer. We say that Whitey is in the drawer because a part of Whitey is in there. Notice also that with some rewording it can be seen that how large a portion of the paper is in the drawer is not crucial. If only a corner of the paper were inside, we would be less likely to say that Whitey is in the drawer when asked where Whitey is. But if asked 'Does Whitey exist inside that drawer?' I think that we would all say 'yes'.

Recognizing that we have this loose way of speaking even when using our three-dimensional picture, it is not surprising that we also have this loose way of speaking when using the four-dimensional picture. Recognizing that such a phrase as 'Whitey exists now' is just loose speaking, we see that, strictly speaking, Whitey only exists within the spatiotemporal region that it exactly fills and regions of which that one is a subregion. To loosely say that Whitey exists now is to strictly say that the present time is within Whitey's temporal boundaries. If there are instantaneous temporal parts, then this is equivalent to saying that Whitey has a temporal part that exists now.

7   Coincidence

One nice consequence of these considerations is that an object and a proper temporal part of that object do not, strictly speaking, exist in the same space at the same time. An object should not be coincident with any of its proper parts. Intuitively, the problem with coincident entities is that of over-crowding. There just is not enough room for them.

On the account provided above, an object and a proper spatiotemporal part of that object do not compete for room. There is a certain spatiotemporal region exactly occupied by the part; the whole object is not in that region. There is only as much of the object there as will fit – namely, the part. This intuitive understanding of the relationship between part and whole is what I intended to capture with my discussion of our loose way of speaking. When we say that Whitey is in the drawer, that is just a loose way of saying that part of Whitey is there. When we say that Whitey exists now, we are only saying that a part of Whitey exists now. Keeping this in mind allows us to avoid being committed to coincident entities.

Let us consider a spatial case. Even adopting a three-dimensional picture, we are not tempted to say that Heller and Heller's left hand are coincident entities. These are not two distinct entities in one place at one time. Strictly speaking, there is only one object in that hand-shaped region of space – my hand. Whatever truth there is in saying that I am in that region can be wholly captured by saying that a part of me is there. The relation between my hand and me is not that of coincidence, but, rather, that of part to whole. Similar points are relevant to cases of spatial overlap. My living room and my dining room share a common wall. But this does not entail that there is a wall-shaped region of space occupied by both my living room and my dining room. That region is occupied by the wall, and that wall happens to be part of both rooms.

If we adopt the four-dimensional view of physical objects, then similar remarks can be made about the relation between an object and its temporal parts. Heller is not coincident with Heller-during-1983. The only truth there is in saying that I occupy that year-long region of time is that I have a part that occupies that region. Strictly speaking, there is only one entity in the relevant spatiotemporal region – my 1983 part. Also, analogous to the case of spatial overlap, there may be cases of temporal overlap. If I were to undergo fission next year, that should not tempt us to say that prior to 1984 there were two objects in the same space at the same time.[13] Rather, we should say that two four-dimensional objects overlapped prior to 1984 – they shared a common temporal part.

Perhaps a less controversial case would be a hunk of gold that is shaped into a ring. The ring then undergoes a gradual replacement of matter until it is entirely composed of silver. Many would be tempted to say that the ring and the hunk of gold were, for a period of time, coincident entities. However, adopting the four-dimensional view, we can say that the gold and the ring temporally overlap. The gold has a ring-shaped temporal part, the ring has a golden temporal part, and the gold's part is identical with the ring's part. The relationship between the part of the one and the part of the other is identity, not coincidence. The relationship between the gold and the ring is that they share a common part; they overlap.[14] Similar considerations would allow an ontology of four-dimensional objects to avoid an attack based on the Ship of Theseus paradox.[15]

In contrast, trying to make sense of temporal parts without shifting to a four-dimensional picture would require a commitment to objectionable coincident entities. On Thomson's account, Heller and Heller-now are, in the strictest and most problematic sense, two distinct entities occupying the same space at the same time.[16] Heller is, at any given time between his birth and his death, complete. My existing now is not merely my having a part that exists now. Right now I exactly fill all of my three-dimensional boundaries. But that supposed temporal part of me, Heller-now, also exactly fills those same boundaries. Yet the two entities are distinct because I have a much longer career than Heller-now. Thomson cannot claim that strictly speaking I am temporally too big to be coincident with my instantaneous temporal part, because she avails herself of only three dimensions along which to measure. Along those dimensions I am now exactly the same size as Heller-now.

8 A Crazy Metaphysic

In fact, Thomson's problem of coincident entities is a symptom of a much deeper problem with trying to explain temporal parts without rejecting the old three-dimensional picture. Let us return to Whitey, the piece of paper. Even given my meaning hypothesis (according to which it is strictly false that Whitey is in the drawer), the old picture has the consequence that it is strictly true that Whitey exists now (because Whitey now fills the relevant boundaries along all three of the available dimensions). Since 'Whitey' names the whole piece of paper, we get the consequence that it is strictly true that the whole piece of paper exists now. If all of Whitey exists now, then Whitey has no parts that do not exist now. Even though Whitey will continue to exist for the next several hours, 'Whitey-

from-(now + one hour)-to-(now + two hours)' does not designate a part of Whitey unless that part exists now. But if there were such a temporal part, it would not yet have come into existence. So Whitey has no temporal parts other than the one that exists now. Indeed, it does not even have that temporal part, since Whitey – all of it – existed an hour ago, and the temporal part that supposedly exists now did not exist then. If one holds the three-dimensional view of physical objects, it is perfectly reasonable to think of an ontology including temporal parts as a 'crazy metaphysic.'[17]

Of course, this is not Thomson's reason for calling it a crazy metaphysic. She does not draw attention to the three-dimensional/four-dimensional distinction at all. Thomson writes:

> I said this seems to me a crazy metaphysic. It seems to me that its full craziness only comes out when we take the spatial analogy seriously. The metaphysic yields that if I have had exactly one bit of chalk in my hand for the last hour, then there is something in my hand which is white, roughly cylindrical in shape, and dusty, something which also has a weight, something which is chalk, which was not in my hand three minutes ago, and indeed, such that no part of it was in my hand three minutes ago. As I hold the bit of chalk in my hand, new stuff, new chalk keeps constantly coming into existence *ex nihilo*. That strikes me as obviously false.[18]

I suggest that this attack on temporal parts depends on accepting the thesis that physical objects are three-dimensional.

Why does Thomson think that temporal parts would come into existence *ex nihilo*? It is obviously not because nothing exists before the temporal part. It is not even because everything that exists before the temporal part continues to exist, for there are prior temporal parts that go out of existence at just the moment that the part in question comes into existence. It may simply be that none of the temporal part's parts exist before the temporal part does, but if that is all, then there is still the question of why this should be objectionable. I suggest that Thomson's objection is founded on the belief that there is no significant material change occurring at the time that the temporal part is supposed to be coming into existence. The piece of chalk does not undergo any alteration. No molecules need be altering their internal structure or their relationship to other molecules. No matter from outside the chalk is added, nor is any matter that was part of chalk released into the surrounding atmosphere. In short, nothing has occurred that would be enough to bring an object into existence. The temporal part just seems to pop into existence without any sufficient cause.

But this argument reflects an unwarranted prejudice in favor of the three-dimensional picture over the four-dimensional picture. If we accept a four-dimensional view of physical objects, then all it is for an object to come into existence at t_0 is for it to have t_0 as its lower temporal boundary. The question of what caused it to come into existence at t_0 is just the question of what causes it to have the lower temporal boundary that it does, and this question is no more or less answerable than the question of what causes a certain object to have the spatial boundaries it does. There seem to be only two reasonable interpretations of such a question: 'What causes those particular boundaries to be the boundaries of an object?' and 'What causes those boundaries to be filled?' Each of these questions is as answerable for temporal parts as for spatial parts.

Recall that it is not built into the concept of a temporal part that every region should contain such a part. Hence, there may be some explanation for why a given part comes into existence at the particular time that it does, an explanation for what causes those particular boundaries to be the boundaries of an object. For instance, we might think of a person as being one object from birth to death. Still there seems a natural division between the person's prepubescent part and postpubescent part. We can explain why the change from prepubescence to postpubescence should mark the beginning of a new object, because that change will have significant ramifications. The boundaries around the person's postpubescent part seem hardly less significant than the boundaries around the person's heart. Accepting the existence of these temporal parts does not commit us to the existence of a part for every subregion of the region the person exactly fills. A separate argument is required in order to get this rather more cluttered view of what parts there are. Such an argument would also provide an explanation for why the boundaries of each of the objects should be the boundaries of an object.

I suspect that much of the initial impression that temporal parts would have to come into existence *ex nihilo* is based on a picture of these physical objects popping into existence merely because of the passage of time. The phrase '*ex nihilo*' suggests a complete independence from previous events. The objects that I am defending do not just pop into existence. It is not as if there is empty space and then, poof, the space is filled. It is the causal mechanisms together with the material configuration of matter at any given time that affect which parts will exist at the next moment. (Whether this is a deterministic relationship is an independent question.) So, for any particular temporal part there is an answer to the question 'What causes its boundaries to be filled?', or at least as much of an answer as there is for spatial parts. The structure of the world at one moment does affect the structure of the world at the next moment.

9 In Favor of Temporal Parts

To support temporal parts and the four-dimensional view of physical objects, recall that earlier in this chapter I argued that thinking of objects as three-dimensional and enduring would commit us to one of the following five unpleasant alternatives:

(a) there is no such physical object as my body,
(b) there is no physical object in the space that we would typically say is now exactly occupied by all of me other than my left hand,
(c) no physical object can undergo a loss of parts,
(d) there can be distinct physical objects exactly occupying the same space at the same time,
(e) identity is not transitive.

We are now in a position to see how viewing objects as four-dimensional allows us to avoid all of these alternatives. Once we adopt the four-dimensional picture, we can deny all five alternatives without having to be committed to:

(3) the thing that, after t, is Body-minus = the thing that, after t, is Body.

The objects claimed to be identical in (3) are distinct and do not, except in a loose sense, occupy the same space at the same time.

Body and Body-minus are distinct four-dimensional objects, since they have different spatial shapes before t. But then, it might be objected, they seem to be distinct but coincident entities – co-occupying a single spatiotemporal region R that begins at t. The response is that, strictly speaking, neither of them is in R. They are both temporally too big. They each take up a spatiotemporal region that is temporally larger than R, because their regions begin before t. Of course, each has a temporal part that is in R, but that does not entail that either Body or Body-minus is in that region. They overlap in R, but neither one exactly fills R.[19]

Perhaps there may be another way of generating the coincident entity problem. Instead of comparing Body with Body-minus, let us compare that part of Body which does exactly fill R with that part of Body-minus which also exactly fills R. It might be claimed that here we have an example of two distinct objects in the same space at the same time. But this again would be a mistake. These temporal parts are not two distinct objects, but, rather, one object under two descriptions. Body and Body-minus have a common temporal part, just as my living room and my dining room have a common spatial part.[20]

The thesis that there are temporal parts allows us to avoid an otherwise troublesome metaphysical puzzle. Moreover, the existence of such objects seems entirely plausible once we are prepared to think of objects as four-dimensional rather than three-dimensional and enduring. However, not everyone agrees about the plausibility of these entities. Their existence becomes especially dubious to some philosophers when considering the case of people. No matter what other objects are like, it might be claimed, we can at least be sure that people do not have temporal parts.

10   Unity of Consciousness

One thing that makes people special as objects is that we are conscious. We can have experiences and we can be aware of ourselves having experiences. Furthermore, there is a unity to our consciousness. The independent experiences of hearing 'the', 'cat', 'is', and 'spotted' can sometimes go together to form a more elaborate experience. It is this unity of consciousness that suggests to Chisholm that people do not have temporal parts.[21] He thinks that in order to have the more elaborate experience of hearing 'the cat is spotted', it must be the self-same thing having each of the parts of the experience. We could not account for the unity of consciousness if the object hearing 'the' were distinct from the one hearing 'cat', or if the one hearing 'th' were distinct from the one hearing 'e', and the one hearing 'c' were distinct from both the one hearing 'a' and the one hearing 't'. (I ask the reader to allow me the convenience of letting letters represent sounds.) The only way to account for the

several short experiences going together to form the longer experience of hearing 'the cat is spotted', it seems, is to suppose that there is a single entity that is having all of the shorter experiences.

Chisholm draws his concept of a temporal part from the writings of Jonathan Edwards.[22] Edwards's notion develops out of his religious theory that God creates the world and all its objects at every moment *ex nihilo*. It is real *ex nihilo* creation that is intended here: The Heller that exists now is a new creation of God's and exists independently of anything (other than God) that existed at any earlier time. Heller-at-time-t_1 is distinct from Heller-at-time-t_2 for the one only exists at t_1, and the other only exists at t_2. Heller, the object that began to exist in 1957 and still exists now, exists merely by divine convention. God treats a certain collection of momentary objects as if they add up (over time) to a single persisting thing. This conception of temporal part can be divorced from its dependence on God. Edwards's religious beliefs are his motivation for adopting his thesis of temporal parts, but they need not be built into the concept. All that is essential to Chisholm's conception of a temporal part is that the momentary objects be ontologically basic, and that longer-lasting objects be 'built up' out of the momentary ones by convention. It may be human convention, rather than divine convention.

Given a concept of temporal part that is committed to purportedly long-lasting entities being conventional constructions out of more basic momentary objects, Chisholm argues that there are no temporal parts. He argues that an ontology that includes such temporal parts must conflict with our experience. Chisholm uses the example of an individual experiencing the bird call 'bobwhite'. When someone has such an experience, he also has the second-order experience of 'bob' and 'white' being part of a single experience. He is experiencing the unity of the 'bobwhite' experience. It seems to be clearly a single object that is experience both 'bob' and 'white'. But an ontology of temporal parts would be committed to one entity experiencing 'bob' and a different entity, a different temporal part of the hearer, experiencing 'white'. Since on the Edwardsian conception of a temporal part the connection between the two experiencing objects would be merely conventional, the two experiences could not be connected in any way that would allow them to form a single experience. He concludes that an ontology of temporal parts must conflict with our experience of a diachronic unity of consciousness.

11 The Fourth Dimension

This argument requires at least that temporal parts be ontologically more basic than the whole that they compose. It is only by convention that the whole exists at all. Our conventions allow us to act as if there are enduring wholes; they allow us to treat certain momentary objects as if they compose an enduring whole, but the world itself does not contain any enduring objects. This is the sort of view that would be expected from an account of temporal parts that is formed against a background supposition of three-dimensionality. Someone might believe that no object can really exist for more than a moment. If one of these instantaneous objects could exist for longer, it would be a three-dimensional enduring object. But there are no such enduring objects. Instead there are collections of these instantaneous objects added together (by convention) to form the objects that we typically talk about. Someone holding such a view would be reasonable to accept the Edwardsian conception of temporal parts. But I do not accept the background supposition of three-dimensionality. On my account, temporal parts and the wholes that they compose are ontologically on a par. I do not need to appeal to conventions, either divine or earthly, as the glue that holds my temporally extended objects together.

It might still be metaphysically interesting to ask how it is that temporal parts go together to compose a whole, but there will be similar interesting questions for any ontology. For instance, an ontology of three-dimensional enduring objects that does not allow for temporal parts must be prepared to explain how it is that I am identical with the person who was called 'Heller' yesterday. Any explanation that might be offered can easily be adapted to serve as an explanation of the corresponding phenomenon on the ontology of four-dimensional objects. For instance, if the professed identity is founded upon some sort of causal flow, then that same causal flow could serve as the glue for my temporal parts. If the supposed identity is founded on the continuity of consciousness, then such a continuity could also explain the unity of my four-dimensional people. Even if identity is held to be an unexplainable, brute property, the four-dimensionalist can equally well hold that the relation between temporal parts that makes them parts of a single person is brute. And if it turns out that a person's identity is claimed to be a matter of convention after all, then I can claim the same for

people on my ontology of four-dimensional objects.

What I will in fact claim is that every filled region of space-time contains a physical object, and which of these objects we count as people is a matter of convention. This claim is based on independent arguments,[23] and is not part of my conception of temporal parts or of four-dimensional objects. Though the parts of a person may hold together in a special way, that special way is not privileged when it comes to existence. So, even though my conception of a temporal part is different from the Edwardsian conception in such a way as to make it invulnerable to Chisholm's attack, my overall ontology will share the Edwardsian thesis that what makes a certain collection of temporal parts a *person* is a matter of convention. So it seems that my ontology stands or falls with the Edwardsian conception of temporal parts after all. Someone could, using my understanding of a temporal part, accept that there were temporal parts and still accept that Chisholm's argument shows that there are no Edwardsian temporal parts. But it would be inconsistent to adopt my whole ontology and to still put stock in Chisholm's argument.

12 A Sketch of an Explanation

Chisholm does not himself explain how it is that we experience a unity of consciousness. Consider the following sketch of one plausible explanation. The experience of 'bobwhite' has two smaller experiences as parts, that of 'bob' and that of 'white'. But a 'white' experience that is immediately preceded by a 'bob' experience is significantly different from a 'white' experience that has no lead-in. Let us call the first of these a white-1 experience and the second a white-2 experience. By focusing just on that feature of these experiences that is most salient, namely the sound 'white', we might fail to notice the dissimilarities. It is those dissimilarities that we should attend to when trying to explain our apparent experience of a unity of consciousness. Perhaps the white-1 experience carries with it a memory trace of the 'bob' experience. Since the white-2 experience does not follow a 'bob' experience, it does not carry such a memory trace. This is why the white-1 experience is itself experienced as the conclusion of a 'bobwhite' experience, whereas the white-2 experience is not perceived in this way.

If this is accurate (as a sketch), then what would happen if someone had a white-1 experience without its being preceded by a 'bob' experience (assuming that this is possible)? It seems that he would still perceive his white-1 experience as the conclusion of a 'bobwhite' experience. He would have a second-order experience of a unity of consciousness even when there really was no such unity. God could create someone *ex nihilo* (truly *ex nihilo*, so that his coming into existence is totally independent of any natural occurence), and create him having a white-1 experience. His experience will include memory traces of a 'bob' experience, even though he was not around to have had the 'bob' experience. The 'white' experience and the memory traces together are enough to make this newly created person perceive himself as having had a unified 'bobwhite' experience. So it seems that the experience of a unity of consciousness does not require that a single object have both a 'bob' experience and a 'white' experience.

Let us turn to a possible sketch of an explanation of how the white-1 and the white-2 experience might get to have different memory traces in typical situations. If someone is having a 'bobwhite' experience, his brain is in a certain state at the beginning of the experience and is in a different state at the end of the experience. The transition from one brain state to the other will correspond to the having of the 'bobwhite' experience. The state that the person is in when he has the 'white' experience will be affected by the fact that he has just had the 'bob' experience. Someone who is having a 'white' experience that is not preceded by a 'bob' experience will have a different brain state corresponding to his 'white' experience. These differences in brain states correspond to differences in memory traces that are included in the experiences. The white-1 brain state will differ from the white-2 brain state in just the way that is relevant for the experiencer's perceiving the white-1 experience as the conclusion of a 'bobwhite' experience. Anyone who is in a white-1 brain state will perceive himself as having the conclusion of a unitary 'bobwhite' experience, even if he did not get in that state by normal means – even if his 'white' experience was not actually preceded by a 'bob' experience.

13   Causal Connections

Even if we deny the existence of temporal parts, the explanation of how someone typically gets into a white-1 brain state will be in terms of the causal connections between the environment and the brain. The sound waves of the 'bob' sound cause (through a complex process) the brain to be in a certain state. The brain in that state is then affected by the sound waves of the 'white' sound, and therefore goes into a white-1 state. If it had not been in the state that it was in, the 'white' sound would not have put it into a white-1 state. This whole story could be put in terms of the configuration of matter at various times and the forces acting on that matter. We do not need to appeal to enduring brains or persisting people. So long as the relevant process occurs, the object that experiences 'white' will be in the white-1 brain state. So long as it is in that brain state, it will have the experience of having had a unified 'bobwhite' experience. It does not matter if the object in question is identical with the one that was in the 'bob' brain state.

This is why it is crucial that temporal parts as I understand them do not truly come into existence *ex nihilo*. The state of a brain-at-t_2 (a temporal part of a brain) is affected by the state of the relevant brain-at-t_1. My assertion of the conventionality of people does not commit me to denying that matter is sometimes configured in the relevant way or that the forces in question sometimes act upon matter configured in that way. I do claim that the connection between two consecutive temporal parts of a single person does not count any more toward identity than does the connection between Heller-during-1968 and Nixon-during-1974. But this claim is consistent with the claim that there is a much stronger connection between the first pair than there is between the second pair. This difference in causal connection results in a difference of unity of consciousness.

It is just a matter of contingent fact that that causal connectedness does lead to a person's experiencing a unity of consciousness. It is that causal connectedness which happens to be responsible for getting the 'bobwhite' hearer into a white-1 brain state. My hearing 'bob' at t_1 would have no effect on your brain state, so your hearing 'white' at t_2 would not be a 'white-1' experience. Hence, there is no unity of consciousness for an object composed of me-at-t_1 and you-at-t_2. But if we had been hard-wired differently, if the relevant causal connections had been different, then the thing composed of me-at-t_1 and you-at-t_2 might have had a unity of consciousness. It might have been that my hearing 'bob' at t_1 would have made your hearing 'white' at t_2 put you into a white-1 state at t_2. In such a case the thing that would have a unity of consciousness would not be what we would typically call a person (though, depending upon your theory of personhood, you might start calling it a person).

My response to Chisholm is that if an individual's experiencing a unity of consciousness or an individual's actually having a unity of consciousness can be explained on an ontology that does not allow for temporal parts, then they can also be explained on an ontology that does allow for temporal parts – even an ontology that holds that what makes any particular collection of temporal parts add up to a person is mere convention. As an example I sketched one possible explanation for an ontology not including temporal parts, and then showed how that same explanation was available to someone holding my ontology. I do not want to argue that this is the correct explanation of why each of us experiences a unity of consciousness. But it is (at least the beginnings of) a plausible explanation. In order for Chisholm's argument to really be successful, he must be prepared to offer an explanation of the phenomenon in question that cannot be adapted by someone who holds my ontology. I do not think this can be done. If it seems to you that it can, then I suggest that you are assuming that my ontology rules out more than it does.[24]

14 Modal Properties

Peter van Inwagen presents a different sort of argument against the thesis that people have temporal parts.[25] His argument does not explicitly depend on any claims about consciousness. The key premise to van Inwagen's argument is that a person could have existed for less time than he does in fact exist. Insofar as such a premise could be generalized to objects other than people, the thesis that those objects have temporal parts would be equally vulnerable to arguments of this type. Actually, van Inwagen's is an argument against the thesis that people have *arbitrary* temporal parts. Van Inwagen suggests that if there are any nonarbitrary temporal parts, they are momentary slices. Personally, I am more certain of the existence of temporally extended temporal parts than I am of momentary ones. The objects that van Inwagen is arguing against are precisely the ones that I include in my ontology. His argument is fairly simple once we grant him his key premise about an individual's modal properties.

Van Inwagen argues by indirect proof. Assume that Descartes has temporal parts. Then there is some thing that begins to exist when Descartes begins to exist and ceases existing exactly one year before Descartes ceases to exist and is exactly the same spatial size that Descartes is for as long as that part exists. Call that object 'Descartes-minus'. Given the premise that Descartes could have lived for a year less than he did, Descartes could have been the same size that Descartes-minus in fact is. If we also accept that Descartes-minus would have been the same size that it is even if Descartes had not existed beyond the time that Descartes-minus in fact exists, then it follows that Descartes and Descartes-minus could have occupied exactly the same spatiotemporal region. But no distinct objects can occupy exactly the same region. So we must deny our assumption that there is such a thing as Descartes-minus.

This argument depends upon the following premises. First, that Descartes could have lived for a year less than he in fact did. Second, that Descartes-minus would have been the same spatiotemporal shape that it in fact is even if Descartes had lived for a year less than he in fact did. And third, that coincident entities are impossible. I accept the last two of these premises. In fact, I would argue for both of them.[26] But I reject the first of his premises. I grant that most of us believe that it is true, but I deny that we are right in our belief or that we even have any very good reason for it. I might reject this premise on the following grounds: It, together with other premises that I accept, has the consequence that there are no temporal parts; but I am more convinced of the existence of temporal parts than I am of the truth of the premise in question; therefore, I conclude that the premise in question is false. I might reject the premise on these grounds, but I do not. I hope that I can present more persuasive grounds.

Notes

1 For instance: Quine, "Identity, ostension, and hypostasis," this volume, ch. 22; John Perry, "Can the self divide?" *Journal of Philosophy* 69 (Sept. 1972), pp. 463–88; David Lewis, "Survival and identity," in

Philosophical Papers, vol. 1 (New York: Oxford University Press, 1983).

2 Lewis, "Survival and identity," p. 76.

3 Judith Jarvis Thomson, "Parthood and identity across time," this volume, ch. 24.

4 In conversation Jim Hudson and Michael Tye have each expressed doubts about whether they even understand the three-dimensional view, and they claim that the four-dimensional view is in fact the standard view. I am not much concerned about what the standard view really is, but I do think that our standard use of language does reflect at least a tendency to treat time as importantly disanalogous with the three spatial dimensions. Quine puts the point this way: "Our ordinary language shows a tiresome bias in its treatment of time" (*Word and Object* (Cambridge, Mass.: MIT Press, 1960), p. 170). Also, I suspect that many philosophical difficulties would never have arisen if it were not for some tendency toward a three-dimensional view.

5 Peter van Inwagen, "The doctrine of arbitrary undetached parts," *Pacific Philosophical Quarterly* 62 (Apr. 1981), pp. 123–37.

6 Thomson, "Parthood and identity across time."

7 Van Inwagen, "Doctrine of arbitrary undetached parts."

8 Roderick Chisholm, 'Parts as essential to their wholes,' *Review of Metaphysics* 26 (1973), pp. 581–603.

9 Peter Geach, "Identity," *Review of Metaphysics* 21 (1967–8), pp. 3–12.

10 See Mark Heller, *The Ontology of Physical Objects* (Cambridge: Cambridge University Press, 1990), ch. 2, sect. 9.

11 See Heller, *Ontology of Physical Objects*, chs 2 and 3.

12 Notice that my claims do not presuppose a description theory of names. I am not merely supposing that 'Whitey' *means* the whole piece of paper. On a causal theory of names 'Whitey' refers to the whole piece of paper if and only if it was the whole piece that was originally indicated when the reference of 'Whitey' was fixed.

13 Compare this to David Lewis's discussion, "Survival and identity."

14 Compare this to John Perry's discussion in "The same *F*," this volume, ch. 8, esp. pp. 97–8.

15 See my "The best candidate approach to diachronic identity," *Australasian Journal of Philosophy* 65 (Dec. 1987), pp. 434–51. On my "strictly speaking" ploy many of our ordinary utterances end up being false unless they are treated as loose speaking. It is strictly false that Whitey is in the drawer and that Whitey exists now. What is strictly true is that part of Whitey is in the drawer and part of Whitey exists now. One might prefer to hold that it is strictly true that Whitey is in the drawer, but that this just means that part of Whitey is in the drawer. Similarly, it is strictly true that Whitey exists now, and this just means that part

of Whitey exists now. (Actually, if now is supposed to be an instant, and if there are no instantaneous objects, then the strict truth is that now is within Whitey's temporal boundaries.) This suggestion agrees with my earlier claims concerning the nonlinguistic facts, but disagrees about the strict/loose distinction. Perhaps the claim that part of Whitey is in the drawer is in fact the strictest interpretation of 'Whitey is in the drawer'. Someone who adopts the present suggestion will be forced to say that my hand and I do occupy the same space at the same time, but he can still accept that we do not have to compete for the space, since my occupying that space just is my having a part (my hand) that occupies it. The sort of coincidence just described is not an objectionable sort of coincidence. It is not the sort of coincidence discussed in the next paragraph of the text.

16 Thomson, "Parthood and identity across time," this volume, p. 306.

17 Thomson calls it "a crazy metaphysic" on pp. 306 and 307.

18 Ibid., p. 307.

19 Jan Cover has suggested to me that on the four-dimensional view both halves of the identity claim in (3) are nonreferring: There is no thing that, after *t*, is Body-minus. But this is to forget that we can refer to a whole object without having the whole object present. Body-minus (the whole four-dimensional object that begins to exist long before *t*) is Body-minus at all times during its existence, including the after-*t* times.

20 It may appear that in order to get this benefit from temporal parts we will have to accept that every moment within Body's existence is the beginning of a new temporal part (since *t* was arbitrarily selected). I do in fact accept this, but all we really need in the present case is that Body and Body-minus be too big to fit in region *R*. We do not need to claim that there is anything that does exactly fill *R*.

21 Chisholm, "Problems of identity," in Milton K. Munitz (ed.), *Identity and Individuation* (New York: New York University Press, 1971), pp. 3–30.

22 Jonathan Edwards, *Doctrine of Original Sin Defended* (1758), cited in Chisholm, "Problems of identity," p. 12.

23 For these arguments see Heller, *Ontology of Physical Objects*.

24 Just as we can divide up a person's experience and attribute different parts of the experience to different temporal parts of the object, we can do the same for beliefs, desires, actions, etc. It may be that there are temporal parts that are too small to have beliefs. There are certainly temporal parts that are too small to utter sentences. But these parts can have parts of beliefs and can utter parts of sentences. On the other hand, many temporal parts are certainly big enough to utter sentences. Suppose that there is just one person in a room and he is talking to a tape recorder. Am I committed to saying that there are actually lots of

talkers in the room? This is just the 'coincident entities' objection back in a new guise. It does not demand a new answer. Strictly speaking, the thing that is uttering a given sentence is just the person's temporal part that has the same temporal boundaries as the act of sentence production. (Actually, it is probably more exact to say that it is some spatial part of that temporal part.)

25 Van Inwagen, "Doctrine of arbitrary undetached parts," pp. 132–5.

26 For the author's argument see Heller, *Ontology of Physical Objects*, ch. 2.

PART VI

The Persistence of the Self

Introduction

Whatever our philosophical views may be about the persistence of material things, we seem to have a strong, perhaps biologically based, feeling that we are continuants, fully present as persons at each moment of our existence, and that we are not "logical constructions" out of some more basic entities, temporal person-stages. This is Roderick Chisholm's view of the persistence of the self, and he argues for it in his "The Persistence of Persons" (chapter 26). According to Chisholm, there is a fact of the matter as to whether we persist from one time to another, and this is not a matter that can be settled by adopting a *convention* about what to count as a single continuing person.

But what makes a person existing at one time the same person as the person existing at another? Or what makes two person-stages stages of the same person? There are two main groups of theories about this question, memory theories and bodily continuity theories, although hybrid theories are also possible. Roughly, memory theories say that the later person must be connected with the earlier person by a chain of remembered experiences. Similarly, the bodily continuity theories say that the later person's body (perhaps her brain) must be continuous with the earlier person's body. Whether or not the continuity of memory alone is sufficient for personal identity, there seems no question that memory is of great importance for personal identity – at least as evidence for identity. In "Persons and their Pasts", (chapter 27), Sydney Shoemaker investigates the conceptual connection between personal identity and memory, defending the view that persons have special epistemic access to their own pasts.

In "The Self and the Future" (chapter 28), Bernard Williams constructs thought-experiments that appear to show that our intuitive judgments about personal identity ("Will he be me?") can conflict with each other. On the one hand, we seem to be able to imagine cases in which the continuity of memory supersedes bodily continu-

ity. On the other, we can construct stories in which memory seems not really relevant (if you are told that you will be tortured at midnight tonight but that your memory will be cleanly and entirely erased just before the torture, would that make a difference to you?). William explores the assumptions underlying our reactions to such imagined cases, and, like Chisholm, rejects conventionalism as a solution to the puzzles.

In "Personal Identity" (chapter 29), Derek Parfit brings new perspectives on personal identity. First, he challenges the idea that personal identity is a determinate matter, that it is an all-or-nothing affair. Second, he distinguishes personal identity from survival, arguing that it is possible to survive without identity (e.g., by multiplying). Parfit develops the concepts of psychological continuity and connectedness, and argues that survival is a matter of degree. Finally, he explores the consequences of his views for certain ethical issues, such as egoism and our interest in our futures.

Richard Swinburne believes that all "empiricist theories" of the persistence of persons, including memory theories and bodily continuity theories, are fundamentally inadequate. To give a correct theory, we must turn away, he argues, from a materialist view of persons. In "Personal Identity: The Dualist Theory" (chapter 30), he develops an account according to which sameness of the soul is the essential element in the persisting person.

In "Human Beings" (chapter 31), Mark Johnston examines some important methodological issues involved in philosophical discussions of personal identity, surveying representative modern approaches to personal identity in this context (including those of Williams, Parfit, and Shoemaker). On his view, the familiar concepts used in discussions of personal identity, such as mental and physical continuity, are properly regarded as evidence of personal identity, not constitutive of it. He argues that any acceptable account of personal identity must do justice to our usual, reliable and unproblematic, practice of identifying and re-identifying persons.

Further reading

Lewis, David, "Survival and identity," repr. in *Philosophical Papers*, vol. 1 (New York: Oxford University Press, 1983).

Lowe, E. J., "Real selves: persons and a substantial kind," in David Cockburn (ed.) *Human Beings* (Cambridge: Cambridge University Press, 1991).

Noonan, Harold, *Personal Identity* (London and New York: Routledge, 1989).

Parfit, Derek, *Reasons and Persons* (Oxford: Clarendon Press, 1984).

Perry, John (ed.), *Personal Identity* (Berkeley and Los Angeles: University of California Press, 1975).

Rorty, Amélie O. (ed.), *Identities of Persons* (Berkeley and Los Angeles: University of California Press, 1976).

Shoemaker, Sydney, and Swinburne, Richard, *Personal Identity* (Oxford: Blackwell, 1984).

Sosa, Ernest, "Subject among other things," *Philosophical Perspectives* 1 (1987), pp. 155–89.

—— 'Surviving matters,' *Nous* 24 (1990), pp. 305–30.

Strawson, P. F., *Individuals* (London: Methuen, 1959).

26

The Persistence of Persons

Roderick M. Chisholm

1 The Persistence of Persons through Time

Am I an *ens per alio* or an *ens per se*?

Consider the simplest of Cartesian facts – say, that I now hope for rain. Hoping for rain is one of those properties that are rooted only in the times at which they are had. And so if I am an *ens per alio*, an *ens successivum*, like our simple table or the Ship of Theseus, then I may be said to hope for rain only in virtue of the fact that my present stand-in hopes for rain. I borrow the property, so to speak, from the thing that constitutes me now.

But surely *that* hypothesis is not to be taken seriously. There is no reason whatever for supposing that *I* hope for rain only in virtue of the fact that some *other* thing hopes for rain – some stand-in that, strictly and philosophically, is not identical with me but happens to be doing duty for me at this particular moment.

If there are thus two things that now hope for rain, the one doing it on its own and the other such that its hoping is done for it by the thing that now happens to constitute it, then I am the former thing and not the latter thing. But this is to say that I am *not* an *ens successivum*.[1]

But might I not be a constituent of an *ens successivum*?

If I am a constituent of an *ens successivum*, then there have been other things that once constituted the same person that I do now and presumably there will be still others in the future. But if this is so, then the things I think I know about my past history may all be false (even though they may be true of the person I happen now to constitute), and I may have no grounds for making any prediction at all about my future. *Is* this the sort of thing I am?

There are certain philosophical data that we have a right to believe about ourselves – that is, propositions that whether or not they are true are such that they should be regarded as innocent, epistemically, until we have positive reason for thinking them guilty. Among these propositions is the fact that we do undergo change and persist through time. Each of us is justified in believing a great variety of things about his past. We are justified in believing these things until we have found some reason to doubt them. It is reasonable to treat these beliefs as being innocent, epistemically, until we have found some positive reason for thinking them guilty.

What would such a positive reason be?

It is important to remind ourselves that we do *not* find any such positive reason in the writings of those philosophers who have professed to be skeptical about the persistence of persons through time.

Consider, for example, Kant's discussion of what he calls 'the third paralogism of transcendental psychology'. For all I can know, Kant there says, the thing that calls itself 'I' at one time may be other than the thing that calls itself 'I' at another

Originally published in *Person and Object* (1976), pp. 104–13, 212–14. Reprinted by permission of Open Court, a division of Carus Publishing.

time. There might be a series of different subjects which make up my biography, each of them passing its thoughts and memories on to its successor – each subject would 'retain the thought of the preceding subject and so hand it over to the subsequent subject'.[2] The relation between the successive subjects, he says, could be like that of a set of elastic balls, one of which impinges on another in a straight line and 'communicates to the latter its whole motion, and therefore its whole state (that is, if we take account only of the positions in space)'. Kant goes on to say:

If, then, in analogy with such bodies, we postulate substances such that the one communicates to the other representations together with the consciousness of them, we can conceive a whole series of substances of which the first transmits its state together with its consciousness to the second, the second its own state with that of the preceding substance to the third, and this in turn the states of all the preceding substances together with its own consciousness and with their consciousness to another. The last substance would then be conscious of all the states of the previously changed substances, as being its own states, because they would have been transferred to it together with the consciousness of them. And yet it would not have been one and the same person in all these states.[3]

Does *this* give us a reason for wondering whether we have in fact persisted through time? Surely not. What Kant has pointed out to us, in these speculations, is simply that the following is logically possible: instead of there being just one person who makes up my biography, there was a succession of different persons, all but the first of them being deluded with respect to its past. It is also logically possible, as Russell pointed out, that the universe came into being three seconds ago with all its ostensible traces and relics of the past. And it is logically possible that a malicious demon is deceiving each of us with respect to what we think are the external physical things around us. But the fact that these are logically possible is itself no reason for thinking that they actually occur.

'Given the transitory nature of the ultimate particles that make up the physical universe, isn't it reasonable to suppose that, if I do persist through time, then my consciousness may be transferred, as John Locke seemed to suggest, from one substance

or individual thing to another? And if my consciousness is thus transferred, wouldn't I, too, be transferred from one substance to another?'

The supposition, I am certain, is not only untenable, but also incoherent. Philosophers have taken it seriously, however, and so we should consider it briefly.

Is it possible to transfer my consciousness from one substance to another with the result that, whereas the former substance but not the latter was I, the latter substance but not the former is now I? In such a case, I could truly say: 'This is other than that, but once I was that and now I'm this.'

Locke said that, 'it being the same consciousness that makes a man be himself to himself, personal identity depends on that only, whether it be annexed solely to one individual substance, or can be continued in a succession of several substances'.[4] The same consciousness, he said, *could* be thus continued in a succession of several substances, if it were 'transferred from one thinking substance to another', and if this does happen, then the different 'thinking substances may make but one person'.[5] And these different thinking substances will all be 'the same self'.[6] (In fairness to Locke, we should note that he does not quite bring himself to say that I might now be identical with this but not with that and then later identical with that but not with this. Although he suggests that it is possible to transfer my consciousness from one substance to another, he does not explicitly say that, whereas the former substance *was* I, the latter substance is *now* I. It may very well be that, like many other philosophers, he was playing loose with 'is'.[7]

A *part* of a thing or an *appendage* to a thing may be transferred to another thing, as an organ may be transplanted from one body to another. The *contents* of a thing may be transferred to another thing, as apples may be moved from one bag to another.

Speaking somewhat more metaphorically, we might also say that the *properties* of one thing may be transferred to another thing. If you are infected by my contagious disease and if I then recover, one *could* say that my sickness, *including my aches and pains*, has been transferred from me to you. But the disease or sickness will not be transferred in the literal sense in which, say, its carriers might be transferred.

My personality traits could be said to be transferred to you if you acquire the kind of complexes and dispositions that are characteristic of me. My beliefs could be said to be transferred to you, if you begin to believe the same things I do. And my memories could even be said to be transferred from me to you, if you remember, or think you remember, the same things I do. (But if I remember or think I remember *my* doing the deed, the content of that memory could *not* be transferred to you.[8]) By thus acquiring my properties – or, more accurately, by thus instantiating some of the properties that I do – you may become so much like me that others will have difficulty in telling us apart – in that they are unable to decide, with respect to certain things that have happened, whether they belong to your biography or to mine. Perhaps the courts will have to make a decree. Perhaps it will even be reasonable for them to decide, with respect to some of the things that only I did in the past, that you and not I are responsible for them, and then they might decide, with respect to the name I formerly had, that you should be the one who bears it.

But none of these possibilities, perplexing as they may be, justifies us in saying that there could be *two* different substances which are such that *I* am transferred from one to the other.[9]

There is still another type of transfer which is quite naturally described in the way in which Locke described 'transfer of self'. This is illustrated in the transfer of a shadow ('the shadow of his hand moved from the wall to the table and became larger but more faint in the process'). But a shadow is an *ens per alio*; it borrows its properties from other things (most notably from shadowed objects). The kind of transfer that is involved in the passage of a shadow from one object to another, to the extent that it differs from the types of transfer we distinguished above, is typical of *entia per alio*. But persons, we have seen, are *entia per se*.

What could it mean, after all, to say that I might be 'annexed to' or 'placed in' a thinking thing or individual substance?

Whatever it might mean, either I am identical with the thinking substance in which I am thus placed or I am not identical with it.

If I am identical with the thinking substance in which I am thus placed, then I cannot be transferred *from* that substance to another thinking substance.

But if I am placed in a certain thinking substance and am not identical with that thinking substance, then there are *two* different things – the thinking substance and I. But if there are two things, which of us does the thinking? There are exactly four possibilities.

(1) Neither of us does the thinking – that is to say, neither of us thinks. But this we know is false.

(2) I think but the thinking substance does not think. Why call the latter a 'thinking' substance, then? (It would be like calling an elevator a thinking substance because it contains someone who thinks.) And what relation do I bear to this thinking substance? I'm not a *property* of it, since properties do not think. Am I a proper *part*, then, of the thinking substance? But proper parts of substances are themselves substances. And so if I am myself a thinking substance, what is the point of saying there is *another* thinking substance in which I am 'placed' or to which I am 'annexed'?

(3) The thinking substance thinks, but I do not. But isn't this absurd? 'It's not really I who think;' it is some *other* thing that thinks in me – some other thing that does what I mistakenly take to be my thinking.' (Or should the latter clause have been: 'some other thing that does what *it* mistakenly takes to be my thinking'?)

(4) Both the thinking substance and I think. Isn't this multiplying thinkers beyond necessity? If I want my dinner, does it follow that two of us want my dinner? Or does the thinking substance want its dinner and not mine?

I think we may reasonably conclude that there is no significant sense in which we may speak of the transfer of a self from one substance or individual thing to another.

2 'Will I Be He?': Truth-conditions and Criteria

Suppose that there is a person x who happens to know, with respect to a certain set of properties, that there is or will be a certain person y who will have those properties at some future time, and x asks himself: 'Will I be he?' Either x is identical with y, or x is diverse from y.

We cannot find the *answer* to the question, 'Is x identical with y?', merely by deciding what would be practically convenient. To be sure, if we lack sufficient evidence for making a decision, it may yet be necessary for the courts to *rule* that x is the same person as y, or that he is not. Perhaps the ruling will have to be based upon practical considerations, and conceivably such considerations may lead the court later to 'defeat' its ruling. But one may always ask of any such ruling 'But is it *correct*, or *true*?' For a ruling to the effect that x is the same person as y will be correct, or true, only if x is identical with y.

We should remind ourselves, however, that the expression 'x is the same person as y' also has a use which is not this strict and philosophical one. Thus there are circumstances in which one might say: 'Mr Jones is not at all the same person he used to be. You will be disappointed. He is not the person that you remember.' We would not say this sort of thing if Mr Jones had changed only slightly. We would say it only if he had undergone changes that were quite basic and thoroughgoing – the kind of changes that might be produced by psychoanalysis, or by a lobotomy, or by a series of personal tragedies. But just *how* basic and thoroughgoing must these changes be if we are to say of Mr Jones that he is a different person? The proper answer would seem to be: 'As basic and thoroughgoing as you would like. It's just a matter of convention. It all depends upon how widely it is convenient for you to construe the expression "He's the same person he used to be". Insofar as the rules of language are in your own hands, you may have it any way you would like.'[10] (Compare 'Jones is not himself today' or 'Jones was not himself when he said that'.)

This, however, is only playing loose with 'same' – or, more accurately, it is playing loose with 'not the same'. When we say, in the above sense, 'Jones is no longer the person he used to be', we do not mean that there is, or was, a certain entity such that Jones was formerly identical with that entity and is no longer so. What we are saying does not imply that there are (or have been) certain entities, x and y, such that at one time x is, or was, identical with y, and at another time x is not identical with y. For this is incoherent, but 'Jones is no longer the person he used to be' is not.

Nor do we mean, when we say 'Jones is no longer the person he used to be', that there *was* a certain entity, the old Jones, which no longer exists, and that there is a certain *different* entity, the new Jones, which somehow has taken his place. We are not describing the kind of change that takes place when one President succeeds another. In the latter case, there is a clear answer to the question 'What happened to the old one?' But when we decide to call Jones a new person, we are not confronted with such questions as: 'What happened, then, to the old Jones? Did he die, or was he annihilated, or disassembled, or did he retire to some other place?'

The old Jones did not die; he was not annihilated or disassembled; and he did not retire to any other

place. He *became* the new Jones. And to say that he 'became' the new Jones is *not* to say that he 'became identical' with something he hadn't been identical with before. For it is only when a thing comes into being that it may be said to become identical with something it hadn't been identical with before. To say that our man 'became the new Jones' is to say that he, Jones, *altered* in a significant way, taking on certain interesting properties he had not had before. (Hence we should contrast the 'became' of 'Jones then became a married man', said when Jones ceased to be a bachelor, with that of 'The President then became a Republican', said when President Johnson retired.) When we say of a thing that *it* has properties that *it* did not have before, we are saying that there is an x such that x formerly had such-and-such properties and x presently has such-and-such other properties.

It will be instructive, I think, to consider two somewhat different examples.

The first is suggested by C. S. Peirce.[11] Elaborating upon his suggestion, let us assume that you are about to undergo an operation and that you still have a decision to make. The utilities involved are, first, financial – you wish to avoid any needless expense – and, secondly, the avoidance of pain, the avoidance, however, just of *your* pain, for pain that is other than yours, let us assume, is of no concern whatever to you. The doctor proposes two operating procedures – one a very expensive procedure in which you will be subjected to total anaesthesia and no pain will be felt at all, and the other of a rather different sort. The second operation will be very inexpensive indeed; there will be no anaesthesia at all, and therefore there will be excruciating pain. But the doctor will give you two drugs: first, a drug just before the operation which will induce complete amnesia, so that while you are on the table you will have no memory whatever of your present life; and, secondly, just after the agony is over, a drug that will make you completely forget everything that happened on the table. The question is: given the utilities involved, namely, the avoidance of needless expense and the avoidance of pain that *you* will feel, other pains not mattering, is it reasonable for you to opt for the less expensive operation?

My own conviction is that it would *not* be reasonable, even if you could be completely certain that both amnesia injections would be successful. *You* are the one who would undergo that pain, even though you, Jones, would not know at the time that it is Jones who is undergoing it, and even though you would never remember it. Consider after all, the hypothesis that it would *not* be you. What would be your status, in such a case, during the time of the operation? Would you have passed away? That is to say, would you have *ceased to be*, but with the guarantee that you – you, yourself – would come into being once again when the agony was over?[12] And what about the person who *would* be feeling the pain? Who would he be?

It may well be that these things would not be obvious to you if in fact you had to make such a decision. But there is one point, I think, that ought to be obvious.

Suppose that others come to you – friends, relatives, judges, clergymen – and they offer the following advice and assurance. 'Have no fear,' they will say. 'Take the cheaper operation and we will take care of everything. We will lay down the convention that the man on the table is not you, Jones, but is Smith.' What *ought* to be obvious to you, it seems to me, is that the laying down of this convention should have no effect at all upon your decision. For you may still ask, 'But won't that person be I?' and, it seems to me, the question has an answer.

I now turn to the second example. Suppose you knew that your body, like that of an amoeba, would one day undergo fission and that you would go off, so to speak, in two different directions. Suppose you also knew, somehow, that the one who went off to the left would experience the most wretched of lives and that the one who went off to the right would experience a life of great happiness and value. If I am right in saying that one's question 'Will that person be I?' or 'Will I be he?' always has a definite answer, then, I think, we may draw these conclusions. There is no possibility whatever that *you* would be *both* the the person on the right and the person on the left. Moreover, there *is* a possibility that you would be *one or the other* of those two persons. And, finally, *you* could be one of those persons and yet have no memory at all of your present existence. In this case, there may well be no *criterion* by means of which you or anyone else could decide which of the two halves was in fact yourself. Yet it would be reasonable of you, if you were concerned with *your* future pleasures and pains, to hope that you would be the one on the right and not the one on the left. It would also be reasonable of you, given such self-concern, to have this hope even if you knew that the one on the right would have no memory of your present existence. Indeed, it would be reasonable of you to

have it even if you knew that the one on the *left* thought he remembered the facts of your present existence. And it seems to me to be absolutely certain that no fears that you might have about being the half on the left could reasonably be allayed by the adoption of a convention, even if our procedure were endorsed by the highest authorities.[13]

In trying to *decide* which one of the two persons, if either, you will be, you will, of course, make use of such *criteria* that you have and are able to apply. As we all know, there are intriguing philosophical questions about the criteria of the identity of persons through time. ('How are we to make sure, or make a reasonable guess, that that person at that time is the same as that person at the other time?'[14]) What are we to do, for example, when bodily criteria and psychological criteria conflict? Suppose we know that the person on the left will have certain *bodily* characteristics that we have always taken to be typical only of you – and that the person on the right will have certain *psychological* characteristics that we have always taken to be typical only of you. In such a case there may be no sufficient reason at all for deciding that you are or that you are not one or the other of the two different persons. But from this it does not follow that you *will* not in fact be one or the other of the two persons.

We should remind ourselves of a very simple and obvious point. When you ask yourself, 'Will I be the person on the right?' your question is *not* 'Will the person on the right satisfy such criteria as I have, or such criteria as someone or other has, for deciding whether or not a given person is I?' To be sure, the best you can do, by way of answering the first question, is to try to answer the second. But the answers to the two questions are logically independent of each other.

What is a *criterion* of personal identity? It is a statement telling what constitutes evidence of personal identity – what constitutes a good reason for saying of a person x that he is, or that he is not, identical with a person y. Now there is, after all, a fundamental distinction between the *truth-conditions* of a proposition and the *evidence* we can have for deciding whether or not the proposition is true. The *truth-conditions* for the proposition that Caesar crossed the Rubicon consist of the fact, if it is a fact, that Caesar did cross the Rubicon. The only *evidence* you and I can have of this fact will consist of certain *other* propositions – propositions about records, memories, and traces. It is only in the case of what is self-presenting (that I hope for rain or that I seem to me to have a headache) that the evidence for a proposition coincides with its truth-conditions. In all other cases, the two are logically independent; the one could be true while the other is false.[15]

The question 'Was it Caesar?' is not the same as the question: 'Do we have good evidence for thinking it was Caesar?' (or 'Have the criteria for saying that it was Caesar been fulfilled?'). This is true despite the fact that the most reasonable way of trying to find the answer to the first question is to try to answer the second.

And analogously for 'Will I be he?'

What I have said may recall this observation made by Leibniz: 'Suppose that some individual could suddenly become King of China on condition, however, of forgetting what he had been, as though being born again, would it not amount to the same practically, or as far as the effects could be perceived, as if the individual were annihilated, and a King of China were at the same instant created in his place? The individual would have no reason to desire this.'[16]

If I am being asked to consider the possibility that there is an *ens successivum* of which I happen to be the present constituent and which will subsequently be constituted by someone who will then be a King of China, then the fate of the later constituent may well be no special concern of mine. But what if Leibniz were not thus playing loose with 'is'?

In such a case, the proper reply to his question is suggested by the following observation in Bayle's *Dictionary*:

> The same atoms which compose water are in ice, in vapours, in clouds, in hail and snow; those which compose wheat are in the meal, in the bread, the blood, the flesh, the bones, etc. Were they unhappy under the figure or form of water, and under that of ice, it would be the same numerical substance that would be unhappy in these two conditions; and consequently all the calamities which are to be dreaded, under the form of meal, concern the atoms which form corn; and nothing ought to concern itself so much about the state or lot of the meal, as the atoms which form the wheat, though they are not to suffer these calamities, under the form of wheat.

Bayle concludes that 'there are but two methods a man can employ to calm, in a rational manner, the fears of another life. One is, to promise himself the felicities of Paradise; the other, to be firmly persuaded that he shall be deprived of sensations of every kind.'[17]

Notes

1 And so if we say that men are mere *entia per alio* and that God is the only *ens per se*, it will follow that I am God and not a man. Compare Bayle's refutation of Spinoza's doctrine according to which men are modifications of God: ' . . . when we say that a man denies, affirms, gets angry, caresses, praises, and the like, we ascribe all these attributes to the substance of his soul itself, and not to his thoughts as they are either accidents or modifications. If it were true then, as Spinoza claims, that men are modalities of God, one would speak falsely when one said, 'Peter denies this, he wants that, he affirms such and such a thing'; for actually, according to this theory, it is God who denies, wants, affirms; and consequently all the denominations that result from the thoughts of all men are properly and physically to be ascribed to God. From which it follows that God hates and loves, denies and affirms the same things at the same time. . . .' from note N of the article 'Spinoza'; the passage may be found in R. H. Popkin (ed.), Pierre Bayle, *Historical and Critical Dictionary: Selections* (Indianapolis: Bobbs-Merrill, 1965) pp. 309–10.

2 Immanuel Kant, *Critique of Pure Reason*, Kemp-Smith edn, p. 342. The passage is from p. 363 of the first edition of the *Kritik*.

3 Ibid., Kemp-Smith edn p. 342; 1st edn, pp. 363–4.

4 John Locke, *Essay Concerning Human Understanding*, II, ch. 23 ('Our complex ideas of substance'); A. C. Fraser edn, p. 451.

5 Ibid., p. 454.

6 Ibid., p. 458.

7 For Chrisholm's notion of playing loose with 'is', see this volume, ch. 21.

8 The defence of this observation may be found in my *Person and Object* (LaSalle, Ill.: Open Court, 1976), ch. 1, sect. 4.

9 Kant at least was clear about this point. When he states that the 'consciousness' of one substance may be transferred to another, as the motion of one ball may be transferred to another, and notes that the last of a series of such substances might be conscious of all the states of the previous substances, he adds that 'it would not have been one and the same person in all

these states' (*Critique of Pure Reason*, Kemp-Smith edn, p. 342; 1 edn of *Kritik*, p. 364).

10 Compare Bernard Williams, *Problems of the Self* (Cambridge: Cambridge University Press, 1973), pp. 2ff.

11 ' "If the power to remember dies with the material body, has the question of any single person's future life after death any particular interest for him?" As you put the question, it is not whether the matter ought rationally to have an interest but whether as a fact it has; and perhaps this is the proper question, trusting as it seems to do, rather to instinct than to reason. Now if we had a drug which would abolish memory for a while, and you were going to be cut for the stone, suppose the surgeon were to say, "You will suffer damnably, but I will administer this drug so that you will during that suffering lose all memory of your previous life. Now you have, of course, no particular interest in your suffering as long as you will not remember your present and past life, you know, have you?" ' (*Collected Papers*, vol. 5 (Cambridge, Mass.: Harvard University Press, 1935), p. 355).

12 See Locke's *Essay*, II, ch. 27, sect. 1: 'One thing cannot have two beginnings of existence.' Compare Thomas Reid, *Essays on the Intellectual Powers of Man*, essay III, ch. 4, in Sir William Hamilton (ed.), *The Works of Thomas Reid, D.D.* (Edinburgh: Maclachlan & Stewart, 1854), p. 346.

13 Some philosophers who have considered this type of situation have not presupposed, as I have, that persons are *entia per se*. Thus Derek Parfit has suggested it is a mistake to believe that in such cases the question 'Will I be he?' has a true answer. He writes: 'If we give up this belief, as I think we should, these problems disappear. We shall then regard the case as like many others in which, for quite unpuzzling reasons, there *is* no answer to a question about identity. (Consider "Was England the same nation after 1066?")' (Derek Parfit, 'Personal identity', this volume, ch. 29; the quotation is on p. 367. P. F. Strawson has expressed a similar scepticism: 'Perhaps I should say, not that I do not understand Professor Chisholm's notion of strict personal identity, but rather that I understand it well enough to think there can be no such thing' (P. F. Strawson, 'Chisholm on identity through time', in H. E. Kiefer and M. K. Munitz (eds), *Language, Belief, and Metaphysics* (Albany: State University of New York Press, 1970), pp. 183–6; the quotation is on p. 186. I think that the conception of persons set forth in Strawson's *Individuals* (London: Methuen, 1957) coheres more readily with the view that persons are *entia per se* than with the view that they are ontological parasites or *entia per alio*.

14 Compare Godfrey Vesey, *Personal Identity* (London: Macmillan, 1974), pp. 8ff, 80ff; Williams, *Problems of the Self*, pp. 8ff, 15ff; and Anthony Quinton, 'The Soul', *Journal of Philosophy* 59 (1962), pp. 393–409, and *idem*, *The Nature of Things* (London and Boston: Routledge & Kegan Paul, 1973); and Richard Taylor, *With Heart and Mind* (New York: St Martin's Press, 1973), pp. 122–33.

15 I have attempted to throw light upon these distinctions in ch. 4 ('The Problem of the Criterion') of *Theory of Knowledge* (Englewood Cliffs, NJ: Prentice-Hall, 1966). Compare the discussion of criteria of self-identity in Sydney Shoemaker, *Self-Knowledge and Self-Identity* (Ithaca, NY: Cornell University Press, 1963), pp. 35–8, 211–12, 255–60.

16 G.W. Leibniz, *Discourse on Metaphysics*, sect. 34 Open Court edn, p. 58. Sydney Shoemaker cited this passage in criticizing an earlier formulation of my views. This earlier formulation, Shoemaker's criticism, and my rejoinder may be found in Norman S. Care and Robert H. Grimm (eds), *Perception and Personal Identity* (Cleveland: Case Western Reserve Press, 1969), pp. 82–139.

17 Pierre Bayle, article 'Lucretius', note Q, in *A General Dictionary, Historical and Critical*, trans. Rev. J. P. Bernard, Rev. Thomas Birch, John Lockeman, et al. (10 vols, London: James Bettenham, 1734–41).

27

Persons and their Pasts

Sydney Shoemaker

Persons have, in memory, a special access to facts about their own past histories and their own identities, a kind of access they do not have to the histories and identities of other persons and other things. John Locke thought this special access important enough to warrant a special mention in his definition of "person," viz., "a thinking, intelligent Being, that has reason and reflection, *and can consider it self as it self, the same thinking thing, in different times and places*..."[1] In this essay I shall attempt to explain the nature and status of this special access and to defend Locke's view of its conceptual importance. I shall also attempt to correct what now seem to me to be errors and oversights in my own previous writings on this topic.

I

As a first approximation, the claim that persons have in memory a special access to their own past histories can be expressed in two related claims, both of which will be considerably qualified in the course of this essay. The first is that it is a necessary condition of its being true that a person remembers a given past event that he, that same person, should have observed or experienced the event, or known of it in some other direct way, at the time of its occurrence. I shall refer to this as the "previous awareness condition" for remembering.[2]

Originally published in *American Philosophical Quarterly* 7 (1970).

The second claim is that an important class of first-person memory claims are in a certain respect immune to what I shall call "error through mis-identification." Consider a case in which I say, on the basis of my memory of a past incident, "I shouted that Johnson should be impeached," and compare this with a case in which I say, again on the basis of my memory of a past incident, "John shouted that Johnson should be impeached." In the latter case it could turn out that I do remember someone who looked and sounded just like John shouting that Johnson should be impeached, but that the man who shouted this was nevertheless not John – it may be that I misidentified the person as John at the time I observed the incident, and that I have preserved this misidentification in memory, or it may be that I subsequently misidentified him as John on the basis of what I (correctly) remembered about him. Here my statement would be false, but its falsity would not be due to a mistake or fault of my memory; my memory could be as accurate and complete as any memory could be without precluding this sort of error. But this sort of misidentification is not possible in the former case. My memory report could of course be mistaken, for one can misremember such incidents, but it could not be the case that I have a full and accurate memory of the past incident but am mistaken in thinking that the person I remember shouting was myself. I shall speak of such memory judgments as being immune to error through misidentification with respect to the first-person pronouns, or other "self-referring" expressions, contained in them.[3]

I do not contend that all memory claims are immune to error through misidentification with respect to the first-person pronouns contained in them. If I say "I blushed when Jones made that remark" because I remember seeing in a mirror someone, whom I took (or now take) to be myself, blushing, it could turn out that my statement is false, not because my memory is in any way incomplete or inaccurate, but because the person I saw in the mirror was my identical twin or double.[4] In general, if at some past time I could have known of someone that he was φ, and could at the same time have been mistaken in taking that person to be myself, then the subsequent memory claims I make about the past occasion will be subject to error through misidentification with respect to the first-person pronouns. But if, as is frequently the case, I could not have been mistaken in this way in the past in asserting what I then knew by saying "I *am* φ," then my subsequent memory claim "I *was* φ" will be immune to error through misidentification relative to "I"; that is, it is impossible in such cases that I should accurately remember someone being φ but mistakenly take that person to be myself. We might express this by saying that where the present-tense version of a judgment is immune to error through misidentification relative to the first-person pronouns contained in it, this immunity is *preserved* in memory.[5] Thus if I claim on the strength of memory that I saw John yesterday, and have a full and accurate memory of the incident, it cannot be the case that I remember someone seeing John but have misidentified that person as myself; my memory claim "I saw John" is subject to error through misidentification with respect to the term "John" (for it could have been John's twin or double that I saw), but not with respect to "I."

II

In his early paper, "Personal identity," H. P. Grice held that the proposition "One can only remember one's own past experiences" is analytic, but pointed out that this would be analytic in only a trivial way "if 'memory' were to be defined in terms of 'having knowledge of one's own past experiences.'" He says that "even if we were to define 'memory' in this sort of way, we should still be left with a question about the proposition, 'one can only have knowledge of one's own past experiences,' which seems to me a necessary proposi-

tion."[6] Now I doubt very much if Grice, or any other philosopher, would now want to hold that it is necessarily true, or that it is true at all, that one's own past experiences are the only past experiences of which one can have knowledge. But one does not have to hold this to hold, with Grice, that it is not just a trivial analytic truth that one's own experiences are the only ones that one can remember, i.e., that it is not the case that the necessity of this truth derives merely from the fact that we refuse to *call* someone's having knowledge of a past experience a case of his remembering it unless the past experience belonged to the rememberer himself.

Grice's remarks are explicitly about memory of past experiences, but they raise an important question about all sorts of "event memory." Supposing it to be a necessary truth that the previous witnessing condition must be satisfied in any genuine case of remembering, is this necessarily true because we would refuse to *count* knowing about a past event as remembering it if the previous awareness condition were not satisfied, or is it necessary for some deeper reason? I think that many philosophers would hold that if this is a necessary truth at all, it is so only in the former way, i.e., in such a way as to make its necessity trivial and uninteresting. Thus G. C. Nerlich, in a footnote to his paper "On evidence for identity," says that it is true only of *our* world, not of all possible worlds, that only by being identical with a witness to past events can one have the sort of knowledge of them one has in memory.[7] On this view it is logically possible that we should have knowledge of past events which we did not ourselves witness, of experiences we did not ourselves have, and of actions we did not ourselves perform, that is in all important respects like the knowledge we have of past events, experiences, and actions in remembering them. If one takes this view, it will seem a matter of small importance, if indeed it is true, that the having of such knowledge could not be called "remembering."

It is of course not absolutely clear just what it means to speak of knowledge as being "in all important respects like" memory knowledge, if this is not intended to imply that the knowledge *is* memory knowledge. Presumably, knowledge of past events that is "just like" memory knowledge must not be inferred from present data (diaries, photographs, rock strata, etc.) on the basis of empirical laws and generalizations. But while this is necessary, it is not sufficient. When a person remembers a past event, there is a correspondence between his present cognitive state and some past cognitive and sensory state of his that existed at the time of the remembered event and consisted in his experiencing the event or otherwise being aware of its occurrence.[8] I shall say that remembering a past event involves there being a correspondence between the rememberer's present cognitive state and a past cognitive and sensory state that was "of" the event.[9] In actual memory this past cognitive and sensory state is always a past state of the rememberer himself. What we need to consider is whether there could be a kind of knowledge of past events such that someone's having this sort of knowledge of an event does involve there being a correspondence between his present cognitive state and a past cognitive and sensory state that was of the event, but such that this correspondence, although otherwise just like that which exists in memory, does not necessarily involve that past state's having been a state of the very same person who subsequently has the knowledge. Let us speak of such knowledge, supposing for the moment that it is possible, as "quasi-memory knowledge," and let us say that a person who has this sort of knowledge of a past event "quasi-remembers" that past event. Quasi-remembering, as I shall use the term, includes remembering as a special case. One way of characterizing the difference between quasi-remembering and remembering is by saying that the former is subject to a weaker previous awareness condition than the latter. Whereas someone's claim to remember a past event implies that he himself was aware of the event at the time of its occurrence, the claim to quasi-remember a past event implies only that someone or other was aware of it. Except when I indicate otherwise, I shall use the expression "previous awareness condition" to refer to the stronger of these conditions.

Our faculty of memory constitutes our most direct access to the past, and this means, given the previous awareness condition, that our most direct access to the past is in the first instance an access to *our own* past histories. One of the main questions I shall be considering in this essay is whether it is conceivable that our most direct access to the past should be a faculty of quasi-remembering which is not a faculty of remembering. Is it conceivable that we should have, as a matter of course, knowledge that is related to past experiences and actions other than our own in just the way in which, as things are, our memory knowledge is related to our own past experiences and actions? In our world all quasi-remembering is remembering; what we must consider is whether

the world could be such that most quasi-remembering is not remembering.

Before going on to consider this question, I should mention two reasons why I think it important. The first is its obvious bearing on the question of the relationship between the concepts of memory and personal identity. If there can be quasi-remembering that is not remembering, and if remembering can be defined as quasi-remembering that is of events the quasi-rememberer was aware of at the time of their occurrence (thus making it a trivial analytic truth that one can remember an event only if one was previously aware of it), then it would seem that any attempt to define or analyze the notion of personal identity in terms of the notion of remembering will be viciously circular. I shall have more to say about this in section V. But this question also has an important bearing on the question of how a person's memory claims concerning his own past are grounded. In previous writings I have claimed, and made a great deal of the claim, that our memory knowledge of our own past histories, unlike our knowledge of the past histories of other things, is not grounded on criteria of identity.[10] Strawson makes a similar claim in *The Bounds of Sense*, saying that "When a man (a subject of experience) ascribes a current or directly remembered state of consciousness to himself, no use whatever of any criteria of personal identity is required to justify his use of the pronoun 'I' to refer to the subject of that experience." He remarks that "it is because Kant recognized this truth that his treatment of the subject is so greatly superior to Hume's."[11] Now it can easily seem that this claim follows immediately from the fact that remembering necessarily involves the satisfaction of the previous awareness condition. If one remembers a past experience, then it has to have been one's own, and from this it may seem to follow that it makes no sense to inquire concerning a remembered experience whether it was one's own and then to try to answer this question on the basis of empirical criteria of identity. But suppose that it were only a trivial analytic truth that remembering involves the satisfaction of the previous awareness condition, and suppose that it were possible to quasi-remember experiences other than one's own. If this were so, one might remember a past experience but not know whether one was remembering it or only quasi-remembering it. Here, it seems, it would be perfectly appropriate to employ a criterion of identity to determine whether the quasi-remembered experience was one's own, i.e., whether one remembered it as opposed to merely quasi-remembering it. Thus the question of whether the knowledge of our own identities provided us by memory is essentially non-critical turns on the question of whether it is possible to quasi-remember past actions and experiences without remembering them.

III

There is an important respect in which my characterization of quasi-remembering leaves that notion inadequately specified. Until now I have been ignoring the fact that a claim to remember a past event implies, not merely that the rememberer experienced such an event, but that his present memory is in some way *due* to, that it came about *because of*, a cognitive and sensory state the rememberer had at the time he experienced the event. I am going to assume, although this is controversial, that it is part of the previous awareness condition for memory that a veridical memory must not only correspond to, but must also stand in an appropriate *causal* relationship to, a past cognitive and sensory state of the rememberer.[12] It may seem that if quasi-memory is to be as much like memory as possible, we should build a similar requirement in to the previous awareness condition for quasi-memory, i.e., that we should require that a veridical quasi-memory must not only correspond to, but must also stand in an appropriate causal relationship to, a past cognitive and sensory state of someone or other. On the other hand, it is not immediately obvious that building such a requirement into the previous awareness condition for quasi-memory would not make it equivalent to the previous awareness condition for memory, and thus destroy the intended difference between memory and quasi-memory. But there is no need for us to choose between a previous awareness condition that includes the causal requirement and one that does not, for it is possible and useful to consider both. In the present section I shall assume that the previous awareness condition for quasi-memory does not include the causal requirement, and that it includes nothing more than the requirement that a quasi-memory must, to be a veridical quasi-memory of a given event, correspond in content to a past cognitive and sensory state that was of that event. In the sections that follow I shall consider the consequences of strengthening this condition to include the causal requirement.

The first thing we must consider is what becomes of the immunity of first-person memory claims to error through misidentification if we imagine the faculty of memory replaced by a faculty of quasi-memory. As things are now, there is a difference between, on the one hand, remembering an action of someone else's – this might consist, for example, in having a memory of seeing someone do the action – and, on the other hand, remembering *doing* an action, which can be equated with remembering *oneself* doing the action. In the case of quasi-remembering, the distinction corresponding to this is that between, on the one hand, the sort of quasi-memory of a past action whose corresponding past cognitive and sensory state belonged to someone who was watching someone else do the action and, on the other hand, the sort of quasi-memory of a past action whose corresponding past cognitive and sensory state belonged to the very person who did the action. Let us call these, respectively, quasi-memories of an action "from the outside" and quasi-memories of an action "from the inside." Now whereas I can remember an action from the inside only if it was my action, a world in which there is quasi-remembering that is not remembering will be one in which it is not true that any action one quasi-remembers from the inside is thereby an action he himself did. So – assuming that ours may be such a world – if I quasi-remember an action from the inside, and say on this basis that I did the action, my statement will be subject to error through misidentification; it may be that my quasi-memory of the action is as accurate and complete as it could be, but that I am mistaken in thinking that I am the person who did it. There is another way in which a first-person quasi-memory claim could be mistaken through misidentification. If there can be quasi-remembering that is not remembering, it will be possible for a person to quasi-remember an action of his own from the outside. That is, one might quasi-remember an action of one's own as it appeared to someone else who observed it; one might, as it were, quasi-remember it through the eyes of another person. But of course, if I were to quasi-remember someone who looks like me doing a certain action, and were to say on that basis that I did the action, I might be mistaken through no fault of my quasi-memory; it might be that the person who did the action was my identical twin or someone disguised to look like me.

What I have just said about the quasi-remembering of past actions also applies to the quasi-remembering of past experiences and of other mental phenomena. If I remember a past pain from the inside – i.e., remember the pain itself, or remember having the pain, as opposed to remembering seeing someone manifest pain behavior – then the pain must have been mine. But the fact that I *quasi*-remember a pain from the inside will be no guarantee that the pain was mine. Any quasi-memory claim to have been in pain on some past occasion, or to have had a certain thought, or to have made a certain decision, will be subject to error through misidentification.

What is shown by the foregoing is that the immunity of first-person memory claims to error through misidentification exists only because remembering requires the satisfaction of the previous awareness condition, and that this feature disappears once we imagine this requirement dropped. Quasi-memory, unlike memory, does not preserve immunity to error through misidentification relative to the first-person pronouns. To consider the further consequences of replacing memory with quasi-memory, I must first say something more about memory.

To refer to an event of a certain sort as one that one remembers does not always uniquely identify it, since one may remember more than one event of a given sort, but it does go some way toward identifying it. In referring to an event in this way, one to a certain extent locates it in space and time, even if the description of the event contains no place-names, no names of objects by reference to which places can be identified, and no dates or other temporal indicators. For in saying that one remembers the event, one locates it within a spatiotemporal region which is defined by one's own personal history. The spatiotemporal region which is "rememberable" by a given person can be charted by specifying the intervals of past time during which the person was conscious and by specifying the person's spatial location, and indicating what portions of his environment he was in a position to witness, at each moment during these intervals. If someone reports that he remembers an event of a certain kind, we know that unless his memory is mistaken, an event of that kind occurred within the spatiotemporal region rememberable by him, and in principle we can chart this region by tracing his history back to its beginning.

Ordinarily, of course, we have far more knowledge than this of the spatiotemporal location of a remembered event, for usually a memory report will fix this position by means of dates, place-names, and other spatial and temporal indicators. But it must be noted that memory claims are subject to error through misidentification with respect to spatial indicators. If a man says "I remember an explosion occurring right in front of that building," it is possible for this to be false even if the memory it expresses is accurate and detailed; the remembered explosion may have occurred, not in front of the building indicated, but in front of another building exactly like it. This remains true no matter how elaborate and detailed we imagine the memory claim to be. For any set of objects that has actually existed in the world, even if this be as extensive as the set of buildings, streets, parks, bridges, etc. that presently make up New York City, it is logically possible that there should somewhere exist, or that there should somewhere and at some time have existed, a numerically different but exactly similar set of objects arranged in exactly the same way. So memory claims are, in principle, subject to error through misidentification even with respect to such place names as "New York City." Here I am appealing to what Strawson has referred to as the possibility of 'massive reduplication.'[13]

When a memory report attempts to fix the location of a remembered event by reference to some landmark, we are ordinarily justified in not regarding it as a real possibility that the claim involves error through misidentification owing to the reduplication of that landmark. Certainly we are so justified if the landmark is New York City. But it is important to see why this is so. It is not that we have established that nowhere and at no time has there existed another city exactly like New York; as a self-consistent, unrestricted, negative existential claim, this is something that it would be impossible in principle for us to establish.[14] What we can and do know is that New York is not reduplicated within any spatiotemporal region of which anyone with whom we converse can have had experience. Whether or not New York is reduplicated in some remote galaxy or at some remote time in the past, we know that the man who claims to remember doing or experiencing something in a New York-like city cannot have been in any such duplicate. And from this we can conclude that if he does remember doing or experiencing something in a New York-like city, then it was indeed in New York, and not in any duplicate of it, that the remembered action or event occurred. But we can conclude this only because remembering involves the satisfaction of the previous awareness condition.

Even when a landmark referred to in someone's memory claim is reduplicated within the spatiotemporal region rememberable by that person, we can often be confident that the claim does not involve error through misidentification. Suppose that someone locates a remembered event, say an explosion, by saying that it occurred in front of his house, and we know that there are many houses, some of which he has seen, that are exactly like his. If he reported that he had simply found himself in front of his house, with no recollection of how he had gotten there, and that after seeing the explosion he had passed out and awakened later in a hospital, we would think it quite possible that he had misidentified the place at which the remembered explosion occurred. But suppose instead that he reports that he remembers walking home from work, seeing the explosion in front of his house, and then going inside and being greeted by his family. Here a misidentification of the place of the explosion would require the reduplication, not merely of his house, but also of his family, his place of work, and the route he follows in walking home from work. We could know that no such reduplication exists within the spatiotemporal region of which he has had experience, and could conclude that his report did not involve an error through misidentification. But again, what would enable us to conclude this is the fact that remembering involves the satisfaction of the previous awareness condition.

Presumably, what justifies any of us in using such expressions as "New York" and "my house" in his own memory reports are considerations of the same kind as those that justify others in ruling out the possibility that claims containing such expressions involve error through misidentification. What justifies one is the knowledge that certain sorts of reduplication do not in fact occur within the spatiotemporal regions of which any of us have had experience. Normally no such justification is needed for the use of "I" in memory reports; this is what is involved in saying that memory claims are normally immune to error through misidentification relative to the first-person pronouns. But what makes such a justification possible in the case of "New York" is the same as what makes it unnecessary in the case of "I": namely, the fact that remembering involves the satisfaction of the previous awareness condition. So it is because of this fact that remembering can provide us, not merely with the information that an event of a certain sort has occurred somewhere or other in the vicinity of persons and things satisfy-

ing certain general descriptions, but with the information that such an event occurred in a certain specified place, in a certain specifiable spatial relationship to events presently observed, and in the vicinity of certain specified persons or things. But this is also to say that it is this fact about remembering that makes it possible for us to know that an object or person to which one remembers something happening is, or is not, identical with an object or person presently observed. And it will emerge later that it is also this fact about remembering that makes it possible to know that different memories are, or are not, of events in the history of a single object or person.

But now let us consider the consequences of replacing the faculty of memory by a faculty of quasi-memory. Quasi-remembering does not necessarily involve the satisfaction of the previous awareness condition, and first-person quasi-memory claims are, as we have seen, subject to error through misidentification. It is a consequence of this that even if we are given that someone's faculty of quasi-memory is highly reliable, in the sense that when he seems to quasi-remember an event of a certain sort he almost always does quasi-remember such an event, nevertheless, his quasi-memory will provide neither him nor us with any positive information concerning the spatial location of the events he quasi-remembers, or with any information concerning the identity, or concerning the history, of any object or person to which he quasi-remembers something happening. The fact that he quasi-remembers an event of a certain sort will not provide us with the information that such an event has occurred within the spatiotemporal region of which he has had experience. But in consequence of this, if he attempts to locate the quasi-remembered event by reference to some object or place known to us, e.g., New York or Mt Everest, it is impossible for us to rule out on empirical grounds the possibility that his claim involves error through misidentification owing to the reduplication of that object or place. To rule this out, we would have to have adequate grounds for asserting, not merely that there is no duplicate of New York (say) in the spatiotemporal region of which he has had experience, but that at no place and time has there been a duplicate of New York. And this we could not have.[15] But this means that in expressing his quasi-memories he could not be justified in using such expressions as "New York" and "Mt Everest," or such expressions as "I," "this," and "here," to refer to the places, persons, and things in or to which he quasi-remembers certain things happening. The most he could be entitled to assert on the basis of his quasi-memories would be a set of general propositions of the form "An event of type φ at some time occurred in the history of an object of type A while it stood in relations $R_1, R_2, R_3 \ldots$ to objects of types B, C, $D \ldots$" And given only a set of propositions of this sort, no matter how extensive, one could not even begin to reconstruct any part of the history of the world; one could not even have grounds for asserting that an object mentioned in one proposition in the set was one and the same as an object mentioned in another proposition of the set.

So far I have been ignoring the fact that the events and actions we remember generally have temporal duration, and the fact that we sometimes remember connected sequences of events and actions lasting considerable lengths of time. What will correspond to this if remembering is replaced with quasi-remembering? If someone says "I remember doing X and then doing Y," it would make no sense to say to him, "Granted that your memory is accurate, and that such a sequence of actions did occur, are you sure that it was one and the same person who did both X and Y?" But now suppose that someone says "I quasi-remember doing X and then doing Y," and that the world is such that there is quasi-remembering that is not remembering. Here it is compatible with the accuracy of the man's quasi-memory that he should be mistaken in thinking that he himself did X and Y. And as I shall now try to show, it must also be compatible with the accuracy of this man's quasi-memories that he should be mistaken in thinking even that one and the same person did both X and Y.

Suppose that at time t_1 a person, call him A, does action Y and has while doing it a quasi-memory from the inside of the immediately previous occurrence of the doing of action X. A's having this quasi-memory of the doing of X is of course compatible with X's having been done by someone other than himself. At t_1 A's cognitive state includes this quasi-memory from the inside of the doing of X together with knowledge from the inside of the doing of Y; we might say that it includes knowledge from the inside of the action sequence X-followed-by-Y. But now suppose that at a later time t_2 someone, call him B, has a quasi-memory corresponding to the cognitive state of A at t_1. It would seem that B's quasi-memory will be a quasi-memory from the inside of the action

sequence X-followed-by-Y. This quasi-memory will be veridical in the sense that it corresponds to a past cognitive state that was itself a state of knowledge, yet its being veridical in this way is compatible with X and Y having been done by different persons. If A were mistakenly to assert at t_1 that X and Y were done by the same person, his mistake would not be due to a faulty quasi-memory. And if B's cognitive state at t_2 corresponds to A's cognitive state at t_1, then if B were mistaken at t_2 in thinking that X and Y were done by the same person, this mistake would not be due to a faulty quasi-memory.

If, as I have been arguing, someone's quasi-remembering from the inside the *action* sequence X-followed-by-Y provides no guarantee that X and Y were done by the same person, then by the same reasoning someone's quasi-remembering the *event* sequence X-followed-by-Y provides no guarantee that X and Y were witnessed by the same person, and therefore no guarantee that they occurred in spatial proximity to one another. But any temporally extended event can be thought of as a succession of temporally and spatially contiguous events; e.g., a stone's rolling down a hill can be thought of as consisting in its rolling half of the way down followed by its rolling the other half of the way. Suppose, then, that someone has a quasi-memory of the following event sequence: stone rolling from top of hill to middle followed by stone rolling from middle of hill to bottom. If we knew this to be a memory, and not just a quasi-memory, we would know that if it is veridical, then one and the same person observed both of these events, one immediately after the other, and this together with the contents of the memory could guarantee that one and the same hill and one and the same stone were involved in both, and that a single stone had indeed rolled all the way down a hill. But the veridicality of this quasi-memory *qua* quasi-memory would be compatible with these events having been observed by different persons, and with their involving different stones and different hills; it would be compatible with no stone's having rolled all of the way down any hill. And since any temporally extended event can be thought of as a succession of temporally and spatially contiguous events, it follows that someone's quasi-remembering what is ostensibly a temporally extended event of a certain kind is always compatible with there actually being no such event that he quasi-remembers, for it is compatible with his quasi-memory being, as it were, compounded out of quasi-memories of a number of different events that were causally unrelated and spatiotemporally remote from one another. The knowledge of the past provided by such a faculty of quasi-memory would be minimal indeed.[16]

IV

But now we must consider the consequences of strengthening the previous awareness condition for quasi-remembering to include the requirement that a veridical quasi-memory must not only correspond to, but must also stand in an appropriate causal relationship to, a past cognitive and sensory state of someone or other. Clearly, much of what I have said about quasi-remembering ceases to hold once its previous awareness condition is strengthened in this way. If, as is commonly supposed, causal chains must be spatiotemporally continuous, then if quasi-memory claims implied the satisfaction of this strengthened previous awareness condition, they would, when true, provide some information concerning the location of the quasi-remembered events and actions. We would know at a minimum that the spatiotemporal relationship between the quasi-remembered event and the making of the quasi-memory claim is such that it is possible for them to be linked by a spatiotemporally continuous causal chain, and if we could trace the causal ancestry of the quasi-memory, we could determine precisely when and where the quasi-remembered event occurred. Thus if we construe the previous awareness condition of quasi-memory as including this causal requirement, it seems that a faculty of quasi-remembering could enable us to identify past events and to reidentify persons and things, and it seems at first glance (though not, I think, on closer examination) that it would enable us to do this without giving us a special access to our own past histories.

It must be stressed that this strengthened previous awareness condition is an improvement on the weaker one *only* on the assumption that causal chains (or at any rate the causal chains that link cognitive and sensory states with subsequent quasi-memories) must be spatiotemporally continuous, or at least must satisfy a condition similar to spatiotemporal continuity. If the sort of causality operating here allowed for action at a spatial or temporal distance, and if there were no limit on the size of the spatial or temporal gaps that could exist in a causal chain linking a cognitive and sensory state

with a subsequent quasi-memory, then the claim that a quasi-memory originated in a corresponding cognitive and sensory state would be as unfalsifiable, and as uninformative, as the claim that it corresponds to a past cognitive and sensory state of someone or other.

To consider the consequences of strengthening the previous awareness condition for quasi-memory in the way just suggested, I shall have to introduce a few technical expressions. First, I shall use the expressions "quasi$_c$-remember" and "quasi$_c$-memory" when speaking of the sort of quasi-remembering whose previous awareness condition includes the causal requirement. Second, I shall use the term "M-type causal chain" to refer to the sort of causal chain that must link a quasi$_c$-memory with a corresponding past cognitive and sensory state if they are to be "of" the same event, or if the former is to be "of" the latter. Since quasi$_c$-remembering is to be as much like remembering as is compatible with the failure of the strong previous awareness condition, M-type causal chains should resemble as much as possible the causal chains that are responsible for actual remembering, i.e., should resemble them as much as is compatible with their sometimes linking mental states belonging to different persons. At any given time a person can be said to have a total mental state which includes his memories or quasi$_c$- memories and whatever other mental states the person has at that time. Let us say that two total mental states, existing at different times, are directly M-connected if the later of them contains a quasi$_c$ memory which is linked by an M-type causal chain to a corresponding cognitive and sensory state contained in the earlier. And let us say, by way of giving a recursive definition, that two total mental states are M-connected if either (1) they are directly M-connected, or (2) there is some third total mental state to which each of them is M-connected.[17]

Now there are two cases we must consider. Either the world will be such, or it will not, that a total mental state existing at a particular time can be M-connected with at most one total mental state existing at each other moment in time. Or, what comes to the same thing, either the world will be such, or it will not, that no two total mental states existing at the same time can be M-connected. Let us begin by considering the case in which the former of these alternatives holds. This is the case that will exist if there is no "branching" of M-type causal chains, i.e., if it never happens that an M-type causal chain branches into two such chains which then produce quasi$_c$-memories belonging to different and simultaneously existing total mental states, and if it never happens that different M-type causal chains coalesce and produce in a single total mental state quasi$_c$-memories whose corresponding past cognitive and sensory states belonged to different and simultaneously existing total mental states. This is presumably the situation that exists in the actual world. And I think that in any world in which this situation exists, M-connected total mental states will be, to use a term of Bertrand Russell's, "copersonal," i.e., states of one and the same person, and quasi$_c$-remembering will reduce to remembering. There seems to me to be at least this much truth in the claim that memory is constitutive of personal identity.[18] (But more about this in section V.)

Now let us consider the case in which M-type causal chains do sometimes branch, and in which, as a result, it can happen that two or more simultaneously existing total mental states are M-connected. Here we cannot claim that if two total mental states are M-connected, they are thereby copersonal without committing ourselves to the unattractive conclusion that a person can be in two different places, and can have two different total mental states, at one and the same time. But it is still open to us to say that if a total mental state existing at time t_1 and a total mental state existing at time t_2 are M-connected, then they are copersonal *unless* the M-type causal chain connecting them branched at some time during the interval $t_1 - t_2$. If we can say this, as I think we can, then even in a world in which there is branching of M-type causal chains, the fact that a person quasi$_c$-remembers a past event or action would create a presumption that he, that same person, experienced the event or did the action, and therefore a presumption that the quasi$_c$-memory was actually a memory. This presumption would stand as long as there was no evidence that the M-type causal chain linking the past action or experience with the subsequent quasi$_c$-memory had branched during the interval between them.

Worlds of the sort we are now considering, i.e., worlds in which M-type causal chains sometimes branch, could be of several kinds. Consider first a world in which people occasionally undergo fission or fusion; i.e., people sometimes split, like amoebas, both offshoots having quasi$_c$-memories of the actions done prior to the fission by the person who underwent it, and two people sometimes coalesce

into a single person who then has quasi$_c$-memories of both of their past histories. Here we cannot say that a person did whatever actions he quasi$_c$-remembers from the inside without running afoul of Leibniz' law and the principle of the transitivity of identity. But we can say something close to this. Suppose that someone, call him Jones, splits into two persons, one of whom is me and the other is someone I shall call Jones II. Both Jones II and I have quasi$_c$-memories from the inside of Jones's past actions, and no one else does. If anyone now alive is identical with Jones, it is either myself or Jones II, and any objection to saying that I am Jones is equally an objection to saying that Jones II is Jones. I think that we can say here that I am identical with Jones if anyone now alive is identical with him. Or suppose that two people, call them Brown and Smith, coalesce, resulting in me. I have quasi$_c$-memories from the inside of Brown's actions and also of Smith's actions. There are serious objections to identifying me with either Brown or Smith, but it seems clear here that if anyone now alive is identical with either Brown or Smith, I am. So in such a world the following principle holds: if at time t a person A quasi$_c$-remembers a past action X from the inside, then A is identical with the person who did X if anyone alive at t is identical with him.[19]

But I think that we can imagine a world in which this principle would not hold. In the case in which two persons coalesce, the M-type causal chains involved might be represented by a river having two "forks" of equal width. Suppose that instead of this we have an M-type causal chain, or a connected set of such causal chains, that could be represented by a river having several small tributaries. For example, suppose, very fancifully, that memories were stored, by some sort of chemical coding, in the blood rather than in the brain cells, and that as a result of being given a blood transfusion, one sometimes acquired quasi$_c$-memories "from the inside" of a few of the actions of the blood donor. Here the blood transfusion would be a "tributary" into what apart from its tributaries would be the sort of M-type causal chain that occurs in the history of a single person. Now I do not think that we would deny that A, existing at time t_2, was the same person as B, who existed at an earlier time t_1, merely because A quasi$_c$-remembers from the inside, as the result of a blood transfusion, an action at t_1 that was not done by B. Nor would we deny that another person C, the blood donor, is the person who did that past action merely because there is someone other than himself, namely A, who quasi$_c$-remembers it from the inside. So here it would not be true that if at time t a person quasi$_c$-remembers a past action from the inside, then he is identical with the person who did it if anyone existing at t is identical with the person who did it.

Yet even in such a world it seems essential that in any total mental state the memories, i.e., the quasi$_c$-memories produced by the past history of the person whose total mental state it is, should outnumber the quasi$_c$-memories produced by any given tributary. If the quasi$_c$-memories produced by a given tributary outnumbered the memories, then surely the tributary would not be a tributary at all, but would instead be the main stream. But this implies that if a person quasi$_c$-remembers an action from the inside, then, in the absence of evidence to the contrary, he is entitled to regard it as more likely that the action was done by him than that it was done by any other given person. And this, taken together with my earlier point that if someone quasi$_c$-remembers an action from the inside, there is a presumption that he is the person who did it, gives us a sense in which quasi$_c$-memory can be said to provide the quasi$_c$-rememberer with "special access" to his own past history. This is of course a much weaker sense of "special access" than that explained in section I – but in this sense it will be true in *any* possible world, and not merely in ours, that people have a special access to their own past histories.

V

In the preceding sections it was assumed that remembering, as opposed to (mere) quasi$_c$-remembering, necessarily involves the satisfaction of the strong previous awareness condition; that is, it was assumed that in any genuine case of event memory the memory must correspond to a past cognitive and sensory state of the rememberer himself. And this is commonly supposed in discussions of memory and personal identity. But it is not really clear that this assumption is correct. For consider again the hypothetical case in which a man's body "splits" like an amoeba into two physiologically identical bodies, and in which both offshoots produce memory claims corresponding to the past life of the original person. Or, to take a case that lies closer to the realm of real possibility, consider the hypothetical case in which a human brain is split,

its two hemispheres are transplanted into the newly vacated skulls of different bodies, and both transplant recipients survive, regain consciousness, and begin to make memory claims that correspond to the past history of the brain "donor."[20] In neither case can we identify both of the physiological offshoots of a person with the original person, unless we are willing to take the drastic step of giving up Leibniz' Law and the transitivity of identity. But is it clear that it would be wrong to say that each of the offshoots remembers the actions, experiences, etc. of the original person? There is, to be sure, an awkwardness about saying that each offshoot remembers *doing* an action done by the original person, for this seems to imply that an action done by one and only one person was done by each of the two nonidentical offshoots. But perhaps we can say that each of the offshoots does remember the action "from the inside." In our world, where such bizarre cases do not occur, the only actions anyone remembers from the inside are those that he himself performed, so it is not surprising that the only idiomatic way of reporting that one remembers an action from the inside is by saying that one remembers doing the action. But this need not prevent us from describing my hypothetical cases by saying that both offshoots do remember the actions of the original person, and it does not seem to me unnatural to describe them in this way. If this is a correct way of describing them, then perhaps my second sort of quasi-remembering, i.e., quasi$_c$-remembering, turns out to be just remembering, and the previous awareness condition for remembering turns out to be the causal requirement discussed in the preceding section rather than the stronger condition I have been assuming it to be.

If the suggestion just made about the conditions for remembering is correct, the logical connection between remembering and personal identity is looser than I have been supposing it to be. Yet adopting this suggestion does not prevent one from defending the claim that remembering is constitutive of and criterial for personal identity; on the contrary, this makes it possible to defend the letter of this claim, and not just its spirit, against the very common objection that any attempt to analyze personal identity in terms of memory will turn out to be circular.

Bishop Butler objected against Locke's account of personal identity that "one should really think it self-evident, that consciousness of personal identity presupposes, and therefore cannot constitute, personal identity, any more than knowledge, in any other case, can constitute truth, which it presupposes."[21] More recently several writers have argued that while "S remembers doing A" entails "S did A" (and so entails "S is identical with the person who did A"), this is only because "S remembers doing A" is elliptical for "S remembers himself doing A."[22] To offer as a partial analysis of the notion of personal identity, and as a criterion of personal identity, the formula "If S remembers (himself) doing action A, S is the same as the person who did A" would be like offering as a partial definition of the word "red," and as a criterion of redness, the formula "If S knows that X is red, then X is red." In both cases the concept allegedly being defined is illicitly employed in the formulation of the defining condition. Likewise, it has been argued that while someone's remembering a past event is a sufficient condition of his being identical with a witness to the event, we cannot use the former as a criterion for the latter, since in order to establish that a person really does remember a given past event, we have to establish that he, that very person, was a witness to the event. And if this is so, the formula "If S remembers E, S is identical with someone who witnessed E" will be circular if offered as a partial analysis of the concept of personal identity.[23]

Such objections assume that remembering involves the satisfaction of the strong previous awareness condition, and they can be avoided on the assumption that the previous awareness condition is weaker than this, e.g., is that given for quasi$_c$-remembering in section IV. Or, better, they can be avoided if we explicitly use "remember" in a "weak" sense ("remember$_w$") rather than in a "strong" sense ("remember$_s$"), the strength of the sense depending on the strength of the associated previous awareness condition. Although there are perhaps other possibilities, let us take "remember$_w$" to be synonymous with "quasi$_c$-remember." Clearly, to establish that S remembers$_w$ event E (or remembers$_w$ action A from the inside) it is not necessary to establish that S himself witnessed E (or did A), for it will be enough if S is the offshoot of someone who witnessed E (did A). And while we cannot claim that statements about what events or actions a man remembers$_w$ logically entail statements about his identity and past history, this does not prevent the truth of the former from being criterial evidence for, and from being partially constitutive of, the truth of the latter. For we can still assert as a logical

truth that if S remembers$_w$ event E (or remembers$_w$ action A from the inside), *and* if there has been no branching of M-type causal chains during the relevant stretch of S's history, then S is one of the witnesses of E (is the person who did A). Here we avoid the circularity that Butler and others have thought to be involved in any attempt to give an account of personal identity, and of the criteria of personal identity, in terms of memory.

In the actual world, people remember$_s$ whatever they remember$_w$ and this makes it difficult to settle the question of whether it is the weak or the strong sense of "remember" that is employed in ordinary discourse. It is possible that this question has no answer; since branching of M-type causal chains does not in fact occur, and is seldom envisaged, people have had no practical motive for distinguishing between the strong and the weak senses of "remember." But I do not think that this question is especially important. We can defend the spirit of the claim that memory is a criterion of personal identity without settling this question, although in order to defend the letter of that claim, we must maintain that in its ordinary use "remember" means "remember$_w$."

At this point I should say something about why it is important to insist on the claim that there is a causal element in the notion of memory. For this claim has recently come under attack.[24] It has been argued that the notion of memory should be analyzed in terms of the *retention*, rather than the causation, of knowledge, and that the notion of retention is not itself a causal notion. Now I have no objection to saying that remembering$_s$ consists in the retention of knowledge. But I believe that unless we understand the notion of retention, as well as that of memory, as involving a causal component, we cannot account for the role played by the notion of memory, or even the concept of similarity, in judgements of personal identity.

Here it will be useful to consider a hypothetical case I have discussed at some length elsewhere.[25] Let us suppose that the brain from the body of one man, Brown, is transplanted into the body of another man, Robinson, and that the resulting creature – I call him "Brownson" – survives and upon regaining consciousness begins making memory claims corresponding to the past history of Brown rather than that of Robinson. We can also suppose that Brownson manifests personality traits strikingly like those previously manifested by Brown and quite unlike those manifested by Robinson. Although Brownson has Robinson's (former) body, I doubt if anyone would want to say that Brownson is Robinson, and I think that most people would want to say that Brownson is (is the same person as) Brown.

But what can we offer as evidence that Brownson is Brown? Clearly the mere correspondence of Brownson's ostensible memories to Brown's past history, and the similarity of Brownson's personality to Brown's, is far from being sufficient evidence. And it is equally clear that the notion of the *retention* of knowledge and traits is of no use here. To be sure, once we take ourselves to have established that Brownson is Brown, we can say that Brownson retains knowledge, and also personality traits, acquired by Brownson in the past. But the latter assertion presupposes the identity of Brownson and Brown, and cannot without circularity be offered as evidence for it. Indeed, the circularity is the same as what would be involved in offering as evidence of this identity the fact that Brownson remembers$_s$ Brown's past experiences and actions.

We do not, however, beg the question about identity if we take Brownson's possession of what used to be Brown's brain, together with the empirical facts about the role played by the brain in memory, as establishing that Brown's ostensible memories are directly M-connected with Brown's past actions and experiences, i.e., are causally related to them in essentially the same ways as people's memories are generally connected with their own past experiences and actions. This in turn establishes that Brownson quasi$_c$-remembers, and so remembers$_w$? Brown's past experiences and actions. And from this in turn, and from the fact that we have good reason to suppose that no other person's memories are M-connected with Brown's past history in this way, i.e., that there has been no 'branching' of M-type causal chains, we can conclude that Brownson is Brown.[26]

We can reason in this way only if we can assert that there is a causal connection between Brownson's past history and Brownson's ostensible memories. And this, it seems to me, we are clearly entitled to do. Given that Brownson has Brown's former brain, there is every reason to think that had Brown's history been different in certain ways, there would (*ceteris paribus*) be corresponding differences in what Brownson ostensibly remembers. I can see no reason for doubting that such counterfactuals assert causal connections. Similar remarks can be made about the similarity between Brownson's and Brown's personality traits. Given that Brownson has Brown's former brain, we have rea-

son to think that had Brown developed a different set of personality traits, Brownson would (*ceteris paribus*) have those personality traits rather than the ones he has. And while we cannot naturally speak of Brown's having a certain trait at one time as causing Brownson to have the same trait at a subsequent time, we can speak of the former as being an important part of a causally sufficient condition for the latter. It is only where we suppose that the traits of things at different times are causally related in this way that we are entitled to take the similarity of something at one time and something at another time as evidence of identity.

VI

We are now in a position to reassess the view, mentioned in section II, that the knowledge of our own pasts and our own identities provided us by memory is essentially "noncriterial." If I remember$_s$ an action or experience from the inside, and know that I do, it makes no sense for me to inquire whether that action or experience was my own. But it seems logically possible that one should remember$_w$ an action or experience from the inside (i.e., quasi$_c$-remember it) without remembering$_s$ it. So if one remembers$_w$ an action or experience from the inside, it can make sense to inquire whether it was one's own (whether one remembers$_s$ it), and it would seem offhand that there is no reason why one should not attempt to answer this question on the basis of criteria of personal identity.

But while an action I remember$_w$ from the inside can fail to be mine, there is only one way in which this can happen: namely, through there having been branching in the M-type causal chain linking it with my present memory. So in asking whether the action was mine, the only question I can significantly be asking is whether there was such branching. If I go on to verify that there was no branching, I thereby establish that a sufficient criterion of personal identity is satisfied. If instead I conclude on inductive grounds that there was no branching, relying on my general knowledge that M-type causal chains seldom or never branch (or that it is physiologically impossible for them to do so), I thereby conclude that a sufficient criterion of personal identity is satisfied. But an important part of what the satisfaction of this criterion consists in, namely my remembering$_w$ the past action from the inside, is not something I establish, and not something I necessarily presuppose in inquiring concerning my relation to the remembered$_w$ action. In cases where one remembers$_w$ a past action from the inside, and knows of it only on that basis, one cannot significantly inquire concerning it whether one does remember$_w$ it – for as I tried to bring out in my discussion of quasi-remembering, there is no way of knowing the past that stands to remembering$_w$ as remembering$_w$ stands to remembering$_s$, i.e., is such that one can know of a past event in this way and regard it as an open question whether in so knowing of it one is remembering$_w$ it. So in such cases the satisfaction of this part of the memory criterion for personal identity is a precondition of one's being able to raise the question of identity, and cannot be something one establishes in attempting to answer that question.

That one remembers$_w$ a past action is not (and could not be) one of the things one remembers$_w$ about it, and neither is the fact that there is no branching in the M-type causal chain linking it with one's memory of it. And normally there is no set of remembered$_w$ features of an action one remembers$_w$ from the inside, or of the person who did the action, by which one identifies the action as one's own and the agent as oneself. If one has not identified a remembered person as oneself on the basis of his remembered$_w$ features, then of course it cannot be the case that one has *mis*identified him on this basis. This is not to say that there is no basis on which one might misidentify a remembered$_w$ person as oneself. If there can, logically, be remembering$_w$ that is not remembering$_s$, then where one remembers$_w$ an action from the inside, one's judgment that one did the action will not be logically immune to error through misidentification in the sense defined in section II – though given the contingent fact that all remembering$_w$ is remembering$_s$, such judgments can be said to have a *de facto* immunity to error through misidentification. But the sort of error through misidentification to which a statement like "I saw a canary" is liable, if based on a memory$_w$ from the inside, is utterly different from that to which a statement like "John saw a canary" is liable when based on a memory$_w$ of the incident reported. If the making of the latter statement involves an error through misidentification, this will be because either (1) the speaker misidentified someone as John at the time the reported incident occurred, and retained this misidentification in memory, or (2) at some subsequent time, perhaps at the time of speaking, the speaker misidentified a remembered$_w$ person as John on the basis of his remembered$_w$ features. But

if I remember$_w$ from the inside someone seeing a canary, and am mistaken in thinking that person to have been myself, it is absurd to suppose that this mistake originated at the time at which the remembered$_w$ seeing occurred. Nor, as I have said, will this be a misidentification based on the remembered$_w$ features of the person who saw the canary. What could be the basis for a misidentification in this case is the mistaken belief that there is no branching in the M-type causal chain linking one's memory with the past incident. But a misidentification on this basis, while logically possible, would be radically unlike the misidentifications that actually occur in the making of third-person reports.

VII

Because I have taken seriously the possibility of worlds in which M-type causal chains sometimes branch, and thus the possibility of quasi$_c$-remembering (remembering$_w$) that is not remembering$_s$, I have had to qualify and weaken my initial claims about the "special access" people have to their own past histories. But if our concern is with the elucidation of our present concept of personal identity, and with personal identity as something that has a special sort of importance for us, then it is not clear that the possibility of such worlds, and the qualifications this requires, should be taken as seriously as I have taken them. For there is reason to think (1) that some of our concepts, perhaps including the concept of a person, would necessarily undergo significant modification in their application to such worlds, and (2) that in such worlds personal identity would not *matter* to people in quite the way it does in the actual world.

There are important connections between the concept of personal identity and the concepts of various "backward-looking" and "forward-looking" mental states. Thus the appropriate objects of remorse, and of a central sort of pride, are past actions done by the very person who is remorseful or proud, and the appropriate objects of fear and dread, and of delighted anticipation, are events which the subject of these emotions envisages as happening to himself. And intentions have as their "intentional objects" actions to be done by the very person who has the intention. It is difficult to see how the notion of a person could be applied, *with these conceptual connections remaining intact*, to a world in which M-type causal chains frequently branch, e.g., one in which persons frequently undergo fission. If I remember$_w$ from the inside a cruel or deceitful action, am I to be relieved of all tendency to feel remorse if I discover that because of fission someone else remembers$_w$ it too? May I not feel proud of an action I remember$_w$ from the inside even though I know that I am only one of several offshoots of the person who did it, and so cannot claim to be identical with him? Am I not to be afraid of horrible things I expect to happen to my future offshoots, and not to view with pleasant anticipation the delights that are in prospect for them? And is it to be impossible, or logically inappropriate, for me knowingly to form intentions, and make decisions and plans, which because of the prospect of immanent fission will have to be carried out by my offshoots rather than by me? To the extent that I can imagine such a world, I find it incredible to suppose that these questions must be answered in the affirmative. The prospect of immanent fission might not be appealing, but it seems highly implausible to suppose that the only rational attitude toward it would be that appropriate to the prospect of immanent death (for fission, unlike death, would be something "lived through"). It seems equally implausible to suppose that a person's concern for the well-being of his offshoots should be construed as altruism; surely this concern would, or at any rate could, be just like the self-interested concern each of us has for his own future well-being. Yet a negative answer to my rhetorical questions would suggest that either the concept of a person or such concepts as those of

pride, remorse, fear, etc. would undergo significant modification in being applied to such a world.[27]

A person's past history is the most important source of his knowledge of the world, but it is also an important source of his knowledge, and his conception, of himself; a person's "self-image," his conception of his own character, values, and potentialities, is determined in a considerable degree by the way in which he views his own past actions. And a person's future history is the primary focus of his desires, hopes, and fears.[28] If these remarks do not express truths about the concept of personal identity, they at least express truths about the *importance* of this concept in our conceptual scheme, or in our "form of life." It seems plausible to suppose that in a world in which fission was common, personal identity would not have this sort of importance. Roughly speaking, the portion of past history that would matter to a person in this special way would be that which it is possible for him to remember$_w$, and not merely that which it is possible for him to remember$_s$. And the focus of people's "self-interested" attitudes and emotions would be the future histories of their offshoots, and of their offshoots' offshoots, and so on, as well as their own future histories. In the actual world it is true both that (1) remembering$_w$ is always remembering$_s$ (and thus that there is special access in the strong sense characterized in section I), and that (2) the primary focus of a person's "self-interested" attitudes and emotions is his own past and future history. It is surely no accident that (1) and (2) go together.

Notes

1 John Locke, *Essay Concerning Human Understanding*, ed. Peter H. Nidditch (Oxford: Clarendon Press, 1975), p. 335 (bk 11, ch. 27, sect. 9); italics added.
2 In their paper "Remembering," (*Philosophical Review* 75 (1966), C. B. Martin and Max Deutscher express what I call the previous awareness condition by saying that "a person can be said to remember something happening or, in general, remember something directly, only if he has observed or experienced it." Their notion of direct remembering seems to be much the same as Norman Malcolm's notion of "personal memory" (see his "Three forms of memory," in *Knowledge and Certainty* (Englewood Cliffs, NJ: Prentice-Hall, 1963), pp. 203–21). To remember that Caesar invaded Britain, I need not have had any experience of the invasion, but no one who lacked such experience could directly or personally remem-

ber that Caesar invaded Britain. In this essay I am primarily concerned with memories that are of events, i.e., of something happening, and do not explicitly consider what Malcolm calls "factual memory," i.e., memories *that* such and such was (or is, or will be) the case; but what I say can be extended to cover all cases of direct or personal memory. Martin and Deutscher hold, and I agree, that remembering something happening is always direct remembering.

There are apparent counterexamples to the previous witnessing condition as I have formulated it. I can be said to remember Kennedy's assassination, which is presumably an event, yet I did not witness or observe it, and the knowledge I had of it at the time was indirect. But while I can be said to remember the assassination, I could hardly be said to remember Kennedy being shot (what I do remember is hearing about it, and the impact this made on me and those around me). Perhaps I can be said to remember the assassination because we sometimes mean by "the assassination" not only the events in Dallas but their immediate effects throughout the nation and world. In any case, when I speak of memories of events in this essay, I mean what Martin and Deutscher speak of as memories of something happening.

3 Although self-reference is typically done with first-person pronouns, it can be done with names, and even with definite descriptions – as when de Gaulle says "De Gaulle intends..." and the chairman of a meeting says "The Chair recognizes...," In such cases these expressions are "self-referring," not merely because their reference is in fact to the speaker, but also because the speaker intends in using them to refer to himself.

4 There is a subtle distinction between this sort of case and cases like the following, which I would not count as a case of error through misidentification. Suppose that Jones says "You are a fool," and I mistakenly think that he is speaking to me. Subsequently I say "I remember Jones calling me a fool," and my statement is false through no fault of my memory. While this is a case of knowing *that* Jones called someone (someone or other) a fool and mistakenly thinking that he was calling me a fool, it is not a case of knowing *of* some particular person that Jones called him a fool but mistakenly identifying that person as oneself. Whereas in the other case we can say, not merely that I know that someone or other blushed, and mistakenly think that it was I, but that I know *of* some particular person (namely the man I saw in the mirror) that he blushed and have mistakenly identified him as myself.

5 I have discussed the immunity to error through misidentification of first-person present-tense statements in Sydney Shoemaker, *Identity, Cause and Mind* (Cambridge: Cambridge University Press, 1984), Essay I. There I made the mistake of associating this feature with the peculiarities of the first-person pronouns. But in fact present-tense statements having the appropriate sorts of predicates are immune to error through misidentification with respect to any expressions that are "self-referring" in the sense of n. 3, above, including names and definite descriptions. If someone says "De Gaulle intends to remove France from NATO," and is using "de Gaulle" to refer to himself, his statement is in the relevant sense immune to error through misidentification, regardless of whether he is right in thinking that his name is "de Gaulle" and that he is the President of France.

6 H. P. Grice, "Personal identity," *Mind* 50 (1941), pp. 330–50, at p. 344.

7 G. C. Nerlich, "On evidence for identity," *Australasian Journal of Philosophy*, 37 (1959), pp. 201–14, at p. 208.

8 I am not here endorsing the view, which I in fact reject, that remembering consists in the having of an

image, or some other sort of mental "representation," in which the memory content is in some way encoded. It is sufficient for the existence at *t* of the "cognitive state" of remembering such and such that it be true of the person at *t* that he remembers such and such; I am not here committing myself to any account of what, if anything, someone's remembering such and such "consists in."

9 I should make it clear that I am not saying that what we remember is always, or even normally, a past cognitive and sensory state. I am not propounding the view, which is sometimes held but which is clearly false, that "strictly speaking" one can remember only one's own past experiences. I am saying only that if a person remembers an event that occurred at time *t*, then at *t* there must have been a corresponding cognitive and sensory state – which the person may or may not remember – that was of that event. It would not be easy to specify just what sort of correspondence is required here, and I shall not attempt to do so. But I take it as obvious that the claim to remember firing a gun requires, for its truth, a different sort of past cognitive and sensory state than the claim to remember hearing someone else fire a gun, and that the latter, in turn, requires a different sort of past cognitive and sensory state than the claim to remember seeing someone fire a gun. Sometimes one remembers a past event but no longer remembers just how one knew of it at the time of its occurrence; in such a case one's memory, because of vagueness and incompleteness, corresponds to a wider range of possible cognitive and sensory states than (say) a memory of seeing the event or a memory of being told about it.

10 See my book *Self-Knowledge and Self-Identity* (Ithaca, NY: Cornell University Press, 1963), esp. ch. 4, and my paper "Personal identity and memory," *Journal of Philosophy* 56 (1959), pp. 868–82.

11 P. F. Strawson, *The Bounds of Sense* (London: Methuen, 1966), p. 165.

12 I owe to Norman Malcolm the point that to be memory knowledge, one's knowledge must be in some way due to, must exist because of, a past cognitive and sensory state of oneself – see his "Three forms of Memory." Malcolm holds that "due to" does not here express a causal relationship, but I have been persuaded otherwise by Martin's and Deutscher's "Remembering." See also my paper "On knowing who one is" (*Common Factor* 4 (1966)), and David Wiggins's *Identity and Spatio-Temporal Continuity* (Oxford: Blackwell, 1967), esp. pp. 50ff. The view that there is a causal element in the concept of memory is attacked by Roger Squires in his recent paper "Memory unchained," *Philosophical Review* 78 (1969), pp. 178–96; I make a very limited reply to this in section V of this essay.

13 P. F. Strawson, *Individuals* (London: Methuen, 1959), p. 20.

14 It will perhaps be objected that the dictum that unrestricted negative existential claims are unverifiable in principle is brought into question by the possibility that we might discover – what some cosmologists hold there is good reason for believing – that space and past time are finite. If we discovered this, why shouldn't we be able, at least in principle, to establish that at no place does there exist, and at no time in the past has there existed, a duplicate of New York?

One way of countering this objection would be to introduce the possibility, which has been argued by Anthony Quinton in his paper "Spaces and times," *Philosophy 57* (1962), pp. 130–41, of there being a multiplicity of different and spatially unrelated spaces. Establishing that there is no duplicate of New York in our space would not establish that there is no space in which there is such a duplicate, and if it is possible for there to be multiplicity of spaces, there would seem to be no way in which the latter could be established.

But we needn't have recourse to such recondite possibilities in order to counter this objection, if it is viewed as an objection to my claim that it is the fact that remembering involves the satisfaction of the previous awareness condition that makes it possible for us to rule out the possibility that memory claims are false through misidentification owing to the reduplication of landmarks. For to discover that space or past time is finite, and that massive reduplication does not occur, one would have to have a vast amount of empirical information about the world, including information about the histories of particular things. But, as I think the remainder of my discussion should make clear, one could not be provided with such information by memory (or by quasi-memory) unless one were *already* entitled in a large number of cases to refer to particular places and things in one's memory reports without having to regard it as possible that one's references were mistaken owing to massive reduplication. So this entitlement would have to precede the discovery that space and past time are finite, and could not depend on it.

15 The point made in the preceding note can now be expressed by saying that even if we, who have the faculty of memory, could establish that at no place and time has there been a duplicate of New York, this could not be established by someone whose faculty of knowing the past was a faculty of quasi-memory.

16 It may be objected that I have overlooked one way in which a quasi-rememberer might begin to reconstruct his own past history, and the histories of other things, from the information provided him by his quasi-memories. The quasi-rememberer's difficulties would be solved if he had a way of sorting out those of his quasi-memories that are of his own past, i.e., are memories, from those that are not. But it may seem that the quasi-rememberer could easily tell which of his quasi-memories of the very recent past are of his own past, namely by noting which of them have contents very similar to the contents of his *present* experiences; e.g., if he quasi-remembers from the inside the very recent seeing of a scene that resembles very closely the scene he presently sees, it may seem that he can justifiably conclude that the quasi-remembered seeing was his own. And it may seem that by starting in this way he could trace back his own history by finding among his quasi-memories a subset of situations that form a spatiotemporally continuous series of situations, that series terminating in the situation he presently perceives.

This objection assumes that the quasi-rememberer can know the degree of recentness of the situations of which he has quasi-memories, but I shall not here question this assumption. What I shall question is the assumption that if the quasi-rememberer knows that a quasi-remembered scene occurred only a moment or so ago, and that it closely resembles the scene he presently sees, he is entitled to believe that it is numerically the same scene as the one he presently sees and that in all probability it was he who saw it. For of course it could be the case that there is somewhere else a duplicate of the scene he sees, and that his quasi-memory is of that duplicate. It will perhaps be objected that while this is logically possible (given the possibility of quasi-remembering that is not remembering), it is highly improbable. But while it may be intrinsically improbable that a highly complicated situation should be reduplicated within some limited spatiotemporal area, it does not seem intrinsically improbable that such a situation should be reduplicated somewhere or other in the universe – unless the universe is finite, which is something the quasi-rememberer could have no reason for believing (see nn. 14 and 15 above). Moreover, one could not be in a position to know how rare or frequent such reduplication is in fact, and therefore how likely or unlikely it is that a given situation is reduplicated, unless one already had a way of reidentifying places and things. So the quasi-rememberer could not be in a position to know this, for he could have a way of reidentifying places and things only if he were already in a position to rule out reduplication as improbable.

17 It is worth mentioning that if quasi$_c$-remembering is to be as much like remembering as possible, then not just any causal chain linking a past cognitive and sensory state with a subsequent quasi$_c$-memory can be allowed to count as an M-type causal chain. For as Martin and Deutscher ("Remembering") point out, there are various sorts of cases in which a man's knowledge of a past event is causally due to his previous experience of it, but in which the causal connection is obviously not of the right kind to permit us to say that he remembers the event. E.g., I have completely forgotten the event, but know of it now because you told me about it, and you came to know

about it through my telling you about it prior to my forgetting it. It is easier to decide in particular cases whether the causal connection is "of the right kind" than it is to give a general account of what it is for the causal connection to be of the right kind, i.e., what it is for there to be an M-type causal chain. I shall not attempt to do the latter here. The notion of an M-type causal chain would of course be completely useless if it were impossible to determine in any particular case whether the causal connection is "of the right kind" without already having determined that the case is one of remembering – but I shall argue in section V that this is not impossible.

18 In his paper "Bodily continuity and personal identity: a reply," *Analysis* 21 (1960), pp. 42–8), B. A. O. Williams says that "identity is a one–one relation, and . . . no principle can be a criterion of identity for things of type *T* if it relies on what is logically a one–many or many–many relation between things of type *T*," and remarks that the relation "being disposed to make sincere memory claims which exactly fit the life of" is a many–one relation and "hence cannot possibly be adequate in logic to constitute a criterion of identity" (pp. 44–5). Now it may seem that my version of the view that memory is a criterion of personal identity is open to the same objection, for if M-type causal chains can branch and coalesce, then the relation "has a quasi-memory which is linked by an M-type causal chain with a cognitive and sensory state of" is not logically a one–one relation. But while this relationship is not logically one–one, the relationship "has a quasi-memory which is linked by a *non-branching* M-type causal chain with a cognitive and sensory state of" is logically one–one, and it is the holding of the latter relationship that I would hold to be a criterion, in the sense of being a sufficient condition, for personal identity.

19 A. N. Prior has defended the view that in cases of fission *both* offshoots can be identified with the original person, although not with each other. This of course involves modifying the usual account of the logical features of identity. See his "'Opposite number'" *Review of Metaphysics* 2 (1957), pp. 196–201 and his "Time, existence and identity," *Proceedings of the Aristotelian Society* pp. (1965–6), pp. 183–92. Roderick Chisholm takes a very different view. Considering the supposition that "you knew that your body, like that of an amoeba, would one day undergo fission and that you would go off, so to speak, in two different directions," he says "it seems to me, first, that there is no possibility whatever that *you* would be *both* the person on the right and the person on the left. It seems to me, secondly, that there *is* a possibility that you would be one or the other of those two persons" ("The loose and popular and the strict and philosophical senses of identity," in Norman S. Care and Robert H. Grimm (eds), *Perception and Personal Identity* (Cleveland: Press of Case Western Reserve University, 1969), p. 106). It is not clear to me whether Chisholm would hold that one (but not both) of the offshoots might be me if the memories of each stood in the same causal relationships to my actions and experiences as the memories of the other, and if each resembled me, in personality, appearance, etc. as much as the other. If so, I would disagree.

20 See Wiggins, *Identity and Spatio-Temporal Continuity*, p. 53, where such a case is discussed.

21 Joseph Butler, "Of personal identity," First Dissertation to the *Analogy of Religion*; repr. in J. Perry (ed.), *Personal Identity* (Berkeley and Los Angeles: University of California Press, 1975).

22 See A. J. Ayer, *The Problem of Knowledge* (Harmondsworth: Penguin, 1956), p. 196, and B. A. O. Williams, "Personal identity and individuation," in *Problems of the Self* (Cambridge: Cambridge University Press, 1973), pp. 3–4.

23 See Williams, "Personal identity and individuation," pp. 4–5, and my "Personal identity and memory," pp. 869–70 and 877. In the latter, and in *Self-Knowledge and Self-Identity*, I attempted to reduce the force of this objection by arguing that it is a "conceptual truth" that memory claims are generally true, and that we can therefore be entitled to say that a person remembers a past event without already having established, or having inductive evidence, that some other criterion of personal identity (one not involving memory) is satisfied. This way of handling the objection no longer seems to me satisfactory.

24 See Squires's "Memory unchained."

25 Shoemaker, *Self-Knowledge and Self-Identity*, pp. 23–5 and 245–7.

26 In *Self-Knowledge and Self-Identity* I held that saying that Brownson is Brown would involve making a "decision" about the relative weights to be assigned to different criteria of personal identity, and that in the absence of such a decision there is no right answer to the question whether Brownson is Brown. I have come to believe that there is a right answer to this question, namely that Brownson is Brown, and that my former view overlooked the importance of the causal component in the notion of memory (see my treatment of this example in "On knowing who one is").

27 On this and related questions, see my exchange with Chisholm in Care and Grimm (eds), *Perception and Personal Identity*, pp. 107–27.

28 This is not to deny the possibility or occurrence of unselfish attitudes and emotions. Even the most unselfish man, who is willing to suffer that others may prosper, does not and cannot regard the pleasures and pains that are in prospect for him in the same light as he regards those that are in prospect for others. He may submit to torture, but he would hardly be human if he could regularly view his own future sufferings with the same detachment (which is not indifference) as he views the future suffering of others.

28

The Self and the Future

Bernard Williams

Suppose that there were some process to which two persons, A and B, could be subjected as a result of which they might be said – question-beggingly – to have *exchanged bodies*. That is to say – less question-beggingly – there is a certain human body which is such that when previously we were confronted with it, we were confronted with person A, certain utterances coming from it were expressive of memories of the past experiences of A, certain movements of it partly constituted the actions of A and were taken as expressive of the character of A, and so forth; but now, after the process is completed, utterances coming from this body are expressive of what seem to be just those memories which previously we identified as memories of the past experiences of B, its movements partly constitute actions expressive of the character of B, and so forth; and conversely with the other body.

There are certain important philosophical limitations on how such imaginary cases are to be constructed, and how they are to be taken when constructed in various ways. I shall mention two principal limitations, not in order to pursue them further here, but precisely in order to get them out of the way.

There are certain limitations, particularly with regard to character and mannerisms, to our ability to imagine such cases even in the most restricted sense of our being disposed to take the later per-

First published in *Philosophical Review* 79 (1970), pp. 161–80. Reprinted by permission of Cornell University.

formances of that body which was previously A's as expressive of B's character; if the previous A and B were extremely unlike one another both physically and psychologically, and if, say, in addition, they were of different sex, there might be grave difficulties in reading B's dispositions in any possible performances of A's body. Let us forget this, and for the present purpose just take A and B as being sufficiently alike (however alike that has to be) for the difficulty not to arise; after the experiment, persons familiar with A and B are just *overwhelmingly struck* by the B-ish character of the doings associated with what was previously A's body, and conversely. Thus the feat of imagining an exchange of bodies is supposed possible in the most restricted sense. But now there is a further limitation which has to be overcome if the feat is to be not merely possible in the most restricted sense, but also is to have an outcome which, on serious reflection, we are prepared to describe as A and B having changed bodies – that is, an outcome where, confronted with what was previously A's body, we are prepared seriously to say that we are now confronted with B.

It would seem a necessary condition of so doing that the utterances coming from that body be taken as genuinely expressive of memories of B's past. But memory is a causal notion; and as we actually use it, it seems a necessary condition of x's present knowledge of x's earlier experiences constituting memory of those experiences that the causal chain linking the experiences and the knowledge should not run outside x's body. Hence if utterances coming from a given body are to be taken as expressive of memories of the experiences of B, there should be some suitable causal link between the appropriate state of the body and the original happening of those experiences to B. One radical way of securing that condition in the imagined exchange case is to suppose, with Shoemaker,[1] that the brains of A and of B are transposed. We may not need so radical a condition. Thus suppose it were possible to extract information from a man's brain and store it in a device while his brain was repaired, or even renewed, the information then being replaced: it would seem exaggerated to insist that the resultant man could not possibly have the memories he had before the operation. With regard to our knowledge of our own past, we draw distinctions between merely recalling, being reminded, and learning again, and those distinctions correspond (roughly) to distinctions between no new input, partial new input, and total new input with regard to the information in question; and it seems clear that the information-parking case just imagined would not count as new input in the sense necessary and sufficient for 'learning again'. Hence we can imagine the case we are concerned with in terms of information extracted into such devices from A's and B's brains and replaced in the other brain; this is the sort of model which, I think not unfairly for the present argument, I shall have in mind.

We imagine the following. The process considered above exists; two persons can enter some machine, let us say, and emerge changed in the appropriate ways. If A and B are the persons who enter, let us call the persons who emerge the *A-body-person* and the *B-body-person*: the *A*-body-person is that person (whoever it is) with whom I am confronted when, after the experiment, I am confronted with that body which previously was A's body – that is to say, that person who would naturally be taken for A by someone who just saw this person, was familiar with A's appearance before the experiment, and did not know about the happening of the experiment. A non-question-begging description of the experiment will leave it open which (if either) of the persons A and B the *A*-body-person is; the description of the experiment as 'persons changing bodies' of course implies that the *A*-body-person is actually B.

We take two persons A and B who are going to have the process carried out on them. (We can suppose, rather hazily, that they are willing for this to happen; to investigate at all closely at this stage why they might be willing or unwilling, what they would fear, and so forth, would anticipate some later issues.) We further announce that one of the two resultant persons, the *A*-body-person and the *B*-body-person, is going after the experiment to be given \$100,000, while the other is going to be tortured. We then ask each of A and B to choose which treatment should be dealt out to which of the persons who will emerge from the experiment, the choice to be made (if it can be) on selfish grounds.

Suppose that A chooses that the *B*-body-person should get the pleasant treatment and the *A*-body-person the unpleasant treatment; and B chooses conversely (this might indicate that they thought that 'changing bodies' was indeed a good description of the outcome). The experimenter cannot act in accordance with both these sets of preferences, those expressed by A and those expressed by B. Hence there is one clear sense in which A and B cannot both get what they want: namely, that if the experimenter, before the experiment, announces to A and B that he intends to carry out the alternative (for example), of treating the *B*-body-person unpleasantly and the *A*-body-person pleasantly – then A can say rightly, 'That's not the outcome I chose to happen', and B can say rightly, 'That's just the outcome I chose to happen'. So, evidently, A and B before the experiment can each come to know either that the outcome he chose will be that which will happen, or that the one he chose will not happen, and in that sense they can get or fail to get what they wanted. But is it also true that when the experimenter proceeds after the experiment to act in accordance with one of the preferences and not the other, *then* one of A and B will have got what he wanted, and the other not?

There seems very good ground for saying so. For suppose the experimenter, having elicited A's and B's preference, says nothing to A and B about what he will do; conducts the experiment; and then, for example, gives the unpleasant treatment to the *B*-body-person and the pleasant treatment to the *A*-body-person. Then the *B*-body-person will not only complain of the unpleasant treatment as such, but will complain (since he has A's memories) that that was not the outcome he chose, since he chose that the *B*-body-person should be well treated; and since A made his choice in selfish spirit, he may add that he precisely chose in that way because he did not want the unpleasant things to happen to *him*. The *A*-body-person meanwhile will express satisfaction both at the receipt of the \$100,000, and also at the fact that the experimenter has chosen to act in the way that he, *B*, so wisely chose. These facts make a strong case for saying that the experimenter has brought it about that *B* did in the outcome get what he wanted and *A* did not. It is therefore a strong case for saying that the *B*-body-person really is *A*, and the *A*-body-person really is *B*; and therefore for saying that the process of the experiment really is that of changing bodies. For the same reasons it would seem that *A* and *B* in our example really did choose wisely, and that it was *A*'s bad luck that the choice he correctly made was not carried out, *B*'s good luck that the choice he correctly made was carried out. This seems to show that to care about what happens to me in the future is not necessarily to care about what happens to *this* body (the one I now have); and this in turn might be taken to show that in some sense of Descartes's obscure phrase, I and my body are 'really distinct' (though, of course, nothing in these considerations could support the idea that I could exist without a body at all).

These suggestions seem to be reinforced if we consider the cases where *A* and *B* make other choices with regard to the experiment. Suppose that *A* chooses that the *A*-body-person should get the money, and the *B*-body-person get the pain, and *B* chooses conversely. Here again there can be no outcome which matches the expressed preferences of both of them: they cannot both get what they want. The experimenter announces, before the experiment, that the *A*-body-person will in fact get the money, and the *B*-body-person will get the pain. So *A* at this stage gets what he wants (the announced outcome matches his expressed preference). After the experiment, the distribution is carried out as announced. Both the *A*-body-person and the *B*-body-person will have to agree that what is happening is in accordance with the preference that *A* originally expressed. The *B*-body-person will naturally express this acknowledgement (since he has *A*'s memories) by saying that this is the distribution he chose; he will recall, among other things, the experimenter announcing this outcome, his approving it as what he choose, and so forth. However, he (the *B*-body-person) certainly does not like what is now happening to him, and would much prefer to be receiving what the *A*-body-person is receiving – namely, $100,000. The *A*-body-person will on the other hand recall choosing an outcome other than this one, but will reckon it good luck that the experimenter did not do what he recalls choosing. It looks, then, as though the *A*-body-person has got

what he wanted, but not what he chose, while the *B*-body-person has got what he chose, but not what he wanted. So once more it looks as though they are, respectively, *B* and *A*; and that in this case the original choices of both *A* and *B* were unwise.

Suppose, lastly, that in the original choice *A* takes the line of the first case and *B* of the second: that is, *A* chooses that the *B*-body-person should get the money and the *A*-body-person the pain, and *B* chooses exactly the same thing. In this case, the experimenter would seem to be in the happy situation of giving both persons what they want – or at least, like God, what they have chosen. In this case, the *B*-body-person likes what he is receiving, recalls choosing it, and congratulates himself on the wisdom of (as he puts it) his choice; while the *A*-body-person does not like what he is receiving, recalls choosing it, and is forced to acknowledge that (as he puts it) his choice was unwise. So once more we seem to get results to support the suggestions drawn from the first case.

Let us now consider the question, not of *A* and *B* choosing certain outcomes to take place after the experiment, but of their willingness to engage in the experiment at all. If they were initially inclined to accept the description of the experiment as 'changing bodies', then one thing that would interest them would be the character of the other person's body. In this respect also, what would happen after the experiment would seem to suggest that 'changing bodies' was a good description of the experiment. If *A* and *B* agreed to the experiment, being each not displeased with the appearance, physique, and so forth of the other person's body; after the experiment the *B*-body-person might well be found saying such things as: 'When I agreed to this experiment, I thought that *B*'s face was quite attractive, but now I look at it in the mirror, I am not so sure'; or the *A*-body-person might say, 'When I agreed to this experiment, I did not know that *A* had a wooden leg; but now, after it is over, I find that I have this wooden leg, and I want the experiment reversed.' It is possible that he might say further that he finds the leg very uncomfortable, and that the *B*-body-person should say, for instance, that he recalls that he found it very uncomfortable at first, but one gets used to it: but perhaps one would need to know more than at least I do about the physiology of habituation to artificial limbs to know whether the *A*-body-person would find the leg uncomfortable: that body, after all, has had the leg on it for some time. But apart from this sort of detail, the general line of the outcome regarded from this point of view seems to confirm our previous conclusions about the experiment.

Now let us suppose that when the experiment is proposed (in non-question-begging terms) *A* and *B* think rather of their psychological advantages and disadvantages. *A*'s thoughts turn primarily to certain sorts of anxiety to which he is very prone, while *B* is concerned with the frightful memories he has of past experiences which still distress him. They each hope that the experiment will in some way result in their being able to get away from these things. They may even have been impressed by philosophical arguments to the effect that bodily continuity is at least a necessary condition of personal identity: *A*, for example, reasons that, granted the experiment comes off, then the person who is bodily continuous with him will not have this anxiety, and while the other person will no doubt have some anxiety—perhaps in some sense his anxiety – at least that person will not be he. The experiment is performed, and the experimenter (to whom *A* and *B* previously revealed privately their several difficulties and hopes) asks the *A*-body-person whether he has got rid of his anxiety. This person presumably replies that he does not know what the man is talking about; he never had such anxiety, but he did have some very disagreeable memories, and recalls engaging in the experiment to get rid of them, and is disappointed to discover that he still has them. The *B*-body-person will react in a similar way to questions about his painful memories, pointing out that he still has his anxiety. These results seem to confirm still further the description of the experiment as 'changing bodies'. And all the results suggest that the only rational thing to do, confronted with such an experiment, would be to identify oneself with one's memories, and so forth, and not with one's body. The philosophical arguments designed to show that bodily continuity was at least a necessary condition of personal identity would seem to be just mistaken.

Let us now consider something apparently different. Someone in whose power I am tells me that I am going to be tortured tomorrow. I am frightened, and look forward to tomorrow in great apprehension. He adds that when the time comes, I shall not remember being told that this was going to happen to me, since shortly before the torture something else will be done to me which will make me forget the announcement. This certainly will not cheer me up, since I know perfectly well that I can forget things, and that there is such a thing as indeed being tortured unexpectedly because I had forgotten or been made to forget a prediction of the torture: that will still be a torture which, so long as I do know about the prediction, I look forward to in fear. He then adds that my forgetting the announcement will be only part of a larger process: when the moment of torture comes, I shall not remember any of the things I am now in a position to remember. This does not cheer me up, either, since I can readily conceive of being involved in an accident, for instance, as a result of which I wake up in a completely amnesiac state and also in great pain; that could certainly happen to me, I should not like it to happen to me, nor to know that it was going to happen to me. He now further adds that at the moment of torture I shall not only not remember the things I am now in a position to remember, but will have a different set of impressions of my past, quite different from the memories I now have. I do not think that this would cheer me up, either. For I can at least conceive the possibility, if not the concrete reality, of going completely mad, and thinking perhaps that I am George IV or somebody; and being told that something like that was going to happen to me would have no tendency to reduce the terror of being told authoritatively that I was going to be tortured, but would merely compound the horror. Nor do I see why I should be put into any better frame of mind by the person in charge adding lastly that the impressions of my past with which I shall be equipped on the eve of torture will exactly fit the past of another person now living, and that indeed I shall acquire these impressions by (for instance) information now in his brain being copied into mine. Fear, surely, would still be the proper reaction: and not because in one did not know what was going to happen, but because in one vital respect at least one did know what was going to happen – torture, which one can indeed expect to happen to oneself, and to be preceded by certain mental derangements as well.

If this is right, the whole question seems now to be totally mysterious. For what we have just been through is of course merely one side, differently represented, of the transaction which we considered before; and it represents it as a perfectly hateful prospect, while the previous considerations represented it as something one should rationally, perhaps even cheerfully, choose out of the options there presented. It is differently presented, of course, and in two notable respects; but when we look at these two differences of presentation, can we really convince ourselves that the second presentation is wrong or misleading, thus leaving the road open to the first version which at the time seemed so convincing? Surely not.

The first difference is that in the second version the torture is throughout represented as going to happen to *me*: 'you', the man in charge persistently says. Thus he is not very neutral. But should he have been neutral? Or, to put it another way, does his use of the second person have a merely emotional and rhetorical effect on me, making me afraid when further reflection would have shown that I had no reason to be? It is certainly not obviously so. The problem just is that through every step of his predictions I seem to be able to follow him successfully. And if I reflect on whether what he has said gives me grounds for fearing that I shall be tortured, I could consider that behind my fears lies some principle such as this: that my undergoing physical pain in the future is not excluded by any psychological state I may be in at the time, with the platitudinous exception of those psychological states which in themselves exclude experiencing pain, notably (if it is a psychological state) unconsciousness. In particular, what impressions I have about the past will not have any effect on whether I undergo the pain or not. This principle seems sound enough.

It is an important fact that not everything I would, as things are, regard as an evil would be something that I should rationally fear as an evil if it were predicted that it would happen to me in the future and also predicted that I should undergo significant psychological changes in the meantime. For the fact that I regard that happening, things being as they are, as an evil can be dependent on factors of belief or character which might themselves be modified by the psychological changes in question. Thus if I am appallingly subject to acrophobia, and am told that I shall find myself on top of a steep mountain in the near future, I shall to that extent be afraid; but if I am told that I shall be psychologically changed in the meantime in such a way as to rid me of my acrophobia (and as with the other prediction, I believe it), then I have no reason to be afraid of the predicted happening, or at least not the same reason. Again, I might look forward to meeting a certain person again with either alarm or excitement because of my memories of our past relations. In some part, these memories operate in connection with my emotion, not only on the present time, but projectively forward: for it is to a meeting itself affected by the presence of those memories that I look forward. If I am convinced that when the time comes I shall not have those memories, then I shall not have just the same reasons as before for looking forward to that meeting with the one emotion or the other. (Spiritualism, incidentally, appears to involve the belief that I have just the same reasons for a given attitude toward encountering people again after I am dead, as I did before: with the one modification that I can be sure it will all be very nice.)

Physical pain, however, the example which for simplicity (and not for any obsessional reason) I have taken, is absolutely minimally dependent on character or belief. No amount of change in my character or my beliefs would seem to affect substantially the nastiness of tortures applied to me; correspondingly, no degree of predicted change in my character and beliefs can unseat the fear of torture which, together with those changes, is predicted for me.

I am not at all suggesting that the *only* basis, or indeed the only rational basis, for fear in the face of these various predictions is how things will be relative to my psychological state in the eventual outcome. I am merely pointing out that this is one component; it is not the only one. For certainly one will fear and otherwise reject the changes themselves, or in very many cases one would. Thus one of the old paradoxes of hedonistic utilitarianism; if one had assurances that undergoing certain operations and being attached to a machine would provide one for the rest of one's existence with an unending sequence of delicious and varied experiences, one might very well reject the option, and react with fear if someone proposed to apply it compulsorily; and that fear and horror would seem appropriate reactions in the second case may help to discredit the interpretation (if anyone has the nerve to propose it) that one's reason for rejecting the option voluntarily would be a consciousness of duties to others which one in one's hedonic state would leave undone. The prospect of contented madness or vegetableness is found by many (not perhaps by all) appalling in ways which are obviously not a function of how things would then be for them, for things would then be for them not appalling. In the case we are at present discussing, these sorts of considerations seem merely to make it clearer that the predictions of the man in charge provide a double ground of horror: at the prospect of torture, and at the prospect of the change in character and in impressions of the past that will precede it. And certainly, to repeat what has already been said, the prospect of the second certainly seems to provide no ground for rejecting or not fearing the prospect of the first.

I said that there were two notable differences between the second presentation of our situation and the first. The first difference, which we have just said something about, was that the man predicted the torture for *me*, a psychologically very changed 'me'. We have yet to find a reason for saying that he should not have done this, or that I really should be unable to follow him if he does; I seem to be able to follow him only too well. The second difference is that in this presentation he does not mention the other man, except in the somewhat incidental role of being the provenance of the impressions of the past I end up with. He does not mention him at all as someone who will end up with impressions of the past derived from me (and, incidentally, with $100,000 as well – a consideration which, in the frame of mind appropriate to this version, will merely make me jealous).

But why *should* he mention this man and what is going to happen to him? My selfish concern is to be told what is going to happen to me, and now I know: torture, preceded by changes of character, brain operations, changes in impressions of the past. The knowledge that one other person, or none, or many will be similarly mistreated may affect me in other ways, of sympathy, greater horror at the power of this tyrant, and so forth; but surely it cannot affect my expectations of torture? But – someone will say – this is to leave out exactly the feature which, as the first presentation of the case showed, makes all the difference: for it is to leave out the person who, as the first presentation showed, will be you. It is to leave out not merely a feature which should fundamentally affect your fears, it is to leave out the very person for whom you are fearful. So of course, the objector will say, this makes all the difference.

But can it? Consider the following series of cases. In each case we are to suppose that after what is described, *A* is, as before, to be tortured; we are also to suppose the person *A* is informed beforehand that just these things followed by the torture will happen to him:

(i) *A* is subjected to an operation which produces total amnesia;
(ii) amnesia is produced in *A*, and other interference leads to certain changes in his character;
(iii) changes in his character are produced, and at the same time certain illusory 'memory'

beliefs are induced in him: these are of a quite fictitious kind and do not fit the life of any actual person;
(iv) the same as (iii), except that both the character traits and the 'memory' impressions are designed to be appropriate to another actual person, *B*;
(v) the same as (iv), except that the result is produced by putting the information into *A* from the brain of *B*, by a method which leaves *B* the same as he was before;
(vi) the same happens to *A* as in (v), but *B* is not left the same, since a similar operation is conducted in the reverse direction.

I take it that no one is going to dispute that *A* has reasons, and fairly straightforward reasons, for fear of pain when the prospect is that of situation (i); there seems no conceivable reason why this should not extend to situation (ii), and the situation (iii) can surely introduce no difference of principle – it just seems a situation which for more than one reason we should have grounds for fearing, as suggested above. Situation (iv) at least introduces the person *B*, who was the focus of the objection we are now discussing. But it does not seem to introduce him in any way which makes a material difference; if I can expect pain through a transformation which involves new 'memory'-impressions, it would seem a purely external fact, relative to that, that the 'memory'-impressions had a model. Nor, in (iv), do we satisfy a causal condition which I mentioned at the beginning for the 'memories' actually being memories; though notice that if the job were done thoroughly, I might well be able to elicit from the *A*-body-person the kinds of remarks about his previous expectations of the experiment – remarks appropriate to the original *B* – which so impressed us in the first version of the story. I shall have a similar assurance of this being so in situation (v), where, moreover, a plausible application of the causal condition is available.

But two things are to be noticed about this situation. First, if we concentrate on *A* and the *A*-body-person, we do not seem to have added anything which from the point of view of his fears makes any material difference; just as, in the move from (iii) to (iv), it made no relevant difference that the new 'memory'-impressions which precede the pain had, as it happened, a model, so in the move from (iv) to (v) all we have added is that they have a model which is also their cause: and it is still difficult to see why that, to him looking forward, could possibly make the difference between expecting pain and not expecting pain. To illustrate that point from the case of character: if A is capable of expecting pain, he is capable of expecting pain preceded by a change in his dispositions – and to that expectation it can make no difference, whether that change in his dispositions is modelled on, or indeed indirectly caused by, the dispositions of some other person. If his fears can, as it were, reach through the change, it seems a mere trimming how the change is in fact induced. The second point about situation (v) is that if the crucial question for A's fears with regard to what befalls the A-body-person is whether the A-body-person is or is not the person B,[2] then that condition has not yet been satisfied in situation (v): for there we have an undisputed B in addition to the A-body-person, and certainly those two are not the same person.

But in situation (vi), we seemed to think, that is finally what he is. But if A's original fears could reach through the expected changes in (v), as they did in (iv) and (iii), then certainly they can reach through in (vi). Indeed, from the point of view of A's expectations and fears, there is less difference between (vi) and (v) than there is between (v) and (iv) or between (iv) and (iii). In those transitions, there were at least differences – though we could not see that they were really relevant differences – in the content or cause of what happened to him; in the present case there is absolutely no difference at all in what happens to him, the only difference being in what happens to someone else. If he can fear pain when (v) is predicted, why should he cease to when (vi) is?

I can see only one way of relevantly laying great weight on the transition from (v) to (vi); and this involves a considerable difficulty. This is to deny that, as I put it, the transition from (v) to (vi) involves merely the addition of something happening to *somebody else*; what rather it does, it will be said, is to involve the reintroduction of A himself, as the B-body-person; since he has reappeared in this form, it is for this person, and not for the unfortunate A-body-person, that A will have his expectations. This is to reassert, in effect, the viewpoint emphasized in our first presentation of the experiment. But this surely has the consequence that A should not have fears for the A-body-person who appeared in situation (v). For by the present argument, the A-body-person in (vi) is not A; the B-body-person is. But the A-body-person in (v) is, in character, history, everything, exactly the same

as the A-body-person in (vi); so if the latter is not A, then neither is the former. (It is this point, no doubt, that encourages one to speak of the difference that goes with (vi) as being, on the present view, the *reintroduction* of A.) But no one else in (v) has any better claim to be A. So in (v), it seems, A just does not exist. This would certainly explain why A should have no fears for the state of things in (v) – though he might well have fears for the path to it. But it rather looked earlier as though he could well have fears for the state of things in (v). Let us grant, however, that that was an illusion, and that A really does not exist in (v); then does he exist in (iv), (iii), (ii), or (i)? It seems very difficult to deny it for (i) and (ii); are we perhaps to draw the line between (iii) and (iv)?

Here someone will say: you must not insist on drawing a line – borderline cases are borderline cases, and you must not push our concepts beyond their limits. But this well-known piece of advice, sensible as it is in many cases, seems in the present case to involve an extraordinary difficulty. It may intellectually comfort observers of A's situation; but what is A supposed to make of it? To be told that a future situation is a borderline one for its being myself that is hurt, that it is conceptually undecidable whether it will be me or not, is something which, it seems, I can do nothing with; because, in particular, it seems to have no comprehensible representation in my expectations and the emotions that go with them.

If I expect that a certain situation, S, will come about in the future, there is of course a wide range of emotions and concerns, directed on S, which I may experience now in relation to my expectation. Unless I am exceptionally egoistic, it is not a condition on my being concerned in relation to this expectation, that I myself will be involved in S – where my being 'involved' in S means that I figure in S as someone doing something at that time or having something done to me, or, again, that S will have consequences affecting me at that or some subsequent time. There are some emotions, however, which I will feel only if I will be involved in S, and fear is an obvious example.

Now the description of S under which it figures in my expectations will necessarily be, in various ways, indeterminate; and one way in which it may be indeterminate is that it leaves open whether I shall be involved in S or not. Thus I may have good reason to expect that one of us five is going to get hurt, but no reason to expect it to be me rather than one of the others. My present emotions will be correspondingly affected by this indeterminacy. Thus, sticking to the egoistic concern involved in fear, I shall presumably be somewhat more cheerful than if I knew it was going to be me, somewhat less cheerful than if I had been left out altogether. Fear will be mixed with, and qualified by, apprehension; and so forth. These emotions revolve around the thought of the eventual determination of the indeterminacy; moments of straight fear focus on its really turning out to be me, of hope on its turning out not to be me. All the emotions are related to the coming about of what I expect: and what I expect in such a case just cannot come about save by coming about in one of the ways or another.

There are other ways in which indeterminate expectations can be related to fear. Thus I may expect (perhaps neurotically) that something nasty is going to happen to me, indeed expect that when it happens, it will take some determinate form, but have no range, or no closed range, of candidates for the determinate form to rehearse in my present thought. Different from this would be the fear of something radically indeterminate – the fear (one might say) of a nameless horror. If somebody had such a fear, one could even say that he had, in a sense, a perfectly determinate expectation: if what he expects indeed comes about, there will be nothing more determinate to be said about it after the event than was said in the expectation. Both these cases of course are cases of *fear* because one thing that is fixed amid the indeterminacy is the belief that it is me to whom the things will happen.

Central to the expectation of S is the thought of what it will be like when it happens – thought which may be indeterminate, range over alternatives, and so forth. When S involves me, there can be the possibility of a special form of such thought: the thought of how it will be for me, the imaginative projection of myself as participant in S.[3] I do not have to think about S in this way, when it involves me; but I may be able to. (It might be suggested that this possibility was even mirrored in the language, in the distinction between 'expecting to be hurt' and 'expecting that I shall be hurt'; but I am very doubtful about this point, which is in any case of no importance.)

Suppose now that there is an S with regard to which it is for conceptual reasons undecidable whether it involves me or not, as is proposed for the experimental situation by the line we are discussing. It is important that the expectation of S is not *indeterminate* in any of the ways we have just

been considering. It is not like the nameless horror, since the fixed point of that case was that it was going to happen to the subject, and that made his state unequivocally fear. Nor is it like the expectation of the man who expects one of the five to be hurt; his fear was indeed equivocal, but its focus, and that of the expectation, was that when S came about, it would certainly come about in one way or the other. In the present case, fear (of the torture, that is to say, not of the initial experiment) seems neither appropriate, nor inappropriate, nor appropriately equivocal. Relatedly, the subject has an incurable difficulty about how he may think about S. If he engages in projective imaginative thinking (about how it will be for him), he implicitly answers the necessarily unanswerable question; if he thinks that he cannot engage in such thinking, it looks very much as if he also answers it, though in the opposite direction. Perhaps he must just refrain from such thinking; but is he just refraining from it, if it is incurably undecidable whether he can or cannot engage in it?

It may be said that all that these considerations can show is that fear, at any rate, does not get its proper footing in this case; but that there could be some other, more ambivalent, form of concern which would indeed be appropriate to this particular expectation, the expectation of the conceptually undecidable situation. There are, perhaps, analogous feelings that actually occur in actual situations. Thus material objects do occasionally undergo puzzling transformations which leave a conceptual shadow over their identity. Suppose I were sentimentally attached to an object to which this sort of thing then happened; it might be that I could neither feel about it quite as I did originally, nor be totally indifferent to it, but would have some other and rather ambivalent feeling towards it. Similarly, it may be said, toward the prospective sufferer of pain, my identity relations with whom are conceptually shadowed, I can feel neither as I would if he were certainly me, nor as I would if he were certainly not, but rather some such ambivalent concern.

But this analogy does little to remove the most baffling aspect of the present case – an aspect which has already turned up in what was said about the subject's difficulty in thinking either projectively or non-projectively about the situation. For to regard the prospective pain-sufferer *just* like the transmogrified object of sentiment, and to conceive of my ambivalent distress about his future pain as just like ambivalent distress about some future damage to such an object, is of course to leave him and me clearly distinct from one another, and thus to displace the conceptual shadow from its proper place. I have to get nearer to him than that. But is there any nearer that I can get to him without expecting his pain? If there is, the analogy has not shown us it. We can certainly not get nearer by expecting, as it were, *ambivalent* pain; there is no place at all for that. There seems to be an obstinate bafflement to mirroring in my expectations a situation in which it is conceptually undecidable whether I occur.

The bafflement seems, moreover, to turn to plain absurdity if we move from conceptual undecidability to its close friend and neighbour, conventionalist decision. This comes out if we consider another description, overtly conventionalist, of the series of cases which occasioned the present discussion. This description would reject a point I relied on in an earlier argument – namely, that if we deny that the *A*-body-person in (vi) is *A* (because the *B*-body-person is), then we must deny that the *A*-body-person in (v) is *A*, since they are exactly similar. 'No', it may be said, 'this is just to assume that we say the same in different sorts of situation. No doubt when we have the very good candidate for being *A* – namely, the *B*-body-person – we call him *A*; but this does not mean that we should not call the *A*-body-person *A* in that other situation when we have no better candidate around. Different situations call for different descriptions.' This line of talk is the sort of thing indeed appropriate to lawyers deciding the ownership of some property which has undergone some bewildering set of transformations; they just have to decide, and in each situation, let us suppose, it has got to go to somebody, on as reasonable grounds as the facts and the law admit. But as a line to deal with a person's fears or expectations about his own future, it seems to have no sense at all. If *A*'s fears can extend to what will happen to the *A*-body-person in (v), I do not see how they can be rationally diverted from the fate of the exactly similar person in (vi) by his being told that someone would have a reason in the latter situation which he would not have in the former for deciding to call another person *A*.

Thus, to sum up, it looks as though there are two presentations of the imagined experiment and the choice associated with it, each of which carries conviction, and which lead to contrary conclusions. The idea, moreover, that the situation after the experiment is conceptually undecidable in the relevant respect seems not to assist, but rather to increase, the puzzlement; while the idea (so often appealed to in these matters) that it is conventionally decidable is even worse. Following from all that, I am not in the least clear which option it would be wise to take if one were presented with them before the experiment. I find that rather disturbing.

Whatever the puzzlement, there is one feature of the arguments which have led to it which is worth picking out, since it runs counter to something which is, I think, often rather vaguely supposed. It is often recognized that there are 'first-personal' and 'third-personal' aspects of questions about persons, and that there are difficulties about the relations between them. It is also recognized that 'mentalistic' considerations (as we may vaguely call them) and considerations of bodily continuity are involved in questions of personal identity (which is not to say that there are mentalistic and bodily criteria of personal identity). It is tempting to think that the two distinctions run in parallel: roughly, that a first-person approach concentrates attention on mentalistic considerations, while a third-personal approach emphasizes considerations of bodily continuity. The present discussion is an illustration of exactly the opposite. The first argument, which led to the 'mentalistic' conclusion that *A* and *B* would change bodies and that each person should identify himself with the destination of his memories and character, was an an argument entirely conducted in third-personal terms. The second argument, which suggested the bodily continuity identification, concerned itself with the first-personal issue of what *A* could expect. That this is so seems to me (though I will not discuss it further here) of some significance.

I will end by suggesting one rather shaky way in which one might approach a resolution of the problem, using only the limited materials already available.

The apparently decisive arguments of the first presentation, which suggested that *A* should identify himself with the *B*-body-person, turned on the extreme neatness of the situation in satisfying, if any could, the description of 'changing bodies'. But this neatness is basically artificial; it is the product of the will of the experimenter to produce a situation which would naturally elicit, with minimum hesitation, that description. By the sorts of methods he employed, he could easily have left off earlier or gone on further. He could have stopped at situation (v), leaving *B* as he was; or he could have gone on and produced two persons each with

A-like character and memories, as well as one or two with *B*-like characteristics. If he had done either of those, we should have been in yet greater difficulty about what to say; he just chose to make it as easy as possible for us to find something to say. Now if we had some model of ghostly persons in bodies, which were in some sense actually moved around by certain procedures, we could regard the neat experiment just as the *effective* experiment: the one method that really did result in the ghostly persons' changing places without being destroyed, dispersed, or whatever. But we cannot seriously use such a model. The experimenter has not in the sense of that model *induced* a change of bodies;

he has rather produced the one situation out of a range of equally possible situations which we should be most disposed to call a change of bodies. As against this, the principle that one's fears can extend to future pain whatever psychological changes precede it seems positively straightforward. Perhaps, indeed, it is not; but we need to be shown what is wrong with it. Until we are shown what is wrong with it, we should perhaps decide that if we were the person *A* then, if we were to decide selfishly, we should pass the pain to the *B*-body-person. It would be risky: that there is room for the notion of a *risk* here is itself a major feature of the problem.

Notes

1 Sydney Shoemaker, *Self-Knowledge and Self-Identity* (Ithaca, NY: Cornell University Press, 1963), pp. 23ff.
2 This of course does not have to be the crucial question, but it seems one fair way of taking up the present objection.
3 For a more detailed treatment of issues related to this, see 'Imagination and the self', in Bernard Williams, *Problems of the Self* (Cambridge: Cambridge University Press, 1973), pp. 38ff.

29

Personal Identity

Derek Parfit

We can, I think, describe cases in which, though we know the answer to every other question, we have no idea how to answer a question about personal identity. These cases are not covered by the criteria of personal identity that we actually use.

Do they present a problem?

It might be thought that they do not, because they could never occur. I suspect that some of them could. (Some, for instance, might become scientifically possible.) But I shall claim that even if they did, they would present no problem.

My targets are two beliefs: one about the nature of personal identity, the other about its importance.

The first is that in these cases the question about identity must have an answer.

No one thinks this about, say, nations or machines. Our criteria for the identity of these do not cover certain cases. No one thinks that in these cases the questions "Is it the same nation?" or "Is it the same machine?" must have answers.

Some people believe that in this respect they are different. They agree that our criteria of personal identity do not cover certain cases, but they believe that the nature of their own identity through time is, somehow, such as to guarantee that in these cases questions about their identity must have answers. This belief might be expressed as

follows: "Whatever happens between now and any future time, either I shall still exist, or I shall not. Any future experience will either be *my* experience, or it will not."

This first belief – in the special nature of personal identity – has, I think, certain effects. It makes people assume that the principle of self-interest is more rationally compelling than any moral principle. And it makes them more depressed by the thought of aging and of death.

I cannot see how to disprove this first belief. I shall describe a problem case. But this can only make it seem implausible.

Another approach might be this. We might suggest that one cause of the belief is the projection of our emotions. When we imagine ourselves in a problem case, we do feel that the question "Would it be me?" must have an answer. But what we take to be a bafflement about a further fact may be only the bafflement of our concern.

I shall not pursue this suggestion here. But one cause of our concern is the belief which is my second target. This is that unless the question about identity has an answer, we cannot answer certain important questions (questions about such matters as survival, memory and responsibility).

Against this second belief my claim will be this. Certain important questions do presuppose a question about personal identity. But they can be freed of this presupposition. And when they are, the question about identity has no importance.

Originally published in *Philosophical Review* 80 (1971), pp. 3–27. Reprinted by permission of the author and Cornell University.

Derek Parfit

I

We can start by considering the much discussed case of the man who, like an amoeba, divides.[1]

Wiggins has recently dramatized this case.[2] He first referred to the operation imagined by Shoemaker.[3] We suppose that my brain is transplanted into someone else's (brainless) body, and that the resulting person has my character and apparent memories of my life. Most of us would agree, after thought, that the resulting person is me. I shall here assume such agreement.[4]

Wiggins then imagined his own operation. My brain is divided, and each half is housed in a new body. Both resulting people have my character and apparent memories of my life.

What happens to me? There seem only three possibilities: (1) I do not survive; (2) I survive as one of the two people; (3) I survive as both.

The trouble with (1) is this. We agreed that I could survive if my brain were successfully transplanted. And people have in fact survived with half their brains destroyed. It seems to follow that I could survive if half my brain were successfully transplanted and the other half were destroyed. But if this is so, how could I *not* survive if the other half were also successfully transplanted? How could a double success be a failure?

We can move to the second description. Perhaps one success is the maximum score. Perhaps I shall be one of the resulting people.

The trouble here is that in Wiggins's case each half of my brain is exactly similar, and so, to start with, is each resulting person. So how can I survive as only one of the two people? What can make me one of them rather than the other?

It seems clear that both of these descriptions – that I do not survive, and that I survive as one of the people – are highly implausible. Those who have accepted them must have assumed that they were the only possible descriptions.

What about our third description: that I survive as both people?

It might be said, "If 'survive' implies identity, this description makes no sense – you cannot be two people. If it does not, the description is irrelevant to a problem about identity."

I shall later deny the second of these remarks. But there are ways of denying the first. We might say, "What we have called 'the two resulting people' are not two people. They are one person. I do survive Wiggins's operation. Its effect is to give me two bodies and a divided mind."

It would shorten my argument if this were absurd. But I do not think it is. It is worth showing why.

We can, I suggest, imagine a divided mind. We can imagine a man having two simultaneous experiences, in having each of which he is unaware of having the other.

We may not even need to imagine this. Certain actual cases, to which Wiggins referred, seem to be best described in these terms. These involve the cutting of the bridge between the hemispheres of the brain. The aim was to cure epilepsy. But the result appears to be, in the surgeon's words, the creation of "two separate spheres of consciousness,"[5] each of which controls one half of the patient's body. What is experienced in each is, presumably, experienced by the patient.

There are certain complications in these actual cases. So let us imagine a simpler case.

Suppose that the bridge between my hemispheres is brought under my voluntary control. This would enable me to disconnect my hemispheres as easily as if I were blinking. By doing this, I would divide my mind. And we can suppose that when my mind is divided, I can, in each half, bring about reunion.

This ability would have obvious uses. To give an example: I am near the end of a maths exam, and see two ways of tackling the last problem. I decide to divide my mind, to work, with each half, at one of two calculations, and then to reunite my mind and write a fair copy of the best result.

What shall I experience?

When I disconnect my hemispheres, my consciousness divides into two streams. But this division is not something that I experience. Each of my two streams of consciousness seems to have been straightforwardly continuous with my one stream of consciousness up to the moment of division. The only changes in each stream are the disappearance of half my visual field and the loss of sensation in, and control over, half my body.

Consider my experiences in what we can call my "right-handed" stream. I remember that I assigned my right hand to the longer calculation. This I now begin. In working at this calculation I can see, from the movements of my left hand, that I am also working at the other. But I am not aware of working at the other. So I might, in my right-handed stream, wonder how, in my left-handed stream, I am getting on.

My work is now over. I am about to reunite my mind. What should I, in each stream, expect? Simply that I shall suddenly seem to remember just having thought out two calculations, in thinking out each of which I was not aware of thinking out the other. This, I submit, we can imagine. And if my mind was divided, these memories are correct.

In describing this episode, I assumed that there were two series of thoughts, and that they were both mine. If my two hands visibly wrote out two calculations, and if I claimed to remember two corresponding series of thoughts, this is surely what we should want to say.

If it is, then a person's mental history need not be like a canal, with only one channel. It could be like a river, with islands, and with separate streams.

To apply this to Wiggins's operation: we mentioned the view that it gives me two bodies and a divided mind. We cannot now call this absurd. But it is, I think, unsatisfactory.

There were two features of the case of the exam that made us want to say that only one person was involved. The mind was soon reunited, and there was only one body. If a mind was permanently divided and its halves developed in different ways, the point of speaking of one person would start to disappear. Wiggins's case, where there are also two bodies, seems to be over the borderline. After I have had his operation, the two "products" each have all the attributes of a person. They could live at opposite ends of the earth. (If they later met, they might even fail to recognize each other.) It would become intolerable to deny that they were different people.

Suppose we admit that they are different people. Could we still claim that I survived as both, using "survive" to imply identity?

We could. For we might suggest that two people could compose a third. We might say, "I do survive Wiggins's operation as two people. They can be different people, and yet be me, in just the way in which the Pope's three crowns are one crown."[6]

This is a possible way of giving sense to the claim that I survive as two different people, using "survive" to imply identity. But it keeps the language of identity only by changing the concept of a person. And there are obvious objections to this change.[7]

The alternative, for which I shall argue, is to give up the language of identity. We can suggest that I survive as two different people without implying that I am these people.

When I first mentioned this alternative, I mentioned this objection: "If your new way of talking does not imply identity, it cannot solve our problem. For that is about identity. The problem is that all the possible answers to the question about identity are highly implausible."

We can now answer this objection.

We can start by reminding ourselves that this is an objection only if we have one or both of the beliefs which I mentioned at the start of this paper.

The first was the belief that to any question about personal identity, in any describable case, there must be a true answer. For those with this belief, Wiggins's case is doubly perplexing. If all the possible answers are implausible, it is hard to decide which of them is true, and hard even to keep the belief that one of them must be true. If we give up this belief, as I think we should, these problems disappear. We shall then regard the case as like many others in which, for quite unpuzzling reasons, there *is* no answer to a question about identity. (Consider "Was England the same nation after 1066?")

Wiggins's case makes the first belief implausible. It also makes it trivial. For it undermines the second belief. This was the belief that important questions turn upon the question about identity. (It is worth pointing out that those who have only this second belief do not think that there must *be* an answer to this question, but rather that we must decide upon an answer.)

Against this second belief my claim is this. Certain questions do presuppose a question about personal identity. And because these questions *are* important, Wiggins's case does present a problem. But we cannot solve this problem by answering the question about identity. We can solve this problem only by taking these important questions and prizing them apart from the question about identity. After we have done this, the question about identity (though we might for the sake of neatness decide it) has no further interest.

Because there are several questions which presuppose identity, this claim will take some time to fill out.

We can first return to the question of survival. This is a special case, for survival does not so much presuppose the retaining of identity as seem equivalent to it. It is thus the general relation which we need to prize apart from identity. We can then consider particular relations, such as those involved in memory and intention.

"Will I survive?" seems, I said, equivalent to "Will there be some person alive who is the same person as me?"

If we treat these questions as equivalent, then the least unsatisfactory description of Wiggins's case is, I think, that I survive with two bodies and a divided mind.

Several writers have chosen to say that I am neither of the resulting people. Given our equivalence, this implies that I do not survive, and hence, presumably, that even if Wiggins's operation is not literally death, I ought, since I will not survive it, to regard it *as* death. But this seemed absurd.

It is worth repeating why. An emotion or attitude can be criticized for resting on a false belief, or for being inconsistent. A man who regarded Wiggins's operation as death must, I suggest, be open to one of these criticisms.

He might believe that his relation to each of the resulting people fails to contain some element which is contained in survival. But how can this be true? We agreed that he *would* survive if he stood in this very same relation to only *one* of the resulting people. So it cannot be the nature of this relation which makes it fail, in Wiggins's case, to be survival. It can only be its duplication.

Suppose that our man accepts this, but still regards division as death. His reaction would now seem wildly inconsistent. He would be like a man who, when told of a drug that could double his years of life, regarded the taking of this drug as death. The only difference in the case of division is that the extra years are to run concurrently. This is an interesting difference. But it cannot mean that there are *no* years to run.

I have argued this for those who think that there must, in Wiggins's case, be a true answer to the question about identity. For them, we might add, "Perhaps the original person does lose his identity. But there may be other ways to do this than to die. One other way might be to multiply. To regard these as the same is to confuse nought with two."

For those who think that the question of identity is up for decision, it would be clearly absurd to regard Wiggins's operation as death. These people would have to think, "We could have chosen to say that I should be one of the resulting people. If we had, I should not have regarded it as death. But since we have chosen to say that I am neither person, I *do*." This is hard even to understand.[8]

My first conclusion, then, is this. The relation of the original person to each of the resulting people contains all that interests us – all that matters – in any ordinary case of survival. This is why we need a sense in which one person can survive as two.[9]

One of my aims in the rest of this paper will be to suggest such a sense. But we can first make some general remarks.

II

Identity is a one–one relation. Wiggins's case serves to show that what matters in survival need not be one–one.

Wiggins's case is of course, unlikely to occur. The relations which matter are, in fact, one–one. It is because they are that we can imply the holding of these relations by using the language of identity.

This use of language is convenient. But it can lead us astray. We may assume that what matters *is* identity and, hence, has the properties of identity.

In the case of the property of being one–one, this mistake is not serious. For what matters is in fact one–one. But in the case of another property, the mistake *is* serious. Identity is all-or-nothing. Most of the relations which matter in survival are, in fact, relations of degree. If we ignore this, we shall be led into quite ill-grounded attitudes and beliefs.

The claim that I have just made – that most of what matters are relations of degree – I have yet to support. Wiggins's case shows only that these relations need not be one–one. The merit of the case is not that it shows this in particular, but that it makes the first break between what matters and identity. The belief that identity *is* what matters is hard to overcome. This is shown in most discussions of the problem cases which actually occur: cases, say, of amnesia or of brain damage. Once Wiggins's case has made one breach in this belief, the rest should be easier to remove.[10]

To turn to a recent debate: most of the relations which matter can be provisionally referred to under the heading "psychological continuity" (which includes causal continuity). My claim is thus that we use the language of personal identity in order to imply such continuity. This is close to the view that psychological continuity provides a criterion of identity.

Williams has attacked this view with the following argument. Identity is a one–one relation. So any criterion of identity must appeal to a relation which is logically one– one. Psychological continuity is not logically one–one. So it cannot provide a criterion.[11]

Some writers have replied that it is enough if the relation appealed to is always in fact one–one.[12]

I suggest a slightly different reply. Psychological continuity is a ground for speaking of identity when it is one–one.

If psychological continuity took a one–many or branching form, we should need, I have argued, to abandon the language of identity. So this possibility would not count against this view.

We can make a stronger claim. This possibility would count in its favor.

The view might be defended as follows. Judgments of personal identity have great importance. What gives them their importance is the fact that they imply psychological continuity. This is why, whenever there is such continuity, we ought, if we can, to imply it by making a judgment of identity.

If psychological continuity took a branching form, no coherent set of judgments of identity could correspond to, and thus be used to imply, the branching form of this relation. But what we ought to do, in such a case, is take the importance which would attach to a judgment of identity and attach this importance directly to each limb of the branching relation. So this case helps to show that judgments of personal identity do derive their importance from the fact that they imply psychological continuity. It helps to show that when we can, usefully, speak of identity, this relation is our ground.

This argument appeals to a principle which Williams put forward.[13] The principle is that an important judgment should be asserted and denied only on importantly different grounds.

Williams applied this principle to a case in which one man is psychologically continuous with the dead Guy Fawkes, and a case in which two men are. His argument was this. If we treat psychological continuity as a sufficient ground for speaking of identity, we shall say that the one man is Guy Fawkes. But we could not say that the two men are, although we should have the same ground. This disobeys the principle. The remedy is to deny that the one man is Guy Fawkes, to insist that sameness of the body is necessary for identity.

Williams's principle can yield a different answer. Suppose we regard psychological continuity as more important than sameness of the body.[14] And suppose that the one man really is psychologically (and causally) continuous with Guy Fawkes. If he is, it would disobey the principle to deny that he is Guy Fawkes, for we have the same important ground as in a normal case of identity. In the case of the two men, we again have the same important ground. So we ought to take the importance from the judgment of identity and attach it directly to this ground. We ought to say, as in Wiggins's case, that each limb of the branching relation is as good as survival. This obeys the principle.

To sum up these remarks: even if psychological continuity is neither logically, nor always in fact, one–one, it can provide a criterion of identity. For this can appeal to the relation of *non-branching* psychological continuity, which is logically one–one.[15]

The criterion might be sketched as follows. "X and Y are the same person if they are psychologically continuous and there is no person who is contemporary with either and psychologically continuous with the other." We should need to explain what we mean by "psychologically continuous" and say how much continuity the criterion requires. We should then, I think, have described a sufficient condition for speaking of identity.[16]

We need to say something more. If we admit that psychological continuity might not be one–one, we need to say what we ought to do if it were not one–one. Otherwise our account would be open to the objections that it is incomplete and arbitrary.[17]

I have suggested that if psychological continuity took a branching form, we ought to speak in a new way, regarding what we describe as having the same significance as identity. This answers these objections.[18]

We can now return to our discussion. We have three remaining aims. One is to suggest a sense of "survive" which does not imply identity. Another is to show that most of what matters in survival are relations of degree. A third is to show that none of these relations needs to be described in a way that presupposes identity.

We can take these aims in the reverse order.

III

The most important particular relation is that involved in memory. This is because it is so easy to believe that its description must refer to identity.[19] This belief about memory is an important cause of the view that personal identity has a special nature. But it has been well discussed by Shoemaker[20] and by Wiggins.[21] So we can be brief.

It may be a logical truth that we can only remember our own experiences. But we can frame a new concept for which this is not a logical truth. Let us call this "q-memory".

To sketch a definition[22] I am q-remembering an experience if (1) I have a belief about a past experience which seems in itself like a memory belief, (2) someone did have such an experience, and (3) my beliefs is dependent upon this experience in the same way (whatever that is) in which a memory of an experience is dependent upon it.

According to (1), q-memories seem like memories. So I q-remember *having* experiences.

This may seem to make q-memory presuppose identity. One might say, "My apparent memory of *having* an experience is an apparent memory of *my* having an experience. So how could I q-remember my having other people's experiences?"

This objection rests on a mistake. When I seem to remember an experience, I do indeed seem to remember *having* it.[23] But it cannot be a part of what I seem to remember about this experience that I, the person who now seems to remember it, am the person who had this experience.[24] That I am is something that I automatically assume. (My apparent memories sometimes come to me simply as the belief that *I* had a certain experience.) But it is something that I am justified in assuming only because I do not in fact have q-memories of other people's experiences.

Suppose that I did start to have such q-memories. If I did, I should cease to assume that my apparent memories must be about my own experiences. I should come to assess an apparent memory by asking two questions: (1) Does it tell me about a past experience? (2) If so, whose?

Moreover (and this is a crucial point) my apparent memories would now come to me *as* q-memories. Consider those of my apparent memories which do come to me simply as beliefs about my past: for example, "I did that." If I knew that I could q-remember other people's experiences, these beliefs would come to me in a more guarded form: for example, "Someone – probably I – did that." I might have to work out who it was.

I have suggested that the concept of q-memory is coherent. Wiggins's case provides an illustration. The resulting people, in his case, both have apparent memories of living the life of the original person. If they agree that they are not this person, they will have to regard these as only q-memories. And when they are asked a question like "Have you heard this music before?", they might have to answer "I am sure that I q-remember hearing it. But I am not sure whether I remember hearing it. I am not sure whether it was I who heard it, or the original person."

We can next point out that on our definition every memory is also a q-memory. Memories are, simply, q-memories of one's own experiences. Since this is so, we could afford now to drop the concept of memory and use in its place the wider concept q-memory. If we did, we should describe the relation between an experience and what we now call a "memory" of this experience in a way which does not presuppose that they are had by the same person.[25]

This way of describing this relation has certain merits. It vindicates the "memory criterion" of personal identity against the charge of circularity.[26] And it might, I think, help with the problem of other minds.

But we must move on. We can next take the relation between an intention and a later action. It may be a logical truth that we can intend to perform only our own actions. But intentions can be redescribed as q-intentions. And one person could q-intend to perform another person's actions.

Wiggins's case again provides the illustration. We are supposing that neither of the resulting people is the original person. If so, we shall have to agree that the original person can, before the operation, q-intend to perform their actions. He might, for example, q-intend, as one of them, to continue his present career, and, as the other, to try something new.[27] (I say "q-intend *as* one of them" because the phrase "q-intend that one of them" would not convey the directness of the relation which is involved. If I intend that someone else should do something, I cannot get him to do it simply by forming this intention. But if I am the original person, and he is one of the resulting people, I can.)

The phrase "q-intend *as* one of them" reminds us that we need a sense in which one person can survive as two. But we can first point out that the concepts of q-memory and q-intention give us our model for the others that we need: thus, a man who can q-remember could q-recognize, and be a q-witness of, what he has never seen; and a man who can q-intend could have q-ambitions, make q-promises, and be q-responsible for.

To put this claim in general terms: many different relations are included within, or are a consequence of, psychological continuity. We describe these relations in ways which presuppose the continued existence of one person. But we could describe them in new ways which do not.

This suggests a bolder claim. It might be possible to think of experiences in a wholly "impersonal" way. I shall not develop this claim here. What I shall try to describe is a way of thinking of our own identity through time which is more flexible, and less misleading, than the way in which we now think.

This way of thinking will allow for a sense in which one person can survive as two. A more important feature is that it treats survival as a matter of degree.

IV

We must first show the need for this second feature. I shall use two imaginary examples.

The first is the converse of Wiggins's case: fusion. Just as division serves to show that what matters in survival need not be one–one, so fusion serves to show that it can be a question of degree.

Physically, fusion is easy to describe. Two people come together. While they are unconscious, their two bodies grow into one. One person then wakes up.

The psychology of fusion is more complex. One detail we have already dealt with in the case of the exam. When my mind was reunited, I remembered just having thought out two calculations. The one person who results from a fusion can, similarly, q-remember living the lives of the two original people. None of their q-memories need be lost.

But some things must be lost. For any two people who fuse together will have different characteristics, different desires, and different intentions. How can these be combined?

We might suggest the following. Some of these will be compatible. These can coexist in the one resulting person. Some will be incompatible. These, if of equal strength, can cancel out, and if of different strengths, the stronger can be made weaker. And all these effects might be predictable.

To give examples – first, of compatibility: I like Palladio and intend to visit Venice. I am about to fuse with a person who likes Giotto and intends to visit Padua. I can know that the one person we shall become will have both tastes and both intentions. Second, of incompatibility: I hate red hair, and always vote Labour. The other person loves red hair, and always votes Conservative. I can know that the one person we shall become will be indifferent to red hair, and a floating voter.

If we were about to undergo a fusion of this kind, would we regard it as death?

Some of us might. This is less absurd than regarding division as death. For after my division the two resulting people will be in every way like me, while after my fusion the one resulting person will not be wholly similar. This makes it easier to say, when faced with fusion, "I shall not survive", thus continuing to regard survival as a matter of all-or-nothing.

This reaction is less absurd. But here are two analogies which tell against it.

First, fusion would involve the changing of some of our characteristics and some of our desires. But only the very self-satisfied would think of this as death. Many people welcome treatments with these effects.

Second, someone who is about to fuse can have, beforehand, just as much "intentional control" over the actions of the resulting individual as someone who is about to marry can have, beforehand, over the actions of the resulting couple. And the choice of a partner for fusion can be just as well considered as the choice of a marriage partner. The two original people can make sure (perhaps by "trial fusion") that they do have compatible characters, desires and intentions.

I have suggested that fusion, while not clearly survival, is not clearly failure to survive, and hence that what matters in survival can have degrees.

To reinforce this claim, we can now turn to a second example. This is provided by certain imaginary beings. These beings are just like ourselves except that they reproduce by a process of natural division.

We can illustrate the histories of these imagined beings with the aid of a diagram (fig. 29.1). The lines on the diagram represent the spatiotemporal paths which would be traced out by the bodies of these beings. We can call each single line (like the double line) a "branch"; and we can call the whole structure a "tree". And let us suppose that each "branch" corresponds to what is thought of as the life of one individual. These individuals are referred to as "A", "B + 1", and so forth.

Now, each single division is an instance of Wiggins's case. So A's relation to both B + 1 and B + 2 is just as good as survival. But what of A's relation to B + 30?

I said earlier that what matters in survival could be provisionally referred to as "psychological continuity". I must now distinguish this relation from another, which I shall call "psychological connectedness".

Let us say that the relation between a q-memory and the experience q-remembered is a "direct" relation. Another "direct" relation is that which holds between a q-intention and the q-intended action. A third is that which holds between different expressions of some lasting q-characteristic.

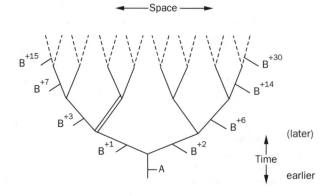

Figure 29.1

"Psychological connectedness", as I define it, requires the holding of these direct psychological relations. "Connectedness" is not transitive, since these relations are not transitive. Thus, if X q-remembers most of Y's life, and Y q-remembers most of Z's life, it does not follow that X q-remembers most of Z's life. And if X carries out the q-intentions of Y, and Y carries out the q-intentions of Z, it does not follow that X carries out the q-intentions of Z.

"Psychological continuity", in contrast, only requires overlapping chains of direct psychological relations. So "continuity" is transitive.

To return to our diagram. A is psychologically continuous with $B + 30$. There are between the two continuous chains of overlapping relations. Thus, A has q-intentional control over $B + 2$, $B + 2$ has q-intentional control over $B + 6$, and so on up to $B + 30$. Or $B + 30$ can q-remember the life of $B + 14$, $B + 14$ can q-remember the life of $B + 6$, and so on back to A.[28]

A, however, need *not* be psychologically connected to $B + 30$. Connectedness requires direct relations. And if these beings are like us, A cannot stand in such relations to every individual in his indefinitely long "tree". Q-memories will weaken with the passage of time, and then fade away. Q-ambitions, once fulfilled, will be replaced by others. Q-characteristics will gradually change. In general, A stands in fewer and fewer direct psychological relations to an individual in his "tree" the more remote that individual is. And if the individual is (like $B + 30$) sufficiently remote, there may be between the two *no* direct psychological relations.

Now that we have distinguished the general relations of psychological continuity and psycholo-

gical connectedness, I suggest that connectedness is a more important element in survival. As a claim about our own survival, this would need more arguments than I have space to give. But it seems clearly true for my imagined beings. A is as close psychologically to $B + 1$ as I today am to myself tomorrow. A is as distant from $B + 30$ as I am from my great-great-grandson.

Even if connectedness is not more important than continuity, the fact that one of these is a relation of degree is enough to show that what matters in survival can have degrees. And in any case the two relations are quite different. So our imagined beings would need a way of thinking in which this difference is recognized.

V

What I propose is this.

First, A can think of any individual, anywhere in his "tree", as "a descendant self". This phrase implies psychological continuity. Similarly, any later individual can think of any earlier individual on the single path[29] which connects him to A as "an ancestral self".

Since psychological continuity is transitive, "being an ancestral self of" and "being a descendant self of" are also transitive.

To imply psychological connectedness, I suggest the phrases "one of my future selves" and "one of my past selves".

These are the phrases with which we can describe Wiggins's case. For having past and future selves is, what we needed, a way of continuing to exist which does not imply identity through time. The original person does, in this sense, survive

Wiggins's operation: the two resulting people are his later selves. And they can each refer to him as "my past self". (They can share a past self without being the same self as each other.)

Since psychological connectedness is not transitive, and is a matter of degree, the relations "being a past self of" and "being a future self of" should themselves be treated as relations of degree. We allow for this series of descriptions: "my most recent self", "one of my earlier selves", "one of my distant selves", "hardly one of *my* past selves (I can only *q*-remember a few of his experiences)," and, finally, "not in any way one of *my* past selves – just an ancestral self."

This way of thinking would clearly suit our first imagined beings. But let us now turn to a second kind of being. These reproduce by fusion as well as by division.[30] And let us suppose that they fuse every autumn and divide every spring. This yields figure 29.2

If A is the individual whose life is represented by the three-lined "branch," the two-lined "tree" represents those lives which are psychologically continuous with A's life. (It can be seen that each individual has his own "tree," which overlaps with many others.)

For the imagined beings in this second world, the phrases "an ancestral self" and "a descendant self" would cover too much to be of much use. (There may well be pairs of dates such that every individual who ever lived before the first date was an ancestral self of every individual who ever will live after the second date.) Conversely, since the lives of each individual last for only half a year, the word "I" would cover too little to do all of the work which it does for us. So part of this work would have to be done, for these second beings, by talk about past and future selves.

We can now point out a theoretical flaw in our proposed way of thinking. The phrase "a past self of" implies psychological connectedness. Being a past self of is treated as a relation of degree, so

that this phrase can be used to imply the varying degrees of psychological connectedness. But this phrase can imply only the degrees of connectedness between different lives. It cannot be used within a single life. And our way of delimiting successive lives does not refer to the degrees of psychological connectedness. Hence there is no guarantee that this phrase, "a past self of," could be used whenever it was needed. There is no guarantee that psychological connectedness will not vary in degree within a single life.

This flaw would not concern our imagined beings. For they divide and unite so frequently, and their lives are in consequence so short, that within a single life psychological connectedness would always stand at a maximum.

But let us look, finally, at a third kind of being.

In this world there is neither division nor union. There are a number of everlasting bodies, which gradually change in appearance. And direct psychological relations, as before, hold only over limited periods of time. This can be illustrated with a third diagram (figure 29.3). In this diagram the two shadings represent the degrees of psychological connectedness to their two central points.

These beings could not use the way of thinking that we have proposed. Since there is no branching of psychological continuity, they would have to regard themselves as immortal. It might be said that this is what they are. But there is, I suggest, a better description.

Our beings would have one reason for thinking of themselves as immortal. The parts of each "line" are all psychologically continuous. But the parts of each "line" are not all psychologically connected. Direct psychological relations hold only between those parts which are close to each other in time. This gives our beings a reason for *not* thinking of

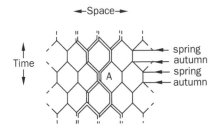

Figure 29.2

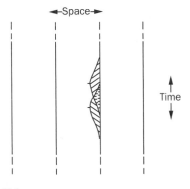

Figure 29.3

each "line" as corresponding to one single life. For if they did, they would have no way of implying these direct relations. When a speaker says, for example, "I spent a period doing such and such," his hearers would not be entitled to assume that the speaker has any memories of this period, that his character then and now are in any way similar, that he is now carrying out any of the plans or intentions which he then had, and so forth. Because the word "I" would carry none of these implications, it would not have for these "immortal" beings the usefulness which it has for us.[31]

To gain a better way of thinking, we must revise the way of thinking that we proposed above. The revision is this. The distinction between successive selves can be made by reference, not to the branching of psychological continuity, but to the degrees of psychological connectedness. Since this connectedness is a matter of degree, the drawing of these distinctions can be left to the choice of the speaker and be allowed to vary from context to context.

On this way of thinking, the word "I" can be used to imply the greatest degree of psychological connectedness. When the connections are reduced, when there has been any marked change of character or style of life, or any marked loss of memory, our imagined beings would say, "It was not I who did that, but an earlier self." They could then describe in what ways, and to what degree, they are related to this earlier self.

This revised way of thinking would suit not only our "immortal" beings. It is also the way in which we ourselves could think about our lives. And it is, I suggest, surprisingly natural.

One of its features, the distinction between successive selves, has already been used by several writers. To give an example, from Proust: "we are incapable, while we are in love, of acting as fit predecessors of the next persons who, when we are in love no longer, we shall presently have become . . ."[32]

Although Proust distinguished between successive selves, he still thought of one person as being these different selves. This we would not do on the way of thinking that I propose. If I say, "It will not be me, but one of my future selves," I do not imply that I will be that future self. He is one of my later selves, and I am one of his earlier selves. There is no underlying person who we both are.

To point out another feature of this way of thinking. When I say, "There is no person who we both are," I am only giving my decision.

Another person could say, "It will be you," thus deciding differently. There is no question of either of these decisions being a mistake. Whether to say "I," or "one of my future selves," or "a descendant self" is entirely a matter of choice. The matter of fact, which must be agreed, is only whether the disjunction applies. (The question "Are X and Y the same person?" thus becomes "Is X *at least* an ancestral (or descendant) self of Y?")

VI

I have tried to show that what matters in the continued existence of a person are, for the most part, relations of degree. And I have proposed a way of thinking in which this would be recognized.

I shall end by suggesting two consequences and asking one question.

It is sometimes thought to be especially rational to act in our own best interests. But I suggest that the principle of self-interest has no force. There are only two genuine competitors in this particular field. One is the principle of biased rationality: do what will best achieve what you actually want. The other is the principle of impartiality: do what is in the best interests of everyone concerned.

The apparent force of the principle of self-interest derives, I think, from these two other principles.

The principle of self-interest is normally supported by the principle of biased rationality. This is because most people care about their own future interests.

Suppose that this prop is lacking. Suppose that a man does not care what happens to him in, say, the more distant future. To such a man, the principle of self-interest can only be propped up by an appeal to the principle of impartiality. We must say, "Even if you don't care, you ought to take what happens to you then equally into account." But for this, as a special claim, there seem to me no good arguments. It can only be supported as part of the general claim, "You ought to take what happens to everyone equally into account."[33]

The special claim tells a man to grant an *equal* weight to all the parts of his future. The argument for this can only be that all the parts of his future are *equally* parts of *his* future. This is true. But it is a truth too superficial to bear the weight of the argument. (To give an analogy: The unity of a nation is, in its nature, a matter of degree. It is therefore only a superficial truth that all of a man's compatriots are *equally* his compatriots. This truth cannot support a good argument for nationalism.)[34]

I have suggested that the principle of self-interest has no strength of its own. If this is so, there is no special problem in the fact that what we ought to do can be against our interests. There is only the general problem that it may not be what we want to do.

The second consequence which I shall mention is implied in the first. Egoism, the fear not of near but of distant death, the regret that so much of one's *only* life should have gone by – these are not, I think, wholly natural or instinctive. They are all strengthened by the beliefs about personal identity which I have been attacking. If we give up these beliefs, they should be weakened.

My final question is this. These emotions are bad, and if we weaken them, we gain. But can we achieve this gain without, say, also weakening loyalty to, or love of, other particular selves? As Hume warned, the "refined reflections which philosophy suggests . . . cannot diminish . . . our vicious passions . . . without diminishing . . . such as are virtuous. They are . . . applicable to all our affections. In vain do we hope to direct their influence only to one side."[35]

That hope *is* vain. But Hume had another: that more of what is bad depends upon false belief. This is also my hope.

Notes

I have been helped in writing this by D. Wiggins, D. F. Pears, P. F. Strawson, A. J. Ayer, M. Woods, N. Newman, and (through his publications) S. Shoemaker.

1 Implicit in John Locke, *Essay Concerning Human Understanding*, ed. John W. Yolton, (London: J.M. Dent and New York: E. P. Dutton, 1961) vol. 2, ch. 27, sect. 18 and discussed by (among others) A. N. Prior in "Opposite number," *Review of Metaphysics* 11 (1957–8), and *idem*, "Time, existence and identity," *Proceedings of the Aristotelian Society* 57 (1965–6); J. Bennett in "The simplicity of the soul," *Journal of Philosophy* 64 (1967); and R. Chisholm and S. Shoemaker in "The loose and popular and the strict and the philosophical senses of identity," in Norman Care and Robert H. Grimm, *Perception and Personal Identity: Proceeding of the 1967 Oberlin Colloquium in Philosophy*, (eds), (Cleveland: Press of Case Western Reserve University, 1967).
2 David Wiggins, *Identity and Spatio-Temporal Continuity* (Oxford: Blackwell, 1967), p. 50.
3 Sydney S. Shoemaker, *Self-Knowledge and Self-Identity* (Ithaca, N.Y: Cornell University Press, 1963), p. 22.
4 Those who would disagree are not making a mistake. For them my argument would need a different case. There must be some multiple transplant, faced with which these people would both find it hard to believe that there must be an answer to the question about personal identity, and be able to be shown that nothing of importance turns upon this question.
5 R. W. Sperry, *Brain and Conscious Experience*, ed. J. C. Eccles (New York: Springer Verlag, 1966), p. 299.
6 Cf. Wiggins, *Identity*, p. 40.
7 Suppose the resulting people fight a duel. Are there there three people fighting, one on each side, and one on both? And suppose one of the bullets kills. Are there two acts, one murder and one suicide? How many people are left alive? One? Two? (We could hardly say, "One and a half".) We could talk in this way. But instead of saying that the resulting people are the original person – so that the pair is a trio – it would be far simpler to treat them as a pair, and describe their relation to the original person in some new way. (I owe this suggested way of talking, and the objections to it, to Michael Woods.)
8 Cf. Sydney Shoemaker, in *Perception and Personal Identity*, p. 54.
9 Cf. Wiggins *Identity*.
10 Bernard Williams's "The self and the future," this volume, ch. 28, is relevant here. He asks the question "Shall I survive?" in a range of problem cases, and he shows how natural it is to believe (1) that this question must have an answer, (2) that the answer must be all-or-nothing, and (3) that there is a "risk" of our reaching the wrong answer. Because these beliefs are so natural, we should need in undermining them to discuss their causes. These, I think, can be found in the ways in which we misinterpret what it is to remember (cf. sect. III) and to anticipate (cf. Williams's "Imagination and the self," *Proceedings of the British Academy* 52 (1966), pp. 105–24); and also in the way in which certain features of our egoistic concern – e.g., that it is simple, and applies to all imaginable cases – are "projected" on to its object. (For another relevant discussion, see Terence Penelhum's *Survival and Disembodied Existence* (New York: Humanities Press, 1970, final chapters.)
11 Bernard Williams, "Personal identity and Individuation," *Proceedings of the Aristotelian Society* 57 (1956–7), pp. 229–53; also his "Bodily continuity and personal identity: a reply," *Analysis* 21 (1960–61), 43–8.
12 J. M. Shorter, "More about bodily continuity and personal identity," *Analysis* 22 (1961–2), pp. 79–85;

and Mrs J. M. R. Jack (unpublished), who requires that this truth be embedded in a causal theory.

13 Williams, "Bodily Continuity," p. 44.

14 For the reasons given by A. M. Quinton in "The soul," *Journal of Philosophy* 59 (1962), pp. 393–409.

15 Cf. S. Shoemaker, "Persons and their pasts," this volume, ch. 27, and *idem*, "Wiggins on identity," *Philosophical Review* 79 (1970), p. 542.

16 But not a necessary condition, for in the absence of psychological continuity, bodily identity might be sufficient.

17 Cf. Williams, "Personal identity and individuation," pp. 240–1, and *idem*, "Bodily continuity," p. 44; and also Wiggins, *Identity*, p. 38: "if coincidence under [the concept] *f* is to be *genuinely* sufficient we must not withhold identity . . . simply because transitivity is threatened."

18 Williams produced another objection to the "psychological criterion," that it makes it hard to explain the difference between the concepts of identity and exact similarity ("Bodily continuity," p. 48). But if we include the requirement of causal continuity, we avoid this objection (and one of those produced by Wiggins in his n. 47).

19 Those philosophers who have held this belief, from Butler onward, are too numerous to cite.

20 Shoemaker, this volume, ch. 27.

21 In a paper on Butler's objection to Locke (not yet published).

22 I here follow Shoemaker's "quasi-memory." Cf. also Penelhum's "retrocognition," in his article on "Personal identity," in Paul Edwards (ed.), *Encyclopedia of Philosophy*.

23 As Shoemaker put it, I seem to remember the experience "from the inside" (this volume, ch. 27).

24 This is what so many writers have overlooked. Cf. Thomas Reid: "My memory testifies not only that this was done, but that it was done by me who now remember it" ("Of identity," in *Essays on the Intellectual Powers of Man*, ed. A. D. Woozley (London: Macmillan, 1941), p. 203). This mistake is discussed by A. B. Palma in "Memory and personal identity," *Australasian Journal of Philosophy* 42 (1964), p. 57.

25 It is not logically necessary that we only *q*-remember our own experiences. But it might be necessary on other grounds. This possibility is intriguingly explored by Shoemaker in his "Persons and their pasts," this volume, ch. 27. He shows that *q*-memories can provide a knowledge of the world only if the observations which are *q*-remembered trace out fairly continuous spatiotemporal paths. If the observations

which are *q*-remembered traced out a network of frequently interlocking paths, they could not, I think, be usefully ascribed to persisting observers, but would have to be referred to in some more complex way. But in fact the observations which are *q*-remembered trace out single and separate paths; so we can ascribe them to ourselves. In other words, it is epistemologically necessary that the observations which are *q*-remembered should satisfy a certain general condition, one particular form of which allows them to be usefully self-ascribed.

26 Cf. Wiggins's paper on Butler's objection to Locke.

27 There are complications here. He could form *divergent q*-intentions only if he could distinguish, in advance, between the resulting people (e.g., as "the left-hander" and "the right-hander"). And he could be confident that such divergent *q*-intentions would be carried out only if he had reason to believe that neither of the resulting people would change their (inherited) mind. Suppose he was torn between duty and desire. He could not solve this dilemma by *q*-intending, as one of the resulting people, to do his duty, and, as the other, to do what he desires. For the one he *q*-intended to do his duty would face the same dilemma.

28 The chain of continuity must run in one direction of time. B + 2 is not, in the sense I intend, psychologically continuous with B + 1.

29 Cf. Wiggins, *Identity*.

30 Cf. Shoemaker in "Persons and their pasts," this volume, ch. 27.

31 Cf. Austin Duncan Jones, "Man's mortality," *Analysis* 28 (1967–8), pp. 65–70.

32 Proust, *Within a Budding Grove* (New York: Modern Library, 1949), vol. 1, p. 226 (my own translation).

33 Cf. Thomas Nagel's *The Possibility of Altruism* (Oxford: Clarendon Press, 1970), in which the special claim is in effect defended as part of the general claim.

34 The unity of a nation we seldom take for more than what it is. This is partly because we often think of nations, not as units, but in a more complex way. If we thought of ourselves in the way that I proposed, we might be less likely to take our own identity for more than what it is. We are, for example, sometimes told, "It is irrational to act against your own interests. After all, it will be you who will regret it." To this we could reply, "No, not me. Not even one of my future selves. Just a descendant self."

35 Hume, "The Sceptic," in "Essays Moral, Political and Literary," *Hume's Moral and Political Philosophy* (New York, 1959), p. 349.

30

Personal Identity: The Dualist Theory

Richard Swinburne

1 Empiricist Theories

There are two philosophical questions about personal identity. The first is: what are the logically necessary and sufficient conditions for a person P_2 at a time t_2 being the same person as a person P_1 at an earlier time t_1,[1] or, loosely, what does it mean to say that P_2 is the same person as P_1? The second is: what evidence of observation and experience can we have that a person P_2 at t_2 is the same person as a person P_1 at t_1 (and how are different pieces of evidence to be weighed against each other)? Many writers about personal identity have, however, needed to give only one account of personal identity, because their account of the logically necessary and sufficient conditions of personal identity was in terms of the evidence of observation and experience which would establish or oppose claims of personal identity. They have made no sharp distinction between the meaning of such claims and the evidence which supported them. Theories of this kind we may call empiricist theories.

In this section I shall briefly survey the empiricist theories which have been offered and argue that they are ultimately unsatisfactory, and so go on to argue that my two questions have very different answers. What we mean when we say that two persons are the same is one thing; the evidence

Originally published in Sydney Shoemaker and Richard Swinburne, *Personal Identity*, pp. 3–34. Reprinted by permission of Blackwell Publishers.

which we may have to support our claim is something very different.

The most natural theory of personal identity which readily occurs to people, is that personal identity is constituted by bodily identity. P_2 is the same person as P_1 if P_2's body is the same body as P_1's body. The person to whom you are talking now and call 'John' is the same person as the person to whom you were talking last week and then called 'John' if and only if he has the same body. To say that the two bodies – call them B_1 and B_2 – are the same is not to say that they contain exactly the same bits of matter. Bodies are continually taking in new matter (by people eating and drinking and breathing in) and getting rid of matter. But what makes the bodies the same is that the replacement of matter is only gradual. The matter which forms my body is organized in a certain way, into parts – legs, arms, heart, liver, etc., which are interconnected and exchange matter and energy in regular ways. What makes my body today the same body as my body yesterday is that most of the matter is the same (although I may have lost some and gained some) and its organization has remained roughly the same.[2]

This bodily theory of personal identity gives a somewhat similar account of personal identity to the account which it is natural to give of the identity of any material object or plant, and which is due ultimately to Aristotle (*Metaphysics*, bk 7). Aristotle distinguished between substances and properties. Substances are the individual things, like tables and chairs, cars and plants, which have properties (such as being square or round or red). Properties are 'universals'; that is, they can be possessed by many different substances; many different substances can be square or red. Substances are the individual substances which they are because of the matter out of which they are made and the form which is given to that matter. By 'the form' is meant those properties (normally of shape and organization), the possession of which is essential if a substance is to be the substance in question, the properties which it cannot lose without ceasing to exist. We thus distinguish between the essential properties of a substance – those which constitute its form – and the accidental properties of a substance. It is among the essential properties of a certain oak tree that it has under normal conditions, a certain general shape and appearance, a certain life cycle (of producing leaves in spring and acorns in autumn); but its exact height, its position and the distribution of leaves on its tallest branch are accidental properties. If the matter of the oak tree is reduced to a heap of planks, the oak tree, lacking its essential properties, has ceased to exist. We think of substances as belonging to different kinds, natural – e.g., oak trees or ferns; or artificial – e.g., cars or desks; and the defining properties of a kind constitute the form of a substance which belongs to it. Normally there is one and only one obvious kind to which we ascribe some given chunk of matter – a particular chunk of matter which we classify as an oak tree we would find it very unnatural to classify as belonging to any other kind – e.g., as a largely green thing more than twenty feet high. Although a substance may have the latter properties, it seems unnatural to think of them as forming a kind, and so of some substance being the substance it is because of its possession of those properties – with the consequence that it would cease to exist if the matter out of which it was made became brown instead. But sometimes a given chunk of matter may be thought of as belonging to one or other kind of thing – e.g., as a car or as a motor vehicle; and so we get a different substance according to the kind of thing we judge the matter to constitute. If the car is transformed into a lorry, the substance which was the car has ceased to exist, but the substance which was the motor vehicle has not.

What makes a substance the same substance as an earlier substance is that its matter is the same, or obtained from the matter of the former substance by gradual replacement, while continuing to possess the essential properties which constitute its form. The table at which I am writing today is the same table at which I was writing yesterday because it consists of the same matter (or at any rate, most of the same matter), organized in the same way – into the form of a table. For inanimate things, however, too much replacement of matter, however gradual, will destroy identity. If I replace the drawer of my desk by another drawer, the desk remains the same desk. But if, albeit gradually, I replace first the drawers and then the sides and then the top, so that there is none of the original matter left, we would say that the resulting desk was no longer the same desk as the original desk. For living things, such as plants, total replacement of matter – so long as it is gradual, and so long as physiology and anatomy also change only gradually if at all – will not destroy identity. The oak tree is the same as the sapling out of which it has grown, because replacement of matter has been gradual, and form (i.e., shape, physiology and behaviour) has been largely preserved while any changes in it have been gradual.[3] This account of the identity of plants is also one which applies to social entities – such as a country or an army or a club. Two armies are the same, so long as any replacement of soldiers has been gradual and new soldiers play similar roles in the organization of the army to the roles played by those who have been replaced.

Persons too are substances. (Men, or human beings, are persons of a certain kind – viz., those with similar anatomy, physiology and evolutionary origin to ourselves. There may be persons, e.g., on another planet, who are not human beings.) If we apply Aristotle's general account of the identity of substances to persons, it follows that for a person to be the same person as an earlier person, he has to have the same matter (or matter obtained from that earlier person by gradual replacement) organized into the form of person. The essential properties which make the form of a person would include, for Aristotle, not merely shape and physiological properties, but a kind of way of behaving and a capacity for a mental life of thought and feeling. For P_2 at t_2 to be the same person as P_1 at t_1, both have to be persons (to have a certain kind of body and mental life) and to be made of the same matter (i.e., to be such that P_2's body is obtained from P_1's by gradual replacement of parts). Such is the bodily theory of personal identity. It does not deny that persons have a mental life, but insists that what makes a person the same as an earlier person is sameness of body.[4]

The difficulty which has been felt by those modern philosophers basically sympathetic to a bodily theory of personal identity is this. One part of the body – viz., the brain – seems to be of crucial importance for determining the characteristic behaviour of the rest. The brain controls not merely the physiology of the body, but the way people behave and talk and think. If a man loses an arm or a leg, we do not think that the subsequent person is in any way different from the original person. If a man has a heart transplant or a liver transplant, again we do not think that the replacement makes a different person. On the other hand, if the brain of a person P_1 were removed from his body B_1 and transplanted into the skull of a body B_2 of a person P_2, from which the brain was removed and then transplanted into the empty skull of B_1 (i.e., if brains were interchanged), we would have serious doubt whether P_1 had any more the same body. We would be inclined to say that the person went where his brain went – viz., that P_1 at first had body B_1, and then, after the transplant, body B_2. The reason why we would say this is that (we have very good scientific reason to believe) the person with B_2's body would claim to be P_1, to have done and experienced the things which we know P_1 to have done, and would have the character, beliefs and attitudes of P_1. What determines my attitude towards a person is not so much the matter out of which his body is made, but who he claims to be, whether he has knowledge of my past life purportedly on the basis of previous acquaintance with me, and more generally what his beliefs about the world are and what are his attitudes towards it. Hence a philosopher seeking a materialist criterion of personal identity, will come to regard the brain, the core of the body, rather than the rest of the body as what matters for personal identity. So this modified bodily theory states: that P_2 is the same person as P_1 if and only if P_2 has the same central organ controlling memory and character, viz., same brain, as P_1. Let us call it the brain theory of personal identity. A theory along these lines (with a crucial qualification, to be discussed shortly) was tentatively suggested by David Wiggins in *Identity and Spatio-temporal Continuity*.[5]

The traditional alternative to a bodily theory of personal identity is the memory-and-character theory. This claims that, given the importance for our attitude towards persons of their memory claims and character, continuity in respect of these would constitute personal identity – whether or not this continuity is caused by continuity of some bodily organ, such as the brain; and the absence of continuity of memory and character in some particular case involves the absence of personal identity, even if there is continuity in respect of that bodily organ which produces such continuity between other persons on other occasions.

The simplest version of this theory was that given by John Locke. According to Locke, memory alone, (or 'consciousness', as he often calls it) constitutes personal identity. Loosely – P_2 at t_2 is the same person as P_1 at an earlier time t_1, if and only if P_2 remembers having done and experienced various things, where these things were in fact done and experienced by P_1[6]

Before expounding Locke's theory further, we need to be clear about the kind of memory which is involved. First, it is what is sometimes called personal memory, i.e., memory of one's own past experiences. It is thus to be distinguished from factual memory, which is memory of some fact known previously, as when I remember that the battle of Hastings was fought in 1066. This is not a memory of a past experience. Personal memory is also to be distinguished from remembering-how (e.g., to swim or to ride a bicycle), which is remembering how to perform some task. Secondly, it is personal memory in the weak sense. In the normal or strong sense of 'remember', one can only remember doing something if one really did it. I may say that I 'remember' going up the Eiffel Tower, but if I didn't do it, it seems natural to say that I cannot really remember having done it. In this sense, just as you can only know what is true, so you can only remember what you really did. However, there is also a weak sense of 'remember' in which a man remembers whatever he believes that he remembers in the strong sense. One's weak memories are not necessarily true ones. Now if the memory criterion defined personal identity in terms of memory in the strong sense, it would not be very useful; for to say that P_2 remembers having done what P_1 did would already entail their being the same person, and anyone in doubt as to whether P_2 was the same person as P_1, would have equal doubt whether P_2 really did remember doing what P_1 did. What the criterion as stated is concerned with is memory in the weak sense, which (because the strong sense is the more natural one) I shall henceforward call apparent memory.

So Locke's theory can now be rephrased as follows: P_2 at t_2 is the same person as P_1 at an earlier time t_1, if and only if P_2 apparently remembers having done and experienced various things when those things were in fact done and experienced by P_1. A person is who he thinks that he is. Note that what a person believes about his identity may be different from what he claims publicly. We only take public memory claims to be evidence of personal identity when we believe them to be honest, to express genuine memory beliefs, i.e., in my stated sense apparent memories. No doubt it is normally right to suppose that memory claims express apparent memories. But there may be circumstances in which it is reasonable to doubt this; e.g., if the subject has a source other than memory of the information which he claims to remember, if it is to his interest to pretend to remember, and if he is known to be deceitful.

Locke is very clear about the nature and consequences of his theory. If I do not apparently remember having done something, then I am not the same person as the person who did it. And if I do apparently remember having done the deeds of some person long since dead, then it follows that I am that person.

> If Socrates and the present mayor of Queenborough agree in [identity of consciousness], they are the same person: if the same Socrates waking and sleeping does not partake of the same consciousness, Socrates waking and sleeping is not the same person. And to punish Socrates waking for what sleeping Socrates thought, and waking Socrates was never conscious of, would be no more right, than to punish one twin for what his brother twin did, whereof he knew nothing.[7]

Locke's theory needs tidying up if we are to avoid absurdity. Consider, first, the following objection made by Thomas Reid:

> Suppose a brave officer to have been flogged when a boy at school for robbing an orchard, to have taken a standard from the enemy in his first campaign, and to have been made a general in advanced life; suppose also, which must be admitted to be possible, that, when he took the standard, he was conscious of his having been flogged at school, and that, when made a general, he was conscious of his taking the standard, but had absolutely lost the consciousness of his flogging. These things being supposed, it follows, from Mr Locke's doctrine, that he who was flogged at school is the same person who took the standard, and that he who took the

standard is the same person who was made a general. Whence it follows if there be any truth in logic, that the general is the same person with him who was flogged at school. But the general's consciousness does not reach so far back as his flogging; therefore according to Mr Locke's doctrine, he is not the same person who was flogged. Therefore the general is, and at the same time is not, the same person with him who was flogged at school.[8]

The objection illustrates the important point that identity is a transitive relation; if a is identical with b and b is identical with c, then necessarily a is identical with c. We can meet the objection by reformulating Locke's theory as follows: P_2 at t_2 is the same person as P_1 at an earlier time t_1 if and only if $either$ P_2 apparently remembers what P_1 did and experienced, or he apparently remembers what some person P' at an intermediate time t' did and experienced, when P' apparently remembers what P_1 did and experienced, or they are linked by some longer intermediate chain. (That is, P_2 apparently remembers what P' did and experienced, P' apparently remembers what P'' did and experienced, and so on until we reach a person who apparently remembers what P_1 did and experienced.) If P_1 and P_2 are linked by such a chain, they are, we may say, linked by continuity of memory. Clearly, the apparent memories of the deeds and experiences of the previous person at each stage in the chain need not be completely accurate memories of what was done and experienced. But they do need to be fairly accurate memories of what was done and experienced, if the later person is to be the person who did and experienced those things.

Secondly, Locke ought to allow that while in general apparent memory guarantees personal identity and so amounts to genuine memory, there are cases where it does not. One kind of case is one to which in effect I have just referred. If a person apparently remembers being the person who did or experienced a certain thing, that apparent memory is not genuine if no one did or experienced that thing. My apparent memory of having led a victorious army against the Russians in battle in 1976 is not genuine if no one did this deed. Also, an apparent memory is not genuine if it is caused by a chain of causes which runs outside the person (e.g., it is caused by some informant). If my apparent memory of having met my great-grandfather at the age of three months was caused by my mother telling me much later in life that I had done this thing, and my having forgotten that she was the sole source of my belief that I had met my great-grandfather, then my apparent memory is not genuine. Finally, if apparent memories are inconsistent (e.g., I apparently remember being in Australia at a certain time and I also apparently remember being in England at exactly that same time), then at least one of them cannot be genuine. Locke can allow that there are these exceptions, and that if any of them are found to hold, we cannot regard an apparent memory as genuine, while insisting that, but for them, apparent memory guarantees personal identity.

Locke's memory theory was a simple theory, and a more complicated version of the theory which takes in other connected points was developed by Hume.[9] It is not only his apparent memory which determines the attitude which others have towards a person. How others treat a person depends also on his beliefs about the world and his attitudes towards it, whether they are changeable or constant, and what leads them to change – that is, on the person's character. Hume brings these in. He is also aware that if memory is not mistaken (and he assumes it normally to be correct), it is a causal relation. If in the strong sense I remember some past experience, this involves my past experience being in part the cause of my having the apparent memory which I do.

Hume regards a person as basically a mental state with a body attached; but the mental state is just a 'bundle or collection of different perceptions', i.e., of thoughts, sensations and images. Some of these are caused by past 'perceptions', and among these are memories, which for Hume are faint copies of past 'perceptions'. The bundle of 'perceptions' C_2, which is my mental state now, is linked to the bundle of perceptions C_1, which we call my mental state yesterday, by the fact that some members of C_2 are caused by and resemble (e.g., include memories of and similar thoughts to) members of C_1, or are linked by a causal chain which passes through similar bundles. (Hume does not say what links 'perceptions' into one bundle – i.e., what makes all the 'perceptions' which I have at one time all mine.) Hume calls that kind of identity 'fictitious', because the 'perceptions' which belong to some bundle are really distinct entities from the 'perceptions' which belong to some other bundle, although linked causally to them; he contrasts it with the real identity which would be possessed by a substance which continued to exist in a perfectly unchanged state.

A number of more recent writers have developed more careful versions of a memory theory of personal identity, including Grice[10] and Quinton.[11]

Many advocates of a memory theory have not always been very clear in their exposition about whether the apparent memories which form the links in the chain of memory need to be actual memories, or whether they need only to be hypothetical memories. By 'actual memories' I mean actual recallings of past experiences. The trouble with the suggestion that actual memories are required is that we do not very often recall our past, and it seems natural to suppose that the deeds and experiences of some moments of a person's life never get recalled. Yet the memory theory, as stated so far, rules out that possibility. If I am not connected by a chain of memories with the deeds and experiences done by a person at a certain time, then I am not identical with that person. It is perhaps better if the theory claims that the apparent memories which form the links need only be hypothetical memories – i.e., what a person would apparently remember if he were to try to remember the deeds and experiences in question, e.g., in consequence of being prompted.[12]

There is however a major objection to any memory theory of personal identity, arising from the possibility of duplication. The objection was made briefly by Reid and at greater length in an influential article by Bernard Williams.[13] Williams imagines the case of a man whom he calls Charles who turns up in the twentieth century claiming to be Guy Fawkes:

> All the events he claims to have witnessed and all the actions he claims to have done point unanimously to the life-history of some one person in the past – for instance Guy Fawkes. Not only do all Charles' memory-claims that can be checked fit the pattern of Fawkes' life as known to historians, but others that cannot be checked are plausible, provide explanations of unexplained facts, and so on.[14]

The fact that memory claims which 'cannot be checked are plausible, provide explanations of unexplained facts, and so on' is evidence that Charles is not merely claiming to remember what he has in fact read in a book about Guy Fawkes, and so leaves us back with the supposition, natural to make in normal cases, that he is reporting honestly his apparent memories. So, by a memory theory, Charles would be Guy Fawkes. But then suppose,

Williams imagines, that another man Robert turns up, who satisfies the memory criteria for being Guy Fawkes equally well. We cannot say that they are both identical with Guy Fawkes, for if they were, they would be identical with each other – which they are not, since they currently live different lives and have different thoughts and feelings from each other. So apparent memory cannot constitute personal identity, although it may be fallible evidence of it.

The objection from the possibility of duplication, together with other difficulties which will be mentioned in later chapters, have inclined the majority of contemporary writers to favour a theory which makes some sort of bodily continuity central to personal identity. As we have seen, the brain theory takes into account the insight of memory-and-character theory into the importance of these factors for personal identity, by selecting the brain, as the organ causally responsible for the continuity of memory and character, as that part of the body, the continuity of which constitutes the continuity of the person.

The trouble is that any brain theory is also open to the duplication objection. The human brain has two very similar hemispheres – a left and a right hemisphere. The left hemisphere plays a major role in the control of limbs of and processing of sensory information from the right side of the body (and from the right sides of the two eyes); and the right hemisphere plays a major role in the control of limbs of and processing of sensory information from the left side of the body (and from the left sides of the two eyes). The left hemisphere plays a major role in the control of speech. Although the hemispheres have different roles in the adult, they interact with each other; and if parts of a hemisphere are removed, at any rate early in life, the roles of those parts are often taken over by parts of the other hemisphere. Brain operations which remove substantial parts of the brain are not infrequent. It might be possible one day to remove a whole hemisphere, without killing the person. There are no logical difficulties in supposing that we could transplant one of P_1's hemispheres into one skull from which a brain had been removed, and the other hemisphere into another such skull, and that both transplants should take, and it may well be practically possible to do so. It is certainly more likely to occur than the Guy Fawkes story told by Williams! If these transplants took, clearly each of the resulting persons would behave to some extent like P_1, and indeed both would

probably have some of the apparent memories of P_1. Each of the resulting persons would then be good candidates for being P_1

After all, if one of P_1's hemispheres had been destroyed and the other remained intact and untransplanted, and the resulting person continued to behave and make memory claims somewhat like those of P_1, we would have had little hesitation in declaring that person to be P_1. The same applies, whichever hemisphere was preserved – although it may well be that the resulting person would have greater capacities (e.g., speech) if one hemisphere was preserved than if the other one was preserved. We have seen earlier good reason for supposing that the person goes where his brain goes, and if his brain consists only of one hemisphere, that should make no difference. So if the one remaining hemisphere is then transplanted, we ought to say that the person whose body it now controls is P_1. Whether that person is P_1 can hardly be affected by the fact that instead of being destroyed, the other hemisphere is also transplanted so as to constitute the brain of a person. But if it is, that other person will be just as good a candidate for being P_1. So a Wiggins-type account might lead us to say that both resulting persons are P_1. But, for the reason given earlier in connection with the Guy Fawkes examples, that cannot be – since the two later persons are not identical with each other. Hence, Wiggins adds to his tentative definition a clause stating that P_2 who satisfies his criterion stated earlier is the same person as P_1, only if there is no other later person who also satisfies the criterion.[15]

But the introduction into any theory, whether a memory theory, a brain theory, or whatever, of a clause stating that a person who satisfies the criterion in question for being the same as an earlier person is the same, only so long as there is no other person who satisfies the criterion also or equally well, does have an absurd consequence. Let us illustrate this for the brain theory. Suppose P_1's left hemisphere is transplanted into some skull and the transplant takes. Then, according to the theory, whether the resulting person is P_1, i.e., whether P_1 survives, will depend on whether the other transplant takes. If it does, since both resulting persons will satisfy the memory and brain continuity criteria equally well, neither will be P_1. But if the other transplant does not take, then since there is only one person who satisfies the criterion, that person is P_1. So whether I survive an operation will depend on what happens in a body entirely different from the body which will be mine, if I do survive. But how can who I am depend on what happens to you? A similar absurd consequence follows when a similar clause forbidding duplication is added to a memory theory.

Yet if we abandon the duplication clause, we are back with the original difficulty – that there may be more than one later person who satisfies any memory criterion or brain criterion, or combination thereof, for being the same person as an earlier person. Our discussion brings to our attention also the fact that both these criteria are criteria which may be satisfied to varying degrees. P_2 can have 90 per cent, or 80 per cent, or less than 50 per cent of the brain of P_1; and likewise the similarity of apparent memory and character may vary along a spectrum. Just how well do criteria have to be satisfied for the later person to be the same person as the earlier person? Any line one might draw seems totally artificial. One might think that it was non-arbitrary to insist on more than 50 per cent of the original brain matter – for only one later person could have more than 50 per cent of the original brain matter (whereas if our criterion demands only a smaller proportion, more than one later person could satisfy it). But would we really want to say that P_6 was the same person as P_1 if P_2 was obtained from P_1 by a transplant of 60 per cent (and so more than half) of P_1's brain matter, P_3 was obtained from P_2 by a transplant of 60 per cent of P_2's brain matter, and so on until we came to P_6. By the criterion of 'more than half of the brain matter', P_6 would be the same person as P_5, P_5 as P_4, and so on, and so by the transitivity of identity, P_6 would be the same person as P_1 – although he would have very little of P_1's brain matter. Any criterion of the proportion of brain matter transferred, to be plausible, would have to take account of whether there had been similar transplants in the past, and the length of the interval between them. And then the arbitrariness of the criterion would stare us in the face.

This problem pushes the thinker towards one of two solutions. The first solution is to say that personal identity is a matter of degree. P_2 is the same person as P_1 to the extent to which there is sameness of brain matter and continuity of memory. After all, survival for inanimate things is a matter of degree. As we gradually replace bits of a desk with new bits, the resulting desk is only more or less the same as the original desk. And if my car is taken to pieces and some of the bits are used to make one new car, and some of the bits used to make another new car, both cars are partly the same

as and partly different from the old car. Why cannot we say the same of people? Normally we are not inclined to talk thus, because brain operations are rare and brain hemisphere transplants never happen. Hence there is normally at most only one candidate for being the same person as an earlier person, and he is normally a very strong candidate indeed – having a more or less identical brain and very great similarities of apparent memory and character. So we tend to think of personal identity as all or nothing. But it is not thus in its logic, the argument goes. There is the logical possibility, which could become an empirical possibility, of intermediate cases – of persons who are to some extent the same as and to some extent different from original persons.

This view has been advocated by Derek Parfit.[16] When a person divides, as a result of a split brain transplant, he 'survives' in part, Parfit holds, as each of two persons. They constitute his later 'selves', neither of whom, to speak strictly, are identical with the original person.

This theory which Parfit calls the complex view,[17] does however, run up against a fundamental difficulty that it commits him to substantial empirical claims which to all appearance could very easily be false. I can bring this out by adopting Bernard Williams's famous mad surgeon story.[18] Suppose that a mad surgeon captures you and announces that he is going to transplant your left cerebral hemisphere into one body, and your right one into another. He is going to torture one of the resulting persons and free the other with a gift of a million pounds. You can choose which person is going to be tortured and which to be rewarded, and the surgeon promises to do as you choose. You believe his promise. But how are you to choose? You wish to choose that you are rewarded, but you do not know which resultant person will be you. Now on the complex theory each person will be you to the extent to which he has your brain and resembles you in his apparent memories and character. It would be in principle empirically ascertainable whether and to what extent persons with right hemisphere transplants resemble their originals in apparent memories and character more or less than persons with left hemisphere transplants. But clearly the difference is not going to be great. So Parfit must say that your choice does not greatly matter. Both subsequent persons will be in part you – although perhaps to slightly different degrees. And so you will – although perhaps to slightly different degrees – in part suffer and in part enjoy what each suffers and enjoys. So you have reason both for joyous expectation and for terrified anticipation. But one problem is: how could you have reason for part joyous expectation and part terrified anticipation, when no one future person is going to suffer a mixed fate?

But even if this notion of partial survival does make sense, the more serious difficulty remains, which is this. We can make sense of the supposition that the victim makes the wrong choice, and has the experience of being tortured and not the experience of being rewarded; or the right choice, and has the experience of being rewarded and not the experience of being tortured. A mere philosophical analysis of the concept of personal identity cannot tell you which experiences will be yours tomorrow. To use Bernard Williams's telling word, any choice would be a 'risk'. But on Parfit's view, no risk would be involved – for knowing the extent of continuity of brain, apparent memory, and character, you would know the extent to which a future person would be you and so the extent to which his experiences would be yours. Although it *may* be the case that if my cerebral hemispheres are transplanted into different bodies, I survive partly as the person whose body is controlled by one and partly as the person whose body is controlled by the other, it may not be like that at all. Maybe I go where the left hemisphere goes; and when my right hemisphere is separated from the left hemisphere and comes to control a body by itself, either a new person is formed, or the resulting organism, although behaving to some extent like a person, is really a very complicated non-conscious machine. As we have noted, the fate of some parts of my body, such as my arms and legs, is quite irrelevant to the fate of me. And plausibly the fate of some parts of my brain is irrelevant – can I not survive completely a minor brain operation which removes a very small tumour? But then maybe it is the same with some larger parts of the brain too. We just don't know. If the mad surgeon's victim took the attitude that it didn't matter which way he chose, we must, I suggest, regard him as taking an unjustifiably dogmatic attitude.

The alternative way out of the duplication problem is to say that although apparent memory and brain continuity are, as they obviously are, evidence of personal identity, they are fallible evidence, and personal identity is something distinct from them. Just as the presence of blood stains and fingerprints matching those of a given man are evidence of his earlier presence at the scene of the crime, and the discovery of Roman-looking coins and buildings is evidence that the Romans lived in some region, so the similarity of P_2's apparent memory to that of P_1, and his having much the same brain matter, is evidence that P_2 is the same person as P_1. Yet blood stains and fingerprints are one thing, and a man's earlier presence at the scene of the crime another. His presence at the scene of the crime is not analysable in terms of the later presence of blood stains and fingerprints. The latter is evidence of the former, because you seldom get blood stains and fingerprints at a place matching those of a given man, unless he has been there leaving them around. But it might happen. So, the suggestion is, personal identity is distinct from, although evidenced by, similarity of memory and continuity of brain.

This account, which for the moment I will follow Parfit in calling the simple view, can meet all the difficulties which have beset the other theories which we have discussed. The difficulty for the complex view was that it seemed very peculiar to suppose that mere logic could determine which of the experiences had by various persons, each of which was to some extent continuous with me in apparent memory and brain matter, would be mine. There seemed to be a further truth – that I would or would not have those experiences – beyond any truths about the extent of similarity in apparent memory and matter of future persons to myself. The simple view claims explicitly that personal identity is one thing, and the extent of similarity in matter and apparent memory another. There is no contradiction in supposing that the one should occur without the other. Strong similarity of matter and apparent memory is powerful evidence of personal identity. I and the person who had my body and brain last week have virtually the same brain matter and such similar apparent memory, that it is well-nigh certain that we are the same person. But where the brain matter is only in part the same and the memory connection less strong, it is only fairly probable that the persons are the same. Where there are two later persons P_2 and P_2^*, each of whom had some continuity with the earlier person P_1, the evidence supports to some extent each of the two hypotheses – that P_2 is the same person as P_1, and that P_2^* is the same person as P_1. It may give more support to one hypothesis than to the other, but the less-well-supported hypothesis might be the true one, or maybe neither hypothesis is true. Perhaps P_1 has ceased to exist, and two different persons have come into existence. So the simple view fully accepts that mere logic cannot determine which experiences will be mine, but it allows that continuity of apparent memory and brain provides fallible evidence about this. And of course the duplication objection that they allow for the two subsequent persons being the same person, which we brought against the brain and the memory theories, has no force against the simple theory. For although there can be equally good evidence that each of two later persons is the same person as an earlier person, that evidence is fallible; and since clearly only one person at one time can be strictly the same person as some person at an earlier time, it follows that in one case the evidence is misleading – although we may not know in which case.

There are, however, other difficulties with the simple view, and to these I shall come in due course. In the next section I will expound and develop the simple view, and show that it amounts to the same as Cartesian dualism – the view that a person consists of two parts, soul, and body. In section 3 I shall attempt to rebut verificationist objections to the simple view, and argue that on the simple view the continuing existence of the person is something of which the subject is aware in his own experience.

The simple view is normally combined with the doctrine that persons are indivisible, in the sense that only one person P_2 at t_2 can be in any degree the same person as P_1 at t_1; and only one person P_1 at t_1 can in any degree be the same person as P_2 at t_2. Not merely is strict identity of one person with two distinct earlier persons or two distinct later persons impossible, but so is partial identity (e.g., Parfit-style 'survival'). Neither fission nor fusion of persons is possible. When a brain is split, at most one of any resulting persons is to any degree the same as the original person; and if hemispheres from separate brains are put together to form the brain of a new person, at most one of the original persons from whose brains the hemispheres were transplanted is to any degree the same as the later person, and any identity is full identity. We have so far noted briefly one argument in favour of the indivisibility thesis (pp. 383–4) – the difficulty of giving any sense to the supposition that a person P_1 about to undergo fission will have in any degree the experiences of both of the two persons P_2 and P_2^* who will in no way have shared each other's experiences. Two later cars or tables can be in part the same as and in part different from an earlier car or table; but cars and tables do not have experiences,

and so this difficulty does not arise for them. We shall consider in due course a brief argument against the possibility of fusion, to back up the argument against fission, and so complete the defence of both parts of the indivisibility thesis, but note that although normally combined with the simple view, the indivisibility thesis can be separated from it. I have made that separation. As I shall understand it, the simple view is simply the view that the truth about personal identity is not analysable in terms of the fallible empirical evidence for it of brain and memory continuity; and my primary concern is with the simple view.

2   The Dualist Theory

The brain transplant considerations of the first section leading to the simple view of personal identity showed that significant continuity of brain and memory was not enough to ensure personal identity. They did not show that continuity of brain or memory were totally dispensable: that P_2 at time t_2 could be the same person as P_1 at an earlier time t_1, even though P_2 had none of the brain matter (or other bodily matter) of P_1 and had no apparent memory of P_1's actions and experiences. A number of more extravagant thought-experiments do, however, show that there is no contradiction in this latter supposition.

There seems no contradiction in the supposition that a person might acquire a totally new body (including a completely new brain) – as many religious accounts of life after death claim that men do. To say that this body, sitting at the desk in my room, is my body is to say two things. First, it is to say that I can move parts of this body (arms, legs, etc.), just like that, without having to do any other intentional action, and that I can make a difference to other physical objects only by moving parts of this body. By holding the door handle and turning my hand, I open the door. By bending my leg and stretching it, I kick the ball and make it move into the goal. But I do not turn my hand or bend my leg by doing some other intentional action; I just do these things.[19] Secondly, it is to say that my knowledge of states of the world outside this body is derived from their effects on this body – I learn about the positions of physical objects by seeing them, and seeing them involves light rays reflected by them impinging on my eyes and setting up nervous impulses in my optic nerve. My body is the vehicle of my agency in the world and my knowledge of the world. But then is it not coherent to suppose that I might suddenly find that my present body no longer served this function, that I could no longer acquire information through these eyes or move these limbs, but might discover that another body served the same function? I might find myself moving other limbs and acquiring information through other eyes. Then I would have a totally new body. If that body, like my last body, was an occupant of the Earth, then we would have a case of reincarnation, as Eastern religions have understood that. If that body, was an occupant of some distant planet, or an environment which did not belong to the same space[20] as our world, then we would have a case of resurrection as, on the whole, Western religions (Christianity, Judaism and Islam) have understood that.

This suggestion of a man acquiring a new body (with brain) may be more plausible, to someone who has difficulty in grasping it, by supposing the event to occur gradually. Suppose that one morning a man wakes up to find himself unable to control the right side of his body, including his right arm and leg. When he tries to move the right-side parts of his body, he finds that the corresponding left-side parts of his body move; and when he tries to move the left-side parts, the corresponding right-side parts of his wife's body move. His knowledge of the world comes to depend on stimuli to his left side and to his wife's right side (e.g., light rays stimulating his left eye and his wife's right eye). The bodies fuse to some extent physiologically as with Siamese twins, while the man's wife loses control of her right side. The focus of the man's control of and knowledge of the world is shifting. One may suppose the process completed as the man's control is shifted to the wife's body, while the wife loses control of it.

Equally coherent, I suggest, is the supposition that a person might become disembodied. A person has a body if there is one particular chunk of matter through which he has to operate on and learn about the world. But suppose that he finds himself able to operate on and learn about the world within some small finite region, without having to use one particular chunk of matter for this purpose. He might find himself with knowledge of the position of objects in a room (perhaps by having visual sensations, perhaps not), and able to move such objects just like that, in the ways in which we know about the positions of our limbs and can move them. But the room would not be, as it were, the person's body; for we may suppose that simply by choosing

to do so he can gradually shift the focus of his knowledge and control, e.g., to the next room. The person would be in no way limited to operating and learning through one particular chunk of matter. Hence we may term him disembodied. The supposition that a person might become disembodied also seems coherent.

I have been arguing so far that it is coherent to suppose that a person could continue to exist with an entirely new body or with no body at all. (And I would also suggest by the way that in the cases cited the subject would in some circumstances have reason to believe, through his memory of what he had just experienced, that this had happened to him.) Could a person continue to exist without any apparent memory of his previous doings? Quite clearly, we do allow not merely the logical possibility, but the frequent actuality of amnesia – a person forgetting all or certain stretches of his past life. Despite Locke, many a person does forget much of what he has done. But, of course, we normally only suppose this to happen in cases where there is the normal bodily and brain continuity. Our grounds for supposing that a person forgets what he has done are that the evidence of bodily and brain continuity suggests that he was the previous person who did certain things, which he now cannot remember having done. And in the absence of both of the main kinds of evidence for personal identity, we would not be justified in supposing that personal identity held. (Character continuity is a minor kind of evidence, hardly of great importance on its own.) For that reason I cannot describe a case where we would have good reason to suppose that P_2 was identical with P_1, even though there was neither brain continuity nor memory continuity between them. However, only given verificationist dogma, is there any reason to suppose that the only things which are true are those of whose truth we can have evidence, and I shall suggest in section 3 that there is no good reason for believing verificationism to be true. We can make sense of states of affairs being true, of which we can have no evidence that they are true. And among them surely is the supposition that the person who acquires another body loses not merely control of the old one, but memories of what he did with its aid. Again, many religions have taken seriously stories of persons passing through the waters of Lethe (a river whose waters made a person forget all his previous life) and then acquiring a new body. Others who have heard these stories may not have believed them true; but they have usually claimed to understand them, and (unless influenced by philosophical dogma) have not suspected them of involving contradiction.

Those who hope to survive their death, despite the destruction of their body, will not necessarily be disturbed if they come to believe that they will then have no memory of their past life on Earth; they may just want to survive and have no interest in continuing to recall life on Earth. Again, apparently, there seems to be no contradiction involved in their belief. It seems to be a coherent belief (whether or not true or justified). Admittedly, there may be stories or beliefs which involve a hidden contradiction when initially they do not seem to do so. But the fact that there seems (and to so many people) to be no contradiction hidden in these stories is good reason for supposing that there is no contradiction hidden in them – until a contradiction is revealed. If this were not a good reason for believing there to be no contradiction, we would have no good reason for believing any sentence at all to be free of hidden contradiction.

Not merely is it not logically necessary that a person have a body made of certain matter, or have certain apparent memories, if he is to be the person which he is; it is not even necessitated by laws of nature.[21] For let us assume that natural laws dictated the course of evolution and the emergence of consciousness. In 4000 million BC the Earth was a cooling globe of inanimate atoms. Natural laws then, we assume, dictated how this globe would evolve, and so which arrangements of matter will be the bodies of conscious men, and just how apparent memories of conscious men depend on their brain states. My point now is that what natural laws in no way determine is which animate body is yours and which is mine. Just the same arrangement of matter and just the same laws could have given to me the body (and so the apparent memories) which are now yours, and to you the body (and so the apparent memories) which are now mine. It needs either God or chance to allocate bodies to persons; the most that natural laws determine is that bodies of a certain construction are the bodies of some person or other, who in consequence of this construction have certain apparent memories. Since the body which is presently yours (together with the associated apparent memories) could have been mine (logic and even natural laws allow), that shows that none of the matter of which my body is presently made (nor the apparent memories) is essential to my being the person I am. That must be determined by something else.

The view that personal identity is something ultimate, unanalysable in terms of such observable and experienceable phenomena as bodily continuity and continuity of memory, was put forward in the eighteenth century by Butler, and, slightly less explicitly, by Reid. In recent years R. M. Chisholm[22] has put forward a similar view.

I could just leave my positive theory at that – that personal identity is unanalysable. But it will, I hope, be useful to express it in another way, to bring out more clearly what it involves and to connect it with another whole tradition of philosophical thought.

In section 1, I set out Aristotle's account of the identity of substances: that a substance at one time is the same substance as a substance at an earlier time if and only if the later substance has the same form as, and continuity of matter (in the sense delineated on p. 378) with, the earlier substance. On this view, a person is the same person as an earlier person if he has the same form as the earlier person (i.e., both are persons) and has continuity of matter with him (i.e., has the same body).

Certainly, to be the same person as an earlier person, a later person has to have the same form – i.e., has to be a person. If my arguments for the logical possibility of there being disembodied persons are correct, then the essential characteristics of a person constitute a narrower set than those which Aristotle would have included. My arguments suggest that all that a person needs to be a person are certain mental capacities – for having conscious experiences (e.g., thoughts or sensations) and performing intentional actions. Thought-experiments of the kind described earlier allow that a person might lose his body, but they describe his continuing to have conscious experiences and his performing or being able to perform intentional actions, i.e., to do actions which he means to do, bring about effects for some purpose.

Yet if my arguments are correct, showing that two persons can be the same, even if there is no continuity between their bodily matter, we must say that in the form stated the Aristotelian account of identity applies only to inanimate objects and plants and has no application to personal identity.[23] We are then faced with a choice either of saying that the criteria of personal identity are different from those for other substances, or of trying to give a more general account than Aristotle's of identity of substances which would cover both persons and other substances. It is possible to widen the Aristotelian account so that we can do the latter. We have only to say that two substances are the same if and only if they have the same form and there is continuity of the stuff of which they are made, and allow that there may be kinds of stuff other than matter. I will call this account of substance identity the wider Aristotelian account. We may say that there is a stuff of another kind, immaterial stuff, and that persons are made of both normal bodily matter and of this immaterial stuff, but that it is the continuity of the latter which provides that continuity of stuff which is necessary for the identity of the person over time.

This is in essence the way of expressing the simple theory which is adopted by those who say that a person living on Earth consists of two parts – a material part, the body, and an immaterial part, the soul. The soul is the essential part of a person, and it is its continuing which constitutes the continuing of the person. While on Earth, the soul is linked to a body (by the body being the vehicle of the person's knowledge of and action upon the physical world). But, it is logically possible, the soul can be separated from the body and exist in a disembodied state (in the way described earlier) or linked to a new body. This way of expressing things has been used in many religious traditions down the centuries, for it is a very natural way of expressing what is involved in being a person once you allow that a person can survive the death of his body. Classical philosophical statements of it are to be found in Plato and, above all, in Descartes. I shall call this view classical dualism.

I wrote that 'in essence' classical dualism is the view that there is more stuff to the person than bodily matter, and that it is the continuing of this stuff which is necessary for the continuing of the person, because a writer such as Descartes did not distinguish between the immaterial stuff, let us call it soul-stuff, and that stuff being organized (with or without a body) as one soul. Descartes and other classical dualists however did not make this distinction, because they assumed (implicitly) that it was not logically possible that persons divide – i.e., that an earlier person could be in part the same person as each of two later persons. Hence they implicitly assumed that soul-stuff comes in essentially indivisible units. That is indeed what one has to say about soul-stuff, if one makes the supposition (as I was inclined to do, in section 1), that it is not logically possible that persons divide. There is nothing odd about supposing that soul-stuff comes in essentially indivisible units. Of any chunk of matter, however small, it is always logically, if not physically, possible that it be divided into two. Yet it is because matter is extended, that one can always make sense of it being divided. For a chunk of matter necessarily takes up a finite volume of space. A finite volume of space necessarily is composed of two half-volumes. So it always makes sense to suppose that part of the chunk which occupies the left half-volume of space to be separated from that part of the chunk which occupies the right half-volume. But that kind of consideration has no application to immaterial stuff. There is no reason why there should not be a kind of immaterial stuff which necessarily is indivisible; and if the supposition of section 1 is correct, the soul-stuff will have that property.

So then – once we modify the Aristotelian understanding of the criteria for the identity of substances, the simple view of personal identity finds a natural expression in classical dualism. The arguments which Descartes gave in support of his account of persons are among the arguments which I have given in favour of the simple theory, and since they take for granted the wider Aristotelian framework, they yield classical dualism as a consequence. Thus Descartes argues:

> Just because I know certainly that I exist, and that meanwhile I do not remark that any other thing necessarily pertains to my nature or essence, excepting that I am a thinking thing, I rightly conclude that my essence consists solely in the fact that I am a thinking thing. And although possibly . . . I possess a body with which I am very intimately conjoined, yet because, on the one side, I have a clear and distinct idea of myself inasmuch as I am only a thinking and unextended thing, and as, on the other, I possess a distinct idea of body, inasmuch as it is only an extended and unthinking thing, it is certain that this I [that is to say, my soul by which I am what I am], is entirely and absolutely distinct from my body, and can exist without it.[24]

Descartes is here saying that he can describe a thought-experiment in which he continues to exist although his body does not. I have also described such a thought-experiment and have argued, as Descartes in effect does, that it follows that his body is not logically necessary for his existence, that it is not an essential part of himself. Descartes can go on 'thinking' (i.e., being conscious) and so existing without it. Now if we take the wider Aristotelian framework for granted that the continuing of a substance involves the continuing of some of the stuff of which it is made, and since the continuing existence of Descartes does not involve the continuing of bodily matter, it follows that there must now be as part of Descartes some other stuff, which he calls his soul, which forms the essential part of Descartes.

Given that for any present person who is currently conscious, there is no logical impossibility, whatever else may be true now of that person, that that person continue to exist without his body, it follows that that person must now actually have a part other than a bodily part which can continue, and which we may call his soul – and so that his possession of it is entailed by his being a conscious thing. For there is not even a logical possibility that if I now consist of nothing but matter and the matter is destroyed, that I should nevertheless continue to exist. From the mere logical possibility of my continued existence there follows the actual fact that there is now more to me than my body; and that more is the essential part of myself. A person's being conscious is thus to be analysed as an immaterial core of himself, his soul being conscious.[25]

So Descartes argues, and his argument seems to me correct – given the wider Aristotelian framework. If we are prepared to say that substances can be the same, even though none of the stuff (in a wide sense) of which they are made is the same, the conclusion does not follow. The wider Aristotelian framework provides a partial definition of 'stuff' rather than a factual truth. To say that a person has an immaterial soul is not to say that if you examine him closely enough under an acute enough microscope you will find some very rarefied constituent which has eluded the power of ordinary microscopes. It is just a way of expressing the point within a traditional framework of thought that persons can – it is logically possible – continue, when their bodies do not. It does, however, seem a very natural way of expressing the point – especially once we allow that persons can become disembodied. Unless we adopt a wider Aristotelian framework, we shall have to say that there can be substances which are not made of anything, and which are the same substances as other substances which are made of matter.

It does not follow from all this that a person's body is no part of him. Given that what we are trying to do is to elucidate the nature of those entities which we normally call 'persons', we must say that arms and legs and all other parts of the living body are parts of the person. My arms and legs are parts of me. The crucial point that Descartes was making is that the body is only, contingently and possibly temporarily, part of the person; it is not an essential part. However, Descartes does seem in a muddle about this. In the passage from the *Meditations* just cited, as elsewhere in his works,[26] he claims sometimes (wrongly) that my body is no part of me, and at other times (correctly) that my body is not an essential part of me.

The other arguments which I have given for the 'simple theory', e.g., that two embodied persons can be the same despite their being no bodily continuity between them, can also, like the argument of Descartes just discussed, if we assume the wider Aristotelian framework, be cast into the form of arguments for classical dualism.

As we have seen, classical dualism is the way of expressing the simple view of personal identity within what I called the wider Aristotelian framework. However, this framework is a wider one than Aristotle himself would have been happy with, allowing a kind of stuff other than Aristotle would have countenanced. There has been in the history of thought a different and very influential way of modifying Aristotle, to take account of the kind of point made by the simple view. This way was due to St Thomas Aquinas (see, e.g., *Summa contra Gentiles*). Aquinas accepted Aristotle's general doctrine that substances are made of matter, organized by a form; the desk is the desk which it is because of the matter of which it is made and the shape which is imposed upon it. The form was normally a system of properties, universals which had no existence except in the particular substances in which they were instantiated. However, Aquinas claimed that for man the form of the body, which he called the soul, was separable from the body and capable of independent existence. The soul of man, unlike the souls of animals or plants, was in Aquinas's terminology, an 'intellectual substance'.

However, if we are going to modify Aristotle to make his views compatible with the simple theory of personal identity, this seems definitely the less satisfactory way of doing so. Properties seem by their very nature to be universals, and so it is hard to give any sense to their existing except when conjoined to some stuff. Above all, it is hard to give sense to their being individual – a universal can be instantiated in many different substances. What makes the substances differ is the different stuff of which they are composed. The form of man can be instantiated in many different men. But

Aquinas wants a form which is a particular, and so could only be combined with one body. All of this seems to involve a greater distortion of Aristotle's system than does classical dualism. Aquinas's system does have some advantages over classical dualism – for example, it enables him to bring out the naturalness of a person being embodied and the temporary and transitory character of any disembodiment – but the disadvantages of taking Aristotle's approach and then distorting it to this unrecognizable extent are in my view very great. Hence my preference for what I have called classical dualism. I shall in future express the simple view in the form of classical dualism, in order to locate this view within the philosophical tradition which seems naturally to express it.

There is, however, one argument often put forward by classical dualists – their argument from the indivisibility of the soul to its natural immortality – from which I must dissociate myself. Before looking at this argument, it is necessary to face the problem of what it means to say that the soul continues to exist. Clearly the soul continues to exist if a person exercises his capacities for experiences and action, by having experiences and performing actions. But can the soul continue to exist when the person does not exercise those capacities? Presumably it can. For we say that an unconscious person (who is neither having experiences or acting) is still a person. We say this on the grounds that natural processes (i.e., processes according with the laws of nature) will, or at any rate may, lead to his exercising his capacities again – e.g., through the end of normal sleep or through some medical or surgical intervention. Hence a person, and so his soul, if we talk thus, certainly exists while natural processes may lead to his exercising those capacities, again. But what when the person is not exercising his capacities, and no natural processes (whether those operative in our present material universe or those operative in some new world to which the person has moved) will lead to his exercising his capacities? We could say that the person and so his soul still exists on the grounds that there is the logical possibility of his coming to

life again. To my mind, the more natural alternative is to say that when ordinary natural processes cannot lead to his exercising his capacities again, a person and so his soul has ceased to exist; but there remains the logical possibility that he may come into existence again (perhaps through God causing him to exist again). One argument against taking the latter alternative is the argument that no substance can have two beginnings of existence. If a person really ceases to exist, then there is not even the logical possibility of his coming into existence again. It would follow that the mere logical possibility of the person coming into existence again has the consequence that a person, once existent, is always existent (even when he has no capacity for experience and action). But this principle – that no substance can have two beginnings of existence – is one which I see no good reason for adopting; and if we do not adopt it, then we must say that souls cease to exist when there is no natural possibility of their exercising their capacities. But that does not prevent souls which have ceased to exist coming into existence again. This way of talking does give substantial content to claims that souls do or do not exist, when they are not exercising their capacities.

Now classical dualists assumed (in my view, on balance, correctly) that souls cannot be divided. But they often argued from this, that souls were indestructible,[27] and hence immortal, or at any rate naturally immortal (i.e., immortal as a result of the operation of natural processes, and so immortal barring an act of God to stop those processes operating). That does not follow. Material bodies may lose essential properties without being divided – an oak tree may die and become fossilized without losing its shape. It does not follow from a soul's being indivisible that it cannot lose its capacity for experience and action – and so cease to be a soul. Although there is (I have been arguing) no logical necessity that a soul be linked to a body, it may be physically necessary that a soul be linked to one body if it is to have its essential properties (of capacity for experience and action) and so continue to exist.

Notes

1 The logically necessary and sufficient conditions for something being so are those conditions such that if they are present, that thing must be so; and if they are absent, that thing cannot be so – all this because of considerations of logic.

2 Some writers have attempted to analyse the notion of 'most of the matter' of yesterday's body being the same as 'most of the matter' of today's body in terms of today's body being composed largely of chunks of matter which are 'spatio-temporally continuous' with

chunks of matter of yesterday's body, i.e., as linked to such chunks by a spatio-temporal chain. Two chunks of matter M_1 at time t_1 and M_2 at time t_2 are spatio-temporally continuous if and only if there is a material object M' identical in quantity and intrinsic properties to both M_1 and M_2 at every temporal instant t' between t_1 and t_2, such that each M' at each t' occupies a place contiguous with the place occupied by the M' at prior and succeeding instants of time if you take instants close enough in time to t'. (More precisely 'such that the place occupied by each M' at each t' is contiguous to places occupied by an M' at some instant t'' later than t' and all instants between t'' and t' and to places occupied by an M' at some instant t''' earlier than t' and all instants between t''' and t''.) It is very plausible to suppose that spatio-temporal continuity is a necessary condition for the identity of chunks of matter – chunks of matter cannot go from one place to another without moving along a path joining the places. But it is not so plausible to suppose that spatio-temporal continuity is a sufficient condition of the identity of chunks of matter, i.e., is enough to ensure that two chunks of matter are the same. It does not seem logically impossible that two qualitatively identical chunks should emerge from a given chunk. Something else than spatio-temporal continuity is needed to ensure that two chunks of matter are the same. On this, see Eli Hirsch, *The Concept of Identity* (New York: Oxford University Press, 1982), esp. ch. 4.

3 Aristotle did not himself go into the problem of how much matter has to continue the same if the substance is to be the same.

4 Aristotle himself seemed to have some hesitation about the applicability of his theory of the identity of substances to the identity of persons. See *De anima* at 413a. He writes, first, 'that, therefore, the soul or certain parts of it, if it is divisible, cannot be separated from the body is quite clear'. But then he qualifies this by writing 'Not that anything prevents at any rate some parts from being separable'. He seems to be supposing that there are some capacities, e.g., for thought, which need no bodily material for their exercise. (For similar remarks see his 403a, 408b, 413b.) Aquinas develops these points into his doctrine that the Aristotle-type soul (the form of the body) is separable from the body. See below, pp. 389ff, for this doctrine and criticism of it.

5 D. Wiggins, *Identity and Spatio-temporal Continuity* (Oxford: Blackwell, 1967). Wiggins is even more tentative in the amended version of the book, *Sameness and Substance* (Oxford: Blackwell, 1980).

6 Although Locke's account of what it is for two persons to be the 'same person' is the simple memory account given above, he complicates it by providing a different account of what it is for two persons to be the 'same man'. This account is basically the bodily account which I have just outlined. P_1 is the same

man as whoever has the same body as P_{11} but the same person as whoever has the same memories as P_1. But Locke regards personal identity (which person, rather than which man, one is) as what is of importance for the way in which we should treat people, e.g., whom we are to reward or punish.

7 John Locke, *An Essay Concerning Human Understanding*, ed. P. H. Nidditch, (Oxford: Clarendon Press, 1975), sect. 19.

8 Thomas Reid, *Essays on the Intellectual Powers of Man* (1785; repr. Cambridge, Mass.: MIT Press, 1969), Essay III, ch. 6.

9 Hume subsequently found this view outlined above and expanded in the main text of the *A Treatise of Human Nature*, ed. L. A. Selbye-Bigge (Oxford: Clarendon Press, 1975), unsatisfactory, as he wrote in his Appendix. But the grounds of his dissatisfaction are not clear. See Barry Stroud, *Hume* (London: Routledge and Kegan Paul, 1977), ch. 6.

10 H. P. Grice, 'Personal identity', *Mind* 50 (1941), pp. 330–50.

11 Anthony Quinton, 'The soul', *Journal of Philosophy* 59 (1962), pp. 393–403.

12 We would need some well-justified theory by means of which we could infer what some person would apparently remember if he were to try, if we were ever to apply our theory to answering particular questions of the form 'Is P_2 identical with P_1?' The theory would need to be established without presupposing which past person, some person who is not now currently recalling anything, was. For although it is reasonable to suppose that such a person would remember many of his recent deeds and experiences, if he were to try, we cannot know which recent deeds and experiences were his until we know what he would apparently remember, according to the memory theory.

13 Bernard Williams, 'Personal identity and individuation', *Proceedings of the Aristotelian Society* 57 (1956–7), pp. 229–52.

14 Ibid., p. 332.

15 He suggests analysing 'person' in such a way that 'coincidence under the concept person logically required the continuance in one organized parcel of all that was causally sufficient and causally necessary to the continuance of essential and characteristic functioning, no autonomously sufficient part achieving autonomous and functionally separate existence' (Wiggins, *Identity*, p. 55).

16 Derek Parfit, 'Personal identity', this volume, ch. 29.

17 He introduces this terminology in his paper 'The importance of self-identity', *Journal of Philosophy* 68 (1971), pp. 683–90.

18 Bernard Williams, 'The self and the future', this volume, ch. 28.

19 Following A. C. Danto 'Basic actions', *American Philosophical Quarterly* 2 (1965), pp. 141–8, philosophers call those intentional actions which we just do,

not by doing some other intentional action, basic actions, and those which we do by doing some other intentional action, mediated actions. An intentional action is one which an agent does, meaning to do. No doubt certain events have to happen in our nerves and muscles if we are to move our arms and legs, but we do not move our arms and legs by intentionally making these events occur.

20 Two objects belong to the same space if they are at some distance from each other, if you can get from one to the other by going along a path in space which joins them. For a fuller account of the meaning of the claim that an object occupies a different space from our space, see Richard Swinburne, *Space and Time*, 2nd edn (London: Macmillan, 1981), chs 1 and 2.

21 I owe this argument to John Knox, 'Can the self survive the death of its mind?', *Religious Studies* 5 (1969), pp. 85–97.

22 R. M. Chisholm, 'The loose and popular and the strict and philosophical senses of identity', in N. S. Care and R. H. Grimm (eds), *Perception, and Personal Identity* (Cleveland: Press of Case Western Reserve University, 1969).

23 I do not discuss the difficult issue of whether the Aristotelian account applies to animals other than man, e.g., whether continuity of matter and form is necessary and sufficient for the identity of a dog at a later time with a dog at an earlier time.

24 Descartes, *Meditations on the First Philosophy*, in *The Philosophical Works of Descartes* vol. 1, trans. E. S. Haldane and G. R. T. Ross (Cambridge: Cambridge University Press, 1911), p. 190. The clause in square brackets occurs only in the French translation, approved by Descartes.

25 It may be useful, in case anyone suspects the argument of this paragraph of committing some modal fallacy, to set it out in a more formal logical shape. I use the usual logical symbols – '.' means 'and', '∼' means 'not', '◊' means 'it is logically possible'. I then introduce the following definitions:

p = 'I am a conscious person, and I exist in 1984'
q = My body is destroyed at the end of 1984
r = I have a soul in 1984
s = I exist in 1985
x ranges over all consistent propositions compatible with (p. q) and describing 1984 states of affairs

('(x)' is to be read in the normal way as 'for all states x . . .')

The argument may now be set out as follows:

p	Premiss (1)
$(x) \diamond (p.q.x.s)$	Premiss (2)
$\sim \diamond (p.q.\sim r.s)$	Premiss (3)

∴ ∼r is not within the range of x.

But since ∼r describes a state of affairs in 1984, it is not compatible with (p.q). But q can hardly make a difference to whether or not r. So p is incompatible with ∼r.

∴ r

The argument is designed to show that r follows from p; and so, more generally, that every conscious person has a soul. Premiss (3) is justified by the wider Aristotelian principle that if I am to continue, some of the stuff out of which I am made has to continue. As I argued in the text, that stuff must be non-bodily stuff. The soul is defined as that non-bodily part whose continuing is essential for my continuing.

Premiss (2) relies on the intuition that whatever else might be the case in 1984, compatible with (p.q), my stream of consciousness could continue thereafter.

If you deny (2) and say that r is a state of affairs not entailed by (p.q), but which has to hold if it is to be possible that s, you run into this difficulty. There may be two people in 1984, Oliver who has a soul, and Fagin, who does not. Both are embodied and conscious, and to all appearances indistinguishable. God (who can do all things logically possible, compatible with how the world is up to now), having forgotten to give Fagin a soul, has, as he annihilates Fagin's body at the end of 1984, no power to continue his stream of thought. Whereas he has the power to continue Oliver's stream of thought. This seems absurd.

26 For examples and commentary, see Brian Smart, 'How can persons be ascribed M-predicates?', *Mind* 86 (1977), pp. 49–66, at pp. 63–6.

27 Thus Berkeley: 'We have shown that the soul is indivisible, incorporeal, unextended, and it is consequently incorruptible' (*Principles of Human Knowledge*, sect. 141).

31

Human Beings

Mark Johnston

Many of us hope for a kind of philosophy that is precise without thereby desiccating its object, so that the results of a philosophical investigation could answer a question still worth asking. So it is with the question: What is it that we are? But much of contemporary philosophical theorizing about personal identity conforms to what could easily become a desiccating analytic paradigm. Cases imaginary and real are produced. Competing accounts of the necessary and sufficient conditions for personal identity are then evaluated simply in accord with how well they jibe with intuitions wrung from these cases.

Compare Gettierology, the search for the analysis of knowledge by means of conjecturing necessary and sufficient conditions for knowledge, followed by confirmation or refutation by appeal to intuitions about cases.[1] Here reliance on the method of cases has a straightforward, if somewhat wooden, justification. We are interested in articulating our concept of knowledge and in charting its relations to other concepts, such as the concepts of believing a proposition, of that proposition's being true, of one's being justified in believing the proposition, of one's employing a reliable method in coming to believe the proposition, and so on. Masters of these concepts by and large agree about when they are to be applied, and so the method of

Originally published in *Journal of Philosophy* 84 (1987), pp. 59–83. © The Journal of Philosophy, Inc. Reprinted by permission of Columbia University.

cases appears well adapted to investigating the relations among them.

But what relations among concepts are being charted when we develop a systematic account of the conditions under which a person survives, continues on, or persists through a period of time? No doubt there is some innocuous sense in which we are employing some nonindividual concept when we judge that Anthony Blunt is the same person as the notorious Maurice or that Orcutt is not the same person as the most cultured spy. No doubt there is some relation between this concept of being the same person and the concepts of mental continuity, of physical continuity, and of the various patterns of causal dependence which could be responsible for such continuities. However, it ought to be controversial that the relation here is the same as the relation between knowledge and, say, true belief. Believing correctly that p is arguably part of what it means to have knowledge that p, whereas the holding of patterns of mental and physical continuity and dependence across a stretch of time seems to be the sort of evidence we might ideally rely upon in justifying our claim that a person survived or continued on through the stretch in question. Why should we think that we could analyze what it means to say that someone has survived in terms of the concepts of the sorts of relations that are *evidence* for survival?

The method of theorizing about personal identity solely or mainly by appeal to our intuitive reactions to puzzle cases which exhibit all sorts of variations in kind and degree of continuity and dependence would be justified if two requirements were satisfied. First, our grasp of the concept of being the same person should be able to be correctly represented as a grasp of necessary and sufficient conditions for the application of the predicate "is the same person," conditions that could be cast in terms of statements about continuity and dependence, statements not themselves to be explained in terms of statements about personal identity. Call this the *reductionist requirement*. Secondly, our intuitive reactions to the puzzle cases should be able to be taken as manifestations of our grasp of those necessary and sufficient conditions, and not as overgeneralizations from the everyday run of cases or manifestations of a particular conception of people, be it a religious conception (e.g., that people are reincarnatable souls) or some more inchoate secular counterpart. But then it should be evident that this second requirement generates a difficulty for the ideology behind the method of cases. Given the enormous variety of apparently conceptually coherent *conceptions* of people which have been entertained, we must assume that our common *concept* of people, if there is such a thing, is quite unspecific; so the topic of personal identity will be the dry articulation of a vague generality compatible with all the more interesting and specific conceptions that have guided practical life.

This difficulty not having been taken seriously, there is a dominant – and as it turns out, fairly specific – philosophical view about people which is defended in large part by the method of cases. The dominant view has it that we are minds – perhaps essentially embodied minds, although no *particular* body or brain is such that its survival is essential to ours. Put in more familiar terms, the dominant view is what we might call, following Derek Parfit, *wide psychological reductionism.*[2] *Psychological reductionism* is the view that truths about personal identity have as necessary and sufficient conditions statements about the holding of relations of mental continuity and connectedness. Connectedness involves the holding of direct psychological connections, such as the persistence of beliefs and desires, the connection between an intention and the later act in which the intention is carried out, and the connection between an experience and a memory of that experience. Connectedness can come in twice over in the statement of the conditions on personal identity. All psychological reductionists require that, if two person-stages are stages of the same person, then psychological continuity, the ancestral of strong or predominant psycholo-

gical connectedness, holds between them. Some psychological reductionists also require that no two such stages be entirely unconnected psychologically. The dominant view is properly called *wide* psychological reductionism because it has it that mental continuity and connectedness can constitute personal identity even if the holding of these relations is not secured by its normal cause, the persistence of a particular human body or brain. Any causal mechanism that operates so that these psychological relations hold will do. The identity over time of any particular human body or brain plays no strictly indispensable role in the identity of a particular person over time. Any particular human body or brain is just one causal means among others for the holding of the relations of psychological continuity and connectedness which constitute a particular person's survival.

David Lewis, Anthony Quinton, and Sydney Shoemaker are among those who have advanced the *wide psychological view.*[3] The view is typically defended by appeal to the intuition that one could discover that one had come to inhabit a new body and that others could confirm this by noticing one's familiar personality manifesting itself in that new body. Sometimes this intuition is wrung from cases like John Locke's case of the prince and the cobbler who appear to swap bodies.[4] Sometimes it is wrung from cases of *Star Trek*-style teletransportation in which a body is scanned at one point and is destroyed by the scanning, while at another point a cell-by-cell duplicate is made in accord with the information got from the scanning.[5] Sometimes it is wrung from cases of brain-state transfer in which a machine wipes one brain "clean," and another brain is caused to go into states which are identical in all respects to the previous states of the first brain.[6]

The body-change intuition generated by each of these fantastic cases is supposed to support the claim that mental continuity and connectedness, however they are caused, are jointly sufficient for personal identity. In support of the necessity of mental continuity and connectedness it is observed that if the processes in question did not secure these psychological relations, we would not be inclined to say that the original person came to inhabit a new body.

The method of cases and the dominant view taken together have a fair claim to constitute the orthodoxy in philosophical discussions of personal identity. Orthodoxies have a tendency to freeze the imagination, so before criticizing this orthodoxy, it may be worthwhile briefly to describe an alternative method and an alternative view.

Suppose that right from the start we give up the reductionist requirement to the effect that statements about personal identity be shown to have the same fact-stating potential as statements about continuity and connectedness. So, in Parfit's terms, we adopt the *further-fact view*, according to which statements about personal identity are made true by facts different from facts about mental and physical continuity and dependence.[7] These latter facts constitute our evidence for personal identity and are not that in which personal identity consists.

Once we make this first departure from the orthodox position, the method of cases will no longer seem to be the primary method of theorizing about personal identity. We can no longer represent our intuitive reactions to puzzle cases described in the language of continuity and connectedness as mere manifestations of our concept of personal identity. Rather, we will regard those intuitive reactions as judgments based upon the evidence available in the cases. And there will be reason to think that these judgments are more unreliable the more bizarre the cases in question are. For many of the bizarre cases involve the severing of just those contingent connections which in everyday life make continuity and connectedness good evidence for identity.

What then will take the primary place of the method of cases? What are the primary phenomena that a philosophical theory of personal identity should aim to save? Here is a suggestion. There is the humble and ubiquitous practice of reidentifying each other over time. Philosophical skepticism aside, this practice is a reliable and mostly unproblematic source of knowledge about particular claims of personal identity. So the primary question for a philosophical theory of personal identity is: What sort of thing is such that things of that sort can be reliably and unproblematically reidentified over time in *just the way* in which we reliably and unproblematically reidentify ourselves and each other over time? Any theory of personal identity, such as the *bare-locus view* discussed below (section 2), which would represent our practice of reidentifying each other over time as extremely problematic so far as generating knowledge of the facts of personal identity goes, is automatically ruled out at this stage. And considerable implausibility attaches to any theory that cannot reconstruct as wholly justified the easy and uncomplicated ways in

which we reidentify people on the basis of their physical appearance and manner.

Of course it may be that a number of competing theories survive this first stage. The surviving competitors may then be evaluated in terms of their compatibility with our reactions to those puzzle cases which provide situations in which the competing theories diverge in their pronouncements. But these intuitive reactions are defeasible judgments, which we can defeat by showing that they are overgeneralizations from the ordinary run of cases or are produced by some distorting influence or are outweighed by other judgments that we have reason to respect. So the alternative treatment of intuitive reactions will make more of comparing cases where intuitions conflict and will look for the underlying explanations of these conflicting intuitions. Sometimes the underlying explanations will discredit the intuitions and the conceptions of people which they appear to support, sometimes not. If equally good competitors still survive at this second stage, then we may be faced with genuine indeterminacy which our philosophical theory of personal identity should articulate.

I shall argue that, if we adopt this alternative method which takes a more critical attitude to the method of cases and relegates it to a secondary role, then our investigations will not converge on the dominant view of personal identity. Rather than see ourselves as minds whose *particular* embodiments are contingent, we will see ourselves as human beings: that is, beings which necessarily are normally constituted by human organisms, and whose conditions of survival deviate from those of their constituting organisms only because a human being will continue on if his mind continues on, so that a human being could be reduced to the condition of a mere brain so long as that brain continues the human being's mental life. Although having all but its brain destroyed is too much for a human organism to survive, a human being might plausibly be held to survive this. But as I (somewhat stipulatively) shall use the term 'human being', no human being could survive teletransportation or like cases of *complete* body transfer.[8]

By way of beginning to displace the orthodox position – the method of cases and the dominant view – I shall present a well-known conundrum about personal identity which, on the face of it, seems to threaten both parts of the orthodox position. A relatively orthodox reaction to the conundrum will be found wanting. In extracting the right morals from the conundrum, I shall employ the alternative methodology outlined above. It will then become evident that the dominant view depends for its appeal upon the exploitation of certain systematically distorting influences on our intuitions about puzzle cases.

1 The Conundrum

The conundrum that threatens both the method of cases and the dominant view derives from Bernard Williams,[9] though I will present it in my own way.

In the fantastic tale that follows we are to suppose that there is a machine which produces the sort of psychological effects that would be produced by transposing patients' brains. When the machine is connected up to two patients, A and B, and turned on, the machine records all features of their brains relevant to the determination of dispositional and occurrent mentality. The machine alters the A-brain so that it comes to have associated with it what appears to be the continuation of B's dispositional and occurrent mentality, and so that the person with the A-body emerges from the machine with what appears to be B's course of experience, memories, character traits, projects, etc. *Mutatis mutandis* for the B-brain. The person with the B-body emerges from the machine with what appears to be A's course of experience, memories, character traits, projects, etc.

Suppose that A is faced with such a procedure. First his psychology is realized in his brain and body. Then the machine is turned on and his psychology appears to be realized in the B-body and brain. *Mutatis mutandis* for B. Before the machine operates, it appears to A that the machine's operation would cause him to swap bodies with B. So if before the machine's operation A were to choose which of the A-body and the B-body is to undergo pain after the machine's operation and choose only from the self-interested point of view, he would choose the A-body. When the case is presented this way, many would agree with A. After all, if the brains of A and B were surgically transposed and the resultant composites survived, then, so many of us believe, A and B would have swapped bodies. The machine seems to produce the same effects without having to transpose brains.

But now suppose that A has to choose whether to undergo a very painful surgical procedure which has a small chance of curing him of some illness.

There is no effective anesthetic or analgesic that will block the pain. But A's doctor tells him that the latest medical technology can be used to "get around" the pain. The doctor explains that he is able to record all the features of A's brain relevant to the determination of dispositional and occurrent mentality, and reorganize those features so that dispositional and occurrent mental features very different from A's will be realized by A's brain. Then and only then will A's body be subjected to the painful surgical intervention. Only after the pain has ceased will the machine reorganize A's brain so that it realizes dispositional and occurrent mentality continuous with A's mentality as it was before the machine first acted on his brain.

Presented with such a prospect and asked to regard the future pain as having no significance from the self-interested point of view, A might reasonably retort that he is being asked to undergo a double assault. First his brain is to be fiddled with in a fairly drastic way so as to produce radical psychological discontinuity, and then he is to be caused to feel severe pain. And this reaction is in accord with the intuition most of us would have about the case. The future pain is A's pain despite the intervening psychological discontinuity. As Williams notes, the concept of a person's future pain is not such that some degree of psychological continuity is required in order to make some future pain his.

So we have two intuitions, the intuition that A would swap bodies and so avoid any pain then undergone by the A-body, and the intuition that A would suffer pain in the A-body despite radical psychological discontinuity. The second intuition counts against the dominant view, which takes psychological continuity to be necessary for personal identity. And, on reflection, a further difficulty emerges. We have two directly conflicting intuitions about what could be taken to be two presentations of the same case. For we may suppose that the medical technology referred to by the doctor is just the machine that appears to transpose minds. What the doctor described was just one side of the body-swapping case followed by another body swap to reinstate A in the A-body and B in the B-body. The doctor refrained from describing B's experiences to A; but just how can this be relevant to the determination of our intuitions in the second presentation of the case?

Taken at face value, the intuition associated with the second presentation: that A would suffer pain in the A-body despite intervening psychological discontinuity of the most radical sort, threatens the dominant view. And on the face of it the two intuitions taken together threaten the method of cases. For how can intuition be reliable if we can be got to react so differently to the very same case?

Robert Nozick has recently offered a diagnosis which, if successful, would save the method of cases and only slightly modify the dominant view. He suggests that our intuitions about personal identity conform to the *closest-continuer schema* according to which the closest of the sufficiently close continuers of a given individual is that individual.[10] This is properly called a "schema" because just which weightings of just which relations are relevant in determining closeness of continuation will vary depending on what kind of individual is in question. The intuition associated with the second presentation can be taken as showing that, when it comes to persons, bodily continuity can make for sufficient continuity in the absence of psychological continuity. This explains our tracing A so that he remains in the same body throughout. The intuition associated with the first presentation can be taken as showing that when bodily continuity and psychological continuity diverge, we give more weight to psychological continuity. This explains why, when told of the adventures of B's psychology as well as A's, we have the intuition that A and B swap bodies. Our intuitive reactions to the two presentations are consistent because the first presentation simply describes a better continuer of A than any continuer of A described in the second presentation. That is why mentioning B and what happens to his brain is relevant. And the dominant view requires only modification. Psychological continuity can be on its own sufficient for personal identity and, in the absence of bodily continuity, necessary for personal identity.

This would be a satisfying orthodox response to the conundrum if it could be shown that our intuitions about personal identity conform in general to the closest-continuer schema interpreted in terms of the modified dominant view. But they do not.

Suppose the brain-state transfer machine is developed further so that it can seem to continue the mentality of a given patient A in each of the bodies of two patients B and C. Typically, the original A-body dies as a result of the machine's operation, and, after the machine operates, the person associated with the B-body and the person associated with the C-body are each sufficiently close psychological continuers of A. Suppose also, however, that typically the person associated with the C-body is a considerably better psychological continuer of A than the person associated with the B-body. Finally, suppose that this extra continuity is more than enough to compensate for the extra ten-minute delay typically involved in "reading" A's psychology into the C-body.

Now imagine that the machine has been operating and A's psychology has been (or seems to have been) "read into" the B-body. The person associated with the B-body gets up and walks around and thinks to himself, "I am A. I did not just come into existence." He sees the machine beginning to "read" A's psychology into the C-body. He knows that if the process is allowed to continue the result will be that the person associated with the C-body will be a better continuer of A than he is. So he turns off the machine. According to the closest-continuer theory, the person associated with the B-body has made it true that he is A and has existed before the operation of the machine as A. But, as against this, surely our intuition is that the B-body person's thought, "I am A. I did not just come into existence," is made true or false by what has happened up to and including the time at which that thought occurs. Surely no subsequent act by the B-body person can make this thought true or false. The closest-continuer schema interpreted in terms of the modified dominant view violates the intuition that the relevant facts are settled before the B-body person decides whether or not to tamper with the machine. To the extent that we have this and like intuitions, we are not to be construed as responding to cases as if we were adherents of the closest-continuer schema, at least as applied to people. To that extent Nozick's reaction to the conundrum, a conundrum which derives from our present responses to two presentations of the same case, is inadequate, *even if it were the case that philosophical theorists should ultimately adopt the closest-continuer schema in some form in the light of all the evidence about personal identity.*

There is another consideration that suggests that Nozick's diagnosis of the conundrum is inadequate. That diagnosis crucially depends upon the second presentation of Williams's case being one-sided, in the sense that the only sufficiently good continuer of A presented in the A-body person. The closest-continuer schema applied in accord with the modified dominant view implies that if the second presentation had included reference to another body who appears to inherit A's psychology, then we would simply have the first presentation and the familiar body-swap intuition. But in fact we easily understand the *stipulation* that *A undergoes* or survives throughout the "reading into" his brain of *B*'s psychology and then suffers severe pain while *B undergoes* the "reading into" his brain of *A*'s psychology. An adequate response to the conundrum has to explain why we can make sense of this *stipulation* even though we respond as we do in the first presentation of Williams's case.

What then can we say about the conundrum? Here is a minimal response. (Competing elaborations of the response will be considered below.) It seems that our reactions to the two presentations indicate that we think of a person as a *locus* of mental life; that is to say, something which typically exhibits psychological continuity and can be traced in terms of it, but something which need not always exhibit psychological continuity, something which can undergo psychological discontinuity of the most radical sort. The first presentation has us trace *A* in terms of psychological continuity, the second presentation encourages us to suppose that *A* undergoes psychological discontinuity. Our reactions are comprehensible if we think of ourselves as loci of mental lives, where this characterization does not in itself require that we think of ourselves as things of such a sort that psychological continuity, however it is secured, is sufficient for our survival. All that needs to be allowed is that it is reasonable to trace a locus of mental life in terms of psychological continuity. It is left open whether a reasonable practice might be leading us wrong in the puzzle case at hand.

Given this way of understanding our reactions to the conundrum, we can take our reaction to the second presentation as prima facie evidence against the wide psychological view (since such a view would make no sense of the stipulation that *A undergoes* radical psychological discontinuity) without automatically taking our reaction to the first presentation as showing that psychological continuity, however it is secured, is sufficient for our survival. At least, this is so if we are able satisfactorily to answer the question: Just what *kind* of locus of mental life are we? in a way that does not imply that psychological continuity, however it is secured, is sufficient for our survival. This is the question that will have to be answered by any theorist of personal identity whether or not he aims for a reduction of the persistence conditions of people in terms of conditions on continuity.

2   What Kind of Locus of Mental Life?

The dominant view, or wide psychological reductionism, amounts to a fairly specific characterization of the kind of thing we are, since it has psychological continuity and connectedness figure as necessary conditions on personal identity. But, given its reliance on the method of cases, the dominant view has no clear right to this necessary condition and consequent degree of specificity. For if the method of cases is taken at face value, we get the result that there are no specific necessary conditions on the survival of a person. That is, William's conundrum and like cases could be taken to show that we are what I will call *bare loci* of mental life, that is, possessors of mental life whose survival requires no amount of either bodily or mental continuity.[11] If the method of cases is taken as *the* method of theorizing about personal identity, such a view can be made to appear quite compelling. It is only when we adopt the alternative method of theorizing about personal identity described above that the bare-locus view can be *shown* to be unacceptable.

The first presentation of Williams's case seems to show that bodily continuity is not necessary for survival, and the second presentation seems to show that psychological continuity is not necessary for survival. We may bolster up these appearances by pointing out that we can imagine many sorts of cases that seem to involve one's ceasing to be associated with a particular human body and human personality. These cases are particularly compelling when imagined "from the inside." So I am to imagine myself undergoing a radical change in my form, e.g., a change like that undergone by Franz Kafka's beetle-man,[12] and perhaps concurrently a wild change in my psychology. There seems to be nothing internally incoherent about such imaginings. None of them exhibit the sort of conceptual deadlock associated with the attempt to imagine a married bachelor or a round square (if anything could be called such an attempt). Nor do such imaginings appear necessarily to embody some religious or secular conception of people which the imaginer has picked up. Rather it seems that such imaginings are not ruled out by, and so are consistent with, our concept of a person. So, given the ideology behind the method of cases, it is difficult to dismiss such imaginings as idle. They will appear to chart the boundaries of our concept of a person and thus indicate the correct theory of personal identity.

But such imaginings are idle. And if this can be shown, then it is plausible to take our pure *concept* of a person, understood as whatever it is that our reactions to these puzzle cases manifest, as being too unspecific to be of much interest, and as unspecific in a way that will typically lead us wrong in many puzzle cases.

Suppose, for example, that our pure concept of a person is *just* the concept of an unspecified kind of locus of (perhaps reflective) mental life, where this is understood, as before, to allow that a locus of mental life can survive radical psychological discontinuity. This concept is unspecific in the sense that it embodies no determinate necessary conditions on the survival of a person. There are no determinate necessary conditions on any tracing of a locus of mental life through any imagined vicissitude. Of course, in the *presence* of imagined bodily or mental continuities, we typically trace in terms of them, but this is just the reflection in our imaginative conceits of our ordinary practice of tracing people. That practice employs such continuities as evidence for the survival of people, and some of our reactions to imagined puzzle cases can be taken as harmless extensions of this practice. But, in the *absence* of imagined bodily or mental continuity, our unspecific conception of people is unconstrained by any evidence for persistence, and we get just the intuitive responses that seem to indicate that we are beings of the kind *bare locus of mental life*, where this characterization is now understood as including all that is necessary and sufficient for our persistence through time, so that we could undergo any sort of physical or mental metamorphosis.

How are we to show that the imaginings that detach me from the human being I appear to be are idle, without begging the question against the bare-locus view? The alternative method outlined above lays down as a first constraint on any theory of personal identity that it enable us to reconstruct our everyday practice of reidentifying people as an unproblematic source of knowledge about personal identity over time. This is a constraint which the bare-locus view flouts.

To see this, consider one of the wilder imaginative conceits which is identity-preserving on the view that I am a bare locus. I can imagine something that might be called my experiencing my body turning to stone. A queer numbness creeps up from my feet. It is as if my body is getting heavier and heavier and less and less tractable to my will. My senses give out, and in the end I am in the grip of panic at what seems like complete paralysis and sensory loss.

If we suppose that I can survive my body turning to stone, we must then face the question of which relations tie me to my body. The supposition that I could survive my body's petrification implies that the relations that tie me to my body are contingent. It cannot be that I am identical with or necessarily constituted by my living body. It seems, then, that the relevant relation can at most involve some actual pattern of causal interaction or some particular channel of causal influence (which may or may not be exploited at any particular time) by which I, a bare locus, get information about and direct changes in some of the states of that body.

The supposition that it is always some actual pattern of causal interaction which ties the bare locus that I am to a particular body can be set aside. If I can survive my body turning to stone because my essence is to be a bare locus of mental life, then surely I could survive my body turning to stone when that body is in deep (dreamless) sleep or rendered unconscious by drugs that work on the brain. For there was nothing in the idea of a locus of mental life as we introduced it which required that such a locus never undergo an interruption in its occurrent mental life. Otherwise the bare-locus view would be at odds with what appear to be the facts about our surviving periods of unconsciousness. Suppose then that, while it was unconscious, the living thing that I call "my body" turned to stone. The contingent relation which held between the bare locus that I am supposed to be and my body before it turned to stone and which ceased to hold when my body turned to stone was not some actual pattern of causal interaction by which that bare locus got information about and directed changes in some of the states of my body. None of that was going on when I was unconscious.

So we are driven back to the suggestion that, according to the bare-locus view, what makes a particular human body my body is a channel of causal influence which holds between the bare locus that I am and the body that I call "my body". But now the epistemological difficulties associated with the bare-locus view come to the fore.

Ordinary judgements that a particular person is in a state of unconsciousness are based on the observed continuity of human bodily life. Such judgements typically constitute knowledge that the particular person still exists though unconscious. If one condition on knowing that p is having evidence that converges on p as opposed to the relevant alternatives to p, then, in cases of unconsciousness, continuity of human bodily life must favour the proposition that a single person's survival is manifested by that bodily life. But then, in typical cases of unconsciousness or sleep, there cannot be a relevant alternative to the effect that people understood as bare loci have been replacing each other behind the stage of one human body's life. For that is an alternative that we are not in a position to rule out when faced with a sleeping or unconscious human body. If such an alternative were relevant, we would have little chance of knowing who was in bed with us at night.

For suppose that one came to accept the bare-locus view, complete with the account of channels of causal influence tying bare loci to particular human bodies. Then the ordinary judgement that a particular person is still in bed even though in deep sleep will have to be construed as the judgement that the same bare locus of mental life is associated with the living body in question via a channel of causal influence which is not then being exploited. But such a judgement brings in its train a host of alternative hypotheses: e.g., that there are two or three or four or many more such loci, perhaps each with its appropriate channel, replacing each other behind the stage of the continuous bodily life that we observe. Given the *metaphysical* picture of a bare locus being tied to a body by a channel of possible causal influence, these *become* relevant alternatives. Let no one suggest that those ignorant of the ways of bare loci can rule out these alternatives by means of an inference to the numerically *simplest explanation* of observed bodily continuity. None of these hypotheses *explain* continuity of a bodily life devoid of mental accompaniments. They are all merely compatible with such continuity. And indeed one should want to know why the simplest hypothesis is not that in deep sleep the bare locus usually tied to a given body has faded away or has simply detached itself from that body to wander where it will, as in the spiritualist's fantasies of astral travel. The relative simplicity of such alternative hypotheses could be reasonably evaluated only in the presence of some account of the typical or natural ways of bare loci.

Suppose there were some empirical theory that one could offer about bare loci, perhaps confirmed by introspection and observation of others or even by revelation, and – the best case – such a theory implied that bare loci did not typically migrate or permute during unconsciousness or sleep. This is roughly what any substance dualist, the bare-locus

theorist included, should take himself to be offering: namely, an empirical theory that fits the facts of human experience.[13] By appeal to the theory, one might have a way of ruling out the relevant alternatives, and so a way of coming to know that a single person is associated with a sleeping or unconscious body over a period of time.

The crucial point is that our ordinary claims to know that our friends and familiars were continuously where their bodies were when they were unconscious or in deep sleep rests on nothing like the employment of any such theory to rule out the possibility that any number of bare loci came to be associated with their bodies during such periods. These are alternatives we just do not consider, let alone rule out. We would boggle if asked to take them seriously. Yet they would be relevant alternatives if the bare-locus view were the correct view of people. So if the bare-locus view is correct, then our ordinary practice of reidentifying people during periods of unconsciousness and deep sleep does not generate knowledge. But, philosophical skepticism aside, we have every reason to think that it does.

One cannot save the bare-locus view by holding that, although it is the true view, in ordinary life we are spared the obligation to rule out the alternatives it makes relevant by our ignorance of the fact that it is the true view. For this sort of ignorance does not make it easier to know. Take just one familiar example. Suppose that my interlocutor and I both see a woman who looks just like Mary steal a book from the library. It is in fact Mary, and in fact I believe this, but I am not in a position to know this because I know that Mary has an identical twin who dresses just like her, so there is a relevant alternative that my observational evidence does not rule out. My interlocutor knows nothing of Mary's twin and claims to know that Mary stole the book on the strength of what we both saw. I take it that our intuition is that, even if it was Mary we both saw, his claim to know is mistaken, for he cannot know and I not know just because he is ignorant of crucially relevant facts.[14]

If this is right, the bare-locus view flouts the first constraint of the alternative method. Given that view, we cannot reconstruct a part of our ordinary practice of reidentifying each other as generating knowledge about personal identity. If the bare-locus view fails, a number of views fail with it. For similar arguments would count against any substance dualist, such as Richard Swinburne, who identifies us with mental substances, even if that substance dualist allows that we have some mental features as permanent or essential properties.[15] On any such view, similar problems will arise with unconsciousness and deep sleep. We do not trace a locus of mental life with a purely mental nature or essence when we trace people through such states.

The bare-locus view is straightforwardly supported by the method of cases. To the extent that we find that view absurd in its consequences, we should have grave doubts about relying simply upon the method of cases. For if we are not bare loci of mental life or activity, then some of our intuitions in puzzle cases simply represent our tracing what is no more than a reification of our unspecific concept of ourselves as *some or other sort* of locus of mental life.[16] But what is the correct specific conception of ourselves, and how could we argue for it without running foul of intuitions generated by a misleading reification of this unspecific concept of ourselves?

3 Human Organisms and Human Beings

Suppose that, instead of engaging in the self-defeating search for truths about ourselves that are both purely conceptual and yet specific enough to be interesting, we start with the specific conception of ourselves as evolved animals of a particular sort, the conception that locates us most easily within the naturalistic framework taken for granted by scientifically validated common sense. We will then try to articulate which aspects of our thought about ourselves could lead us to displace or modify this conception. The point of departure is then the position that we are essentially organisms of a particular animal species, namely *Homo sapiens*, so that the locus of mental life that we reidentify when we reidentify a person over time is just an instance of a biological kind, a kind whose members typically exhibit a complex mental life.

That we must depart from this position is, I think, the upshot of the case first introduced into philosophical discussion by Sydney Shoemaker:

It is now possible to transplant certain organs ...it is at least conceivable...that a human body could continue to function normally if its brain were replaced by one taken from another human body...Two men, a Mr Brown and a Mr Robinson, had been operated on for brain tumors, and brain extractions had been performed on both of them. At the end of the operations, however, the assistant inadvertently put Brown's brain in Robinson's head, and Robinson's brain in Brown's head. One of these men immediately dies, but the other, the one with Robinson's head and Brown's brain, eventually regains consciousness. Let us call the latter "Brownson"...When asked his name he automatically replies "Brown." He recognizes Brown's wife and family..., and is able to describe in detail events in Brown's life...of Robinson's past life he evidences no knowledge at all.[17]

The predominant reaction to this case is to suppose that Brownson is Brown and that during the brain-switching operation Brown survives as his denuded or debodied brain. This intuition is robust in the sense that it remains even if we modify the case by supposing that Brown's debrained body – call it "Brownless" – is provided with enough in the way of transplanted brain-stem tissue to keep it alive indefinitely. Although the transplanted brain-stem tissue does not subserve consciousness, Brownless is alive. Blood is coursing through Brownless, compounds in that blood are being metabolized, breath is being drawn into the lungs of Brownless, wastes are being expelled, and so on. Brownless is a living though badly mutilated human organism. And it seems bizarre to suppose that the organism Brownless came into being only after Brown's brain was taken out of Brown's body. Instead it seems that Brownless is the same organism as Brown. If we trace Brown's original organic life, we find Brownless realizing most of this life after Brown's brain is transplanted into Robinson's debrained body. We can allow a sense in which Brown's mental life may seem to continue on in Brownson. But, given the predominance of basic life functions that continue on in Brownless, we cannot count Brownson as the same human organism as Brown *and* think of human organisms as instances of purely *biological* kinds: i.e., individuals whose persistence through time is constituted by continuous biological life, so that the relative importance of life functions (including mental functioning) in tracing such an individual is determined by the relative contribution that those functions make to maintaining continuous life. For in this respect metabolism is more important than mentation. So if 'human organism' is taken to pick out a purely biological kind, Brownless and not Brownson is the same human organism as Brown. Hence if Brown survives as Brownson, neither Brown nor his kind-mates (those essentially the same as he) are essentially human organisms.[18]

Usually, what I've called the "predominant" reaction to Shoemaker's case, viz., the fact that most judge that Brownson is Brown, is taken as establishing that Brownson is Brown. But this is just another example of uncritical reliance on the method of cases. Indeed, the predominant reaction can be explained in terms of the distorting influences described below as the psychological- and social-continuer effects. *We* need a principled reason, consonant with the alternative method, for taking seriously the judgment that Brownson is Brown and thereby departing from the straightforward naturalistic conception of ourselves as essentially human organisms.

The alternative method requires that we represent ourselves as things of a kind such that the easy and uncomplicated ways in which we ordinarily trace people are well adapted to tracing things of that kind. Now, in tracing oneself backwards in time, one typically relies upon experiential memory. The deliverances of experiential memory are propositions involving claims about personal identity, viz., that the one who is now having the memory experience is the one whose experience is being remembered. That is, experiential memory does not leave us at a halfway house short of a full-blooded belief about personal identity. It does not leave us with some inference to make to arrive at the belief that it was none other than the one who is now having the memory who had the experience being presently remembered. Moreover, it seems that, even if one were in the Cartesian predicament of having suspended belief in anything external to one's own mind, experiential memory could still deliver knowledge about personal identity.

This raises a difficulty. Once it is admitted that among the necessary conditions on personal identity are certain bodily conditions having to do with the survival of an organism or crucial parts of it, the question arises how experiential memory, i.e., something whose internal phenomenology makes it seem like a faculty suited to picking up only mental connections between earlier and later mental states, could deliver any more than conclusions of the form: the same *mind* that had the remembered experience is the mind that is now remembering. For how could such a faculty directly pick up the fact that some bodily condition on personal identity is satisfied? And if it could not do this, by

what right are its deliverances properly taken to involve claims about personal identity as opposed to claims about mere mental identity?

The way out of this difficulty for the reconstructive program that is the alternative method is to realize that, if anything deserves the name of a conceptual truth about the relation between persons and minds, it is the claim that a person cannot be outlived by (what once was) his own mind. It is not a temporary feature of my mind that it is my mind. Nor could it be. No situation could deserve a description to the effect that the very mind that is my mind has been or will come to be the mind of someone else. Talk of a particular mind is just talk about a particular person's mental functioning. So, in delivering the conviction (and typically the knowledge) that the mind that had the remembered experience is the same mind that is now remembering, experiential memory is *eo ipso* delivering the conviction (and typically the knowledge) that the person who had the remembered experience is the same person as the person who is now remembering.

If this is so, then, whenever we have reason to say that a single mind has continued on, we have reason to say that a single person has continued on. But if we now adopt a properly naturalistic view of our mental functioning, i.e., see our mental functioning as the characteristic functioning of our brains, then it will be difficult, albeit not impossible, to resist the idea that one's mind would continue on if only one's brain were kept alive and functioning. Given the conceptual connection between people and minds, this amounts to the conclusion that one would go where one's brain goes and that one could survive as a mere brain. And now we have not just a brute intuition but an argument for the predominant reaction to Shoemaker's case from a principle that must hold if experiential memory is to be reconstructed as a faculty that could deliver knowledge about personal (as opposed to merely mental) identity. Applying the alternative method and attempting to reconstruct our reidentifications of others, things go most smoothly if we understand ourselves as tracing human organisms. But once we try to reconstruct our reidentifications of ourselves via memory, we see that it is human beings that we trace, i.e., beings that could outlive the human organisms they are invariably constituted by if their minds were to continue on.

Focusing on intuitions about brain-transfer cases and, in particular, the intuition that during such processes one survives as a mere brain has led some philosophers to take seriously a view floated for discussion by Thomas Nagel and J. L. Mackie, the view that we are essentially human brains, so that, for example, 'I' in my mouth picks out a pink, spongy thing inside my skull.[19] This extraordinary view is of the same ilk as William James's notion that his true self was located somewhere near the back of his throat and G. E. Moore's conviction that he was closer to his hands than to his feet. Rather than argue directly against the view that I am my brain and its strange implications (e.g., that when I report my weight as 150 pounds, I am like a driver of a heavy truck who says to a bridge attendant "I weigh 3 tons"), it is better to show that what is correct in the motivation for the view can be accommodated without needless paradox or wriggling out of paradox. The plausible observation behind the Nagel/Mackie view is that the survival of one's brain can be sufficient for one's survival and may well be necessary for it. But this does not show that we are of the kind *human brain*, i.e., that in our normal unmutilated condition we are pinkish-grey, spongy organs awash in cerebrospinal fluid. For the conditions under which one of us might be held to survive as a mere brain are just the conditions where it would make sense to talk of a *radically mutilated* human being, one reduced to the condition of a mere brain. The concept of mutilation must be respected here; we cannot determine the characteristic extent and form of a human being by determining how much mutilation it *can* undergo. The characteristic extent and form of a human being is that of an unmutilated human being, and that is the extent and form of an unmutilated human organism. This obvious claim is in no way threatened by the observation that each human being has a proper part, his brain, which is such that the survival of that part may constitute his survival in a radically mutilated condition and which is such that he would not survive the destruction of that part.

Hence allowing that in cases like Shoemaker's one would go where one's brain goes does not imply that one is of the kind *human brain*, but only that one is of a kind such that its members survive if their mental life continues on as a result of the survival of their organ of mentation. The kind *human being* is such a kind if the tracing of the life of a human being gives primary importance to mental functioning among the various life functions exhibited by human beings. In this sense 'human being' names a partly psychological kind, whereas 'human organism', as we were understanding it, names a purely biological kind, a kind such that mental functioning is given no special persistence-guaranteeing status among the various life functions exhibited by the instances of that kind. Nevertheless, these kinds are intimately related. So far, in every actual case a human being is constituted by a particular human organism, and so the survival of the organism is for all practical purposes a necessary condition of the survival of the human being. There are possible cases, such as Shoemaker's, in which a human being can come to be constituted by a mere brain and then by another organism which comes to have that brain as its organ of mentation. But it is crucial to the tracing of a human being that there be something that is the continued functioning of that human being's brain, and so a human being cannot survive teletransportation and the like. The fact that teletransportation secures certain causal dependencies between earlier and later mental states should not seduce us into thinking that these are states of the same mind. A human mind is neither an independently traceable substance nor some bundle theorist's ersatz for such a substance. A human mind is just a mode of functioning of a natural unit (e.g., a human organism or a human brain) whose conditions of persistence are statable in nonmental terms.[20] This is the sense in which talk of a mind is overly reified talk of an aspect of some minded thing.

4 The Conundrum Again

We have some final work to do on Williams's conundrum. If we are essentially human beings, we can undergo radical psychological discontinuity as a result of having our brains tampered with, but we cannot switch bodies without brain transplantation. So the view that we are essentially human beings is incompatible with the intuition generated by the first presentation of Williams's case. What is going on here?

We have found good reason to suspect intuitions that show that one or another form of continuity is not necessary for survival; for such intuitions may simply be generated by an unspecific concept of ourselves as some or other kind of locus of mental life. That having been said, it should be noted that, in the first presentation of Williams's case, we trace A in terms of psychological continuity even though we have the option of tracing A in terms of bodily continuity. This is not to be explained simply in terms of the employment of an unspecific concept of ourselves as loci of mental life. Why do we favor psychological continuity over bodily continuity? Is it that we are implicitly committed to the wide psychological view?

I think not. Our tendency to trace people in terms of psychological continuity in those puzzle cases in which such continuity comes apart from bodily continuity can be accounted for more satisfactorily as an understandable overgeneralization from the ordinary run of things. Let us say that X is an excellent continuer of Y if X's occurrent mental life evolves out of Y's occurrent mental life and X's dispositional psychology (character traits, quasi-memories, beliefs, and desires) evolves out of and is very similar to Y's dispositional psychology, so that X will experience and be disposed to do what Y would have experienced and have been disposed to do. Now in everyday life the normal concomitant of death is the loss of any very good continuer of oneself. When one dies, there is no one to take one's place in the world, to draw on one's memories and experiences, to act on one's intentions, to do the things one would have done in just the way one would have done them. And the normal concomitant of survival is having over the short term a unique and excellent continuer, namely oneself.

Now if we are essentially human beings, it will be possible to imagine cases in which a person ceases to be and yet nonetheless has a unique excellent continuer and also cases in which a person continues to exist while another becomes his unique, excellent continuer. Parfit's teletransportation case will be a case of the first sort, whereas Williams's first presentation depicts a case of the second sort. If such cases are described simply in terms of continuities, we will be liable to be misled by the normal psychological concomitants of survival and so trace individuals in terms of psychological continuity. By means of an understandable overgeneralization from the ordinary run of cases, we will be led to trace individuals in accord with the wide psychological criterion. We could call this overgeneralization *the psychological-continuer effect*.

This can only be part of the explanation. The question remains why, in reacting to the first presentation of Williams's case, we do not instead generalize from another typical "concomitant" of survival, namely, the fact that in everyday life one has the same body throughout any process that one

survives. Part of the answer is that people *can* be got to react this way to the first presentation of Williams's case if it is described immediately after cases that highlight the importance of bodily continuity. But when I described the first presentation, I followed Williams and deliberately assimilated it to a brain-transplanting case, describing it as a case that produces the same psychological effects as brain transplanting without the surgical messiness of an actual brain swap. Given the concurrent presentation of a brain-swap case, the sort of bodily continuity that is typical of survival in everyday life is made less salient, and the psychological-continuer effect tends to operate. But in my experience it is difficult to get the uninitiated to come up with the body-swap intuition in response to the first presentation of Williams's case when the first presentation comes immediately after cases that emphasize the importance of bodily continuity. Such inconstancy in our intuitive reactions itself suggests that our ordinary capacity to make correct judgments about personal identity is not well engaged by such bizarre cases. We are bewildered, and in our bewilderment we opt for one or another partial extension of our ordinary practice of reidentification.

It must be admitted, however, that there is a tendency among some people to respond to the first presentation of Williams's case with the body-swap intuition, even when the first presentation is delivered on its own and without any suggestion about which other cases it should be assimilated to. This is especially so when, in the case presented, B, the recipient of what seems like A's psychology, is like A in most bodily respects. The question remains why for some, in such a case, the psychological-continuer effect still predominates over the bodily-continuer effect.

Two factors may play a role. First, our practical interests in the relation of personal identity: in everyday-life the persistence of a person typically guarantees that over the short term there will continue to be some occupant of the particular complex of detailed and manifold social roles (father, lover, friend, leader, supporter, colleague, nemesis, regular customer, etc.) which made up that person's social life. Let us say then that personal identity typically guarantees that one will have over the short term a unique *social continuer*. Whereas gross bodily continuity without psychological continuity does not provide a social continuer, the massive psychological continuity described in the first presentation of Williams's case is plausibly taken to provide a social continuer, especially when the bodies involved are alike. So a tendency to trace *A* through a body swap rather than in accord with continuity of bodily life represents a fixation on the important *practical* concomitants of personal identity. Reinforcing the psychological-continuer effect, we have the social-continuer effect, i.e., the tendency to trace a person in terms of his social continuer. This too will be a potentially distorting effect so long as we are not essentially occupants of complexes of social roles. The wide psychological view is thus parasitic upon the psychological- and social-continuer effects; it gives roughly correct conditions for the persistence of "persons" – psychological and social continuers of developed persons – but persons antedate, outlive, and may sometimes be outlived by their personas.

Secondly, if there is such a thing as the pure or merely determinable concept of personal identity, the concept of a persisting person as some or other unspecified kind of persisting locus of reflective mental life, and if the psychological-continuer effect leads us to trace such loci along lines of psychological continuity in cases in which bodily and psychological continuity come apart, then it is a short step to a more or less inchoate conception of ourselves as souls, i.e., primarily psychological and so not essentially physical loci of reflective mental life. That is, some of the primary intuitions supporting the wide psychological view may well depend upon a residual tendency to trace ourselves as nonphysical souls, a tendency which survives conversion to a secular world view, since it is at least partly born of the interaction between the pure concept of personal identity and the psychological-continuer effect, a tendency which

should be at least mildly embarrassing to those physicalists who have advanced the wide psychological view.

None of this is to give a direct argument against the wide psychological view, but only to point out why the arguments for it should not carry conviction. There may be more direct arguments against the wide psychological view, but if they are needed, they are best left for another time.[21] For to give them here would be to distract from the upshot of the present discussion, namely that the wide psychological view relies for its appeal on an analytical method which we have no reason to respect, and indeed upon a method which if thoroughly pursued delivers the bare-locus view instead. If that is right, it is hard to see how the wide psychological view could now be rehabilitated. Indeed, it is hard to see why one would want to rehabilitate it, given the availability of the view that we are essentially human beings. For if we take ourselves to be essentially human beings, we are able to locate ourselves in a broadly naturalistic conception of the world and find nothing problematic in our everyday practice of reidentifying ourselves and others on the strength of the continuous mental and physical functioning of the human organisms we encounter. Weighed against these advantages, we have no real costs, but merely the deliverances of unconstrained imaginative conceits, deliverances which have misled the orthodox as a result of their uncritical overreliance on the method of cases, deliverances which actually show only that the concept of personal identity common to the adherents of particular and divergent conceptions of personal identity is just the unilluminating because merely determinable concept of some or other unspecified kind of locus of mental life.

Notes

In writing this paper I have been helped by conversations with Rogers Albritton, Paul Benacerraf, Philippa Foot, David Kaplan, Saul Kripke, David Lewis, Derek Parfit, Warren Quinn, and Michael Smith. My indebtedness to the works of Bernard Williams on personal identity should be obvious.

1 For an extensive survey of this material, see Robert K. Shope, *The Analysis of Knowing* (Princeton: Princeton University Press, 1983). I do not mean to suggest that the method of cases is entirely unproblematic in epistemology, only that it is even more problematic when it comes to personal identity.

2 Derek Parfit, *Reasons and Persons* (New York: Oxford University Press, 1984), pp. 207–8.

3 See David Lewis, "Survival and identity," in Amelie O. Rorty (ed.), *The Identities of Persons* (Berkeley: University of California Press, 1976); Anthony Quinton, "The soul," *Journal of Philosophy* 49/15 (19 July 1962), pp. 393–409; Sydney Shoemaker with Richard Swinburne, *Personal Identity* (Oxford: Blackwell, 1984). Shoemaker clearly had some sympathy for the view that bodily continuity is constitutive of personal identity when he wrote *Self-Knowledge and Self-Identity* (Ithaca, NY: Cornell University Press, 1963), although he allowed that in exceptional cases the

bodily criterion of personal identity could be over-
ridden by the memory criterion. He decisively aban-
dons the bodily criterion in "Persons and their pasts,"
this volume, ch. 27. The most notable opponents of
the dominant view have been Bernard Williams, "Are
persons bodies?," "Bodily continuity and personal
identity: a reply," "Personal identity and individuation," "The self and the future," all repr. in *Problems
of the Self* (New York: Cambridge University Press,
1973), the last in this volume, ch. 28; and David
Wiggins, "Personal identity," *Sameness and Substance*
(New York: Oxford University Press, 1980), ch. 6.
My differences with Wiggins are indicated in n. 17
below.

4 Quinton, "The Soul." The Locke example occurs in
An Essay Concerning Human Understanding, bk II, ch.
17, sect. 15.

5 Derek Parfit introduces teletransportation on pp.
119–20 of *Reasons and Persons*, and discusses it further
on pp. 282–7. Parfit, however, claims only that teletransportation is as good as survival. The claim (1) on
p. 216, which seems to imply otherwise, is just misleadingly formulated (personal communication).

6 Shoemaker discusses the brain-state transfer device in
Personal Identity, pp. 108–11.

7 Notice, however, that the account that follows is in no
way committed to the view that we are "separately
existing" (Parfit's phrase) entities distinct from
human brains and bodies. Instead I argue that we
are human beings, and that human beings are constituted by human bodies. Thus the present paper can
be read as an extended refutation of Parfit's claim
(*Reasons and Persons*, p. 216) that if we believe that
personal identity is a further fact, we must also believe
we are separately existing entities. This claim is crucial to the argument of Part Three of *Reasons and
Persons*. Parfit argues directly against the view that
we are separately existing entities. But, when it comes
to arguing for revisions in our practical attitudes, he
takes himself to have established that personal identity is never a further fact. If we are essentially human
beings in the sense of the present paper, then Parfit's
revisionary arguments are broken-backed. Moreover,
we can allow Parfit that in some puzzle cases personal
identity might well be an indeterminate matter, without accepting his revisionary arguments. I elaborate
these claims in "Reasons and reductionism" (forthcoming).

8 Although, for the purposes of this paper the possibility is set aside to avoid complications, I do not rule out
a kind of relativism about personal identity which
allows that acculturated human animals blamelessly
could have had or could come to have a conception of
personal identity according to which "they" could
survive teletransportation. (Whether the scare quotes
can be taken off ' "they" ' is of course a moot point.)
The main claim of the present paper is that there is no
reason to think that our actual conception of personal

identity is such as to allow us to survive teletransportation. The main impact of relativism about personal
identity and the possibility of refiguring our conception of ourselves will not be that we are not of the kind
human being, but that this kind may not strictly be a
substance kind, i.e., may not fix in an absolutely invariant way what kind of changes we could survive. However, on the assumption that the radical changes in
our thought and attitudes required for refiguring
our conception of ourselves will not take place, we
may treat the kind *human being* as if it were our
substance kind and so as if it determined our essence.
On these matters see my "Relativism and the self,"
forthcoming.

9 Bernard Williams, "The self and the future," this
volume, ch. 28.

10 Robert Nozick, *Philosophical Explanations* (Cambridge, Mass.: Harvard University Press, 1981), pp.
29–70.

11 Geoffrey Maddel argues, in *The Identity of the Self*
(Edinburgh: Edinburgh University Press, 1981), that
our survival requires no amount of either mental or
bodily continuity, taking himself to be arguing in the
tradition of Butler, Reid, and McTaggart. See especially pp. 117–40. I hesitate, however, to attribute the
bare-locus view to Maddel, since he insists that people
are not objective entities at all, but rather thoroughly
"subjective" in the sense of Thomas Nagel, "Subjective and objective," in *Mortal Questions* (New York:
Cambridge University Press, 1979). It may be that
this idea of ourselves as subjective is a seductive Idea
of Reason in something like the Kantian sense, an idea
which derives its apparent plausibility from the fact
that the only conception of ourselves that reflective
"I"-thought appears to underwrite is the unspecific
conception of ourselves as some or other sort of
locus of reflective mental life. See what follows and
n. 16.

12 Franz Kafka, *The Metamorphosis (Die Verwandlung)*,
trans. Willa and Edwin Muir, (New York: Schocken
Books, 1968).

13 That is, I reject attempts to rule out every form of
substance dualism a priori in the fashion of P. F.
Strawson, *Individuals* (London: Methuen; New
York: Doubleday, 1964), pp. 90–103, or, more
recently, Jay Rosenberg, *Thinking Clearly about
Death* (Englewood Cliffs, NJ: Prentice-Hall, 1984).
On this see Sydney Shoemaker, "Two kinds of dualism," in his collected papers, *Identity, Cause and Mind*
(New York: Cambridge University Press 1984). On
Donald Davidson's attempt to rule out a priori a
dualism of mental and physical events, see my "Why
having a mind matters," in Ernest Lepore and Brian
McLaughlin (eds), *Actions and Events: Perspectives on
the Philosophy of Donald Davidson* (New York: Blackwell, 1985).

14 For similar cases and a discussion of relevant alter-
atives, see Alvin Goldman, "Discrimination and per-

ceptual knowledge," *Journal of Philosophy* 73/20 (18 Nov. 1976), pp. 771–91, and Marshall Swain, "Reasons, causes, and knowledge," *Journal of Philosophy* 75 (May 1978): 229–49.

15 See Richard Swinburne, "Personal identity," *Proceedings of the Aristotelian Society* 74, (1973/4), pp. 231–47, and Shoemaker and Swinburne, *Personal Identity*.

16 Compare Kant's diagnosis in the Paralogisms (B427) of the Cartesian mistake: "I think myself on behalf of a possible experience, at the same time abstracting from all actual experience, and I conclude therefrom that I can be conscious of my existence even apart from experience and its empirical conditions. In so doing I am confusing a possible abstraction from my empirically determined existence with the supposed consciousness of a possible separate existence of my thinking self, and I thus come to believe that I have knowledge that what is substantial in me is the transcendental subject."

17 Shoemaker, *Self-Knowledge and Self-Identity*, pp. 23–4.

18 Hence Shoemaker's case raises problems for David Wiggins's account of human persons in *Sameness and Substance*. Wiggins suggests, "a person is any animal that is such by its kind to have the biological capacities to enjoy fully the psychological capacities enumerated," and extracts this consequence: "There would be no one real essence of person as such, but every person could still have the real essence of a certain kind of animal. Indirectly this would be the real essence in virtue of which he was a person" (p. 172). If Brown is not the same human organism as Brownson, then he is not the same animal as Brownson. So if Brown survives as Brownson, then the animal kind *human animal* does not capture Brown's essence. Similar remarks apply to Peter van Inwagen's claim that persons are organisms, a centerpiece of his *Material Beings* (Ithaca, NY: Cornell University Press, 1987).

19 Thomas Nagel, "Are you your brain?," paper delivered to Princeton Philosophy Colloquium and APA Pacific Division, 1984. J. L. Mackie, "The transcendental 'I'," in Zak van Straaten (ed.), *Philosophical Subjects: Essays Presented to P. F. Strawson* (New York: Oxford University Press, 1980).

20 The defense of this claim and the task of giving an acceptable account of constitution, persistence, and kinds I leave for another occasion. On the matter of kinds, all that is needed for present purposes is that all actual and possible members of a kind share the same general conditions of persistence through time and the same possible types of constitution over time.

21 See "Reasons and reductionism."

Causation

Introduction

The world is not a mere assemblage of objects, events, and facts, but a structure in which things are related in significant ways. Or at least, that is the way we think. Among the relations that can generate structure, causation perhaps has the preeminent status, having received serious attention from philosophers at least since the time of Aristotle. The importance of causation can be seen in many ways. First, causal concepts are ubiquitous: they are present not only when we use words that obviously express causal concepts, such as "produce," "yield," "generate," "result," and the like, but also in countless other familiar expressions. For example, to kill something involves causing that thing to die; to break something is to cause its parts to separate from one another; and so on. If we cleansed our language of all expressions that involve causal concepts, we would be left with an extremely impoverished skeleton of a language manifestly inadequate for our needs. Second, causation is intimately tied to explanation: to explain why or how an event occurred is often, if not always, to identify its cause, an event or condition that brought it about. More, it seems likely that we cannot make sense of the notions of important ethical concepts, like moral responsibility and legal liability, without the use of causal concepts. Presumably one cannot be held responsible or liable for events or conditions that one didn't cause, or with which one is not causally involved in some way. Finally, knowledge of causal relations seems essential to our ability to make predictions about the future and control the course of natural events. It is not for nothing that Hume called causation "the cement of the universe."

In "Causes and Conditions" (chapter 32), J. L. Mackie offers an analysis of causation as an "INUS condition," a form of the regularity approach to causation (an exact interpretation of Mackie on this point depends on his conceptions of sufficiency and necessity). On this approach, a singular causal relation – that is, the causal relation between two individual events – must be covered by a lawful regularity between kinds of events under which the cause and effect fall. According to Mackie, a cause is a condition that, though *insufficient* in itself for its effect, is a *necessary* part of a condition that is *unnecessary* (since there often are alternative causes) but *sufficient* for the effect. If this sounds complicated, you will see that Mackie provides perspicuous examples and explanations.

Donald Davidson's aim in his "Causal Relations" (chapter 33) is not to offer an analysis of causation (although a nomic regularity approach lurks in the background), but to clarify some important issues that are prior to such an analysis. One such issue concerns the *relata* of causal relations – what sort of entities are linked by causal relations. For Davidson, causation is an extensional binary relation between concrete individual events, regardless of how these events are described. In this sense, causation differs from explanation, which is sensitive to how events are represented. Another important distinction which Davidson emphasizes is one between a partial description of an event and a part of that event, and he shows how ignoring this distinction has led to much confusion.

In "Causation", (chapter 34), David Lewis presents an account of causation in terms of counterfactual dependency. It is a development of the familiar idea that a cause is a *sine qua non* condition for its effect – a condition without which the effect would not have occurred. He argues that his approach resolves many of the difficulties that beset the nomic regularity approach. (Lewis develops his approach further, and discusses many new points in his several substantial postscripts to this paper; see his *Philosophical Papers*.[1]

Wesley C. Salmon argues, in "Causal Connections" (chapter 35), that the traditional view according to which the causal relation holds between individual events covered by a law is fundamentally mistaken. According to him, processes, rather than events, must be taken as fundamental in understanding causation, and the basic problem of causation, or "Hume's challenge," is to provide a principled distinction between genuine causal processes and pseudo-processes, processes that, although they exhibit regular, even lawlike, connections between their elements (like the successive shadows cast by a moving car), are not real causal processes. The main question for Salmon then is this: What distinguishes causal processes from pseudo-processes? As an answer to this question, he develops the idea that causal processes are those that are able to "transmit a mark."

In "The Nature of Causation: A Singularist Account" (chapter 36), Michael Tooley rejects the assumption underlying most attempts at an analysis of causation: namely, that causal facts supervene on noncausal facts – that is to say, once all noncausal facts (including laws of nature) of a world are fixed, that fixes all the causal facts as well. Indeed, he argues against the view that causal relations between individual events must always be subsumed, or covered, by general regularities. Instead Tooley proposes a "singularist" account, an account that allows a pair of events to be related as cause to effect without being covered by any law.

Note

1 David Lewis, *Philosophical Papers*, vol. 2 (Oxford and New York: Oxford University Press, 1986).

Further reading

Anscombe, G. E. M., "Causality and determination," in *Metaphysics and the Philosophy of Mind* (Minneapolis: University of Minnesota Press, 1981); repr. in Sosa and Tooley, *Causation*.

Cartwright, Nancy, *Nature's Capacities and their Measurement* (Oxford: Clarendon Press, 1989).

Ducasse, C. J., *Causation and the Types of Necessity* (Seattle: University of Washington Press, 1924; Dover reprint, 1969).

Ehring, Douglas, *Causation and Persistence* (New York: Oxford University Press, 1997).

Fales, Evan, *Causation and Universals* (New York and London: Routledge, 1990).

Harré, Rom, and Madden, E. H., *Causal Powers: A Theory of Natural Necessity* (Totowa, NJ: Rowman and Littlefield, 1975).

Humphreys, Paul, *The Chances of Explanation* (Princeton: Princeton University Press, 1989).

Kim, Jaegwon, "Epiphenomenal and supervenient causation," in *Supervenience and Mind* (Cambridge: Cambridge University Press, 1993).

Mackie, J. L., *The Cement of the Universe* (Oxford: Clarendon Press, 1974).

Rosenberg, Alexander, and Beauchamp, Tom L., *Hume and the Problem of Causation* (Oxford and New York: Oxford University Press, 1981).

Sosa, Ernest, and Tooley, Michael, (eds)., *Causation* (Oxford: Oxford University Press, 1993).

Suppes, Patrick, *A Probabilistic Theory of Causality* (Amsterdam: North-Holland Publishing Company, 1970).

Tooley, Michael, *Causation: A Realist Approach* (Oxford: Clarendon Press, 1987).

von Wright, Georg, *Explanation and Understanding* (Ithaca, NY: Cornell University Press, 1971).

Yablo, Stephen, "Cause and essence," *Synthese* 93 (1992), pp. 403–49.

32

Causes and Conditions

J. L. Mackie

Asked what a cause is, we may be tempted to say that it is an event which precedes the event of which it is the cause, and is both necessary and sufficient for the latter's occurrence; briefly, that a cause is a necessary and sufficient preceding condition. There are, however, many difficulties in this account. I shall try to show that what we often speak of as a cause is a condition not of this sort, but of a sort related to this. That is to say, this account needs modification, and can be modified, and when it is modified, we can explain much more satisfactorily how we can arrive at much of what we ordinarily take to be causal knowledge; the claims implicit within our causal assertions can be related to the forms of the evidence on which we are often relying when we assert a causal connection.

1   Singular Causal Statements

Suppose that a fire has broken out in a certain house, but has been extinguished before the house has been completely destroyed. Experts investigate the cause of the fire, and they conclude that it was caused by an electrical short circuit at a certain place. What is the exact force of their statement that this short circuit caused this fire? Clearly the experts are not saying that the short circuit was a necessary condition for this house's catching fire at

Originally published in *American Philosophical Quarterly* 2 (1965), pp. 245–64.

this time; they know perfectly well that a short circuit somewhere else, or the overturning of a lighted oil stove, or any one of a number of other things might, if it had occurred, have set the house on fire. Equally, they are not saying that the short circuit was a sufficient condition for this house's catching fire; for if the short circuit had occurred, but there had been no inflammable material nearby, the fire would not have broken out, and even given both the short circuit and the inflammable material, the fire would not have occurred if, say, there had been an efficient automatic sprinkler at just the right spot. Far from being a condition both necessary and sufficient for the fire, the short circuit was, and is known to the experts to have been, neither necessary nor sufficient for it. In what sense, then, is it said to have caused the fire?

At least part of the answer is that there is a set of conditions (of which some are positive and some are negative), including the presence of inflammable material, the absence of a suitably placed sprinkler, and no doubt quite a number of others, which combined with the short circuit constituted a complex condition that was sufficient for the house's catching fire – sufficient, but not necessary, for the fire could have started in other ways. Also, of *this* complex condition, the short circuit was an indispensable part: the other parts of this condition, conjoined with one another in the absence of the short circuit, would not have produced the fire. The short circuit which is said to have caused the fire is thus an indispensable part of a complex sufficient (but not necessary) condition of the fire. In this case, then, the so-called cause is, and is known to be, an *insufficient* but *necessary* part of a condition which is itself *unnecessary* but *sufficient* for the result. The experts are saying, in effect, that the short circuit is a condition of this sort, that it occurred, that the other conditions which conjoined with it form a sufficient condition were also present, and that no other sufficient condition of the house's catching fire was present on this occasion. I suggest that when we speak of the cause of some particular event, it is often a condition of this sort that we have in mind. In view of the importance of conditions of this sort in our knowledge of and talk about causation, it will be convenient to have a short name for them: let us call such a condition (from the initial letters of the words italicized above), an INUS condition.[1]

This account of the force of the experts' statement about the cause of the fire may be confirmed by reflecting on the way in which they will have reached this conclusion, and the way in which anyone who disagreed with it would have to challenge it. An important part of the investigation will have consisted in tracing the actual course of the fire; the experts will have ascertained that no other condition sufficient for a fire's breaking out and taking this course was present, but that the short circuit did occur, and that conditions were present which in conjunction with it were sufficient for the fire's breaking out and taking the course that it did. Provided that there is some necessary and sufficient condition of the fire – and this is an assumption that we commonly make in such contexts – anyone who wanted to deny the experts' conclusion would have to challenge one or another of these points.

We can give a more formal analysis of the statement that something is an INUS condition. Let 'A' stand for the INUS condition – in our example, the occurrence of a short circuit at that place – and let 'B' and '$\bar{C}$' (that is, 'not-C', or the absence of C) stand for the other conditions, positive and negative, which were needed along with A to form a sufficient condition of the fire – in our example, B might be the presence of inflammable material, $\bar{C}$ the absence of a suitably placed sprinkler. Then the conjunction '$AB\bar{C}$' represents a sufficient condition of the fire, and one that contains no redundant factors; that is, $AB\bar{C}$ is a minimal sufficient condition for the fire.[2] Similarly, let $D\bar{E}F$, $\bar{G}\bar{H}I$, etc. be all the other minimal sufficient conditions of this result. Now provided that there is some necessary

and sufficient condition for this result, the disjunction of all the minimal sufficient conditions for it constitutes a necessary and sufficient condition.[3] That is, the formula "$AB\bar{C}$ or $D\bar{E}F$ or $\bar{G}\bar{H}I$ or ..." represents a necessary and sufficient condition for the fire; each of its disjuncts, such as '$AB\bar{C}$', represents a minimal sufficient condition; and each conjunct in each minimal sufficient condition, such as 'A', represents an INUS condition. To simplify and generalize this, we can replace the conjunction of terms conjoined with 'A' (here $B\bar{C}$') by the single term 'X', and the formula representing the disjunction of all the other minimal sufficient conditions – here '$D\bar{E}F$ or $\bar{G}\bar{H}I$ or ...' – by the single term 'Y'. Then an INUS condition is defined as follows:

> A is an INUS condition of a result P if and only if, for some X and for some Y, (AX or Y) is a necessary and sufficient condition of P, but A is not a sufficient condition of P, and X is not a sufficient condition of P.

We can indicate this type of relation more briefly if we take the provisos for granted and replace the existentially quantified variables 'X' and 'Y' by dots. That is, we can say that A is an INUS condition of P when (A ... or ...) is a necessary and sufficient condition of P.

(To forestall possible misunderstandings, I would fill out this definition as follows.[4] First, there could be a set of minimal sufficient conditions of P, but no necessary conditions, not even a complex one; in such a case, A might be what Marc-Wogau calls a moment in a minimal sufficient condition, but I shall not call it an INUS condition. I shall speak of an INUS condition only where the disjunction of all the minimal sufficient conditions is also a necessary condition. Secondly, the definition leaves it open that the INUS condition A might be a conjunct in each of the minimal sufficient conditions. If so, A would be itself a necessary condition of the result. I shall still call A an INUS condition in these circumstances: it is not part of the definition of an INUS condition that it should *not* be necessary, although in the standard cases, such as that sketched above, it is not in fact necessary.[5] Thirdly, the requirement that X by itself should not be sufficient for P insures that A is a nonredundant part of the sufficient condition AX; but there is a sense in which it may not be strictly necessary or indispensable even as a part of *this* condition, for it may be replaceable: for example KX might be another minimal sufficient condition of P.[6] Fourthly, it *is* part of the definition that the minimal sufficient condition, AX, of which A is a nonredundant part, is not also a necessary condition, that there is another sufficient condition Y (which may itself be a disjunction of sufficient conditions). Fifthly, and similarly, it *is* part of the definition that A is not by itself sufficient for P. The fourth and fifth of these points amount to this: I shall call A an INUS condition only if there are terms which actually occupy the places occupied by 'X' and 'Y' in the formula for the necessary and sufficient condition. However, there may be cases where there is only one minimal sufficient condition, say AX. Again, there may be cases where A is itself a minimal sufficient condition, the disjunction of all minimal sufficient conditions being (A or Y); again, there may be cases where A itself is the only minimal sufficient condition, and is itself both necessary and sufficient for P. In any of these cases, as well as in cases where A is an INUS condition, I shall say that A is *at least an INUS condition*. As we shall see, we often have evidence which supports the conclusion that something is *at least* an INUS condition; we may or may not have other evidence which shows that it is *no more than* an INUS condition.)

I suggest that a statement which asserts a singular causal sequence, of such a form as "A caused P", often makes, implicitly, the following claims:

(i) A is at least an INUS condition of P – that is, there is a necessary and sufficient condition of P which has one of these forms: (AX or Y), (A or Y), AX, A.
(ii) A was present on the occasion in question.
(iii) The factors represented by the 'X', if any, in the formula for the necessary and sufficient condition were present on the occasion in question.
(iv) Every disjunct in 'Y' which does not contain 'A' as a conjunct was absent on the occasion in question. (As a rule, this means that whatever 'Y' represents was absent on this occasion. If 'Y' represents a single conjunction of factors, then it was absent if at least one of its conjuncts was absent; if it represents a disjunction, then it was absent if each of its disjuncts was absent. But we do not wish to exclude the possibility that 'Y' should be, or contain as a disjunct, a conjunction one of whose conjuncts is A, or to require that *this* conjunction should have been absent.[7]

I do not suggest that this is the whole of what is meant by "A caused P" on any occasion, or even that it is a part of what is meant on every occasion: some additional and alternative parts of the meaning of such statements are indicated below.[8] But I am suggesting that this is an important part of the concept of causation; the proof of this suggestion would be that in many cases the falsifying of any one of the above-mentioned claims would rebut the assertion that A caused P.

This account is in fairly close agreement, in substance if not in terminology, with at least two accounts recently offered of the cause of a single event.

Konrad Marc-Wogau sums up his account thus:

> when historians in singular causal statements speak of a cause or the cause of a certain individual event β, then what they are referring to is another individual event α which is a moment in a minimal sufficient and at the same time necessary condition *post factum* β.[9]

He explained his phrase "necessary condition *post factum*" by saying that he will call an event a_1 a necessary condition *post factum* for x if the disjunction "a_1 or a_2 or $a_3 \ldots$ or a_n" represents a necessary condition for x, and of these disjuncts only a_1 was present on the particular occasion when x occurred.

Similarly Michael Scriven has said:

> Causes are *not* necessary, even contingently so, they are not sufficient – but they are, to talk that language, *contingently sufficient*. . . . They are part of *a* set of conditions that does guarantee the outcome, and they are non-redundant in that the rest of *this* set (which does not include all the other conditions present) is not alone sufficient for the outcome. It is not even true that they are relatively necessary, i.e., necessary with regard to that set of conditions rather than the total circumstances of their occurrence, for there may be several possible replacements for them which happen not to be present. There remains a ghost of necessity; a cause is a factor from a set of possible factors the presence of one of which (*any* one) is necessary in order that a set of conditions actually present be sufficient for the effect.[10]

There are only slight differences between these two accounts, or between each of them and that offered above. Scriven seems to speak too strongly when he says that causes are not necessary: it is, indeed, not part of the definition of a cause of this sort that it should be necessary, but, as noted above, a cause, or an INUS condition, may be necessary, either because there is only one minimal sufficient condition or because the cause is a moment in each of the minimal sufficient conditions. On the other hand, Marc-Wogau's account of a minimal sufficient condition seems too strong. He says that a minimal sufficient condition contains "only those moments relevant to the effect" and that a moment is relevant to an effect if "it is a necessary condition for $\beta : \beta$ would not have occurred if this moment had not been present". This is less accurate than Scriven's statement that the cause only needs to be nonredundant.[11] Also, Marc-Wogau's requirement, in his account of a necessary condition *post factum*, that only one minimal sufficient condition (the one containing α) should be present on the particular occasion, seems a little too strong. If two or more minimal sufficient conditions (say a_1 and a_2) were present, but α was a moment in each of them, then though neither a_1 nor a_2 was necessary *post factum*, α would be so. I shall use this phrase "necessary *post factum*" to include cases of this sort: that is, α is a necessary condition *post factum* if it is a moment in every minimal sufficient condition that was present. For example, in a cricket team the wicket-keeper is also a good batsman. He is injured during a match, and does not bat in the second innings, and the substitute wicket-keeper drops a vital catch that the original wicket-keeper would have taken. The team loses the match, but it would have won if the wicket-keeper had *both* batted *and* taken that catch. His injury was a moment in two minimal sufficient conditions for the loss of the match; either his not batting, or the catch's not being taken, would on its own have insured the loss of the match. But we can certainly say that his injury caused the loss of the match, and that it was a necessary condition *post factum*.

This account may be summed up, briefly and approximately, by saying that the statement "*A* caused *P*" often claims that *A* was necessary and sufficient for *P* in the circumstances. This description applies in the standard cases, but we have already noted that a cause is nonredundant rather than necessary even in the circumstances, and we shall see that there are special cases in which it may be neither necessary nor nonredundant.

2 Difficulties and Refinements[12]

Both Scriven and Marc-Wogau are concerned not only with this basic account, but with certain difficulties and with the refinements and complications that are needed to overcome them. Before dealing with these, I shall introduce, as a refinement of my own account, the notion of a causal field.[13]

This notion is most easily explained if we leave, for a time, singular causal statements and consider general ones. The question "What causes influenza?" is incomplete and partially indeterminate. It may mean "What causes influenza in human beings in general?" If so, the (full) cause that is being sought is a difference that will mark off cases in which human beings contract influenza from cases in which they do not; the causal field is then the region that is to be thus divided, *human beings in general*. But the question may mean, "Given that influenza viruses are present, what makes some people contract the disease whereas others do not?" Here the causal field is *human beings in conditions where influenza viruses are present*. In all such cases, the cause is required to differentiate, within a wider region in which the effect sometimes occurs and sometimes does not, the sub-region in which it occurs: this wider region is the causal field. This notion can now be applied to singular causal questions and statements. "What caused this man's skin cancer?"[14] may mean "Why did this man develop skin cancer now when he did not develop it before?" Here the causal field is the career of this man: it is within this that we are seeking a difference between the time when skin cancer developed and times when it did not. But the same question may mean "Why did this man develop skin cancer, whereas other men who were also exposed to radiation did not?" Here the causal field is the class of men thus exposed to radiation. And what is the cause in relation to one field may not be the cause in relation to another. Exposure to a certain dose of radiation may be the cause in relation to the former field: it cannot be the cause in relation to the latter field, since it is part of the description of that field, and being present throughout that field it cannot differentiate one sub-region of it from another. In relation to the latter field, the cause may be, in Scriven's terms, "Some as-yet-unidentified constitutional factor".

In our first example of the house which caught fire, the history of this house is the field in relation to which the experts were looking for the cause of the fire: their question was "Why did this house catch fire on this occasion, and not on others?" However, there may still be some indeterminacy in this choice of a causal field. Does this house, considered as the causal field, include all its features, or all its relatively permanent features, or only some of these? If we take all its features, or even all of its relatively permanent ones, as constituting the field, then some of the things that we have treated as conditions – for example, the presence of inflammable material near the place where the short circuit occurred – would have to be regarded as parts of the field, and we could not then take them also as conditions which in relation to this field, as additions to it or intrusions into it, are necessary or sufficient for something else. We must therefore take the house, in so far as it constitutes the causal field, as determined only in a fairly general way, by only some of its relatively permanent features, and we shall then be free to treat its other features as conditions which do not constitute the field, and are not parts of it, but which may occur within it or be added to it. It is in general an arbitrary matter whether a particular feature is regarded as a condition (that is, as a possible causal factor) or as part of the field, but it cannot be treated in both ways at once. If we are to say that something happened to this house because of, or partly because of, a certain feature, we are implying that it would still have been *this* house, the house in relation to which we are seeking the cause of this happening, even if it had not had this particular feature.

I now propose to modify the account given above of the claims often made by singular causal statements. A statement of such a form as "*A* caused *P*" is usually elliptical, and is to be expanded into "*A* caused *P* in relation to the field *F*." And then in place of the claim stated in (i) above, we require this:

(i a)   *A* is at least an INUS condition of *P* in the field *F* – that is, there is a condition which, given the presence of whatever features characterize *F* throughout, is necessary and sufficient for *P*, and which is of one of these forms: (AX or Y), (A or Y), AX, A.

In analysing our ordinary causal statements, we must admit that the field is often taken for granted or only roughly indicated, rather than specified precisely. Nevertheless, the field in relation to which we are looking for a cause of this effect, or saying that such-and-such is a cause, may be definite enough for us to be able to say that certain facts or possibilities are irrelevant to the particular causal problem under consideration, because they would constitute a shift from the intended field to a different one. Thus if we are looking for the cause, or causes, of influenza, meaning its cause(s) in relation to the field *human beings*, we may dismiss, as not directly relevant, evidence which shows that some proposed cause fails to produce influenza in rats. If we are looking for the cause of the fire in *this house*, we may similarly dismiss as irrelevant the fact that a proposed cause would not have produced a fire if the house had been radically different, or had been set in a radically different environment.

This modification enables us to deal with the well-known difficulty that it is impossible, without including in the cause the whole environment, the whole prior state of the universe (and so excluding any likelihood of repetition), to find a genuinely sufficient condition, one which is "by itself, adequate to secure the effect".[15] It may be hard to find even a complex condition which is absolutely sufficient for this fire because we should have to include, as one of the negative conjuncts, such an item as the earth's not being destroyed by a nuclear explosion just after the occurrence of the suggested INUS condition; but it is easy and reasonable to say simply that such an explosion would, in more senses than one, take us outside the field in which we are considering this effect. That is to say, it may be not so difficult to find a condition which is sufficient in relation to the intended field. No doubt this means that causal statements may be vague, in so far as the specification of the field is vague, but this is not a serious obstacle to establishing or using them, either in science or in everyday contexts.[16]

It is a vital feature of the account I am suggesting that we can say that *A* caused *P*, in the sense described, without being able to specify exactly the terms represented by '*X*' and '*Y*' in our formula. In saying that *A* is at least an INUS condition for *P* in *F*, one is *not* saying what other factors, along with *A*, were both present and nonredundant, and one is *not* saying what other minimal sufficient conditions there may be for *P* in *F*. One is not even claiming to be able to say what they are. This is in no way a difficulty: it is a readily recognizable fact about our ordinary causal statements, and one which this account explicitly and correctly reflects.[17] It will be shown (in section 5) that this elliptical or indeterminate character of our causal statements is closely connected with some of our characteristic ways of discovering and confirming causal relationships: it is precisely for statements that are thus "gappy" or indeterminate that we can obtain fairly direct evidence from quite modest ranges of observation. On this analysis, causal statements implicitly contain existential quantifications; one can assert an existentially quantified statement without asserting any instantiation of it, and one can also have good reason for asserting an existentially quantified statement without having the information needed to support any precise instantiation of it. I can know that there is someone at the door even if the question. "Who is he?" would floor me

Marc-Wogau is concerned especially with cases where "there are two events, each of which independently of the other is a sufficient condition for another event". There are, that is to say, two minimal sufficient conditions, both of which actually occurred. For example, lightning strikes a barn in which straw is stored, and a tramp throws a burning cigarette butt into the straw at the same place and at the same time. Likewise for a historical event there may be more than one "cause", and each of them may, on its own, be sufficient.[18] Similarly Scriven considers a case where

> ... conditions (perhaps unusual excitement plus constitutional inadequacies) [are] present at 4.0 P.M. that guarantee a stroke at 4.55 P.M. and consequent death at 5.0 P.M.; but an entirely unrelated heart attack at 4.50 P.M. is still correctly called the cause of death, which, as it happens, does occur at 5.0. P.M..[19]

Before we try to resolve these difficulties, let us consider another of Marc-Wogau's problems: Smith and Jones commit a crime, but if they had not done so, the head of the criminal organization would have sent other members to perform it in their stead, and so it would have been committed anyway.[20] Now in this case, if 'A' stands for the actions of Smith and Jones, what we have is that AX is one minimal sufficient condition of the result (the crime), but $\bar{A}\,Z$ is another, and both X and Z are present. A combines with one set of the standing conditions to produce the result by one route: but the absence of A would have combined with another set of the standing conditions to produce the same result by another route. In this case we *can* say that A was a necessary condition *post factum*. This sample satisfies the requirements of Marc-Wogau's analysis, and of mine, of the statement that A caused this result; and this agrees with

what we would ordinarily say in such a case. (We might indeed add that there was *also* a deeper cause – the existence of the criminal organization, perhaps – but this does not matter: our formal analyses do not insure that a particular result will have a unique cause, nor does our ordinary causal talk require this.) It is true that in this case we cannot say what will usually serve as an informal substitute for the formal account, that the cause, here A, was necesary (as well as sufficient) in the circumstances; for $\bar{A}$ would have done just as well. We cannot even say that A was nonredundant. But this shows merely that a formal analysis may be superior to its less formal counterparts.

Now in Scriven's example, we might take it that the heart attack prevented the stroke from occurring. If so, then the heart attack *is* a necessary condition *post factum*: it is a moment in the only minimal sufficient condition that was present in full, for the heart attack itself removed some factor that was a necessary part of the minimal sufficient condition which has the excitement as one of its moments. This is strictly parallel to the Smith and Jones case. Again it is odd to say that the heart attack was in any way necessary, since the absence of the heart attack would have done just as well: this absence would have been a moment in that other minimal sufficient condition, one of whose other moments was the excitement. Nevertheless, the heart attack was necessary *post factum*, and the excitement was not. Scriven draws the distinction, quite correctly, in terms of continuity and discontinuity of causal chains: "the heart attack was, and the excitement was not the cause of death because the 'causal chain' between the latter and death was interrupted, while the former's 'went to completion'." But it is worth nothing that a break in the causal chain corresponds to a failure to satisfy the logical requirements of a moment in a minimal sufficient condition that is also necessary *post factum*.

Alternatively, if the heart attack did not prevent the stroke, then we have a case parallel to that of the straw in the barn, or of the man who is shot by a firing squad, and two bullets go through his heart simultaneously. In such cases the requirements of my analysis, or of Marc-Wogau's, or of Scriven's, are not met: each proposed cause *is* redundant and not even necessary *post factum*, though the disjunction of them is necessary *post factum* and nonredundant. But this agrees very well with the fact that we *would* ordinarily hesitate to say, of either bullet, that it caused the man's death, or of either the lightning or the cigarette butt that it caused the fire, or of either the excitement or the heart attack that it was the cause of death. As Marc-Wogau says, "in such a situation as this we are unsure also how to use the word 'cause'." Our ordinary concept of cause does not deal clearly with cases of this sort, and we are free to decide whether or not to add to our ordinary use, and to the various more or less formal descriptions of it, rules which allow us to say that where more than one at-least-INUS-condition, and its conjunct conditions are present, each of them caused the result.[21]

The account thus far developed of singular causal statements has been expressed in terms of statements about necessity and sufficiency; it is therefore incomplete until we have added an account of necessity and sufficiency themselves. This question is considered in Section 4 below. But the present account is independent of any particular analysis of necessity and sufficiency. Whatever analysis of these we finally adopt, we shall use it to complete the account of what it is to be an INUS condition, or to be at least an INUS condition. But in whatever way this account is completed, we can retain the general principle that at least part of what is often done by a singular causal statement is to pick out, as the cause, something that is claimed to be at least an INUS condition.

3 General Causal Statements

Many general causal statements are to be understood in a corresponding way. Suppose, for example, that an economist says that the restriction of credit causes (or produces) unemployment. Again, he will no doubt be speaking with reference to some causal field; this is now not an individual object, but a class, presumably economies of a certain general kind; perhaps their specification will include the feature that each economy of the kind in question contains a large private enterprise sector with free wage-earning employees. The result, unemployment, is something which sometimes occurs and sometimes does not occur within this field, and the same is true of the alleged cause, the restriction of credit. But the economist is not saying that (even in relation to this field) credit restriction is either necessary or sufficient for unemployment, let alone both necessary and sufficient. There may well be other circumstances which must be present along with credit restric-

tion, in an economy of the kind referred to, if unemployment is to result; these other circumstances will no doubt include various negative ones, the absence of various counteracting causal factors which, if they were present, would prevent this result. Also, the economist will probably be quite prepared to admit that in an economy of this kind, unemployment could be brought about by other combinations of circumstances in which the restriction of credit plays no part. So once again the claim that he is making is merely that the restriction of credit is, in economies of this kind, a non-redundant part of one sufficient condition for unemployment: that is, an INUS condition. The economist is probably assuming that there is some condition, no doubt a complex one, which is both necessary and sufficient for unemployment in this field. This being assumed, what he is asserting is that, for some X and for some Y, (AX or Y) is a necessary and sufficient condition for P in F, but neither A nor X is sufficient on its own, where 'A' stands for the restriction of credit, 'P' for unemployment, and 'F' for the field, economies of such-and-such a sort. In a developed economic theory the field F may be specified quite exactly, and so may the relevant combinations of factors represented here by 'X' and 'Y'. (Indeed, the theory may go beyond statements in terms of necessity and sufficiency to ones of functional dependence, but this is a complication which I am leaving aside for the present.) In a preliminary or popular statement, on the other hand, the combinations of factors may either be only roughly indicated or be left quite undetermined. At one extreme we have the statement that (AX or Y) is a necessary and sufficient condition, where 'X' and 'Y' are given definite meanings; at the other extreme we have the merely existentially quantified statement that this holds for *some* pair X and Y. Our knowledge in such cases ordinarily falls somewhere between these two extremes. We can use the same convention as before, deliberately allowing it to be ambiguous between these different interpretations, and say that in any of these cases, where A is an INUS condition of P in F, ($A \ldots$ or $\ldots$) is a necessary and sufficient condition of P in F.

A great deal of our ordinary causal knowledge is of this form. We know that the eating of sweets causes dental decay. Here the field is human beings who have some of their own teeth. We do not know, indeed it is not true, that the eating of sweets by any such person is a sufficient condition for dental decay: some people have peculiarly resistant teeth, and there are probably measures which, if taken along with the eating of sweets, would protect the eater's teeth from decay. All we know is that sweet-eating combined with a set of positive and negative factors which we can specify, if at all, only roughly and incompletely, constitutes a minimal sufficient condition for dental decay – but not a necessary one, for there are other combinations of factors, which do not include sweet-eating, which would also make teeth decay, but which we can specify, if at all, only roughly and incompletely. That is, if 'A' now represents sweet-eating, 'P' dental decay, and 'F' the class of human beings with some of their own teeth, we can say that, for some X and Y, $(AX$ or $Y)$ is necessary and sufficient for P in F, and we *may* be able to go beyond this merely existentially quantified statement to at least a partial specification of the X and Y in question. That is, we can say that $(A \ldots$ or $\ldots)$ is a necessary and sufficient condition, but that A itself is only an INUS condition. And the same holds for many general causal statements of the form "A causes (or produces) P". It is in this sense that the application of a potential difference to the ends of a copper wire produces an electric current in the wire; that a rise in the temperature of a piece of metal makes it expand; that moisture rusts steel; that exposure to various kinds of radiation causes cancer, and so on.

However, it is true that not all ordinary general causal statements are of this sort. Some of them are implicit statements of functional dependence. Functional dependence is a more complicated relationship of which necessity and sufficiency can be regarded as special cases. Here too what we commonly single out as causing some result is only one of a number of factors which jointly affect the result. Again, some causal statements pick out something that is not only an INUS condition, but also a necessary condition. Thus we may say that the yellow fever virus is the cause of yellow fever. (This statement is not, as it might appear to be, tautologous, for the yellow fever virus and the disease itself can be independently specified.) In the field in question – human beings – the injection of this virus is not by itself a sufficient condition for this disease, for persons who have once recovered from yellow fever are thereafter immune to it, and other persons can be immunized against it. The injection of the virus, combined with the absence of immunity (natural or artificial), and perhaps combined with some other factors, constitutes a sufficient condition for the disease. Beside this, the

injection of the virus is a necessary condition of the disease. If there is more than one complex sufficient condition for yellow fever, the injection of the virus into the patient's bloodstream (either by a mosquito or in some other way) is a factor included in every such sufficient condition. If 'A' stands for this factor, the necessary and sufficient condition has the form $(A \ldots$ or $A \ldots$ etc.), where A occurs in every disjunct. We sometimes note the difference between this and the standard case by using the phrase "the cause". We may say not merely that this virus *causes* yellow fever, but that it is *the cause* of yellow fever; but we would say only that sweet-eating *causes* dental decay, not that it is *the cause* of dental decay. But about an individual case we could say that sweet-eating was *the cause* of the decay of this person's teeth, meaning (as in section 1 above) that the only sufficient condition present here was the one of which sweet-eating is a nonredundant part. Nevertheless, there will not in general be any one item which has a unique claim to be regarded as *the cause* even of an individual event, and even after the causal field has been determined. Each of the moments in the minimal sufficient condition, or in each minimal sufficient condition, that was present can equally be regarded as the cause. They may be distinguished as predisposing causes, triggering causes, and so on, but it is quite arbitrary to pick out as "main" and "secondary", different moments which are equally nonredundant items in a minimal sufficient condition, or which are moments in two minimal sufficient conditions each of which makes the other redundant.[22]

4 Necessity and Sufficiency

One possible account of general statements of the forms "S is a necessary condition of T" and "S is a sufficient condition of T" – where 'S' and 'T' are general terms – is that they are equivalent to simple universal propositions. That is, the former is equivalent to "All T are S" and the latter to "All S are T". Similarly, "S is necessary for T in the field F" would be equivalent to "All FT are S", and "S' is sufficient for T in the field F" to "All FS are T". Whether an account of this sort is adequate is, of course, a matter of dispute; but it is not disputed that these statements about necessary and sufficient conditions at least *entail* the corresponding universals. I shall work on the assumption that this account is adequate, that general statements of necessity and sufficiency are equivalent to universals: it will be worthwhile to see how far this account will take us, how far we are able, in terms of it, to understand how we use, support, and criticize these statements of necessity and sufficiency.

A directly analogous account of the corresponding singular statements is not satisfactory. Thus it will not do to say that "A short circuit here was a necessary condition of a fire in this house" is equivalent to "All cases of this house's catching fire are cases of a short circuit occurring here", because the latter is automatically true if this house has caught fire only once and a short circuit has occurred on that occasion, but this is not enough to establish the statement that the short circuit was a necessary condition of the fire; and there would be an exactly parallel objection to a similar statement about a sufficient condition.

It is much more plausible to relate singular statements about necessity and sufficiency to certain kinds of non-material conditionals. Thus "A short circuit here was a necessary condition of a fire in this house" is closely related to the counter factual conditional "If a short circuit had not occurred here this house would not have caught fire", and "A short circuit here was a sufficient condition of a fire in this house" is closely related to what Goodman has called the factual conditional, "Since a short circuit occurred here, this house caught fire".

However, a further account would still have to be given of these non-material conditionals themselves. I have argued elsewhere[23] that they are best considered as condensed or telescoped *arguments*, but that the statements used as premises in these arguments are no more than simple factual universals. To use the above-quoted counterfactual conditional is, in effect, to run through an incomplete argument: "Suppose that a short circuit did not occur here, then the house did not catch fire." To use the factual conditional is, in effect, to run through a similar incomplete argument: "A short circuit occurred here; therefore the house caught fire." In each case the argument might in principle be completed by the insertion of other premises which, together with the stated premiss, would entail the stated conclusion. Such additional premisses may be said to *sustain* the non-material conditional. It is an important point that someone can use a non-material conditional without completing or being able to complete the argument, without being prepared explicitly to assert premisses that would sustain it, and similarly that we can understand such a conditional without knowing exactly how the argument would or could be completed. But to say that a short circuit here was a necessary condition of a fire in this house is to say that there is some set of true propositions which would sustain the above-stated counterfactual, and to say that it was a sufficient condition is to say that there is some set of true propositions which would sustain the above-stated factual conditional. If this is conceded, then the relating of singular statements about necessity and sufficiency to nonmaterial conditionals leads back to the view that they refer indirectly to certain simple universal propositions. Thus if we said that a short circuit here was a necessary condition for a fire in this house, we should be saying that there are true universal propositions from which, together with true statements about the characteristics of this house, and together with the supposition that a short circuit did not occur here, it would follow that the house did not catch fire. From this we could infer the universal proposition which is the more obvious, but unsatisfactory, candidate for the analysis of this statement of necessity, "All cases of this house's catching fire are cases of a short circuit occurring here", or, in our symbols, "All FP are A". We can use this to represent approximately the statement of necessity, on the understanding that it is to be a consequence of some set of wider universal propositions, and is not to be automatically true merely because there is only this one case of an FP, of this house's catching fire.[24] A statement that A was a sufficient condition may be similarly represented by "All FA are P". Correspondingly, if all that we want to say is that $(A \ldots \text{or} \ldots)$ was necessary and sufficient for P in F, this will be represented approximately by the pair of universals "All FP are $(A \ldots \text{or} \ldots)$ and all $F(A \ldots \text{or} \ldots)$ are P", and more accurately by the statement that there is some set of wider universal propositions from which, together with true statements about the features of F, this pair of universals follows. This, therefore, is the fuller analysis of the claim that in a particular case A is an INUS condition of P in F, and hence of the singular statement that A caused P. (The statement that A is *at least* an INUS condition includes other alternatives, corresponding to cases where the necessary and sufficient condition is $(A \text{ or} \ldots)$, $A \ldots$, or A.)

Let us go back now to general statements of necessity and sufficiency and take F as a class, not as an individual. On the view that I am adopting, at least provisionally, the statement that Z is a necessary and sufficient condition for P in F is equivalent to "All *FP* are *Z* and all *FZ* are *P*". Similarly, if we cannot completely specify a necessary and sufficient condition for *P* in *F*, but can only say that the formula "(*A* . . . or . . .)" represents such a condition, this is equivalent to the pair of incomplete universals, "All *FP* are (*A* . . . or . . .) and all *F* (*A* . . . or . . .) are *P*". In saying that our general causal statements often do no more than specify an INUS condition, I am therefore saying that much of our ordinary causal knowledge is knowledge of such pairs of incomplete universals, of what we may call elliptical or *gappy* causal laws.

[Sections 5–7 omitted]

8 The Direction of Causation

This account of causation is still incomplete, in that nothing has yet been said about the direction of causation, about what distinguishes *A* causing *P* from *P* causing *A*. This is a difficult question, and it is linked with the equally difficult question of the direction of time. I cannot hope to resolve it completely here, but I shall state some of the relevant considerations.[25]

First, it seems that there is a relation which may be called *causal priority*, and that part of what is meant by "*A* caused *P*" is that this relation holds in one direction between *A* and *P*, not the other. Secondly, this relation is not identical with temporal priority; it is conceivable that there should be evidence for a case of backward causation, for *A* being causally prior to *P* whereas *P* was temporally prior to *A*. Most of us believe, and I think with good reason, that backward causation does not occur, so that we can and do normally use temporal order to limit the possibilities about causal order; but the connection between the two is synthetic. Thirdly, it could be objected to the analysis of "necessary" and "sufficient" offered in section 4 above that it omits any reference to causal order, whereas our most common use of "necessary" and "sufficient" in causal contexts includes such a reference. Thus "*A* is (causally) sufficient for *B*" says "If *A*, then *B*, and *A* is causally prior to *B*", but "*B* is (causally) necessary for *A*" is not equivalent to this: it says "If *A*, then *B*, and *B* is causally prior to *A*". However, it is simpler to use "necessary" and "sufficient" in senses which exclude this causal priority, and to introduce the assertion of priority separately into our accounts of "*A* caused *P*" and "*A* causes *P*." Fourthly, although "*A* is (at

least) an INUS condition of *P*" is not synonymous with "*P* is (at least) an INUS condition of *A*", this difference of meaning cannot exhaust the relation of causal priority. If it did exhaust it, the direction of causation would be a trivial matter, for, given that there is some necessary and sufficient condition of *A* in the field, it can be proved that if *A* is (at least) an INUS condition of *P*, then *P* is also (at least) an INUS condition of *A*: we can construct a minimal sufficient condition of *A* in which *P* is a moment.[26]

Fifthly, it is often suggested that the direction of causation is linked with controllability. If there is a causal relation between *A* and *B*, and we can control *A* without making use of *B* to do so, and the relation between *A* and *B* still holds, then we decide that *B* is not causally prior to *A* and, in general, that *A* is causally prior to *B*. But this means only that if one case of causal priority is known, we can use it to determine others: our rejection of the possibility that *B* is causally prior to *A* rests on our knowledge that our action is causally prior to *A*, and the question how we know the latter, and even the question of what causal priority is, have still to be answered. Similarly, if one of the causally related kinds of event, say *A*, can be randomized, so that occurrences of *A* are either not caused at all, or are caused by something which enters this causal field *only* in this way, by causing *A*, we can reject both the possibility that *B* is causally prior to *A* and the possibility that some common cause is prior both to *A* and separately to *B*, and we can again conclude that *A* is causally prior to *B*. But this still means only that we can infer causal priority in one place if we first know that it is absent from another place. It is true that our knowledge of the direction of causation in ordinary cases is thus based on what we find to be controllable, and on what we either find to be random or find that we can randomize; but this cannot without circularity be taken as providing a full account either of what we mean by causal priority or of how we know about it.

A suggestion put forward by Popper about the direction of time seems to be relevant here.[27] If a stone is dropped into a pool, the entry of the stone will explain the expanding circular waves. But the reverse process, with contracting circular waves, "would demand a vast number of distant coherent generators of waves the coherence of which, to be explicable, would have to be shown . . . as originating from one centre". That is, if *B* is an occurrence which involves a certain sort of "coherence" between a large number of separated items, whereas A is a single event, and A and B are causally connected, A will explain B in a way in which B will not explain A unless some other single event, say C, first explains the coherence in B. Such examples give us a *direction of explanation*, and it may be that this is the basis, or part of the basis, of the relation I have called causal priority.

9 Conclusions

Even if Mill was wrong in thinking that science consists mainly of causal knowledge, it can hardly be denied that such knowledge is an indispensable element in science, and that it is worthwhile to investigate the meaning of causal statements and the ways in which we can arrive at causal knowledge. General causal relationships are among the items which a more advanced kind of scientific theory explains, and is confirmed by its success in explaining. Singular causal assertions are involved in almost every report of an experiment: doing such and such *produced* such and such an effect. Materials are commonly identified by their causal properties: to recognize something as a piece of a certain material, therefore, we must establish singular causal assertions about it, that this object affected that other one, or was affected by it, in such and such a way. Causal assertions are embedded in both the results and the procedures of scientific investigation.

The account that I have offered of the force of various kinds of causal statements agrees both with our informal understanding of them and with accounts put forward by other writers: at the same time it is formal enough to show how such statements can be supported by observations and experiments, and thus to throw a new light on philosophical questions about the nature of causation and causal explanation and the status of causal knowledge.

One important point is that, leaving aside the question of the direction of causation, the analysis has been given entirely within the limits of what can still be called a regularity theory of causation, in that the causal laws involved in it are no more than straightforward universal propositions, although their terms may be complex and perhaps incompletely specified. Despite this limitation, I have been able to give an account of the meaning of statements about singular causal sequences, regardless of whether such a sequence is or is not

of a kind that frequently recurs: repetition is not essential for causal relation, and regularity does not here disappear into the mere fact that this single sequence has occurred. It has, indeed, often been recognized that the regularity theory could cope with single sequences if, say, a unique sequence could be explained as the resultant of a number of laws each of which was exemplified in many other sequences; but my account shows how a singular causal statement can be interpreted, and how the corresponding sequence can be shown to be causal, even if the corresponding complete laws are not known. It shows how even a unique sequence can be directly recognized as causal.

One consequence of this is that it now becomes possible to reconcile what have appeared to be conflicting views about the nature of historical explanation. We are accustomed to contrast the "covering-law" theory adopted by Hempel, Popper, and others with the views of such critics as Dray and Scriven who have argued that explanations and causal statements in history cannot be thus assimilated to the patterns accepted in the physical sciences.[28] But while my basic analysis of singular causal statements in sections 1 and 2 agrees closely with Scriven's, I have argued in section 4 that this analysis can be developed in terms of complex and elliptical universal propositions, and this means that wherever we have a singular causal statement we shall still have a covering law, albeit a complex and perhaps elliptical one. Also, I have shown in section 5, and indicated briefly, for the functional dependence variants, in section 7, that the evidence which supports singular causal statements also supports general causal statements or covering laws, though again only complex and elliptical ones. Hempel recognized long ago that historical accounts can be interpreted as giving incomplete "explanation sketches", rather than what he would regard as full explanations, which would require fully stated covering laws, and that such sketches are also common outside history. But in these terms what I am saying is that explanation sketches and the related elliptical laws are often all that we can discover, that they play a part in all sciences, that they can be supported and even established without being completed, and do not serve merely as preliminaries to or summaries of complete deductive explanations. If we modify the notion of a covering law to admit laws which not only are complex but also are known only in an elliptical form, the covering-law theory can accommodate many of the points that have been made in criticism of it, while preserving the structural similarity of explanation in history and in the physical sciences. In this controversy, one point at issue has been the symmetry of explanation and prediction, and my account may help to resolve this dispute. It shows, in agreement with what Scriven has argued, how the actual occurrence of an event in the observed circumstances may be a vital part of the evidence which supports an explanation of that event, which shows that it was A that caused P on this occasion. A prediction on the other hand cannot rest on observation of the event predicted. Also, the gappy law which is sufficient for an explanation will not suffice for a prediction (or for a retrodiction): a statement of initial conditions together with a gappy law will not entail the assertion that a specific result will occur, though of course such a law may be, and often is, used to make tentative predictions the failure of which will not necessarily tell against the law. But the recognition of these differences between prediction and explanation does not affect the covering-law theory as modified by the recognition of elliptical laws.

Although what I have given is primarily an account of physical causation, it may be indirectly relevant to the understanding of human action and mental causation. It is sometimes suggested that our ability to recognize a single occurrence as an instance of mental causation is a feature which distinguishes mental causation from physical or "Humean" causation.[29] But this suggestion arise's from the use of too simple a regularity account of physical causation. If we first see clearly what we mean by singular causal statements in general, and how we can support such a statement by observation of the single sequence itself, even in a physical

case, we shall be better able to contrast with this our awareness of mental causes, and to see whether the latter has any really distinctive features.

This account also throws light on both the form and the status of the "causal principle", the deterministic assumption which is used in any application of the methods of eliminative induction. These methods need not presuppose determinism in general, but only that each specific phenomenon investigated by such a method is deterministic. Moreover, they require not only that the phenomenon should have some cause, but that there should be some restriction of the range of possibly relevant factors (at least to spatio-temporally neighbouring ones). Now the general causal principle, that every event has some cause, is so general that it is peculiarly difficult either to confirm or to disconfirm, and we might be tempted either to claim for it some a priori status, to turn it into a metaphysical absolute presupposition, or to dismiss it as vacuous. But the specific assumption that this phenomenon has some cause based somehow on factors drawn from this range, or even that this phenomenon has some neighboring cause, is much more open to empirical confirmation and disconfirmation: indeed, the former can be conclusively falsified by the observation of a positive instance of P, and a negative case in which P does not occur, but where each of the factors in the given range is either present in both or absent from both. This account, then, encourages us to regard the assumption as something to be empirically confirmed or disconfirmed. At the same time it shows that there must be some principle of the confirmation of hypotheses other than the eliminative methods themselves, since each such method rests on an empirical assumption.

Notes

1 This term was suggested by D. C. Stove, who has also given me a great deal of help criticizing earlier versions of this article.

2 The phrase "minimal sufficient condition" is borrowed from Konrad Marc-Wogau, "On historical explanation," *Theoria* 28 (1962), pp. 213–33. This article gives an analysis of singular causal statements, with special reference to their use by historians, which is substantially equivalent to the account I am suggesting. Many further references are made to this article, especially in n. 9 below.

3 Cf. p. 227, n. 8, where it is pointed out that in order to infer that the disjunction of all the minimal sufficient conditions will be a necessary condition, "it is necessary to presuppose that an arbitrary event C, if it occurs, must have sufficient reason to occur." This presupposition is equivalent to the presupposition that there is some (possibly complex) condition that is both necessary and sufficient for C.

It is of some interest that some common turns of speech embody this presupposition. To say "Nothing but X will do," or "Either X or Y will do, but nothing else will," is a natural way of saying that X, or the disjunction (X or Y), is a *necessary* condition for whatever result we have in mind. But taken literally, these remarks say only that there is no sufficient condition for this result other than X, or other than (X or Y). That is, we use to mean "a necessary condition" phrases whose literal meanings would be "the only sufficient condition," or "the disjunction of all sufficient conditions." Similarly, to say that Z is "all that's needed" is a natural way of saying that Z is a sufficient condition, but taken literally, this remark says that Z is the only necessary condition. But, once again, that the only necessary condition will also be a sufficient one follows only if we presuppose that some condition is both necessary and sufficient.

4 I am indebted to the referees appointed by *American Philosophical Quarterly*, in which this material was first published, for the suggestion that these points should be clarified.

5 Special cases where an INUS condition is also a necessary one are mentioned at the end of sect. 3.

6 This point, and the term "nonredundant", are taken from Michael Scriven's review of Nagel's *The Structure of Science*, in *Review of Metaphysics* (1964). See esp. the passage on p. 408 quoted below.

7 See example of the wicket-keeper discussed below.

8 See sects 7, 8.

9 See Marc-Wogau, "On historical explanation", pp. 226–7. Marc-Wogau's full formulation is as follows:

Let 'msc' stand for minimal sufficient condition and 'nc' for necessary condition. Then suppose we have a class K of individual events a_1, a_2, $...a_n$. (It seems reasonable to assume that K is finite; however, even if K were infinite, the reasoning below would not be affected.) My analysis of the singular causal statement: α is the cause of β, where α and β stand for individual events, can be summarily expressed in the following statements:

(1) $(EK)(K = \{a_1, a_2, \ldots, a_n\})$;
(2) $(x)(x \in K \equiv x \text{ msc } \beta)$;
(3) $(a_1 \lor a_2 \lor \ldots a_n) \text{ nc } \beta$;
(4) $(x)((x \in Kx \neq a_1) \supset x$ is not fulfilled when α occurs);
(5) α is a moment in a_1.

(3) and (4) say that a_1 is a necessary condition *post factum* for β. If a_1 is a necessary condition *post factum* for β, then every moment in a_1 is a necessary condition *post factum* for β, and therefore also α. As has been mentioned before (n. 6) there is assumed to be a temporal sequence between α and β; β is not itself an element in K.

10 Scriven, review, p. 408.

11 However, Marc-Wogau "On historical explanation," pp. 222–3, n. 7, draws attention to the difficulty of giving an accurate definition of "a moment in a sufficient condition". Further complications are involved in the account given in sect. 5 of "clusters" of factors and the progressive localization of a cause. A condition which is minimally sufficient in relation to one degree of analysis of factors may not be so in relation to another degree of analysis.

12 This section is something of an aside: the main argument is resumed in sect. 3.

13 This notion of a causal field was introduced by John Anderson. He used it, e.g., in "The problem of causality," first published in the *Australasian Journal of Psychology and Philosophy* 16 (1938), and repr. in *Studies in Empirical Philosophy* (Sydney: Angus and Robertson, 1962), pp. 126–36, to overcome certain difficulties and paradoxes in Mill's account of causation. I have also used this notion to deal with problems of legal and moral responsibility, in "Responsibility and language," *Australasian Journal of Philosophy* 33 (1955), pp. 143–59.

14 These examples are borrowed from Scriven, review, pp. 409–10. Scriven discusses them with reference to what he calls a "contrast class", the class of cases where the effect did not occur with which the case where it did occur is being contrasted. What I call the causal field is the logical sum of the case (or cases) in which the effect is being said to be caused with what Scriven calls the contrast class.

15 Cf. Bertrand Russell, "On the notion of cause," in *Mysticism and Logic* (London: Allen & Unwin, 1917), p. 187. Cf. also Scriven's first difficulty, review, p. 409: "First, there are virtually no known sufficient conditions, literally speaking, since human or accidental interference is almost inexhaustibly possible, and hard to exclude by specific qualification without tautology." The introduction of the causal field also automatically covers Scriven's third difficulty and third refinement, that of the contrast class and the relativity of causal statements to contexts.

16 J. R. Lucas, "Causation", R. J. Butler (ed.), *Analytical Philosophy* (Oxford: Blackwell, 1962), pp. 57–9, resolves this kind of difficulty by an informal appeal to what amounts to this notion of a causal field: "...these circumstances [cosmic cataclysms, etc.]... destroy the whole causal situation in which we had been looking for Z to appear... predictions are not expected to come true when quite unforeseen emergencies arise."

17 This is related to Scriven's second difficulty, review, p. 409: "there still remains the problem of saying what the other factors are which, with the cause, make up the sufficient condition. If they can be stated, causal explanation is then simply a special case of subsumption under a law. If they cannot, the analysis is surely mythological." Scriven correctly replies that "a combination of the thesis of macro-determinism... and observation-plus-theory frequently gives us the very best of reasons for saying that a certain factor combines with an unknown sub-set of the conditions present into a sufficient condition for a particular effect." He gives a statistical example of such evidence, but the whole of my account of typical sorts of evidence for causal relationships in sects 5 and 7 is an expanded defence of a reply of this sort.

18 Marc-Wogau, "On historical explanation", pp. 228–33.

19 Scriven, review, pp. 410–11: this is Scriven's fourth difficulty and refinement.

20 Marc-Wogau, "Oh historical explanation", p. 232: the example is taken from P. Gardiner, *The Nature of Historical Explanation* (Oxford: Oxford University Press, 1952), p. 101.

21 Scriven's fifth difficulty and refinement are concerned with the direction of causation. This is considered briefly in sect. 8 below.

22 Cf. Marc-Wogau's concluding remarks, "On historical explanation", pp. 232–3.

23 J. L. Mackie, "Counterfactuals and causal laws", R. J. Butler (ed.) *Analytical Philosophy* (Oxford: Blackwell, 1962), pp. 66–80.

24 This restriction may be compared with one which Nagel imposes on laws of nature: "the vacuous truth of an unrestricted universal is not sufficient for counting it a law; it counts as a law only if there is a set of other assumed laws from which the universal is logically derivable" (Ernest Nagel, *The Structure of Science* (New York: Harcourt, Brace and World, 1961), p. 60). It might have been better if he had added "or if there is some other way in which it is supported (ultimately) by empirical evidence". Cf. my remarks in "Counterfactuals and causal laws", pp. 72–4, 78–80.

25 As was mentioned in n. 21, Scriven's fifth difficulty and refinement are concerned with this point (review, pp. 411–12), but his answer seems to me inadequate. Lucas touches on it ('Causation', pp. 51–3). The problem of temporal asymmetry is discussed, e.g., by J. J. C. Smart, *Philosophy and Scientific Realism* (London: Routledge and Kegan Paul, 1963), pp. 142–8, and by A. Grünbaum in the article cited in n. 28 below.

26 I am indebted to one of the referees of *American Philosophical Quarterly* for correcting an inaccurate statement on this point in an earlier version.

27 Karl Popper, "The arrow of time", *Nature* 177 (1956), p. 538; also vol. 178, p. 382 and vol. 179, p. 1297.

28 See e.g., C. G. Hempel, "The function of general laws in history", *Journal of Philosophy*, 39 (1942), repr. in H. Feigl and W. Sellars (eds), *Readings in Philosophical Analysis* (New York, Appletan-Century-Crofts, 1949), pp. 459–71; C. G. Hempel and P. Oppenheim, "Studies in the logic of explanation", *Philosophy of Science* 15 (1948), repr. in H. Feigl and M. Brodbeck (eds), *Readings in the Philosophy of Science* (New York: Appleton-Century-Crofts, 1953), pp. 319–52; K. R. Popper, *Logik der Forschung* (Vienna: J. Springer, 1934), trans. as *The Logic of Scientific Discovery* (New York: Harper & Row, 1959), pp. 59–60, also *The Open Society* (London: Routledge and Kegan Paul, 1952), vol. 2, p. 262; W. Dray, *Laws and Explanation in History* (Oxford: Oxford University Press, 1957); N. Rescher, 'On prediction and explanation', *British Journal for the Philosophy of Science* 9, (1958), pp. 281–90; various papers in H. Feigl and G. Maxwell (eds), *Minnesota Studies in the Philosophy of Science*, vol. 3 (Minneapolis: University of Minnesota Press, 1962); A. Grünbaum, "Temporally-asymmetric principles, parity between explanation and prediction, and mechanism versus teleology", *Philosophy of Science*, 29 (1962), pp. 146–70.

Dray's criticisms of the covering-law theory include the following: we cannot state the law used in a historical explanation without making it so vague as to be vacuous (*Laws*, esp. pp. 24–37) or so complex that it covers only a single case and is trivial on that account (p. 39); the historian does not come to the task of explaining an event with a sufficient stock of laws already formulated and empirically validated (pp. 42–3); historians do not need to replace judgement about particular cases with deduction from empirically validated laws (pp. 51–2). It will be clear that my account resolves each of these difficulties. Grünbaum draws an important distinction between (1) an asymmetry between explanation and prediction with regard to the grounds on which we claim to know that the explanandum is true, and (2) an asymmetry with respect to the logical relation between the explanans and the explanandum; he thinks that only the former sort of asymmetry obtains. I suggest that my account of the use of gappy laws will clarify both the sense in which Grünbaum is right (since an explanation and a tentative prediction can use similarly gappy laws which are similarly related to the known initial conditions and the result) and the sense in which, in such a case, we may contrast an entirely satisfactory explanation with a merely tentative prediction. Scriven (in his most recent statement, the review cited in n. 10 above) says that "we often pin down a factor as a cause by excluding other possible causes. Simple – but disastrous for the covering-law theory of explanation, because we can eliminate causes only for something *we know has occurred*. And if the grounds for our explanation of an event *have* to include knowledge of that event's occurrence, they cannot be used (without circularity) to predict the occurrence of that event" (p. 414). That is, the observation of this event in these circumstances may be a vital part of the evidence that justifies the particular causal explanation that we give of this event: it may itself go a long way toward establishing the elliptical law in relation to which we explain it (as I have shown in sect. 5), whereas a law used for prediction cannot thus rest on the observation of the event predicted. But as my account also shows, this does not introduce an asymmetry of Grünbaum's second sort, and is therefore not disastrous for the covering-law theory.

29 See, e.g., G. E. M. Anscombe, *Intention* (Oxford: Blackwell, 1957), esp. p. 16; J. Teichmann, "Mental cause and effect", *Mind*, 70 (1961), pp. 36–52. Teichmann speaks (p. 36) of "the difference between them

and ordinary (or 'Humean') sequences of cause and effect", and says (p. 37) "it is sometimes in order for the person who blinks to say absolutely dogmatically that the cause is such-and-such, and to say this independently of his knowledge of any previously established correlations," and again, "if the noise is a cause it seems to be one which is known to be such in a special way. It seems that while it is necessary for an observer to have knowledge of a previously established correlation between noises and Smith's jumpings, before he can assert that one causes the other, it is not necessary for Smith himself to have such knowledge."

33

Causal Relations

Donald Davidson

What is the logical form of singular causal statements like: 'The flood caused the famine', 'The stabbing caused Caesar's death', 'The burning of the house caused the roasting of the pig'? This question is more modest than the question how we know such statements are true, and the question whether they can be analyzed in terms of, say, constant conjunction. The request for the logical form is modest because it is answered when we have identified the logical or grammatical roles of the words (or other significant stretches) in the sentences under scrutiny. It goes beyond this to define, analyze, or set down axioms governing, particular words or expressions.

I

According to Hume, "we may define a cause to be an object, followed by another, and where all the objects similar to the first are followed by objects similar to the second." This definition pretty clearly suggests that causes and effects are entities that can be named or described by singular terms; probably events, since one can follow another. But in the *Treatise*, under "rules by which to judge of causes and effects," Hume says that "where several different objects produce the same effect, it must be by means of some quality, which we discover to

Originally published in *Journal of Philosophy* 64 (1967), pp. 691–703. Copyright © by Donald Davidson. Reprinted by permission of the author and Columbia University.

be common amongst them. For as like effects imply like causes, we must always ascribe the causation to the circumstances, wherein we discover the resemblance." Here it seems to be the "quality" or "circumstances" of an event that is the cause rather than the event itself, for the event itself is the same as others in some respects and different in other respects. The suspicion that it is not events, but something more closely tied to the descriptions of events, that Hume holds to be causes, is fortified by Hume's claim that causal statements are never necessary. For if events were causes, then a true description of some event would be 'the cause of *b*', and, given that such an event exists, it follows logically that the cause of *b* caused *b*.

Mill said that the cause "is the sum total of the conditions positive and negative taken together ... which being realized, the consequent invariably follows." Many discussions of causality have concentrated on the question whether Mill was right in insisting that the "real Cause" must include all the antecedent conditions that jointly were sufficient for the effect, and much ingenuity has been spent on discovering factors, pragmatic or otherwise, that guide and justify our choice of some "part" of the conditions as the cause. There has been general agreement that the notion of cause may be at least partly characterized in terms of sufficient and (or) necessary conditions.[1] Yet it seems to me we do not understand how such characterizations are to be applied to particular causes.

Take one of Mill's examples: some man, say Smith, dies, and the cause of his death is said to be that his foot slipped in climbing a ladder. Mill would say we have not given the whole cause, since having a foot slip in climbing a ladder is not always followed by death. What we were after, however, was not the cause of death in general but the cause of Smith's death: does it make sense to ask under what conditions Smith's death invariably follows? Mill suggests that part of the cause of Smith's death is "the circumstance of his weight," perhaps because if Smith had been light as a feather, his slip might not have injured him. Mill's explanation of why we don't bother to mention this circumstance is that it is too obvious to bear mention, but it seems to me that if it was Smith's fall that killed him, and Smith weighed twelve stone, then Smith's fall was the fall of a man who weighed twelve stone, whether or not we know it or mention it. How could Smith's actual fall, with Smith weighing, as he did, twelve stone, be any more efficacious in killing him than Smith's actual fall?

The difficulty has nothing to do with Mill's sweeping view of the cause, but attends any attempt of this kind to treat particular causes as necessary or sufficient conditions. Thus Mackie asks, "What is the exact force of [the statement of some experts] that this short circuit caused this fire?" And he answers, "Clearly the experts are not saying that the short circuit was a necessary condition for this house's catching fire at this time; they know perfectly well that a short circuit some-where else, or the overturning of a lighted oil stove... might, if it had occurred, have set the house on fire."[2] Suppose the experts know what they are said to; how does this bear on the question whether the short circuit was a necessary condition of this particular fire? For a short circuit elsewhere could not have caused *this* fire, nor could the over-turning of a lighted oil stove.

To talk of particular events as conditions is bewildering, but perhaps causes aren't events (like the short circuit, or Smith's fall from the ladder), but correspond rather to sentences (perhaps like the fact that this short circuit occurred, or the fact that Smith fell from the ladder). Sentences can express conditions of truth for others – hence the word 'conditional'.

If causes correspond to sentences rather than singular terms, the logical form of a sentence like:

(1) The short circuit caused the fire

would be given more accurately by:

(2) *The fact that* there was a short circuit *caused it to be the case that* there was a fire.

In (2) the italicized words constitute a sentential connective like 'and' or 'if...then...'. This approach no doubt receives support from the idea that causal laws are universal conditionals, and singular causal statements ought to be instances of them. Yet the idea is not easily implemented. Suppose, first, that a causal law is (as it is usually said Hume taught) nothing but a universally quantified material conditional. If (2) is an instance of such, the italicized words have just the meaning of the material conditional, 'If there was a short circuit, then there was a fire'. No doubt (2) entails this, but not conversely, since (2) entails something stronger: namely, the conjunction 'There was a short circuit *and* there was a fire'. We might try treating (2) as the conjunction of the appropriate law and 'There was a short circuit and there was a fire' – indeed, this seems a possible interpretation of Hume's definition of cause quoted above – but then (2) would no longer be an instance of the law. And aside from the inherent implausibility of this suggestion as giving the logical form of (2) (in contrast, say, to giving the grounds on which it might be asserted), there is also the oddity that an inference from the fact that there was a short circuit and there was a fire, and the law, to (2) would turn out to be no more than a conjoining of the premises.

Suppose, then, that there is a non-truth-func-tional causal connective, as has been proposed by many.[3] In line with the concept of a cause as a condition, the causal connective is conceived as a conditional, though stronger than the truth-func-tional conditional. Thus Arthur Pap writes, "The distinctive property of causal implication as com-pared with material implication is just that the falsity of the antecedent is no ground for inferring the truth of the causal implication."[4] If the connective Pap had in mind were that of (2), this remark would be strange, for it is a property of the connective in (2) that the falsity of either the "ante-cedent" or the "consequent" is a ground for infer-ring the falsity of (2). That treating the causal connective as a kind of conditional unsuits it for the work of (1) or (2) is perhaps even more evident from Burks's remark that "p is causally sufficient for q is logically equivalent to $\sim q$ is causally suffi-cient for $\sim p$."[5] Indeed, this shows not only that Burks's connective is not that of (2), but also that it is not the subjunctive causal connective would cause. My tickling Jones would cause him to laugh, but his not laughing would not cause it to be the case that I didn't tickle him.

These considerations show that the connective of (2), and hence by hypothesis of (1), cannot, as is often assumed, be a conditional of any sort, but they do not show that (2) does not give the logical form of singular causal statements. To show this needs a stronger argument, and I think there is one, as follows.

It is obvious that the connective in (2) is not truth-functional, since (2) may change from true to false if the contained sentences are switched. Nevertheless, substitution of singular terms for others with the same extension in sentences like (1) and (2) does not touch their truth-value. If Smith's death was caused by the fall from the ladder and Smith was the first man to land on the moon, then the fall from the ladder was the cause of the death of the first man to land on the moon. And if the fact that there was a fire in Jones's house caused it to be the case that the pig was roasted, and Jones's house is the oldest building on Elm Street, then the fact that there was a fire in the oldest building on Elm Street caused it to be the case that the pig was roasted. We must accept the principle of extensional substitution, then. Surely also we cannot change the truth-value of the likes of (2) by substituting logically equivalent sentences for sentences in it. Thus (2) retains its truth if for 'there was a fire' we substitute the logically equivalent '$\hat{x}(x = x$ & there was a fire$) = \hat{x}(x = x)$'; retains it still if for the left side of this identity we write the coextensive singular term '$\hat{x}(x = x$ & Nero fiddled)'; and still retains it if we replace '$\hat{x}(x = x$ & Nero fiddled$) = \hat{x}(x = x)$' by the logically equivalent 'Nero fiddled' Since the only aspect of 'there was a fire' and 'Nero fiddled' that matters to this chain of reasoning is the fact of their material equivalence, it appears that our assumed principles have led to the conclusion that the main connective of (2) is, contrary to what we supposed, truth-functional.[6]

Having already seen that the connective of (2) cannot be truth-functional, it is tempting to try to escape the dilemma by tampering with the principles of substitution that led to it. But there is another, and, I think, wholly preferable way out: we may reject the hypothesis that (2) gives the logical form of (1), and with it the ideas that the 'caused' of (1) is a more or less concealed sentential connective, and that causes are fully expressed only by sentences.

II

Consider these six sentences:

(3) *It is a fact that* Jack fell down.
(4) Jack fell down *and* Jack broke his crown.
(5) Jack fell down *before* Jack broke his crown.
(6) Jack fell down, *which caused it to be the case that* Jack broke his crown.
(7) *Jones forgot the fact that* Jack fell down.
(8) *That* Jack fell down *explains the fact that* Jack broke his crown.

Substitution of equivalent sentences for, or substitution of coextensive singular terms or predicates in, the contained sentences, will not alter the truth-value of (3) or (4): here extensionality reigns. In (7) and (8), intensionality reigns, in that similar substitution in or for the contained sentences is not guaranteed to save truth. (5) and (6) seem to fall in between; for in them substitution of coextensive singular terms preserves truth, whereas substitution of equivalent sentences does not. However this last is, as we just saw with respect to (2), and hence also (6), untenable middle ground.

Our recent argument would apply equally against taking the 'before' of (5) as the sentential connective it appears to be. And of course we don't interpret 'before' as a sentential connective, but rather as an ordinary two-place relation true of ordered pairs of times; this is made to work by introducing an extra place into the predicates ('x fell down' becoming 'x fell down at t') and an ontology of times to suit. The logical form of (5) is made perspicuous, then, by:

(5′) There exist times t and t' such that Jack fell down at t, Jack broke his crown at t' and t preceded t'.

This standard way of dealing with (5) seems to me essentially correct, and I propose to apply the same strategy to (6), which then comes out:

(6′) There exist events e and e' such that e is a falling down of Jack, e' is a breaking of his crown by Jack, and e caused e'.

Once events are on hand, an obvious economy suggests itself: (5) may as well be construed as about events rather than times. With this, the canonical version of (5) becomes just (6′), with 'preceded' replacing 'caused'. Indeed, it would be difficult to make sense of the claim that causes precede, or at least do not follow, their effects if (5) and (6) did not thus have parallel structures. We will still want to be able to say when an event occurred, but with events this requires an ontology of pure numbers only. So 'Jack fell down at 3 p.m.' says that there is an event e that is a falling down of Jack, and the time of e, measured in hours after noon, is three; more briefly, $(\exists e)\ (F\ (\text{Jack},\ e)\ \&\ t(e) = 3)$.

On the present plan, (6) means some fall of Jack's caused some breaking of Jack's crown; so (6) is not false if Jack fell more than once, broke his crown more than once, or had a crown-breaking fall more than once. Nor, if such repetitions turned out to be the case, would we have grounds for saying that (6) referred to one rather than another of the fracturings. The same does not go for 'The short circuit caused the fire' or 'The flood caused the famine' or 'Jack's fall caused the breaking of Jack's crown'; here singularity is imputed. ('Jack's fall', like 'the day after tomorrow', is no less a singular term because it may refer to different entities on different occasions.) To do justice to 'Jack's fall caused the breaking of Jack's crown' what we need is something like. 'The one and only falling down of Jack caused the one and only breaking of his crown by Jack'; in some symbols of the trade, '$(\imath)\ F\ (\text{Jack},\ e)$ caused $(\imath)\ B\ (\text{Jack's crown},\ e)$'.

Evidently (1) and (2) do not have the same logical form. If we think in terms of standard notations for first-order languages, it is (1) that more or less wears its form on its face; (2), like many existentially quantified sentences, does not (witness 'Somebody loves somebody'). The relation between (1) and (2) remains obvious and close: (1) entails (2), but not conversely.[7]

III

The salient point that emerges so far is that we must distinguish firmly between causes and the features we hit on for describing them, and hence between the question whether a statement says truly that one event caused another and the further question whether the events are characterized in such a way that we can deduce, or otherwise infer, from laws or other causal lore, that the relation was causal. "The cause of this match's lighting is that it was struck. – Yes, but that was only *part* of the cause; it had to be a dry match, there had to be adequate oxygen in the atmosphere, it had to

be struck hard enough, etc." We ought now to appreciate that the "Yes, but" comment does not have the force we thought. It cannot be that the striking of this match was only part of the cause, for this match was in fact dry, in adequate oxygen, and the striking was hard enough. What is partial in the sentence "The cause of this match's lighting is that it was struck" is the *description* of the cause; as we add to the description of the cause, we may approach the point where we can deduce, from this description and laws, that an effect of the kind described would follow.

If Flora dried herself with a coarse towel, she dried herself with a towel. This is an inference we know how to articulate, and the articulation depends in an obvious way on reflecting in language an ontology that includes such things as towels: if there is a towel that is coarse and was used by Flora in her drying, there is a towel that was used by Flora in her drying. The usual way of doing things does not, however, give similar expression to the similar inference from 'Flora dried herself with a towel on the beach at noon' to 'Flora dried herself with a towel', or for that matter, from the last to 'Flora dried herself'. But if, as I suggest, we render 'Flora dried herself' as about an event, as well as about Flora, these inferences turn out to be quite parallel to the more familiar ones. Thus if there was an event that was a drying by Flora of herself and that was done with a towel, on the beach, at noon, then clearly there was an event that was a drying by Flora of herself – and so on.

The mode of inference carries over directly to causal statements. If it was a drying she gave herself with a coarse towel on the beach at noon that caused those awful splotches to appear on Flora's skin, then it was a drying she gave herself that did it; we may also conclude that it was something that happened on the beach, something that took place at noon, and something that was done with a towel, that caused the tragedy. These little pieces of reasoning seem all to be endorsed by intuition, and it speaks well for the analysis of causal statements in terms of events that on that analysis the arguments are transparently valid.

Mill, we are now in better position to see, was wrong in thinking we have not specified the whole cause of an event when we have not wholly specified it. And there is not, as Mill and others have maintained, anything elliptical in the claim that a certain man's death was caused by his eating a particular dish, even though death resulted only because the man had a particular bodily constitution, a particular state of present health, and so on. On the other hand Mill was, I think, quite right in saying that "there certainly is, among the circumstances that took place, some combination or other on which death is invariably consequent ... the whole of which circumstances perhaps constituted in this particular case the conditions of the phenomenon ... ".[8] Mill's critics are no doubt justified in contending that we may correctly give the cause without saying enough about it to demonstrate that it was sufficient; but they share Mill's confusion if they think every deletion from the description of an event represents something deleted from the event described.

The relation between a singular causal statement like 'The short circuit caused the fire' and necessary and sufficient conditions seems, in brief, to be this. The fuller we make the description of the cause, the better our chances of demonstrating that it was sufficient (as described) to produce the effect, and the worse our chances of demonstrating that it was necessary; the fuller we make the description of the effect, the better our chances of demonstrating that the cause (as described) was necessary, and the worse our chances of demonstrating that it was sufficient. The symmetry of these remarks strongly suggests that in whatever sense causes are correctly said to be (described as) sufficient, they are as correctly said to be necessary. Here is an example. We may suppose there is some predicate '$P(x, y, e)$' true of Brutus, Caesar, and Brutus's stabbing of Caesar and such that any stab (by anyone of anyone) that is P is followed by the death of the stabbed. And let us suppose further that this law meets Mill's requirements of being *unconditional* – it supports counterfactuals of the form 'If Cleopatra had received a stab that was P, she would have died'. Now we can prove (assuming a man dies only once) that Brutus's stab was sufficient for Caesar's death. Yet it was not the cause of Caesar's death, for Caesar's death was the death of a man with more wounds than Brutus inflicted, and such a death could not have been caused by an event that was P ('P' was chosen to apply only to stabbings administered by a single hand). The trouble here is not that the description of the cause is partial, but that the event described was literally (spatio temporally) only part of the cause.

Can we then analyze 'a caused b' as meaning that a and b may be described in such a way that the existence of each could be demonstrated, in the light of causal laws, to be a necessary and sufficient condition of the existence of the other? One objec-

tion, foreshadowed in previous discussion, is that the *analysandum* does, but the *analysans* does not, entail the existence of a and b. Suppose we add, in remedy, the condition that either a or b, as described, exists. Then on the proposed analysis one can show that the causal relation holds between any two events. To apply the point in the direction of sufficiency, imagine some description '$(\imath x)Fx$' under which the existence of an event a may be shown sufficient for the existence of b. Then the existence of an arbitrary event c may equally be shown sufficient for the existence of b: just take as the description of c the following: '$(\imath y)(y = c \ \& \ (\exists! x)Fx)$'.[9] It seems unlikely that any simple and natural restrictions on the form of allowable descriptions would meet this difficulty, but since I have abjured the analysis of the causal relation, I shall not pursue the matter here.

There remains a legitimate question concerning the relation between causal laws and singular causal statements that may be raised independently. Setting aside the abbreviations successful analysis might authorize, what form are causal laws apt to have if from them, and a premise to the effect that an event of a certain (acceptable) description exists, we are to infer a singular causal statement saying that the event caused, or was caused by, another? A possibility I find attractive is that a full-fledged causal law has the form of a conjunction:

$$(L) \begin{cases} (S) & (e)(n)((Fe \ \& \ t(e) = n) \rightarrow \\ & (\exists! f)(Gf \ \& \ t(f) = n + \epsilon \ \& \\ & C(e,f))) \ \text{and} \\ (N) & (e)(n)((Ge \ \& \ t(e) = n + \epsilon) \rightarrow \\ & (\exists! f)(Ff \ \& \ t(f) = n \ \& \ C(f,e))) \end{cases}$$

Here the variables 'e' and 'f' range over events, 'n' ranges over numbers, F and G are properties of events, '$C(e, f)$' is read 'e causes f', and 't' is a function that assigns a number to an event to mark the time the event occurs. Now, given the premise:

(P) $(\exists! e)(Fe \ \& \ t(e) = 3)$

(C) $(\imath e)(Fe \ \& \ t(e) = 3)$ caused
$(\imath e)(Ge \ \& \ t(e) = 3 + \epsilon)$

It is worth remarking that part (N) of (L) is as necessary to the proof of (C) from (P) as it is to the proof of (C) from the premise '$(\exists! e)(Ge \ \& \ t(e) = 3 + \epsilon))$'. This is perhaps more reason for holding that causes are, in the sense discussed above, necessary as well as sufficient conditions.

Explaining "why an event occurred," on this account of laws, may take an instructively large number of forms, even if we limit explanation to the resources of deduction. Suppose, for example, we want to explain the fact that there was a fire in the house at 3:01 p.m. Armed with appropriate premises in the form of (P) and (L), we may deduce: that there was a fire in the house at 3:01 p.m.; that it was caused by a short circuit at 3:00 p.m.; that there was only one fire in the house at 3:01 p.m.; that this fire was caused by the one and only short circuit that occurred at 3:00 p.m. Some of these explanations fall short of using all that is given by the premises; and this is lucky, since we often know less. Given only (S) and (P), for example, we cannot prove there was only one fire in the house at 3:01 p.m., though we can prove there was exactly one fire in the house at 3:01 p.m. that was caused by the short circuit. An interesting case is where we know a law in the form of (N), but not the corresponding (S). Then we may show that, given that an event of a particular sort occurred, there must have been a cause answering to a certain description, but, given the same description of the cause, we could not have predicted the effect. An example might be where the effect is getting pregnant.

If we explain why it is that a particular event occurred by deducting a statement that there is such an event (under a particular description) from a premise known to be true, then a simple way of explaining an event, for example the fire in the house at 3:01 p.m., consists in producing a statement of the form of (C); and this explanation makes no use of laws. The explanation will be greatly enhanced by whatever we can say in favor of the truth of (C); needless to say, producing the likes of (L) and (P), if they are known true, clinches the matter. In most cases, however, the request for explanation will describe the event in terms that fall under no full-fledged law. The device to which we will then resort, if we can, is apt to be redescription of the event. For we can explain the occurrence of any event a if we know (L), (P), and the further fact that $a = (\imath e)(Ge \ \& \ t(e) = 3 + \epsilon)$. Analogous remarks apply to the redescription of the cause, and to cases where all we want, or can, explain is the fact that there was *an* event of a certain sort.

The great majority of singular causal statements are not backed, we may be sure, by laws in the way (C) is backed by (L). The relation in general is rather this: if 'a caused b' is true, then there are descriptions of a and b such that the result of substituting them for 'a' and 'b' in 'a caused b' is entailed by true premises of the form of (L) and (P); and the converse holds if suitable restrictions are put on the descriptions.[10] If this is correct, it does not follow that we must be able to dredge up a law if we know a singular causal statement to be true; all that follows is that we know there must be a covering law. And very often, I think, our justification for accepting a singular causal statement is that we have reason to believe an appropriate causal law exists, though we do not know what it is. Generalizations like 'If you strike a well-made match hard enough against a properly prepared surface, then, other conditions being favorable, it will light' owe their importance not to the fact that we can hope eventually to render them untendentious and exceptionless, but rather to the fact that they summarize much of our evidence for believing that full-fledged causal laws exist covering events we wish to explain.[11]

If the story I have told is true, it is possible to reconcile, within limits, two accounts thought by their champions to be opposed. One account agrees with Hume and Mill to this extent: it says that a singular causal statement 'a caused b' entails that there is a law to the effect that "all the objects similar to a are followed by objects similar to b" and that we have reason to believe the singular statement only in so far as we have reason to believe there is such a law. The second account (persuasively argued by C. J. Ducasse[12]) maintains that singular causal statements entail no law and that we can know them to be true without knowing any relevant law. Both of these accounts are entailed, I think, by the account I have given, and they are consistent (I therefore hope) with each other. The reconciliation depends, of course, on the distinction between knowing there is a law "covering" two events and knowing what the law is: in my view, Ducasse is right that singular causal statements entail no law; Hume is right that they entail there is a law.

IV

Much of what philosophers have said of causes and causal relations is intelligible only on the assumption (often enough explicit) that causes are individual events, and causal relations hold between events. Yet, through failure to connect this basic *aperçu* with the grammar of singular causal judgments, these same philosophers have found themselves pressed, especially when trying to put causal statements into quantificational form, into trying to express the relation of cause to effect by a sentential connective. Hence the popularity of the utterly misleading question: can causal relations be expressed by the purely extensional material conditional, or is some stronger (non-Humean) connection involved? The question is misleading because it confuses two separate matters: the logical form of causal statements and the analysis of causality. So far as form is concerned, the issue of nonextensionality does not arise, since the relation of causality between events can be expressed (no matter how "strong" or "weak" it is) by an ordinary two-place predicate in an ordinary, extensional first-order language. These plain resources will perhaps be outrun by an adequate account of the form of causal laws, subjunctives, and counterfactual conditionals, to which most attempts to analyze the causal relation turn. But this is, I have urged, another question.

This is not to say there are no causal idioms that directly raise the issue of apparently non-truthfunctional connectives. On the contrary, a host of statement forms, many of them strikingly similar, at least at first view, to those we have considered, challenge the account just given. Here are samples: 'The failure of the sprinkling system caused the fire', 'The slowness with which controls were applied caused the rapidity with which the inflation developed', 'The collapse was caused, not by the fact that the bolt gave way, but by the fact that it gave way so suddenly and unexpectedly', 'The fact that the dam did not hold caused the flood'. Some

of these sentences may yield to the methods I have prescribed, especially if failures are counted among events, but others remain recalcitrant. What we must say in such cases is that in addition to, or in place of, giving what Mill calls the "producing cause," such sentences tell, or suggest, a causal story. They are, in other words, rudimentary causal explanations. Explanations typically relate statements, not events. I suggest therefore that the 'caused' of the sample sentences in this paragraph is not the 'caused' of straightforward singular causal statements, but is best expressed by the words 'causally explains'.[13]

A final remark. It is often said that events can be explained and predicted only in so far as they have repeatable characteristics, but not in so far as they are particulars. No doubt there is a clear and trivial sense in which this is true, but we ought not to lose sight of the less obvious point that there is an important difference between explaining the fact that there was *an* explosion in the broom closet and explaining the occurrence of *the* explosion in the broom closet. Explanation of the second sort touches the particular event as closely as language can ever touch any particular. Of course this claim is persuasive only if there are such things as events to which singular terms, especially definite descriptions, may refer. But the assumption, ontological and metaphysical, that there are events, is one without which we cannot make sense of much of our most common talk; or so, at any rate, I have been arguing. I do not know any better, or further, way of showing what there is.

Notes

I am indebted to Harry Lewis and David Nivison, as well as to other members of seminars at Stanford University to whom I presented the ideas in this paper during 1966/67, for many helpful comments. I have profited greatly from discussion with John Wallace of the questions raised here; he may or may not agree with my answers. My research was supported in part by the National Science Foundation.

1 For a recent example, with reference to many others, see J. L. Mackie, "Causes and conditions," this volume, ch. 32.

2 Ibid., p. 413.

3 For example by: Mackie, ibid., p. 421; Arthur Burks, "The logic of causal propositions," *Mind*, 60/239 (July 1951), pp. 363–82; and Arthur Pap, "Disposition concepts and extensional logic," in H. Feigl, M.

Scriven, and G. Maxwell (eds), *Minnesota Studies in the Philosophy of Science*, vol. 2, (Minneapolis: University of Minnesota Press, 1958), pp. 196–224.

4 Pap, "Disposition concepts," p. 212.

5 Burks, "Logic of causal propositions," p. 369.

6 This argument is closely related to one spelled out by Dagfinn Føllesdal, in "Quantification into causal contexts" in R. S. Cohen and M. W. Wartofsky (eds), *Boston Studies in the Philosophy of Science*, vol. 2 (New York: Humanities Press, 1966), pp. 263–74, to show that unrestricted quantification into causal contexts leads to difficulties. His argument is in turn a direct adaptation of Quine's (*Word and Object* (Cambridge, Mass.: MIT Press, 1960), pp. 197–8) to show that (logical) modal distinctions collapse under certain natural assumptions. My argument derives directly from Frege.

7 A familiar device I use for testing hypotheses about logical grammar is translation into standard quantificational form; since the semantics of such languages is transparent, translation into them is a way of providing a semantic theory (a theory of the logical form) for what is translated. In this employment, canonical notation is not to be conceived as an improvement on the vernacular, but as a comment on it.

For elaboration and defense of the view of events sketched in this section, see my "The logical form of action sentences," in Nicholas Rescher (ed.), *The Logic of Action and Preference*, (Pittsburgh: Pittsburgh University Press, 1967).

8 J. S. Mill, *A System of Logic* (orig. pub. 1843; London: Routledge & Sons, 1872), bk III, ch. 5, sect. 3.

9 Here I am indebted to Professor Carl Hempel, and in the next sentence to John Wallace.

10 Clearly this account cannot be taken as a definition of the causal relation. Not only is there the inherently vague quantification over expressions (of what language?), but there is also the problem of spelling out the "suitable restrictions."

11 The thought in these paragraphs, like much more that appears here, was first adumbrated in my "Actions, reasons, and causes," *Journal of Philosophy* 60/23 (7 Nov. 1963), pp. 685–700, esp. pp. 696–9; repr. in Bernard Berofsky (ed.), *Free Will and Determinism*, (New York: Harper & Row, 1966). This conception of causality was subsequently discussed and, with various modifications, employed by Samuel Gorovitz, "Causal judgments and causal explanations," *Journal of Philosophy* 62/23 (2 Dec. 1965), pp. 695–711, and by Bernard Berofsky, "Causality and general laws," *Journal of Philosophy*, 63/6 (17 Mar. 1966), pp. 148–57.

12 See C. J. Ducasse, "Critique of Hume's conception of causality," *Journal of Philosophy* 63/6 (17 Mar. 1966); pp. 141–8; *idem, Causation and the Types of Necessity* (Seattle: University of Washington Press, 1924); *idem, Nature, Mind, and Death* (La Salle, Ill.: Open Court, 1951), pt 2. I have omitted from my "second account" much that Ducasse says that is not consistent with Hume.

13 Zeno Vendler has ingeniously marshaled the linguistic evidence for a deep distinction, in our use of 'cause', 'effect', and related words, between occurrences of verb-nominalizations that are fact-like or propositional, and occurrences that are event-like. (See Zeno Vendler, "Effects, results and consequences," in R. J. Butler (ed.), *Analytic Philosophy* (New York: Barnes & Noble, 1962), pp. 1–15.) Vendler concludes that the 'caused' of 'John's action caused the disturbance' is always flanked by expressions used in the propositional or fact-like sense, whereas 'was an effect of' or 'was due to' in 'The shaking of the earth was an effect of (was due to) the explosion' is flanked by expressions in the event-like sense. My distinction between essentially sentential expressions and the expressions that refer to events is much the same as Vendler's and owes much to him, though I have used more traditional semantic tools and have interpreted the evidence differently.

My suggestion that 'caused' is sometimes a relation, sometimes a connective, with corresponding changes in the interpretation of the expressions flanking it, has much in common with the thesis of J. M. Shorter's "Causality, and a method of analysis," in *Analytic Philosophy*, II, 1965, pp. 145–57.

34

Causation

David Lewis

Hume defined causation twice over. He wrote: "we may define a cause to be *an object followed by another, and where all the objects, similar to the first, are followed by objects similar to the second.* Or, in other words, *where, if the first object had not been, the second never had existed.*"[1]

Descendants of Hume's first definition still dominate the philosophy of causation: a causal succession is supposed to be a succession that instantiates a regularity. To be sure, there have been improvements. Nowadays we try to distinguish the regularities that count – the "causal laws" – from mere accidental regularities of succession. We subsume causes and effects under regularities by means of descriptions they satisfy, not by overall similarity. And we allow a cause to be only one indispensable part, not the whole, of the total situation that is followed by the effect in accordance with a law. In present-day regularity analyses, a cause is defined (roughly) as any member of any minimal set of actual conditions that are jointly sufficient, given the laws, for the existence of the effect.

More precisely, let C be the proposition that c exists (or occurs), and let E be the proposition that e exists. Then c causes e, according to a typical regularity analysis,[2] iff (1) C and E are true; and (2) for some nonempty set $\mathfrak{L}$ of true law-propositions and some set $\mathfrak{F}$ of true propositions of part-

icular fact, $\mathfrak{L}$ and $\mathfrak{F}$ jointly imply $C \supset E$, although $\mathfrak{L}$ and $\mathfrak{F}$ jointly do not imply E, and $\mathfrak{F}$ alone does not imply $C \supset E$.[3]

Much needs doing, and much has been done, to turn definitions like this one into defensible analyses. Many problems have been overcome. Others remain: in particular, regularity analyses tend to confuse causation itself with various other causal relations. If c belongs to a minimal set of conditions jointly sufficient for e, given the laws, then c may well be a genuine cause of e. But c might rather be an effect of e: one which could not, given the laws and some of the actual circumstances, have occurred otherwise than by being caused by e. Or c might be an epiphenomenon of the causal history of e: a more or less inefficacious effect of some genuine cause of e. Or c might be a preempted potential cause of e: something that did not cause e, but that would have done so in the absence of whatever really did cause e.

It remains to be seen whether any regularity analysis can succeed in distinguishing genuine causes from effects, epiphenomena, and preempted potential causes – and whether it can succeed without falling victim to worse problems, without piling on the epicycles, and without departing from the fundamental idea that causation is instantiation of regularities. I have no proof that regularity analyses are beyond repair, nor any space to review the repairs that have been tried. Suffice it to say that the prospects look dark. I think it is time to give up and try something else.

A promising alternative is not far to seek. Hume's "other words" – that if the cause had not

Originally published in *Journal of Philosophy* 70 (1973), pp. 556–67. Copyright © by David Lewis. Reprinted by permission of the author and Columbia University Press.

been, the effect never had existed – are no mere restatement of his first definition. They propose something altogether different: a counterfactual analysis of causation.

The proposal has not been well received. True, we do know that causation has something or other to do with counterfactuals. We think of a cause as something that makes a difference, and the difference it makes must be a difference from what would have happened without it. Had it been absent, its effects – some of them, at least, and usually all – would have been absent as well. Yet it is one thing to mention these platitudes now and again, and another thing to rest an analysis on them. That has not seemed worthwhile.[4] We have learned all too well that counterfactuals are ill understood, wherefore it did not seem that much understanding could be gained by using them to analyze causation or anything else. Pending a better understanding of counterfactuals, moreover, we had no way to fight seeming counterexamples to a counterfactual analysis.

But counterfactuals need not remain ill understood, I claim, unless we cling to false preconceptions about what it would be like to understand them. Must an adequate understanding make no reference to unactualized possibilities? Must it assign sharply determinate truth-conditions? Must it connect counterfactuals rigidly to covering laws? Then none will be forthcoming. So much the worse for those standards of adequacy. Why not take counterfactuals at face value: as statements about possible alternatives to the actual situation, somewhat vaguely specified, in which the actual laws may or may not remain intact? There are now several such treatments of counterfactuals, differing only in details.[5] If they are right, then sound foundations have been laid for analyses that use counterfactuals.

In this paper, I shall state a counterfactual analysis, not very different from Hume's second definition, of some sorts of causation. Then I shall try to show how this analysis works to distinguish genuine causes from effects, epiphenomena, and preempted potential causes.

My discussion will be incomplete in at least four ways. Explicit preliminary settings-aside may prevent confusion.

(1)   I shall confine myself to causation among *events*, in the everyday sense of the word: flashes, battles, conversations, impacts, strolls, deaths, touchdowns, falls, kisses, and the like. Not that events are the only things that can cause or be caused; but I have no full list of the others, and no good umbrella-term to cover them all.

(2)   My analysis is meant to apply to causation in particular cases. It is not an analysis of causal generalizations. Presumably those are quantified statements involving causation among particular events (or non-events), but it turns out not to be easy to match up the causal generalizations of natural language with the available quantified forms. A sentence of the form "C-events cause E-events," for instance, can mean any of

(a)   For some c in C and some e in E, c causes e.

(b)   For every e in E, there is some c in C such that c causes e.

(c)   For every c in C, there is some e in E such that c causes e.

not to mention further ambiguities. Worse still, "Only C-events cause E-events" ought to mean

(d)   For every c, if there is some e in E such that c causes e, then c is in C.

if "only" has its usual meaning. But no; it unambiguously means (b) instead! These problems are not about causation, but about our idioms of quantification.

(3)   We sometimes single out one among all the causes of some event and call it "the" cause, as if there were no others. Or we single out a few as the "causes," calling the rest mere "causal factors" or "causal conditions." Or we speak of the "decisive" or "real" or "principal" cause. We may select the abnormal or extraordinary causes, or those under human control, or those we deem good or bad, or just those we want to talk about. I have nothing to say about these principles of invidious discrimination.[6] I am concerned with the prior question of what it is to be one of the causes (unselectively speaking). My analysis is meant to capture a broad and nondiscriminatory concept of causation.

(4)   I shall be content, for now, if I can give an analysis of causation that works properly under determinism. By determinism I do not mean any thesis of universal causation, or universal predictability-in-principle, but rather this: the prevailing laws of nature are such that there do not exist any two possible worlds which are exactly alike up to some time, which differ thereafter, and in which those laws are never violated. Perhaps by ignoring indeterminism I squander the most striking advantage of a counterfactual analysis over a regularity analysis: that it allows undetermined events

to be caused.[7] I fear, however, that my present analysis cannot yet cope with all varieties of causation under indeterminism. The needed repair would take us too far into disputed questions about the foundations of probability.

Comparative Similarity

To begin, I take as primitive a relation of *comparative overall similarity* among possible worlds. We may say that one world is *closer to actuality* than another if the first resembles our actual world more than the second does, taking account of all the respects of similarity and difference and balancing them off one against another.

(More generally, an arbitrary world w can play the role of our actual world. In speaking of our actual world without knowing just which world is ours, I am in effect generalizing over all worlds. We really need a three-place relation: world w_1 is closer to world w than world w_2 is. I shall henceforth leave this generality tacit.)

I have not said just how to balance the respects of comparison against each other, so I have not said just what our relation of comparative similarity is to be. Not for nothing did I call it primitive. But I have said what *sort* of relation it is, and we are familiar with relations of that sort. We do make judgments of comparative overall similarity – of people, for instance – by balancing off many respects of similarity and difference. Often our mutual expectations about the weighting factors are definite and accurate enough to permit communication. I shall have more to say later about the way the balance must go in particular cases to make my analysis work. But the vagueness of overall similarity will not be entirely resolved. Nor should it be. The vagueness of similarity does infect causation, and no correct analysis can deny it.

The respects of similarity and difference that enter into the overall similarity of worlds are many and varied. In particular, similarities in matters of particular fact trade off against similarities of law. The prevailing laws of nature are important to the character of a world; so similarities of law are weighty. Weighty, but not sacred. We should not take it for granted that a world that conforms perfectly to our actual laws is *ipso facto* closer to actuality than any world where those laws are violated in any way at all. It depends on the nature and extent of the violation, on the place of the violated laws in the total system of laws of nature, and on

the countervailing similarities and differences in other respects. Likewise, similarities or differences of particular fact may be more or less weighty, depending on their nature and extent. Comprehensive and exact similarities of particular fact throughout large spatiotemporal regions seem to have special weight. It may be worth a small miracle to prolong or expand a region of perfect match.

Our relation of comparative similarity should meet two formal constraints. (1) It should be a weak ordering of the worlds: an ordering in which ties are permitted, but any two worlds are comparable. (2) Our actual world should be closest to actuality, resembling itself more than any other world resembles it. We do *not* impose the further constraint that for any set A of worlds there is a unique closest A-world, or even a set of A-worlds tied for closest. Why not an infinite sequence of closer and closer A-worlds, but no closest?

Counterfactuals and Counterfactual Dependence

Given any two propositions A and C, we have their *counterfactual* $A \mathbin{\square\!\!\rightarrow} C$: the proposition that if A were true, then C would also be true. The operation $\mathbin{\square\!\!\rightarrow}$ is defined by a rule of truth, as follows. $A \mathbin{\square\!\!\rightarrow} C$ is true (at a world w) iff either (1) there are no possible A-worlds (in which case $A \mathbin{\square\!\!\rightarrow} C$ is *vacuous*), or (2) some A-world where C holds is closer (to w) than is any A-world where C does not hold. In other words, a counterfactual is nonvacuously true iff it takes less of a departure from actuality to make the consequent true along with the antecedent than it does to make the antecedent true without the consequent.

We did not assume that there must always be one or more closest A-worlds. But if there are, we can simplify: $A \mathbin{\square\!\!\rightarrow} C$ is nonvacuously true iff C holds at all the closest A-worlds.

We have not presupposed that A is false. If A is true, then our actual world is the closest A-world, so $A \mathbin{\square\!\!\rightarrow} C$ is true iff C is. Hence $A \mathbin{\square\!\!\rightarrow} C$ implies the material conditional $A \supset C$; and A and C jointly imply $A \mathbin{\square\!\!\rightarrow} C$.

Let $A_1, A_2, \ldots$ be a family of possible propositions, no two of which are compossible; let $C_1, C_2, \ldots$ be another such family (of equal size). Then if all the counterfactuals $A_1 \mathbin{\square\!\!\rightarrow} C_1$, $A_2 \mathbin{\square\!\!\rightarrow} C_2, \ldots$ between corresponding propositions in the two families are true, we shall say that the C's *depend counterfactually* on the A's. We can say it like this in ordinary language: whether C_1 or C_2 or ... depends (counterfactually) on whether A_1 or A_2 or ....

Counterfactual dependence between large families of alternatives is characteristic of processes of measurement, perception, or control. Let $R_1, R_2, ...$ be propositions specifying the alternative readings of a certain barometer at a certain time. Let $P_1, P_2, ...$ specify the corresponding pressures of the surrounding air. Then, if the barometer is working properly to measure the pressure, the R's must depend counterfactually on the P's. As we say it: the reading depends on the pressure. Likewise, if I am seeing at a certain time, then my visual impressions must depend counterfactually, over a wide range of alternative possibilities, on the scene before my eyes. And if I am in control over what happens in some respect, then there must be a double counterfactual dependence, again over some fairly wide range of alternatives. The outcome depends on what I do, and that in turn depends on which outcome I want.[8]

Causal Dependence among Events

If a family $C_1, C_2, ...$ depends counterfactually on a family $A_1, A_2, ...$ in the sense just explained, we will ordinarily be willing to speak also of causal dependence. We say, for instance, that the barometer reading depends causally on the pressure, that my visual impressions depend causally on the scene before my eyes, or that the outcome of something under my control depends causally on what I do. But there are exceptions. Let $G_1, G_2, ...$ be alternative possible laws of gravitation, differing in the value of some numerical constant. Let M_1 $M_2, ...$ be suitable alternative laws of planetary motion. Then the M's may depend counterfactually on the G's, but we would not call this dependence causal. Such exceptions as this, however, do not involve any sort of dependence among distinct particular events. The hope remains that causal dependence among events, at least, may be analyzed simply as counterfactual dependence.

We have spoken thus far of counterfactual dependence among propositions, not among events. Whatever particular events may be, presumably they are not propositions. But that is no problem, since they can at least be paired with propositions. To any possible event e, there corres-ponds the proposition $O(e)$ that holds at all and only those worlds where e occurs. This $O(e)$ is the proposition that e occurs.[9] (If no two events occur at exactly the same worlds – if, that is, there are no absolutely necessary connections between distinct events – we may add that this correspondence of events and propositions is one to one.) Counterfactual dependence among events is simply counterfactual dependence among the corresponding propositions.

Let $c_1, c_2, ...$ and $e_1, e_2, ...$ be distinct possible events such that no two of the c's and no two of the e's are compossible. Then I say that the family $e_1, e_2, ...$ of events *depends causally* on the family $c_1, c_2, ...$ iff the family $O(e_1), O(e_2), ...$ of propositions depends counterfactually on the family $O(c_1), O(c_2), ...$. As we say it: whether e_1 or e_2 or... occurs depends on whether c_1 or c_2 or ... occurs.

We can also define a relation of dependence among single events rather than families. Let c and e be two distinct possible particular events. Then e *depends causally* on c iff the family $O(e)$, $\sim O(e)$ depends counterfactually on the family $O(c), \sim O(c)$. As we say it: whether e occurs or not depends on whether c occurs or not. The dependence consists in the truth of two counterfactuals: $O(c) \rightarrow O(e)$ and $\sim O(c) \rightarrow \sim O(e)$. There are two cases. If c and e do not actually occur, then the second counterfactual is automatically true because its antecedent and consequent are true: so e depends causally on c iff the first counterfactual holds. That is, iff e would have occurred if c had occurred. But if c and e are actual events, then it is the first counterfactual that is automatically true. Then e depends causally on c iff, if c had not been, e never had existed. I take Hume's second definition as my definition not of causation itself, but of causal dependence among actual events.

Causation

Causal dependence among actual events implies causation. If c and e are two actual events such that e would not have occurred without c, then c is a cause of e. But I reject the converse. Causation must always be transitive; causal dependence may not be; so there can be causation without causal dependence. Let c, d, and e be three actual events such that d would not have occurred without c, and e would not have occurred without d. Then c is a cause of e even if e would still have occurred (otherwise caused) without c.

We extend causal dependence to a transitive relation in the usual way. Let $c, d, e, \ldots$ be a finite sequence of actual particular events such that d depends causally on c, e on d, and so on throughout. Then this sequence is a *causal chain*. Finally, one event is a *cause* of another iff there exists a causal chain leading from the first to the second. This completes my counterfactual analysis of causation.

Counterfactual versus Nomic Dependence

It is essential to distinguish counterfactual and causal dependence from what I shall call *nomic dependence*. The family $C_1, C_2, \ldots$ of propositions depends nomically on the family $A_1, A_2, \ldots$ iff there are a nonempty set $\mathfrak{L}$ of true law-propositions and a set $\mathfrak{F}$ of true propositions of particular fact such that $\mathfrak{L}$ and $\mathfrak{F}$ jointly imply (but $\mathfrak{F}$ alone does not imply) all the material conditionals $A_1 \supset C_1$, $A_2 \supset C_2, \ldots$ between the corresponding propositions in the two families. (Recall that these same material conditionals are implied by the counterfactuals that would comprise a counterfactual dependence.) We shall say also that the nomic dependence holds *in virtue* of the premise sets $\mathfrak{L}$ and $\mathfrak{F}$.

Nomic and counterfactual dependence are related as follows. Say that a proposition B is *counterfactually independent* of the family $A_1, A_2, \ldots$ of alternatives iff B would hold no matter which of the A's were true – that is, iff the counterfactuals $A_1 \Box\!\!\rightarrow B$, $A_2 \Box\!\!\rightarrow B, \ldots$ all hold. If the C's depend nomically on the A's in virtue of the premise sets $\mathfrak{L}$ and $\mathfrak{F}$, and if in addition (all members of) $\mathfrak{L}$ and $\mathfrak{F}$ are counterfactually independent of the A's, then it follows that the C's depend counterfactually on the A's. In that case, we may regard the nomic dependence in virtue of $\mathfrak{L}$ and $\mathfrak{F}$ as explaining the counterfactual dependence. Often, perhaps always, counterfactual dependences may be thus explained. But the requirement of counterfactual independence is indispensable. Unless $\mathfrak{L}$ and $\mathfrak{F}$ meet that requirement, nomic dependence in virtue of $\mathfrak{L}$ and $\mathfrak{F}$ does not imply counterfactual dependence, and, if there is counterfactual dependence anyway, does not explain it.

Nomic dependence is reversible, in the following sense. If the family $C_1, C_2, \ldots$ depends nomically on the family $A_1, A_2, \ldots$ in virtue of $\mathfrak{L}$ and $\mathfrak{F}$, then also $A_1, A_2, \ldots$ depends nomically on the family $AC_1, AC_2, \ldots$, in virtue of $\mathfrak{L}$ and $\mathfrak{F}$, where A is

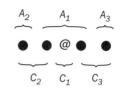

Figure 34.1

the disjunction $A_1 \vee A_2 \vee \ldots$. Is counterfactual dependence likewise reversible? That does not follow. For, even if $\mathfrak{L}$ and $\mathfrak{F}$ are independent of $A_1, A_2, \ldots$ and hence establish the counterfactual dependence of the C's on the A's, still they may fail to be independent of $AC_1, AC_2, \ldots$, and hence may fail to establish the reverse counterfactual dependence of the A's on the AC's. Irreversible counterfactual dependence is shown in figure 34.1: @ is our actual world, the dots are the other worlds, and distance on the page represents similarity "distance."

The counterfactuals $A_1 \Box\!\!\rightarrow C_1$, $A_2 \Box\!\!\rightarrow C_2$, and $A_3 \Box\!\!\rightarrow C_3$ hold at the actual world; wherefore the C's depend on the A's. But we do not have the reverse dependence of the A's on the AC's, since instead of the needed $AC_2 \Box\!\!\rightarrow A_2$ and $AC_3 \Box\!\!\rightarrow A_3$ we have $AC_2 \Box\!\!\rightarrow A_1$ and $AC_3 \Box\!\!\rightarrow A_1$.

Just such irreversibility is commonplace. The barometer reading depends counterfactually on the pressure – that is as clear-cut as counterfactuals ever get – but does the pressure depend counterfactually on the reading? If the reading had been higher, would the pressure have been higher? Or would the barometer have been malfunctioning? The second sounds better: a higher reading would have been an incorrect reading. To be sure, there are actual laws and circumstances that imply and explain the actual accuracy of the barometer, but these are no more sacred than the actual laws and circumstances that imply and explain the actual pressure. Less sacred, in fact. When something must give way to permit a higher reading, we find it less of a departure from actuality to hold the pressure fixed and sacrifice the accuracy, rather than vice versa. It is not hard to see why. The barometer, being more localized and more delicate than the weather, is more vulnerable to slight departures from actuality.[10]

We can now explain why regularity analyses of causation (among events, under determinism) work as well as they do. Suppose that event c causes event e according to the sample regularity analysis that I gave at the beginning of this paper, in virtue of premise sets $\mathfrak{L}$ and $\mathfrak{F}$. It follows that $\mathfrak{L}$, $\mathfrak{F}$, and $\sim O(c)$ jointly do not imply $O(e)$. Strengthen this: suppose further that they do imply $\sim O(e)$. If so, the family $O(e)$, $\sim O(e)$ depends nomically on the family $O(c)$, $\sim O(c)$ in virtue of $\mathfrak{L}$ and $\mathfrak{F}$. Add one more supposition: that $\mathfrak{L}$ and $\mathfrak{F}$ are counterfactually independent of $O(c)$, $\sim O(c)$. Then it follows according to my counterfactual analysis that e depends counterfactually and causally on c, and hence that c causes e. If I am right, the regularity analysis gives conditions that are almost but not quite sufficient for explicable causal dependence. That is not quite the same thing as causation; but causation without causal dependence is scarce, and if there is inexplicable causal dependence we are (understandably!) unaware of it.[11]

Effects and Epiphenomena

I return now to the problems I raised against regularity analyses, hoping to show that my counterfactual analysis can overcome them.

The *problem of effects*, as it confronts a counterfactual analysis, is as follows. Suppose that c causes a subsequent event e, and that e does not also cause c. (I do not rule out closed causal loops a priori, but this case is not to be one.) Suppose further that, given the laws and some of the actual circumstances, c could not have failed to cause e. It seems to follow that if the effect e had not occurred, then its cause c would not have occurred. We have a spurious reverse causal dependence of c on e, contradicting our supposition that e did not cause c.

The *problem of epiphenomena*, for a counterfactual analysis, is similar. Suppose that e is an epiphenomenal effect of a genuine cause c of an effect f. That is, c causes first e and then f, but e does not cause f. Suppose further that, given the laws and some of the actual circumstances, c could not have failed to cause e; and that, given the laws and others of the circumstances, f could not have been caused otherwise than by c. It seems to follow that if the epiphenomenon e had not occurred, then its cause c would not have occurred and the further effect f of that same cause would not have occurred either. We have a spurious causal dependence of f on e, contradicting our supposition that e did not cause f.

One might be tempted to solve the problem of effects by brute force: insert into the analysis a stipulation that a cause must always precede its effect (and perhaps a parallel stipulation for causal dependence). I reject this solution. (1) It is worthless against the closely related problem of epiphenomena, since the epiphenomenon e does precede its spurious effect f. (2) It rejects a priori certain legitimate physical hypotheses that posit backward or simultaneous causation. (3) It trivializes any theory that seeks to define the forward direction of time as the predominant direction of causation.

The proper solution to both problems, I think, is flatly to deny the counterfactuals that cause the trouble. If e had been absent, it is not that c would have been absent (and with it f, in the second case). Rather, c would have occurred just as it did but would have failed to cause e. It is less of a departure from actuality to get rid of e by holding c fixed and giving up some or other of the laws and circumstances in virtue of which c could not have failed to cause e, rather than to hold those laws and circumstances fixed and get rid of e by going back and abolishing its cause c. (In the second case, it would of course be pointless not to hold f fixed along with c.) The causal dependence of e on c is the same sort of irreversible counterfactual dependence that we have considered already.

To get rid of an actual event e with the least overall departure from actuality, it will normally be best not to diverge at all from the actual course of events until just before the time of e. The longer we wait, the more we prolong the spatiotemporal region of perfect match between our actual world and the selected alternative. Why diverge sooner rather than later? Not to avoid violations of laws of nature. Under determinism *any* divergence, soon or late, requires some violation of the actual laws. If the laws were held sacred, there would be no way to get rid of e without changing all of the past; and nothing guarantees that the change could be kept negligible except in the recent past. That would mean that if the present were ever so slightly different, then all of the past would have been different – which is absurd. So the laws are not sacred. Violation of laws is a matter of degree. Until we get up to the time immediately before e is to occur, there is no general reason why a later divergence to avert e should need a more severe violation than an earlier one. Perhaps there are special reasons in special cases – but then these may be cases of backward causal dependence.

Preemption

Suppose that c_1 occurs and causes e; and that c_2 also occurs and does not cause e, but would have caused

e if c_1 had been absent. Thus c_2 is a potential alternate cause of e, but is preempted by the actual cause c_1. We may say that c_1 and c_2 overdetermine e, but they do so asymmetrically.[12] In virtue of what difference does c_1 but not c_2 cause e?

As far as causal dependence goes, there is no difference: e depends neither on c_1 nor on c_2. If either one had not occurred, the other would have sufficed to cause e. So the difference must be that, thanks to c_1 there is no causal chain from c_2 to e; whereas there is a causal chain of two or more steps from c_1 to e. Assume for simplicity that two steps are enough. Then e depends causally on some intermediate event d, and d in turn depends on c_1. Causal dependence is here intransitive: c_1 causes e

via d even though e would still have occurred without c_1.

So far, so good. It remains only to deal with the objection that e does *not* depend causally on d, because if d had been absent, then c_1 would have been absent, and c_2, no longer preempted, would have caused e. We may reply by denying the claim that if d had been absent, then c_1 would have been absent. That is the very same sort of spurious reverse dependence of cause on effect that we have just rejected in simpler cases. I rather claim that if d had been absent, c_1 would somehow have failed to cause d. But c_1 would still have been there to interfere with c_2 so e would not have occurred.

Notes

I thank the American Council of Learned Societies, Princeton University, and the National Science Foundation for research support.

1 David Hume, *An Enquiry Concerning Human Understanding*, sec. 7.
2 Not one that has been proposed by any actual author in just this form, so far as I know.
3 I identify a *proposition*, as is becoming usual, with the set of possible worlds where it is true. It is not a linguistic entity. Truth-functional operations on propositions are the appropriate Boolean operations on sets of worlds; logical relations among propositions are relations of inclusion, overlap, etc. among sets. A sentence of a language *expresses* a proposition iff the sentence and the proposition are true at exactly the same worlds. No ordinary language will provide sentences to express all propositions; there will not be enough sentences to go around.
4 One exception: Ardon Lyon, "Causality," *British Journal for the Philosophy of Science*, 18/1 (May 1967), pp. 1–20.
5 See, for instance, Robert Stalnaker, "A theory of conditionals," in Nicholas Rescher (ed.), *Studies in Logical Theory* (Oxford: Blackwell, 1968); and my *Counterfactuals* (Oxford: Blackwell, 1973).
6 Except that Morton G. White's discussion of causal selection, in *Foundations of Historical Knowledge* (New York: Harper & Row, 1965), pp. 105–81, would meet my needs, despite the fact that it is based on a regularity analysis.
7 That this ought to be allowed is argued in G. E. M. Anscombe, *Causality and Determination: An Inaugural Lecture* (Cambridge: Cambridge University Press, 1971); and in Fred Dretske and Aaron Snyder, "Causal irregularity," *Philosophy of Science*, 39/1 (Mar. 1972), pp. 69–71.

8 Analyses in terms of counterfactual dependence are found in two papers of Alvin I. Goldman: "Toward a theory of social power," *Philosophical Studies* 23 (1972), pp. 221–68; and "Discrimination and perceptual knowledge," presented at the 1972 Chapel Hill Colloquium.
9 Beware: if we refer to a particular event e by means of some description that e satisfies, then we must take care not to confuse $O(e)$, the proposition that e itself occurs, with the different proposition that some event or other occurs which satisfies the description. It is a contingent matter, in general, what events satisfy what descriptions. Let e be the death of Socrates – the death he actually died, to be distinguished from all the different deaths he might have died instead. Suppose that Socrates had fled, only to be eaten by a lion. Then e would not have occurred, and $O(e)$ would have been false; but a different event would have satisfied the description "the death of Socrates" that I used to refer to e. Or suppose that Socrates had lived and died just as he actually did, and afterwards was resurrected and killed again and resurrected again, and finally became immortal. Then no event would have satisfied the description. (Even if the temporary deaths are real deaths, neither of the two can be *the* death.) But e would have occurred, and $O(e)$ would have been true. Call a description of an event e *rigid* iff (1) nothing but e could possibly satisfy it, and (2) e could not possibly occur without satisfying it. I have claimed that even such commonplace descriptions as "the death of Socrates" are nonrigid, and in fact I think that rigid descriptions of events are hard to find. That would be a problem for anyone who needed to associate with every possible event e a sentence $\Phi(e)$ true at all and only those worlds where e occurs. But we need no such sentences – only propositions, which may or may not have expressions in our language.

10 Granted, there are contexts or changes of wording that would incline us the other way. For some reason, "If the reading had been higher, that would have been because the pressure was higher" invites my assent more than "If the reading had been higher, the pressure would have been higher." The counterfactuals from readings to pressures are much less clear-cut than those from pressures to readings. But it is enough that some legitimate resolutions of vagueness give an irreversible dependence of readings on pressures. Those are the resolutions we want at present, even if they are not favored in all contexts.

11 I am not here proposing a repaired regularity analysis. The repaired analysis would gratuitously rule out inexplicable causal dependence, which seems bad. Nor would it be squarely in the tradition of regularity analyses any more. Too much else would have been added.

12 I shall not discuss symmetrical cases of overdetermination, in which two overdetermining factors have equal claim to count as causes. For me these are useless as test cases because I lack firm naïve opinions about them.

35

Causal Connections

Wesley C. Salmon

Basic Problems

As a point of departure for the discussion of causality, it is appropriate for us to take a look at the reasons that have led philosophers to develop theories of explanation that do not require causal components. To Aristotle and Laplace it must have seemed evident that scientific explanations are inevitably causal in character. Laplacian determinism is causal determinism, and I know of no reason to suppose that Laplace made any distinction between causal and noncausal laws.

It might be initially tempting to suppose that all laws of nature are causal laws, and that explanation in terms of laws is *ipso facto* causal explanation. It is, however, quite easy to find law-statements that do not express causal relations. Many regularities in nature are not direct cause–effect relations. Night follows day, and day follows night; nevertheless, day does not cause night, and night does not cause day. Kepler's laws of planetary motion describe the orbits of the planets, but they offer no causal account of these motions.[1] Similarly, the ideal gas law

$$PV = nRT$$

relates pressure (P), volume (V), and temperature (T) for a given sample of gas, and it tells how these quantities vary as functions of one another, but it says nothing whatever about causal relations among them. An increase in pressure might be brought about by moving a piston so as to decrease the volume, or it might be caused by an increase in temperature. The law itself is entirely noncommittal concerning such causal considerations. Each of these regularities – the alternation of night with day; the regular motions of the planets; and the functional relationship among temperature, pressure, and volume of an ideal gas – can be *explained* causally, but they do not *express* causal relations. Moreover, they do not afford causal explanations of the events subsumed under them. For this reason, it seems to me, their value in providing scientific explanations of particular events is, at best, severely limited. These are regularities that need to be explained, but that do not, by themselves, do much in the way of explaining other phenomena.

To untutored common sense, and to many scientists uncorrupted by philosophical training, it is evident that causality plays a central role in scientific explanation. An appropriate answer to an explanation-seeking why-question normally begins with the word "because," and the causal involvements of the answer are usually not hard to find.[2] The concept of causality has, however, been philosophically suspect ever since David Hume's devastating critique, first published in 1739 in his *Treatise of Human Nature*. In the "Abstract" of that work, Hume wrote:

> Here is a billiard ball lying on the table, and another ball moving toward it with rapidity.

Originally published in *Scientific Explanation and the Causal Structure of the World* (1984). Copyright © by Princeton University Press. Reprinted by permission of Princeton University Press.

They strike; the ball which was formerly at rest now acquires a motion. This is as perfect an instance of the relations of cause and effect as any which we know either by sensation or reflection. Let us therefore examine it. It is evident that the two balls touched one another before the motion was communicated, and that there was no interval betwixt the shock and the motion. *Contiguity* in time and place is therefore a requisite circumstance to the operation of all causes. It is evident, likewise, that the motion which was the cause is prior to the motion which was the effect. *Priority* in time is, therefore, another requisite circumstance in every cause. But this is not all. Let us try any other balls of the same kind in a like situation, and we shall always find that the impulse of the one produces motion in the other. Here, therefore, is a *third* circumstance, viz., that of *constant conjunction* betwixt the cause and the effect. Every object like the cause produces always some object like the effect. Beyond these three circumstances of contiguity, priority, and constant conjunction I can discover nothing in this cause.[3]

This discussion is, of course, more notable for factors Hume was unable to find than for those he enumerated. In particular, he could not discover any 'necessary connections' relating causes to effects, or any 'hidden powers' by which the cause 'brings about' the effect. This classic account of causation is rightly regarded as a landmark in philosophy.

In an oft-quoted remark that stands at the beginning of a famous 1913 essay, Bertrand Russell warns philosophers about the appeal to causality:

All philosophers, of every school, imagine that causation is one of the fundamental axioms or postulates of science, yet, oddly enough, in advanced sciences such as gravitational astronomy, the word "cause" never occurs. . . . To me it seems that . . . the reason why physics has ceased to look for causes is that, in fact, there are no such things. The law of causality, I believe, like much that passes muster among philosophers, is a relic of a bygone age, surviving, like the monarchy, only because it is erroneously supposed to do no harm.[4]

It is hardly surprising that, in the light of Hume's critique and Russell's resounding condemnation,

philosophers with an empiricist bent have been rather wary of the use of causal concepts. By 1927, however, when he wrote *The Analysis of Matter*,[5] Russell recognized that causality plays a fundamental role in physics; in *Human Knowledge*, four of the five postulates he advanced as a basis for all scientific knowledge make explicit reference to causal relations.[6] It should be noted, however, that the causal concepts he invokes are *not* the same as the traditional philosophical ones he had rejected earlier.[7] In contemporary physics, causality is a pervasive ingredient.[8]

Two Basic Concepts

A standard picture of causality has been around at least since the time of Hume. The general idea is that we have two (or more) distinct events that bear some sort of cause – effect relations to one another. There has, of course, been considerable controversy regarding the nature of both the relation and the relata. It has sometimes been maintained, for instance, that facts or propositions (rather than events) are the sorts of entities that can constitute relata. It has long been disputed whether causal relations can be said to obtain among individual events, or whether statements about cause–effect relations implicitly involve assertions about classes of events. The relation itself has sometimes been taken to be that of sufficient condition, sometimes necessary condition, or perhaps a combination of the two.[9] Some authors have even proposed that certain sorts of statistical relations constitute causal relations.

The foregoing characterization obviously fits J. L. Mackie's sophisticated account in terms of INUS conditions – that is, *insufficient* but *nonredundant* parts of *unnecessary* but *sufficient* conditions.[10] The idea is this. There are several different causes that might account for the burning down of a house: careless smoking in bed, an electrical short circuit, arson, being struck by lightning. With certain obvious qualifications, each of these may be taken as a sufficient condition for the fire, but none of them can be considered necessary. Moreover, each of the sufficient conditions cited involves a fairly complex combination of conditions, each of which constitutes a nonredundant part of the particular sufficient condition under consideration. The careless smoker, for example, must fall asleep with his cigarette, and it must fall upon something flammable. It must not awaken the smoker by burning him before it falls from his hand. When the smoker does become aware of the fire, it must have progressed beyond the stage at which he can extinguish it. Any one of these necessary components of some complex sufficient condition can, under certain circumstances, qualify as a cause. According to this standard approach, events enjoy the status of fundamental entities, and these entities are 'connected' to one another by cause–effect relations.

It is my conviction that this standard view, in all of its well-known variations, is profoundly mistaken, and that a radically different notion should be developed. I shall not, at this juncture, attempt to mount arguments against the standard conception. Instead, I shall present a rather different approach for purposes of comparison. I hope that the alternative will stand on its own merits.

There are, I believe, two fundamental causal concepts that need to be explicated, and if that can be achieved, we will be in a position to deal with the problems of causality in general. The two basic concepts are *propagation* and *production*, and both are familiar to common sense. When we say that the blow of a hammer drives a nail, we mean that the impact produces penetration of the nail into the wood. When we say that a horse pulls a cart, we mean that the force exerted by the horse produces the motion of the cart. When we say that lightning ignites a forest, we mean that the electrical discharge produces a fire. When we say that a person's embarrassment was due to a thoughtless remark, we mean that an inappropriate comment produced psychological discomfort. Such examples of causal production occur frequently in everyday contexts.

Causal propagation (or transmission) is equally familiar. Experiences that we had earlier in our lives affect our current behavior. By means of memory, the influence of these past events is transmitted to the present.[11] A sonic boom makes us aware of the passage of a jet airplane overhead; a disturbance in the air is propagated from the upper atmosphere to our location on the ground. Signals transmitted from a broadcasting station are received by the radio in our home. News or music reaches us because electromagnetic waves are propagated from the transmitter to the receiver. In 1775, some Massachusetts farmers – in initiating the American Revolutionary War – "fired the shot heard 'round the world."[12] As all of these examples show, what happens at one place and time can have significant influence upon what happens at other places and times. This is possible because causal influence can be propagated through time and space. Although causal production and causal propagation are intimately related to one another, we should, I believe, resist any temptation to try to reduce one to the other.

Processes

One of the fundamental changes that I propose in approaching causality is to take processes rather than events as basic entities. I shall not attempt any rigorous definition of processes; rather, I shall cite examples and make some very informal remarks. The main difference between events and processes is that events are relatively localized in space and time, while processes have much greater temporal duration, and in many cases, much greater spatial extent. In space-time diagrams, events are represented by points, while processes are represented by lines. A baseball colliding with a window would count as an event; the baseball, traveling from the bat to the window, would constitute a process. The activation of a photocell by a pulse of light would be an event; the pulse of light, traveling, perhaps from a distant star, would be a process. A sneeze is an event. The shadow of a cloud moving across the landscape is a process. Although I shall deny that all processes qualify as causal processes, what I mean by a process is similar to what Russell characterized as a causal line:

> A causal line may always be regarded as the persistence of something – a person, a table, a photon, or what not. Throughout a given causal line, there may be constancy of quality, constancy of structure, or a gradual change of either, but not sudden changes of any considerable magnitude.[13]

Among the physically important processes are waves and material objects that persist through time. As I shall use these terms, even a material object at rest will qualify as a process.

Before attempting to develop a theory of causality in which processes, rather than events, are taken as fundamental, I should consider briefly the scientific legitimacy of this approach. In Newtonian mechanics, both spatial extent and temporal duration were absolute quantities. The length of a rigid rod did not depend upon a choice of frame of reference, nor did the duration of a process (such as the length of time between the creation and destruction of a material object). Given two events, in Newtonian mechanics, both the spatial distance and the temporal separation between them were absolute magnitudes. A 'physical thing ontology' was thus appropriate to classical physics. As everyone knows, Einstein's special theory of relativity changed all that. Both the spatial distance and the temporal separation were relativized to frames of reference. The length of a rigid rod and the duration of a temporal process varied from one frame of reference to another. However, as Minkowski showed, there is an invariant quantity – the space-time interval between two events. This quantity is independent of the frame of reference; for any two events, it has the same value in each and every inertial frame of reference. Since there are good reasons for according a fundamental physical status to invariants, it was a natural consequence of the special theory of relativity to regard the world as a collection of events that bear space-time relations to one another. These considerations offer support for what is sometimes called an 'event ontology'.

There is, however, another way (originally developed by A. A. Robb) of approaching the special theory of relativity; it is done entirely with paths of light pulses. At any point in space-time, we can construct the Minkowski light cone – a two-sheeted cone whose surface is generated by the paths of all possible light pulses that converge upon the point (past light cone) and the paths of all possible light pulses that could be emitted from the point (future light cone). When all of the light cones are given, the entire space-time structure of the world is determined.[14] But light pulses, traveling through space and time, are processes. We can, therefore, base special relativity upon a 'process ontology'. Moreover, this approach can be extended in a natural way to general relativity by taking into account the paths of freely falling material particles; these moving gravitational test particles are also processes.[15] It is, consequently, entirely legitimate to approach the space-time structure of the physical world by regarding physical processes as the basic types of physical entities. The theory of relativity does not mandate an 'event ontology'.

Whether one adopts the event-based approach or the process-based approach, causal relations must be accorded a fundamental place in the special theory of relativity. As we have seen, any given event E_0 occurring at a particular space-time point

P_0, has an associated double-sheeted light cone. All events that could have a causal influence upon E_0 are located in the interior or on the surface of the past light cone, and all events upon which E_0 could have any causal influence are located in the interior or on the surface of the future light cone. All such events are *causally connectable* with E_0. Those events that lie on the surface of either sheet of the light cone are said to have a *lightlike separation* from E_0 those that lie within either part of the cone are said to have a *timelike separation* from E_0, and those that are outside of the cone are said to have a *spacelike separation* from E_0. The Minkowski light cone can, with complete propriety, be called "the cone of causal relevance," and the entire space-time structure of special relativity can be developed on the basis of causal concepts.[16]

Special relativity demands that we make a distinction between *causal processes* and *pseudo-processes*. It is a fundamental principle of that theory that light is a *first signal* – that is, no signal can be transmitted at a velocity greater than the velocity of light in a vacuum. There are, however, certain processes that can transpire at arbitrarily high velocities – at velocities vastly exceeding that of light. This fact does not violate the basic relativistic principle, however, for these 'processes' are incapable of serving as signals or of transmitting information. Causal processes are those that are capable of transmitting signals; pseudo-processes are incapable of doing so.

Consider a simple example. Suppose that we have a very large circular building – a sort of super-Astrodome, if you will – with a spotlight mounted at its center. When the light is turned on in the otherwise darkened building, it casts a spot of light upon the wall. If we turn the light on for a brief moment, and then off again, a light pulse travels from the light to the wall. This pulse of light, traveling from the spotlight to the wall, is a paradigm of what we mean by a causal process. Suppose, further, that the spotlight is mounted on a mechanism that makes it rotate. If the light is turned on and set into rotation, the spot of light that it casts upon the wall will move around the outer wall in a highly regular fashion. This 'process' – the moving spot of light – seems to fulfill the conditions Russell used to characterize causal lines, but it is not a causal process. It is a paradigm of what we mean by a pseudo-process.

The basic method for distinguishing causal processes from pseudo-processes is the criterion of mark transmission. A causal process is capable of transmitting a mark; a pseudo-process is not. Consider, first, a pulse of light that travels from the spotlight to the wall. If we place a piece of red glass in its path at any point between the spotlight and the wall, the light pulse, which was white, becomes and remains red until it reaches the wall. A single intervention at one point in the process transforms it in a way that persists from that point on. If we had not intervened, the light pulse would have remained white during its entire journey from the spotlight to the wall. If we do intervene locally at a single place, we can produce a change that is transmitted from the point of intervention onward. We shall say, therefore, that the light pulse constitutes a causal process whether it is modified or not, since in either case it is capable of transmitting a mark. Clearly, light pulses can serve as signals and can transmit messages; remember Paul Revere, "One if by land and two if by sea."

Now, let us consider the spot of light that moves around the wall as the spotlight rotates. There are a number of ways in which we can intervene to change the spot at some point; for example, we can place a red filter at the wall with the result that the spot of light becomes red at that point. But if we make such a modification in the traveling spot, it will not be transmitted beyond the point of interaction. As soon as the light spot moves beyond the point at which the red filter was placed, it will become white again. The mark can be made, but it will not be transmitted. We have a 'process', which, in the absence of any intervention, consists of a white spot moving regularly along the wall of the building. If we intervene at some point, the 'process' will be modified *at that point*, but it will continue on beyond that point just as if no intervention had occurred. We can, of course, make the spot red at other places if we wish. We can install a red lens in the spotlight, but that does not constitute a *local* intervention at an isolated point in the process itself. We can put red filters at many places along the wall, but that would involve *many* interventions rather than a single one. We could get someone to run around the wall holding a red filter in front of the spot continuously, but that would not constitute an intervention *at a single point* in the 'process'.

This last suggestion brings us back to the subject of velocity. If the spot of light is moving rapidly, no runner could keep up with it, but perhaps a mechanical device could be set up. If, however, the spot moves too rapidly, it would be physically impossible to make the filter travel fast enough to keep pace. No material object, such as the filter, can travel at a velocity greater than that of light, but no such limitation is placed upon the spot on the wall. This can easily be seen as follows. If the spotlight rotates at a fixed rate, then it takes the spot of light a fixed amount of time to make one entire circuit around the wall. If the spotlight rotates once per second, the spot of light will travel around the wall in one second. This fact is independent of the size of the building. We can imagine that without making any change in the spotlight or its rate of rotation, the outer walls are expanded indefinitely. At a certain point, when the radius of the building is a little less than 50,000 kilometers, the spot will be traveling at the speed of light (300,000 km/sec). As the walls are moved still farther out, the velocity of the spot exceeds the speed of light.

To make this point more vivid, consider an actual example that is quite analogous to the rotating spotlight. There is a pulsar in the Crab nebula that is about 6,500 light-years away. This pulsar is thought to be a rapidly rotating neutron star that sends out a beam of radiation. When the beam is directed toward us, it sends out radiation that we detect later as a pulse. The pulses arrive at the rate of 30 per second; that is the rate at which the neutron star rotates. Now, imagine a circle drawn with the pulsar at its center, and with a radius equal to the distance from the pulsar to the earth. The electromagnetic radiation from the pulsar (which travels at the speed of light) takes 6,500 years to traverse the radius of this circle, but the 'spot' of radiation sweeps around the circumference of this circle in 1/30th of a second; at that rate, it is traveling at about 4×10^{13} times the speed of light. There is no upper limit on the speed of pseudo-processes.[17]

Another example may help to clarify this distinction. Consider a car traveling along a road on a sunny day. As the car moves at 100 km/hr, its shadow moves along the shoulder at the same speed. The moving car, like any material object, constitutes a causal process; the shadow is a pseudo-process. If the car collides with a stone wall, it will carry the marks of that collision – the dents and scratches – along with it long after the collision has taken place. If, however, only the shadow of the car collides with the stone wall, it will be deformed momentarily, but it will resume its normal shape just as soon as it has passed beyond the wall. Indeed, if the car passes a tall building that cuts it off from the sunlight, the shadow will be obliterated, but it will pop right back into existence as soon as the car has returned to the direct sunlight. If, however, the car is totally obliterated – say, by an atomic bomb blast – it will not pop back into existence as soon as the blast has subsided.

A given process, whether it be causal or pseudo, has a certain degree of uniformity – we may say, somewhat loosely, that it exhibits a certain structure. The difference between a causal process and a pseudo-process, I am suggesting, is that the causal process transmits its own structure, while the pseudo-process does not. The distinction between processes that do and those that do not transmit their own structures is revealed by the mark criterion. If a process – a causal process – is transmitting its own structure, then it will be capable of transmitting certain modifications in that structure.

In *Human Knowledge*, Russell placed great emphasis upon what he called "causal lines," which he characterized in the following terms:

A "causal line," as I wish to define the term, is a temporal series of events so related that, given some of them, something can be inferred about the others whatever may be happening elsewhere. A causal line may always be regarded as the persistence of something – a person, table, a photon, or what not. Throughout a given causal line, there may be constancy of quality, constancy of structure, or gradual change in either, but not sudden change of any considerable magnitude.[18]

He then goes on to comment upon the significance of causal lines:

That there are such more or less self-determined causal processes is in no degree logically necessary, but is, I think, one of the fundamental postulates of science. It is in virtue of the truth of this postulate – if it is true – that we are able to acquire partial knowledge in spite of our enormous ignorance.[19]

Although Russell seems clearly to intend his causal lines to be what we have called causal processes, his characterization may appear to allow pseudo-processes to qualify as well. Pseudo-processes, such as the spot of light traveling around the wall of our Astrodome, sometimes exhibit great uniformity, and their regular behavior can serve as a basis for inferring the nature of certain parts of the pseudo-process on the basis of observation of other parts. But pseudo-processes are not self-determined; the spot of light is determined by the behavior of the beacon and the beam it sends out. Moreover, the inference from one part of the pseudo-process to another is *not* reliable *regardless of what may be happening elsewhere*, for if the spotlight is switched off or covered with an opaque hood, the inference will go wrong. We may say, therefore, that our observations of the various phenomena going on in the world around us reveal processes that exhibit considerable regularity, but some of these are genuine causal processes and others are pseudo-processes. The causal processes are, as Russell says, self-determined; they transmit their own uniformities of qualitative and structural features. The regularities exhibited by the pseudo-processes, in contrast, are parasitic upon causal regularities exterior to the 'process' itself – in the case of the Astrodome, the behavior of the beacon; in the case of the shadow traveling along the roadside, the behavior of the car and the sun. The ability to transmit a mark is the criterion that distinguishes causal processes from pseudo-processes, for if the modification represented by the mark is propagated, the process is transmitting its own characteristics. Otherwise, the 'process' is not self-determined, and is not independent of what goes on elsewhere.

Although Russell's characterization of causal lines is heuristically useful, it cannot serve as a fundamental criterion for their identification for two reasons. First, it is formulated in terms of our ability to infer the nature of some portions from a knowledge of other portions. We need a criterion that does not rest upon such epistemic notions as knowledge and inference, for the existence of the vast majority of causal processes in the history of the universe is quite independent of human knowers. This aspect of the characterization could, perhaps, be restated nonanthropocentrically in terms of the persistence of objective regularities in the process. The second reason is more serious. To suggest that processes have regularities that persist "whatever may be happening elsewhere" is surely an overstatement. If an extremely massive object should happen to be located in the neighborhood of a light pulse, its path will be significantly altered. If a nuclear blast should occur in the vicinity of a mail truck, the letters that it carries will be totally destroyed. If sunspot activity reaches a high level, radio communication is affected. Notice that, in each of these cases, the factor cited does not occur or exist on the world line of the process in question. In each instance, of course, the disrupting factor initiates processes that intersect with the process in question, but that does not undermine the objection to the claim that causal processes transpire in their self-determined fashion regardless of what is happening elsewhere. A more acceptable statement might be that a causal process would persist even if it were isolated from external causal influences. This formulation, unfortunately, seems at the very least to flirt with circularity, for external causal influences must be transmitted to the locus of the process in question by means of other processes. We shall certainly want to keep clearly in mind the notion that causal processes are not parasitic upon other processes, but it does not seem likely that this rough idea could be transformed into a useful basic criterion.

It has often been suggested that the principal characteristic of causal processes is that they transmit energy. While I believe it is true that all and only causal processes transmit energy, there is, I think, a fundamental problem involved in employing this fact as a basic criterion – namely, we must have some basis for distinguishing situations in which energy is transmitted from those in which it merely appears in some regular fashion. The difficulty is easily seen in the 'Astrodome' example. As a light pulse travels from the central spotlight to the wall, it carries radiant energy; this energy is present in the various stages of the process as the pulse travels from the lamp to the wall. As the spot of light travels around the wall, energy appears at the places occupied by the spot, but we do not want to say that this energy is transmitted. The problem is to distinguish the cases in which a given bundle of energy is transmitted through a process from those in which different bundles of energy are appearing in some regular fashion. The key to this distinction is, I believe, the mark method. Just as the detective makes his mark on the murder weapon for purposes of later identification, so also do we make marks in processes so that the energy present at one space-time locale can be identified when it appears at other times and places.

A causal process is one that is self-determined and not parasitic upon other causal influences. A causal process is one that transmits energy, as well as information and causal influence. The fundamental criterion for distinguishing self-determined energy-transmitting processes from pseudo-processes is the capability of such processes of transmitting marks. In the next section, we shall deal with the concept of transmission in greater detail.

Our main concern with causal processes is their role in the propagation of causal influences; radio broadcasting presents a clear example. The transmitting station sends a carrier wave that has a certain structure – characterized by amplitude and frequency, among other things – and modifications of this wave, in the form of modulations of amplitude (AM) or frequency (FM), are imposed for the purpose of broadcasting. Processes that transmit their own structures are capable of transmitting marks, signals, information, energy, and causal influence. Such processes are the means by which causal influence is propagated in our world. Causal influences, transmitted by radio, may set your foot to tapping, or induce someone to purchase a different brand of soap, or point a television camera aboard a spacecraft toward the rings of Saturn. A causal influence transmitted by a flying arrow can pierce an apple on the head of William Tell's son. A causal influence transmitted by sound waves can make your dog come running. A causal influence transmitted by ink marks on a piece of paper can gladden one's day or break someone's heart.

It is evident, I think, that the propagation or transmission of causal influence from one place and time to another must play a fundamental role in the causal structure of the world. As I shall argue next, causal processes constitute precisely the causal connections that Hume sought, but was unable to find.

The 'At-At' Theory of Causal Propagation

In the preceding section, I invoked Reichenbach's mark criterion to make the crucial distinction between causal processes and pseudo-processes. Causal processes are distinguished from pseudo-processes in terms of their ability to transmit marks. In order to qualify as causal, a process need not actually be transmitting a mark; the requirement is that it be capable of doing so.

When we characterize causal processes partly in terms of their ability to transmit marks, we must deal explicitly with the question of whether we have violated the kinds of strictures Hume so emphatically expounded. He warned against the uncritical use of such concepts as 'power' and 'necessary connection'. Is not the *ability to transmit* a mark an example of just such a mysterious power? Kenneth Sayre expressed his misgivings on this score when, after acknowledging the distinction between causal interactions and causal processes, he wrote:

> The causal process, continuous though it may be, is made up of individual events related to others in a causal nexus . . . . it is by virtue of the relations among the members of causal series that we are enabled to make the inferences by which causal processes are characterized. . . . if we do not have an adequate conception of the relatedness between individual members in a causal series, there is a sense in which our conception of the causal process itself remains deficient.[20]

The 'at-at' theory of causal transmission is an attempt to remedy this deficiency.

Does this remedy illicitly invoke the sort of concept Hume proscribed? I think not. Ability to transmit a mark can be viewed as a particularly important species of constant conjunction – the sort of thing Hume recognized as observable and admissible. It is a matter of performing certain kinds of experiments. If we place a red filter in a light beam near its source, we can observe that the mark – redness – appears at all places to which the beam is subsequently propagated. This fact can be verified by experiments as often as we wish to perform them. If, contrariwise (returning to our Astrodome example of the preceding section), we make the spot on the wall red by placing a filter in the beam at one point just before the light strikes the wall (or by any other means we may devise), we will see that the mark – redness – is not present at all other places in which the moving spot subsequently appears on the wall. This, too, can be verified by repeated experimentation. Such facts are straightforwardly observable.

The question can still be reformulated. What do we mean when we speak of *transmission*? How does the process *make* the mark appear elsewhere within it? There is, I believe, an astonishingly simple answer. The transmission of a mark from point A in a causal process to point B in the same process *is* the fact that it appears at each point between A and B *without further interactions*. If A is the point at which the red filter is inserted into the beam going from the spotlight to the wall, and B is the point at which the beam strikes the wall, then only the interaction at A is required. If we place a white card in the beam at any point between A and B, we will find the beam red at that point.

The basic thesis about mark transmission can now be stated (in a principle I shall designate MT for "mark transmission") as follows:

MT: *Let P be a process that, in the absence of interactions with other processes, would remain uniform with respect to a characteristic Q, which it would manifest consistently over an interval that includes both of the space-time points A and B ($A \neq B$). Then, a mark (consisting of a modification of Q into Q'), which has been introduced into process P by means of a single local interaction at point A, is transmitted to point B if P manifests the modification Q' at B and at all stages of the process between A and B without additional interventions.*

This principle is clearly counterfactual, for it states explicitly that the process P would have continued to manifest the characteristic Q if the specific marking interaction had not occurred. This subjunctive formulation is required, I believe, to overcome an objection posed by Nancy Cartwright (in conversation) to previous formulations. The problem is this. Suppose our rotating beacon is casting a white spot that moves around the wall, and that we mark the spot by interposing a red filter at the wall. Suppose further, however, that a red lens has been installed in the beacon just a tiny fraction of a second earlier, so that the spot on the wall becomes red at the moment we mark it with our red filter, but it remains red from that point on because of the red lens. Under these circumstances, were it not for the counterfactual condition, it would appear that we had satisfied the requirement formulated in MT, for we have marked the spot by a single interaction at point A, and the spot remains red from that point on to any other point B we care to designate, without any additional interactions. As we have just mentioned, the installation of the red lens on the spotlight does not constitute a marking of the spot on the wall. The counterfactual stipulation given in the first sentence of MT blocks situations, of the sort mentioned by Cartwright, in which we would most certainly want to deny that any mark transmission occurred via the spot moving around the wall. In this case, the moving spot would have turned red because of the lens even if no marking interaction had occurred locally at the wall.

A serious misgiving arises from the use of counterfactual formulations to characterize the distinction between causal processes and pseudo-processes; it concerns the question of objectivity. The distinction is fully objective. It is a matter of fact that a light pulse constitutes a causal process, while a shadow is a pseudo-process. Philosophers have often maintained, however, that counterfactual conditionals involve unavoidably pragmatic aspects. Consider the famous example about Verdi and Bizet. One person might say, "If Verdi had been a compatriot of Bizet, then Verdi would have been French," whereas another might maintain, "If Bizet had been a compatriot of Verdi, then Bizet would have been Italian." These two statements seem incompatible with one another. Their antecedents are logically equivalent; if, however, we accept both conditionals, we wind up with the conclusion that Verdi would be French, that Bizet would be Italian, and they would still not be compatriots. Yet both statements can be true. The first person could be making an unstated presupposition that the nationality of Bizet is fixed in this context, while the second presupposes that the nationality of Verdi is fixed. What remains fixed and what is subject to change – which are established by pragmatic features of the context in which the counterfactual is uttered – determine whether a counterfactual is true or false. It is concluded that counterfactual conditional statements do not express objective facts of nature; indeed, van Fraassen[21] goes so far as to assert that science contains no counterfactuals. If that sweeping claim were true (which I seriously doubt),[22] the foregoing criterion MT would be in serious trouble.

Although MT involves an explicit counterfactual, I do not believe that the foregoing difficulty is insurmountable. Science has a direct way of dealing with the kinds of counterfactual assertions we require: namely, the experimental approach. In a well-designed controlled experiment, the experimenter determines which conditions are to be fixed for purposes of the experiment and which allowed to vary. The result of the experiment establishes some counterfactual statements as true and others as false under well-specified conditions. Consider the kinds of cases that concern us; such counterfactuals can readily be tested experimentally. Suppose we want to see whether the beam traveling from the spotlight to the wall is capable of transmitting the red mark. We set up the following experiment. The light will be turned on and off one hundred times. At a point midway between the spotlight and the wall, we station an experimenter with a random number generator. Without communicating with the experimenter who turns the light on and off, this second experimenter uses his device to make a random selection of fifty trials in which he will make a mark and fifty in which he will not. If all and only the fifty instances in which the marking interaction occurs are those in which the spot on the wall is red, as well as all the intervening stages in the process, then we may conclude with reasonable certainty that the fifty cases in which the beam was red subsequent to the marking interaction are cases in which the beam would not have been red if the marking interaction had not occurred. On any satisfactory analysis of counterfactuals, it seems to me, we would be justified in drawing such a conclusion. It should be carefully noted that I am *not* offering the foregoing experimental procedure as an analysis of counterfactuals; it is, indeed, a result that we should expect any analysis to yield.

A similar experimental approach could obviously be taken with respect to the spot traversing the wall. We design an experiment in which the beacon will rotate one hundred times, and each traversal will be taken as a separate process. We station an experimenter with a random number generator at the wall. Without communicating with the experimenter operating the beacon, the one at the wall makes a random selection of fifty trials in which to make the mark and fifty in which to refrain. If it turns out that some or all of the trials in which no interaction occurs are, nevertheless, cases in which the spot on the wall turns red as it passes the second experimenter, then we know that we are *not* dealing with cases in which the process will not turn from white to red if no interaction occurs. Hence, if in some cases the spot turns red and remains red after the mark is imposed, we know we are not entitled to conclude that the mark has actually been transmitted.

The account of mark transmission embodied in principle MT – which is the proposed foundation for the concept of propagation of causal influence – may seem too trivial to be taken seriously. I believe such a judgment would be mistaken. My reason lies in the close parallel that can be drawn between the foregoing solution to the problem of mark transmission and the solution of an ancient philosophical puzzle.

About 2,500 years ago, Zeno of Elea enunciated some famous paradoxes of motion, including the well-known paradox of the flying arrow. This paradox was not adequately resolved until the early part of the twentieth century. To establish an intimate connection between this problem and our problem of causal transmission, two observations are in order. First, a physical object (such as the arrow) moving from one place to another constitutes a causal process, as can be demonstrated easily by application of the mark method – for example, initials carved on the shaft of the arrow before it is shot are present on the shaft after it hits its target. And there can be no doubt that the arrow propagates causal influence. The hunter kills his prey by releasing the appropriately aimed arrow; the flying arrow constitutes the causal connection between the cause (release of the arrow from the bow under tension) and the effect (death of a deer). Second, Zeno's paradoxes were designed to prove the absurdity not only of motion, but also of every kind of process or change. Henri Bergson expressed this point eloquently in his discussion of what he called "the cinematographic view of becoming." He invites us to consider any process, such as the motion of a regiment of soldiers passing in review. We can take many snapshots – static views – of different stages of the process, but, he argues, we cannot really capture the movement in this way, for,

> every attempt to reconstitute change out of states implies the absurd proposition, that movement is made out of immobilities.
>
> Philosophy perceived this as soon as it opened its eyes. The arguments of Zeno of Elea, although formulated with a very different intention, have no other meaning.
>
> Take the flying arrow.[23]

Let us have a look at this paradox. At any given instant, Zeno seems to have argued, the arrow is where it is, occupying a portion of space equal to itself. During the instant it cannot move, for that would require the instant to have parts, and an instant is *by definition* a minimal and indivisible element of time. If the arrow did move during the instant, it would have to be in one place at one part of the instant and in a different place at another part of the instant. Moreover, for the arrow to move during the instant would require that during that instant it must occupy a space larger than itself, for otherwise it has no room to move. As Russell said:

> It is never moving, but in some miraculous way the change of position has to occur *between* the instants, that is to say, not at any time whatever.

This is what M. Bergson calls the cinematographic representation of reality. The more the difficulty is meditated, the more real it becomes.[24]

There is a strong temptation to respond to this paradox by pointing out that the differential calculus provides us with a perfectly meaningful definition of instantaneous velocity, and that this quantity *can* assume values other than zero. Velocity is change of position with respect to time, and the derivative dx/dt furnishes an expression that can be evaluated for particular values of t. Thus an arrow can be at rest at a given moment – that is, dx/dt may equal 0 for that particular value of t. Or it can be in motion at a given moment – that is, dx/dt might be 100 km/hr for another particular value of t. Once we recognize this elementary result of the infinitesimal calculus, it is often suggested, the paradox of the flying arrow vanishes.

This appealing attempt to resolve the paradox is, however, unsatisfactory, as Russell clearly realized. The problem lies in the definition of the derivative; dx/dt is defined as the limit as Δt approaches 0 of $\Delta x/\Delta t$, where Δt represents a nonzero interval of time and Δx may be a nonzero spatial distance. In other words, instantaneous velocity is defined as the limit, as we take decreasing time intervals, of the noninstantaneous average velocity with which the object traverses what is – in the case of nonzero values – a nonzero stretch of space. Thus in the definition of instantaneous velocity, we employ the concept of noninstantaneous velocity, which is precisely the problematic concept from which the paradox arises. To put the same point in a different way, the concept of instantaneous velocity does not genuinely characterize the motion of an object at an isolated instant all by itself, for the very definition of instantaneous velocity makes reference to neighboring instants of time and neighboring points of space. To find an adequate resolution of the flying arrow paradox, we must go deeper.

To describe the motion of a body, we express the relation between its position and the moments of time with which we are concerned by means of a mathematical function; for example, the equation of motion of a freely falling particle near the surface of the earth is

$$(1) \quad x = f(t) = 1/2gt^2$$

where $g = 9.8 \text{m/sec}^2$. We can therefore say that this equation furnishes a function $f(t)$ that relates the position x to the time t. But what is a mathematical function? It is a set of pairs of numbers; for each admissible value of t, there is an associated value of x. To say that an object moves in accordance with equation (1) is simply to say that *at* any given moment t it is *at* point x, where the correspondence between the values of t and of x is given by the set of pairs of numbers that constitute the function represented by equation (1). To move from point A to point B is simply to be *at* the appropriate point of space *at* the appropriate moment of time – no more, no less. The resulting theory is therefore known as "the 'at-at' theory of motion." To the best of my knowledge, it was first clearly formulated and applied to the arrow paradox by Russell.

According to the 'at-at' theory, to move from A to B is simply to occupy the intervening points at the intervening instants. It consists in being *at* particular points of space *at* corresponding moments. There is no *additional* question as to how the arrow *gets from* point A *to* point B; the answer has already been given – by being at the intervening points at the intervening moments. The answer is emphatically *not* that it gets from A to B by zipping through the intermediate points at high speed. Moreover, there is no additional question about how the arrow gets from one intervening point to another – the answer is the same, namely, by being at the points between them at the corresponding moments. And clearly, there can be no question about how the arrow gets from one point to the next, for in a continuum there is no next point. I am convinced that Zeno's arrow paradox is a profound problem concerning the nature of change and motion, and that its resolution by Russell in terms of the 'at-at' theory of motion represents a distinctly nontrivial achievement.[25] The fact that this solution can – if I am right – be extended in a direct fashion to provide a resolution of the problem of mark transmission is an additional laurel.

The 'at-at' theory of mark transmission provides, I believe, an acceptable basis for the mark method, which can in turn serve as the means to distinguish causal processes from pseudo-processes. The world contains a great many types of causal processes – transmission of light waves, motion of material objects, transmissions of sound waves, persistence of crystalline structure, and so forth. Processes of any of these types may occur without having any mark imposed. In such instances, the processes still qualify as causal. *Ability* to transmit a mark is the criterion of causal processes; processes that are *actually* unmarked may be causal. Unmarked processes exhibit some sort of persistent structure, as Russell pointed out in his characterization of causal lines; in such cases, we say that the structure is transmitted within the causal process. Pseudo-processes may also exhibit persistent structure; in these cases, we maintain that the structure is *not transmitted* by means of the 'process' itself, but by some other external agency.

The basis for saying that the regularity in the causal process is transmitted via the process itself lies in the ability of the causal process to transmit a modification in its structure – a mark – resulting from an interaction. Consider a brief pulse of white light; it consists of a collection of photons of various frequencies, and if it is not polarized, the waves will have various spatial orientations. If we place a red filter in the path of this pulse, it will absorb all photons with frequencies falling outside of the red range, allowing only those within that range to pass. The resulting pulse has its structure modified in a rather precisely specifiable way, and the fact that this modification persists is precisely what we mean by claiming that the mark is transmitted. The counterfactual clause in our principle MT is designed to rule out structural changes brought about by anything other than the marking interaction. The light pulse could, alternatively, have been passed through a polarizer. The resulting pulse would consist of photons having a specified spatial orientation instead of the miscellaneous assortment of orientations it contained before encountering the polarizer. The principle of structure transmission (ST) may be formulated as follows:

ST: *If a process is capable of transmitting changes in structure due to marking interactions, then that process can be said to transmit its own structure.*

The fact that a process does not transmit a particular type of mark, however, does not mean that it is not a causal process. A ball of putty constitutes a causal process, and one kind of mark it will transmit is a change in shape imposed by indenting it with the thumb. However, a hard rubber ball is equally a causal process, but it will not transmit the same sort of mark, because of its elastic properties. The fact that a particular sort of structural modification does not persist, because of some inherent tendency of the process to resume its earlier structure, does not mean it is not transmitting its own structure; it means only that we have not found the appropriate sort of mark for that kind of process. A hard rubber ball can be marked by painting a spot on it, and that mark will persist for a while.

Marking methods are sometimes used in practice for the identification of causal processes. As fans of Perry Mason are aware, Lieutenant Tragg always placed 'his mark' upon the murder weapon found at the scene of the crime in order to be able to identify it later at the trial of the suspect. Radioactive traces are used in the investigation of physiological processes – for example, to determine the course taken by a particular substance ingested by a subject. Malodorous substances are added to natural gas used for heating and cooking in order to ascertain the presence of leaks; in fact, one large chemical manufacturer published full-page color advertisements in scientific magazines for its product "La Stink."

One of the main reasons for devoting our attention to causal processes is to show how they can transmit causal influence. In the case of causal processes used to transmit signals, the point is obvious. Paul Revere was caused to start out on his famous night ride by a light signal sent from the tower of the Old North Church. A drug, placed surreptitiously in a drink, can cause a person to lose consciousness because it retains its chemical structure as it is ingested, absorbed, and circulated through the body of the victim. A loud sound can produce a painful sensation in the ears because the disturbance of the air is transmitted from the origin to the hearer. Radio signals sent to orbiting satellites can activate devices aboard because the wave retains its form as it travels from earth through space. The principle of propagation of causal influence (PCI) may be formulated as follows:

PCI: *A process that transmits its own structure is capable of propagating a causal influence from one space-time locale to another.*

The propagation of causal influence by means of causal processes *constitutes*, I believe, the mysterious connection between cause and effect which Hume sought.

In offering the 'at-at' theory of mark transmission as a basis for distinguishing causal processes from pseudo-processes, we have furnished an account of the transmission of information and propagation of causal influence without appealing to any of the 'secret powers' which Hume's account of causation soundly proscribed. With this account we see that the mysterious connection between causes and effects is not very mysterious after all.

Our task is by no means finished, however, for this account of transmission of marks and propagation of causal influence has used the unanalyzed notion of a causal interaction that produces a mark. Unless a satisfactory account of causal interaction and mark production can be provided, our theory of causality will contain a severe lacuna.[26] Nevertheless, we have made significant progress in explicating the fundamental concept, introduced at the beginning of the chapter, of *causal propagation* (or *transmission*).

This chapter is entitled "Causal Connections," but little has actually been said about the way in which causal processes provide the connection between cause and effect. Nevertheless, in many common-sense situations, we talk about causal relations between pairs of spatiotemporally separated events. We might say, for instance, that turning the key causes the car to start. In this context we assume, of course, that the electrical circuitry is intact, that the various parts are in good working order, that there is gasoline in the tank, and so forth, but I think we can make sense of a cause–effect relation only if we can provide a *causal connection* between the cause and the effect. This involves tracing out the causal processes that lead from the turning of the key and the closing of an electrical circuit to various occurrences that eventuate in the turning over of the engine and the ignition of fuel in the cylinders. We say, for another example, that a tap on the knee causes the foot to jerk. Again, we believe that there are neutral impulses traveling from the place at which the tap occurred to the muscles that control the movement of the foot, and processes in those muscles that lead to movement of the foot itself. The genetic relationship between parents and offspring provides a further example. In this case, the molecular biologist refers to the actual process of information transmission via the DNA molecule employing the 'genetic code'.

In each of these situations, we analyze the cause–effect relations in terms of three components – an event that constitutes the cause, another event that constitutes the effect, and a causal process that connects the two events. In some cases, such as the starting of the car, there are many intermediate events, but in such cases, the successive intermediate events are connected to one another by spatiotemporally continuous causal processes. A splendid example of multiple causal connections was provided by David Kaplan. Several years ago, he paid a visit to Tucson, just after completing a boat trip through the Grand Canyon with his family. The best time to take such a trip, he remarked, is when it is very hot in Phoenix. What is the causal connection to the weather in Phoenix, which is about 200 miles away? At such times, the air-conditioners in Phoenix are used more heavily, which places a greater load on the generators at the Glen Canyon Dam (above the Grand Canyon). Under these circumstances, more water is allowed to pass through the turbines to meet the increased demand for power, which produces a greater flow of water down the Colorado River. This results in a more exciting ride through the rapids in the Canyon.

In the next chapter,[27] we shall consider events – especially causal interactions – more explicitly. It will then be easier to see how causal processes constitute precisely the physical connections between causes and effects that Hume sought – what he called "the cement of the universe." These causal connections will play a vital role in our account of scientific explanation.

It is tempting, of course, to try to reduce causal processes to chains of events; indeed, people fre-

quently speak of causal chains. Such talk can be seriously misleading if it is taken to mean that causal processes are composed of discrete events that are serially ordered so that any given event has an immediate successor. If, however, the continuous character of causal processes is kept clearly in mind, I would not argue that it is philosophically incorrect to regard processes as collections of events. At the same time, it does seem heuristically disadvantageous to do so, for this practice seems almost inevitably to lead to the puzzle (articulated by Sayre in the quotation given previously) of how these events, which make up a given process, are causally related to one another. The point of the 'at-at' theory, it seems to me, is to show that no such question about the causal relations among the constituents of the process need arise – for the same reason that, aside from occupying intermediate positions at the appropriate times, there is no further question about how the flying arrow gets from one place to another. With the aid of the 'at-at' theory, we have a complete answer to Hume's penetrating question about the nature of causal connections. For this heuristic reason, then, I consider it advisable to resist the temptation always to return to formulations in terms of events.

Notes

1 It might be objected that the alternation of night with day, and perhaps Kepler's "laws," do not constitute genuine lawful regularities. This consideration does not really affect the present argument, for there are plenty of regularities, lawful and nonlawful, that do not have explanatory force, but that stand in need of causal explanation.

2 Indeed, in Italian, there is one word, *perche*, which means both "why" and "because." In interrogative sentences it means "why," and in indicative sentences it means "because." No confusion is engendered as a result of the fact that Italian lacks two distinct words.

3 David Hume, *An Inquiry Concerning Human Understanding* (Indianapolis: Bobbs-Merrill, 1955), which also contains "An abstract of *A Treatise of Human Nature*," pp. 186–7.

4 Bertrand Russell, *Mysticism and Logic* (New York: W. W. Norton, 1929), p. 180.

5 Bertrand Russell, *The Analysis of Matter* (London: George Allen and Unwin, 1927).

6 Bertrand Russell, *Human Knowledge, Its Scope and Limits* (New York: Simon and Schuster, 1948), pp. 487–96.

7 In ibid., regrettably, Russell felt compelled to relinquish empiricism. I shall attempt to avoid such extreme measures.

8 Patrick Suppes, *A Probabilistic Theory of Causality* (Amsterdam: North-Holland, 1970), pp. 5–6.

9 See J. L. Mackie, *The Cement of the Universe* (Oxford: Clarendon Press, 1974), for an excellent historical and systematic survey of the various approaches.

10 Ibid., p. 62.

11 Deborah A. Rosen, "An argument for the logical notion of a memory trace," *Philosophy of Science* 42 (1975), pp. 1–10.

12 Ralph Waldo Emerson, "Hymn sung at the completion of the battle monument, Concord."

13 Russell, *Human Knowledge*, p. 459.

14 See John Winnie, "The causal theory of space-time," in John Earman, Clark Glymour, and John Stachel (eds), *Minnesota Studies in the Philosophy of Science*, vol. 8 (Minneapolis: University of Minnesota Press, 1977), pp. 134–205.

15 See Adolf Grünbaum, *Philosophical Problems of Space and Time*, 2nd edn (Dordrecht: D. Reidel, 1973), pp. 735–50.

16 Winnie, "Causal theory."

17 Milton A. Rothman, "Things that go faster than light," *Scientific American* 203/1 (July 1960), pp. 142–52, contains a lively discussion of pseudo-processes.

18 Russell, *Human Knowledge*, p. 459.

19 Ibid.

20 Kenneth M. Sayre, "Statistical models of causal relations," *Philosophy of Science* 44 (1977), pp. 203–14, at p. 206.

21 Bas C. van Fraassen, *The Scientific Image* (Oxford: Clarendon Press, 1980), p. 118.

22 For example, our discussion of the Minkowski light cone made reference to paths of possible light rays; such a path is one that would be taken by a light pulse if it were emitted from a given space-time point in a given direction. Special relativity seems to be permeated with reference to possible light rays and possible causal connections, and these involve counterfactuals quite directly. See Wesley C. Salmon, "Foreword," in Hans Reichenbach, *Laws, Modalities, and Counterfactuals* (Berkeley/Los Angeles/London: University of California Press, 1976), pp. vii–xlii, for further elaboration of this issue, not only with respect to special relativity but also in relation to other domains of physics. A strong case can be made, I believe, for the thesis that counterfactuals are scientifically indispensable.

23 Henri Bergson, *Creative Evolution* (New York: Holt, Reinhart and Winston, 1911), p. 308.

24 Russell, *Mysticism and Logic*, p. 187.

25 Zeno's arrow paradox and its resolution by means of the 'at-at' theory of motion are discussed in Wesley C. Salmon, *Space, Time, and Motion* (Encino, Calif.: Dickenson, 1975; 2nd edn, Minneapolis: University of Minnesota Press, 1980), ch. 2. Relevant writings by Bergson and Russell are reprinted in *idem, Zeno's Paradoxes* (Indianapolis: Bobbs-Merrill, 1970); the introduction to this anthology also contains a discussion of the arrow paradox.

26 Salmon offers an account of these notions in his *Scientific Explanation and the Causal Structure of the World* (Princeton: Princeton University Press, 1984), ch. 6.

27 Ibid.

36

The Nature of Causation: A Singularist Account

Michael Tooley

Is a singularist conception of causation coherent? That is to say, is it possible for two events to be causally related, without that relationship being an instance of some causal law, either basic or derived, and either probabilistic or non-probabilistic? Since the time of Hume, the overwhelmingly dominant philosophical view has been that such a conception of causation is not coherent. In this paper, I shall attempt to show that that view is incorrect.

The paper has three main sections. In the first, I argue that, although some traditional arguments in support of a singularist conception of causation are problematic, there are good reasons for trying to develop a singularist account.

Then, in the second section, I consider a Humean objection to a singularist conception of causation. My central contention there is that while the argument has considerable force against any reductionist account, it leaves untouched the possibility of a realist approach according to which causal relations are neither observable, nor reducible to observable properties and relations.

Finally, in the third section, I turn to the task of actually setting out a satisfactory singularist account of the nature of causation. There I shall offer both a general recipe for constructing a singularist account, and a specific version that incorporates my own views on the direction of causation.

Originally published in *Canadian Journal of Philosophy*, suppl. vol. 16 (1990), pp. 271–322. Reprinted by permission of University of Calgary Press.

1 Arguments in Support of a Singularist Conception of Causation

A. Two problematic arguments in support of a singularist account

What grounds might be offered for thinking that it is possible for one event to cause another, without the causal relation being an instance of any causal law? There are, I think, at least six lines of argument that are worth mentioning. Two of these I shall set aside as dubious. The other four, however, appear to be sound.

Immediate knowledge of causal relations? One consideration that might be advanced starts out by appealing to the possibility of knowledge that two events are causally related, which is based upon nothing beyond perception of the two events and their more or less immediate surroundings. The thrust of the argument is then that, since experience of such a very limited sort can surely not provide one with any knowledge of the existence of a law, it must be possible to know that two events are causally related without knowing that there is any law of which that relation is an instance. But if that is possible, then is it not also reasonable to suppose that it is possible for two events to be causally related, even if there is no corresponding law?

This general line of argument comes in different versions, corresponding to four slightly different claims concerning knowledge of causal relations. First, there is the claim that causal relations can be given in immediate experience, in the strong sense of actually being part of an experience itself. Second, there is the claim that, even if causal relations are not given in immediate experience, one can certainly have non-inferential knowledge that states of affairs are causally related. Third, there is the claim that causal relations are at least observable in many cases. Finally, there is the claim that there are situations where observation of a single case can provide one with grounds for believing that two events are causally related, and that it can do so even in the absence of any prior knowledge of causal laws. These four claims give rise to different arguments. But, while I shall not attempt to establish it here, I think that it is very doubtful that any of them can be sustained.

The appeal to intuition A second line of thought involves the claim that if one simply examines one's ordinary concept of causation – of one event's bringing about, or giving rise to, another – one does not find any reference to the idea of a law. One's ordinary concept of causation is simply that of a relation between two events – that is to say, a relation that involves only two events, together with whatever causal intermediaries there may be, and nothing else. It cannot matter, therefore, what is the case in other parts of the universe, or what laws obtain.

Is there anything in this argument? Perhaps. For if it is true that, no matter how carefully one inspects one's ordinary concept of causation, one cannot see any reason why only events that fall under laws can be causally related, then that may provide *some* support for a singularist conception. But it would seem that that support must be, at best, very limited. For, given the great difficulty, not only in arriving at a satisfactory analysis of the concept of causation, but even in determining the correct direction in which to look, the fact that no connection with laws is immediately apparent when one introspectively examines one's ordinary concept of causation can hardly provide much of a basis for concluding that no such connection exists.

B. More promising lines of argument

In this section, I want to mention four considerations that, though by no means compelling, constitute much more substantial reasons for accepting a singularist conception of causation. The four arguments consist of three that I have set out elsewhere, in a detailed way,[1] plus a natural variant.

My discussion of them here, consequently, will be comparatively brief.

The four arguments all attempt to establish a singularist conception of causation by offering reasons for rejecting the alternatives. We need to consider, therefore, just what the alternatives are. The place to begin, clearly, is with the dominant, supervenience view. According to it, events cannot be causally related unless that relation is an instance of some law. Moreover, whether or not two events are causally related is logically determined by the non-causal properties of the two events, and the non-causal relations between them, together with the causal laws that there are in the world. The supervenience view of causal relations involves, in short, the following two theses:

1 Causal relations presuppose corresponding causal laws;
2 Causal relations are logically supervenient upon causal laws plus the non-causal properties of, and relations between, events.

Traditionally, the supervenience view and the singularist view have been treated as the only alternatives on offer with respect to the question of the relation between causal relations and causal laws. It is clear, however, that there is a third alternative, since the first of the above theses is compatible with the denial of the second. There is, accordingly, a view that is intermediate between the singularist position and the supervenience position – the view, namely, that causal relations presuppose corresponding causal laws, even though causal relations are *not* logically supervenient upon causal laws together with the non-causal properties of, and relations between, events.

The relevance of this for the present arguments is that each argument involves two distinct parts – one directed against the supervenience view and the other directed against the intermediate view. In the case of the supervenience alternative, the strategy is to describe a logically possible situation that is a counterexample to the supervenience account. The counterexamples have no force, however, against the intermediate view, so some other line of argument is called for, and what I shall argue is that the singularist view is to be preferred to the intermediate view on grounds of simplicity.

The argument from the possibility of indeterministic laws The first argument starts out from the plausible – though by no means indubitable –

assumption that indeterministic causal laws are logically possible. Granted that assumption, consider a world with only two basic causal laws:

For any x, x's having property P is causally sufficient to bring it about that either x has property Q or x has property R;

For any x, x's having property S is causally sufficient to bring it about that either x has property Q or x has property R.

In such a world, if an object has property P, but not property S, and then acquires property Q, but not property R, it must be the case that the acquisition of property Q was caused by the possession of property P. Similarly, if an object has property S, but not property P, and then acquires property Q, but not property R, it must be the case that the acquisition of property Q was caused by the possession of property S. But what if an object has both property P and property S? If the object acquires only property Q, there will be no problem: it will simply be a case of causal overdetermination. Similarly, if it acquires only property R. But what if it acquires *both* property Q and property R? Was it the possession of property P that caused the acquisition of property Q, and the possession of property S that caused the possession of property R, or was it the other way around? Given a supervenience view of causation, no answer is possible, for the causal laws in question, together with the non-causal properties of the objects, do not entail that it was one way rather than the other.

Can an advocate of a supervenience view argue successfully that this case is not really a counterexample? One try would be to say that in the case where an object has both property P and property S, and then acquires properties Q and R, there are *no* causal relations at all involved. But that won't do, since the first law, for example, implies that the possession of property P always causes something.

Another attempted escape would be to argue that there are causal relations in the situation, but they are not quite as determinate as one might initially assume. Thus it is not the case either that the possession of property P causes the possession of property Q, or that it causes the possession of property R. What is true is that the possession of property P causes the state of affairs which involves either the possession of property Q, or the possession of property R.

But this, I believe, will not do either. The reason is that causal relations hold between states of affairs, and, while one may use disjunctive expressions to pick out states of affairs, states of affairs in themselves can never be disjunctive in nature. Accordingly, if the situation described is to involve causal relations falling under the relevant laws, it must be the case either that the possession of property P caused the acquisition of property Q, or that it caused the acquisition of property R, and similarly for property S.

It would seem, then, that the possibility of indeterministic causal laws gives rise to a very strong objection to the supervenience view of causal relations. But what of the intermediate view? Obviously, the above argument leaves it unscathed, since, in the situation being considered, all of the causal relations fall under causal laws. So if the intermediate view is to be rejected, some other argument is needed.

The only possibility that I can see here is a somewhat modest argument which turns upon the fact that the intermediate view involves a somewhat richer ontology than the other views. For consider, first, the supervenience view. Given that, according to it, causal relations between states of affairs are logically supervenient upon causal laws plus non-causal states of affairs, the only basic causal facts that need to be postulated are those that correspond to causal laws. (According to the view of causal laws that I have defended elsewhere, such facts are to be identified with certain contingent relations between universals.[2])

Second, consider the singularist view. According to it, it is causal relations that are in some sense primary, rather than causal laws. So the singularist view is certainly committed to postulating basic causal facts which involve states of affairs standing in causal relations. But what account is to be offered of causal laws? If a regularity view of laws were tenable, nothing would be needed beyond regularities involving the relation of causation. However, as a number of philosophers have argued, regularity accounts of the nature of laws are exposed to very strong objections.[3] Let us suppose, therefore, that a singularist account of causation is combined with the view that laws are relations among universals. The result will be that a singularist approach involves, in the case of any world that contains causal laws, the postulation of two sorts of basic causal facts – consisting, on the one hand, of relations between particular states of affairs, and, on the other, of relations between universals.

At first glance, then, the singularist approach might seem to have a more luxuriant ontology than the supervenience approach, since the latter postulates only one type of causal fact, whereas the former postulates two. But I think that further reflection undermines that conclusion. The reason is that both approaches need to leave room for the possibility of *non-causal* laws. When this is taken into account, it can be seen that both approaches need to postulate exactly two fundamental sorts of facts, in the general area of laws and causation. For, on the one hand, the supervenience view needs to postulate two special types of facts in order to distinguish between causal laws and non-causal laws, while, on the other, the singularist approach can also account for everything while postulating only two special sorts of facts. For although it cannot reduce causal laws to causal relations between states of affairs, it can analyse the concept of a causal law in terms of the concept of a law – causal or otherwise – together with the concept of causal relations.

In short, the situation is this. Both approaches need an account of the nature of laws. Given that, the supervenience view then goes on to explain what it is that distinguishes causal laws from non-casual laws, and then uses the notion of a causal law to offer an analysis of what it is for two states of affairs to be causally related. The singularist view, on the other hand, has to explain what it is for two states of affairs to be causally related, and it then uses that concept, in conjunction with that of a law, to explain what a causal law is. The two approaches would seem, therefore, to be on par with respect to overall simplicity.

But what of the intermediate account? The answer is that it is necessarily more complex. Since it denies that causal relations between events are logically supervenient upon causal laws together with the totality of non-causal facts, it is committed, like the singularist approach, to postulating a special relation that holds between states of affairs. But, unlike the singularist approach, it cannot go on to analyse causal laws as laws that involve the relation of causation. For the latter sort of analysis makes it impossible to offer any reason why it should be the case that events can be causally related only if they fall under some law. Accordingly, if the exclusion of anomic causation is to be comprehensible, given an intermediate view, one needs to offer a separate account of the nature of causal laws.[4] The upshot is that an intermediate account needs to postulate three special sorts of facts: those corresponding to non-causal laws, those corresponding to causal laws, and those corresponding to causal relations between states of affairs. An intermediate account therefore involves a somewhat richer ontology than either a singularist approach or a supervenience approach.

This completes the argument. For we have seen, first, that there are only two alternatives to a singularist conception of causation – namely, the supervenience view and the intermediate view. Second, one of the alternatives – the supervenience view – is ruled out by certain logically possible cases involving indeterministic causal laws. Third, the other alternative – the intermediate view – is ontologically less economical than the singularist view. Other things being equal, therefore, the singularist approach is to be preferred.

The argument from the possibility of uncaused events and probabilistic laws The second argument is, in a sense, a simpler version of the previous one. It does involve however, two additional assumptions – namely, that both probabilistic laws and uncaused events are possible.

Given those two assumptions, the argument runs as follows. Imagine a world where objects sometimes acquire property Q without there being any cause of that occurrence. Suppose, further, that the following is a law:

For any x, x's having property P causally brings it about, with probability 0.75, that x has property Q.

If objects sometimes acquire property Q even though there is no cause of their doing so, then why shouldn't this also be possible in cases where an object happens to have property P? Indeed, might there not be an excellent reason for thinking that there were such cases? For suppose that objects having property P went on to acquire property Q 76 per cent of the time, rather than 75 per cent of the time. That would not necessarily be grounds for entertaining doubts concerning the above law, since that law might be derived from a very powerful, simple, and well-confirmed theory.

In that situation, one would have reason for believing that, over the long term, of the 76 out of 100 cases when an object with property P acquires property Q, 75 will be ones where the acquisition of property Q is caused by the possession of property P, while the other will be one where property Q is spontaneously acquired. But if one adopts a supervenience view, what state of affairs serves to differentiate the two sorts of cases? No answer can be forthcoming, since, by hypothesis, there are no differences with respect to non-causal properties or relations. The above possibility is a counter-example, therefore, to a supervenience view of causal relations.

The argument from the possibility of exact replicas of causal situations The third argument runs as follows. Suppose that event P causes event M. There will, in general, be nothing impossible about there also being an event M^* which has precisely the same properties[5] as M, both intrinsic and relational, but which is not caused by P. But is it logically possible for it to be the case that, in addition, either (1) the only relation between P and M is that of causation, or else (2) any other relation that holds between P and M also holds between P and M^*?

If either of these situations can obtain, we have a counterexample to the supervenience view. For assume that the supervenience approach is correct. That means that P's causing M is logically supervenient upon the non-causal properties of, and the non-causal relations between, P and M, together with the causal laws. But if M^* has precisely the same non-causal properties as M, and also stands to P in the same non-causal relations as M does, then the supervenience thesis entails that P must also cause M^*, contrary to our hypothesis.

An advocate of the supervenience view might well challenge, of course, the assumption that situations of the above sort are possible. But I believe that the assumption can be sustained, and elsewhere I have advanced three sorts of cases in support of it,[6] two of which I shall mention here. The first involves two assumptions; first, that there could be immaterial minds that were not located in space, but which could be causally linked – say, by 'telepathy'; second, that there could also be two such minds that were in precisely the same state at every instant. Granted these assumptions, one has a counterexample of the desired sort to the supervenience view: a case, namely, where a mind P is causally linked to a mind, M, but not to a qualitatively indistinguishable mind, M^*.

A second sort of case involves the following three assumptions: first, that it is logically possible for there to be worlds that exhibit, at least some of the time, rotational symmetry; second, that enduring objects have temporal parts, and that it is causal relations between those parts that unite them into

enduring objects; third, that the only external relations that hold between complete temporal slices of a universe, or between parts of different complete temporal slices, are causal and temporal ones. Given those assumptions, consider, for example, a Newtonian world that contains only two neutrons, endlessly rotating in the same direction around their centre of gravity. Choose any time, t, and let U be the temporal part that contains events at t, together with all prior events, while V contains all later events. The thrust of the argument is then that the rotational symmetry that characterizes such a world at every moment means that a supervenience view cannot give a satisfactory account of the causal connections between the two temporal parts. For if P and P^* are the earlier temporal parts of the two neutrons, and M and M^* the later temporal parts, it will be impossible, given a supervenience view, to hold that P is causally linked to M, but not to M^*, since M and M^* have the same properties, both intrinsic and relational, and there is no non-causal relation that holds between P and M, but not between P and M^*.

If the subsidiary assumptions can be defended in either or both of these cases – and I believe that they can[7] – then one has another sort of counter-example to the supervenience view.

The argument from the possibility of inverted universes Let us say that two possible worlds are inverted twins if they are exactly the same except for the direction of time and for any properties or relations that involve the direction of time. Whether a possible world has an inverted twin depends upon what the laws of nature are. Some laws will exclude inversion; others will not.

Consider, for example, any world that is governed by the laws of Newtonian physics. For any instantaneous temporal slice, S, of that world, there will be another possible Newtonian world that contains an instantaneous temporal slice, T such that T involves precisely the same distribution of particles as S, but with velocities that are exactly reversed. Given that the laws of Newtonian physics are symmetric with respect to time, the course of events in the one world will be exactly the opposite of that in the other world. Any Newtonian world necessarily has, therefore, an inverted twin.

Imagine, then, for purposes of illustration, that our world is a Newtonian world. There will then be a possible world that is just like our world, except that the direction of time, and the direction of causation, are, so to speak, reversed. That is to say, if we let *A* and *B* be any two complete temporal slices of our world, such that *A* is causally and temporally prior to *B*, then the other world will contain temporal slices *A** and *B** such that, first, *A** and *B** are indistinguishable from *A* and *B*, respectively, except with respect to properties that involve the direction of time, and second, *B** is causally and temporally prior to *A**. So there will be, for example, a complete temporal slice of the twin world that is just like a temporal slice of our own world in the year AD 1600 except that all properties that involve the direction of time – such as velocity – will be reversed. Similarly, there will be a complete temporal slice that corresponds, in the same way, to a temporal slice of our own world in the year AD 1700. But both the causal and the temporal orderings will be flipped over, with the 1700-style slice both causally prior to, and earlier than, the 1600-style slice.

The question now is this. What makes it the case that, in our world, *A* causes *B*, whereas in the inverted twin world, *B** causes *A**? If one adopts a supervenience account, then, in view of the fact that the two worlds have, by hypothesis, the same laws, the difference must be a matter either of some difference between *A* and *A**, or between *B* and *B**, with respect to non-causal properties, or else of some non-causal relation that holds between *A* and *B*, but not between *A** and *B**. Can such a difference be found?

One difference is that while *A* is earlier than *B*, *A** is later than *B**, rather than earlier. But is this a non-causal difference? The answer depends upon the correct theory of the nature of time. In particular, it depends upon whether the direction of time is to be analysed in terms of the direction of causation. If, as I am inclined to believe, it is, then the causal difference between the two worlds cannot be grounded upon the temporal difference. But this, in turn, also means that *A* and *A** cannot differ with respect to their non-causal properties, and similarly for *B* and *B**. For, by hypothesis, *A* differs from *A** only with respect to those properties that involve the direction of time, and those differences will not be non-causal differences if the direction of time is to be defined in terms of the direction of causation.

The crux of this fourth and final argument, in short, is the assumption that the direction of time is to be analysed in terms of the direction of causation. If that assumption cannot be sustained, the argument collapses. But if it can be sustained, the argument appears to go through, since *A* will not

then differ from *A** with respect to any non-causal properties, nor *B* from *B**, nor will there be any non-causal relation that holds between *A* and *B* but not between *A** and *B**. The possibility of inverted universes will thus constitute another counter-example to the supervenience view of causation.

To sum up, the four arguments that I have set out in this section constitute, I believe, a very strong case against the supervenience view. As we have seen, however, this is not to say that there is an equally strong case for the singularist conception of causation. For there is a third alternative – the intermediate view – which escapes the objections to which the supervenience account is exposed. Nevertheless, with the field thus narrowed, there is at least some reason for preferring the singularist view, since it involves a more economical ontology.

2 Arguments against a Singularist Account?

I have argued that, other things being equal, the singularist view is to be preferred. But are other things equal, or are there, on the contrary, strong objections to a singularist conception of causation?

Given that very few philosophers indeed have embraced a singularist view, it is natural to suppose that very strong objections, if not out and about, must at least be lurking on the sidelines. But is that so? Perhaps, instead, it has simply been taken for granted that a singularist view cannot be right, that causal relations must fall under laws? That certainly seem to have been the feeling of Elizabeth Anscombe, as the following, somewhat caustic comment on Davidson, and others, testifies:

Meanwhile in non-experimental philosophy it is clear enough what are the dogmatic slumbers of the day. It is over and over again assumed that any singular causal proposition implies a universal statement running 'Always when this, then that'; often assumed that true singular causal statements are derived from such 'inductively believed' universalities. Examples indeed are recalcitrant, but that does not seem to disturb. Even a philosopher acute enough to be conscious of this, such as Davidson, will say, without offering any reason at all for saying it, that a singular causal statement implies *that there is* such a true universal statement – though perhaps we can never have knowledge of it.

Such a thesis needs some reason for believing it![8]

Such a thesis does indeed need support. However, I believe that Anscombe is wrong in suggesting that the widespread philosophical acceptance of the view that causal relations presuppose laws does not rest upon any argument. For it seems to me that the reason that one rarely encounters any arguments bearing upon this thesis is that most philosophers have generally been convinced by Hume's argumentation on the matter, regardless of whether they have accepted or rejected his positive account of the nature of causation.

We need to consider, therefore, the Humean line of argument. It has, in effect, two parts. The first involves the claim that causal relations are not observable in the relevant technical sense of being immediately given in experience. The second involves the claim that causal relations are not analytically reducible to observable properties and relations *unless* one looks beyond the individual case.

How might it be argued that causal relations are not immediately given in experience? A standard empiricist argument might run as follows. First, to say that a property or relation is immediately given in an experience is to say that it is part of the experience itself, and where the latter is so understood that a property or relation can be part of an experience E only if it would also have to be part of any experience that was qualitatively indistinguishable from E. Second, given any experience E whatever – be it a perception of external events, or an introspective awareness of some mental occurrence, such as an act of willing, or a process of thinking – it is logically possible that appropriate, direct stimulation of the brain might produce an experience, E^*, which was qualitatively indistinguishable from E, but which did not involve any causally related elements. So, for example, it might seem to one that one was engaging in a process of deductive reasoning, when, in fact, there was not really any direct connection at all between the thoughts themselves – all of them being caused instead by something outside of oneself. It then follows, from these two premises, that causal relations cannot be immediately given in experience in the sense indicated.

But what is the significance of this conclusion? The answer is that it then follows, according to traditional empiricism, that the concept of causation cannot be analytically basic. For one of the central tenets of empiricism is that not all ideas can be treated as primitive. In particular, an idea can be treated as analytically basic only if it serves to pick out some property or relation with which one is directly acquainted. But what properties and relations can be objects of direct acquaintance? Within traditional empiricism, the answer is that one can be directly acquainted only with properties and relations that can be given within immediate experience. It therefore follows that if traditional empiricist views concerning what concepts can be treated as analytically basic are sound, the concept of causation cannot be treated as analytically basic. It stands in need of analysis.

Is traditional empiricism right on these matters? I believe that it is. Arguing for that view would, however, take us rather far afield. For the way that I would want to proceed is by showing, first, that, *pace* Wittgenstein, a private language is unproblematic, and second, that while concepts that involve the ascription of secondary qualities to external objects can be analysed in terms of concepts that involve the ascription of qualia to experiences, analysis in the opposite direction is impossible.

This brings us to the second stage of the Humean argument – the part which is directed to showing that a singularist conception of causation makes it impossible to analyse causation in terms of observable properties and relations. Hume's argument here involves asking one to try to identify, in any case where one event causes another, what it is that constitutes the causal connection. He suggests that when we do so, we will see, first, that the effect comes after the cause, and second, that cause and effect are contiguous, both temporally and spatically. But these two relations, surely, are not enough. Something more is needed, if events are to be causally related. But what can that something more possibly be?

In response to this question, Hume argues that, regardless of what sort of instance one considers – be it a case of one object's colliding with another, or a case of a person's performing some action – one will find that there is neither any further property, either of the cause or of the effect, nor any further relation between the two events, to which one can point. Hume therefore concludes that if one is to find something that answers to our concept of causation, one has to look beyond any single instance, and he then goes on to argue that if one has to look beyond single instances, the only situations that could possibly be relevant are ones involving events of similar sorts, similarly conjoined.

Thus one is led, in the end, to the conclusion that our idea of causation is in some way necessarily linked with the idea of regularities, of constant conjunctions of events.[9]

How might one attempt to rebut this argument? One line, which appears to be embraced by Anscombe,[10] involves the attempt to move from the claim that causation is observable to the conclusion that the concept of causation can be treated as basic, and thus as not in need of any analysis in terms of other ideas. But it seems very unlikely that this response can be sustained. For, on the one hand, the fact that something is observable in the ordinary, non-technical sense of that term provides no reason at all for concluding that the relevant concept can be taken as analytically basic: electrons are, for example, observable in cloud chambers, but that does not mean that the term 'electron' does not stand in need of analysis. And, on the other hand, if one shifts to a technical sense of 'observation' that does license that inference – namely, that according to which a property or relation is observable only if it can be given in immediate experience – then, as was argued above, causation is not observable in that sense.

Another possible singularist response is that advanced by C. J. Ducasse, who attempted to show that causation could be analysed in terms of relations which Hume granted are observable in the individual instance – the relations, namely, of spatial and temporal contiguity, and of temporal priority. Thus, according to Ducasse, to say that C caused K, where C and K are changes, is just to say:

1 The change C occurred during a time and through a space terminating at the instant I at the surface S.
2 The change K occurred during a time and through a space beginning at the instant I at the surface S.
3 No change other than C occurred during the time and through the space of C, and no change other than K during the time and through the space of K.[11]

But this proposal cannot be sustained. One problem with it, which Ducasse himself discusses, is that causation is not just a relation between the totality of states of affairs existing during some interval, and terminating at some surface at some instant, and the totality of states of affairs beginning at that surface and at that instant, and existing throughout some interval. Causation is a relation that holds between different parts of two such totalities. Thus, to use Ducasse's own illustration, if a brick strikes a window at the same time that sound waves emanating from a canary do so, one wants to be able to say that it is the brick's striking the window that causes it to shatter. But this is precluded by Ducasse's analysis.[12]

Ducasse's account is open to a number of other objections. Is it not logically possible, for example, for there to be spatio-temporal events which are uncaused? And is it not possible for there to be immaterial minds that have no spatial location, but who can communicate with one another 'telepathically'? Ducasse's account appears to exclude such possibilities. The objection that I wish to focus upon here, however, concerns the question of whether there can be causal action at a distance – i.e., whether two events that are separated, either spatially, or temporally, or both, can be causally related even if there is no intervening causal process that bridges the spatial and/or temporal gap between the two events. Ducasse's account implies that causal action at a distance is logically impossible. But is that really so?

Ducasse's account is by no means the only one which entails that causal action at a distance is logically impossible, since Hume's own account, for example, has precisely the same implication. But other, more recent accounts of the concept of causation – such as Wesley Salmon's – also involve the idea that gappy causal processes are logically impossible.[13] But though this idea has been embraced by various philosophers, it seems clearly untenable. For, as I have argued elsewhere, one can surely imagine, for example, a world where the laws governing the transmission of light waves entail that light particles will exist only at some of the places along the line of travel. Insert a mirror at certain points, and the light ray would be reflected. Insert it at other points, and there would be no effect at all. Nor would there be any other ways of intervening at those points which would interfere in any way with the transmission of the wave.[14]

My reason for mentioning this objection to Ducasse's analysis is that the fact that discontinuous causal processes are logically possible adds force to Hume's objection to a singularist conception of causation. To see why, consider the responses that can be made to Hume's argument. Two possible replies have already been mentioned, and rejected – the response, namely, that causation is itself a directly observable relation, so that the whole idea that an analysis is needed is wrong, and the response that causation *is* just succession plus continguity, contrary to what Hume contends. But if neither of these replies is satisfactory, what, then, is left?

One idea is to uncover what Hume himself failed to find – that is, some further observable property or relation. It is at this point that the possibility of discontinuous causal processes is relevant. For while the situation does not seem very promising if one assumes, with Hume, that there cannot be any spatial or temporal gap between a cause and its effect, it surely looks desperate indeed if an event at one time can cause an event at a much later time, in a remote part of the universe, with no intervening causal process. If causal situations can be as unconstrained as this, what observable relation – beyond that of temporal priority – can possibly hold between two causally related events?

The prospects for a singularist account of causation may well seem hopeless at this point. It may seem that, if one is to find an account of causation, one *must* look beyond a given pair of causally related events. But if causation is simply a relation between two individual events, this possibility is precluded. It would seem, therefore, that a singularist conception of causation must be rejected.

This conclusion is, however, mistaken. To see why, one needs only to get clear about precisely what the Humean argument establishes. In the first place, then, it shows, I believe, that causation is not directly observable in the relevant technical sense, and therefore that it cannot be a primitive, unanalysable relation between events. In the second place, it makes it at least immensely plausible – especially when one considers the possibility of radical causal gaps – that causation cannot be reduced to observable properties of, and relations between, individual pairs of events. These two conclusions, however, do not suffice to rule out a singularist conception of causation. For one possibility remains: the possibility, namely, that causation is simply a relation between individual events, but one that is neither observable, nor reducible to observable properties and relations.

Hume's line of argument therefore requires supplementation, if a singularist conception of causation is to be refuted. Specifically, one must either show that there is something special about causation which makes it the case that only a reductionist account will do, or else one must defend the completely general thesis that all properties and relations are either observable or else reducible to observable properties and relations. But neither route seems at all promising. For as regards the former, the problem is that there just do not seem to be any arguments of that sort, while, as regards the latter, the thesis that there are no theoretical properties or relations at all is not tremendously plausible in itself, and the arguments that have been offered in support of it all seem to appeal, either openly or covertly, to some form of verificationism.

The conclusion, accordingly, is that a Humean argument does not refute a singularist approach to causation. It shows at most that a singularist account needs to be combined with the view that causation is a theoretical relation between events.

Should an advocate of a singularist account of causation be troubled by this conclusion? Not if the arguments advanced in section 1.B are correct. For those arguments are not only arguments in support of a singularist conception of causation: they are also arguments against any reductionist approach to causation, and indeed, more powerful ones, since a reductionist approach to causation is incompatible with *both* singularist accounts and intermediate accounts of causal relations.

The case against a reductionist approach to causation does not rest, however, simply upon the arguments advanced in section 1.B. For, as I have argued elsewhere, there are other very strong reasons for holding that no reductionist account of causation can be tenable, and reasons that are *completely independent* of whether a singularist account of causation is correct.[15]

In a passage quoted earlier, Anscombe says that contemporary philosophers, in holding that causal relations presuppose laws, are guilty of dogmatic slumber. Now even if she were right in thinking that philosophers were slumbering here, the characterization of that as 'dogmatic' would not be fair, since the most that would be involved would be an assumption which philosophers had not in fact examined, rather than one which they were unwilling to examine. But, as the discussion in the present section has shown, Anscombe is not right on this matter. For the idea that a singularist account of causation is untenable is not an assumption that philosophers have made without any supporting argument. There is an argument, and one that goes back to Hume's discussion. It is, moreover, an argument that is very difficult to resist, *unless* one has a viable account of the meaning of theoretical terms – something that, in addition to being unavailable to Hume, has become available only in this century.

It is true, nevertheless, that there is an unexamined assumption that is endemic in the philosophy of causation, but Anscombe has misdiagnosed its location. For, rather than its being the idea that causal relations presuppose causal laws, it is, instead, an assumption that Anscombe herself shares with those whom she criticizes – the assumption, namely, that causal relations, rather than being theoretical relations, are either themselves observable, or else reducible to other properties and relations that are.

3   The Positive Theory

In the first part of this paper, I have tried to do two main things: first, to show that a singularist account of causation is preferable to the alternatives; second, to determine in what general direction one should look in attempting to develop such an account.

My argument in support of the preferability of a singularist account involved three main points. First, supervenience accounts of causation must be set aside, since they are exposed to decisive counterexamples. Second, other things being equal, singularist accounts of causation are preferable to intermediate accounts, since the latter necessarily involve a more complicated ontology. Third, the Humean objection to singularist accounts – an objection that may initially appear very strong indeed – turns out to rest upon an unexamined assumption, and one which, I have argued elsewhere, will not stand up under critical scrutiny – the assumption, namely, that causal relations are reducible to non-causal properties and relations.

What form should a singularist account take? The main points that emerged with respect to this question were these. First, causation cannot be treated as a primitive relation, for it is not directly observable in the relevant sense. Second, a singularist theory of causation cannot attempt to reduce causation to non-causal properties and relations, since, although the Humean argument is not successful in ruling out a singularist account, it is, I believe, a very plausible argument for the conclusion that if causation is conceived of in singularist terms, then no reductionist account is possible. Therefore, third, the only hope for a viable singularist account of causation involves treating causal relations as theoretical relations between events. But, fourth, there is nothing disturbing about this conclusion, since there are independent grounds for holding that no reductionist account of causation can be satisfactory.

A.   The basic strategy, and the underlying ideas

How is the concept of causation to be analysed? If causal relations are theoretical relations, then the starting point must be some *theory* that can plausibly be viewed as *implicitly defining* the concept of causation. Given such a theory, the next task will then be to convert the implicit definition that the theory provides into an explicit analysis.

Exactly how the latter task is best carried out need not concern us at this point. What is relevant is simply that no method of analysing any theoretical term can be employed until a relevant theory involving that term is at hand. We need to develop, accordingly, a theory of causation.

The relevant theory of causation must, in addition, be analytically true. For the goal is to set out an analysis of the *concept* of causation, and not merely to offer an account that is true of causation as it is in the actual world. The theory must be true of causation in all possible worlds. So none of the statements in the theory can be merely contingently true.

The remainder of the present section will be concerned with isolating the basic ideas that can be used to construct an appropriate, analytically true theory of causation. The material is organized as follows. I begin by raising the question of precisely which causal relation, or relations, one should focus upon. Is there a single, basic causal relation, to which all other causal relations can be reduced? Or does one have to recognize distinct causal relations that are equally basic?

Having determined which causal relation (or relations) one should focus upon, I then go on to consider the formal properties of the basic causal relation (or relations) in question. That might appear, initially, to be a relatively straightforward task, but we shall see that that is not entirely so. In any case, given a decision as to the formal properties possessed by some basic causal relation, the idea is that the analytically true statements in question can form part of the desired theory of that relation.

Those formal properties will not suffice, however, to differentiate the causal relation in question from a number of non-causal relations. Nor, if it turns out that there is more than one basic causal relation, will the formal properties provide one with any account of what it is that makes all of those distinct relations causal relations. Something more is needed, then, before one has a theory that suffices to capture the concept of a causal relation, and the crucial question is what that something more is.

If one were setting out a non-singularist account of causation, a natural move at this point would be to appeal to the idea that events cannot be causally related unless the relation is an instance of some law, and then to try to exploit this connection between causal relations and causal laws in order to construct a sufficiently strong theory. But this avenue is closed if it is a singularist account that one is after. So what can one appeal to at this point?

The more one reflects upon this problem of developing a theory of causation for the singularist case, the more intractable it is likely to seem. But there is, I believe, a possible solution. Suppose that a singularist view of causation is correct, so that it is logically possible for there to be causally related events that do not fall under any law. It is then very tempting to think that it must be possible to characterize causation as it is in itself, without any reference to laws of nature. But perhaps this is a mistake. Perhaps our grasp of causation is inextricably tied to the distinction between causal laws and non-causal laws, so that causal relations just are those relations which are such that any laws involving them have certain properties – properties not possessed by non-causal laws.

The idea, in short, is that it may be that the only way we have of characterizing causal relations is an *indirect* one, and one that involves the concept of a law of nature. If so, then the concept of causation is parasitic upon the concept of a law of nature. But this sort of conceptual dependence need not entail any ontological dependence. Events could still be causally related without falling under any relevant law.

To implement this general idea, one needs to be able to point to a difference between laws that involve causal relations and laws that do not. One needs to find some further condition, T – beyond that of involving causal relations – such that it is an analytic truth that a law is a causal law if and only if it satisfies T. For given such a condition, one would then be able to characterize causal relations as those relations such that any laws involving them must satisfy condition T. Moreover, such a characterization would be perfectly compatible with the possibility of there being events that were causally related, even though the relation was not an instance of any law, since the fact that the intrinsic

nature of some relation is such that any laws involving it *would* necessarily have certain properties does not entail that, in order for the relation to be instantiated, there need be any laws involving it.

Given this general strategy, the basic challenge is to come up with a plausible candidate for condition T. The specific suggestion that I shall advance is one that I have defended elsewhere, in connection with supervenience and intermediate accounts of causal laws.

Fundamental causal relations Before attempting to set out a theory of causation, one needs to get clear about which causal relation or relations should feature in the theory. Is there a single basic causal relation, to which all causal relations, in all possible worlds, can be reduced? Or is it necessary to recognize distinct causal relations that are equally basic?

How might one attempt to reduce all causal relations to a single, basic, causal relation? Two possibilities immediately come to mind. One involves treating direct causation as the basic relation, and then defining other causal relations – such as indirect causation, and causation in general – in terms of it. The other involves treating causation in general as the basic relation, and then defining both direct causation and indirect causation in terms of it.

Would either of these reductions be satisfactory? I think not. In the case of the first, the problem is that any acceptable account of causation must apply to continuous causal processes, and this will not be the case for any theory in which all causal relations are to be reduced to direct causation. For in a continuous causal process, there are no events standing in the relation of direct causation, and therefore no relation that is definable in terms of direct causation can be instantiated in such a process.

But what about the reduction of all causal relations to the relation of causation in general? Initially, this programme may seem more promising, since it might seem to be a straightforward matter to define both the concept of a continuous causal process and the concept of direct causation, given the concept of causation in general. But this, I think, is a mistake. One way of seeing the problem is by noticing that there are two rather different concepts of direct causation. According to one, a sufficient condition of A's being a direct cause of B is that A is a cause of B and there is no causally intermediate event. Direct causation, so conceived, can be reduced to the relation of causation in

implicates of an effective if not finite set of axioms – then certainly we can get arithmetical reinterpretations of the predicates.[3] But that is not what we are about. We are concerned rather to accommodate all the *truths* of θ – all the sentences, regardless of axiomatizability, that were true under the original interpretation of the predicates of θ. There is, under the Löwenheim–Skolem theorem, a reinterpretation that carries all these truth into truths about natural numbers; but there may be no such interpretation in arithmetical terms. There will be if θ admits of complete axiomatization, of course, and there will be under some other circumstances, but not under all. In the general case the most that can be said is, again, that the numerical reinterpretations are expressible in the notation of arithmetic plus the truth predicate for θ.[4]

So on the whole the reduction to a Pythagorean ontology exacts a price in ideology whether we invoke the truth predicate directly or let ourselves be guided by the argument of the Löwenheim–Skolem theorem. Still there is a reason for preferring the latter, longer line. When I suggested simply translating S as 'Tx' with x as Gödel number of S, I was taking advantage of the liberal standard: reduction was just any effective and truth-preserving mapping of closed sentences on closed sentences. Now the virtue of the longer line is that it works also for a less liberal standard of reduction. Instead of accepting just any and every mapping of closed sentences on closed sentences so long as it is effective and truth-preserving, we can insist rather that it preserve predicate structure. That is, instead of mapping just whole sentences of θ on sentences, we can require that each of the erstwhile primitive predicates of θ carry over into a predicate or open sentence about the new objects (the natural numbers).

Whatever its proof and whatever its semantics, a doctrine of blanket reducibility of ontologies to natural numbers surely trivializes most further ontological endeavor. If the universe of discourse of every theory can as a matter of course be standardized as the Pythagorean universe, then apparently the only special ontological reduction to aspire to in any particular theory is reduction to a finite universe. Once the size is both finite and specified, of course, ontological considerations lose all force; for we can then reduce all quantifications to conjunctions and alternations and so retain no recognizably referential apparatus.

Some further scope for ontological endeavor does still remain, I suppose, in the relativity to

ideology. One can try to reduce a given theory to the Pythagorean ontology without stepping up its ideology. This endeavor has little bearing on completely axiomatized theories, however, since they reduce to pure arithmetic, or elementary number theory.[5]

Anyway we seem to have trivialized most ontological contrasts. Perhaps the trouble is that our standard of ontological reduction is still too liberal. We narrowed it appreciably when we required that the predicates be construed severally. But we still did not make it very narrow. We continued to allow the several predicates of a theory θ to go over into any predicates or open sentences concerning natural numbers, so long merely as the truth-values of closed sentences were preserved.

Let us return to the Carnap case of impure number for a closer look. We are initially confronted with a theory whose objects include place-times x and impure numbers α and whose primitive predicates include 'H'. We reduce the theory to a new one whose objects include place-times and pure numbers, and whose predicates include 'H_c'. The crucial step consists of explaining '$H(x, n°C)$' as '$H_c(x, n)$'.

Now this is successful, if it is, because three conditions are met. One is, of course, that '$H_c(x, n)$' under the intended interpretation agrees in truth-value with '$H(x, n°)C$', under its originally intended interpretation, for all values of x and n. A second condition is that, in the original theory, all mention of impure numbers α was confined or confinable to the specific form of context '$H(x, \alpha)$'. Otherwise the switch to '$H_c(x, n)$' would not eliminate such mention. But if this condition were to fail, through there being further predicates (say a predicate of length or of density) and further units (say meters) along with 'H' and degrees, we could still win through by just treating them similarly. A third condition, finally, is that an impure number α can always be referred to in terms of a pure number and a unit: thus $n°C$, n meters. Otherwise explaining '$H(x, n°C)$' as '$H_c(x, n)$' would not take care of '$H(x, \alpha)$'.

This third condition is that we be able to specify what I shall call a *proxy function*: a function which assigns one of the new things, in this example a pure number, to each of the old things – each of the impure numbers of temperature. In this example the proxy function is the function 'how many degrees centigrade' – the function f such that $f(n°C) = n$. It is not required that such a function be expressible in the original theory θ to which 'H'

belonged, much less that it be available in the final theory θ' to which 'H_c' belongs. It is required rather of *us*, out in the metatheory where we are explaining and justifying the discontinuance of θ in favor of θ', that we have some means of expressing a proxy function. Only upon us, who explain '$H(x, \alpha)$' away by '$H_c(x, n)$', does it devolve to show how every α that was intended in the old θ determines an n of the new θ'.

In these three conditions we have a further narrowing of what had been too liberal a standard of what to count as a reduction of one theory or ontology to another. We have in fact narrowed it to where, as it seems to me, the things we should like to count as reduction do so count and the rest do not. Carnap's elimination of impure number so counts; likewise Frege's and von Neumann's reduction of natural arithmetic to set theory; likewise the various essentially Dedekindian reductions of the theory of real numbers. Yet the general trivialization of ontology fails; there ceases to be any evident way of arguing, from the Löwenheim–Skolem theorem, that ontologies are generally reducible to the natural numbers.

The three conditions came to us in an example. If we restate them more generally, they lose their tripartite character. The standard of reduction of a theory θ to a theory θ' can now be put as follows. We specify a function, not necessarily in the notation of θ or θ', which admits as arguments all objects in the universe of θ' and takes values in the universe of θ'. This is the proxy function. Then to each n-place primitive predicate of θ, for each n, we effectively associate an open sentence of θ' in n free variables, in such a way that the predicate is fulfilled by an n-tuple of arguments of the proxy function always and only when the open sentence is fulfilled by the corresponding n-tuple of values.

For brevity I am supposing that θ has only predicates, variables, quantifiers, and truth functions. The exclusion of singular terms, function signs, abstraction operators, and the like is no real restriction, for these accessories are reducible to the narrower basis in familiar ways.

Let us try applying the above standard of reduction to the Frege case: Frege's reduction of number to set theory. Here the proxy function f is the function which, applied, e.g., to the 'genuine' number 5, gives as value the class of all five-member classes (Frege's so-called 5). In general, fx is describable as the class of all x-member classes.

When the real numbers are reduced (by what I called the first method) to classes of ratios, fx is the class of all ratios less than the 'genuine' real number x.

I must admit that my formulation suffers from a conspicuous element of make-believe. Thus, in the Carnap case I had to talk as if there *were* such things as $x°C$, much though I applaud Carnap's repudiation of them. In the Frege case I had to talk as if the 'genuine' number 5 were really something over and above Frege's, much though I applaud his reduction. My formulation belongs, by its nature, in an inclusive theory that admits the objects of θ, as unreduced, and the objects of θ' on an equal footing.

But the formulation seems, if we overlook this imperfection, to mark the boundary we want. Ontological reductions that were felt to be serious do conform. Another that conforms, besides those thus far mentioned, is the reduction of an ontology of place-times to an ontology of number quadruples by means of Cartesian coordinates. And at the same time any sweeping Pythagoreanization on the strength of the Löwenheim–Skolem theorem is obstructed. The proof of the Löwenheim–Skolem theorem is such as to enable us to give the predicates of the numerical model; but the standard of ontological reduction that we have now reached requires more than that. Reduction of a theory θ to natural numbers – true reduction by our new standard, and not mere modeling – means determining a proxy function that actually assigns numbers to all the objects of θ and maps the predicates of θ into open sentences of the numerical model. Where this can be done, with preservation of truthvalues of closed sentences, we may well speak of reduction to natural numbers. But the Löwenheim–Skolem argument determines, in the general case, no proxy function. It does not determine which numbers are to go proxy for the respective objects of θ. Therein it falls short of our standard of ontological reduction.

It emerged early in this paper that what justifies an ontological reduction is, vaguely speaking, preservation of relevant structure. What we now perceive is that this relevant structure runs deep; the objects of the one system must be assigned severally to objects of the other.

Goodman argued along other lines to this conclusion and more;[6] he called for isomorphism, thereby requiring one-to-one correspondence between the old objects and their proxies. I prefer to let different things have the same proxy. For instance, n is wanted as proxy for both $n°C$ and n meters. Or again, consider hidden inflation.[7] Relieving such inflation is a respectable brand of ontological reduction, and it consists precisely in taking one thing as proxy for all the things that were indiscriminable from it.[8]

Notes

1 Rudolf Carnap, *Physikalische Begriffsbildung* (Karlsruhe: G. Brawn, 1926).

2 See A. Tarski, *Logic, Semantics, Metamathematics*, (Oxford: Clarendon Press, 1956), p. 273. There are exceptions where θ is especially weak; see J. R. Myhill, 'A complete theory of natural, rational, and real numbers', *Journal of Symbolic Logic* 15 (1950), pp. 185–96, at p. 194.

3 See Hao Wang, 'Arithmetic models for formal systems', *Methodos* 3 (1951), pp. 217–32; also S. C. Kleene, *Introduction to Metamathematics* (New York: Van Nostrand, 1952), pp. 389–98 and more particularly p. 431. For exposition see also my 'Interpretations of sets of conditions', *Journal of Symbolic Logic* 19 (1954), pp. 97–102.

4 This can be seen by examining the general construction in sect.1 of my 'Interpretations of sets of conditions'.

5 Thus far in this paper I have been recording things that I said in the Shearman Lectures at University College, London, February 1954. Not so from here on.

6 Nelson Goodman, *The Structure of Appearance* (Cambridge, Mass.: Harvard University Press, 1951), pp. 5–19.

7 For details see W. V. Quine, 'Necessary truth', in *The Ways of Paradox* (New York: Random Hause, 1966).

8 I am indebted for this observation to Paul Benacerraf. On such deflation see further my discussion of identification of indiscernibles in *Word and Object* (Cambridge, Mass.: MIT Press, 1960), p. 230; in *From a Logical Point of View* (Cambridge, Mass.: Harvard University Press, 1953), pp. 71f; and in 'Reply to Professor Marcus', in Quine, *Ways of Paradox*.

39

Special Sciences

Jerry A. Fodor

A typical thesis of positivistic philosophy of science is that all true theories in the special sciences should reduce to physical theories in the 'long run'. This is intended to be an empirical thesis, and part of the evidence which supports it is provided by such scientific successes as the molecular theory of heat and the physical explanation of the chemical bond. But the philosophical popularity of the reductionist program cannot be explained by reference to these achievements alone. The development of science has witnessed the proliferation of specialized disciplines at least as often as it has witnessed their elimination, so the widespread enthusiasm for the view that there will eventually be only physics can hardly be a mere induction over past reductionist successes.

I think that many philosophers who accept reductionism do so primarily because they wish to endorse the generality of physics *vis-à-vis* the special sciences: roughly, the view that all events which fall under the laws of any science are physical events and hence fall under the laws of physics.[1] For such philosophers, saying that physics is basic science and saying that theories in the special sciences must reduce to physical theories have seemed to be two ways of saying the same thing, so that the latter doctrine has come to be a standard construal of the former.

Originally published in *Synthese* 28 (1974), pp. 77–115, appearing under the title 'Special sciences, or The disunity of science as a working hypothesis.' Copyright © by Kluwer Academic Publishers. Reprinted by permission of the author and the publisher.

In what follows, I shall argue that this is a considerable confusion. What has traditionally been called 'the unity of science' is a much stronger, and much less plausible, thesis than the generality of physics. If this is true, it is important. Though reductionism is an empirical doctrine, it is intended to play a regulative role in scientific practice. Reducibility to physics is taken to be a *constraint* upon the acceptability of theories in the special science, with the curious consequence that the more the special sciences succeed, the more they ought to disappear. Methodological problems about psychology, in particular, arise in just this way: The assumption that the subject matter of psychology is part of the subject matter of physics is taken to imply that psychological theories must reduce to physical theories, and it is this latter principle that makes the trouble. I want to avoid the trouble by challenging the inference.

Reductionism is the view that all the special sciences reduce to physics. The sense of 'reduce to' is, however, proprietary. It can be characterized as follows.[2]

Let formula (1) be a law of the special science *S*.

(1) $S_1 x \rightarrow S_2 y$

Formula (1) is intended to be read as something like 'all events which consist of *x*'s being S_1 bring about events which consist of *y*'s being S_2'. I assume that a science is individuated largely by reference to its typical predicates (see n. 2), hence that if S is a special science, 'S_1' and 'S_2' are not predicates of basic physics. (I also assume that the 'all' which quantifies laws of the special sciences needs to be taken with a grain of salt. Such laws are typically *not* exceptionless. This is a point to which I shall return at length.) A necessary and sufficient condition for the reduction of formula (1) to a law of physics is that the formulae (2) and (3) should be laws, and a necessary and sufficient condition for the reduction

(2a) $S_1x \leftrightarrow P_1x$

(2b) $S_2y \leftrightarrow P_2y$

(3) $P_1x \rightarrow P_2y$

of S to physics is that all its laws should be so reduced.[3]

'P_1' and 'P_2' are supposed to be predicates of physics, and formula (3) is supposed to be a physical law. Formulae like (2) are often called 'bridge' laws. Their characteristic feature is that they contain predicates of both the reduced and the reducing science. Bridge laws like formula (2) are thus contrasted with 'proper' laws like formulae (1) and (3). The upshot of the remarks so far is that the reduction of a science requires that any formula which appears as the antecedent or consequent of one of its proper laws must appear as the reduced formula in some bridge law or other.[4]

Several points about the connective '$\rightarrow$' are now in order. First, whatever properties that connective may have, it is universally agreed that it must be transitive. This is important, because it is usually assumed that the reduction of some of the special sciences proceeds via bridge laws which connect their predicates with those of intermediate reducing theories. Thus, psychology is presumed to reduce to physics via, say, neurology, biochemistry, and other local stops. The present point is that this makes no difference to the logic of the situation so long as the transitivity of '$\rightarrow$' is assumed. Bridge laws which connect the predicates of S to those of $S*$ will satisfy the constraints upon the reduction of S to physics so long as there are other bridge laws which, directly or indirectly, connect the predicates of $S*$ to physical predicates.

There are, however, quite serious open questions about the interpretation of '$\rightarrow$' in bridge laws. What turns on these questions is the extent to which reductionism is taken to be a physicalist thesis.

To begin with, if we read '$\rightarrow$' as 'brings about' or 'causes' in proper laws, we will have to have some other connective for bridge laws, since bringing about and causing are presumably asymmetric, while bridge laws express symmetric relations. Moreover, unless bridge laws hold by virtue of the *identity* of the events which satisfy their antecedents with those that satisfy their consequents, reductionism will guarantee only a weak version of physicalism, and this would fail to express the underlying ontological bias of the reductionist program.

If bridge laws are not-identity statements, then formulae like (2) claim at most that, by law, x's satisfaction of a P predicate and x's satisfaction of an S predicate are causally correlated. It follows from this that it is nomologically necessary that S and P predicates apply to the same things (i.e., that S predicates apply to a subset of the things that P predicates apply to). But, of course, this is compatible with a nonphysicalist ontology, since it is compatible with the possibility that x's satisfying S should not itself be a physical event. On this interpretation, the truth of reductionism does *not* guarantee the generality of physics *vis-à-vis* the special sciences, since there are some events (satisfactions of S predicates) which fall in the domain of a special science (S) but not in the domain of physics. (One could imagine, for example, a doctrine according to which physical and psychological predicates are both held to apply to organisms, but where it is denied that the event which consists of an organism's satisfying a psychological predicate is, in any sense, a physical event. The upshot would be a kind of psychophysical dualism of a non-Cartesian variety, a dualism of events and/or properties rather than substances.)

Given these sorts of considerations, many philosophers have held that bridge laws like formula (2) ought to be taken to express contingent event identities, so that one would read formula (2a) in some such fashion as 'every event which consists of an x's satisfying S_1 is identical to some event which consists of that x's satisfying P_1 and vice versa'. On this reading, the truth of reductionism would entail that every event that falls under any scientific law is a physical event, thereby simultaneously expressing the ontological bias of reductionism and guaranteeing the generality of physics *vis-à-vis* the special sciences.

If the bridge laws express event identities, and if every event that falls under the proper laws of a special science falls under a bridge law, we get classical reductionism, a doctrine that entails the truth of what I shall call 'token physicalism'. Token physicalism is simply the claim that all the events that the sciences talk about are physical events. There are three things to notice about token physicalism.

First, it is weaker than what is usually called 'materialism'. Materialism claims *both* that token physicalism is true *and* that every event falls under the laws of some science or other. One could therefore be a token physicalist without being a materialist, though I don't see why anyone would bother.

Second, token physicalism is weaker than what might be called 'type physicalism', the doctrine, roughly, that every *property* mentioned in the laws of any science is a physical property. Token physicalism does not entail type physicalism, if only because the contingent identity of a pair of events presumably does not guarantee the identity of the properties whose instantiation constitutes the events; not even when the event identity is nomologically necessary. On the other hand, if an event is simply the instantiation of a property, then type physicalism does entail token physicalism; two events will be identical when they consist of the instantiation of the same property by the same individual at the same time.

Third, token physicalism is weaker than reductionism. Since this point is, in a certain sense, the burden of the argument to follow, I shan't labor it here. But, as a first approximation, reductionism is the conjunction of token physicalism with the assumption that there are natural kind predicates in an ideally completed physics which correspond to each natural kind predicate in any ideally completed special science. It will be one of my morals that reductionism cannot be inferred from the assumption that token physicalism is true. Reductionism is a sufficient, but not a necessary, condition for token physicalism.

To summarize: I shall be reading reductionism as entailing token physicalism, since, if bridge laws state nomologically necessary contingent event identities, a reduction of psychology to neurology would require that any event which consists of the instantiation of a psychological property is identical with some event which consists of the instantiation of a neurological property. Both reductionism and token physicalism entail the generality of physics, since both hold that any event which falls within the universe of discourse of a special science will also fall within the universe of discourse of physics. Moreover, it is a consequence of both doctrines that any prediction which follows from the laws of a special science (and a statement of initial conditions) will follow equally from a theory which consists only of physics and the bridge laws (together with the statement of initial conditions). Finally, it is assumed by both reductionism and token physicalism that physics is the *only* basic science; viz., that it is the only science that is general in the sense just specified.

I now want to argue that reductionism is too strong a constraint upon the unity of science, but that, for any reasonable purposes, the weaker doctrine will do.

Every science implies a taxonomy of the events in its universe of discourse. In particular, every science employs a descriptive vocabulary of theoretical and observation predicates, such that events fall under the laws of the science by virtue of satisfying those predicates. Patently, not every true description of an event is a description in such a vocabulary. For example, there are a large number of events which consist of things having been transported to a distance of less than three miles from the Eiffel Tower. I take it, however, that there is no science which contains 'is transported to a distance of less than three miles from the Eiffel Tower' as part of its descriptive vocabulary. Equivalently, I take it that there is no natural law which applies to events in virtue of their instantiating the property is *transported to a distance of less than three miles from the Eiffel Tower* (though I suppose it is just conceivable that there is some law that applies to events in virtue of their instantiating some distinct but coextensive property). By way of abbreviating these facts, I shall say that the property *is transported* . . . does not determine a *(natural) kind*, and that predicates which express that property are not (natural) kind predicates.

If I knew what a law is, and if I believed that scientific theories consist just of bodies of laws, then I could say that '*P*' is a kind predicate relative to *S* if *S* contains proper laws of the form '*P*$_x$ → . . . *y*' or '. . . *y* → *P*$_x$': roughly, the kind predicates of a science are the ones whose terms are the bound variables in its proper laws. I am inclined to say this even in my present state of ignorance, accepting the consequence that it makes the murky notion of a kind viciously dependent on the equally murky notions of *law* and *theory*. There is no firm footing here. If we disagree about what a kind is, we will probably also disagree about what a law is, and for the same reasons. I don't know how to break out of this circle, but I think that there are some interesting things to say about which circle we are in.

For example, we can now characterize the respect in which reductionism is too strong a construal of the doctrine of the unity of science. If reductionism is true, then *every* kind is, or is coextensive with, a physical kind. (Every kind *is* a physical kind if bridge statements express nomologically necessary property identities, and every kind is coextensive with a physical kind if bridge statements express nomologically necessary event identities.) This follows immediately from the reductionist premise that every predicate which appears as the antecedent or consequent of a law of a special science must appear as one of the reduced predicates in some bridge law, together with the assumption that the kind predicates are the ones whose terms are the bound variables in proper laws. If, in short, some physical law is related to each law of a special science in the way that formula (3) is related to formula (1), then every kind predicate of a special science is related to a kind predicate of physics in the way that formula (2) relates 'S_1' and 'S_2' to 'P_1' and 'P_2' respectively.

I now want to suggest some reasons for believing that this consequence is intolerable. These are not supposed to be knock-down reasons; they couldn't be, given that the question of whether reductionism is too strong is finally an *empirical* question. (The world could turn out to be such that every kind corresponds to a physical kind, just as it could turn out to be such that the property *is transported to a distance of less than three miles from the Eiffel Tower* determines a kind in, say, hydrodynamics. It's just that, as things stand, it seems very unlikely that the world *will* turn out to be either of these ways.)

The reason it is unlikely that every kind corresponds to a physical kind is just that (a) interesting generalizations (e.g., counterfactual supporting generalizations) can often be made about events whose physical descriptions have nothing in common; (b) it is often the case that *whether* the physical descriptions of the events subsumed by such generalizations have anything in common is, in an obvious sense, entirely irrelevant to the truth of the generalizations, or to their interestingness, or to their degree of confirmation, or, indeed, to any of their epistemologically important properties; and (c) the special sciences are very much in the business of formulating generalizations of this kind.

I take it that these remarks are obvious to the point of self-certification; they leap to the eye as soon as one makes the (apparently radical) move of taking the existence of the special sciences at all

seriously. Suppose, for example, that Gresham's 'law' really is true. (If one doesn't like Gresham's law, then any true and counterfactual supporting generalization of any conceivable future economics will probably do as well.) Gresham's law says something about what will happen in monetary exchanges under certain conditions. I am willing to believe that physics is general *in the sense that it implies that any event which consists of a monetary exchange* (hence any event which falls under Gresham's law) *has a true description in the vocabulary of physics and in virtue of which it falls under the laws of physics*. But banal considerations suggest that a physical description which covers all such events must be wildly disjunctive. Some monetary exchanges involve strings of wampum. Some involve dollar bills. And some involve signing one's name to a check. What are the chances that a disjunction of physical predicates which covers all these events (i.e., a disjunctive predicate which can form the right-hand side of a bridge law of the form 'x is a monetary exchange $\leftrightarrow \ldots$') expresses a physical kind? In particular, what are the chances that such a predicate forms the antecedent or consequent of some proper law of physics? The point is that monetary exchanges have interesting things in common; Gresham's law, if true, says what one of these interesting things is. But what is interesting about monetary exchanges is surely not their commonalities under *physical* description. A kind like a monetary exchange *could* turn out to be coextensive with a physical kind; but if it did, that would be an accident on a cosmic scale.

In fact, the situation for reductionism is still worse than the discussion thus far suggests. For reductionism claims not only that all kinds are coextensive with physical kinds, but that the coextensions are nomologically necessary: bridge laws are *laws*. So, if Gresham's law is true, it follows that there is a (bridge) law of nature such that 'x is a monetary exchange $\leftrightarrow x$ is P' is true for every value of x, and such that P is a term for a physical kind. But, surely, there is no such law. If there were, then P would have to cover not only all the systems of monetary exchange that there *are*, but also all the systems of monetary exchange that there *could be*; a law must succeed with the counterfactuals. What physical predicate is a candidate for P in 'x is a nomologically possible monetary exchange iff P_x'?

To summarize: An immortal econophysicist might, when the whole show is over, find a predicate in physics that was, in brute fact, coextensive with 'is a monetary exchange'. If physics is general – if the ontological biases of reductionism are true – then there must *be* such a predicate. But (a) to paraphrase a remark Professor Donald Davidson made in a slightly different context, nothing but brute enumeration could convince us of this brute coextensivity, and (b) there would seem to be no chance at all that the physical predicate employed in stating the coextensivity would be a physical kind term, and (c) there is still less chance that the coextension would be lawful (i.e., that it would hold not only for the nomologically possible world that turned out to be real, but for any nomologically possible world at all).[5]

I take it that the preceding discussion strongly suggests that economics is not reducible to physics in the special sense of reduction involved in claims for the unity of science. There is, I suspect, nothing peculiar about economics in this respect; the reasons why economics is unlikely to reduce to physics are paralleled by those which suggest that psychology is unlikely to reduce to neurology.

If psychology is reducible to neurology, then for every psychological kind predicate there is a coextensive neurological kind predicate, and the generalization which states this coextension is a law. Clearly, many psychologists believe something of the sort. There are departments of psychobiology or psychology and brain science in universities throughout the world whose very existence is an institutionalized gamble that such lawful coextensions can be found. Yet, as has been frequently remarked in recent discussions of materialism, there are good grounds for hedging these bets. There are no firm data for any but the grossest correspondence between types of psychological states and types of neurological states, and it is entirely possible that the nervous system of higher organisms characteristically achieves a given psychological end by a wide variety of neurological means. It is also possible that given neurological structures subserve many different psychological functions at different times, depending upon the character of the activities in which the organism is engaged.[6] In either event, the attempt to pair neurological structures with psychological functions could expect only limited success. Physiological psychologists of the stature of Karl Lashley have held this sort of view.

The present point is that the reductionist program in psychology is clearly *not* to be defended on ontological grounds. Even if (token) psychological events are (token) neurological events, it does not follow that the kind predicates of psychology are coextensive with the kind predicates of any other discipline (including physics). That is, the assumption that every psychological event is a physical event does not guarantee that physics (or, *a fortiori*, any other discipline more general than psychology) can provide an appropriate vocabulary for psychological theories. I emphasize this point because I am convinced that the make-or-break commitment of many physiological psychologists to the reductionist program stems precisely from having confused that program with (token) physicalism.

What I have been doubting is that there are neurological kinds coextensive with psychological kinds. What seems increasingly clear is that, even if there are such coextensions, they cannot be lawful. For it seems increasingly likely that there are nomologically possible systems other than organisms (viz., automata) which satisfy the kind predicates of psychology but which satisfy no neurological predicates at all. Now, as Putnam has emphasized,[7] if there are any such systems, then there must be vast numbers, since equivalent automata can, in principle, be made out of practically anything. If this observation is correct, then there can be no serious hope that the class of automata whose psychology is effectively identical to that of some organism can be described by *physical* kind predicates (though, of course, if token physicalism is true, that class can be picked out by some physical predicate or other). The upshot is that the classical formulation of the unity of science is at the mercy of progress in the field of computer simulation. This is, of course, simply to say that that formulation was too strong. The unity of science was intended to be an empirical hypothesis, defeasible by possible scientific findings. But no one had it in mind that it should be defeated by Newell, Shaw, and Simon.

I have thus far argued that psychological reductionism (the doctrine that every psychological natural kind is, or is coextensive with, a neurological natural kind) is not equivalent to, and cannot be inferred from, token physicalism (the doctrine that every psychological event is a neurological event). It may, however, be argued that one might as well take the doctrines to be equivalent, since the only possible *evidence* one could have for token physicalism would also be evidence for reductionism: viz., that such evidence would have to consist in the discovery of type-to-type psychophysical correlations.

A moment's consideration shows, however, that this argument is not well taken. If type-to-type psychophysical correlations would be evidence for token physicalism, so would correlations of other specifiable kinds.

We have type-to-type correlations where, for every *n*-tuple of events that are of the same psychological kind, there is a correlated *n*-tuple of events that are of the same neurological kind.[8] Imagine a world in which such correlations are *not* forthcoming. What is found, instead, is that for every *n*-tuple of type-identical psychological events, there is a spatiotemporally correlated *n*-tuple of type-*distinct* neurological events. That is, every psychological event is paired with some neurological event or other, but psychological events of the same kind are sometimes paired with some neurological events of different kinds. My present point is that such pairings would provide as much support for token physicalism as type-to-type pairings do *so long as we are able to show that the type-distinct neurological events paired with a given kind of psychological event are identical in respect of whatever properties are relevant to type identification in psychology*. Suppose, for purposes of explication, that psychological events are type-identified by reference to their behavioral consequences.[9] Then what is required of all the neurological events paired with a class of type-homogeneous psychological events is only that they be identical in respect of their behavioral consequences. To put it briefly, type-identical events do not, of course, have *all* their properties in common, and type-distinct events must nevertheless be identical in *some* of their properties. The empirical confirmation of token physicalism does not depend on showing that the neurological counterparts of type-identical psychological events are themselves type-identical. What needs to be shown is just that they are identical in respect of those properties which determine what kind of *psychological* event a given event is.

Could we have evidence that an otherwise heterogeneous set of neurological events have those kinds of properties in common? Of course we could. The neurological theory might itself explain why an *n*-tuple of neurologically type-distinct events are identical in their behavioral consequences, or, indeed, in respect of any of indefinitely many other such relational properties. And, if the neurological theory failed to do so, some science more basic than neurology might succeed.

My point in all this is, once again, not that correlations between type-homogeneous psychological states and type-heterogeneous neurological states would prove that token physicalism is true.

It is only that such correlations might give us as much reason to be token physicalists as type-to-type correlations would. If this is correct, then epistemological arguments from token physicalism to reductionism must be wrong.

It seems to me (to put the point quite generally) that the classical construal of the unity of science has really badly misconstrued the *goal* of scientific reduction. The point of reduction is *not* primarily to find some natural kind predicate of physics coextensive with each kind predicate of a special science. It is, rather, to explicate the physical mechanisms whereby events conform to the laws of the special sciences. I have been arguing that there is no logical or epistemological reason why success in the second of these projects should require success in the first, and that the two are likely to come apart *in fact* wherever the physical mechanisms whereby events conform to a law of the special sciences are heterogeneous.

I take it that the discussion thus far shows that reductionism is probably too strong a construal of the unity of science; on the one hand, it is incompatible with probable results in the special sciences, and, on the other, it is more than we need to assume if what we primarily want, from an ontological point of view, is just to be good token physicalists. In what follows, I shall try to sketch a liberalized version of the relation between physics and the special sciences which seems to me to be just strong enough in these respects. I shall then give a couple of independent reasons for supposing that the revised doctrine may be the right one.

The problem all along has been that there is an open empirical possibility that what corresponds to the kind predicates of a reduced science may be a heterogeneous and unsystematic disjunction of predicates in the reducing science. We do not want the unity of science to be prejudiced by this possibility. Suppose, then, that we allow that bridge statements may be of this form,

$$(4) \quad Sx \leftrightarrow P_1 x \lor P_2 x \lor \cdots \lor P_n x$$

where $P_1 \lor P_2 \lor \cdots \lor P_n$ is *not* a kind predicate in the reducing science. I take it that this is tantamount to allowing that at least some 'bridge laws' may, in fact, not turn out to be laws, since I take it that a necessary condition on a universal generalization being lawlike is that the predicates which constitute its antecedent and consequent should be kind predicates. I am thus assuming that it is enough, for purposes of the unity of science, that every law of the special sciences should be reducible to physics by bridge statements which express true empirical generalizations. Bearing in mind that bridge statements are to be construed as species of identity statements, formula (4) will be read as something like 'every event which consists of x's satisfying S is identical with some event which consists of x's satisfying some or other predicate belonging to the disjunction $P_1 \vee P_2 \cdots \vee P_n$.'

Now, in cases of reduction where what corresponds to formula (2) is not a law, what corresponds to formula (3) will not be either, and for the same reason: viz., the predicates appearing in the antecedent and consequent will, by hypothesis, not be kind predicates. Rather, what we will have is something that looks like figure 39.1. That is, the antecedent and consequent of the reduced law will each be connected with a disjunction of predicates in the reducing science. Suppose, for the moment, that the reduced law is exceptionless, viz., that no S_1 events satisfy P'. Then there will be laws of the reducing science which connect the satisfaction of *each* member of the disjunction associated with the antecedent of the reduced law with the satisfaction of some member of the disjunction associated with the consequent of the reduced law. That is, if $S_1x \rightarrow S_2y$ is exceptionless, then there must be some proper law of the reducing science which either states or entails that $P_1x \rightarrow P^*$ for some P^*, and similarly for P_2x through P_nx. Since there must be such laws, and since each of them is a 'proper law' in the sense which we have been using that term, it follows that

each disjunct of $P_1 \vee P_2 \vee \cdots \vee P_n$ is a kind predicate, as is each disjunct of $P_1 \vee P_2^* \vee \cdots \vee P_n^*$.

This, however, is where push comes to shove. For it might be argued that if each disjunct of the P disjunction is lawfully connected to some disjunct of the P^* disjunction, then it follows that formula (5) is itself a law.

$$(5) \quad P_1x \vee P_2x \vee \cdots \vee P_nx \rightarrow P_1^*y \vee P_2^*y \vee \\ \cdots \vee P_n^*y.$$

The point would be that the schema in figure 39.1 implies $P_1x \rightarrow P_2^*y$, $P_2x \rightarrow P_n^*y$, etc., and the argument from a premise of the form $(P \supset R)$ and $(Q \supset S)$ to a conclusion of the form $(P \vee Q) \supset (R \vee S)$ is valid.

What I am inclined to say about this is that it just shows that 'it's a law that —' defines a non-truth-functional context (or, equivalently for these purposes, that not all truth functions of kind predicates are themselves kind predicates); in particular, that one may not argue from: 'it's a law that P brings about R' and 'it's a law that Q brings about S' to 'it's a law that P or Q brings about R or S'. Though, of course, the argument from those premises to 'P or Q brings about R or S *simpliciter* is fine.) I think, for example, that it is a law that the irradiation of green plants by sunlight causes carbohydrate synthesis, and I think that it is a law that friction causes heat, but I do not think that it is a law that (either the irradiation of green plants by sunlight or friction) causes (either carbohydrate synthesis or heat). Correspondingly, I doubt that 'is either

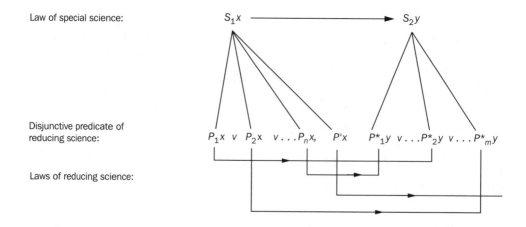

Law of special science: $S_1x \longrightarrow S_2y$

Disjunctive predicate of reducing science: $P_1x \vee P_2x \vee \ldots P_nx, \quad P'x \qquad P^*_1y \vee \ldots P^*_2y \vee \ldots P^*_my$

Laws of reducing science:

Figure 39.1 Schematic representation of the proposed relation between the reduced and the reducing science on a revised account of the unity of science. If any S_1 events are of the type P′, they will be exceptions to the law $S_1x \rightarrow S_2y$.

carbohydrate synthesis or heat' is plausibly taken to be a kind predicate.

It is not strictly mandatory that one should agree with all this, but one denies it at a price. In particular, if one allows the full range of truth-functional arguments inside the context 'it's a law that —', then one gives up the possibility of identifying the kind predicates of a science with the ones which constitute the antecedents or consequents of its proper laws. (Thus formula (5) would be a proper law of physics which fails to satisfy that condition.) One thus inherits the need for an alternative construal of the notion of a kind, and I don't know what that alternative would be like.

The upshot seems to be this. If we do not require that bridge statements must be laws, then either some of the generalizations to which the laws of special sciences reduce are not themselves lawlike, or some laws are not formulable in terms of kinds. Whichever way one takes formula (5), the important point is that the relation between sciences proposed by figure 39.1 is weaker than what standard reductionism requires. In particular, it does not imply a correspondence between the kind predicates of the reduced and the reducing science. Yet it does imply physicalism given the same assumption that makes standard reductionism physicalistic: viz., that bridge statements express token event identities. But these are precisely the properties that we wanted a revised account of the unity of science to exhibit.

I now want to give two further reasons for thinking that this construal of the unity of science is right. First, it allows us to see how the laws of the special sciences could reasonably have exceptions, and, second, it allows us to see why there are special sciences at all. These points in turn.

Consider, again, the model of reduction implicit in formulae (2) and (3). I assume that the laws of basic science are strictly exceptionless, and I assume that it is common knowledge that the laws of the special sciences are not. But now we have a dilemma to face. Since '$\rightarrow$' expresses a relation (or relations) which must be transitive, formula (1) can have exceptions only if the bridge laws do. But if the bridge laws have exceptions, reductionism loses its ontological bite, since we can no longer say that every event which consists of the satisfaction of an S predicate consists of the satisfaction of a P predicate. In short, given the reductionist model, we cannot consistently assume that the bridge laws and the basic laws are exceptionless while assuming that the special laws are not. But we cannot accept

the violation of the bridge laws unless we are willing to vitiate the ontological claim that is the main point of the reductionist program.

We can get out of this (*salve* the reductionist model) in one of two ways. We can give up the claim that the special laws have exceptions, or we can give up the claim that the basic laws are exceptionless. I suggest that both alternatives are undesirable – the first because it flies in the face of fact. There is just no chance at all that the true, counterfactual supporting generalizations of, say, psychology, will turn out to hold in strictly each and every condition where their antecedents are satisfied. Even when the spirit is willing, the flesh is often weak. There are always going to be behavioral lapses which are physiologically explicable but which are uninteresting from the point of view of psychological theory. But the second alternative is not much better. It may, after all, turn out that the laws of basic science have exceptions. But the question arises whether one wants the unity of science to depend on the assumption that they do.

On the account summarized figure 39.1, however, everything works out satisfactorily. A nomologically sufficient condition for an exception to $S_1x \rightarrow S_2y$ is that the bridge statements should identify some occurrence of the satisfaction of S_1 with an occurrence of the satisfaction of any P^* predicate which is not itself lawfully connected to the satisfaction of any P^* predicate (i.e., suppose S_1 is connected to P' such that there is no law which connects P' to any predicate which bridge statements associate with S_2. Then any instantiation of S_1 which is contingently identical to an instantiation of P' will be an event which constitutes an exception to $S_1x \rightarrow S_2y$). Notice that, in this case, we need assume no exceptions to the laws of the *reducing* science, since, by hypothesis, formula (5) is not a law.

In fact, strictly speaking formula (5) has no status in the reduction at all. It is simply what one gets when one universally quantifies a formula whose antecedent is the physical disjunction corresponding to S_1 and whose consequent is the physical disjunction corresponding to S_2. As such, it will be true when $S_1x \rightarrow S_2y$ is exceptionless and false otherwise. What does the work of expressing the physical mechanisms whereby n-tuples of events conform, or fail to conform, to $S_1x \rightarrow S_2y$ is not formula (5) but the laws which severally relate elements of the disjunction $P_1 \vee P_2 \vee \cdots \vee P_n$ to elements of the disjunction $P_1^* \vee P_2^* \vee \cdots \vee P_m^*$ Where there *is* a law which relates an event that satisfies one of the P disjuncts to an event which satisfies one of the P^* disjuncts, the pair of events so related conforms to $S_1 x \rightarrow S_2 y$. When an event which satisfies a P predicate is not related by law to an event which satisfies a P^* predicate, that event will constitute an exception to $S_1 x \rightarrow S_2 y$. The point is that none of the laws which effect these several connections need themselves have exceptions in order that $S_1 x \rightarrow S_2 y$ should do so.

To put this discussion less technically: We could, if we liked, *require* the taxonomies of the special sciences to correspond to the taxonomy of physics by insisting upon distinctions between the kinds postulated by the former whenever they turn out to correspond to distinct kinds in the latter. This would *make* the laws of the special sciences exceptionless if the laws of basic science are. But it would also likely lose us precisely the generalizations which we want the special sciences to express. (If economics were to posit as many *kinds* of monetary systems as there are physical realizations of monetary systems, then the generalizations of economics *would* be exceptionless – but, presumably, only vacuously so, since there would be no generalizations left for economists to state. Gresham's law, for example, would have to be formulated as a vast, open disjunction about what happens in monetary system$_1$ or monetary system$_n$ under conditions which would themselves defy uniform characterization. We would not be able to say what happens in monetary systems *tout court* since, by hypothesis, 'is a monetary system' corresponds to no kind of predicate of physics.)

In fact, what we do is precisely the reverse. We allow the generalizations of the special sciences to *have* exceptions, thus preserving the kinds to which the generalizations apply. But since we know that the *physical* descriptions of the members of these kinds may be quite heterogeneous, and since we know that the physical mechanisms which connect the satisfaction of the antecedents of such generalizations to the satisfaction of their consequents may be equally diverse, we expect both that there will be exceptions to the generalizations and that these will be 'explained away' at the level of the reducing science. This is one of the respects in which physics really is assumed to be bedrock science; exceptions to *its* generalizations (if there are any) had better be random, because there is nowhere 'further down' to go in explaining the mechanism whereby the exceptions occur.

This brings us to why there are special sciences at all. Reductionism, as we remarked at the outset,

flies in the face of the facts about the scientific institution: the existence of a vast and interleaved conglomerate of special scientific disciplines which often appear to proceed with only the most casual acknowledgment of the constraint that their theories must turn out to be physics 'in the long run'. I mean that the acceptance of this constraint often plays little or no role in the practical validation of theories. Why is this so? Presumably, the reductionist answer must be *entirely* epistemological. If only physical particles weren't so small (if only brains were on the *outside*, where one can get a look at them), *then* we would do physics instead of paleontology (neurology instead of psychology, psychology instead of economics, and so on down). There is an epistemological reply: viz., that even if brains were out where they could be looked *at*, we wouldn't, as things now stand, know what to look *for*. We lack the appropriate theoretical apparatus for the psychological taxonomy of neurological events.

If it turns out that the functional decomposition of the nervous system corresponds precisely to its neurological (anatomical, biochemical, physical) decomposition, then there are only epistemological reasons for studying the former instead of the latter. But suppose that there is no such correspondence? Suppose the functional organization of the nervous system cross-cuts its neurological organization. Then the existence of psychology depends not on the fact that neurons are so depressingly small, but rather on the fact that neurology does not posit the kinds that psychology requires.

I am suggesting, roughly, that there are special sciences not because of the nature of our epistemic relation to the world, but because of the way the world is put together: not all the kinds (not all the classes of things and events about which there are important, counterfactual supporting generalizations to make) are, or correspond to, physical kinds. A way of stating the classical reductionist view is that things which belong to different physical kinds *ipso facto* can have none of their projectable descriptions in common:[10] that if x and y differ in those descriptions by virtue of which they fall under the proper laws of physics, they must differ in those descriptions by virtue of which they fall under any laws at all. But why should we believe that this is so? Any pair of entities, however different their physical structure, must nevertheless converge in indefinitely many of their properties. Why should there not be, among those convergent properties, some whose lawful interrelations support the generalizations of the special sciences? Why, in short, should not the kind predicates of the special sciences *cross-classify* the physical natural kinds?

Physics develops the taxonomy of its subject matter which best suits its purposes: the formulation of exceptionless laws which are basic in the several senses discussed above. But this is not the only taxonomy which may be required if the purposes of science in general are to be served: e.g., if we are to state such true, counterfactual supporting generalizations as there are to state. So there are special sciences, with their specialized taxonomies, in the business of stating some of these generalizations. If science is to be unified, then all such taxonomies must apply to *the same things*. If physics is to be basic science, then each of these things had better be a physical thing. But it is not further required that the taxonomies which the special sciences employ must themselves reduce to the taxonomy of physics. It is not required, and it is probably not true.

Notes

1 For expository convenience, I shall usually assume that sciences are about events in at least the sense that it is the occurrence of events that makes the laws of a science true. Nothing, however, hangs on this assumption.

2 The version of reductionism I shall be concerned with is a stronger one than many philosophers of science hold, a point worth emphasizing, since my argument will be precisely that it is too strong to get away with. Still, I think that what I shall be attacking is what many people have in mind when they refer to the unity of science, and I suspect (though I shan't try to prove it) that many of the liberalized versions of reductionism suffer from the same basic defect as what I shall take to be the classical form of the doctrine.

3 There is an implicit assumption that a science simply is a formulation of a set of laws. I think that this assumption is implausible, but it is usually made when the unity of science is discussed, and it is neutral so far as the main argument of this chapter is concerned.

4 I shall sometimes refer to 'the predicate which constitutes the antecedent or consequent of a law'. This is shorthand for 'the predicate such that the antecedent or consequent of a law consists of that predicate, together with its bound variables and the quantifiers which bind them'...

5 P. Oppenheim and H. Putnam, "Unity of science as a working hypothesis," in H. Feigl, M. Scriven, and G. Maxwell (eds), *Minnesota Studies in the Philosophy of Science*, vol. 2 (Minneapolis: University of Minnesota Press, 1958), pp. 3–36, argue that the social sciences probably *can* be reduced to physics assuming that the reduction proceeds via (individual) psychology. Thus, they remark, "in economics, if very weak assumptions are satisfied, it is possible to represent the way in which an individual orders his choices by means of an individual preference function. In terms of these functions, the economist attempts to explain group phenomena, such as the market, to account for collective consumer behavior, to solve the problems of welfare economics, etc." (p. 17). They seem not to have noticed, however, that even if such explanations can be carried through, they would not yield the kind of *predicate-by-predicate* reduction of economics to psychology that Oppenheim and Putnam's own account of the unity of science requires.

Suppose that the laws of economics hold because people have the attitudes, motives, goals, needs, strategies, etc., that they do. Then the fact that economics is the way it is can be explained by reference to the fact that people are the way that they are. But it doesn't begin to follow that the typical predicates of economics can be reduced to the typical predicates of psychology. Since bridge laws entail biconditionals, P_1 reduces to P_2 only if P_1 and P_2 are at least coextensive. But while the typical predicates of economics subsume (e.g.) monetary systems, cash flows, commodities, labor pools, amounts of capital invested, etc., the typical predicates of psychology subsume stimuli, responses, and mental states. Given the proprietary sense of 'reduction' at issue, to reduce economics to psychology would therefore involve a very great deal more than showing that the economic behavior of groups is determined by the psychology of the individuals that constitute them. In particular, it would involve showing that such notions as *commodity, labor pool*, etc., can be reconstructed in the vocabulary of stimuli, responses, and mental states, and that, moreover, the predicates which affect the reconstruction express psychological kinds (viz., occur in the proper laws of psychology). I think it's fair to say that there is no reason at all to suppose that such reconstructions can be provided: prima facie there is every reason to think that they cannot.

6 This would be the case if higher organisms really are interestingly analogous to general-purpose computers. Such machines exhibit no detailed structure-to-function correspondence over time: rather, the function subserved by a given structure may change from instant to instant depending upon the

character of the program and of the computation being performed.

7 H. Putnam, "Minds and machines," in S. Hook (ed.), *Dimensions of Mind* (New York, New York University Press, (1960), pp. 138–64.

8 To rule out degenerate cases, we assume that n is large enough to yield correlations that are significant in the statistical sense.

9 I don't think there is any chance at all that this is true. What is more likely is that type identification for psychological states can be carried out in terms of the 'total states' of an abstract automation which models the organism whose states they are.

10 For the notion of projectability, see N. Goodman, *Fact, Fiction and Forecast* (Indianapolis: Bobbs-Merrill, 1965).

40

Multiple Realization and the Metaphysics of Reduction

Jaegwon Kim

1 Introduction

It is part of today's conventional wisdom in philosophy of mind that psychological states are "multiply realizable," and are in fact so realized, in a variety of structures and organisms. We are constantly reminded that any mental state, say pain, is capable of "realization," "instantiation," or "implementation" in widely diverse neural-biological structures in humans, felines, reptiles, molluscs, and perhaps other organisms further removed from us. Sometimes we are asked to contemplate the possibility that extraterrestrial creatures with a biochemistry radically different from the earthlings', or even electromechanical devices, can "realize the same psychology" that characterizes humans. This claim, to be called hereafter "the Multiple Realization Thesis" ("MR,"[1] for short), is widely accepted by philosophers, especially those who are inclined to favor the functionalist line on mentality. I will not here dispute the truth of MR, although what I will say may prompt a reassessment of the considerations that have led to its nearly universal acceptance.

And there is an influential and virtually uncontested view about the philosophical significance of MR. This is the belief that MR refutes psychophysical reductionism once and for all. In particu-

lar, the classic psychoneural identity theory of Feigl and Smart, the so-called type physicalism, is standardly thought to have been definitively dispatched by MR to the heap of obsolete philosophical theories of mind. At any rate, it is this claim, that MR proves the physical irreducibility of the mental, that will be the starting point of my discussion.

Evidently, the current popularity of anti-reductionist physicalism is owed, for the most part, to the influence of the MR-based anti-reductionist argument originally developed by Hilary Putnam and elaborated further by Jerry Fodor[2] – rather more so than to the "anomalist" argument associated with Donald Davidson.[3] For example, in their elegant paper on nonreductive physicalism,[4] Geoffrey Hellman and Frank Thompson motivate their project in the following way:

> Traditionally, physicalism has taken the form of reductionism – roughly, that all scientific terms can be given explicit definitions in physical terms. Of late there has been growing awareness, however, that reductionism is an unreasonably strong claim.

But why is reductionism "unreasonably strong"? In a footnote Hellman and Thompson explain, citing Fodor's "Special Sciences":

> Doubts have arisen especially in connection with functional explanation in the higher-level sciences (psychology, linguistics, social theory,

Originally published in *Philosophy and Phenomenological Research* 52 (1992), pp. 309–35. Reprinted by permission of Brown University, Providence, 1992.

etc.). Functional predicates may be physically realizable in heterogeneous ways, so as to elude physical definition.

And Ernest Lepore and Barry Loewer tell us this:

It is practically received wisdom among philosophers of mind that psychological properties (including content properties) are not identical to neurophysiological or other physical properties. The relationship between psychological and neurophysiological properties is that the latter *realize* the former. Furthermore, a single psychological property might (in the sense of conceptual possibility) be realized by a large number, perhaps infinitely many, of different physical properties and even by non-physical properties.[5]

They then go on to sketch the reason why MR, on their view, leads to the rejection of mind–body reduction:

If there are infinitely many physical (and perhaps nonphysical) properties which can realize F, then F will not be reducible to a basic physical property. Even if F can only be realized by finitely many basic physical properties, it might not be reducible to a basic physical property since the disjunction of these properties might not itself be a basic physical property (i.e., occur in a fundamental physical law). We will understand "multiple realizability" as involving such irreducibility.[6]

This anti-reductionist reading of MR continues to this day; in a recent paper, Ned Block writes:

Whatever the merits of physiological reductionism, it is not available to the cognitive science point of view assumed here. According to cognitive science, the essence of the mental is computational, and any computational state is "multiply realizable" by physiological or electronic states that are not identical with one another, and so content cannot be identified with any one of them.[7]

Considerations of these sorts have succeeded in persuading a large majority of philosophers of mind[8] to reject reductionism and type physicalism. The upshot of all this has been impressive: MR has not only ushered in "nonreductive physicalism" as

the new orthodoxy on the mind–body problem, but in the process has put the very word "reductionism" in disrepute, making reductionisms of all stripes an easy target of disdain and curt dismissals.

I believe a reappraisal of MR is overdue. There is something right and instructive in the anti-reductionist claim based on MR and the basic argument in its support, but I believe that we have failed to follow out the implications of MR far enough, and have as a result failed to appreciate its full significance. One specific point that I will argue is this: the popular view that psychology constitutes an *autonomous special science*, a doctrine heavily promoted in the wake of the MR-inspired anti-reductionist dialectic, may in fact be inconsistent with the real implications of MR. Our discussion will show that MR, when combined with certain plausible metaphysical and methodological assumptions, leads to some surprising conclusions about the status of the mental and the nature of psychology as a science. I hope it will become clear that the fate of type physicalism is not among the more interesting consequences of MR.

2 Multiple Realization

It was Putnam, in a paper published in 1967,[9] who first injected MR into debates on the mind–body problem. According to him, the classic reductive theories of mind presupposed the following naïve picture of how psychological kinds (properties, event and state types, etc.) are correlated with physical kinds:

For each psychological kind M there is a unique physical (presumably, neurobiological) kind P that is *nomologically coextensive* with it (i.e., as a matter of law, any system instantiates M at t iff that system instantiates P at t).

(We may call this "the Correlation Thesis.") So take pain: the Correlation Thesis has it that pain as an event kind has a neural substrate, perhaps as yet not fully and precisely identified, that, as a matter of law, always co-occurs with it in all pain-capable organisms and structures. Here there is no mention of species or types of organisms or structures: the neural correlate of pain is invariant across biological species and structure types. In his 1967 paper, Putnam pointed out something that, in retrospect, seems all too obvious:

Consider what the brain-state theorist has to do to make good his claims. He has to specify a physical-chemical state such that any organism (not just a mammal) is in pain if and only if (a) it possesses a brain of a suitable physical-chemical structure; and (b) its brain is in that physical-chemical state. This means that the physical-chemical state in question must be a possible state of a mammalian brain, a reptilian brain, a mollusc's brain (octopuses are mollusca, and certainly feel pain), etc. At the same time, it must not be a possible brain of any physically possible creature that cannot feel pain.[10]

Putnam went on to argue that the Correlation Thesis was *empirically false*. Later writers, however, have stressed the multiple realizability of the mental as a *conceptual* point: it is an a priori, conceptual fact about psychological properties that they are "second-order" physical properties, and that their specification does not include constraints on the manner of their physical implementation.[11] Many proponents of the functionalist account of psychological terms and properties hold such a view.

Thus, on the new, improved picture, the relationship between psychological and physical kinds is something like this: there is no single neural kind N that "realizes" pain across all types of organisms or physical systems; rather, there is a multiplicity of neural-physical kinds, $N_h, N_r, N_m, \ldots$ such that N_h realizes pain in humans, N_r realizes pain in reptiles, N_m realizes pain in Martians, etc. Perhaps, biological species as standardly understood are too broad to yield unique physical-biological realization bases; the neural basis of pain could perhaps change even in a single organism over time. But the main point is clear: any system capable of psychological states (that is, any system that "has a psychology") falls under some structure type T such that systems with structure T share the same physical base for each mental state-kind that they are capable of instantiating (we should regard this as relativized with respect to time to allow for the possibility that an individual may fall under different structure types at different times). Thus physical realization bases for mental states must be relativized to species or, better, physical structure types. We thus have the following thesis:

If anything has mental property M at time t, there is some physical structure type T and physical property P such that it is a system of type T at t and has P at t, and it holds as a matter of law that all systems of type T have M at a time just in case they have P at the same time.

We may call this "the Structure-Restricted Correlation Thesis" (or "the Restricted Correlation Thesis" for short).

It may have been noticed that neither this nor the correlation thesis speaks of "realization."[12] The talk of "realization" is not metaphysically neutral: the idea that mental properties are "realized" or "implemented" by physical properties carries with it a certain ontological picture of mental properties as derivative and dependent. There is the suggestion that when we look at concrete reality, there is nothing over and beyond instantiations of physical properties and relations, and that the instantiation on a given occasion of an appropriate physical property in the right contextual (often causal) setting simply *counts as*, or *constitutes*, an instantiation of a mental property on that occasion. An idea like this is evident in the functionalist conception of a mental property as *extrinsically* characterized in terms of its "causal role," where what fills this role is a physical (or, at any rate, nonmental) property (the latter property will then be said to "realize" the mental property in question). The same idea can be seen in the related functionalist proposal to construe a mental property as a "second-order property" consisting in the having of a physical property satisfying certain extrinsic specifications. We will recur to this topic later; however, we should note that someone who accepts either of the two correlation theses need not espouse the "realization" idiom. That is, it is prima facie a coherent position to think of mental properties as "first-order properties" in their own right, characterized by their intrinsic natures (e.g., phenomenal feel), which, as it happens, turn out to have nomological correlates in neural properties. (In fact, anyone interested in defending a serious dualist position on the mental should eschew the realization talk altogether and consider mental properties as first-order properties on a par with physical properties.) The main point of MR that is relevant to the anti-reductionist argument it has generated is just this: *mental properties do not have nomically coextensive physical properties, when the latter are appropriately individuated.* It may be that properties that are candidates for reduction must be thought of as being realized, or implemented, by properties in the prospective reduction base;[13] that is, if we think of certain properties as having their own intrinsic characterizations that are entirely independent of another set of properties, there is no hope of *reducing* the former to the latter. But this point needs to be argued, and will, in any case, not play a role in what follows.

Assume that property M is realized by property P. How are M and P related to each other and, in particular, how do they covary with each other? Lepore and Loewer say this:

> The usual conception is that e's being P realizes e's being F iff e is P and there is a strong connection of some sort between P and F. We propose to understand this connection as a necessary connection which is *explanatory*. The existence of an explanatory connection between two properties is stronger than the claim that $P \rightarrow F$ is physically necessary since not every physically necessary connection is explanatory.[14]

Thus, Lepore and Loewer require only that the realization base of M be *sufficient* for M, not both necessary and sufficient. This presumably is in response to MR: if pain is multiply realized in three ways as above, each of N_h, N_r, and N_m will be sufficient for pain, and none necessary for it. This I believe is not a correct response, however; the correct response is not to weaken the joint necessity and sufficiency of the physical base, but rather to *relativize* it, as in the Restricted Correlation Thesis, with respect to species or structure types. For suppose we are designing a physical system that will instantiate a certain psychology, and let $M_1 \ldots, M_n$ be the psychological properties required by this psychology. The design process must involve the specification of an n-tuple of physical properties, $P_1 \ldots, P_n$, all of them instantiable by the system, such that for each i, P_i constitutes a *necessary and sufficient* condition *in this system* (and others of relevantly similar physical structure), not merely a sufficient one, for the occurrence of M_i. (Each such n-tuple of physical properties can be called a "physical realization" of the psychology in question.[15]) That is, for each psychological state we must design into the system a nomologically coextensive physical state. We must do this *if we are to control both the occurrence and nonoccurrence of the psychological states involved*, and control of this kind is necessary if we are to ensure that the physical device will properly instantiate the psychology. (This is especially clear if we think of building a computer; computer

analogies loom large in our thoughts about "realization.")

But isn't it possible for multiple realization to occur "locally" as well? That is, we may want to avail ourselves of the flexibility of allowing a psychological state, or function, to be instantiated by alternative mechanisms within a single system. This means that P_i can be a *disjunction* of physical properties; thus, M_i is instantiated in the system in question at a time if and only if at least one of the disjuncts of P_i is instantiated at that time. The upshot of all this is that Lepore and Loewer's condition that $P \rightarrow M$ holds as a matter of law needs to be upgraded to the condition that, *relative to the species or structure type in question (and allowing P to be disjunctive)*, $P \leftrightarrow M$ holds as a matter of law.[16]

For simplicity let us suppose that pain is realized in three ways as above, by N_h in humans, N_r in reptiles, and N_m in Martians. The finitude assumption is not essential to any of my arguments: if the list is not finite, we will have an infinite disjunction rather than a finite one (alternatively, we can talk in terms of "sets" of such properties instead of their disjunctions). If the list is "open-ended," that's all right, too; it will not affect the metaphysics of the situation. We allowed above the possibility of a realization base of a psychological property itself being disjunctive; to get the discussion going, though, we will assume that these Ns, the three imagined physical realization bases of pain, are not themselves disjunctive – or, at any rate, that their status as properties is not in dispute. The propriety and significance of "disjunctive properties" is precisely one of the principal issues we will be dealing with below, and it will make little difference just at what stage this issue is faced.

3 Disjunctive Properties and Fodor's Argument

An obvious initial response to the MR-based argument against reducibility is "the disjunction move": Why not take the disjunction $N_h \lor N_r \lor N_m$ as the single physical substrate of pain? In his 1967 paper, Putnam considers such a move but dismisses it out of hand: "Granted, in such a case the brain-state theorist can save himself by ad hoc assumptions (e.g., defining the disjunction of two states to be a single 'physical–chemical state'), but this does not have to be taken seriously."[17] Putnam gives no hint as to why he thinks the disjunction strategy does not merit serious consideration.

If there is something deeply wrong with disjunctions of the sort involved here, that surely isn't obvious; we need to go beyond a sense of unease with such disjunctions and develop an intelligible rationale for banning them. Here is where Fodor steps in, for he appears to have an argument for disallowing disjunctions. As I see it, Fodor's argument in "Special Sciences" depends crucially on the following two assumptions:

(1) To reduce a special-science theory T_M to physical theory T_r, each "kind" in T_M (presumably, represented by a basic predicate of T_M) must have a nomologically coextensive "kind" in T_i:

(2) A disjunction of heterogeneous kinds is not itself a kind.

Point (1) is apparently prompted by the derivational model of intertheoretic reduction due to Ernest Nagel:[18] the reduction of T_2 to T_1 consists in the derivation of laws of T_2 from the laws of T_1, in conjunction with "bridge" laws or principles connecting T_2-terms with T_1-terms. Although this characterization does not in general require that each T_2-term be correlated with a *coextensive* T_1-term, the natural thought is that the existence of T_1-coextensions for T_2-terms would in effect give us definitions of T_2-terms in T_1-terms, enabling us to rewrite T_2-laws exclusively in the vocabulary of T_1; we could then derive these rewrites of T_2-laws from the laws of T_1 (if they cannot be so derived, we can add them as additional T_1-laws – assuming both theories to be true).

Another thought that again leads us to look for T_1-coextensions for T_2-terms is this: for genuine reduction, the bridge laws must be construed as *property identities*, not mere *property correlations* – namely, we must be in a position to identify the property expressed by a given T_2-term (say, water solubility) with a property expressed by a term in the reduction base (say, having a certain molecular structure). This of course requires that each T_2-term have a nomic (or otherwise suitably modalized) coextension in the vocabulary of the reduction base. To put it another way, ontologically significant reduction requires the reduction of higher-level *properties*, and this in turn requires (unless one takes an eliminativist stance) that they be identified with complexes of lower-level properties. Identity of properties of course requires, at a minimum, an appropriately modalized coextensivity.[19]

So assume M is a psychological kind, and let us agree that to reduce M, or to reduce the psychological theory containing M, we need a physical coextension, P, for M. But why should we suppose that P must be a physical "kind"? But what is a "kind," anyway? Fodor explains this notion in terms of *law*, saying that a given predicate P is a "kind predicate" of a science just in case the science contains a law with P as its antecedent or consequent.[20] There are various problems with Fodor's characterization, but we don't need to take its exact wording seriously; the main idea is that kinds, or kind predicates, of a science are those that figure in the laws of that science.

To return to our question, why should "bridge laws" connect kinds to kinds, in this special sense of "kind"? To say that bridge laws are "laws" and that, by definition, only kind predicates can occur in laws is not much of an answer. For that only invites the further question why "bridge laws" ought to be "laws" – what would be lacking in a reductive derivation if bridge laws were replaced by "bridge principles" which do not necessarily connect kinds to kinds.[21] But what of the consideration that these principles must represent property identities? Does this force on us the requirement that each reduced kind must find a coextensive kind in the reduction base? No; for it isn't obvious why it isn't perfectly proper to reduce kinds by identifying them with properties expressed by non-kind (disjunctive) predicates in the reduction base.

There is the following possible argument for insisting on kinds: if M is identified with non-kind Q (or M is reduced via a biconditional bridge principle "$M \leftrightarrow Q$," where Q is a non-kind), M could no longer figure in special science laws; e.g., the law "$M \rightarrow R$" would in effect reduce to "$Q \rightarrow R$," and therefore lose its status as a law on account of containing Q, a non-kind.

I think this is a plausible response – at least, the beginning of one. As it stands, though, it smacks of circularity: "$Q \rightarrow R$" is not a law because a non-kind, Q, occurs in it, and Q is a non-kind because it cannot occur in a law and "$Q \rightarrow R$," in particular, is not a law. What we need is an *independent* reason for the claim that the sort of Q we are dealing with under MR, namely a badly heterogeneous disjunction, is unsuited for laws.

This means that point (1) really reduces to point (2) above. For, given Fodor's notion of a kind, (2) comes to this: disjunctions of heterogeneous kinds are unfit for laws. What we now need is an *argument* for this claim; to dismiss such disjunctions as "wildly disjunctive" or "heterogeneous and unsystematic" is to label a problem, not to offer a diagnosis of it.[22] In the sections to follow, I hope to take some steps toward such a diagnosis and draw some implications which I believe are significant for the status of mentality.

4 Jade, Jadeite, and Nephrite

Let me begin with an analogy that will guide us in our thinking about multiply realizable kinds.

Consider *jade*: we are told that jade, as it turns out, is not a mineral kind, contrary to what was once believed; rather, jade comprises two distinct minerals with dissimilar molecular structures, *jadeite* and *nephrite*. Consider the following generalization:

(L) Jade is green.

We may have thought, before the discovery of the dual nature of jade, that (L) was a law, a law about jade; and we may have thought, with reason, that (L) had been strongly confirmed by all the millions of jade samples that had been observed to be green (and none that had been observed not to be green). We now know better: (L) is really a conjunction of these two laws:

(L₁) Jadeite is green.
(L₂) Nephrite is green.

But (L) itself might still be a law as well; is that possible? It has the standard basic form of a law, and it apparently has the power to support counterfactuals: if anything were jade – that is, if anything were a sample of jadeite or of nephrite – then, in either case, it would follow, by law, that it was green. No problem here.

But there is another standard mark of lawlikeness that is often cited, and this is "projectibility," the ability to be confirmed by observation of "positive instances." Any generalized conditional of the form "All Fs are G" can be confirmed by the *exhaustion* of the class of Fs – that is, by eliminating all of its potential falsifiers. It is in this sense that we can verify such generalizations as "All the coins in my pockets are copper" and "Everyone in this room is either first-born or an only child." Lawlike generalizations, however, are thought to have the following further property: observation of positive instances, Fs that are Gs, can strengthen our credence in the next F's being G. It is this kind of instance-to-instance accretion of confirmation that is supposed to be the hallmark of lawlikeness; it is what explains the possibility of confirming a generalization about an indefinitely large class of items on the basis of a finite number of favorable observations. This rough characterization of projectibility should suffice for our purposes.

Does (L), "Jade is green," pass the projectibility test? Here we seem to have a problem.[23] For we can imagine this: on re-examining the records of past observations, we find, to our dismay, that all the positive instances of (L), that is, all the millions of observed samples of green jade, turn out to have been samples of jadeite, and none of nephrite! If this should happen, we clearly would not, and should not, continue to think of (L) as well confirmed. All we have is evidence strongly confirming (L₁), and none having anything to do with (L₂). (L) is merely a conjunction of two laws, one well confirmed and the other with its epistemic status wholly up in the air. But all the millions of green jadeite samples *are* positive instances of (L): they satisfy both the antecedent and the consequent of (L). As we have just seen, however, (L) is not confirmed by them, at least not in the standard way we expect. And the reason, I suggest, is that jade is a true disjunctive kind, a disjunction of two heterogeneous nomic kinds which, however, is not itself a nomic kind.[24]

That disjunction is implicated in this failure of projectibility can be seen in the following way: inductive projection of generalizations like (L) with disjunctive antecedents would sanction a cheap, and illegitimate, confirmation procedure. For assume that "All Fs are G" is a law that has been confirmed by the observation of appropriately numerous positive instances, things that are both F and G. But these are also positive instances of the generalization "All things that are F *or* H are G," for any H you please. So, if you in general permit projection of generalizations with a disjunctive antecedent, this latter generalization will also be well confirmed. But "All things that are F *or* H are G" logically implies "All Hs are G." Any statement implied by a well-confirmed statement must itself be well confirmed.[25] So "All Hs are G" is well confirmed – in fact, it is confirmed by the observation of Fs that are Gs!

One might protest: "Look, the very same strategy can be applied to something that is a genuine law. We can think of any nomic kind – say, being an emerald – as a disjunction, being an African emerald or a non-African emerald. This would make 'All emeralds are green' a conjunction of two laws, 'All African emeralds are green' and 'All non-African emeralds are green'. But surely this doesn't show there is anything wrong with the lawlikeness of 'All emeralds are green.'" Our reply is obvious: the disjunction "being an African emerald or non-African emerald" does not denote some heterogeneously disjunctive, nonnomic kind; it denotes a perfectly well-behaved nomic kind, that of being an emerald! There is nothing wrong with disjunctive predicates as such; the trouble arises when the kinds denoted by the disjoined predicates are heterogeneous, "wildly disjunctive," so that instances falling under them do not show the kind of "similarity," or unity, that we expect of instances falling under a single kind.

The phenomenon under discussion, therefore, is related to the simple maxim sometimes claimed to underlie inductive inference: "similar things behave in similar ways," "same cause, same effect," and so on. The source of the trouble we saw with instantial confirmation of "All jade is green" is the fact, or belief, that samples of jadeite and samples of nephrite do not exhibit an appropriate "similarity" with respect to each other to warrant inductive projections from the observed samples of jadeite to unobserved samples of nephrite. But similarity of the required sort presumably holds for African emeralds and non-African emeralds – at least, that is what we believe, and that is what makes the "disjunctive kind," being an African emerald or a non-African emerald, a single nomic kind. More generally, the phenomenon is related to the point often made about disjunctive properties: disjunctive properties, unlike conjunctive properties, do not guarantee similarity for instances falling under them. And similarity, it is said, is the core of our idea of a property. If that is your idea of a property, you will believe that there are no such things as disjunctive properties (or "negative properties"). More precisely, though, we should remember that properties are not inherently disjunctive or conjunctive any more than classes are inherently unions or intersections, and that any property can be expressed by a disjunctive predicate. Properties of course can be conjunctions, or disjunctions, *of* other properties. The point about disjunctive properties is best put as a closure condition on properties: the class of properties is not closed under disjunction (presumably, or under negation). Thus, there may well be properties P and Q such that P *or* Q is also a property,

but its being so doesn't follow from the mere fact that P and Q are properties.[26]

5 Jade and Pain

Let us now return to pain and its multiple realization bases, N_h, N_r, and N_m. I believe the situation here is instructively parallel to the case of jade in relation to jadeite and nephrite. It seems that we think of jadeite and nephrite as distinct kinds (and of jade not as a kind) because they are different chemical kinds. But why is their being distinct as chemical kinds relevant here? Because many important properties of minerals, we think, are supervenient on, and explainable in terms of, their microstructure, and chemical kinds constitute a microstructural taxonomy that is explanatorily rich and powerful. Microstructure is important, in short, because macrophysical properties of substances are determined by microstructure. These ideas make up our "metaphysics" of microdetermination for properties of minerals and other substances, a background of partly empirical and partly metaphysical assumptions that regulate our inductive and explanatory practices.

The parallel metaphysical underpinnings for pain, and other mental states in general, are, first, the belief, expressed by the Restricted Correlation Thesis, that pain, or any other mental state, occurs in a system when, and only when, appropriate physical conditions are present in the system, and, second, the corollary belief that significant properties of mental states, in particular nomic relationships amongst them, are due to, and explainable in terms of, the properties and causal-nomic connections among their physical "substrates." I will call the conjunction of these two beliefs "the Physical Realization Thesis."[27] Whether or not the micro-explanation of the sort indicated in the second half of the thesis amounts to a "reduction" is a question we will take up later. Apart from this question, though, the Physical Realization Thesis is widely accepted by philosophers who talk of "physical realization," and this includes most functionalists; it is all but explicit in Lepore and Loewer, for example, and in Fodor.[28]

Define a property, N, by disjoining N_h, N_r, and N_m; that is, N has a disjunctive definition, $N_h \lor N_r \lor N_m$. If we assume, with those who endorse the MR-based anti-reductionist argument, that N_h, N_r, and N_m are a heterogeneous lot, we cannot make the heterogeneity go away merely by introducing a simpler expression, "N"; if there is a problem with certain disjunctive properties, it is not a *linguistic* problem about the form of expressions used to refer to them.

Now, we put the following question to Fodor and like-minded philosophers: If pain is nomically equivalent to N, the property claimed to be wildly disjunctive and obviously nonnomic, *why isn't pain itself equally heterogeneous and nonnomic as a kind?* Why isn't pain's relationship to its realization bases, N_h, N_r, and N_m, analogous to jade's relationship to jadeite and nephrite? If jade turns out to be nonnomic on account of its dual "realizations" in distinct microstructures, why doesn't the same fate befall pain? After all, the group of actual and nomologically possible realizations of pain, as they are described by the MR enthusiasts with such imagination, is far more motley than the two chemical kinds comprising jade.

I believe we should insist on answers to these questions from those functionalists who view mental properties as "second-order" properties, i.e., properties that consist in having a property with a certain functional specification.[29] Thus, pain is said to be a second-order property in that it is the *property of having some property with a certain specification* in terms of its typical causes and effects and its relation to other mental properties; call this "specification H." The point of MR, on this view, is that there is more than one property that meets specification H – in fact, an open-ended set of such properties, it will be said. But pain itself, it is argued, is a more abstract but well-behaved property at a higher level, namely the property of having one of these properties meeting specification H. It should be clear why a position like this is vulnerable to the questions that have been raised. For the property of having property P is exactly identical with P, and the property of having *one* of the properties, P_1, P_2, ..., P_n is exactly identical with the disjunctive property, $P_1 \lor P_2 \lor \ldots \lor P_n$. On the assumption that N_h, N_r, and N_m are all the properties satisfying specification H, the property of having a property with H, namely pain, is none other than the property of having either N_h or N_r or N_m[30] – namely, the *disjunctive* property, $N_h \lor N_r \lor N_m$! We cannot hide the disjunctive character of pain behind the second-order *expression* "the property of having a property with specification H." Thus, on the construal of mental properties as second-order properties, mental properties will in general turn out to be disjunctions of their physical realization

bases. It is difficult to see how one could have it both ways – that is, to castigate N_h, $\lor N_r$, $\lor N_m$ as unacceptably disjunctive while insisting on the integrity of pain as a scientific kind.

Moreover, when we think about making projections over pain, very much the same worry should arise about their propriety as did for jade. Consider a possible law: "Sharp pains administered at random intervals cause anxiety reactions." Suppose this generalization has been well confirmed for humans. Should we expect *on that basis* that it will hold also for Martians whose psychology is implemented (we assume) by a vastly different physical mechanism? Not if we accept the Physical Realization Thesis, fundamental to functionalism, that psychological regularities hold, to the extent that they do, in virtue of the causal-nomological regularities at the physical implementation level. The reason the law is true for humans is due to the way the human brain is "wired"; the Martians have a brain with a different wiring plan, and we certainly should not expect the regularity to hold for them just because it does for humans.[31] "Pains cause anxiety reactions" may turn out to possess no more unity as a scientific law than does "Jade is green."

Suppose that in spite of all this Fodor insists on defending pain as a nomic kind. It isn't clear that would be a viable strategy. For he would then owe us an explanation of why the "wildly disjunctive" N, which after all is equivalent to pain, is not a nomic kind. If a predicate is nomically equivalent to a well-behaved predicate, why isn't that enough to show that it, too, is well behaved, and expresses a well-behaved property? To say, as Fodor does,[32] that "it is a law that ..." is "intensional" and does not permit substitution of equivalent expressions ("equivalent" in various appropriate senses) is merely to locate a potential problem, not to resolve it.

Thus, the nomicity of pain may lead to the nomicity of N; but this isn't very interesting. For, given the Physical Realization Thesis and the priority of the physical implicit in it, our earlier line of argument, leading from the nonnomicity of N to the nonnomicity of pain, is more compelling. We must, I think, take seriously the reasoning leading to the conclusion that pain, and other mental states, might turn out to be nonnomic. If this turns out to be the case, it puts in serious jeopardy Fodor's contention that its physical irreducibility renders psychology an autonomous special science. If pain fails to be nomic, it is not the sort of property in terms of which laws can be formulated;

and "pain" is not a predicate that can enter into a scientific theory that seeks to formulate causal laws and causal explanations. And the same goes for all multiply realizable psychological kinds – which, according to MR, means *all* psychological kinds. There are no scientific theories of jade, and we don't need any; if you insist on having one, you can help yourself with the *conjunction* of the theory of jadeite and the theory of nephrite. In the same way, there will be theories about human pains (instances of N_h), reptilian pains (instances of N_r), and so on; but there will be no unified, integrated theory encompassing all pains in all pain-capable organisms, only a conjunction of pain theories for appropriately individuated biological species and physical structure types. Scientific psychology, like the theory of jade, gives way to a conjunction of structure-specific theories. If this is right, the correct conclusion to be drawn from the MR-inspired anti-reductionist argument is not the claim that psychology is an irreducible and autonomous science, but something that contradicts it: namely, that it cannot be a science with a unified subject matter. This is the picture that is beginning to emerge from MR when combined with the Physical Realization Thesis.

These reflections have been prompted by the analogy with the case of jade; it is a strong and instructive analogy, I think, and suggests the possibility of a general argument. In the following section I will develop a direct argument, with explicit premises and assumptions.

6 Causal Powers and Mental Kinds

One crucial premise we need for a direct argument is a constraint on concept formation, or kind individuation, in science that has been around for many years; it has lately been resurrected by Fodor in connection with content externalism.[33] A precise statement of the constraint may be difficult and controversial, but its main idea can be put as follows:

[Principle of Causal Individuation of Kinds] Kinds in science are individuated on the basis of causal powers; that is, objects and events fall under a kind, or share in a property, insofar as they have similar causal powers.

I believe this is a plausible principle, and it is, in any case, widely accepted.

We can see that this principle enables us to give a specific interpretation to the claim that N_h, N_r, and N_m are *heterogeneous* as kinds: the claim must mean that they are *heterogeneous as causal powers* – that is, they are diverse as causal powers and enter into diverse causal laws. This must mean, given the Physical Realization Thesis, that pain itself can show no more unity as a causal power than the disjunction, $N_h \lor N_r \lor N_m$. This becomes especially clear if we set forth the following principle, which arguably is implied by the Physical Realization Thesis (but we need not make an issue of this here):

[The Causal Inheritance Principle] If mental property M is realized in a system at t in virtue of physical realization base P, the causal powers of *this instance of M* are identical with the causal powers of P.[34]

It is important to bear in mind that this principle only concerns the causal powers of *individual instances of M*; it does not identify the causal powers of mental property M *in general* with the causal powers of some physical property P; such identification is precluded by the multiple physical realizability of M.

Why should we accept this principle? Let us just note that to deny it would be to accept *emergent* causal powers: causal powers that magically emerge at a higher level and of which there is no accounting in terms of lower-level properties and their causal powers and nomic connections. This leads to the notorious problem of "downward causation" and the attendant violation of the causal closure of the physical domain.[35] I believe that a serious physicalist would find these consequences intolerable.

It is clear that the Causal Inheritance Principle, in conjunction with the Physical Realization Thesis, has the consequence that mental kinds cannot satisfy the Causal Individuation Principle, and this effectively rules out mental kinds as scientific kinds. The reasoning is simple: instances of M that are realized by the same physical base must be grouped under one kind, since *ex hypothesi* the physical base is a causal kind; and instances of M with different realization bases must be grouped under distinct kinds, since, again *ex hypothesi*, these realization bases are distinct as causal kinds. Given that mental kinds are realized by diverse physical causal kinds, therefore, it follows that mental kinds are not causal kinds, and hence are disqualified as proper scientific kinds. Each mental kind is sundered into as many kinds as there are physical realization bases for it, and psychology as a science with disciplinary unity turns out to be an impossible project.

What is the relationship between this argument and the argument adumbrated in our reflections based on the jade analogy? At first blush, the two arguments might seem unrelated: the earlier argument depended chiefly on epistemological considerations, considerations on inductive projectibility of certain predicates, whereas the crucial premise of the second argument is the Causal Individuation Principle, a broadly metaphysical and methodological principle about science. I think, though, that the two arguments are closely related, and the key to seeing the relationship is this: causal powers involve laws, and laws are regularities that are projectible. Thus, if pain (or jade) is not a kind over which inductive projections can be made, it cannot enter into laws, and therefore cannot qualify as a causal kind; and this disqualifies it as a scientific kind. If this is right, the jade-inspired reflections provide a possible rationale for the Causal Individuation Principle. Fleshing out this rough chain of reasoning in precise terms, however, goes beyond what I can attempt here.

7 The Status of Psychology: Local Reductions

Our conclusion at this point, therefore, is this: If MR is true, psychological kinds are not scientific kinds. What does this imply about the status of psychology as a science? Do our considerations show that psychology is a pseudo-science like astrology and alchemy? Of course not. The crucial difference, from the metaphysical point of view, is that psychology has physical realizations, but alchemy does not. To have a physical realization is to be physically grounded and explainable in terms of the processes at an underlying level. In fact, if each of the psychological kinds posited in a psychological theory has a physical realization for a fixed species, the theory can be "locally reduced" to the physical theory of that species, in the following sense. Let S be the species involved; for each law L_m of psychological theory $T_m, S \rightarrow L_m$ (the proposition that L_m holds for members of S) is the "S-restricted" version of L_m: and $S \rightarrow T_m$ is the S-restricted version of T_m, the set of all S-restricted laws of T_m. We can then say that T_m is "locally reduced" for species S to an underlying theory,

T_p, just in case $S \rightarrow T_m$ is reduced to T_p. And the latter obtains just in case each S-restricted law of $T_m, S \rightarrow L_m$,[36] is derivable from the laws of the reducing theory T_p, taken together with bridge laws. What bridge laws suffice to guarantee the derivation? Obviously, an array of S-restricted bridge laws of the form, $S \rightarrow (M_i \leftrightarrow P_i)$, for each mental kind M_i. Just as unrestricted psychological bridge laws can underwrite a "global" or "uniform" reduction of psychology, species- or structure-restricted bridge laws sanction its "local" reduction.

If the same psychological theory is true of humans, reptiles, and Martians, the psychological kinds posited by that theory must have realizations in human, reptilian, and Martian physiologies. This implies that the theory is locally reducible in three ways, for humans, reptiles, and Martians. If the dependence of the mental on the physical means anything, it must mean that the regularities posited by this common psychology must have divergent physical explanations for the three species. The very idea of physical realization involves the possibility of physically explaining psychological properties and regularities, and the supposition of multiple such realizations, namely MR, involves a commitment to the possibility of multiple explanatory reductions of psychology.[37] The important moral of MR we need to keep in mind is this: *if psychological properties are multiply realized, so is psychology itself.* If physical realizations of psychological properties are a "wildly heterogeneous" and "unsystematic" lot, psychological theory itself must be realized by an equally heterogeneous and unsystematic lot of physical theories.

I am inclined to think that multiple local reductions, rather than global reductions, are the rule, even in areas in which we standardly suppose reductions are possible. I will now deal with a possible objection to the idea of local reduction, at least as it is applied to psychology. The objection goes like this: given what we know about the differences among members of a single species, even species are too wide to yield determinate realization bases for psychological states, and given what we know about the phenomena of maturation and development, brain injuries, and the like, the physical bases of mentality may change even for a single individual. This throws into serious doubt, continues the objection, the availability of species-restricted bridge laws needed for local reductions.

The point of this objection may well be correct as a matter of empirical fact. Two points can be made in reply, however. First, neurophysiological research goes on because there is a shared, and probably well-grounded, belief among the workers that there are not huge individual differences within a species in the way psychological kinds are realized. Conspecifics must show important physical-physiological similarities, and there probably is good reason for thinking that they share physical realization bases to a sufficient degree to make search for species-wide neural substrates for mental states feasible and rewarding. Researchers in this area evidently aim for neurobiological explanations of psychological capacities and processes that are generalizable over all or most ("normal") members of a given species.

Second, even if there are huge individual differences among conspecifics as to how their psychology is realized, that does not touch the metaphysical point: as long as you believe in the Physical Realization Thesis, you must believe that every organism or system with mentality falls under a physical structure type such that its mental states are realized by determinate physical states of organisms with that structure. It may be that these structures are so finely individuated and so few *actual* individuals fall under them that research into the neural bases of mental states in these structures is no longer worthwhile, theoretically or practically. What we need to recognize here is that the scientific possibility of, say, human psychology is a contingent fact (assuming it is a fact); it depends on the fortunate fact that individual humans do not show huge physiological-biological differences that are psychologically relevant. But if they did, that would not change the metaphysics of the situation one bit; it would remain true that the psychology of each of us was determined by, and locally reducible to, his neurobiology.

Realistically, there are going to be psychological differences among individual humans: it is a commonsense platitude that no two persons are exactly alike – either physically or psychologically. And individual differences may be manifested not only in particular psychological facts but in psychological regularities. If we believe in the Physical Realization Thesis, we must believe that our psychological differences are rooted in, and explainable by, our physical differences, just as we expect our psychological similarities to be so explainable. Humans probably are less alike among themselves than, say, tokens of a Chevrolet model.[38] And psychological laws for humans, at a certain level of specificity, must be expected to be statistical in character, not deterministic – or, if you prefer,

"ceteris paribus laws" rather than "strict laws." But this is nothing peculiar to psychology; these remarks surely apply to human psychology and anatomy as much as human psychology. In any case, none of this affects the metaphysical point being argued here concerning microdetermination and microreductive explanation.

8 Metaphysical Implications

But does local reduction have any interesting philosophical significance, especially in regard to the status of mental properties? If a psychological property has been multiply locally reduced, does that mean that the property itself has been reduced? Ned Block has raised just such a point, arguing that species-restricted reductionism (or species-restricted-type physicalism) "sidesteps the main metaphysical question: 'What is common to the pains of dogs and people (and all other species) in virtue of which they are pains?'"[39]

Pereboom and Kornblith elaborate on Block's point as follows:

> ... even if there is a single type of physical state that normally realizes pain in each type of organism, or in each structure type, this does not show that pain, *as a type of mental state*, is reducible to physical states. Reduction, in the present debate, must be understood as reduction of types, since the primary object of reductive strategies is explanations and theories, and explanations and theories quantify over types.... The suggestion that there are species-specific reductions of pain results in the claim that pains in different species have nothing in common. But this is just a form of eliminativism.[40]

There are several related but separable issues raised here. But first we should ask: Must all pains have "something in common" in virtue of which they are pains?

According to the phenomenological conception of pain, all pains do have something in common: they all *hurt*. But as I take it, those who hold this view of pain would reject any reductionist program, independently of the issues presently on hand. Even if there were a species-invariant uniform bridge law correlating pains with a single physical substrate across all species and structures, they would claim that the correlation holds as a brute, unexplainable matter of fact, and that pain as a qualitative event, a "raw feel," would remain irreducibly distinct from its neural substrate. Many emergentists apparently held a view of this kind.

I presume that Block, and Pereboom and Kornblith, are speaking not from a phenomenological viewpoint of this kind but from a broadly functionalist one. But from a functionalist perspective, it is by no means clear how we should understand the question "What do all pains have in common in virtue of which they are all pains?" Why should all pains have "something in common"? As I understand it, at the core of the functionalist program is the attempt to explain the meanings of mental terms *relationally*, in terms of inputs, outputs, and connections with other mental states. And on the view, discussed briefly earlier, that mental properties are second-order properties, pain is the property of having a property with a certain functional specification H (in terms of inputs, outputs, etc.). This yields a short answer to Block's question: what all pains have in common is the pattern of connections as specified by H. The local reductionist is entitled to that answer as much as the functionalist is. Compare two pains, an instance of N_h and one of N_m; what they have in common is that each is an instance of a property that realizes pain – that is, they exhibit the same pattern of input–output–other internal state connections, namely the pattern specified by H.

But some will say: "But H is only an *extrinsic* characterization; what do these instances of pain have in common that is *intrinsic* to them?" The local reductionist must grant that on his view there is nothing intrinsic that all pains have in common in virtue of which they are pains (assuming that N_h, N_r, and N_m, "have nothing intrinsic in common"). But that is also precisely the consequence of the functionalist view. That, one might say, is the whole point of functionalism: the functionalist, especially one who believes in MR, would not, and should not, look for something common to all pains over and above H (the heart of functionalism, one might say, is the belief that mental states have no "intrinsic essence").

But there is a further question raised by Block et al.: What happens to properties that have been locally reduced? Are they still with us, distinct and separate from the underlying physical-biological properties? Granted: human pain is reduced to N_h, Martian pain to N_m, and so forth, but what of *pain itself*? It remains unreduced. Are we still stuck with the dualism of mental and physical properties?

I will sketch two possible ways of meeting this challenge. First, recall my earlier remarks about the functionalist conception of mental properties as second-order properties: pain is *the property of having a property with specification H*, and, given that N_h, N_r, and N_m are the properties meeting H, pain turns out to be the disjunctive property, $N_h \lor N_r \lor N_m$, If you hold the second-order property view of mental properties, pain has been reduced to, and survives as, this disjunctive physical kind. Quite apart from considerations of local reduction, the very conception of pain you hold commits you to the conclusion that pain is a disjunctive kind, and if you accept any form of respectable physicalism (in particular, the Physical Realization Thesis), it is a disjunctive *physical* kind. And even if you don't accept the view of mental properties as second-order properties, as long as you are comfortable with disjunctive kinds and properties, you can, in the aftermath of local reduction, identify pain with the disjunction of its realization bases. On this approach, then, you have another, more direct, answer to Block's question: what all pains have in common is that they all fall under the disjunctive kind, $N_h, \lor N_r \lor N_m$.

If you are averse to disjunctive kinds, there is another more radical, and in some ways more satisfying, approach. The starting point of this approach is the frank acknowledgment that MR leads to the conclusion that pain as a property or kind must go. Local reduction after all is reduction, and to be reduced is to be eliminated as an *independent* entity. You might say: global reduction is different in that it is also *conservative* – if pain is globally reduced to physical property P, pain survives as P. But it is also true that under local reduction, pain survives as N_h in humans, as N_r in reptiles, and so on. It must be admitted, however, that pain as a kind does not survive multiple local reduction. But is this so bad?

Let us return to jade once again. Is jade a *kind*? We know it is not a mineral kind; but is it any kind of a kind? That of course depends on what we mean by "kind." There are certain shared criteria, largely based on observable macroproperties of mineral samples (e.g., hardness, color, etc.), that determine whether something is a sample of jade, or whether the predicate "is jade" is correctly applicable to it. What all samples of jade have in common is just these observable macrophysical properties that define the applicability of the predicate "is jade." In this sense, speakers of English who have "jade" in their repertoire associate the same *concept* with "jade"; and we can recognize the existence of the concept of jade and at the same time acknowledge that the concept does not pick out, or answer to, a property or kind in the natural world.

I think we can say something similar about pain and "pain": there are shared criteria for the application of the predicate "pain" or "is in pain," and these criteria may well be for the most part functionalist ones. These criteria generate for us a *concept of pain*, a concept whose clarity and determinacy depend, we may assume, on certain characteristics (such as explicitness, coherence, and completeness) of the criteria governing the application of "pain." But the concept of pain, on this construal, need not pick out an objective kind any more than the concept of jade does.

All this presupposes a distinction between concepts and properties (or kinds). Do we have such a distinction? I believe we do. Roughly, concepts are in the same ball park as predicates, meanings (perhaps, something like Fregean *Sinnen*), ideas, and the like; Putnam has suggested that concepts be identified with "synonymy classes of predicates,"[41] and that comes close enough to what I have in mind. Properties and relations, on the other hand, are "out there in the world"; they are features and characteristics of things and events in the world. They include fundamental physical magnitudes and quantities, like mass, energy, size, and shape, and are part of the causal structure of the world. The property of being water is arguably identical with the property of being H_2O, but evidently the concept of water is distinct from the concept of H_2O (Socrates had the former but not the latter). Most of us would agree that ethical predicates are meaningful, and that we have the concepts of "good," "right," etc.; however, it is a debatable issue, and has lately been much debated, whether there are such properties as goodness and rightness.[42] If you find that most of these remarks make sense, you understand the concept–property distinction that I have in mind. Admittedly, this is all a little vague and programmatic, and we clearly need a better-articulated theory of properties and concepts; but the distinction is there, supported by an impressively systematic set of intuitions and philosophical requirements.[43]

But is this second approach a form of mental eliminativism? In a sense it is: as I said, on this approach no properties in the world answer to general, species-unrestricted mental concepts. But remember: there still are pains, and we sometimes are in pain, just as there still are samples of jade.

We must also keep in mind that the present approach is not, in its ontological implications, a form of the standard mental eliminativism currently on the scene.[44] Without elaborating on what the differences are, let us just note a few important points. First, the present view does not take away species-restricted mental properties, e.g., human pain, Martian pain, canine pain, and the rest, although it takes away "pain as such." Second, while the standard eliminativism consigns mentality to the same ontological limbo to which phlogiston, witches, and magnetic effluvia have been dispatched, the position I have been sketching views it on a par with jade, tables, and adding machines. To see jade as a non-kind is not to question the existence of jade, or the legitimacy and utility of the concept of jade. Tables do not constitute a scientific kind; there are no laws about tables as such, and being a table is not a causal-explanatory kind. But that must be sharply distinguished from the false claim that there are no tables. The same goes for pains. These points suggest the following difference in regard to the status of psychology: the present view allows, and in fact encourages, "species-specific psychologies," but the standard eliminativism would do away with all things psychological – species-specific psychologies as well as global psychology.

To summarize, then, the two metaphysical schemes I have sketched offer these choices: either we allow disjunctive kinds and construe pain and other mental properties as such kinds, or else we must acknowledge that our general mental terms and concepts do not pick out properties and kinds in the world (we may call this "mental property irrealism"). I should add that I am not interested in promoting either disjunctive kinds or mental irrealism, a troubling set of choices to most of us. Rather, my main interest has been to follow out the consequences of MR and try to come to terms with them within a reasonable metaphysical scheme.

I have already commented on the status of psychology as a science under MR. As I argued, MR seriously compromises the disciplinary unity and autonomy of psychology as a science. But that does not have to be taken as a negative message. In particular, the claim does not imply that a scientific study of psychological phenomena is not possible or useful; on the contrary, MR says that psychological processes have a foundation in the biological and physical processes and regularities, and it opens the possibility of enlightening explanations of psychological processes at a more basic level. It is only that at a deeper level, psychology becomes sundered by being multiply locally reduced. However, species-specific psychologies, e.g., human psychology, Martian psychology, etc., can all flourish as scientific theories. Psychology remains scientific, though perhaps not a *science*. If you insist on having a global psychology valid for all species and structures, you can help yourself with that, too; but you must think of it as a *conjunction* of species-restricted psychologies and be careful, above all, with your inductions.

Notes

This paper is descended from an unpublished paper, "The disunity of psychology as a working hypothesis?," which was circulated in the early 1980s. I am indebted to the following persons, among others, for helpful comments: Fred Feldman, Hilary Kornblith, Barry Loewer, Brian McLaughlin, Joe Mendola, Marcelo Sabates, and James Van Cleve.

1 On occasion, "MR" will refer to the *phenomenon* of multiple realization rather than the *claim* that such a phenomenon exists; there should be no danger of confusion.

2 Jerry Fodor, "Special sciences," this volume, ch. 39.

3 Donald Davidson, "Mental events," repr. in *Essays on Actions and Events* (Oxford: Oxford University Press, 1980).

4 Geoffrey Hellman and Frank Thompson, "Physicalism: Ontology, Determination, and Reduction," this volume, ch. 41; the two quotations are from pp. 531 and 537.

5 Ernest Lepore and Barry Loewer, "More on making mind matter," *Philosophical Topics* 17 (1989), pp. 175–92, at p. 179.

6 Ibid., p. 180.

7 Ned Block, "Can the mind change the world?," in George Boolos (ed.), *Meaning and Method: Essays in Honor of Hilary Putnam* (Cambridge: Cambridge University Press, 1990), p. 146.

8 They include Richard Boyd, "Materialism without reductionism: what physicalism does not entail," in Block (ed.), *Readings in Philosophy of Psychology*, vol. 1 (Cambridge, Mass.: Harvard University Press, 1980); Block, in "Introduction: what is functionalism?," in his anthology just cited, pp. 178–9; John Post, *The Faces of Existence* (Ithaca, NY: Cornell University Press, 1987); Derk Pereboom and Hilary Kornblith, "The metaphysics of irreducibility," *Philosophical Studies* 63 (1991), pp. 125–45. One philosopher who is not impressed by the received view of MR is David Lewis; see his "Review of Putnam," in Block (ed.), *Readings in Philosophy of Psychology*, vol. 1.

9 Hilary Putnam, "Psychological predicates," in W. H. Capitan and D. D. Merrill (eds), *Art, Mind, and Religion* (Pittsburgh: University of Pittsburgh Press, 1967); repr. with a new title, "The nature of mental states," in Block (ed.), *Readings in Philosophy of Psychology*.

10 Putnam, "Nature of mental states," p. 228.

11 Thus, Post says, "Functional and intentional states are defined without regard to their physical or other realizations" (*Faces of Existence*, p. 161). Also compare the earlier quotation from Block.

12 As far as I know, the term "realization" was first used in something like its present sense by Hilary Putnam in "Minds and machines," in Sydney Hook (ed.), *Dimensions of Mind* (New York: New York University Press, 1960).

13 On this point see Robert Van Gulick, "Nonreductive materialism and intertheoretic constraints", in Ansgar Beckermann, Hans Flohr, and Jaegwon Kim (eds), *Emergence or Reduction?* (Berlin: De Gruyter, 1992).

14 Lepore and Loewer, "More on making mind matter," p. 179.

15 Cf. Hartry Field, "Mental representation," in Block (ed.), *Readings in Philosophy of Psychology* (Cambridge, Mass.: Harvard University Press, 1981), vol. 2.

16 What of Lepore and Loewer's condition (ii), the requirement that the realization basis "explain" the realized property? Something like this explanatory relation may well be entailed by the realization relation; however, I do not believe it should be part of the definition of "realization"; that such an explanatory relation holds should be a consequence of the realization relation, not constitutive of it.

17 Putnam, "Nature of mental states," p. 228.

18 Ernest Nagel, *The Structure of Science* (New York: Harcourt, Brace & World, 1961), ch. 11.

19 My remarks here and in the preceding paragraph assume that the higher-level theory requires no "correction" in relation to the base theory. With appropriate caveats and qualifications, they should apply to models of reduction that allow such corrections, or models that only require the deduction of a suitable analogue, or "image," in the reduction base – as long as the departures are not so extreme as to warrant talk of replacement or elimination rather than reduction. Cf. Patricia Churchland, *Neurophilosophy* (Cambridge, Mass.: MIT Press, 1986), ch. 7.

20 See Fodor, "Special sciences," this volume, ch. 39, p. 506.

21 Fodor appears to assume that the requirement that bridge laws must connect "kinds" to "kinds" is part of the classic positivist conception of reduction.

I don't believe there is any warrant for this assumption, however.

22 See Pereboom and Kornblith, "Metaphysics of irreducibility," in which it is suggested that laws with disjunctive predicates are not "explanatory." I think, though, that this suggestion is not fully developed there.

23 The points to follow concerning disjunctive predicates were developed about a decade ago; however, I have just come across some related and, in some respects similar, points in David Owens's interesting paper "Disjunctive laws," *Analysis* 49 (1989), pp. 197–202. See also William Seager, "Disjunctive laws and supervenience," *Analysis* 51 (1991), pp. 93–8.

24 This can be taken to define one useful sense of kind heterogeneity: two kinds are heterogeneous with respect to each other just in case their disjunction is not a kind.

25 Note: this doesn't say that for any *e*, if *e* is "positive evidence" for *h* and *h* logically implies *j*, then *e* is positive evidence for *j*. About the latter principle there is some dispute; see Carl G. Hempel, "Studies in the logic of confirmation," repr. in Hempel, *Aspects of Scientific Explanation* (New York: Free Press, 1965), esp. pp. 30–5; Rudolf Carnap, *Logical Foundations of Probability* (Chicago: University of Chicago Press, 1950), pp. 471–6.

26 On issues concerning properties, kinds, similarity, and lawlikeness, see W. V. Quine, "Natural kinds," this volume, ch. 18; David Lewis, "New work for a theory of universals," this volume, ch. 17; D. M. Armstrong, *Universals* (Boulder, Colo.: Westview Press, 1989).

27 This term is a little misleading since the two subtheses have been stated without the term "realization" and may be acceptable to those who would reject the "realization" idiom in connection with the mental. I use the term since we are chiefly addressing philosophers (mainly functionalists) who construe the psychophysical relation in terms of realization, rather than, say, emergence or brute correlation.

28 See E. Lepore and B. Loewer, "Making mind matter more," *Philosophical Topics* 17 (1989), pp. 59–79, and Fodor "Special Sciences," this volume, ch. 39.

29 See, e.g., Block, "Can the mind change the world?," p. 155.

30 We might keep in mind the close relationship between disjunction and the existential quantifier standardly noted in logic textbooks.

31 It may be a complicated affair to formulate this argument within certain functionalist schemes; if, for example, mental properties are functionally defined by Ramseyfying a total psychological theory, it will turn out that humans and Martians cannot share any psychological state unless the same total psychology (including the putative law in question) is true (or held to be true) for both.

32 Fodor, "Special sciences," this volume, ch. 39.

33 See, e.g., Carl G. Hempel, *Fundamentals of Concept Formation in Empirical Science* (Chicago: University of Chicago Press, 1952); Quine, "Natural kinds," this volume, ch. 18. Fodor gives it an explicit statement in *Psychosemantics* (Cambridge, Mass.: MIT Press, 1988), ch. 2. A principle like this is often invoked in the current externalism/internalism debate about content; most principal participants in this debate seem to accept it.

34 A principle like this is sometimes put in terms of "supervenience" and "supervenience base" rather than "realization" and "realization base." See my "Epiphenomenal and supervenient causation," in Jaegwon Kim, *Supervenience and Mind* (Cambridge: Cambridge University Press, 1993), ch. 6. Fodor appears to accept just such a principle of supervenient causation for mental properties in ch. 2 of his *Psychosemantics*. In "Metaphysics of irreducibility," Pereboom and Kornblith appear to reject it.

35 For more details see my "'Downward causation' in emergentism and nonreductive Physicalism," in Beckermann, et al. (eds), *Emergence or Reduction?*, and "The nonreductivist's troubles with mental causation," in Kim, *Supervenience and Mind*, ch. 17.

36 Or an appropriately corrected version thereof (this qualification applies to the bridge laws as well).

37 In "Special sciences" and "Making mind matter more" Fodor appears to accept the local reducibility of psychology and other special sciences. But he uses the terminology of local *explanation*, rather than reduction, of psychological regularities in terms of underlying microstructure. I think this is because his preoccupation with Nagelian uniform reduction prevents him from seeing that this is a form of intertheoretic reduction if anything is.

38 Compare J. J. C. Smart's instructive analogy between biological organisms and superheterodyne radios, in *Philosophy and Scientific Realism* (London: Routledge & Kegan Paul, 1963), pp. 56–7. Smart's conception of the relation between physics and the special sciences, such as biology and psychology, is similar in some respects to the position I am defending here.

39 Block, "Introduction: what is functionalism?" pp. 178–9.

40 Pereboom and Korablith, "Metaphysics of irreducibility." See also Ronald Endicott, "On physical multiple realization," *Pacific Philosophical Quarterly* 70 (1989), pp. 212–24. In personal correspondence Earl Conee and Joe Mendola have raised similar points. There is a useful discussion of various metaphysical issues relating to MR in Cynthia Macdonald, *Mind–Body Identity Theories* (London and New York: Routledge, 1989).

41 Putnam, "Nature of mental states."

42 I of course have in mind the controversy concerning moral realism; see essays in Geoffrey Sayre-McCord

(ed.) *Essays on Moral Realism* (Ithaca, NY: Cornell University Press, 1988).

43 On concepts and properties, see, e.g., Hilary Putnam, "On properties," this volume, ch. 19; Mark Wilson, "Predicate meets property," *Philosophical Review* 91 (1982), pp. 549–90, esp. sect. 3.

44 Such as the versions favored by W. V. Quine, Stephen Stich, and Paul Churchland.

41

Physicalism: Ontology, Determination, and Reduction

Geoffrey Hellman and Frank Thompson

Mathematical physics, as the most basic and comprehensive of the sciences, occupies a special position with respect to the overall scientific framework. In its loosest sense, physicalism is a recognition of this special position. Traditionally, physicalism has taken the form of reductionism – roughly, that all scientific terms can be given explicit definitions in physical terms.[1] Of late there has been a growing awareness, however, that reductionism is an unreasonably strong claim.[2] Along with this has come recognition that reductionism is to be distinguished from a purely ontological thesis concerning the sorts of entities of which the world is constituted. This separation is important: even if physical reductionism is unwarranted, what may be called "emergence" of higher-order phenomena is allowed for without departing from the physical ontology. (In particular, anti-reductionist arguments are seen as lending no support whatever to Cartesian dualism as an ontological claim.) Moreover, there has been a tendency to suppose that reduction of terminology entails reduction of ontology, but this is mistaken. It is thus necessary to consider just how to state a reasonably precise physicalist ontological position. This is the burden of section I.

Although a purely ontological thesis is a necessary component of physicalism, it is insufficient, in that it makes no appeal to the power of physical law. In section II, we seek to develop principles of *physical determination* that spell out rather precisely the underlying physicalist intuition that the physical facts determine all the facts. The goal is then to show that these principles do not imply physical reductionism. The main task here is to avoid the effects of the well-known definability theorem of Beth, to which end a natural solution is proposed.

Physicalism, so construed, consists in two sorts of principles, one ontological, the other the principles of physical determination, together compatible with the falsity of reductionism. Yet physicalism without reductionism does not rule out endless lawful connections between higher-level and basic physical sciences.[3] Both ontological and determinationist principles have the character of higher-order empirical hypotheses and are not immune from revision. Nor are they intended as final claims, for it is recognized that physical science is a changing and growing body of theory. Nevertheless, these sorts of principles can be adopted at various stages of development to assert the tentative adequacy of a physical basis for ontology and determination.

I

A. Ontology and reduction

Pre-systematically, the physicalist ontological position is simply put: "Everything is physical." However, unless 'physical' is spelled out, the claim is hopelessly vague. Yet, as soon as the attempt is

Originally published in *Journal of Philosophy* 72 (1975), pp. 551–64. Reprinted by permission of Columbia University.

made to identify 'is physical' with satisfaction of any predicate on some list of clearly physical predicates (drawn, say, from standard physics texts), it is discovered that the simple formula, $(\forall x)$ (x satisfies some predicate on the list), fails of its purpose. Unless closure of the list under some fairly complex operations were specified, predicates of ordinary macroscopic objects would not appear, and the claim would be trivially false. Indeed, one seems already forced into the reductionist position of defining – at least in the sense of finding extensional equivalents for – all predicates in terms of the basic list. What started as a bald ontological assertion seems to involve dubious claims as to the defining power of a language. When it is contemplated, moreover, that, no matter how sophisticated the list and the "defining machinery," there are bound to be entities composed of "randomly selected" parts of other entities which elude description in the physical language, then it is evident that something is wrong with this whole approach.

There is another approach. As a preliminary, it should be stated here that no sharp distinction between physics and mathematics is being presupposed. Since we are interested in physicalism *vis-à-vis* the mind–body problem and the relations among the sciences, we do not wish any physicalist theses that we formulate to turn on views concerning abstract entities. For the purposes of this discussion we will assume an object language L containing a stock of mathematical-physical predicates, including those which might be drawn from texts concerning elementary particles, field theory, space-time physics, etc.,[4] as well as identity, the part–whole relation, "$<$" of the calculus of individuals, and a full stock of mathematical predicates (which, for convenience we may suppose are built up within set theory from '$\in$'). The metalanguage in which we work includes L (and enough to express the (referential) semantics of L). Henceforth, we shall use 'physics' to mean "physics plus mathematics" and shall speak indifferently of "physical" or "mathematical-physical" predicates.

Now a thesis that qualifies as ontological physicalism not involving any appeal to the defining power of L (or any language) asserts, roughly, that everything is *exhausted* – in a sense to be explained – by mathematical-physical entities, where these are specified as anything satisfying any predicate in a list of basic positive physical predicates of L. Such a list might include, e.g., '— is a neutrino', '— is an electromagnetic field', '— is a four-dimensional manifold', '— and — are

related by a force obeying the equations (Einstein's, say) listed', etc. There are no doubt many ways of developing such a list, depending on how physical theory is formulated. The fundamental requirement for a *basic positive physical predicate at a place* is that satisfaction of it at that place constitutes a sufficient condition for being a physical entity, clearly enough to be granted by physicalists and nonphysicalists alike.[5] Clearly, negations of primitive predicates of physics do not qualify; hence we say "positive" physical predicates. However, it is clear that certain predicates, even primitives, do not meet the fundamental requirement just stated at any place. For example, to include '$=$' in the list would beg the question: any nonphysicalist will agree that everything is exhausted by all the entities in the extension of this predicate! The same goes for the part–whole relation '$<$', and for set membership '$\in$', since what are regarded as among the relata of these predicates depends quite directly on one's ontological position. Finally, we must exclude predicates of location of the form 'is at space-time point p', since it would be question-begging to say that merely having location is sufficient for being a physical object.

Assume, then, that requisite exclusions of this kind have been made and we have a list, Γ, of basic positive physical predicates with the concrete places specified. In terms of Γ we now sketch a physicalist ontology. Since '$\in$' is not in Γ, special provision must be made for mathematical entities. The alternative we favor consists in an iterative set-theoretic hierarchy built on a ground level of concrete physical entities (plus the null set). Since the mathematical objects required by physical science can be developed within set theory, we may concentrate on the members of Γ at their concrete places (where they apply only to objects in space-time). Thus, stipulating that

$V[\Gamma](x)$ iff
x belongs to the extension at a concrete place of some predicate of Γ

we may apply notions of the calculus of individuals[6] to objects x such that $V[\Gamma](x)$. In particular, where Δ is any set of predicates, it is assumed there is a unique individual that exhausts all objects satisfying $V[\Delta]$; that is,

$$(\exists!x)(\forall y)((\exists z)(z < y \ \& \ z < x) \leftrightarrow$$
$$(\exists z)(\exists w)(V[\Delta](z) \ \& \ w < z \ \& \ w < y))$$

general. But there is another possibility. Causation might, so to speak, be quantized, so that there were cases where A caused B, and where, rather than its merely happening to be the case that there was no causal intermediary between A and B, the causal relationship that obtained between A and B was itself such as to *preclude* there being any causally intermediate event.[16] This latter situation involves a stronger type of direct causation, and one that is not, it would seem, reducible to the relation of causation in general. For suppose that one offered the following account: A causes B directly if and only if the general relation of causation obtains between A and B, and the world is such that it is a law that if the general relation of causation holds between events X and Y, there is no event Z such that the general relation of causation holds both between X and Z and between Z and Y. That definition would secure the right formal properties for the relation of direct causation, but it would suffer from two defects. First, the relation of causation in general is necessarily transitive, whereas in the above definition of direct causation one is postulating a law which entails that causation in general is not transitive. Second, this definition of direct causation entails that in a world where some events are directly caused by others, absolutely *all* causal relations must be quantized. It therefore would preclude the possibility of a world where some causal relations were quantized, and others not.

Given that the strong relation of direct causation – which precludes the existence of causally intermediate events – cannot be reduced to the relation of causation in general, or vice versa, the prospects for reducing all causal relations to some single, basic causal relation do not seem promising. It seems to me that one must recognize the possibility of at least two basic causal relations: first, that of direct causation, of the strong, quantized sort, and second, that of causation of the sort involved in continuous causal processes – what might be referred to as non-discrete causation.

The approach that I shall adopt, accordingly, will be to set out a theory of causation that, rather than focusing upon some specific causal relation, functions simply to explain what it is to be a causal relation. Any specific causal relation can then be defined in terms of the additional properties that serve to distinguish it from other causal relations.

Formal properties of causal relations What properties distinguish one causal relation from another? A natural answer is that certain formal properties do so. Thus, it might seem to be true by definition, for example, that the relation of non-discrete causation is a *dense* relation, whereas the relation of direct, quantized causation is not. That is to say, for any states of affairs X and Y, if X stands in the relation of non-discrete causation to Y, then there must be some state of affairs, Z, such that X stands in that relation to Z, and similarly for Z and Y. Similarly, it might also seem to be a necessary truth that non-discrete causation is transitive, while direct, quantized causation is not.

The idea that different causal relations are to be individuated by reference to their differing formal properties may seem plausible. Some care is needed, however, on this matter. Consider, first, the question of transitivity. Is it really the case that non-discrete causation is transitive? Initially, an affirmative answer may seem obviously correct. But there is a somewhat subtle objection that can be directed against the proposition that non-discrete causation is transitive – an objection that is perhaps best developed by considering an analogous case. Suppose that the correct account of laws is in terms of relations among universals, and that, in particular, there is some second-order relation N such that if N holds between properties P and Q, then it is a law that anything with property P has property Q. Suppose, further, that N holds between P and Q, and between Q and R. Then it will be a law that everything with property P has property Q and also that everything with property Q has property R. But if so, it must also be a law that everything with property P has property R. Does this mean that properties P and R must also stand in relation N? It is not easy to see any reason why this need be so. The conjunctive state of affairs consisting of P and Q's standing in relation N, together with Q and R's standing in relation N, would seem perfectly sufficient to make it a law that anything with property P has property R.

This view may very well be correct in the case of laws. But if so, should not one adopt the same view in the case of the relation of non-discrete causation? That is to say, assume that that relation holds between events P and Q, and also between Q and R. Is not that conjunctive fact sufficient to make it true to say that P caused R, without one's having to postulate that events P and R are themselves united by the relevant causal relation?

This objection, though initially plausible, cannot be sustained. For, first of all, notice that one cannot maintain that whenever P causes R via some other event Q, the relevant causal relation cannot hold between P and R. For that would entail that in a continuous causal process there would be *no* events that were causally related. There must, accordingly, be cases of three events – P, Q, and R – where there is a causal relation that holds between P and Q, between Q and R, and also between P and R.

Second, in such a case, how is one to think of the three instances of the causal relation? As three states of affairs that are unrelated except as involving the same individuals, and the same causal relation? This is not, I suggest, plausible, for it fails to capture the fact that the third state of affairs is logically supervenient upon the other two. A much more natural view, and one that does capture that supervenience, is to view the third state of affairs as containing the other two states of affairs as parts.

An analogy may be helpful. Consider the relation between two points when there is some pathway connecting them, and suppose that points A and C are connected because, and only because, A is connected to B, and B to C. Then the path from A to C can be broken down into two parts, one of which is the path from A to B, and the other the path from B to C. In similar fashion, I am suggesting that when P causes R because, and only because, P causes Q, and Q causes R, the right way to think of the situation is to view the causal connection between P and R as decomposable into two parts – the causal connection of P to Q, and that of Q to R.

But if, in a given case, the relation of non-discrete causation is thus decomposable into parts, then it would seem that composition of appropriately related parts should also result in an instance of the relation in question. That is to say, if the relation of non-discrete causation holds between P and Q, and between Q and R, then it must also hold between P and R, since the latter state of affairs need be nothing over and above the combination of the other two states of affairs. Non-discrete causation, considered as a real relation, as a genuine universal, must therefore be transitive.

The relation of direct causation, on the other hand, obviously need not be transitive. But is it also true that it *cannot* be transitive? The problem with the latter claim is that there does not seem to be any reason why P's being a direct cause of Q, together with Q's being a direct cause of R, should be incompatible with P's also being a direct cause of R. For why might not one event cause another

event both directly and indirectly? But if this can sometimes be the case, then it would seem that there must be possible worlds in which it is always the case, and in which, therefore, direct causation is transitive. So transitivity will not always serve to distinguish between non-discrete causation and direct causation.

But while transitivity itself will not do, the idea of there being, so to speak, different causal pathways connecting two states of affairs suggests that a slightly different property will serve to distinguish between direct causation and non-discrete causation. Consider some state of affairs in virtue of which event X stands in the relation of non-discrete causation to event Y, and where the state of affairs has no proper part that has that property, and similarly, a minimal state of affairs in virtue of which event Y stands in the relation of non-discrete causation to event Z. Then the combination of those two states of affairs necessarily makes it the case that event X stands in the relation of non-discrete causation to event Z. The relation of non-discrete causation has what I shall refer to as the property of being *intrinsically transitive*. Direct causation, by contrast, lacks this property: the combination of a minimal state of affairs in virtue of which X directly causes Y with one in virtue of which Y directly causes Z is never in itself a state of affairs in virtue of which X directly causes Z. Direct causation can never be intrinsically transitive.

What about the other property mentioned above – namely, that of being a dense relation? Will it serve to distinguish between the two causal relations? That non-discrete causation is necessarily dense seems unproblematic. But what about direct, quantized causation? Does it necessarily lack that property?

The situation appears to be the same as with transitivity. That is to say, it would seem that while direct causation need not be a dense relation, one can describe possible worlds in which it would, as a matter of fact, have that property. But here, too, one can shift to a slightly different notion – that of being *intrinsically dense* – where to say that a relation R is intrinsically dense is to say that any state of affairs, S, in virtue of which X stands in relation R to Y, can always be divided into proper parts, S_1 and S_2, such that, for some Z, X stands in relation R to Z, and Z in relation R to Y, in virtue of S_1 and S_2, respectively. One can then say that non-discrete causation is an intrinsically dense relation, whereas direct causation is not.

It seems plausible, then, that different causal relations can be distinguished by reference to their different formal properties. But can a consideration of formal properties also play a role in the construction of the general account of what it is to be a causal relation? If this is to be so, there will presumably have to be formal properties that are *common* to all causal relations.

That there are certain formal properties that any causal relation must necessarily possess is, I think, both a rather natural view, and one quite widely accepted in philosophical discussions of causation. In particular, I think that it is tempting to hold that all causal relations must have the following three formal properties. First, causal relations are irreflexive: no state of affairs can ever be the cause of itself. Second, causal relations are asymmetric: if A causes B, then it cannot be the case that B causes A. Third, causal loops are impossible. There cannot, for example, be three events, A, B, and C such that A causes B, B causes C, and C causes A.

But this view can certainly be challenged. One way of doing so is by arguing that time-travel into the past is logically possible, and that if it is, then local causal loops must also be logically possible. For if Mary can travel back into the past, what prevents her from, say, marrying her maternal grandfather, and then later giving birth to her own mother?[17] Alternatively, one can argue that global causal loops are possible – that is to say, that there could be a world where the total state of the universe at one time – call it A – would causally give rise to a sequence of total states which, though all qualitatively distinct for perhaps a very long time indeed, would lead, in the end, to a state that was not only qualitatively indistinguishable from A, but identical to it.[18]

On the other hand, a number of philosophers, such as Antony Flew, Max Black, David Pears, Richard Swinburne, Hugh Mellor and others, have tried to show either that the idea of backwards causation is not coherent – thus ruling out the possibility of local causal loops – or, alternatively, that no causal loops at all are possible, be they local or global.[19] Some of the arguments appear either to be question-begging or to depend upon the assumption that a tensed view of time is correct, but others are both neutral on the question of the nature of time and more promising. Nevertheless, I think it is very doubtful whether any of the arguments succeeds in establishing the desired conclusion.

I cannot defend that judgement here, but let me illustrate it by reference to one of the more interesting arguments – that advanced by Hugh Mellor. The thrust of Mellor's argument is that the impossibility of backwards causation can be established by appealing to the proposition that a cause must raise the probability of its effect. An initial objection to this argument is that there are counterexamples to the general thesis that causes raise the probabilities of their effects.[20] This first objection, however, can be gotten around, since it is possible to set out postulates for causal laws that will enable one to derive modified versions of the claim that causes are positively relevant to their effects – versions which will not be exposed to any straightforward counterexamples, and which will still provide the basis for a proof that causal loops are impossible.[21] But now another objection can be pressed, for it can be argued that, if causal loops are possible, then one of the crucial postulates that is needed to establish the probability claim is not acceptable.[22] So the issue then becomes whether it is possible to offer grounds for accepting that postulate which will not beg the question of the possibility of causal loops.

I shall not pursue this issue here. For while I think that the question of the possibility of causal loops is a fundamental one, it does not seem crucial with respect to the theory of causation that I am setting out here. For my general approach can, I believe, be tailored to either view.

What I shall do, accordingly, is to adopt the position that seems to me most plausible – namely, the view that causal loops are not possible – and set out the account that is appropriate, given that assumption. I shall then indicate how the account would need to be modified, if it turned out that that assumption was incorrect.

The problem of completing the theory In what follows it will be assumed, then, that all causal relations are irreflexive, asymmetric, and such as cannot enter into causal loops. These formal properties do not suffice, of course, to distinguish causal relations from a number of other relations. Consider, for example, the relation of temporal priority. If causal relations have the above formal properties, then I think it is plausible to hold that temporal priority does so as well. Or consider the inverse of any causal relation – such as the relation of being caused by. Since the inverse of any relation possessing the above properties must also possess those properties, the relation of being caused by must also be irreflexive, asymmetric, and such as cannot enter into loops.

What, then, can we add to the theory of causation so that it is satisfied by causal relations, but not by their inverses, or by any other relation? This is not an easy question, but one way of approaching it is by asking what account is to be given of the *direction* of causation, since, in distinguishing between causal relations and their inverses, the theory must necessarily incorporate some explanation of the direction of causation.

Elsewhere, I have surveyed the main accounts that have been offered of the direction of causation, and I have argued that none of them is tenable.[23] But there is another account that can be offered – an account to which I shall be turning shortly – which is, I believe, satisfactory. For in addition to escaping the objections to which other accounts fall prey, it rests upon an underlying idea which has a strong intuitive basis, it can generate the desired formal properties for causal relations and causal laws, and it provides the basis for a satisfactory account of the epistemological justification of our causal claims.

In *Causation*, I was only able to show how the alternative approach to the direction of causation could be carried through for the supervenience and intermediate views, for none of the avenues that I explored in an attempt to develop a singularist account proved successful. The problem was, however, that I was implicitly assuming that if causal relations do not presuppose causal laws, then an analysis of what it is to be a causal relation should not involve the concept of a law. But while this is a rather natural assumption, it is in fact false, and once it is set aside, there is no longer any barrier to developing a singularist account.

Causal relations and causal laws: exploiting the conceptual link The objective is to find a set of analytical truths involving the concept of causation that, taken together, will constitute a theory which implicitly defines what it is to be a causal relation. Some analytical truths are already at hand – namely, those concerning the formal properties of causation. But as they are obviously not sufficient, the problem is how to supplement them.

As I indicated earlier, the solution that I am proposing is as follows. First, if a singularist account of causation is correct, then there is a connection between the concept of a causal law and that of causal relations. For on a singularist view, causal laws are nothing more than laws that involve causal relations. As a consequence, given a singularist view, one can characterize causal relations as those relations whose presence in a law makes that law a causal one.

Such a characterization will not, of course, shed any light upon causal relations if one cannot say anything about causal laws beyond the fact that they are laws involving causal relations. My second point, however, is that that is not the case. For one can specify an independent constraint T, such that something is a causal law if and only if it satisfies T.

If the latter point can be sustained, then it will be possible to set out an analysis of the concept of causation. For causal relations will simply be those relations that have certain formal properties, and which are such that any laws involving them must satisfy condition T.

Causal laws: the underlying intuition The problem of setting out a singularist analysis of causation reduces, therefore, to that of finding an appropriate constraint upon causal laws. But if that is right, then the prospects for a singularist account of causation would seem promising. For once one is dealing with causal *laws*, it would appear to be a straightforward matter to modify the basic account that I have offered elsewhere in the case of supervenience and intermediate approaches to causation.

What is it that makes something a *causal* law? Reflection upon certain simplified situations suggests, I believe, a very plausible answer. Imagine, for example, the following possible world. It contains two radioactive elements, P and Q, that, in every sort of situation but one, exhibit half-lives of five minutes and ten minutes respectively. However, in one special sort of environment – characterized by some property R – an atom of type P undergoes radioactive decay *when and only when* one of type Q also decays. Now, given such facts, a natural hypothesis would be that the events in question are causally connected. Either (1) the decay of an atom of type P is, in the presence of property R, both causally sufficient and causally necessary for the decay of an atom of type Q, or (2) the decay of an atom of type Q, in the presence of property R, is both causally sufficient and causally necessary for the decay of an atom of type P, or (3) there is some property S which is, given property R, causally sufficient and causally necessary both for the decay of an atom of type P and for the decay of one of type Q. But which of these causal connections obtains? Given only the above information, there is no reason for preferring one causal hypothesis to the others. But suppose that the following is also the case: in the presence of property R, both element P and element Q have a half-life of five minutes. Then surely one has good grounds for thinking that, given the presence of property R, it is the decay of an atom of type P that is both causally sufficient and causally necessary for the decay of an atom of type Q, rather than vice versa, and rather than there being some other property that is involved. Conversely, if it turned out that, in the special situation, each element had a half-life of ten minutes, one would have good grounds for thinking instead that it was the decay of an atom of type Q that, given the presence of property R, was both causally sufficient and causally necessary for the decay of an atom of type P.

In the former case, the observed facts suggest that atoms of type P have the same probability of decaying in a given time period in the special situation that they have in all other situations, while atoms of type Q do not. On the contrary, atoms of type Q appear to have, in the special situation, precisely the same probability of decay as atoms of type P. So the probability of decay has, so to speak, been transferred from atoms of type P to atoms of type Q. It is this, I suggest, that makes it natural to say, in that case, that it is the decay of atoms of type P that is, in the presence of property R, both causally sufficient and causally necessary for the decay of atoms of type Q. The direction of causation coincides, therefore, with the direction of transmission of probabilities.

The basic idea, accordingly, is to characterize causal laws in terms of the transmission of probabilities. Talk about the 'transmission of probabilities' is, of course, a metaphor, and one needs to show that that metaphor can be cashed out in precise terms. I shall turn to that task in the next section.

B. The theory

A brief recap may be helpful at this point, so that the overall structure of my approach is clear. If a singularist account of causation is to succeed, causation must be treated as a theoretical relation between events. We need, accordingly, a theory of causation. That theory, moreover, must consist of analytically true statements, if it is to provide the basis for an analysis of the *concept* of causation.

The basic theory which I shall be proposing – at least in its initial formulation – will involve two

sorts of elements: first, statements concerning the formal properties of causal relations; second, statements that place constraints upon causal laws, by connecting causal laws with probabilities. Causal relations can then be defined as those relations that satisfy the theory question.

Causal laws: capturing the intuition How can we express, in a precise way, the intuitive idea presented in the previous section concerning the relation between causal laws and relevant probabilities? The answer is provided, I believe, by the postulates described below.[24]

In setting out those postulates, I think it will be best to proceed in two steps. First, I shall formulate a set of postulates that captures, in a simple and natural way, the fundamental intuition concerning causal laws. Second, I shall show how those postulates can be modified slightly to produce postulates that are equally natural, but more powerful.

The first set of postulates would appear to be adequate for our purposes. For when combined with appropriate statements concerning the formal properties of causal relations, the result is a theory that can be used to explain what it is to be a causal relation. But the second set of postulates provides, I believe, an account that is in a certain respect more satisfying, since it allows one to dispense with any explicit reference to the formal properties that are shared by all causal relations.

In order to set out the postulates in a more perspicuous fashion, it will be helpful to use a little notation. First, we need a way of representing the fact that two states of affairs (or events) are causally related. I shall use the term 'C' as the relevant predicate, and, to represent a state of affairs, I shall place square brackets around a sentence describing that state of affairs.[25] So, for example, the sentence '$C[Pa][Qb]$' will say that the state of affairs (or event) that consists of a's having property P causes the state of affairs (or event) that consists of b's having property Q.

Next, we need to have a perspicuous way of representing causal laws. Now on a singularist approach to causation, in contrast to a supervenience one, statements expressing causal laws involve reference to some causal relation, so that a typical statement of a causal law might be: 'It is a law that if anything, x, has property P, then x's having P causes it to be the case that there is some other thing, y, such that y stands in relation R to x, and y has the intrinsic property I.' If we use standard logical notation, plus '$\square$' as an abbreviation for 'it is a law that', together with the notation just introduced for the representation of causal relations between states of affairs, the preceding statement could be expressed as:

$$\Box(x)(Px \supset C[Px][\exists y)(y \neq x \;\&\; Ryx \;\&\; Iy)]).$$

But this is still very cumbersome. One way of improving things is to introduce predicates that attribute relational properties to individuals. Thus, if one defines 'Qx' as equivalent to

$$(\exists y)(y \neq x \;\&\; Ryx \;\&\; Iy),$$

the above statement can be rewritten as:

$$\Box(x)(Px \supset C[Px][Qx]).$$

Even with this simplification, however, the postulates needed for causal laws will still be rather messy. But further simplification is obviously possible, since all that the relevant expression really needs to do is to indicate that we are dealing with a statement of a causal law, and to refer to the intrinsic property P, and to the relational property Q. I shall, accordingly, employ the expression '$P \rightarrow Q$' as an abbreviation of the above statement. This will enable me to set out the postulates for causal laws in a considerably more perspicuous fashion.

Not all causal laws need have the same fine-grained logical structure as that of the above. There can, for example, be causal laws where the state of affairs that is the cause involves a number of individuals, having various intrinsic properties, and standing in various relations to one another. But statements of such laws can easily be viewed as having the same basic logical form as the above. For the individuals over which the variable, 'x', ranges need not, of course, be simple entities. They may, instead, be complex individuals, consisting of a large number of simpler individuals.

Another possibility is that of causal laws of the following form:

$$\Box(x)(Px \supset C[Px][\exists y)(y \neq x \;\&\; Iy)]).$$

Here, in contrast to the type of causal law considered above, there is no specification of how x and y are related. But this does not make any difference with respect to the basic logical form of the statement, since by defining 'Qx' as equivalent to

$$(\exists y)(y \neq x \;\&\; Iy),$$

the above statement can be seen to have the form:

$$\Box(x)(Px \supset C[Px][Qx]).$$

A final possibility worth mentioning is that of causal laws of the following form:

$$\Box(x)(Px \supset C[Px][Ix]).$$

Here, in contrast to the previous cases, the same individual is involved in the effect as in the cause: an individual's having property P causes it to have property I. But this, too, does not affect the basic logical form. For in the first place, one could simply allow property Q to be either a relational property or an intrinsic one. Alternatively – and this is the approach that I favour – one can argue that, properly viewed, laws of the present sort also involve relational properties. For, although I cannot defend these claims here, I believe that it can be shown, first, that a cause can never be simultaneous with its effect, and second, that enduring individuals are reducible to causally related, momentary individuals. If these two claims can be sustained, then causal relations between states of affairs involving a single enduring individual are, at bottom, causal relations between states of affairs that involve different temporal parts of that individual.

A third thing that is needed is a way of referring to relations of logical probability. I shall use the expression '$\mathrm{Prob}(Px, E) = k$' to do that. It is to be interpreted as saying that the logical probability that x has property P, given only evidence E, is equal to k.

Finally, we need to refer to information of a certain restricted sort – specifically, information that is either tautological, or that concerns only what causal laws there are. I shall use the term 'L' for that purpose.

Given the above notation, one natural formulation of the desired postulates for causal laws is this:

$$
\begin{aligned}
(C_1):\ &\mathrm{Prob}(Px, P \rightarrow Q \;\&\; L) = \mathrm{Prob}(Px, L) \\
(C_2):\ &\mathrm{Prob}(Qx, P \rightarrow Q \;\&\; L) \\
&= \mathrm{Prob}(Px, L) + \mathrm{Prob}(\sim Px, L) \\
&\quad \times \mathrm{Prob}(Qx, \sim Px \;\&\; P \rightarrow Q \;\&\; L) \\
(C_3):\ &\mathrm{Prob}(Qx, \sim Px \;\&\; P \rightarrow Q \;\&\; L) \\
&= \mathrm{Prob}(Qx, \sim Px \;\&\; L) \\
(C_4):\ &\mathrm{Prob}(Qx, P \rightarrow Q \;\&\; L) \\
&= \mathrm{Prob}(Px, L) + \mathrm{Prob}(\sim Px \;\&\; L) \\
&\quad \times \mathrm{Prob}(Qx, \sim Px \;\&\; L)
\end{aligned}
$$

These postulates are essentially somewhat simplified versions of ones that I set out elsewhere in developing a supervenience account of causation. There I discussed, in a fairly detailed way, the line of thinking that leads to the specific postulates in question.[26] So perhaps it will suffice here simply to note the central considerations.

Postulate (C_1) states that if the prior probability that some individual will have property P, given only information that is restricted to logical truths and statements of causal laws, has a certain value, then the posterior probability of that individual's having property P, given the additional information that the possession of property P causally gives rise to the possession of property Q, must have precisely the same value. Postulate (C_1) therefore asserts, in effect, that the posterior probability of a state of affairs of a given type is, in the situation described, not a function of the prior probability of any state of affairs of a type to which states of affairs of the first type causally give rise.

Postulates (C_2), (C_3), and (C_4) deal with the posterior probability of a state of affairs, given information to the effect that it is a state of affairs of a type that is causally brought about by states of affairs of some other type, together with prior information that is restricted in the way indicated above. The first of these three postulates asserts that, given the additional information that the possession of property P causally gives rise to the possession of property Q, the posterior probability that some individual has property Q is, in the way indicated, a function of the prior probability that that individual has property P.

Postulate (C_2) does not, however, express that dependence in the clearest way, since it involves, on the right-hand side, a probability that is also conditional upon the information that the possession of property P gives rise to the possession of property Q. It is for this reason that postulate (C_3) is part of the theory, for it makes it possible to derive a statement in which the relevant posterior probability is expressed in terms of prior probabilities alone.

Postulate (C_3) asserts that if the prior probability that some individual will have property Q, given only information that is either tautologous or else restricted to statements of causal laws, has a certain value, then the posterior probability of that individual's having property Q – given the additional information both that the possession of property P causally gives rise to the possession of property Q, and that the individual does *not* have property P

– must have precisely the same value as the prior probability. (C_3), together with (C_2), then entails (C_4), which does express the posterior probability that an individual will have property Q in a way that involves only prior probabilities.

The crucial content of the above theory of causal laws is expressed, accordingly, by postulates (C_1) and (C_4). For (C_1) expresses the fact that the logical probability that a given state of affairs will obtain, given information about the types of states of affairs that *are caused by* states of affairs of that type, does not differ from the prior probability, upon evidence of a certain restricted sort, that the state of affairs in question will obtain. Its posterior logical probability cannot, therefore, be a function of the prior logical probabilities of states to which it causally gives rise. But by contrast, as is indicated by postulate (C_4), the posterior logical probability of a given state of affairs is a function of the prior logical probability of any state of affairs of such a type that states of affairs of that type *causally give rise* to states of affairs of the first type. The relation between posterior probabilities and prior probabilities is, in short, different for causes than for effects.

The above theory of causal laws could be formulated more economically. For not only does (C_4) follow from (C_2) and (C_3), as was noted above, but, in addition, (C_2) is not an independent postulate either, since it follows from (C_1) by means of the probability calculus. One could, therefore, cut back to postulates (C_1) and (C_3) if one wanted a more succinct formulation. However, it seems to me that, in the present context, explicit expression of the basic ideas is more important than economy.

I have attempted to motivate postulates (C_1) through (C_4) by appealing to the idea that there is a connection between the direction of causation and what I have referred to as the direction of transmission of probabilities. But as I mentioned earlier, the case for those postulates does not rest upon that intuition alone, for there are at least three other grounds of support. First, reductionist accounts of the direction of causation are open to decisive objections – objections that an account based on postulates (C_1) through (C_4) totally avoids. Second, those postulates – or, rather, the strengthened versions of them that I shall be setting out shortly – generate the desired formal properties for causal relations. Third, the above postulates also serve to explain how justified beliefs concerning causal relations are possible.

It will not be possible here to discuss these considerations in a detailed way. I shall, however, touch upon the second and third points in later sections.[27]

I mentioned earlier that, although the postulates just set out appear to provide a perfectly sound basis for an account of causal relations, a strengthening of those postulates makes possible an analysis that is in a certain respect more satisfying. In addition, the strengthened postulates will help to make it clearer precisely how the theory that I am setting out would need to be modified if one decided that, contrary to what I am assuming, causal relations need not be asymmetrical. So let me indicate, very briefly, how the postulates can be strengthened.

The basic idea is simply this. Postulates (C_1) through (C_4) all refer to laws expressed by statements of the following form:

$$\Box(x)(Px \supset C[Px][Qx]).$$

Suppose, however, that one considers, instead, laws expressed by statements of the following form:

$$\Box(x)(Px \supset (\exists P_1)(C[Px][P_1x] \And C[P_1x][Qx])).$$

It seems clear that postulates that are comparable to (C_1) through (C_4) should hold when references to laws of the former sort are replaced by references to laws of the latter sort. For after all, in a world where causal processes exhibit continuity, the connection between x's having property P and x's having the relational property Q will involve causally intermediate states of affairs. But if the existence of causal intermediaries does not, in the case of laws of the simpler sort, block the transmission of probabilities, then it would seem that law-statements of the slightly more complex sort, where there is an explicit reference to a two-step causal chain, should also enter into corresponding postulates dealing with the relation between posterior probabilities and prior probabilities.

Granted this, the next point is that there is, of course, nothing special about two-step causal processes. If the appeal to continuity in the case of the simplest laws justifies the conclusion that there must be corresponding postulates for law-statements that involve explicit reference to a two-link causal chain, then it must equally justify the corresponding conclusion for law-statements that involve explicit reference to causal chains containing an indefinite number of links.

The natural way of representing laws of the latter sort is by introducing a predicate – say, 'C^*'

– associated with *the ancestral* of the causal relation in question. The idea then is that there should be postulates that are comparable to (C_1) through (C_4) except that they concern laws expressed by statements of the following form:

$$\Box(x)(Px \supset C^*[Px][Qx]).$$

Here, as before, it will make the postulates more perspicuous if we have an abbreviated way of expressing the law-statements in question. I shall use the expression '$P \rightarrow^* Q$' to do so. The required postulates can then be formulated as follows:

(C_1^*): $\mathrm{Prob}(Px, P \rightarrow^* Q \And L) = \mathrm{Prob}(Px, L)$

(C_2^*): $\mathrm{Prob}(Qx, P \rightarrow^* Q \And L)$
$\qquad = \mathrm{Prob}(Px, L) + \mathrm{Prob}(\sim Px, L)$
$\qquad \times \mathrm{Prob}(Qx, \sim Px \And P \rightarrow^* Q \And L)$

(C_3^*): $\mathrm{Prob}(Qx, \sim Px \And P \rightarrow^* Q \And L)$
$\qquad = \mathrm{Prob}(Qx, \sim Px \And L)$

(C_4^*): $\mathrm{Prob}(Qx, P \rightarrow^* Q \And L)$
$\qquad = \mathrm{Prob}(Px, L) + \mathrm{Prob}(\sim Px, L)$
$\qquad \times \mathrm{Prob}(Qx, \sim Px \And L)$

Though (C_1^*) through (C_4^*) are stronger than (C_1) through (C_4), it seems to me that the case for accepting them, if one accepts (C_1) through (C_4), is very strong indeed. For expressed very briefly, it is simply this. If all causal relations must satisfy (C_1) through (C_4), then the ancestral of a given causal relation could fail to satisfy (C_1) through (C_4) only if the ancestral was not itself a causal relation. But if the ancestral of a given causal relation satisfies (C_1) through (C_4), then (C_1^*) through (C_4^*) must be true of the relation in question. Therefore, if all causal relations must satisfy (C_1) through (C_4), the only way that any of them can fail to satisfy (C_1^*) through (C_4^*) as well is if there are causal relations whose ancestrals are not causal relations.

An analysis of the concept of causation It is now a straightforward matter to set out an analysis of the concept of causation. For by combining statements concerning the formal properties of causal relations with, for example, the first set of postulates for causal laws set out above, one has a theory of causation that consists entirely of analytically true statements, and, given such a theory, one need merely appeal to whatever one takes to be the correct method of defining theoretical terms in order to generate an analytical account of what it is to be a causal relation.

The method of analysing theoretical terms that seems to me correct is that suggested by F. P. Ramsey's approach to theories, and later developed in detail by David Lewis.[28] Let me briefly indicate, therefore, how things proceed if one adopts a Ramsey/Lewis approach.[29]

The basic idea is to define causal relations as those relations that satisfy a certain open sentence. We need, therefore, to transform the above theory of causation into a single sentence, containing occurrences of an appropriate variable. Doing so involves three steps. First, the individual sentences of the theory are all conjoined, so that one has a single sentence. Second, wherever the theory involves an expression of the form 'Cst' – which says that a certain causal relation holds between state of affairs s and state of affairs t – one replaces the expression by an ontologically more explicit one that contains some term – say, 'c' – that *denotes* the causal relation in question. The new expression will thus say that the causal relation in question obtains between s and t. This shift to terms that *refer* to the causal relation then makes possible the third and final step, which involves replacing all the occurrences of 'c' by occurrences of some variable – say, 'v'. With that replacement, one has arrived at the open formula that one needs, and one can then define a causal relation as any relation that satisfies that open formula.

The open formula depends, of course, on precisely what one incorporates into the theory of causation. One possibility is to include statements expressing *all* of the formal properties that are common to all causal relations, together with the first set of postulates for causal laws. In that case, if we let T be the open sentence that results when the above procedure is applied only to the relevant postulates for causal laws – that is, to statements (C_1) through (C_4) – we would have the following account of what it is to be a causal relation:

A causal relation is any relation between states of affairs which is irreflexive and asymmetric, which excludes loops, and which satisfies the open sentence, T.

But this account can obviously be simplified, since if a relation cannot enter into loops, then it must be asymmetric and irreflexive. So the above analysis can be expressed more succinctly as follows:

A causal relation is any relation between states of affairs which cannot enter into loops, and which satisfies the open sentence, T.

Can the analysis be condensed even more? The answer is that it can be, provided that one shifts to the second, and stronger set of postulates, (C_1^*) through (C_4^*). For, then, if T^* is the open sentence that results when the above procedure is applied to postulates (C_1^*) through (C_4^*), all reference to the formal properties that are shared by all causal relations can be dropped, and the following analysis can be offered:

A causal relation is any relation between states of affairs which satisfies the open sentence, T^*.

How does the shift to postulates (C_1^*) through (C_4^*) make possible this simplified formulation? The answer lies in an argument whose structure is as follows. First, it can be argued that any genuine relation is necesarily 'directly irreflexive'. Second, assume that there is some causal relation that is not asymmetric. Since any relation is directly irreflexive, it follows that there is some causal relation that is not anti-symmetric – where a relation R is anti-symmetric just in case one cannot have both xRy and yRx unless x is identical with y. But third, if there is some causal relation that is not anti-symmetric, then it must be possible for there to be causal laws that are not anti-symmetric. However, it can be shown, fourth, that any laws that satisfy postulates (C_1^*) through (C_4^*) must be anti-symmetric. So the assumption that there is some causal relation that is not asymmetric leads to a contradiction, and hence must be rejected. Fifth, a precisely parallel argument can be used to show that no causal relation can enter into loops. That is to say, the assumption that some causal relation can enter into loops leads to the conclusion that causal laws can enter into loops – something which is also ruled out by postulates (C_1^*) through (C_4^*). In short, it follows from the above account of what it is to be a causal relation that causal relations must be asymmetric, and that they cannot enter into causal loops.

I shall not attempt to develop this argument in a detailed way, but let me comment briefly on some of the steps involved. The first one involves the claim that any genuine relation is necessarily directly irreflexive. What does this claim come to, and what reason is there for accepting it? As regards the content, I need to explain what is meant by a genuine relation, and what it is for a relation to be directly irreflexive. First, then, the concept of a genuine relation. This is tied up with a distinction between concepts and universals – where the latter, rather than being mind-dependent entities, are features of the world which are the basis of objective, qualitative identity. Given this distinction, one can ask whether it need be the case that, corresponding to any given concept, there is a *single* universal. The answer, surely, is that this need not be so: a given concept may be applicable to something in virtue of any number of distinct properties. But if this is so, then, in some of the cases where one speaks of a relation, there will be a relational *concept*, but no single universal corresponding to that concept. When I refer to a genuine relation, I am referring to something which is a universal, and not to a relational concept.

Now it is sometimes claimed that all genuine relations are necessarily irreflexive[30] – a contention that might be supported by an argument along the following lines. Consider a relational *concept* that is reflexive, such as that of simultaneity. If E and F are distinct events, and if E is simultaneous with F, then the latter state of affairs may well involve a dyadic universal. By contrast, the state of affairs that consists of E's being simultaneous with itself surely does not involve the instantiation of any dyadic universal: the mere existence of E itself is sufficient to guarantee that it is simultaneous with itself.

But this argument, tempting though it is, is flawed, as can be shown by a simple example. Consider the relation – call it spatial accessibility – that obtains between two locations, A and B, when there is a path along which one can move from A to B. Now every location, of course, is trivially accessible from itself, in virtue of the path of zero length consisting of the location in question. But a location may also be spatially accessible from itself in virtue of a path leading to some other point, together with a path – possibly the same one, possibly a different one – leading back to the original point. So a point may be accessible from itself in a way that is not trivial, and which might well involve the instantiation of a dyadic universal.

In general, the objection to the thesis that all genuine relations are necessarily irreflexive is that it would seem that there could well be genuine relations that are transitive but not asymmetric, and in such cases something could well stand in a genuine relation to itself.

But while this refutes the original thesis, it also points towards a revision that avoids the objection.

What one needs to do is to draw a distinction between a relation's being irreflexive and its being *directly* irreflexive, where to say that a relation R is directly irreflexive is to say that it can be the case that xRx only if xRx holds in virtue of the fact that R is transitive, together with the fact that there is some y such that both xRy and yRx. It can then be claimed – plausibly, I believe – that genuine relations are, necessarily, directly irreflexive.

The second step in the argument involves assuming that there can be a causal relation that is not necessarily asymmetric – the intention being to show that that assumption leads to a contradiction. Given this assumption, it immediately follows, in view of the thesis that all genuine relations are directly irreflexive, that there can be a causal relation that is not necessarily anti-symmetric. For if state of affairs S causes state of affairs U, and vice versa, it will follow, unless S is identical with U, that the relation is not anti-symmetric. But if S is identical with U, then in virtue of the property of direct irreflexivity, there must be a state of affairs T that is distinct from S, such that S causes T and T causes S. So regardless of whether S is identical with U or not, the causal relation in question will be anti-symmetric.

To assume that some causal relation is not necessarily asymmetric forces one to assume, therefore, that there can be distinct properties, P and Q, and an individual, a, such that the state of affairs [Pa] causes the state of affairs [Qa], and vice versa. But if there can be such a world, then it would seem that there could be a world where, first, there were a large number of things with property P, and second, every state of affairs of the form [Px] caused a state of affairs [Qx], and vice versa.

If one is a realist about laws, of course, the truth of a generalization, even one involving a very large number of instances, does not ensure the existence of a corresponding law. However, if laws are relations among universals, then it would seem that if there can be worlds where certain generalizations are all true, and where none of the generalizations involve essential reference to individuals, or 'gruesome' predicates, etc., then there can also be worlds where the same generalizations are not only true, but true in virtue of underlying relations among universals, and so express laws.

If this is right, then the possibility of a world where there are a large number of things with property P, and where every state of affairs of the form [Px] causes [Qx], and vice versa, entails the possibility of a world where it is a causal law that, for all x, x's having property P causes x to have property Q, and also a causal law that for all x, x's having property Q causes x to have property P.

What has been shown, therefore, is that the assumption that there can be a causal *relation* that is not asymmetric leads to the conclusion that causal *laws* need not be characterized by anti-symmetry.

But – and this brings me to the fourth step in the argument – the above theory of causation asserts that all causal laws must satisfy postulates (C_1^*) through (C_4^*). The question then becomes whether those postulates are compatible with anti-symmetry's not holding for laws. The answer is that they are not. For I have shown elsewhere, for a set of postulates that are weaker than postulates (C_1^*) through (C_4^*) in all respects that are relevant to the proof, that any laws satisfying the postulates in question must be anti-symmetric.[31]

The assumption that some causal relation might not be asymmetric leads, therefore, to a contradiction. Any causal relation that satisfies postulates (C_1^*) through (C_4^*) must be asymmetric.

A parallel argument can be offered with respect to the possibility of causal loops. That is to say, if one assumes that there is some causal relation that can enter into causal loops, one can argue that it follows that it must be possible for there to be a world where there are causal laws that exhibit a loop structure. It can be shown, however, that postulates (C_1^*) through (C_4^*) entail that such loops, involving causal laws, are impossible.[32] It therefore follows that no causal relation which satisfies postulates (C_1^*) through (C_4^*) can enter into causal loops.

Finally, the fact that causal loops are impossible, together with the fact that all genuine relations are directly irreflexive, entails that all causal relations are irreflexive.

The conclusion, accordingly, is that if causal relations are defined as above, namely,

A causal relation is any relation between states of affairs which satisfies the open sentence, T^*,

then, although all explicit references to the formal properties of causal relations have been eliminated from the analysis, it can be shown that causal relations must possess certain formal properties: they must be irreflexive and asymmetric, and they cannot enter into causal loops.

In short, the formal properties shared by all causal relations follow from the analytical con-straints upon causal laws, together with the fact that what distinguishes causal laws from non-causal laws is that the former involve causal relations. This is, I think, an appealing result. For if there could be other relations which satisfied the postulates for causal laws, but whose formal properties differed from those that are common to causal relations, one would be left with the somewhat puzzling question of what those other relations were.

Earlier, in the first part of section 3, A, I considered the question of whether all causal relations are reducible to a single, basic, causal relation, and I argued that one must allow for the possibility of at least two distinct, basic causal relations – namely, the relation of direct, quantized causation and that of non-discrete causation. I then went on to discuss what properties serve to distinguish those two relations, and settled, in the end, upon the properties of intrinsic transitivity and intrinsic denseness. If those conclusions are sound, one can offer the following accounts of those specific, basic causal relations:

C is the relation of non-discrete causation if and only if C is a causal relation that is intrinsically dense and intrinsically transitive.

D is the relation of direct, quantized causation if and only if D is a causal relation that is neither intrinsically dense nor intrinsically transitive.

Finally, the above analyses have all been predicated on the assumption that causal relations are necessarily irreflexive and asymmetric, and such as cannot enter into loops. How would the above approach need to be reformulated if it turned out, as some have contended, that that assumption is mistaken?

Given that any relation that satisfies the open sentence, T^*, corresponding to postulates (C_1^*) through (C_4^*), must, for example, be irreflexive, those postulates would have to be abandoned. The basic idea would then be to reformulate the account in terms of the open sentence, T, that corresponds to the weaker postulates, (C_1^*) through (C_4^*). That in itself will not be sufficient, however, since, as I indicated earlier, if all causal relations satisfy T, they must also satisfy T^*, provided that the ancestral of any causal relation is also a causal relation. But this difficulty can be avoided if one holds that only *basic* causal relations need satisfy T.

Given those two modifications, the proofs that causal relations are irreflexive, asymmetric, and such as cannot enter into loops will no longer go through. But on the other hand, the contrast between postulates (C_1) and (C_4) will still capture the crucial idea of the direction of causation. The general approach would therefore seem to be compatible with different views concerning the formal properties of causal relations.

C. The epistemological question

A crucial question for any account of causation, and especially for one that treats causation as a theoretical relation, is whether it is compatible with our everyday views concerning the possibility of causal knowledge, and concerning the sorts of evidence that serve to confirm causal claims. The analysis just offered fares very well, I believe, in those respects. For, so far as I can see, any evidence that we normally take to be relevant to causal claims turns out to be relevant on the present account.

The grounds for this view are as follows. First, I have argued elsewhere that in the case of both intermediate and supervenience approaches to causation which are based upon the idea of relating causation to the transmission of probabilities, all of the things that we normally take to be evidence for causal claims can be shown to be evidence given the analyses in question.[33] Thus it can be shown, for example, that such things as the direction of irreversible processes, both entropic and non-entropic, the direction of open forks, especially those of high complexity, and the direction of apparent control, all provide good evidence for claims about causal relations.

Second, this situation is not altered when one jettisons the intermediate and supervenience accounts in favour of a singularist conception based upon the same idea of the transmission of probabilities. For it can be shown – though I have not attempted to do so here – that even if one adopts a singularist conception of causation, one is never justified in believing that two events are causally connected unless one is also justified in believing that there is some causal law of which the relation in question is an instance.[34]

4   Summing Up

In this paper I have tried to show that there is a singularist account of the nature of causation that is not only coherent, but plausible. My argument in support of this contention involved the following steps. First, I argued that, other things being equal, a singularist account is preferable to both intermediate accounts and supervenience accounts. For intermediate accounts suffer from greater complexity, while supervenience accounts are exposed to decisive counterexamples.

Second, I argued that it is only if causation is treated as a theoretical relation that there is any hope of finding a successful singularist account. For in the first place, the relation of causation cannot be given in immediate experience. And in the second place, a Humean-style argument, especially when supplemented with the idea of possible worlds where causation is gappy, appears to make it very unlikely that a reductionist analysis can be given for causation if causal relations do not presuppose causal laws. But in addition, there appear to be very strong reasons for thinking that causation must be treated as a theoretical relation, regardless of whether a singularist account is correct.

I then went on to develop a theory which enables one to provide an account of the nature of causal relations. That theory involved two central ideas. The first was that the fact that a theory of causation involves the concept of a law of nature does not mean that it cannot provide an account of causal relations according to which events can be causally related even in worlds where there are no causal laws. The second was that the correct account of causal laws is one that captures, in a precise way, the idea of the transmission of probabilities. For, among other things, such an account both escapes the objections to which competing accounts of causal laws are exposed, and it has, in addition, a very plausible intuitive basis.

The outcome was a characterization of causal relations as those relations which satisfy the appropriate open sentence corresponding to the analytical theory of causation set out above. Given that definition, it then follows that causal relations have the formal properties they are normally taken to have, that they are epistemologically accessible relations between events, and that events can be causally related even in worlds where there are no causal laws.[35]

Notes

1 Michael Tooley, 'Laws and causal relations', in P. A. French, T. E. Uehling and H. K. Wettstein (eds), *Midwest studies in Philosophy*, vol. 9 (Minneapolis: University of Minnesota Press, 1984), pp. 93–112, and *idem, Causation – A Realist Approach* (Oxford: Oxford University Press, 1988), ch. 6.

2 Tooley, *Causation*, ch. 8.

3 Fred I. Dretske, 'Laws of nature', *Philosophy of Science* 44 (1977), pp. 248–68; David M. Armstrong, *What is a Law of Nature?* (Cambridge: Cambridge University Press, 1983), esp. chs 1–5; and my own discussions in 'The nature of Laws', (*Canadian Journal of Philosophy* 7/4 (1977), pp. 667–98, and in *Causation*, sect. 2.1.1.

4 For a more detailed discussion, see Tooley, *Causation*, pp. 268–74.

5 The only restriction upon properties here is that they must not involve particulars.

6 Tooley, 'Laws and causal relations', pp. 99–107.

7 Some axiomatic formulations of Newtonian spacetime involve the postulate of a generalized betweenness relation that, rather than being restricted to locations at a given time, can hold between spacetime points belonging to different temporal slices. See, e.g., Hartry Field's *Science without Numbers* (Princeton: Princeton University Press, 1980), pp. 52–3. But the idea that such a spatio-temporal relation can be basic is, I believe, very dubious.

8 G. E. M. Anscombe, 'Causality and determination', in E. Sosa (ed.), *Causation and Conditionals* (Oxford: Oxford University Press, 1975), pp. 63–81, at p. 81.

9 David Hume, *A Treatise of Human Nature*, pt 2, sect. 14, and *An Inquiry Concerning Human Understanding*, sect. 7.

10 Anscombe, 'Causality and determination', pp. 67–9.

11 C. J. Ducasse, 'The nature and the observability of the causal relation', *Journal of Philosophy* 23 (1926), pp. 57–67, repr. in Sosa (ed.), *Causation and Conditionals*, pp. 114–25; see p. 116.

12 Ibid., p. 122. Ducasse thought he could get around this difficulty, but as Ernest Sosa and others have shown, Ducasse's response is unsatisfactory. See, e.g., Sosa's discussion in the introduction to *Causation and Conditionals*, pp. 8–10.

13 Wesley Salmon, 'Theoretical explanation', in S. Korner (ed.), *Explanation* (Oxford: Oxford University Press, 1975), pp. 118–43, at pp. 128ff.

14 A more extended discussion can be found in Tooley, *Causation*, pp. 235–6.

15 Ibid., esp. pp. 247–50.

16 I am indebted to David Armstrong for pointing out the possibility of quantized causal relations.

17 Compare David Lewis's 'The paradoxes of time travel', *American Philosophical Quarterly* 13 (1976), pp. 145–52.

18 Adolf Grünbaum, 'Carnap's views on the foundations of geometry', in Paul A. Schilpp (ed.), *The Philosophy of Rudolf Carnap* (La Salle, Ill: Open Court, 1963), pp. 599–684; see pp. 614–15.

19 See, e.g., Antony Flew, 'Can an effect precede its cause?', *Proceedings of the Aristotelian Society*, suppl. vol. 28 (1954), pp. 45–62; Max Black, 'Why cannot an effect precede its cause?', *Analysis* 16 (1955–6), pp. 49–58; David Pears, 'The priority of causes,' *Analysis* 17 (1956–7), pp. 54–63; Richard Swinburne, *Space and Time* (London: Macmillan, 1968), p. 109; D. H. Mellor, *Real Time* (Cambridge: Cambridge University Press, 1981), ch. 9.

20 See, e.g., my discussion in *Causation*, pp. 234–5.

21 The relevant proofs are set out in ibid., pp. 277–80 and 325–35.

22 The postulate in question is the second of the six postulates set out in ibid., p. 262.

23 Ibid., ch. 7.

24 The intuitive idea set out in the previous section applies to both probabilistic and non-probabilistic causal laws. For my purposes here, however, it will suffice to consider only the case of non-probabilistic causal laws. The extension to the case of probabilistic laws is straightforward, and is discussed in ibid., pp. 291–6.

25 Compare the slightly different notation proposed by Jaegwon Kim in his article 'Causes and events: Mackie on causation,' *Journal of Philosophy* 68 (1971), pp. 426–41, repr. in Sosa (ed.), *Causation and Conditionals*, pp. 48–62: 'we shall use the notation "[x, P, t]" to refer to the event of x's exemplifying property P at time t' (p. 60).

26 Tooley, *Causation*, pp. 256–62.

27 The problems that confront reductionist accounts of the direction of causation are discussed at length in ibid., esp. ch. 7 and the first section of ch. 8.

28 F. P. Ramsey, 'Theories', in R. B. Braithwaite (ed.), *The Foundations of Mathematics* (Paterson, NJ: Littlefield, Adams & Co., 1960), pp. 212–36; David Lewis, 'How to define theoretical terms', *Journal of Philosophy* 67 (1970), pp. 427–46.

29 For a fuller discussion of this method, see Tooley, *Causation*, pp. 13–25.

30 See, e.g., David Armstrong's *Universals and Scientific Realism*, vol. 2 (Cambridge: Cambridge University Press, 1978), pp. 91–3.

31 For the proof, see Tooley, *Causation*, pp. 278–9.

32 For a proof of a stronger theorem, from comparable postulates, see ibid., pp. 328–35.

33 Ibid., pp. 296–303.

34 This thesis needs to be qualified slightly, since it assumes that there are no 'confirmation machines', and if this were false, it would be possible to have reason to believe that there were causally related events that did not fall under any law. For the relevant

argument, see Edward Erwin, 'The confirmation machine', in *Boston Studies in the Philosophy of Science*, vol. 8 (Dordrecht: D. Reidel, 1971), pp. 306–21.

35 I am indebted to David Armstrong, to Evan Fales, to Ernest Sosa, and to two anonymous referees of the *Canadian Journal of Philosophy* for detailed written comments on an earlier draft, and to John Burgess, Lloyd Humberstone, Peter Menzies, Robert Pargetter, Philip Pettit, Michael Smith, Neil Tennant and Aubrey Townsend for their comments on earlier versions which I read at Monash University and at the Australian National University.

PART VIII

Emergence, Reduction, Supervenience

Introduction

Causation perhaps is not the only "cement of the universe." There may well be other relations that generate structure for events, facts, properties, and things of this world. Consider, for example, the part–whole ("mereological") relation: the properties of a whole seem entirely determined by the properties and relations that characterize its parts – in that if you build, say, two tables from parts that are exactly identical and configure them in an exactly identical structure, you would have two tables that are indistinguishable – the same shape, the same weight, the same functionality, and even the same aesthetic qualities.

Modern science encourages a metaphysical picture of the world in which the basic building blocks of all things are unobservable microscopic particles (atoms, elementary particles, quarks, or whatever), with everything else – tables and chairs, trees and animals, the planets and stars – being wholly composed of them. Given that a macro-object is decomposable into micro-parts without remainder, what is the relationship between its (the whole's) properties and the properties and relations holding for its parts? C. D. Broad, in his "Mechanism and Emergentism" (chapter 37) discusses two major alternatives: *mechanism*, according to which the properties of a whole can be deduced or predicted from the properties of its parts, and *emergentism*, which affirms that some properties of a whole are "emergent" in the sense that they cannot be so deduced or predicted. According to Broad, there are emergent properties in this sense, and this is a position that has been, and still is, quite popular with philosophers and with scientists in many fields. It is a widely shared view that complex systems often exhibit characteristics that are irreducible to, and not deducible from, those of their simpler constituent systems. What Broad calls "mechanism" is now standardly called "reductionism" or "micro-reductionism."

Although the main topic of Quine's "Ontological Reduction and the World of Numbers" (chapter 38) is the reduction in the abstract domain of numbers and other mathematical objects, what he has to say is directly relevant to broader metaphysical issues of ontological reduction – that is, reduction of ontological domains.

Jerry Fodor's "Special Sciences" (chapter 39) deploys the so-called 'multiple realizability' of higher-level kinds and properties, first explicitly discussed by Hilary Putnam,[1] as a powerful and influential argument against their reducibility to lower-level properties. The Putnam/Fodor argument has been primarily responsible for the decline of various reductionisms in philosophy. In "Multiple Realization and the Metaphysics of Reduction", (chapter 40) Jaegwon Kim subjects the phenomenon of multiple realization to close scrutiny, and reaches conclusions at variance with those of Putnam and Fodor – in particular, concerning reductionism and the scientific/nomic status of multiply realizable properties.

In "Physicalism: Ontology, and Determination, and Reduction" (chapter 41), Geoffrey Hellman and Frank Thompson attempt to develop a position that is physicalist in its ontology, but which makes sense of the priority and basicness of physics without, however, embracing reductionism. They develop their ideas by the use of formal model theory, but these ideas turn out to be closely related to the idea of "supervenience." Many nonreductive physicalists look upon supervenience as a relation that enables a perspicuous formulation of physicalism that is nonreductive: all the facts supervene on the physical facts in the sense that physical facts determine all the facts, but this does not imply that all facts are reducible to physical facts. Kim's "Supervenience as a Philosophical Concept" (chapter 42) surveys the main results in this area and discusses the controversial and complicated relationship between supervenience and reduction.

Note

1 In "The nature of mental states," in *Philosophical Papers*, vol. 2 (Cambridge: Cambridge University Press, 1975; first pub. 1967).

Further reading

Bonevac, Daniel A., *Reduction in the Abstract Sciences* (Indianapolis: Hackett, 1982).

Causey, Robert L., *Unity of Science* (Dordrecht: Reidel, 1977).

Churchland, Patricia, *Neurophilosophy* (Cambridge, Mass.: MIT Press, 1986), ch. 7.

Dupré, John, *The Disorder of Things* (Cambridge, Mass.: Harvard University Press, 1993).

Humphreys, Paul W., "How properties emerge," *Philosophy of Science* 64 (1997), pp. 1–17.

Kim, Jaegwon, "Concepts of supervenience," in *Supervenience and Mind* (Cambridge: Cambridge University Press, 1993).

—— "Making sense of emergence," *Philosophical Studies*, forthcoming.

McLaughlin, Brian, "The rise and fall of British emergentism," in Ansgar Beckermann, Hans Flohr, and Jaegwon Kim (eds), *Emergence or Reduction* (Berlin: De Gruyter, 1992).

—— "Varieties of supervenience", in Savellos and Yalcin, *Supervenience: New Essays*.

Morgan, Lloyd C., *Emergent Evolution* (London: William & Norgate, 1923).

Nagel, Ernest, *The Structure of Science* (New York: Harcourt, Brace & World, 1961), ch. 11.

Oppenheim, Paul, and Putnam, Hilary "Unity of science as a working hypothesis," in H. Feigl, M. Scriven, and G. Maxwell (eds), *Minnesota Studies in the Philosophy of Science*, vol. 2 (Minneapolis: University of Minnesota Press, 1958), pp. 3–36.

Paull, Cranston, and Sider, Theodore, "In defense of global supervenience," *Philosophy and Phenomenological Research* 32 (1992), pp. 830–45.

Post, John F., *The Faces of Existence* (Ithaca, NY: Cornell University Press, 1987).

Rosenberg, Alexander, *Instrumental Biology, or the Disunity of Science* (Chicago: University of Chicago Press, 1994).

Savellos, Elias, and Yalcin, Umit (eds), *Supervenience: New Essays* (Cambridge: Cambridge University Press, 1995).

Stalnaker, Robert, "Varieties of supervenience," *Philosophical Perspectives* 10 (1996), pp. 221–41.

37

Mechanism and Emergentism

C. D. Broad

I want to consider some of the characteristic differences which there seem to be among material objects, and to enquire how far these differences are ultimate and irreducible. On the face of it, the world of material objects is divided pretty sharply into those which are alive and those which are not. And the latter seem to be of many different kinds, such as oxygen, silver, etc. The question which is of the greatest importance for our purpose is the nature of living organisms, since the only minds that we know of are bound up with them. But the famous controversy between Mechanists and Vitalists about living organisms is merely a particular case of the general question: Are the apparently different kinds of material objects irreducibly different?

It is this general question which I want to discuss at present. I do not expect to be able to give a definite answer to it; and I am not certain that the question can ever be settled conclusively. But we can at least try to analyse the various alternatives, to state them clearly, and to see the implications of each. Once this has been done, it is at least possible that people with an adequate knowledge of the relevant facts may be able to answer the question with a definite Yes or No; and, until it has been done, all controversy on the subject is very much in the air. I think one feels that the disputes between Mechanists and Vitalists are unsatisfactory for two reasons. (i) One is never quite sure what is meant

From *The Mind and its Place in Nature,* published by Routledge and Kegan Paul, London, 1925.

by 'Mechanism' and by 'Vitalism'; and one suspects that both names cover a multitude of theories which the protagonists have never distinguished and put clearly before themselves. And (ii) one wonders whether the question ought not to have been raised long before the level of life. Certainly living beings behave in a very different way from non-living ones; but it is also true that substances which interact chemically behave in a very different way from those which merely hit each other, like two billiard-balls. The question: Is chemical behaviour ultimately different from dynamical behaviour? seems just as reasonable as the question: Is vital behaviour ultimately different from non-vital behaviour? And we are much more likely to answer the latter question rightly if we see it in relation to similar questions which might be raised about other apparent differences of kind in the material realm.

The Ideal of Pure Mechanism

Let us first ask ourselves what would be the ideal of a mechanical view of the material realm. I think, in the first place, that it would suppose that there is only one fundamental kind of stuff out of which every material object is made. Next, it would suppose that this stuff has only one intrinsic quality, over and above its purely spatio-temporal and causal characteristics. The property ascribed to it might, e.g., be inertial mass or electric charge. Thirdly, it would suppose that there is only one

487

fundamental kind of change, viz., change in the relative positions of the particles of this stuff. Lastly, it would suppose that there is one fundamental law according to which one particle of this stuff affects the changes of another particle. It would suppose that this law connects particles by pairs, and that the action of any two aggregates of particles as wholes on each other is compounded in a simple and uniform way from the actions which the constituent particles taken by pairs would have on each other. Thus the essence of Pure Mechanism is (a) a single kind of stuff, all of whose parts are exactly alike except for differences of position and motion; (b) a single fundamental kind of change, viz., change of position. Imposed on this there may of course be changes of a higher order, e.g., changes of velocity, of acceleration, and so on; (c) a single elementary causal law, according to which particles influence each other by pairs; and (d) a single and simple principle of composition, according to which the behaviour of any aggregate of particles, or the influence of any one aggregate on any other, follows in a uniform way from the mutual influences of the constituent particles taken by pairs.

A set of gravitating particles, on the classical theory of gravitation, is an almost perfect example of the ideal of Pure Mechanism. The single elementary law is the inverse-square law for any pair of particles. The single and simple principle of composition is the rule that the influence of any set of particles on a single particle is the vector-sum of the influences that each would exert taken by itself. An electronic theory of matter departs to some extent from this ideal. In the first place, it has to assume at present that there are two ultimately different kinds of particle, viz., protons and electrons. Secondly, the laws of electromagnetics cannot, so far as we know, be reduced to central forces. Thirdly, gravitational phenomena do not at present fall within the scheme; and so it is necessary to ascribe masses as well as charges to the ultimate particles, and to introduce other elementary forces beside those of electromagnetics.

On a purely mechanical theory, all the apparently different kinds of matter would be made of the same stuff. They would differ only in the number, arrangement and movements of their constituent particles. And their apparently different kinds of behaviour would not be ultimately different. For they would all be deducible by a single simple principle of composition from the mutual influences of the particles taken by pairs; and these mutual influences would all obey a single law which

is quite independent of the configurations and surroundings in which the particles happen to find themselves. The ideal which we have been describing and illustrating may be called 'Pure Mechanism'.

When a biologist calls himself a 'Mechanist', it may fairly be doubted whether he means to assert anything so rigid as this. Probably all that he wishes to assert is that a living body is composed only of constituents which do or might occur in non-living bodies, and that its characteristic behaviour is wholly deducible from its structure and components and from the chemical, physical and dynamical laws which these materials would obey if they were isolated or were in non-living combinations. Whether the apparently different kinds of chemical substance are really just so many different configurations of a single kind of particles, and whether the chemical and physical laws are just the compounded results of the action of a number of similar particles obeying a single elementary law and a single principle of composition, he is not compelled as a biologist to decide. I shall later on discuss this milder form of 'Mechanism', which is all that is presupposed in the controversies between mechanistic and vitalistic biologists. In the meanwhile I want to consider how far the ideal of Pure Mechanism could possibly be an adequate account of the world as we know it.

Limitations of pure mechanism

No one of course pretends that a satisfactory account even of purely physical processes in terms of Pure Mechanism *has* ever been given; but the question for us is: How far, and in what sense, *could* such a theory be adequate to all the known facts? On the face of it, external objects have plenty of other characteristics beside mass or electric charge, e.g., colour, temperature, etc. And, on the face of it, many changes take place in the external world beside changes of position, velocity, etc. Now of course many different views have been held about the nature and status of such characteristics as colour; but the one thing which no adequate theory of the external world can do is to ignore them altogether. I will state here very roughly the alternative types of theory, and show that none of them is compatible with Pure Mechanism as a complete account of the facts.

(1) There is the naïve view that we are in immediate cognitive contact with parts of the sur-

faces of external objects, and that the colours and temperatures which we perceive quite literally inhere in those surfaces independently of our minds and of our bodies. On this view, Pure Mechanism breaks down at the first move, for certain parts of the external world would have various properties different from and irreducible to the one fundamental property which Pure Mechanism assumes. This would not mean that what scientists have discovered about the connection between heat and molecular motion, or light and periodic motion of electrons, would be wrong. It might be perfectly true, so far as it went; but it would certainly not be the whole truth about the external world. We should have to begin by distinguishing between 'macroscopic' and 'microscopic' properties, to use two very convenient terms adopted by Lorentz. Colours, temperatures, etc. would be macroscopic properties; i.e., they would need a certain minimum area or volume (and perhaps, as Dr Whitehead has suggested, a certain minimum duration) to inhere in. Other properties, such as mass or electric charge, might be able to inhere in volumes smaller than these minima and even in volumes and durations of any degree of smallness. Molecular and electronic theories of heat and light would then assert that a certain volume is pervaded by such and such a temperature or such and such a colour if and only if it contains certain arrangements of particles moving in certain ways. What we should have would be laws connecting the macroscopic qualities which inhere in a volume with the number, arrangement and motion of the microscopic particles which are contained in this volume.

On such a view, how much would be left of Pure Mechanism? (i) It would of course not be true of macroscopic properties. (ii) It might still be true of the microscopic particles in their interactions with each other. It might be that there is ultimately only one kind of particle, that it has only one non-spatio-temporal quality, that these particles affect each other by pairs according to a single law, and that their effects are compounded according to a single law. (iii) But, even if this were true of the microscopic particles in their relations *with each other*, it plainly could not be the *whole truth* about them. For there will also be laws connecting the presence of such and such a configuration of particles, moving in such and such ways, in a certain region, with the pervasion of this region by such and such a determinate value of a certain macroscopic quality, e.g., a certain shade of red or a temperature of 57° C. These will be just as much laws of the external

world as are the laws which connect the motions of one particle with those of another. And it is perfectly clear that the one kind of law cannot possibly be reduced to the other, since colour and temperature are irreducibly different characteristics from figure and motion, however close may be the causal connection between the occurrence of the one kind of characteristic and that of the other. Moreover, there will have to be a number of different and irreducible laws connecting microscopic with macroscopic characteristics; for there are many different and irreducible determinable macroscopic characteristics, e.g., colour, temperature, sound, etc. And each will need its own peculiar law.

(2)   A second conceivable view would be that in perception we are in direct cognitive contact with parts of the surfaces of external objects, and that, so long as we are looking at them or feeling them, they do have the colours or temperatures which they then seem to us to have; but that the inherence of colours and temperatures in external bodies is dependent upon the presence of a suitable bodily organism, or a suitable mind, or of both, in a suitable relation to the external object.

On such a view it is plain that Pure Mechanism cannot be an adequate theory of the external world of matter. For colours and temperatures would belong to external objects on this view, though they would characterize an external object only when very special conditions are fulfilled. And evidently the laws according to which, e.g., a certain shade of colour inheres in a certain external region when a suitable organism or mind is in suitable relations to that region cannot be of the mechanical type.

(3)   A third conceivable view is that physical objects can seem to have qualities which do not really belong to any physical object; e.g., that a pillar-box can seem to have a certain shade of red, although really no physical object has any colour at all. This type of theory divides into two forms. (a) It might be held that, when a physical object seems to have a certain shade of red, there really is *something* in the world which has this shade of red, although this something cannot be a physical object or literally a part of one. Some would say that there is a red mental state – a 'sensation'; others that the red colour belongs to something which is neither mental nor physical. (b) It might be held that *nothing* in the world really has colour, though certain things *seem* to have certain colours. The

relation of 'seeming to have' is taken as ultimate. On either of these alternatives it would be conceivable that Pure Mechanism was the whole truth about matter considered in its relations with matter. But it would be certain that it is not the whole truth about matter when this limitation is removed. Granted that bits of matter only *seem* to be red or to be hot, we still claim to know a good deal about the conditions under which one bit of matter will seem to be red and another to be blue and about the conditions under which one bit of matter will seem to be hot and another to be cold. This knowledge belongs partly to physics and partly to the physiology and anatomy of the brain and nervous system. We know little or nothing about the mental conditions which have to be fulfilled if an external object is to seem red or hot to a percipient; but we can say that this depends on an unknown mental factor x and on certain physical conditions a, b, c, etc., partly within and partly outside the percipient's body, about which we know a good deal. It is plain then that, on the present theory, physical events and objects do not merely interact mechanically with each other; they also play their part, along with a mental factor, in causing such and such an external object to seem to such and such an observer to have a certain quality which really no physical object has. In fact, for the present purpose, the difference between theories (2) and (3) is simply the following. On theory (2) certain events in the external object, in the observer's body, and possibly in his mind, cause a certain quality to inhere in the external object so long as they are going on. On theory (3) they cause the same quality to *seem* to inhere in the same object, so long as they are going on, though *actually* it does not inhere in any physical object. Theory (1), for the present purpose, differs from theory (2) only in taking the naïve view that the body and mind of the observer are irrelevant to the *occurrence* of the sensible quality in the external object, though of course it would admit that these factors are relevant to the *perception* of this quality by the observer. This last point is presumably common to all three theories.

I will now sum up the argument. The plain fact is that the external world, as perceived by us, seems not to have the homogeneity demanded by Pure Mechanism. If it *really* has the various irreducibly different sensible qualities which it *seems* to have, Pure Mechanism cannot be true of the whole of the external world and cannot be the whole truth about any part of it. The best that we can do for Pure

Mechanism on this theory is to divide up the external world first on a macroscopic and then on a microscopic scale; to suppose that the macroscopic qualities which pervade any region are causally determined by the microscopic events and objects which exist within it; and to hope that the latter, in their interactions with *each other* at any rate, fulfil the conditions of Pure Mechanism. We must remember, moreover, that there is no a priori reason why microscopic events and objects should answer the demands of Pure Mechanism even in their interactions with each other; that, so far as science can tell us at present, they do not; and that, in any case, the laws connecting them with the occurrence of macroscopic qualities *cannot* be mechanical in the sense defined.

If, on the other hand, we deny that physical objects have the various sensible qualities which they seem to us to have, we are still left with the fact that some things *seem* to be red, others to be blue, others to be hot, and so on. And a complete account of the world must include some explanation of such events as 'seeming red to me', 'seeming blue to you', etc. We can admit that the ultimate physical objects may all be exactly alike, may all have only one non-spatio-temporal and non-causal property, and may interact with each other in the way which Pure Mechanism requires. But we must admit that they are also cause-factors in determining the *appearance*, if not the *occurrence*, of the various sensible qualities at such and such places and times. And, in these transactions, the laws which they obey *cannot* be mechanical.

We may put the whole matter in a nutshell by saying that the appearance of a plurality of irreducible sensible qualities forces us, no matter what theory we adopt about their status, to distinguish two different kinds of law. One may be called 'intra-physical' and the other 'trans-physical'. The intra-physical laws may be, though there seems no positive reason to suppose that they are, of the kind required by Pure Mechanism. If so, there is just one ultimate elementary intra-physical law and one ultimate principle of composition for intra-physical transactions. But the trans-physical laws cannot satisfy the demands of Pure Mechanism; and, so far as I can see, there must be at least as many irreducible trans-physical laws as there are irreducible determinable sense-qualities. The nature of the trans-physical laws will of course depend on the view that we take about the status of sensible qualities. It will be somewhat different for each of the three alternative types of theory which I have mentioned, and it will differ according to which form of the third theory we adopt. But it is not necessary for our present purpose to go into further detail on this point.

The Three Possible Ways of Accounting for Characteristic Differences of Behaviour

So far, we have confined our attention to pure qualities, such as red, hot, etc. By calling these 'pure qualities' I mean that, when we say 'This is red', 'This is hot', and so on, it is no part of the meaning of our predicate that 'this' stands in such and such a relation to something else. It is *logically* possible that this should be red even though 'this' were the only thing in the world; though it is probably not *physically* possible. I have argued so far that the fact that external objects seem to have a number of irreducibly different pure qualities makes it certain that Pure Mechanism cannot be an adequate account of the external world. I want now to consider differences of *behaviour* among external objects. These are not differences of pure quality. When I say 'This combines with that', 'This eats and digests', and so on, I am making statements which would have no meaning if 'this' were the only thing in the world. Now there are apparently extremely different kinds of behaviour to be found among external objects. A bit of gold and a bit of silver behave quite differently when put into nitric acid. A cat and an oyster behave quite differently when put near a mouse. Again, all bodies which would be said to be 'alive', behave differently in many ways from all bodies which would be said not to be 'alive'. And, among non-living bodies, what we call their 'chemical behaviour' is very different from what we call their 'merely physical behaviour'. The question that we have now to discuss is this: 'Are the differences between merely physical, chemical and vital behaviour ultimate and irreducible or not? And are the differences in chemical behaviour between oxygen and hydrogen, or the differences in vital behaviour between trees and oysters and cats, ultimate and irreducible or not?' I do not expect to be able to give a conclusive answer to this question, as I do claim to have done to the question about differences of pure quality. But I hope at least to state the possible alternatives clearly, so that people with an adequate knowledge of the relevant empirical facts may know exactly what we want them to discuss, and may not beat the air in the regrettable way in which they too often have done.

We must first notice a difference between vital behaviour, on the one hand, and chemical behaviour, on the other. On the macroscopic scale, i.e., within the limits of what we can perceive with our unaided senses or by the help of optical instruments, *all* matter seems to behave chemically from time to time, though there may be long stretches throughout which a given bit of matter has no chance to exhibit any marked chemical behaviour. But only a comparatively few bits of matter *ever* exhibit vital behaviour. These are always very complex chemically; they are always composed of the same comparatively small selection of chemical elements; and they generally have a characteristic external form and internal structure. All of them after a longer or shorter time cease to show vital behaviour, and soon after this they visibly lose their characteristic external form and internal structure. We do not know how to make a living body out of non-living materials; and we do not know how to make a once living body, which has ceased to behave vitally, live again. But we know that plants, so long as they are alive, do take up inorganic materials from their surroundings and build them up into their own substance; that all living bodies maintain themselves for a time through constant change of material; and that they all have the power of restoring themselves when not too severely injured, and of producing new living bodies like themselves.

Let us now consider what general types of view are possible about the fact that certain things behave in characteristically different ways.

(1) Certain characteristically different ways of behaving may be regarded as absolutely unanalysable facts which do not depend *in any way* on differences of structure or components. This would be an absurd view to take about vital behaviour, for we know that all living bodies have a complex structure even on the macroscopic scale, and that their characteristic behaviour depends *in part* at least on their structure and components. It would also be a foolish view to take about the chemical behaviour of non-living substances which are known to be compounds and can be split up and re-synthesized by us from their elements. But it was for many years the orthodox view about the chemical elements. It was held that the characteristic differences between the behaviour of oxygen and hydrogen are due in no way to

differences of structure or components, but must simply be accepted as ultimate facts. This first alternative can hardly be counted as one way of *explaining* differences of behaviour, since it consists in holding that there are certain differences which cannot be explained, even in part, but must simply be swallowed whole with that philosophic jam which Professor Alexander calls 'natural piety'. It is worthwhile to remark that we could never be logically compelled to hold this view, since it is always open to us to suppose that what is macroscopically homogeneous has a complex microscopic structure which wholly or partly determines its characteristic macroscropic behaviour. Nevertheless, it is perfectly possible that this hypothesis is not true in certain cases, and that there are certain ultimate differences in the material world which must just be accepted as brute facts.

(2) We come now to types of theory which profess to explain, wholly or partly, differences of behaviour in terms of structure or components or both. These of course all presuppose that the objects that we are dealing with are at any rate microscopically complex; a hypothesis, as I have said, which can never be conclusively refuted. We may divide up these theories as follows. (a) Those which hold that the characteristic behaviour of a certain object or class of objects is in part dependent on the presence of a peculiar *component* which does not occur in anything that does not behave in this way. This is of course the usual view to take about the characteristic chemical behaviour of compounds. We say that silver chloride behaves differently from common salt because one contains silver and the other sodium. It is always held that differences of microscopic *structure* are also relevant to explaining differences of macroscopic chemical behaviour. For example, the very marked differences between the chemical behaviour of acetone and propion aldehyde, which both consist of carbon, hydrogen and oxygen in exactly the same proportions, are ascribed to the fact that the former has the structure symbolized by

$$CH_3 - C - CH_3$$
$$\overset{\|}{O}$$

and that the latter has the structure symbolized by

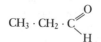

The doctrine which I will call 'Substantial Vitalism' is logically a theory of this type about vital behaviour. It assumes that a necessary factor in explaining the characteristic behaviour of living bodies is the presence in them of a peculiar component, often called an 'Entelechy', which does not occur in inorganic matter or in bodies which were formerly alive but have now died. I will try to bring out the analogies and differences between this type of theory as applied to vital behaviour and as applied to the behaviour of chemical compounds. (i) It is not supposed that the presence of an entelechy is *sufficient* to explain vital behaviour; as in chemistry, the structure of the complex is admitted to be also an essential factor. (ii) It is admitted that entelechies cannot be isolated, and that perhaps they cannot exist apart from the complex which is a living organism. But there is plenty of analogy to this in chemistry. In the first place, elements have been recognized, and the characteristic behaviour of certain compounds has been ascribed to their presence, long before they were isolated. Secondly, there are certain groups, like CH_3 and C_6H_5 in organic chemistry, which cannot exist in isolation, but which nevertheless play an essential part in determining the characteristic behaviour of certain compounds. (iii) The entelechy is supposed to exert some kind of directive influence over matter which enters the organism from outside. There is a faint analogy to this in certain parts of organic chemistry. The presence of certain groups in certain positions in a benzene nucleus makes it very easy to put certain other groups and very hard to put others into certain positions in the nucleus. There are well-known empirical rules on this point.

Why then do most of us feel pretty confident of the truth of the chemical explanation and very doubtful of the formally analogous explanation of vital behaviour in terms of entelechies? I think that our main reasons are the following, and that they are fairly sound ones. (i) It is true that some elements were recognized and used for chemical explanations long before they were isolated. But a great many other elements had been isolated, and it was known that the process presented various degrees of difficulty. No entelechy, or anything like one, has ever been isolated; hence an entelechy is a *purely* hypothetical entity in a sense in which an as yet unisolated but suspected chemical element is not. If it be said that an isolated entelechy is from the nature of the case something which could not be perceived, and that this objection is therefore unreasonable, I can only answer (as I should to the similar assertion that the physical phenomena of mediumship can happen only in darkness and in the presence of sympathetic spectators) that it may well be true but is certainly very unfortunate. (ii) It is true that some groups which cannot exist in isolation play a most important part in chemical explanations. But they are *groups* of known composition, not mysterious simple entities; and their inability to exist by themselves is not an isolated fact but is part of the more general, though imperfectly understood, fact of valency. Moreover, we can at least pass these groups from one compound to another, and can note how the chemical properties change as one compound loses such a group and another gains it. There is no known analogy to this with entelechies. You cannot pass an entelechy from a living man into a corpse and note that the former ceases and that latter begins to behave vitally. (iii) Entelechies are supposed to differ in kind from material particles; and it is doubtful whether they are literally in space at all. It is thus hard to understand what exactly is meant by saying that a living body is a compound of an entelechy and a material structure; and impossible to say anything in detail about the structure of the total complex thus formed.

These objections seem to me to make the doctrine of Substantial Vitalism unsatisfactory, though not impossible. I think that those who have accepted it have done so largely under a misapprehension. They have thought that there was no alternative between Biological Mechanism (which I shall define a little later) and Substantial Vitalism. They found the former unsatisfactory, and so they felt obliged to accept the latter. We shall see in a moment, however, that there is another alternative type of theory, which I will call 'Emergent Vitalism', borrowing the adjective from Professors Samuel Alexander and C. Lloyd Morgan. Of course, positive arguments have been put forward in favour of entelechies, notably by Hans Driesch. I do not propose to consider them in detail. I will merely say that Driesch's arguments do not seem to me to be in the least conclusive, even against Biological Mechanism, because they seem to forget that the smallest fragment which we can make of an organized body by cutting it up may contain an enormous number of similar microscopic structures, each of enormous complexity. And, even if it be held that Driesch has conclusively *dis*proved Biological Mechanism, I cannot see that his arguments have the least tendency to *prove* Substantial

Vitalism rather than the Emergent form of Vitalism which does not assume entelechies.

(b) I come now to the second type of theory which professes to explain, wholly or partly, the differences of behaviour between different things. This kind of theory denies that there need be any peculiar *component* which is present in all things that behave in a certain way and is absent from all things which do not behave in this way. It says that the components may be exactly alike in both cases, and it tries to explain the difference of behaviour wholly in terms of difference of structure. Now it is most important to notice that this type of theory can take two radically different forms. They differ according to the view that we take about the laws which connect the properties of the components with the characteristic behaviour of the complex wholes which they make up. (i) On the first form of the theory the characteristic behaviour of the whole *could* not, even in theory, be deduced from the most complete knowledge of the behaviour of its components, taken separately or in other combinations, and of their proportions and arrangements in this whole. This alternative, which I have roughly outlined and shall soon discuss in detail, is what I understand by the 'Theory of Emergence'. I cannot give a conclusive example of it, since it is a matter of controversy whether it actually applies to anything. But there is no doubt, as I hope to show, that it is a logically possible view with a good deal in its favour. I will merely remark that, so far as we know at present, the characteristic behaviour of common salt cannot be deduced from the most complete knowledge of the properties of sodium in isolation, or of chlorine in isolation, or of other compounds of sodium, such as silver chloride. (ii) On the second form of the theory, the characteristic behaviour of the whole is not only completely *determined by* the nature and arrangement of its components; in addition to this, it is held that the behaviour of the whole could, in theory at least, be *deduced* from a sufficient knowledge of how the components behave in isolation or in other wholes of a simpler kind. I will call this kind of theory 'Mechanistic'. A theory may be 'mechanistic' in this sense without being an instance of Pure Mechanism, in the sense defined earlier in this chapter. For example, if a biologist held that all the characteristic behaviour of living beings could be deduced from an adequate knowledge of the physical and chemical laws which its components would obey in isolation or in non-living complexes, he would be called a 'Biological Mechanist', even though he believed that the different chemical elements are ultimately different kinds of stuff and that the laws of chemical composition are not of the type demanded by Pure Mechanism.

The most obvious examples of wholes to which a mechanistic theory applies are artificial machines. A clock behaves in a characteristic way. But no one supposes that the peculiar behaviour of clocks depends on their containing as a component a peculiar entity which is not present in anything but clocks. Nor does anyone suppose that the peculiar behaviour of clocks is simply an emergent quality of that kind of structure and cannot be learnt by studying anything but clocks. We know perfectly well that the behaviour of a clock can be deduced from the particular arrangement of springs, wheels, pendulum, etc. in it, and from general laws of mechanics and physics which apply just as much to material systems which are not clocks.

To sum up: We have distinguished three possible types of theory to account wholly or partly for the characteristic differences of behaviour between different kinds of material object: viz., the Theory of a Special Component, the Theory of Emergence, and the Mechanistic Theory. We have illustrated these, so far as possible, with examples which everyone will accept. In the special problem of the peculiar behaviour of living bodies these three types of theory are represented by Substantial Vitalism, Emergent Vitalism and Biological Mechanism. I have argued that Substantial Vitalism, though logically possible, is a very unsatisfactory kind of theory, and that probably many people who have accepted it have done so because they did not recognize the alternative of Emergent Vitalism. I propose now to consider in greater detail the emergent and the mechanistic types of theory.

Emergent theories

Put in abstract terms, the emergent theory asserts that there are certain wholes, composed (say) of constituents A, B and C in a relation R to each other; that all wholes composed of constituents of the same kind as A, B and C in relations of the same kind as R have certain characteristic properties; that A, B and C are capable of occurring in other kinds of complex where the relation is not of the same kind as R; and that the characteristic properties of the whole R(A, B, C) cannot, even in theory, be deduced from the most complete knowledge of the properties of A, B and C in isolation or in other

wholes which are not of the form R(A, B, C). The mechanistic theory rejects the last clause of this assertion.

Let us now consider the question in detail. If we want to explain the behaviour of any whole in terms of its structure and components, we *always* need two independent kinds of information. (a) We need to know how the parts would behave separately. And (b) we need to know the law or laws according to which the behaviour of the separate parts is compounded when they are acting together in any proportion and arrangement. Now it is extremely important to notice that these two bits of information are quite independent of each other in every case. Let us consider, e.g., the simplest possible case. We know that a certain tap, when running by itself, will put so many cubic centimetres of water into a tank in a minute. We know that a certain other tap, when running by itself, will put so many cubic centimetres of water into this tank in the same time. It does not follow logically from these two bits of information that, when the two taps are turned on together, the sum of these two numbers of cubic centimetres will be added to the contents of the tank every minute. This might not happen for two reasons. In the first place, it is quite likely that, if the two taps came from the same pipe, less would flow from each when both were turned on together than when each was turned on separately; i.e., the separate factors do not behave together as they would have behaved in isolation. Again, if one tap delivered hot water and the other cold water, the simple assumption about composition would break down although the separate factors continued to obey the same laws as they had followed when acting in isolation. For there would be a change of volume on mixture of the hot and cold water.

Next let us consider the case of two forces acting on a particle at an angle to each other. We find by experiment that the actual motion of the body is the vector-sum of the motions which it would have had if each had been acting separately. There is not the least possibility of deducing this law of composition from the laws of each force taken separately. There is one other fact worth mentioning here. As Mr Russell pointed out long ago, a vector-sum is not a sum in the ordinary sense of the word. We cannot strictly say that each force is doing what it would have done if it had been alone, and that the result of their joint action is the sum of the results of their separate actions. A velocity of 5 miles an hour in a certain direction does not literally contain as parts a velocity of 3 miles an hour in a certain other direction and a velocity of 4 miles an hour in a direction at right angles to this. All that we can say is that the effect of several forces acting together is a fairly simple mathematical function of the purely hypothetical effects which each would have had if it had acted by itself, and that this function reduces to an algebraical sum in the particular case where all the forces are in the same line.

We will now pass to the case of chemical composition. Oxygen has certain properties, and hydrogen has certain other properties. They combine to form water, and the proportions in which they do this are fixed. Nothing that we know about oxygen by itself or in its combinations with anything but hydrogen would give us the least reason to suppose that it would combine with hydrogen at all. Nothing that we know about hydrogen by itself or in its combinations with anything but oxygen would give us the least reason to expect that it would combine with oxygen at all. And most of the chemical and physical properties of water have no known connection, either quantitative or qualitative, with those of oxygen and hydrogen. Here we have a clear instance of a case where, so far as we can tell, the properties of a whole composed of two constituents could not have been predicted from a knowledge of the properties of these constituents taken separately, or from this combined with a knowledge of the properties of other wholes which contain these constituents.

Let us sum up the conclusions which may be reached from these examples before going further. It is clear that in *no* case could the behaviour of a whole composed of certain constituents be predicted *merely* from a knowledge of the properties of these constituents, taken separately, and of their proportions and arrangements in the particular complex under consideration. Whenever this *seems* to be possible, it is because we are using a suppressed premiss which is so familiar that it has escaped our notice. The suppressed premiss is the fact that we have examined other complexes in the past and have noted their behaviour; that we have found a general law connecting the behaviour of these wholes with that which their constituents would show in isolation; and that we are assuming that this law of composition will hold also of the particular complex whole at present under consideration. For purely dynamical transactions this assumption is pretty well justified, because we have found a simple law of composition and have verified it very fully for wholes of very different

composition, complexity and internal structure. It is therefore not particularly rash to expect to predict the dynamical behaviour of any material complex under the action of any set of forces, however much it may differ in the details of its structure and parts from those complexes for which the assumed law of composition has actually been verified.

The example of chemical compounds shows us that we have no right to expect that the same simple law of composition will hold for chemical as for dynamical transactions. And it shows us something further. It shows us that, if we want to know the chemical (and many of the physical) properties of a chemical compound, such as silver chloride, it is absolutely necessary to study samples of *that particular compound*. It would of course (on any view) be useless merely to study silver in isolation and chlorine in isolation; for that would tell us nothing about the law of their conjoint action. This would be equally true even if a mechanistic explanation of the chemical behaviour of compounds were possible. The essential point is that it would also be useless to study chemical compounds in general and to compare their properties with those of their elements in the hope of discovering a *general* law of composition by which the properties of *any* chemical compound could be foretold when the properties of its separate elements were known. So far as we know, there is no general law of this kind. It is useless even to study the properties of other compounds of silver and of other compounds of chlorine in the hope of discovering one general law by which the properties of silver compounds could be predicted from those of elementary silver and another general law by which the properties of chlorine compounds could be predicted from those of elementary chlorine. No doubt the properties of silver chloride are completely *determined* by those of silver and of chlorine, in the sense that whenever you have a whole composed of these two elements in certain proportions and relations, you have something with the characteristic properties of silver chloride, and that nothing has these properties except a whole composed in this way. But the law connecting the properties of silver chloride with those of silver and of chlorine and with the structure of the compound is, so far as we know, a *unique* and *ultimate* law. By this I mean (a) that it is not a special case which arises through substituting certain determinate values for determinable variables in a general law which connects the properties of *any* chemical compound with those of its separate elements and with its structure. And (b) that it is not a special case which arises by combining two more general laws, one of which connects the properties of *any* silver compound with those of elementary silver, whilst the other connects the properties of *any* chlorine compound with those of elementary chlorine. So far as we know, there are no such laws. It is (c) a law which could have been discovered *only* by studying samples of silver chloride itself, and which can be extended inductively *only* to other samples of the same substance.

We may contrast this state of affairs with that which exists where a mechanistic explanation is possible. In order to predict the behaviour of a clock, a man need never have seen a clock in his life. Provided he is told how it is constructed, and that he has learnt from the study of *other* material systems the general rules about motion and about the mechanical properties of springs and of rigid bodies, he can foretell exactly how a system constructed like a clock must behave.

The situation with which we are faced in chemistry, which seems to offer the most plausible example of emergent behaviour, may be described in two alternative ways. These may be theoretically different, but in practice they are equivalent. (i) The first way of putting the case is the following. What we call the 'properties' of the chemical elements are very largely propositions about the compounds which they form with other elements under suitable conditions. For example one of the 'properties' of silver is that it combines under certain conditions with chlorine to give a compound with the properties of silver chloride. Likewise, one of the 'properties' of chlorine is that under certain conditions it combines with silver to give a compound with the properties of silver chloride. These 'properties' cannot be deduced from any selection of the other properties of silver or of chlorine. Thus we may say that we do not know all the properties of chlorine and of silver until they have been put in the presence of each other; and that no amount of knowledge about the properties which they manifest in other circumstances will tell us what property, if any, they will manifest in these circumstances. Put in this way, the position is that we do not know all the properties of any element, and that there is always the possibility of their manifesting unpredictable properties when put into new situations. This happens whenever a chemical compound is prepared or discovered for the first time. (ii) The other way to put the matter is to confine the name 'property' to those charac-

teristics which the elements manifest when they do not act chemically on each other: i.e., the physical characteristics of the isolated elements. In this case we may indeed say, if we like, that we know all the properties of each element; but we shall have to admit that we do not know the laws according to which elements, which have these properties in isolation, together produce compounds having such and such other characteristic properties. The essential point is that the behaviour of an as yet unexamined compound cannot be predicted from a knowledge of the properties of their other compounds; and it matters little whether we ascribe this to the existence of innumerable 'latent' properties in each element, each of which is manifested only in the presence of a certain other element, or to the lack of any general principle of composition, such as the parallelogram law in dynamics, by which the behaviour of any chemical compound could be deduced from its structure and from the behaviour of each of its elements in isolation from the rest.

Let us now apply the conceptions, which I have been explaining and illustrating from chemistry, to the case of vital behaviour. We know that the bits of matter which behave vitally are composed of various chemical compounds arranged in certain characteristic ways. We have prepared and experimented with many of these compounds apart from living bodies, and we see no obvious reason why some day they might not all be synthesized and studied in the chemical laboratory. A living body might be regarded as a compound of the second order, i.e., a compound composed of compounds; just as silver chloride is a compound of the first order, i.e., one composed of chemical elements. Now it is obviously possible that, just as the characteristic behaviour of a first-order compound could not be predicted from any amount of knowledge of the properties of its elements in isolation or of the properties of other first-order compounds, so the properties of a second-order compound could not be predicted from any amount of knowledge about the properties of its first-order constituents taken separately or in other surroundings. Just as the only way to find out the properties of silver chloride is to study samples of silver chloride, and no amount of study of silver and of chlorine taken separately or in other combinations will help us; so the only way to find out the characteristic behaviour of living bodies may be to study living bodies as such. And no amount of knowledge about how the constituents of a living body behave in isolation or in other and non-living wholes might suffice to enable us to predict the characteristic behaviour of a living organism. This possibility is perfectly compatible with the view that the characteristic behaviour of a living body is completely determined by the nature and arrangement of the chemical compounds which compose it, in the sense that any whole which is composed of such compounds in such an arrangement will show vital behaviour and that nothing else will do so. We should merely have to recognize, as we had to do in considering a first-order compound like silver chloride, that we are dealing with a *unique* and *irreducible* law, and not with a special case which arises by the substitution of particular values for variables in a more general law, nor with a combination of several more general laws.

We could state this possibility about living organisms in two alternative but practically equivalent ways, just as we stated the similar possibility about chemical compounds. (i) The first way would be this. Most of the properties which we ascribe to chemical compounds are statements about what they do in presence of various chemical reagents under certain conditions of temperature, pressure, etc. These various properties are not deducible from each other; and, until we have tried a compound with every other compound and under every possible condition of temperature, pressure, etc., we cannot possibly know that we have exhausted all its properties. It is therefore perfectly possible that, in the very special situation in which a chemical compound is placed in a living body, it may exhibit properties which remain 'latent' under all other conditions. (ii) The other, and practically equivalent, way of putting the case is the following. If we confine the name 'property' to the behaviour which a chemical compound shows in isolation, we may perhaps say that we know all the 'properties' of the chemical constituents of a living body. But we shall not be able to predict the behaviour of the body unless we also know the laws according to which the behaviour which each of these constituents *would have* shown in isolation is compounded when they are acting together in certain proportions and arrangements. We can discover such laws only by studying complexes containing these constituents in various proportions and arrangements. And we have no right to suppose that the laws which we have discovered by studying non-living complexes can be carried over without modification to the very different case of living complexes. It may be that the only way to

discover the laws according to which the behaviour of the separate constituents combines to produce the behaviour of the whole in a living body is to study living bodies as such. For practical purposes it makes little difference whether we say that the chemical compounds which compose a living body have 'latent properties' which are manifested only when they are parts of a whole of this peculiar structure; or whether we say that the properties of the constituents of a living body are the same whether they are in it or out of it, but that the law according to which these separate effects are compounded with each other is different in a living whole from what it is in any non-living whole.

This view about living bodies and vital behaviour is what I call 'Emergent Vitalism'; and it is important to notice that it is quite different from what I call 'Substantial Vitalism'. So far as I can understand them, I should say that Driesch is a Substantial Vitalist, and that Dr J. S. Haldane is an Emergent Vitalist. But I may quite well be wrong in classifying these two distinguished men in this way.

Mechanistic theories

The mechanistic type of theory is much more familiar than the emergent type, and it will therefore be needless to consider it in great detail. I will just consider the mechanistic alternative about chemical and vital behaviour, so as to make the emergent theory still clearer by contrast. Suppose it were certain, as it is very probable, that all the different chemical atoms are composed of positive and negative electrified particles in different numbers and arrangements; and that these differences of number and arrangement are the only ultimate difference between them. Suppose that all these particles obey the same elementary laws, and that their separate actions are compounded with each other according to a single law which is the same no matter how complicated may be the whole of which they are constituents. Then it would be *theoretically* possible to deduce the characteristic behaviour of any element from an adequate knowledge of the number and arrangement of the particles in its atom, without needing to observe a sample of the substance. We could, *in theory*, deduce what other elements it would combine with and in what proportions; which of these compounds would be stable to heat, etc.; and how the various compounds would react in the presence of each other under given conditions of temperature, pressure, etc. And all this should be *theoretically* possible without needing to observe samples of these compounds.

I want now to explain exactly what I mean by the qualification 'theoretically'. (1) In the first place the mathematical difficulties might be overwhelming in practice, even if we knew the structure and the laws. This is a trivial qualification for our present purpose, which is to bring out the *logical* distinction between mechanism and emergence. Let us replace Sir Ernest Rutherford by a mathematical archangel, and pass on. (2) Secondly, we cannot directly perceive the microscopic structure of atoms, but can only infer it from the macroscopic behaviour of matter in bulk. Thus, in practice, even if the mechanistic hypothesis were true and the mathematical difficulties were overcome, we should have to start by observing enough of the macroscopic behaviour of samples of each element to infer the probable structure of its atom. But, once this was done, it should be possible to deduce its behaviour in macroscopic conditions under which it has never yet been observed. That is, if we could infer its microscopic structure from a *selection* of its observed macroscopic properties, we could henceforth *deduce* all its other macroscopic properties from its microscopic structure without further appeal to observation. The difference from the emergent theory is thus profound, even when we allow for our mathematical and perceptual limitations. If the emergent theory of chemical compounds be true, a mathematical archangel, gifted with the further power of perceiving the microscopic structure of atoms as easily as we can perceive hay stacks, could no more predict the behaviour of silver or of chlorine or the properties of silver chloride without having observed samples of those substances than we can at present. And he could no more deduce the rest of the properties of a chemical element or compound from a selection of its properties than we can.

Would there be any theoretical limit to the deduction of the properties of chemical elements and compounds if a mechanistic theory of chemistry were true? Yes. Take any ordinary statement, such as we find in chemistry books: e.g., 'Nitrogen and hydrogen combine when an electric discharge is passed through a mixture of the two. The resulting compound contains three atoms of hydrogen to one of nitrogen; it is a gas readily soluble in water, and possessed of a pungent and characteristic smell.' If the mechanistic theory be true, the archangel could deduce from his knowledge of the microscopic structure of atoms all these facts but the last. He would know exactly what the microscopic structure of ammonia must be; but he would be totally unable to predict that a substance with this structure must smell as ammonia does when it gets into the human nose. The utmost that he could predict on this subject would be that certain changes would take place in the mucous membrane, the olfactory nerves and so on. But he could not possibly know that these changes would be accompanied by the appearance of a smell in general or of the peculiar smell of ammonia in particular, unless someone told him so or he had smelled it for himself. If the existence of the so-called secondary qualities, or the fact of their appearance, depends on the microscopic movements and arrangements of material particles which do not have these qualities themselves, then the laws of this dependence are certainly of the emergent type.

The mechanistic theory about vital behaviour should now need little explanation. A man can hold it without being a mechanist about chemistry. The minimum that a Biological Mechanist need believe is that, *in theory*, everything that is characteristic of the behaviour of a living body could be deduced from an adequate knowledge of its structure, the chemical compounds which make it up, and the properties which these show in isolation or in non-living wholes.

38

Ontological Reduction and the World of Numbers

W. V. Quine

One conspicuous concern of analytical or scientific philosophy has been to reduce some notions to others, preferably to less putative ones. A familiar case of such reduction is Frege's definition of number. Each natural number n became, if I may speak in circles, the class of all n-member classes. As is also well known, Frege's was not the only good way. Another was von Neumann's. Under it, if I may again speak in circles, each natural number n became the class of all numbers less than n.

In my judgment we have satisfactorily reduced one predicate to others, certainly, if in terms of these others we have fashioned an open sentence that is *coextensive* with the predicate in question as originally interpreted; i.e., that is satisfied by the same values of the variables. But this standard does not suit the Frege and von Neumann reductions of number; for these reductions are both good, yet not coextensive with each other.

Again, consider Carnap's clarification of measure, or impure number, where he construes 'the temperature of x is $n°$C' in the fashion 'the temperature-in-degrees-Centigrade of x is n' and so dispenses with the impure numbers $n°$C in favor of the pure numbers n.[1] There had been, we might say, a two-place predicate 'H' of temperature such

that '$H(x, \alpha)$' meant that the temperature of x was α. We end up with a new two-place predicate 'H_0' of temperature in degrees Centigrade. '$H(x, n°$ C)' is explained away as '$H_c(x, n)$'. But 'H' is not coextensive with 'H_c', or indeed with any surviving open sentence at all; 'H' had applied to putative things α, impure numbers, which come to be banished from the universe. Their banishment was Carnap's very purpose. Such reduction is in part *ontological*, as we may say, and coextensiveness here is clearly not the point.

The definitions of numbers by Frege and von Neumann are best seen as ontological reductions too. Carnap, in the last example, showed how to skip the impure numbers and get by with pure ones. Just so, we might say, Frege and von Neumann showed how to skip the natural numbers and get by with what we may for the moment call *Frege classes* and *von Neumann classes*. There is only this difference of detail: Frege classes and von Neumann classes simulate the behavior of the natural numbers to the point where it is convenient to call them natural numbers, instead of saying that we have contrived to dispense with the natural numbers as Carnap dispensed with impure numbers.

Where reduction is in part ontological, we see, coextensiveness is not the issue. What then is? Consider again Frege's way and von Neumann's of construing natural number. And there is yet a third well-known way, Zermelo's. Why are these all good? What have they in common? Each is a structure-preserving model of the natural numbers. Each preserves arithmetic, and that is

Originally published in *Journal of Philosophy* 61 (1964), pp. 209–16; the substantially revised version reprinted here is from my *The Ways of Paradox* (New York: Random House, 1966). I am grateful to Kenneth F. Schaffner for a letter of inquiry that sparked the revision.

enough. It has been urged that we need more: we need also to provide for translating mixed contexts in which the arithmetical idioms occur in company with expressions concerning physical objects and the like. Specifically, we need to be able to say what it means for a class to have n members. But in fact this is no added requirement. We can say what it means for a class to have n members no matter how we construe the numbers, as long as we have them in order. For to say that a class has n members is simply to say that the members of the class can be correlated with the natural numbers up to n, whatever they are.

The real numbers, like the natural numbers, can be taken in a variety of ways. The Dedekind cut is the central idea, but you can use it to explain real numbers either as certain classes of ratios, or as certain relations of natural numbers, or as certain classes of natural numbers. Under the first method, if I may again speak in circles, each real number x becomes the class of all ratios less than x. Under the second method, x becomes this relation of natural numbers: m bears the relation to n if m stands to n in a ratio less than x. For the third version, we change this relation of natural numbers to a class of natural numbers by mapping the ordered pairs of natural numbers into the natural numbers.

All three alternatives are admissible, and what all three conspicuously have in common is, again, just the relevant structure: each is a structure-preserving model of the real numbers. Again it seems that no more is needed to assure satisfactory translation also of any mixed contexts. When real numbers are applied to magnitudes in the physical world, any model of the real numbers could be applied as well.

The same proves true when we come to the imaginary numbers and the infinite numbers, cardinal and ordinal: the problem of construing comes to no more, again, than modeling. Once we find a model that reproduces the formal structure, there seems to be no difficulty in translating any mixed contexts as well.

These cases suggest that what justifies the reduction of one system of objects to another is preservation of relevant structure. Since, according to the Löwenheim–Skolem theorem, any theory that admits of a true interpretation at all admits of a model in the natural numbers, G. D. W. Berry concluded that only common sense stands in the way of adopting an all-purpose Pythagorean ontology: natural numbers exclusively.

There is an interesting reversal here. Our first examples of ontological reduction were Frege's and von Neumann's reductions of natural number to set theory. These and other examples encouraged the thought that what matters in such reduction is the discovery of a model. And so we end up saying, in view of the Löwenheim–Skolem theorem, that theories about objects of any sort can, when true, be reduced to theories of natural numbers. Instead of reducing talk of numbers to talk of sets, we may reduce talk of sets – and of all else – to talk of natural numbers. And here there is an evident again, since the natural numbers are relatively clear and, as infinite sets go, economical.

But is it true that all that matters is a model? Any interpretable theory can, in view of the Löwenheim–Skolem theorem, be *modeled* in the natural numbers, yes; but does this entitle us to say that it is once and for all *reducible* to that domain, in a sense that would allow us thenceforward to repudiate the old objects for all purposes and recognize just the new ones, the natural numbers? Examples encouraged in us the impression that modelling assured such reducibility, but we should be able to confirm or remove the impression with a little analysis.

What do we require of a reduction of one theory to another? Here is a complaisant answer: any effective mapping of closed sentences on closed sentences will serve if it preserves truth. If we settle for this, then what of the thesis that every true theory θ can be reduced to a theory about natural numbers? It can be proved, even without the Löwenheim–Skolem theorem. For we can translate each closed sentence S of θ as 'Tx' with x as the Gödel number of S and with 'T' as the *truth predicate* for θ, a predicate satisfied by all and only the Gödel numbers of true sentences of θ.

Of this trivial way of reducing an ontology to natural numbers, it must be said that whatever it saves in ontology it pays for in *ideology*: we have to strengthen the primitive predicates. For we know from Gödel and Tarski that the truth predicate of θ is expressible only in terms that are stronger in essential ways than any originally available in θ itself.[2]

Nor is this a price that can in general be saved by invoking the Löwenheim–Skolem theorem. I shall explain why not. When, in conformity with the proof of the Löwenheim – Skolem theorem, we reinterpret the primitive predicates of a theory θ so as to make them predicates of natural numbers, we do not in general make them arithmetical predicates. That is, they do not in general go over into predicates that can be expressed in terms of sum, product, equality and logic. If we are modeling merely the *theorems* of a deductive system – the

where '$<$' is the part–whole relation of the calculus of individuals, here understood as "spatiotemporal part." We designate this individual $F(\Delta)$. The hierarchy is defined thus:

$$R(0) = \{x|x = \phi \vee x < F(\Gamma)\}$$
$$R(\alpha') = \text{Power set } (R(\alpha)) \quad (\alpha' \text{successor of} \alpha)$$
$$R(\lambda) = \cup_\beta < \lambda\, R(\beta), \text{limit ordinals } \lambda$$

These are just like the ranks, defined by transfinite induction, in set theory, except here rank 0 contains, in addition to the null set, all parts of the fusion of concrete basic positive physical predicates (as ur-elements). This hierarchy admits all required mathematical constructions, both pure and applied (i.e., defined on physical systems). In terms of this hierarchy, ontological physicalism takes the following simple form:[7]

(1) $(\forall x)(\exists \alpha)(x \in R(\alpha))$

The crucial step is in the use of '$x < F(\Gamma)$' in the definition of $R(0)$. Recall that, like '$\in$', '$<$' is not on the basic list Γ. Its use enables one to say, without begging any questions, that everything concrete is *exhausted* by basic physical objects, without thereby implying that everything is in the extension of a basic physical predicate. (1) ensures that the only further entities are sets built on $R(0)$, and may be appropriately dubbed the *Principle of Physical Exhaustion* (not to be confounded with mental exhaustion!).

There is, in addition to Physical Exhaustion, an allied principle that merits attention under the heading of purely ontological theses. It may be called the *Identity of Physical Indiscernibles* and corresponds to one reading of the basic physicalist intuition, "no difference without a physical difference." Letting ϕ range over physical predicates and using u and v to range over arbitrary n-tuples of objects, we may express the Identity of Physical Indiscernibles thus:

(2) $(\forall u)(\forall v)((\forall \phi)(\phi u \leftrightarrow \phi v) \to u = v)$

Let ψ range over all nonphysical predicates (all predicates outside L needed to describe any phenomena in any branch of science). Then, in the presence of (a certain formulation of) Leibniz's laws, (2) is equivalent to

(3) $(\forall \psi)(\forall u)(\forall v)(\exists \phi)(\psi u\, \& \sim \psi v \to \phi u$
     $\& \sim \phi v)$

i.e., for every nonphysical predicate and every distinction it makes, there is a physical predicate that makes that distinction.[8]

By appropriately restricting the range of ϕ, (2) and (3) come very close to implying (1): they imply that there can be at most one entity discrete from the sum of all basic physical entities. (Details are omitted for lack of space. Suffice it to say, evidently monotheism was an advance on polytheism after all, provided God has no proper parts!) However, (2) and (3) are essentially stronger than Physical Exhaustion: the physical might exhaust everything, though physical language might be too weak to distinguish nonidenticals. What is most significant, however, is that, regardless of the appeal (2) and (3) make to the power of physical language, *none* of the principles (1)–(3) says anything about reduction or even accidental extensional equivalence between nonphysical and physical predicates. While ruling out Cartesian dualism, epiphenomenalism, and their ilk, the principle of Physical Exhaustion (like (2) or (3)) is compatible with there being no physical predicate, no matter how complex, which even accidentally picks out the extension of any nonphysical predicate, even those of biology, not to mention psychology. Insofar as reductionism has been motivated by a desire to restrict ontological commitment to the physical, it has made necessity out of a virtue.[9]

B. The status of the ontological principles

Let us take physical reductionism to be the claim that, in the theory consisting of all the lawlike truths of science (stated in an adequate language), including, of course physical theory, every scientific predicate is definable in physical terms. That is, for every n-place predicate P, the laws of science entail a formula of the form

$$(\forall x_1) \ldots (\forall x_n)(Px_1 \ldots x_n \leftrightarrow A)$$

where A is a (finite) sentence containing only physical vocabulary as nonlogical terms and occurrences of n distinct variables, $x_1, \ldots, x_n$. This is a "strong" form of reductionism because it asserts not merely that the extensions of all scientific predicates are physically expressible, but also that the equivalences are lawlike. The equivalences are provable in scientific theory and are therefore logical consequences of its laws. Yet even this strong form of reductionism is compatible with ontological dualism.

To see this, consider a very simple theory, Σ, containing just two nonlogical one-place predicates, P and Q, and the following nonlogical axioms:

$$(\exists x)(\exists y)(x \neq y \ \& \ (\forall z)(z = x \ \lor \ z = y))$$
$$(\exists x)(Px \ \& \ (\forall y)(Py \rightarrow y = x))$$
$$(\exists x)(Qx \ \& \ (\forall y)(Qy \rightarrow y = x))$$
$$(\forall x)(Px \lor Qx)$$

That is, Σ asserts that there are exactly two objects and that exactly one object is a P and exactly one object is a Q and everything is either a P or a Q. Now in Σ, the following is provable:

$$(\forall x)(Qx \leftrightarrow \sim Px)$$

In other words, Q is definable in terms of P. Yet, this doesn't guarantee that all objects are, or are exhausted by, P-type things. In fact, in every model of Σ, there are two disjoint subsets of entities, one P-type, the other Q-type.[10]

Although the Principle of Physical Exhaustion is a necessary component of physicalism, it is hardly sufficient, in that it says nothing about the scope or power of physical laws. The same may be said for the Identity of Physical Indiscernibles, since quantification therein is restricted to the actual world.[11] All these principles are too weak in that they give no expression to the fundamental physicalist claim that physical phenomena *determine* all phenomena.

II

The intuitive notion to be explicated, then, is that of one realm of facts determining another. A relation of determination has been thought to hold in many cases of scientific interest, such as between facts about the past and facts about the future, the natural and the ethical, the instrumental or observational and the theoretical, and elsewhere, including (as we here urge) the physical and all facts. Although frequently identified with definability or reduction (save the case of past and future), determination, as will be seen, is an independent matter.

A. Determination

If one kind or realm of facts determines another, then, at a minimum, the truth-values of sentences

expressing facts in the latter realm cannot vary without variance of the truth-values of sentences expressing facts of the former kind. What cannot happen happens under no scientifically possible circumstances. Circumstances are possible if they are compatible with what is fixed. A model-theoretic characterization of determination is in order.[12]

For generality, assume we are working within a family of languages such that any term appearing in more than one has the same interpretation in each. Let ϕ and ψ stand for various sets of nonlogical terms and let α be a set of structures representing scientific possibilities. We may now formulate the notion of a complete ϕ characterization of the world uniquely determining a complete ψ characterization. Recall that two models are elementarily equivalent – m eleq m' – if the same sentences are true or valid in each, and that the restriction or reduct of a model m to a certain vocabulary $L - m|$ $L -$ is the structure derived from m by omitting the interpretation of all terms not in L. Thus we have

(4) In α structures, ϕ truth determines ψ truth iff

$$(\forall m)(\forall m')((m, m' \in \alpha \ \& \ m|\phi \ \text{eleq} \ m'|\phi) \rightarrow m|\psi \ \text{eleq} \ m'|\psi).$$

The intuitive appeal of this notion is clear. Given a full characterization of things in ϕ terms, one and only one full characterization in ψ terms is correct. Once the ϕ facts have been established, so are the ψ facts.[13]

This notion of determination has a number of trivial and uninteresting applications which it would be tedious to discuss explicitly or exclude. In the interesting cases, α is a specifiable subset of the models of a theory T which consists of lawlike truths, ϕ and ψ are each subsets of the vocabulary in which T is stated, and ψ is not a subset of ϕ. More strongly, T will contain sentences with essential occurrences of terms of both ϕ and $\psi - \phi$. Thus the theory T *connects* the ϕ terms and the ψ terms, which is to say that determination involves "bridge laws" connecting the determining phenomena with the phenomena determined. Notice that determination would hold trivially if all models of the theory T were elementarily equivalent or, even more strongly, if T were categorical.

Thus far we have spoken of the determination of one kind of fact or one kind of truths by another.

Can we come closer to the world? Precisely the same sentences can be true in two structures that differ enormously in other respects, for example in cardinality. Reference determines truth, as common sense assumes and Frege and Tarski clarified, but truth does not determine reference. In reference different terms differentially correspond to the world, determining truths that fail differentially so to correspond.

It is natural to maintain that, just as models are indistinguishable with respect to truth if the same sentences are true in each, i.e., if they are elementarily equivalent, structures are indistinguishable with respect to reference if each term has the same reference in each, i.e., if they are identical.[14] Thus corresponding to (4) we have

(5) In α structures, ϕ reference determines

ψ reference iff

$(\forall m)(\forall m')((m, m' \in \alpha \ \& \ m|\phi = m'|\phi)$
$\rightarrow m|\psi = m'|\psi).$

That is, if any two structures in α agree on the references they assign to the ϕ terms; i.e., their restrictions to the ϕ vocabulary are identical; then they agree on the references they assign to the ψ terms; i.e., their restrictions to the ψ vocabulary are identical.[15]

A question concerning the relative strength of these notions remains: What is the connection between (4) and (5)? Perhaps surprisingly, the answer is "none." As they stand, they are model-theoretically independent: there are α, ϕ, and ψ such that, in α structures, ϕ reference determines ψ reference but ϕ truth does not determine ψ truth. The commonplace about reference determining truth does not here apply. Yet, for an extremely important class of structures, those sets consisting of all and only the models of some theory T, (5) so restricted does imply (4).

If ϕ is construed as the vocabulary of mathematical physics, ψ as *all* the vocabulary by means of which truths can be stated, and α as a set of structures representing scientific possibility, then (4) and (5) constitute *Principles of Physical Determination*.

If α is to represent scientific possibility, it must at least be the case that every member of α models all the laws of science. The question can then be raised whether this condition is sufficient as well as necessary. If it were, we could in every occurrence simply replace 'α' by '$\{m : m$ models $T\}$',

where T is the whole of scientific theory, or (more elegantly) reformulate our principles of physical determination directly to refer to this body of theory.

In the next section we shall argue that there is reason to believe that scientific theory, at least insofar as it is formulable without recourse to an infinitary language, has models which would *violate* principles of physical determination and which therefore, assuming as we do that principles of physical determination hold, must be excluded by other means. Fortunately, simple means are available to this end which allow us to construct (instead of assume as an unanalyzed primitive) the requisite notion of scientific possibility.

B. *Reduction and determination*

If for simplicity we assume that our language contains only predicates as nonlogical terms (an assumption which can easily be relaxed), then

A primitive n-place predicate P is definable in terms of a vocabulary ϕ in α structures
iff
there is a (finite) sentence A containing no nonlogical terms not in ϕ and with occurrences of n distinct variables, $x_1, \ldots, x_n$, such that every structure in α models $(\forall x_1) \ldots (\forall x_n)$ $(Px_1 \ldots x_n \leftrightarrow A)$.[16]

It should be noted that definability claims are not *per se* claims of synonymy. Definability is a clear notion; synonymy is not. But neither are they simply claims of coextensiveness. As before, α is to be a set of structures representing scientific possibility; at a minimum, every member of α is a model of the laws of science. Definability is thus a kind of lawlike coextensiveness.

The notion of reducibility with which we are here concerned is that obtaining when all the terms of the vocabulary to be reduced are definable in the reducing vocabulary. That is,

(6) In α structures, ϕ reduces ψ iff

$(\forall P)(P \in \psi \rightarrow P$ is definable in terms

of ϕ *in* α *structures*).[17]

If ϕ is construed as the vocabulary of mathematical physics, ψ as *all* the vocabulary by means of which truths can be stated, and α as a set of structures representing scientific possibility, then (6) constitutes the Principle of Physical Reductionism. (A more stringent notion, which one might call "effective reducibility," would require that every term in the reduced vocabulary be definable in a recursively enumerable set of definitions.)

Although some assumption as to the mathematical-physical determination of all truth and, probably, all reference is a regulative principle of scientific theory construction, a general assumption of the reducibility of all terms (and thus, all theory) to mathematical-physical terms (and thus, theory) is unwarranted and probably false. The physicalism that appears plausible has two components: ontological physicalism – the Principle of Physical Exhaustion – and Physical Determinationism, a unified thesis which we choose to call *Physicalist Materialism*.

A word is here in order extending our earlier point that ontological physicalism is formally independent from reductionism. As a moment's reflection on "parallelism" will verify, ontological physicalism is likewise independent from physical determinationism. This will, however, give no comfort to dualists. In the absence of positive arguments for extra entities, Occam's razor (sound scientific procedure) will dictate commitment to the sparser ontology. And, physical determination being given, such positive arguments would seem difficult if not impossible to find.

This is not the place to argue the truth of this version of physicalism. The aim is to characterize the position so as to make evident its plausibility and consistency, and, further, to make clear the independence of any and all these principles (ontological and determinationist) from physical reductionism and even from the mere coextensiveness of nonphysical with physical terms. Therewith it will have been demonstrated that anti-reductionist arguments are irrelevant to the truth of physicalism.

That such a position has not been previously, to our knowledge, presented in the relevant literature, is surprising. Ontological physicalism and anti-physical reductionism are both widely held, and many have hinted at notions like physical determinationism. To be sure, there is an argument, based on an application of Beth's renowned definability theorem, which might appear to render simultaneous support for determinationism and anti-reductionism impossible. But it seems unlikely that his argument has dissuaded many,

since, once again to our knowledge, this argument has not been previously noticed.

Beth's theorem shows the equivalence of what logicians have long distinguished as implicit and explicit definability in a theory. All the terms in ψ are *implicitly defined* by the terms in ϕ, in a theory T, just in case

$$(\forall m)(\forall m')((m, m' \text{ model } T \ \& \ m|\phi = m'|\phi) \rightarrow m|\psi = m'|\psi)$$

that is, just in case

$$(\forall m)(\forall m')((m, m' \in \{m : m \text{ models } T\} \ \& \ m|\phi = m'|\phi) \rightarrow m|\psi = m'|\psi$$

This is of course an instance of (5), and thus equivalent to

(7) In $\{m : m \text{ models } T\}$ structures,
ϕ reference determines ψ reference.

All the terms in ψ are *explicitly defined* by the terms in ϕ, in a theory T, just in case

(8) In $\{m : m \text{ models } T\}$ structures,
ϕ reduces ψ.

Thus what Beth's theorem shows is that (7) and (8) are model-theoretically equivalent (where T is a first-order theory of a noninfinitary language), that is, that with respect to sets of structures which are all and only the models of (such) a theory, determination of reference is equivalent to reducibility.

But, in the general case in which the set of structures α is not necessarily all and only the models of some theory T, determination of reference is not equivalent to reducibility. Although (6) entails (5), the converse does not obtain. Thus if one holds that some models of the laws of science are "nonstandard" models that do not represent scientific possibilities, then one can endorse principles of physical determinationism including determination of reference without claiming that all scientific facts are reducible to the mathematical-physical.

Nor does such a position commit one to accepting the notion of scientific possibility as an unexplicated primitive. One can specify α as that subset of the models of the laws of science in which certain predicates receive standard interpretations. One can require, for example, that the vocabulary of pure arithmetic receive its standard interpretation, thus specifying a set of structures representing scientific possibility which, as is well known, is not capturable as all and only the models of a first-order theory in a noninfinitary language, even when the theory itself fails to be recursively enumerable in virtue of containing every truth of arithmetic.

Which models of the laws of science must be excluded in order to delineate a set of structures representing scientific possibility is itself a scientific question. Further mathematical notions, e.g., set-theoretic, may plausibly be held standard, likewise resulting in a set of structures not capturable as all and only the models of a theory.[18]

The syntactically specifiable notion of a theory plays a crucial role in the Beth theorem and hence in the subcase in which determination and reducibility are equivalent. The absence of a general equivalence between determination and reducibility is somewhat clarified if it is noticed that the notion of reducibility is essentially tied to that of theory but determination is not. Reduction requires the existence of syntactic entities, the definitions, which license the elimination in principle of certain theory and description.[19]

Determination, in contrast to reducibility, has nothing directly to do with the existence of a theory containing or permitting the proof of certain kinds of sentences. To emphasize the extreme, the determination of ψ reference by ϕ reference in α structures is compatible with *no* term in ψ being even *accidentally* coextensional with a term constructed out of the ϕ vocabulary. That is, (5) does not entail that an instance of (6) holds where α in the latter formula is replaced by a reference to (the unit set of) some member of α.

In summary, it has been shown how to construct both the ontological principle of physical exhaustion and independent principles of physical determination which together, it is submitted, constitute the major claims of physicalism. The principle of the physical determination of reference threatened to collapse to reducibility in view of Beth's definability theorem. However, as the work of Gödel and others would suggest, the power of our symbolic systems is such that full theoretical characterization of scientific possibility in any manner that would license the inference from determination to reduction is not to be expected.

For some purposes, the prevalence of nonstandard interpretation, the powerlessness of our most useful theories directly to pin down the possible, are grounds for discouragement. From a certain perspective, however, the present case is entirely the opposite. Physicalism in no way dictates the course of progress in the higher-level sciences. Reductions are indeed frequently constitutive of such progress. But the truth of physicalism is compatible with the utter absence of lawlike or even accidental generalized biconditionals connecting any number of predicates of the higher-level sciences with those of physics.

Finally, without specifying the forms of laws to be sought by the higher-order sciences, the principles of physicalism here sketched do, it is suggested, play a regulative role. They do so by incorporating certain standards of adequacy – exhaustiveness of ontology, and determination of truth and reference – by which the claims of a physics as a comprehensive and most fundamental level of scientific theory may be assessed. These principles constitute a substantive and realistic sense for the goal of unity of science.

Notes

For helpful comments on an earlier draft of this paper, the authors are grateful to Hector Castañeda, Hartry Field, Nelson Goodman, Richard Grandy, W. V. Quine, and Paul Teller.

1 Of course, there are different reductionist positions here, as elsewhere, corresponding to different criteria of definition.

2 Doubts have arisen especially in connection with functional explanation in the higher-level sciences (psychology, linguistics, social theory, etc.). Functional predicates may be physically realizable in heterogeneous ways, so as to elude physical definition.

Cf. H. Putnam, "Reductionism and the nature of psychology," *Cognition* 2/1 (1973), pp. 131–46; J. Fodor, *Psychological Explanation* (New York: Random House, 1968), ch. 3, and *idem, The Language of Thought* (New York: Crowell, 1975).

3 Our position appears thus to be at odds with Donald Davidson's "anomalism." Cf. his "Mental events" in L. Foster and J. Swanson (eds), *Experience and Theory* (Amherst: University of Massachusetts Press, 1970).

4 Obviously, there are many alternative formulations of physical theory. Nothing of present concern will turn on the specific choice of vocabulary in any way that is not obvious from the context.

5 Thus, for example, magnitude-signs are typically concrete at certain places (satisfied by concreta) and abstract at others (satisfied by abstracta, e.g., real numbers).

6 For an exposition of the calculus of individuals, see Nelson Goodman, *The Structure of Appearance* (Indianapolis: Bobbs-Merrill, 1966), ch. 2.

7 Note that properties and relations are not taken as entities on the ground level, thereby avoiding any hidden reductionist claim behind the simple assertion that everything is identical with some physical entity. In a sequel to this paper, "Physicalist materialism," *Nous* 11 (1977), pp. 309–45, it will be shown how to construe properties and relations of any scientific sort without exceeding the physical ontology.

8 N.B. (3) corresponds to one reading of "no difference without a physical difference"; another vastly different reading corresponds to the result of rewriting (3) with '$(\exists\phi)$' preceding '$(\forall u)(\forall v)$'. This (call it (3')) says that, for any nonphysical predicate, there is a physical predicate that makes all the distinctions it does. By first-order quantifier logic, (3') implies $(\forall\psi)(\exists\phi)(\forall u)(\psi u \leftrightarrow \phi u)$, provided ψ is neither universal nor null, i.e., that every such nonphysical predicate is extensionally equivalent to a physical predicate – a weak form of reductionism! (3), however, is much weaker, implying no form of reductionism. A better example of the value of logical paraphrase would be hard to find!

9 Failure to recognize the independence of ontological and reductionist theses undermines much work in philosophy, particularly in the philosophy of mind. The psychophysical identity thesis is the ontological claim that every psychological entity is a physical entity, i.e., that every former entity is identical with some latter entity. This is entirely compatible with the irreducibility of psychology to physics and with psychological properties not being physical properties (although being mathematical-physical *entities*). This point is elaborated in our "Physicalist materialism."

10 Of course, an even simpler theory with the same property is '$(\forall x)(Qx \leftrightarrow \sim Px)$' itself.

N.B. Nothing essential turns on there being only two predicates. If use is made of certain relative terms, clearly within physical vocabulary as conceived by traditional reductionist positions, e.g., predicates of location, then parallel arguments can be constructed for theories containing any finite number of predicates.

11 Cf. Carnap's explication of determination in his *Introduction to Symbolic Logic and its Applications* (New York: Dover, 1958), p. 211.

12 For details on model theory relevant to what follows, see J. Shoenfield, *Mathematical Logic* (Reading, Mass.: Addison-Wesley, 1967), ch. 5; G. Boolos and R. Jeffrey, *Computability and Logic* (New York: Cambridge University Press, 1974), chs 17–19, 23, 24; and M. A. Dickmann, *Model Theory of Infinitary Languages*, vol. 1, Aarhus Lecture Notes Series no. 20 (1968/9), ch. 1.

13 This and following notions of determination have a number of interesting applications, explored in our "Physicalist materialism." Determinism in physics is not a special case of (4), but rather of a somewhat more general principle, here omitted for lack of space. See ibid.

14 If α is closed under automorphic images, then (5) is equivalent to the condition that any bijective map between domains of m amd m' which is a ϕ-isomorphism is a ψ-isomorphism. Otherwise the latter requirement may be stronger, depending on α. An analogous point has been noted by J. Earman in his discussion of Montague's treatment of determinism in physics in "Laplacian determinism, or Is this any way to run a universe?," *Journal of Philosophy* 68, 21 (4 Nov. 1971), pp. 729–44, at p. 738, n. 11.

15 One further type of determination principle along these lines is interesting, that of ϕ-reference determining ψ-truth in α structures. This is weaker than (4) but still makes a substantial determination claim. It allows us to exploit our presumed confidence in the scientific respectability of the determining vocabulary ϕ – confidence that its terms clearly refer to elements in a well-understood part of our ontology – without our needing to grant a similar respect for the vocabulary of ψ. We grant that the vocabulary of ψ can be used to state truths, truths which are determined by the referential facts in ϕ terms, without claiming that the references of the ϕ terms precisely determine references for the ψ terms as well.

16 The order of the quantifiers should be noted: It is not simply that, in each structure in α, P is coextensive with *some* primitive or complex term formulated in ϕ terms; rather, more strongly, there is a term formulated in the ϕ vocabulary such that P is coextensive with it in *every* structure in α.

17 Although this notion of reduction applies directly to the linguistic primitives of the language reduced, it extends in a natural way also to the sentences, including the laws, formulated in that language: If in α structures, ϕ reduces ψ, then every law formulated in whole or in part in ψ terms (including the "bridge" laws) is a definitional equivalent of a law formulated in purely ϕ terms. Thus reduction of terms implies reduction of laws, and thus, for example, physicalist reduction is incompatible with nonontological "emergence" these which claim that, although evolution adds no nonphysical entities to the universe, it does introduce lawlike regularities that can be captured only by nonphysical laws. (A weaker "epistemological" emergence thesis, which claims only that the physical reductions of laws formulated in the nonphysical vocabulary will be independent of the physics previously known, is not excluded.)

18 There is an obvious connection between this issue and those raised by Saul Kripke concerning rigid designa-

tion and David Lewis concerning counterparts. Cf. above n. 14.

19 Thus, if in α structures, ϕ reduces ψ, there is an easily specifiable theory (not necessarily recursively enumerable) within which every definition composing the reduction of ψ to ϕ is provable. This is true whether or not α, the set of structures to which the reduction is relativized, is itself directly specifiable as the models of such a theory. Given α, we can specify the theory

$$\cap \{\gamma : (\exists m)(m \in \alpha \ \& \ m \text{ models } \gamma)\}$$

that is, the intersection of the theories of each of the models in α, a theory which contains every definition required for the reduction of ψ to ϕ. In fact, (6) is *equivalent* to

$$\text{In } \{m : m \text{ models} \cap \{\gamma : (\exists m')(m' \in \alpha \ \& \ m' \text{ models } \gamma)\}\}, \phi \text{ reduces } \psi.$$

That is, if reducibility holds for a set of structures, then, and only then, it holds for the set of models for all sentences true in each member of that set of structures, even though the former may be a proper subset of the latter. No such principle holds for determination; determination with respect to α can coexist with indetermination with respect to the set of all structures modeling every sentence true in every member of α.

42

Supervenience as a Philosophical Concept

Jaegwon Kim

1 Supervenience in Philosophy

Supervenience is a philosophical concept in more ways than one. First of all, like such concepts as cause and rationality, it is often used in the formulation of philosophical doctrines and arguments. Thus, we have the claim that ethical predicates are "supervenient predicates," or that the characteristics of a whole supervene on those of its parts. And arguments have been advanced to show that the supervenience of moral properties undermines moral realism, or that, on the contrary, moral supervenience shows ethical judgements are "objective" after all. And, again like causality and rationality, the concept of supervenience itself has become an object of philosophical analysis and a matter of some controversy.

But unlike causality, supervenience is almost exclusively a philosopher's concept, one not likely to be encountered outside philosophical dissertations and disputations. The notion of cause, on the other hand, is an integral part of our workaday language, a concept without which we could hardly manage in describing our experiences and observations, framing explanations of natural events, and

Delivered as the Third Metaphilosophy Lecture at the Graduate School, City University of New York, in May 1989. Originally published in *Metaphilosophy* 21 (1990), pp. 1–27, and reprinted in *Supervenience and Mind* (Cambridge: Cambridge University Press, 1993).

assessing blame and praise. Something similar can be said about the notion of being rational as well, although this concept is not as ubiquitous in ordinary discourse as that of cause. Supervenience of course is not unique in being a technical philosophical concept; there are many others, such as "haecceity" and "possible world" in metaphysics, "analyticity" in the theory of meaning, and the currently prominent concepts of "wide" and "narrow" content.

But this isn't to say that the word "supervenience" is a philosopher's neologism; on the contrary, it has been around for some time, and has had a respectable history. The OED lists 1594 for the first documented occurrence of the adjective "supervenient" and 1647–8 for the verb "supervene"; the noun "supervenience" occurred as early as 1664. In these uses, however, "supervene" and its derivatives were almost without exception applied to concrete events and occurrences in the sense of "coming upon" a given event as something additional and extraneous (perhaps as something unexpected), or coming shortly after another occurrence, as in "Upon a sudden supervened the death of the king" (1647–8) and "The king was bruised by the pommel of his saddle; fever supervened, and the injury proved fatal" (1867). There is also this entry from Charlotte Brontë's *Shirley* (1849): "A bad harvest supervened. Distress reached its climax." In common usage supervenience usually implies temporal order: the supervenient event occurs after the event upon which it supervenes, often as an effect. It is clear that even though the vernacular meaning of "supervenience" is not entirely unrelated to its current philosophical sense, the relationship is pretty tenuous, and unlikely to provide any helpful guide for the philosophical discussion of the concept.

I noted that supervenience is like haecceity and narrow content in that they are specifically philosophical concepts, concepts introduced by philosophers for philosophical purposes. But in one significant respect supervenience differs from them: haecceity and narrow content are notions used within a restricted area of philosophy, to formulate distinctions concerning a specific domain of phenomena, or for the purpose of formulating doctrines and arguments concerning a specific topic. Thus, the notion of haecceity arises in connection with the problem of identity and the essence of things; and the concepts of narrow and broad content emerge in the discussion of some problems about meaning and propositional attitudes. In contrast, supervenience is not subject-specific. Although the idea of supervenience appears to have originated in moral theory,[1] it is a general, methodological concept in that it is entirely topic-neutral, and its use is not restricted to any particular problem or area of philosophy. It is this subject-neutral character of supervenience that distinguishes it from the usual run of philosophical concepts and makes it an appropriate object of metaphilosophical inquiry. Supervenience is a topic of interest from the point of view of philosophical methodology.

In undertaking a philosophical study of supervenience, we quickly run into the following difficulty. Because the term is rarely used outside philosophy, there is not a body of well-established usage in ordinary or scientific language that could generate reliable linguistic intuitions to guide the inquiry; there are few linguistic or conceptual data against which to test one's speculations and hypotheses. This means that for supervenience there are not the usual constraints on the "analysis" of a concept; in a sense, there is no preexisting concept to be analyzed. As we shall see, earlier philosophical uses of the concept do set some broad constraints on our discussion; however, when it comes to matters of detail, supervenience is going to be pretty much what we say it is. That is, within limits we are free to define it to suit the purposes on hand, and the primary measure of success for our definitions is their philosophical usefulness. This, I believe, is the principal explanation of the multiplicity of supervenience concepts currently on the scene.

Perhaps, the concept of a possible world is also like this. If we want to use this concept in a serious way, we would need to explain what we mean, either by explicitly defining it or by providing appropriately chosen examples and applications. However this is done, we need not be bound, in any significant way, by previous usage; there is not a common body of philosophical usage to which one's conception of a possible world must answer. The only criterion of success here is pragmatic: how useful and fruitful the introduced concept is in clarifying modal concepts, systematizing our modal intuitions, and helping us sharpen our metaphysical opinions.

There is a long tradition of philosophical discussion of modal concepts, the notions of necessity and possibility, of essential and contingent properties, of essences and haecceities, and so on. In contrast, supervenience is a concept of a comparatively recent origin. R. M. Hare is usually credited with having introduced the term "supervenience" into contemporary discussion, and our present use of the term appears historically continuous with Hare's use of it in *The Language of Morals* (1952).[2] More than thirty years later, in his Inaugural Address, "Supervenience" (1984), to the Aristotelian Society,[3] Hare wonders who first used the term in its current philosophical sense, being quite sure that he was not that person. Hare says that he first used the term in an unpublished paper written in 1950, but is not able to name any particular philosopher who had used it before he did. In any case, Hare's introduction of the term didn't exactly start a stampede. There were, to be sure, isolated appearances of the concept in the ethical literature during the two decades following the publication of *The Language of Morals*,[4] but they were not marked by any real continuity, or an awareness of its potential and significance as a general philosophical concept. An idea related to supervenience, that of "universalizability" or "generality" of moral judgments, was much discussed in moral philosophy during this period, but the debate remained pretty much one of local concern within ethics.

It would be an error, however, to think that moral theorists had a monopoly on supervenience. On the contrary, early in this century, "supervenience" and its derivatives were used with some regularity by the emergentists, and their critics, in the formulation and discussion of the doctrine of "emergent evolution," and it seems possible that Hare and others got "supervenience," directly or indirectly, from the emergentist literature. Many of the leading emergentists were British (for example, G. H. Lewes, Samuel Alexander, C. Lloyd Morgan, C. D. Broad), and the emergence debate was robust and active in the 1930s and 1940s. The doctrine of emergence, in brief, is the claim that when basic physicochemical processes achieve a certain level of complexity of an appropriate kind, genuinely novel characteristics, such as mentality, appear as "emergent" qualities. Lloyd Morgan, a central theoretician of the emergence school, appears to have used "supervenient" as an occasional stylistic variant of "emergent," although the latter remained the official term associated with the philosophical position, and the concept he intended with these terms seems surprisingly close to the supervenience concept current today.[5]

The emergence debate, however, has by and large been forgotten, and appears to have had negligible effects on the current debates in metaphysics, philosophy of mind, and philosophy of science, except perhaps in some areas of philosophy of biology.[6] This is to be regretted, because some of the issues that were then discussed concerning the status of emergent qualities are highly relevant to the current debate on mental causation and the status of psychology in relation to the biological and physical sciences.[7] In any case, the present interest in supervenience was kindled by Donald Davidson in the early 1970s when he used the term in his influential and much discussed paper "Mental events"[8] to formulate a version of nonreductive physicalism. What is noteworthy is that the term has since gained quick currency, especially in discussions of the mind–body problem; and, more remarkably, the term seems by now to have acquired, among philosophers, a pretty substantial shared content. "Supervene" and its derivatives are now regularly encountered in philosophical writings, and often they are used without explanation, signaling an assumption on the part of the writers that their meaning is a matter of common knowledge.

And during the past decade or so attempts have been made to sharpen our understanding of the concept itself. Various supervenience relations have been distinguished, their mutual relationships worked out, and their suitability for specific philosophical purposes scrutinized. This has led David Lewis to complain about an "unlovely proliferation" of supervenience concepts, which he believes has weakened its core meaning.[9] I disagree with the "unlovely" part of Lewis's characterization, but he is certainly right about the proliferation. I think this is a good time to take stock of the current state of the supervenience concept, and reflect on its usefulness as a philosophical concept. That is my aim in this essay.

2 Covariance, Dependence, and Nonreducibility

The first use of the term "supervene" (actually, the Latin *supervenire*) I have found in a philosophical text is by Leibniz. In connection with his celebrated doctrine concerning relations, Leibniz wrote:

> Relation is an accident which is in multiple subjects; it is what results without any change made in the subjects but supervenes from them; it is the thinkability of objects together when we think of multiple things simultaneously.[10]

There has been much interpretive controversy concerning Leibniz's doctrine of relations – in particular, whether or not it was a reducibility thesis, to the effect that relations are reducible, in some sense, to "intrinsic denominations" of things. Leibniz's use of "supervene" in this context seems not inappropriate in our light: his thesis could be interpreted as the claim that relations supervene on the intrinsic properties of their relata. Such a claim would certainly be an interesting and important metaphysical thesis.

But Leibniz's use of "supervene" may well have been an isolated event; although I cannot say I have done anything like an exhaustive or systematic search, I have not found any other occurrence of the term since then, until we come well into the present century. However, the idea of supervenience, or something very close to it, if not the term "supervenience," was clearly present in the writings of the British Moralists. There is, for example, the following from Sidgwick:

> There seems, however, to be this difference between our conceptions of ethical and physical objectivity: that we commonly refuse to admit in the case of the former – what experience compels us to admit as regards the latter – variations for which we can discover no rational explanation. In the variety of coexistent physical facts we find an accidental or arbitrary element in which we have to acquiesce, ... But within the range of our cognitions of right and wrong, it will generally be agreed that we cannot admit a similar unexplained variation. We

cannot judge an action to be right for A and wrong for B, unless we can find in the nature or circumstances of the two some difference which we can regard as a reasonable ground for difference in their duties.[11]

Sidgwick is saying that moral characteristics must necessarily *covary* with certain (presumably nonmoral) characteristics, whereas there is no similar covariance requirement for physical properties. In terms of supervenience the idea comes to this: moral properties, in particular, the rightness or wrongness of an action, are supervenient on their nonmoral properties (which could provide reasons for the rightness or wrongness).

Concerning the concept of "intrinsic value," G. E. Moore said this:

> . . . if a given thing possesses any kind of intrinsic value in a certain degree, then not only must that same thing possess it, under all circumstances, in the same degree, but also anything *exactly like it*, must, under all circumstances, possess it in exactly the same degree.[12]

Likeness of things is grounded, presumably, in their descriptive, or "naturalistic" properties – that is, their nonevaluative properties. Thus, Moore's point amounts to the statement that the intrinsic value of a thing supervenes on its descriptive, nonevaluative properties.

Hare, introducing the term "supervenience" into moral philosophy for the first time, said this:

> First, let us take that characteristic of "good" which has been called its supervenience. Suppose that we say, "St Francis was a good man." It is logically impossible to say this and to maintain at the same time that there might have been another man placed exactly in the same circumstances as St Francis, and who behaved in exactly the same way, but who differed from St Francis in this respect only, that he was not a good man.[13]

It is clear that both Moore and Hare, like Sidgwick, focus on the characteristic of moral properties or ethical predicates that has to do with their *necessary covariation* with descriptive – nonmoral and nonevaluative – properties or predicates. The attribution of moral properties, or the ascription of ethical predicates, to an object is necessarily constrained, in a specific way, by the nonethical properties

attributed to that object. For Moore the constraint has the modal force of "must';' for Hare, the violation of the constraint amounts to the contravention of logical consistency.

The basic idea of supervenience we find in Sidgwick, Moore, and Hare, therefore, has to do with property covariation: properties of one kind must covary with properties of another kind in a certain way. As Lewis put it, "no difference of one sort without differences of another sort",[14] and a change in respect of properties of one sort cannot occur unless accompanied by a change in respect of properties of another sort. If you have qualms about properties as entities, the same idea can be expressed in terms of predicates; if you think the predicates in question do not express properties, in something like the way ethical noncognitivists regard ethical predicates, you could express the idea in terms of "ascriptions" of predicates or the making of ethical judgements.[15]

Hare spoke of ethical and other evaluative predicates as "supervenient predicates," apparently taking supervenience as a *property* of expressions. But it is evident that the fundamental idea involves a *relation* between two sets of properties, or predicates, and that what Hare had in mind was the supervenience *of* ethical predicates *in relation to* nonethical, or naturalistic, predicates. In fact, that was precisely the way Lloyd Morgan used the term, in the 1920s, some three decades before Hare; he used "supervenience" to denote a general relation, speaking of the supervenience of physical and chemical events "on spatiotemporal events,"[16] and of deity as a quality that might be supervenient "on reflective consciousness."[17] As I said, Morgan used "supervene" and "emerge" as stylistic variants, and this means that supervenience is as much a general relation as emergence is.

Thus, Morgan and other emergentists were the first, as far as I know, to develop a generalized concept of supervenience as a relation, and their concept turns out to be strikingly similar to that in current use, especially in philosophy of mind. They held that the supervenient, or emergent, qualities necessarily manifest themselves when, and only when, appropriate conditions obtain at the more basic level; and some emergentists[18] took great pains to emphasize that the phenomenon of emergence is consistent with determinism. But in spite of that, the emergents are not reducible, or reductively explainable, in terms of their "basal" conditions. In formulating his emergentism, Morgan thought of himself as defending a reasonable naturalistic alternative to both mechanistic reductionism and such anti-naturalisms as vitalism and Cartesianism. Thus, Morgan's position bears an interesting similarity to the supervenience thesis Davidson has injected into philosophy of mind, and to many currently popular versions of nonreductive materialism which Davidson has helped inspire. In a passage that has become a bench-mark to the writers on supervenience and nonreductive materialism, Davidson wrote:

> Although the position I describe denies there are psychophysical laws, it is consistent with the view that mental characteristics are in some sense dependent, or supervenient, on physical characteristics. Such supervenience might be taken to mean that there cannot be two events alike in all physical respects but differing in some mental respects, or that an object cannot alter in some mental respects without altering in some physical respects. Dependence or supervenience of this kind does not entail reducibility through law or definition: if it did, we could reduce moral properties to descriptive, and this there is good reason to *believe* cannot be done.[19]

Both Morgan and Davidson seem to be saying that mental phenomena are supervenient on physical phenomena and yet not reducible to them.

What Davidson says about the supervenience relation between mental and physical characteristics is entirely consonant with the idea of property covariation we saw in Sidgwick, Moore, and Hare. But he did more than echo the idea of the earlier writers: in this paragraph Davidson explicitly introduced two crucial new ideas, earlier adumbrated in the emergence literature, that were to change the complexion of the subsequent philosophical thinking about supervenience. First, supervenience is to be a relation of *dependence*: that which is supervenient is dependent on that on which it supervenes. Second, it is to be a *nonreductive* relation: supervenient dependency is not to entail the reducibility of the supervenient to its subvenient base.[20]

Davidson had his own reasons for attaching these two ideas to supervenience. The quoted paragraph occurs in his "Mental events" just after he has advanced his "anomalous monism," the doctrine that mental events are identical to physical events even though there are no laws connecting mental and physical properties. In writing this

passage, he is trying to mitigate the likely impression that anomalous monism permits no significant relationships between mental and physical attributes, positing two isolated, autonomous domains. His psychophysical anomalism, the thesis that there are no laws connecting the mental with the physical, has sundered the two domains; with the supervenience thesis he is trying to bring them back together. But not so close as to revive the hope, or threat, of psychophysical reductionism.

In any event, these two ideas, dependency and nonreductiveness, have become closely associated with supervenience. In particular, the idea that supervenience is a dependency relation has become firmly entrenched, so firmly that it has by now acquired the status of virtual analyticity. But I think it is useful to keep these three ideas separate; so let us summarize the three putative components, or desiderata, of supervenience:

Covariance: Supervenient properties covary with their subvenient, or base, properties. In particular, indiscernibility in respect of the base properties entails indiscernibility in respect of the supervenient properties.

Dependency: Supervenient properties are dependent on, or are determined by, their base properties.

Nonreducibility: Supervenience is to be consistent with the irreducibility of supervenient properties to their base properties.

Obviously, covariance is the crucial component; any supervenience concept must include this condition in some form. The main issue, then, concerns the relationship between covariance and the other two components, and here there are two principal questions. First, can covariance yield dependence, or must dependence be considered an independent component of supervenience? Second, is there an interpretation of covariance that is strong enough to sustain supervenience as a dependency relation but weak enough not to imply reducibility? More broadly, there is this question: In what ways can these three desiderata be combined to yield coherent and philosophically interesting concepts of supervenience? I will not be offering definitive answers to these questions here; for I don't have the answers. What follows is a kind of interim report on the ongoing work by myself and others on these and related issues.

3 Types of Covariance

In the passage quoted above, Davidson writes as though he held that property covariation of the sort he is specifying between mental and physical properties *generated* a dependency relation between them. That is, mental properties are dependent on physical properties *in virtue of* the fact that the two sets of properties covary as indicated. Is this idea sound? But what precisely is covariance, to begin with?

It turns out that the simple statement of covariance in terms of indiscernibility has at least two distinct interpretations, one stronger than the other, depending on whether things chosen for comparison in respect of indiscernibility come exclusively from one possible world, or may come from different worlds. We can call them "weak" and "strong" covariance. Let A and B be two sets of properties, where we think of A as supervenient and B as subvenient. I state two definitions for each type of covariance:

Weak covariance I: No possible world contains things, x and y, such that x and y are indiscernible in respect of properties in B ("B-indiscernible") and yet discernible in respect of properties in A ("A-discernible").

Weak covariance II: Necessarily, if anything has property F in A, there exists a property G in B such that the thing has G, and everything that has G has F.

Strong covariance I: For any objects x and y and any worlds w_i and w_j, if x in w_j is B-indiscernible from y in w_i (that is, x has in w_j precisely those B-properties that y has in w_j), then x in w_i is A-indiscernible from y in w_j.

Strong covariance II: Necessarily, if anything has property F in A, there exists a property G in B such that the thing has G, and *necessarily* everything with G has F.

For both weak and strong covariance, the two versions are equivalent under certain assumptions concerning property composition.[21] However, it will be convenient to have both versions. The sole difference between strong covariance II and weak covariance II lies in the presence of the second modal expression "necessarily" in the former; this ensures that the G–F correlation holds across possible worlds and is not restricted to the given

world under consideration. I have elsewhere called the two types of covariance "weak supervenience" and "strong supervenience" respectively; I am using the "covariance" terminology here since I am trying to keep the idea of covariance and that of dependence separate. This is a purely terminological decision; if we liked, we could continue to use the supervenience terminology here, and then raise the question concerning the relationship between supervenience and dependence.

How should we understand the modal term "necessarily," or quantification over possible worlds, that occurs in the statements of covariance? I believe that a general characterization of covariance, or supervenience, should leave this term as an unfixed parameter to be interpreted to suit specific supervenience claims. The standard options in this area include metaphysical, logico-mathematical, analytic, and nomological necessity.

Hare's and Davidson's original statements of supervenience seem neutral with respect to weak and strong covariance. Interestingly, however, both have since come out in favor of weak covariance: Hare for moral supervenience and Davidson for psychophysical supervenience. In his Inaugural Address "Supervenience," Hare says that "what I have always had in mind is not what Kim now calls 'strong' supervenience. It is nearer to his 'weak' supervenience"[22]

Davidson has recently given an explicit account of the notion of supervenience that he says he had earlier in mind:

> The notion of supervenience, as I have used it, is best thought of as a relation between a predicate and a set of predicates in a language: a predicate *p* is supervenient on a set of predicates *s* if for every pair of objects such that *p* is true of one and not of the other there is a predicate of *s* that is true of one and not of the other.[23]

We can easily verify that this is equivalent to weak covariance II, of the unit set consisting of *p* on the set *s*.

Hare and Davidson are not alone in their preference for weak covariance. Simon Blackburn, who has used normative supervenience as a premise in his argument against moral realism, opts for weak covariance as his favored form of supervenience, at least for the case of moral properties.[24] On his account, if property F supervenes on a set G of properties, the following holds: in every possible world, if something has F, its total or maximal G-property, G^*, is such that anything with G^* has F, Blackburn stresses that this last universal conditional, "Everything with G^* has F," is to be taken as a material conditional with no modal force,[25] which makes his concept exactly fit our weak covariance II.

4 Covariance and Dependence

As may be recalled, Davidson has said that the mental is "supervenient, or dependent" on the physical; here he seems to be using "supervenient" and "dependent" interchangeably, or perhaps the former as specifying a sense of the latter. We have just seen that it is weak covariance that he says he had in mind when he spoke of supervenience. So there is the following substantive question: Can weak covariance give us a sense of dependence? Or equivalently: Can weak covariance be a form of supervenience if supervenience is to be a dependency relation?

Weak covariance does place a constraint on the distribution of supervenient properties relative to the distribution of their base properties. The question is whether this constraint is strong enough to warrant our considering it a form of dependence or determination. As I have argued elsewhere,[26] the answer must be in the negative. For concreteness consider the weak covariance of mental on physical properties; this covariance is consistent with each of the following situations:

1   In a world that is just like this one in the distribution of physical properties, no mentality is present.
2   In a world that is just like this one in all physical details, unicellular organisms are all fully conscious, while no humans or other primates exhibit mentality.
3   In a world that is just like this one in all physical details, everything exhibits mentality in the same degree and kind.

These are all possible under weak covariance because its constraint works only *within* a single world at a time: *the fact that mentality is distributed in a certain way in one world has absolutely no effect on how it might be distributed in another world*. Intra-world consistency of the distribution of mental properties relative to the distribution of physical properties is the only constraint imposed by weak covariance.

This evidently makes weak covariance unsuitable for any dependency thesis with modal or subjunctive force. And modal force is arguably a necessary aspect of any significant dependency claim. Thus, when we say that the mental is dependent on the physical, we would, I think, want to exclude each of the possibilities, (1)–(3).[27]

Not so with strong covariance: property-to-property connections between supervenient and subvenient properties carry over to other worlds. That is obvious from both versions of strong covariance. Consider version II: When applied to the psychophysical case, it says that if anything has a mental property M, then there is some physical property P such that the "P → M" conditional holds across all possible worlds. This supports in a straightforward way the assertion that the psychological character of a thing is entailed, or necessitated, by its physical nature. The strength of entailment, or necessitation, in this statement depends on how the modal term "necessarily" is interpreted, or alternatively, what possible worlds are involved in our quantification over them (e.g., whether we are talking about all possible worlds, or only physically or nomologically possible worlds, etc.).

But does strong covariance give us dependence or determination? If the mental strongly covaries with the physical, does this mean that the mental is dependent on, or determined by, the physical? As we saw, strong covariance is essentially a relation of entailment or necessitation. We notice this initial difference between necessitation and dependence: dependence, or determination, is usually understood to be asymmetric whereas entailment or necessitation is neither symmetric nor asymmetric. We sometimes speak of "mutual dependence" or "mutual determination"; however, when non-reductive physicalists appeal to supervenience as a way of expressing the dependence of the mental on the physical, they pretty clearly have in mind an asymmetric relation: they would say that their thesis automatically excludes the converse dependence of the physical on the mental. "Functional dependence," in the sense that the two state variables of a system are related by a mathematical function, may be neither symmetric nor asymmetric; however, what we want is *metaphysical* or *ontic* dependence or determination, not merely the fact that values of one variable are determined as a mathematical function of those of another variable.

It isn't difficult to think of cases in which strong covariance fails to be asymmetric: think of a domain of perfect spheres.[28] The surface area of each sphere strongly covaries with its volume, and conversely, the volume with the surface area. And we don't want to say either determines, or depends on, the other, in any sense of these terms that implies an asymmetry. There is only a functional determination, and dependence, both ways; but we would hesitate to impute a metaphysical or ontological dependence either way.

Could we get a relation of dependency by requiring that the subvenient properties not also strongly covary with the supervenient properties? Let us consider the following proposal:[29]

A-properties depend on B-properties just in case A strongly covaries with B, but not conversely; that is, any B-indiscernible things are A-indiscernible, but there are A-indiscernible things that are B-discernible.

In most cases of asymmetric dependence this condition appears to hold; for example, the mental strongly covaries with the physical, but the physical does not strongly covary with the mental; and similarly for the evaluative and the descriptive. Moreover, all of these examples involve large and comprehensive systems of properties. So the idea would be that when an asymmetric strong covariance obtains for two comprehensive systems of properties, a dependency relation may be imputed to them.

It isn't clear that this proposal states a necessary condition for dependence. For consider this: chemical kinds (e.g., water, gold, etc.) and their microphysical compositions (at least, at one level of description) seem to strongly covary with each other, and yet it is true, presumably, that natural kinds are asymmetrically dependent on microphysical structures. Here our mereological intuition, that macrophysical properties are asymmetrically dependent on microphysical structures, seems to be the major influence on our thinking, canceling out the fact that the converse strong covariance may also be present. I admit that this is not a clear-cut example; for one thing, the converse strong covariance could perhaps be defeated by going to a deeper micro-level description; for another, one might argue that there is here no dependence either way, since being a certain chemical kind just *is* having a certain microstructure.

It is even less clear whether the proposal states a sufficient condition for dependence. There is reason to think it does not. For what does the added second condition that B not covary with A really contribute? What is clear is this: the absence of strong covariance from B to A guarantees that B does not depend on A. For that means that there are objects with identical A-properties but with different B-properties. So the net effect of this added condition is just that B does not depend on A. The question then is this: Can we count on A to depend on B whenever A strongly covaries with B and B does not depend on A?

One might argue for an affirmative answer as follows: "Strong covariance between A and B requires an explanation, and it is highly likely that any explanation must appeal to an asymmetric relation of dependence. So either A depends on B or B depends on A; but the failure of strong covariance from B to A shows that B doesn't depend on A. Hence, A depends on B."

What this argument neglects, rather glaringly, is the possibility that an explanation of the covariance from A to B may be formulated in terms of a third set of properties. It seems clearly possible for there to be three sets of properties A, B, and C, such that A and B each depend on C, A covaries with B but B does not covary with A, and A does not depend on B.[30] Something like this could happen if, although both A and B covary with C, B makes finer discriminations than A, so that indiscernibility in regard to B-properties entails indiscernibility with respect to A, but not conversely.

As a possible example consider this: I've heard that there is a correlation between intelligence as measured by the IQ test and manual dexterity. It is possible that both manual dexterity and intelligence depend on certain genetic and developmental factors, and that intelligence strongly covaries with manual dexterity but not conversely. If such were the case, we would not consider intelligence to be dependent on, or determined by, manual dexterity.

Although the argument, therefore, has a serious flaw, it is not without value. Observed correlations of properties, especially between two comprehensive systems of properties, cry out for an explanation, and when no third set of properties is in the offing that might provide an appropriate ("common cause") explanation, it may be reasonable to posit a direct dependency relation between the two property families. The proposed criterion of dependent covariation says that if B fails to covary with A, that rules out the possibility that B depends on A, leaving A's dependency on B as the only remaining possibility. So the criterion may be of some use in certain situations; however, it cannot be regarded – at least, in its present form – as an "analysis" of supervenient dependence, since the needed further condition (i.e., that there not be a set C on which both A and B severally depend) itself makes use of the concept of dependence.

Trying to define dependence in terms of covariance is not likely to meet with complete and unambiguous success. Consider the case of causal dependence. Experience has taught us that we are not likely to succeed in defining an asymmetric relation of causal dependence, or causal directionality, in terms only of nomological covariations between properties or event kinds.[31] Unless, that is, we make a direct appeal to some relation that is explicitly asymmetric, like temporal precedence. We are not likely to do any better with supervenient dependence; the proposal above, with the further proviso that the strong covariation holds for two *comprehensive* sets of properties, may be close to the best that can be done to generate dependence out of covariation. All this points to the conclusion that the idea of dependence, whether causal or supervenient, is metaphysically deeper and richer than what can be captured by property covariance, even when the latter is supplemented with the usual modal notions.[32]

Much of the philosophical interest that supervenience has elicited lies in the hope that it is a relation of dependency; many philosophers saw in it the promise of a new type of dependency relation that seemed just right, neither too strong nor too weak, allowing us to navigate between reductionism and outright dualism. And it is the dependency aspect of supervenience, not the covariation component, that can sanction many of the usual philosophical implications drawn from, or associated with, supervenience these concerning various subject matters. Often it is thought, and claimed, that a thing has a supervenient property *because*, or *in virtue of the fact that*, it has the corresponding base property, or that its having the relevant base property *explains* why it has the supervenient property. All these relations are essentially asymmetric, and are in the same generic family of relations that includes dependence and determination. Clearly, property covariation by itself does not warrant the use of "because," "in virtue of," etc., in describing the relationship any more than it warrants the attribution of dependence. Thus, if we want to promote the doctrine of psychophysical supervenience, intending it to include a claim of psychophysical dependence, we had better be prepared to produce an independent justification of the dependency claim which goes beyond the mere fact of covariance between mental and physical properties.

Property covariation *per se* is metaphysically neutral; dependence, and other such relations, suggest ontological and explanatory directionality – that upon which something depends is ontologically and explanatorily prior to, and more basic than, that which depends on it. In fact, we can think of the dependency relation as explaining or grounding property covariations: e.g., one might say that mental properties covary with physical properties because the former are dependent on the latter. Direct dependence, however, is not the only possible explanation; as we saw, two sets of properties may covary because each is dependent on a common third set.

The upshot, therefore, is this: it is best to separate the covariation element from the dependency element in the relation of supervenience. Our discussion shows that property covariation alone, even in the form of "strong asymmetric covariance," does not by itself give us dependency; in that sense, dependency is an additional component of supervenience. But the two components are not entirely independent; for it seems that the following is true: for there to be property dependence, there must be property covariation. We can, therefore, distinguish between two forms of dependence, each based on one of the two covariation relations. Thus, "strong dependence" requires strong covariation, while "weak dependence" can do with weak covariation. What must be added to covariation to yield dependence is an interesting, and metaphysically deep, question. It's analogous, in certain ways, to J. L. Mackie's question as to what must be added to mere causal connectedness to generate "causal priority," or "causal directionality." Mackie and others have sought a single, uniform account of that in which causal priority consists; however, it isn't at all obvious that our question concerning dependence admits of a single answer. Evidently, dependency requires different explanations in different cases, and for any given case there can be competing accounts of why the dependency holds. Among the most important cases of supervenient dependence are instances of part–whole dependence ("mereological supervenience"), and these may constiue a special basic category of dependence. Concerning the supervenience of the moral on the naturalistic, the classic ethical naturalist will formulate an explanation in terms of meaning dependence or priority; the noncognitivist's account may involve considerations of the function of moral language and why its proper fulfillment requires consistency, in an appropriate sense, of moral avowals in relation to descriptive judgments. These cases seem fundamentally different from one another metaphysically, and any "analysis" of dependence that applies to all varieties of dependence, I think, is unlikely to throw much light on the nature of dependence. We will briefly return to these issues in a later section.

5   Covariance and Reducibility

As previously noted, Davidson has been chiefly responsible for the close association of supervenience with both the idea of dependency and that of nonreducibility. Nonreducibility, however, has been less firmly associated with supervenience than dependency has been; and there has been some controversy as to whether supervenience is in fact a nonreductive relation. Also, it seems that the association of nonreducibility with supervenience has come about from the historical happenstance that Moore and Hare, who are well known for their supervenience thesis concerning the moral relative to the naturalistic, also formulated classic and influential arguments against ethical naturalism, the doctrine that the moral is definitionally reducible to the naturalistic.[33] So why not model a nonreductive psychophysical relation on supervenience? If the moral could be supervenient on the naturalistic without being reducible to it, couldn't the mental be supervenient on the physical without being reducible to it?[34] But, it is possible that the sense of reduction Moore had in mind when he argued against the reducibility of the moral is very different from the concept of reducibility that is now current in philosophy of mind; and it is also possible that Moore was just mistaken in thinking that he could have supervenience without reducibility.

Moore's so-called "open question" argument suggests that the sort of naturalistic reduction he was trying to undermine is a *definitional* reductionism – the claim that ethical terms are analytically definable in naturalistic terms. Moreover, the argument is effective only against the claim that there is an *overt synonymy* relation between an ethical term and its purported naturalistic definition. For consider what the open question is intended to test: for any pair of expressions X and Y, we are supposed to determine whether "Is everything that is X also

Y?" can be used to ask an intelligible and significant question. The idea is that if X is definable as Y (that is, if X and Y are synonymous), the question would not be an intelligible one (consider: "Is everyone who is a bachelor also a male?" and "Does everything that is a cube also have twelve edges?"). It is clear that the logical equivalence of X and Y, or the fact that in some philosophical sense X can be "analyzed" as Y, etc., would not make the question necessarily unintelligible or lack significance. The nomological equivalence between X and Y probably was the furthest thing from Moore's mind; he pointedly says that even if we found a "physical equivalent" of the color yellow, certain "light-vibrations" as Moore puts it,[35] these light-vibrations are not what the term "yellow" *means*. So Moore's anti-naturalism was the denial of the definitional reducibility of ethical terms to naturalistic terms, where the notion of definition itself is extremely narrowly construed.

The kind of reduction Davidson had in mind in "Mental events" is considerably wider than definitional reduction of the Moorean sort: the main focus of his anti-reductionist arguments is *nomological* reduction, reduction underwritten by contingent empirical laws correlating, and perhaps identifying, properties being reduced with those in the reduction base. Davidson's argument is two-pronged: the demise of logical behaviorism shows the unavailability of a definitional reduction of the mental, and his own psychophysical anomalism, the doctrine that there are no laws correlating mental with physical properties, shows that a nomological reduction isn't in the cards either.[36] Moore would have been unconcerned about nomological reducibility; his anti-naturalism apparently permitted strong, necessary synthetic, a priori relationships between the moral and the nonmoral.

I earlier noted that the issue of reducibility seemed less central to supervenience than that of dependence. It is somewhat ironic that covariance seems more intimately connected with reduction than it is with dependence. But before getting into the details, we must know what we mean by reduction. Reduction is standardly understood as a relation between *theories*, where a theory is understood to consist of a distinctive theoretical vocabulary and a set of laws formulated in this vocabulary. The reduction of one theory to another is thought to be accomplished when the laws of the reduced theory are shown to be derivable from the laws of the reducer theory, with the help of "bridge principles" connecting terms of the reduced theory with those of the reducer.[37] Just what bridge laws are required obviously depends on the strength of the two theories involved, and there seems very little that is both general and informative to say about this. The only requirement on the bridge laws that can be explicitly stated, independently of the particular theories involved, is the following, which I will call "the condition of strong connectibility".[38]

> Each primitive predicate P of the theory being reduced is connected with a coextensive predicate Q of the reducer in a biconditional law of the form: "for all x, Px iff Qx"; and similarly for all relational predicates.

If this condition is met, then no matter what the content of the two theories may be, derivational reduction is guaranteed; for these biconditional laws would allow the rewriting of the laws of the theory being reduced as laws of the reducer, and if any of these rewrites is not derivable from the preexisting laws of the reducer, it can be added as an additional law (assuming both theories to be true). In discussing reduction and covariance, therefore, we will focus on this condition of strong connectibility.[39]

To begin, weak covariance obviously does not entail strong connectibility. Weak covariance lacks an appropriate modal force to generate laws, as noted, the correlations entailed by weak covariance between supervenient and subvenient properties have no modal force, being restricted to particular worlds.

What then of strong covariance? Here the situation is different; for consider strong covariance II: it says that whenever a supervening property P is instantiated by an object, there is a subvenient property Q such that the instantiating object has it and the following conditional holds: necessarily if anything has Q, then it has P. So the picture we have is that for supervenient property P, there is a set of properties, $Q_1, Q_2 \ldots$ in the subvenient set such that each Q_1 is necessarily sufficient for P. Assume that this list contains all the subvenient properties each of which is sufficient for P. Consider then their disjunction: Q_1 or Q_2 or ... (or UQ_i for short). This disjunction may be infinite; however, it is a well-defined disjunction, as well defined as the union of infinitely many sets. It is easy to see that this disjunction is necessarily coextensive with P.

First, it is clear enough that UQ_i entails P, since each disjunct does. Second, does P entail UQ_i?

Suppose not: something then, say b, has P but not UQ_i. According to strong covariance, b has some property in the subvenient set, say S, such that necessarily whatever has S also has P. But then S must be one of the Q_i and since b has S, b must have UQ_i. So P entails UQ_i. So P and UQ_i are necessarily coextensive, and whether the modality here is metaphysical, logical, or nomological, it should be strong enough to give us a serviceable "bridge law" for reduction.

So does this show that the strong connectibility is entailed by strong covariance, and hence that the supervenience relation incorporating strong covariance entails reducibility? Some philosophers will resist this inference.[40] Their concern will focus on the way the nomological coextension for P was constructed in the subvenient set – in particular, the fact that the constructional procedure made use of disjunction.[41] There are two questions, and only two as far as I can see, that can be raised here: (1) Is disjunction a proper way of forming properties out of properties? (2) Given that disjunction is a permissible property-forming operation, is it proper to form infinite disjunctions? I believe it is easy to answer (2): the answer has to be a yes. I don't see any special problem with an infinite procedure here, any more than in the case of forming infinite unions of sets or the addition of infinite series of numbers. We are not here talking about predicates, or linguistic expressions, but properties; I am not saying that we should accept predicates of infinite length, although I don't know if anything would go astray if we accepted infinite disjunctive predicates that are finitely specified (we could then introduce a simple predicate to abbreviate it). So the main question is (1).

Is disjunction a permissible mode of property composition? One might argue as follows for a negative answer, at least in the present context: Bridge laws are laws and must connect nomological kinds or properties (so their predicates must be "lawlike," "projectible," and so on). However, from the fact that M and N are each nomic, it does not follow that their disjunction, M or N, is also nomic. Consequently, our constructional procedure fails to guarantee the nomologicality of the generated coextensions.

One might try to buttress this point by the following argument: the core concept of a property is *resemblance* – that is, the sharing of a property must ensure resemblance in some respect. We can now see that the disjunctive operation does not preserve this crucial feature of propertyhood (nor does complementation, one might add). Round objects resemble one another and so do red objects; but we cannot count on objects with the property of being *round or red* to resemble each other. This is why "conjunctive properties" present no difficulties, but "disjunctive properties," and also "negative properties," are problematic.

I do not find these arguments compelling. It isn't at all obvious that we must be bound by such a narrow and restrictive conception of what nomic properties, or properties in general, must be in the present context. When reduction is at issue, we are talking about theories, theories couched in their distinctive theoretical vocabularies. And it seems that we allow, and ought to allow, freedom to combine and recombine the basic theoretical predicates and functors by the usual logical and mathematical operations available in the underlying language, without checking each step with something like the resemblance criterion; that would work havoc with free and creative scientific theorizing. What, after all, is the point of having these logical operations on predicates? When we discuss the definitional reducibility of, say, ethical terms to naturalistic terms, it would be absurd to disallow definitions that make use of disjunctions, negations, and what have you; why should we deny ourselves the use of these operations in forming reductive bridges of other sorts? Moreover, it may well be that when an artificial-looking predicate proves useful, or essential, in a fecund and well-corroborated theory and gets entrenched, we will come to think of it as expressing a robust property, an important respect in which objects and events can resemble each other. In certain situations, that recognizing something as a genuine property would make reduction possible may itself be a compelling reason for doing so![42]

Let me make a final point about this. The fact that for each supervenient property, a coextension – a qualitative coextension if not a certifiably nomic one – exists in the subvenient base properties means that there is at least the possibility of our developing a theory that will give a perspicuous theoretical description of this coextension, thus providing us with strong reason for taking the coextension as a nomic property. At least in this somewhat attenuated sense, strong covariance can be said to entail the possibility of reducing the supervenient to the subvenient. And we should note this: if we knew strong covariance to fail, that would scotch the idea of reduction once and for all.

We should briefly look at "global supervenience," or "global covariance," as a nonreductive supervenience relation. For this idea has been touted by many philosophers as an appropriate dependence relation between the mental and the physical which is free of reductive implications.[43] The basic idea of global supervenience is to apply the indiscernibility considerations globally to "worlds" taken as units of comparison. Standardly the idea is expressed as follows:

> Worlds that are indiscernible in respect of subvenient properties are indiscernible in respect of supervenient properties.

> Worlds that coincide in respect of truths involving subvenient properties coincide in respect of truths involving supervenient properties.

For our present purposes we may think of indiscernibility of worlds in respect of a given set of properties (say, physical properties) as consisting in the fact that these properties are distributed over their individuals in the same way (for simplicity we may assume that the worlds have the same individuals).

It is known that this covariance relation does not imply property-to-property correlations between supervenient and subvenient properties; thus, it does not imply what I have called strong connectibility.[44] So global supervenience, along with weak supervenience, can qualify as a nonreductive relation. But this is a signal that global covariance may be quite weak, perhaps too weak to sustain a dependency relation of significance.[45]

As I have argued elsewhere,[46] this can be seen in at least two ways. First, this form of covariance permits worlds that differ minutely in subvenient properties to differ drastically in respect of supervenient properties. Thus, global covariance of the mental with respect to the physical is consistent with there being a world that differs from this world in some insignificant physical detail (say, it contains one more hydrogen atom) but which differs radically in psychological respects (say, it is wholly void of mentality). Second, global covariance as explained fails to imply weak covariance; that is, it can hold where weak covariance fails. This means that psychophysical global covariance can be true in a world that contains exact physical duplicates with divergent psychological characteristics; it permits the existence in the actual world of an exact physical replica of you who, however, has the mentality of a fruit fly. There certainly is reason to wonder whether a supervenience relation whose property covariance requirement is this weak can qualify as a dependency relation. As I argued earlier, property covariance alone, even "strong covariance," does not yield dependence, and in that sense dependence must be considered an independent component of supervenience in any case. However, again as I argued, dependence does require an appropriate relation of property covariance. This raises the following question: Is global covariance strong enough to ground a respectable supervenience relation? We may well wonder whether a supervenience relation based on global covariance might not turn out to be incongruous in that, given this is what it requires of property covariance, the dependency component makes little sense.

I suggest, however, that we keep an open mind about this, and adopt an attitude of "Let one hundred supervenience concepts bloom!" Each may have its own sphere of application, serving as a useful tool for formulating and evaluating philosophical doctrines of interest. And this does not mean that we must discard the core idea of supervenience captured by the maxim "No difference of one kind without a difference of another kind." It's just that we now recognize that this core idea can be explained in distinct but interestingly related ways, and that what we want to say about a supervenience claim about a specific subject matter may depend on the interpretation of supervenience appropriate to the context. I think this is philosophical progress.

6 Grounds of Supervenience

It has been argued that supervenience is a mysterious and unexplained relation, and hence that any philosophical argument couched in the vocabulary of supervenience is a retrogressive and obfuscating maneuver incapable of yielding any illumination for the issue on hand. For example, Stephen Schiffer takes a dim view of those who appeal to supervenience:

> How could being told that non-natural moral properties stood in the supervenience relation to physical properties make them any more palatable? On the contrary, invoking a special primitive metaphysical relation of supervenience to explain how non-natural moral properties were related to physical properties was just

to add mystery to mystery, to cover one obscurantist move with another. I therefore find it more than a little ironic, and puzzling, that supervenience is nowadays being heralded as a way of making nonpleonastic, irreducibly non-natural properties cohere with an acceptably naturalistic solution to the mind – body problem ... the appeal to a special primitive relation of "supervenience," as defined above, is obscurantist in the extreme.[47]

The supervenience relation Schiffer refers to "as defined above" is in effect our strong covariance II, with the further proviso that the relationship "necessarily everything with G has F" is an unexplainable "brute metaphysical fact."

There perhaps have been philosophers who deserve Schiffer's excoriations; however, we need to separate Schiffer's editorial comment that supervenience is a "brute metaphysical" fact from a mere claim of supervenience concerning a given topic. Schiffer's addition is a nontrivial further claim, which someone advocating a supervenience thesis might or might not wish to make, that goes beyond the claim of supervenient covariance or dependence. For there is nothing in the concept of covariance or dependence that forces us to view supervenience as invariably involving unexplainable relationships. In fact, when a supervenience claim is made, it makes perfectly good sense to ask for an *explanation* of why the supervenience relation holds. Why does the moral supervene on the nonmoral? Why do facts about wholes supervene, if they do, on facts about their parts? Why does the mental supervene on the physical?

It may well be that the only answer we can muster for some of these questions is that, as far as we can tell, it is a brute fact. But that need not be the only kind of answer; we should, and can, hope to do better. This is evident from the following fact alone: supervenience, whether in the sense of co-variation or in the sense that includes dependence, is transitive. This means that it is possible, at least in certain situations, to answer the question "Why does X supervene on Y?" by saying that, as it turns out, X supervenes on Z, and Z in turn supervenes on Y. The interpolation of another supervenient tier may well explain why X-to-Y supervenience holds. (Compare: Why does X cause Y? Answer: X causes Z, and Z causes Y.) As Schiffer says, Moore gave a sort of "brute fact" account of moral supervenience, and given his metaethical theory he probably had no other choice: we "intuit" necessary synthetic a priori connections between nonnatural moral properties and certain natural properties. But it isn't just ethical intuitionists like Moore who accept moral supervenience; Hare, whose metaethics radically diverges from Moore's, too has championed moral supervenience. And we also have Blackburn, a "projectivist" moral antirealist, who professes belief in moral supervenience, not to mention John Post,[48] who is an objectivist about ethical judgments. As I take it, these philosophers would give different accounts of why moral supervenience obtains; as we noted in our earlier discussion of dependence as a component of supervenience, Hare would presumably give an account in terms of some consistency requirement on the use of language of prescription. And Blackburn has argued against "moral realism" on the ground that it, unlike his own projectivist "quasi-realism," is unable to give a satisfactory explanation of moral supervenience.[49]

We may distinguish between two kinds of request for a "ground" of a supervenience relation. One concerns *general* claims of supervenience: why a given family of properties, say mental properties, supervene on another family, say neurobiological properties. Why does the mental supervene on the physical, and why does the normative supervene on the nonnormative? These are perfectly good, intelligible questions, which may or may not have informative answers. The second type of request concerns the relationship between *specific* supervenient properties and their base properties: Why is it that pain supervenes on the activation of A-delta and C-fibers? Why doesn't, say, itch or tickle supervene on it? Why doesn't pain supervene on, say, the excitation of A-and B-fibers?

The potential for supplying explanations for specific supervenience relationships varies for different mind–body theories. Both the behaviorist and the functionalist could formulate a plausible meaning-based explanation (I mean, plausible *given* their basic doctrines): pain, not itch, supervenes on physicalistic condition P because of an analytic, semantic connection between "pain" and the standard expression for P. For the behaviorist, the connection is a direct one of definability. The functionalist will appeal to an additional empirical fact, saying something like this: "pain," as a matter of meaning, designates a certain causal-functional role, and it turns out, as a contingent empirical fact, that condition P occupies this causal role (in organisms or structures of a given kind). The function-

alist can push ahead with his search for explanations and ask: why does condition P occupy this causal role in these organisms? This question is an empirical scientific question, and may be given an evolution-based answer, or one based in engineering considerations (in the case of artifacts); and there may be answers of other types.

There are philosophers who have a fundamentally physicalist outlook on the mind–body problem and yet would reject any analytic, definitional relationships between mental and nonmental expressions. Many of them would accept a thoroughgoing dependence of the mental on the physical grounded in lawlike type–type correlations between the two domains. Epiphenomenalism is such a position; so is the classic nonfunctionalist type-identity theory based on the supposed existence of pervasive psychophysical correlations. It seems that someone holding a physicalist position like these has no choice but to view the relationship between say, pain and C-fiber activation as a brute fact that is not further explainable, something like the way G. E. Moore viewed the relationship between the nonnatural property of goodness and the natural property on which it supervenes. In this respect, the position of a physicalist who accepts psychophysical supervenience, especially of the "strong covariance" sort, but rejects a physicalist rendering of mental expressions, is much like that of those emergentists who regarded the phenomena of emergence as not susceptible of further explanation; that is, it is not further explainable why mentality emerges just when these physicochemical conditions are present, but not otherwise. Samuel Alexander, a leading emergentist, recommended that we accept these emergence relationships "with natural piety"; Lloyd Morgan, referring to Alexander, announced, "I accept this phrase."[50]

Is this a serious blemish on nonfunctionalist physicalism? This is an interesting, and difficult, question. Its proponents might insist that all of us must accept certain brute facts about this world, and that it is necessary to count fundamental psychophysical correlations among them in order to develop a plausible theory of mind, all things considered. This is only an opening move in what is likely to be a protracted dialectic between them and the functionalists, something we must set aside.[51] I will conclude with some brief remarks concerning explanations of general supervenience claims.

I think that the only direct way of explaining why a general supervenience relation holds, e.g., why the mental supervenes on the physical, is to appeal to the presence of specific supervenience relations – that is, appropriate correlations between specific supervenient properties and their subvenient bases. If these specific correlations are themselves explainable, so much the better; but whether or not they are, invoking them would constitute the first necessary step. Moreover, such correlations seem to be the best, and the most natural, *evidential ground* for supervenience claims – often the only kind of solid evidence we could have for *empirical* supervenience claims. Even the nonfunctionalist physicalist has an explanation of sorts for psychophysical supervenience: it holds because a pervasive system of lawlike psychophysical correlations holds. These correlations are logically contingent and empirically discovered; though they are not further explainable, they constitute our ground, both evidential and explanatory, of the supervenience of the mental on the physical.

This shows why a global supervenience claim *unaccompanied by the corresponding strong supervenience (or covariance) claim* can be so unsatisfying:

we are being asked, it seems to me, to accept a sweeping claim about *all possible worlds*, say, that no two worlds could differ mentally without differing physically, on faith as a brute fact. In the absence of specific psychophysical correlations, and some knowledge of them, such a supervenience claim should strike us as a mere article of faith seriously lacking in motivation both evidentially and explanatorily; it would assert as a fact something that is apparently unexplainable and whose evidential status, moreover, is unclear and problematic. The attitude of the friends of global psychophysical supervenience is not unlike that of Samuel Alexander and Lloyd Morgan toward emergence: we must accept it "with natural piety"! But there is this difference: the emergentists could at least point to the observed lawful correlations between specific mental and biological processes as evidence for the presence of a general system of such correlations encompassing all mental processes, and point to the latter as the ground of the general thesis of mental emergence.

Notes

1 However, see below on emergence and n. 5.

2 R. M. Hare, *The Language of Morals* (London: Oxford University Press, 1952).

3 R. M. Hare, "Supervenience," *Proceedings of the Aristotelian Society*, suppl. vol. 58 (1984), pp. 1–16.

4 In *Moral Notions* (London: Routledge and Kegan Paul, 1967), pp. 158–9, Julius Kovesi points to the same characteristic of "good" that Hare called supervenience, but without using the supervenience terminology. Kovesi mentions that this characteristic is had by many nonethical expressions as well, e.g., "tulip"; however, he does not develop this point in any detail.

5 See especially Morgan's *Emergent Evolution* (London: Williams and Norgate, 1923). Others who used "supervenience" in connection with the doctrine of emergence include Stephen C. Pepper, "Emergence," *Journal of Philosophy* 23 (1926), pp. 241–5; and Paul Meehl and Wilfrid Sellars, "The concept of emergence," in Herbert Feigl and Michael Scriven (eds), *Minnesota Studies in the Philosophy of Science*, vol. 1 (Minneapolis: University of Minnesota Press, 1956).

6 See, e.g., Ernest Nagel, *The Structure of Science* (New York: Harcourt Brace & World, 1961); F. J. Ayala and T. Dobzhansky (eds), *Studies in the Philosophy of Biology: Reduction and Related Problems* (Berkeley and Los Angeles: University of California Press, 1974).

7 I discuss the doctrine of emergence in relation to the currently popular doctrine of nonreductive physicalism in " 'Downward causation' in emergentism and nonreductive physicalism," in A. Beckermann, H. Flohr, and J. Kim (eds), *Emergence or Reduction?* (Berlin: De Gruyter, 1992).

8 Donald Davidson, "Mental events," repr. in *Essays on Actions and Events* (Oxford: Oxford University Press, 1980); originally published in 1970.

9 David Lewis, *On the Plurality of Worlds* (Oxford: Basil Blackwell, 1986), p. 14.

10 *Die Leibniz-Handschriften der koeniglichen oeffentlichen Bibliothek zu Hannover*, ed. E. Bodemann (Hanover, 1895), VII, c, p. 74. Quoted by Hide Ishiguro in her *Leibniz's Philosophy of Logic and Language* (Ithaca, NY: Cornell University Press, 1972), p. 71, n. 3. The Latin text reads: "Relatio est accidents quod est in pluribus subjects estque resultans tantum seu nulla mutatione facta ab iis supervenit, si plura simul cogitantur, est concogitabilitas."

11 Henry Sidgwick, *The Method of Ethics* (London: Macmillan, 1874), pp. 208–9; quoted by Michael DePaul in his "Supervenience and moral dependence," *Philosophical Studies* 51 (1987), pp. 425–39.

12 G. E. Moore, *Philosophical Studies* (London: Routledge and Kegan Paul, 1922), p. 261.

13 Hare, *Language of Morals*, p. 145.

14 Lewis, *On the Plurality of Worlds*, p. 14.

15 See James Klagge, "Supervenience: ontological and ascriptive," *Australasian Journal of Philosophy* 66 (1988), pp. 461–70.

16 Morgan, *Emergent Evolution*, p. 9.

17 Ibid., p. 30. I should add that Morgan was here expounding Samuel Alexander's doctrine of emergence, and that he is skeptical about these two supervenience theses.

18 See Arthur O. Lovejoy's distinction between "indeterminist" and "determinist" theories of emergent evolution in his "The meaning of 'emergence' and its modes," in *Proceedings of the Sixth International Congress of Philosophy* (New York, 1927), pp. 20–33.

19 Davidson, "Mental events," p. 214.

20 Note that "nonreductive" is also consistent with reducibility. Thus, "nonreductive" is to be understood as indicting a neutral, noncommittal position with regard to reducibility, not as an affirmation of irreducibility.

21 See my "Concepts of supervenience" and "'Strong' and 'global' supervenience revisited," in Jaegwon Kim, *Supervenience and Mind* (Cambridge: Cambridge University Press, 1993), chs 4, 5 respectively.

22 Hare, "Supervenience," p. 4. Hare's actual definition of supervenience, ibid., pp. 4–5, is a little difficult to interpret in terms of our present scheme, in part because he still does not explicitly relativize supervenience, treating "supervenient" as a one-place predicate of properties. But there is little question that his definition of "F is a supervenient property" comes to "F is weakly covariant with respect to (G, not-G)" (it isn't wholly clear to me whether G is to be thought of as existentially quantified, or contextually indicated).

23 Davidson, in his "Replies to essays X–XII," in Bruce Vermazen and Merrill B. Hintikka (eds) *Essays on Davidson: Actions and Events* (Oxford: Clarendon Press, 1985), p. 242.

24 See Simon Blackburn, "Supervenience revisited," in Ian Hacking (ed.) *Exercises in Analysis* (Cambridge: Cambridge University Press, 1985). His (S), on p. 49, corresponds to weak covariance II; his (?), on p. 50, to strong covariance II. His argument against moral realism depends on accepting (S), not (?), as the appropriate form of moral supervenience. In "The supervenience argument against moral realism," *Southern Journal of Philosophy* 30 (1992), pp. 13–38, James Dreier urges a reading of Blackburn's argument on which it is committed to strong covariance.

25 Blackburn's (S), which he takes to characterize his notion of supervenience, is a little more complicated; it contains the relational predicate "x underlies y." However, I believe what he has in mind with (S) is best read, and restated, as a definition of "underlie," that is, the converse of "supervene."

26 E.g., in "Concepts of supervenience."

27 For some interesting considerations in defense of weak covariance in connection with materialism, see William Seager, "Weak supervenience and materialism," *Philosophy and Phenomenological Research* 48 (1988), pp. 697–709.

28 This example is similar to the one used by Lawrence Lombard in his interesting and helpful discussion of covariance and dependence in *Events: A Metaphysical Study* (London: Routledge & Kegan Paul, 1986), pp. 225ff. My discussion here is indebted to Lombard, and also to Michael R. DePaul, "Supervenience and moral dependence," and Thomas R. Grimes, "The myth of supervenience," *Pacific Philosophical Quarterly* 69 (1988), pp. 152–60.

29 In "The myth of supervenience" Grimes considers a criterion of this form and rejects it as neither necessary nor sufficient. The possible counterexamples I consider below are consistent with Grimes's argument; however, only schematic examples are presented by Grimes.

30 Grimes makes a similar point, ibid., p. 157.

31 For further discussion see J. L. Mackie, *The Cement of the Universe* (Oxford: Oxford University Press, 1974), ch. 7; David H. Sanford, "The direction of causation and the direction of conditionship," *Journal of Philosophy* 73 (1976), pp. 193–207, and *idem*, "The direction of causation and the direction of time," in *Midwest Studies in Philosophy* 9 (1984): pp. 53–75; Tom Beauchamp and Alexander Rosenberg, *Hume and the Problem of Causation* (New York and Oxford: Oxford University Press, 1981), ch. 6.

32 Could counterfactuals help? Perhaps; see, e.g., David Lewis, "Causation," this volume, ch. 34; but also Grimes, "Myth of supervenience."

33 There may also have been the influence of the emergentist doctrine that emergent properties are irreducible to their "basal" conditions.

34 For further discussion of supervenience in relation to nonreductive physicalism see my "The myth of nonreductive materialism," in Kim, *Supervenience and Mind*, ch. 14.

35 Moore, *Principia Ethica*, p. 10.

36 For details see Davidson's "Mental events."

37 This is the model of derivational reduction developed by Ernest Nagel in *The Structure of Science*. Whether this is the most appropriate model to be used in the present context could be debated; on this issue see William C. Wimsatt, "Reductive explanation: a functional account," in R. S. Cohen et al., (eds), *PSA 1974* (East Lansing, Mich.: Philosophy of Science Association, 1974), pp. 671–710.

38 Restricting ourselves to theories formulated in first-order languages.

39 There are various plausible considerations for thinking that derivational reduction as characterized isn't enough (and that it may not even be necessary). One line of consideration seems to show that we need *identities* of entities and properties rather than correlations; another line of consideration argues that the reduction must exhibit some underlying "mechanism," preferably at a micro-level, that explains how

the higher processes work. We must bypass these issues here.

40 See Paul Teller, "Comments on Kim's paper," and John Post, "Comment on Teller," both in *Southern Journal of Philosophy* 22 (1983), *The Spindel Conference Supplement* ("Supervenience"), pp. 57–62, 163–7.

41 This in part meets an objection that John Post has raised (in his "Comment on Teller") against my earlier construction of these coextensions (in "Concepts of supervenience") which made use of other property-forming operations. Post's specific objection was aimed at property complementation (or negation). On this issue see also William Seager, "Weak supervenience and materialism," and James Van Cleve, "Supervenience and closure," *Philosophical Studies* 58 (1990), pp. 225–38. Some remarks to follow in the main text are relevant to Post's point.

42 I wonder how "natural" the quantity $1/2$ (mv^2) looked before it was identified as kinetic energy.

43 See, e.g., Terence Horgan, "Supervenience and microphysics," *Pacific Philosophical Quarterly* 63 (1982), pp. 29–43; David Lewis, "New work for a theory of universals," this volume, ch. 17. Also Geoffrey Hellman and Frank Thompson, "Physicalism: ontology, determination, and reduction," this volume, ch. 41.

44 See, e.g., Bradford Petrie, "Global supervenience and reduction," *Philosophy and Phenomenological Research* 48 (1987), pp. 119–30. (Added 1993: for further discussion of this issue, see "Postcripts on supervenience," sect. 3, in this volume.)

45 I believe this indeed is the case with psychophysical global supervenience; for details see my " 'Strong' and 'global' supervenience revisited" and "Myth of non-reductive materialism."

46 Kim, " 'Strong' and 'global' supervenience revisited."

47 Stephen Schiffer, *Remnants of Meaning* (Cambridge, Mass.: MIT Press, 1987), pp. 153–4.

48 See John Post, "On the determinacy of valuation," *Philosophical Studies* 45 (1984), pp. 315–33.

49 See Simon Blackburn, "Supervenience revisited." For discussion of Blackburn's argument see James Klagge, "An alleged difficulty concerning moral properties," *Mind* 93 (1984), pp. 370–80; Dreier, "Supervenience argument against moral realism."

50 Morgan, *Emergent Evolution*, p. 36.

51 See for further discussion Terence Horgan and Mark Timmons, "Troubles on moral Twin Earth: moral queerness revisited," *Synthese* 92 (1992), pp. 221–60. Ernest Sosa has pointed out to me that appeals to meaning and analyticity, too, might involve appeals to brute facts in the end.

PART IX

Realism/Antirealism

Introduction

Contemporary debates on realism/antirealism have arisen largely from considerations of the semantics of languages. One central use of language is to make *statements*, e.g., that snow is white, that the average high temperature in New York during July is 85 ° F, that necessarily 7 + 5 = 12, that it is wrong to cause gratutious pain, and so on. Some statements we make are true; the rest are false – or, at any rate, not true. But what makes a statement true or false? Is it some mind-and knowledge-independent reality, or is it something other than that? Is truth dependent, in some ways, on evidence that we have, or can have, or is it evidence-transcendent?

In "Realism" (chapter 43), Michael Dummett, who is one of the philosophers who have played a major role in reintroducing the problem of realism into contemporary philosophy, gives a wide-ranging discussion of the variegated issues involved. As Dummett conceives it, realism with respect to a class of statements is a semantic thesis to the effect that what renders a statement of that class true is some reality existing independently of our knowledge, or belief. He argues that realism about a class of statements has two important consequences: first, the principle of bivalence for these statements (i.e., they must each be either true or false), and, second, a truth-conditional meaning theory (i.e., the meaning of a statement is its "truth-condition," a condition that obtains if and only if the statement is true). Dummett then surveys in detail possible antirealist options, discussing what each involves.

In "Pragmatic Realism" (chapter 44), Hilary Putnam defends a combination of realism and conceptual relativism. For him, realism is the thesis that ordinary objects such as tables and chairs exist; conceptual relativism is the thesis that questions about what objects exist and what genuine properties there are have meaning only relative to a scheme of concepts. Such a scheme generates conditions for being an object and for being a genuine property. Putnam also calls his position "internal realism," which he contrasts with "metaphysical realism," a position he rejects.

Sosa's "Putnam's Pragmatic Realism" (chapter 45) examines three arguments Putnam has offered for his pragmatic realism. The first is based on the supposed perspectival character of causation; the second begins with the premise that it is unlikely that science will converge on a finished theory that will provide an objective and absolute conception of reality; the third argument is from the non-absoluteness of objecthood and existence. Sosa feels that there is a case to be made for a view suggested by Putnam's third argument, although that argument is wrapped in a problematic linguistic garb.

William Alston's "Yes, Virginia, There Is a Real World" (chapter 46) is a defense of realism. He takes realism to be the position that what there is is independent of whether or how cognizers know or think of it. Alston argues that the available antirealist arguments are unconvincing, and that the antirealist is unable to produce a coherent conception of *truth* for propositions or sentences.

In "Morals and Modals" (chapter 47), Simon Blackburn outlines a general antirealist approach ("quasi-realism") to discourses that apparently commit us to a range of problematic facts. Unlike standard varieties of antirealism, quasi-realism does not advocate rejection or reconstruction of the target discourse; rather, sentences of the target discourse are treated as tools for "projection": moral sentences, for example, are used to project our conative attitudes, and the attribution of "necessity" to a sentence projects our sense of inability to "do anything" with the truth of that sentence. Blackburn examines the latter case, modal quasi-realism, in some detail, discussing how it differs from moral quasi-realism.

In "Realism, Antirealism, Irrealism, Quasi-Realism" (chapter 48), Crispin Wright surveys and discusses an array of possible antirealist alternatives – Dummettian antirealism, irrealism, quasi-realism, and a new version of antirealism that Wright outlines. Both Dummettian antirealism and Blackburn's quasi-realism come in for close scrutiny, and are found wanting. Wright suggests a new way of conducting debates over realism/antirealism: Investigate the notion of truth appropriate to the discourse in question. Grant that the notion of truth is applicable, but look into how substantial a concept it is. Wright discusses some specific questions to be asked in this context.

Further reading

Blackburn, Simon, *Spreading the Word* (Oxford: Clarendon Press, 1984).

Devitt, Michael, "The metaphysics of nonfactualism," *Philosophical Perspectives* 10 (1996), pp. 159–76.

——, *Realism and Truth*, 2nd edn (Oxford: Blackwell, 1991).

Dummett, Michael, *The Seas of Language* (Oxford: Clarendon Press, 1993).

——, *Truth and Other Enigmas* (Cambridge, Mass: Harvard University Press, 1978).

Haldane, John, and Wright, Crispin (eds), *Reality, Representation, and Projection* (New York and Oxford: Oxford University Press, 1993).

Horwich, Paul, "Realism and truth," *Philosophical Perspectives* 10 (1996), pp. 187–99.

McCormick, Peter (ed.), *Starmaking: Realism, Anti-Realism, and Irrealism* (Cambridge, Mass.: MIT Press, 1996).

Putnam, Hilary, *Realism and Reason: Philosophical Papers*, vol. 3 (Cambridge: Cambridge University Press, 1983).

——, *Reason, Truth, and History* (Cambridge: Cambridge University Press, 1981).

Tennant, Neil, *Anti-realism and Logic* (Oxford: Clarendon Press 1987).

Van Cleve, James, "Semantic supervenience and referential indeterminacy," *Journal of Philosophy* 89 (1992), pp. 344–61.

Wright, Crispin, *Truth and Objectivity* (Cambridge, Mass.: Harvard University Press, 1992).

43

Realism

Michael Dummett

The term 'realism' is constantly used by philosophers, in various connections, to characterize certain philosophical views; but it is rare for them to attempt to explain what they mean by calling a view realistic or non-realistic. I here attempt to analyse the concept of realism.

It is clear that one can be a realist about one subject-matter, and not about another: though someone may have a general inclination towards realistic views, it is plain that there is no coherent philosophical position which consists in being a realist *tout court*. This may be expressed by saying that one may be a realist about certain entities – mental states, possible worlds, mathematical objects – and not about others. But it seems preferable to say that realism is a view about a certain class of *statements* – for instance, statements in the future tense, or ethical statements – since certain kinds of realism, for instance realism about the future or about ethics, do not seem readily classifiable as doctrines about a realm of entities. So, in every case, we may regard a realistic view as consisting in a certain interpretation of statements in some class, which I shall call 'the given class'.

So construed, realism is a *semantic* thesis, a thesis about what, in general, renders a statement in the given class true when it is true. The very minimum that realism can be held to involve is that statements in the given class relate to some reality that

Originally published in *Synthese* 52 (1982), pp. 55–112. Reprinted with permission of Kluwer Academic Publishers.

exists independently of our knowledge of it, in such a way that that reality renders each statement in the class determinately true or false, again independently of whether we know, or are even able to discover, its truth-value. Thus realism involves acceptance, for statements of the given class, of the principle of bivalence, the principle that every statement is determinately either true or false. Acceptance of bivalence is not, as we shall see, sufficient for realism, but it is necessary to it. It follows that, on a realistic interpretation of some class of statements, the classical logical constants can always be intelligibly applied to those statements; for instance, classical negation or existential quantification, classically construed. Realism does not, of itself, exclude the possibility of intelligibly applying to statements of the given class some non-classical logical operators. For instance, realism concerning mathematical statements is usually called Platonism: and a Platonist, although he admits non-constructive mathematical reasoning as valid, may quite legitimately take an interest in whether or not a proof is constructive – legitimately so, because a constructive proof gives more information than a non-constructive one. Having this interest, he could, if he liked, introduce symbols for constructive disjunction and constructive existential quantification into his mathematical language. Where 'OR' is constructive, and 'or' classical, a proof of '*A* OR *B*' must not merely prove '*A* or *B*', but must also provide an effective method of finding a proof either of '*A*' or of '*B*', a proof of 'For each natural number *n*, *A(n)* OR *B(n)*' must supply an effective method for finding, for each value k of 'n', a proof of '$A(k)$' or a proof of '$B(k)$'; where 'SOME' is constructive and 'some' classical, a proof of 'For SOME natural number n, $A(n)$' must supply an effective method for finding a number k and a proof of '$A(k)$'. These constructive logical constants plainly do not obey the classical laws: for instance, 'A OR not A', the law of excluded middle, cannot in all cases be asserted. The admission of these non-classical logical constants does not, in itself, in the least impair the realistic interpretation of mathematical statements – at least, of those that do not contain such logical constants. What *would* rule out a realistic interpretation would be the view that the constructive logical constants were the only ones that could intelligibly be used in a mathematical context, that classical disjunction and classical existential quantification could not intelligibly be applied to mathematical statements. It is not the admissibility of non-classical logical operations, but the inadmissibility of classical ones, that entails a rejection of realism.

Rejection of the principle of bivalence for statements of some given class always involves a repudiation of a realistic interpretation of them; and adoption of an anti-realistic view often turns critically upon such a rejection of bivalence. But sometimes it is not the principle of bivalence that is the crucial question. To have a realistic view, it is not enough to suppose that statements of the given class are determined, by the reality to which they relate, either as true or as false; one has also to have a certain conception of the manner in which they are so determined. This conception consists essentially in the classical two-valued semantics: and this, in turn, embodies an appeal to the notion of reference as an indispensable notion of the semantic theory. Statements of the given class will ordinarily include ones containing expressions of generality: and, within the two-valued semantics, there will be associated with such expressions a definite domain of objects. Reference is a relation between a singular term, of a kind that can occur within statements of the given class, and some one object within the domain. We might, in a particular case, be concerned with a class of statements that contained no (closed) singular terms, but only expressions of generality; but that will not affect the crucial role within the semantic theory of the notion of reference. It will not do so because of the characteristic way in which, within the two-valued semantics, the truth-value of a statement involving generality – universal or existential quantification –

is conceived of as being determined. The truth-value of a quantified statement is, on this conception, determined by the truth-values of its instances, so that the instances stand to the quantified statement just as the constituent subsentences of a complex sentence whose principal operator is a sentential connective stand to the complex sentence: the truth-value of the quantified statement is a truth-function of the truth-values of its instances, albeit an infinitary one if the domain is infinite. The truth-value of a universally quantified statement is the logical product of the truth-values of its instances, that of an existentially quantified statement the logical sum of the truth-values of its instances. These operations, these possibly infinitary truth-functions, are conceived of as being everywhere defined, that is, as having a value in every case: in other words, the application of the operation of universal or of existential quantification to any predicate that is determinately true or false of each object in the domain will always yield a sentence that is itself determinately either true or false, independently of whether we are able to come to know its truth-value or not. (Thus, on this semantic theory, it is correct, on the *semantic* level, to say that universal quantification amounts to infinite conjunction, existential quantification to infinite disjunction; such a remark ceases to be true only at the level of *meaning* (sense), since to know the meaning of a quantified statement, it is not necessary to know the meanings of all its instances.) Here, of course, by an *instance* of a quantified statement is simply meant the result of filling the argument-place of the predicate with a singular term, that is, of removing the quantifier and replacing each occurrence of the variable that was bound by that quantifier by that singular term.

Now, in an actual language, there may not be, for every object in the domain, a singular term referring to that object. We can handle such a language in either of two ways. On what is essentially Frege's approach, instead of constructing a semantic theory for that language, we construct one for an expansion of it: this expanded language is obtained by enriching the original language by adding sufficiently many singular terms for there to be, for each object in the domain, a term referring to it. A semantic account of how the sentences of this expanded language are determined as true or as false will, of course, cover all the sentences of the original language; and, in this account, the notion of reference plays a crucial role. It does so precisely because the semantics is such that, once the truth-values of all the atomic statements are given, the truth-value of every complex statement, built up from the atomic ones by means of the sentential operators and the quantifiers, is thereby also determined; and the determination of the truth-value of an atomic statement, formed by inserting singular terms in the argument-place or argument-places of a one-place or many-place predicate, goes via the referents of the singular terms.

The other approach is that of Tarski. On this approach, we regard complex sentences as, in general, built up, not necessarily from atomic sentences properly so called, but from atomic *open sentences*, that is, from expressions that resemble sentences save that *free* variables may occur where, in an actual (closed) sentence, a singular term might stand. Just as the Fregean approach required consideration of a language expanded from the original one, so the Tarskian approach may require modification of the original language. It is being presupposed that, in that language, generality is expressed by means of the notation of quantifiers and variables (or, at any rate, that the language has first been modified to that extent in order to apply classical semantics to it). This presupposition entails that *bound* variables occur in some sentences of the language; but there is no necessity that the original language should admit any such device as *free* variables, nor, therefore, even allow the formation of open sentences. However this may be, the manner in which a quantified sentence is determined as true or false is explained, on the Tarskian approach, not in terms of the truth-values of its various instances, but in terms of the open sentence that results from removing the quantifier and replacing each occurrence of the variable that it bound by a free variable. In order to do this, we have to invoke the notion of the truth or falsity of an open sentence under an assignment of some object in the domain to the free variable, or of objects to the various distinct free variables, when there is more than one; this is often expressed as the notion of the *satisfaction* of the open sentence by an object or sequence of objects from the domain. Instead of considering the replacement of the bound variable by different singular terms, each with a fixed reference to one particular object, we consider its replacement by a single free variable, regarded as capable of receiving different assignments to it of an object from the domain. It is plain, however, that this is a mere variation on the idea embodied in the Fregean approach. Under any one particular assignment, the free variable

behaves exactly as if it were a singular term having the assigned object as its referent. Save in a very special case, we shall still need to introduce the notion of reference in addition to that of an assignment of values to the free variables. Suppose that the language contains some individual constants (proper names) and some function-symbols (like '+') or functional expressions (like 'the wife of . . .'). The individual constants or proper names must be taken as having references in the usual way; to the functional expressions will correspond functions, of appropriate degree, over the domain. We shall then have to explain, inductively, the notion of the reference of a simple or complex singular term, which may be either open or closed, that is, may or may not contain free variables, under any given assignment to the free variables, as follows: what a free variable refers to, under the assignment, is the object assigned to it; what an individual constant refers to, under the assignment, is simply the object it refers to; what a complex term, say $f(t_1, t_2)$, formed by means of a function-symbol, refers to under the assignment is the value of the corresponding function for those objects as arguments to which the constituent terms (here t_1 and t_2) refer under the assignment. The only case in which we can dispense altogether with the notion of reference in favour of that of an assignment is that in which the language contains neither any individual constants or proper names nor any function-symbols or other device for forming complex terms; and, even in this case, the notion of reference is being surreptitiously appealed to, since the possible assignments to a free variable are, in effect, different interpretations of it as an individual constant. Thus, even if our original language does not actually contain any (closed) singular terms, and even if we formulate the semantic theory in Tarski's manner, in terms of satisfaction, the notion of reference still plays a crucial role in the theory.

A semantic theory is not itself a theory of meaning, since it does not concern itself with what is known by a speaker and constitutes his grasp of the use of an expression: a knowledge of the meaning of a predicate does not consist in knowing of which objects it is true and of which it is false, and a knowledge of the meaning of a sentence does not consist in knowing its truth-value. But a semantic theory is plausible only in so far as it provides a base on which a theory of meaning can be constructed. The semantic theory seeks to exhibit the manner in which a sentence is determined as true, when it is true, in accordance with its composition, its internal structure. It does so by specifying, for each type of expression, what has to be associated with an expression of that type in order that, for every true sentence in which the expression occurs, we can exhibit the manner in which that sentence is determined as true in accordance with its composition. Let us say that, for any particular expression of any given type, that which must, according to the semantic theory, be so associated with it is its *semantic value*.

Now some semantic theories do not admit that every well-formed sentence with a definite sense is, independently of our knowledge, determined either as true or as not true. A characteristic way in which this comes about is illustrated by the intuitionistic semantic theory for mathematical statements sketched by Heyting. In this semantics, the semantic values of the component expressions of a sentence jointly determine a decidable relation between that sentence and an arbitrary mathematical construction which obtains just in case that construction constitutes a proof of that sentence. A sentence may then be said to be true if and only if there exists a construction that constitutes a proof of it: but, since the phrase 'there exists', in this definition, is itself interpreted constructively, we may not assert, for an arbitrary mathematical statement with a well-defined meaning, that there either does or does not exist a construction which is a proof of it, not, therefore, that it either is true or is not true. Within such a semantic theory, we cannot say that the semantic values of the components of a sentence determine that sentence either as true or as not true, but only that they determine what, if there be such a thing, will render it true.

A semantic theory of this kind is, evidently, a highly non-realistic one, since it involves rejecting the principle of bivalence. A realistic theory, on the other hand, incorporates the principle of bivalence, the principle that every meaningful sentence is determined as true or as false, and so entails the weaker principle, namely that every meaningful sentence is determined as true or as not true. Without at present enquiring more closely into the rationale that may be offered for admitting a distinction between a statement's failing to be true and its actually being false, let us say that a semantic theory which involves the weaker principle is an *objectivist* semantics: a realistic semantics is necessarily objectivist, but an objectivist semantics need not be realistic. An objectivist semantics incorporates a notion of truth which is not closely linked to

the possibility of our recognizing a statement as true: on such a semantic theory, a statement may be true even though we have not recognized it as such, and, possibly, even though we have no means of doing so. By contrast, in such a semantic theory as that of Heyting for mathematical statements, intuitionistically interpreted, the only admissible notion of truth is one directly connected with our capacity for recognizing a statement as true: the supposition that a statement is true is the supposition that there is a mathematical construction constituting a proof of that statement.

In any objectivist semantic theory, it will be possible to regard the semantic values of the components of any sentence as jointly determining it either as true or as not true; and so we may describe such a semantic theory as specifying, for each type of expression, what has to be associated with an expression of that type in order that every sentence in which the expression occurs should be determined as true or otherwise. Thus, in particular, according to the classical two-valued semantics, there must be associated with each proper name or other singular term an object from the domain, with each one-place predicate a mapping from the domain into the set of the two truth-values, *true* and *false*, with a sentential connective a truth-function, with a sentence, considered as capable of serving as a constituent in a more complex sentence, a truth-value, and so forth.

An understanding of a sentence must involve a grasp of how it is determined as true, if it is true, in accordance with its composition: hence a theory of meaning must ascribe to a speaker of the language an implicit grasp of the underlying semantic theory. A grasp of the meaning of a specific expression will thus involve a knowledge of the kind of semantic value it may have, in virtue of the linguistic type or category to which it belongs. It will not, in general, amount, in any straightforward way, to a knowledge of the semantic value of the expression, since, on any objectivist semantic theory, once we know the semantic values of all the component expressions in some sentence, we are in a position to say whether that sentence is or is not true, whereas we can understand the sentence without being in any such position. It is natural to say that whether or not a sentence is true depends both on its meaning and on the way the world is, on the constitution of external reality; and, since the semantic values of the component expressions together determine whether or not the sentence is true, it is plain that, in associating particular semantic values with these expressions, we have already taken the contribution of external reality into account. But, given the way the world is, whether a sentence is or is not true depends upon its meaning; so, given the way the world is, the semantic value of an expression depends only on its meaning. It follows that a grasp of the meaning of a specific expression must be something which, taken together with the way the world is, determines the particular semantic value that it has. Thus meaning must be something that determines semantic value: in Frege's terminology, sense determines reference. (For Frege, the notion of reference applies not only to singular terms, as I am here taking it, but to expressions of all categories; it thus coincides with what I am here calling semantic value, at least within the two-valued semantic theory, which Frege of course advocated.) To say that meaning determines semantic value does not just mean that, if the meanings of two expressions coincide, so do their semantic values. Rather, its having any particular semantic value is to be *explained* in terms of its having a certain sort of meaning. A grasp of its meaning just is the conception of its having a semantic value that depends in a certain way on how the world is: on an objectivist semantic theory, to know the meaning of an expression consists in knowing the condition for it to have any given semantic value. In Frege's terminology, the sense of the expression is the mode under which its reference is presented to us; to keep the metaphor, but employ the terminology being used here, its meaning is the manner in which its semantic value is given to us. It is in this way that a semantic theory, while not itself being a theory of meaning, forms a base for such a theory, and is plausible only if a viable theory of meaning can be constructed on it as base. To vary the metaphor, it provides a framework for a theory of meaning; it lays down the terms in which such a theory must provide a model for that in which the understanding of an expression of any given category must consist.

If, in particular, our semantic theory is an objectivist one, then any theory of meaning that can be erected on it as base will be one under which a knowledge of the meaning of a sentence will consist in a grasp of what has to be the case for it to be true, where, in general, truth is regarded as determinately attaching to certain statements and failing to attach to others independently of our knowledge. It is important to notice, however, that this observation holds good only as regards that understanding of a sentence which is sufficient to yield a comprehension of its significance when it forms a complete utterance – of what, for example, is the content of an assertion made by means of it. A knowledge of the condition that must hold for a sentence to be true need not suffice for an understanding of the sentence as it might occur as a constituent in a more complex sentence, that is, of the contribution it makes to determining the condition under which that more complex sentence is true: for that, we may need to know more than simply under what conditions the constituent sentence is true. For instance, if the language contains modal operators, explained in terms of a semantics of possible worlds, the semantic theory may allow that a grasp of the content of some sentence, considered as a complete utterance, amounts to a knowledge of what has to be the case for it to be true: but constituent subsentences will not contribute to determining this solely in virtue of whether or not they are true, that is, true in the actual world, but also in virtue of their being true or false in various possible worlds. It is characteristic of the two-valued semantics, however, that, according to it, that understanding of a sentence which is enough to supply a grasp of its content when it serves as a complete utterance suffices also for an understanding of its significance when it occurs as a constituent in a more complex sentence. From this it follows that no distinction can be made between a sentence's failing to be true and its being false; hence the relatively weak principle common to all objectivist semantic theories, that every statement is determinately either true or not true, can be strengthened to the principle of bivalence, that every statement is determinately either true or false. In any case, a theory of meaning for which the two-valued semantics serves as a base is a *truth-conditional* meaning-theory; one according to which to grasp the meaning of a sentence consists in a knowledge of the condition that has to obtain for it to be true.

Now some interpretations of the statements in some given class fail to be realistic, not because they involve a repudiation of the principle of bivalence, but because they diverge from a theory of meaning of this kind. This may be because they are not truth-conditional in form, that is, not constructed on the basis of an objectivist semantics: they deny that an understanding of the statements in question is to be explained in terms of a grasp of the condition for such a statement to be true. Alternatively, they may accept this general characterization of that in which an understanding of a

Michael Dummett

statement consists, but reject the account embodied in the two-valued semantics of the mechanism whereby a statement is determined as true or false; they may, for instance, repudiate the conception whereby a determination of the truth-value of a statement containing a singular term proceeds via an identification of an object as the referent of that term. An example of a rejection of realism on both counts would be Wittgenstein's view of statements ascribing inner sensations to people. In one passage of the *Philosophical Investigations* (I. 352), Wittgenstein does, it is true, inveigh against the principle of bivalence for such statements (or, rather, against the law of excluded middle, which, for him, accepting as he did the redundancy theory of truth, amounted to the same thing). He writes:

> Here it happens that our thinking plays us a queer trick. We want, that is, to quote the law of excluded middle and to say: 'Either such an image is in his mind, or it is not; there is no third possibility!' ... when it is said, 'Either he has this experience, or not' – what primarily occurs to us is a picture which by itself seems to make the sense of the expressions *unmistakable*: 'Now you know what is in question' – we should like to say. And that is precisely what it does not tell him.

But, in fact, Wittgenstein is not particularly interested in denying the principle of bivalence for ascriptions of inner sensations or images, save in queer cases, such as if someone says that the stove is in pain. The thrust of the argument is not that bivalence fails: it is, rather, first, that we cannot employ the notion of reference to explain how expressions for inner sensations function ('if we construe the grammar of the expression of sensation on the model of "object and name", the object drops out of consideration as irrelevant" (I. 293)), and, secondly, that an understanding of ascriptions of inner sensation cannot be explained as consisting in a knowledge of the condition for them to be true. The condition for an ascription of pain to someone to be true is plainly not that he manifests pain-behaviour. Hence, if we attempt to give a truth-conditional account of the meaning of such ascriptions, we are forced to resort to the conception whereby I understand the word 'pain' in the first instance from my own case, namely by giving myself a private ostensive definition of the word, and then transfer it to the experiences of others by analogy: the condition which I apprehend as being

that under which 'Henry is in pain' is true is then, on this conception, that it should be with Henry as it is with me when I am in pain. Having, as I think successfully, but at least to his own satisfaction, exposed the chimerical nature both of the private ostensive definition and of the supposed analogical transference, Wittgenstein concludes that the understanding of pain-ascriptions is not to be represented on the model of a grasp of truth-conditions. Our philosophical perplexities arise, according to him, precisely from the use of this model: for, if we use it, we are forced to choose between two alternatives. One is to seek for conclusive and publicly accessible grounds for ascribing pain to someone, and to declare the existence of such grounds to be that which renders such an ascription true; this is behaviourism. The other is to deny the possibility of any publicly accessible and absolutely conclusive grounds, and, on that score, to hold that what renders a pain-ascription true is something inaccessible to any but the one to whom the pain is ascribed, and hence that our understanding of pain-ascriptions rests on our grasp of what it is for such an in principle inaccessible state of affairs to obtain. The solution is to abandon the attempt to give a truth-conditional account of the meanings of statements of this form. We have, rather, to accept that an understanding of pain-ascriptions consists in a mastery of their actual use. This involves knowing that the presence of a pain-stimulus and the manifestation of pain-behaviour together supply an entitlement for an ascription of pain; knowing when one of these does, and when it does not, supply such an entitlement in the apparent or demonstrable absence of the other; and knowing what justifies withdrawing an ascription of pain for which there had been such an entitlement. (To display pity for the sufferer and to gloat over his sufferings are two possible manifestations of a belief that he is in pain: but, in view of the callousness which is also a prevalent human attitude, it seems difficult to maintain that such a belief is incompatible with behaviour no different from that towards a broken chair.) It is, on this account, part of our understanding of the word 'pain' that we recognize that a report by a speaker that he is himself in pain does not require grounds or justification, but also that it is to be assessed like any other pain-behaviour. It is not that the speaker attaches a private meaning to the word 'pain' under which he knows that he is in pain, as he understands 'pain'. Rather, the significance of his utterance depends upon his use of the word as part of the public language, and so on his grasp of the connections between, pain, pain-stimuli, and pain-behaviour; for instance, an apparently sincere declaration on his part that he did not in the least mind being in pain would call in question the meaning, and thereby the truth, of his report.

The rejection of a realistic view of statements of some given class has often been associated with the maintenance of a reductionist thesis concerning them. Reductionism, properly so called, is the thesis that there exists a translation of statements of the given class into those of some other class, which I shall call the reductive class. This translation is proposed, not merely as preserving truth-values, but as part of an account of the meanings of statements of the given class: it is integral to the reductionist thesis that it is by an implicit grasp of the scheme of translation that we understand those statements. The most celebrated example of a reductionist thesis is that embodied in classical phenomenalism: the given class here consists of statements about material objects, and the reductive class of statements about sense-data. Reductionism in this sense may indeed afford a ground for rejecting realism concerning statements of the given class, even when it does not provide any reason for repudiating the principle of bivalence as applied to them. To take an example of Frege's, suppose that we have a method for translating statements containing terms for and quantification over directions into ones containing only terms for and quantification over straight lines, and that a grasp of this scheme of translation is accepted as being integral to our understanding of statements about directions. In the *Grundlagen der Arithmetik*, Frege claimed that the necessity to invoke such a translation in order to explain the meanings of statements about directions would not render it improper to ascribe a reference to terms for directions, since it is only in the context of a sentence that a word has a meaning. Provided that an expression really does function logically as a singular term, that is, that certain patterns of inference govern sentences containing it, and provided that we have laid down determinate truth-conditions for sentences containing that expression, then, according to Frege, it is entirely proper to ascribe a reference to that expression (a reference to an object); any question that may remain as to whether it actually has such a reference will not be a semantic question, but a factual one, namely a question as to the truth of an existential sentence of the kind for which we have laid down the truth-

conditions. In the example, we have laid down the truth-conditions of statements about directions precisely by means of the translation, provided, of course, that it is assumed that statements about lines already have determinate truth-conditions. Hence according to Frege, the setting up of such a translation actually supplies a justification for ascribing reference to terms for directions, or, in another terminology, for admitting directions into our ontology: no better justification can be required for acknowledging the existence of abstract objects than that we know what must hold good if sentences concerning them are to be true.

Even in the *Grundlagen*, this was, for Frege, a merely hypothetical case: for rather special reasons, he did not in fact think that it was possible to translate statements about directions into statements about lines. Furthermore, his stance on this matter in his later writings is somewhat unclear. But, in *Grundlagen* at any rate, his espousal of the hypothetical thesis is unequivocal: *if* we had such a translation, then we should, by that very fact, be justified in ascribing a reference to terms for directions.

I do not wish to controvert this thesis: given an acceptance of the scheme of translation as providing a correct account of the meanings of statements about directions, nothing is gained by a philosophical protest to the effect that 'there are not really any such things as directions'. Such a protest springs, however, from the perception of a genuine and important fact: the fact, namely, that adoption of this form of explanation for statements about directions represents the abandonment of a realistic view of such statements. Realism is abandoned, not because a truth-conditional account of the meanings of the statements is impossible, nor, necessarily, because there is any reason to repudiate the principle of bivalence as applied to them, but because the notion of reference no longer plays any role in the account of their meanings. Even if, relying on Frege's principle that a term has reference only in the context of a sentence, we continue to ascribe reference to terms for directions, we do not need to invoke the notion of reference, as applied to such terms, in order to explain how a sentence containing such a term is determined as true or false: the determination of the truth-value of the sentence does not proceed via the identification of an object as the referent of the term. Indeed, just because it is only in the context of a sentence that such a term is conceived of as having a reference, the notion of reference, as applied to that term, has not been explained by the use of anything characterized as identifying an object as its referent; and, for all that has been said, there may be no process that can legitimately be so characterized. Suppose that we have the simplest kind of statement about a direction, a sentence formed by inserting in the argument-place of a suitable one-place predicate a term for a direction. Then, under the given account of the meanings of statements about directions, the canonical means by which we establish the atomic sentence as true or as false is not by identifying some direction as being that to which the term refers, and then determining that the predicate is true of it; it is by first translating the sentence into a statement about lines, and then determining, by whatever are the appropriate means, the truth-value of the resulting statement. In this process, the notion of reference as applied to terms for lines may need to be invoked, if we have a realistic theory of meaning for statements about lines which here form our reductive class: but the notion of reference as applied to terms for directions, however defensible, plays no role in the account of the meaning of the original sentence. And, because this is so for atomic sentences about directions, it is so also for sentences involving quantification over directions: we shall determine such sentences as true or as false not by considering their truth-values as the values of infinitary truth-functions whose arguments are the truth values of their instances, but by first applying our translation scheme to obtain some statement about lines, and then determining the resulting statement as true or as false.

It may be for reasons of this kind that phenomenalism was always reckoned to stand in opposition to realism concerning statements about material objects; but I think that another, imperfectly apprehended, reason underlay this classification. I have emphasized that realism concerning a given class of statements requires adherence in all respects to a certain pattern of explanation for statements of the given class, a certain style of meaning-theory for those statements: any divergence from that pattern constitutes an abandonment of realism in its full-fledged form. A very radical type of divergence is involved when, as with Wittgenstein's view of statements ascribing inner sensations, it is denied that it is possible to give a truth-conditional account of the meanings of the given statements; if this is denied, it becomes relatively unimportant whether the principle of bivalence is abandoned or not. On the other hand, when the divergence takes

the form of dispensing with the notion of reference, as playing a crucial role in the semantic account of statements of the given class, perhaps because of the acceptance of a reductionist thesis concerning those statements, and does not involve either a rejection of a truth-conditional account of their meanings or a repudiation of bivalence, we have only a comparatively mild species of anti-realism. Probably the great majority of anti-realistic views are ones whose most characteristic expression consists in a rejection of the principle of bivalence: very plain examples are a constructivist view of mathematical statements, under which a mathematical statement is true only if we are in possession of a proof of it, and false only if we are in possession of a refutation; and neutralism concerning the future, under which future-tense statements are not in general determinately true or false.

Now although there is just one logic, the familiar classical logic, which accords with an acceptance of the principle of bivalence, there is no one logic which accords with its rejection: to reject the principle of bivalence is, in itself, merely to adopt a negative position, and is compatible with the acceptance of a variety of semantic theories and a variety of resulting logics. In some cases, the semantic theory advocated by the anti-realist will involve, not merely the rejection of bivalence, but the abandonment of a truth-conditional theory of meaning, because the semantic theory underlying his theory of meaning is not of the objectivist type: he does not admit, for statements of the given class, any notion of truth under which each statement is determinately either true or not true, independently of our knowledge. In other cases, the semantic theory he advocates, although not embodying the principle of bivalence, will remain objectivist in character, and therefore compatible with a theory of meaning under which a grasp of the meaning of a sentence consists in a knowledge of the condition that has to obtain for it to be true. In the former case, we are concerned with an anti-realist view of a very thoroughgoing kind; in the latter, with a less radical type of anti-realism, although one more radical than a view which leaves the principle of bivalence intact, but merely calls in question the role of the notion of reference in the meaning-theory.

There are other cases, however, in which the opponent of realism does not actually take the step of rejecting the principle of bivalence, but in which it appears that his position would be strengthened were he to do so: and these cases are rather hard to classify. It has already been remarked that opposition to realism is frequently associated with acceptance of a reductionist thesis, and not incorrectly so. But it has often been associated also with acceptance of a weaker form of thesis, which I shall call a *reductive* thesis. A reductive thesis, like a full-fledged reductionist thesis, is concerned with the relation between two classes of statements, the given class and the reductive class. A reductionist thesis claims the existence of a translation from statements in the given class into statements in the reductive class; a reductive thesis more modestly claims only that no statement of the given class can be true unless some suitable statement or statements of the reductive class are true, and, conversely, that the truth of those statements of the reductive class guarantees the truth of the corresponding statement of the given class. It is, once again, essential that the reductive thesis be advanced, not as a mere observation concerning a connection between the truth-conditions of statements of the two classes, but as part of an account of the meanings of statements of the given class: the proponent of the thesis holds that an understanding of those statements involves an implicit grasp of their relation to statements of the reductive class, that is, an implicit acceptance of the reductive thesis.

In order to bring out the difference between a reductionist thesis and the weaker philosophical proposition I have labelled a reductive thesis, it is worth while to consider the different possible reasons an adherent of the weaker thesis might have for not advancing the stronger one.

(1) He might hold that, for any particular statement A of the given class, there will in general be infinitely many statements of the reductive class the truth of any one of which will guarantee the truth of A, and such that the truth of A requires the truth of one of those statements. If the language does not contain a mechanism whereby we can form a statement, belonging to the reductive class, tantamount to the disjunction of those infinitely many statements, then it will be impossible actually to translate A into a statement of the reductive class. Alternatively, he might hold that the truth of A entailed the simultaneous truth of the statements in some infinite subset of the reductive class, and was guaranteed only by the truth of all of them: and, again, if the language contained no device for forming a sentence tantamount to the infinite conjunction of the statements in that set, it

would be impossible actually to give a translation of A. Or, again, he might combine these views: the truth of A might guarantee, and might require, the truth of all the statements in some one out of infinitely many infinite subsets of the reductive class, so that a translation of A could be given only as an infinite disjunction of infinite conjunctions of statements of the reductive class. Just such a reason as this has been advanced by some philosophers as a ground for denying the possibility of translating statements about material objects into statements about sense-data, while admitting the correctness of a weaker reductive thesis concerning these two classes of statements.

(2) Quite a different ground has been given for denying the possibility of an actual scheme of translation. This is, namely, that it is impossible to introduce a vocabulary adequate for expressing statements of the reductive class without thereby introducing one adequate for the expression of statements of the given class. This need not mean that the given class becomes a subclass of the reductive class, thereby rendering the reductive thesis entirely nugatory: the reductive class may be characterized in such a way that, although the entire vocabulary by means of which statements of the given class are expressed may occur in statements of the reductive class, it does so only in a restricted type of context. Nevertheless, when the two classes are related in this way, there can be no question of a translation of statements of the given class in a manner that eliminates its characteristic vocabulary. An example might be a reductive thesis concerning mathematical statements, the thesis, namely, that a mathematical statement A can be true only if the statement ⌜We possess a proof that A⌝ is true: the given class consists of mathematical statements, the reductive class of statements to the effect that we have proofs of such statements. Such a reductive thesis is quite compatible with the view that, for any given mathematical statement, there is no way in which to express the general notion of something's being a proof of that statement that does not require the use of that statement itself as a subordinate clause, or, more generally, that there is no way of characterizing all possible proofs of a given statement without employing a vocabulary adequate for the expression of the statement in question. Accordingly, a reductionist thesis could not be maintained: there could be no scheme for translating mathematical statements into statements about our possession of proofs of them.

Another example would be a reductive thesis, such as has been advanced by some philosophers (Łukasiewicz, C. I. Lewis, and, at one time, A. J. Ayer) concerning statements in the past tense, to the effect that such a statement cannot be true unless some statement about the existence of present (or perhaps also future) evidence and memories is also true; if every trace of the occurrence of the alleged past event has disappeared, the statement that it occurred is devoid of truth. This reductive thesis could be maintained even though it was denied that there could be any translation of past-tense statements into ones in the present and future tense, on the ground that any such translation would require allusion to memories, and that there is no way to characterize a memory of an event without the use of the past tense. A similar ground has also been given for denying the possibility of translating material-object statements into ones about perceptual experience: our perceptual experience is, on this view, so coloured by our interpretation of our sense-impressions as revealing to us the constitution of material objects and their disposition in three-dimensional space that there can be no way of characterizing that experience without the use of a vocabulary already adequate for the expression of material-object statements.

This second type of ground for rejecting reductionism while accepting a reductive thesis deserves a closer scrutiny. It might be objected that the overlap of vocabulary is no impediment to a translation. We might still be supposed to be capable in principle of understanding statements of the reductive class in advance of understanding those of the given class: at such a stage, our understanding of the vocabulary needed for expressing statements of the given class would be only partial, for we should understand it only in those restricted contexts in which it occurs in statements of the reductive class. For instance, we might understand a mathematical vocabulary only within contexts governed by 'a proof that . . .'; or we might understand the past tense only in contexts governed by '. . . remembers that . . .'. If this assumption were made, there would be no obstacle to an informative translation of statements of the given class: we should be translating statements in which certain expressions occurred in a context of one kind into statements in which they occurred only in contexts of another kind. And, it might be urged, the possibility of such a translation is implicit in the claim that the reductive thesis forms part of an account of the *meanings* of the statements of the given class: if

we could not understand statements of the reductive class antecedently to a knowledge of the meanings of those of the given class, how could the reductive thesis operate as an explanation of those meanings?

This objection is perfectly reasonable, so far as our present characterization of this second ground for resisting reductionism while accepting a reductive thesis goes. It shows, however, that we have not yet fully characterized that ground. In a case of this kind, the reductive thesis is not intended to be understood as a partial explanation of the meanings of statements of the given class after the manner of a reductionist thesis and, perhaps, of other reductive theses. That is to say, the reductive thesis is not intended to explain the meanings of statements of the given class by formulating their truth-conditions in terms that can be understood antecedently to an understanding of those statements, as a reductionist thesis is certainly intended to do. It is precisely because, in a case of this sort, it is *not* supposed that statements of the reductive class are even in principle intelligible in advance of an understanding of those of the given class that the reductionist thesis is rejected. The reductive thesis makes an important contribution to circumscribing the form which a theory of meaning for statements of the given class must take, namely by saying something about the appropriate notion of truth for statements of that class; but it is not intended to offer an explanation of those statements in terms of other statements regarded as capable of being antecedently understood.

(3) A third ground for rejecting reductionism while accepting a reductive thesis is very seldom appealed to: it is that, while, for any statement *A* of the given class there must be a statement *B* of the reductive class in the truth of which the truth of *A* consists, we have no effective means of identifying, for each statement *A*, the corresponding statement *B*. This appears to be Donald Davidson's reason for denying the possibility of translating psychological into neurophysiological statements: I know of no other actual example of an appeal to such a ground for denying a reductionist thesis.

Very often maintenance of any reductive thesis is taken as constituting in itself a rejection of realism for statements of the given class. This is, however, a mistake. A reductive thesis does not, of itself, imply that we cannot give a truth-conditional account of the meanings of statements of the given class; it does not imply that bivalence fails for those statements; it does not even imply that the notion of reference does not play its standard role in the explanation of how those statements are determined as true or as false. An example might be the reductive thesis, for psychological statements, embodied in so-called central-state materialism: the reductive class, in this case, consists of statements about the states of the central nervous system. Such a thesis has no tendency to cast doubt upon whether any specific statement ascribing a psychological state to an individual is determinately either true or false: rather, it tends to reinforce the presumption that it will be one or the other, since it is assumed that his central nervous system either is or is not in the corresponding state at any given time. It does not even call in question the ascription of reference to terms for particular psychological states, since these can be construed as referring, in a certain manner, to the corresponding neurophysiological states. In fact, we can see that, in this example, we do not arrive at an anti-realist position even if the reductive thesis is strengthened to a full-fledged reductionism: if there is a one–one correspondence between describable psychological states and describable neurophysiological states, then terms for the former can be construed as referring, in a particular manner, to the latter. What, in the example concerning directions and lines, deprived the notion of reference of any significant role in the account of the meanings of statements about directions was that we tacitly assumed that, in the process of translating such statements into statements about lines, we did not simply replace a term for a direction by a term for a line, or by a term of any other kind, but effected a transformation under which that term disappeared altogether. If we had been concerned with a translation under which a term for a direction was replaced by a term for, say, a maximal class of parallel lines, then we should not have said that the notion of reference, as applied to terms for directions, no longer had any part to play in the meaning-theory: we should have said, rather, that terms for directions were being construed as referring to classes of parallel lines. In this latter case, therefore, we should have a reductionist thesis that in no way impugned a realistic interpretation of statements about directions. Reductionism is, therefore, not intrinsically anti-realist: it depends on the character of the translation proposed. *A fortiori*, a reductive thesis does not in itself involve any rejection of realism.

The principal reason why philosophers have often confused an advocacy of a reductive thesis with the repudiation of realism is that the reductive thesis frequently represents a first step in an argument leading to the rejection of bivalence. For instance, it is first claimed that a mathematical statement can be true only if there exists a proof of it; and then the second step is taken, namely to observe that there is no ground for assuming that, for any intelligible mathematical statement, we must be able to construct either a proof or a disproof of it of the kind that we are able to grasp. It then follows that we have no entitlement to assert that every mathematical statement is either true or false. In general, a reductive thesis may lead to a rejection of bivalence if the correspondence between the given class and the reductive class is of a particular kind; given the reductive thesis, the second step in the argument may be cogent even though a realistic interpretation is allowed for statements of the reductive class. The general form of the second step consists in pointing out that, for any particular statement A of the given class, there is no guarantee that there should be any true statement, or set of true statements, of the reductive class whose truth would entail the truth of A or would entail the truth of $\ulcorner$Not A$\urcorner$, the given class being taken to be one closed under negation; where the falsity of A is identified with the truth of its negation, as it is usually natural to do, it follows, given the reductive thesis, that a statement of the given class cannot be assumed to be either true or false.

This second step, leading to a rejection of bivalence, and, therefore, of realism concerning the given class of statements, often very naturally follows upon the reductive thesis. For instance, if statements about the past are considered as needing to be rendered true, when they are true, by what lies in the present or the future, it will inevitably be inferred that a past-tense statement need not be either true or false. Or, again, to take an example not so far used, if a psychological statement is regarded as requiring to be rendered true by corresponding behaviour on the part of the individual concerned, if it is to be true at all, it is almost equally natural to conclude that a psychological statement will not in all cases be either true or false: the individual may not behave in such a way as to render either that statement or its negation true. It is, however, a mistake to suppose that a reductive thesis leads inevitably to a rejection of bivalence, or that it always represents a repudiation of realism. We have to look at the particular case to see whether, given the reductive thesis, the second step can be taken: the relation between the given class and the reductive class may be such that – given a realistic interpretation of the reductive class – for any statement A of the given class, we are assured that either there will be some true statement B of the reductive class such that A is true in virtue of the truth of B, or there will be some true statement C of the reductive class such that the negation of A is true in virtue of the truth of C. We have already considered a case in which it is natural to say this, namely when the given class consists of psychological statements, and the reductive class consists, not of statements about behaviour, but of neurophysiological ones.

Realism about a certain class of statements is thus compatible with acceptance of a reductive thesis concerning that class: and we may label a realistic view that is combined with, and, perhaps, even rests on, a reductive thesis *sophisticated realism*. In this sense, central-state materialism represents a form of sophisticated realism concerning psychological statements. Opposed to all reductive theses applied to a given class of statements is what we may call an *irreducibility thesis*: the thesis, namely, that no reductive thesis holds good for that class. In characterizing the general notion of a reductive thesis, I did not need to place any restrictions on the two classes of statements considered: if the two classes can be chosen in such a way that the reductive thesis becomes trivially true and hence philosophically unilluminating, that is no objection to the concept of a reductive thesis. Probably, however, in order to give a clear explanation of what I intend by speaking of an irreducibility thesis, I ought to circumscribe the type of class for which such a thesis can be propounded, and the type of class about which the irreducibility thesis asserts that it cannot serve as a reductive class for the given class. To state such restrictions accurately is, however, not easy to do, and I shall therefore leave the notion of an irreducibility thesis to this extent incompletely specified: I do not think that any serious misunderstanding will result. A reductive thesis offers an informative general answer to the question 'What makes a statement of the given class true, when it is true?' or 'In virtue of what is such a statement true, if it is true?' An irreducibility thesis is, conversely, to the effect that, for a statement of the given class, no non-trivial answer can be given to this question; or, at least, that no non-trivial general answer is possible.

A trivial answer to the question what makes a statement A true, if it is true, is one that consists, actually or in effect, of simply repeating the statement; and a trivial general answer to the question what makes any statement of a certain class true, when it is true, is one that amounts to no more than saying, 'That statement's being true'. For instance, a constructivist has an informative general answer to the question 'What, in general, makes a true mathematical statement true?': namely, 'The existence of a proof of that statement'. A Platonist, on the other hand, that is, one who adopts a realistic interpretation of mathematical statements, can give no answer to the question 'What makes Goldbach's conjecture true, if it is true?', save 'Every even number's being the sum of two primes', that is, by formulating Goldbach's conjecture; and, to the general question 'What makes a mathematical statement true, when it is true?' he can do no better than to reply, 'The constitution of mathematical reality'. Since mathematical reality is composed of mathematical facts, that reply is quite uninformative: it amounts to saying that each true mathematical statement is rendered true by the fact which it states. An informative answer to the question what makes a statement of some class true, when it is true, sheds light on the notion of truth appropriate for statements of that class, and gives an indication of the type of semantic theory, and therefore the type of meaning-theory, required for them: it is therefore desirable when it can be attained. But we cannot expect in each case to be able to find an informative answer; in some cases, only a trivial answer may be possible.

As already explained, a realistic interpretation of a certain class of statements does not require the maintenance of an irreducibility thesis concerning them. It is, however, characteristic of a number of disputes over the tenability of a realistic interpretation that the critic of realism maintains a reductive thesis, while its defender rejects not only that, but any conceivable, reductive thesis, and so propounds an irreducibility thesis. The term 'naïve realism' is well known from philosophical literature, although it is sometimes difficult to grasp what is intended by it. For the present, let us say that *naïve realism* concerning statements of a given class consists in the combination of a realistic interpretation of them with an irreducibility thesis; how far this agrees with the accepted use of the term we shall enquire later.

Now an interesting distinction between reductive theses can be drawn by asking whether subjunctive conditionals are admitted as belonging to the reductive class. In some cases, the plausibility of the reductive thesis depends heavily upon their admission. Notoriously, for instance, the first step in the phenomenalist translation of material-object statements into sense-data statements was supposed, in most cases, to consist in the formation of a subjunctive conditional the antecedent of which would state the condition for a suitable observation to be made and the consequent of which would state the making of a positive observation: the celebrated prototype was the rendering of 'There is a table in the next room' by 'If anyone were to go into the next room (and switch on the light), he would see a table'. Of course, this was only a first step, since at this stage both antecedent and consequent are expressed in material-object vocabulary: they would then be subjected to further transformations, in order to obtain equivalents couched solely in sense-datum vocabulary; but, in the process, the subjunctive conditional form would persist. The need for the admission of the subjunctive conditional form in statements of the reductive class arose from the fact that the phenomenalists were not prepared to be sufficiently tough-minded as to declare only those material-object statements true which have actually been observed to be true. A similar inclusion of subjunctive conditionals among the statements of the reductive class is very characteristic of a number of reductive theses. A behaviourist wants to assert an intrinsic connection between the concept of knowledge or of expectation and that of its manifestation, between the concept of belief and that of its avowal, between that of intention or of emotion and its expression. But he hardly wants to deny that a man may have knowledge which he does not display, an expectation that he never manifests, and so forth: so he is disposed to say that 'X expects E to happen' is true provided that X would show surprise if he were to discover that E had not occurred, that to ascribe an intention to someone is to say that he would act in accordance with it were the occasion to arise, and the like. Other reductive theses, on the other hand, make no appeal to subjunctive conditionals. One who takes a constructivist view of mathematical statements does not hold that such a statement is true provided that there *would be* a proof of it under favourable conditions; he is content to say that it is true only if there actually *is* such a proof. Even in the mathematical case, however, there are contexts in which it is natural to appeal to subjunctive con-

ditionals. A constructivist may be more or less radical: he may be content, like the intuitionists, to appeal to procedures that could in principle be effectively carried out, or he may, like the strict finitists, rely only on procedures that can in practice be carried out. A constructivist of the less radical variety would accept a computation procedure that would in principle effectively decide the application of some predicate to any natural number as imposing a determinate meaning on that predicate, of such a kind as to make it true or false of every natural number: for instance, by factorization we can decide whether or not a number is prime, or is square-free. A radical constructivist will object that, for sufficiently large numbers, we could not in fact decide the application of the predicate by that means: the less radical one may then be tempted to reply that, nevertheless, the predicate is true of such a number provided that, if we *were* to apply the decision procedure, we *should* obtain an affirmative result. A case in which an appeal to subjunctive conditionals is completely out of the question is that of a reductive thesis concerning statements about the past. For an anti-realist about the past, a past-tense statement can be true only if there is present evidence for its truth. He may well allow that it may be true, given such evidence, even if we are unaware of that evidence: but there is no plausible but non-trivial thesis to the effect that it is true just in case, under such-and-such conditions, there *would be* present evidence for its truth.

If subjunctive conditionals are excluded from the reductive class, it will usually be fairly obvious whether or not the reductive thesis entails a rejection of bivalence for statements of the given class. When subjunctive conditionals are admitted to the reductive class, however, it is a great deal more delicate to decide whether, given the reductive thesis, bivalence will fail: it depends on how many subjunctive conditionals are considered as holding good. This problem was particularly acute for the phenomenalist. For the naïve realist, or for any realist who rejected the phenomenalist reduction, any significant statement about the physical universe, for example, 'There are living organisms on some planet in the Andromeda galaxy', must be determinately true or false, at least within the limits imposed by the vagueness of some of the terms occurring in it. From the truth of such a statement, the truth of a subjunctive conditional concerning the results of observation under suitable conditions, in our case, 'If we were to travel to the

Andromeda galaxy and inspect all the planets in it, we should observe at least one on which there were living organisms', would follow; from its falsity, the truth of the opposite subjunctive conditional would follow, where the opposite of any conditional is that conditional having the same antecedent and the contradictory consequent. The realist therefore had good ground for holding that, of any pair of such opposite subjunctive conditionals, one must be true and the other false. The phenomenalist, however, was in a different position. For him, the affirmative subjunctive conditional was not a *consequence* of the material-object statement, but equivalent to it in meaning: it represented the first step in the translation of that statement. The phenomenalist could not, therefore, argue, as the realist could, that, *because* the material-object statement was either true or false, so one or other of the pair of opposite subjunctive conditionals must be true. For him, a decision on whether the material-object statement had to be either true or false must depend upon a prior decision as to whether it was necessary that one or other of the two subjunctive conditionals must be true.

Now one who adopted a realistic interpretation of material-object statements could well afford to hold a reductive thesis concerning subjunctive conditionals. On such a view, for any subjunctive conditional, we can always give an informative answer, even if a rather complicated one, to the question in virtue of what it is true, if it is true: such an answer would allude to general laws and, perhaps, to tendencies, intentions, and the like. If the phenomenalist likewise accepted a reductive thesis concerning subjunctive conditionals, he would be more or less forced to grant that material-object statements, understood in his way, did not satisfy the principle of bivalence. For the realist, an essential ingredient in an informative answer to the question what renders the subjunctive condition, 'If we were to inspect the planets in the Andromeda galaxy, we should observe one on which there were living organisms', true, if it is true, would be 'There being living organisms on some planet in the Andromeda galaxy'. But, for the phenomenalist, this could not be part of an *informative* answer to that question, since, for him, it is simply to reiterate the subjunctive conditional in a disguised form: the phenomenalist had, as it were, a much more slender basis of categorical truths on which to support those subjunctive conditionals which he could consider true. For the phenomenalist who accepted a reductive thesis concerning subjunctive conditionals, a subjunctive conditional could not be true in virtue of the truth of some material-object statement whose truth we might never know: it could be true only in virtue of some actual reports of observation, expressible as sense-datum statements, together with laws stating observed or at least observable regularities connecting our observations. On such a basis, it would be quite implausible that, for any material-object statement, either the subjunctive conditional which represented the first step in its translation, or the opposite one, would have to be true: and so the consequence would be a denial of the principle of bivalence for material-object statements, and, therefore, a thoroughgoing repudiation of realism.

What is surprising is that, in the actual historical development, very few phenomenalists appear to have taken that position. Rather, they appear to have rejected any reductive thesis concerning subjunctive conditionals, while continuing to maintain a reductionist view of material-object statements. To reject a reductive thesis concerning a certain class of statements does not, of itself, afford any ground for accepting the principle of bivalence as applied to them: it merely disposes of one argument to show that bivalence fails. Independently of any reductive thesis concerning subjunctive conditionals, for example, it would be hard to maintain that they satisfy the principle of bivalence, if the falsity of a subjunctive conditional be equated with the truth of the opposite conditional. Few could be found to hold that such a subjunctive conditional as 'If the next Pope to be elected were an Englishman, he would take the name Adrian' must, in this sense, be determinately be true or false, that is, that either it or its opposite must be true. It could, indeed, be argued that this is not the natural way to understand the word 'false' as applied to subjunctive conditionals, that it should, instead, be so taken that the falsity of the foregoing subjunctive conditional would involve the truth only of 'If the next Pope to be elected were an Englishman, he would not necessarily take the name Adrian', rather than that of the opposite conditional 'If the next Pope to be elected were an Englishman, he would not take the name Adrian'. On this latter way of understanding the notion of the falsity of a subjunctive conditional, the opinion that subjunctive conditionals are determinately either true or false would be much more widespread. Let us speak of *strong* bivalence for subjunctive conditionals when the falsity of a conditional is equated with the truth of its opposite, and of *weak* bivalence when its falsity is equated with the truth of the statement resulting from inserting 'not necessarily' in the consequent. The appropriate application of 'false' to subjunctive conditionals is not, however, to the present point. If we call subjunctive conditionals with 'might', 'would perhaps', or 'would not necessarily' in their consequents *permissive* conditionals, and those with plain 'would' or 'would not' in their consequents *straightforward* conditionals, it is plain that the first step in the phenomenalist translation of a material-object statement will always yield a straightforward, not a permissive, subjunctive conditional; this will normally be the case under any reductionist thesis admitting subjunctive conditionals in the reductive class. In particular, the phenomenalist translation of the negation of a material-object statement A will be the opposite subjunctive conditional to that which is the translation of A. Hence, for the phenomenalist, the question whether the principle of bivalence holds for material-object statements is the question whether strong bivalence holds for subjunctive conditionals of the kind which serve as their translations into the sense-datum language: it makes no difference whether strong bivalence is or is not what 'bivalence' should be taken to mean when applied to subjunctive conditionals.

Now it is impossible to hold that subjunctive conditionals satisfy the principle of strong bivalence quite generally. The reason is that there are obvious cases in which it is neither true to say that, if it had been the case that A, then it would have been the case that B, nor true to say that, if it had been the case that A, then it would not have been the case that B. A very wide class of such cases is provided by those in which an additional condition is required to determine the consequent: that is, where, for some additional statement C, we can truly say (1) that, if it had been the case that A, it might or might not also have been the case that C, (2) that, if it had been the case that A and that C, then it would have been the case that B, and (3) that, if it had been the case that A but not C, then it would not have been the case that B. Now, since subjunctive conditionals cannot be held to be generally subject to strong bivalence, the most that can be claimed is that strong bivalence holds for some restricted range of subjunctive conditionals. The most characteristic reason for supposing this is the belief that there is some underlying class of categorical statements such that, for any subjunctive conditional in the given range, there is some categorical statement in the underlying class that

would support it, and that these categorical statements are subject to bivalence. For instance, we may have a test T for the possession of some property P by a body. The statement 'The body x possesses the property P' then gives support to the subjunctive conditional 'If x were to be subjected to the test T, it would pass that test'. If statements ascribing the property P to a body are realistically interpreted, they will be regarded as subject to bivalence: at any given time, any particular body either has the property P or does not have it. It will then follow that, for any subjunctive conditional of the form 'If x were to be (have been) subjected to the test T, it would pass (have passed) it', either it or the opposite conditional must be true. This assurance reflects the fact that a realistic interpretation has been adopted for statements of the form 'x has property P': we could say that the belief that subjunctive conditionals of this form satisfy strong bivalence simply expresses acceptance of a realistic view of statements ascribing the property P to a body.

The phenomenalists appear, however, not merely to have rejected a reductive thesis for subjunctive conditionals, but, further, to have retained the belief, natural for anyone taking a realistic view of material-object statements, that strong bivalence holds good for the subjunctive conditionals resulting from the phenomenalist translation. This belief on the part of the phenomenalist could not have the same basis as the corresponding belief held by a realist. For the phenomenalist, such a subjunctive conditional would not *rest on* the corresponding material-object statement; that is, it would not be true in virtue of the truth of that statement, together with the laws of nature, since it would be a translation of it. In so far as the phenomenalist rejected a reductive thesis for subjunctive conditionals, they need not rest on anything at all: there need be no non-trivial answer to the question in virtue of what such a statement was true.

This extraordinary situation reveals how close the classical phenomenalist actually was to his opponent, the realist. In terms of the analysis of the concept of realism I am here putting forward, a phenomenalist of this kind diverged from a realistic view of material-object statements neither in repudiating the principle of bivalence as applied to them nor in rejecting a truth-conditional account of their meanings. Indeed, in only one respect could he be said to diverge from realism, as I have analysed it, namely if he denied that the notion of reference, as applied to names of material objects, played any role in the account of how a statement containing such names was to be determined as true or as false. Whether he could be said to deny this would depend upon the details of his translation into the sense-datum language, details which were, notoriously, never forthcoming: specifically, on whether, in the process of translation, a name for a material object would be replaced by a term for some complex of sense-data, or whether it would be dissolved altogether so that no corresponding term remained in the sense-datum sentence. It thus becomes highly dubious whether a classical phenomenalist can properly be described as having held an anti-realist view at all. His principal disagreement with those who called themselves realists lay in his acceptance of a reductionist thesis concerning material-object statements; and, as we have seen, neither a reductive nor even a reductionist thesis is sufficient for a rejection of realism. It would be better to say that the distinction between those who called themselves realists and those who called themselves phenomenalists was that the former were naïve realists, at least as I earlier explained the term 'naïve realism', while the latter were sophisticated realists, concerning material objects.

An outcome which involves that a philosophical view like phenomenalism that would ordinarily be taken as a prototype of anti-realism is better regarded as a sophisticated version of realism may seem to be a *reductio ad absurdum* of my proposed analysis of the concept of realism; but I do not think so. The disposition to classify phenomenalism as an outstanding example of anti-realism is partly to be explained as due to a failure to distinguish clearly between anti-realism, properly so called, and advocacy of a reductive thesis. But it is not wholly due to that confusion. It springs also from a perception of the irrationality of the classical phenomenalist's position: he had neither ground nor motive for accepting strong bivalence for the subjunctive conditionals resulting from his translation of material-object statements. We can reasonably regard his having done so as due to a lingering attachment to a realistic view of material-object statements; and, so regarded, he was not genuinely an anti-realist. But we can equally view him as having failed to pursue his ideas to their natural conclusion. Given his reductionist thesis about material-object statements, the natural line for him to have taken was to accept a reductive thesis for subjunctive conditionals generally, and, on that very ground, to have rejected strong bivalence for the subjunctive conditionals resulting from his

translation; he would then have had to reject the principle of bivalence for material-object statements. Had he taken such a position, he would, on the present analysis of the concept of realism, have been an anti-realist of a fairly thoroughgoing kind; and it was surely an imperfect perception that this was the natural consequence of his principal contention that made it seem so obviously correct to classify the phenomenalist as an opponent of realism.

For all that, philosophers have frequently failed to distingush between a reductive thesis and the repudiation of a truth-conditional meaning-theory of the standard kind; it is the latter which is constitutive of anti-realism. Not only is a reductive thesis by itself insufficient for a rejection of realism: it is also unnecessary. Realism requires us to hold both that, for statements of the given class, we have a notion of truth under which each statement is determinately either true or false, and also that an understanding of those statements consists in a knowledge of the conditions under which they are true. Either proposition may be denied without appeal to a reductive thesis. To speak more exactly, almost any anti-realist doctrine seems to lend itself to expression by means of a reductive thesis: but, in some cases, this thesis proves to be only a loose and inessential formulation of the doctrine, while in others it plays an essential role.

To illustrate this, let us examine in more detail the case of neutralism with regard to the future. The neutralist does not believe that there is any definite future course of events which renders every statement in the future tense determinately either true or false. There is a wide variety of different forms of neutralism; but it is common to a great many of them that, if a future-tense statement is (now) true, then it can be so only in virtue of something that lies in the present. This is, as it stands, a reductive thesis; but it is only a very rare type of neutralist who will combine this thesis with the view that it is solely by grasping how a future-tense statement is determined as having present truth that we attain an understanding of such statements. A neutralist of this type (an example of which is provided by Peter Geach) in effect holds that the only intelligible use we have for the future tense is that in which it expresses present tendencies; there is therefore no difficulty whatever for him in allowing that something was going to happen, but is now no longer going to happen. There can be no disputing that we do have such a use of the future tense, exemplified by a newspaper announcement reading 'The marriage arranged between X and Y will not now take place'; a Geachian neutralist differs from everyone else in maintaining that it is the *only* coherent use of the future tense that we have. He is thus in some difficulty how to explain the use of the future tense to make bets; it is not apparent why, on his view, a bet about what will happen in two years' time should not be settled immediately.

If the present truth or falsity of a future-tense statement depends only on what lies in the present, the possibility is open that such a statement may be true at one time but not at another; or, to speak more precisely, it is possible that some future-tense statement, made at some time, is rightly assessed at that time as not being true then, although, when made at another time, is then rightly assessed as being true at *that* time. If a sentence contains only an indexical temporal indicator, such as 'a week from today', and the identity of the statement made by means of it is taken as fixed by the identity of the sentence used, then, of course, this possibility will be admitted by everyone, whatever his metaphysical view of the future; but a neutralist admits the possibility even for a statement made by means of a sentence containing a non-indexical temporal indicator like 'in the year 2001'. Most neutralists will, however, wish to place some restriction upon such possibilities; and, if any restriction is imposed, and if an awareness of that restriction is essential to an understanding of the future tense, it ceases to hold good that an understanding of future-tense statements consists solely in a knowledge of what will confer on them present truth. Typically, a neutralist will hold that, once a future-tense statement is true, it cannot at any later time cease to be true. Such a neutralist will regard a future-tense statement as acquiring truth only at a time at which there is something more than a mere *tendency* for things to go that way, something that confers a certain kind of physical necessity upon the statement. (Necessity of this kind is thought of as possessed by all true present-tense and past-tense statements, but only by some future-tense ones, those, namely, which follow from some true present-tense statements together with some general laws of nature.) On his conception, a future-tense statement that is not at present either true or false may later become true, either at the time to which it refers or at some intervening time; but, unlike a Geachian neutralist, he does not allow that a future-tense statement may be true now, but later cease to be true or even become false. For such a

neutralist, then, in order to understand statements in the future tense, one must indeed know the sort of thing that can confer on them present truth, namely physical necessity; but one must know more besides. One must also know that, if a future-tense statement is now true, it is *necessarily* true, in the relevant sense of 'necessarily'; that is, one must know the connection between what may render such a statement true now and what may render it true at a later time, and, in particular, at the time to which it refers; and one must know that, by the time to which it refers, it will have become determinately either true or false. (We are here considering only statements whose reference is to a definite future time.) An admission by a speaker of the possibility that a future-tense statement, although now true, might later cease to be true would serve, on this view, to show that he did not fully understand the central use of the future tense, even if he rightly judged of the present truth or otherwise of any such statement. From this it follows that, for such a neutralist, an understanding of future-tense statements does not consist solely in knowing what is required to confer on them present truth; one must also know the connection between their truth at one time and their truth at a later time.

A neutralist of this kind diverges from a realistic view of statements about the future not only, and not principally, because he rejects the principle of bivalence for them, but because he holds that, for an understanding of them, we need to appeal, not to the notion of a statement's simply being true, but to that of its being true at one or another time. He is a believer in variable truth-value in a sense stronger than that in which this can be said of one who accepts that there is a definite future course of events, but employs a tense logic. A tense logic differs from a representation of temporal indicators as arguments for predicates in that the temporal indicators, figuring as sentential operators in the tense logic, can be indefinitely iterated. This requires that a sentence – that to which such an operator can be applied – be regarded, not as being simply true or false, but as being true at certain times and false at others, the atomic sentences thus being taken as present-tensed. The metaphysical implications of this device for handling temporal reference, considered in itself, are, however, minimal. It appears as no more than a recognition of the indexical character of some temporal indicators, which makes iteration significant in the way that compound tenses like the future perfect and pluperfect are significant; when the temporal reference is non-indexical, the tense logic may admit the sentence to be either true at all times or false at all times, or, in other words, simply true or simply false. A neutralist of the kind we are considering may also be said to believe in variable truth-value in a sense more serious than that in which a Geachian neutralist does so. A Geachian neutralist allows that a sentence in the future tense, with a non-indexical temporal indicator, may be used at one time to say something true and at another time to say something false; but, just because, on his view, there is no constraint on the different truth-values the sentence may have at different times, there is no serious sense in which he is taking it to make the same statement on the different occasions of utterance.

A neutralist of our kind can be said to hold a reductive thesis; but it is quite wrong to compare him with an anti-realist who derives from a reductive thesis the failure of bivalence, since the neutralist does not regard the meanings of future-tense statements as given by the conditions under which they are (now) true. A better representation of the theory of meaning he favours for future-tense statements is a variant on a semantic theory in terms of possible worlds. A 'world' here consists of the actual present state and past history of the world, together with some complete possible future history of it, where the notion of possibility is correlative to that of necessity as employed by the neutralist: a future event is possible if it does not follow from the present state of the world, taken together with the laws of nature, that it will not occur. The central notion for such a semantic theory is not that of a statement's being true absolutely, but of its being true in a 'world'. The set of possible 'worlds' continually diminishes with the passage of time; that is to say, the various 'worlds' may be regarded as forming paths in a (mathematical) tree, the nodes of the tree – the points at which the paths diverge – corresponding to a state of a 'world' at a particular time, each state being common to many 'worlds'. A statement may therefore be said to be true in a 'world' W at a particular time t just in case it is true in every 'world' V such that the state of V at t is the same as the state of W at t. It is the basic contention of the neutralist that no one 'world' is the actual world; there is no *actual* future course of events. But, at any time, we may pick out an actual state as being the state-of-the-world at that time: hence, at any time, we may characterize as assertable those statements which are true at that time in any 'world' of which the actual state is a state. When the meaning-theory of our neutralist is represented in such a manner, no reductive thesis can be attributed to him at all: he cannot even formulate a reductive thesis, since he admits no notion of absolute truth, but only the notions of being true in a 'world', being true in a 'world' at a time, and being actually true at present. He cannot, therefore, strictly speaking, be said to reject the principle of bivalence, which requires the notions of absolute truth and falsity for its formulation; we can, indeed, loosely describe him as rejecting it, on the ground that, while he holds each statement to be either true or false in each 'world', he denies that, for each particular time, each statement is either true in a given 'world' at that time or false in that 'world' at that time, and hence, in particular, that each statement is actually either true or false at present. His rejection of realism is more accurately described as consisting in a repudiation of two-valued semantics that results from his having discarded altogether the notion of a statement's being absolutely true.

One form which an anti-realistic view may take is, thus, the replacement of the notion of absolute truth-value by a notion of relativized truth-values. The resultant semantic theory may still be objectivist, in that the (relativized) truth-value of a statement need not depend on our knowledge of it or our capacity to know it: in the foregoing example, there may be many statements that are actually now true even though we do not know that they are and perhaps can never know. Another type of anti-realism, perhaps the most interesting, consists in rejecting an objectivist semantics, even though it may still be allowed that to understand a statement is to know the condition for it to be true. The notion of truth admitted in such a meaning-theory will be one closely linked to our recognition of truth. Now this tendency is already evident in many reductive theses that afford a ground for rejecting bivalence. The reductive thesis is often arrived at by considering on what basis we are accustomed to assert a statement of the given class, and then declaring that such a statement can be true only if there is such a basis for an assertion of it. Thus, we assert subjunctive conditionals on the basis of general laws; we make assertions about the past on the basis of memories, records, and other present traces; we make psychological statements on the basis of behaviour; and we make statements about the physical world on the basis of observation. The thought underlying the reductive thesis is that, since our use of statements of the given class is governed by a knowledge of the kind of basis on which they may be asserted, a grasp of their meaning could not involve a notion of truth as attaching to them independently of such a basis. But, in most of these cases, the reductive thesis, while leading to a rejection of bivalence, does not call in question an objectivist theory of meaning; a statement of the given class may still be considered as determinately either true or not true. The mere existence of a basis for asserting a particular statement, the existence of something such that, if we knew it, we should take ourselves as entitled to assert that statement, is sufficient for its truth; it is not required that we should know that there is such a basis, or even be in a position to discover the fact. If, then, statements of the reductive class – statements to the effect that there is a basis for assertion – are themselves realistically interpreted, it will follow that each statement of the given class will be determinately either true or not true.

Sometimes, however, it does not work in this way. Consider, once again, the case of mathematical statements. A Platonist will admit that, for a given statement, there may be neither a proof nor a disproof of it to be found; but there is no intelligible anti-realist notion of truth for mathematical statements under which a statement is true only if there is a proof of it, but may be true because such a proof exists, even though we do not know it, shall never know it, and have no effective means of discovering it. The reason is evident: we can introduce such a notion only by appeal to some Platonistic conception of proofs as existing independently of our knowledge, that is, as abstract objects not brought into being by our thought. But, if we admit such a conception of proofs, we can have no objection to a parallel conception of mathematical objects such as natural numbers, real numbers, metric spaces, etc.; and then we shall have no motivation for abandoning a realistic, that is, Platonist, interpretation of mathematical statements in the first place.

If we wish to say that a mathematical statement can be true only if there exists a proof of it, we have, therefore, only two choices. We can interpret 'exists' as meaning concrete existence, our actual possession of a proof; in this case 'is true' becomes a tensed predicate of mathematical statements, a statement being able to change from not being true to being true, although not conversely. Each statement is then either true or not true at any given time, although it may be neither true nor false, where its falsity involves the existence of a disproof; but there will be no question of its being objectively true, although we (collectively) are unaware of its truth. Alternatively, we may construe 'exists' and therefore 'is true', as tenseless. We shall, in this case, have to interpret 'exists' constructively; we can then rule out the possibility of a statement's being neither true nor false, since its not being true would be tantamount to its being false, but we cannot assert, in advance of a proof or disproof of a statement, or an effective method of finding one, that it is either true or false. Because, on this second interpretation, 'exists' is understood constructively, we shall still be unable to conceive of a statement as being true although we shall never know it to be true, although we can suppose true a statement as yet unproved.

Instead of allowing ourselves to be entangled in these difficulties, it seems better to represent a constructivist theory of meaning for mathematical statements as dispensing with the notion of truth altogether. This notion is replaced, as the central concept of the meaning-theory, by that of something's being a proof of a statement, as explained earlier in connection with Heyting's semantics for intuitionistic mathematics in terms of constructions. In the present context, what is important about such a shift is that it no longer appears that a first step towards this anti-realistic interpretation of mathematical statements consisted in the adoption of a reductive thesis: just as with the neutralist, no reductive thesis can even be formulated, since the notion of truth is unavailable. The difference is that the neutralist meaning-theory remained objectivist in the modified sense that there may be something, of which we are not aware, which would justify the assertion of some future-tense statement if we were aware of it; whereas the only thing which will justify the assertion of a mathematical statement is the existence of a proof, and, when 'existence' is not interpreted Platonistically, this is something of which we cannot be unaware.

The possibility of stating the anti-realist view of mathematics without formulating a reductive thesis at all is closely connected with there being an objection, of the second of the types we listed, to a proposal to translate mathematical statements into statements about proofs. We listed three generic types of objection to reductionism: one of the second type rested on the claim that statements of the reductive class are not intelligible antecedently to those of the given class; for example, that statements about mathematical proofs cannot be

Michael Dummett

understood independently of the statements proved. A case in which this objection does not appear to arise is that of a reductive thesis about psychological statements, the reductive class consisting of statements about behaviour. Here it seems natural to say that statements reporting someone's behaviour can be understood independently of statements ascribing to him a mental state or psychological character: we can even state the quality of an action, as brave, generous, prudent, or the like, without presuming an understanding of an ascription of the corresponding character-trait to an individual. An actual theory of meaning for psychological statements, based on the reductive thesis, will require a detailed scheme for assigning, to each psychological statement, a range of statements about behaviour, or of sets of such statements, the truth of any one of which would establish the truth of the psychological statement; this would hold good even if the thesis did not amount to a full-fledged reductionism, so that an actual translation was not in question. Such a scheme might be very complicated and very hard to construct; it would remain that, in so far as our interest lay in explaining psychological statements, we could, in constructing it, take a theory of meaning for statements about behaviour as already given, just because they were assumed to be intelligible in advance of the psychological statements.

When, as in the mathematical case, the meanings of statements of the reductive class cannot be taken as given in advance of those of the given class, the problem of giving a meaning-theory for the latter is quite different. We have, in such a case, simultaneously to devise theories of meaning for statements of the reductive class and for those of the given class. For instance, we have, for each mathematical statement A, to characterize what, in general, is to count as a proof of A: this will obviously depend, in some systematic manner, on the composition of the statement A, on its internal structure. What we have to do, therefore, is first to lay down, for each atomic statement, what is to count as a proof of it, and then to give, by means of a stipulation relating to each mode of sentence-composition – the use of the various sentential operators and of each type of quantifier – an inductive characterization of what is to count as a proof of a complex statement. For each mode of sentence-composition, we shall assume it known what is to count as a proof of the immediate constituents of a sentence so formed (in the case of a quantified sentence, of its instances); and we shall, in terms

of that, state what is to count as a proof of such a sentence. A simple example would be the stipulation that a proof of an existential statement $\exists x A$ (x) is to be a proof of some statement of the form A (t), where t is a term, together with a proof that t stands for some element of the domain of the variable x.

We shall, by this procedure, have gone a long way towards explaining the meanings, not only of statements of the reductive class, but of those of the given class itself. In the general case, we shall have explained what it means to say that something is a ground for asserting an arbitrary statement of the given class. If the reductive thesis is to the effect that a statement of the given class is true if and only if there exists a ground for asserting it, and if a statement that there exists such a ground is regarded as determinately true or false, or at any rate as capable of being true independently of our knowledge, what remains will be to explain the meaning, that is, the truth-conditions, of such an existential statement: when this has been done, we shall have explained simultaneously the meanings of statements of the reductive class and of the given class. In the mathematical case, however, this final step is redundant, because we are not considering a proof as something that may exist independently of our having constructed it or having an effective method of constructing it. Hence, once we have laid down, for an arbitrary mathematical statement, what is to count as a proof of it, we have, from the constructivist standpoint, thereby determined the meanings of all mathematical statements. Constructively regarded, the meaning of such a statement is given as soon as we know when we are entitled to assert it. We shall be entitled to assert it just in case we possess a proof of it; and, for each statement, it has been inductively stipulated what is to count as such a proof. It is for this reason that, in a case of this kind, the reductive thesis falls away as irrelevant. There are not, in a case like this, two separate tasks, to explain the meanings of statements of the reductive class and to explain, in terms of them, the meanings of statements of the given class. There is only one task, to explain simultaneously the meanings of statements of both kinds; and, in executing this task, we do not need to appeal to or to introduce any notion of truth for statements of the given class – in the example, for mathematical statements – considered as attaching to them independently of our being aware of grounds for asserting them.

The constructivist's view of mathematical statements can be formulated by enunciating, as a first step in his argument, a reductive thesis concerning them, and it is quite natural to express it in this way. But what makes it natural is the analogy with anti-realist views of other classes of statements; and this analogy we have seen to be in part misleading. What makes it misleading is that we do not end up with any objectivist notion of truth for mathematical statements; for that very reason, the reductive thesis is not an essential ingredient of the constructivist view. It follows that, just as a reductive thesis need not lead to an anti-realistic interpretation of statements of the given class, so an anti-realist view need not incorporate any reductive thesis. An anti-realist view can be arrived at by means of an argument intended to show directly, without the mediation of a reductive thesis, that, for statements of the given class, we possess no legitimate objectivist notion of truth, no notion of truth transcending our capacity to recognize such statements as true, and, *a fortiori*, no notion of truth subject to the principle of bivalence. It must be admitted that, save in relation to mathematics, an anti-realist view resting on a non-objectivist semantics has seldom been formulated; but that may be largely because the distinction between the different possible forms that a rejection of realism may take was unclear to those who were disposed to reject it.

We can at least conceive of a version of anti-realism of this kind for statements about physical reality, one that does not rest upon any reductive thesis in the sense in which a constructivist interpretation of mathematical statements does not really rest upon a reductive thesis. Even if such a view has never been adopted, even if no one ever does adopt it, it will remain of philosophical interest to consider how it might be rebutted, just as philosophers concern themselves with the refutation of solipsism or other extreme sceptical opinions. Phenomenalism embodied a reductionist thesis, and it was therefore integral to it to maintain that sense-datum statements could be understood antecedently to the material-object statements that were to be translated into them. It was, indeed, this ingredient of phenomenalism that was subject to the heaviest criticisms, criticisms that eventually brought about its downfall. But an anti-realism about the physical world which did not rest upon a reductive thesis would adopt just the opposite view: there would be no reductive class of statements intelligible independently of material-object statements. Instead, the claim would be that a theory of meaning for statements about physical reality would have to take, as its central notion, not

that of the truth of such a statement, but that of conclusive ground for asserting it. The meaning of such a statement would have to be given by specifying, in accordance with its composition, what was to count as such a ground. Such a specification would have to relate to our faculties of observation; but, since not every statement about physical reality is capable of serving as a report of observation, it would have to relate also to those means of establishing such statements as true which involve inference, either deductive or inductive. Very likely, since we do not often expect to attain certainty about the truth of statements concerning the physical world, it would be necessary to consider the meanings of such statements as given, not in terms only of what counted as a *conclusive* ground for asserting them, but in terms of a ground of the strongest attainable kind: given such a ground for asserting a given statement, we can rule out the possibility that we shall subsequently be presented with stronger contrary grounds, but cannot rule out the possibility that we shall meet with contrary grounds of equal strength. Or perhaps we might have to invoke some weaker notion yet. It is not to my purpose here to go into the difficulties which would attend the construction of a theory of meaning of this kind. My intention is only to indicate the possibility of such a position, which represents a form of anti-realism not vulnerable to many of the objections successfully brought against phenomenalism. In the present context, an important feature of it is that, since, unlike mathematical statements, statements about physical reality have grounds of so various a kind that we have no single word for them corresponding to 'mathematical proof', it would be highly unnatural to express an anti-realist view of this kind by means of a reductive thesis. The most important point is that, natural or unnatural, such a way of expressing it would be to a high degree misleading.

We saw that there are two genera of realists, those that accept an irreducibility thesis for statements of the given class, whom we termed *naïve realists*, and those that propound some reductive thesis for them, whom we termed *sophisticated realists*. In just the same way, there are two principal genera of anti-realists, though many species within each genus. One genus consists of those who arrive at their anti-realist position via some reductive thesis, which constitutes an indispensable ingredient of their theory of meaning for statements of the given class. Such anti-realists we may term *reductive anti-realists*; examples are phenomenalists and behaviourists. The other genus consists of those whose anti-realist view does not rest upon any reductive thesis; these we might term *outright anti-realists*. Various as they are, there belong to this genus most neutralists about the future, mathematical intuitionists, and adherents of Wittgenstein's account of ascriptions of inner sensations. By and large, their views tend to be more interesting than those of reductive anti-realists.

I have taken realism as requiring acceptance, in all its details, of a classical two-valued semantics and of a truth-conditional theory of meaning based on that semantics. This might be objected to, on two counts. It might be said, first, that what is essential to realism is that the meaning of a sentence be regarded as given in terms of what has to hold for it to be true, absolutely and timelessly, where the notion of truth is understood in an objectivist way: but that the mechanism whereby the condition for the truth of a sentence is determined in accordance with its composition is, in some respects at least, metaphysically irrelevant. Granted that, if we are to have a realistic interpretation, this mechanism must involve the notion of reference, there is no necessity that the sentential operators be truth-functional in the sense of being definable by two-valued truth-tables. There is a weaker and a stronger sense in which someone may be said to know the meaning of a sentence. In the weaker sense, all that is required is that he know its content when used as a complete utterance, for instance that he grasp the significance of an assertion made by uttering just that sentence. If the meaning of the sentence is to be explained in truth-conditional terms, then, in order to know its meaning in this weaker sense, it is sufficient that someone should know no more than under what conditions it is true and under what conditions it is not true. In the stronger sense, however, a speaker may be said to know the meaning of a sentence only when he also knows the contribution which that sentence makes to the meaning of a more complex sentence of which it is a constituent, that is, the contribution that it makes to determining the condition for the more complex sentence to be true. It does not, however, violate the general principle of a truth-conditional meaning-theory that the knowledge, in the weaker sense, of the meaning of a sentence should not suffice for the knowledge of its meaning in the stronger sense. There is no reason why a subsentence of a complex sentence should contribute to determining the condition for the truth of the complex sentence only via the condition for the subsentence to be true or not to be true: it may well contribute in some more complicated way. The truth or otherwise of the complex sentence may depend, not just on whether or not the subsentence is true, but on whether it fails to be true for a reason of one kind or for a reason of another kind. When this is so, we shall need a many-valued semantics to explain the sentential operators or other devices for forming complex sentences: the different undesignated values will represent different ways in which a sentence may fail to be true; if there are also distinct designated values, they will represent different ways in which a sentence may succeed in being true. Whether or not a complex sentence is true will then depend, not just on whether its constituents are true or not, that is, on whether they have designated or undesignated values, but on the different ways in which they succeed in being or fail to be true, in other words, on the specific values that they have. It will remain that, to know the meaning of any sentence in the weaker sense, that is, to grasp its content when it stands on its own, it is necessary to know only the condition for it to have some designated value, the condition, namely, for it to be true; if we want to know the meaning of the sentence only in this weaker sense, we shall not need to know the conditions for it to have specific undesignated values or specific designated ones. Now our objector's claim is that, in order to have a realistic interpretation of a class of sentences, all that need be assumed is that to know the meaning of a sentence in the weaker sense, to know its content, is to know the condition for it to be true: the details of the mechanism by which this condition is determined in accordance with the way the sentence is put together out of atomic sentences are of no metaphysical importance.

The second prong of this objection is a protest against the assumption that I have hitherto made, that realism demands an unqualified assent to the principle of bivalence. A formulation of the principle invokes not only the concept of truth but also that of falsity; and, it is objected, while the concept of truth usually has a fairly natural application to the statements of any given class, that of falsity depends for its application on much more *ad hoc* conventions. In most cases that I have here discussed, in fact in all save that of subjunctive conditionals, I equated the falsity of a statement with the truth of its negation, that is, of what looks at first sight like its negation. The reductive thesis then led to the conclusion that not every statement need be either true or false. But, the objector says, this same conclusion could have been expressed less dramatically by saying that what looked like the negation was not the real negation; and, if we so expressed it, we should have no reason for claiming any departure from realism. Since whether or not someone is a realist cannot depend on the partly arbitrary question how he chooses to apply the word 'false', it follows that not every repudiation of the principle of bivalence is incompatible with realism: we have to distinguish those grounds for rejecting bivalence which are compatible with realism from those which are genuinely incompatible with it. One type of violation of bivalence that would be perfectly compatible with realism would occur if we adopted a many-valued semantics, of the kind which the first part of the objection maintained to be consistent with realism, but gave the name 'falsity' to just one out of several undesignated values. A motive for doing so might be to enable us to identify some unary sentential operator as a negation operator, one that converted every true sentence into a false one and every false sentence into a true one. In any case, the objector may add, it is foolish to attach much importance, when treating of sentences of natural language, to the principle that a sentence is false just in case its negation is true, or, at least, to treat it as a guide to when a sentence should be called 'false'. The reason is that we do not, in natural language, have a sentential negation operator; we cannot, therefore, be guided mechanically by syntactic form in deciding what is the negation of any sentence, but have to reflect. The principle connecting falsity and negation can serve only to guide us what to take the negation of some sentence to be, once we have already decided when to call it 'false': it cannot serve the converse purpose.

This two-pronged objection expresses opinions that I once held. I used to think that one could classify semantic theories involving departures from the principle of bivalence into those which did and those which did not entail a rejection of realism. I no longer think that this can be done by appeal just to the form of the semantic theory: *any* modification of the principle of bivalence, or, more generally, of the standard two-valued semantics, involves potentially a rejection of some realistic view. Anti-realism, which, as we have seen, can assume a wide variety of forms, is, as such, a negative doctrine: it is correlative to a corresponding species of realism. Where we are disposed to interpret sentences of a certain range in accordance

with a two-valued semantics, any divergent way of understanding them will appear to us an anti-realist doctrine; where we have no such inclination, the observation that some departure from the two-valued semantics is called for will not seem anti-realist in character, but will appear merely to be a comment on the underlying semantic mechanism of those sentences. There need be no difference, however, in the form of the semantic theory proposed in each case: the difference may lie solely in our having had, in the one case but not in the other, a disposition to treat those sentences at their face-value, as it were, that is, to apply to them the simplest form of semantic theory, the two-valued one. Whenever some non-classical semantics or some non-truth-conditional meaning-theory is proposed, there is a possible form of realism to which the proposal stands in opposition, which would be embodied in a truth-conditional meaning-theory based on a two-valued semantics. In some cases, this possible realistic view would lack all plausibility; in others, it may be merely out of fashion; and in others again, it may be a live alternative. It will depend on which of these states of affairs obtains whether the proposal strikes us as anti-realist in character: but the question is external to the form of meaning-theory that has been proposed.

Admittedly, we need to reflect in order to decide what is the negation of a sentence of a given form: for this reason, to equate the falsity of a sentence with the truth of its negation is not to appeal to a mere syntactic criterion, but, rather, to what we intuitively regard as the condition for the sentence to be false, since the principle that the negation of a statement is true if and only if the statement is false is what guides us in deciding what to recognize as being the negation of a given statement. But, for that very reason, an appeal to the concept of negation, as applied to sentences of natural language, is an appeal to our intuitive conception of the conditions under which they are rightly said to be false. Hence, if some reductive thesis has the consequence that some sentence need not be either true or false, when its falsity is equated with the truth of what is ordinarily taken to be its negation, that result does not merely reflect an arbitrary decision to apply the word "false" to that sentence in a particular way; rather, it undermines a realistic interpretation which we are unreflectively disposed to adopt for that and similar sentences. In any case, the fact that natural language does not possess a sentential negation operator ought not to be overstressed. Natural language does possess a regular means for negating a predicate, a means which breaks down principally in the presence of modal auxiliaries like 'must' and 'may'. Reflection is needed to decide what is the negation of a quantified sentence: but, when we have what is apparently a singular term as the grammatical subject, there is normally no difficulty in saying what would ordinarily be taken as the negation of that sentence, namely the result of negating the predicate. If we accept some reductive thesis for a class of statements that yields an objectivist semantics for those statements, we could indeed propose to use the word 'false' so that a statement was false just in case it was not true, thus saving the principle of bivalence at the cost of divorcing the concept of falsity from that of the truth of what would ordinarily be taken as the negation of the statement. Contrary to what the objector maintains, however, such a proposal would not enable us to preserve a realistic interpretation of statements of that class. If what appears to be the negation of a singular statement is declared not to be its real negation, this can be explained in either of two ways: either what was apparently a singular term is not genuinely one, and then we must abandon a semantic account which involves assigning a reference to that expression; or the operator which apparently negated the predicate does not function in an ordinary two-valued manner. In either case, although we have formally preserved the principle of bivalence, we shall have had in some way to diverge from the two-valued semantics; and we shall thus have abandoned a purely realistic interpretation of statements of the given class. We shall, in particular, have opened the way for the introduction of a 'genuine' negation operator which carries a sentence in the given class into one not in that class, i.e. one under which the given class is not closed; and it was integral to the realistic account of statements of that class to suppose it closed under negation.

The distinction between any form of objectivist semantics and a non-objectivist semantics is, indeed, the most important one: an adherent of a non-objectivist semantics could not count as a realist from any perspective, whereas an adherent of an objectivist semantics is an anti-realist only to the extent that a straightforward two-valued semantics holds any attraction. Consider someone who believes that there is no *one* intended model for set theory, so that the central notion for a semantics for set-theoretical statements is not that of simply being true, but that of being true in a model belonging to some class K; a set-theoretical statement will be absolutely true only if it is true in all models belonging to K, so that there will be some set-theoretical statements that are neither absolutely true nor absolutely false. The sentential operators and quantifiers are to be interpreted in the two-valued manner relatively to each model. Compared with the intuitionists' account of mathematical statements, a proponent of such a view is very little removed from an out-and-out Platonist; for him, each set-theoretical statement is determinately either true or false in each particular model, independently of our knowledge. There is, however, nothing to distinguish this conception formally from that of a neutralist about the future, who thinks that there is no *one* actual future course of events, but is prepared to treat the sentential operators and quantifiers occurring in a future-tense statement as to be interpreted in a two-valued manner relatively to each possible future course of events. In both cases, we shall have a classical logic for set-theoretical statements and for future-tense statements respectively, since, in each case, the semantic values which a sentence may assume form a Boolean algebra, although not the two-element one: in both cases, therefore, the law of excluded middle will hold, although not the principle of bivalence as stated in terms of absolute truth and absolute falsity. We shall certainly regard the neutralist as an anti-realist, since the conception under which every statement about the future already has a determinate truth-value exerts a strong attraction. The idea that there is some one intended model of set theory has less power; but the view proposed is, nevertheless, an anti-realist one when contrasted with a wholly realistic view of set theory, one according to which every set-theoretical statement is absolutely true or absolutely false, because, in making such statements, we have in mind some one particular abstract structure, even though we have not fully succeeded in characterizing it, and, perhaps, cannot ever do so.

Whenever we allow that the truth-condition of a complex sentence depends on more than the conditions for its constituent sentences to be true or not to be true, we create the possibility for a disagreement between a realistic and a non-realistic interpretation. We shall have a realistic interpretation whenever it is held that the mechanism whereby the truth-condition of a sentence is determined could be explained by means of the two-valued semantics, with, perhaps, some slight adjustment of the syntactic analysis of the sentence. It was already remarked that a tense logic, when not founded upon any neutralist view of the future or any anti-realist view of the past, does not involve any divergence from realism, even though it requires a non-two-valued semantics, namely a semantics in terms of relativized truth-values, of a sentence's being true or false at each particular time. This, we saw, was because the tense logic could be viewed as a variation upon a two-valued semantics for a language in which temporal indicators appeared as arguments of predicates. What makes this possible is that we should treat the temporal indicators in such a language as genuinely having reference: so the tense logic does not appear to involve any genuine departure from realism. Now, formally speaking, a semantics for a language containing modal operators appears very similar: we again employ a notion of relativized truth-values, relativized in this case to possible worlds rather than to times. When this kind of semantics was first introduced, therefore, it might have seemed natural to say that it did not involve any departure from realism either. In line with the objection we are considering, it might have been claimed that this semantics embodied a divergence from two-valued semantics with no metaphysical implications: obviously, the truth-condition of a modal statement could not depend solely on the conditions for its constituent subsentences simply to be true; but that would not affect the fact that we were regarding their meanings as determined by their truth-conditions, with respect to a notion of truth under which each was determinately either true or false. But, in saying this, we should have been wrong. A semantics of possible worlds brings with it the possibility of a new form of realism, concerning possible worlds, as advocated, for example, by David Lewis. To be a realist about possible worlds, to believe that there really are such things as possible worlds, is, as Lewis says, to treat the adverb 'actually' as indexical, as indicating position in modal space in the way that 'here' indicates position in physical space. And to do this is to regard modal logic as strictly comparable with tense logic. To treat modal statements in terms of a semantics of possible worlds is, on this view, no more than a variation on a treatment of them by means of a two-valued semantics for a language in which each predicate has an additional argument-place for a possible world; in such a language, a variable ranging over possible worlds would need to be explained in the same way as any

other sort of individual variable, namely by ultimate appeal to the notion of reference to a possible world. To reject realism about possible worlds is, in effect, to deny that a straightforward two-valued semantic theory could be given for such a language: to speak of possible worlds is only a *façon de parler*, and there is no such thing as reference to a possible world. To know whether or not we have a realistic interpretation of some class of statements, it is necessary to look, not merely at the formal structure of the semantic theory, but at the entire meaning-theory constructed on it as foundation. Even then, we shall not classify a given interpretation as anti-realistic unless there is some form of realism with which to contrast it. The mere possibility of a view compared to which a given interpretation would be anti-realistic supplies no guarantee that such a view will ever actually be proposed: probably, when the semantics of possible worlds was first introduced, it appeared unthinkable that anyone would adopt a realistic view of possible worlds. But we can be secure that our interpretation of some class of statements will never appear an anti-realistic one, when compared with some other view, only if that interpretation embodies a completely unmodified two-valued semantic theory.

What is sound about the objection is that it is not the mere adherence to or rejection of the principle of bivalence that marks the difference between a realistic and an anti-realistic interpretation. Impressed by the fact that many philosophical views which involved rejecting some form of realism turned on, or at least naturally led to, a repudiation of bivalence, I have been guilty in the past of speaking as though what characterizes anti-realism is the rejection of bivalence, so that, provided one accepts bivalence, one is a realist. The price of adopting this excessively simple criterion was to be forced to distinguish between metaphysically significant and metaphysically insignificant grounds for rejecting bivalence: for instance, it did not appear that one who, like Frege and Strawson, held that a singular statement containing an empty proper name was neither true nor false need be any less of a realist than one who, like Russell, declared that it was false, on the ground that the proper name was a disguised definite description, to be interpreted according to Russell's theory of descriptions. Another price of adopting bivalence as the shibboleth for discriminating realists from anti-realists was the necessity to admit different senses of 'realism', since some philosophical debates over certain forms of realism (for example, the realism concerning universals which is opposed by nominalism) patently did not involve any disagreement about bivalence. The mistake lay in concentrating on only one feature of the two-valued semantics. There really is nothing to choose between the Russell view and the Frege–Strawson view of sentences containing empty proper names in respect of realism. This is not, however, because the topic is metaphysically neutral. Both views stand in opposition to a realism of a Meinongian kind, which would take all proper names as referring to objects, whether existent or non-existent, and would construe statements of the form '*a* is *F*' as meaning '*a* exists and is *F*'. Russell's theory departs from Meinong's idea that reference can be ascribed to every proper name by declaring that ordinary proper names are not, as they appear, genuine singular terms, and, being definite descriptions, are not to be explained in terms of the notion of reference at all. The Frege–Strawson account departs from it by invoking the distinction between sense and reference to explain how a genuine singular term may lack a reference, and by repudiating bivalence. We do not see either theory as anti-realist, because we no longer take Meinongian realism seriously, and our attention is concentrated upon the disagreement between Russell on the one hand and Frege and Strawson on the other. But it is a mistake to say that the dispute has nothing to do with any question concerning realism; and still more of a mistake to say that we can recognize this to be so from some formal characteristics of the competing views.

We have, up to now, been considering realism solely as a *semantic* doctrine, a doctrine about the sort of thing that makes our statements true when they are true: the fundamental thesis of realism, so regarded, is that we really do succeed in referring to external objects, existing independently of our knowledge of them, and that the statements we make about them carry a meaning of such a kind that they are rendered true or false by an objective reality the constitution of which is, again, independent of our knowledge. Very often, however, realism, or, to speak more exactly, naïve realism, is taken as also having an epistemological component: it is considered to be part of a naïve realist view that we have a direct acquaintance with the external objects about which we speak. It is readily understandable how this epistemological thesis comes to be associated with naïve realism. Naïve realism, as I characterized it above, embodies an irreducibility

thesis, to the effect that there can be no informative answer to the question what, in general, makes a statement of the given class true, when it is true. We certainly cannot expect that, for any statement or class of statements we choose to consider, there will be an informative answer to this question. But, when it is possible only to give a trivial answer to the question, there must be a non-trivial answer to the further question in what our knowledge of the condition for such a statement to be true consists. If this question, too, admitted only a trivial answer, then we should have no account of the meanings of such statements, that is, no account of what a speaker knows when he understands statements of this class; and this would be absurd, because a knowledge that we are able to acquire must be a knowledge of which we can give an account. Now realism is primarily a semantic doctrine; but, as we have seen, this should not be interpreted as meaning that a realistic interpretation of some class of statements consists simply in the adoption of a certain semantic theory, in the sense in which logicians speak of a semantic theory. A semantic theory in this sense gives an outline sketch of the manner in which a sentence is determined as true, when it is true, in accordance with its composition; it is plausible only in so far as it is possible to construct, on the semantic theory as base, a complete theory of meaning. A theory of meaning must do much more than simply analyse the way in which a sentence is determined as true, when it is true, in accordance with its composition: it has, among other things, to say what a speaker knows when he understands an expression of the language, and to explain how the speaker's understanding of an expression determines it as having whatever semantic value it has, its semantic value being that whereby it contributes to determining the truth or otherwise of any sentence in which it occurs. Hence, in so far as the meaning-theory takes a truth-conditional form, in so far as it equates the understanding of a sentence with a knowledge of the condition that must obtain for the sentence to be true, it has to explain in what a speaker's knowledge of that condition consists. When it is possible to give a non-trivial answer to the question in virtue of what a sentence of a certain form is true, if it is true, we have already an explanation of what a speaker must know in knowing the condition for a sentence of that form to be true. But, when no non-trivial answer can be given, a further explanation must be supplied by the meaning-theory. The simplest way in which the meaning-theory can do this will consist in attributing to the speaker a capacity, in favourable circumstances, to recognize the condition as obtaining or not obtaining. Just because we cannot state informatively what will render the sentence true, when it is true, the faculty of recognition thus attributed to the speaker will be a faculty of *unmediated* recognition; neither the speaker nor the meaning-theorist can say *whereby* he recognizes the condition as obtaining. That which renders the sentence true is the very thing of which we are directly aware when we recognize it as being true.

Now the claim that we possess such a faculty for direct recognition of a condition of a certain kind is an epistemological one; and we see, from this, why epistemology enters into the matter. Realism and anti-realism are metaphysical doctrines; and it has been an implicit contention of the present analysis of the concept of realism that metaphysical questions, at least ones of this type, are at root questions belonging to the theory of meaning. It is impossible, however, to keep the theory of meaning sterilized from all epistemological considerations, because meaning is, ultimately, a matter of *knowledge*. The meaning of an expression is what a speaker must know if he is to be said to understand that expression; the meaning-theory for a language displays what anyone must know if he is to be said to know, or to be able to speak, that language. For this reason, the purely semantic explanation previously given of what naïve realism consists in does not completely tally with the way in which the term 'naïve realism' has traditionally been used: it stated only part of what has usually been taken as involved in being a naïve realist. For example, a realistic interpretation of statements about the past involves accepting the principle of bivalence as applied to them: they are determinately true or false, independently of whether we know their truth-values or, in a particular case, have any means of knowing. Anyone who takes this view – and very few philosophers have dared to contradict it – is unlikely to admit any reductive thesis for statements about the past, considered as a class; there will be no non-trivial answer to the question what, in general, renders a past-tense statement true if it is true. By our original criterion, therefore, the standard view of statements about the past should count as a naïvely realistic one. It would usually be thought, however, that more was required for naïve realism about the past: namely, a view to the effect that we are directly acquainted with past states of affairs, that memory affords us direct contact with them.

It is not altogether easy to see what this additional epistemological component of naïve realism, as ordinarily understood, amounts to. It might be said that our knowledge of the past in memory is indeed direct, in the sense that a report of memory is not ordinarily the conclusion of an inference: I do not conclude to the truth of the past-tense statement because that is the most plausible explanation of the memory-experience that I have. On occasion, indeed, something like this may happen. I may have the impression that I remember a certain event, then feel uncertain that I have not made a mistake of memory, and finally conclude that I must have remembered correctly, on the ground, say, that I have hardly ever made mistakes of that particular kind, or that I should be unlikely to have thought of such a curious event had I not actually witnessed it. But a case of this kind must necessarily be exceptional: we could not suppose ourselves to know enough about the past to make any such inferences if we did not take most of our memories to be correct; in fact, if all memory is called in question, we are left without any knowledge of the past at all. The claim that, in memory, we are in direct contact with the past event must, however, mean more than just that reports of memory are not, in general, based on inference, since the same may be said of knowledge based on the testimony of others. On many occasions, I may doubt whether someone else is to be trusted in what he asserts; he does not know enough about the subject, he has proved unreliable in the past, he is not always veracious. On other occasions, I may at first entertain such doubts, and then set them at rest by some particular consideration: the individual in question is unlikely to lie to *me*, and, although he has made mistakes, he has always been right on questions of this specific kind. In such a case, I may be said to conclude to the truth of what he says on the basis of an inductive inference. But the normal case is not of that kind: for, if I call in doubt the truth of everything for which I have only the authority of others, I should simply know far too little about the world to be able to judge, on an inductive basis, of the reliability of any but a very few of the things that are said to me. It is our normal practice to accept other people's assertions, just as it is our normal practice to take what we remember to have happened as having happened. Just as it is only when we have a special reason for mistrusting our own memories that we look for further grounds for supposing things to have been as we remember them, so it is only when we have a special reason for doubting the truth of what someone else says that we look for further grounds for accepting it. This is not due to laziness, or because 'life is too short': without its being ordinary practice to take what another asserts as true, we could not have a language; part of what a child has to learn in learning language is to accept and act on what other people say. Lying subverts the institution of language: if most members of a society started to lie most of the time, they would cease to be able to communicate. For the same reason, it is a priori impossible that most assertions should be mistaken.

For present purposes, the point is that 'direct knowledge', as the naïve realist speaks of it, must mean more than 'knowledge not arrived at as the conclusion of an inference'. When I accept a statement on the testimony of another, I am not normally concluding to its truth on the strength of an inference: nevertheless, that is the prime case of knowing something indirectly, of knowing it 'not of my own knowledge', as the lawyers say. What the naïve realist appears to mean in speaking of direct knowledge is that a Cartesian doubt is excluded. If my knowledge of the past, in memory, is the outcome of a direct contact that I now make with the past event, then it must be *senseless* to suppose that I should have this memory even though the past event did not occur. Thus, for the naïve realist, the connection between that which renders a statement true and our knowledge of its truth is an intimate one, just as it is for the anti-realist: from what it is like to know it to be true, we see just what it is for it to be true. Only, they draw opposite conclusions. The anti-realist draws the conclusion that the statement cannot be true unless we know it to be true, at least indirectly, or unless we have the means to arrive at such knowledge, or at least unless there exists that which, if we were aware of it, would yield such knowledge. The naïve realist believes that the statement must be determinately true or false, regardless of whether we are able, in the particular case, to perceive that which renders it true or false; but it is our capacity, in favourable circumstances, to perceive directly that which renders true or false other statements of the same type that constitutes our understanding of what it is for the given statement to be true or to be false.

The naïve realist faces a twofold difficulty. He has, first, a problem to explain how we ever come to make a mistake in making a judgement on the favoured basis: if memory is a direct contact with past events, how can a mistake of memory occur?

Secondly, he has a problem about the connection between our mode of coming to know the truth of a statement and the consequences we take it to have: if memory is a direct contact with a past event, which must, therefore, still exist in some manner if I am to be able now to apprehend it, how can I know that that event has not changed somewhat since it originally occurred? The question is, of course, senseless: but it is difficult to argue it to be senseless without, at the same time, rendering senseless the notion of a direct contact with past events.

A realist who is not, in my sense, a sophisticated realist, that is, who does not accept any reductive thesis for statements of the given class, but who also does not accept the epistemological component of naïve realism, is in an intermediate position: we might call him a *semi-naïve realist*. The semi-naïve realist has difficulties of his own. He has to explain in what our knowledge of the condition for a statement of the given class to be true consists; he cannot, for this purpose, invoke even our most straightforward means of knowing such statements to be true in the way that the anti-realist and the naïve realist do; at least, he cannot assign it such a leading role. He usually has recourse to some type of analogy; we are supposed to transfer to statements of the given class some feature of our understanding of some more primitive class of statements, where our understanding of these more primitive statements can be explained in a naïve realist fashion. But I do not wish to go further into the debate between the protagonists of the different metaphysical (or metaphysico-epistemological) positions. My sole aim has been to characterize them; that is, to explain the concept of realism as applying to philosophical views which may be adopted on a wide variety of different questions.

Cartesian doubt has two features. It is doubt entertained in the teeth of the best possible evidence, unimpaired by any contrary evidence; and it is all-encompassing. Descartes wished to entertain every doubt that is not by its nature *senseless*; and he wished to doubt simultaneously every proposition which, taken by itself, it would be possible to doubt. The naïve realist's response is to declare the doubt senseless; even Cartesian doubt is then excluded. It is this which gives its special character to his conception of *immediate* knowledge, knowledge by direct apprehension of that which renders the proposition true. Without a grasp of this curious idea, we cannot understand much that is to be found in empiricist epistemology. Consider, for instance, Locke's doctrine of secondary qualities. Locke says, of colours, that they 'are nothing in the objects themselves but powers to produce various sensations in us'. Ayer, in his *The Central Questions of Philosophy*,[1] attributes to Locke the view that 'colour is nothing in the object itself', without adding the phrase 'but powers...'. At first sight, this is as unwarranted as if someone, accused of being nothing but a social climber, should say, 'He said that I was nothing': we should naturally construe Locke as saying that colours, in the objects, are only powers to produce sensations, and, in a later passage, he does precisely so express himself. Ayer is not misrepresenting Locke, however; for Locke also says, in yet another passage, that colours 'are not really in' the bodies. Now how does it come about that Locke makes this seemingly unjustifiable transition from his own doctrine? If, in the objects, colours are powers, then the colours are presumably in the objects, though, indeed, only as powers: why, then, does Locke contradict himself by saying that the colours are not in the objects? It seems that Locke is offering an analysis of the concept of a colour, considered, at least, as a property of an opaque surface, as being a disposition of a particular type, namely a power: what more is added to this analysis by remarking that the colours are not in the objects? Are the powers, then, not in the objects? It is, after all, the body that has the power: the power is not floating independently in space, at a location where the body happens to be; when the body moves, the power moves with it, for the power, on Locke's formulation, is a power *of the body* to produce sensations in us. If, then, the colour is a power, and the power is in the body, what can possibly be meant by saying that the colour is not in the body?

Not surprisingly, it is easy to feel totally baffled by this notion of Locke's that colours, and other secondary qualities, are not *in* the physical objects. It cannot be understood unless we bear in mind the epistemological component of naïve realism, the notion of direct contact with, or immediate awareness of, the object and its properties. Locke wishes to depart from naïve realism, so far as secondary qualities are concerned: but he is attracted to it. A naïve realist about the physical world supposes that, in perception, we are in direct contact with physical objects: we know them as they really are. When, under normal conditions, I perceive an object, a Cartesian doubt is impossible, according to the naïve realist: it would be senseless, given my

perceptual state, to suppose that the object was not present or was otherwise than I perceive it to be; mistakes occur only because perception does not always take place under normal conditions. My ability to judge the truth of material-object statements on the basis of observation constitutes, for the naïve realist, my knowledge of what has to be the case for those statements to be true: so the very meaning of an ascription of perceptible qualities to an object is given by reference to the process of perceptual recognition of those qualities, and can only be so given. Now a disposition of any kind is not a quality of which we can be directly aware in such a way; a disposition is something that is manifested on some occasions and not on others, and may be variously manifested in differing circumstances. For instance, our concept of colour, as a property of an opaque surface, is not to be explained, as the naïve realist is forced to suppose, solely in terms of the appearance of a surface 'under normal conditions'; it is not irrelevant to that concept that there is a connection between the colour of a surface and its appearance under various abnormal conditions, under a coloured light, under excessive or inadequate illumination, or from too far away to allow resolution into its differently coloured regions. Now, as Locke understands the word 'colour', a colour is a disposition, and is really in the object. But, as a naïve realist understands the word 'colour', a colour cannot be a disposition, for then perception, under normal conditions, would not be an immediate awareness of the object as it really is: so, as the naïve realist understands 'colour', Locke's view entails that objects do not have colours. It is the conflation of these two conceptions of what the word 'colour' means that produces Locke's contradictory remarks.

The naïve realist's notion of immediate awareness, consisting in a direct contact between the knowing subject and the object of his knowledge, is probably in all cases incoherent: it is certainly extremely difficult to formulate it intelligibly. The proper response to Cartesian doubt is to deny, not the meaningfulness of each individual expression of doubt, but the possibility of professing simultaneously every doubt which, taken by itself, is meaningful, if neurotic: it is the generality of Cartesian doubt, not its contempt for evidence, which is the point at which it should be attacked. Bertrand Russell maintained that we could not know for certain that the world was not created two minutes ago, complete with all our apparent memories and with all the apparent traces of past events. Most philosophers do not trouble themselves with a Cartesian doubt of this kind; it is too absurd to entertain seriously, but they tacitly agree with Russell that, if someone succumbed to it, philosophy could do nothing to dispel it. Many years ago, I heard Professor Anscombe argue that what makes such thoroughgoing Cartesian doubt absurd is that, if we came across a society of people in whose language there was an inflexion of the verb such that we could establish no correlation between the sentences containing verbs in this inflexion to which they assented and what had previously happened, we could not intelligibly suppose that this inflexion represented their past tense, but that their memories were hopelessly astray. This argument was being advanced from a Wittgensteinian standpoint, but it agrees equally with that of Quine and many others; and it is surely fundamentally correct. Naïve realism, as traditionally understood, was a doctrine advanced by philosophers to whom epistemological considerations were of paramount importance, and one of whose primary objectives was to defeat scepticism; being an incoherent doctrine, it failed as a weapon in this particular battle, and this led to too easy a victory for idealism. In more recent philosophy, it has been realism, in a semi-naïve or sophisticated form, which has, for the most part, attained too easy a victory. Many of the problems expressible as disputes for and against one or another species of realism are still live issues, or ought to be. In tackling them, we need a clear formulation of what realism consists in, and a clear view also of the various forms which it can take, and the various forms which a denial of realism can take. In most of these disputes, naïve realism, as traditionally conceived with its epistemological component, is no longer a serious contender. This very fact may, but ought not to be allowed to, obscure the importance of the distinction between the sophisticated realist and what, in the later part of this essay, I have been calling the semi-naïve realist; above all, it should not lead us to mistake the sophisticated realist for the anti-realist.

Note

1 A. J. Ayer, *The Central Questions of Philosophy* (London: Weidenfeld and Nicholson, 1973).

44

Pragmatic Realism

Hilary Putnam

Lecture I: Is There Still Anything to Say about Reality and Truth?

The man on the street, Eddington reminded us, visualizes a table as 'solid' – that is, as *mostly* solid matter. But physics has discovered that the table is mostly empty space: that the distance between the particles is immense in relation to the radius of the electron or the nucleus of one of the atoms of which the table consists. One reaction to this state of affairs, the reaction of Wilfrid Sellars,[1] is to deny that there are tables at all as we ordinarily conceive them (although he chooses an ice cube rather than a table as his example). The commonsense conception of ordinary middle-sized material objects such as tables and ice cubes (the 'manifest image') is simply *false* in Sellars's view (although not without at least some cognitive value – there are real objects that the 'tables' and 'ice cubes' of the manifest image 'picture', according to Sellars, even if these real objects are not the layman's tables and ice cubes). I don't agree with this view of Sellars's, but I hope he will forgive me if I use it, or the phenomenon of its appearance on the philosophical scene, to highlight certain features of the philosophical debate about 'realism'.

First of all, this view illustrates the fact that Realism with a capital 'R' doesn't always deliver what the innocent expect of it. If there is any appeal of Realism which is wholly legitimate, it is the appeal to the commonsense feeling that *of course* there are tables and chairs, and any philosophy that tell us that there really aren't – that there are really only sense data, or only 'texts', or whatever, is more than slightly crazy. In appealing to this commonsense feeling, Realism reminds me of the Seducer in the old-fashioned melodrama. In the melodramas of the 1890s the Seducer always promised various things to the Innocent Maiden which he failed to deliver when the time came. In this case the Realist (the evil Seducer) promises common sense (the Innocent Maiden) that he will rescue her from her enemies (Idealists, Kantians and Neo-Kantians, Pragmatists, and the fearsome self-described 'Irrealist' Nelson Goodman) who (the Realist says) want to deprive her of her good old ice cubes and chairs. Faced with this dreadful prospect, the fair Maiden naturally opts for the company of the commonsensical Realist. But when they have traveled together for a little while, the 'Scientific Realist' breaks the news that what the Maiden is going to get *isn't* her ice cubes and tables and chairs. In fact, all there *really* is – the Scientific Realist tells her over breakfast – is what 'finished science' will say there is – whatever that may be. She is left with a promissory note for She Knows Not What, and the assurance that even if there *aren't* tables and chairs, still there are some *Dinge an sich* that her 'manifest image' (or her 'folk physics', as some Scientific Realists put it) 'picture'. Some will say that the lady has been had.

Originally published in *The Many Faces of Realism* (1987), pp. 3–40, 87–8. Reprinted by permission of Open Court, a division of Carus Publishing.

Thus, it is clear that the name 'Realism' can be claimed by or given to at least two very different philosophical attitudes (and, in fact, to many). The philosopher who claims that only scientific objects 'really exist' and that much, if not all, of the commonsense world is mere 'projection' claims to be a 'realist', but so does the philosopher who insists that there *really are* chairs and ice cubes (and some of these ice cubes really are *pink*), and these two attitudes, these two images of the world, can lead to and have led to many different programs for philosophy.

Husserl[2] traces the first line of thought, the line that denies that there 'really are' commonsense objects, back to Galileo, and with good reason. The present Western world view depends, according to Husserl, on a new way of conceiving 'external objects' – the way of mathematical physics. An external thing is conceived of as a congeries of particles (by atomists) or as some kind of extended disturbance (in the seventeenth century, a 'vortex', and later, a collection of 'fields'). Either way, the table in front of me (or the object that I 'picture as' a table) is described by 'mathematical formulas', as Husserl says. And this, he points out, is what above all came into Western thinking with the Galilean revolution: the idea of the 'external world' as something whose true description, whose description 'in itself', consists of mathematical formulas.

It is important to this way of thinking that certain familiar properties of the table – its size and shape and location – are 'real' properties, describable, for example, in the language of Descartes' analytic geometry. Other properties, however, the so-called 'secondary' properties, of which *color* is a chief example, are *not* treated as real properties in the same sense. No 'occurrent' (non-dispositional) property of that swarm of molecules (or that space-time region) recognized in mathematical physics can be said to be what we all along called its *color*.

What about dispositional properties? It is often claimed that color is simply a function of *reflectancy*, that is, of the disposition of an object (or of the surface of an object) to selectively absorb certain wavelengths of incident light and reflect others. But this doesn't really do much for the reality of colors. Not only has recent research shown that this account is much too simple (because changes of reflectancy across edges turn out to play an important role in determining the colors we see), but reflectancy itself does not have one uniform physical explanation. A red star and a red apple and a reddish glass of colored water are red for quite different physical reasons. In fact, there may well be an infinite number of different physical conditions which could result in the disposition to reflect (or emit) red light and absorb light of other wavelengths. A dispositional property whose underlying non-dispositional 'explanation' is so very non-uniform is simply incapable of being represented as a mathematical function of the dynamical variables. And these – the dynamical variables – are the parameters that this way of thinking treats as the 'characteristics' of 'external' objects.

Another problem[3] is that *hues* turn out to be much more subjective than we thought. In fact, any shade on the color chart in the green part of the spectrum will be classed as 'standard green' by some subject – even if it lies at the extreme 'yellow-green' end or the extreme 'blue-green' end.

In sum, no 'characteristic' recognized by this way of thinking – no 'well-behaved function of the dynamical variables' – corresponds to such a familiar property of objects as *red* or *green*. The idea that there is a property all red objects have in common – the same in all cases – and another property all green objects have in common – the same in all cases – is a kind of illusion, on the view we have come more and more to take for granted since the age of Descartes and Locke.

However, Locke and Descartes did give us a sophisticated substitute for our pre-scientific notion of color; a substitute that has, perhaps, come to seem mere 'post-scientific common sense' to most people. This substitute involves the idea of a sense datum (except that, in the seventeenth- and eighteenth-century vocabulary, sense data were referred to as 'ideas' or 'impressions'). The red sweater I see is not red in the way I thought it was (there is no 'physical magnitude' which is its redness), but it does have a disposition (a Power, in the seventeenth- and eighteenth-century idiom) to affect me in a certain way – to cause me to have sense data. And these, the sense data, do truly have a simple, uniform, non-dispositional sort of 'redness'.

This is the famous picture, the dualistic picture of the physical world and its primary qualities, on the one hand, and the mind and its sense data, on the other, that philosophers have been wrangling over since the time of Galileo, as Husserl says. And it is Husserl's idea – as it was the idea of William James, who influenced Husserl – that this picture is disastrous.

But why should we regard it as disastrous? It was once shocking, to be sure, but as I have already said, it is by now widely accepted as 'post-scientific common sense'. What is *really* wrong with this picture?

For one thing, *solidity* is in much the same boat as color. If objects do not have color as they 'naively' seem to, no more do they have solidity as they 'naively' seem to.[4] It is this that leads Sellars to say that such commonsense objects as ice cubes do not really exist at all. What *is* our conception of a typical commonsense object if not of something solid (or liquid) which exhibits certain colors? What there really are, in Sellars's scientific metaphysics, are objects of mathematical physics, on the one hand, and 'raw feels', on the other. This is precisely the picture I have just described as 'disastrous'; it is the picture that denies precisely the common man's kind of realism, his realism about tables and chairs.

The reply to me (the reply a philosopher who accepts the post-Galilean picture will make) is obvious: 'You are just nostalgic for an older and simpler world. This picture works; our acceptance of it is an "inference to the best explanation". We cannot regard it as an objection to a view that it does not preserve everything that laymen once falsely believed.'

If it is an inference to the best explanation, it is a strange one, however. How does the familiar explanation of what happens when I 'see something red' go? The light strikes the object (say, a sweater), and is reflected to my eye. There is an image on the retina (Berkeley knew about images on the retina, and so did Descartes, even if the wave aspect of light was not well understood until much later). There are resultant nerve impulses (Descartes knew there was some kind of transmission along the nerves, even if he was wrong about its nature – and it is not clear we know its nature either, since there is again debate about the significance of chemical, as opposed to electrical, transmissions from neuron to neuron.) There are events in the brain, some of which we understand thanks to the work of Hubel and Wiesel, David Marr, and others. And then – this is the mysterious part – there is somehow a 'sense datum' or a 'raw feel'. *This* is an *explanation*?

An 'explanation' that involves connections of a kind we do not understand at all ('nomological danglers', Herbert Feigl called them[5]) and concerning which we have not even the sketch of a theory is an explanation through something more obscure than the phenomenon to be explained. As has been pointed out by thinkers as different from one another as William James, Husserl, and John Austin, every single part of the sense datum story is supposition – theory – and theory of a most peculiar kind. Yet the epistemological role 'sense data' are supposed to play by traditional philosophy required them to be what is 'given', to be *what we are absolutely sure of independently of scientific theory*. The kind of scientific realism we have inherited from the seventeenth century has not lost all its prestige even yet, but it has saddled us with a disastrous picture of the world. It is high time we looked for a different picture.

Intrinsic properties: dispositions

I want to suggest that the problem with the 'Objectivist' picture of the world (to use Husserl's term for this kind of scientific realism) lies deeper than the postulation of 'sense data'; sense data are, so to speak, the visible symptoms of a systemic disease, like the pock marks in the case of smallpox. The deep systemic root of the disease, I want to suggest, lies in the notion of an 'intrinsic' property, a property something has 'in itself', apart from any contribution made by language or the mind.

This notion, and the correlative notion of a property that is merely 'appearance', or merely something we 'project' onto the object, has proved extremely robust, judging by its appeal to different kinds of philosophers. In spite of their deep disagreements, all the strains of philosophy that accepted the seventeenth-century circle of problems – subjective idealists as well as dualists and materialists – accepted the distinction, even if they disagreed over its application. A subjective idealist would say that there are only sense data (or minds and sense data, in some versions), and that 'red' is an intrinsic property of these objects, while persistence (being there even when we don't look) is something we 'project'; a dualist or a materialist would say the 'external' objects have persistence as an intrinsic property, but red is, in their case, something we 'project'. But all of these philosophers *have* the distinction. Even Kant, who expresses serious doubts about it in the first Critique (to the point of saying that the notion of a 'Ding an sich' *may* be 'empty'), makes heavy use of it in the second Critique.

Putting aside the Berkeleyan view (that there aren't really any external objects at all) as an aberrant form of the seventeenth-century view, we may say that the remaining philosophers all accept the account of 'redness' and 'solidity' that I have been describing; these are not 'intrinsic properties' of the external things we ascribe them to, but rather (in the case of external things) dispositions to affect us in certain ways – to produce certain sense data in us, or, the materialist philosophers would say, to produce certain sorts of 'states' in our brains and nervous systems. The idea that these properties are 'in' the things themselves, as intrinsic properties, is a spontaneous 'projection'.

The Achilles' heel of this story is the notion of a disposition. To indicate the problems that arise – they have preoccupied many first-rate philosophical minds, starting with Charles Peirce's – let me introduce a technical term (I shall not introduce much terminology in this lecture, I promise!). A disposition that something has to do something *no matter what*, I shall call a *strict disposition*. A disposition to do something under 'normal conditions', I shall call an *'other things being equal' disposition*. Perhaps it would be wise to give examples.

The disposition of bodies with non-zero rest mass to travel at sub-light speeds is a *strict* disposition; it is physically impossible for a body with non-zero rest mass to travel at the speed of light. Of course, the notion of a 'strict disposition' presupposes the notion of 'physical necessity', as this example illustrates, but this is a notion I am allowing the 'scientific realist', at least for the sake of argument. What of the disposition of sugar to dissolve in water?

This is not a strict disposition, since sugar which is placed in water which is already saturated with sugar (or even with other appropriate chemicals) will not dissolve. Is the disposition of sugar to dissolve in *chemically pure water*, then, a strict disposition?

'This is also not a strict disposition'; the first counterexample I shall mention comes from thermodynamics. Suppose I drop a sugar cube in water and the sugar cube dissolves. Consider sugar which is in water, but in such a way that while the situation is identical with the situation I just produced (the sugar is dissolved in the water) with respect to the position of each particle, and also with respect to the numerical value of the momentum of each particle, all the momentum vectors have the exactly opposite directions from the ones they now have. This is a famous example: what happens in the example is that the sugar, instead of staying dissolved, simply forms a sugar cube which spontaneously leaps out of the water! Since every normal state (every state in which sugar dissolves) can be paired with a state in which it 'undissolves', we see that there are infinitely many physically possible conditions in which sugar 'undissolves' instead of staying in solution. Of course, these are all states in which entropy decreases; but that is not impossible, only extremely improbable!

Shall we say, then, that sugar has a strict disposition to dissolve unless the condition is one in which an entropy decrease takes place? No, because if sugar is put in water and there is immediately a flash freeze, the sugar will not dissolve if the freezing takes place fast enough. . . .

The fact is that what we can say is that under *normal* conditions sugar will dissolve if placed in water. And there is no reason to think that all the various abnormal conditions (including bizarre quantum-mechanical states, bizarre local fluctuations in the space-time, etc.) under which sugar would not dissolve if placed in water could be summed up in a closed formula in the language of fundamental physics.

This is exactly the problem we previously observed in connection with redness and solidity! If the 'intrinsic' properties of 'external' things are the ones that we can represent by formulas in the language of fundamental physics, by 'suitable functions of the dynamical variables', then *solubility* is also not an 'intrinsic' property of any external thing. And, similarly, neither is any 'other things being equal' disposition. The Powers, to use the seventeenth-century language, have to be set over against, and carefully distinguished from, the properties the things have 'in themselves'.

Intrinsic properties: intentionality

Well, what of it? Why should we not say that dispositions (or at least 'other things being equal' dispositions, such as solubility) are also not 'in the things themselves' but rather something we 'project' onto those things? Philosophers who talk this way rarely if ever stop to say what *projection* itself is supposed to be. Where in the scheme does the ability of the mind to 'project' anything onto anything come in?

Projection is thinking of something as having properties it does not have, but that we can imagine (perhaps because something else we are acquainted with really does have them), without being conscious that this is what we are doing. It is thus a species of *thought* – thought about something. Does the familiar 'Objectivist' picture have anything to tell us about thought (or, as philosophers say, about 'intentionality', that is, about *aboutness*)?

Descartes certainly intended that it should. His view was that there are two fundamental substances – mind and matter – not one, and, correspondingly there should be two fundamental sciences: physics and psychology. But we have ceased to think of mind as a separate 'substance' at all. And a 'fundamental science' of psychology which explains the nature of thought (including how thoughts can be true or false, warranted or unwarranted, about something or not about something) never did come into existence, contrary to Descartes' hopes. So to explain the features of the commonsense world, including color, solidity, causality – I include causality because the commonsense notion of 'the cause' of something is a 'projection' if dispositions are 'projections'; it depends on the notion of 'normal conditions' in exactly the same way – in terms of a mental operation called 'projection' is to explain just about every feature of the commonsense world in terms of *thought*.

But wasn't that what idealists were accused of doing? This is the paradox that I pointed out at the beginning of this lecture. So far as the commonsense world is concerned (the world we experience ourselves as *living* in, which is why Husserl called it the *Lebenswelt*), the effect of what is called 'realism' in philosophy is to deny objective reality, to make it all simply *thought*. It is the philosophers who in one way or another stand in the Neo-Kantian tradition – James, Husserl, Wittgenstein – who claim that commonsense tables and chairs and sensations and electrons are *equally real*, and not the metaphysical realists.

Today, some metaphysical realists would say that we don't need a perfected science of psychology to account for thought and intentionality, because the problem is solved by some philosophical theory; while others claim that a perfected 'cognitive science' based on the 'computer model' will solve the problem for us in the near or distant future. I obviously do not have time to examine these suggestions closely today, but I shall indicate briefly why I believe that none of them will withstand close inspection.

Why intentionality is so intractable

The problem, in a nutshell, is that thought itself has come to be treated more and more as a 'projection' by the philosophy that traces its pedigree to the seventeenth century. The reason is clear: we have not succeeded in giving the theory that thought is just a primitive property of a mysterious 'substance', mind, any content. As Kant pointed out in the first Critique, we have no theory of this substance or its powers and no prospect of having one. If, *unlike* the Kant of the first Critique (as I read the *Critique of Pure Reason*), we insist on sticking to the fundamental 'Objectivist' assumptions, the only line we can then take is that *mental phenomena must be highly derived physical phenomena in some way*, as Diderot and Hobbes had already proposed. By the 'fundamental Objectivist assumptions', I mean (1) the assumption that there is a clear distinction to be drawn between the properties things have 'in themselves' and the properties which are 'projected by us' and (2) the assumption that the fundamental science – in the singular, since only physics has that status today – tells us what properties things have 'in themselves'. (Even if we were to assume, with Wilfrid Sellars, that 'raw feels' – fundamental sensuous qualities of experience – are not going to be reduced to physics, but are in some way going to be added to fundamental science in some future century, it would not affect the situation much; Sellars does not anticipate that *intentionality* will turn out to be something we have to add to physics in the same way, but rather supposes that a theory of the 'use of words' is all that is needed to account for it.)

Modern Objectivism has simply become Materialism. And the central problem for Materialism is 'explaining the emergence of mind'. But if 'explaining the emergence of mind' means solving Brentano's problem, that is, saying in *reductive* terms what 'thinking there are a lot of cats in the neighborhood' *is*, and what 'remembering where Paris is' *is*, etc., why should we now think *that*'s possible? If reducing color or solidity or solubility to fundamental physics has proved impossible, why should this vastly more ambitious reduction program prove tractable?

Starting in the late 1950s, I myself proposed a program in the philosophy of mind that has become widely known under the name 'Functionalism'. The claim of my 'Functionalism' was that thinking beings are *compositionally plastic* – that is, that there is no one physical state or event (i.e., no necessary and sufficient condition expressible by a finite formula in the language of first-order fundamental physics) for being even a *physically possible* (let alone 'logically possible' or 'metaphysically possible') occurrence of a thought with a given propositional content, or of a feeling of anger, or of a pain, etc. *A fortiori*, propositional attitudes, emotions, feelings, are not *identical* with brain states, or even with more broadly characterized physical states. When I advanced this claim, I pointed out that thinking of a being's mentality, affectivity, etc. as aspects of its *organization to function* allows one to recognize that all sorts of logically possible 'systems' or beings could be conscious, exhibit mentality and affect, etc. in exactly the same sense without having the same matter (without even consisting of 'matter' in the sense of elementary particles and electromagnetic fields at all). For beings of many different physical (and even 'non-physical') constitutions could have the same functional organization. The thing we want insight into is the nature of human (and animal) functional organization, not the nature of a mysterious 'substance', on the one hand, or merely additional physiological information on the other.

I also proposed a theory as to what our organization to function is, one I have now given up – this was the theory that our functional organization is that of a Turing machine. I have given this up because I believe that there are good arguments to show that mental states are not only compositionally plastic but also *computationally plastic*. What I mean by this is that physically possible creatures who believe that there are a lot of cats in the neighborhood, or whatever, may have an *indefinite number of different 'programs'*. The hypothesis that there is a necessary and sufficient condition for the presence of a given believe in computational (or computational *cum* physical) terms is unrealistic in just the way that the theory that there is a necessary and sufficient condition for the presence of a table in phenomenalistic terms is unrealistic. Such a condition would have to be infinitely long, and not constructed according to any effective rule, or even according to a non-effective prescription that we could state without using the very terms to be reduced. I do not believe that even all *humans* who have the same belief (in different cultures, or with different bodies of knowledge and different conceptual resources) have in common a physical *cum* computational feature which could be 'identified with' that belief. The 'intentional level' is simply not reducible to the 'computational level' any more than it is to the 'physical level'.[6]

If this is right, then the Objectivist will have to conclude that intentionality *too* must be a mere 'projection'. But how can any philosopher think this suggestion has even the semblance of making

sense? As we saw, the very notion of 'projection' *presupposes* intentionality!

Strange to say, the idea that thought *is* a mere projection is being defended by a number of philosophers in the United States and England, in spite of its absurdity. The strength of the 'Objectivist' tradition is so strong that some philosophers will abandon the deepest intuitions we have about ourselves-in-the-world, rather than ask (as Husserl and Wittgenstein did) whether the whole picture is not a mistake. Thus it is that in the closing decades of the twentieth century we have intelligent philosophers[7] claiming that intentionality itself is something we project by taking a 'stance' to some parts of the world (as if 'taking a stance' were not itself an intentional notion!), intelligent philosophers claiming that no one really has propositional attitudes (beliefs and desires), that 'belief' and 'desire' are just notions from a false theory called 'folk psychology', and intelligent philosophers claiming there is no such property as 'truth' and no such relation as reference, that 'is true' is just a phrase we use to 'raise the level of language'. One of these – Richard Rorty – a thinker of great depth – sees that he is committed to rejecting the intuitions that underly every kind of realism[8] (and not just metaphysical realism), but most of these thinkers write as if they were *saving* realism (in its Materialist version) by abandoning intentionality! It's as if it were all right to say 'I don't deny that there is an external world; I just deny that we *think* about it'! Come to think of it, this is the way Foucault wrote, too. The line between relativism *à la française* and Analytic Philosophy seems to be thinner than anglophone philosophers think! Amusingly enough, the dust-jacket of one of the latest attacks on 'folk psychology'[9] bears an enthusiastic blurb in which a reviewer explains the importance of the book inside the dust-jacket by saying that most people *believe* that there are such things as beliefs!

'The trail of the human serpent is over all'

If seventeenth-century Objectivism has led twentieth-century philosophy into a blind alley, the solution is neither to fall into extreme relativism, as French philosophy has been doing, nor to deny our commonsense realism. There *are* tables and chairs and ice cubes. There are also electrons and space-time regions and prime numbers and people who are a menace to world peace and moments of beauty and transcendence and many other things. My old-fashioned story of the Seducer and the

Innocent Maiden was meant as a double warning; a warning against giving up commonsense realism and, simultaneously, a warning against supposing that the seventeenth-century talk of 'external world' and 'sense impressions', 'intrinsic properties', and 'projections', etc., was in any way a Rescuer of our commonsense realism. Realism with a capital 'R' is, sad to say, the foe, not the defender, of realism with a small 'r'.

If this is hard to see, it is because the task of overcoming the seventeenth-century world picture is only begun. I asked – as the title of this lecture – whether there is still anything to say, anything really new to say, about reality and truth. If 'new' means 'absolutely unprecedented', I suspect the answer is 'no'. But if we allow that William James might have had something 'new' to say – something new to *us*, not just new to his own time – or, at least, might have had a program for philosophy that is, in part, the right program, even if it has not been properly worked out yet (and may never be completely 'worked out'); if we allow that Husserl and Wittgenstein and Austin may have shared something of the same program, even if they too, in their different ways, failed to state it properly; then there is still something new, something *unfinished and important* to say about reality and truth. And that is what I believe.

The key to working out the program of preserving commonsense realism while avoiding the absurdities and antinomies of metaphysical realism in all its familiar varieties (Brand X: Materialism: Brand Y: Subjective Idealism; Brand Z: Dualism . . .) is something I have called *internal realism*. (I should have called it pragmatic realism!) Internal realism is, at bottom, just the insistence that realism is *not* incompatible with conceptual relativity. One can be *both* a realist *and* a conceptual relativist. Realism (with a small 'r') has already been introduced; as was said, it is a view that takes our familiar commonsense scheme, as well as our scientific and artistic and other schemes, at face value, without helping itself to the notion of the thing 'in itself'. But what is conceptual relativity?

Conceptual relativity sounds like 'relativism', but has none of the 'there is no truth to be found . . . "true" is just a name for what a bunch of people can agree on' implications of 'relativism'. A simple example will illustrate what I mean. Consider 'a world with three individuals' (Carnap often used examples like this when we were doing inductive logic together in the early 1950s), X_1, X_2, X_3. How many *objects* are there in this world?

Well, I *said* 'Consider a world with just three individuals', didn't I? So mustn't there be three objects? Can there be non-abstract entities which are not 'individuals'?

One possible answer is 'no'. We can identify 'individual', 'object', 'particular', etc., and find no absurdity in a world with just three objects which are independent, unrelated 'logical atoms'. But there are perfectly good logical doctrines which lead to different results.

Suppose, for example, that, like some Polish logicians, I believe that for every two particulars there is an object which is their sum. (This is the basic assumption of 'mereology', the calculus of parts and wholes invented by Lezniewski.) If I ignore, for the moment, the so-called null object, then I will find that the world of 'three individuals' (as Carnap might have had it, at least when he was doing inductive logic) actually contains *seven* objects:

WORLD 1	WORLD 2
x_1, x_2, x_3	x_1, x_2, x_3, $x_1 + x_2$, $x_1 + x_3$, $x_2 + x_3$, $x_1 + x_2 + x_3$
(A world *à la* Carnap)	('Same' world *à la* Polish logician)

Some Polish logicians would also say that there is a 'null object', which they count as a part of every object. If we accepted this suggestion, and added this individual (call it **O**), then we would say that Carnap's world contains *eight* objects.

Now, the classic metaphysical realist way of dealing with such problems is well known. It is to say that there is a single world (think of this as a piece of dough) which we can slice into pieces in different ways. But this 'cookie cutter' metaphor founders on the question, 'What are the "parts" of this dough?' If the answer is that O, x_1, x_2, x_3, $x_1 + x_2$, $x_1 + x_3$, $x_2 + x_3$, $x_1 + x_2 + x_3$ are all the different 'pieces', then we have not a *neutral* description, but rather a *partisan* description – just the description of the Warsaw logician! And it is no accident that metaphysical realism cannot really recognize the phenomenon of conceptual relativity – for that phenomenon turns on the fact that *the logical primitives themselves, and in particular the notions of object and existence, have a multitude of different uses rather than one absolute 'meaning'.*

An example which is historically important, if more complex than the one just given, is the ancient dispute about the ontological status of the

Euclidean plane. Imagine a Euclidean plane. Think of the points in the plane. Are these *parts* of the plane, as Leibniz thought? Or are they 'mere limits', as Kant said?

If you say, in *this* case, that these are 'two ways of slicing the same dough', then you must admit that what is a *part* of space, in one version of the facts, is an abstract entity (say, a set of convergent spheres – although there is not, of course, a *unique* way of construing points as limits) in the other version. But then you will have conceded that which entities are 'abstract entities' and which are 'concrete objects', at least, is version-relative. Metaphysical realists to this day continue to argue about whether points (space-time points, nowadays, rather than points in the plane or in three-dimensional space) are individuals or properties, particulars or mere limits, etc. My view is that God himself, if he consented to answer the question, 'Do points really exist or are they mere limits?', would say 'I don't know'; not because his omniscience is limited, but because there is a limit to how far questions make sense.

One last point before I leave these examples: *given* a version, the question 'How many objects are there?' has an answer, namely 'three' in the case of the first version ('Carnap's world') and 'seven' (or 'eight') in the case of the second version ('The Polish logician's world'). Once we make clear how we are using 'object' (or 'exist'), the question 'How many objects exist?' has an answer that is not at all a matter of 'convention'. That is why I say that this sort of example does not support *radical* cultural relativism. Our concepts may be culturally relative, but it does not follow that the truth or falsity of everything we say using those concepts is simply 'decided' by the culture. But the idea that there is an Archimedean point, or a use of 'exist' inherent in the world itself, from which the question 'How many objects *really* exist?' makes sense, is an illusion.

If this is right, then it may be possible to see how it can be that what is in one sense the 'same' world (the two versions are deeply related) can be described as consisting of 'tables and chairs' (and these described as colored, possessing dispositional properties, etc.) in one version *and* as consisting of space-time regions, particles and fields, etc. in other versions. To require that all of these *must* be reducible to a single version is to make the mistake of supposing that 'Which are the real objects?' is a question that makes sense *independently of our choice of concepts.*

What I am saying is frankly programmatic. Let me close by briefly indicating where the program leads, and what I hope from it.

Many thinkers have argued that the traditional dichotomy between the world 'in itself' and the concepts we use to think and talk about it must be given up. To mention only the most recent examples, Davidson has argued that the distinction between 'scheme' and 'content' cannot be drawn; Goodman has argued that the distinction between 'world' and 'versions' is untenable; and Quine has defended 'ontological relativity'. Like the great pragmatists, these thinkers have urged us to reject the spectator point of view in metaphysics and epistemology. Quine has urged us to accept the existence of abstract entities on the ground that these are indispensable in mathematics,[10] and of microparticles and space-time points on the ground that these are indispensable in physics; and what better justification is there for accepting an ontology than its indispensability in our scientific practice?, he asks. Goodman has urged us to take seriously the metaphors that artists use to restructure our worlds, on the ground that these are an indispensable way of understanding our experience. Davidson has rejected the idea that talk of propositional attitudes is 'second class', on similar grounds. These thinkers have been somewhat hesitant to forthrightly extend the same approach to our moral images of ourselves and the world. Yet what can giving up the spectator view in philosophy mean if we don't extend the pragmatic approach to the most indispensable 'versions' of ourselves and our world that we possess? Like William James (and like my teacher Morton White[11]), I propose to do exactly that. In the remaining lectures, I shall illustrate the standpoint of pragmatic realism in ethics by taking a look at some of our moral images, and particularly at the ones that underlie the central democratic value of *equality*. Although reality and truth are old, and to superficial appearances 'dry', topics, I shall try to convince you in the course of these lectures that it is the persistence of obsolete assumptions about these 'dry' topics that sabotages philosophical discussion about all the 'exciting' topics, not to say the possibility of doing justice to the reality and mystery of our commonsense world.

Lecture II: Realism and Reasonableness

Some questions in philosophical logic are able to divide philosophers into warring camps. Since the middle of the twentieth century, this has been the case with the question of the status of dispositional statements (and with the closely related question of the status of counterfactual conditionals). For some philosophers, dispositions are simply part of 'the furniture of the universe'; for others, the use of a dispositional notion in a philosophical analysis is a sign of 'low standards', of willingness to 'explain the obscure by the still more obscure'; while for still others (perhaps the silent majority), dispositional notions are unavoidable in what we do but troubling to the conscience. This is a relatively new state of affairs: the writers who make up the canon of 'Modern Philosophy' (or at least of seventeenth-century to mid-nineteenth-century philosophy) all availed themselves of the notion of a Power (i.e., a dispositional property) without any visible pangs of conscience.

Perhaps this is not surprising, as it is only since the appearance of mathematical logic that we have realized how hard it is to give an interpretation of counterfactual conditionals and of dispositional predicates in truth-functional[12] terms. But, in a way, it should have been realized a long time ago that the talk of Powers in 'modern' philosophy was problematical, for such talk is a hang-over from medieval philosophy, not something that belongs in its own right to the new picture. The heart of the new picture is the new conception of the 'external' world, the conception of the external world as governed by *strict* laws of the form with which we are familiar from the work of Newton and his successors. It is this conception that motivates the division of properties into primary and secondary, or into intrinsic properties of the external things and powers to affect the mind of the observer. A world governed by a system of differential equations is one thing; a medieval (or an Aristotelian) world governed by Substantial Forms which manifest themselves as 'tendencies' rather than as exceptionless laws is something else. The Cartesian picture is confused. It exhibits both modern physicalist and medieval 'tendency-ist' forms of explanation in an unhappy coexistence. The new image of nature – the World Machine – ought to have no place for the classical 'tendencies'.

In the previous lecture this was argued with the aid of the example of the color predicate 'red'. Something is red if it has a certain tendency – the tendency to produce certain 'sense impressions' (according to the seventeenth- and eighteenth-century story), or a certain 'brain state' (an alternative to the dualist story that goes back at least as far as

Diderot if not to Hobbes), or (in a story which is overly simple but at least avoids the mind–body problem) if it has the tendency to selectively absorb and reflect certain wavelengths of light. But what does 'have the tendency' mean? Tendencies, as I said in yesterday's lecture, do not exemplify the operation of strict laws (in the modern sense of 'strict law'); they are sloppy things, that manifest themselves 'under normal conditions'. To analyze the dispositional idiom, we need an analysis of the phrase 'under normal conditions', or something similar, and, in fact, the attempts to produce a theory which have been made by contemporary authors[13] involve such notions as the 'similarity' of a whole possible world with another whole world – notions which attempt to express, or at least to substitute for, the desired notion of a 'normal' state of affairs. But the currently most fashionable of these – the notion of 'similarity' of possible worlds – only illustrates the distance of counterfactual (and dispositional) talk from the world picture of physics – illustrates it by introducing a metaphysical primitive which sticks out like a sore thumb.

Other philosophers content themselves with introducing dispositional predicates one by one, as needed, without any attempt to analyze or account for the general dispositional idiom. Sometimes this can be justified (from an 'Objectivist' point of view) by showing that the predicate so introduced is coextensive with a non-dispositional (perhaps a structural) predicate. But most dispositional notions – e.g., 'red', 'poisonous', 'tending to say *da* if the linguist says *gavagai* and both of them are watching a rabbit' – are almost certain not to be coextensive with predicates definable in the language of fundamental physics.

Certain other philosophers have suggested that dispositional predicates are not, in general, the sorts of predicates for which one ought to expect there to be necessary and sufficient conditions. Perhaps such a word as 'poisonous' is only partly defined; perhaps when we encounter a new substance that human beings are capable of ingesting or breathing or touching, we just extend the notion of being poisonous as we extend our other notions (including the notion of what is 'normal') in the given circumstances.[14] Other philosophers have suggested that such dispositional statements as '*X* is poisonous' do not predicate a *property* at all; they are ways in which we perform the speech act of *licensing an inference*. As the late J. L. Mackie put it, such statements can be assertible under appropriate conditions without possessing any property a realist would recognize as 'truth'. (They are 'not simply true', he claimed.[15]) What many of these theories have in common is a denial that the semantics of dispositional sentences is the classical bivalent truth-conditional semantics. Either dispositional sentences aren't 'simply true' and 'simply false' at all, these authors say, or else they are true and false only in certain cases (the cases in which the dispositional predicate has been defined), and remain to be given a truth-value in all other cases. (On either form of the view, the dispositional predicate lacks a well-defined extension.)

As I mentioned in the last lecture, similar issues arise in connection with the notions of *causality* and of *explanation* (conceived of as a relation between events or between 'situations', rather than as a relation between statements). Like dispositions, causal and explanatory relations may be strict (the event or 'situation' described as the cause may be connected by strict laws with the event or situation which is taken to be the effect) or may be loose (the event or situation described as the cause may bring about the effect only 'under suitable circumstances'). And the loose causal relations are, once again, an embarrassment from the point of view of the 'Objectivist' picture – the picture of nature as the World Machine.

If we could define in physicalistic terms what it is for a feature of a situation to be only an 'attendant circumstance', we might be able to explain '*X* brought about *Y*' as meaning that *given the attendant circumstances*, it followed from physical laws that *Y* would happen if *X* did; but unfortunately, an intrinsic distinction between situations which are capable of being 'bringers about' and situations which are only attendant 'circumstances' has much more to do with medieval (and Aristotelian) notions of 'efficient causation' than with post-Newtonian ones. And once again, some philosophers have proposed either to *reject* the loose causal and explanatory relations altogether,[16] while others have proposed that the loose causal and explanatory relations[17] have only 'assertibility conditions' and not 'truth conditions'.

My own view – the view I began to sketch out for you in the last lecture – differs from all of these. These authors all assume we can make the distinction between what is 'simply true' and what has only 'assertibility conditions', or the cut between what is already true or false and what is an 'extension of previous use' (albeit one that we all make the same way), or between what is a 'projection' and what is an independent and unitary property of

things in themselves. I think that, epistemically at least, the attempt to draw this distinction, to make this cut, has been a total failure. The time has come to try the methodological hypothesis that no such cut can be made.

I recall a conversation with Noam Chomsky many years ago in which he suggested that philosophers often take perfectly sensible continua and get in trouble by trying to convert them into dichotomies. Consider, for example, the continuum between the relatively 'subjective' (or, at least, interest- and culture-relative) and the relatively 'objective' (or, at least, interest- and culture-independent). Prephilosophically, most of us would probably agree on the ordering of the following properties along this continuum:

1 Being very amusing (as in 'the behavior of young babies is often very amusing').
2 Being a region of space which contains at least one hydrogen atom (assume classical physics for this one – no relativity or quantum mechanics, please!).
3 Being soluble.
4 A single case counterfactual conditional – e.g., the property we predicate of a particular match at a particular time when we say it *would have* lit *if* it *had been* struck at that time.
5 Meaning 'Do you speak French?' (predicated of a particular utterance).

I suppose the average person might rank these predications as follows (taking the left-hand end of the line to represent the 'subjective' and the right-hand end to represent the 'objective'):

Being amusing   Counter-factual   Meaning '...'   Being soluble   Contains hydrogen

(A plausible objective-subjective ranking)

Yet as soon as we are asked to make a 'Dedekind cut' – to turn this ranking into a dichotomy – we find that there is no agreement at all in our philosophical intuitions. Quine, for example, would put the cut between (5) and (3) – counting both dispositional predicates (such as 'soluble') and non-dispositional predicates from fundamental physics as 'objective' and all the others as more or less subjective (or 'second class', in his terminology). Some philosophers might disagree with me on the position of the meaning-assignment (5) – some counting it as more 'objective' than the assignment of *solubility* to a substance – and draw the line after

(1), (4), and (3). Philosophers who are 'comfortable' with counterfactuals would make still another choice for the location of the 'cut', placing it immediately after (1) – i.e., counting 'amusing' as subjective and all the rest as 'objective'. But my own view, as I have said (and perhaps Chomsky's as well, if I understood him aright) is that the enterprise isn't worth the candle. The game is played out. We can make a rough sort of rank ordering (although even here there are disagreements), but the idea of a 'point at which' subjectivity ceases and Objectivity-with-a-capital-O begins has proved chimerical.

If this is right, then a number of other famous dichotomies must be abandoned. Two of these have already been mentioned, namely:

Projection/Property of the thing in itself

and

'Power'/Property of the thing in itself

The rejection of these three dichotomies is the essence of the 'internal realism' I have been defending over the years.

My rejection of these dichotomies will trouble many, and it should. Without the constraint of trying to 'save the appearances', philosophy becomes a game in which anyone can – and, as a rule does – say just about *anything*. Unless we take our intuitions seriously, we cannot do *hard* philosophy at all. So I respect philosophers who insist that the traditional dichotomies are deeply intuitive, and who 'need a lot of convincing' before they will give them up.

But if philosophy which simply scorns our intuitions is not worth the candle, philosophy which tries to preserve *all* of them becomes a vain attempt to have the past over again. There are phenomena which really do challenge our intuitions – the phenomenon Husserl described in *Crisis of the European Sciences*, the breakdown of the great seventeenth-century project of trying to turn physics into metaphysics ('Objectivism') – the breakdown I described in the preceding lecture – is one such. On the one hand, seventeenth-century science succeeded in smashing the medieval foundations of knowledge – and not just of knowledge, but of religion, politics, and morality as well. On the other hand, the line of thinking that said, 'Well, if science smashed all that, well and good. Science will give us better in its place,' now looks tired. (It

already seemed tired to Kant – and not because Kant was a foe of science or Enlightenment; on the contrary, he was a great scientist and a great man of the Enlightenment.) Science is wonderful at destroying metaphysical answers, but incapable of providing substitute ones. Science takes away foundations without providing a replacement. Whether we want to be there or not, science has put us in the position of having to live without foundations. It was shocking when Nietzsche said this, but today it is commonplace; *our* historical position – and no end to it is in sight – is that of having to philosophize without 'foundations'.

The impossibility of imagining what credible 'foundations' might look like is one phenomenon, but not the only phenomenon, that challenges our 'intuitions'. Since the end of the nineteenth century science itself has begun to take on a 'non-classical' – that is, a non-seventeenth-century appearance. In the last lecture I described the phenomenon of conceptual relativity – one which has simple illustrations, like the ones I used, but which has become pervasive in contemporary science. That there are ways of describing what are (in some way) the 'same facts' which are (in some way) 'equivalent' but also (in some way) 'incompatible' is a strikingly non-classical phenomenon. Yet contemporary logicians and meaning-theorists generally philosophize as if it did not exist. If claiming to abandon *all* our 'intuitions' is mere show, retaining all of them would require us to philosophize as if the phenomena I just reminded you of did not exist. The task of the philosopher, as I see it, is to *see which* of our intuitions we can responsibly retain and which we must jettison in a period of enormous and unprecedented intellectual, as well as material, change.

If I reject the dichotomies I depicted, it is not, then, because I fail to recognize their intuitive appeal, or because that intuitive appeal counts for nothing in my eyes. It is rather because these dichotomies have become distorting lenses which prevent us from seeing real phenomena – the phenomena I have been describing – in their full extent and significance.

Yet I still term myself a 'realist' – even if I spell it all in lower case – and *can* one be any sort of a realist without the dichotomies? In particular, is not the dichotomy between what is a 'human projection' – what is not 'simply true', what has 'assertibility conditions' rather than 'realist truth conditions' – and what is in the things 'in themselves' *constitutive* of realism?

Part of my answer to that question was given in the first lecture. Far from being constitutive of *commonsense* realism, that dichotomy tends to undermine it, as I tried to show. But another part of the answer must consist in showing that the rejection of this dichotomy is not a simple capitulation to garden-variety cultural relativism, or to the idea that every conceptual scheme is as good as every other.

What is strange about the fear that only the Metaphysical Realist can save fair Common Sense from Demon Relativism is that even Metaphysical Realists recognize that the writ of rationality runs farther than what they are pleased to call 'realist truth'. Mackie did not think that ordinary-language causal statements, e.g., 'The failure of the safety valve caused the boiler to explode', are 'simply true', but he would certainly have distinguished between 'reasonable' and 'unreasonable' ones. Perhaps such statements have only 'assertibility' conditions rather than 'truth' conditions, perhaps they are used to issue 'inference licenses' rather than to 'describe', but that does not make them arbitrary. If we license one another to expect X to dissolve when put in water when X is a piece of sugar, this is part of a practice whose success we can explain; and if we issued the same license when X was a piece of steel, nature would show us our mistake. In the same way, Quine denies that 'X means *Do you speak French?* states a 'fact', even when X is the familiar French utterance, *Parlez-vous français?*; but he would certainly answer the question 'What does *Parlez-vous français?* mean?' with 'It means *Do you speak French?* and not with 'It means *Coachman, stop, the road is jerky; look out! you will lose the turkey*'. That one answer to this sort of question has 'heuristic' value and the other does not is something he himself points out. (I am not claiming that Quine is a 'metaphysical realist', in my sense, since he does not accept the correspondence theory of truth; but his 'robust realism' has an important feature in common with metaphysical realism – namely, the existence of a sharp line between what there is a 'fact of the matter' about, and what has only 'heuristic' value, or value when our interests are less than 'theoretical'.)

In sum, my own position involves the denial of yet another dichotomy:

(TYPE OF STATEMENT)

Possesses only assertibility vs Possesses truth
  conditions   conditions

We can know that it is 'true', speaking with the vulgar, that the water would have boiled if I had turned on the stove, without having the slightest idea whether this 'truth' is 'realist truth' (Mackie's 'simply true') or only an idealization of 'warranted assertibility'. Nor need we suppose the question makes sense. Rejecting the dichotomy *within* kinds of 'truth' – kinds of truth in the common-sense world – is not the same thing as saying 'anything goes'.

Reality without the dichotomies

How can one assure oneself that this is not sheer linguistic idealism? Perhaps the best place to start is with the explanation of internal realism that I gave in the first lecture. That explanation certainly sounds like 'linguistic idealism'; according to me, how many objects there are in the world (and even whether certain objects – individual space-time points, in the second of the examples I used – exist at all as individual 'particulars') is relative to the choice of a conceptual scheme. How can one propound this sort of relativistic doctrine and still claim to believe that there is anything to the idea of 'externality', anything to the idea that there is something 'out there' independent of language and the mind?

Well, it really isn't so hard. Look again at the picture I showed you:

WORLD 1	WORLD 2
x_1, x_2, x_3	$x_1, x_2, x_3, x_1 + x_2,$
	$x_1 + x_3, x_2 + x_3,$
	$x_1 + x_2 + x_3$
(A world *à la* Carnap)	('Same' world *à la* Polish logician)

How we go about answering the question 'How many objects are there?' – the method of 'counting', or the notion of what constitutes an 'object' – depends on our choice (call this a 'convention'); but the *answer* does not thereby become a matter of convention. If I choose Carnap's language, I must say there are three objects because *that is how many there are*. If I choose the Polish logician's language (this is the language of a Polish logician who has not yet invented the 'null object' O, remember), I must say there are seven objects, *because that is how many objects* (in the Polish logician's sense of 'object') *there are*. There are 'external facts', and we can *say what they are*. What we *cannot* say – because it makes no sense – is what the facts are *independent of all conceptual choices*.

A metaphor which is often employed to express this is the metaphor of the 'cookie cutter'. The things independent of all conceptual choices are the dough; our conceptual contribution is the shape of the cookie cutter. Unfortunately, this metaphor is of no real assistance in understanding the phenomenon of conceptual relativity. Take it seriously, and you are at once forced to answer the question, 'What are the various parts of the dough?' If you answer, that (in the present case) the 'atoms' of the dough are x_1, x_2, x_3, and the other parts are the mereological sums containing more than one 'atom', then you have simply *adopted* the Polish logician's version. Insisting that this is the correct view of the metaphysical situation is just another way of insisting that mereological sums *really* exist. But internal realism denies that this is *more* the 'right' way to view the situation than is insisting that only Carnap's 'individuals' really exist. The metaphysician who takes the latter view can also explain the success of the Polish logician's version, after all: he can say that when the Polish logician says, as it might be, that

(I) There is at least one object which is partly red and partly black,

this is to be understood as a useful *façon de parler*, rather than as something which is 'literally true'. Under an adequate translation scheme (and such a scheme can be easily given in a recursive way, in the case of the kind of first-order language that Carnap had in mind in these simple examples), (I) turns out to say no more than

(II) There is at least one red object and there is at least one black object

says when written in the Carnapian language. (To verify this, assuming that 'red' and 'black' are predicates of Carnap's language, observe that the only way a Polish logician's object – a mereological sum – can be partly red is by containing a red atom, and the only way it can be partly black is by containing a black atom. So if (I) is true in the Polish logician's language, then there is at least one red atom and at least one black atom – which is what (II) says in Carnap's language. Conversely, if there is at least one black atom and at least one red atom, then their mereological sum is an 'object' – in the Polish logician's sense – which is partly red and partly black.) To claim that such a translation scheme

shows what is 'really going on' is just a way of insisting that mereological sums *don't* 'really exist'.

The cookie cutter metaphor *denies* (rather than explaining) the phenomenon of conceptual relativity. The other way of dealing with our little example – producing a translation scheme which *reinterprets the logical connectives (in this case, existence)*, in such a way that each statement in the 'richer' language can be 'translated' into the more 'parsimonious' language – may also be used to deny the phenomenon of conceptual relativity; but it is, nonetheless, more sophisticated than the cookie cutter metaphor. The cookie cutter metaphor assumes that all existence statements that we count as true in our several versions really are true; it's just that the variables of quantification pick out different mereological sums as their ranges in the case of different languages. The device of *reinterpretation* goes beyond this in recognizing that one person's 'existence' claim may be another person's something else.

Sometimes it is suggested that in such cases we should *not* be 'neutrals'; we should always adopt the more parsimonious version. 'If we don't have to postulate such strange discontinuous objects as mereological sums, then should't we take that as a reason for concluding that they don't really exist, that they are just (at best) a *façon de parler*?'

To this metaphysical move there is, inevitably, an equally metaphysical rejoinder: 'Aren't almost all the "objects" we talk about – chairs and tables, our own bodies, countries, not to mention such scientific objects as solar systems and galaxies – "strange discontinuous objects"? It hardly follows that they don't really exist. Yet, if my body exists, if this chair exists, if the solar system exists, then why should we not say that the discontinuous object consisting of *my nose and the Eiffel Tower* also exists? This is an unnatural object to talk about, to be sure, but what has the "naturalness" of an object to do with its *existence*?'

What is right with the second of the ways we considered of reconciling the two versions or 'worlds' – reinterpreting the existential quantifier – is that the notions of 'object' and 'existence' are not treated as sacrosanct, as having just one possible use. It is very important to recognize that the existential quantifier itself can be used in different ways – ways consonant with the rules of formal logic. What would be wrong, were we to do it, would be to accept this idea, and then go on to single out *one* use of the existential quantifier – the use in Carnap's version – as the only metaphysically *serious* one. But go one step farther: take the position that one may *either* treat Carnap's version as 'correct' and interpret the Polish logician's version as a *façon de parler* in the manner illustrated by the reinterpretation of (I) as (II), or treat the Polish logician's version as 'correct' and interpret Carnap's version as a language in which the range of the individual variables is restricted to atoms (as suggested by the cookie cutter metaphor). That is, take the position that one will be equally 'right' in either case. Then you have arrived at the position I have called 'internal realism'!

What is wrong with the notion of objects existing 'independently' of conceptual schemes is that there are no standards for the use of even the logical notions apart from conceptual choices. What the cookie cutter metaphor tries to preserve is the naïve idea that at least one Category – the ancient category of Object or Substance – has an absolute interpretation. The alternative to this idea is not the view that, in some inconceivable way, it's all *just* language. We can and should insist that some facts are there to be discovered and not legislated by us. But this is something to be said when one has adopted a way of speaking, a language, a 'conceptual scheme'. To talk of 'facts' without specifying the language to be used is to talk of nothing; the word 'fact' no more has its use fixed by Reality Itself than does the word 'exist' or the word 'object'.

Of course, the adoption of internal realism is the renunciation of the notion of the 'thing in itself'. And here lies the connection between the almost trivial example we have been discussing and the profound metaphysical dichotomies (or would-be dichotomies) we discussed earlier. Internal realism says that the notion of a 'thing in itself' makes no sense; and *not* because 'we cannot know the things in themselves'. This was Kant's reason, but Kant, although admitting that the notion of a thing in itself *might* be 'empty', still allowed it to possess a formal kind of sense. Internal realism says that we don't know what we are talking about when we talk about 'things in themselves'. And that means that the dichotomy between 'intrinsic' properties and properties which are not intrinsic also collapses – collapses because the 'intrinsic' properties were supposed to be just the properties things have 'in themselves'. The thing in itself and the property the thing has 'in itself' belong to the same circle of ideas, and it is time to admit that what the circle encloses is worthless territory.

A dichotomy whose relation to these notions may be somewhat less evident is the dichotomy between 'truth-conditional semantics' and 'assertibility-conditional semantics'. Yet what could ground the claim that certain sorts of statements, for example, 'If I *had* put a pan of water on the stove and turned on the flame, the water *would have* boiled', have only 'assertibility conditions' and not 'truth conditions'? What, that is, but a preconceived idea of what is and is not 'ontologically queer', that is, what is and is not capable of being a part of the world as the world as the world is 'in itself'? As I argued in yesterday's lecture, the problem with that preconceived idea, in its Humean as well as in its Cartesian version, was its inability to tell any story about the mind (or, if you prefer, about 'intentionality') which was not riddled with contradictions or saddled with arbitrary and unconvincing posits; and I argued that this remains its problem today.

What does the world look like without the dichotomies? It looks both familiar and different. It looks familiar, insofar as we no longer try to divide up mundane reality into a 'scientific image' and a 'manifest image' (or our evolving doctrine into a 'first-class' and a 'second-class' conceptual system). Tables and chairs (and yes, pink ice cubes) exist just as much as quarks and gravitational fields, and the fact that this pot of water would have boiled if I had put it on the stove and turned on the flame is as much a 'fact' as is the circumstance that the water weights more than eight ounces. The idea that most of mundane reality is illusion (an idea which has haunted Western philosophy since Plato, in spite of Aristotle's valiant counterattack) is given up once and for all. But mundane reality looks different, in that we are forced to acknowledge that many of our familiar descriptions reflect our interests and choices.

Imagine that the escape valve on a pressure cooker sticks and the pressure cooker explodes. We say – and the conceptual relativist regards this as a perfectly 'true' statement, without making any fuss about whether it is 'simply true' or only a 'good inference license' – 'The stuck valve caused the pressure cooker to explode'. We do not say 'The presence of Δ caused the pressure cooker to explode', where Δ is, say, an arbitrary irregularly shaped piece of the surface of the cooker, 0.1 cm in area. Yet, in the physics of the explosion, the role played by the stuck valve is exactly the same as the role of Δ: the absence of either would have permitted the steam to escape, bringing down the pressure and averting the explosion.

Why, then, do we speak of one of these things and not the other as 'causing' the explosion? Well, we know that the valve 'should have' let the steam escape – that is its 'function', what it was designed to do. On the other hand, the surface element Δ was not doing anything 'wrong' in preventing the steam from escaping; containing the steam is the 'function' of the surface of which Δ is a part. So when we ask 'Why did the explosion take place?', knowing what we know and having the interests we do have, our 'explanation space' consists of the alternatives:

(1) Explosion taking place
(2) Everything functioning as it should

What we want to know, in other words, is why (1) is what happened, *as opposed to* (2). We are simply not interested in why (1) is what happened *as opposed to* such alternatives as:

(3) The surface element Δ is missing, and no explosion takes place.

This 'explanatory relativity' is parallelled by a relativity in our use of such locutions as 'caused' and 'the cause'. Since the question 'Why did the pressure cooker explode?' assumes an explanation space which does not include the alternative (3), or similar alternatives, we understand such factors as the presence of Δ to be 'background conditions' and not 'causes'.

This relativity of causes to interests, and to background conditions not mentioned in the 'hard science' explanation of the event in question, does not make causation something we simply legislate. Given our interests and what we regard as the relevant background conditions, it would be simply false to say that it was the wall of the pressure cooker that caused the explosion (unless it happened to be defective, and it should happen to be the defect and not the condition of the valve that 'explains' the explosion). Our conceptual scheme restricts the 'space' of descriptions available to us; but it does not predetermine the answers to our questions.

It is understandable, however, that many philosophers should read a different moral into this story. Does not the situation lend itself naturally to a dichotomy? Should we not regard the 'hard science' description of the situation ('The pressure increased in the closed container until a certain coefficient was exceeded. The material then rup-

tured . . .') with its exact laws and numerical coefficients as the description of the 'objective facts', and regard the singling out of the bit of material, or whatever, that kept the valve from working as 'the cause' as semi-magical Stone Age thinking? If we want to be generous and leave a place for this useful way of speaking, while denying that there exists a distinction between 'causes' and 'background conditions' in Nature itself, we can just say that causal statements have 'assertibility' conditions in ordinary language but not, strictly speaking, 'truth conditions'.

The problem with all this – the problem I discussed in the first lecture – is that if the causes/background conditions distinction is fundamentally subjective, not descriptive of the world in itself, then current philosophical explanations of the metaphysical nature of *reference* are bankrupt. John Barwise and John Perry, for example, tell us that what links certain states of affairs to certain mental states is that the states of affairs *cause* those states; this is the intentional link, at least in certain metaphysically basic cases. Clark Glymour and Michael Devitt (independently) both tell us that words are connected to their referents by 'causal connection'. Richard Boyd tells us that 'the causal theory of reference is correct because the causal theory of knowledge is correct'. But the notions on which causal theories of knowledge and reference depend – the difference between a cause and a mere background condition, the legitimacy of counterfactuals – are precisely what is called into question by the 'inference licence' interpretation of causal statements and counterfactuals. If these notions are 'saved' only to the extent of being treated as heuristics (as 'projections', in the terminology of the first lecture), then it cannot also be held that they explain how reference comes to exist in the world as the world is 'in itself'.

Nor would dualism help, if we were willing to adopt it. For what description do we have of the mind 'in itself'? Kant's exposure of the bankruptcy of 'rational psychology' still stands.

Rather than succumb to the temptation to repeat verbatim all the proposals of the seventeenth and eighteenth centuries, we have to recognize that such familiar statements as the statement that the stuck valve caused the pressure cooker to explode reflect both the way things are and our interests and assumptions about the way things are *without* giving in to the temptation to suppose that the philosophically relevant description of 'the way things are' is something *other* than 'the valve stuck and caused the pressure cooker to explode' (or whatever the example may be). *Given* a language, we can describe the 'facts' that make the sentences of that language true and false in a 'trivial' way – using the sentences of that very language; but the dream of finding a well-defined Universal Relation between a (supposed) totality of *all* facts and an arbitrary true sentence in

an arbitrary language is just the dream of an absolute notion of a fact (or of an object') and of an absolute relation between sentences and the facts (or the objects) 'in themselves'; the very dream whose hopelessness I hoped to expose with the aid of my little example involving three Carnapian individuals and seven non-empty mereological sums.

Notes

1 Wilfrid Sellars, *Science, Perception, and Reality* (Atlantic Highlands, NJ: Humanities Press, 1963).

2 Edmund Husserl, *The Crisis of the European Sciences and Transcendental Phenomenology*, trans. David Carr (Evanston, Ill.: Northwestern University Press, 1970).

3 See C. L. Hardin's 'Are "Scientific" objects colored?', *Mind*, 93/22 (Oct. 1964), pp. 491–500.

4 The commonsense notion of 'solidity' should not be confused with the physicist's notion of being in 'the solid state'. For example, a sand dune is in the 'solid state' but is not solid in the ordinary sense of the term, while a bottle of milk may be solid, but most of its contents are not in the solid state.

5 Herbert Feigl, 'The "mental" and the "physical" ', in Feigl, Scriven, and Maxwell (eds), *Minnesota Studies in the Philosophy of Science*, vol. 2: *Concepts, Theories and the Mind–Body Problem* (Minneapolis: University of Minnesota Press, 1958), pp. 370–497.

6 This is argued in my *Representation and Reality* (Cambridge, Mass.: MIT Press, 1988).

7 D. C. Dennett, *Content and Consciousness* (Atlantic Highlands, NJ: Humanities Press, 1969).

8 Richard Rorty, *Philosophy and the Mirror of Nature* (Princeton: Princeton University Press, 1979).

9 Stephen Stich, *From Folk Psychology to Cognitive Science: The Case Against Belief* (Cambridge, Mass.: MIT Press, 1983).

10 W. V. Quine, 'On what there is', this volume, ch. 1.

11 White has advocated doing this early and late: *Toward Reunion in Philosophy* (Cambridge, Mass.: Harvard University Press, 1956); *What Is and What Ought to Be Done* (Oxford: Oxford University Press, 1981).

12 In logic a way of connecting statements is called 'truth-functional' if the truth-value of the resulting statement can be determined given just the truth-values of the components. Counterfactual conditionals all have false antecedents, and typically they have false consequents as well; yet some of them are true and some false. Thus the counterfactual is not a truth-function of its parts.

13 David Lewis, *Counterfactuals* (Cambridge, Mass.: Harvard University Press, 1973).

14 This idea was implicit in Carnap's treatment of dispositional predicates via 'reduction sentences' in 'Testability and meaning', *Philosophy of Science* 3 (1936) pp. 420–68, 4 (1937) pp. 1–40.

15 J. L. Mackie, *The Cement of the Universe* (New York: Oxford University Press, 1974).

16 E.g., Hempel proposed to count as complete 'explanations' only those explanations which fit his strict Deductive-Nomological Model. (Cf. Hempel and C. P. Oppenheim, 'The logic of scientific explanation', repr. in H. Feigl and M. Brodbeck (eds), *Readings in the Philosophy of Science*. (New York: Appleton-Century-Crofts, 1953), pp. 319–52.

17 Mackie (*Cement of the Universe*) referred to the notion we use in these as our 'paleolithic' notion of causation.

45

Putnam's Pragmatic Realism

Ernest Sosa

Exceptional among contemporary philosophers, Hilary Putnam has long defended a philosophy sane enough to hold not only water, but also people and even values. Having once championed hard realism, he has moved steadily away from any scientism that would have physical science determine fully our world view and its ontology to the detriment of our lifeworld. In several fascinating papers and books, he has developed an alternative realism called first "internal" and more recently "pragmatic."

Putnam has been at pains to distinguish his view from Rortean relativism and from the excesses of recent French philosophy, but he has also warned repeatedly against naïve belief in a ready-made world with "in-itself" categories. According to his own preferred *via media*, the mind and the world jointly constitute *both* the mind and the world. It is not immediately obvious what this amounts to in prosaic detail, however, and there is no better way to find out than to examine his arguments.

Putnam argues against "metaphysical realism" and in favor of his own "internal (or pragmatic) realism." Both the view and the arguments, however, have provoked much controversy. Donald Davidson,[1] for example, finds Putnam's version of antirealism objectionable, and indeed incoherent. By 'internal realism' Putnam seems to have in

mind not just that the truth of sentences or utterances is relative to a language. That much is, as Davidson indicates, "familiar and trivially correct." But, Davidson continues, "Putnam seems to have more in mind – for example that a sentence of yours and a sentence of mine may contradict each other, and yet each be true 'for the speaker'. It is hard to think in what language this position can be coherently, much less persuasively, expressed."[2] What argument might lead to such a view?

Putnam has several arguments, actually, but four stand out. First, the "model-theoretic" argument; second, the argument from the nonobjectivity of reference and of the sort of causation involved in contemporary accounts of reference; third, the argument from the unlikelihood of scientific convergence on a finished science that provides an objective and absolute conception of reality; and, finally, the argument from the nonabsoluteness of objecthood and of existence.

The model-theoretic argument has been most extensively discussed and has elicited much criticism. It seems to me that on this argument we have reached an impasse. The critics charge that whatever it is that constitutes reference can on its own secure reference between our words and the pertinent items in the objective, independent world: for example, if a certain causal relation is what constitutes reference, then the existence of that causal relation between a word of ours and a certain item would be sufficient on its own to bring it about that the reference relation holds between the word and the item. Most emphatically, according to the

Originally published in *Journal of Philosophy* 90 (1993), pp. 605–26. Copyright © by Ernest Sosa and the Journal of Philosophy, Inc. Reprinted by permission of the author and Columbia University.

critics, it is not required, as Putnam seems to believe, that we accept a theory about the relevant causal relation and about how it constitutes reference, a theory about which one could then with Putnam raise questions concerning how *its* words secure their reference, how the word 'causation' in it, for example, acquires its own reference. Putnam for his part accuses his critics of begging the question in supposing that the relevant causal relation can on its own, objectively and independently, secure reference relations between our words and corresponding items in ready-made reality. And he accuses his critics of superstitious belief in essentialism, and in a magical theory of reference.

Here I shall put that controversy aside, as one with little prospect of any new progress or insight beyond what is already contained in the extensive journal literature about it.[3] In what follows, I would like to discuss instead, and in turn, the other three arguments that sustain Putnam's pragmatic realism.

1 Perspectival Causation, Reference, Truth, and Reality

One place where this argument is presented in detail by Putnam is his paper "Why there isn't a ready-made world."[4] Here is a thumbnail sketch:

P 1 Truth depends on, and is constituted by, reference (at least in part).
2 Reference depends on, and is constituted by, causation (at least partly).
3 Causation is radically perspectival.
4 Reference is radically perspectival (from 2, 3).
5 Truth is radically perspectival (from 1, 4).
6 Reality is "internal" to one's perspective (from 5).

This can be spelled out a bit further as follows. When a belief or a sentence is true, that depends on and derives from what that belief or that sentence refers to. But when a belief or sentence refers to something, it does so, surely, in virtue of some appropriate causal relation holding between it and its referent. Causation is not an absolute relation, however, not a relation that holds in metaphysical reality independently of any perspective. For Earthians it may be a discarded cigarette that causes a forest fire, while for Martians it is the presence of oxygen. Strictly speaking 'X causes Y' is true or false not absolutely, but only relative

to perspective. At least that seems clear with regard to the less-than-total causation needed for an appropriate pairing of referents with referring terms. For example, we need to pair the term 'window' with windows and the term 'draft' with drafts, so we cannot stop with the *total* causation that relates, on one side, *both* the felt draft and the seen window (and much else) and, on the other, your utterance of 'Please close the window'.

If the sort of causation constitutive of reference is thus radically perspectival (perspective-relative), however, then reference is similarly perspectival, and so then must truth be, since reference is in turn constitutive of truth. But in that case reality itself must be also perspectival, also relative to perspective, and in that sense "internal" to perspective, and not wholly external.

What seems most questionable in that argument, put briefly and bluntly, is the move from the perspectival character of truth to the perspectival character of reality itself. Consider for comparison our vocabulary of indexicals and the associated perspectival concepts of oneself and of the temporal present. It may well be that these are important and ineliminable components of any adequate conceptual scheme (adequate for us limited humans, anyhow). Suppose that our *concepts* and our *conceptual scheme* are thus importantly perspectival. Would it follow that reality itself must be similarly perspectival? This seems implausible when we consider the following.

Take a world W defined by two people (Paul and Mary) and the postural state (standing, not-standing) of each, such that in W Paul is standing while Mary is sitting. In W, therefore, the sentence 'I am standing' is true relative to Paul, but false relative to Mary. And, more generally: whatever is true in a certain world W relative to a certain perspective and whatever is false in W relative to a certain perspective is as it is in that world as a necessary consequence of how things are in that world absolutely and nonperspectivally.

It is true that our talk and even, granted, our *thought* is in fact largely perspectival. It may well be, moreover, that the perspectival character of our thought is not eliminable except (at best) with a very high practical and intellectual cost. But from the fundamentally and ineliminably perspectival character of our thought it does not follow that reality itself is fundamentally perspectival. Everything that is true relative to a perspective and everything that is false relative to a perspective may be as it is as a necessary consequence of the absolute and nonperspectival character of things.

Perhaps it is true that our concepts of reference and truth are ineliminably perspectival. Even so, it still would not follow that reality itself could not be largely as it is independently of us and our thought, in the sense that plenty of reality could have existed propertied and interrelated very extensively just as it is in fact propertied and interrelated even if we had never existed to have any thoughts, and even if no other finite thinkers had taken our place. What is more, our perspectival references and truths may be seen to derive necessarily from absolute and unperspectival reality.

2 Objectivity, Absoluteness, and the Many Faces of Realism

What the metaphysical realist holds is that we can think and talk about things as they are, independently of our minds, and that we can do this by virtue of a 'correspondence' relation between the terms in our language and some sorts of mind-independent entities.[5]

But reference, like causality, is a flexible, interest-relative notion [and so, therefore, is correspondence]: what we count as *referring* to something depends on background knowledge and our willingness to be charitable in interpretation. To read a relation so deeply human and so pervasively intentional into the world and to call the resulting metaphysical picture satisfactory (never mind whether or not it is 'materialist') is absurd.[6]

But, again, why must the metaphysical realist "read into the world" any such relation of reference or of correspondence (or of causal explanation)? What the metaphysical realist is committed to holding is that there is an in-itself reality independent of our minds and even of our existence, and that we can talk about such reality and its constituents by virtue of correspondence relations between our language (and/or our minds), on the one hand, and things-in-themselves and their intrinsic properties (including their relations), on the other. This does not commit the metaphysical realist to holding that reference itself (or correspondence, or causal explanation) is among the objective properties constitutive of in-itself reality.

Bernard Williams[7] apparently reaches just that conclusion and adopts the view that it opens up. Putnam responds as follows:

... Williams's suggestion is that the intentional (or the "semantic") is itself perspectival, and the absolute conception will someday explain why this kind of talk is useful (as it explains why talk of "grass" and "green" is useful, even though "grass" and "green" are not notions that figure in the absolute conception of the world). But ... the absolute conception of the world was *defined* in terms of the idea that some statements describe the world with a minimum of "distortion," that they describe it "as it is," that they describe it "independently of perspective" – and what does any of this talk mean, unless something like a correspondence theory of truth is in place? Williams tacitly assumes a correspondence theory of truth when he *defines* the absolute conception, and then forgets that he did this when he suggests that we do not need to assume that such semantic notions as the "content" of a sentence will turn out to figure in the absolute conception itself.[8]

It is hard to see this bit of reasoning as anything more than a fallacy. From the fact that the absoluteness that applies to conceptions is a perspectival concept, it simply does not follow that any absolute conception itself must include any perspectival concept, not even the concept of absoluteness. (My copy of *Principia Mathematica is mine*, and the concept of what is one's own is a perspectival concept, but it does not follow that my copy of *PM* must include the concept of what is one's own.)

Putnam does argue further that Williams must make room in his absolute conception itself for notions of reference and correspondence (and of absoluteness itself). Putnam writes that "if, as Williams believes, the fact that we are 'fated' to accept the sentence 'Snow is white' is *explained* by something 'out there', then the correspondence too must be 'out there'."[9] And his argument here seems to turn on an assumption that only an objective, nonperspectival correspondence could do the explanatory work that Williams requires. Only such an objective relation of correspondence could possibly explain why it is that we accept certain truths, and why it is that they are rightly assertible, when all this is so *because* the truths in question correspond to the way things (mind-independently) are. This seems inconclusive, however.

Prima facie, it would seem I can explain why I return a book to you by saying that it is *yours*. I can explain why I reach for some water by saying that *I* am thirsty. And so on. Why assume that perspectival concepts have no legitimate place in explanations?

There is nevertheless an argument open to Putnam against William's view if the latter includes commitment to "objectivism," which is defined by Putnam in *The Many Faces of Realism* (TMFR)[10] as *the view that what really has a place in objective reality is only what is included in the ontology and the ideology of "finished science," only what the absolute conception recognizes*.[11] It is not at all clear that Williams himself would accept objectivism, but in Putnam's own mind objectivism and absolutism are closely connected, as emerges clearly in *TMFR*. In any case, the argument against objectivism is as follows. The objectivist believes that only what would be reflected in finished science is truly real (the rest will amount at most to heuristically or practically valuable talk, and cannot truly represent reality). But, as we have seen, perspectival concepts like those of reference, correspondence, and causal explanation will not be reflected in finished science, in the science to be converged upon by all determined inquirers, whatever their perspective or context. So the objectivist seems committed by Putnam's reasoning to holding that he is not really thinking at all, nor referring to anything (assuming, again, that Putnam's reasoning about reference, correspondence, and causal explanation is correct). Thus Putnam's complaint in TMFR: "It's as if it were all right to say 'I don't deny that there is an external world; I just deny that we [truly really] *think* about it'!"[12]

In *TMFR*, Putnam also returns to his argument against metaphysical realism via appeal to intentionality, aboutness, reference, and correspondence. And again his reasoning goes in outline like this:

(a) The only viable form of metaphysical realism is objectivism (or materialism or scientific realism).

(b) For objectivism only properties that figure in strict and exceptionless laws are real properties of things in themselves (and these are presumably laws that would be part of finished science) – though perhaps we might admit also properties based on strict laws in the way strict dispositional properties might be so based.

(c) But clearly there is little prospect that the mind can be viewed as constituted or characterized by such properties. Sensa have no place in any actual science, much less in finished science.[13] If we think of (some) mental properties in terms of dispositions, and of these in terms of conditionals, we find that the conditionals involved are all "in normal conditions," *ceteris paribus* sorts of conditionals; and none of these has a place in finished science.[14] As for reference, aboutness, and correspondence, the most promising account of these acceptable to an objectivist (materialist, scientific realist) is in terms of causation. But the causation involved would be relative to interests and background conditions (in the way we have seen in earlier discussion) and hence perspectival in a way antithetical to finished science.[15]

Let us now consider this line of reasoning, which connects realism thus with objectivism.

In *TMFR*, four dichotomies are decisively rejected. First these three:

D1 Subjective (interest- and culture-relative) versus objective (interest- and culture-independent).

D2 Projection [property attributed falsely, etc.] versus property of the thing in itself.

D3 Power [dispositional property] versus property of the thing in it-self.[16]

About these we are told: "The rejection of these three dichotomies is the essence of ... 'internal realism'."[17] And then a fourth dichotomy is also targeted:

D4 Statement possessing only assertibility conditions versus statement possessing truth conditions.[18]

How are we to understand the technical terms used in the formulation of these four dichotomies? Here is a proposal:

(i) ϕ is a subjective property $=_{Df}$ ϕ is postulated by a particular language or conceptual scheme.

(ii) ϕ is a property of the thing in itself (an intrinsic, objective property) $=_{Df}$ ϕ is a property that is not just subjective but would be postulated by finished science.

(iii) x is a subjective individual $=_{Df}$ x is among the individuals or is a member of a kind of individual postulated by some particular language or conceptual scheme.

(iv) x is a thing in itself (an objective individual) $=_{Df}$ x is among the individuals or is a member of a kind of individual postulated by finished science.

(v) Statement σ has assertibility conditions in a particular language or conceptual scheme L $=_{Df}$ L contains criteria or rules that specify conditions within which σ would be correctly assertible.

(vi) Statement σ has truth conditions $=_{Df}$ σ has assertibility conditions within finished science (i.e., σ attributes an intrinsic, objective property with respect to things in themselves or objective individuals).

We can understand the emphasis that Putnam places on rejection of these dichotomies above, and on how that rejection defines his own internal or pragmatic realism, if we focus on how all four of them involve the notion of an intrinsic property of things-in-themselves, about which Putnam has this to say: "The deep systemic root of the disease [of objectivism or scientific realism, and hence of metaphysical realism], I want to suggest, lies in the notion of an 'intrinsic' property, a property something has 'in itself', apart from any contribution made by language or the mind."[19]

Perhaps our definitions may help clarify Putnam's rationale for rejecting the four dichotomies, and the content and motivation for his own internal or pragmatic realism, as well as his emphasis on conceptual relativity, as put, for example, in the following passage: "The key to working out the program of preserving commonsense realism while avoiding the absurdities and antinomies of metaphysical realism in all its familiar varieties ... is something I have called *internal realism*. (I should have called it pragmatic realism!) Internal realism is, at bottom, just the insistence that realism is *not* incompatible with conceptual relativity."[20]

Putnam's rejection of the dichotomies derives, on the present suggestion, from his rejection of the possibility that there are things-in-themselves with intrinsic properties. For if there is no possibility that there are any such things or properties, then there are no objective things-in-themselves, no intrinsic, objective properties of things-in-themselves, and no statements with truth conditions. All this may be seen through the definitions above. And it then follows that none of the dichotomies is real: they are all necessarily empty on one side.

But just how does Putnam refute the possibility that there are things-in-themselves with intrinsic, objective properties. He has argued explicitly as follows:

[If] ... it is simply a matter of how we formalize our language whether we say (with Saul Kripke) that stones, animals, persons, and so on are *not* identical with mereological sums at all, or say (as suggested by Lewis) that they *are* mereological sums (and take care of Kripke's difficulty by claiming that when we say that "the" stone consists of different particle-slices in different possible worlds, then what that means is that the various modal "counterparts" of the stone in different possible worlds consists of different particle slices, and not that the self-identical stone consists of different particle slices in different possible worlds) – and to me this certainly looks like a mere choice of a formalism, and not a question of fact – we will be forced to admit that it is partly a matter of our conceptual choice which scientific object a given commonsense object – a stone or a person – is identified with ... Nor is the situation any better in theoretical physics. At the level of space-time geometry, there is the well-known fact that we can take points to be individuals or we can take them to be mere limits ... Not only do single theories have a bewildering variety of alternative rational reconstructions (with quite different ontologies), but there is no evidence at all for the claim (which is essential to ... an "absolute conception of the world") that science converges to a *single* theory ... We simply do not have the evidence to justify speculation as to whether or not science is "destined" to converge to some one definite theoretical picture ... Yet, without the postulate that science converges to a single definite theoretical picture with a unique ontology and a unique set of theoretical predicates, the whole notion of "absoluteness" collapses [and indeed is] ... incoherent. Mathematics and physics, as well as ethics and history and politics, show our conceptual choices; the world is not going to impose a single language upon us, no matter what we choose to talk about.[21]

And that suggests the following argument against things-in-themselves with intrinsic properties.

(a) There is no real possibility of a finished science.

(b) Things-in-themselves are by definition the things in the ontology of finished science, and intrinsic, objective properties are by definition those in the ideology of finished science.

(c) Hence, there is no possibility that there are things-in-themselves with intrinsic, objective properties.

When we take stock, now, we see that we must learn to live with unfinished science: when we affirm that there are certain things with certain properties, our affirmation must be viewed as relative to a particular language or conceptual scheme. It may then be viewed as one that, if correct, is correct by the assertibility rules or criteria of that language or scheme. I shall return to this form of reasoning below.

Putnam has further reasoning behind his rejection of objective or absolute reality, however; I mean his arguments from the nonabsoluteness of existence itself. To this reasoning I turn next.

3 Nonabsolute Existence and Conceptual Relativity

Suppose a world with just three individuals x_1, x_2, x_3. Such a world is held by some "mereologists" to have in it a total of seven things or entities or objects, namely, x_1, x_2, x_3, $x_1 + x_2$, $x_1 + x_3$, $x_2 + x_3$, $x_1 + x_2 + x_3$. Antimereologists by contrast prefer the more austere ontology that recognizes only the three individuals as objects that *really* exist in that world. Talk of the existence of $x_1 + x_2$ and its ilk is just convenient abbreviation of a more complex discourse that refers to nothing but the three individuals. Thus, suppose x_1 is wholly red and x_2 is wholly black. And consider

(1) There is an object that is partly red and partly black.

(2) There is an object that is red and an object that is black.

For the antimereologist, statement 1 is not true, if we assume that x_3 is also wholly red or wholly black. It is at best a convenient way of abbreviating the likes of 2.

Putnam has now joined Rudolf Carnap in viewing our controversy as follows:

... the question is one of the choice of language. On some days it may be convenient to use [antimereological language]; ... on other days it may be convenient to use [mereological] language.[22]

Take the question

How many objects with a volume of at least 6 cubic centimeters are there in this container?

This question can have no absolute answer on the Carnap–Putnam view, even in a case where the container contains a vacuum except for three marbles each with a volume of 6 cubic centimeters. The antimereologist may say

(3) There are three objects in the box.

But the mereologist will reply:

(4) There are at least seven objects in the box.

The Carnap–Putnam line is now this: *which statement we accept* – (3) or (4) – *is a matter of linguistic convenience.* The language of mereology has criteria of existence and identity according to which sums of individuals are objects. The language of antimereology rejects such criteria, and may even claim that by its criteria only individuals are objects.

There is a valuable insight here, I believe, but I am puzzled by the linguistic wrapping in which it is offered. After all, none of (1)–(4) mentions any language or any piece of language, nor does any of them say that we shall or shall not or should or should not use any language or bit of language. So I do not see how our decision actually to use or not to use any or all of the sentences (1)–(4) can settle the question of whether what these sentences *say* is true or false. And if the point is that these sentences do not really *say* anything, then how can they be incompatible in the first place so that a conflict or problem can arise that requires resolution? Also, it is not clear how we gain by replacing questions about atoms (or the like) with questions about *sentences* and *our* relations to some specific ones of these sentences. This is all very puzzling, and we should pause to peer more closely.

What does the proposed linguistic relativity amount to? Can it be spelled out more fully and prosaically? Here, for a start, is a possibility:

LR1: In order to say *anything* you must adopt a language. So you must "adopt a meaning" even for so basic a term as 'object'. And you might have adopted another. Thus you might adopt Carnap language (CL) or you might adopt Polish logician language (PL). What you say, i.e., the utterances you make, the sentences you affirm, are not true or false absolutely, but are true or false only relative to a given language. Thus, if you say "There are three objects in this box," your utterance or sentence may be true understood as a statement of CL while it is false understood as a statement in PL.

But under this interpretation linguistic relativity seems trivially true. Who could deny that inscriptions of shapes and emissions of sounds are not true or false independently of their meaning, independently of all relativization to language or idiolect? Of course, you must "adopt a language" in order to speak (though such "adoption" need not be a conscious and voluntary act), and indeed you might have adopted another. And it seems quite uncontroversial that an utterance of yours might be true relative to one language while it is false relative to another.

Perhaps then the point is rather this:

LR2: When we say 'There are 3 objects here, not 8' we are really saying: 'The following is assertible as true in our CL: "There are 3 objects here, not 8." '

This is indeed in the spirit of Carnap's philosophy, whose *Logical Syntax of Language*,[23] published in English in 1937, defends the following theses:

(i) Philosophy, when cognitive at all, amounts to the logical syntax of scientific language.
(ii) But there can be alternative such languages and we are to choose between them on grounds of convenience.
(iii) A language is completely characterized by its formation and transformation rules.

In that book Carnap also distinguishes between:

(s1) Object sentences: e.g., 'Five is a prime number', 'Babylon was a big town'.
(s2) Pseudo–object sentences: e.g., 'Five is not a thing but a number', 'Babylon was treated of in yesterday's lecture'.

(s3) Syntactical sentences: e.g., ' "Five" is not a thing-word but a number-word', ' "Babylon" occurred in yesterday's lecture'.

And he defends the thesis that (s2) sentences seem deceptively like (s1) sentences but are really (s3) sentences in "material mode" disguise.

It was W. V. Quine who in 1934 suggested "material mode" to Carnap (as Quine himself reports in the section on "Semantic Ascent" in *Word and Object*[24]). Quine agrees that a kind of "semantic ascent" is possible, as when we shift from talk of miles to talk of 'mile', but he thinks this kind of semantic ascent is *always* trivially available, not just in philosophy but in science generally and even beyond. Thus, we can paraphrase 'There are wombats in Tasmania' as ' "Wombat" is true of some creatures in Tasmania'. Quine does grant that semantic ascent tends to be especially useful in philosophy. But he explains why as follows:

> The strategy of semantic ascent is that it carries the discussion into a domain where both parties are better agreed on the objects (viz., words) and on the main terms concerning them. Words, or their inscriptions, unlike points, miles, classes, and the rest, are tangible objects of the size so popular in the marketplace, where men of unlike conceptual schemes communicate at their best ... No wonder it helps in philosophy.[25]

The use of this strategy, however, is clearly limited to discourse about recondite entities of controversial status. No relevant gain is to be expected from semantic ascent when the subject matter is the inventory of the marketplace itself. Tables and chairs are no more controversial than words: in fact, they seem less so, by a good margin. No general internal realism, with its conceptual or linguistic relativity, can be plausibly supported by the semantic ascent strategy offered by Quine.

In addition, questions of coherence arise concerning LR2. When we say something of the form 'The following is assertible in our CL: ...' can we rest with a literal interpretation that does not require ascent and relativization? If not, where does ascent stop? Are we then *really* saying 'The following is assertible in our CL: "The following is assertible in our CL: ..." '. This way lies vicious regress. But if we *can* stop the regress with our metalinguistic reference to our sentences of CL (and to ourselves), why can we not stop it with our references to tables and chairs and other medium-sized dry goods?

An additional interpretation of Putnam's linguistic or conceptual relativism would have it say this:

LR3: When we see that finished science might well be a chimera, that our best attitude to it is that of agnosticism, we must not assert the claims of our present, unfinished science as if they amounted to truths about an in-itself reality and its intrinsic properties (which would require us to know that our claims would be found also in finished science – and who could possibly know about that?). Rather, we should rest content with the assertibility of our assertions in our unfinished conceptual or linguistic frameworks. But of course what is assertible in one framework may not be so in another. So we have to learn to live with our relativism. It is all pretty much like our claim that one must drive on the right, whose assertibility in the relevant American frameworks is not impugned by the fact that the opposite is assertible in the relevant British frameworks, nor by the absence of any "finished millenary legal system" that would include driving on the right as one of its requirements.

There is much to be discussed about this form of argument. But I would like to focus on one main presupposition required if it is put forward as a form of reasoning that would apply quite generally, whatever sphere may be involved. The argument, which I shall call *Putnam's master argument* (PMA) against realism, runs more simply as follows:

PMA 1 Realism (in general) is acceptable only if scientific realism is acceptable.

2 Scientific realism is not acceptable, if only because of the history of science induction, which precludes any reasonable expectation of convergence on one final ontology and ideology.

3 Therefore, realism is unacceptable: we cannot accept that there are any things-in-themselves with intrinsic properties; we can accept at best a view of things constitutive of our present conceptual or linguistic framework, but we must not suppose that this would gain conver-

gence among persistent, undefective inquirers, etc.

Here again there is much to be discussed, for example, about the relation between convergence and the existence of things-in-themselves, independently of the mind, with intrinsic properties in no way contributed by any speakers or thinkers. In any case, one premise of the argument that seems immediately dubious is the first. A large fragment of our commonsense view of ourselves and things around us seems quite safe from anything like the history of science induction. Surely, there is a great deal in our ordinary outlook that we share in common with groups widely divergent from us in place, time, and culture. Concerning all of that, nothing like the history of science induction stands in the way of convergence. Suppose we granted that the acceptability of (the certainty or at least the likelihood of) convergence *is* relevant to the acceptability of ordinary realism. And suppose we granted further that, given the history of science induction, we *cannot* plausibly expect that there would be any relevant sort of convergence in science: that here we must remain at best agnostic. Even so, that would not establish internal realism with its conceptual or linguistic relativity, as presently understood in line with interpretation LR3 above.[26]

There is hence reason to doubt the linguistic turn taken by Carnap and now Putnam. We have found no very plausible way to conceive of the turn so that it discloses an attractive new direction in metaphysics. The only direction that seems certainly right and clearly defensible is that provided by our first interpretation above (interpretation LR1), but that also seemed trivially right, and not something anyone would deny, not even the most hard-line metaphysical realist. Nevertheless, it still seems to me that there is a valuable insight in Putnam's now repeated appeal to the contrast between the Carnapian conceptual scheme and that of the Polish logician. But, given our recent reflections, I would like to put the insight without appeal to language or to any linguistic relativity.

The artifacts and even the natural objects that we recognize as existing at a time are normally composed of stuff or of parts in certain ways, and those which we see as enduring for an interval are normally not only thus composed of stuff or of parts at each instant of their enduring; but also the stuff or parts thus composing them right up to t must be related in certain restricted ways to the stuff or parts that compose them right after t, for any time t within the history of such an enduring object.

Thus, the existence of a snowball at a time t and location 1 requires that there be a round quantity of snow at 1 and t sufficiently separate from other snow, etc.; and for that snowball to endure through an interval I, it is required that for every division of I into a sequence of subintervals $I1, I2, \ldots$, there must be a corresponding sequence of quantities of snow $Q1, Q2, \ldots$, related in certain restricted ways. By all this I mean to point to our "criteria of existence and perdurance for snowballs."

I spoke of a snowball, its existence and perdurance, and what that requires of its sequence of constituent quantities of snow. In place of these, I might have talked of chains and constituent links, of boxes and constituent sides, or of a great variety of artifacts or natural entities such as hills or trees; or even – especially – of persons and their constituent bodies. In every case, there are criteria of existence and of perdurance for an entity of the sort in question such that necessarily an entity of the sort exists at t (perdures through I) if and only if its criteria of existence are satisfied at t (its criteria of perdurance are satisfied relative to I). Thus, necessarily a snowball exists at t if and only if at t a quantity of snow is round and separate from other snow; and a snowball perdures through I if and only if for any subdivision of I into a sequence of subintervals $I1, I2, \ldots$, there must be a corresponding sequence of round, etc., quantities of snow $Q1, Q2, \ldots$, such that, for all i, Qi satisfies the conditions for being successor of $Qi - 1$ in the constitution of the "life" of a snowball. And similarly for chains, boxes, hills, trees, and persons.

I am supposing a snowball to be constituted by a certain piece of snow as constituent matter and the shape of (approximate) roundness as constituent form. That particular snowball exists at that time because of the roundness of that piece of snow. More, if at that time that piece of snow were to lose its roundness, then at that time that snowball would go out of existence.

Compare now with our ordinary concept of a snowball, the concept of a snowdiscall, defined as an entity constituted by a piece of snow as matter and as form any shape between being round and being disc-shaped. At any given time, therefore, any piece of snow that constitutes a snowball constitutes a snowdiscall, but a piece of snow might at a time constitute a snowdiscall without then constituting a snowball. For every round piece of snow is also in shape between disc-shaped and round (inclusive), but a disc-shaped piece of snow is of course not round.

Any snowball SB must hence be constituted by a piece of snow PS which also then constitutes a snowdiscall SD. Now, SB is distinct (a different entity) from PS, since PS would survive squashing and SB would not. By similar reasoning, SD also is distinct from PS. And, again by similar reasoning, SB must also be distinct from SD, since enough partial flattening of PS will destroy SB but not SD. Now, there are infinitely many shapes $S1, S2, \ldots$, between roundness and flatness of a piece of snow, and, for each i, having a shape between flatness and Si would give the form of a distinctive kind of entity to be compared with snowballs and snowdiscalls. Whenever a piece of snow constitutes a snowball, therefore, it constitutes infinitely many entities all sharing its place with it.

Under a broadly Aristotelian conception, therefore, the barest flutter of the smallest leaf hence creates and destroys infinitely many things, and ordinary reality suffers a sort of "explosion."

We might perhaps resist this "explosion" of our ordinary world by embracing conceptual relativism. Constituted, supervenient entities do not just objectively supervene on their requisite, constitutive matters and forms, outside all conceptual schemes, with absolute independence from the categories recognized by any person or group. Perhaps snowballs do exist relative to all actual conceptual schemes ever, but not relative to all conceivable conceptual schemes. Just as we are not willing to countenance the existence of snowdiscalls, just so another culture might have been unwilling to countenance snowballs. We do not countenance snowdiscalls, because our conceptual scheme does not give to the snowdiscall form (being in shape between round and disc-shaped) the status required for it to be a proper constitutive form of a separate sort of entity – at least not with snow as underlying stuff.

That would block the explosion of reality, but the price is conceptual relativity. Supervenient, constituted entities do not just exist or not in themselves, free of any dependence on or relativity to conceptual scheme. What thus exists relative to one conceptual scheme may not do so relative to another. In order for such a sort of entity to exist relative to a conceptual scheme, that conceptual scheme must recognize its constituent form as an appropriate way for a separate sort of entity to be constituted.

Must we now conceive of the existence even of the conceptual scheme itself and of its framers and users as also relative to that conceptual scheme? And are we not then caught in a vicious circle? The framers exist only relative to the scheme, and this they do in virtue of the scheme's giving their constituent form-cum-matter the required status. But to say that the scheme gives to this form-cum-matter the required status – is that not just to say that the *framers* of that scheme do so? Yet are not the framers themselves dependent on the scheme for their existence relative to it?

Answer: existence *relative* to a conceptual scheme is *not* equivalent to existence *in virtue* of that conceptual scheme. Relative to scheme C the framers of C exist *in virtue* of their constitutive matter and form, and in virtue of how these satisfy certain criteria for existence and perdurance of such subjects (among whom happen to be the framers themselves). This existence of theirs is in that way relative to C but not in virtue of C. There is hence no vicious circularity.

The picture then is roughly this. Each of us acquires and develops a view of things that includes criteria of existence and perdurance for categories of objects. When we consider whether an object of a certain sort exists, the specification of the sort will entail the relevant criteria of existence and perdurance. And when we correctly recognize that an object of that sort does exist, our claim is elliptical for "…exists relative to *this* our conceptual scheme."

Again, this is *not* the only conceivable view of the matter. We could try to live with the explosion. And that does seem almost inevitable if we view it this way: a sort of object O – a constituted, supervenient sort – comes with a sort of constituent matter M, or sorts of constituent matters $M1$, $M2, \ldots$, and a sort of constituent form F. These – M (or $M1$, $M2, \ldots$) and F – we may take to be given independently of any acceptance by anyone of any criteria of existence or perdurance. For the sake of argument, then, we are accepting as given the sorts of items – $M1$, $M2, \ldots$ – that will play the role of constituent matters, and also the property or relation – F – that will play the role of constituent form. And presumably whether or not any particular sequence of matters $(m1, m2, \ldots)$ of sorts $M1$, $M2, \ldots$, respectively, does or does not satisfy form F is also generally independent of whether or not we accept any criteria of existence or perdurance, and indeed independent of whether *anyone* does so.

Suppose there is a time t when our conceptual scheme C first recognizes the appropriate criteria of existence and perdurance. According to our conceptual relativism, prior to that time t there were, relative to C, no objects of sort O, and in particular object o did not exist. But if there were no objects of sort O, such as o, relative to our scheme C, then why complicate our own scheme by supplementing it with criteria of existence and perdurance which do give standing to objects of sort O? After all, it is not as though we would fail to recognize the existence of something already in existence. By hypothesis *there are no objects of sort O*, not right up to that time t, anyhow.

On the other side, there is the threat of exploding reality, however. If we allow the satisfaction by any sequence S of any form F of the appropriate polyadicity and logical form to count as a criterion of existence for a corresponding sort of object, then reality right in us, before us, and all around us is unimaginably richer and more bizarre than we have ever imagined. And anyway we shall still face the problem of giving some explanation for why we focus so narrowly on the objects we do attend to, whose criteria of existence and perdurance we do recognize, to the exclusion of the plethora of other objects all around and even in the very same place.

A third option is a disappearance or elimination theory that refuses to countenance supervenient, constituted objects. But then most if not all of ordinary reality will be lost. Perhaps we shall allow ourselves to continue to use its forms of speech "…but only as a convenience or abbreviation." But in using those forms of speech, in speaking of snowballs, chains, boxes, trees, hills, or even people, we shall *not* believe ourselves to be seriously representing reality and its contents. "As a convenience": to *whom* and for what *ends*? "As an abbreviation": of *what*?

With alternatives so grim, we are encouraged to return to our relativistic reflections. Our conceptual scheme encompasses criteria of existence and of perdurance for the sorts of objects that it recognizes. Shall we say now that a sort of object O exists (has existed, exists now, or will exist) relative to a scheme C at t if and only if, at t, C recognizes sort O by allowing the corresponding criteria? But surely there are sorts of objects that our present conceptual scheme does not recognize, such as artifacts yet uninvented and particles yet undiscovered, to take only two obvious examples. Of course, we allow there might be and probably are many such things. Not that there could be any such entities relative to our *present* conceptual scheme, however, for by hypothesis it does not recognize them. So are there sorts of objects – constituted sorts among them, as are the artifacts at least – such that they exist but not relative to our present scheme C? In that case we are back to our problem. What is it for there to be such objects? Is it just the in-itself satisfaction of constitutive forms by constitutive matters? That yields the explosion of reality.

Shall we say then that a constituted, supervenient sort of object O exists relative to our present scheme C if and only if O is recognized by C directly or recognized by it indirectly through being recognized by some predecessor or successor scheme? That, I fear, cannot suffice, since there might be sorts of particles that always go undiscovered by us, and sorts of artifacts in long disappeared cultures unknown to us, whose conceptual schemes are not predecessors of ours.

Shall we then say that what exists relative to our present scheme C is what it recognizes directly, what it recognizes indirectly through its predecessors or successors, and what it *would* recognize if we had developed appropriately or were to do so now, and had been or were to be appropriately situated? This seems the sort of answer required, but it obviously will not be easy to say what appropriateness amounts to in our formula, in its various guises.

Regardless of whatever success may await any further specification of our formula, there is the following further objection. Take a sort of object O recognized by our scheme C, with actual instances $o_1, o_2, \ldots$; for example, the sort Planet, with various particular planets as instances: Mercury, Venus, etc. Its instances, say we, exist, which amounts to saying that they exist relative to our scheme. But if we had not existed, there would have been no scheme of ours for anything to exist relative to; nor would there have been our actual scheme C either. For one thing, we may just assume the contingent existence of our actual scheme to depend on people's actually granting a certain status to certain constitutive forms. If we had not existed, therefore, the constitutive form for the sort Planet would not have had, relative to our conceptual scheme, the status required for it to be possible that there be instances of that sort, particular planets. And from this it apparently follows that if we had not existed there would have been no planets: no Mercury, no Venus, etc.

This objection conceptual relativism can rebut as follows. While existing in the actual world x we now have a conceptual scheme Cx relative to which

we assert existence, when we assert it at all. Now, we suppose a possible world w in which we are not to be found, in which indeed no life of any sort is to be found. Still we may, in x: (a) consider alternative world w and recognize that our absence there would have no effect on the existence or course of a single planet or star, that Mercury, Venus, and the rest, would all still make their appointed rounds just as they do in x; while yet (b) this recognition, which after all takes place in x, is still relativized to Cx, so that the existence in w of whatever exists in w relative to Cx need not be affected at all by the absence from w of Cx, and indeed of every conceptual scheme and of every being who could have a conceptual scheme. For when we suppose existence in w, or allow the possibility of existence in w, *we* do so *in x*, and we do so there still relative to Cx, to our present conceptual scheme, and what it recognizes directly or indirectly, or ideally.

If I am right, we have three choices:

Eliminativism: a disappearance view for which our ordinary talk is so much convenient abbreviation. Problem: we still need to hear: "abbreviation" of what, and "convenient" for what ends and whose ends? Most puzzling of all is how we are to take this "abbreviation" – not literally, surely.

Absolutism: Snowballs, hills, trees, planets, etc. are all constituted by the in-itself satisfaction of certain conditions by certain chunks of matter, and the like, and all this goes on independently of any thought or conceptualization on the part of anyone. Problem: this leads to the "explosion of reality."

Conceptual relativism: We recognize potential constituted objects only relative to our implicit conceptual scheme with its criteria of existence and of perdurance. Problem: is there not much that is very small, or far away, or long ago, or yet to come, which surpasses our present acuity and acumen? How can we allow the existence of such sorts at present unrecognized by our conceptual scheme?

Right now I cannot decide which of these is least disastrous. But is there any other option?

4 Conclusion

I have considered four lines of reasoning used by Putnam in favor of his pragmatic realism. Of these, the fourth seems to me deepest, most richly suggestive, and most effective. The first, the model-theoretic argument, we put aside. The interest of the second resides mainly in its exploration of (a) the sort of causation that is required for a realist account of reference, and (b) consequences of this for the perspectival nature of reference and of truth. My questions arise mainly with the last step of the argument, where the move is made from the perspectival status of truth to a correspondingly perspectival character of reality itself, its internality to conceptual scheme. As for the third line of reasoning, it merges with the second to some extent but is separable, and emphasizes a requirement of scientific convergence or absolutism. According to this line, the very idea of in-itself reality with intrinsic properties is tied together with the notion of an absolute conception of the world to be provided by finished science: an ontology and ideology that would attract convergence by all persistent and undefective inquirers, given sufficient time and resources. To the extent that we must remain agnostic with regard to the possibility or likelihood of such convergence, therefore, to that extent must we be equally agnostic with regard to the very idea of things-in-themselves with their mind-independent, intrinsic properties. There is much to discuss about this whole approach, but one main focus of serious doubt is its assumption that realism (in general, even commonsense realism about observable reality) can be upheld only if scientific realism can be upheld. This runs up against a problem: *the history of science induction that feeds doubt against scientific convergence is inapplicable to our commonsense conception of ordinary reality or anyhow to a substantial enough portion of it.*

I also discussed a fourth line of reasoning used by Putnam, one that leads to a sort of conceptual relativity. I questioned the linguistic turn taken by Putnam's actual reasoning, since there seemed no good interpretation on which it would avoid both triviality and absurdity. Nevertheless, the considerations adduced by this line of reasoning contain important insights worth exploring. And in fact they eventually open a fascinating menu of ontological possibilities.[27] By extending Putnam's reasoning, we reach a set of options in contemporary ontology that presents us with a rather troublesome trilemma. Which shall we opt for: eliminativism, absolutism, or conceptual relativism? Putnam's own pragmatic realism is built around the case that he makes against both eliminativism and absolutism, and in favor of his special sort of conceptual relativism.

Of the four Putnamian arguments for pragmatic realism – the model-theoretic argument; the argument from the perspectival character of causation, reference, and truth; the argument from agnosticism regarding scientific convergence upon a finished science; and the argument for conceptual relativity – this fourth and last of them seems to me far the most powerful and persuasive. It raises a threefold issue – the choice between eliminativism, absolutism, and relativism – still wide open on the philosophical agenda, and a most exciting issue before us today.

Notes

This paper grew (extensively) from one presented at a conference, The Philosophy of Hilary Putnam, organized by the Instituto de Investigaciones Filosóficas, National University of Mexico. I am very pleased to have been included in this conference on Hilary Putnam's work and in his honor.

1 Donald Davidson, "The structure and content of truth," *Journal of Philosophy* 87/6 (June 1990), pp. 279–328.

2 Ibid., p. 307.

3 But see the excellent paper by James Van Cleve, "Semantic supervenience and referential indeterminacy," *Journal of Philosophy* 89/7 (July 1992), pp. 344–61.

4 Hilary Putnam, "Why there isn't a ready-made world," in his *Realism and Reason* (New York: Cambridge University Press, 1983), pp. 205–28. Similar reasoning may also be found in the more recent *Realism with a Human Face* (Cambridge, Mass.: Harvard University Press, 1991); see, e.g., ch. 11, "Objectivity and the science/ethics distinction," and also ch. 5, "The causal structure of the physical," on p. 88 of which we find: "... an *epistemic* distinction between a 'cause' and a 'background condition'. How does the mind get to be able to *refer* to the mind-independent world? Answer 'via the relation of causal connection', and you have slipped back to treating causation as something 'out there' and not simply 'epistemic'." Here again it is the last move that seems false, and in step with the misstep to be discussed here.

5 Putnam, "Why there isn't a ready-made world," p. 205.

6 Ibid., p. 225.

7 Bernard Williams, *Descartes: The Project of Pure Inquiry* (New York: Penguin, 1978) and *idem, Moral Luck* (New York: Cambridge University Press, 1981), esp. ch. 11.

8 Putnam, *Realism with a Human Face*, p. 174.

9 Ibid., pp. 172–3.

10 Putnam, *The Many Faces of Realism* (La Salle, Ill: Open Court, 1987).

11 Ibid., p. 4.

12 Ibid., p. 16.

13 Ibid., pp. 7–8.

14 Ibid., pp. 8–11.

15 Ibid., pp. 11–16, 39–40; also p. 7.

16 Ibid., pp. 27–31.

17 Ibid., p. 28.

18 Ibid., p. 31.

19 Ibid., p. 8.

20 Ibid., p. 17.

21 Putnam, *Realism with a Human Face*, pp. 170–1.

22 Putnam, "Truth and convention: on Davidson's refutation of conceptual relativism," *Dialectica* 41 (1987), pp. 69–77 at p. 75.

23 Rudolf Carnap, *Logical Syntax of Language* (New York: Harcourt Brace, 1937).

24 W. V. Quine, *Word and Object*, (Cambridge, Mass.: MIT Press, 1960).

25 Ibid., p. 272.

26 To mention only one attractive possibility, one might, with C. Bas van Fraassen, combine both agnosticism toward theoretical science and common-sense realism toward observable reality; see, e.g., his *The Scientific Image* (New York: Oxford University Press, 1980).

27 Closely related issues are explored in my "Subjects among other things: persons and other beings," *Philosophical Perspectives* 1 (1987), pp. 155–89.

46

Yes, Virginia, There Is a Real World

William P. Alston

My topic this evening is realism, which I come not to bury but to praise. More specifically, I shall be casting a critical eye on some recent divagations from the straight and narrow path of realism, and I shall be considering whether these tempting by-ways do really exist. My contention shall be that there is, in truth, but the one path through the forest, and that what have been taken as alternative routes, are but insubstantial phantoms.

I

But first I must explain what view this is that will be so earnestly commended. Many a position wears the name of "realism," and with most of them I shall not be concerned.

As a first shot, let's say that Realism is here being understood as the view that whatever there is, is what it is regardless of how we think of it. Even if there were no human thought, even if there were no human beings, whatever there is other than human thought (and what depends on that, causally or logically) would still be just what it actually is.

As just stated, the position is quite compatible with there being nothing except human thought and what depends on that. So watery a potion is unsuitable for this high occasion. Let's turn it into

wine by a codicil to the effect that there is something independent of human thought.

Realism, so stated, is a bit hard to get hold of. It will prove useful to concentrate instead on a certain consequence around which many of the historic battles have raged. If there is a reality independent of our thought, it obviously behooves us to find out as much about it as possible. This means that our thought and discourse will be (largely) directed to thinking (saying) it like it is. Believing (saying) what is true rather than what is false will be the primary goal of cognition; *where we have said what is true iff what we were talking about is as we have said it to be.*[1] I shall call this the realistic conception of truth, and where 'true' and its cognates are used in the sequel without further qualification, this is the intended meaning. So the consequence in question is: *The primary goal of human thought and discourse is to believe (say) what is true in the realistic sense.* Although this is the full statement of the consequence, I shall be working with a somewhat less inflated form:

> Our statements are issued with a (realistic) truth claim (a claim to truth in the realist sense).

I agree with Hilary Putnam[2] that a distinguishing feature of the realistic sense of 'true' is that it is logically possible for even the best attested statement to be false, where the attestation is in terms of "internal" criteria like coherence with the total system of beliefs, being self-evident, being a report of current experience, or being the best explanation of something or other. That is what is "realistic"

Originally published in *Proceedings and Addresser of the American Philosophical Association* 52/6 (1979), pp. 779–808. Reprinted by permission of the author and the American Philosophical Association.

about this concept of truth. In the final analysis what makes our statement true or false is the way things are (the things the statement is about); not the reasons, evidence, or justification we have for it.

Our thesis is marked by exemplary modesty. It only requires that we hold our statements subject to assessment in terms of truth and falsity. A bolder thesis would be that we sometimes succeed in making statements that are true rather than false. I shall not be so rash this evening; it will not be necessary, since the issues I will be considering concern the viability of the realistic *concept* of truth and its attempted substitutes. Therefore it will be sufficient to consider whether we can, and whether we must, make statements with that kind of claim.

But even within this ambit we can distinguish more and less modest claims. Let me illustrate this point with respect to singular subject–predicate statements. Suppose I assert that this cup is empty. According to the above formulation of the realist thesis, that statement is true or false, depending on whether what the statement is about is as it is said to be. That formulation *presupposes* that I have succeeded at least to the extent of picking out a particular referent about which to make a statement. But even if I had failed in that referential task (there is nothing that I would be prepared to recognize as what I was saying to be empty), I would still be saying something intelligible that could be assessed for its success in "saying it like it is." There is, notoriously, controversy over whether, in that case, I said anything that could be evaluated as true or false. Be that as it may, a realistic thesis more modest than ours could be formulated as follows: a statement is put forward with the claim that what it is about, if there is anything it is about, is as it is said to be. I shall not carry modesty to those lengths in this paper; I shall be rash enough to assume that we often do succeed in making a statement about something. If anyone feels that this unfairly begs an important question against the anti-realist, he may substitute the more guarded formulation without disrupting the ensuing discussion.

Here are a few additional exegetical notes:

(1)   I have presented the thesis in terms both of thought and discourse (beliefs and statements). To sharpen the focus, I shall henceforward restrict the discussion to statements. I do this not because I consider statement more fundamental than belief;

my bent is the opposite one. It is rather that statements are more "out in the open" and, hence, the structure is more readily identified and denominated.

(2)   My formulation is limited to statements that can be said to be about something(s). This will take in a wider territory than is sometimes supposed, e.g., not only singular statements but also universal and existential generalizations if we can think of the latter as being "about" all the values of the variables. Other kinds of statements, e.g., subjunctive conditionals, will be harder to fit into this model. But enough statements clearly do fit to give our discussion a point.

(3)   Whether my version of realism boils down to a "correspondence" theory of truth depends on how that term is construed. If correspondence theory of truth merely holds that the truth-value of a statement depends on how it is with what the statement is about, rather than on, e.g., its relations to other statements, then of course this is a (the) correspondence theory. But that term is often reserved for theories that take truth to consist in some structural isomorphism, or mirroring or picturing relation between statements (propositions) and facts. Nothing of that sort is implied by my thesis.

(4)   In espousing realism in this fundamental sense I am not committed to acknowledging the independent reality of any particular kinds of entities – material substances, numbers, classes, properties, facts, propositions, quanta, angels, or whatever. The thesis is quite neutral as to what is real; it merely holds that our attempts at knowledge are to be evaluated in terms of whether we succeed in picking out something(s) real and saying them to be as they are. Thus it is not tied to most of the views called "realism" – "Platonic" realism about abstract objects, perceptual realism about commonsense physical objects, "scientific" realism about theoretical entities, and so on. These are all much more specific doctrines than the one being defended here.

Because of this my thesis is not necessarily opposed to many of the positions with which realism is commonly contrasted – idealism (in most uses of that term), phenomenalism, verificationism, even conventionalism as applied to some restricted domain, such as scientific theories. If idealism is the view that reality is basically mental or spiritual in character, whether this be a Berkeleyan, Leibnizian, or Hegelian[3] version of that thesis, then idealism allows particular statements (about spirits, monads, the Absolute, or whatever) to be true or false in a realistic sense. If you're attributing to the Absolute characteristics it really has, you are speaking truly; if not, not.

I note in this connection that in the March 1979 issue of the *Journal of Philosophy* an excellent article by Colin McGinn, entitled "An a priori argument for realism" begins with the sentence:

> Except in the vulgar sense, one is not a realist *tout court*; one is a realist with respect to some or other type of subject matter – or better, with respect to particular classes of statements.

As Thomas Reid said, in connection with Hume's contract between the vulgar and the philosophical opinions concerning the immediate objects of perception, "In this division, to my great humiliation, I find myself classed with the vulgar."

Realism, as I have defined it, may seem to the uninitiated to be so minimal as to be trivially true. But notoriously, even so minimal a doctrine as this has been repeatedly denied; and the denials supported by elaborate and ingenious argumentation. Nineteenth-century idealism and pragmatism were in good part devoted to attacking realism and searching for an alternative. Thus F. H. Bradley tells us that truth is "that which satisfies the intellect,"[4] "an ideal expression of the Universe, at once coherent and comprehensive,"[5] and Brand Blanshard that a proposition is true if it coheres with an all comprehensive and fully articulated whole.[6] From the pragmatist side, C. S. Peirce's well-known view is that "the opinion which is fated to be ultimately agreed to by all who investigate, is what we mean by the truth,"[7] while William James writes that "true ideas are those that we can assimilate, validate, corroborate, and verify."[8] John Dewey holds true ideas to be those that are instrumental to "an active reorganization of the given environment, a removal of some specific trouble and perplexity."[9] These philosophers would make the truth of the statement that snow is white to consist in something other than snow's *being* white. More recently, Hilary Putnam, who for years had been presenting a highly visible target to the anti-realist, has now been kind enough to turn the other cheek and present an equally prominent target to the realist. In his recent Presidential Address to the Eastern Division,[10] he argues that it is incoherent to suppose that a theory that satisfies all epistemic criteria might be false.

After having dominated the field for some time, the idealist and pragmatist movements provoked a vigorous realist reaction in the late nineteenth and early twentieth century in the redoubtable persons of Frege, Husserl, Moore, and Russell. It is not my intention this evening to do an instant replay of these epic battles, even though it might result in changing some earlier calls by the arbiters of philosophic fashion. Rather, I shall look at some recent anti-realist tendencies. Though these are by no means unconnected with their distinguished precedents, they also present some apparently new features.

My procedure will be as follows. First, I shall look at some anti-realist arguments, or trends of thought, and find them lacking in merit. Second, I shall consider some attempts to work out a non-realist position, and conclude that no coherent alternative has been provided. At that point the defense will rest.

II

A

Under the first rubric I will begin by taking a very brief look at the Quinean theses of indeterminacy of translation and inscrutability of reference. I have no time to enter the formidable thickets of Quinean exegesis, and so I refrain from asking whether Quine is a realist, or whether Quine himself takes these theses to have an anti-realist thrust. But they have frequently been so taken, a tendency encouraged by Quine's use of the label "ontological relativism." Just what bearing do these celebrated doctrines have on the matter? It seems to me somewhat less direct than ordinarily supposed. They don't exactly contradict realism; rather, they strike at a presupposition of the question for which realism is one possible answer. They make, or seem to make, it impossible to raise the question. What indeterminacy of translation and inscrutability of reference most directly imply is that our thought and discourse is irremediably indeterminate in a throughgoing and shocking fashion. To wit, there is no particular determinate content to any assertion. Because of the indeterminacy of translation, there are indefinitely many versions of what it is I am saying about an object in any assertion I make. And because of inscrutability of reference, there are indefinitely many versions of what I would be saying it about if there were any particular thing I were saying. Viewed in a larger context, this is simply an extreme version of forms of indeterminacy that have long been recognized as affecting much of our speech. It is uncontroversial that people frequently use words in an ambiguous or confused manner, so that there is no precise answer to the question: "What is he saying?" And again it is uncontroversial that there are breakdowns in reference in which it is in principle indeterminate to what the speaker meant to be referring. Quine is simply holding, with what justice I shall not inquire, that such indeterminacies ineluctably affect all speech. Now it has long been recognized by realists that a statement will have a definite truth-value only to the extent that it has a definite content. If I am not saying anything definite, it will be correspondingly indefinite whether what I say is true or false. If, e.g., the meaning of 'religion' does not involve precise necessary and sufficient conditions for something's being a religion, then there is no definite answer to the question whether the Ethical Culture movement is a religion. Since the Quinean doctrines under consideration imply that all our utterances are in this condition, they imply that the issue of realism cannot arise anywhere in human discourse. Anti-realism goes down the drain along with realism. For the remainder of this section I shall concentrate on arguments that have been thought to support an anti-realist answer to the question to which realism is another answer.

B

Next let's take a brief look at some echoes of nineteenth-century idealism – the attack on the "Given." This familiar theme of Hegelianism and pragmatism has reappeared in partially novel garb in the work of Quine, Sellars, and others. As in the previous century, it is denied that there are any fixed immutable certainties, any statements totally immune to revision or rejection, any points at which an objective fact itself is directly given to us, so that all we need to do is to note it. Since it is assumed, wrongly in my opinion, that unless a statement satisfies these descriptions it cannot be justified save by its support from other statements, these denials issue in some form of a coherence or contextualist epistemology. Insofar as there is novelty in the recent attack on fixed, isolated, intuitive certainties, it comes from the "linguistic turn," e.g., the resting of epistemic status on conditions of assertability in a language community.

So far this is epistemology. What does it have to do with truth and reality? Not all the recent opponents of the given have followed their idealist and pragmatist forebears in rejecting a realist conception of truth. The story of where Sellars, e.g., stands on this matter is too complex to be gone into here. But at least one contemporary thinker has drawn anti-realist morals from this epistemology. In his book, *Philosophy and the Mirror of Nature*, Richard Rorty writes:

> Shall we take ... "S knows non-inferentially that P" ... as a remark about the status of S's reports among his peers, or shall we take it as a remark about the relation between nature and its mirror?[11] The first alternative leads to a pragmatic view of truth ... (on) the second alternative ... truth is something more than what Dewey called "warranted assertability": more than what our peers will, *ceteris paribus*, let us get away with saying ... To choose between these approaches is to choose between truth as "what it is good for us to believe" and truth as "contact with reality."[12]

Why should we suppose realism to depend on the existence of fixed intuitive certainties? Perhaps the argument goes like this. If we are to have any reason for supposing that any of our statements are realistically true, there must be some points at which we have direct access to the way things are in themselves. If some objective states of affairs are directly presented to consciousness, so that here we have the fact itself and not just our own "interpretation," then at those points at least, we can tell whether a statement is telling it like it is. But if we never enjoy any such intuitive apprehensions of objective reality, how could we ever tell whether any statement is or is not in accord with the facts. And if it is in principle impossible to determine this, it is idle, meaningless, or empty, to claim such an accord or to wonder whether it obtains.

This argument is in two stages. (1) Without fixed intuitive certainties we have no way of telling whether any statement is realistically true. (2) Hence it is unintelligible, or otherwise out of order, to employ this dimension of evaluation. Both steps seem to me unwarranted.

The first stage is, at best, question begging. The basic issue here is the status and evaluation of epistemic principles. The argument obviously assumes that a valid (reasonable, justified) set of epistemic principles might be such that a statement could satisfy sufficient conditions for acceptability without our having any reason to think it realistically true. But that is just what a realist would deny. From a realist point of view, epistemic justification is intimately connected with truth; not necessarily so closely connected that justification entails truth, but at least so closely connected that justification entails a considerable probability of truth. An epistemic principle that laid down sufficient principles of justification such that we could know that a statement satisfied them while having no reason to think it true, would *ipso facto* be unacceptable.

Another way of putting this last point: this first stage of the argument is one form of the old contention that "we can't get outside our thought and experience to compare it with reality." Therefore we had better renounce any ambition to make our thought conform to "reality" and concentrate instead on tidying up its internal structure. But from a realist point of view this picture of being trapped inside our own thought, unable to get a glimpse of what it is like outside, is radically misleading – even if we do lack fixed intuitive certainties. For whenever we have knowledge, that is *ipso facto* a case of getting a glimpse of the reality "outside." However we get this knowledge, it wouldn't be knowledge unless the belief in question were conformed to its referent(s).[13] It is unfortunate picture-thinking to suppose that only some specially direct or intuitive knowledge constitutes finding out what something is really like.

The second stage of the argument is plain unvarnished verificationism. If there is no way of telling whether a given statement is realistically true, then we can attach no sense (or, if you prefer, no cognitive or factual meaning) to the supposition that it is true. It would be pleasant to suppose that verificationism is now in such ill repute that to tar the argument with this brush would be condemnation enow. But, alas, such is not the case. The verificationist criterion has conclusively and repeatedly been found wanting; but perhaps excessive attention to technical details has obscured the basic point of these criticisms. If the underlying causes of the disease are not clearly identified, relapses are to be expected. The basic point is simply this. Except for such statements as are directly testable, no statement can be empirically tested in isolation. We must conjoin it with other statements if we are to derive any directly testable consequences. And for any sentence, no matter how meaningless, we can find some set of sentences that together with the former will yield observation sentences not derivable from that set alone. Thus the capacity of a sentence to contribute to the generation of directly testable consequences completely fails to discriminate between the meaningful and the meaningless. We do, of course, make distinctions between those sentences that do, and those that do not, enter *fruitfully* into empirically testable systems, though it is either very difficult or impossible to formulate precise criteria for this. But this distinction also fails to coincide with the distinction between meaningful and meaningless, as is shown by the fact that one and the same statement, e.g., "Matter is composed of tiny indivisible particles," will enter into such combinations fruitfully at one period but not at another.[14]

C

Rorty's argument can be generally characterized as moving from epistemology to ontology, from considerations concerning the epistemic status of statements to conclusions concerning their capacity to "reveal" reality. I now want to consider some further arguments of this general sort, which differ from the argument just discussed in being of a relativistic character. Although Rorty's argument depends on rejecting classical foundationalism, it does not question (1) the existence of a single set of epistemological principles that (2) yield a unique result in each individual instance. The two lines of thought I shall now consider each deny one of these assumptions.

The first assumption is rejected by, e.g., the language-game approach that stems from the later work of Wittgenstein and is found full-blown in Peter Winch and D. Z. Phillips. Here the idea is that there are radically different criteria of justification and rationality for different spheres of discourse – commonsense talk about the physical environment, talk about personal agents, moral discourse, religious discourse, scientific theorizing, reports of dreams, experiential reports, etc. Observation is crucial for physical-object talk, the authority of sacred books and holy persons for religious discourse, and the sincere asseveration of the subject for reports of experience. It is a piece of outrageous imperialism to suppose that any single requirement for justification applies across the board.

What bearing is this supposed to have on realism? Well, first there is a straight verificationist argument from the fact that different language-games have different criteria of truth to the conclusion that they employ different concepts of truth. This argument presupposes a stronger form of verificationism. Rorty's argument only required us to suppose that being empirically testable is a necessary condition of meaningfulness for sentences. But here we need the additional assumption that the mode of verification constitutes the meaning. We need this stronger thesis if we are to infer a difference in the meaning of 'true' in different language-games from differences in the *way* of verifying truth-ascriptions in different language-games. This stronger verificationist thesis can hardly be in a more favorable position than the weaker one, since it entails the latter.

The language-game approach also generates arguments of a more distinctive sort, though I cannot see that they fare any better.

(1)   The irreducible plurality of language-games militates against the realist position in another way. The ontologies of different language-games do not all fit into any single scheme. There is no place in physical space for minds, sense-data, or God. Agency cannot be located in the interstices of the physiological causal network. Nor is there any overarching neutral position from which particular language-games can be criticized and their subject matters integrated into a single framework. Therefore it seems quite unjustified to suppose that the success of a statement in some particular language-game depends on whether it conforms to the constitution of something called "reality."

This argument also depends on verificationism. It argues from our inability to see whether, or how, different sorts of entities fit into one scheme, to the unintelligibility of supposing that they do. But, more basically, the argument suffers from a naïvely simplistic conception of reality. Why suppose that reality, if there be such, must fall into some single pattern? Why shouldn't reality be as many-mansioned as you like? Why should there not be even more kinds of entities in heaven and earth than are dreamt of in our language-games? And if there is some significant degree of unity to it all, why should we expect to be able to discern it? Even if we can't integrate agency and physical causation in a single "space," they may, for all that, be what they are apart from our attempts to conceptualize them. The argument suffers from a grievous lack of ontological imagination.

(2)   We find in the writings of Sprachspielists, as well as in their historical relativist forebears, the insistence that *our* concepts of truth and reality are rooted in *our* forms of life, *our* practices – linguistic and non-linguistic. From this the inference is drawn that truth cannot consist in conformity to the way things are "outside" our thought and practice. But this is just the old question-begging argument that we "can't get outside our own thought and experience to compare it with reality." Of course, when we use the term 'true' or any other term, we are using *our* language, if we know what we are talking about. Who else's language might we be using? (I could have been speaking French or Bantu instead, but that is presumably not to the point.) But this has absolutely no implications for the *content* of what I am saying, or for the ways in which it is properly evaluated. The fact that when I say anything I am using the language I am using, which is rooted in the social practices it is rooted in, is a miserable truism that has no bearing on our problem. It leaves completely open the question of whether, in saying what I say, I am claiming to refer to something that exists independent of our discourse, and whether this is an intelligible or reasonable claim to make.[15]

D

Although Sprachspielism is relativistic in the sense that it takes any particular cognitive success to be relative to some particular language-game, it is not so relativistic as to suppose that different language-games yield mutually incompatible results. On the contrary, it considers different language-games to be too different to be in competition for the same prize. We now turn to a more extreme relativism, which denies the second of the assumptions listed earlier – that our epistemological principles yield a unique result in each application.

This line of thought has taken many forms from the ancient Greek sophists to the present. Its most prominent recent incarnation is in the work of Feyerabend and Kuhn. Here is a highly oversimplified version. In the development of a science we have a succession of "theoretical (or conceptual) frameworks" or "paradigms." Each of these paradigms is self-enclosed in something like the way Winch and Phillips think of a language-game as being self-enclosed. The constituent terms get their meanings by their place in the framework; observations are conceptualized and reported in these terms; and hypotheses are evaluated in terms of how well they explain data so construed, and in terms of how well they solve the problems generated by that paradigm. Hence we are unable to choose between rival theoretical frameworks in terms of one or another contestant.

The position is usually not held in so extreme a form, but I wanted to present it as such so as to see what bearing it would have on realism. The obvious argument is this. All our conclusions are relative to the assumptions and conceptual framework of a given paradigm, which has indefinitely many alternatives. Therefore we can never have reason to think that any of our conclusions are in conformity with reality itself. Hence the realist notion of truth is inapplicable to our discourse. Clearly this is but another rerun of the same old verificationist argument. And again the same comments are applicable.

These, I take it, are the epistemological arguments against realism that are most prominent on the current scene. I have not contested their epistemological premises, though I do not accept them in every case, but instead have concentrated on showing that even with these premises the arguments are far from cogent.

E

Finally, there is the direct application of verificationism to the crucial implication of realism mentioned above, viz., that however well confirmed, justified, or rationally acceptable a statement may be, it is logically possible that it be false. The argument is very simple. We have, *ex hypothesi*, ruled out any possible reason for supposing the statement false. Therefore we cannot attach any meaning to the denial that it is true. This is clearly not just an argument against realism, but also an argument for the equation of 'true' and 'justified' (or 'could be justified'), or at least for the substitution of the latter for the former. In only slightly different garb it is the main argument of Peirce, James, and Dewey for their several pragmatic conceptions of truth. It is given a fancy logical dress in Hilary Putnam's recent Presidential Address to the Eastern Division, but the verificationist underpinning is the same in all its versions. And about this enough has been said.

I conclude from this discussion that the recent opponents of realism have failed to shake our commonsense confidence in that doctrine. They have not done significantly better than Hegel, Bradley, James, and Dewey; in fact, their arguments turn out to be warmed-over scraps from the idealist, pragmatist and positivist traditions,

masked by a few ingenious sauces from La Nouvelle Cuisine.

III

However, on this solemn occasion I am not content with simply shooting down the arguments of opponents. A more fitting aspiration would be to show that there is no coherent alternative to realism. Unfortunately, I can see no way to do this other than by examining all sufficiently promising alternatives. This is, of course, a very large task, and I shall only be able to make a start.

The most obvious move for the anti-realist is to *define* truth in terms of whatever he takes to be the appropriate standards for accepting a statement. A common thread in the arguments we have been considering is the verificationist objection to the idea that there is something involved in a statement's *being* true over and above the grounds we can have for regarding it as true. Such arguments naturally lead to an identification of a statement's being true with there being adequate grounds for taking it to be true (not, of course, with anyone's seeing that there are adequate grounds). Thus the truth of a statement, S, will be identified with S's cohering with the rest of one's beliefs, with S's leading, or having the capacity to lead, to fruitful consequences, with S's satisfying the standards of the particular language-game in which it is a move, with S's being one of the survivors at the ideal limit of scientific inquiry, or whatever.[16]

Instead of proposing a non-realist analysis of 'true', the anti-realist may instead (more candidly, in my view) propose that we abandon the concept of truth and talk instead of justification, confirmation, or verification. Thus Dewey once advocated dropping 'true' in favor of 'warrantedly assertable'. It will be easier to focus the discussion if I stick with the version in which some non-realist analysis of 'true' is given.

As is implicit in the list just given, these non-realist theories differ along various dimensions. They may be atomistic or holistic; i.e., they may attach justification conditions to individual statements or only to larger systems; in the latter case what it is for a particular statement to be true is to belong to a system that, as a whole, satisfies certain constraints. Again, they may seek to give a single account of justification for *all* statements, like the traditional coherence theories, or they may hold, like Sprachspielism, that different accounts are to be given for different realms of discourse. The question I want to explore is whether *any* verificationist account of truth can be intelligibly and coherently spelled out (while not completely losing touch with its subject matter), without involving or presupposing the realist concept of truth.

A

The first place a realist will look for a chink in the armor is the status of the higher-level epistemic judgments like S_1 – 'S would be included in the ultimate scientific theory'.[17] Isn't Peirce implicitly thinking of this as true in the realist sense? In asserting S, isn't he thinking that it is really the case that if scientific inquiry were pushed to the limit, S would still be there? If so, we have extruded (real) truth from first-level statements, only to have it reappear on a second level.[18] But suppose that Peirce retorts that he is prepared to treat these second-level statements in the same way, i.e., hold their truth to consist in their membership in the ultimate scientific theory. In that case he will be faced with an infinite regress. For this will set up a still higher-level statement S_2 – 'S_1 would be included in the ultimate scientific theory'. And if that in turn is treated in the same way . . . .

I am uncertain as to the force of this realist criticism. It is unclear to me whether this regress is any more vicious than a variety of other infinite regresses with which we are saddled anyway, e.g., the regress of truth levels, or the regress of levels of justification. Hence I will pass on to difficulties that seem to me to be clearly fatal.

B

The real crusher for the anti-realist is the question "How are we to interpret the statements to which you apply your concept of truth?" What is crushing about this question? Well, the point is that on a natural, intuitive way of understanding statement content (of specifying what is being asserted in a given statement), that content carries with it the applicability of the realist concept of truth. Let's continue to restrict the discussion to those statements that can plausibly be thought of as being "about something(s)." For such a statement, the natural way of specifying content, of making explicit what statement it is, is to specify the referent(s), and to make explicit what is being asserted of that referent(s). But if that is what makes the statement

the statement it is, then there is no alternative to supposing that the statement is true *iff* the referent(s) is as it is being said to be. If what I did in a certain utterance was to refer to snow and say of it that it is white, what alternative is there to holding that my statement is true *iff* snow is white?[19] You can't in one and the same breath construe the statement as a commitment to X's being Φ, and also deny that the statement is true *iff* X is Φ. To understand statement content in this familiar way *is* to subject it to realistic truth-conditions. It is incoherent to say "What I asserted was that snow is white (or what I did in my assertion was to refer to snow and say of it that it is white), but the truth of my assertion does not ride on whether snow *is* white." This is to take away with one hand what was offered with the other. The realistic concept of truth is indissolubly bound up with this familiar way of specifying statement content.[20] If I am correct in this, the anti-realist will have to provide some other way of specifying *what* is being asserted – other than "The speaker referred to snow and said of it that it is white."

If we ask whether anti-realists have recognized the necessity for an alternative reading, the picture appears to be a mixed one. I believe that idealists in the Hegelian tradition have generally been alive to the issue. Consider Bradley's view of the nature of judgment, as involving a separation of the 'that' and the 'what', and a vain attempt to reunite them in the forms of predication, together with the view that the essential aim of thought is to produce a comprehensive, coherent totality that would be identical with reality. This is an attempt to give an account of what we are up to in statement making that is fundamentally different from the familiar account and that is in harmony with a coherence account of the nature of truth. Again, we can see Dewey's emphasis on the "instrumental" function of ideas and judgments as the germ of a different kind of alternative account. If what we are up to in statement making is not attempting to tell it like it is with particular referents or classes thereof, but rather providing effective guidance to our active commerce with the environment (allowing, as I would not, that the latter can be separated from the former), then it might be not incoherent to hold that the fundamental dimension of evaluation for statements is their effectiveness in this role. In many cases, however, one is left with the impression that the anti-realist takes individual statements in the same old way, but simply proposes to change the account of what it is for them to be *true*. If the above argument is correct, this is just what she cannot do.

A thoroughgoing anti-anti-realist argument would involve a careful scrutiny of all the noteworthy attempts, actual and possible, to devise a mode of statement-interpretation suitable for their purposes. However, I fear that an examination of such darkly labyrinthine authors as Bradley and Dewey would be beyond the bounds of this lecture even if we were at the beginning rather than, as I hasten to assure you, in the latter half. Instead, I shall consider some moves that are more in accord with the dominant temper of Anglo-American philosophy of the last half-century, moves that might well tempt anti-realists, and in some cases actually have.

(1)   The anti-realist may try to turn the above argument back on her opponent in the following manner. "The argument depends on the claim that statemental content is tied to truth-conditions. Well and good; two can play at this game. If a realist construal of statements yields realist truth-conditions, then non-realist truth-conditions can be associated with a corresponding mode of assigning statement-content. If what it takes for a statement, S, to be true is that it belong to the ultimate scientific theory (call that 'T') then we will simply assign to S the content – *S belongs to T*."

However tempting this may sound in the abstract, as soon as it is stated explicitly, it clearly displays its absurdity. How could it be that asserting that S is asserting that S has some property or other? How could S *be* some higher-level statement about S, i.e., be a higher-level statement than itself? How can a statement be a statement about itself, rather than itself?

A contemporary anti-realist like Dummett, or (the most recent) Putnam, would not be moved by this. They would just take it as illustrating the futility of working with *statements* or *propositions* as our basic units, instead of sentences in a language. Of course, we can't regard a statement as being a statement about itself, instead of being itself. But we do not find the same absurdity in the suggestion that each of our statements makes a claim about a certain sentence, even the very sentence used to make that statement. Let's follow recent fashion and take a theory to consist of a set of sentences. Then we may formulate the following Peircean view of statement interpretation. When I assertorically utter "Lead melts at 327 degrees F," what I am claiming is: "The sentence 'Lead melts at 327

degrees F' will (would) be included in the final scientific theory, T."[21]

But though this escapes the absurdity of denying that a statement is identical with itself, it suffers the same unhappy fate that befalls other attempts to substitute sentences for beliefs, propositions, or statements. Here, as elsewhere, it turns out that even the closest possible statement about language will fail to have the same force as the original. In this case (passing over the *parochiality* involved in supposing that the *ultimate* scientific theory will consist of English sentences) the difficulty is that whether the sentence in question figures in T depends, *inter alia*, on what that sentence will mean by the time the final consummation is achieved. If the sentence means something different from what it means now, it may not be included, even if T does include a statement to the effect that lead melts at 327 degrees F. Thus, on this interpretation, when we assert "Lead melts at 327 degrees F," we are, in part, making a claim about the future history of the English language. This radically distorts our intent. Sometimes we are talking about language, but most of the time we are not.

Of course, this view may be so construed that our statement has to do not with a mere phonological string (which might receive various semantic interpretations) but with the semantically interpreted sentence "Lead melts at 327 degrees F." But that is to throw us back on the absurdities of treating a statement as being about itself. For a semantic interpretation of an assertoric sentence is precisely designed to determine a statement-content; it specifies *what* is asserted when the sentence is used assertorically. Therefore this latest proposal amounts to assigning two different contents to the statement: the one determined by the presupposed semantic interpretation, and the one built on that – to the effect that the sentence used to express the first content will be in T. Again we lapse into incoherence.

(2)   The moral of this story is that we can't identify a statement with a statement about *itself*, whether about its epistemic status or about the sentence used to make it. But the diagnosis suggests a simple remedy. Why not take S to be, not the statement that S satisfies certain epistemic conditions, but rather the statement of those conditions themselves? For each statement, S, we will choose conditions the satisfaction of which will guarantee that the statement has the desired

epistemic status; but we will construe S not as the statement that S has that status, but rather as the affirmation of those conditions.

It would seem that this kind of first-level interpretation is not available for holistic theories that identify the truth of S with the way it fits into some system – the final scientific theory, the most coherent and comprehensive theory of truth, or the ongoing enterprise of coping with the environment. Here a blanket statement that makes reference to S (to the way S fits into some system) is all we have to work with. But an empirical verifiability theory of truth looks more promising. If we can specify conditions under which S would be verified, why not identify what is stated by S with the satisfaction of those conditions?

Interpretations like this were prominent in twentieth-century phenomenalism and in early logical positivism. ("The meaning of a statement is its method of verification.")[22] And recently Michael Dummett has suggested the possibility of replacing (realist) truth-conditions with "verification-conditions" in giving a semantic description of a language. Let's use as our example an oversimplified statement of C. I. Lewis's version of phenomenalism.[23] A singular attribution of a property to a physical object, like 'This container is made of glass', is to be construed as the assertion of an indefinitely large conjunction of subjunctive conditionals like the following:

1 If I were to seem to dash this container to the floor, I would seem to see the container shattering.
2 If I were to seem to thump this container with my finger, I would hear a certain kind of ringing sound.

Each of these "terminating judgments" is supposed to have the virtue of being decisively verified or falsified by "sensory presentations." And the verification of the whole set would *be* the verification of the original statement, since they are one and the same.[24]

It has been frequently argued and, I think, to good effect, that projects like Lewis's cannot be carried out, that no purely phenomenalistic statement is equivalent to any physical-object statement. I don't want to get into all of that. I merely want to ask whether, assuming that some such project can be carried through, it enables us to avoid the realistic concept of truth. And here I am not asking whether the concept of verification can be cut loose from dependence on the concept of

truth, as it would have to be if it is to be used in an analysis of truth. Clearly the ordinary meaning of 'verify' is simply *show (ascertain) to be true*. But this is not to the present point, since the second-level concept of verification does not enter into the proposed interpretation of first-level statements like 'This container is made of paper'.

The crucial point, rather, is this. Let's say that S is taken to be the assertion that p, q, ..., where these are verifying conditions, whether stated in Lewis's way or in some other. We have given a propositional content to S that differs from the familiar one. But in giving it this new content, are we not thereby committed to realistic truth-conditions for *that* content as firmly as we were with the earlier one? Instead of simply attributing a property to the object referred to by 'this container', we are asserting a number of contingencies in sense experience. But with respect to each of those contingencies are we not asserting that it in fact obtains – that if I were to seem to dash this container to the floor, it would seem to break? But if so, then again I am saying something that is true *iff* that consequence would result from that activity.[25] Once more, I cannot both be making that claim and denying that whether the claim is true rides on whether things would come out that way under those conditions. In fact, this is the way in which the matter has been viewed by most phenomenalists and other verificationists. They were far from wanting to jettison the realistic concept of truth. They simply wanted to put restrictions on what sorts of statements are susceptible of (realistic) truth and falsity.

One might think that the failure to slough off realistic truth-conditions comes from making the verificationist interpretation match the original too closely. By insisting on conditions of conclusive verification, we have guaranteed that the translation says just the same as the original, and that is why we wind up with realistic truth claims after all. This suggests that we should follow the pilgrimage of logical positivism from conclusive verification to "confirmation." Perhaps we should interpret our statements in terms of what would provide (more or less strong) confirmation, rather than in terms of what would conclusively verify. But this suggestion is even more incoherent than its predecessor. We cannot judge a certain condition to be merely providing some evidence for S, rather than conclusively verifying it, except against the background of a conception of what would render S *true* or, if you like, of what would conclusively verify S. Why do we suppose that determining that X is malleable is only some evidence for X's being gold, but does not conclusively establish that it is gold? Because we have enough of an idea of what it is for X to *be* gold to see that it is possible for something to be malleable and yet not be gold.

Contrariwise, if we simply take some "confirmation condition" as giving the content of a statement, then it follows that we can't be taking it to be merely non-conclusively confirming. If what I am asserting when I utter 'X is gold' is that X is malleable, then it cannot be denied that the malleability of X makes my assertion true. A set of conditions cannot be merely confirming evidence, and also constitute the content of what was said.

Nor will it be more efficacious to construe our interpretation as made up of conditions of "acceptance." Again, if we mean to contrast conditions of acceptance with conditions of truth or verification, we still have the latter in the background; we have neither eliminated them, nor dissolved their tie with statement content. If, on the other hand, we are serious in taking our so-called conditions of acceptance to specify statement-content, we are thereby precluded from regarding them as conditions of acceptance rather than of truth.

Thus these verificationist moves are to no avail. When we identify statement-content in terms of test, verification, or confirmation conditions, we do not evade realistic truth-conditions; rather, we introduce certain restrictions on what can be asserted, thereby generating parallel restrictions on what it takes to make statements true. When all the smoke has cleared, it is still a matter of what is talked about being as it is said to be.

The language-game, and other relativistic approaches such as Quine's "ontological relativism," may *seem* to provide a different way out. Instead of trying to get away from interpreting statements in terms of the familiar machinery of reference, predication, and truth, we simply hang onto all that, but regard it, in each instance, as relative to a certain language-game (paradigm, scheme of translation). In a normal utterance of 'Snow is white', we are, indeed, referring to snow and predicating whiteness of it; and so what we say is true *iff* snow is white. But this is all relative to the "commonsense physical world language-game." We can only pick out a referent, identify a property predicated, and adjudge truth by the standards internal to that language-game. There is no way in which we can raise the question, absolutely, as to what is referred to in that statement, or as to the conditions under which it is true. All such semantic notions exist only in relativized forms. When we try to drop the qualification, the concept dissolves.

But what does it mean to say that 'Snow is white' is true *in the commonsense physical world language-game*, rather than just true *tout court?*

(1) There is an innocuous interpretation according to which it is in L that S is true, because L is where S is. That is, S is constructed from the conceptual resources of L; that statement-content emerges from that conceptual practice. Clearly on this interpretation 'S is true in L' will be true for some L, for any true statement, S, assuming that every statement can be assigned to at least one language-game. But this is innocuous because the relativity does not affect the notion of truth. On this reading 'S is true in L' is just a conjunction of 'S is in L' and 'S is true (*tout court*)'.

(2) It could mean – we're just pretending, rather than claiming that S is *really* true, as in "It is true that Bunter is Lord Peter's butler in Dorothy Sayer's mysteries." But presumably this is not what is intended, for this reading depends on a contrast with "really true" (absolutely) – not to mention the fact that a Sprachspielist would not be prepared to assimilate all language-games to fiction.

(3) What is left to us? Only the obvious, straightforward suggestion that 'S is true in L' means – 'S passes the tests of L for being true'. But the second occurrence of 'true' has to be taken as employing the *verboten* absolute concept. For if we try to make that occurrence express a relativistic concept of truth in some L, that will require a similar explanation, and an infinite regress looms.

These all too brief considerations indicate that notions like 'true' and 'refers' stubbornly resist relativization. Once admitted, they point inevitably to what there is, whatever webs of thought we weave.

(3) The non-realist interpretations that emerge from currently fashionable modes of thought have all backfired. The moral I draw from this cautionary tale is that most non-realists have seriously underestimated the magnitude of their task. They have failed to appreciate how violent a break is required with our customary ways of viewing thought and discourse. They have failed to grasp the central point that if they are to abandon the realistic concept of truth, they must give up

thinking of our thought and discourse in terms of reference, and the other semantic notions based on that – saying this or that *of* what is referred to, quantification over what is (or could be) referred to, and so on. They have supposed that they can continue to construe discourse in these terms, while attaching a relativistic rider to these semantic notions, or by substituting some specially tailored propositional content for the more familiar ones. But it just doesn't work. To repeat the main point once more, so long as we think of our utterances as being about something(s), there is no escape from the realistic truth formula. So long as it is correct to say that you are talking about this container, or dogs, or the quality of mercy, then there is no escape from the recognition that what you say is true *iff* what you are talking about is as you say it to be. If, on the other hand, it could be made out that it is a mistake to think of statemental utterances as being *about* anything, then clearly the realistic truth concept does not apply. If there is nothing I am talking about, my utterance can hardly be evaluated in terms of whether what it is about is as I say it to be. If the non-realist is to make her position stick, she will have to find some adequate non-referential account of statemental discourse.

How might this be done? Well, there is the Bradleian idea that the aim of thought is to develop a comprehensive, coherent system of concepts, where this aim is so conceived that if it were fully realized, the system would *be* Reality as a whole. Here the relation with reality is not secured by way of reference to particular objects in each judgment (belief, statement), but rather by way of the fact that Reality is what would constitute the complete fulfillment of the aim of thought. Whether this is a radically non-referential conception depends on whether we can understand the incomplete stages of this quest without thinking of ourselves as referring either to the concepts themselves, or to their

extensions or instances. A still more radical alternative would be an explicitly non-intentionalistic account of speech as complexly conditioned behavior, as in B. F. Skinner's book *Verbal Behavior*. Whether *this* is really a radically non-referential account will depend, *inter alia*, on whether the account itself can be an account of speech without itself being about something, viz., speech.

Obviously I can't discuss these putatively non-referential accounts at the tag-end of this paper. I shall have to confine myself to the following remark. Even if doubts of the sort just expressed could be stilled, and one or more such accounts could be formulated without embodying or presupposing references at some point, the question would still remain whether reference is being sold at too dear a price. We would have to give up such cherished ideas so that we can pick out objects of various sorts and characterize them, correctly and incorrectly, and that in the course of this enterprise we sometimes communicate information about the world that guides our behavior as well as satisfies our intellectual curiosity. Unless the arguments against realism are considerably stronger than I found them to be earlier in this essay, the game, clearly, is not worth the candle.

IV

Yes, Virginia, there is a real world. Not, or not only, in the hearts and minds of men. Not, or not only, in the language-games we play, in the schemes of translation we devise, or in the epistemic standards we acknowledge. But in that ineluctable, circumambient web of fact to the texture of which we must needs do homage, lest, though we speak with the tongues of men and of angels, and have not truth, our logos is become as sounding symbols or as tinkling paradigms.

Notes

Presidential Address delivered before the Seventy-Seventh Annual Western Division Meeting of the American Philosophical Association in Denver, Colorado, 20 May, 1979.

1 I take this to be simply a slightly more explicit formulation of the view classically expressed by Aristotle in *Metaphysics* (1011b, 27) as "... to say of what is that it is, and of what is not that it is not, is true."

2 See Hilary Putnam, "Realism and reason," *Proceedings and Addresses of the American Philosophical Association* 50 (1977), p. 485.

3 To be sure, Hegel's philosophy as a whole contains elements that are incompatible with realism in my sense. Here I am only concerned with the Hegelian or "absolute" version of the particular thesis that reality is basically spiritual in character.

4 F. H. Bradley, *Essays on Truth and Reality* (Oxford: Clarendon Press, 1914), p. 1.

5 F. H. Bradley, *Essays on Truth and Reality* (Oxford: Clarendon Press, 1914) p. 223.

6 Brand Blanshard, *The Nature of Thought* (London: George Allen & Unwin Ltd., 1939), vol. 2, p. 264.

7 C. S. Peirce, "How to make our ideas clear," in C. Hartshorne and P. Weiss (eds), *Collected Papers* (Cambridge, Mass.: Harvard University Press, 1934), p. 268.

8 William James, *Pragmatism* (Cambridge, Mass.: Harvard University Press, 1975), p. 97.

9 John Dewey, *Reconstruction in Philosophy* (New York: Henry Holt & Co., 1920), p. 156.

10 Putnam, "Realism and reason."

11 This last is Rorty's picturesque way of saying, "taking it as involving an immediate awareness that *p*, or as involving the fact that *p*'s being directly presented to consciousness.

12 Richard Rorty, *Philosophy and the Mirror of Nature* (Princeton: Princeton University Press, 1979), pp. 175–6.

13 Hence the well-advised tendency of some anti-realists to renounce the concept of knowledge for justified belief, or warranted assertability.

14 In this connection we may note that the verifiability criterion forces us into a caricature of the process of scientific inquiry. Often this involves generating some hypothesis ('Electric current is a flow of tiny particles') and then looking around for some way to test it. Free of verificationist blinders, it seems obvious that this process is guided throughout by our understanding of the hypothesis we do not yet see how to test. (We haven't yet found a promising way of embedding it in a larger system that will generate directly testable consequences.) But verificationism would have it that what we were doing was looking for a meaning to bestow on a certain sentence! And if that were what we were doing, why should it matter which of indefinitely many empirically respectable meanings we chose?

15 We might also note that though this argument is found principally in the writings of Sprachspielists, it does not in any way depend on the multiplicity of language-games. These truisms would be equally true if our discourse were restricted to a single language-game.

16 It may be suggested that I should have taken "redundancy" or "disappearance" theories as equally obvious alternatives for the anti-realist. These theories deny that the statement 'It is true that S' has any more "cognitive" or "assertoric" content (makes any further truth claim!) than S. The function of 'It's true' is simply to endorse someone else's statement that S, or to assert that S in a specially emphatic way, or the like. But the relation of the redundancy theory to realism is unclear. It does *look* anti-realist; if we aren't asserting anything (over and above S) in saying 'It's true that S', then we aren't asserting, among other things, that what S is about is as it is said to be

in asserting S. Nevertheless, the opposition might be only skin deep. If the redundancy theory is merely a view as to how the *word* 'true' or phrases like 'It's true' are used, then it is quite compatible with the view that realism is right about the primary aim of thought, and about the most fundamental dimension of evaluation of statements; the disagreement would only be over whether the word 'true' is properly used to express this.

17 We might also raise questions about the status of epistemic principles like "The ultimate scientific theory must satisfy the following constraints ..."

18 This realist rejoinder is reminiscent of a variety of *tu quoque*'s in which one who denies that there are X's is charged with assuming X's himself. Thus the skeptic who denies that anyone knows anything is charged with himself claiming to know something – viz., that no one knows anything. Again, the mechanist or behaviorist who writes books to prove that men are not actuated by purposes, is charged with displaying an example of what he is claiming not to exist. It is generally true in these cases that the denial of X's on a first level is held to involve the admission of X's on a higher level.

19 The use of the Tarskian paradigm is not inadvertent. Unlike those who see the whole Tarskian treatment of truth as a series of technical gimmicks, I feel that Tarski's criterion of adequacy embodies a fundamental feature of our concept of truth. But I read it somewhat differently from many other admirers. The fact that 'S is true *iff* S' is a conceptual truth is often taken to show that the former doesn't say anything more than the latter, and that truth-talk is eliminable. But in opposition to this reductive reading, I prefer to concentrate on the other direction of equivalence and give it an inflationary reading. That is, the notion of what it takes for the statement to be true is already embodied, implicitly, in the statement-content; in explicitly saying that S is true, we are just bringing to light what is already embedded in the first-level statement.

20 This contention can be rerun for the question "What is it to *understand* a given statement or to know what statement is being made on a given occasion?" For what one has to know to know that is precisely what we have been calling statement-content. So again we cannot say: "In order to know what statement P asserted at *t*, what we have to know is that P referred to snow and said of it that it was white; and yet the truth of what P said does not ride on whether snow is white."

21 Hilary Putnam considers an interpretation like this in the second of his John Locke lectures, *Meaning and the Moral Sciences* (London: Routledge and Kegan Paul, 1978).

22 To be sure, the mid-twentieth-century advocates of this mode of interpretation were not concerned to reject a realist theory of truth, and rightly so, as we

shall see. Nevertheless, their verificationist brand of statement-interpretation might well appear attractive to an anti-realist who is grappling with the problem currently under consideration.

23 See C. I. Lewis, *Analysis of Knowledge and Valuation* (La Salle, Ill.: Open Court, 1946), ch. 8.

24 Of course, there are many alternative ways of stating verification-conditions for statements. They may be stated in terms of what would have to be experienced in order to verify it, or, as with Lewis, in terms of the experiencing of it. On the former alternative the con-

ditions may be phenomenalistic or physicalistic. They may or may not be such as to provide a practicable possibility of complete verification or falsification. And so on.

25 It must be admitted that conditionals, especially subjunctive conditions, pose special difficulties for the determination of realistic truth-conditions. But these are problems that arise for any view that allows conditionals (and how can they be avoided?). It is just that subjunctive conditionals loom much larger on the view under discussion.

47

Morals and Modals

Simon Blackburn

1 Introduction

Conclusions properly drawn must be true when the premisses are; events must unfold in accordance with natural law; people must obey the moral laws. Why do we find it so tricky to give a satisfactory philosophy of these necessities? In the first part of this essay, I suggest that it is because we have a rooted, and inadequate, conception of what is needed to establish such an understanding. This conception dominates the philosophy of modality, just as it does other areas, but it makes a genuine advance in understanding impossible. The diagnosis here is quite simple, but it is not so simple to disentangle ourselves from its influence, and to become practised with tools that are better suited to the problem.

What would a philosophical theory of logical, natural, or moral necessity be? By making judgements, of necessity, we say things, and these things are true or false. Perplexity arises because we think there must therefore be something which *makes* them so, but we cannot quite imagine or understand what this is. Nor do we understand how we know about whatever this is: we do not understand our own must-detecting faculty. Elucidating the truth-condition, and our access to it, is *the* goal of philosophy, to which its techniques and controversies are essentially directed. Not only is this so, but

surely it has to be so, for the philosophical itch is that of finding the nature of the facts strange and incomprehensible, of failing to imagine what could make true the relevant judgements. The problem is that of the fugitive fact, and the solution is to capture the nature of the fact in an intelligible way. This answer would tell us what such truths *consist in*: the answer would be obtained by establishing the *truth-conditions* for such judgements. It would give us an 'account' of the states of affairs in which their truth consists, or of what it is that *makes* them true. The account would have an explanatory role as well: fully established, it would explain why it is necessary that twice two is four, or how it can be that natural laws exist, or why we must be nice to one another. The most direct technique would be analysis, showing, it might be hoped, that the judgements are made true by some state of affairs relatively familiar and unproblematic (by whichever standards prompted the perplexity). Another technique would be more aggressive: to suggest that the concepts involved in the judgements are defective and due for replacement, so that the fugitive 'facts' were not really such, not really worth chasing after all.

Within this conception of the philosopher's quest, there is room for disagreement over detail – for instance, whether the description of the state of affairs finally fixed upon as making true the original modal judgement has to be synonymous with that judgement; whether one range of arguments or another succeeds in showing some concepts to be defective, or over what would count as an admissible reduction class for the modal claims.

Originally published in Crispin Wright and Graham Macdonald (eds), *Fact, Science and Value* (Oxford: Blackwell, 1987). Reprinted by permission of the author.

It is to the twists of this detail that we naturally turn when faced with the embarrassment that the head-on search for truth-conditions for modal assertions has turned up nothing at all promising. Where else is there to turn? For rejecting the problem is too much like ignoring the itch.

The modal concepts need a theory. But I do not think that they need or could possibly get a theory described, however remotely, in the terms suggested so far. In other words, I think that we have completely misinterpreted the *kind* of solution the philosophical problem needs. This may seem surprising, for I posed the problem and the kind of solution in terms deliberately bland – the kind of terms that would go quite unremarked as a preface to discussions. But I shall argue that they mislead us, and that a better way to approach the matter exists.

2 The Quasi-realist Alternative

Let us call the direct approach the truth-conditions approach. Here is a dilemma that attends it, and that I shall exhibit quite generally for moral, natural, or logical necessity. If we ask what makes it so that A must be the case, we may be given a local proof, a proof of A from B. This is satisfactory if we already understand why B must be so (if our topic is logical necessity, there is also the status of the proof to consider). But if our concern is with the whole area, then we turn to scrutinize that understanding. Attention shifts to why B must be the case, for our philosophical concern is with necessity in general, not with A in particular. Suppose an eventual answer cites some truth F, and so takes the form: '$\Box A$ because F'. ('Because' here is taken to include constitutive variants: the truth that $\Box A$ consists in F, is made so by F, etc.)

Now, either F will claim just that something *is* so, or it will claim that something *must* be so. If the latter, there is no problem about the *form* of the explanation, for one necessity can well explain another. But, as we have seen, there will be the same bad residual 'must': the advance will be representable as 'if we see why *this* must be so, we can now see why *that* must be as well'. And there is no escape from the overall problem that way. Suppose instead that F just cites that something *is* so. If whatever it is does not *have to be* so, then there is strong pressure to feel that the original necessity has not been explained or identified, so much as undermined. For example, suppose a

theorist claims that twice two must be four because of a linguistic convention, or that particles must attract each other thus because of some ongoing cosmic setup, or that we must be nice to one another because that is what God wants. Suppose it is denied that there is any residual necessity, that we *must* make just those conventions, that laws determine the consequences and continuation of the cosmic setup, or that God's wants ought to be heeded. Then in each case there is a principled difficulty about seeing how the kind of fact cited could institute or be responsible for the necessity. This is because the explanation, if good, would undermine the original modal status: if that's all there is to it, then twice two does not have to be four, particles don't have to attract each other, and we don't have to be nice to each other, even if it would be unwise not to. This is, of course, a generalization of the famous Euthyphro dilemma. Either the explanandum shares the modal status of the original, and leaves us dissatisfied, or it does not, and leaves us equally dissatisfied.

So why is the truth-conditional approach so dominant – why is this dilemma not universally recognized? Partly at least because it leaves room for work. The circle can be virtuous and explanatory. In other words, there is no embargo on finding theories of the form '$\Box p$ because F' where F stays *within* the modal sphere in question – '$\Box p$ because in all possible worlds p'; '$\Box p$ because there is a relation of necessitation between certain universals', or '$\Box p$ because $\sim p$ is impermissible', for example. Such theories can and do uncover important aspects of our thought: making the logic of modality intelligible, for instance. But from the standpoint that prompts the original problem – the dissatisfaction with the fugitive fact – by staying within the family in question, the analyses cannot do more than postpone things. Of course, at one level this is perfectly well known, for everyone agrees that it is one thing to have a possible-worlds approach to modality, for example, and quite another to have a theory of the metaphysics or epistemology of the things we say about possible worlds.

The poor prospects of the truth-conditional approach would be easier to tolerate if there were another approach. Fortunately, there is. The truth-conditional approach looks for another way of characterizing the 'layer of reality' that makes true modal utterances. The alternative starts (and, I shall urge, ends) with our making of those utterances: the thing we intend by insisting upon a necessity or allowing a possibility. We could call it a 'conceptual role' or even a 'use' approach, but neither title is quite happy, for neither makes plain the contrast with truth-conditional approaches that is needed. The conceptual role of use of a modal idiom might be just that of expressing belief in the fugitive layer of fact! If the best that can be said about our commitments is that they are those of people who believe in particular distributions of possibilities – logical, natural, or moral – then we are silenced again. But this may not be the best that there is to say: we can approach the commitments differently.

This alternative is familiar under the heading of projectivism (or sometimes, which is worse, 'noncognitivism') in ethics: this is why in setting the scene I have included moral musts. It has been pioneered in the philosophy of natural law by Ramsey and Ayer, and my aim is to make it a recognized option in the metaphysics of modality.

Notice that this is *not* the alternative of saying that 'there are no laws of nature' (or no possible worlds), any more than projective theory of ethics involves the 'eccentric' view that there are no obligations. Instead, this approach gives its own account of what it is to say that there *are*, and, if the commitments are valuable, *why it is correct* to do so. The account has two stages. It starts with a theory of the mental state expressed by commitments in the area in question: the habits, dispositions, attitudes they serve to express. It is these that are voiced when we express such commitments in the ordinary mode: when we say that there exists this possibility, that necessity, this obligation. The second stage (which I called quasi-realism) explains on this basis the propositional behaviour of the commitments – the reason why they become objects of doubt or knowledge, probability, truth, or falsity. The aim is to see these propositions as constructions that stand at a needed point in our cognitive lives – they are the objects to be discussed, rejected, or improved upon when the habits, dispositions, or attitudes need discussion, rejection, or improvement. Their truth corresponds to correctness in these mental states, by whichever standards they have to meet. Such a theory only collapses back into realism if we are reduced to saying that correctness in modal or moral judgement is simply representing the modal or moral facts as they are. But according to my direction of theorizing, we can better than that, and what we can do involves no irreducible appeal to a moral or modal reality. It is here that the

opposition to realism lies, although I shall try to make it plain that the interest of the approach remains even if, as I also believe, there is no very coherent realism for it to be 'anti'.

It is tempting to characterize this anti-realism as an 'as-if' philosophy: we talk as if there exist moral or modal facts, when in fact there are none. This makes it sound as though, according to this approach, some *error* of expression or thought is involved in such talk – for we talk as if *p*, when in fact *p* is false. This consequence of an as-if characterization is especially tempting when we remember other areas in philosophy where such projections are supposed to be responsible for mistakes we make – pathetic fallacies, for instance. Spinoza, for example, believed that what we take to be contingency in the world is merely a reflection of our ignorance, and this diagnoses a *mistaken* belief that we have.[1] Most writers on projective theories of morals and modals mention Hume, of course, and then continue with some version of this:

> Hume's view is that we then make a mistake: we project something essentially 'inner' onto the external world, and come to the mistaken belief that the concept of necessity we have applies to propositions in virtue of the objective properties of ideas and, as a consequence of this, we mistakenly believe that modal judgements can be true or false.[2]

There is excuse for the interpretation, for Hume is not as clear as one might wish. The first passage in which he appeals to the metaphor of the mind spreading itself on external objects is in the context of diagnosing a mistake – the 'contrary bias' that leads people to ridicule his philosophy of causation, to suppose that, by making the 'efficacy of causes lie in the determination of the mind', Hume is reversing the order of nature.[3] But this does not show Hume admitting that, by talking of causes (or obligations or necessary relations of ideas) as we do, we make any mistake. The theorist may misinterpret the nature of our judgements, their origins, and the standards that justify them. But the first-order user of the vocabulary makes no mistake: there is decisive evidence that Hume thought he made none. This is clearest in the moral case, of course, for Hume's philosophy of natural belief is infected by the background problem that our belief in the external world in any case involves a mistake – natural and inevitable propensities of the mind that must lead us to falsehood. But there is no further mistake involved in 'causalizing' – in finding causal order in the world we take ourselves to inhabit – any more than there is in moralizing as a reaction to characters and actions.

Hume's position is best explained by separating two different applications of the notion of projection. In the one use (which I prefer) we 'project' when we use the ordinary propositional expressions of our commitments, saying that there is this causal relation, that natural law, this other obligation. In the other we project only when we adopt, as philosophers, a particular 'realist' explanation of the sphere in question. This is a quite different thing, and it is what gave the contrary bias of which Hume is indeed complaining. The space between the two uses is easily missed, especially by philosophers coming with a realist bias in the first place. For they will be only too apt to suppose that the ordinary use has, as it were, done their work for them, so that a realist ontology is the only possible explanation of the first-order usage. But this, in Hume's view and mine, is not so. And this view must be given a hearing.

How can a projective theory accompany the view that no mistake is made in talking as we do? We would only make a mistake in saying that things ought to be done, or have to be so, if *these judgements have a false content*. But if their content arises as the projectivist + quasi-realist story maintains, they do not. No error occurs in moralizing or modalizing, even if philosophers have mistaken the kind of content these judgements have. Error exists only if there is a real *mismatch* between the truth about the nature of the claims and their content or what we make them do in our theories of things. But no mismatch exists in the thought that '1 + 1 = 2', that bees cause stings, and so on.

Quite apart from the implication that we make some kind of mistake, an as-if description of the theory makes it appear inadequate to the depth of our commitments. It looks refutable by a kind of phenomenological reminder of the strength of our belief that there *really are* possibilities, necessities, etc. Don't you believe that there *really are* natural laws, iron proofs, genuine duties? It is not just that we talk as if there are such things! But a quasi-realist will properly say: it is not simply that we think and behave *as if* there are necessities: there *are*. And we are right to think that there are. The commitment, and its correct expression, should not be in question.

What, then, is the mistake in describing such a philosophy as holding that 'we talk as if there are

necessities when really *there are none*'? It is the failure to notice that the quasi-realist need allow no sense to what follows the 'as if' except one in which it is true. And conversely, he need allow no sense to the contrasting proposition in which it in turn is true. He no more need allow such sense than (say) one holding Locke's theory of colour need accept the view that we talk as if there are colours, when there are actually none. This is doubly incorrect, because nothing in the Lockean view forces us to allow any sense to 'there are colours' except one in which it is true; conversely, neither need it permit a sense to 'there are actually none' in which *that* is true. Theorists *may* construct such senses: for instance, a sense in which 'there are colours' implies that colours do some work of physical explanation, or could be apprehended by more than one sense, and of course the Lockean will deny anything implying such a thing. But if the words retain an uncorrupted, English sense, then the Lockean, and similarly the quasi-realist, holds not just that we talk and think as if there are . . . , but that there are.[4]

Then the objection might be rephrased: according to the quasi-realist, we think and talk as if there were real moral and modal *facts*, but there are none. However, this too, although it points in a better direction, invites misunderstanding. It cannot stand as an accurate diagnosis of a position, for the word 'fact' also has an uncorrupted English sense: it is a fact that there are colours, and there are many facts about them. Certainly, there is a sense in which the quasi-realist is opposed to giving an ontological status to moral and modal facts, but according to him you cannot read off this status just from the nature of our commitments, their modes of expression, or their genuine place in our thinking, even if that thinking goes on invoking talk of facts. The appearance tempts philosophers to ontological quests, puzzles, and errors, but the mistake lies with the theorist who succumbs to the temptation.

Of what then is the quasi-realist suspicious? We can see now how the problem of characterizing either realism or anti-realism becomes acute. Suppose, for instance, we are satisfied with a quasi-realist construction of modality: we see what we are doing when we modalize, and why talking of possibilities or possible worlds is a legitimate form for these commitments to take. So when a writer such as Lewis maintains the irreducible nature of the modal idiom and expresses his commitments in that idiom, he is doing no more than a quasi-realist allows. What *more* does he intend by deeming himself a realist? How is there to be space, as it were, for some extra content in any such claim? One might see illegitimate content: if a theorist held that alternative possibilities are real in the sense that we can find them in space or hold them responsible for causing various results, or if he took comfort in the thought that he could model apprehension of possibilities upon sensory apprehension. But theorists, including Lewis, call themselves modal realists without accepting any such theses. It begins to look as if there is no way of framing an ontological or metaphysical opposition. Saying 'I believe in possible worlds, and I am (or: I am not) a realist about them' would amount to no more than accepting irreducible modal idioms, and in either form the last conjunct is quite idle.

Universal harmony is desirable, but it does not come quite so cheaply. The difficulty of characterizing the dispute shows that it is up to anyone who takes pride in announcing himself in this style to make sure that the last conjunct has a content. And in my view, many philosophers who take pleasure in calling themselves 'moral realists' have failed badly in this obligation. They have either been content to pour cold water on revisionary anti-realism of John Mackie's kind, or content to insist on the surface appearances, or content to generalize what is mistakenly seen as a late Wittgensteinian lesson, to the effect that every indicative sentence shares the same role – that of describing an aspect of the world ('our world'). The existence of the kind of theory I am describing should undercut this. But there is still room for disagreement, specifically about what in the commitments needs explaining, and about the kind of explaining modal and moral facts can themselves do.

Realist theorizing is apt to pay too little attention to the first and to make too much of the second. It worries too little about the curious place that moral and modal commitments have, about what notion of truth can be appropriate to them, about why it matters, and about how the commitments blend with others that we have. It worries less about these issues because if these commitments are beliefs, then their aim is simple truth, and this is proper depiction of the modal or moral realm. This is an application of the second tendency: to make much of the explanatory powers of the moral or modal states of affairs. A realist may betray himself, for instance, by relying upon metaphors of perception or vision to explain how we become acquainted with moral or modal fact, or by entering false theses

about the creation or destruction of such facts and their dependence on others, or by supposing that the existence of such facts explains other genuine states of affairs, in the way in which one state of affairs can explain another. To suppose, for instance, that the world exists as it does because it ought to do so might be the privilege of the moral realist. To suppose that the world exists because God made it is the privilege of the theological realist. If this kind of belief is intrinsic to first-order theorizing (as in the theological case), then the kind of diagnosis of the commitments offered by a projectivist will indeed find error in the everyday practice, as well as in various philosophical interpretations of it; this is why a 'Wittgensteinian' protection of religious belief is a kind of cheat. Ordinary religious belief, thought of in an expressive way, involves the mismatch referred to above. This is also why there is very doubtfully any space for a genuine realist versus anti-realist debate about explanatory physics. But first-order theories are notably silent about the explanatory role of possible worlds or moral duties; it is left to the philosophers to inject good or bad views about that.[5]

Once the explanations are agreed, not much is left in the words. So the universal harmony is better approached in a case like that of colour, where we feel reasonably confident of the underlying facts and the way they relate to colour perception. And then indeed it is no great matter whether we say that there are colours (and I am a realist about them) or that there are not (and I am not). The space for dispute has shrunk away and can only be resurrected if false implications are read into the parenthetical remarks. It is no great trick to announce oneself in either style; the work comes in earning a right to do so. But to achieve this harmony in the modal case involves the hard work of showing how to explain modalizing in the first place, and this remains to be done.

At the risk of appearing moralistic, I shall close this section by illustrating how truth-conditional theorizing dominates our philosophical imaginations. One of the clearest expressive approaches to commitment to natural law is that of Ramsey and Ayer. Here is Ayer:

> In short I propose to explain the distinction between generalizations of law and generalizations of fact, and thereby to give some account of what a law of nature is, by the indirect method of analysing the distinction between

treating a generalization as a statement of law and treating it as a statement of fact.[6]

It is, however, a little unclear from this way of setting it up quite how Ayer conceives the step from a theory of what it is to treat something as a law of nature to giving 'some account of what a law of nature is' – the ontological overtone of this suggests that the truth-conditional theory is not quite exorcized. For if the expressive theory is successful, there is no last chapter to write on what a modal fact or state of affairs is. We would know what we do and why we are correct to do it when we commit ourselves to necessities of logic, nature, or action, and that would be the end. Ayer's nod towards truth-conditional hankerings is wholesale prostration in other writers. A recent example is David Armstrong. After observing that inference from the observed to the unobserved is central to our whole life as human beings, and that if there were no laws, those inferences would be unreliable, he continues: 'hence the notion of law is, or should be, a central concept for epistemology. If so we will also want to enquire into its ontology. We will want to know what a law of nature is.'[7] The grip of the truth-conditional approach appears when Armstrong considers the alternative to this, which he identifies as the 'truly eccentric view...which denies that there are any Laws'.[8]

Even writers as cautious as Edward Craig and Crispin Wright find it straightforward to agree on the point that, in effect, closes off projectivism + quasi-realism. The context here is that Craig had demonstrated decisively the imaginative block that faces us when we try to conceive, in proper detail, of a counter-arithmetical reality. The projectivist is then poised to see this imaginative block as something expressed when we insist upon the necessity of arithmetic. But Wright commented, 'If as Craig makes plausible, we are unable to conceive of how any alternative determination might be viable, then that is how things are with us; it is a further, tendentious step to inflate our imaginative limitations into a metaphysical discovery.'[9] And Craig, acknowledging that he and Wright agree that we should not ask the imagination to do too much, concedes immediately: 'It certainly is a further step.'[10] Is it so clear that there is this further step? Only if claims of necessity are 'metaphysical discoveries', and this the projectivist will query. Again, the position is clear if we revert to the moral case: a projectivist will see commitment to

an obligation as a distinctive mental state – call it a sentiment – but he will not accept any charge that we tendentiously inflate our sentiments into metaphysical discoveries (discoveries about the independent structure of the world of obligations), precisely because he denies that in our awareness of duty and obligation we are in fact making any such discoveries. (I return later to Craig's reasons, which were good, for thinking there is *a* further step – only it is not this one.)

There are aspects of the work of making quasi-realism attractive that I shall not repeat in this paper. These include its distinction from naïve subjectivism, its moves to accommodate the propositional nature of ethical claims, its explanation of the syntax and semantics that go with that, and the basis for constructing a working notion of truth. My concern here is to see how this shape of theory fares with one of the other two 'musts': that of logic.

3 Policies versus Needs

We allow possibilities, rule out impossibilities, and insist upon necessities. This is not describing anything. As in Wittgenstein, attributing necessity to a proposition is not making a true or false claim about it – or at least is not to be understood that way.[11] It is more like adopting a norm, or a policy or a rule that a thesis be put 'in the archives', above the hurly-burly of empirical determination. The decision dictates how we shall treat recalcitrant evidence. This accords with the parallel with morals. The one kind of rule makes courses of thought intellectually obligatory; the other makes courses of action so. But there is a major problem: to identify any space for this rule-making. Modalizing, like moralizing, does not feel optional: it feels as though we regard '$1 + 1 = 2$' as necessary simply because we *must* do so, not because we have chosen to do so. Its status is more naturally seen as a product of our inability to conceive otherwise, or to *do* anything with a counter-arithmetical judgement. If the necessity of propositions is in any sense conferred by us, it is still unnatural to see it as reflecting anything in which we had a choice. So notwithstanding Wittgenstein, a projectivist will be wise to look for the mental set that gains expression outside the realms of the optional (and it is vital to notice that he can do this – (the denial of metaphysical realism does not usher in a 1950s embrace of free choice and conventionalism).

If attributing modal value reflected free policies and choices, it would be unclear why we should go in for it. The right attitude would seem to be that which Wright attributes to his imagined 'Cautious Man'.[12] This is the character who agrees with us on all empirical truth. He agrees with us too in accepting proofs; in arithmetic or logic, or in any more apparently metaphysical commitments, such as those determining our basic ascriptions of temporal, spatial, or causal categories, this character agrees with us. But he refuses to make modal assignments. As far as he is concerned, it is enough that we accept, say, that $1 + 1 = 2$. It is unwise to go further and ascribe necessity to the proposition.

The challenge is reminiscent of Quine: would it not be better simply to register our stronger attachment to some propositions than others, and then to leave market forces to determine which ones maintain our loyalty? Even if we abandon the self-image of decision-makers, we confront essentially the same problem. What would be lost if we simply did not modalize? Is it not foolish to elevate mere imaginative limitations into iron necesssities?

Quine thinks that even in the case of logic we would be better off doing no such thing. Of course, in the context of positivism, Quine's strength lay not so much in opposition to modal discrimination in itself, as in his insistence that coming to the problem with notions of meaning or convention is coming with dirty hands: there can be no modally innocent appeal to conventions, or concepts or meanings or rules or languages, giving us an anterior understanding from which to explain or justify those discriminations. In other words, even if we can *say* things like 'analytic propositions are true in virtue of meaning/concepts/constraints on the application of concepts...', this is no help. It is no help because there is no identification of concepts, meanings, etc. which does not itself involve knowing the modal liaisons of propositions in which the concepts occur – what must be, may be, or cannot be true, if they are so. Hence, any such appeal cannot explain or justify our modal commitments: in a frequent metaphor, it keeps us within the same circle.

It may have been naïve of the positivists to think that by retreating to questions of meaning we obtained a clean-handed empiricist approach to modality. But overthrowing that is not the same as overthrowing the modal. Indeed, the 'dirty-hands' argument is entirely two-edged: by showing how deeply the modal is entrenched in any 'conceptual scheme', it makes it less likely that modal-izing is left an unprotected optional extra in our thought. But so far as the present essay goes, the point to insist upon is that there is clearly an antecedent problem for any naturalistic sanitizing of the modal. This is to explain the way in which we make modal judgements – the ease with which we non-collusively agree upon them. Obviously, before we recommend that we abandon modalizing, we want to know what it involves and why we do it. Our capacity to make non-collusive modal discriminations requires explanation, whether or not it is regrettable that we do so. But curiously enough (since the task is one of naturalized epistemology), Quine's philosophy of the modal is incapable of meeting this eminently naturalistic request, and when it is buttressed to do so, it loses its appeal, doing better by becoming quasi-realistic. Or so I shall argue.

4 Explaining Modalizing

Quine's consistent position has been that even when we think of the most elementary trivialities of truth-functional logic, the best we can say is that they are *obvious*. It is sometimes said that he changed his mind about this, and that, discussing translation from allegedly pre-logical or alternative-logical tongues, he conceded some very special status to truth-functional logic, in the determination with which we would reinterpret others as conforming to it. But in Quine's view this is no shift. It is just a consequence of the fact that we always translate so as to save the obvious.[13]

Of course, not all truths naïvely called necessary are at all obvious, but Quine can and does extend the explanation to those which can be proved by obvious means from obvious starting points. Here we have the famous Quinean picture in which the truths naïvely called necessary are those which are obvious enough to lie far away from the theatres of war in which empirical forces mould and break theories. It substitutes the one-dimensional web of belief, with only a vague and pragmatic boundary between propositions that face the test of experience routinely ('contingent') and those that at worst would only face it in periods of exceptional theoretical turbulence ('necessary'). And at first sight it gives Quine his answer to the problem of explaining our non-collusive application of the notion. When we deem a proposition necessary, we express our apprehension of its obvious character.

But a little thought shows that this is quite inadequate. For a great many truths are in Quine's central reservation, but would simply be classed as contingent. These are truths that are *central, certain, obvious* to everyone – that there exist trees and rocks, that houses keep off the rain, and so on. There is no prospect of these being rocked by scientific change, nor of recalcitrant experience casting doubt upon them. But we unhesitatingly class them as contingent. How is Quine to explain this difference in the modal reaction, if they are in the scientific archive, beyond the struggles of falsification and modification?

Quine admits that logic is 'built into translation more fully than other systematic departments of science. It is in the incidence of the obviousness that the difference lies. . . .'[14] It looks as if this is to be developed when he contrasts '1 + 1 = 2', which is 'obvious outright', with 'it is raining', which is 'obvious in particular circumstances'. But the point he apparently has in mind is just that 'every logical truth is obvious, actually or potentially: each, that is to say, is either obvious as it stands or can be reached from obvious truths by a sequence of individually obvious steps'.[15] This is the extension referred to above. But it is not at all clear how it relates to the incidence of the obviousness. And in any event, in a well-developed theoretical science, obviousness can similarly transmit from obvious data through obvious principles of interpretation and explanation, to bring hitherto unobvious conclusions into the fold. There is no diagnosis of our different reactions to '1 + 1 = 2' and 'there exist trees and rocks' here.

Quine's first thought about the contrast was the best: it is indeed in the incidence of the obviousness that the difference lies: 'it is raining' is obvious *only* in particular circumstances; '1 + 1 = 2' is 'obvious outright'. But 'obvious in particular circumstances' versus 'obvious outright' is a dangerously suggestive contrast: not far from 'assertible only in the light of particular experience' versus 'assertible by conceptual means alone', or a posteriori versus a priori. If the best theory of the incidence of the obviousness is that in the one case but not the other it varies with particular *contingencies*, we are left with our judgement that the truth of the one does so vary, and the truth of the other does not. This once more is what common sense would say: 'there are trees' is obvious in the light of something that, we know, could have been otherwise; not so '1 + 1 = 2'. Another way of putting it is that common sense allows that recalcitrant experience is

possible in the one case but not the other: we could tell a story in which it came to appear to us as if there were not trees, but not one in which 1 + 1 is anything other than 2. But Quine cannot appeal to entrenched modal intuitions to explain the division within the obvious.

The problem, remember, is that Quine is to *explain* our modal tendencies before dismissing or sanitizing them – showing that nothing in the making of them licenses epistemology to draw any grander distinction than his. He is therefore quite within his rights to call upon his list of theoretical defects here. Perhaps it is because we are in the grip of mythical theories of ideas, or molecular theories of meaning, or use–mention confusion, that we distinguish between equally certain or obvious judgements, identically remote from the threat of overthrow: there being trees and 1 + 1 being 2. But is it clear from a naturalist perspective that *only* a defect is involved – that there is no legitimate point and purpose in the distinction, within the overall class of certainties, between those that are necessary and those that are contingent? Surely not, and a better explanation of our propensities is easy to produce. Let us consider the matter from the opposite point of view. It is usually necessity that is the bugbear, but if we suppose that it is the distinction between the necessary and the contingent that requires understanding, we also can ask what we miss if we lack the capacity to deem propositions contingent. This direction of approach must be equally legitimate. In fact, I suspect there is some evidence that contingency needs more explanation to children than necessity: the initial tendency is to take everything that is so as having to be so. Suppose someone who is modally blind in this way: he sees no point or purpose in accepting any notion of *contingency*. Running the metaphysics and the epistemology in tandem, we can suppose that epistemologically he can make nothing of the idea that a particular judgement is a posteriori.[16] So he can make nothing of the idea that although there are trees there might not have been, nor that there being trees is obvious only in the light of particular experience, so that if the experience were different (or had been different), as it might be, the opposite judgement would have seemed right.

What does he miss? The case is still underspecified. This person may, perhaps like Leibniz or Spinoza, have a background theory that all apparent contingency is disguised necessity. In that case, in the marketplace, or talking with the vulgar, he could use a perfectly good surrogate for contingency – perhaps one that he may regard as suited for finite beings. Or perhaps he is like the Cautious Man, and claims to find some kind of hubris in expressing verdicts in modal language, although he makes the same distinctions and the same use of them (for instance, in distinguishing valid from invalid proofs, or reflecting on alternative possibilities) that we do. This is theoretical or philosophical scepticism, and, like its counterparts elsewhere, is supposed to coexist with normal living. Such theorists draw the same distinctions as the rest of us, except that when they think such things as that there might not have been trees, they will (as it were) preface their assent with a universal qualification: contingency becomes some species of *apparent* contingency, or not the real thing. This is scepticism, or perhaps idealism, about modality, and not what I intend. I want instead someone who does not even recognize the need for a reinterpretation, for he cannot begin by recognizing even apparent contingency as such.

It seems plain that blindness to the a posteriori status of propositions is catastrophic. To such a person, failure to realize that it is raining here now is *like* failure to realize that $1 + 1 = 2$, an incomprehensible defect. He is unable to make anything of a mode of thinking in which it is not realized that p, when p is true, in just the way that we are unable to when p represents an elementary necessity. But what does he make of (for instance) sleep, of blindness, of his own need for telephone directories or testimony, or of the difference that different spatial and temporal position causes to his own information gathering? How does he think of his own failures of omniscience or conceive of his own changes of knowledge as he goes about the world? There seems no way of answering these questions without stripping the subject of massive quantities of ordinary, non-modal, *empirical* understanding – simple understanding about the variation of belief with circumstance. It would be possible to fill out the way in which the deficiency disqualifies him from interpreting others reliably: he cannot rationalize them, seeing why various beliefs seem right to them, because he has no way of seeing how belief varies with point of view, with use of the senses, with skill or luck. But ignorance of these things in this context is just a *species* of ignorance of the way one thing varies with another. The person who cannot understand how the cat's awareness of the bird varies with whether it can see it seems little better than one who cannot

understand how the leaf's motion varies with the wind.

Conversely, if the subject has this understanding, he is in a position at least to *imitate* modal discriminations. Crucially, he can do better than Quine suggests in making distinctions within the class of the obvious. He can make something of a way of thought in which it is not realized that there are trees, just as he can make something of a way of thought in which it is not appreciated that it is raining here now. Long-term confinement to treeless zones is a kind of position he can understand, and whose impact upon a belief system he could appreciate. He can say something *better* about 'it is raining here now' and '$1 + 1 = 2$' than that they are equally obvious. He can say something of what makes the former obvious, and describe people to whom it would not be obvious; he can appreciate how there could be, or make something of, a way of describing the world in which it is denied. Suppose he is set our task of discriminating, among obvious truths, between those which are intuitively necessary and those which are contingent; then he can at least approximate to our division, by simply classing as contingent those which satisfy this condition: he can make something of ways of thought in which, for various reasons, they are either not accepted or are even denied. Here 'make something of' will include being able to explain how such a way of thought might arise, knowing how it might be rectified, understanding the practices of those whose thought it is, and so on. This will give the subject a sense of what would count as recalcitrant experience, and what would have counted as such, even for entrenched, obvious, but contingent, certainties. And, given that there is a residual class of apparent beliefs where he cannot do this, he will have a working substitute for the necessary and the impossible.

The upshot is that blindness to the a posteriori character of beliefs seems impossible in subjects who have virtually any comprehension of the world. Now naturalized epistemology is largely a study of the variation of belief with circumstance. It can be done by us only when we can make something of the variation of belief involved. In some cases we can; in residual cases such as logic and mathematics we characteristically cannot. This difference can be used naturalistically to explain our tendency to make modal divisions, and it gives the explanation that Quine left himself without.

Is it an explanation that can be taken over by Quine? I believe so. Quine has no reason to oppose our discrimination of contingency; it is the remainder he dislikes. So his best path would be to accept the explanation of our propensity to modalize, but to warn us against making too much of the imaginative differences it cites. This would be to join forces with Wright's Cautious Man: our imaginative limitations are facts about us; they may gain expression in our modalizing and explain our discriminations, but they ought not to be taken as any guide to what is necessarily the case.

5 Refining Imagination

The players, then, seem to align themselves into two teams. Both admit the existence and centrality of imaginative blocks – of the fact that there are propositions of whose falsity we can make nothing. The one side, encompassing Craig, Wright, this new Quine, Forbes, and probably most others, finds something distinctive about the Cautious Man, who goes this far, but refuses to modalize. Quine recommends his modesty; Forbes thinks it would be a mistake to project imaginative limitations. Craig does not go quite so far. He indeed thinks there is a further step if we take our imaginative limitations as guides to what must be the case, namely the step of supposing that the world is transparent to our intelligence. He points out that in particular philosophical climates the belief that the world is thus transparent, or the goal of making it thus transparent, may be much more appealing than in others. In particular in the twentieth-century pragmatic climate that Quine inhabits, this belief is less prominent: it becomes enough that theory should enable us to 'anticipate and control perceivable events', and genuine intelligibility is no longer a first priority.[17] In modalizing we are being incautious, and even if Craig finds much to admire in the old ideology that prompted us to be so, the sense remains that sobriety requires the more Quinean attitude. This side then thinks that the Cautious Man is distinctive in not modalizing. Either he does not possess a set of concepts that we, somewhat unaccountably, do, or he exercises proper caution in not making judgements with them.

The other side, where I feel rather isolated, queries the central doctrine of these thinkers. When we understand what the Cautious Man lacks, we shall be pleased that we have it. The central doctrine of the other team is, in Craig's words, that 'we should not infer any absolute impossibility from the limitations of our own ima-

ginations'.[18] With modifications, I suggest that there is a quite proper move or inference here; that what looks like intellectual hubris is in fact not so. The shared doctrine of the other team is that there is a chasm which the Cautious Man is admirable for not crossing. My claim is that it is only in the shadows cast by illicit hankering after a realistic, truth-conditional account of modalizing that the crossing seems so dangerous.

Craig thinks that there might be two sources for the idea that the crossing can be made. One is that meanings are sufficiently transparent to our minds, that we can know just by introspection that what we mean by some sentence can never come out false. As he rightly says, nobody can succumb to that with a clear conscience these days. The other is the assumption that our mental powers are perfectly in tune with reality, and as he again rightly says, that can only be credible within a specific philosophical climate. My source is different: I am sceptical about the assumption that we know what we mean by 'absolute necessity', or the real distribution of possibilities, in a way that allows us to contrast them wholesale with the blocks that our only ways of thinking meet. I am sceptical because I detect the influence of realism at just this point.

This scepticism will, I hope, appear less extravagant if we remember the other, easier, fields on which projectivism + quasi-realism fought. The equivalent of the Craig–Wright–Quine team over morals would say: 'we should not infer any ("absolute") obligations from the direction of our own sentiments' (for example). The equivalent of the Cautious Man would be someone who, while conducting his practical reasoning in every respect as the rest of us do, eschews the 'inference' to the proposition that we have, for instance, an obligation to our children. He can make the same deprecatory remarks about our right to think ourselves in tune with metaphysical moral reality. He can even cite theological and philosophical climates in which this pride would have seemed natural, but which no longer obtain. My reaction is that he has mistaken the nature of the judgement: by thinking of it as 'made true' by some possibly alien state of affairs, he has made his scepticism inevitable; by seeing the proper function of the proposition, we avoid it. On a realist account, his caution is correct, as is his refusal to moralize. But as it is, he is actually missing nothing (as I put it in 'Errors and the phenomenology of value', 'shmoralizing' – conducting practical reasoning properly without a realistic backdrop – is just moralizing). Again, the colour case provides an easier but slightly more distant analogy: we would be wrong to be cautious over whether using our eyes tunes us to the real divisions and distributions of colours, because our only concept of the reality of those divisions comes from proper use of our eyes.

However, the other team has another weapon, again wielded powerfully by Craig. Following the passage agreeing with Wright that it is a 'tendentious step' to inflate our imaginative limitations into a metaphysical discovery, Craig writes:

> It certainly is a further step. In the first place, it is clear that there is a group of possibilities which no argument from premises about what we can and can't imagine could ever rule out. We might, for instance, come to be able to imagine what we can't now imagine, there may be other beings who can imagine what we can't and never will be able to imagine, and so on. . . . [I]f we close our minds to these possibilities then we make assumptions about our present imaginative capacities for which we have no warrant.[19]

To address this, we need to make distinctions within the class of the 'unimaginable'. I wrote above of propositions whose truth we cannot imagine in the sense that we could make nothing of ways of thought in which they are asserted. Now this is to be taken fairly strictly, and so taken it does not quite correspond to 'unimaginable' on an untutored reading. Suppose, for instance, I announce that I am able to show you a new primary colour, quite distinct from any mixture or shade of previous colours. You may doubt me, and you would certainly be unable to imagine what I was going to show you, if my claim is true. You might even express yourself by saying that it is impossible, but you would be unwise to have much confidence in this claim, for in some sense you can 'make something of' the possibility that I am going to do what I said. It is not as if I had said I would show you a circle with straight sides, or a true contradiction.

Let us distinguish a proposition's being 'unimaginable', in the sense that we cannot present to ourselves a sense of what it is like to experience it as true, from its being 'inconceivable', where this involves the kind of block just indicated, in which we can do nothing with the thought of its truth. It is frequently pointed out that unimaginability is a poor symptom of inconceivability, and this is correct. The cases one would adduce include these: the extra colour, the existence of infinite totalities, the bounded and shaped nature of space or time, the existence of extra dimensions, perhaps the operation of backward causation. Then there is the unimaginability of entities like the self, or of the will, and in some frames of mind, we cannot imagine the possibility even of rule-following, intentionality, and so on. The lack of fit works the other way round as well – propositions might be properly classed as impossible, although the imagination freely allows them: notoriously, the alleged possibility that I might have been Napoleon, or that Fermat's theorem might be true (or false), one of which is imaginable, although impossible.

Our imaginative powers change and develop. The child cannot imagine the beliefs of the adult; those unacquainted with them cannot imagine the taste of claret or the work of Rembrandt. These conditions can be altered, which immediately gives us a sense of potential ways in which our own imaginations are partial. Our experience is limited, and our imaginations not much better. Just as people of limited experience have impoverished imaginations compared with us, so we must accept that there are many things of various kinds which we cannot now imagine – tastes, smells, insights, and presumably truths. This, of course, accords well with Craig's caution: it is not just a modal sceptic, but all of us, who will beware of inferring impossibility from just any imaginative failure.

Using unimaginability as a good indication of impossibility is also a mistake because it depends upon too simple a notion of the relation between experience and thought. It asks, as it were, that we should be able to see any truth in a single picture. So, for instance, if we want to think of a theoretical notion, such as that of force acting at a distance, we try to visualize the process, and, failing, are apt to find the notion suspicious. We find it hard to accept that full intelligibility can be earned by a proper place in a theory, even if we cannot visualize the happenings of the processes. Consider, for another example, the shape of space. Children find it incredible to think that space has a shape, because they try to visualize it, or in other words imagine themselves *looking* at it, which is what we normally do to observe the shape of things, and the thought experiment collapses, for the observer cannot find a standpoint from which the whole of space can be observed. But using that failure as a reason for concluding that space must be infinite would be a mistake, for it would ignore other ways in which a shape of space might be certified – ways like those a man might use to find the shape of a container in which he is confined. If these procedures certify that only certain routes in space are possible, then the right conclusion may be that space is bounded and has a shape, and we can explain why the enterprise of trying to visualize it fails. Visualizing is a poor guide to states of affairs, because not all states of affairs reveal themselves in a picture. Similarly, things may be impossible although naïve imagination allows them, because naïve imagination does not tell us how to describe the scenes it re-creates; this is why it is so dangerous to use imagination as a guide to the metaphysics of the self.

Here we have explanations of failures of imagination. And we can conceive of superior positions from which some of our imaginative limitations could analogously be explained. When we can do that, we will not take imaginative limitations as a guide to impossibility. Now Craig in particular notices all this. This is a difference, he writes, between the case of the extra colour or difficult intermediate cases like that of extra spatial dimensions and full-blown cases like that of a deviant arithmetic: 'An explanation of our inability to imagine the arithmetically deviant along the lines that served for colour and spatial dimensions doesn't get started; so nothing checks our tendency to project our incapacity and suppose that reality just *couldn't be like that*.'[20] But Craig does not highlight the good use the projectivist can make of this difference.

Consider again the parallel with moral projectivism. We do not find it trivial to cross from a sentiment to a moral judgement. Only certain sentiments – those of a certain strength, or with certain objects, or those accompanied by sentiments about others who do not share them – form a jumping-off point. We are also conscious that there are doubtless flaws and failures in our sentiments, which are perhaps capable of explanation in the same way that we explain the defects of those who are worse than ourselves. But when the sentiments are strong and nothing on the cards explains them by the presence of defects, we go ahead and moralize. We may be aware that our opinion is fallible, but that is because we can do something with the thought of an improved perspective, even when we are fairly certain that one will not be found, and here as elsewhere commitment can coexist with knowledge that we may be wrong. The 'step' from a fully integrated sentiment of sufficient strength

to the moral expression now becomes no step at all: the moral is just the vocabulary in which to express that state. Avoiding it would not be an exercise in modesty, but an impoverishing idiosyncrasy of expression.

Why should it not be like this with logical necessity? We have arrived at the residual class of propositions of whose truth we can make nothing. We cannot see our failure to make anything of them as the result of a contingent limitation in our own experience, nor of a misapprehension making us think that their truth should be open to display in a way in which it need not be. We express ourselves by saying that they cannot be true – that their negations are necessary. There is the bare possibility of being shown wrong – perhaps our search into the causes of our imaginative block was inadequate, or perhaps we were under a misapprehension of what it might be for the proposition to be true. We may be uncomfortably aware of even great philosophers who mistakenly projected what turned out to be rectifiable limitations of imagination – the a priori has a bad history. But as Wright notices, we should have no wish to make ourselves infallible when deeming things a priori. We make the commitment in the light of the best we can do. There is no step, and no illusion.

6 Naturalism and Quasi-realism

On this account, part of what it is for us to make nothing of the truths that we deem impossible is that we cannot explain *naturalistically* our own failure to see what it would be for them to be true. When we can see how, if a proposition were true, we might nevertheless be in bad circumstances to appreciate how it might be, we release it from impossibility. It does not deserve ruling out any more. But we cannot see how, if contradictions were true or if $1 + 1 = 3$, we might be in bad circumstances to appreciate how it might be. We could have not even a sketch of a natural story of the block we face, because we can make nothing of the starting point.

This provides a kind of catch-22 in our attempts to theorize about the modal. If we can see our tendency to rule out p as the outcome of a contingent limitation, we are already making something of the thought that p might be true, but that if it were, nevertheless we would not appreciate it because of something or other. And this undermines any original commitment to its impossibility.

When someone starts: 'if there were an extra colour, then...', perhaps we can understand how it might be contingent limitations that make the hypothesis hard to contemplate – but if that is all there is to it, we lose any right to regard it as impossible. On the other hand, when someone says 'if $1 + 1 = 3$, then...' and essays to show how, if this were true, we would be in a bad position to appreciate it, the thought experiment breaks down, for we cannot properly work through what is being supposed and how we might be in a world of which it is true. But this means that there is bound to be a residual 'surd': our incapacity to make anything of the thought that some propositions are true has to be resistant to natural explanation, if it remains a good candidate for modal commitment.

The fear of an inexplicable core motivates attempts, such as the positivists gave, to remove any content from necessary truths. But we have accepted that the dirty-hands argument shows that we will not explain this incapacity by invoking uncontaminated knowledge of meaning, concepts, rules. We now find that if *any* natural explanation of our imaginative block can be given, this attacks our right to make the commitment. I think that here we get an alternative, or perhaps supplementary, explanation to that offered by Craig, of the late twentieth-century opposition to the modal. It can arise not only from a changed conception of what theories need to do, but also from a conviction that nothing escapes naturalistic explanation.

When we have thoroughly tested the sense of a hypothesis and make nothing of it, this is, in Wright's words, how things are with us. As Craig says, if the quasi-experiment of working through how it would be if p is done on ourselves, now, and if our attempts to work with p being true fail, then 'for any logical guarantee we have, that may be as far as it goes'.[21] But it goes a little further, for in the light of what we have said, it will also be so that we cannot see the incapacity as *just* one we happen to be subject to; we cannot deem it a *mere* fact about ourselves, here, now. If we could see it in that light, then that itself would destroy the modal commitment. This is why there is something bogus in Kant's theory that it is the forms of inner and outer sense that determine our a priori commitments. This looks illuminating because it looks sufficiently parallel to the natural explanation we might give of the imaginative limitations we can accept as no indication of impossibility – the colour limitation, for example. But it is not really parallel,

for if we can make nothing of the possibility of other forms of sense, the 'fact' that ours is one way or another is not intelligible as a genuine explanatory truth. Seeing it like that would require thinking the other side of the boundary: understanding how it might be, for instance, that although it is compulsory for us to use classical arithmetic, with a different cast of mind it might have been compulsory to use another arithmetic. And this we cannot do.

The residual surd marks a large asymmetry between the moral and the modal. In the case of moralizing, nothing stands in the way of a complete naturalistic story of what it is, why we do it, and, quasi-realistically, why we are right to do it. But the genesis of the way of thought is similar. The moralist insists upon obligations. He rules out those who flout them, refusing approval, ignoring contrary temptations, bending his actions to conform. The modalist insists upon necessities. He rules out ways of thought that flout them, refuses theories that involve them, bends his thoughts to conform. The moralist could just issue rules and penalties, but if he becomes self-conscious he needs the moral proposition to stand as a focus for discussion and reflection, and he contemplates its truth as a way of doing so. The self-conscious modalist needs the same. But the moralist can be quite completely aware of the genesis and justification of his activity, whereas if what we have just said is true, the modalist cannot be. In the case of the modal, the phenomenon is anti-naturalistic at its core.

Or is this unduly pessimistic? Some relief might be got by teasing out more aspects of the core inability to 'make anything of' a way of thought that accepts a putative impossibility. Obviously, there are enterprises of thinking through what modifications in logic are possible or what would be missing in a way of thought that consistently tried to make $1 + 1 = 3$. The business, for instance, of thinking through how a science might be built around denial of double negation, or of the distributive laws of logic (from P and $Q \vee R$, infer $(P \& Q) \vee (P \& R)$) proceeds under the stimulus of constructivism, or of quantum mechanics, respectively. So it ought to be possible to hold both that these laws are necessarily true and that we *can* 'make something of' ways of thought that lead people to deny them. This is not a serious obstacle to the direction of this essay. What we do is take a proposed deviation and follow it until either the way of thought seems possible – and we no longer modalize against it – or it breaks down. But 'breaks down' will mean: offends against something that we suppose essential to any scheme of thought (such as some distinction of truth and falsity, some stability of content, some embargo on contradiction). Eventually we voice an inability to make anything of transgression against these norms: this is the surd that remains. If the thought processes of the deviants are eventually seen to break down, then we can get a deeper understanding of our own commitments: it is no longer so that we face an entirely blank wall when we try to explain our own attachment to these laws. This reveals the genuine scope for explanatory work, and it may do a little to moderate the anti-naturalistic pessimism. We can certainly hope to show why a way of thought that is committed (say) to non-contradiction, or to supposing that not all propositions are true, or to other elementary necessities, is also committed (say) to '$1 + 1 = 2$', since we can hope to prove (relying, inevitably, on moves that we find inescapable) that if they are necessary, then so is this. This would give a complete bill of health to the modal if, as the positivists hoped, the propositions finally bearing the burden were free of genuine content, or owed their truth to some naturalistically explicable fact about us – a decision or convention, for instance. But these escapes no longer appear, and in default of a leap outside the system of necessities, the final surd seems set to remain.

Addendum

In this essay I do not press an argument against Lewis's modal realism that I did express in *Spreading the Word*; this argument nevertheless hovers in the background. This argument is that, as well as problems of saying how we get as far as possible worlds, the realist has a problem of getting us back from them: when we use a counterfactual, for instance, in pursuit of a concern with the actual world, why should we be interested if things are thus and so in a neighbouring world, or in all neighbouring worlds? It sounds like a change of subject. This argument was assailed by Bob Hale in his review.[22] Hale in effect plays the equation between 'this wire might have been live' and 'there is a possible world in which this wire is live' backwards, pointing out that since we have excellent reason to be interested in the former, and since according to the modal realist the latter

means the same, we have excellent reason to be interested in the latter.

This mistakes the nature of the problem. My concern, as usual, was explanation, and the point is that a realist construction of the neighbouring-possible-world proposition plays absolutely no role in explaining why we should be interested in the 'might have been' proposition with which it is identified. If anything, it seems to make such an interest strange or even inexplicable. It is no good replying that we are after all interested in the 'might' proposition, so we can expect the possible-world proposition to inherit that interest: the point is that the interest is not explained, and becomes harder to explain, if we give each of the claims other-worldly truth-conditions. There is an immaculate treatment of this by the late Ian McFetridge in the collection of his papers, *Logical Necessity*.[23] McFetridge also correctly breaks the alleged parallel with Kripke's notorious argument against Lewis's counterpart theory.

Another puzzle with modal realism that I do not develop is that the realism seems to take the modality out. 'Necessarily $2 + 2 = 4$' and '$2 + 2 = 4$ *everywhere*' do not mean the same. But, says the realist, what if 'everywhere' means 'in all possible worlds'? The question is ambiguous. If the collection of all possible worlds were given extensionally ($w_1, w_2, \cdots$), then again the identity would be lost: someone might think that $2 + 2 = 4$ in all those worlds, without thinking of 'all those worlds' as exhausting the possible worlds. If the totality were given under some heading other than modality, the modal content would be lost. It is only if the collection is given *under the heading* of modality that the two mean the same, but we are not any further in understanding what it is to think of a set of worlds under that heading. This is no objection to using possible-worlds talk, but it shows that the idea that when we do so we refer to real things just like the actual world provides no explanation of the nature of modal commitment.

It is natural to worry whether the use of the idea of an imaginative block is a fig leaf, disguising what must ultimately be thought of in more conventionalist terms, as for example adherence to a rule of language. In a way, and for the purposes of this essay, I do not mind very much whether this is so (it would matter much more to Craig, whose campaign has been directly concerned with refuting conventionalism). In the last few lines of the essay I do indeed express pessimism for the prospects of *any* theory of why we face the blocks we do when we set about thinking in terms of impossibilities. But for my purpose it is more important that this block is identified and properly located as the source of our propensity to modalize.

Notes

1 Spinoza, *The Ethics*, pt II, prop. 44. I owe the reference to Al McKay.

2 Graeme Forbes, *The Metaphysics of Modality* (Oxford: Oxford University Press, 1985), p. 218.

3 David Hume, *A Treatise on Human Nature*, bk I, pt III, sect. 14, ed. L. A. Selby-Bigge (Oxford: Oxford University Press), p. 167.

4 I do not have a fixed opinion on what Locke himself thought about the existence of colour. See P. A. Boghossian and J. D. Velleman, 'Colour as a secondary quality', *Mind* 97 (1989).

5 Obviously in this paragraph I ignore the possibility of the generalized quasi-realist move introduced in 'Truth, realism, and the regulation of theory', in Simon Blackburn, *Essays in Quasi-realism* (New York and Oxford: Oxford University Press, 1993), ch. 1: the move that allows even the use of a concept in explanatory roles, but still defends an anti-realist construction of it. It is not that I changed my mind between the two papers, or between then and now, but that for the purposes of this paper it is the different *direction* of a quasi-realist story that is important. Even if explanatory contexts eventually fall within the quasi-realist net, it is not right to start with them.

6 A. J. Ayer, 'What is a law of nature?', in *The Concept of Person* (London: Macmillan, 1963), pp. 230–1.

7 D. Armstrong, *What is a Law of Nature?* (Cambridge: Cambridge University Press, 1983), p. 5.

8 Ibid., p. 5.

9 Crispin Wright, *Wittgenstein on the Foundations of Mathematics* (London: Duckworth, 1980), p. 439.

10 E. J. Craig, 'Arithmetic and fact', in Ian Hacking (ed.), *Exercises in Analysis* (Cambridge: Cambridge University Press, 1985), p. 90.

11 E.g., Ludwig Wittgenstein, *Remarks on the Foundations of Mathematics* (Oxford: Blackwell, 1956), V. 6, 4–5, p. 163. Wittgenstein *constantly* appeals to hidden difference of role underlying superficial descriptive appearances. See also Blackburn, 'Errors and the phenomenology of value', in *Essays in Quasi-realism*, ch. 8, n. 13.

12 Wright, *Wittgenstein on the Foundations of Mathematics*, ch. 23.

13 In 'Carnap and logical truth' (1954; repr. in W. V. Quine, *The Ways of Paradise and Other Essays* (New York: Random House, 1966), pp. 105–6) promoting the dirty-hands argument, he wrote 'The considerations which were adduced in *1, to show the naturalness of the linguistic doctrine, are likewise seen to be empty when scrutinized in the present spirit. One was the circumstances that alternative logics are inseparable practically from mere change in usage of logical words. Another was that illogical cultures are indistinguishable from ill-translated ones. But both of these circumstances are adequately accounted for by mere obviousness of logical principles, without help of a linguistic doctrine of logical truth. For, there can be no stronger evidence of a change in usage than the repudiation of what had been obvious, and no stronger evidence of bad translation than that it translates earnest affirmations into obvious falsehoods.' And in *Philosophy of Logic* (Englewood Cliffs, NJ: Prentice-Hall, 1970), in the same context, again insisting upon the inevitability of our imputing classical logic to a translatee, he offers almost identical terms: 'Being thus built into translation is not an exclusive trait of logic. If the natives are not prepared to assent to a certain sentence in the rain, then equally we have reason not to translate the sentence as 'It is raining'. Naturally the native's unreadiness to assent to a certain sentence gives us reason not to construe the sentence as saying something whose truth should be obvious to the native at the time. Data of this sort are all we have to go on ...'

14 Quine, *Philosophy of Logic*, p. 82.

15 Ibid., pp. 82–3.

16 It is beyond the scope of this paper to explore the distinction between necessity and a prioricity, where the one is thought as logical or metaphysical, and the other as epistemological. I believe that an 'attitude'-based theory of necessity is able to explain Kripkean intuitions about the distinction, although the story is not altogether straightforward. The difficult phenomenon to explain would be the alleged conferring of necessity upon truths that were clearly arrived at a posteriori. But it should be all right that, after we have discovered something ('water is H_2O'), we should 'archive it' at least for *some* purposes: we do not of course regard such things as truths of logic, nor can we 'make nothing of' the thought processes of one who would deny them.

17 Craig, 'Arithmetic and fact', p. 92.

18 Ibid., p. 110.

19 Ibid., p. 90.

20 Ibid., p. 106.

21 Ibid., p. 91.

22 Robert Hale, 'The compleat projectivist', *Philosophical Quarterly* 36 (1986), pp. 65–84.

23 Ian McFetridge, *Logical Necessity* (London: Aristotelian Society Monographs, 1990), pp. 144–6.

48

Realism, Antirealism, Irrealism, Quasi-realism

Crispin Wright

I

It is, as is familiar, difficult to be precise about what is involved in realism. The realist in us wants to hold to a certain sort of very general view about our place in the world, a view that, as I have put it elsewhere, mixes modesty with presumption.[1] On the one hand, it is supposed, modestly, that how matters stand in the world, what opinions about it are true, is settled independently of whatever germane beliefs are held by actual people.[2] On the other, we presume to think that we are capable of arriving at the right concepts with which to capture at least a substantial part of the truth, and that our cognitive capacities can and do very often put us in position to know the truth, or at least to believe it with ample justification. The unique attraction of realism is the nice balance of feasibility and dignity that it offers to our quest for knowledge. Greater modesty would mean doubts about the capacity of our cognitive procedures to determine what is true – or even about our capacity to conceptualize the truth – and, so, would be a slide in the direction of skepticism. Greater presumption would mean calling into question, one way or another, the autonomy of truth, and, so, would be a slide in the direction of idealism. To the extent that we are serious about the pursuit of truth, we are unlikely to be attracted by either of these tendencies. We

want the mountain to be climbable, but we also want it to be a real mountain, not some sort of reification of aspects of ourselves.

It is a remarkable phenomenon that an issue of this degree of abstractness, whose proper formulation is unclear to the point where it is prima facie hazy what shape a relevant debate about it might assume, can so command intellectual curiosity. The conviction that a real issue is being presented is the conviction that metaphysics, in the most traditional sense, is possible: that there are genuine questions about the objectivity of human intellectual endeavor, and about the constitution of reality, which it falls to the traditional philosophical methods of critical reflection and analysis to resolve, if resolution is possible. This conviction may be baseless, and may yet be shown to be so by the application of just those methods. But we should work very hard before drawing that conclusion. The intellectual satisfaction associated with properly formulating and responding to these questions will be far greater than that of a repudiation of them, however well motivated.

In any case, it is evident that progress can be consequent only on some clarifications, perhaps in unexpected directions. One deservedly influential attempt at such a clarification has been Michael Dummett's.[3] I shall begin by indicating certain causes for dissatisfaction with Dummett's proposal, and will then try to consider what more generally apt analysis of realism may be appropriate if the metaphysical issues are to emerge both as reasonably definite in content and as (at least

Originally published in *Midwest Studies in Philosophy* 12 (1988), pp. 25–49. Reprinted by permission of University of Minnesota Press.

potentially) tractable. I am bound to confess to a certain pessimism about the ultimate possibility of this project. But my suggestions here must, in any case, be sketchy. And the thought is always consoling that, often in philosophy, it is more instructive to travel than to get anywhere.

II

No one has to be a realist, or not *tout court*. It is open to us to regard only some of our commitments as apt to engage with reality in the appropriate way. Realism about theoretical science, for example, need not commit one to realism about pure mathematics – and, indeed, one may wish to be only eclectically realist within science, taking an antirealist view of quantum theory, for instance. Dummett's original view was that the distinctive and proper thesis of realism about a particular genre of statements is that each of them is determinately either true or false – that the principle of bivalence holds good for them. The point of the proposal is best appreciated if we concentrate on a class of statements – say, those concerning the past beyond living memory – for whose truth-values we cannot guarantee to be able to get evidence one way or the other. Holding that bivalence is valid for such statements is holding that each is, nevertheless, guaranteed to be true or false. It would appear to follow that what confers truth or falsity on such a statement must be something separate from and independent of whatever makes for the availability of evidence for the statement's truth-value – if anything does. Hence, in particular, such a statement's being true cannot be the same thing as its meeting even our most refined criteria for its truth. The truth is, thus, independent of human opinion, which is the key realist notion.[4]

This line of thought has its problems,[5] but here I shall assume that it is in good order as far as it goes. That, however, does not seem to be far enough. One drawback of Dummett's proposal, remarked by a number of commentators, is that a Dummettian 'realist' about a given class of statements may also be a reductionist about them. Someone who held, for instance, that statements about the mental may be exhaustively analyzed in behavioral terms could also consistently hold that the analysis would be bivalence-preserving; anyway, they would have to hold, presumably, that the analysis would respect the lack of any guarantee of available evidence, one way or the other, for such statements.

But, such a view would hardly involve what we think of as realism about the *mental*. Dummett, it should be emphasized, has never been under any illusions about this,[6] and would be content to add, I think, that realism must be a view about what makes for the truth of statements when they are literally and nonreductively construed. But a more serious worry concerns vagueness. If the members of the germane class of statements are vague, then we precisely do not want to hold that each of them is guaranteed to be determinately either true or false. At the same time, vague statements are capable of truth and falsity, and a realist conception ought to be possible, it seems, of what makes for the state of affairs when they do possess determinate truth-values.[7]

One response would be to suggest that, when bivalence is inappropriate for this sort of reason, Dummett's proposal should reduce, in effect, to the claim that truth may be *evidence-transcendent*: The truth of a statement, vague or otherwise, need have no connection with the availability of any ground, even in principle, for believing it to be true. I believe that the appropriateness of so construing truth is the deep question that Dummett's writings on the topic raise, and that such a construal is, indeed, a cardinal feature of certain realist positions, notably the Cartesian philosophy of mind, the Platonist philosophy of mathematics, and certain forms of scientific realism. But it leaves the realist with no opinion to hold when it comes to statements for which evidence, one way or the other, can be guaranteed to be available – effectively decidable mathematical statements, for instance, or a statement concerning the observable outcome of an experiment. More important still, it represents as the distinctive realist thesis something that someone might well want to oppose, though still wishing to endorse the spirit of realism. *Antirealism*, in the sense associated with Dummett's work, is exactly the view that the notion of truth cannot intelligibly be evidentially unconstrained – or the view, at least, that once it is so unconstrained, it is no longer in terms of *truth*-conditions that the meanings of the statements in question can be interpreted. But someone who believes that has, so far, no motive to forswear all use of the notion of truth (whatever exactly that would involve), unless it is supposed that truth is always and essentially epistemically unconstrained – a supposition that falls foul of evident fact that, for a great many types of statements, we can make no sense of the idea of their being true if we have to suppose that evidence for their truth is not, at least in principle, available. Indeed, in contrast to the direction of much of Dummett's work on this topic, it is not clear that a general antirealist semantics must be other than truth-conditional, provided the truth of a statement is always taken to require the availability of evidence for its truth. The point remains that it ought to be possible to take a realist view of what makes for the truth or falsity of statements whose truth-values are not conceived as evidence-transcendent. Dummett's antirealist, who wishes to urge that truth-value should never be so conceived, seems to have no motive to reject realism in this more basic sense.

But what is the more basic sense? It would pass for a platitude, I think, that whether or not a statement, envisaged as uttered on a particular occasion, would express a truth is a function only of the content it would have on that occasion and the state of the world in relevant respects. The more basic kind of realism involves, I suggest, the assumption of a sort of *mechanical* view of this Platitude. Truth-values are, so to speak, ground out on the interface between language and reality. What thought a particular sentence would express in a particular context depends only on the semantics of the language and germane features of the context. Whether that thought is true depends only on which thought it is and germane features of the world. At neither point does human judgment or response come into the picture. To be sure, the semantics of the language depends on institution; it is we who built the machine. But, once built, it runs by itself. Thus, of any particular statement of sufficiently definite sense, it is determinate whether it expresses a truth in any particular context, irrespective of any judgment we may make about the matter. A basic realist thought is that wherever there is truth, it is, in this way, *investigation-independent*.

Since this conception builds no epistemic constraints into the factors that determine truth, it will no doubt come easily to someone who subscribes to it to suppose that truth can transcend all evidence. And since no provision seems to be made whereby reality can fail to determine truth-values, so long as the statements concerned are of sufficiently definite sense, bivalence, too, will be a natural adjunct. But the conception is completely general, available both for the class of statements whose truth we conceive as requiring the availability of evidence for their truth and for its complement. And it does nothing to alter the essential character of this conception of truth to superimpose whatever verificationist constraints we please.

The conception remains very much at the level of metaphor. But at least it is clear that realism, as characterized by it, has two quite distinct areas of obligation. The belief that a class of statements are apt to possess investigation-independent truth-values depends on regarding meaning as strongly objective: What constitutes correct use of an expression in particular circumstances has to be thought of as settled somehow independently of anyone's actual dispositions of response to those circumstances. What fits the meaning is one thing; what, if anything, we are inclined to say is another; and any correspondence between the two is merely contingent. Naturally, one feels there has to be something to this thought, that if the notion of meaning, and with it the notions of truth and error, are not to collapse, there must be space for *some* kind of contrast between proper use of an expression and that use to which people may actually incline. But it is quite another question whether only a realist conception of the objectivity of meaning can avoid such a collapse. Wittgenstein[8] assimilated the relationship between meaning and practice to that between character and behavior. The parallel is suggestive: It is quite consistent with our attaching sense to the idea of someone's action being out of character to regard what it is true to say about character – as we do – as a function of the way the subject is actually inclined to behave. But I shall not consider further what notion of the objectivity of meaning may be appropriate to the realist's purpose.[9] My point is merely that someone who inclines to the 'more basic' realism owes an account of the matter.

A philosopher who had no qualms about the objectivity of meaning as such, however, might still be dissatisfied with this kind of realism about a particular class of statements. If there are to be things that it would be correct to say, irrespective of what anyone is actually inclined to say, then – in accordance with the Platitude – a contribution is called for from 'the state of the world in relevant respects'. Historically, the various forms of antirealism, in different areas of philosophy, have been fueled mainly by doubts about the capacity of the world to make the necessary contribution. One class of such proposals is associated with more or less austere, empiricism-inspired theories of concept-formation. Hume, for instance, believed that there is no way whereby we can form a properly perspicuous notion of causation except at the cost of not including all the features that popular thought attributes to it. Hence, understood as popularly intended, statements involving the notion of causation are of insufficiently definite sense, in the Humean view, to take on determinate truth-values. Since they, nevertheless, play a relatively determinate role in our ordinary thought and language, the proper account must be that their role is not to 'correspond to the facts' – we can attain no satisfactory conception of the relevant 'facts' – but is a nondescriptive one. The instrumentalism about scientific-theoretical statements espoused by many positivists had an essentially similar rationale: A preferred theory of meaning – here, the conviction that all significant descriptive language must ultimately be analyzable into a vocabulary of sense experience – transpired not to have the resources to accommodate such statements within the sanctuary of fact-stating respectability.

This kind of proposal has its primary motivation in the theory of meaning. The reality of causation, or of certain sorts of theoretical entities, is called into question only because it is doubted that we can form any genuine concepts of what such things could be. A second kind of proposal, to similar effect, has a more basic ontological motivation. Although it is true that nondescriptive theories of moral and aesthetic valuation, for instance, can be and were stimulated by positivistic views about meaning, they have, nevertheless, retained an attraction for many who find no virtue in positivism. Such philosophers simply find it metaphysically incredible, as it were, that the world might actually contain objective values to which our moral, aesthetic, and other value judgments may be seen as some sort of cognitive response. It is thought baffling what kind of thing an objective value could be – in what the objective value of a situation could reside – and what part of our nature might justifiably be considered sensitive to such a commodity. The alternative to so murky and pretentious a view of, for example, moral language is, again, to account for what appear to be its genuine assertions in terms of their possession of some other nondescriptive role.[10]

There are, no doubt, other kinds of motives for similar tendencies. The general conception to which they give rise is that the range and variety of our declarative discourse somehow outstrips the categories of states of affairs that are genuinely exemplified by reality. We apparently talk as if there were moral, or scientific-theoretical, or pure mathematical states of affairs, but in truth there are

not. One response to that conviction, of course, would be to dismiss the 'language games' in question as mythology. What is common to the forms of antirealism in which we are interested here is that they eschew that response: What might be taken to be mythological descriptions are credited, instead, with some sort of different but valid role. I shall reserve the term *irrealism* as a marker for these tendencies in general, preferring 'projectivism' for a proper subclass of irrealist proposals with which we shall be concerned later. What opposes irrealism with respect to a particular class of statements is the view that the world is furnished to play the part in the determination of their truth-values, which the Platitude calls for, that there really are states of affairs of the appropriate species.[11]

III

Our concern, then, is with the philosophical topology of irrealism. What precisely are the commitments of irrealism concerning a particular class of statements? How best might it be supported? Is it ultimately coherent? For a time, during the hegemony of so-called linguistic philosophy, the irrealist tendency seemed to be channeled exclusively into various forms of *expressive* theory. Expressive theories were proposed not merely of judgments of value, but of claims about truth and about causation, professions of knowledge, descriptions of actions as voluntary, and much else.[12] The point of the notion of 'expression' here is precisely its contrast with and exclusion of assertion, properly so regarded. When one expresses something in this sense, the intention was, one makes no claim about reality,[13] even though the syntax of the utterance is superficially that of a genuine assertion, apt to agree or to fail to agree with some putative state of affairs.

The principal difficulties encountered by these theories were twofold. First, many of the positive suggestions concerning *what* was being expressed, or more generally what, in enunciating an 'expression', people were doing, were actually quite consistent with holding that the relevant kind of sentence effected an assertion. For example, those who held that to characterize an action as voluntary was to express one's willingness to hold the subject responsible for the consequences said something that no realist about the distinction between voluntary and involuntary action would have wanted to deny. Not that this has to be an objection to the expressivist's positive claim. The point is, rather, that if the positive account offered by an expressive theory nowhere goes beyond what an opponent would acknowledge as aspects of the 'pragmatics' of the relevant class of utterances, then the theoretical obligation remains to explain why it is that these pragmatic aspects actually *exhaust* the use of the relevant sentences and are not merely consequences of their possession of a genuinely assertoric role. Historically, this obligation has not, by and large, been properly met.

Second, the syntactic similarities between the sorts of 'expression' listed and what the theorists would have been content to regard as genuine assertions are actually far from superficial. Sentences, for instance, which, according to emotivism, are apt merely for the expression of evaluative attitudes, display all the syntactic possibilities enjoyed by, for example, descriptions of the weather. They allow, for instance, a full range of tenses, appraisal as "true," "false," "exaggerated," "justified," and so on; they may feature embedded in the ascription of propositional attitudes; and they admit of compounding under the full range of logical operations. In connection with the last, Peter Geach[14] argued, in an influential note, that expressive theories have no resources with which to explain the permissible occurrence of, for example, moral sentences as the antecedents of conditionals. If "Stealing is wrong" serves only to express moral disapprobation, how do we construe its role in "If stealing is wrong, encouraging people to steal is wrong also"?

Expressivism can give no answer to this question unless it is possible to construe the antecedent of such a conditional as doing something other than hypothesizing its *truth*. Dummett has suggested that it is.[15] Each kind of sentence for which expressive theories have been proposed is used to mark the speaker's undertaking of a certain sort of commitment. Accordingly, rather than view the conditional just as a device for focusing attention of the range of circumstances in which its antecedent is true, we can see it, more generally, as a device for articulating the consequences of acceptance of the commitment that, if someone were to avow the antecedent on its own, they would undertake. For instance, the effect of the conditional at the conclusion of the preceding paragraph would be, roughly:

If I were (to be brought to) to express a commitment to the wrongness of stealing, I should also

(be willing to?) express a commitment to the wrongness of encouraging others to steal.[16]

Geach's point, it could be claimed, would hardly be philosophically fundamental, in any case. If moral irrealism did, indeed, have absolutely no prospect of a satisfactory construal of conditionals with moral antecedents, that could hardly be decisive. Rather, whatever case there was for moral irrealism would become potentially revisionary of our ordinary and moral linguistic practice – compare the relation between classical mathematics and the philosophical views of the intuitionists. But such radical revisionism – in effect, the proscription of all compound moral sentences – is best avoided, and Dummett's proposal, though in some respects imprecise, at least indicates a strategy for avoiding it in the present case.

The strategy has been taken further by Simon Blackburn[17] in connection with what he styles the general program of *quasi-realism*. This program comes into play by way of supplement to the irrealist (for Blackburn, 'projectivist') view of some given class of statements. Quasi-realism's goal is to show how the irrealist account of the content of these statements need not be revisionary. It proceeds by attempting to supply alternative analyses of what appear, from an irrealist point of view, to be problematic modes of construction – conditionals, embeddings within propositional attitudes, even the truth predicate itself, and so on – which are to harmonize with what the irrealist wants to say about the basic statements in the class in question. In particular, therefore, the *quasi-realist* constructions have to proceed without any assignment of truth-conditions to these basic statements.

Actually, there a number of significant differences between Dummett and Blackburn. Dummett's proposal consisted essentially in calling attention to the potential utility of a conditional construction that – unlike the ordinary conditional – hypothesizes not the truth of its antecedent, but its utterance with a particular recognized illocutionary force. What is contemplated is a range of conditionals with antecedents like "if I were to be brought to ask whether P . . . ," "if I were to be brought to assert that P . . .," "if I were to command that P . . .," and so on. The consequents of such conditionals may, then, either describe a further such utterance or may simply say something about the circumstances that would prevail if the speech act characterized in the antecedent were to be performed. This suggests, though it is not conclusive, that Dummett was tacitly viewing expressive theories as holding 'expression' to be an illocutionary operation on a thought, just as are assertion, wish, question, and command. Undoubtedly, this is one possible view. It promises perhaps the tidiest explanation of how 'expressions' fail candidacy for truth-value – one directly modeled on the corresponding failure of, for instance, an indicative sentence used to express a command. Of course, if one attempts to view 'expression' in this way, then there has to *be* an embedded thought, just as there is in the case of the command (namely, the thought whose truth it is commanded should be brought about). So, an account will be owing of what are the genuine, truth-value-bearing thoughts that are so embedded in, for instance, moral evaluation – a possible source of difficulty if the case is an example like "Stealing is wrong," rather than "You were wrong to steal that money."

Whether or not this was Dummett's perception of the matter, Blackburn's seems different. If an apparent assertion is not a genuine assertion, that is, a claim that something is true, it may be a different mode of illocution of something apt to be true; but it may also be construed as a different kind of speech act altogether, no sort of operation on a thought. Blackburn's reaction to the problem of construing moral compounds, and especially conditionals with moral antecedents, is in keeping with this second conception. For Dummett, such conditionals emerge as genuine assertions. Blackburn, in contrast, has it that a conditional such as

> If stealing is wrong, encouraging others to steal is wrong

is *itself* an evaluation; to wit, a positive evaluation of combining a negative evaluation of stealing with a negative evaluation of encouraging others to steal.

How do these proposals cope with Geach's challenge to explain the validity of such an inference as

> Stealing is wrong;
> If stealing is wrong, encouraging others to steal is wrong;
> So: encouraging others to steal is wrong?

On Dummett's account, the conditional premise becomes something like:

> If I ever (am brought to) negatively evaluate stealing, then I also (will be willing to) negatively evaluate encouraging others to steal.

If that conditional is true, then if I so perform as to realize its antecedent – that is, I endorse the first premise – then it follows that I thereby endorse, or at least that I will be willing to endorse, the wrongness of encouraging others to steal. So, it looks as though, modulo its inexactness, Dummett's proposal may well have the means to validate Geach's example. One might wonder, though, about whether the inference, even if valid as so construed, is properly represented by Dummett's account. The gist of the second premise ought to be not a description of a performance that I will actually (be ready to) carry out in certain circumstances, but rather, something *normative*: It is that a negative evaluation of stealing *ought* to be accompanied by a negative evaluation of the practice of encouraging others to steal.

In this respect, Blackburn's strategy of construing the conditional as itself an evaluation seems superior. But what, now, does the validity of the inference consist in – when it cannot be that the truth of the premises guarantees that of the conclusion?[18] Anything worth calling the validity of an inference has to reside in the inconsistency of accepting its premises but denying its conclusion. Blackburn does indeed speak of the 'clash of attitudes' involved in endorsing the premises of the *modus ponens* example, construed as he construes it, but in failing to endorse the conclusion. But nothing worth regarding as *inconsistency* seems to be involved. Those who do that merely fail to have every combination of attitudes of which they themselves approve. That is a *moral* failing, not a logical one.[19]

Generally, there is no difficulty in making out a notion of inconsistency for speech acts other than assertion, provided they represent genuine modes of illocutionary force, that is, operations on a thought. Commands, for instance, are inconsistent just in case the thoughts are inconsistent whose truth they command be brought about; questions are inconsistent just in case the thoughts of whose truth they inquire are inconsistent; and so on. Even in these cases, the notion of inconsistency need not carry the stigma associated with assertoric case. Issuing inconsistent commands is irrational – at least if one intends that they be obeyed. But asking inconsistent questions is not. And, in any case, this seems to be, as noted, the wrong model for Blackburn's purposes. Evaluation, as he seems to conceive it, is not a mode of illocutionary force.[20]

Neither account, then, seems to cope entirely happily with the *modus ponens* inference. Dummett's account fails to reflect the normativity of the conditional premise; Blackburn's fails to respect the powerful prejudice that the failing of one who accepted the premises but repudiated the conclusion would not be merely moral. But there is, to my mind, a deeper cause for dissatisfaction with both approaches. What they have in common is that they see the presence of a certain kind of vocabulary – that of moral or aesthetic evaluation, for instance, or that of logical necessity and modality in general – as marking the performance of a certain kind of speech act, distinct from assertion (at least when the latter is properly regarded as the purported depiction of truth). It does not matter, now, whether the speech act in question is strictly a mode of illocutionary force or whether it is something else. In neither case are the materials at hand, it seems, for an explanation of the role of *iterated* applications of the vocabulary in question.[21] So neither proposal promises any sort of satisfactory account of the kind of applications that we seem, intelligibly enough, to be able to make of notions like logical necessity and logical possibility to statements in which such modal notions are themselves the principal operators. Such applications may not be very important in ordinary inferential contexts; but they are tremendously important in modal logic, and they are, it should be stressed, apparently intelligible. If, in contrast, affirming 'necessarily P' is some kind of projection from my inability to imagine the opposite, or marks the adoption of P as some kind of linguistic rule, or expresses my resolve to count nothing as falsification of P – or whatever the preferred expressive account is – no space seems to have been left for a construal of 'necessarily: necessarily P'.

Blackburn himself is strongly committed to the progressive character of the projectivist/quasi-realist research program with respect to modal idiom,[22] but the point is not (merely) *ad hominem*. It is that modality undoubtedly raises the same kinds of problems, in this context, as does morality. There is the same kind of difficulty in seeing our judgements, modal or moral, as responses to objective features of the world. In both cases, we feel the want of a satisfactory account of the confidence that, on occasion anyway, we repose in such judgements; in both cases, philosophers have been tempted to invoke special cognitive faculties, sensitive to states of affairs of the problematic kind, as our ordinary senses are sensitive to many of the characteristics of our physical environment. In neither case has any account of this kind achieved

anything but mystery. This is not to say that an irrealist account of either can be satisfactory only if it handles both equally well. But it is to suggest that the general form of an irrealist account of morals should at least be a starter in the case of modal discourse also. There may, in the end, be good reason for rejecting the irrealist account of either or both. But we can hardly suppose that we are entertaining the strongest possible version of such an account until it is fashioned in such a way that it can be adapted to any of the areas of discourse about which an irrealist (or, more specifically, projectivist) tale may seem worth telling.

The proper response to the foregoing considerations, it seems to me, is to recognize that the step in the direction of expressive, or more generally non-assertoric accounts of those areas of discourse that, for various reasons, have inspired irrealist suspicions, is a *faux pas*. The irrealist should seek not to explain away the assertoric appearance, but to sever the connection between assertion and the realism, which he wishes to oppose. This direction has been largely passed over, no doubt, because of the intimate connection between assertion and truth: To assert a statement is to present it as true. So if moral or modal judgements rank as assertions, we are bound to countenance, it seems, some notion of moral or modal truth. If this seems a fatal step from a would-be irrealist point of view, it can only be because it is being assumed that where there is truth at all, realism is correct. But that is an error. Realism, even when characterized as impressionistically as above, evidently intends a conception of truth that should be understood along the line traditionally favoured by 'correspondence' theorists. What else could be the point of the play with the idea of an 'independent' reality, one that 'confers' truth-values independently of our judgements? By contrast, it has yet to be understood why the notion of truth, which essentially engages with that of assertion, may not be the thinnest possible, merely 'disquotational' notion.

To assert a statement is to present it as true, but there need be no supposition that the notion of truth is uniform across all regions of assertoric discourse. The proper focus for the dispute between realist and irrealist tendencies in moral philosophy, the philosophy of science, the philosophy of mathematics, and elsewhere is on the notion of truth appropriate to these various kinds of statements. Actually, this is the conclusion to which Blackburn's quasi-realist program must, if successful, lead. The goal of the quasi-realist is to explain how *all* the features of some problematic region of discourse that might inspire a realist construal of it can be harmonized with objectivism. But if this program succeeds, and provides *inter alia* – as Blackburn himself anticipates – an account of what appear to be ascriptions of truth and falsity to statements in the region, then we shall wind up – running the connection between truth and assertion in the opposite direction – with a rehabilitation of the notion that such statements rank as assertions, with truth-conditions, after all. Blackburn's quasi-realist thus confronts a rather obvious dilemma. Either his program fails – in which case he does not, after all, explain how the projectivism that inspires it can satisfactorily account for the linguistic practices in question – or it succeeds, in which case it makes good all the things the projectivist started out wanting to deny: that the discourse in question is genuinely assertoric, aimed at truth, and so on. The dilemma is fatal unless what the projectivist originally wanted to maintain is actually consistent with the admission that the statements in question are, indeed, assertions, apt to be true or false in the sense, but only in the sense, that the quasi-realist explains. But if that is right, then the route through the idea that such statements are not genuinely assertoric but are 'expressive', or, one way or another, constitute some other kind of speech act, emerges as a detour. Working with that idea, and pursuit of the quasi-realist program on its basis, may help us to focus on the notion of truth that *is* appropriate to the statements in question. But once that focus is achieved, we have to drop the idea – and it hardly seems credible that only by this somewhat circuitous route can the requisite focus be gained.[23]

IV

Naturally, it is questionable whether the notion of truth can, indeed, be divided up in the manner that the foregoing considerations anticipate, and also, if it can, whether reasonably definite criteria can emerge for determining which notion is applicable within which areas of discourse. And correspondence accounts, should they prove to be the stuff of realism, have their familiar problems.[24] But, still, I think there is a program here, and that the beginnings of some germane distinctions can be sketched.

How 'thin' can something worth regarding as a notion of truth be? We do not have a truth pre-

dicate if we merely have a device of 'disquotation', since such a device could as well be applied to utterances that are not assertions. And, it may seem, it will hardly do to say that a predicate that functions disquotationally just for assertions is a truth predicate; that account, if it is not to be circular, will require us to separate assertions from speech acts of other kinds without appeal to the notion of truth, an unpromising project. Actually, I believe the commitment to avoid circularity of this kind would be an impossible burden in the quest for an account of truth. But, in any case, one essential aspect omitted by a bare disquotational account of truth is *normativity*: Truth is what assertions aim for. Now, if aiming at truth is to supply a substantial constraint on assertoric practice, an assertion's being true cannot be guaranteed simply by the assertor's taking it to be true. A constraint is substantial only if we can make sense of the idea of a misapprehension about whether or not it is satisfied, or of its being satisfied independently of any particular subject's opinion about the matter. The normativity of truth is respected by an assertoric practice only if a role is provided within that practice for the notions of ignorance, error, and improved assessment.

This, I think, is the least that must be asked. Nor is it very much. What is called for is only some *sort* of notion of a proper pedigree for an assertion, and correspondingly proper grounds for criticism of assertions. We do, indeed, practice these distinctions in all the areas of discourse about which philosophers have been drawn to an irrealistic point of view. Even the sort of affective judgements – concerning what is funny, or revolting, and so on – about which almost everybody's antecedent prejudice is irrealist are allowed to be capable of being better and worse made. Judgements about what is funny, for instance, may be in bad taste, or idiosyncratic, or insincere, or just plain wrong. (There is nothing funny about what happened at Chernobyl.)

There is a connection, here, with Geach's point. We should have, in general, no use for conditional or disjunctive compounds of such judgements unless it was sometimes possible to appraise the truth-values of the compounds independently of any knowledge of those of their constituents. Otherwise, knowledge of such a compound could never be of any practical inferential use, and its assertion would always violate Gricean 'co-operative' constraints. It is, thus, a condition of practically significant embedding of the kind Geach focused on that ignorance be possible concerning the status of the embedded statements. And ignorance is possible only if there is, indeed, a contrast in content between the claim that P is true and the claim that any particular subject assents to P – the contrast that, I have just suggested, is prerequisite for paying proper heed to the normativity of truth.

It appears, then – if I am permitted a somewhat swift conclusion – that truth, assertion, ignorance, error, and significant embedding constitute a package deal. We get all of them off the ground together, or none of them. And the real significance of Geach's antiexpressivist point is that they are 'off the ground' in all the familiar cases where expressivists wanted to look away from the notion of assertion and to characterize practices in other terms. The question, then, is: What can, nevertheless, be missing? What may a region of discourse lack, even when it has all this, which may inspire doubts about its factuality?

The answer, in one unhelpful word, is "objectivity." I think that a number of separable ideas jostle each other here, and I have space only to advert to three of the more important. The first has to do with what I shall call the *rational command* of truth. The second concerns the distinction between (human) responses that, respectively, are and are not properly regarded as *cognitive*. The third I shall touch on at the end of this paper.

By the 'rational command' of truth, I mean the idea that truth commands the assent of any subject who has an appropriate cognitive endowment and uses it appropriately. Associated with this is the notion that belief is not an operation of the will. We do not choose our beliefs, but come to them involuntarily – though not necessarily, of course, as a result of involuntary processes – by putting ourselves at the mercy, so to speak, of our reason, our senses, any other cognitive receptors' we may have, and the external world. Truth, then, according to this feature of the concept, is what is at the origin of the beliefs we form when we function as, cognitively, we ought.

In describing this as part of our 'concept' of truth, I mean only that it is a feature of the way we ordinarily think about truth. One of the oldest philosophical lessons is that there are other, potentially destructive elements within the notion – elements that traditional skeptical arguments exploit – that threaten to reduce the correspondence, if any, between what is true and the deliverances of our better cognitive natures to inscrutable contingency. Even prescinding from skepticism, realists in the

sense of Dummett will want to insist that we can understand, for at least a significant number of kinds of statements, how their truth might altogether fail to connect with any disposition on our part to believe them, no matter how meticulous and extensive our investigation. And, in the other direction, everyone must acknowledge that what we are induced to believe by meticulous and extensive investigation may still not be the truth in any examples where no such finite investigation can encompass all the material, as it were, in which evidence of untruth might be found. Explicitly unrestricted, contingent generalizations, and any statement that – like many ascriptions of dispositions – implicitly contains such a generality, are the obvious instances.

One response, which would continue to allot a dominant role to the aspect of rational command, would be to move in the direction of a Peircean conception of truth: We can mean by 'truth' only that which is fated to be agreed on by all who pursue rational enquiry sufficiently far, a "final opinion . . . independent not indeed of thought in general, but of all that is arbitrary and individual in thought."[25] Such a conception dismisses the total or partial epistemological absolutism involved in skepticism and in Dummettian realism. And it relaxes the sense in which the truth of an unrestricted generalization must command the assent of a rational investigator: A well-founded investigation may, indeed, mislead, but if such a generalization is true, all rational investigators will, sooner or later, come justifiably to believe that it is.

This has been an influential construal of the notion of truth. But, insofar as some sort of preconception about the failure of certain statements to exemplify rational command is at work in the motivation for some kinds of irrealism, it is questionable whether the Peircean construct gets it quite right. For one thing, it very much *is* a philosophers' construct, building on but going a good way past anything that might plausibly be regarded as our intuitive understanding of truth. For another, the thought that only Peircean truths are true in the substantial sense we seek may seem to hold out too many hostages to fortune. If, for instance, Quine's famous thesis of the underdetermination of scientific theory by empirical data is true (fated to be agreed by all rational investigators?), then it seems that the hypotheses of such theories cannot pass the Peircean test. That would be too swift a resolution of the debate about scientific realism. Worse, any statement whose conditions of justifiable assent are a function of what else a subject believes are at risk in the same way. If whether you ought to believe a particular statement depends on what you already believe, Peircean convergence could be expected only among rational investigators who set out with the same baggage, as it were. And it has yet to be explained why their rationality alone should tend to ensure that that is so. Yet, almost all our contingent beliefs appear to be in this situation.

A Peircean can reply. The possibility adverted to is the possibility that there may be rationally incommensurable alternative systems of belief. If that is so, we can either retain the idea that one such system might contain the truth at the expense of the others, or we can drop the idea. To retain it is to render the connection between truth and rational inquiry utterly fortuitous. To drop it is to abandon or to relativize the notion of an accurate representation of the world. In neither case is room left for the idea that the truth is what commands the assent of an appropriately cognitively endowed, rational investigator. So the Peircean development of the notion of rational command should not be faulted on the ground that it cannot accommodate the possible consequences of the underdetermination thesis or of justificational holism. The fact is that whatever notion of truth survives for statements that fall prey to those consequences simply cannot have the feature of rational command. My own opinion is that not very much of what we are pleased to regard as factual discourse will actually fall prey to those consequences. In particular, a holistic conception of confirmation poses a global threat only if, at some level, the selection of background beliefs is unconstrained. There is no reason to suppose that this must be so, but the matter raises very large issues, which I shall not attempt to broach here.

Even so, I think the intuition of rational command should be explained along other than Peircean lines. For it is an intuition that coexists with our inclination (however unfortunate) to allow that truth may be evidence-transcendent. So, the intuitive point is not that what is true ultimately commands the assent of the rational. It is, I suggest, that what it is correct to think about any statement that is apt to be, in the appropriately substantial sense, true or false is something about which rational investigators have no option at *any given stage of investigation*. It is, more specifically, determinate of any given body of evidence whether it supports such a statement, or supports its negation, or

neither. Even that is too simple. Vague statements, for instance, may nevertheless be factual. But their vagueness consists precisely in the existence of a range of cases where rational subjects may permissibly and irreducibly disagree about their status in point of justification. A similar point applies to statements, vague or not, for which the evidence is probabilistic. Different subjects may, without putting their rationality in jeopardy, have different probability thresholds, so to speak. One may require a higher probability than another before being prepared to work on the expectation that a hypothesis is true. But, so far as I can see, only in these two respects is qualification necessary. If a pair of subjects disagree about the credibility of a particular statement, and if the explanation of the disagreement concerns neither of the qualifications just noted, then either they are operating on the basis of different pools of evidence – states of information – or one (perhaps both) is misrating the evidence they share. If the states of information are different, and neither is misrating the state of information, then one state must be superior to the other: Either it must contain bona fide data that the other lacks, or it must omit spurious data that the other contains. Accordingly, we may lay down the following as a criterion for the inclusion of a statement, or range of statements within the category of those apt to be true in the substantial sense – the sense which incorporates the aspects of rational command: Disagreements about the status of such statements, where not attributable to vagueness or permissibly differing probability thresholds, can be explained only if fault is found with one of the protagonist's assessment of his or her data, or with the data being assessed. The data must be in some way faulty or incomplete, or, if not, they must have suffered a prejudiced response.

It follows that reason to think that other kinds of explanation of disagreement are possible is reason to think that the statements disagreed about are not objective in the relevant sense, and so not apt to be substantially true or false. This is one of the primary motives that have fueled expressive theories. It is surely, for instance, the mainspring of the thought that judgments about what is funny are not genuinely factual: None of the envisaged explanations may be appropriate in the case of a disagreement about humor – it may be, as we say, that the subjects have different 'senses of humor'. It is for the same reason that importance is attached, in the debates about moral and aesthetic realism, to the (much exaggerated) cultural variability of moral standards and the often idiosyncratic character of standards of aesthetic excellence.

It is another question, though, how one would actually set about showing that a given region of discourse failed to pass the test. A model dispute must be constructed whose explanation falls within none of the alternatives noted: It is not, that is to say, to be owing to vagueness in the statement(s) disputed about, nor to permissibly different probability thresholds, nor to faulty data – including inferential or observational error – nor to one of the subject's possession of a relatively inferior state of information, nor to a prejudiced assessment of agreed data.[26] But the question is, of course, what, for these purposes, counts as 'a state of information' or 'data'? What will tend to happen when this construction is attempted for a particular problematic class of statements – about humor, or value, or logical necessity, for instance – is that it will be relatively easy to construct a dispute that fits the bill, provided the 'data' are restricted to statements of *other* kinds whose factuality is not at issue. It is often possible, for instance, to give reasons for or against the judgment that some situation is funny, but, as just remarked, it seems perfectly conceivable that a pair of subjects may have an irreducible disagreement about such a judgment, although neither is under any misapprehension about any pertinent facts, or knows more than the other, or is somehow prejudicially over- or under-rating the facts that they agree about. But this way of describing the matter explicitly takes it that the 'facts' exclude whether or not the situation in question is funny. A similar possibility obtains in the case of logical necessity.[27] And it does not seem unlikely that moral evaluations, for instance, are in a like situation, although I shall not pause here to consider the construction of an appropriate dispute.

In any such case, it is open to the realist to accept the proposed criterion but to insist that the germane data may not legitimately be taken to exclude facts of the very species that the problematic of statements serve to record. The comic realist,[28] for instance, may accommodate the model dispute that the opponent constructs by insisting that misappraisal of the data must, indeed, be at the root of it; it is just that the data misappraised may irreducibly concern the humor, or lack of it, in the situation.

The *structure* of this maneuver is not unreasonable. Plainly, it cannot always be the case that, for any particular class of statements whose factuality is not disputed, they would pass the test even if we restricted our attention to 'data' that excluded them; not all genuinely factual disagreements have to be owing to mistakes, or ignorance, or prejudice about other matters. But the upshot is not that the proposed test is useless, but merely that it has a part to play only in the first stage of a dialectic, which must now be pressed further. The test connects failure to agree about judgments that are apt to be substantially true or false with failure of *ideal cognitive performance*. Accordingly, the realist who responds in the way described now owes something by way of explanation of what ideal cognitive performance might be with respect to the *sui generis* states of affairs to which, as such a realist now contends, our judgments of humor, or value, or modality, or whatever, are responsive. We require to be told *how* it is possible for us to be in touch with states of affairs of the relevant kind. What is it about them, and about us, that makes them – at least ideally – accessible to us? It is no answer, of course, merely to introduce a word or phrase for some putative kind of special cognitive faculty – the sense of humor', 'conscience', 'the reason' – that is to play the appropriate part. It is true that some of our judgments must be, so to speak, *primitively* factual, from the point of view of the test. But that is not to say that we have *carte blanche* to regard in this way any class of judgments that would otherwise fail the test. Where there is cognition, there must be at least the possibility of a satisfactory theoretical account of how it is accomplished.

The first preconception about a substantial notion of truth was its possession of the feature of rational command. Now we have, in effect, arrived at the second: Statements are apt to be substantially true or false only if it is possible to provide a satisfactory account of the kind of cognitive powers that a mind would have to have in order to be in touch with the states of affairs that they purportedly describe.[29] But what should 'a satisfactory account' mean here? I take it that it would not be necessary to trouble ourselves with the question if it could be shown that the judgments that the realist wishes to take as expressive of special abilities could actually be satisfactorily simulated, without collusion, by a subject who had only cognitive powers that both the realist and his irrealist opponent are agreed about. Thus, if, for instance, assertibility conditions could be laid down for judgments of logical necessity that someone could recognize to obtain, whose cognitive faculties embraced only the capacity for empirical judgments and so excluded anything sensitive to logical necessity as such, it would be, on the face of it, simply a bad explanation of our handling of such judgments to view it as expressive of anything additional. *Facultates non fingendae sunt praeter necessitatem.*[30]

The irrealist, however, may not easily be able to make out such a case. This will be the situation when the ability to make acceptable, or at any rate, sincere and apparently well-understood, judgments of the kind in question will depend on the subject's capacity to be *affected* in some distinctive way: to be amused, for instance, or revolted. If possessing such affective capacities is a necessary condition of full competence with the judgments in question, the irrealist's question has to be, rather, why see such affection as cognition? And the thought is, of course, that no 'satisfactory account' either of the affective response itself or of its causes can be given that will legitimate the realist's view. Contrast the sort of story that can be told about our perceptual knowledge of our immediate environment. Our theories of the nature of matter and of the workings of our sense organs and brains are hardly complete. But we know enough to tell an elaborate story about my perception of the telephone on my desk – about the kind of object it is, and the kind of creature I am, and about why, accordingly, I am able to be aware of its being there in the way in which I am. However, we have not the slightest idea how to extend this prototype to the cases of value or humor or logical necessity. And, though that is so, it is perfectly idle to claim that, in our judgments of these various kinds, we express cognitive responses to objective states of affairs.

The likely realist reply will be to suggest that the kind of explanatory model invoked is question-begging. In insisting that the epistemology of a certain putative range of states of affairs ultimately be accounted for in terms of existing fields of natural science, the irrealist loads the dice in favor of a naturalistic ontology. The states of affairs that pass the test implicitly imposed can only be those to which natural science assigns a causal role. Accordingly, as before, it is open to the realist to claim that the suggested criterion – that a class of judgments is apt to be substantially true or false only if a satisfactory account of the (ideal) epistemology can be given – is in itself acceptable, but that it is being applied here in a tendentiously restricted way. The moral realist can urge, for instance, that just as the 'data' that figured in the statement of the first criterion should be allowed to include moral data, so a 'satisfactory account', as the notion fig-

ures in the second criterion, should be allowed to proceed by reference to a framework that includes not only natural science, but also, *inter alia*, moral judgment.

Does this help? Well, it might be supposed that once moral judgments themselves are allowed to be explanatorily primitive, the account of our cognition of the truth of some particular moral judgment may straightforwardly proceed by inducing the kinds of consideration that incline us to that particular judgment, namely, a moral argument based on both moral and nonmoral premises. This, though, will hardly do. Such a model explanation of moral 'knowledge' would no doubt overestimate the extent to which our convictions on particular questions are principled, and would be inapplicable, besides, to at least some of the moral premises that applications of it would be likely to involve. But what is most basically wrong is that no real analogy is constructed with the perceptual case. It is not to our *knowledge* of neurophysiology and physics, for instance, that the explanation of my capacity to perceive the telephone would appeal, but to relevant hypotheses *within* those disciplines themselves. By contrast, the kind of 'explanation' of our moral knowledge, just canvassed explicitly, does appeal, not to certain moral premises, but to our knowledge of them. So it cannot provide what was being requested: an explanation of what it is about us, and about the moral realm, that makes for the possibility of cognitive relations at all.

In general, then, though it would be, I think, a fair complaint by an evaluative realist, for instance, that the original, explicitly naturalistic version of the second test is unfairly loaded, the prospects for the position do not seem to become much brighter if we grant, for the sake of argument, that *moral* theory be permitted to figure in the explanans. Indeed, prescinding from the confusion just discussed, it is unclear what, for these purposes, moral 'theory' might be taken to be, and how it might be exploited by a more liberal style of explanation. Matters look hardly more promising for modal and comic realism, but I cannot attempt a more detailed appraisal here.

V

Blackburn writes:

> Suppose we say that we *project* an attitude or habit or other commitment which is not

descriptive on to the world, when we speak and think as though there were a property of things which our sayings describe, which we can reason about, be wrong about, and so on. Projecting is what Hume refers to when he talks of "gilding and staining all natural objects with the colours borrowed from internal sentiment", or of the mind "spreading itself on the world."[31]

I have spoken more often of 'irrealism' than of 'projectivism'. The latter, it seems, is best reserved for those species of irrealism that concern commitments – to borrow Blackburn's term – founded on some specific mode of 'internal sentiment' or affective phenomenology. The root projectivist notion is the Humean one that we have a tendency to seem to ourselves to find in the world qualities that, properly, are predicated of our responses to it; more specifically, that the range of our responses that we tend to talk about as though they were cognitive, apt to disclose real features of the world, is actually much broader than the range of those which really deserve to be so regarded. Projectivism is, thus, a possible and natural form for the irrealist cause to assume in the three areas – morality, modality, and humor – that this discussion has mainly had in view.[32] Irrealism about scientific theory, by contrast, is not, in any version worthy of attention, projectivist. The most powerful arguments against scientific realism concern not whether any appropriately local response we have to scientific theory is cognitive – there is no such local response – but whether theoretical statements can survive the first of the two tests adumbrated: Must disagreements about scientific theory, insofar as they are not attributable to vagueness in the concepts involved, or to rationally permissible variations in standards of evidence, invariably be explicable in terms of prejudiced assessment of agreed data, or faulty data, or ignorance? Not if the underdetermination thesis is accepted. And not, perhaps, if the received wisdom is correct that the acceptability of any report of observation is invariably theoretically conditioned. For, then, the acceptability of any pool of data comes to depend on one's background theory. And that means that the data can exhibit the feature of rational command only if the ingredients in the background theories do. How is that to be provided for, if any data by which such theories might, in turn, be assessed will be theoretically conditioned in the same sense?[33]

In Blackburn's hands, as we have seen, projectivism starts out as an 'expressive' or nonassertoric thesis. I have suggested that this element of the view should be abandoned. The real question concerns what notion of truth is applicable to the 'projections'. The projectivist/irrealist thesis should be that only the thinnest possible notion is appropriate; we have seen, by contrast, two ways in which the notion of truth applicable to a class of commitments might, on the contrary, be 'thick'. I shall conclude by noting a potential instability in the projectivist position, and a third potentially germane distinction on the thinness/thickness scale.

The instability afflicts, paradoxically, just those cases where the projectivist line is intuitively most appealing. These are the classes of commitment that, like judgments about what is funny, seem to be most intimately associated with a well-defined kind of response, which we are already inclined to regard as affective rather than detective. The problem is that any such response can be construed as potentially detective – can be 'cognitivized', as it were – if the relevant projected 'quality' will sustain construal as a *disposition*. Suppose, for instance, that some such biconditional as this holds:

X is funny iff X is disposed to amuse many/most/normal people in many/most/normal circumstances.

There is, obviously, scope for consideration about which version of such a biconditional might be most plausible, about whether some reference to right-mindedness, or the like, might be wanted, and so on. But if *any* such biconditional construal provides the resources for a reasonably accurate descriptive account of the relevant parts of our linguistic practice, there can be no objection to the idea that judgments of humor do have the substantial truth-conditions that the biconditional describes. And the relevant response – being amused – will take on cognitive status only insofar as finding oneself so affected will constitute a defeasible ground for the assertion that the right-hand side of the biconditional is realized.

A defensible form of projectivism, then, in making good the claim that a certain class of judgments is based on a response that is better not regarded as cognitive, has to interpose sufficient distance, as it were, between the judgments and the response to prevent a dispositional construal. And this will be possible only to the extent that the original project-ivist image – that we make such judgments merely by way of reading back into the world features that properly belong to our response to it – is strictly misplaced. Projectivism has, therefore, a delicate balancing act to perform. If it stays too close to the image, it is liable to be undermined by a dispositional construal; if it departs too far from it, it may become unclear in what sense the response in question provides the *basis* for the relevant class of judgments, and why an argument for an irrealist view of those judgments may properly proceed from the noncognitive character of the response. The difficulty is well illustrated, I think, by the case of moral judgments. It is prima facie very implausible to construe moral qualities as dispositions to produce moral sentiments – not least because the ascription of such a disposition does not seem to have the reason-giving force that properly belongs to a moral judgment.[34] But just for that reason, the belief that moral passion is not properly viewed as a state of cognition seems to have no very direct connection with moral irrealism.

Consider, finally, a case where such a dispositional analysis seems appropriate anyway: the case of secondary qualities.[35] To be red, for instance, consists in being disposed to induce a certain kind of visual experience in the normally sighted, under normal circumstances. (I prescind from the considerations to do with trans-galactic Doppler effect, and so on.) So, we have a biconditional comparable to those mooted for 'funny' above:

X is red iff X would be seen as red by normally functioning observers in normal circumstances.

Now, there is a question about how 'normality' is to be understood for the purposes of the biconditional. Suppose we understand it statistically: Normally functioning observers function like most of us actually do most of the time; normal circumstances are relevantly similar to those which actually prevail most of the time. So understood, the statement on the right-hand side of the biconditional would still qualify as apt for substantial truth by both the tests earlier considered. Disagreement about such a statement might well be owing to vagueness in its constituent concepts, or to personal probability thresholds – the disputants might, for example, each have used statistical sampling techniques. But it seems impossible to understand how there could be a disagreement that could not

be explained along those lines and yet owe nothing to prejudice, ignorance, or misinformation. As for the second test, the sort of direction that an account of the ideal epistemology of such a judgment should take is, prima facie at least, clear. Nevertheless, to interpret the relevant notion of normality in this way is to impose a certain kind of reading on the biconditional – at least if it is held to be true a priori. In effect, we give priority to the right-hand side. What *makes* something red is how we, most of us, respond to it in the conditions that usually obtain.

It is possible to elicit a third and stronger respect in which the notion of truth may be substantial if we contrast with this right-to-left reading of such a biconditional an interpretation that assigns priority, instead, to the left-hand side. Such an interpretation would see redness as a property of things in themselves, connecting at best contingently with any effect induced in us under statistically normal circumstances. Accordingly, to give priority to the left-hand side of the biconditional, while retaining its a priori status, would be to impose a different interpretation on the normality provisos. The essential characteristic of a normally functioning observer will now be: one suffering from no internal impediment to the proper functioning of the capacity to *detect* red. And normal circumstances will be those in which there is no external impediment to the proper functioning of this same capacity.

I owe to Mark Johnston the suggestion of the possibility of these alternative readings of such biconditionals; he characterized them as 'projective' and 'detective' respectively.[36] I would rather reserve 'projective' and 'projectivism' in the way I have indicated. The distinction, if it can be properly elucidated, is nevertheless very important and does correspond, it seems to me, to a further aspect of our intuitive preconceptions about factuality and substantial truth. An interesting suggestion, which I suspect is not quite right, is that it also corresponds to the distinction between secondary and primary qualities. Primary qualities will sustain biconditionals for which the proper reading is detective; the biconditionals appropriate to secondary qualities, by contrast, will be properly read from right to left. However that may be, there is a distinction here – roughly, between our responses *making it true* that so-and-so is the case and their merely *reflecting* that truth – that the contrast between two ways of reading an appropriate biconditional, interpreted as holding a priori, seems to capture nicely. And this, as noted, is a distinction that comes into play for judgments that pass the tests earlier considered and are accordingly apt for truth in more than the thinnest sense. Of any such class of judgments, we can ask whether an appropriate biconditional does, indeed, hold a priori, and if so, to which side belongs the priority. If the way I introduced the distinction is appropriate, this is a question to be decided by reflection on the proper interpretation of the normality provisos. But that is

not the only possible way of proceeding, and it may prove not to be best. I wish merely to suggest the thought that one important class of intuitions about objectivity – those reflected, in particular, in the attempt to draw a distinction between primary and secondary qualities – have no proper place in the disputes between realism and irrealism. Rather, when the dialectic is set up in the way I have suggested it should be, they are internal to realism.[37, 38]

Notes

1 In the introduction to my *Realism, Meaning and Truth* (Oxford: Blackwell, 1986). This introduction elaborates many of the themes of parts I and II of this paper.

2 A qualification even of this formulation would be necessary to make space for realism about self-intimating mental states.

3 See especially essays 1, 10, 14, and 21 in his *Truth and Other Enigmas* (Cambridge, Mass.: Harvard University Press, 1978); ch. 20 of his *The Interpretation of Frege's Philosophy* (Cambridge, Mass.: Harvard University Press, 1981); and "What is a theory of meaning (II)," in G. Evans and J. McDowell (eds), *Truth and Meaning* (Oxford: Clarendon Press, 1976), pp. 67–137.

4 Again, a qualification is called for, to make space for realism about statements that *concern* human opinion.

5 As it stands, it involves a *non sequitur*, generated by substituting into an opaque context: 'it is guaranteed that P' and 'it is not guaranteed that Q' do not entail the falsity of the biconditional: $P \leftrightarrow Q$. See my *Realism, Meaning and Truth*, ch. 11, sect. 1.

6 See, e.g., Dummett, *Truth and Other Enigmas*, chs 10, 21.

7 Dummett notes the problems posed by vagueness for his original account of realism in *Interpretation of Frege's Philosophy*, ch. 20, p. 440. This chapter substantially qualifies the original account (though for somewhat different reasons). For a useful discussion of the new account, see the appendix to S. Rasmussen and J. Ravnkinde, "Realism and logic," *Synthese* 52 (1982), pp. 379–439.

8 Ludwig Wittgenstein, *Remarks on the Foundations of Mathematics* (Oxford: Blackwell, 1956), I, 13.

9 For more on the objectivity of meaning, see my "Rule-following, meaning and constructivism," in C. Travis (ed.), *Meaning and Interpretation* (Oxford: Blackwell, 1986), pp. 271–97, and "On making up one's mind: Wittgenstein on intention," in P. Weingartner and G. Schurz (eds), *Logic, Philosophy of Science and Epistemology* (Vienna, 1987), pp. 391–404.

To avoid misunderstanding, let me emphasize that I see no commitment to the objectivity of meaning issu-

ing from acceptance of the platitude as such: It all depends on what we see as determining the contents that, with assistance from the world and in accordance with the Platitude, determine truth-values. See "Rule-following, meaning and constructivism," pp. 273–4.

10 A fascinating recent example of the second sort of proposal is provided, of course, by Saul Kripke's interpretation of Wittgenstein on rule-following and meaning in his *Wittgenstein on Rules and Private Language* (Cambridge, Mass.: Harvard University Press, 1982).

11 However, someone who so opposes irrealism (about a particular class of statements) need not endorse the objectivity of meaning unless, contrary to my own belief, the Platitude requires it, so need not be a realist in the 'more basic' sense described in sect. II.

12 Thus, Austin on knowledge: "saying 'I know' is taking a new plunge. But it is *not* saying 'I have performed a specially striking feat of cognition, superior, in the same scale as believing and being sure, even to being merely quite sure': for there *is* nothing in that scale superior to being quite sure. Just as promising is not something superior, in the same scale as hoping and intending, even to merely fully intending: for there *is* nothing in that scale superior to fully intending. When I say 'I know', I *give others my word*: I *give others my authority for saying* that 'S is P'" (J. L. Austin, *Philosophical Papers*, 2nd edn (Oxford: Oxford University Press, 1970), p. 99).

Compare Strawson on truth: "The sentence 'What the policeman said is true' has no use *except* to confirm the policeman's story; but . . . [it] . . . does not say anything further *about* the policeman's story. . . . It is a device for confirming the story without telling it again. So, in general, in using such expressions we are confirming, underwriting, agreeing with, what somebody has said; but . . . we are not making any assertion additional to theirs; and are *never* using 'is true' to talk *about* something which is *what they said*, or the sentences they used in saying it" (P. F. Strawson, "Truth," *Analysis* 9 (1949), p. 93).

But the classic example is Ayer on morals: "If I say to someone, 'You acted wrongly in stealing that money', I am not stating anything more than if I had simply said, 'You stole that money'. In adding that this action is wrong, I am not making any further statement about it. I am simply evincing my moral disapproval of it. It is as if I had said, 'You stole that money', in a peculiar tone of horror, or written it with the addition of some special exclamation marks" (A. J. Ayer, *Language, Truth and Logic* (London, 1962), p. 107).

13 More accurately: no *additional* claim beyond the clause embedded within the expressive vocabulary if – as, for instance, in each of the examples cited in n. 12 – there is one.

14 P. T. Geach, "Ascriptivism," *Philosophical Review* 69 (1960), pp. 221–5.

15 Michael Dummett, in his *Frege: Philosophy of Language* (New York: Harper & Row, 1973), ch. 10.

16 Ibid., pp. 351–4.

17 Simon Blackburn, *Spreading the Word* (Oxford: Clarendon Press, 1984), ch. 6, and "Morals and Modals," this volume, ch. 47.

18 That still is the character of the inference when the conditional is construed in Dummett's way. The result is something on the model of:

I hereby ask whether Q;
If I ask whether Q, I expect an answer;
So: I expect an answer.

19 Bob Hale, in his excellent critical study ("The compleat projectivist," *Philosophical Quarterly* 36 (1986), pp. 65–84) of *Spreading the Word*, notes that Blackburn's construal of the conditional is, in any case, inapposite for examples like

If Jones stole that money, he should be punished,

whose role cannot possibly be to evaluate a combination of evaluations, since the antecedent is not evaluative. His ingenious alternative proposal is, first, to refashion the account of

If stealing is wrong, encouraging others to steal is wrong

as a *negative* evaluation of combining a negative evaluation of stealing with *the lack of* a negative evaluation of encouraging others to steal; and, second, to include not just evaluations, but beliefs (and presumably propositional attitudes in general) within the scope of such second-order evaluations. The conditional about Jones would then emerge as a negative evaluation of the combinations of believing that Jones stole the money but fail to approve of (positively evaluate) his punishment.

No question but that this improves Blackburn's account, and may well indicate the only viable direction for it to follow. But, notwithstanding some suggestive remarks by Hale ("Compleat projectivist," pp. 73–4), I do not think it deflects the criticism bruited that Blackburn must misconstrue the failing of one who accepts the premises of the *modus ponens* example, but does not accept the conclusion. Certainly, the character of the 'inconsistency' changes: It is now a matter not of *failing* to have every combination of evaluations of which one approves, but of *actually having* a combination – a negative evaluation of stealing and the lack of a negative evaluation of encouraging others to steal – of which one *disapproves*. However, though such conduct – "doing what you boo," as Hale describes it – is naturally described as 'inconsistent', it remains that this is *moral* inconsistency: conduct that is not true to moral principle. Someone who rejects Geach's inference is being, in addition, *irrational* – and this additional failing, separate from the moral one, is just as evident if he merely rejects the conditional:

Provided that stealing is wrong, and that, if stealing is wrong, encouraging others to steal is wrong, then encouraging others to steal is wrong

without endorsing any particular evaluation of the conjuncts in its antecedent.

A related worry (acknowledged by Hale in correspondence) is whether a projectivist who follows Hale's direction can, once having construed 'mixed' conditionals as evaluations, avoid so construing *all* conditionals. Of course, expressive theories of the conditional have their supporters, too. But there is something unhappy about being pushed toward such an account quite generally, merely by the conviction that morals are of limited objectivity.

20 Actually, and independently of the illocutionary status of evaluation, there is, of course, a notion of inconsistency for evaluations quite similar to that mooted for commands: A set of evaluations, positive and negative, is inconsistent just in case no possible world realizes all the positives but avoids realizing all the negatives. But this is of no obvious help in the present case. Whether the conditional is construed as originally by Blackburn, or as proposed by Hale (see n. 19), one who endorses both 'Stealing is wrong' and 'If stealing is wrong, encouraging others to steal is wrong', but denies 'Encouraging others to steal is wrong', commits himself to no such inconsistent set of evaluations. There is, I have urged, a logical inconsistency in such a performance, different from both the forms of moral inconsistency that, respectively, are disclosed by the Blackburn/Hale proposals. But neither the logical inconsistency nor those types of moral inconsistency are instances of this interevaluational species of inconsistency. The former has essentially nothing to do with the values the subject actually accepts (compare n. 19). And the latter concern not

the relations among his values, but those between his values and his conduct.

21 The point is made by Hale, "Compleat projectivist," pp. 78–9.

22 See, e.g., his "Morals and modals," this volume, ch. 47.

23 For pursuit of these misgivings, see my review of *Spreading the Word* in *Mind* 94 (1985), pp. 310–19.

24 Of which the foremost is probably Frege's regress argument, given in his paper "Thoughts," trans. P. T. Geach, in G. Frege, *Logical Investigations* (New Haven: Yale University Press, 1977), pp. 3–4. See Peter Carruthers's discussion, "Frege's regress," *Proceedings of the Aristotelian Society* 82 (1981–2), pp. 17–32. For a very illuminating analysis of the issues between correspondence and disquotational or 'deflationary' accounts of truth, see the contributions by Hartry Field ("The deflationary concept of truth") and Graeme Forbes ("Truth, correspondence and redundancy") in G. MacDonald and C. Wright (eds), *Fact, Science and Morality* pp. 55–117 and 27–54, respectively.

25 From *Charles S. Peirce: Selected Writings (Values in a World of Chance)*, ed. Philip P. Wiener (New York, 1966), p. 82.

26 And 'dispute' here means, of course: genuine dispute. There must be no material misunderstanding.

27 For details of how such a dispute might run, see the dialogue with the Cautious Man in ch. 3 of my *Wittgenstein on the Foundations of Mathematics* (Cambridge, Mass.: Harvard University Press, 1980). Compare my "Inventing logical necessity," in J. Butterfield (ed.), *Language, Mind and Logic* (Cambridge: Cambridge University Press, 1986), pp. 187–209.

28 Not all realists are comic, of course.

29 I try to deploy this feature of substantial truth in the context of a strategy against traditional epistemological skepticism in "Facts and certainty," *Proceedings of the British Academy* 71 (1985), pp. 429–72.

30 Compare my *Wittgenstein on the Foundations of Mathematics*, ch. 23, pp. 456–60.

31 Blackburn, *Spreading the Word*, pp. 170–1.

32 There are important internal differences. The relation between moral sentiment and moral judgment is much more complicated than that between amusement and judgment about what is funny. For one thing, though we may wish to allow that certain moral sentiments are natural in the sense that they are untrained, the capacity for *moral* sentiment arguably presupposes possession of moral concepts. An infant's distress at his older brother's punishment is not yet a moral response. By contrast, possession of the concept of humor is not a prerequisite for the capacity to be amused. For another, judging that a certain hypothetical state of affairs would be funny involves an element of prediction missing from the corresponding moral judgment, and is defeasible by subsequent apathetic responses in a way that moral judgment need not be. Third, both moral and modal judgments are disciplined by principle: Moral sentiment, and the phenomena of conviction and unintelligibility involved, for example, in the ratification of mathematical proofs, are quite often quashed by appeal to what it is independently considered correct, morally or mathematically, to think. Humor affords a parallel to this only insofar as we moralize about it, by introducing, for example, the notion of a joke in bad taste.

33 For pursuit of this line of thought, see my "Scientific realism, observation and the verification principle," in MacDonald and Wright (eds), *Fact, Science and Morality*, pp. 247–74.

34 But perhaps only prima facie. See the remarks on the 'Moral Sense Theory' in Michael Smith's "Should we believe in emotivism?," in MacDonald and Wright (eds), *Fact, Science and Morality*, pp. 289–310.

35 The distinction I wish to use the case to illustrate is actually appreciable independently of the belief that a dispositional analysis is here appropriate, so it does not matter if the reader does not share that belief.

36 In graduate classes on ethics in Princeton, spring 1986. However, the explanation of the contrast in terms of the alternative interpretations of the normality provisos demanded if the biconditional is to hold a priori is mine and may not coincide with his own preferred account. I should emphasize that I do not, at present, regard the contrast as unproblematic.

37 Johnston wanted to commend the question whether appropriate such biconditionals for moral judgements should be read right to left as the pivotal issue for moral realism. Certainly, we need a more detailed examination of the relations among the three criteria of the capacity for substantial truth than I have here been able to attempt. But my present belief, to stress, is that the first two criteria are prior, and that the third comes into play only for judgments that satisfy them. However, that does not entail that Johnston was in error to lay emphasis on the third criterion. For the capacity to sustain the truth of *some* such biconditional may be regarded as the litmus test of whether a type of statement is apt for substantial truth at all – so, unapt for irrealism – with the first two criteria providing tests in turn – perhaps not the only tests – of this capacity. The correctness of such a view is one among a number of very interesting questions here in prospect.

38 I would like to acknowledge the stimulus of conversations on these matters with Mark Johnston, David Lewis, and Michael Smith, and to thank Simon Blackburn, Bob Hale, Mark Johnston, and Peter Railton for extensive and very helpful comments on a previous draft, most of which the deadline has prevented me from responding to as I would have wished.

Name Index

Subject Index

Subject Index

constancy, 157
constructivism, 579, 580–1
contingency, 189, 263, 264, 641–2
contingent identity, 72, 73, 76, 79, 81–5, 114, 120–3, 125; as categorical indiscernibility, 121–3; and concrete things, 124; and dispositional properties, 112–13; and essentialism, 110–11; and functionalism, 124–5; modeling, 123; and necessity, 100; objections to, 107–10; and persistence criteria, 101–2; and reference, 100; and violation of Liebniz' Law, 107–8
contracted worlds, 187, 188–9
coordinate systems, 53
copy theory, 45
core cluster theory, 263, 264–5
correlation: theses, 516–18; type-to-type, 508–9, 553
Correlation Thesis, 516–17
counterfactuals, 78, 83–4, 88, 106, 112–13, 201, 218, 223, 437, 443, 451–2, 601, 605; see also conditionals
counterparts, 87–8, 114, 133, 155, 156–7, 159, 166–8, 169, 647
covariance, 542–3, 555; and dependence, 546–9; global, 551–2; property, 548; and reducibility, 549–52; weak/strong, 545–6, 548, 550, 553; see also supervenience
covering-law theory, 250, 294–5, 296–7, 423–4, 426
cross-world identity, 104, 106

data, 20
dependence, 544; causal, 439–41, 548; counterfactual, 411, 438–9, 440–1; and covariance, 546–9; see also supervenience
description(s), 6–7, 9, 29–30, 41–2, 73–5, 83, 86–7, 100–1; ambiguous, 30; definite, 30–5, 41–2
determinism, 218, 437–8, 534–7, 538
difference, 66–7
directionality, 548
dirty-hands argument, 640, 646, 648
disjunction, 201, 518–21, 522, 526–7, 529, 550–1
dispositions, 112–13, 231, 238–9, 241, 592, 593–4, 599–600, 661–2, 665; equal, 594; strict, 594
divergence, 162, 163, 217–18
dualism, 531, 592; and personal identity, 385–90

effects, 435, 441
egoism, 375
eliminativism, 616, 617, 618
elliptical laws, 423–4
emergence, emergent, 485, 493, 494–7, 538, 541–2, 543–4
empiricism, 13

endurance, 160–1
entities, 106; abstract, 18–21; acceptance of a kind of, 17–18; existence/reality of, 14–17
entrenchment, 233
epiphenomena, 441, 553
epistemology, 623–4, 625, 632, 639, 660
equivalence, 248, 251
ersatzism, 155, 156–7
essence, 80–1, 86, 87, 115, 117–18, 119, 126, 127, 140, 141, 151–2; and being necessarily true, 143–5; and identity, 110–11, 124; and the mathematical cyclist, 145–7; modeling, 118–20; and the number of apostles, 142–3; paradox of, 116–17; and set-theoretical reduction, 141–2
ethics, 543
evaluation, 654, 664–5
events, 253; causal dependence among, 439, 442
existence, 3–4, 25–9, 33–5, 119, 127, 616; internal/external questions, 14–17
existence-facts, 27
experience, 85
explanation, 593, 600, 605, 638, 647, 660; causal, 423, 425, 434, 444
explanation/prediction distinction, 426
expression, 51, 652–5, 658
extensionalism, 248–9

facts, 26–7, 185, 604, 634, 636, 637, 659; molecular, 27
family resemblances, 202
'Fido'-principle, 19
first-order/second-order properties, see primary and secondary qualities
first-personal/third-personal questions, 363
fission, 275
formalism, 9, 10
four-dimensional objects, 271, 312, 322, 325; boundaries of, 314; difference from three-dimensional objects, 317–18; refinement of, 314–16; spatiotemporal parts, 316–17
functional states, 248, 249
functionalism, 124–5, 553, 595
functions, 7
fundamental magnitudes, 244–6, 249–52
fusion principle, 275, 295–9, 301–2, 305, 371

games, 202
gappy law, 418, 422, 424, 426
general causal statements, 419–20, 423; of necessity and sufficiency, 420–2

geometry, 200
Gettierology, 393

haecceitism, 133, 157, 187–8, 541
higher-order phenomenon, 531
homophonic rule, 52
human beings, 401–5
human organisms, 401–5
hypothetical properties, 121, 122, 127

idealism, 225, 621–2, 623, 623–4
identity, 5, 65, 73, 74–6, 79, 85, 88, 128, 189, 190, 246, 259, 261, 263; absolute, 94; and coincidence, 124; distinction between necessity and, 135–8; and essence, 124; good questions and bad, 154–7; and object/occurrence of a kind, 95; and overlap, 157–64; and possible words, 149–53; relative, 90–8, 99; restricted, 93–4, 99; and substitutability, 92, 96; and word types/tokens, 93–7; see also personal identity
identity of indiscernibles, 66–71, 175, 286–7, 533; almost indiscernible twins arguments, 177–9; dispersal arguments against, 176–7
identity over time, 164; and alteration, 274; and change, 284–5; feigning, 277–81; loose and popular sense, 275–7, 282–3; and parthood, 301–11; relative, 276; and scattered objects, 291–9; Ship of Theseus, 273–5; and spatiotemporal spread, 285–90; transitive, 273, 274
imagination, 643–5
incomplete symbols, 30, 35
indeterminacy, 162, 622–3
indiscernibles: identity of, 66–71, 175–9, 286–7, 533; qualitative, 183
individuals, 5, 108–9, 110–11, 112–13, 184, 185; alien, 186–7
individuation 47, 243, 523–4
induction, 237–8
influence, 450–6
inheritance principle, 523
inscrutability of reference, 48, 49–50, 52–4, 622–3
instantiation, 161, 198–201, 205–6, 207, 264
intensionalism, 249
intentionality, 225, 594–5, 604; as intractable, 595–6
internal relations, 140
internal/external questions, 14–17, 18, 19–20, 54–5
interpretation, eligible, 224–5
intra-physical laws, 490
intrinsic properties, 543, 593–5, 604, 611
intrinsic/extrinsic distinction, 216, 230

Subject Index